United States Department of State

Treaties in Force

A List of Treaties and Other International Agreements of the United States in Force on January 1, 2017

This publication lists treaties and other international agreements of the United States on record in the Department of State on January 1, 2017, which had not expired by their own terms or which had not been denounced by the parties, replaced, superseded by other agreements, or otherwise definitely terminated.

Compiled by the Treaty Affairs Staff,
Office of the Legal Adviser,
U.S. Department of State

Foreword

Treaties in Force is prepared by the Department of State for the purpose of providing information on treaties and other international agreements to which the United States has become a party and which are carried on the records of the Department of State as being in force as of its stated publication date, January 1, 2017.

The electronic edition of *Treaties in Force* may be updated periodically throughout the year on the Treaty Affairs webpage. It is presented in Adobe Acrobat PDF, which allow text searches and printing of the entire document or selections from it.

The print edition of *Treaties in Force* is published annually in limited quantities to meet the needs of certain users who are not able to consult the on-line version. The print edition lists only those treaties on record at the time of publication as being in force for the United States on January 1 of each year. Because the print edition is only updated annually, the electronic edition, in most cases, will better reflect the current status of U.S. treaties and international agreements. A number of format and other changes were introduced in the 2016 edition of *Treaties in Force*. A description of those changes may be found in the Foreword to the 2016 edition.

Arrangement

Treaties in Force is arranged in two sections. **Section 1** includes bilateral treaties and other international agreements listed by country or other international entity with subject headings under each entry. Arrangements with territorial possessions of a country appear at the end of the entry for that country. In some cases, treaties and international agreements applicable to a territory prior to its independence are included in the entry for that country on the basis of its assumption of treaty obligations upon becoming independent, as noted at the beginning of the entry for that country. For convenience, some treaties and agreements concluded with countries whose name or statehood status has changed continue to be listed under the name in use at the time the agreement was concluded, if the title of the treaty or agreement has not been formally amended.

Section 2 lists multilateral treaties and other international agreements to which the United States is a party, arranged by subject. The depositary is the authoritative source for a current list of parties and information on other matters concerning the status of the agreement, and status information often changes. Information is provided on the depositary for the agreement in question, and contact information, including an Internet site is provided for the depositary where available.

Scope

Treaties in Force uses the term "treaty" in the generic sense as defined in the Vienna Convention on the Law of Treaties, that is, an international agreement "governed by international law, whether embodied in a single instrument or in two or more related instruments and whatever its particular designation." The term "treaty" as a matter of U.S. constitutional law denotes international agreements made by the President with the advice and consent of the Senate in accordance with Article II, section 2 of the Constitution of the United States. In addition to such "treaties", this publication covers international agreements in force that have been concluded by the Executive (a) pursuant to or in accordance with existing legislation or a prior treaty; (b) subject to congressional approval or implementation, and/or (c) under and in accordance with the President's constitutional powers.

Treaties in Force includes those treaties and other international agreements entered into by the United States which, as of the specified date, had not expired by their own terms, been denounced by the parties, replaced or superseded by other agreements, or otherwise definitely terminated. Certain agreements, particularly those concerned with World War II and the immediate postwar period, which contain continuing provisions or which have not been clearly terminated in their entirety are included even though operations under the agreements may have ceased. While all efforts are made to ensure the accuracy of this publication, the presence or absence of a particular agreement, as well as the details cited regarding a listed agreement, should not be regarded as determinative of the status of the agreement. Some categories of agreements, such as those implementing certain other agreements, are deliberately omitted from this publication even though they constitute binding international agreements. If there is a question about the status or details of a particular agreement, the text of the agreement itself always should be consulted in the first instance. Please bring any suspected errors or omissions to the attention of the Office of Treaty Affairs at the U.S. Department of State.

References

Bevans	*Treaties and Other International Agreements of the United States of America 1776-1949,* compiled under the direction of Charles I. Bevans.
EAS	*Executive Agreement Series*, issued singly in pamphlets by the Department of State (until replaced in 1945 by the TIAS).
Foreign Relations	Foreign Relations of the United States.
F.R.	*Federal Register.*
H.Doc.	House Document.
ILM	*International Legal Materials.*
LNTS	*League of Nations Treaty Series.*
Miller	*Treaties and other International Acts of the United States of America*, edited by Hunter Miller.
NP	Not Printed in *Treaties and Other International Acts Series.*
Stat.	*United States Statutes at Large.*
T. Doc.	Senate Treaty Document.
TIAS	*Treaties and Other International Acts Series*, issued singly in pamphlets by the Department of State.
TS	*Treaty Series,* issued singly in pamphlets by the Department of State (replaced in 1945 by *Treaties and Other International Acts Series*).
UNTS	*United Nations Treaty Series.*
UST	*United States Treaties and Other International Agreements* (volumes published on a calendar-year basis beginning as of January 1, 1950).

Category Crosswalk

The current category system according to which treaties are organized in this publication was introduced in the 2016 edition of *Treaties in Force*. In editions prior to 2016, a different category system, containing a larger number of categories, was used. The table below lists the new categories, and indicates how categories used in the pre-2016 editions have been consolidated into the current system.

1. Agriculture •Food and Agriculture Organization •Poplar Commission	*2. Antarctica and Arctic*
3. Arms Control •Arms Limitation •Gas Warfare •Biological Weapons •Nuclear Test Limitation •Chemical Weapons •Open Skies •Environmental Modification •Weather Modification	*4. Atomic Energy** •Nuclear Accidents •Nuclear Waste •Nuclear Safety
5. Boundaries & Boundary Waters •Boundaries •Sewage Disposal System •Boundary Waters	*6. Canals*
8. Civil Affairs, Emergencies & Defense •Civil Affairs •Civil Defense •Crisis Management •Disaster Assistance •Emergency Management •Emergency Preparedness •Evacuation •Police Equipment	*7. Claims and Dispute Resolution* •Afghanistan Settlement •Pacific Settlement of Disputes •Arbitration •Reparations •Investment Disputes •Trust Territory of the Pacific Islands
9. Commodities •Coffee •Copper •Timber	*10. Consular Affairs* •Nationality •Passports •Visas
11. Cultural Exchanges, Property and Cooperation •Campobello •Cemeteries •Cultural Heritage •Cultural Property •Cultural Relations •Tourism •Peace Corps •World Heritage •Cultural and Educational Relations •Military Cemeteries and Monuments	*12. Defense* •Geodetic Survey •Mapping •Missions, Military •Missions, Technical •Mutual Security •North Atlantic Treaty (NATO)
13. Diplomatic & Consular Relations •Consular Conventions •Friendship •General Relations	*14. Education*
15. Employment	*16. Energy* •Petroleum •Pipelines
17. Environment & Conservation •Conservation •Marine Pollution •Desertification •Polar Bears •Environmental Cooperation •Pollution •Forestry	*18. Finance* •Financial Institutions •All Financial Organizations and Development Funds (World Bank, IMF, IRBD, etc.)
19. Fisheries •Whaling	*20. Foreign Assistance* •Agricultural Commodities •Food Aid •Development Assistance •Humanitarian Assistance •Economic Assistance •Relief Supplies and Packages •Economic and Technical Cooperation •Informational Media Guarantees
21. Health and Medical Cooperation •Chemical Safety •Health and Sanitation •Drugs •Medical Assistance •Health •Shellfish	*22. Human Rights* •Child Rights •Torture •Genocide •Traffic in Women and Children •Racial Discrimination •Women – Political Rights •Slavery
23. Intellectual Property •Copyright •Phonograms •Industrial Property •Trademarks •Patents	*24. Labor*
25. Law Enforcement •Extradition •Organized Crime •Bribery •Prisoner Transfer •Corruption •Smuggling •Judicial Assistance •Stolen Property •Narcotic Drugs •Terrorism •Computer Crime (Renamed "Cybersecurity") •Customs (CMAA's – Relating to Law Enforcement and Monitoring)	*26. Maritime Matters* •Containers •Bills of Lading •Collisions at Sea •Load Lines •Maritime Interdiction •Law of the Sea •Naval Vessels •Marine Science •Shipping •Marine Pollution •International Maritime Organization •Tonnage

27. *Migration & Refugees* •International Tracing Service •Refugee Relief •Migratory Workers •Repatriation •Refugees	28. *Nonproliferation** •Nuclear Free Zone •Technology Transfer •Nuclear Test Ban •Nuclear Weapons – Non-Proliferation
29. *Occupation & Peacekeeping* •Occupation Costs •Occupied Territory	30. *Peace* •Amani Islands •Germany •Amity •Korea •Armistice Agreements •Laos •Atlantic Charter •Peace Treaties •Austria •Ryukyu Islands •Bonin Islands •Vietnam •Cambodia •WWII
31. *Pollution* •Oil Pollution	32. *Postal Matters* •Postal Arrangements
33. *Private International Law* •Maintenance (Child Support) •Marriage	34. *Publications*
35. *Property* •Diplomatic Property •Lend-Lease Settlement •Embassy Sites •Property, Real and Personal •Interests Sections •Surplus Property •Lend-Lease	36. *Regional Issues* •Compact of Free Association •Regional Commissions •Organization of American States •South Pacific Commission
37. *Regulatory Cooperation & Standardization* •Weights and Measures	38. *Rules of War* •Red Cross Conventions •States, Rights and Duties •Renunciation of War •War Crimes
39. *Scientific & Technical Cooperation* •Aerospace Disturbances •Oceanography •Hydrography •Remote Sensing •Marine Science •Scientific Cooperation •Meteorology •Weather Stations •Meteorological Research •World Meteorological Organization	40. *Social Security*
41. *Space* •Astronauts •Space Cooperation •Tracking Stations	42. *Taxation*
43. *Telecommunications* •Television	44. *Territorial Issues* •Insular Possessions •Territorial Sovereignty •Spitzbergen •Territorial Status •Territorial Acquisition •Trusteeships
45. *Trade & Investment* •Investment •Trade and Commerce •Grains •Wheat •Liquor •Wine •Customs (Relating to Tariffs and Protections)	46. *Transportation* •Automotive Traffic •Highways •Aviation •Driver's Licenses •International Civil Aviation Organization •Pan-American Highway
47. *Treaty Law* •Treaty Obligations •Treaty Succession	48. *UN & Related Organizations* •International Court of Justice •International Criminal Court
49. *Weapons**	

*In the pre-2016 system, categories involving atomic energy, nuclear weapons and control of the movement of nuclear material included varied subjects titled Atomic Energy, Nuclear Material, Nuclear Matters, Nuclear Risk Reduction, and several separate weapons categories. These have all been reorganized under three new categories: ***Atomic Energy***, which will comprise all civil aspects of nuclear power (fuel, research, peaceful uses agreements, IAEA, safety, etc.); ***Nonproliferation,*** which will include trafficking, prevention, detection and monitoring agreements, and ***Weapons,*** which include storage and safety, monitoring and control, and disarmament.

Contents

SECTION 1:

BILATERAL TREATIES AND OTHER AGREEMENTS

This page intentionally left blank.

A

AFGHANISTAN

CULTURAL EXCHANGES, PROPERTY & COOPERATION

Agreement concerning cultural relations.
Exchange of notes at Washington June 26, 1958.
Entered into force June 26, 1958.
9 UST 997; TIAS 4069; 321 UNTS 67

Agreement relating to the establishment of a Peace Corps program in Afghanistan.
Exchange of notes at Kabul September 6 and 11, 1962.
Entered into force September 11, 1962.
13 UST 2100; TIAS 5169; 461 UNTS 169

DEFENSE

Agreement relating to the deposit by Afghanistan of ten percent of the value of grant military assistance furnished by the United States.
Exchange of notes at Kabul May 24 and June 29, 1972.
Entered into force June 29, 1972; effective May 24, 1972.
23 UST 1219; TIAS 7389; 853 UNTS 153

Agreement regarding grants under the Foreign Assistance Act of 1961, as amended, or successor legislation, and the furnishing of defense articles, defense services and related training, including pursuant to the United States International Military and Education Training Program (IMET), from the United States of America to the Afghanistan Interim Administration.
Exchange of notes at Kabul April 6 and 13, 2002.
Entered into force April 13, 2002.
TIAS 02-413

Enduring strategic partnership agreement.
Signed at Kabul May 2, 2012.
Entered into force July 4, 2012.
TIAS 12-704.

Acquisition agreement, with annexes.
Signed at Kabul December 30, 2012.
Entered into force December 30, 2012.
TIAS 12-1230

Acquisition and cross-servicing agreement, with annexes.
Signed at Kabul and Tampa February 22 and March 20, 2014.
Entered into force March 20, 2014.
NP

Security and defense cooperation agreement, with annexes.
Signed at Kabul September 30, 2014.
Entered into force January 1, 2015.
TIAS

DIPLOMATIC & CONSULAR RELATIONS

Provisional agreement in regard to friendship and diplomatic and consular representation.
Signed at Paris March 26, 1936.
Entered into force March 26, 1936.
49 Stat. 3873; EAS 88; 5 Bevans 1; 168 LNTS 143

EDUCATION

Agreement for financing certain educational exchange programs.
Signed at Kabul August 20, 1963.
Entered into force August 20, 1963.
14 UST 1218; TIAS 5421; 488 UNTS 41

FINANCE

Investment incentive agreement, with appendix.
Signed at Kabul April 17, 2004.
Entered into force April 17, 2004.
TIAS 04-417

Agreement regarding the consolidation and rescheduling of debts owed to, guaranteed by, or insured by the United States government or its agencies, with annexes.
Signed at Washington September 26, 2006.
Entered into force March 16, 2007.
NP

Agreement regarding the reduction of certain debts owed to, guaranteed by, or insured by the United States or its agencies, with annexes.
Signed at Kabul March 10, 2008.
Entered into force July 14, 2008.
NP
Amendment:
July 27 and August 8, 2009 (NP)

Agreement regarding the reduction of certain debts owed to the United States by the Islamic Republic of Afghanistan.
Signed at Kabul July 22, 2010.
Entered into force September 20, 2010.
NP

FOREIGN ASSISTANCE

General agreement for technical cooperation.
Signed at Kabul February 7, 1951.
Entered into force February 7, 1951.
2 UST 592; TIAS 2210; 132 UNTS 265
Amendment:
January 2 and 24, 1952 (3 UST 4683; TIAS 2624; 177 UNTS 341)

Agreement relating to a loan for the purchase of wheat and flour for famine relief in Afghanistan.
Exchange of notes at Washington January 8, 1953.
Entered into force January 8, 1953.
4 UST 2941; TIAS 2896

Agreement relating to duty-free entry and defrayment of inland transportation charges on relief supplies and packages to Afghanistan.
Exchange of notes at Kabul April 29 and May 29, 1954.
Entered into force May 29, 1954.
5 UST 1533; TIAS 3030; 234 UNTS 3

Amendment

December 27, 1960, and January 12, 1961 (12 UST 52; TIAS 4673; 402 UNTS 319)

Agreement providing development assistance to Afghanistan.
Exchange of notes at Kabul June 23, 1956.
Entered into force June 23, 1956.
7 UST 2047; TIAS 3606; 271 UNTS 295

Agreement providing for an informational media guaranty program.
Exchange of notes at Kabul January 26 and February 15, 1961.
Entered into force February 15, 1961.
12 UST 378; TIAS 4726; 406 UNTS 235

AGENCY FOR INTERNATIONAL DEVELOPMENT

Strategic objective grant agreement for a thriving economy led by the private sector, with attachments.
Signed September 19, 2005.
Entered into force September 19, 2005.

Amendments:

September 30, 2009 (NP)
December 15, 2009 (NP)
July 26, 2010 (NP)
July 22, 2011 (NP)
February 18, 2012 (NP)
July 21, 2012 (NP)
August 6, 2012 (NP)
August 28, 2012 (NP)

Strategic objective grant agreement for a better educated and healthier population, with attachments.
Signed September 19, 2005.
Entered into force September 19, 2005.

Amendments:

July 21, 2009 (NP)
September 30, 2009 (NP)
December 15, 2009 (NP)
July 26, 2010 (NP)
July 22, 2011 (NP)
February 18, 2012 (NP)

Strategic objective grant agreement for a democratic government with broad citizen participation, with attachments.
Signed September 19, 2005.
Entered into force September 19, 2005.

Amendments:

April 19, 2009 (NP)
September 30, 2009 (NP)
December 15, 2009 (NP)
July 22, 2011 (NP)
July 21, 2012 (NP)

Strategic objective grant agreement to provide support for programs to achieve strategic development objectives, with attachments.
Signed September 19, 2005.
Entered into force September 19, 2005.

Amendments:

July 30, 2009 (NP)
September 30, 2009 (NP)
December 15, 2009 (NP)
February 26, 2010 (NP)
July 26, 2010 (NP)
July 22, 2011 (NP)
February 18, 2012 (NP)

INTERNATIONAL CRIMINAL COURT

Agreement regarding the surrender of persons to the International Criminal Court.
Signed at Washington September 20, 2002.
Entered into force August 23, 2003.
TIAS 03-823

LAW ENFORCEMENT

Agreement concerning the prohibition of opium poppy cultivation in the project area of the Central Helmand drainage project (phase II).
Signed at Kabul August 29, 1977.
Entered into force August 29, 1977.
29 UST 2481; TIAS 8951

Agreement concerning the prohibition of opium poppy cultivation in the project area of the integrated wheat development project.
Signed at Kabul September 29, 1977.
Entered into force September 29, 1977.
29 UST 2479; TIAS 8950

Letter of agreement on police, justice and counter-narcotics programs.
Signed at Kabul February 19, 2003.
Entered into force February 19, 2003.
NP

Letter of agreement on police, criminal justice, and counter-narcotics support programs.
Signed at Kabul March 9, 2006.
Entered into force March 9, 2006.
NP

Amendment:

September 23, 2010

PUBLICATIONS

Agreement relating to the exchange of official publications.
Exchange of notes at Kabul February 29, 1944.
Entered into force February 29, 1944.
58 Stat. 1393; EAS 418; 5 Bevans 3; 106 UNTS 247

TELECOMMUNICATION

Agreement for the establishment and operation of United States radio transmitting facilities in Afghanistan, with annexes.
Signed at Washington October 3, 2002.
Entered into force October 3, 2002.
TIAS 02-1003.1
Amendment:
May 4, 2006 (TIAS 02-1003.1)

TRANSPORTATION

Memorandum of agreement for the provision of assistance in developing and modernizing the civil aviation infrastructure in Afghanistan.
Signed August 20 and 27, 2003.
Entered into force August 27, 2003.
NP
Amendment:
October 21 and December 1, 2010

AFRICAN DEVELOPMENT BANK

FINANCE

Cooperation agreement.
Signed at New York May 29, 1986.
Entered into force May 29, 1986.
TIAS 11363

AFRICAN UNION

DEFENSE

Agreement regarding grants under the Foreign Assistance Act of 1961, as amended, or successor legislation, and the furnishing of defense articles, related training and other defense services from the United States of America to the African Union.
Exchange of notes at Addis Ababa August 27 and September 6, 2004.
Entered into force September 6, 2004.
NP

ALBANIA

CLAIMS & DISPUTE RESOLUTION

Arbitration treaty.
Signed at Washington October 22, 1928.
Entered into force February 12, 1929.
45 Stat. 2728; TS 770; 5 Bevans 14; 92 LNTS 217

Treaty of conciliation.
Signed at Washington October 22, 1928.
Entered into force February 12, 1929.
45 Stat. 2732; TS 771; 5 Bevans 17; 92 LNTS 223

Agreement on the settlement of certain outstanding claims, with agreed minute.
Signed at Tirana March 10, 1995.
Entered into force April 18, 1995.
TIAS 12611
Amendment:
November 18, 2005, and April 27, 2006 (TIAS 06-427)

CONSULAR AFFAIRS

Agreement relating to waiver of passport visa fees for nonimmigrants.*
Exchange of notes at Tirana May 7, 1926.
Operative June 1, 1926.
5 Bevans 12
Note
* The status of this agreement is under review.

CULTURAL EXCHANGES, PROPERTY & COOPERATION

Agreement concerning the program of the Peace Corps in the Republic of Albania.
Signed at Tirana July 22, 2003.
Entered into force October 9, 2003.
TIAS 03-1009

Agreement on the protection and preservation of certain cultural properties.
Signed at Washington July 12, 2004.
Entered into force November 2, 2009.
TIAS 09-1102.1

DEFENSE

Basic exchange and cooperative agreement for topographic mapping, nautical and aeronautical charting and information, geodesy and geophysics, digital data and related mapping, charting and geodesy materials.
Signed at Tirana March 25, 1994.
Entered into force March 25, 1994.
NP

Agreement regarding grants under the Foreign Assistance Act of 1961, as amended, and the furnishing of defense articles, related training and other defense services from the United States to Albania.
Exchange of notes at Tirana April 27 and May 6, 1994.
Entered into force May 6, 1994.
TIAS 12272

Agreement concerning the status of U.S. military personnel and civilian employees of the Department of Defense who may be present in Albania in connection with the Search and Rescue (SAREX) joint military exercise.
Exchange of notes at Tirana January 17 and 24, 1995.
Entered into force January 24, 1995.
NP

Security agreement.
Signed at Washington October 16, 1995.
Entered into force October 16, 1995.
TIAS 12244

Agreement regarding grants under the Foreign Assistance Act of 1961, as amended, and the furnishing of defense articles, related training and other defense services from the United States to Albania (SEEBRIG).
Exchange of notes at Tirana October 15 and December 4, 2002.
Entered into force December 4, 2002.
NP

Supplementary agreement to the "Agreement among member countries of the North Atlantic Treaty and other participating states in the Partnership for Peace regarding the status of their forces" on the status of the forces of the United States of America in the Republic of Albania.
Signed at Tirana March 31, 2004.
Entered into force August 19, 2004.
TIAS 04-819

Acquisition and cross-servicing agreement, with annexes.
Signed at Tirana and Patch Barracks August 26 and September 23, 2015.
Entered into force September 23, 2015.
NP

DIPLOMATIC & CONSULAR RELATIONS

Memorandum of understanding concerning the re-establishment of diplomatic relations.
Signed at Washington March 15, 1991.
Entered into force March 15, 1991.
TIAS 12428

EMPLOYMENT

Agreement relating to the employment of dependents of official government employees.
Exchange of notes at Washington August 30 and September 30, 1993.
Entered into force September 30, 1993.
TIAS

Amendment:
December 10, 2010 and February 8, 2011 (TIAS 11-208)

FINANCE

Investment incentive agreement.
Signed at Washington November 19, 1991.
Entered into force March 18, 1993.
TIAS 12441

FOREIGN ASSISTANCE

Agreement concerning economic, technical and related assistance.
Signed at Tirana June 10, 1992.
Entered into force June 10, 1992.
TIAS 12456

INTERNATIONAL CRIMINAL COURT

Agreement regarding the surrender of persons to the International Criminal Court.
Signed at Tirana May 2, 2003.
Entered into force July 7, 2003.
TIAS 03-707.2

LAW ENFORCEMENT

Treaty of extradition.
Signed at Tirana March 1, 1933.
Entered into force November 14, 1935.
49 Stat. 3313; TS 902; 5 Bevans 22; 166 LNTS 195

Agreement for the exchange of terrorism screening information.
Signed at Tirana April 14, 2016.
Entered into force September 14, 2016.
TIAS 16-914.1

POSTAL MATTERS

Convention for the exchange of money orders.
Signed at Washington June 18, 1932.
Entered into force October 1, 1932.
NP

Express mail agreement, with detailed regulations.
Signed at Tirana and Washington June 26 and July 15, 1996.
Entered into force September 15, 1996.
NP

TRADE & INVESTMENT

Agreement concerning most-favored-nation treatment and passports.
Exchange of notes at Tirana June 23 and 25, 1922.
Entered into force June 25, 1922.
Foreign Relations, 1925, Vol. I, p. 511; 5 Bevans 9

Agreement on trade relations, with exchange of letters.
Signed at Washington May 14, 1992.
Entered into force November 2, 1992.
TIAS 12454

Treaty concerning the reciprocal protection of investment, with annex and protocol.
Signed at Washington January 11, 1995.
Entered into force January 4, 1998.
TIAS 98-104

TRANSPORTATION

Air transport agreement, with annexes.
Signed at Washington September 24, 2003.
Entered into force April 5, 2004.
TIAS 04-405

ALGERIA

NOTE: For the "Declarations of the Government of the Democratic and Popular Republic of Algeria ..." initialed at Algiers January 19, 1981, see IRAN — CLAIMS & DISPUTE RESOLUTION.

CULTURAL EXCHANGES, PROPERTY & COOPERATION

Agreement on cultural cooperation.
Signed at Algiers June 2, 1987.
Entered into force October 3, 1988.
TIAS 12016; 2244 UNTS 33

DEFENSE

Agreement with respect to articles and services provided from the Government of the United States of America to the Government of Algeria pursuant to the Trans Sahara Counterterrorism Initiative.
Exchange of notes at Algiers March 20, May 31, and June 20, 2006.
Entered into force May 31, 2006.
NP

DIPLOMATIC & CONSULAR RELATIONS

Consular convention.
Signed at Washington January 12, 1989.
Entered into force July 30, 1997.
TIAS

EDUCATION

Agreement regarding the opening of an American International School in Algiers.
Signed at Washington December 29, 2015.
Entered into force April 14, 2016.
TIAS 16-414

FINANCE

Investment incentive agreement.
Signed at Washington June 22, 1990.
Entered into force December 4, 1990.
TIAS 12075

Agreement regarding the consolidation and rescheduling or refinancing of certain debts owed to, guaranteed by or insured by the United States Government and its agencies, with annexes.
Signed at Algiers December 15, 1994.
Entered into force February 8, 1995.
NP

Agreement regarding the consolidation and rescheduling of certain debts owed to, guaranteed by, or insured by the United States Government and its agencies, with annexes.
Signed at Algiers March 27, 1996.
Entered into force June 24, 1996.
NP

FOREIGN ASSISTANCE

Agreement establishing the United States-Algerian Joint Commission for economic, technical and technological cooperation.
Signed at Washington April 17, 1985.
Entered into force April 17, 1985.
TIAS 11998

INTERNATIONAL CRIMINAL COURT

Agreement regarding the surrender of persons to international tribunals.
Exchange of notes at Algiers April 6 and 13, 2004.
Entered into force April 13, 2004.
TIAS 04-413

LAW ENFORCEMENT

Agreement for mutual assistance in connection with the investigation of activities of International Systems and Controls Corporation and International Telephone and Telegraph Company, their affiliates and subsidiaries.
Exchange of letters at Washington May 22, 1980.
Entered into force May 22, 1980.
32 UST 1411; TIAS 9780; 1234 UNTS 339
Related Agreement:
December 18, 1980 (32 UST 4491; TIAS 9960; 1266 UNTS 378)

POSTAL MATTERS

International express mail agreement, with detailed regulations.
Signed at Algiers and Washington June 25 and July 26, 1994.
Entered into force September 1, 1994.
NP

SCIENTIFIC & TECHNICAL COOPERATION

Memorandum of understanding concerning scientific and technical cooperation in the earth sciences, with annexes.
Signed at Algiers February 21, 2000.
Entered into force February 21, 2000.
TIAS 13081

Agreement on science and technology cooperation, with annexes.
Signed at Algiers January 18, 2006.
Entered into force August 14, 2007.
TIAS 07-814

ANDORRA

EDUCATION

Memorandum of understanding on the Fulbright Exchange Program.
Signed at Ordino February 2, 2015.
Entered into force December 1, 2015.
TIAS 15-1201

LAW ENFORCEMENT

Agreement regarding the sharing of confiscated proceeds and instrumentalities of crimes.
Signed at Washington February 14, 2013.
Entered into force October 16, 2013.
TIAS 13-1016

ANGOLA

DEFENSE

Agreement concerning the provision of training to military and related civilian personnel of foreign countries under the United States International Military Education and Training (IMET) Program.
Exchange of notes at Luanda September 21, 1995, and January 24, 1996.
Entered into force January 24, 1996.
NP

FINANCE

Investment incentive agreement.
Signed at Luanda July 27, 1994.
Entered into force August 18, 1994.
TIAS 12189

FOREIGN ASSISTANCE

Economic, technical and related assistance agreement.
Signed at Luanda April 9, 1996.
Entered into force April 9, 1996.
TIAS 12741

INTERNATIONAL CRIMINAL COURT

Agreement regarding the surrender of persons to international tribunals.
Signed at Washington May 2, 2005.
Entered into force October 6, 2005.
TIAS 05-1006

POSTAL MATTERS

International express mail agreement, with detailed regulations.
Signed at Luanda and Washington December 29, 1993, and October 17, 1994.
Entered into force December 1, 1994.
NP

ANTIGUA AND BARBUDA

On November 1, 1981, Antigua and Barbuda became an independent state from the United Kingdom, and an independent state in the British Commonwealth of Nations. In a note dated November 4, 1981, to the Secretary-General of the United Nations, the Deputy Prime Minister and Minister of Foreign Affairs made a statement reading in part as follows:

I have the honour to inform you that Antigua and Barbuda became an independent nation on 1st November, 1981, and is now ready to participate with other nations in fulfilling obligations under international law with respect to treaties to which this Government succeeded upon independence. However, it is necessary to examine in depth such treaties to ascertain whether or not under customary international law any may have lapsed. Until this has been done the Government of Antigua and Barbuda wish:

(a) that it be presumed that each Treaty has been legally succeeded to by Antigua and Barbuda; and

(b) that future action be based on the presumption in (a) above.

You will be notified in due course of those treaties this Government regards as having lapsed and those treaties which this Government wishes to terminate. Notice of lapse or termination in an appropriate form will also be given to the country or countries that is or are party to those treaties.

CULTURAL EXCHANGES, PROPERTY & COOPERATION

Agreement relating to the establishment of a Peace Corps program in Antigua.
Exchange of notes at Bridgetown and Antigua December 19 and 28, 1966.
Entered into force December 28, 1966.
18 UST 25; TIAS 6195; 681 UNTS 137

DEFENSE

Agreement concerning the provision of training related to defense articles under the United States International Military Education and Training (IMET) Program.
Exchange of notes at St. John's December 7 and 10, 1981.
Entered into force December 10, 1981.
33 UST 4411; TIAS 10311

Agreement regarding articles, services, and associated training transferred to the Government of Antigua and Barbuda for antinarcotics purposes.
Exchange of notes at Bridgetown and St. John's November 13 and 25, 1998.
Entered into force November 25, 1998.
NP

Agreement regarding the Caribbean Basin Security Initiative and the provision of technical support for maritime security forces (Technical Assistance Field Team).
Exchange of notes at Bridgetown and St. John's June 29 and December 19, 2012.
Entered into force December 19, 2012.
TIAS 12-1219

DIPLOMATIC & CONSULAR RELATIONS

Consular convention between the United States and the United Kingdom.
Signed at Washington June 6, 1951.
Entered into force September 7, 1952.
3 UST 3426; TIAS 2494; 165 UNTS 121

EMPLOYMENT

Agreement relating to the employment of dependents of official government employees.
Exchange of notes at Bridgetown and St. John's December 23, 1997, and January 27, 1998.
Entered into force January 27, 1998.
TIAS 12926

FINANCE

Agreement relating to investment guaranties.
Signed at St. John's October 9, 1968.
Entered into force October 9, 1968.
19 UST 6060; TIAS 6567; 702 UNTS 253

Agreement regarding the consolidation and rescheduling of certain debts owed to, guaranteed by, or insured by the United States Government or its agencies, with annexes.
Signed at St. John's February 28, 2011.
Entered into force April 28, 2011.
NP

FOREIGN ASSISTANCE

General agreement for economic, technical, and related assistance.
Signed at St. John's June 17, 1983.
Entered into force June 17, 1983.
35 UST 1523; TIAS 10742; 2006 UNTS 335

INTELLECTUAL PROPERTY

Declaration by the United States and the United Kingdom affording reciprocal protection to trade-marks.
Signed at London October 24, 1877.
Entered into force October 24, 1877.
20 Stat. 703; TS 138; 12 Bevans 198

INTERNATIONAL CRIMINAL COURT

Agreement regarding the surrender of persons to the International Criminal Court.
Exchange of notes at Washington September 29, 2003.
Entered into force September 29, 2003.
TIAS 03-929

LAW ENFORCEMENT

Extradition treaty.
Done at St. John's June 3, 1996.
Entered into force July 1, 1999.
TIAS 99-701.1

Treaty on mutual legal assistance in criminal matters, with exchange of notes.
Signed at St. John's October 31, 1996.
Entered into force July 1, 1999.
TIAS 99-701

Arial intercept assistance agreement.
Exchange of notes done at Bridgetown and St. John October 7, 2011 and April 18, 2012.
Entered into force April 18, 2012.
TIAS 12-418

MARITIME MATTERS

Agreement concerning maritime counter-drug operations.
Signed at St. John's April 19, 1995.
Entered into force April 19, 1995.
TIAS 12763

Amendments
June 3, 1996 (TIAS 12763)
September 30, 2003 (TIAS 03-930)

NONPROLIFERATION

Agreement concerning cooperation to suppress the proliferation of weapons of mass destruction, their delivery systems, and related materials by sea.
Signed at St. John's April 26, 2010.
Entered into force September 27, 2010.
TIAS 10-927

OCCUPATION & PEACEKEEPING

Agreement for the furnishing of commodities and services in connection with the peacekeeping force for Grenada.
Exchange of notes at Bridgetown and St. John's November 30, 1983, and January 27, 1984.
Entered into force January 27, 1984.
35 UST 4334; TIAS 10934; 2015 UNTS 127

Related Agreement:
December 16, 1985, and January 28, 1986 (TIAS 11172; 2126 UNTS 155)

POSTAL MATTERS

Convention for the exchange of postal money orders with Antigua.
Signed at Antigua and Washington December 5, 1956, and March 22, 1957.
Entered into force December 1, 1957.
11 UST 1425; TIAS 4482

PROPERTY

Convention between the United States and the United Kingdom relating to the tenure and disposition of real and personal property.
Signed at Washington March 2, 1899.
Applicable to Antigua June 17, 1901.
31 Stat. 1939; TS 146; 12 Bevans 246

Supplementary convention relating to the tenure and disposition of real and personal property of March 2, 1899.
Signed at Washington May 27, 1936.
Entered into force March 10, 1941.
55 Stat. 1101; TS 964; 5 Bevans 140; 203 LNTS 367

SPACE

Agreement between the United States and the United Kingdom concerning the establishment and operation of a space vehicle tracking and communications station on Antigua.
Exchange of notes at Washington January 17 and 23, 1967.
Entered into force January 23, 1967.
18 UST 112; TIAS 6207

TAXATION

Agreement for the exchange of information with respect to taxes.
Signed at Washington December 6, 2001.
Entered into force February 10, 2003.
TIAS 13178

TELECOMMUNICATION

Agreement between the United States and the United Kingdom relating to the reciprocal granting of authorizations to permit licensed amateur radio operators of either country to operate their stations in the other country.
Exchange of notes at London November 26, 1965.
Applicable to Antigua December 11, 1969.
16 UST 2047; TIAS 5941; 561 UNTS 193

Agreement between the United States and the United Kingdom extending to certain territories the application of the agreement of November 26, 1965, relating to the reciprocal granting of authorizations to permit licensed amateur radio operators of either country to operate their stations in the other country.
Exchange of notes at London December 11, 1969.
Entered into force December 11, 1969.
20 UST 4089; TIAS 6800; 732 UNTS 334

Memorandum of understanding providing for a radio relay facility in Antigua for relaying Voice of America programs to areas in the Caribbean.
Signed at St. John's September 12, 1980.
Entered into force September 12, 1980.
33 UST 1541; TIAS 10130; 1560 UNTS 409

Arrangement relating to radio communications between amateur stations on behalf of third parties.
Exchange of notes at St. John's April 30 and May 24, 1982.
Entered into force June 23, 1982.
34 UST 1103; TIAS 10395; 1566 UNTS 117

TRANSPORTATION

Agreement between the United States and the United Kingdom concerning air services, with annexes and exchange of letters.
Signed at Bermuda July 23, 1977.
Entered into force July 23, 1977.
28 UST 5367; TIAS 8641

Amendments:
April 25, 1978 (29 UST 2680; TIAS 8965)
December 4, 1980 (33 UST 655; TIAS 10059)
August 19 and October 7, 1991 (TIAS 11794)

ARGENTINA

ATOMIC ENERGY

Agreement providing for a grant to assist in the acquisition of certain nuclear research and training equipment and materials.
Exchange of notes at Buenos Aires September 9, 1959, and May 23, 1960.
Entered into force May 23, 1960.
11 UST 1628; TIAS 4508; 377 UNTS 3

Agreement providing for equipment to be used in nuclear research and training programs at La Plata University, Argentina.
Exchange of notes at Buenos Aires November 8, 1962, and November 30, 1963.
Entered into force November 30, 1963.
14 UST 1907; TIAS 5504; 505 UNTS 131

Agreement for cooperation concerning peaceful uses of nuclear energy, with annex and agreed minute.
Signed at Buenos Aires February 29, 1996.
Entered into force October 16, 1997.
TIAS 12730

Implementing arrangement for technical exchange and cooperation in the area of peaceful uses of nuclear energy.
Signed at Buenos Aires October 16, 1997.
Entered into force October 16, 1997.
TIAS 12892

Arrangement for the exchange of technical information and cooperation in regulatory and safety research matters, with addenda.
Signed at Rockville and Buenos Aires December 4 and 28, 2007.
Entered into force December 28, 2007.
TIAS 07-1228.3

Arrangement for the exchange of technical information and cooperation in regulatory and safety research matters, with addenda and annex.
Signed at Vienna and Buenos Aires September 17 and 30, 2013.
Entered into force September 30, 2013.
TIAS 13-930.1

CONSULAR AFFAIRS

Agreement relating to the reciprocal waiver of nonimmigrant passport visa fees.*
Exchange of notes at Buenos Aires April 15, 1942.
Operative June 1, 1942.
56 Stat. 1578; EAS 266; 5 Bevans 117; 103 UNTS 307
Note:
* The status of this agreement is under review.

CULTURAL EXCHANGES, PROPERTY & COOPERATION

Agreement on the development and facilitation of tourism.
Signed at Buenos Aires September 25, 1990.
Entered into force September 25, 1990.
TIAS 12420

Agreement establishing a Peace Corps program in Argentina.
Exchange of notes at Buenos Aires July 18 and August 30, 1991.
Entered into force August 30, 1991.
TIAS 12102

DEFENSE

Agreement relating to the transfer to Argentina of certain United States naval vessels, with memorandum of understanding.
Exchange of notes at Washington January 4 and 8, 1951.
Entered into force January 8, 1951.
3 UST 2735; TIAS 2442; 165 UNTS 89

Agreement for a United States Air Force Mission to the Argentine Republic.
Signed at Buenos Aires October 3, 1956.
*Entered into force October 3, 1956.**
7 UST 2571; TIAS 3652; 279 UNTS 13
Amendment:
October 16, 1959 (10 UST 1978; TIAS 4363; 361 UNTS 358)

Note:
* Article 17 suspended by agreement of November 27, 1972 (24 UST 279; TIAS 7550).

Agreement relating to the appointment of officers to constitute a United States Army Mission to Argentina.
Signed at Buenos Aires August 2, 1960.
Entered into force August 2, 1960.
11 UST 1964; TIAS 4546; 384 UNTS 105
Amendment:
January 8 and June 7, 1962 (13 UST 1376; TIAS 5098; 458 UNTS 354)

Agreement relating to a military assistance program, with memorandum of understanding.
Exchange of notes at Buenos Aires May 10, 1964.
Entered into force May 10, 1964.
15 UST 719; TIAS 5594; 527 UNTS 77

Armed forces cooperative projects agreement.
Exchange of notes at Buenos Aires May 5, 1970.
Entered into force May 5, 1970.
21 UST 1297; TIAS 6881; 752 UNTS 25

Agreement relating to the deposit by Argentina of ten percent of the value of grant military assistance furnished by the United States.
Exchange of notes at Buenos Aires April 4 and June 8, 1972.
Entered into force June 8, 1972.
23 UST 1324; TIAS 7414

Agreement relating to cooperation and mutual assistance in cartography and geodesy, with annex.
Signed at Buenos Aires July 11, 1983.
Entered into force July 11, 1983.
35 UST 1310; TIAS 10730; 1578 UNTS 91

Memorandum of understanding on the exchange of officers between the U.S. Marine Corps and the Argentine Marine Corps.
Signed at Washington October 7 and December 3, 1987.
Entered into force December 3, 1987.
TIAS 11559

Agreement concerning nautical cartography and geodesy, with annexes.
Signed at Buenos Aires and Fairfax November 28, 1990, and June 18, 1991.
Entered into force June 18, 1991.
NP

Memorandum of understanding on the exchange of service personnel between the United States Navy and Argentine Navy and on the general conditions which will apply to the exchange of such personnel.
Signed at Washington July 13, 1992.
Entered into force July 13, 1992.
NP

Agreement concerning exchange of research and development information, with appendix.
Signed at Washington July 22, 1998.
Entered into force July 22, 1998.
TIAS
Amendment:
October 17, 2000

Agreement concerning security measures for the protection of classified military information.
Signed at Washington January 12, 1999.
Entered into force January 12, 1999.
TIAS 13017

Basic exchange and cooperative agreement concerning geospatial information and services cooperation, with annex.
Signed at Buenos Aires March 5, 2001.
Entered into force March 5, 2001.
NP

Agreement concerning health care for military members and their dependents.
Signed at Washington March 15, 2006.
Entered into force June 13, 2006.
NP
Extension:
March 5 and 18, 2010

Memorandum of understanding concerning the inter-American Naval telecommunications network.
Signed October 9 and November 8, 2006.
Entered into force November 8, 2006.
TIAS 06-1108

Agreement regarding the assignment of liaison officers, with annex.
Signed at Washington February 7 and April 17, 2007.
Entered into force April 17, 2007.
NP

Acquisition and cross-servicing agreement, with annexes.
Signed at Buenos Aires March 27, 2009.
Entered into force March 27, 2009.
NP

Agreement concerning health care for military members and their dependents.
Signed at Washington February 17 and March 7, 2016.
Entered into force March 7, 2016, with effect from February 1, 2016.
NP

Memorandum of agreement regarding the assignment of liaison officers, with annexes.
Signed at Buenos Aires and Miami June 28, 2016.
Entered into force June 28, 2016.
NP

EDUCATION

Agreement for financing certain educational exchange programs.
Signed at Buenos Aires August 21, 1963.
Entered into force August 21, 1963.
14 UST 1236; TIAS 5423; 488 UNTS 61
Amendment:
January 18 and March 20, 2000 (TIAS 13086)

EMPLOYMENT

Agreement relating to the employment of dependents of official government employees.
Exchange of notes at Buenos Aires May 28 and December 15, 1986.
Entered into force December 15, 1986.
TIAS 11414

ENVIRONMENT & CONSERVATION

Agreement for cooperation in the Global Learning and Observations to Benefit the Environment Program, with appendices.
Signed at Buenos Aires June 28, 1995.
Entered into force June 28, 1995.
TIAS 12671

FINANCE

Agreement relating to investment guaranties under section 413(b)(4) of the Mutual Security Act of 1954, as amended.
Signed at Buenos Aires December 22, 1959.
Entered into force provisionally December 22, 1959; definitively May 5, 1961.
12 UST 955; TIAS 4799; 411 UNTS 41

Agreement regarding the consolidation and rescheduling of certain debts owed to, guaranteed by or insured by the United States Government and its agencies, with annexes.
Signed at Buenos Aires April 8, 1986.
Entered into force May 19, 1986.
NP

Swap agreement between the United States Treasury and the Central Bank of the Argentine Republic/Government of the Argentine Republic, with related letter and amendment.
Signed at Washington and Buenos Aires February 23, 1988.
Entered into force February 23, 1988.
TIAS

Swap agreement between the United States Treasury, the Central Bank of the Argentine Republic/Government of the Argentine Republic, with memorandum of understanding.
Signed at Washington and Buenos Aires October 19, 1988.
Entered into force October 19, 1988.
TIAS

Agreement regarding the consolidation and rescheduling or refinancing of certain debts owed to, guaranteed by, or insured by the United States Government and its agencies, with annexes.
Signed at Buenos Aires December 14, 1989.
Entered into force January 22, 1990.
NP

Agreement regarding the consolidation and rescheduling of certain debts owed to, guaranteed by, or insured by the United States Government and its agencies, with annexes.
Signed at Buenos Aires December 5, 1990.
Entered into force January 16, 1991.
NP

Agreement regarding the consolidation and rescheduling or refinancing of certain debts owed to, guaranteed by or insured by the United States Government and its agencies, with annexes.
Signed at Washington December 6, 1991.
Entered into force February 10, 1992.
NP

Agreement regarding the reduction of certain debts related to foreign assistance owed to the Government of the United States and its agencies, with appendices.
Signed at Washington and Buenos Aires January 13 and 15, 1993.
Entered into force February 14, 1993.
NP

Agreement regarding the consolidation and rescheduling of certain debts owed to, guaranteed by or insured by the United States Government and its agencies, with annexes.
Signed at Washington January 13, 1993.
Entered into force March 8, 1993.
NP

Agreement regarding the clearance of arrears owed to, guaranteed by, or insured by the United States government including its agencies, with annexes.
Signed at Buenos Aires February 26, 2015.
Entered into force April 13, 2015.
TIAS 15-413

FOREIGN ASSISTANCE

General agreement for a program of technical cooperation.
Signed at Buenos Aires June 3, 1957.
Entered into force June 3, 1957.
8 UST 811; TIAS 3840; 291 UNTS 61

Agreement concerning the establishment of an Americas Fund and Administering Commission.
Signed at Buenos Aires September 27, 1993.
Entered into force September 27, 1993.
TIAS 12507

INTELLECTUAL PROPERTY

Copyright arrangement.
Exchanges of notes at Buenos Aires April 28, July 28, August 28, and September 3, 1934.
Entered into force August 23, 1934.
5 Bevans 72; 160 LNTS 57

LAW ENFORCEMENT

Memorandum of understanding on cooperation in the narcotics field.
Signed at Buenos Aires September 15, 1972.
Entered into force September 15, 1972.
23 UST 2620; TIAS 7450; 852 UNTS 97

Cooperation agreement for reducing demand, preventing abuse, and combatting illicit production and traffic of drugs and psychotropic substances.
Signed at Buenos Aires May 24, 1989.
Entered into force March 5, 1992.
TIAS

Treaty on mutual legal assistance in criminal matters, with attachments.
Signed at Buenos Aires December 4, 1990.
Entered into force February 9, 1993.
TIAS

Treaty on extradition.
Signed at Buenos Aires June 10, 1997.
Entered into force June 15, 2000.
TIAS 12866; 2159 UNTS 129

MARITIME MATTERS

Memorandum of understanding regarding certain maritime matters.
Signed at Buenos Aires March 31, 1978.
Entered into force January 30, 1979.
30 UST 1054; TIAS 9239; 1152 UNTS 227

NONPROLIFERATION

Memorandum of understanding on the transfer and protection of strategic technology.
Signed at Buenos Aires February 12, 1993.
Entered into force February 12, 1993.
TIAS 12487

Agreement concerning cooperation to prevent the illicit trafficking in nuclear and other radioactive material, with agreed minute.
Signed at Washington April 13, 2010.
Entered into force April 13, 2010.
TIAS 10-413

POSTAL MATTERS

Agreement for the exchange of insured parcel post packages.
Signed at Buenos Aires February 28 and at Washington April 8, 1939.
Entered into force October 1, 1938.
53 Stat. 2223; Post Office Department print; 198 LNTS 55

International express mail agreement, with detailed regulations.
Signed at Buenos Aires and Washington September 4 and 26, 1980.
Entered into force January 1, 1981.
33 UST 2509; TIAS 10193; 1529 UNTS 269

Memorandum of understanding concerning the operation of the INTELPOST field trial, with details of implementation.
Signed at Washington and Buenos Aires August 24, September 16, and October 12, 1982.
Entered into force November 1, 1982.
TIAS 10526; 1777 UNTS 355

PUBLICATIONS

Agreement relating to the exchange of official publications.
Exchange of notes at Buenos Aires September 30 and October 17, 1939.
Entered into force October 17, 1939.
54 Stat. 1855; EAS 162; 5 Bevans 83; 201 LNTS 273

SCIENTIFIC & TECHNICAL COOPERATION

Agreement for scientific and technical cooperation.
Signed at Buenos Aires April 7, 1972.
Entered into force August 11, 1972.
23 UST 2534; TIAS 7442; 852 UNTS 77

Agreement on scientific and technical cooperation for a global telemetered seismograph network.
Signed at Reston and San Juan December 28 and 29, 1987.
Entered into force December 29, 1987.
TIAS 12054

Memorandum of understanding concerning scientific and technical cooperation in the earth sciences, with annexes.
Signed at Buenos Aires and Reston December 26, 1996 and July 15, 1997.
Entered into force July 15, 1997.
TIAS 97-715

Memorandum of understanding for cooperation in the use of U.S. land remote sensing satellite data, with annexes.
Signed at Buenos Aires and Reston November 30, 2012 and February 15, 2013.
Entered into force February 15, 2013.
TIAS 13-215

SOCIAL SECURITY

Agreement relating to the payment of old-age, survivors, and disability benefits to beneficiaries residing abroad.
Exchange of notes at Buenos Aires September 15, 1972.
Entered into force September 15, 1972.
23 UST 2660; TIAS 7458; 852 UNTS 91

SPACE

Agreement relating to a cooperative program for the optical satellite tracking station at Villa Dolores, Argentina.
Exchange of notes at Buenos Aires March 16, 1962.
Entered into force March 16, 1962.
13 UST 1385; TIAS 5100; 454 UNTS 3

Memorandum of understanding concerning the Scientific Applications Satellite C Earth Observation Mission.
Signed at Washington October 28, 1996.
Entered into force October 28, 1996.
TIAS

Framework agreement on cooperation in the peaceful uses of outer space, with annex.
Signed at Buenos Aires October 25, 2011.
Entered into force July 30, 2013.
TIAS 13-730

TAXATION

Agreement for relief from double taxation on earnings derived from operation of ships and aircraft.
Exchange of notes at Washington July 20, 1950.
Entered into force July 20, 1950.
1 UST 473; TIAS 2088; 89 UNTS 63

TELECOMMUNICATION

Agreement relating to the reciprocal granting of authorizations to permit licensed amateur radio operators of either country to operate their stations in the other country.
Exchange of notes at Buenos Aires March 31, 1967.
Entered into force April 30, 1967.
18 UST 361; TIAS 6243; 636 UNTS 95

Agreement relating to radio communications between amateur stations on behalf of third parties.
Exchange of notes at Buenos Aires March 31, 1967.
Entered into force April 30, 1967.
18 UST 365; TIAS 6244; 636 UNTS 103

Agreement concerning the provision of satellite facilities and the transmission and reception of signals to and from satellites for the provision of satellite services to users in the United States of America and the Argentine Republic, with protocol.
Signed at Washington June 5, 1998.
Entered into force June 5, 1998.
TIAS 12960

TERRITORIAL ISSUES

Treaty for the free navigation of the rivers Parana and Uruguay.
Signed at San Jose de Flores July 10, 1853.
Entered into force December 20, 1854.
10 Stat. 1001; TS 3; 5 Bevans 58

TRADE & INVESTMENT

Treaty of friendship, commerce and navigation.
Signed at San Jose July 27, 1853.
Entered into force December 20, 1854.
10 Stat. 1005; TS 4; 5 Bevans 61

Trade agreement with exchanges of notes.
Signed at Buenos Aires October 14, 1941.
Entered into force provisionally November 15, 1941; definitively January 8, 1943.
56 Stat. 1685; EAS 277; 5 Bevans 102; 119 UNTS 193.

Agreement relating to the effectiveness of United States schedules to the trade agreement of October 14, 1941.
Exchange of notes at Buenos Aires July 24, 1963.
Entered into force July 24, 1963.
14 UST 1046; TIAS 5402; 487 UNTS 183.

Amendment

December 18 and 27, 1967 (18 UST 3102; TIAS 6402; 693 UNTS 370).

Treaty concerning the reciprocal encouragement and protection of investment, with protocol.
Signed at Washington November 14, 1991.
Entered into force October 20, 1994.
TIAS

Amendment:

August 24 and November 6, 1992

Trade and investment framework agreement, with annex.
Signed at Buenos Aires March 23, 2016.
Entered into force March 23, 2016.
TIAS

TRANSPORTATION

Air transport services agreement, with annexes.
Signed at Buenos Aires October 22, 1985.
Entered into force provisionally October 22, 1985; definitively December 29, 1986.
TIAS 11262
Amendments:
October 26 and November 24, 2000 (TIAS 00-1124).
July 3, 2007 (TIAS 00-1124)

Memorandum of agreement to provide technical assistance in developing and modernizing Argentina's civil aviation.
Signed June 4 and November 5, 1986.
Entered into force November 5, 1986.
NP

Agreement relating to the reciprocal acceptance of airworthiness certifications.
Exchange of notes at Buenos Aires June 22, 1989.
Entered into force June 22, 1989.
TIAS 11669; 2190 UNTS 383

ARMENIA

For agreements prior to December 31, 1991, see UNION OF SOVIET SOCIALIST REPUBLICS.

CULTURAL EXCHANGES, PROPERTY & COOPERATION

Agreement concerning the program of the Peace Corps in Armenia.
Signed at Washington September 24, 1992.
Entered into force September 24, 1992.
TIAS 12082

DEFENSE

Agreement regarding grants under the Foreign Assistance Act of 1961, as amended, or successor legislation, and the furnishing of defense articles, defense services and related training, including pursuant to the United States International Military Education and Training (IMET) Program.
Exchange of notes at Yerevan May 10 and July 31, 2002.
Entered into force July 31, 2002.
NP

Acquisition and cross-servicing agreement, with annex.
Signed at Stuttgart and Yerevan February 5 and March 11, 2015.
Entered into force November 3, 2015.
NP

EMPLOYMENT

Agreement on employment of dependents of members of diplomatic missions and consular posts, with a related note.
Exchange of notes at Yerevan September 20, December 30, 2005, and January 26, 2006.
Entered into force October 16, 2006.
TIAS 06-1016

FINANCE

Investment incentive agreement.
Signed at Washington April 2, 1992.
Entered into force April 2, 1992.
TIAS 12451

FOREIGN ASSISTANCE

Agreement regarding cooperation to facilitate the provision of humanitarian and technical economic assistance.
Signed at Yerevan December 15, 1992.
Entered into force December 15, 1992.
TIAS 12483

INTERNATIONAL CRIMINAL COURT

Agreement regarding the surrender of persons to the International Tribunals.
Signed at Yerevan October 16, 2004.
Entered into force March 17, 2005.
TIAS 05-317

SCIENTIFIC & TECHNICAL COOPERATION

Agreement on science and technology cooperation, with annexes.
Signed at Washington November 3, 2009.
Entered into force March 11, 2010.
TIAS 10-311.1

Memorandum of understanding concerning scientific and technical cooperation in the earth sciences.
Signed at Reston and Yerevan June 4, 2010 and July 29, 2011.
Entered into force July 29, 2011.
TIAS 11-729

TRADE & INVESTMENT

Agreement on trade relations, with related exchanges of letters.
Signed at Washington April 2, 1992.
Entered into force April 7, 1992.
TIAS

Treaty concerning the reciprocal encouragement and protection of investment, with annex.
Signed at Washington September 23, 1992.
Entered into force March 29, 1996.
TIAS

TRANSPORTATION

Air transport agreement, with annexes.
Signed at Washington November 21, 2008.
Entered into force June 16, 2009.
TIAS 09-616

WEAPONS

Agreement concerning cooperation in the area of prevention of proliferation of technology, pathogens, and expertise that could be used in the development of biological weapons.
Signed at Washington and Yerevan September 3 and 16, 2010.
Entered into force January 14, 2011.
TIAS 11-114

ASIAN DEVELOPMENT BANK

FINANCE

Agreement relating to the United States contribution to the Multi-Purpose Special Fund of the Asian Development Bank.
Signed at Manila April 19, 1974.
Entered into force April 19, 1974.
25 UST 1672; TIAS 7903
Amendment:
December 23, 1974, and April 1, 1975 (26 UST 897; TIAS 8074)

ASSOCIATION OF SOUTHEAST ASIAN NATIONS (ASEAN)

AGRICULTURE

Agreement regarding the establishment of an ASEAN Agricultural Development and Planning Center.
Exchange of notes at Kuala Lumpur June 28, 1980.
Entered into force June 28, 1980.
32 UST 1371; TIAS 9778; 1234 UNTS 399

FOREIGN ASSISTANCE

Agreement concerning cooperation in economic development, education, culture, and narcotics.
Signed at Denpasar and Kuala Lumpur July 2 and October 24, 1979.
Entered into force October 24, 1979.
TIAS

AUSTRALIA

ATOMIC ENERGY

Agreement for cooperation concerning technology for the separation of isotopes of uranium by laser excitation, with annexes, agreed minute and related exchange of letters.
Signed at Washington October 28, 1999.
Entered into force May 24, 2000.
TIAS 00-524; 2117 UNTS 243

Agreement concerning the application of non-proliferation assurances to Australian uranium to be transferred to the United States of America for enrichment and retransfer to Taiwan, with annex.
Exchange of notes at Washington July 31, 2001.
Entered into force May 17, 2002.
TIAS; 2208 UNTS 497

Agreement concerning peaceful uses of nuclear energy, with agreed minute.
Signed at New York May 4, 2010.
Entered into force December 22, 2010.
TIAS 10-1222

CLAIMS & DISPUTE RESOLUTION

Treaty amending in their application to Australia certain provisions of the treaty for the advancement of peace between the United States and the United Kingdom signed at Washington September 15, 1914.
Signed at Washington September 6, 1940.
Entered into force August 13, 1941.
55 Stat. 1211; TS 974; 5 Bevans 143

CONSULAR AFFAIRS

Agreement relating to the reciprocal waiver of visa fees for nonimmigrants.*
Exchange of notes at Canberra February 10, 1950.
Entered into force February 10, 1950; operative March 1, 1950.
1 UST 457; TIAS 2082; 51 UNTS 167

Agreement concerning reciprocal changes in immigration regulations relating to nonimmigrant visas.*
Exchanges of notes at Canberra July 29 and August 9, 17 and 20, 1955.
Entered into force August 20, 1955; operative September 1, 1955.
6 UST 6225; TIAS 3472; 268 UNTS 133
Note:
* The status of these agreements is under review.

Agreement relating to the relaxation of nonimmigrant visa requirements.
Exchange of notes at Canberra March 13, June 1 and August 19, 1959.
Entered into force August 19, 1959.
11 UST 2049; TIAS 4561; 388 UNTS 183

Agreement for the sharing of visa and immigration information.
Signed at Canberra August 27, 2014.
Entered into force December 12, 2014.
TIAS 14-1212

DEFENSE

Cooperative mapping agreement.
Approved by Australia March 6, 1947, and by the United States April 4, 1947.
Entered into force April 4, 1947.
5 Bevans 183

Mutual defense assistance agreement.
Exchange of notes at Washington February 1 and 20, 1951.
Entered into force February 20, 1951.
2 UST 644; TIAS 2217; 132 UNTS 297

Agreement relating to the furnishing of certain supplies and services to naval vessels.
Exchange of notes at Canberra December 19 and 31, 1956.
Entered into force January 26, 1957.
8 UST 9; TIAS 3729; 266 UNTS 89
Amendment:
March 28, 1963 (14 UST 347; TIAS 5319; 474 UNTS 338)

Agreement for cooperation regarding atomic information for mutual defense purposes.
Signed at Washington July 12, 1957.
Entered into force August 14, 1957.
8 UST 1339; TIAS 3881; 290 UNTS 139

Mutual weapons development program agreement.
Signed at Washington August 23, 1960.
Entered into force August 23, 1960.
11 UST 2089; TIAS 4565; 388 UNTS 232

Agreement regarding mutual weapons development data exchange concerning weapons of mass destruction threat reduction technologies.
Signed January 25, 1962.
Entered into force January 25, 1962.
TIAS
Amendment:
August 14, 2006

Agreement concerning the status of United States forces in Australia with protocol.
Signed at Canberra May 9, 1963.
Entered into force May 9, 1963.
14 UST 506; TIAS 5349; 469 UNTS 55

Agreement relating to the establishment of a joint defense space research facility.
Signed at Canberra December 9, 1966.
Entered into force December 9, 1966.
17 UST 2235; TIAS 6162; 607 UNTS 83
Amendments and Extensions:
October 19, 1977 (29 UST 2759; TIAS 8969)
November 16, 1988 (TIAS 12266)
June 4, 1998 (2171 UNTS 89) (TIAS 12959)

Agreement relating to the establishment of a joint defense space communications station in Australia.
Signed at Canberra November 10, 1969.
Entered into force November 10, 1969.
20 UST 3097; TIAS 6788; 729 UNTS 17
Amendments and Extensions:
November 16, 1988 (TIAS 12267)

Memorandum of understanding regarding the exchange training program of units from both forces.
Signed at Washington November 4, 1976.
Entered into force November 4, 1976.
28 UST 8237; TIAS 8757; 1095 UNTS 91

Agreement relating to operation of United States military flights through RAAF Base Darwin.
Exchange of notes at Canberra March 11, 1981.
Entered into force March 11, 1981.
33 UST 1300; TIAS 10112

Memorandum of understanding concerning the exchange of service personnel between the U.S. Marine Corps and the Royal Australian Air Force.
Signed at Washington April 13, 1984.
Entered into force April 13, 1984.
TIAS 11131

Memorandum of arrangement relating to the provision of NOMAD aircraft and related services, with attachment.
Signed at Washington April 2, 1987.
Entered into force April 2, 1987.
TIAS 11317

Memorandum of understanding on the exchange of professional military education (PME).
Signed at Washington July 23 and August 5, 1987.
Entered into force August 5, 1987.
NP

Memorandum of understanding concerning exchange of service personnel between the U.S. Marine Corps and the Australian Army.
Signed at Canberra and Washington August 31 and September 16, 1987.
Entered into force September 16, 1987.
TIAS 11550

Agreement concerning cooperation in defense logistic support.
Signed at Sydney November 4, 1989.
Entered into force November 4, 1989.
TIAS 13-1001; 1571 UNTS 167
Amendments and Extensions:
August 7, 2000 and July 30, 2001 (TIAS 13-1001)
October 13 and December 9, 2011 (TIAS 13-1001)

Agreement concerning cooperation in radar activities, with project arrangements.
Signed at Salisbury March 3, 1992.
Entered into force March 3, 1992.
TIAS 12270; 1679 UNTS 251

Arrangement for the exchange of military personnel between the Royal Australian Navy and the U.S. Coast Guard.
Signed at Washington July 27, 1992.
Entered into force July 27, 1992.
NP

Agreement concerning cooperative and collaborative research, development and engineering, with appendix.
Signed at Washington October 21, 1994.
Entered into force October 21, 1994.
TIAS 12271; 1856 UNTS 291

Agreement concerning reciprocal defense procurement.
Signed at Washington April 19, 1995.
Entered into force April 19, 1999.
TIAS

Agreement concerning the establishment of certain mutual defense commitments.
Exchange of notes at Sydney and Canberra December 1, 1995.
Entered into force December 1, 1995.
TIAS 12704; 1945 UNTS 263
Amendment:
December 4, 2008

Agreement concerning security measures for the protection of classified information, with exchange of notes.
Signed at Canberra June 25, 2002.
Entered into force November 7, 2002.
TIAS 02-1107; 2208 UNTS 481

Agreement concerning the cooperative framework for system development and demonstration of the joint strike fighter, with annexes.
Signed at Washington October 31, 2002.
Entered into force November 14, 2002.
TIAS 02-1114

Acquisition and cross-servicing agreement, with annexes.
Signed at Canberra April 27, 2010.
Entered into force August 9, 2010.
NP

Agreement relating to the operation of and access to an Australian Naval Communication Station at North West Cape in Western Australia.
Signed at Washington July 16, 2008.
Entered into force November 24, 2011.
TIAS 11-1124

Treaty concerning defense trade cooperation.
Signed at Sydney September 5, 2007.
Entered into force May 16, 2013.
NP

The force posture agreement.
Signed at Sidney August 12, 2014.
Entered into force March 31, 2015.
NP

DIPLOMATIC & CONSULAR RELATIONS

Convention to regulate commerce (article IV) between the United States and the United Kingdom.
Signed at London July 3, 1815.
Entered into force July 3, 1815.
8 Stat. 228; TS 110; 12 Bevans 49

EDUCATION

Agreement for financing certain educational and cultural exchange programs.
Signed at Canberra August 28, 1964.
Entered into force August 28, 1964.
15 UST 1689; TIAS 5643; 510 UNTS 201
Amendments:
May 12, 1967 (18 UST 493; TIAS 6255; 638 UNTS 300)
February 20 and 21, 1992 (TIAS 12449; 1680 UNTS 502)

EMPLOYMENT

Agreement relating to employment of dependents of official government employees, with related notes.
Exchange of notes at Canberra November 5 and 9, 1984.
Entered into force November 9, 1984.
TIAS 11138

ENERGY

Memorandum of understanding relating to coal information exchange in the areas of health, safety and environment.
Signed at Canberra October 24 and 25, 1978.
Entered into force November 23, 1978.
30 UST 2208; TIAS 9328

ENVIRONMENT & CONSERVATION

Memorandum of understanding for cooperation in the Global Learning and Observations to Benefit the Environment (GLOBE) Program, with appendices.
Signed at Canberra April 21, 1995.
Entered into force April 21, 1995.
TIAS 12634

FISHERIES

Agreement concerning fishing by United States vessels in waters surrounding Christmas Island and Cocos/Keeling Islands pursuant to the treaty on fisheries between the United States and certain Pacific Island states.
Exchange of notes at Port Moresby April 2, 1987.
Entered into force April 2, 1987.
TIAS 11295

FOREIGN ASSISTANCE

Agreement relating to training and other technical services to be furnished by the Bureau of Reclamation, Department of the Interior, in connection with proposed projects of the Australian Snowy Mountains Hydroelectric Authority.
Exchange of notes at Washington November 16, 1951.
Entered into force November 16, 1951.
3 UST 2836; TIAS 2456; 168 UNTS 75

INTELLECTUAL PROPERTY

Agreement to facilitate the interchange of patent rights and technical information for defense purposes, with exchange of notes.
Signed at Washington January 24, 1958.
Entered into force January 24, 1958.
9 UST 5; TIAS 3974; 307 UNTS 105

Agreement approving the procedures for reciprocal filing of classified patent applications.
Exchange of notes at Washington September 13 and October 2, 1961.
Entered into force October 2, 1961.
12 UST 1359; TIAS 4857; 421 UNTS 318

LAW ENFORCEMENT

Treaty on extradition.
Signed at Washington May 14, 1974.
Entered into force May 8, 1976.
27 UST 957; TIAS 8234

Procedures for mutual assistance in administration of justice in connection with the Lockheed Aircraft Corporation matter.
Signed at Washington September 13, 1976.
Entered into force September 13, 1976.
27 UST 3424; TIAS 8372

Protocol amending the treaty on extradition of May 14, 1974.
Signed at Seoul September 4, 1990.
Entered into force December 21, 1992.
1736 UNTS 344

Treaty on mutual assistance in criminal matters, with related exchange of notes.
Signed at Washington April 30, 1997.
Entered into force September 30, 1999.
TIAS 99-930; 2117 UNTS 157

POSTAL MATTERS

Parcel post agreement and detailed regulations of execution.
Signed at Melbourne May 16 and at Washington May 27, 1952.
Entered into force August 1, 1952.
3 UST 4305; TIAS 2580; 178 UNTS 113

Memorandum of understanding for the exchange of international express mail, with details of implementation.
Signed at Washington and Victoria June 5 and 16, 1981.
Entered into force July 1, 1981.
33 UST 3872; TIAS 10266; 1543 UNTS 89

PRIVATE INTERNATIONAL LAW

Agreement for the enforcement of maintenance (support) obligations.
Signed at Canberra December 12, 2002.
Entered into force December 12, 2002.
TIAS 02-1212; 2208 UNTS 469

PROPERTY

Convention between the United States and Great Britain relating to tenure and disposition of real and personal property.
Signed at Washington March 2, 1899.
Entered into force for Australia April 3, 1902.
TS 146; 31 Stat. 1939; 12 Bevans 246

Supplementary convention extending the time within which notifications may be given of the accession of British colonies or foreign possessions to the convention of March 2, 1899.
Signed at Washington January 13, 1902.
Entered into force April 2, 1902.
TS 402; 32 Stat. 1914; 12 Bevans 261

Supplementary convention relating to the tenure and disposition of real and personal property.
Signed at Washington May 27, 1936, by the United States, the United Kingdom, Australia, and New Zealand.
Entered into force March 10, 1941.
55 Stat. 1101; TS 964; 5 Bevans 140; 203 LNTS 367

Agreement relating to the principles applying to the provision of aid in the prosecution of the war.
Exchange of notes at Washington September 3, 1942.
Entered into force September 3, 1942.
56 Stat. 1608; EAS 271; 5 Bevans 146; 24 UNTS 195

Agreement on settlement for lend-lease, reciprocal aid, surplus war property, and claims.
Signed at Washington June 7, 1946.
Entered into force June 7, 1946.
60 Stat. 1707; TIAS 1528; 5 Bevans 164; 4 UNTS 237

Agreement relating to the investment of a portion of the trust account established under the lend-lease settlement agreement of June 7, 1946, and the Fulbright agreement of November 26, 1949.*
Exchange of notes at Canberra July 9 and August 25, 1952.
Entered into force August 25, 1952.
5 UST 650; TIAS 2954; 229 UNTS 262

Note:

* November 26, 1949, agreement (TIAS 1994) superseded by agreement of August 28, 1964 (TIAS 5643). See under EDUCATION.

SCIENTIFIC & TECHNICAL COOPERATION

Agreement providing for the construction and operation of a weather station on Nauru Island.
Exchange of notes at Canberra February 19 and 25, 1958.
Entered into force February 25, 1958.
9 UST 266; TIAS 4001; 317 UNTS 153

Agreement concerning the transfer to the Australian National University of the facility for research on aerospace disturbances at Amberley, Queensland.
Exchange of notes at Canberra January 31 and February 26, 1975.
Entered into force February 26, 1975.
26 UST 446; TIAS 8043; 992 UNTS 139

Agreement regarding the management and operation of the joint geological and geophysical research station at Alice Springs, Australia.
Exchange of notes at Canberra February 28, 1978.
Entered into force March 2, 1978.
29 UST 3040; TIAS 8995; 1120 UNTS 67.
Amendment:
February 17, 1984 (35 UST 4421; TIAS 10946)

Agreement concerning the use of Australian facilities by the National Aeronautics and Space Administration for the conduct of scientific balloon flights for civil research purposes.
Exchange of notes at Canberra February 16, 2006.
Entered into force February 16, 2006.
TIAS 06-216
Extension:
August 26, 2011 and April 24, 2012 (TIAS 12-424)

Agreement on cooperation in science and technology for homeland domestic security matters, with annex.
Signed at Washington December 21, 2005.
Entered into force February 16, 2007.
TIAS 07-216

Agreement relating to scientific and technical cooperation, with annexes.
Signed at Canberra February 28, 2006.
Entered into force February 17, 2007.
TIAS 07-217

Memorandum of understanding concerning scientific and technical cooperation in the earth sciences.
Signed at Reston and Sydney February 2 and 25, 2009.
Entered into force February 25, 2009.
TIAS 09-225

SOCIAL SECURITY

Agreement on social security, with administrative arrangement.
Signed at Canberra September 27, 2001.
Entered into force October 1, 2002.
TIAS 13169; 2208 UNTS 435

SPACE

Agreement providing for the establishment and operation in Australia of a tracking station in connection with the transit navigational satellite program.
Exchange of notes at Canberra June 5, 1961.
Entered into force June 5, 1961.
12 UST 789; TIAS 4779; 409 UNTS 279

Agreement relating to the establishment, maintenance and operation of a solar observatory at Learmonth, Western Australia.
Exchange of notes at Canberra October 14 and 27, 1977.
Entered into force October 27, 1977.
29 UST 2747; TIAS 8968

Agreement concerning space vehicle tracking and communications facilities.
Exchange of notes at Canberra May 29, 1980.
Entered into force May 29, 1980; effective February 26, 1980.
32 UST 1417; TIAS 9781; 1217 UNTS 237
Amendment and Extensions:
July 21, 1981 (TIAS 10198)
January 17 and May 2, 1990 (TIAS 12413)
August 4, 2000 (2171 UNTS 139)
February 25, 2010
August 19, 2011 and January 11, 2012
November 18 and 21, 2013

TAXATION

Convention for the avoidance of double taxation and the prevention of fiscal evasion with respect to taxes on gifts.*
Signed at Washington May 14, 1953.
Entered into force December 14, 1953.
4 UST 2264; TIAS 2879; 205 UNTS 237

Convention for the avoidance of double taxation and the prevention of fiscal evasion with respect to taxes on the estates of deceased persons.*
Signed at Washington May 14, 1953.
Entered into force January 7, 1954.
5 UST 92; TIAS 2903; 205 UNTS 277

Convention for the avoidance of double taxation and the prevention of fiscal evasion with respect to taxes on income.
Signed at Sydney August 6, 1982.
Entered into force October 31, 1983.
35 UST 1999; TIAS 10773

Protocol amending the convention of August 6, 1982 for the avoidance of double taxation and the prevention of fiscal evasion with respect to taxes on income.
Signed at Canberra September 27, 2001.
Entered into force May 12, 2003.
TIAS 13164
Note:
* Applicable to Norfolk Island.

Agreement to improve international tax compliance and to implement the Foreign Account Tax Compliance Act, with annexes.
Signed at Canberra April 28, 2014.
Entered into force June 30, 2014.
TIAS 14-630

TELECOMMUNICATION

Agreement relating to the reciprocal granting of authorizations to permit licensed amateur radio operators of either country to operate their stations in the other country.
Exchange of notes at Canberra June 25, 1965.
Entered into force June 25, 1965.
16 UST 973; TIAS 5836; 541 UNTS 155

Arrangement relating to radio communications between amateur stations on behalf of third parties.
Exchange of notes at Canberra May 21 and 26, 1982.
Entered into force June 25, 1982.
34 UST 1109; TIAS 10396; 1566 UNTS 133

Agreement concerning the agreement of December 16, 1988, and January 20, 1989, and the transfer to the Government of Australia of the high frequency diplomatic radio communications facility in Uriarra.
Exchange of notes at Canberra December 19, 1994, and March 22, 1995.
Entered into force March 22, 1995.
TIAS 12201

TRADE & INVESTMENT

Agreement relating to cooperation on antitrust matters.
Signed at Washington June 29, 1982.
Entered into force June 29, 1982.
34 UST 388; TIAS 10365; 1369 UNTS 43

Agreement on mutual antitrust enforcement assistance, with annex.
Signed at Washington April 27, 1999.
Entered into force November 5, 1999.
TIAS 13033; 2117 UNTS 203

United States–Australia free trade agreement, with annexes and related exchange of letters.
Signed at Washington May 18, 2004.
Entered into force January 1, 2005.
TIAS

TRANSPORTATION

Air service agreement relating to facilities at Eagle Farm and Amberley, Queensland.
Signed at Canberra March 10, 1947.
Entered into force March 10, 1947.
61 Stat. 3843; TIAS 1732; 5 Bevans 181; 10 UNTS 89

Agreement relating to the reciprocal acceptance of airworthiness certifications.
Exchange of notes at Washington December 24, 1974, and June 11, 1975.
Entered into force June 11, 1975.
26 UST 1665; TIAS 8126; 1006 UNTS 241

Agreement on the promotion of aviation safety.
Signed at Canberra June 21, 2005.
Entered into force November 28, 2006.
TIAS 06-1128

Air transport agreement, with annexes.
Signed at Washington March 31, 2008.
Entered into force June 18, 2013.
TIAS 13-618
Amendment:
May 30 and June 18, 2013 (TIAS 13-618)

AUSTRIA

CLAIMS & DISPUTE RESOLUTION

Arbitration treaty.
Signed at Washington August 16, 1928.
Entered into force February 28, 1929.
45 Stat. 2752; TS 776; 5 Bevans 353; 88 LNTS 95

Treaty of conciliation.
Signed at Washington August 16, 1928.
Entered into force February 28, 1929.
45 Stat. 2756; TS 777; 5 Bevans 356; 88 LNTS 101

Agreement regarding settlement for war accounts and claims incident to the operations of United States forces in Austria from April 9, 1945 to June 30, 1947, inclusive.
Signed at Vienna June 21, 1947.
Entered into force June 21, 1947.
61 Stat. 4168; TIAS 1920; 5 Bevans 380; 67 UNTS 89

Agreement providing for settlement of certain claims under Article 26 of the Austrian State Treaty of May 15, 1955.
Exchange of notes at Vienna May 8, 15 and 22, 1959.
Entered into force May 22, 1959.
10 UST 1158; TIAS 4253; 347 UNTS 3

Agreement concerning the Austrian Fund "Reconciliation, Peace and Cooperation" (Reconciliation Fund), with annexes.
Signed at Vienna October 24, 2000.
Entered into force December 1, 2000.
TIAS 13122; 2162 UNTS 3
Related agreement:
January 21, 2001 (TIAS 13143; 2170 UNTS 279)

CONSULAR AFFAIRS

Agreement relating to the waiver of passport visas and passport visa fees.*
Exchange of notes at Vienna June 10, June 28, and July 12, 1949.
Entered into force July 12, 1949; operative July 15, 1949.
63 Stat. 2740; TIAS 1988; 5 Bevans 426; 84 UNTS 291
Note
* The status of this agreement is under review.

DEFENSE

Agreement relating to the assurances required under the Mutual Security Act of 1951.
Exchange of notes at Vienna December 14, 1951, and January 5, 1952.
Entered into force January 5, 1952.
3 UST 4525; TIAS 2600; 179 UNTS 73

Agreement relating to the purchase by Austria of certain military equipment, materials and services.
Exchange of notes at Washington August 9, 1957.
Entered into force August 9, 1957.
8 UST 1241; TIAS 3875; 288 UNTS 299

Acquisition and cross-servicing agreement, with annexes.
Signed at Patch Barracks and Vienna March 15, 2000.
Entered into force March 15, 2000.
NP

DIPLOMATIC & CONSULAR RELATIONS

Treaty establishing friendly relations.
Signed at Vienna August 24, 1921.
Entered into force November 8, 1921.
42 Stat. 1946; TS 659; 5 Bevans 215; 7 LNTS 156

EDUCATION

Agreement for financing certain educational exchange programs.
Signed at Vienna June 25, 1963.
Entered into force June 25, 1963.
14 UST 957; TIAS 5386; 479 UNTS 223

ENVIRONMENT & CONSERVATION

Agreement for cooperation in the Global Learning and Observations to Benefit the Environment (GLOBE) Program, with appendices.
Signed at Vienna April 20, 1995.
Entered into force April 20, 1995.
TIAS 12631

FINANCE

See also PROPERTY

Agreement relating to the funding of the indebtedness of Austria to the United States.
Signed at Washington May 8, 1930.
Operative January 1, 1928.
Treasury Department print; 5 Bevans 365

Agreement modifying the debt funding agreement of May 8, 1930.
Signed at Washington September 14, 1932.
Entered into force July 1, 1931.
Treasury Department print; 5 Bevans 376

Agreement relating to guaranties authorized by Section 111(b)(3) of the Economic Cooperation Act of 1948, as amended.
Exchange of notes at Washington February 14 and 16, 1952.
Entered into force February 20, 1952.
3 UST 3874; TIAS 2516; 177 UNTS 299
Amendment:
October 23, 1958 (9 UST 1345; TIAS 4127; 336 UNTS 336)

Agreement regarding certain bonds of Austrian issue denominated in dollars, with annex and protocol.
Signed at Washington November 21, 1956.
Entered into force September 11, 1957.
8 UST 1457; TIAS 3903; 290 UNTS 181

ERP Counterpart Settlement Agreement, with related exchange of notes of March 10 and 28, 1961.
Signed at Vienna March 29, 1961.
Entered into force July 12, 1962.
13 UST 1838; TIAS 5133; 459 UNTS 45

Agreement to supplement the ERP Counterpart Settlement Agreement of March 29, 1961.
Signed at Vienna April 30, 2004.
Entered into force August 1, 2004.
TIAS 04-801

FOREIGN ASSISTANCE

Economic cooperation agreement and supplementary note.
Signed at Vienna July 2, 1948.
Entered into force July 2, 1948.
62 Stat. 2137; TIAS 1780; 5 Bevans 404; 21 UNTS 29
Amendments:
October 21 and November 30, 1949, and February 20, 1950 (1 UST 145; TIAS 2020; 79 UNTS 288)
January 16 and March 7, 1951 (2 UST 1315; TIAS 2283; 141 UNTS 372)
May 11 and 15, 1951 (2 UST 2569; TIAS 2380; 139 UNTS 79)
July 1 and 31, 1952 (3 UST 5042; TIAS 2685; 181 UNTS 326)
October 15 and December 6, 1952 (3 UST 5300; TIAS 2731; 185 UNTS 322)

Agreement relating to duty-free entry of relief goods and packages and standard packs and for defrayment of transportation charges.
Exchange of notes at Vienna February 3 and 11, 1949.
Entered into force February 11, 1949.
63 Stat. 2420; TIAS 1922; 5 Bevans 419; 79 UNTS 113

LAW ENFORCEMENT

Arrangement for the direct exchange of information regarding the traffic in narcotic drugs.
Exchange of notes at Vienna April 10 and July 24, 1931.
Entered into force July 24, 1931.
5 Bevans 373

Agreement regarding mutual assistance between the customs services of the United States and Austria.
Signed at Vienna September 15, 1976.
Entered into force July 3, 1978.
29 UST 1011; TIAS 8863
Amendment:
April 2, 1986

Treaty on mutual legal assistance in criminal matters, with attachments.
Signed at Vienna February 23, 1995.
Entered into force August 1, 1998.
TIAS 98-801; 2029 UNTS 153

Extradition treaty.
Signed at Washington January 8, 1998.
Entered into force January 1, 2000.
TIAS 12916

Protocol to the extradition treaty of January 8, 1998, as contemplated by Article 3(2) of the agreement on extradition between the United States of America and the European Union signed June 25, 2003.
Signed at Vienna July 20, 2005.
Entered into force February 1, 2010.
TIAS 10-201.2

Protocol to the treaty of February 23, 1995, as contemplated by Article 3(2) of the Agreement on Mutual Legal Assistance between the United States of America and the European Union signed June 25, 2003.
Signed at Vienna July 20, 2005.
Entered into force February 1, 2010.
TIAS 10-201.24

Agreement concerning the sharing of confiscated proceeds of crimes.
Signed at Vienna June 29, 2010.
Entered into force March 15, 2011.
TIAS 11-315

Agreement on enhancing cooperation in preventing and combating serious crime, with annex.*
Signed at Vienna November 15, 2010.
Entered into force May 4, 2012.
TIAS 12-504.1

Note:

* Agreement entered into force May 4, 2012, with the exception of Articles 7 through 9. In accordance with Article 27, Articles 7 through 9 may enter into force in the future under conditions specified in Article 27.

OCCUPATION & PEACEKEEPING

Agreement relating to occupation costs of United States forces in Austria subsequent to June 30, 1947.
Signed at Vienna June 21, 1947.
Entered into force July 1, 1947.
61 Stat. 4171; TIAS 1921; 5 Bevans 383; 67 UNTS 99

POSTAL MATTERS

Parcel post convention.
Signed at Vienna February 16 and at Washington March 1, 1928.
Entered into force March 1, 1928.
45 Stat. 2468; Post Office Department print

Agreement for collection-delivery service.
Signed at Vienna November 8 and at Washington December 11, 1929.
Entered into force December 1, 1929.
46 Stat. 2427; Post Office Department print

Agreement relating to international express mail with memorandum of understanding.
Exchange of letters at Washington and Vienna August 6 and September 4, 1986.
Entered into force February 2, 1987.
TIAS 11391

PROPERTY

Agreement concerning the disposition of certain United States property in Austria.
Signed at Vienna September 26, 1955.
Entered into force September 26, 1955.
7 UST 223; TIAS 3499; 272 UNTS 31.

Agreement regarding the return of Austrian property, rights and interests, with schedule and annex.
Signed at Washington January 30, 1959.
Entered into force May 19, 1964.
15 UST 439; TIAS 5577; 511 UNTS 145

PUBLICATIONS

Agreement for the exchange of official publications.
Exchange of notes at Washington March 11 and 23, 1949.
Entered into force March 23, 1949.
63 Stat. 2434; TIAS 1927; 5 Bevans 422; 43 UNTS 127

SOCIAL SECURITY

Agreement on social security, with administrative arrangement.
Signed at Vienna July 13, 1990.
Entered into force November 1, 1991.
TIAS 12037

Amendment:
October 5, 1995 (TIAS 12696; 1974 UNTS 470)

TAXATION

Convention for the avoidance of double taxation and the prevention of fiscal evasion with respect to taxes on estates, inheritances, gifts and generation-skipping transfers.
Signed at Vienna June 21, 1982.
Entered into force July 1, 1983.
TIAS 10570

Convention for the avoidance of double taxation and the prevention of fiscal evasion with respect to taxes on income, with memorandum of understanding.
Signed at Vienna May 31, 1996.
Entered into force February 1, 1998.
TIAS; 2009 UNTS 309

Agreement for cooperation to facilitate the implementation of the Foreign Account Tax Compliance Act, with annexes.
Signed at Vienna April 29, 2014.
Entered into force December 9, 2014.
TIAS 14-1209.3.

TELECOMMUNICATION

Agreement relating to the operation of amateur radio stations.
Signed at Vienna November 21, 1967.
Entered into force December 21, 1967.
18 UST 2878; TIAS 6378; 634 UNTS 43

TRADE & INVESTMENT

Treaty of friendship, commerce and consular rights.
Signed at Vienna June 19, 1928.
Entered into force May 27, 1931.
47 Stat. 1876; TS 838; 5 Bevans 341; 118 LNTS 241

Supplementary agreement to the treaty of friendship, commerce and consular rights of June 19, 1928.
Signed at Vienna January 20, 1931.
Entered into force May 27, 1931.
47 Stat. 1899; TS 839; 5 Bevans 372; 118 LNTS 259

TRANSPORTATION

Agreement for reciprocal acceptance of certificates of airworthiness for imported aircraft.
Exchange of notes at Washington April 30, 1959.
Entered into force April 30, 1959.
10 UST 796; TIAS 4219; 343 UNTS 41

Memorandum of agreement relating to the provision of flight inspection services.
Signed at Washington and Vienna March 10 and June 22, 1978.
Entered into force June 22, 1978; effective April 1, 1978.
30 UST 288; TIAS 9200

Air services agreement, with annexes.*
Signed at Vienna March 16, 1989.
Entered into force June 2, 1989.
TIAS 11265

Amendment:
June 14, 1995 (TIAS 11503)*

Note:
* This agreement is suspended for the duration of provisional application of the U.S. – E.U. Air Transport Agreement signed April 25 and 30, 2007.

AZERBAIJAN

For agreements prior to December 31, 1991, see UNION OF SOVIET SOCIALIST REPUBLICS.

CULTURAL EXCHANGES, PROPERTY & COOPERATION

Agreement concerning the program of the Peace Corps in the Republic of Azerbaijan.
Signed at Baku October 8, 2003.
Entered into force February 3, 2004.
TIAS 04-203.

DEFENSE

Agreement concerning the provision of training relating to defense articles under the United States International Military Education and Training (IMET) Program.
Exchange of notes at Baku May 8 and June 14, 2002.
Entered into force June 14, 2002.
TIAS 02-614

Acquisition and cross-servicing agreement, with annexes.
Signed at Baku and Stuttgart October 14 and October 30, 2013.
Entered into force January 23, 2014.
NP

EDUCATION

Agreement on educational cooperation.
Signed at Baku June 19, 2008.
Entered into force June 22, 2010.
TIAS 10-622

EMPLOYMENT

Agreement relating to the employment of dependents of official government employees.
Exchange of notes at Washington February 10 and March 8, 1995.
Entered into force March 8, 1995.
TIAS 12608

FINANCE

Investment incentive agreement.
Signed at Washington September 28, 1992.
Entered into force January 17, 1995.
TIAS

FOREIGN ASSISTANCE

Agreement regarding cooperation to facilitate the provision of assistance.
Signed at Baku May 11, 2000.
Entered into force August 21, 2000.
TIAS 13093

INTERNATIONAL CRIMINAL COURT

Agreement regarding the surrender of persons to the International Criminal Court.
Signed at Washington February 26, 2003.
Entered into force August 28, 2003.
TIAS 03-828

LAW ENFORCEMENT

Agreement on mutual assistance and cooperation in customs matters.
Signed at Baku February 7, 2007.
Entered into force June 25, 2007.
TIAS 07-625

NONPROLIFERATION

Implementing arrangement for cooperation in the prevention of illicit trafficking in nuclear and other radioactive material.
Signed at Baku December 8, 2005.
Entered into force December 8, 2005.
TIAS 05-1208

POSTAL MATTERS

Postal money order agreement.
Signed at Baku and Washington April 3 and May 17, 1996.
Entered into force May 17, 1996.
NP

PROPERTY

Agreement concerning the acquisition and retention of diplomatic and consular properties in the United States of America and the Republic of Azerbaijan.
Signed at Baku March 5 and April 21, 1999.
Entered into force June 8, 1999.
TIAS

TAXATION

Agreement to improve international tax compliance and to implement the Foreign Account Tax Compliance Act, with annexes.
Signed at Baku September 9, 2015.
Entered into force November 5, 2015.
TIAS 15-1105.

TRADE & INVESTMENT

Agreement on trade relations, with exchanges of letters.
Signed at Washington April 12, 1993.
Entered into force April 21, 1995.
TIAS

Treaty concerning the encouragement and reciprocal protection of investment, with annex.
Signed at Washington August 1, 1997.
Entered into force August 2, 2001.
TIAS 01-802
Amendment:
August 8 and 25, 2000 (TIAS 01-802)

TRANSPORTATION

Agreement for the provision of technical assistance in developing, modernizing, operating and maintaining the civil aviation infrastructure in the Republic of Azerbaijan.
Signed at Washington and Baku September 10 and 18, 2013.
Entered into force September 18, 2013.
NP

Air transport agreement.
Signed at Baku April 6, 2016.
Entered into force June 14, 2016.
TIAS 16-614

WEAPONS

Agreement concerning cooperation in the area of counter-proliferation of weapons of mass destruction and defense activities.
Signed at Washington September 28, 1999.
Entered into force May 7, 2003.
TIAS 03-507
Amendment:
December 29, 2011(TIAS 03-507)

Agreement concerning cooperation in preventing the proliferation of weapons of mass destruction.
Signed at Baku January 2, 2004.
Entered into force January 2, 2004.
TIAS 04-102
Amendments:
September 29 and October 28, 2004 (TIAS 04-102)
August 1 and 26, 2005 (TIAS 04-102)
June 28 and July 11, 2006 (TIAS 04-102)
March 7 and April 24, 2007 (TIAS 04-102)
February 18 and March 5, 2008 (TIAS 04-102)
April 13 and May 8, 2009 (TIAS 04-102).

Agreement concerning cooperation in the area of prevention of proliferation of technology, pathogens and expertise that could be used in the development of biological weapons.
Signed at Baku and Washington May 6 and June 6, 2005.
Entered into force June 6, 2005.
TIAS 05-606
Amendments:
June 12 and 23, 2006 (TIAS 05-606)
February 28 and March 6, 2007 (TIAS 05-606)
September 12 and October 5, 2007 (TIAS 05-606)
February 13 and March 5, 2008 (TIAS 05-606)
April 13 and August 13, 2009 (TIAS 05-606)

B

THE BAHAMAS

On July 10, 1973, The Bahamas became an independent state. In a note dated July 10, 1973, to the Secretary-General of the United Nations, the Prime Minister made a statement reading in part as follows:

I have the honour, further to inform you that the Government of the Commonwealth of The Bahamas, conscious of the desirability of maintaining existing legal relationships, and conscious of its obligations under international law to honour its treaty commitments, acknowledges that many treaty rights and obligations of the Government of the United Kingdom in respect of The Bahamas were succeeded to by the Commonwealth of The Bahamas upon Independence by virtue of customary international law.

Since, however, it is likely that in virtue of customary international law certain treaties may have lapsed at the date of Independence of the Commonwealth of The Bahamas, it seems essential that each treaty should be subjected to legal examination. It is proposed, after this examination has been completed, to indicate which, if any, of the treaties which may have lapsed by customary international law the Government of the Commonwealth of The Bahamas wishes to treat as having lapsed.

It is desired that it be presumed that each treaty has been legally succeeded to by the Commonwealth of The Bahamas and that action be based on this presumption until a decision is reached that the treaty should be regarded as having lapsed. Should the Government of the Commonwealth of The Bahamas be of the opinion that it has legally succeeded to a treaty, and wishes to terminate the operation of the treaty, it will in due course give notice of termination in the terms thereof.

DEFENSE

Arrangement between the United States and the United Kingdom relating to naval and air bases.
Exchange of notes at Washington September 2, 1940.
Entered into force September 2, 1940.
54 Stat. 2405; EAS 181; 12 Bevans 551; 203 LNTS 201

Agreement between the United States and the United Kingdom regarding leased naval and air bases, and exchanges of notes.
Signed at London March 27, 1941.
Entered into force March 27, 1941.
55 Stat. 1560; EAS 235; 12 Bevans 560; 204 LNTS 15

Agreement between the United States and the United Kingdom amending articles IV and VI of the leased bases agreement of March 27, 1941.
Exchange of notes at Washington July 19 and August 1, 1950.
Entered into force August 1, 1950.
1 UST 585; TIAS 2105; 88 UNTS 273

Agreement between the United States and the United Kingdom for the establishment of oceanographic research stations in the Bahama Islands.
Signed at Washington November 1, 1957.
Entered into force November 1, 1957.
8 UST 1741; TIAS 3927; 299 UNTS 167

Amendment:
May 12, 1960 (11 UST 1405; TIAS 4479; 372 UNTS 364)

Agreement between the United States and the United Kingdom concerning the establishment in the Bahama Islands of a long range aid to navigation station.
Signed at Washington June 24, 1960.
Entered into force June 24, 1960.
11 UST 1587; TIAS 4502; 377 UNTS 63

Understanding between the United States and the United Kingdom relating to the use by Bahamian organizations of certain land at the United States Navy Base, Georgetown, Great Exuma Island, with map and schedule.
Exchange of notes at Nassau June 19, September 12, and November 2, 1972.
Entered into force November 2, 1972.
23 UST 3688; TIAS 7514

Agreement concerning United States defense facilities in The Bahamas, with annex, agreed minute, exchanges of notes and implementing arrangement, with maps.
Signed at Washington April 5, 1984.
Entered into force April 5, 1984; effective January 26, 1983.
TIAS 11058; 2034 UNTS 189

Amendment:
September 22 and October 7, 1992

Note:
See also agreement of April 5, 1984, under UNITED KINGDOM — DEFENSE.

Agreement regarding grants under the Foreign Assistance Act of 1961, as amended, or successor legislation, and the furnishing of defense articles, defense services and related training, including pursuant to the United States International Military and Education Training (IMET) Program.
Exchange of notes at Nassau July 11 and September 13, 2006.
Entered into force September 13, 2006.
NP

Agreement regarding the Caribbean Basin Security Initiative and the provisions of technical support for maritime security forces (Technical Assistance Field Team).
Effected by Exchange of Notes at Nassau October 15, 2012 and June 11, 2013.
Entered into force June 11, 2013.
TIAS 13-611

DIPLOMATIC & CONSULAR RELATIONS

Consular convention between the United States and the United Kingdom.
Signed at Washington June 6, 1951.
Entered into force September 7, 1952.
3 UST 3426; TIAS 2494; 165 UNTS 121

EMPLOYMENT

Agreement relating to the employment of dependents of official government employees.
Exchange of notes at Nassau April 7 and 8, 2005.
Entered into force April 8, 2005.
TIAS 05-408

FINANCE

Agreement on investment insurance and guaranties.
Exchange of notes at Nassau April 5, 1983, and September 27, 1984.
Entered into force September 27, 1984.
TIAS 10997; 2021 UNTS 333

INTELLECTUAL PROPERTY

Declaration by the United States and the United Kingdom affording reciprocal protection to trademarks.
Signed at London October 24, 1877.
Entered into force October 24, 1877.
20 Stat. 703; TS 138; 12 Bevans 198

LAW ENFORCEMENT

Agreement between the United States and the United Kingdom relating to the prevention of abuses of customs privileges at certain leased naval and air bases.
Exchange of notes at Washington January 18 and February 21, 1946.
Entered into force February 21, 1946.
61 Stat. 2637; TIAS 1592; 12 Bevans 739; 6 UNTS 137

Agreement for the interdiction of narcotics trafficking.
Signed at Nassau March 6, 1985.
Entered into force March 6, 1985.
TIAS 11123; 2120 UNTS 75

Agreement on the control of narcotic drugs and psychotropic substances, with appendix.
Signed at Nassau February 17, 1989.
Entered into force February 17, 1989.
TIAS 11602; 2190 UNTS 363

Treaty on mutual assistance in criminal matters.
Signed at Nassau June 12 and August 18, 1987.
Entered into force July 18, 1990.
TIAS

Agreement correcting the text of the treaty on mutual assistance in criminal matters of June 12 and August 18, 1987, with attachments.
Exchange of notes at Nassau January 27 and February 4, 1988.
Entered into force February 4, 1988.
TIAS

Extradition treaty.
Signed at Nassau March 9, 1990.
Entered into force September 22, 1994.
TIAS

MARITIME MATTERS

Agreement relating to jurisdiction over vessels utilizing the Louisiana Offshore Oil Port.
Exchange of notes at Nassau September 23 and October 5, 1982.
Entered into force October 5, 1982.
35 UST 3842; TIAS 10888; 2014 UNTS 451

Agreement concerning cooperation in maritime law enforcement.
Signed at Nassau June 29, 2004.
Entered into force June 29, 2004.
TIAS 04-629

POSTAL MATTERS

Money order agreement.
Signed at Washington June 22, 1921, and at Nassau July 7, 1921.
Operative August 1, 1921.
NP

Agreement concerning the exchange of parcel post, with regulations of execution.
Signed at Nassau October 29, 1936, and at Washington December 21, 1936.
Operative November 1, 1936.
50 Stat. 1472; Post Office Department print; 176 LNTS 411

International express mail agreement, with detailed regulations.
Signed at Nassau and Washington June 24 and July 17, 1985.
Entered into force September 9, 1985.
TIAS 11153; 2126 UNTS 177.

Memorandum of understanding concerning the INTELPOST service, with details of implementation.
Signed at Nassau and Washington September 15 and October 7, 1987.
Entered into force November 1, 1987.
TIAS 11544

PROPERTY

Convention between the United States and the United Kingdom relating to tenure and disposition of real and personal property.
Signed at Washington March 2, 1899.
Applicable to the Bahamas February 9, 1901.
31 Stat. 1939; TS 146; 12 Bevans 246

Supplementary convention relating to the tenure and disposition of real and personal property.
Signed at Washington May 27, 1936.
Entered into force March 10, 1941.
55 Stat. 1101; TS 964; 5 Bevans 140; 203 LNTS 367

SCIENTIFIC & TECHNICAL COOPERATION

Agreement relating to the continuation of a cooperative meteorological program in the Bahama Islands with memoranda of arrangement.
Exchange of notes at Nassau October 14, 1982, and August 25, 1983.
Entered into force August 25, 1983; effective July 2, 1982.
35 UST 3570; TIAS 10868; 2014 UNTS 457

SOCIAL SECURITY

Agreement relating to United States participation in the national insurance scheme of The Bahamas, with related note.
Exchange of notes at Nassau October 27, 1976, May 6 and September 23, 1977.
Entered into force September 23, 1977; effective October 7, 1974.
29 UST 2423; TIAS 8946

TAXATION

Agreement concerning the reciprocal exemption from income tax of income derived from the international operation of ships and aircraft.
Exchange of notes at Washington June 26 and July 16, 1987.
Entered into force July 16, 1987.
TIAS 11276; 2174 UNTS 371

Agreement to implement the Foreign Account Tax Compliance Act, with annexes and exchange of correcting notes.
Signed at Nassau November 3, 2014.
Entered into force September 17, 2015.
TIAS 15-917.1

TELECOMMUNICATION

Agreement between the United States and the United Kingdom relating to the reciprocal granting of authorizations to permit licensed amateur radio operators of either country to operate their stations in the other country.
Exchange of notes at London November 26, 1965.
Applicable to the Bahamas December 11, 1969.
16 UST 2047; TIAS 5941; 561 UNTS 193

Agreement between the United States and the United Kingdom extending to certain territories the application of the agreement of November 26, 1965, relating to the reciprocal granting of authorizations to permit licensed amateur radio operators of either country to operate their stations in the other country.
Exchange of notes at London December 11, 1969.
Entered into force December 11, 1969.
20 UST 4089; TIAS 6800; 732 UNTS 334

Agreement relating to pre-sunrise operations of certain standard broadcasting stations.
Exchange of notes at Nassau January 30 and September 4, 1974.
Entered into force September 4, 1974.
25 UST 2478; TIAS 7929

TRANSPORTATION

Agreement between the United States and the United Kingdom relating to air services.
Signed at Bermuda February 11, 1946.
Entered into force February 11, 1946.
60 Stat. 1499; TIAS 1507; 12 Bevans 726; 3 UNTS 253

Agreement on preclearance for entry into the United States, with annex.
Signed at Nassau April 23, 1974.
Entered into force April 23, 1974.
25 UST 646; TIAS 7816
Related Agreement:
December 28, 1977, and January 10, 1978 (29 UST 4645; TIAS 9072)

Memorandum of agreement for the provision of assistance in developing and modernizing the civil aviation infrastructure of The Bahamas.
Signed at Washington and Nassau December 14, 1998, and January 8, 1999.
Entered into force January 8, 1999.
NP

Memorandum of agreement concerning the deployment of air marshals, with attachment.
Signed at Nassau and Washington October 5 and 20, 2011.
Entered into force October 20, 2011.
TIAS 11-1020

BAHRAIN

CULTURAL EXCHANGES, PROPERTY & COOPERATION

Agreement relating to the establishment of a Peace Corps program in Bahrain.
Exchange of notes at Manama April 24 and June 12, 1973.
Entered into force June 12, 1973.
24 UST 1762; TIAS 7684

DEFENSE

General security of military information agreement.
Signed at Manama January 17, 1988.
Entered into force January 17, 1988.
TIAS

Agreement regarding grants under the Foreign Assistance Act of 1961, as amended, and the furnishing of defense articles, related training and other defense services from the United States to Bahrain.
Exchange of notes at Manama July 18, August 8, August 19, and August 29, 1992.
Entered into force August 29, 1992.
TIAS

Cross servicing agreement, with annexes.
Signed at Washington January 20, 1994.
Entered into force January 20, 1994.
TIAS 12259
Amendments:
November 17, 2001
November 21, 2003, and January 6, 2004

EMPLOYMENT

Agreement concerning bilateral work agreement for dependents of officials serving in Bahrain.
Exchange of notes at Manama February 26 and 27, 2007.
Entered into force February 27, 2007.
TIAS 07-227

ENVIRONMENT & CONSERVATION

Agreement for cooperation in the Global Learning and Observations to Benefit the Environment (GLOBE) Program, with appendices.
Signed at Manama June 16, 2001.
Entered into force June 16, 2001.
TIAS 13154

FINANCE

Investment incentive agreement.
Signed at Manama April 25, 1987.
Entered into force April 25, 1987.
TIAS 12091

LAW ENFORCEMENT

Agreement regarding mutual assistance between customs administrations.
Signed at Washington November 5, 2010.
Entered into force July 2, 2013.
TIAS 13-702

POSTAL MATTERS

International express mail agreement, with detailed regulations.
Signed at Bahrain and Washington April 22 and July 28, 1982.
Entered into force August 1, 1982.
34 UST 1883; TIAS 10469; 1750 UNTS 477

TAXATION

Agreement to exempt from income tax certain income derived from the international operation of a ship or ships and aircraft.
Exchange of notes at Manama September 1 and 12, 1999.
Entered into force September 12, 1999.
TIAS 13059

TRADE & INVESTMENT

Treaty concerning the encouragement and reciprocal protection of investment, with annex.
Signed at Washington September 29, 1999.
Entered into force May 30, 2001.
TIAS 13065

Agreement on the establishment of a free trade area, with annexes and related exchange of letters.
Signed at Washington September 14, 2004.
Entered into force August 1, 2006.
TIAS

TRANSPORTATION

Civil aviation security agreement.
Signed at Manama November 15, 1992.
Entered into force November 15, 1992.
TIAS 11912

Air transport agreement, with annexes.
Signed at Washington May 24, 1999.
Entered into force July 6, 2001.
TIAS 13035

BANGLADESH

CULTURAL EXCHANGES, PROPERTY & COOPERATION

Agreement concerning the establishment of a Peace Corps program in Bangladesh.
Signed at Washington July 13, 1978.
Entered into force July 13, 1978.
30 UST 1734; TIAS 9283; 1153 UNTS 95

DEFENSE

Memorandum of understanding concerning an exchange of officers.
Signed at Dhaka May 18, 1989.
Entered into force May 18, 1989.
TIAS 11680

Memorandum of understanding to specify the legal status of the United States Pacific Command Disaster Relief Task Force.
Signed at Dhaka May 20, 1991.
Entered into force May 20, 1991.
NP

Agreement regarding military assistance under the Foreign Assistance Act of 1961, as amended, and the furnishing of defense articles, related training and other defense services from the United States to Bangladesh.
Exchange of notes at Dhaka September 18 and October 3, 1994.
Entered into force October 3, 1994.
TIAS 12273

Memorandum of understanding international concerning exercise Cope South.
Signed at Dhaka August 5 and September 14, 1998.
Entered into force September 14, 1998.
TIAS

ENVIRONMENT & CONSERVATION

Agreement for cooperation in the Global Learning and Observations to Benefit the Environment (GLOBE) Program, with appendices.
Signed at Dhaka October 4, 2000.
Entered into force October 4, 2000.
TIAS 00-1004

FINANCE

Agreement relating to establishment of a trust account for payment by Bangladesh of certain development assistance program expenses, with related letter.
Signed at Dhaka July 1, 1974.
Entered into force July 1, 1974.
TIAS 7918; 25 UST 2403

Agreement relating to consolidation and rescheduling of certain debts owed to the United States, with annexes.
Signed at Washington March 3, 1976.
Entered into force May 11, 1976.
27 UST 4020; TIAS 8423; 1059 UNTS 21

Investment incentive agreement.
Signed at Washington May 19, 1998.
Entered into force May 19, 1998.
TIAS 12954

Agreement regarding the reduction of certain debt related to agricultural trade owed to the Government of the United States and its agencies, with appendix.
Signed at Washington September 12, 2000.
Entered into force September 12, 2000.
NP

Agreement concerning the establishment of a Tropical Forest Fund and a Tropical Forest Conservation Board.
Signed at Washington September 12, 2000.
Entered into force September 12, 2000.
TIAS
Amendment:
August 15, 2002, and January 13, 2003

FOREIGN ASSISTANCE

Economic, technical and related assistance agreement, with related letter.
Signed at Dhaka May 21, 1974.
Entered into force May 21, 1974.
25 UST 1454; TIAS 7877

AGENCY FOR INTERNATIONAL DEVELOPMENT

Agreement for disaster reconstruction and mitigation, with annex.
Signed September 11 and 29, 2008.
Entered into force September 29, 2008.
Amendments:
September 29, 2008 (NP)
May 21, 2009 (NP)
September 6, 2009 (NP)
September 15, 2009 (NP)

INTERNATIONAL CRIMINAL COURT

Agreement regarding the surrender of persons to the International Criminal Court.
Signed at Washington August 18, 2003.
Entered into force March 29, 2004.
TIAS 04-329

POSTAL MATTERS

International express mail memorandum of understanding, with detailed regulations.
Signed at Dhaka and Washington April 9 and 17, 1987.
Entered into force June 1, 1987.
TIAS 11303

Memorandum of understanding concerning operation of the INTELPOST service, with details of implementation.
Signed at Dhaka and Washington May 16 and 24, 1989.
Entered into force June 15, 1989.
TIAS 11682

TAXATION

Convention for the avoidance of double taxation and the prevention of fiscal evasion with respect to taxes on income, with exchange of notes.
Done at Dhaka September 26, 2004.
Entered into force August 7, 2006.
TIAS 06-807

TRADE & INVESTMENT

Treaty concerning the reciprocal encouragement and protection of investment, with annex, protocol and exchange of letters.
Signed at Washington March 12, 1986.
Entered into force July 25, 1989.
TIAS

TRANSPORTATION

Agreement on aviation security.
Exchange of notes at Dhaka November 23, 1992, and August 23, 1993.
Entered into force August 23, 1993.
TIAS 12160

Memorandum of agreement for the provision of technical assistance in further developing, modernizing, operating, or maintaining the civil aviation infrastructure in Bangladesh.
Signed August 25 and November 4, 2010.
Entered into force November 4, 2010.
NP

BARBADOS

On November 30, 1966, Barbados became an independent state. In a note dated February 10, 1967, to the Secretary-General of the United Nations, the Prime Minister and Minister of External Affairs made a statement reading in part as follows:

I have the honour to inform you that the Government of Barbados, conscious of the desirability of maintaining existing legal relationships, and conscious of its obligation under international law to honour its treaty commitments, acknowledges that many treaty rights and obligations of the Government of the United Kingdom in respect of Barbados were succeeded to by Barbados upon independence by virtue of customary international law.

2. Since, however, it is likely that by virtue of customary international law certain treaties may have lapsed at the date of independence of Barbados, it seems essential that each treaty should be subjected to legal examination. It is proposed after this examination has been completed, to indicate which, if any, of the treaties which may have lapsed by customary international law the Government of Barbados wishes to treat as having lapsed.

3. It is desired that it be presumed that each treaty has been legally succeeded to by Barbados and that action be based on this presumption until a decision is reached that it should be regarded as having lapsed. Should the Government of Barbados be of the opinion that it has legally succeeded to a treaty and wishes to terminate the operation of the treaty, it will in due course give notice of termination in the terms thereof.

CULTURAL EXCHANGES, PROPERTY & COOPERATION

Agreement relating to the establishment of a Peace Corps program in Barbados.
Exchange of notes at Bridgetown May 10 and June 8, 1982.
Entered into force June 8, 1982.
34 UST 1257; TIAS 10413

DEFENSE

Agreement concerning the provision of training related to defense articles under the United States International Military Education and Training (IMET) Program.
Exchange of notes at Bridgetown March 6 and April 3, 1980.
Entered into force April 3, 1980.
32 UST 960; TIAS 9743; 1234 UNTS 321

Agreement regarding articles, services and associated training transferred to the Government of Barbados for anti-narcotics purposes.
Exchange of notes at Bridgetown November 13, 1998, and June 30, 1999.
Entered into force June 30, 1999.
TIAS

Agreement regarding the Caribbean Basin Security Initiative and the provision of technical support for maritime security forces (Technical Assistance Field Team).
Effected by Exchange of Notes at Bridgetown June 29, 2012 and June 27, 2013.
Entered into force June 27, 2013.
TIAS 13-627.1

DIPLOMATIC & CONSULAR RELATIONS

Consular convention between the United States and the United Kingdom.
Signed at Washington June 6, 1951.
Entered into force September 7, 1952.
3 UST 3426; TIAS 2494; 165 UNTS 121

Agreement continuing in force between the United States and Barbados the consular convention of June 6, 1951, between the United States and the United Kingdom.
Exchange of notes at Bridgetown September 14, 1972, and May 10, 1973.
Entered into force May 10, 1973.
24 UST 1803; TIAS 7693

FINANCE

Agreement relating to investment guaranties.
Signed at Bridgetown March 11, 1968.
Entered into force March 11, 1968.
19 UST 4692; TIAS 6463; 698 UNTS 87

FOREIGN ASSISTANCE

General agreement for economic, technical and related assistance.
Signed at Bridgetown September 14, 1983.
Entered into force September 14, 1983.
35 UST 2943; TIAS 10829; 1590 UNTS 153

INTELLECTUAL PROPERTY

Declaration by the United States and the United Kingdom affording reciprocal protection to trademarks.
Signed at London October 24, 1877.
Entered into force October 24, 1877.
20 Stat. 703; TS 138; 12 Bevans 198

LAW ENFORCEMENT

Extradition treaty.
Signed at Bridgetown February 28, 1996.
Entered into force March 3, 2000.
TIAS 00-303

Treaty on mutual legal assistance in criminal matters, with forms.
Signed at Bridgetown February 28, 1996.
Entered into force March 3, 2000.
TIAS 00-303.1

MARITIME MATTERS

Agreement concerning cooperation in suppressing illicit maritime drug trafficking.
Signed at Bridgetown June 25, 1997.
Entered into force October 11, 1998.
TIAS 12872

OCCUPATION & PEACEKEEPING

Agreement for the furnishing of commodities and services in connection with the peacekeeping force for Grenada.
Exchange of notes at Bridgetown November 25, 1983, and January 12, 1984.
Entered into force January 12, 1984.
35 UST 4245; TIAS 10922; 2015 UNTS 115

POSTAL MATTERS

Convention for the exchange of postal money orders.
Signed at Washington September 27 and at Bridgetown November 30, 1933.
Operative October 1, 1933.
NP

Agreement for the exchange of parcels by parcel post, and detailed regulations.
Signed at Washington and Bridgetown August 14 and September 13, 1939.
Entered into force November 1, 1939.
54 Stat. 1838; Post Office Department print; 199 LNTS 375

International express mail agreement, with detailed regulations.
Signed at Hamburg June 27, 1984.
Entered into force October 1, 1984.
TIAS 11006; 2021 UNTS 343

Memorandum of understanding concerning the operation of the INTELPOST service, with details of implementation.
Signed at Bridgetown and Washington October 18 and 26, 1989.
Entered into force February 15, 1990.
TIAS 11704

PROPERTY

Convention between the United States and the United Kingdom relating to the tenure and disposition of real and personal property.
Signed at Washington March 2, 1899.
Applicable to Barbados February 9, 1901.
31 Stat. 1939; TS 146; 12 Bevans 246

Supplementary convention relating to the tenure and disposition of real and personal property.
Signed at Washington May 27, 1936.
Entered into force March 10, 1941.
55 Stat. 1101; TS 964; 5 Bevans 140; 203 LNTS 367

SCIENTIFIC & TECHNICAL COOPERATION

Agreement between the United States and the United Kingdom providing for a tropical meteorological research program (including Project Harp) in Barbados.
Exchange of notes at Bridgetown January 7 and 15, 1963.
Entered into force January 15, 1963.
14 UST 109; TIAS 5276; 466 UNTS 181

Agreement relating to a cooperative program for operation and maintenance of a rawinsonde station at Seawell Airport, Barbados.
Exchange of notes at Bridgetown October 13, 1975.
Entered into force October 13, 1975;effective July 1, 1970.
26 UST 2557; TIAS 8174; 1028 UNTS 37

TAXATION

Agreement for the exchange of information with respect to taxes.
Signed at Washington November 3, 1984.
Entered into force November 3, 1984.
TIAS 11203; 2143 UNTS 277

Convention for the avoidance of double taxation and the prevention of fiscal evasion with respect to taxes on income, with exchange of notes.*
Signed at Bridgetown December 31, 1984.
Entered into force February 28, 1986.
TIAS 11090; 2120 UNTS 197

Protocol amending the convention for the avoidance of double taxation and the prevention of fiscal evasion with respect to taxes on income signed December 31, 1984, with exchange of notes and understandings.*
Signed at Washington December 18, 1991.
Entered into force December 29, 1993.
TIAS

Note:
* With reservation.

Second protocol amending the convention of December 31, 1984, as amended, for the avoidance of double taxation and the prevention of fiscal evasion with respect to taxes on income.
Signed at Washington July 14, 2004.
Entered into force December 20, 2004.
TIAS

Agreement to improve international tax compliance and to implement the Foreign Account Tax Compliance Act, with annexes.
Signed at Bridgetown November 17, 2014.
Entered into force September 25, 2015.
TIAS 15-925

TELECOMMUNICATION

Agreement relating to the reciprocal granting of authorizations to permit licensed amateur radio operators of either country to operate their stations in the other country.
Exchange of notes at Bridgetown September 10 and 12, 1968.
Entered into force September 12, 1968.
19 UST 5994; TIAS 6553; 702 UNTS 175

TRANSPORTATION

Air transport agreement.
Signed at Bridgetown May 5, 2015.
Entered into force May 5, 2015.
TIAS 15-505

BELARUS

For agreements prior to December 31, 1991, see UNION OF SOVIET SOCIALIST REPUBLICS.

ATOMIC ENERGY

Agreement regarding assurances concerning the provision of technical assistance that may be provided by the Government of the United States, through the Department of Energy, to support the transfer of fresh and spent nuclear fuel from the Joint Institute for Physics and Nuclear Research at Minsk, Republic of Belarus to the Russian Federation, and security enhancement of the reactor site and nuclear materials stored at the site.
Exchange of notes at Minsk July 5 and October 1, 2010.
Entered into force October 1, 2010.
TIAS 10-1001.1

EMPLOYMENT

Agreement relating to the employment of dependents of official government employees.
Exchange of notes at Washington June 14 and July 26, 1996.
Entered into force July 26, 1996.
TIAS 12786

FINANCE

Investment incentive agreement.
Signed at Minsk June 24, 1992.
Entered into force June 24, 1992.
TIAS 12460

FOREIGN ASSISTANCE

Agreement regarding cooperation to facilitate the provision of assistance.
Signed at Minsk July 18, 1996.
Entered into force provisionally July 18, 1996; definitively December 21, 2001.
TIAS

LAW ENFORCEMENT

Agreement regarding cooperation and mutual assistance between their customs services.
Exchange of notes at Minsk January 14, 1994.
Entered into force January 14, 1994.
TIAS 12531

POSTAL MATTERS

International express mail agreement, with detailed regulations.
Signed at Minsk and Washington September 21 and November 8, 1993.
Entered into force January 1, 1994.
NP

TAXATION

Agreement to improve international tax compliance and to implement the Foreign Account Tax Compliance Act, with annexes.
Signed at Minsk March 18, 2015.
Entered into force July 29, 2015.
TIAS 15-729

TRADE & INVESTMENT

Agreement on trade relations.
Exchange of notes at Minsk January 6 and February 16, 1993.
Entered into force February 16, 1993.
TIAS 12488

WEAPONS

Agreement concerning control, accounting and physical protection of nuclear material to promote the prevention of nuclear weapons proliferation.
Signed at Minsk June 23, 1995.
Entered into force June 23, 1995.
TIAS

BELGIUM

ATOMIC ENERGY

Arrangement for the exchange of technical information and cooperation in nuclear safety matters, with addenda and annex.
Signed at Vienna September 24, 2014.
Entered into force September 24, 2014.
TIAS 14-924

CLAIMS & DISPUTE RESOLUTION

Treaty of arbitration.
Signed at Washington March 20, 1929.
Entered into force August 25, 1930.
46 Stat. 2790; TS 823; 5 Bevans 547; 109 LNTS 267

Treaty of conciliation.
Signed at Washington March 20, 1929.
Entered into force August 25, 1930.
46 Stat. 2794; TS 824; 5 Bevans 549; 109 LNTS 261

Agreement relating to reciprocity on indemnification for war damages to private property.
Exchanges of notes at Brussels December 5, 1949, March 17 and December 1, 1950, and March 12, 1951.
Entered into force March 12, 1951.
2 UST 943; TIAS 2248; 93 UNTS 109

Arrangement on the settlement of claims for indexing pensions, with annexes.
Signed at Washington September 15, 2015.
Entered into force September 15, 2015.
TIAS 15-915

CONSULAR AFFAIRS

Agreement relating to the reciprocal waiver of visas and visa fees.*
Exchange of notes at Brussels May 3 and 23, 1962.
Entered into force May 23, 1962; operative June 22, 1962.
13 UST 1246; TIAS 5071; 434 UNTS 133
Amendment:
March 9 and April 20, 1971 (22 UST 678; TIAS 7124; 778 UNTS 227)

Note
* The status of this agreement is under review.

CULTURAL EXCHANGES, PROPERTY & COOPERATION

Agreement concerning American military cemeteries, and related note of December 24, 1959.
Signed at Brussels November 27, 1959.
Entered into force November 27, 1959.
10 UST 2124; TIAS 4383; 366 UNTS 331
Amendment:
January 8, 1962, and October 24, 1963 (14 UST 1542; TIAS 5455; 489 UNTS 393)

DEFENSE

Mutual defense assistance agreement.
Signed at Washington January 27, 1950.
Entered into force March 30, 1950.
1 UST 1; TIAS 2010; 51 UNTS 213

Agreement relating to the assurances required under the Mutual Security Act of 1951.
Exchange of notes at Brussels January 7, 1952.
Entered into force January 7, 1952.
3 UST 4529; TIAS 2601; 179 UNTS 81

Agreement concerning export licenses for goods bought in the Belgo-Luxembourg Economic Union for common defense effort under the offshore procurement program.
Exchange of notes at Brussels June 18, 1953.
Entered into force June 18, 1953.
4 UST 1; TIAS 2760; 222 UNTS 3

Agreement relating to offshore procurement with exchange of notes.
Signed at Brussels September 2, 1953.
Entered into force July 22, 1954.
5 UST 1311; TIAS 3000; 200 UNTS 127

Agreement approving the standard offshore procurement contract with Belgium.
Signed at Brussels November 19, 1953.
Entered into force July 22, 1954.
5 UST 1334; TIAS 3001; 233 UNTS 310
Amendment:
May 13 and July 19, 1954 (5 UST 2254; TIAS 3085; 237 UNTS 342)

Agreement relating to the disposal of redistributable and excess property furnished in connection with the mutual defense assistance program.
Signed at Brussels November 17, 1953.
Entered into force March 10, 1955.
6 UST 495; TIAS 3182; 251 UNTS 105

Agreement concerning the participation of the Belgian forces in United Nations operations in Korea.
Signed at Washington July 15, 1955.
Entered into force July 15, 1955.
6 UST 2829; TIAS 3325; 223 UNTS 3

Agreement relating to a weapons production program.
Exchange of notes at Brussels April 6 and 22, 1960.
Entered into force April 22, 1960.
11 UST 1368; TIAS 4472; 372 UNTS 277

Arrangement pursuant to the mutual defense assistance agreement of January 27, 1950, relating to the disposition of equipment and materials furnished under the mutual defense assistance program.
Exchange of notes at Brussels July 7, 1961.
Entered into force July 7, 1961.
12 UST 1174; TIAS 4830; 416 UNTS 301

Agreement for cooperation on the use of atomic energy for mutual defense purposes.
Signed at Brussels May 17, 1962.
Entered into force September 5, 1962.
13 UST 1995; TIAS 5157; 461 UNTS 3

Agreement concerning certain communications facilities.
Signed at Brussels April 19, 1963.
Entered into force April 19, 1963.
14 UST 414; TIAS 5334; 476 UNTS 29

Memorandum of understanding concerning the principles governing mutual cooperation in the research, development, production, procurement and logistic support of defense equipment.
Signed at Brussels December 12, 1979.
Entered into force December 12, 1979.
NP

Agreement concerning provision of mutual logistic support, with annexes.
Signed at Brussels and Stuttgart May 6 and 11, 1982.
Entered into force May 11, 1982.
TIAS 12275
Amendments:
July 1 and 10, 1991 (TIAS 12275)
May 1 and 22, 1992 (TIAS 12275)
October 27 and 30, 1997

Memorandum of understanding on the exchange of officers between the United States and Belgian air forces.
Signed at Brussels and Washington September 22 and November 2, 1983.
Entered into force November 2, 1983.
35 UST 2417; TIAS 10804

Agreement concerning the status of a U.S. ground launched cruise missile (GLCM) unit to be located in Belgium.
Exchange of notes at Brussels February 13, 1984.
Entered into force February 13, 1984.
35 UST 4407; TIAS 10943

Basic exchange and cooperative agreement concerning mapping, charting and geodesy cooperation.
Signed at Fairfax March 1, 1994.
Entered into force March 1, 1994.
NP

Agreement regarding the status of a category of United States personnel.
Signed at Brussels July 13, 2012.
Entered into force March 26, 2015.
TIAS 15-326

DIPLOMATIC & CONSULAR RELATIONS

Arrangement relating to the granting to diplomatic and consular personnel, on a reciprocal basis, of exemption from duties and import taxes on merchandise imported for their personal use.
Exchange of notes at Brussels February 26 and May 28, 1948.
Entered into force May 28, 1948.
5 Bevans 670

Consular convention with exchanges of notes.
Signed at Washington September 2, 1969.
Entered into force January 5, 1974.
25 UST 41; TIAS 7775

EDUCATION

Agreement for the financing of certain academic and cultural exchanges and programs in the field of education.
Signed at Brussels December 12, 1968.
Entered into force May 13, 1971.
22 UST 1538; TIAS 7175; 806 UNTS 231

EMPLOYMENT

Agreement on the gainful occupation of certain dependents of diplomatic and consular personnel.
Exchange of notes at Brussels February 19 and March 18, 2004.
Entered into force June 1, 2006.
TIAS 06-601

FINANCE

Debt funding agreement.
Signed at Washington August 18, 1925.
Operative June 15, 1925.
Treasury Department print; 5 Bevans 531

Agreement modifying the debt funding agreement of August 18, 1925.
Signed at Washington June 10, 1932.
Operative July 1, 1931.
Treasury Department print; 5 Bevans 561

Agreement relating to guaranties authorized by Section 111(b)(3) of the Economic Cooperation Act of 1948, as amended.
Exchange of notes at Washington May 7 and 12, 1952.
Entered into force May 12, 1952.
3 UST 4285; TIAS 2575; 179 UNTS 15

FOREIGN ASSISTANCE

Economic cooperation agreement.
Signed at Brussels July 2, 1948.
Entered into force July 29, 1948.
62 Stat. 2173; TIAS 1781; 5 Bevans 678; 19 UNTS 127

Amendments
November 22 and 29, 1948 (62 Stat. 3776; TIAS 1906; 5 Bevans 703; 31 UNTS 485)
June 29, 1950 (1 UST 510; TIAS 2093; 76 UNTS 250)
September 10, 1951 (2 UST 2057; TIAS 2334; 140 UNTS 428)
December 11, 1952, and March 5, 1953 (4 UST 435; TIAS 2790; 207 UNTS 316)

INTELLECTUAL PROPERTY

Agreement to facilitate the interchange of patent rights and technical information for defense purposes.
Signed at Brussels October 12, 1954.
Entered into force October 12, 1954.
5 UST 2318; TIAS 3093; 202 UNTS 289

Agreement approving the procedures for reciprocal filing of classified patent applications.
Exchange of notes at Brussels May 6 and 18, 1960.
Entered into force May 18, 1960.
11 UST 1464; TIAS 4488

LAW ENFORCEMENT

Convention for the prevention of smuggling of alcoholic beverages into the United States.
Signed at Washington December 9, 1925.
Entered into force January 11, 1928.
45 Stat. 2456; TS 759; 5 Bevans 539; 72 LNTS 171

Arrangement for the direct exchange of certain information regarding the traffic in narcotic drugs.
Exchange of notes at Brussels February 6 and June 13, 1928.
Entered into force June 13, 1928.
5 Bevans 545

Agreement regarding mutual assistance between customs services.
Signed at Brussels June 26, 1991.
Entered into force May 1, 1993.
TIAS 12111

Procedures for mutual assistance in the administration of justice in connection with the Lockheed Aircraft Corporation matter.
Signed at Washington May 21, 1976.
Entered into force May 21, 1976.
27 UST 1966; TIAS 8292

Extradition treaty.
Signed at Brussels April 27, 1987.
Entered into force September 1, 1997.
TIAS 97-901; 2093 UNTS 263

Treaty on mutual legal assistance in criminal matters, with attachment.
Signed at Washington January 28, 1988.
Entered into force January 1, 2000.
TIAS; 2096 UNTS 3

Instrument as contemplated by Article 3(2) of the agreement on extradition between the United States of America and the European Union signed June 25, 2003, as to the application of the extradition treaty of April 27, 1987, with annex.
Signed at Brussels December 16, 2004.
Entered into force February 1, 2010.
TIAS 10-201.3.

Instrument as contemplated by Article 3(2) of the agreement on mutual legal assistance between the United States of America and the European Union signed June 25, 2003, as to the application of the treaty on mutual legal assistance in criminal matters signed January 28, 1988, with annex.
Signed at Brussels December 16, 2004.
Entered into force February 1, 2010.
TIAS 10-201.25

Agreement on enhancing cooperation in preventing and combating serious crime, with annex.
Signed at Brussels September 20, 2011.
Entered into force May 22, 2014, with the exception of Articles 7 through 9, *
TIAS 14-522

Note:

* In accordance with Article 25, Articles 7 through 9 may enter into force in the future under conditions specified in Article 25.

MARITIME MATTERS

Agreement relating to jurisdiction over vessels utilizing the Louisiana Offshore Oil Port.
Exchange of notes at Washington December 1 and 9, 1983.
Entered into force December 9, 1983.
35 UST 3244; TIAS 10853; 2015 UNTS 19

Agreement relating to the agreement of August 14, 1987, on the resolution of practical problems with respect to deep seabed mining areas.*
Exchange of notes at Brussels August 14, 1987.
Entered into force August 14, 1987.
TIAS 11438

Note:

* Parties to the multilateral agreement of August 14, 1987, are Belgium, Canada, Italy, the Netherlands, and the Union of Soviet Socialist Republics.

POSTAL MATTERS

Agreement concerning the exchange of parcel post, and regulations of execution.
Signed at Washington January 5, 1939.
Entered into force May 1, 1939.
53 Stat. 2100; Post Office Department print; 199 LNTS 321

Memorandum of understanding relating to the initiation of express mail/datapost service.
Signed at Washington and Brussels March 6 and 28, 1975.
Entered into force March 28, 1975; effective April 1, 1975.
29 UST 95; TIAS 8796

PROPERTY

Preliminary agreement regarding principles applying to mutual aid in the prosecution of the war against aggression.
Signed at Washington June 16, 1942.
Entered into force June 16, 1942.
56 Stat. 1504; EAS 254; 5 Bevans 571; 105 UNTS 159

Agreement relating to principles applying to the provision of aid to the armed forces of the United States.
Exchange of notes at Washington April 17 and 19, 1945.
Operative June 16, 1942.
59 Stat. 1642; EAS 481; 5 Bevans 606; 139 UNTS 279

Agreement relating to supplies and services, with memorandum of interpretation and exchanges of notes.
Signed at Washington April 17, April 19, and May 19, 1945.
Entered into force April 17, 1945.
59 Stat. 1642; EAS 481; 5 Bevans 594; 139 UNTS 279

Memorandum of understanding regarding settlement for lend-lease, reciprocal aid, Plan A, surplus property and claims. Agreement relating to the transfer of United States surplus property in Belgium.
Signed at Washington September 24, 1946.
Entered into force September 24, 1946.
62 Stat. 3984; TIAS 2064; 5 Bevans 631; 132 UNTS 80

Amendments:

May 12, 1949 (63 Stat. 2837; TIAS 2070; 5 Bevans 708; 132 UNTS 126)
January 20 and April 2, 1954 (5 UST 647; TIAS 2953; 229 UNTS 304)

Memorandum of agreement regarding the purchase of Belgian francs for use by United States armed forces.
Signed at Washington September 24, 1946.
Entered into force September 24, 1946.
62 Stat. 3984; TIAS 2064; 5 Bevans 631; 132 UNTS 80

SCIENTIFIC & TECHNICAL COOPERATION

Memorandum of understanding concerning the furnishing of balloon launching and associated services.
Signed at Washington June 8 and 15, 1983.
Entered into force June 15, 1983.
35 UST 1653; TIAS 10754; 2011 UNTS 87

SOCIAL SECURITY

Agreement on social security, with final protocol.
Signed at Washington February 19, 1982.
Entered into force July 1, 1984.
TIAS 11175; 2129 UNTS 495

Additional protocol and administrative agreement for the implementation of the agreement on social security of February 19, 1982.
Signed at Brussels November 23, 1982.
Entered into force July 1, 1984.
TIAS 11175; 2131 UNTS 238

TAXATION

Agreement relating to relief from taxation of United States expenditures in Belgium for common defense.
Exchange of notes at Brussels March 18 and April 7, 1952.
Entered into force April 7, 1952.
3 UST 5245; TIAS 2719; 205 UNTS 3

Agreement concerning relief from double taxation on income derived from the operation of ships and aircraft.
Exchange of notes at Washington October 14, 1987, and March 21, 1988.
Entered into force March 21, 1988.
TIAS 11571; 2185 UNTS 267

Convention for the avoidance of double taxation and the prevention of fiscal evasion with respect to taxes on income, with protocol.
Signed at Brussels November 27, 2006.
Entered into force December 28, 2007.
TIAS 07-1228.2

Agreement to improve international tax compliance and to implement the Foreign Account Tax Compliance Act, with annexes.
Signed at Brussels April 23, 2014.
Entered into force December 23, 2016.
TIAS 16-1223

TELECOMMUNICATION

Agreement relating to the reciprocal granting of authorizations to permit licensed amateur radio operators of either country to operate their stations in the other country.
Exchange of notes at Brussels June 15 and 18, 1965.
Entered into force June 18, 1965.
16 UST 869; TIAS 5824; 549 UNTS 95

TRADE & INVESTMENT

Convention in addition to the treaty of July 17, 1858, with annexed declaration.*
Signed at Brussels May 20, 1863.
Entered into force June 27, 1864.
13 Stat. 647; TS 22; 5 Bevans 468

Note:
* Articles I and IV remain in force perpetually; remaining articles terminated July 1, 1875, with termination of the 1858 treaty (12 Stat. 1043; TS 20; 5 Bevans 454).

Treaty providing for the extinguishment of the Scheldt dues.
Signed at Brussels July 20, 1863.
Entered into force June 27, 1864.
13 Stat. 655; TS 23; 5 Bevans 471

Treaty of friendship, establishment and navigation, with protocol.
Signed at Brussels February 21, 1961.
Entered into force October 3, 1963.
14 UST 1284; TIAS 5432; 480 UNTS 149

TRANSPORTATION

Agreement regarding the facilitation of road travel in the United States for holders of Belgian driving permits and in Belgium for holders of United States driving permits.
Exchange of notes at Brussels February 4 and 12, 1971.
Entered into force February 12, 1971.
22 UST 1525; TIAS 7172; 806 UNTS 281

Agreement relating to the reciprocal acceptance of airworthiness certifications.
Exchange of notes at Brussels February 12 and May 14, 1973.
Entered into force May 14, 1973.
24 UST 1720; TIAS 7675

Air transport agreement.*
Exchange of notes at Washington October 23, 1980.
Entered into force October 23, 1980.
32 UST 3515; TIAS 9903; 1275 UNTS 103

Amendments:
September 22 and November 12, 1986
November 5, 1993, and January 12, 1994

Note:
* This agreement is suspended for the duration of provisional application of the U.S. – E.U. Air Transport Agreement signed April 25 and 30, 2007.

Memorandum of agreement concerning assistance in developing and modernizing Belgium's civil aviation infrastructure.
Signed at Washington and Brussels June 19 and July 30, 1998.
Entered into force July 30, 1998.
NP

BELIZE

On September 21, 1981, Belize became an independent state. In a letter dated September 29, 1982, to the Secretary General of the United Nations, the Prime Minister and Minister of Foreign Affairs of Belize made a statement reading in part as follows:

I have the honour to inform you that the Government of Belize has decided to continue to apply provisionally and on the basis of reciprocity, all treaties to which the Government of the United Kingdom of Great Britain and Northern Ireland was a party, the application of which was extended either expressly or by necessary implication to the then dependent territory of Belize.

Such provisional application would subsist until Belize otherwise notifies Your Excellency, the depository (in the case of a multilateral treaty), or the state party (in the case of a bilateral treaty.)

On October 14, 2009, the U.S. Department of State sent a diplomatic note to the Government of Belize which included a "list of multilateral treaties that continued to apply provisionally and on the basis of reciprocity between the United States and Belize upon Belize's independence and thereafter…" as well as "a list of bilateral treaties and other international agreements that are carried on the records of the Department of State as being in force between the United States and Belize as of January 1, 2009...".

AGRICULTURE

Agreement confirming the cooperative agreement for the prevention of foot-and-mouth disease and rinderpest in British Honduras.
Signed at Belize September 6 and 12, 1972.
Entered into force September 12, 1972.
23 UST 2592; TIAS 7447

Memorandum of understanding relating to cooperative efforts to protect crops from plant pest damage and plant diseases.
Signed at Washington December 8, 1976.
Entered into force December 8, 1976.
28 UST 8703; TIAS 8767

CULTURAL EXCHANGES, PROPERTY & COOPERATION

Agreement relating to the establishment of a Peace Corps program in British Honduras.
Exchange of notes at Belize July 26 and August 15, 1962.
Entered into force August 15, 1962.
13 UST 1868; TIAS 5137; 580 UNTS 189

Memorandum of understanding concerning the imposition of import restrictions on categories of archaeological material representing the cultural heritage of Belize from the pre-ceramic (approximately 9000 B.C.), pre classic, classic, and post-classic periods of the pre-Columbian era through the early and late colonial periods.
Signed at Belize City February 27, 2013.
Entered into force February 27, 2013.
TIAS 13-227

DEFENSE

Agreement regarding grants under the Foreign Assistance Act of 1961, as amended, or successor legislation, and the furnishing of defense articles, defense services and related training, including pursuant to the United States International Military Education and Training (IMET) Program.
Exchange of notes at Belmopan May 22 and August 8, 2007.
Entered into force August 8, 2007.
NP

Agreement regarding the status of members of the armed forces of the United States and civilian personnel of the United States Department of Defense temporarily present in Belize in connection with military training, exercises, humanitarian activities and other agreed purposes.
Exchange of notes at Belmopan July 2 and October 29, 2007.
Entered into force October 29, 2007.
TIAS 07-1029

Acquisition and cross-servicing agreement with annexes.
Signed at Belmopan and Miami February 28, 2013 and May 13, 2013.
Entered into force May 13, 2013.
NP

DIPLOMATIC & CONSULAR RELATIONS

Consular convention between the United States and the United Kingdom.
Signed at Washington June 6, 1951.
Entered into force September 7, 1952.
3 UST 3426; TIAS 2494; 165 UNTS 121

FINANCE

Agreement relating to investment guaranties.
Signed at Belize February 8, 1966.
Entered into force February 8, 1966.
17 UST 347; TIAS 5983; 685 UNTS 47

Agreement regarding a debt-for-nature swap to prepay and cancel certain debt owed by the Government of Belize to the Government of the United States of America and its agencies, with attachments.
Signed at Washington August 2, 2001.
Entered into force August 22, 2001.
NP

FOREIGN ASSISTANCE

Agreement relating to economic and technical cooperation.
Signed at Belmopan March 8, 1983.
Entered into force March 8, 1983.
TIAS 10670; 2001 UNTS 39

INTELLECTUAL PROPERTY

Declaration by the United States and the United Kingdom affording reciprocal protection to trade-marks.
Signed at London October 24, 1877.
Entered into force October 24, 1877.
20 Stat. 703; TS 138; 12 Bevans 198

INTERNATIONAL CRIMINAL COURT

Agreement regarding the surrender of persons to the International Criminal Court.
Exchange of notes at Washington December 8, 2003.
Entered into force December 8, 2003.
TIAS 03-1208

LAW ENFORCEMENT

Mutual cooperation for reducing demand, preventing illicit use and combatting illicit production and traffic of drugs.
Signed at Belmopan February 9, 1989.
Entered into force February 9, 1989.
TIAS 11600; 2190 UNTS 355

Extradition treaty, with schedule.
Signed at Belize March 30, 2000.
Entered into force March 27, 2001.
TIAS 13089

Treaty for the return of stolen vehicles, with annexes and protocol.
Signed at Belmopan October 3, 1996.
Entered into force August 16, 2002.
TIAS 02-816

Treaty on mutual legal assistance in criminal matters, with exchange of notes.
Signed at Belize September 19, 2000.
Entered into force July 2, 2003.
TIAS 13116

Agreement regarding the Cooperating Nation Information Exchange System.
Exchange of notes at Belize City June 20 and 21, 2005.
Entered into force June 21, 2005.
TIAS 05-621.2

MARITIME MATTERS

Agreement concerning maritime counter-drug operations.
Signed at Belmopan December 23, 1992.
Entered into force December 23, 1992.
TIAS 11914

NONPROLIFERATION

Agreement concerning cooperation to suppress the proliferation of weapons of mass destruction, their delivery systems, and related materials by sea.
Signed at Washington August 4, 2005.
Entered into force October 19, 2005.
TIAS 05-1019

POSTAL MATTERS

Money order agreement.
Signed at Washington August 1 and at Belize August 17, 1906.
Operative October 1, 1906.
NP

Parcel post agreement, with details of implementation.
Signed at Belize City and Washington September 14 and 28, 1982.
Entered into force January 1, 1983.
TIAS 10512; 1777 UNTS 373

International express mail agreement, with detailed regulations.
Signed at Belize and Washington October 28 and November 13, 1992.
Entered into force December 14, 1992.
TIAS 11906

PROPERTY

Convention between the United States and the United Kingdom relating to the tenure and disposition of real and personal property.
Signed at Washington March 2, 1899.
Applicable to Belize February 9, 1901.
31 Stat. 1939; TS 146; 12 Bevans 246

Supplementary convention relating to the tenure and disposition of real and personal property of March 2, 1899.
Signed at Washington May 27, 1936.
Entered into force March 10, 1941.
55 Stat. 1101; TS 964; 5 Bevans 140; 203 LNTS 367

SCIENTIFIC & TECHNICAL COOPERATION

Agreement relating to the establishment, operation and maintenance of an upper air (rawinsonde) observation station at Belize International Airport, with memorandum of arrangement.
Exchange of letters at Belize and Belmopan August 26, 1981.
Entered into force August 26, 1981.
33 UST 3709; TIAS 10253; 1541 UNTS 71

TELECOMMUNICATION

Agreement between the United States and the United Kingdom relating to the reciprocal granting of authorizations to permit licensed amateur radio operators of either country to operate their stations in the other country.
Exchange of notes at London November 26, 1965.
Applicable to Belize December 11, 1969.
16 UST 2047; TIAS 5941; 561 UNTS 193

Agreement between the United States and the United Kingdom extending to certain territories the application of the agreement of November 26, 1965, relating to the reciprocal granting of authorizations to permit licensed amateur radio operators of either country to operate their stations in the other country.
Exchange of notes at London December 11, 1969.
Entered into force December 11, 1969.
20 UST 4089; TIAS 6800; 732 UNTS 334

Arrangement relating to radio communications between amateur stations on behalf of third parties.
Exchange of notes at Belmopan and Belize May 3 and 23, 1984.
Entered into force June 22, 1984.
TIAS 11198

TRANSPORTATION

Agreement between the United States and the United Kingdom concerning air services, with annexes and exchange of letters.
Signed at Bermuda July 23, 1977.
Entered into force July 23, 1977.
28 UST 5367; TIAS 8641

Amendments:
April 25, 1978 (29 UST 2680; TIAS 8965)
December 27, 1979 (32 UST 524; TIAS 9722)
December 4, 1980 (33 UST 655; TIAS 10059)

BENIN

CULTURAL EXCHANGES, PROPERTY & COOPERATION

Agreement concerning the program of the Peace Corps in Benin.
Signed at Cotonou October 30, 2013.
Entered into force October 30, 2013.
TIAS 13-1030

DEFENSE

Agreement relating to the furnishing of military equipment, materials and services to Dahomey (Benin) to help assure its security and independence.
Exchange of notes at Cotonou June 5 and 13, 1962.
Entered into force June 13, 1962.
13 UST 1285; TIAS 5078; 458 UNTS 219

Agreement concerning the provision of training related to defense articles under the United States International Military Education and Training (IMET) Program.
Exchange of notes at Cotonou May 15 and October 15, 1984.
Entered into force October 15, 1984.
TIAS 10988; 2021 UNTS 345

Agreement regarding military assistance under the Foreign Assistance Act of 1961, as amended, and the furnishing of defense articles, related training and other defense services from the United States to Benin.
Exchange of notes at Cotonou September 26 and October 3, 1994.
Entered into force October 3, 1994.
TIAS 12276

Agreement on the establishment of a joint commission for military cooperation.
Signed at Cotonou January 19, 1996.
Entered into force January 19, 1996.
TIAS 12720

Agreement regarding the provision of commodities, services and related training to assist the Republic of Benin's forces participating in the African Crisis Response Initiative.
Exchange of notes at Cotonou June 24 and July 23, 1998.
Entered into force July 23, 1998.
TIAS

Agreement regarding the status of U.S. military personnel and civilian employees of the U.S. Department of Defense temporarily present in Benin in connection with the African Crisis Response Initiative and other activities.
Exchange of notes at Cotonou June 24 and July 29, 1998.
Entered into force July 29, 1998.
TIAS

EMPLOYMENT

Agreement relating to the employment of dependents of official government employees.
Exchange of notes at Washington September 22 and December 3, 1998.
Entered into force December 3, 1998.
TIAS

ENVIRONMENT & CONSERVATION

Agreement regarding the Global Learning and Observations to Benefit the Environment (GLOBE) Program, with appendices.
Signed at Cotonou April 28, 1995.
Entered into force April 28, 1995.
TIAS 12639

FINANCE

Agreement regarding the consolidation and rescheduling of certain debts owed to, guaranteed by, or insured by the United States Government and its agency, with annexes.
Signed at Cotonou November 20, 1989.
Entered into force December 28, 1989.
NP

Investment incentive agreement.
Signed at Washington November 30, 1998.
Entered into force November 30, 1998.
TIAS 13002

FOREIGN ASSISTANCE

Agreement relating to economic, technical and related assistance.
Exchange of notes at Cotonou May 27, 1961.
Entered into force May 27, 1961.
13 UST 347; TIAS 4989; 455 UNTS 23

INTERNATIONAL CRIMINAL COURT

Agreement regarding the surrender of persons to international tribunals.
Signed at Cotonou July 25, 2005.
Entered into force August 25, 2005.
TIAS

POSTAL MATTERS

International express mail agreement, with detailed regulations.
Signed at Cotonou and Washington July 6 and 26, 1988.
Entered into force September 15, 1988.
TIAS 11590

BHUTAN

EMPLOYMENT

Agreement relating to the employment of dependents of official government employees.
Exchange of notes at New York September 22, 2004.
Entered into force September 22, 2004.
TIAS 04-922

INTERNATIONAL CRIMINAL COURT

Agreement regarding the surrender of persons to the International Criminal Court.
Signed at Washington May 2, 2003.
Entered into force August 16, 2004.
TIAS 04-816

POSTAL MATTERS

International express mail agreement.
Signed at Thimphu and Washington June 3 and July 6, 1993.
Entered into force August 1, 1993.
NP

BOLIVIA

CLAIMS & DISPUTE RESOLUTION

Treaty looking to the advancement of the cause of general peace.
Signed at Washington January 22, 1914.
Entered into force January 8, 1915.
38 Stat. 1868; TS 606; 5 Bevans 740

CONSULAR AFFAIRS

Agreement relating to the revision, on a reciprocal basis, the issuance of and fees for nonimmigrant visas.*
Exchange of notes at La Paz July 21, September 9 and 22, 1955.
Entered into force September 22, 1955.
TIAS
Note:
* The status of this agreement is under review.

CULTURAL EXCHANGES, PROPERTY & COOPERATION

Memorandum of understanding concerning the imposition of import restrictions on archaeological material from the Pre-Columbian cultures and certain ethnological material from the Colonial and Republican periods of Bolivia.
Signed at Washington December 4, 2001.
Entered into force December 4, 2001.
TIAS 01-1204
Extensions:
November 27 and 29, 2006 (TIAS 01-1204)
October 31 and November 10, 2011 (TIAS 01-1204)

DEFENSE

Agreement for establishment of an Air Force Mission to Bolivia.
Signed at La Paz June 30, 1956.
Entered into force June 30, 1956.
7 UST 2017; TIAS 3604; 271 UNTS 243
Amendment:
April 2 and 3, 1959 (10 UST 742; TIAS 4209; 342 UNTS 356)

Agreement for the establishment of an Army Mission to Bolivia.
Signed at La Paz June 30, 1956.
Entered into force June 30, 1956.
7 UST 2033; TIAS 3605; 271 UNTS 269
Amendment:
April 2 and 3, 1959 (10 UST 742; TIAS 4209; 342 UNTS 356)

Military assistance agreement.
Exchange of notes at La Paz March 21 and April 22, 1958.
Entered into force April 22, 1958.
9 UST 953; TIAS 4061; 317 UNTS 209

Agreement relating to the furnishing of defense articles and services to Bolivia.
Exchange of notes at La Paz April 26, 1962.
Entered into force April 26, 1962.
13 UST 2294; TIAS 5197; 461 UNTS 105

Agreement relating to the deposit by Bolivia of ten percent of the value of grant military assistance and excess defense articles furnished by the United States.
Exchange of notes at La Paz March 27 and May 2, 1972.
Entered into force May 2, 1972; effective February 7, 1972.
23 UST 892; TIAS 7352

Cooperative arrangement for the production of topographic maps of Bolivia, with annexes.
Signed at Washington and La Paz April 21 and 30, 1986.
Entered into force April 30, 1986.
TIAS 11375.

Agreement concerning the activities of United States civilian and military personnel in Bolivia.
Exchange of notes at La Paz July 27 and August 1, 2007.
Entered into force August 1, 2007.
TIAS 07-801

Agreement regarding grants under the Foreign Assistance Act of 1961, as amended, or successor legislation, and the furnishing of defense articles, defense services and related training, including pursuant to the United States International Military Education and Training (IMET) Program.
Exchange of notes at La Paz September 12 and 16, 2008.
Entered into force September 16, 2008.
NP

EMPLOYMENT

Agreement relating to the employment of dependents of official government employees.
Exchange of notes at La Paz May 9 and 30, 2005.
Entered into force May 30, 2005.
TIAS 05-530

ENVIRONMENT & CONSERVATION

Agreement concerning cooperation in the Global Learning and Observations to Benefit the Environment (GLOBE) Program, with appendices.
Signed at La Paz April 22, 1995.
Entered into force April 22, 1995.
TIAS 12636

FINANCE

Agreement relating to investment guaranties under section 413 (b)(4) of the Mutual Security Act of 1954, as amended.
Exchange of notes at La Paz September 23, 1955.
Entered into force September 23, 1955.
6 UST 3948; TIAS 3404; 256 UNTS 275

Related Agreements:
March 4, 1964 (15 UST 260; TIAS 5548; 524 UNTS 312)
December 19, 1985 (TIAS 12042)
May 20, 1992 (TIAS 12042)

Agreement regarding the consolidation and rescheduling of certain debts owed to, guaranteed by or insured by the United States Government and its agencies, with annexes.
Signed at La Paz March 27, 1987.
Entered into force May 6, 1987.
NP

Agreement regarding the consolidation and rescheduling of certain debts owed to, guaranteed by, or insured by the United States Government and its agencies, with annexes.
Signed at La Paz May 15, 1989.
Entered into force June 23, 1989.
NP

Swap agreement between the United States Treasury and the Central Bank of Bolivia/Government of Bolivia, with related letter.
Signed at La Paz and Washington July 11, 1989.
Entered into force July 11, 1989.
TIAS

Swap agreement between the United States Treasury and the Central Bank of Bolivia/Government of Bolivia, with related letter.
Signed at La Paz and Washington September 14 and 15, 1989.
Entered into force September 15, 1989.
TIAS

Extension:
December 15, 1989

Swap agreement between the United States Treasury and the Central Bank of Bolivia/Government of Bolivia, with related letter.
Signed at Washington and La Paz December 27, 1989.
Entered into force December 27, 1989.
TIAS

Agreement regarding the consolidation and rescheduling of certain debts owed to, guaranteed by, or insured by the United States Government and its agencies, with annexes.
Signed at La Paz November 27, 1990.
Entered into force February 6, 1991.
NP

Agreement regarding the consolidation and rescheduling or refinancing of certain debts owed to, guaranteed by, or insured by the United States Government and its agencies, with annexes.
Signed at La Paz October 13, 1992.
Entered into force December 3, 1992.
NP

Amendments:
March 2 and April 13, 1994 (NP)
August 9 and October 21, 1994 (NP)

Agreement regarding the consolidation and rescheduling of certain debts owed to, guaranteed by, or insured by the United States Government and its agencies, with annexes.
Signed at La Paz January 23, 1996.
Entered into force March 7, 1996.
NP

Agreement regarding the reduction and reorganization of certain debts owed to, guaranteed by, or insured by the United States Government and its agencies.
Signed at La Paz November 27, 1996.
Entered into force April 7, 1997.
NP

Agreement regarding the reduction and reorganization of certain debts owed to, guaranteed by, or insured by the United States Government and its agencies, with annexes.
Signed at Santa Cruz December 2, 1999.
Entered into force February 23, 2000.
NP

Agreement regarding the consolidation of debt owed to, guaranteed by, or insured by the United States Government and its agencies, with annexes.
Signed at La Paz November 27, 2002.
Entered into force January 6, 2003.
NP

FOREIGN ASSISTANCE

General agreement for technical cooperation.
Signed at La Paz March 14, 1951.
Entered into force March 14, 1951.
2 UST 671; TIAS 2221; 132 UNTS 319

Amendments:
December 14, 1951, and January 2, 7 and 8, 1952 (3 UST 4686; TIAS 2625; 180 UNTS 346)
August 27, 1953, and January 15, 1954 (5 UST 518; TIAS 2944; 229 UNTS 213)

Agreement providing economic assistance to Bolivia.
Signed at La Paz November 6, 1953.
Entered into force November 6, 1953.
4 UST 2297; TIAS 2883; 222 UNTS 41

Amendment:
August 24 and November 11, 1959 (10 UST 3023; TIAS 4395; 367 UNTS 319)

Agreement providing for payment by the United States of ocean freight costs on relief shipments to Bolivia, and duty and tax-free entry and payment of inland transportation to point of distribution by Bolivia.
Exchange of notes at La Paz June 3 and 16, 1954.
Entered into force June 16, 1954.
5 UST 1547; TIAS 3033; 234 UNTS 35
Amendment:
December 14 and 30, 1970 (22 UST 211; TIAS 7051; 781 UNTS 312)

Agreement providing for an informational media guaranty program.
Exchange of notes at La Paz February 27 and March 10, 1956.
Entered into force March 10, 1956.
7 UST 440; TIAS 3528; 270 UNTS 199

AGENCY FOR INTERNATIONAL DEVELOPMENT

Strategic objective agreement concerning licit economy in coca-growing and associated areas increasingly sustainable, with annexes.
Signed June 3, 2005.
Entered into June 3, 2005.
NP
Amendments
August 2, 2006 (NP)
September 21, 2007 (NP)

LAW ENFORCEMENT

Treaty on the execution of penal sentences.
Signed at La Paz February 10, 1978.
Entered into force August 17, 1978.
30 UST 796; TIAS 9219; 1150 UNTS 11

Agreement concerning cooperation to combat narcotics trafficking, with annexes and related letter.
Exchange of notes at La Paz February 24, 1987.
Entered into force August 13, 1987.
TIAS 12053
Amendment:
May 9, 1990

Treaty on extradition.
Signed at La Paz June 27, 1995.
Entered into force November 21, 1996.
TIAS 96-1121

Agreement concerning security assistance matters and the provision of articles, services and associated military education and training by the United States Government for anti-narcotics purposes.
Exchange of notes at La Paz October 27 and November 5, 1998.
Entered into force November 5, 1998.
NP

POSTAL MATTERS

International express mail agreement, with detailed regulations.
Signed at La Paz and Washington August 10 and November 21, 1988.
Entered into force December 15, 1988.
TIAS 11635

Postal money order agreement.
Signed at La Paz and Washington February 26 and March 11, 1993.
Entered into force June 1, 1993.
NP

PUBLICATIONS

Agreement relating to the exchange of official publications.
Exchange of notes at La Paz January 26 and 31, 1942.
Entered into force January 31, 1942.
56 Stat. 1436; EAS 242; 5 Bevans 753; 101 UNTS 138

SCIENTIFIC & TECHNICAL COOPERATION

Memorandum of understanding concerning the installation and operation of a real-time seismic station.
Signed at La Paz and Reston September 7, 1983, and June 14, 1984.
Entered into force June 14, 1984.
TIAS 11250

Memorandum of understanding for scientific and technical cooperation in the earth sciences.
Signed at La Paz and Reston April 24 and May 29, 1985.
Entered into force May 29, 1985.
TIAS 11214
Amendment and Extension:
November 20, 1991 (TIAS 11828)

TAXATION

Agreement concerning reciprocal exemption from income tax of income derived from the international operation of ships and aircraft.
Exchange of notes at Washington July 21 and November 23, 1987.
Entered into force November 23, 1987.
TIAS 11542; 2191 UNTS 217

TELECOMMUNICATION

Agreement relating to radio communications between amateur stations on behalf of third parties.
Exchange of notes at La Paz October 23, 1961.
Entered into force November 22, 1961.
12 UST 1695; TIAS 4888; 424 UNTS 93

Agreement relating to the reciprocal granting of authorization to permit licensed amateur radio operators of either country to operate their stations in the other country.
Exchange of notes at La Paz March 16, 1965.
Entered into force April 15, 1965.
16 UST 165; TIAS 5777; 542 UNTS 209

TRADE & INVESTMENT

Treaty of peace, friendship, commerce and navigation.*
Signed at La Paz May 13, 1858.
Entered into force November 9, 1862.
12 Stat. 1003; TS 32; 5 Bevans 721
Note:
* Article 34 terminated by the United States, effective July 1, 1916, in accordance with the Seamen's Act (38 Stat. 1164).

TRANSPORTATION

Agreement relating to the sending of a technical mission to Bolivia to assist in the development of Bolivian civil aviation.
Exchange of notes at La Paz August 26 and November 3, 1947.
Entered into force November 3, 1947.
61 Stat. 3863; TIAS 1739; 5 Bevans 778; 51 UNTS 33

Air transport agreement.
Signed at La Paz September 29, 1948.
Entered into force November 4, 1948.
14 UST 2209; TIAS 5507; 505 UNTS 139
Amendments:
May 4 and 17, 1967 (18 UST 2362; TIAS 6340)
June 28 and August 23, 1988 (TIAS 11642; 2204 UNTS 252)

Memorandum of agreement concerning assistance in developing and modernizing Bolivia's civil aviation system, with annex.
Signed at Washington and La Paz March 1 and June 8, 1988.
Entered into force June 8, 1988.
TIAS 11587; 2192 UNTS 35

BOSNIA AND HERZEGOVINA

On April 5, 1992, Bosnia and Herzegovina became an independent state. For agreements prior to the independence of Bosnia and Herzegovina, see YUGOSLAVIA.

CULTURAL EXCHANGES, PROPERTY & COOPERATION

Agreement concerning the program of the Peace Corps in Bosnia and Herzegovina.
Signed at Sarajevo February 26, 2001.
Entered into force February 26, 2001.
TIAS 01-226

Agreement on the protection and preservation of certain cultural properties.
Signed at Sarajevo July 2, 2002.
Entered into force September 30, 2010.
TIAS 10-930

DEFENSE

Agreement related to the provision of defense articles, related training or other defense services from the United States to Bosnia, with related exchange of notes.
Exchange of notes at Sarajevo January 6 and 7, 1996.
Entered into force January 7, 1996.
TIAS 12716
Amendment:
March 15 and November 28, 2006

Agreement on status protections and access to and use of facilities and areas in Bosnia and Herzegovina.
Signed at Washington November 22, 2005.
Entered into force November 28, 2006.
TIAS 06-1128.1

Acquisition and cross-servicing agreement.
Signed at Stuttgart and Sarajevo June 1 and 9, 2015.
Entered into force June 9, 2015.
NP

EMPLOYMENT

Agreement relating to the employment of dependents of official government employees.
Exchange of notes at Washington March 7 and 15, 1995.
Entered into force March 15, 1995.
TIAS 12614

FINANCE

Investment incentive agreement.
Signed at Sarajevo July 12, 1996.
Entered into force December 10, 1996.
TIAS 12780

Agreement regarding the consolidation, reduction and rescheduling of certain debts owed to, guaranteed by, or insured by the United States Government and its agencies, with annexes.
Signed at Sarajevo August 19, 1999.
Entered into force October 21, 1999.
NP

FOREIGN ASSISTANCE

Agreement concerning economic, technical and related assistance for Bosnia and Herzegovina, with related letters.
Signed at Sarajevo May 3, 1996.
Entered into force May 3, 1996.
TIAS 12749

INTERNATIONAL CRIMINAL COURT

Agreement regarding the surrender of persons to the International Criminal Court.
Signed at Sarajevo May 16, 2003.
Entered into force July 7, 2003.
TIAS 03-707.3

POSTAL MATTERS

Express mail service agreement, with detailed regulations.
Signed at Sarajevo and Washington March 29, 2000, and January 4, 2001.
Entered into force February 1, 2001.
NP

TELECOMMUNICATION

Agreement relating to radio communications between amateur stations on behalf of third parties.
Exchange of notes at New York September 24 and October 14, 1993.
Entered into force October 14, 1993.
TIAS 12511

TRANSPORTATION

Air transport agreement, with annexes.
Signed at Washington November 22, 2005.
Entered into force November 22, 2005.
TIAS 05-1122.1

BOTSWANA

On September 30, 1966, Bechuanaland Protectorate became the independent state of Botswana.

In a note dated October 6, 1966, to the Secretary-General of the United Nations the President of Botswana made a statement reading in part as follows:

As regards bilateral treaties validly concluded by the Government of the United Kingdom on behalf of the former Bechuanaland Protectorate, or validly applied or extended by the said Government to the territory of the former Bechuanaland Protectorate, the Government of Botswana is willing to continue to apply within its territory, on a basis of reciprocity, the terms of all such treaties for a period of twenty-four months from the date of independence (i.e., until October 1, 1968) unless abrogated or modified earlier by mutual consent. At the expiry of that period, the Government of Botswana will regard such of these treaties which could not by the application of the rules of customary international law be regarded as otherwise surviving, as having terminated.

It is the earnest hope of the Government of Botswana that during the aforementioned period of twenty-four months, the normal processes of diplo-matic negotiations will enable it to reach satisfactory accord with the States concerned upon the possibility of the continuance or modification of such treaties.

The Government of Botswana is conscious that the above declaration applicable to bilateral treaties cannot with equal facility be applied to multilateral treaties. As regards these, therefore, the Government of Botswana proposes to review each of them individually and to indicate to the depositary in each case what steps it wishes to take in relation to each such instrument whether by way of confirmation of termination, confirmation of succession or accession. During such interim period of review any party to a multilateral treaty which has, prior to independence, been applied or extended to the former Bechuanaland Protectorate, may, on a basis of reciprocity, rely as against Botswana on the terms of such treaty."

ARMS CONTROL

Agreement concerning the operation of a seismic monitoring station in Botswana.
Signed at Washington and Lobatse October 14, 1999, and February 16, 2000.
Entered into force February 16, 2000.
TIAS 00-216

CULTURAL EXCHANGES, PROPERTY & COOPERATION

Agreement relating to the establishment of a Peace Corps Program in Botswana.
Exchange of notes at Gaborone May 14, 1971.
Entered into force May 14, 1971.
22 UST 1025; TIAS 7145; 797 UNTS 13

DEFENSE

Agreement concerning the provision of training related to defense articles under the United States International Military Education and Training (IMET) Program.
Exchange of notes at Gaborone February 26 and March 21, 1980.
Entered into force March 21, 1980.
32 UST 957; TIAS 9742; 1221 UNTS 217

Agreement regarding grants under the Foreign Assistance Act of 1961, as amended, and the furnishing of defense articles, related training and other defense services from the United States to Botswana.
Exchange of notes at Gaborone May 21 and June 17, 1992.
Entered into force June 17, 1992.
TIAS 12277.

Agreement regarding matters related to U.S. military and civilian personnel of the U.S. Department of Defense temporarily present in Botswana for the purpose of carrying out exercises, training, humanitarian assistance, or other activities.
Exchange of notes at Gaborone January 22 and February 13, 2001.
Entered into force February 13, 2001.
TIAS

Acquisition and cross-servicing agreement.
Signed at Gaborone and Stuttgart June 20 and July 6, 2016.
Entered into force July 6, 2016.
NP

EMPLOYMENT

Agreement relating to the employment of dependents of official government employees.
Signed at Gaborone June 15, 1984.
Entered into force June 15, 1984.
TIAS 11134
Amendment:
August 16, 1999, and December 1, 2000 (TIAS 13130)

Agreement concerning interpretation of the agreement of June 15, 1984, relating to the employment of dependents of official government employees.
Exchange of notes at New York March 14 and April 27, 1989.
Entered into force April 27, 1989.
TIAS

FINANCE

Investment incentive agreement.
Signed at Gaborone December 12, 1997.
Entered into force March 12, 1998.
TIAS 12911

Agreement regarding the reduction of certain debts owed to the Government of the United States and its agencies, with attachment.
Signed at Gaborone October 5, 2006.
Entered into force November 19, 2006.
NP

Agreement concerning the establishment of a Tropical Forest Conservation Fund and a Tropical Forest Conservation Board, with annex.
Signed at Gaborone October 5, 2006.
Entered into force November 19, 2006.
TIAS 06-1119

FOREIGN ASSISTANCE

Regional assistance program framework agreement.
Signed at Gaborone September 27, 1995.
Entered into force September 27, 1995.
TIAS

INTERNATIONAL CRIMINAL COURT

Agreement regarding the surrender of persons to international tribunals.
Signed at Gaborone June 30, 2003.
Entered into force September 28, 2003.
TIAS 03-928

LAW ENFORCEMENT

Agreement concerning an International Law Enforcement Academy.
Signed at Gaborone July 24, 2000.
Entered into force July 24, 2000.
TIAS 13106

POSTAL MATTERS

International express mail agreement, with detailed regulations.
Signed at Gaborone and Washington October 24 and December 29, 1988.
Entered into force January 16, 1989.
TIAS 11624

SCIENTIFIC & TECHNICAL COOPERATION

Memorandum of understanding concerning the development, installation and operation of a seismic data acquisition system.
Signed at Reston and Gaborone June 16 and August 13, 1986.
Entered into force August 13, 1986.
TIAS 11361

TELECOMMUNICATION

Agreement relating to the reciprocal granting of authorizations to permit licensed amateur radio operators of either country to operate their stations in the other country.
Exchange of notes at Gaborone November 7, 1978, and September 26, 1979.
Entered into force September 26, 1979.
32 UST 1357; TIAS 9776; 1221 UNTS 211

Agreement concerning the construction, operation and maintenance of a Voice of America radio relay facility in Botswana, with appendix.
Signed at Gaborone September 5, 1985.
Entered into force September 5, 1985.
TIAS 11126

TRANSPORTATION

Air transport agreement, with annex
Signed at Gaborone May 23, 2014.
Entered into force May 23, 2014.
TIAS 14-523

BRAZIL

ATOMIC ENERGY

Agreement providing for a grant to assist in the acquisition of a subcritical assembly for the Aeronautical Institute of Technology.
Exchange of notes at Rio de Janeiro October 20, 1959, and February 27, 1960.
Entered into force February 27, 1960.
11 UST 1977; TIAS 4547; 384 UNTS 131

Agreement providing for a grant to assist in the acquisition of certain nuclear research and training equipment and materials.
Exchange of notes at Rio de Janeiro October 10, 1960, and March 17, 1961.
Entered into force March 17, 1961.
12 UST 381; TIAS 4727; 406 UNTS 241

Agreement providing for a grant for assistance in obtaining materials and equipment for use in developing the Instituto de Biofisica da Universidade de Brasil radio-biological and research program.
Exchange of notes at Rio de Janeiro October 10, 1962, and March 29, 1963.
Entered into force March 29, 1963.
14 UST 424; TIAS 5337; 476 UNTS 67

Agreement for cooperation concerning peaceful uses of nuclear energy, with annex and agreed minute.
Signed at Brasilia October 14, 1997.
Entered into force September 15, 1999.
TIAS 12888

Arrangement for the exchange of technical information and cooperation in regulatory and safety research matters, with addenda.
Signed at Rio de Janeiro and Rockville August 1 and 28, 2014.
Entered into force August 28, 2014.
TIAS 14-828

CLAIMS & DISPUTE RESOLUTION

Arbitration convention.
Signed at Washington January 23, 1909.
Entered into force July 26, 1911.
37 Stat. 1535; TS 562; 5 Bevans 818

Treaty looking to the advancement of the cause of general peace.
Signed at Washington July 24, 1914.
Entered into force October 28, 1916.
39 Stat. 1698; TS 627; 5 Bevans 820

CONSULAR AFFAIRS

Agreement relating to the waiver of nonimmigrant passport visa fees.*
Exchange of notes at Rio de Janeiro December 16 and 17, 1937.
Operative January 1, 1938.
5 Bevans 874; 186 LNTS 413

Agreement relating to the reciprocal issuance of nonimmigrant visas free of charge to diplomatic, consular, and administrative officers and employees serving in diplomatic missions, and career consular officers, as well as officers and employees of governmental agencies of both countries.*
Exchange of notes at Rio de Janeiro May 26, 1965.
Entered into force July 25, 1965.
16 UST 1006; TIAS 5843; 549 UNTS 125

Note:

* The status of these agreements are under review.

CULTURAL EXCHANGES, PROPERTY & COOPERATION

Agreement relating to the establishment of a Peace Corps program in Brazil.
Exchange of notes at Brasilia June 18, 1973.
Entered into force June 18, 1973.
24 UST 1650; TIAS 7669

DEFENSE

Agreement relating to the presence of military personnel of the United States in Brazil and the presence of military personnel of Brazil in the United States.
Exchange of notes at Rio de Janeiro December 15, 1947, and February 2, 1948.
Entered into force February 2, 1948.
62 Stat. 1957; TIAS 1759; 5 Bevans 1045; 67 UNTS 109

Agreement relating to the transfer to Brazil of certain United States naval vessels.
Exchange of notes at Washington January 4, 1951, with memorandum of understanding dated January 9, 1951.
Entered into force January 4, 1951.
3 UST 2738; TIAS 2443; 165 UNTS 97

Military assistance agreement.*
Signed at Rio de Janeiro March 15, 1952.
Entered into force May 19, 1953.
4 UST 170; TIAS 2776; 199 UNTS 221

Note:

* Terminated March 11, 1977, except that the safeguard clauses to which articles I and III refer remain in force.

Understanding relating to military assistance.
Exchange of notes at Rio de Janeiro January 30, 1964.
Entered into force January 30, 1964.
15 UST 163; TIAS 5534; 511 UNTS 77

Agreement relating to the deposit by Brazil of ten percent of the value of grant military assistance furnished by the United States.
Exchange of notes at Brasilia February 28 and June 27, 1972.
Entered into force June 27, 1972; effective February 7, 1972.
23 UST 1222; TIAS 7390

Memorandum of understanding relating to the acquisition of military aircraft with annexes.
Signed September 24, 1973.
Entered into force September 24, 1973.
27 UST 2810; TIAS 8350; 1066 UNTS 119

Master data exchange arrangement for the mutual development of military equipment.
Signed at Washington November 14, 1984.
Entered into force November 14, 1984.
TIAS 11164; 2126 UNTS 285

Agreement concerning the provision of training related to defense articles under the United States International Military Education and Training (IMET) Program.
Exchange of notes at Brasilia April 19, 1988, and March 27, 1989.
Entered into force March 27, 1989.
NP

Agreement regarding grants under the Foreign Assistance Act of 1961, as amended, and the furnishing of defense articles from the United States of America to the Government of the Federative Republic of Brazil.
Exchange of notes at Washington June 2, 2000.
Entered into force October 19, 2000.
TIAS 13097

Understanding regarding the exchange of military personnel, with annexes.
Signed at Brasila April 25, 2007.
Entered into force April 25, 2007.
NP

Agreement regarding the assignment of foreign liaison officers, with annex.
Signed at Rio de Janeiro and Washington April 12 and 28, 2010.
Entered into force April 28, 2010.
NP

Memorandum of understanding regarding the assignment of foreign liaison officers, with annex.
Signed at Rio de Janeiro January 16, 2013.
Entered into force January 16, 2013.
NP

Memorandum of understanding regarding the exchange of military personnel, with annex.
Signed at Rio de Janeiro January 16, 2013.
Entered into force January 16, 2013.
NP

Agreement concerning security measures for the protection of classified military information.
Signed at Santa Cruz November 21, 2010.
Entered into force June 26, 2015.
TIAS 15-626.1
Amendment:
June 8 and 9, 2015 (TIAS 15-626.1)

Defense cooperation agreement.
Signed at Washington April 12, 2012.
Entered into force June 26, 2015.
TIAS 15-626

Arrangement regarding the exchange of military personnel, with annexes.
Signed July 10 and 13, 2015.
Entered into force July 13, 2015.
NP

Basic exchange and cooperation agreement concerning geospatial information, with annexes.
Signed at Springfield March 9, 2016.
Entered into force March 9, 2016.
NP

DIPLOMATIC & CONSULAR RELATIONS

Agreement granting reciprocal customs privileges for Foreign Service personnel.
Exchange of notes at Rio de Janeiro October 11, 1940.
Entered into force October 11, 1940.
54 Stat. 2419; EAS 185; 5 Bevans 897; 203 LNTS 261

Memorandum of understanding concerning consultations on matters of mutual interest.
Signed at Brasilia February 21, 1976.
Entered into force February 21, 1976.
27 UST 1034; TIAS 8240

EDUCATION

Agreement for educational and cultural exchange programs.
Signed at Brasilia May 27, 2008.
Entered into force November 17, 2009.
TIAS 09-1117

EMPLOYMENT

Agreement relating to the employment of dependents of official government employees, with exchange of letters.
Exchange of notes at Brasilia July 8, 1987.
Entered into force July 8, 1987.
TIAS 11529
Amendments and Extensions:
July 6 and 8, 2005 (TIAS 05-708)
March 18 and 19, 2011 (TIAS 05-708)

FINANCE

Agreement relating to investment guaranties.
Signed at Washington February 6, 1965.
Entered into force September 17, 1965.
18 UST 1807; TIAS 6327; 719 UNTS 3

Agreement regarding the consolidation and rescheduling of certain debts owed to, guaranteed by or insured by the United States Government and its agencies, with annexes.
Signed at Brasilia April 15, 1985.
Entered into force May 28, 1985.
NP

Swap agreement between the United States Treasury and the Central Bank of Brazil/Government of Brazil, with memorandum of understanding.
Signed at Washington and Rio de Janeiro July 15, 1988.
Entered into force July 15, 1988.
TIAS

Agreement regarding the consolidation and rescheduling of certain debts owed to, guaranteed by, or insured by the United States Government and its agencies, with annexes.
Signed at Brasilia March 14, 1990.
Entered into force April 19, 1990.
NP

Agreement regarding the consolidation and rescheduling of certain debts owed to, guaranteed by or insured by the United States Government and its agencies, with annexes.
Signed at Brasilia December 20, 1991.
Entered into force March 9, 1992.
NP

Agreement regarding the consolidation and rescheduling or refinancing of certain debts owed to, guaranteed by, or insured by the United States Government and its agencies, with annexes.
Signed at Washington September 23, 1992.
Entered into force November 9, 1992.
NP

Agreement regarding the reduction of debt in support of conservation and sustainable management of tropical forests, with attachments.
Signed at Brasilia August 12, 2010.
Entered into force September 27, 2010.
TIAS 10-927.1

FOREIGN ASSISTANCE

Agreement relating to the mobilization of productive resources of Brazil.
Exchange of notes at Washington March 3, 1942.
Entered into force March 3, 1942.
57 Stat. 1314; EAS 370; 5 Bevans 913; 105 UNTS 99

Agreement relating to technical cooperation.
Exchange of notes at Rio de Janeiro December 19, 1950.
Entered into force December 19, 1950.
2 UST 845; TIAS 2239; 141 UNTS 3
Amendment:
January 8, 1952 (3 UST 4693; TIAS 2626; 200 UNTS 306)

Special services program agreement.
Signed at Rio de Janeiro May 30, 1953.
Entered into force provisionally May 30, 1953; definitively November 3, 1959.
13 UST 1061; TIAS 5049; 460 UNTS 89
Extension:
December 27 and 30, 1963 (15 UST 99; TIAS 5520; 511 UNTS 308)

Agreement on the cooperation for the promotion of economic and social development in the Brazilian Northeast, with exchange of letters.
Signed at Washington April 13, 1962.
Entered into force April 13, 1962.
13 UST 356; TIAS 4990; 445 UNTS 227

INTELLECTUAL PROPERTY

Agreement for the protection of the marks of manufacture and trade.
Signed at Rio de Janeiro September 24, 1878.
21 Stat. 659; TS 36; 5 Bevans 807

Agreement providing for reciprocal copyright protection of literary, artistic and scientific works.
Exchange of notes at Washington April 2, 1957.
Entered into force April 2, 1957.
8 UST 418; TIAS 3793; 290 UNTS 119

LAW ENFORCEMENT

Treaty of extradition.
Signed at Rio de Janeiro January 13, 1961.
Entered into force December 17, 1964.
15 UST 2093; TIAS 5691; 532 UNTS 177

Additional protocol to the treaty of extradition.
Signed at Rio de Janeiro June 18, 1962.
Entered into force December 17, 1964.
15 UST 2112; TIAS 5691; 532 UNTS 198

Mutual cooperation agreement for reducing demand, preventing illicit use and combatting illicit production and trafficking of drugs.
Signed at Brasilia April 12, 1995.
Entered into force April 24, 1997.
TIAS; 1990 UNTS 27

Treaty on mutual legal assistance in criminal matters.
Signed at Brasilia October 14, 1997.
Entered into force February 21, 2001.
TIAS 12889

Agreement regarding mutual assistance between their customs administrations.
Signed at Brasilia June 20, 2002.
Entered into force February 1, 2005.
TIAS 05-201

MARITIME MATTERS

Agreement relating to establishment of a mechanism for consultation on maritime transportation problems.
Exchange of notes at Rio de Janeiro September 18 and 20, 1968.
Entered into force September 20, 1968.
19 UST 6017; TIAS 6559; 702 UNTS 227

Agreement on maritime transport.
Signed at Washington September 30, 2005.
Entered into force April 27, 2011.
TIAS 11-427

PEACE

Treaty of peace, friendship, commerce and navigation.*
Signed at Rio de Janeiro December 12, 1828.
Entered into force March 18, 1829; operative December 12, 1828.
8 Stat. 390; TS 34; 5 Bevans 792
Note:
* All articles terminated December 12, 1841, except those relating to peace and friendship.

POSTAL MATTERS

Memorandum of understanding concerning the operation of the INTELPOST field trial, with attachment and details of implementation.
Signed at Brasilia and Washington December 18 and 28, 1984.
Entered into force January 7, 1985.
TIAS 11004; 2022 UNTS 209

International express mail agreement, with detailed regulations.
Signed at Brasilia and Washington April 7 and May 11, 1988.
Entered into force May 11, 1988.
TIAS 11654

PROPERTY

Agreement on the disposition of lend-lease supplies in inventory or procurement in the United States.
Signed at Washington June 28, 1946.
Entered into force June 28, 1946.
60 Stat. 1797; TIAS 1537; 5 Bevans 1019; 6 UNTS 327

Agreement concerning the acquisition and retention of diplomatic and consular properties in the United States and Brazil.
Exchange of notes at Brasilia June 1, 2007.
Entered into force January 18, 2008.
TIAS 08-118

PUBLICATIONS

Agreement relating to the exchange of official publications.
Exchange of notes at Washington June 15 and 24, 1940.
Entered into force June 24, 1940.
54 Stat. 2329; EAS 176; 5 Bevans 883; 203 LNTS 227
Amendment:
May 16 and 23, 1950 (3 UST 387; TIAS 2402; 151 UNTS 141)

SCIENTIFIC & TECHNICAL COOPERATION

Agreement relating to cooperation in science and technology.
Signed at Brasilia February 6, 1984.
Entered into force May 15, 1986.
TIAS 10990
Amendment and Extension:
March 21, 1994 (TIAS 12537)

Memorandum of understanding concerning scientific and technical cooperation in the earth sciences.
Signed at Reston January 17 and 31, 1997.
Entered into force January 31, 1997.
TIAS 12829

Memorandum of understanding concerning scientific and technical cooperation in the earth sciences.
Signed at Brasilia and Natal June 22, 2007.
Entered into force June 22, 2007.
TIAS 07-622

SPACE

Memorandum of understanding for flight of the Humidity Sounder for Brazil (HSB) instrument on NASA's Earth Observing System PM–1 spacecraft.
Signed at Washington December 5, 1996.
Entered into force December 5, 1996.
TIAS 12820

Framework agreement on cooperation in peaceful uses of outer space, with annex.
Signed at Brasilia March 1, 1996.
Entered into force July 9, 1997.
TIAS 97-709
Extensions:
February 21 and June 6, 2008 (TIAS 97-709)
January 5 and 29, 2009 (TIAS 97-709)
December 10, 2009 and January 5, 2010 (TIAS 97-709)
February 3 and May 3, 2012 (TIAS 97-709)

Implementing arrangement for the design, development, operation and use of flight equipment and payloads for the International Space Station Program.
Signed at Brasilia October 14, 1997.
Entered into force October 14, 1997.
TIAS 12890

TAXATION

Agreement for the exchange of information relating to taxes.
Signed at Brasilia March 20, 2007.
Entered into force March 19, 2013.
TIAS 13-319.1

Agreement to improve international tax compliance and to implement the Foreign Account Tax Compliance Act, with annexes.
Signed at Brasilia September 23, 2014.
Entered into force June 26, 2015.
TIAS 15-626.2

TELECOMMUNICATION

Agreement relating to a program of joint participation in intercontinental testing in connection with experimental communications satellites.
Exchange of notes at Rio de Janeiro October 27, 1961.
Entered into force October 27, 1961.
12 UST 3145; TIAS 4917; 433 UNTS 113

Agreement relating to radio communications between amateur stations on behalf of third parties.
Exchange of notes at Washington June 1, 1965.
Entered into force June 1, 1965.
16 UST 821; TIAS 5816; 546 UNTS 195

Agreement relating to the reciprocal granting of authorizations to permit licensed amateur radio operators of either country to operate their stations in the other country.
Exchange of notes at Rio de Janeiro and Brasilia January 26 and June 19, 1970.
Entered into force June 19, 1970.
21 UST 1960; TIAS 6936; 756 UNTS 109

TRADE & INVESTMENT

Joint communique relating to trade, investment and financial matters.
Issued at Brasilia May 11, 1976.
Entered into force May 11, 1976.
27 UST 4121; TIAS 8435; 1066 UNTS 131

Agreement relating to the establishment of a United States Trade Center in Sao Paulo, with note of guarantee.
Exchange of notes at Brasilia June 22 and October 20, 1976.
Entered into force October 20, 1976.
28 UST 8146; TIAS 8748

Agreement on steel trade liberalization, with appendices and related letter.
Exchange of letters at Washington February 26 and March 5, 1990.
Entered into force March 5, 1990.
TIAS

Agreement regarding cooperation between their competition authorities in the enforcement of their competition laws.
Signed at Washington October 26, 1999.
Entered into force March 25, 2003.
TIAS 13068

Memorandum of understanding regarding a fund for technical assistance and capacity building with respect to the cotton dispute (WT/DS267) in the World Trade Organization.
Signed at Punta del Este April 20, 2010.
Entered into force April 20, 2010.
TIAS 10-420

Agreement regarding certain distinctive products.
Exchange of letters April 9, 2012.
Entered into force April 9, 2012.
TIAS 12-409

TRANSPORTATION

Agreement relating to reciprocal acceptance of airworthiness certifications.
Exchange of notes at Brasilia June 16, 1976.
Entered into force June 16, 1976.
27 UST 3700; TIAS 8384; 1054 UNTS 181

Agreement on air transport, with annexes.
Signed at Brasilia March 21, 1989.
Entered into force January 13, 1992.
TIAS 11780; 1668 UNTS 59

Agreement replacing annexes I and II to the air transport agreement of March 21, 1989, as amended.
Exchange of notes at Brasilia September 2, 1997.
Entered into force September 2, 1997; effective April 1, 1996.
TIAS 12879

Memorandum of cooperation for mutual cooperation in the promotion and development of civil aviation, with letter of understanding.
Signed at Washington and Brasilia January 18 and February 9, 2000.
Entered into force February 9, 2000.
TIAS

Agreement for promotion of aviation safety.
Signed at Brasilia March 22, 2004.
Entered into force February 27, 2006.
TIAS 06-227

BRUNEI

On January 1, 1984, the former British protected state of Brunei gained full independence. In a letter dated January 1, 1984, to the Secretary General of the United Nations, the Sultan made a statement reading in part as follows:

"The Government of Brunei Darussalam recognises that it is desirable to maintain to the fullest extent compatible with the resumption by Brunei Darussalam of its status and emergence on 1st January 1984 as a fully independent and sovereign nation, legal continuity in treaty relations between Brunei Darussalam and other states. Accordingly, the Government of Brunei Darussalam makes the following declaration:

"1] As regards bilateral treaties validly concluded by the United Kingdom on behalf of Brunei Darussalam or validly applied or extended by the former to the latter, the Government of Brunei Darussalam is willing to accept, on a basis of reciprocity, the rights and obligations under the terms of all such treaties for a period of five years from 1st January 1984 until 31st December 1988 unless abrogated or modified earlier by mutual consent. At the expiry of that period, the Government of Brunei Darussalam will regard such of those treaties which could not by the application of the rules of customary international law be regarded as otherwise surviving, as having terminated.

"2] The Government of Brunei Darussalam acknowledges that the above declaration applicable to bilateral treaties cannot with equal facility be applied to multilateral treaties. As regards these, therefore, the Government of Brunei Darussalam proposes to examine each of them individually and to indicate to the depositary in each case what steps it wishes to take in relation to each such instrument — whether by confirmation of termination, confirmation of succession or accession. During the period of examination the Government of Brunei Darussalam will on a basis of reciprocity accept all treaty rights and obligations accruing and arising under all multilateral treaties which were prior to independence validly applied or extended to Brunei Darussalam."

DEFENSE

Acquisition and cross-servicing agreement, with annexes.
Signed at Brunei July 30, 2010.
Entered into force July 30, 2010.
NP

DIPLOMATIC & CONSULAR RELATIONS

Consular convention between the United States and the United Kingdom.
Signed at Washington June 6, 1951.
Entered into force September 7, 1952.
3 UST 3426; TIAS 2494; 165 UNTS 121

FOREIGN ASSISTANCE

Economic cooperation agreement between the United States and the United Kingdom.
Signed at London July 6, 1948.
Applicable to Brunei October 26, 1949.
62 Stat. 2596; TIAS 1795; 12 Bevans 874; 22 UNTS 263

Amendments:

January 3, 1950 (1 UST 184; TIAS 2036; 86 UNTS 304)
May 25, 1951 (2 UST 1292; TIAS 2277; 99 UNTS 308)
February 25, 1953 (4 UST 1528; TIAS 2815; 172 UNTS 332)

INTELLECTUAL PROPERTY

Declaration by the United States and the United Kingdom affording reciprocal protection to trademarks.
Signed at London October 24, 1877.
Entered into force October 24, 1877.
20 Stat. 703; TS 138; 12 Bevans 198

INTERNATIONAL CRIMINAL COURT

Agreement regarding the surrender of persons to international tribunals.
Exchange of notes at Bandar Seri Begawan February 3 and March 3, 2004.
Entered into force March 3, 2004.
TIAS 04-303

POSTAL MATTERS

International express mail agreement, with detailed regulations.
Signed at Bandar Seri Begawan and Washington December 15, 1990, and January 8, 1991.
Entered into force February 18, 1991.
TIAS 11785

TRADE & INVESTMENT

Treaty of peace, friendship, commerce and navigation.
Signed at Brunei June 23, 1850.
Entered into force July 11, 1853.
10 Stat. 909; TS 33; 5 Bevans 1080

TRANSPORTATION

Air transport agreement, with annexes.*
Signed at Washington June 20, 1997.
Entered into force June 20, 1997.
TIAS 12870

*This agreement is suspended so long as the Multilateral Agreement on the Liberalization of International Air Transportation, signed May 1, 2001, remains in force between the United States and Brunei.

BULGARIA

ATOMIC ENERGY

Arrangement for the exchange of technical information and cooperation in nuclear safety matters, with addenda.
Signed at Rockville and Sofia November 21, 2011 and January 10, 2012.
Entered into force January 10, 2012.
TIAS 12-110

CLAIMS & DISPUTE RESOLUTION

Treaty of arbitration.
Signed at Washington January 21, 1929.
Entered into force July 22, 1929.
46 Stat. 2332; TS 792; 5 Bevans 1094; 93 LNTS 337

Treaty of conciliation.
Signed at Washington January 21, 1929.
Entered into force July 22, 1929.
46 Stat. 2334; TS 793; 5 Bevans 1097; 93 LNTS 331

CULTURAL EXCHANGES, PROPERTY & COOPERATION

Agreement concerning the establishment of a Peace Corps program in Bulgaria.
Signed at Washington September 27, 1990.
Entered into force September 27, 1990.
TIAS 11498

Agreement on the protection and preservation of certain cultural properties.
Signed at Washington December 5, 2002.
Entered into force November 30, 2009.
TIAS 09-1130

Memorandum of understanding concerning the imposition of import restrictions on categories of archaeological and ecclesiastical ethnological material of the Republic of Bulgaria.
Signed at Sofia January 14, 2014.
Entered into force January 14, 2014.
TIAS 14-114

DEFENSE

Agreement concerning the provision of training related to defense articles under the United States International Military Education and Training (IMET) Program.
Exchange of notes at Sofia February 11 and April 7, 1992.
Entered into force April 7, 1992.
NP

Agreement regarding grants under the Foreign Assistance Act of 1961, as amended, and the furnishing of defense articles, related training and other defense services from the United States to Bulgaria.
Exchange of notes at Sofia May 4 and December 5, 1994.
Entered into force December 5, 1994.
TIAS 12279

Agreement concerning the protection of classified military information.
Signed at Sofia February 1, 1995.
Entered into force February 1, 1995.
TIAS 12280

Basic exchange and cooperative agreement for topographic mapping, nautical and aeronautical charting, safety to flight and sea navigation information, geodesy and gravimetrics, digital data, and related global geospatial information and services.
Signed at Washington May 13, 1998.
Entered into force May 13, 1998.
NP

Acquisition and cross-servicing agreement, with annexes.
Signed at Sofia February 21, 2001.
Entered into force February 21, 2001.
NP

Agreement concerning overflight, and transit through, and presence in the territory of the Republic of Bulgaria of U.S. forces, personnel and contractors in support of Operation Enduring Freedom.
Exchange of notes at Sofia November 12, 2001.
Entered into force November 16, 2001.
TIAS

Agreement on defense cooperation, with annexes.
Signed at Sofia April 28, 2006.
Entered into force June 12, 2006.
TIAS 06-612

Memorandum of agreement regarding the exchange of military personnel (MPEP).
Signed at Washington and Varna August 30 and October 25, 2010.
Entered into force October 25, 2010.
NP

DIPLOMATIC & CONSULAR RELATIONS

Consular convention, with agreed memorandum and exchange of letters.
Signed at Sofia April 15, 1974.
Entered into force May 29, 1975.
26 UST 687; TIAS 8067

EDUCATION

Agreement concerning the Bulgarian-American Commission for Educational Exchange.
Signed at Sofia December 3, 2003.
Entered into force July 1, 2004.
TIAS 04-701

EMPLOYMENT

Agreement relating to the employment of dependents of official government employees.
Exchange of notes at Sofia October 8 and 29, 1991.
Entered into force October 29, 1991.
TIAS 11983

ENVIRONMENT & CONSERVATION

Agreement for cooperation in the Global Learning and Observations to Benefit the Environment (GLOBE) Program, with appendices.
Signed at Sofia September 8, 1998.
Entered into force September 8, 1998.
TIAS 12984

FINANCE

Investment incentive agreement.
Signed at Sofia June 7, 1991.
Entered into force September 30, 1991.
TIAS 11500

FOREIGN ASSISTANCE

Agreement concerning economic, technical and related assistance.
Signed at Sofia July 27, 1998.
Entered into force February 1, 1999.
TIAS 12979

LAW ENFORCEMENT

Agreement regarding mutual assistance between customs administrations.
Signed at Sofia November 6, 2000.
Entered into force April 1, 2004.
TIAS 13126

Extradition treaty, with exchange of rectifying notes.
Signed at Sophia September 19, 2007.
Entered into force May 21, 2009.
TIAS 09-521

Agreement on certain aspects of mutual legal assistance in criminal matters, with annex.
Signed at Sofia September 19, 2007.
Entered into force February 1, 2010.
TIAS 10-201.26

Agreement on enhancing cooperation in preventing and combating serious crime.
Signed at Sofia October 10, 2012.
Entered into force March 26, 2013, with the exception of Articles 7 through 9.
TIAS 13-326

Agreement for the exchange of terrorism screening information.
Signed at Washington March 19, 2014.
Entered into force March 19, 2014.
TIAS 14-319

MARITIME MATTERS

Agreement on maritime transport, with exchange of letters.
Signed at Sofia February 19, 1981.
Entered into force February 19, 1981.
TIAS 10098

Amendment and Extension:
February 7 and 13, 1984 (TIAS 10942)

NONPROLIFERATION

Agreement to facilitate the provision of assistance for nuclear nonproliferation purposes.
Signed at Sofia March 25, 2008.
Entered into force March 25, 2008.
TIAS 08-325

POSTAL MATTERS

Parcel post convention.
Signed at Sofia August 2, 1922, and at Washington August 26, 1922.
Operative November 11, 1919.
42 Stat. 2205; Post Office Department print

Memorandum of understanding concerning the operation of the INTELPOST service, with details of implementation.
Signed at Sofia and Washington April 20 and June 13, 1990.
Entered into force June 25, 1990.
TIAS 11763

International express mail agreement, with detailed regulations.
Signed at Sofia and Washington April 5 and May 20, 1991.
Entered into force June 17, 1991.
TIAS 11811

SCIENTIFIC & TECHNICAL COOPERATION

Agreement on scientific and technological cooperation, with annexes.
Signed at Washington February 9, 1978.
Entered into force February 9, 1978.
TIAS

Agreement for scientific and technological cooperation, with annexes.
Signed at Washington January 4, 2008.
Entered into force June 17, 2008.
TIAS 08-617

TAXATION

Convention for the avoidance of double taxation and the prevention of fiscal evasion with respect to taxes on income, with protocol.
Signed at Washington February 23, 2007.
Entered into force December 15, 2008; effective January 1, 2009.
TIAS 08-1215.1

Protocol amending the convention of February 23, 2007 for the avoidance of double taxation and the prevention of fiscal evasion with respect to taxes on income.
Signed at Sofia February 26, 2008.
Entered into force December 15, 2008.
TIAS 08-1215.1

Agreement to improve international tax compliance and to implement the Foreign Account Tax Compliance Act, with annexes.
Signed at Sofia December 5, 2014.
Entered into force June 30, 2015.
TIAS 15-630

TRADE & INVESTMENT

Agreement for the reciprocal waiving of legalization on certificates of origin accompanying merchandise.
Exchange of notes at Sofia January 5, 1938.
Entered into force January 5, 1938.
52 Stat. 1509; EAS 124; 5 Bevans 1105; 191 LNTS 207

Agreement on trade relations, with exchanges of letters.
Signed at Washington April 22, 1991.
Entered into force November 22, 1991.
TIAS

Treaty concerning the encouragement and reciprocal protection of investment, with annex, protocol and exchange of letters.
Signed at Washington September 23, 1992.
Entered into force June 2, 1994.
TIAS

Additional protocol amending the treaty concerning the encouragement and reciprocal protection of investment of September 23, 1992.
Signed at Brussels September 22, 2003.
Entered into force January 16, 2007.
TIAS

TRANSPORTATION

Civil aviation security agreement.*
Signed at Sofia April 24, 1991.
Entered into force April 24, 1991.
TIAS 11984
Note:
* This agreement is suspended for the duration of provisional application of the U.S. – E.U. Air Transport Agreement signed April 25 and 30, 2007.

WEAPONS

Agreement concerning cooperation in the area of the prevention of proliferation of weapons of mass destruction.
Signed at Washington June 17, 2008.
Entered into force January 29, 2009.
TIAS 09-129

BURKINA FASO

CULTURAL EXCHANGES, PROPERTY & COOPERATION

Agreement on general conditions for the employment of Peace Corps volunteers.
Signed at Ouagadougou February 6, 1975.
Entered into force February 6, 1975.
26 UST 2681; TIAS 8183; 1052 UNTS 221

DEFENSE

Arrangement relating to a geodetic survey along the 12th parallel arc.
Exchange of notes at Ouagadougou June 28 and August 21, 1967.
Entered into force August 21, 1967.
18 UST 2848; TIAS 6374; 700 UNTS 297

Agreement concerning the provision of training related to defense articles under the United States International Military Education and Training (IMET) Program.
Exchange of notes at Ouagadougou June 23 and August 29, 2006.
Entered into force August 29, 2006.
NP

Agreement regarding the status of United States personnel who may be temporarily present in Burkina Faso.
Exchange of notes at Ouagadougou February 20, 2006, and August 16, 2007.
Entered into force August 16, 2007.
TIAS 07-816

Acquisition and cross-servicing agreement, with annexes.
Signed at Ouagadougou and Stuttgart July 16 and August 6, 2008.
Entered into force August 6, 2008.
NP

FINANCE

Agreement relating to investment guaranties.
Exchange of notes at Ouagadougou June 18, 1965.
Entered into force June 18, 1965.
16 UST 1068; TIAS 5847; 549 UNTS 133

FOREIGN ASSISTANCE

Agreement providing for the furnishing of economic, technical and related assistance.
Exchange of notes at Ouagadougou June 1, 1961.
Entered into force June 1, 1961.
12 UST 867; TIAS 4787; 410 UNTS 223

INTERNATIONAL CRIMINAL COURT

Agreement regarding the surrender of persons to the International Criminal Court.
Signed at Ouagadougou October 2 and 5, 2003.
Entered into force October 14, 2003.
TIAS 03-1014

POSTAL MATTERS

International express mail agreement, with detailed regulations.
Signed at Ouagadougou and Washington October 12 and November 5, 1987.
Entered into force December 5, 1987.
TIAS 11567

TRANSPORTATION

Air transport agreement, with annexes.
Signed at Washington July 27, 2000.
Entered into force July 27, 2000.
TIAS 13109

BURMA

On January 4, 1948, Burma became a fully independent sovereign state. The treaty between the Government of the United Kingdom and the Provisional Government of Burma, signed at London October 17, 1947, provides in article 2 that "All obligations and responsibilities heretofore devolving on the Government of the United Kingdom which arise from any valid international instrument shall henceforth, insofar as such instrument may be held to have application to Burma, devolve upon the Provisional Government of Burma. The rights and benefits heretofore enjoyed by the Government of the United Kingdom in virtue of the application of any such international instrument to Burma shall henceforth be enjoyed by the Provisional Government of Burma."

CULTURAL EXCHANGES, PROPERTY & COOPERATION

Agreement concerning the program of the peace corps in the Republic of the Union of Myanmar.
Signed at Nay Pyi Taw November 11, 2014.
Entered into force November 11, 2014.
TIAS 14-1111

DEFENSE

Agreement concerning the provision of training related to defense articles under the United States International Military Education and Training (IMET) Program.
Exchange of notes at Rangoon April 8 and May 27, 1980.
Entered into force May 27, 1980.
32 UST 968; TIAS 9745; 1222 UNTS 337

DIPLOMATIC & CONSULAR RELATIONS

Convention to regulate commerce (article IV) between the United States and the United Kingdom.
Signed at London July 3, 1815.
Entered into force July 3, 1815.
8 Stat. 228; TS 110; 12 Bevans 49

EDUCATION

Agreement providing for the United States Educational Foundation.
Signed at Rangoon December 22, 1947.
Entered into force December 22, 1947.
62 Stat. 1814; TIAS 1685; 5 Bevans 1108; 25 UNTS 27

Amendments:

December 18, 1948, and May 12, 1949 (63 Stat. 2704; TIAS 1976; 5 Bevans 1119; 80 UNTS 312)
August 29, 1961 (12 UST 1195; TIAS 4834; 418 UNTS 326)

FINANCE

Agreement on the use of kyats accrued under Title I of the Agricultural Trade Development and Assistance Act of 1954, as amended.
Signed at Rangoon June 1, 1966.
Entered into force June 1, 1966.
17 UST 788; TIAS 6034; 580 UNTS 253

Investment incentive agreement.
Signed at Washington May 21, 2013.
Entered into force May 21, 2013.
TIAS 13-521

FOREIGN ASSISTANCE

Agreement relating to an informational media guaranty program in Burma.
Exchange of notes at Rangoon October 8 and 23, 1956.
Entered into force October 23, 1956.
7 UST 3165; TIAS 3695; 282 UNTS 37

Agreement providing special assistance to Burma on a grant basis to finance preliminary engineering and architectural surveys for two proposed construction projects.
Exchange of notes at Rangoon June 24, 1959.
Entered into force June 24, 1959.
10 UST 1730; TIAS 4325; 358 UNTS 91

Agreement for technical cooperation.
Signed at Nay Pyi Taw June 27, 2013.
Entered into force June 27, 2013.
TIAS 13-627

INTELLECTUAL PROPERTY

Declaration by the United States and the United Kingdom affording reciprocal protection to trademarks.
Signed at London October 24, 1877.
Entered into force October 24, 1877.
20 Stat. 703; TS 138; 12 Bevans 198

LAW ENFORCEMENT

Extradition treaty between the United States and the United Kingdom.
Signed at London December 22, 1931.
Applicable to Burma from November 1, 1941.
47 Stat. 2122; TS 849; 12 Bevans 482; 163 LNTS 59

Agreement relating to the provision of helicopters and related assistance by the United States to help Burma in suppressing illegal narcotic drug production and traffic.
Exchange of notes at Rangoon June 29, 1974.
Entered into force June 29, 1974.
25 UST 1518; TIAS 7887

PROPERTY

Convention between the United States and the United Kingdom relating to tenure and disposition of real and personal property.
*Signed at Washington March 2, 1899.**
31 Stat. 1939; TS 146; 12 Bevans 246

Supplementary convention between the United States and the United Kingdom extending the time within which notifications may be given of the accession of British colonies or foreign possessions to the convention of March 2, 1899.
*Signed at Washington January 13, 1902.**
32 Stat. 1914; TS 402; 12 Bevans 261

Note:
* Applicable to Burma after separation from India on April 1, 1937.

PUBLICATIONS

Agreement for the exchange of official publications.
Exchange of notes at Rangoon January 26 and April 5, 1948.
Entered into force April 5, 1948.
62 Stat. 1892; TIAS 1744; 5 Bevans 1116; 73 UNTS 73

TRANSPORTATION

Air transport agreement.
Signed at Rangoon September 28, 1949.
Entered into force September 28, 1949.
63 Stat. 2716; TIAS 1983; 5 Bevans 1121; 55 UNTS 3

BURUNDI

CULTURAL EXCHANGES, PROPERTY & COOPERATION

Agreement relating to the establishment of a Peace Corps program in Burundi.
Exchange of notes at Bujumbura August 31, 1982.
Entered into force August 31, 1982.
34 UST 1845; TIAS 10465; 1751 UNTS 105

DEFENSE

Agreement regarding grants under the Foreign Assistance Act of 1961, as amended, or successor legislation, and the furnishing of defense articles, defense services and related training, including pursuant to the United States International Military Education and Training (IMET) Program.
Exchange of notes at Bujumbura June 13, 2006, and August 8, 2007.
Entered into force August 8, 2007.
NP

Agreement regarding the status of United States personnel in the Republic of Burundi.
Signed at Bujumbura April 14, 2014.
Entered into force April 22, 2014.
TIAS 14-422

FINANCE

Agreement relating to investment guaranties.
Exchange of notes at Bujumbura May 6, 1969.
Entered into force May 6, 1969.
21 UST 829; TIAS 6852; 753 UNTS 35

FOREIGN ASSISTANCE

General agreement for special development assistance.
Exchange of notes at Bujumbura February 13 and 18, 1970.
Entered into force February 18, 1970.
21 UST 589; TIAS 6843; 740 UNTS 233

Agreement on economic and technical cooperation.
Signed at Bujumbura December 12, 2007.
Entered into force December 12, 2007.
TIAS 07-1212

INTERNATIONAL CRIMINAL COURT

Agreement regarding the surrender of persons to international tribunals.
Signed at Bujumbura July 5, 2003.
Entered into force July 24, 2003.
TIAS 03-724

POSTAL MATTERS

International express mail agreement, with detailed regulations.
Signed at Bujumbura and Washington November 10 and December 13, 1989.
Entered into force January 15, 1990.
TIAS 11895

TRANSPORTATION

Memorandum of agreement relating to assistance in developing and modernizing Burundi's civil aviation infrastructure.
Signed March 19 and 26, 2010.
Entered into force March 26, 2010.
NP

C

CABO VERDE

DEFENSE

Agreement concerning the provision of training related to defense articles under the United States International Military Education and Training (IMET) Program.
Exchange of notes at Praia December 9 and 16, 1987.
Entered into force December 16, 1987.
NP

Agreement regarding grants under the Foreign Assistance Act of 1961, as amended, or successor legislation, and the furnishing of defense articles, related training and other defense services.
Exchange of notes at Praia July 24 and 31, 2007.
Entered into force July 31, 2007.
NP

Acquisition and cross-servicing agreement, with annexes.
Signed at Praia March 24, 2014.
Entered into force March 24, 2014.
NP

EMPLOYMENT

Agreement relating to the employment of dependents of official government employees.
Exchange of notes at Praia February 15 and 18, 2005.
Entered into force June 14, 2005.
TIAS 05-614

ENVIRONMENT & CONSERVATION

Agreement for cooperation in the Global Learning and Observations to Benefit the Environment (GLOBE) Program, with appendices.
Signed at Praia August 9, 2000.
Entered into force August 9, 2000.
TIAS 13110

FOREIGN ASSISTANCE

Millennium Challenge Compact, with annexes.
Signed at Praia February 10, 2012.
Entered into force November 30, 2012.
TIAS 12-1130.1

INTERNATIONAL CRIMINAL COURT

Agreement regarding the surrender of persons to international tribunals.
Signed at Washington April 16, 2004.
Entered into force November 19, 2004.
TIAS 04-1119

POSTAL MATTERS

Postal money order agreement.
Signed at Washington and Praia April 17 and June 17, 1991.
Entered into force August 26, 1991.
TIAS 11818

International express mail agreement, with detailed regulations.
Signed at Praia and Washington December 27, 1991, and February 25, 1992.
Entered into force March 7, 1992.
TIAS 11855

TAXATION

Agreement for reciprocal exemption of taxes on income from the international operation of a ship or ships or aircraft.
Signed at Praia March 16, 2005.
Entered into force June 21, 2005.
TIAS 05-621

TRANSPORTATION

Agreement relating to the provision of site test, commissioning and/or periodic flight checks of air navigation aids by the Federal Aviation Administration.
Signed at Washington and Praia October 13 and November 19, 1976.
Entered into force November 19, 1976.
28 UST 8086; TIAS 8742; 1087 UNTS 111
Extensions and Amendments:
August 17 and October 18, 1977 (29 UST 5893; TIAS 9158)
March 10 and April 4, 1978 (29 UST 5895; TIAS 9158)

Civil aviation security agreement.
Signed at Washington October 11, 1989.
Entered into force October 11, 1989.
TIAS 11705; 2208 UNTS 213

Memorandum of agreement for the provision of technical assistance in developing and modernizing the civil aviation infrastructure of Cape Verde.
Signed at Washington and Praia November 20 and December 18, 2001.
Entered into force December 18, 2001.
NP
Amendment:
December 9, 2002, and June 14, 2004

Air transport agreement, with annexes.
Signed at Praia January 14, 2003.
Entered into force January 14, 2003.
TIAS 03-114

CAMBODIA

CLAIMS & DISPUTE RESOLUTION

Agreement concerning the settlement of certain property claims.
Signed at Washington October 6, 1994.
Entered into force October 6, 1994.
TIAS 12193

CULTURAL EXCHANGES, PROPERTY & COOPERATION

Agreement concerning the program of the Peace Corps in Cambodia.
Signed at Washington October 3, 1994.
Entered into force October 3, 1994.
TIAS 12569

Memorandum of understanding concerning the imposition of import restrictions on Khmer archaeological material from Cambodia from the Bronze Age through the Khmer Era.
Signed at Phnom Penh September 19, 2003.
Entered into force September 19, 2003.
TIAS 03-919
Amendment and Extension:
August 14 and 26, 2008 (TIAS 03-919)
July 18 and August 6, 2013 (TIAS 13-806.1)

DEFENSE

Agreement relating to mutual mapping assistance between the Khmer Geographic Service and the American Mapping Service.
Signed at Phnom Penh October 17, 1957.
Entered into force October 17, 1957.
8 UST 1761; TIAS 3929; 299 UNTS 203

Agreement relating to the provision of defense articles to Cambodia.
Exchange of notes at Phnom Penh August 20, 1970.
Entered into force August 20, 1970.
21 UST 2178; TIAS 6965; 764 UNTS 233

Memorandum of understanding for airfield upgrading at Ream, Pochentong and Battambang.
Signed at Phnom Penh August 12, 1972.
Entered into force August 12, 1972.
23 UST 3144; TIAS 7491; 898 UNTS 161

Agreement concerning payment to the United States of net proceeds from the sale of defense articles furnished under the military assistance program.
Exchange of notes at Phnom Penh May 14 and June 19, 1974.
Entered into force July 1, 1974.
25 UST 1668; TIAS 7902

Agreement regarding the status of United States military personnel and civilian employees of the Department of Defense who may be temporarily present in Cambodia in connection with military assistance activities and other official duties.
Exchange of notes at Phnom Penh October 12, 1995, and January 22, 1996.
Entered into force January 22, 1996.
NP

Agreement regarding grants under the Foreign Assistance Act of 1961, as amended, or successor legislation, and the furnishing of defense articles, defense services and related training, including pursuant to the United States International Military Education and Training Program (IMET), from the United States of America to the Kingdom of Cambodia.
Exchange of notes at Phnom Penh May 18 and July 14, 2006.
Entered into force July 14, 2006.
NP

FINANCE

Investment incentive agreement.
Signed at Phnom Penh August 4, 1995.
Entered into force March 25, 1996.
TIAS

FOREIGN ASSISTANCE

Economic, technical and related assistance agreement.
Signed at Phnom Penh October 25, 1994.
Entered into force October 25, 1994.
TIAS 12573

AGENCY FOR INTERNATIONAL DEVELOPMENT

Agreement for improved health services in HIV/AIDS and infectious diseases as well as in maternal, child and reproductive health, with annex.
Signed September 11, 2003.
Entered into force September 11, 2003.
NP
Amendments:
September 18, 2006 (NP)
September 21, 2012 (NP)
February 5, 2014 (NP)

INTERNATIONAL CRIMINAL COURT

Agreement regarding the non-surrender of persons to the International Criminal Court.
Signed at Phnom Penh June 27, 2003.
Entered into force June 29, 2005.
TIAS 05-629

POSTAL MATTERS

International express mail agreement, with detailed regulations.
Signed at Phnom Penh and Washington April 27 and October 28, 1994.
Entered into force January 1, 1995.
NP

PUBLICATIONS

Agreement relating to the exchange of official publications.
Exchange of notes at Phnom Penh July 15, 1960.
Entered into force July 15, 1960.
11 UST 1923; TIAS 4540; 380 UNTS 129

TRADE & INVESTMENT

Agreement on trade relations and intellectual property rights protection, with exchanges of notes.
Signed at Washington October 4, 1996.
Entered into force October 25, 1996.
TIAS

Trade and investment framework agreement, with annex.
Signed at Washington July 14, 2006.
Entered into force July 14, 2006.
TIAS 06-714

CAMEROON

CULTURAL EXCHANGES, PROPERTY & COOPERATION

Agreement relating to the establishment of a Peace Corps program in Cameroon.
Exchange of notes at Yaounde July 23 and September 10, 1962.
Entered into force September 10, 1962.
13 UST 2114; TIAS 5171; 461 UNTS 177

DEFENSE

Agreement regarding the status of U.S. military personnel in connection with their duties.
Exchange of notes at Yaounde December 28, 1999 and February 24, 2000.
Entered into force September 22, 2015, with effect from February 24, 2000.
TIAS 15-922.2

Agreement regarding grants under the Foreign Assistance Act of 1961, as amended, or successor legislation, and the furnishing of defense articles, defense services and related training, including pursuant to the United States International Military Education and Training (IMET) Program.
Exchange of notes at Yaounde March 8 and August 3, 2007.
Entered into force August 3, 2007.
NP

Acquisition and cross-servicing agreement.
Signed at Stuttgart and Yaounde April 6 and August 31, 2015.
Entered into force August 31, 2015.
NP

EMPLOYMENT

Agreement relating to the employment of dependents of official government employees.
Exchange of notes at Washington May 7, 1992, and January 15, 1993.
Entered into force January 15, 1993.
TIAS 11916

ENVIRONMENT & CONSERVATION

Agreement for cooperation in the Global Learning and Observations to Benefit the Environment (GLOBE) Program, with appendices.
Signed at Yaounde November 6, 1998.
Entered into force November 6, 1998.
TIAS 12993

FINANCE

Agreement relating to investment guaranties.
Exchange of notes at Washington March 7, 1967.
Entered into force March 7, 1967.
18 UST 292; TIAS 6231; 688 UNTS 315

Agreement regarding the phased discharge of certain debts owed to the Government of the United States, with annexes.
Signed at Yaounde January 3, 1990.
Entered into force January 3, 1990.
NP

Agreement regarding the consolidation and rescheduling of certain debts owed to, guaranteed by, or insured by the United States Government and its agencies, with annexes.
Signed at Yaounde January 3, 1990.
Entered into force February 12, 1990.
NP

Agreement regarding the consolidation and rescheduling or refinancing of certain debts owed to, guaranteed by or insured by the United States Government and its agencies, with annexes.
Signed at Yaounde August 19, 1992.
Entered into force October 12, 1992.
NP

Agreement regarding the consolidation and rescheduling or refinancing of certain debts owed to, guaranteed by or insured by the United States Government and its agencies, with annexes.
Signed at Yaounde September 12, 1994.
Entered into force December 5, 1994.
NP

Agreement regarding the consolidation and rescheduling of certain debts owed to, guaranteed by, or insured by the United States Government and its agencies, with annexes.
Signed at Yaounde May 6, 1996.
Entered into force July 31, 1996.
NP

Agreement regarding the consolidation, reduction and rescheduling of certain debts owed to, guaranteed by, or insured by the United States Government and its agencies, with annexes.
Signed at Yaounde July 29, 1998.
Entered into force September 10, 1998.
NP

Agreement regarding the consolidation, reduction, and rescheduling of certain debts owed to, guaranteed by, or insured by the United States Government and its agencies, with annexes.
Signed at Yaounde February 5, 2002.
Entered into force March 21, 2002.
NP
Amendment:
February 22 and March 31, 2006

Agreement regarding the reduction of certain debts owed to, guaranteed by, or insured by the United States Government and its agencies, with annexes.
Signed at Yaounde January 17, 2007.
Entered into force April 26, 2007.
NP

FOREIGN ASSISTANCE

Agreement providing for the furnishing of economic, technical and related assistance.
Exchange of notes at Yaounde May 26, 1961.
Entered into force May 26, 1961.
12 UST 967; TIAS 4801; 413 UNTS 195
Amendment:
December 8, 1961 (13 UST 282; TIAS 4973; 445 UNTS 367)

INTERNATIONAL CRIMINAL COURT

Agreement regarding the surrender of persons to international tribunals.
Signed at Yaounde December 1, 2003.
Entered into force December 1, 2003.
TIAS 03-1201

POSTAL MATTERS

International express mail agreement, with detailed regulations.
Signed at Yaounde and Washington April 25 and June 22, 1990.
Entered into force August 1, 1990.
TIAS 11762

SCIENTIFIC & TECHNICAL COOPERATION

Memorandum of understanding concerning scientific and technical cooperation in the earth sciences, with annexes.
Signed at Reston and Yaounde July 11 and September 10, 2001.
Entered into force September 10, 2001.
TIAS

TRADE & INVESTMENT

Treaty concerning the reciprocal encouragement and protection of investment.
Signed at Washington February 26, 1986.
Entered into force April 6, 1989.
TIAS

TRANSPORTATION

Memorandum of agreement for the provision of technical assistance in developing, modernizing, operating, or maintaining the civil aviation infrastructure in Cameroon, with annex.
Signed at Washington and Yaounde December 20 and 28, 2012.
Entered into force December 28, 2012.
NP

CANADA

AGRICULTURE

Agreement relating to the participation of the provinces of New Brunswick and Quebec in the northeastern interstate forest fire protection compact.
Exchange of notes at Washington January 29, 1970.
Entered into force January 29, 1970.
21 UST 415; TIAS 6825; 753 UNTS 43

Agreement concerning cooperation in the detection and suppression of forest fires along the boundary between the Yukon Territory and Alaska, with memorandum of agreement.
Exchange of notes at Washington June 1, 1971.
Entered into force June 1, 1971.
22 UST 721; TIAS 7132; 793 UNTS 77

Arrangement on mutual assistance in fighting forest fires.
Exchange of notes at Ottawa May 4 and 7, 1982.
Entered into force May 7, 1982.
34 UST 1557; TIAS 10436

ANTARCTICA & ARCTIC

Agreement on Arctic cooperation.
Signed at Ottawa January 11, 1988.
Entered into force January 11, 1988.
TIAS 11565; 1852 UNTS 59

ATOMIC ENERGY

Agreement for cooperation on civil uses of atomic energy.
Signed at Washington June 15, 1955.
Entered into force July 21, 1955.
6 UST 2595; TIAS 3304; 235 UNTS 175

Amendments and Extension*:
June 26, 1956 (8 UST 275; TIAS 3771; 279 UNTS 318)
June 11, 1960 (11 UST 1780; TIAS 4518; 377 UNTS 412)
May 25, 1962 (13 UST 1400; TIAS 5102; 453 UNTS 362)
April 23, 1980 (32 UST 1079; TIAS 9759; 1228 UNTS 425)
June 23, 1999 (TIAS 13049)

Note
* See also agreement of May 22, 1959, for cooperation on uses of atomic energy for mutual defense purposes (10 UST 1293; TIAS 4271).

Agreement regarding participation in the USNRC international piping integrity research group.
Signed at Ottawa and Bethesda April 28 and May 20, 1987.
Entered into force May 20, 1987.
TIAS 12227

Agreement concerning cooperation on the application of non-proliferation assurances to Canadian uranium to be transferred from Canada to the U.S. for enrichment and fabrication into fuel and retransferred to Taiwan for use in nuclear reactors, with annex.
Exchange of letters at Washington February 24 and March 5, 1993.
Entered into force March 5, 1993.
TIAS 12490; 1914 UNTS 209

BOUNDARIES & BOUNDARY WATERS

(See also PEACE, MARITIME MATTERS and POLLUTION)

Convention between the United States and the United Kingdom respecting fisheries, boundary and the restoration of slaves.
Signed at London October 20, 1818.
Entered into force January 30, 1819.
8 Stat. 248; TS 112; 12 Bevans 57

Treaty between the United States and the United Kingdom to settle and define the boundaries between the territories of the United States and the possessions of Her Britannic Majesty in North America; for the final suppression of the African slave trade, and for the giving up of criminals, fugitive from justice, in certain cases (Webster-Ashburton Treaty).*
Washington August 9, 1842.
Entered into force October 13, 1842.
8 Stat. 572; TS 119; 12 Bevans 82

Notes:
* Article 10 supplemented by convention of July 12, 1889 (See under CANADA — EXTRADITION).

Treaty between the United States and the United Kingdom establishing the boundary in the territory on the northwest coast of America lying westward of the Rocky Mountains (Oregon Treaty).
Signed at Washington June 15, 1846.
Entered into force July 17, 1846.
9 Stat. 869; TS 120; 12 Bevans 95

Declaration adopting maps of boundary prepared by the Joint Commission of the Northwest Boundary for surveying and marking the boundaries between the United States and British possessions on the forty-ninth parallel of north latitude, under the first article of the treaty of June 15, 1846 between the United States and the United Kingdom.
Signed at Washington February 24, 1870.
Entered into force February 24, 1870.
TS 129; 12 Bevans 157

Protocol between the United States and the United Kingdom of a conference respecting the northwest water boundary.
Signed at Washington March 10, 1873.
Entered into force March 10, 1873.
18 Stat. 369; TS 135; 12 Bevans 190

Convention providing for the settlement of questions between the United States and the United Kingdom with respect to the boundary line between the territory of Alaska and the British possessions in North America.*
Signed at Washington January 24, 1903.
Entered into force March 3, 1903.
32 Stat. 1961; TS 419; 12 Bevans 263

Notes:
* Obsolete except for first paragraph of article VI.

Acceptance of the report of the commissioners to complete the award under the convention of January 24, 1903, respecting the boundary line between Alaska and the British North American possessions.
Exchange of notes at Washington March 25, 1905.
Entered into force March 25, 1905.
TS 476; 12 Bevans 269

Convention providing for the surveying and marking out upon the ground of the 141st degree of west longitude where said meridian forms the boundary line between Alaska and the British possessions in North America.*
Signed at Washington April 21, 1906.
Entered into force August 16, 1906.
34 Stat. 2948; TS 452; 12 Bevans 276

Notes:
* Obsolete except for article II.

Treaty between the United States and the United Kingdom concerning the Canadian international boundary.
Signed at Washington April 11, 1908.
Entered into force June 4, 1908.
35 Stat. 2003; TS 497; 12 Bevans 297

Treaty relating to the boundary waters and questions arising along the boundary between the United States and Canada.*
Signed at Washington January 11, 1909.
Entered into force May 5, 1910.
36 Stat. 2448; TS 548; 12 Bevans 319

Note:
* Paragraphs 3, 4, and 5 of article V terminated October 10, 1950, upon the entry into force of the treaty relating to uses of waters of the Niagara River, signed February 27, 1950 (1 UST 694; TIAS 2130; 132 UNTS 223).

Treaty concerning the boundary line in Passamaquoddy Bay.
Signed at Washington May 21, 1910.
Entered into force August 20, 1910.
36 Stat. 2477; TS 551; 12 Bevans 341

Treaty in regard to the boundary between the United States and Canada.
Signed at Washington February 24, 1925.
Entered into force July 17, 1925.
44 Stat. 2102; TS 720; 6 Bevans 7; 43 LNTS 239

Convention to regulate the level of the Lake of the Woods, with an accompanying protocol and an agreement.
Signed at Washington February 24, 1925.
Entered into force July 17, 1925.
44 Stat. 2108; TS 721; 6 Bevans 14; 43 LNTS 251

Amendment:
February 21 and June 19, 1979 (30 UST 5998; TIAS 9534; 1180 UNTS 77)

Arrangement relating to the level of Lake Memphremagog.
Exchange of notes at Ottawa September 20 and November 6, 1935.
Entered into force November 6, 1935.
Foreign Relations, 1935, Vol. II, p. 53; 6 Bevans 71

Convention providing for emergency regulation of the level of Rainy Lake and of certain other boundary waters.
Signed at Ottawa September 15, 1938.
Entered into force October 3, 1940.
54 Stat. 1800; TS 961; 6 Bevans 115; 203 LNTS 207

Arrangement relating to the early development of certain portions of the Great Lakes-St. Lawrence Basin project (Long Lac-Ogoki Works).
Exchange of notes at Washington October 14 and 31 and November 7, 1940.
Entered into force November 7, 1940.
54 Stat. 2426; EAS 187; 6 Bevans 199; 203 LNTS 267

Agreement relating to the temporary raising of level of Lake St. Francis during low-water periods.
Exchange of notes at Washington November 10, 1941.
Entered into force November 10, 1941.
56 Stat. 1832; EAS 291; 6 Bevans 236; 23 UNTS 280

Extension:
August 31 and September 7, 1944 (58 Stat. 1437; EAS 424; 105 UNTS 310)

Agreement relating to the Upper Columbia River Basin.
Exchange of notes at Ottawa February 25 and March 3, 1944.
Entered into force March 3, 1944.
58 Stat. 1236; EAS 399; 6 Bevans 342; 109 UNTS 191

Treaty relating to uses of waters of the Niagara River.
Signed at Washington February 27, 1950.
Entered into force October 10, 1950.
1 UST 694; TIAS 2130; 132 UNTS 223

Related Agreements:
September 13, 1954 (5 UST 1979; TIAS 3064; 236 UNTS 382)
April 17, 1973 (24 UST 895; TIAS 7599)

Agreement relating to the St. Lawrence seaway project for the construction of certain navigation facilities.
Exchange of notes at Washington June 30, 1952.
Entered into force June 30, 1952.
5 UST 1788; TIAS 3053; 234 UNTS 199

Agreement establishing the St. Lawrence River Joint Board of Engineers.
Exchange of notes at Washington November 12, 1953.
Entered into force November 12, 1953.
5 UST 2538; TIAS 3116; 234 UNTS 97

Agreement relating to the St. Lawrence seaway project for the construction of certain navigation facilities.
Exchange of notes at Ottawa August 17, 1954.
Entered into force August 17, 1954.
5 UST 1784; TIAS 3053; 234 UNTS 210

Related Agreements:
February 21 and 22, 1955 (NP)
October 24, 1956 (7 UST 2865; TIAS 3668; 281 UNTS 281)
November 7 and December 4, 1956 (7 UST 3271; TIAS 3708)
July 23 and October 26, 1956, and February 26, 1957 (8 UST 279; TIAS 3772; 279 UNTS 179)
November 30, 1956, and April 8 and 9, 1957 (8 UST 637; TIAS 3814; 283 UNTS 217)
May 19, 1955, and February 27, 1959 (10 UST 383; TIAS 4199; 341 UNTS 3)
October 17, 1961 (12 UST 1284; TIAS 4851; 426 UNTS 201)
June 8, 1959, and October 17, 1961 (12 UST 1669; TIAS 4883; 424 UNTS 101)

Agreement governing tolls on the St. Lawrence Seaway.
Exchange of notes at Ottawa March 9, 1959.
Entered into force March 9, 1959.
10 UST 323; TIAS 4192; 340 UNTS 295

Amendments:
July 3 and 13, 1962 (13 UST 1763; 5117 TIAS)
March 31, 1964 (15 UST 271; 5551 TIAS; 527 UNTS 318)
June 30, 1964 (15 UST 1390; TIAS 5608; 530 UNTS 364)
March 31, 1967 (18 UST 321; TIAS 6236; 688 UNTS 380)
July 5, 1968 (NP)
July 27, 1972 (23 UST 1304; TIAS 7408; 851 UNTS 279)
March 20, 1978 (29 UST 3165; TIAS 9003)
October 7, 1980 (32 UST 2893; TIAS 9883)
March 18, 1982 (34 UST 364; TIAS 10363)
November 13 and 16, 1984 (TIAS 11061; 1884 UNTS 457)
May 3, 1985 (TIAS 11309; 1466 UNTS 436)
April 9 and 11, 1986 (TIAS 11309)
May 7 and December 22, 1987 (TIAS 11884)
April 21 and August 10, 1988 (TIAS 11776)
March 30 and August 1, 1989 (TIAS 11966)
April 26 and May 1, 1991 (TIAS 11885)
December 12 and 20, 1991 (TIAS 11866)
June 15 and 30, 1992 (TIAS 11866)
June 10 and July 12, 1994 (TIAS 12697; 2030 UNTS 41)
August 9 and October 18, 1995 (TIAS 12697; 2030 UNTS 30)

Treaty relating to cooperative development of the water resources of the Columbia River Basin.
Signed at Washington January 17, 1961.
Entered into force September 16, 1964.
15 UST 1555; TIAS 5638; 542 UNTS 244

Related Agreements:
January 22, 1964 (TIAS; 5638; 542 UNTS 292)
September 16, 1964 (15 UST 1555; TIAS 5638; 542 UNTS 312)
October 4, 1965 (16 UST 1263; TIAS 5877; 592 UNTS 272)

Agreement relating to the construction of a sewage line from Dunseith, North Dakota to Boissevain, Manitoba.
Exchange of notes at Ottawa January 13, April 22 and June 9, 1966.
Entered into force June 9, 1966.
17 UST 810; TIAS 6037; 580 UNTS 263

Treaty relating to the Skagit River and Ross Lake, and the Seven Mile Reservoir on the Pend d'Oreille River, with annex.
Signed at Washington April 2, 1984.
Entered into force December 14, 1984.
TIAS 11088; 1469 UNTS 309

Agreement concerning cooperation in flood control, with construction plan.
Exchange of notes at Ottawa and Washington August 29 and 30, 1988.
Entered into force August 30, 1988.
TIAS 11641

Agreement for water supply and flood control in the Souris River Basin, with annexes.
Signed at Washington October 26, 1989.
Entered into force October 26, 1989.
TIAS 11731

Amendments:
December 20 and 22, 2000 (TIAS 00-1222)
January 14 and June 9, 2005(TIAS 00-1222)

Agreement for the sale of Canada's entitlement to downstream power benefits within the United States, with attachment.
Exchange of notes at Washington March 31, 1999.
Entered into force March 31, 1999.
TIAS 13027

CIVIL AFFAIRS, EMERGENCIES & DEFENSE

Agreement on emergency management cooperation, with annex.
Signed at Washington December 12, 2008.
Entered into force July 7, 2009.
TIAS 09-707

CLAIMS & DISPUTE RESOLUTION

Convention for the establishment of a tribunal to decide questions of indemnity arising from the operation of the smelter at Trail, British Columbia.
Signed at Ottawa April 15, 1935.
Entered into force August 3, 1935.
49 Stat. 3245; TS 893; 6 Bevans 60; 162 LNTS 73

Treaty amending in their application to Canada certain provisions of the treaty for the advancement of peace between the United States and the United Kingdom signed at Washington
September 15, 1914.
Signed at Washington September 6, 1940.
Entered into force August 13, 1941.
55 Stat. 1214; TS 975; 6 Bevans 190

Agreement relating to claims arising out of traffic accidents involving vehicles of the armed forces of the United States and Canada.
Exchange of notes at Ottawa March 1 and 23, 1944.
Entered into force March 23, 1944.
60 Stat. 1948; TIAS 1581; 6 Bevans 345; 125 UNTS 345

Agreement relating to reciprocal waiver of maritime claims involving government vessels.
Exchange of notes at Washington September 28 and November 13 and 15, 1946.
Entered into force November 15, 1946.
61 Stat. 2520; TIAS 1582; 6 Bevans 422; 7 UNTS 141

Agreement relating to the settlement of certain war accounts and claims.
Exchange of notes at Washington March 14, 1949.
Entered into force March 14, 1949.
63 Stat. 2432; TIAS 1925; 6 Bevans 482; 82 UNTS 3

Agreement supplementary to the convention signed April 15, 1935, for the establishment of a tribunal to decide questions of indemnity and future regime arising from the operation of the smelter at Trail, British Columbia.
Exchange of notes at Washington November 17, 1949, and January 24, 1950.
Entered into force January 24, 1950.
3 UST 539; TIAS 2412; 151 UNTS 171

Treaty to submit to binding dispute settlement the delimitation of the maritime boundary in the Gulf of Maine Area, with annexed agreements, as amended.
Signed at Washington March 29, 1979.
*Entered into force November 20, 1981.**
33 UST 2797; TIAS 10204; 1288 UNTS 27

Related Agreement:
March 29, 1979 (33 UST 2797; 1288 UNTS 33

Notes:
* For the subsequent judgment of the International Court of Justice of October 12, 1984, see Case concerning Delimitation of the Maritime Boundary in the Gulf of Maine Area. 1984 I.C.J. Reports 246.
With the implementation of the special agreement to submit the dispute to a chamber of the I.C.J., the agreement for possible submission to a court of arbitration never entered into force.

CONSULAR AFFAIRS

Agreement for the sharing of visa and immigration information.
Signed at Ottawa December 13, 2012.
Entered into force November 21, 2013.
TIAS 13-1121

CULTURAL EXCHANGES, PROPERTY & COOPERATION

Agreement relating to the establishment of the Roosevelt Campobello International Park.
Signed at Washington January 22, 1964.
Entered into force August 14, 1964.
15 UST 1504; TIAS 5631; 530 UNTS 89

DEFENSE

Agreement relating to naval forces on the American Lakes (Rush-Bagot Agreement).
Exchange of notes at Washington April 28 and 29, 1817.
Entered into force April 29, 1817.
8 Stat. 231; TS 110 1/2; 12 Bevans 54

Agreement relating to the construction of naval vessels on the Great Lakes (interpretation of the Rush-Bagot Agreement).
Exchange of notes at Ottawa June 9 and 10, 1939.
Entered into force June 10, 1939.
61 Stat. 4069; TIAS 1836; 6 Bevans 149; 149 UNTS 332

Declaration by the Prime Minister of Canada and the President of the United States of America regarding the establishing of a Permanent Joint Board on Defense.
Made at Ogdensburg, New York, August 18, 1940.
Department of State Bulletin, Vol. III, No. 61, August 24, 1940, p. 154; 6 Bevans 189; Canada Treaty Series, 1940, No. 14

Arrangement relating to naval and air bases.
Exchange of notes at Washington September 2, 1940.
Entered into force September 2, 1940.
54 Stat. 2405; EAS 181; 12 Bevans 551; 203 LNTS 201

Agreement relating to the armament of naval vessels to be incapable of immediate use (interpretation of the Rush-Bagot Agreement).
Exchange of notes at Ottawa October 30 and November 2, 1940.
Entered into force November 2, 1940.
61 Stat. 4077; TIAS 1836; 6 Bevans 196; 149 UNTS 350

Agreement regarding leased naval and air bases, and exchanges of notes.
Signed at London March 27, 1941.
Entered into force March 27, 1941.
55 Stat. 1560; EAS 235; 12 Bevans 560; 204 LNTS 15
Amendment:
May 22, 1985

Protocol concerning the defense of Newfoundland.
Signed at London March 27, 1941.
Entered into force March 27, 1941.
55 Stat. 1599; EAS 235; 12 Bevans 560; 204 LNTS 70

Arrangement relating to visits in uniform by members of defense forces, with exchange of notes.
Exchange of notes at Ottawa August 28 and September 4, 1941.
Entered into force September 11, 1941.
55 Stat. 1551; EAS 233; 6 Bevans 231; 119 UNTS 285

Agreement relating to payment for certain defense installations in Canada and at Goose Bay (Labrador).
Exchange of notes at Washington June 23 and 27, 1944.
Entered into force June 27, 1944.
58 Stat. 1290; EAS 405; 6 Bevans 360; 101 UNTS 273

Agreement relating to naval vessels for training naval reserve personnel (interpretation of the Rush-Bagot Agreement).
Exchange of notes at Washington November 18 and December 6, 1946.
Entered into force December 6, 1946.
61 Stat. 4082; TIAS 1836; 6 Bevans 426; 149 UNTS 3

United States-Canadian Permanent Joint Board on Defense to continue collaboration for security purposes.
Announced in Ottawa and in Washington February 12, 1947.
Department of State Bulletin, Vol. XVI, No. 399, February 23, 1947, p. 361; 6 Bevans 430; Canada Treaty Series, 1947, No. 43

Agreement relating to the leased naval base at Argentia, Newfoundland.
Exchange of notes at London August 13 and October 23, 1947.
Entered into force October 23, 1947.
61 Stat. 4065; TIAS 1809; 12 Bevans 827; 66 UNTS 277
Amendment:
May 22, 1985

Agreement relating to cooperation between the United States and Canada in air search and rescue operations along the common boundary.
Exchange of notes at Washington January 24 and 31, 1949.
Entered into force January 31, 1949.
63 Stat. 2328; TIAS 1882; 6 Bevans 478; 43 UNTS 119

Agreement establishing a Joint Industrial Mobilization Committee.
Exchange of notes at Ottawa April 12, 1949.
Entered into force April 12, 1949.
63 Stat. 2331; TIAS 1889; 6 Bevans 486; 206 UNTS 241

Agreement relating to a final settlement for all war surplus property disposed of pursuant to the agreements effected by exchanges of notes of November 22 and December 20, 1944; March 30, 1946; and July 11 and 15, 1946.
Exchange of notes at Ottawa June 17 and 18, 1949.
Entered into force June 18, 1949.
2 UST 2272; TIAS 2352; 200 UNTS 258

Agreement relating to economic cooperation for defense.
Exchange of notes at Washington October 26, 1950.
Entered into force October 26, 1950.
1 UST 716; TIAS 2136; 132 UNTS 247

Agreement relating to the extension and coordination of the continental radar defense system.*
Exchange of notes at Washington August 1, 1951.
Entered into force August 1, 1951.
5 UST 1721; TIAS 3049; 233 UNTS 109
Related Agreements:
May 25, 1964 (15 UST 665; TIAS 5587; 526 UNTS 251)
September 30, 1966 (17 UST 1416; TIAS 6102; 616 UNTS 193)
June 30, 1971 (22 UST 1449; TIAS 7154; 797 UNTS 303)
March 22, 1974 (25 UST 283; TIAS 7799; 944 UNTS 173)

Note:
* Provisions are terminated to the extent that they are inconsistent with the agreement of August 16, 1971 (TIAS 7173). See also agreements of June 13, 1955 (TIAS 3452), June 15, 1955 (TIAS 3453), and September 27, 1961 (TIAS 4859).

Agreement modifying the leased bases agreement of March 27, 1941, with the United Kingdom concerning bases in Canada.
Exchange of notes at Washington February 13 and March 19, 1952.
Entered into force March 19, 1952.
3 UST 4271; TIAS 2572; 174 UNTS 267

Agreement relating to the application of the NATO status of forces agreement to U.S. forces in Canada, including those at the leased bases in Newfoundland and Goose Bay, Labrador except for certain arrangements under the leased bases agreement.
Exchange of notes at Washington April 28 and 30, 1952.
Entered into force September 27, 1953.
5 UST 2139; TIAS 3074; 235 UNTS 269

Agreement on the establishment and operation of a distant early warning system between the United States and Canada, with annex.
Exchange of notes at Washington May 5, 1955.
*Entered into force May 5, 1955.**
6 UST 763; TIAS 3218; 241 UNTS 179

Note:
* See also agreements of April 13, 1959 (TIAS 4208), and July 13, 1959 (TIAS 4264).

Agreement relating to the establishment and operation of certain radar stations in the Newfoundland-Labrador area.*
Exchange of notes at Ottawa June 13, 1955.
Entered into force June 13, 1955.
6 UST 6045; TIAS 3452; 268 UNTS 87

Note:
* See also agreements of August 1, 1951 (TIAS 3049), June 15, 1955 (TIAS 3453), September 27, 1961 (TIAS 4859), and August 16, 1971 (TIAS 7173).

Agreement for cooperation regarding atomic information for mutual defense purposes.
Signed at Washington June 15, 1955.
Entered into force July 22, 1955.
6 UST 2607; TIAS 3305; 235 UNTS 201

Agreement relating to the construction and operation of certain radar stations in British Columbia, Ontario, and Nova Scotia.*
Exchange of notes at Ottawa June 15, 1955.
Entered into force June 15, 1955.
6 UST 6051; TIAS 3453; 268 UNTS 101

Note:
* See also agreements of August 1, 1951 (TIAS 3049), June 13, 1955 (TIAS 3452), September 27, 1961 (TIAS 4859), and August 16, 1971 (TIAS 7173).

Agreement relating to the construction of a petroleum products pipeline between the United States Air Force dock at St. John's, Newfoundland, and Pepperrell Air Force Base, Newfoundland, with annex.
Exchange of notes at Ottawa September 22, 1955.
Entered into force September 22, 1955.
6 UST 3899; TIAS 3392; 256 UNTS 227

Agreement providing for the establishment of a Canada-United States Committee on Joint Defense.
Exchange of notes at Ottawa August 29 and September 2, 1958.
Entered into force September 2, 1958.
9 UST 1159; TIAS 4098; 335 UNTS 249

Agreement relating to communications facilities at Cape Dyer, Baffin Island to support the Greenland extension of the distant early warning system.*
Exchange of notes at Ottawa April 13, 1959.
Entered into force April 13, 1959; operative January 15, 1959.
10 UST 739; TIAS 4208; 342 UNTS 43

Note:
* See also agreements of May 5, 1955 (TIAS 3218), and July 13, 1959 (TIAS 4264).

Agreement relating to the establishment, maintenance and operation of short range tactical air navigation (TACAN) facilities in Canada, with annex.
Exchange of notes at Ottawa May 1, 1959.
Entered into force May 1, 1959.
10 UST 790; TIAS 4218; 343 UNTS 27

Amendment:
September 19 and 23, 1961 (12 UST 1357; TIAS 4856; 421 UNTS 79)

Agreement for cooperation on uses of atomic energy for mutual defense purposes.
Signed at Washington May 22, 1959.
Entered into force July 27, 1959.
10 UST 1293; TIAS 4271; 354 UNTS 63

Agreement relating to the establishment of a ballistic missile early warning system.*
Exchange of notes at Ottawa July 13, 1959.
Entered into force July 13, 1959.
10 UST 1260; TIAS 4264; 353 UNTS 237

Note:
* See also agreements of May 5, 1955 (TIAS 3218), and April 13, 1959 (TIAS 4208).

Agreement relating to the disposal of surplus United States property in Canada.
Exchange of notes at Ottawa August 28 and September 1, 1961.
Entered into force September 1, 1961.
12 UST 1228; TIAS 4841; 421 UNTS 199.

Amendment
December 21, 1983, and March 14, 1984 (TIAS 11063; 1466 UNTS 443)

Agreement relating to the extension and strengthening of the continental air defense system (CADIN).*
Exchange of notes at Ottawa September 27, 1961.
Entered into force September 27, 1961.
12 UST 1375; TIAS 4859; 421 UNTS 85

Amendments:
May 6, 1964 (15 UST 427; TIAS 5574; 524 UNTS 324)
November 24, 1965 (16 UST 1768; TIAS 5907; 573 UNTS 330)

Note:
* See also agreements of August 1, 1951 (TIAS 3049), June 13, 1955 (TIAS 3452), June 15, 1955 (TIAS 3453), and August 16, 1971 (TIAS 7173).

Agreement relating to the safeguarding of classified information.
Exchange of notes at Washington January 30, 1962.
Entered into force January 30, 1962.
TIAS

Agreement concerning the establishment, operation and maintenance of the torpedo test range in the Strait of Georgia and the installation and utilization of an advanced underwater acoustic measurement system at Jervis Inlet, with annex.
Exchange of notes at Ottawa May 12, 1965.
Entered into force May 12, 1965.
16 UST 753; TIAS 5805

Amendments and extension:
January 13, and April 14, 1976 (27 UST 3723; TIAS 8386)
June 3 and 17, 1986 (TIAS 11368; 2194 UNTS 298)

Agreement concerning the establishment, operation and maintenance of certain ground-to-air communications facilities in northern Canada, with annex.
Exchange of notes at Ottawa December 1, 1965.
Entered into force December 1, 1965.
16 UST 1789; TIAS 5911; 574 UNTS 37

Agreement relating to the establishment of a ferry service between North Sydney, Nova Scotia and Argentia, Newfoundland, with annex.
Exchange of notes at Washington June 6 and 10, 1966.
Entered into force June 10, 1966.
17 UST 792; TIAS 6035; 639 UNTS 13

Agreement relating to the winter maintenance of the Haines Road.
Exchange of notes at Ottawa May 10 and June 23, 1967.
Entered into force June 23, 1967.
18 UST 1244; TIAS 6274; 685 UNTS 410

Agreement relating to the use of certain facilities at the United States Air Force Pinetree radar site at Hopedale, Labrador.
Exchange of notes at Ottawa June 11, September 19, 1969, and February 24, 1970.
Entered into force February 24, 1970.
21 UST 596; TIAS 6844; 740 UNTS 241

Agreement relating to the transfer of the Redcliff site to Canada.
Exchange of notes at Ottawa May 10, 1971.
Entered into force May 10, 1971.
22 UST 1778; TIAS 7217

Agreement relating to new financial arrangements to govern the operation and maintenance of Pinetree radar stations in Canada, with annex.*
Exchange of notes at Ottawa August 16, 1971.
Entered into force August 16, 1971; operative August 1, 1971.
22 UST 1529; TIAS 7173; 807 UNTS 19

Note:
* See also agreements of August 1, 1951 (TIAS 3049), June 13, 1955 (TIAS 3452), and June 15, 1955 (TIAS 3453).

Agreement relating to the purchase by Canada of eighteen Lockheed P-3 long-range patrol aircraft, with related notes.
Exchange of letters at Washington July 6 and 7, 1976.
Entered into force July 7, 1976.
27 UST 3732; TIAS 8388

Agreement relating to the use of facilities at Goose Bay airport by the United States, with annex.
Exchange of notes at Ottawa November 10 and 24, 1976.
Entered into force November 24, 1976; effective October 1, 1976.
27 UST 4322; TIAS 8454

Memorandum of understanding concerning region operations control center.
Signed at Ottawa and Washington March 5 and April 11, 1977.
Entered into force April 11, 1977.
29 UST 1075; TIAS 8869

Agreement relating to performance evaluation of a variable depth sonar system in conjunction with a high speed surface vessel, with annexes (Project Hytow).
Signed at Washington and Ottawa September 12 and October 12, 1977.
Entered into force October 12, 1977.
29 UST 5561; TIAS 9129

Agreement concerning the test and evaluation of United States defense weapons systems in Canada.
Exchange of notes at Washington February 10, 1983.
Entered into force February 10, 1983.
TIAS 10659; 1469 UNTS 275

Mutual logistical support agreement, with annexes.
Signed at Stuttgart February 11, 1983.
Entered into force February 11, 1983.
TIAS 10658; 2001 UNTS 17

Master data exchange arrangement.
Signed at Brussels April 10, 1984.
Entered into force April 10, 1984.
TIAS

Memorandum of understanding on the exchange of service personnel between the United States Marine Corps and Canadian Forces.
Signed at Washington September 19, 1984.
Entered into force September 19, 1984.
TIAS 11135; 2126 UNTS 143

Agreement regarding modernization of the North American Air Defense System, with memorandum of understanding.
Exchange of notes at Quebec March 18, 1985.
Entered into force March 18, 1985.
TIAS 12260

Memorandum of understanding on aviation cooperation.
Signed at Washington and Ottawa March 20 and April 9, 1987.
Entered into force April 9, 1987.
TIAS 11294

Agreement concerning cooperative testing and evaluation of defense systems.
Exchange of notes at Washington February 10, 1993.
Entered into force February 10, 1993.
TIAS 12262; 1914 UNTS 193

Agreement concerning the establishment of certain mutual defense commitments.
Exchange of notes at Washington and Ottawa March 4 and August 19, 1994.
Entered into force August 19, 1994.
TIAS 12526; 2028 UNTS 97

Memorandum of understanding concerning the measures to be taken for the transfer, security and safeguarding of technical information and equipment to the Department of National Defence for use in the Canadian arctic subsurface surveillance system.
Signed at Washington and Ottawa May 31 and September 23, 1994.
Entered into force September 23, 1994.
TIAS 12264

Memorandum of understanding concerning counterterrorism research and development, with annex.
Signed at Washington and Ottawa June 12 and 23, 1995.
Entered into force June 23, 1995.
TIAS
Amendments:
May 27 and June 23, 2004
June 19 and 22, 2007

Agreement on a full and final settlement of all claims for costs of environmental clean-up at former U.S. military installations in Canada.
Exchange of notes at Washington October 7 and 9, 1996.
Entered into force October 9, 1996.
TIAS 12806; 2025 UNTS 341

Agreement on the North American Aerospace Defense Command.
Signed at Ottawa April 28, 2006.
Entered into force May 12, 2006.
TIAS 06-512

Agreement relating to the establishment of integrated lines of communications to ensure logistic support for the Canadian Armed Forces and the Armed Forces of the United States of America.
Signed at Washington April 23, 2008.
Entered into force September 5, 2008.
TIAS 08-905

DIPLOMATIC & CONSULAR RELATIONS

Convention to regulate commerce (article IV) between the United States and the United Kingdom.
Signed at London July 3, 1815.
Effective July 3, 1815.
8 Stat. 228; TS 110; 12 Bevans 49

Arrangement relating to visits of consular officers to citizens of their own country serving sentences in penal institutions.
Exchange of notes at Ottawa July 29 and September 19, 1935.
Entered into force September 19, 1935.
Foreign Relations, 1935, Vol. II, p. 57; 6 Bevans 65

Agreement concerning the privileges and immunities of members of the administrative and technical staffs of the Embassy of Canada in the United States and the Embassy of the United States in Canada.
Exchange of notes at Ottawa August 26 and September 2, 1993.
Entered into force September 21, 1993.
TIAS 12506

EDUCATION

Agreement for the establishment of a binational educational exchange foundation.
Signed at Washington November 15, 1999.
Entered into force November 15, 1999.
TIAS 13070
Amendments:
July 29, 2003 (TIAS 13070)
May 8 and 22, 2009 (TIAS 09-1023)

EMPLOYMENT

Arrangement relating to the employment of dependents of government employees.
Exchange of notes at Washington June 4 and 12, 1980.
Entered into force June 12, 1980.
TIAS 10693; 2005 UNTS 95
Amendment:
October 3 and November 13, 1997 (TIAS 12898)

ENERGY

Agreement concerning transit pipelines.
Signed at Washington January 28, 1977.
Entered into force October 1, 1977.
28 UST 7449; TIAS 8720

Agreement on principles applicable to a northern natural gas pipeline, with annexes.
Signed at Ottawa September 20, 1977.
Entered into force September 20, 1977, with respect to certain provisions; entered into force July 24, 1978, with respect to remaining provisions.
29 UST 3581; TIAS 9030; 1230 UNTS 311
Amendment:
June 6, 1978 (29 UST 3621; TIAS 9030; 1230 UNTS 340)

ENVIRONMENT & CONSERVATION

Convention for the protection of migratory birds in the United States and Canada.
Signed at Washington August 16, 1916.
Entered into force December 7, 1916.
39 Stat. 1702; TS 628; 12 Bevans 375
Amendment:
December 14, 1995 (TIAS 12721)

Arrangement prohibiting the importation of raccoon dogs.
Exchange of letters at Ottawa and Washington September 1 and 4, 1981.
Entered into force September 4, 1981.
33 UST 3764; TIAS 10259; 1541 UNTS 129

Agreement on the conservation of the Porcupine Caribou Herd, with annex.
Signed at Ottawa July 17, 1987.
Entered into force July 17, 1987.
TIAS 11259; 2174 UNTS 267

FINANCE

Agreement relating to exemptions from exchange control measures.
Exchange of notes at Ottawa June 18, 1940.
Entered into force June 18, 1940.
54 Stat. 2317; EAS 174; 6 Bevans 182; 203 LNTS 41

FISHERIES

Agreement adopting, with certain modifications, the rules and method of procedure recommended in the award of September 7, 1910, of the North Atlantic Coast Fisheries Arbitration.
Signed at Washington July 20, 1912.
Entered into force November 15, 1912.
37 Stat. 1634; TS 572; 12 Bevans 357

Agreement providing for cooperative efforts to be directed toward sanitary control of the shellfish industry.
Exchange of notes at Washington March 4 and April 30, 1948.
Entered into force April 30, 1948.
62 Stat. 1898; TIAS 1747; 6 Bevans 472; 77 UNTS 191

Convention for the extension to halibut fishing vessels of port privileges on the Pacific Coasts of the United States of America and Canada.
Signed at Ottawa March 24, 1950.
Entered into force July 13, 1950.
1 UST 536; TIAS 2096; 200 UNTS 211

Convention for the preservation of the halibut fishery of the Northern Pacific Ocean and Bering Sea.
Signed at Ottawa March 2, 1953.
Entered into force October 28, 1953.
5 UST 5; TIAS 2900; 222 UNTS 77
Amendment:
March 29, 1979 (32 UST 2483; TIAS 9855)

Convention on Great Lakes fisheries.
Signed at Washington September 10, 1954.
Entered into force October 11, 1955.
6 UST 2836; TIAS 3326; 238 UNTS 97
Amendment:
April 5, 1966, and May 19, 1967 (18 UST 1402; TIAS 6297)

Treaty on Pacific Coast albacore tuna vessels and port privileges, with annexes.
Signed at Washington May 26, 1981.
Entered into force July 29, 1981.
33 UST 615; TIAS 10057; 1274 UNTS 247
Amendments:
October 3 and 9, 1997 (TIAS 12887)
July 17 and August 13, 2002 (TIAS 04-528)
August 21 and September 10, 2002 (TIAS 04-528)
June 12, 2009 (TIAS 10-308)
June 17 and 18, 2013 (TIAS 14-225)

Treaty concerning Pacific salmon, with annexes and memorandum of understanding.
Signed at Ottawa January 28, 1985.
Entered into force March 18, 1985.
TIAS 11091; 1469 UNTS 357
Amendments and Related Agreements:
July 9, 1998
July 24 and August 12, 1998 (TIAS 98-812)
June 30, 1999 (TIAS 99-630)
December 4, 2002 (TIAS 02-1204)
April 26 and June 17, 2005 (TIAS 05-617)
June 16, 2006 (TIAS 06-616.1)
December 23, 2008 (TIAS 09-101)
December 21, 2010 (TIAS 10-1221)

Agreement on fisheries enforcement.
Signed at Ottawa September 26, 1990.
Entered into force December 16, 1991.
TIAS 11753

Agreement on the establishment of a mediation procedure regarding the Pacific Salmon Treaty.
Signed at Montreal September 11, 1995.
Entered into force September 11, 1995.
TIAS 12689; 2029 UNTS 307

Agreement on Pacific Hake/Whiting.
Signed at Seattle November 21, 2003.
Entered into force June 25, 2008.
TIAS 08-625

FOREIGN ASSISTANCE

Agreement relating to post-war economic settlements.
Exchange of notes at Washington November 30, 1942.
Entered into force November 30, 1942.
56 Stat. 1815; EAS 287; 6 Bevans 292; 119 UNTS 305

Memorandum of understanding on cooperation in the field of housing and urban affairs.
Signed at Ottawa June 28, 1977.
Entered into force June 28, 1977.
29 UST 2363; TIAS 8942

HEALTH & MEDICAL COOPERATION

Arrangement concerning quarantine inspection of vessels entering Puget Sound and waters adjacent thereto or the Great Lakes via the St. Lawrence River.
Exchange of notes at Ottawa October 10 and 23, 1929.
Entered into force October 23, 1929.
47 Stat. 2573; EAS 1; 6 Bevans 35; 96 LNTS 167

Memorandum of understanding on the monitoring of food, beverage and sanitary services provided on common carriers operating between the United States and Canada.
Signed at Ottawa and at Washington August 20 and September 8, 1975.
Entered into force September 8, 1975.
28 UST 884; TIAS 8485

INTELLECTUAL PROPERTY

Arrangement relating to the admission to practice before patent offices.
Exchange of notes at Washington December 3 and 28, 1937, and January 24, 1938.
Operative January 1, 1938.
52 Stat. 1475; EAS 118; 6 Bevans 97; 187 LNTS 27

Agreement relating to the mutual interchange of patent rights in connection with RDX and other explosives.
Exchange of notes at Washington September 3 and 27, 1946.
Entered into force September 27, 1946.
61 Stat. 2949; TIAS 1628; 6 Bevans 419; 21 UNTS 3

LABOR

Agreement relating to unemployment insurance benefits.
Exchange of notes at Ottawa March 6 and 12, 1942.
Entered into force April 12, 1942.
56 Stat. 1451; EAS 244; 6 Bevans 257; 119 UNTS 295
Amendments:
July 31 and September 11, 1951 (3 UST 2812; TIAS 2452; 206 UNTS 311)
October 29, 1984, and June 21, 1985 (TIAS 11334)

Agreement relating to workmen's compensation and unemployment insurance in connection with construction projects in Canada.
Exchange of notes at Ottawa November 2 and 4, 1942.
Entered into force November 4, 1942.
56 Stat. 1770; EAS 279; 6 Bevans 284; 24 UNTS 217

Agreement relating to the extension of the Canadian Unemployment Insurance Act to Canadian employees of the United States Armed Services in Canada.
Exchange of notes at Washington December 20, 1955, and April 23, 1956.
Entered into force April 23, 1956.
8 UST 1879; TIAS 3933; 300 UNTS 29

LAW ENFORCEMENT

Convention to suppress smuggling.
Signed at Washington June 6, 1924.
Entered into force July 27, 1925.
44 Stat. 2097; TS 718; 6 Bevans 1; 43 LNTS 225

Treaty on extradition, as amended by exchange of notes of June 28 and July 9, 1974.*
Signed at Washington December 3, 1971.
Entered into force March 22, 1976.
27 UST 983; TIAS 8237
Amendments:
January 11, 1988 (1853 UNTS 407)
January 12, 2001(TIAS 03-430)

Procedures for mutual assistance in the administration of justice in connection with the Boeing Company matter.
Signed at Washington March 15, 1977.
Entered into force March 15, 1977.
28 UST 2463; TIAS 8567

Treaty on the execution of penal sentences.
Signed at Washington March 2, 1977.
Entered into force July 19, 1978.
30 UST 6263; TIAS 9552

Agreement regarding mutual assistance and cooperation between customs administrations.
Signed at Quebec June 20, 1984.
Entered into force January 8, 1985.
TIAS 11253; 1469 UNTS 319

Treaty on mutual legal assistance in criminal matters, with annex.
Signed at Quebec March 18, 1985.
Entered into force January 24, 1990.
TIAS

Agreement regarding the sharing of forfeited assets and equivalent funds.
Signed at Ottawa March 22, 1995.
Entered into force March 22, 1995.
TIAS 12618; 2028 UNTS 335

MARITIME MATTERS

Treaty providing for reciprocal rights for United States and Canada in matters of conveyance of prisoners and wrecking and salvage.
Signed at Washington May 18, 1908.
Entered into force June 30, 1908.
35 Stat. 2035; TS 502; 12 Bevans 314

Load line convention.
Signed at Washington December 9, 1933.
Entered into force July 26, 1934.
49 Stat. 2685; TS 869; 6 Bevans 54; 152 LNTS 39

Agreement relating to reciprocal recognition of load-line regulations for vessels engaged in international voyages on the Great Lakes.
Exchanges of notes at Ottawa April 29, August 24, and October 22, 1938, September 2 and October 18, 1939, and January 10 and March 4, 1940.
Entered into force March 4, 1940.
54 Stat. 2300; EAS 172; 6 Bevans 171; 202 LNTS 429

Search and rescue agreement, with attachment.
Signed at Ottawa and Washington September 12 and October 25, 1974.
Entered into force October 25, 1974.
TIAS 11963

Memorandum of understanding concerning reciprocal recognition of Great Lakes load lines.
Signed at Ottawa November 21, 1977.
Entered into force November 21, 1977.
29 UST 4948; TIAS 9088; 1230 UNTS 345

Agreement for a cooperative vessel traffic management system for the Juan de Fuca region, with annex.
Exchange of notes at Ottawa December 19, 1979.
Entered into force December 19, 1979.
32 UST 377; TIAS 9706; 1221 UNTS 67

Agreement relating to coordination between the United States and Canadian Coast Guards of icebreaking operations in the Great Lakes and St. Lawrence Seaway system.
Exchange of notes at Ottawa October 28 and December 5, 1980.
Entered into force December 5, 1980.
32 UST 4334; TIAS 9950; 1266 UNTS 87
Extensions:
December 4 and 5, 2000 (TIAS 00-1205)
December 5, 2005 (TIAS 00-1205)
November 30 and December 2, 2010 (TIAS 00-1205)

Memorandum of understanding concerning cooperation in marine transportation technology and systems research and development.
Signed at Ottawa June 18, 1981.
Entered into force June 18, 1981.
33 UST 2082; TIAS 10172; 1529 UNTS 483

Agreement relating to the agreement of August 14, 1987, on the resolution of practical problems with respect to deep seabed mining areas.*
Exchange of notes at Ottawa August 14, 1987.
Entered into force August 14, 1987.
TIAS 11438
Note:
* Parties to the multilateral agreement of August 14, 1987, are Belgium, Canada, Italy, Netherlands and Union of Soviet Socialist Republics.

Framework agreement on integrated cross-border maritime law enforcement operations.
Signed at Detroit May 26, 2009.
Entered into force October 11, 2012.
TIAS 12-1011

MIGRATION & REFUGEES

Agreement for cooperation in the examination of refugee status claims from nationals of third countries.
Signed at Washington December 5, 2002.
Entered into force December 29, 2004.
TIAS 04-1229

PEACE

Treaty of amity, commerce and navigation between the United States and Great Britain (Jay Treaty).*
Signed at London November 19, 1794.
Entered into force October 28, 1795.
8 Stat. 116; TS 105; 12 Bevans 13
Note:
* Only article 3 so far as it relates to the right of Indians to pass across the border, and articles 9 and 10 appear to remain in force. But see Akins v. U.S., 551 F.2d 1222 (1977).

Explanatory article to article 3 of the November 19, 1794, treaty of amity, commerce and navigation between the United States and Great Britain.*
Signed at Philadelphia May 4, 1796.
Entered into force October 6, 1796.
8 Stat. 130; TS 106; 12 Bevans 34

Treaty of peace and amity between the United States and Great Britain.
Signed at Ghent December 24, 1814.
Entered into force February 17, 1815.
8 Stat. 218; TS 109; 12 Bevans 41

Treaty for an amicable settlement of all causes of differences between the United States and Great Britain (Treaty of Washington).*
Washington May 8, 1871.
Entered into force June 17, 1871.
17 Stat. 863; TS 133; 12 Bevans 170
Note:
* Articles I-XVII and XXXIV-XLII have been executed; articles XVIII-XXV, XXX, and XXXII terminated July 1, 1885; articles XXVIII and XXIX not considered in force.

POLLUTION

Agreement relating to the establishment of a Canada-United States committee on water quality in the St. John River and its tributary rivers and streams which cross the Canada-United States boundary, with annex.
Exchange of notes at Ottawa September 21, 1972.
Entered into force September 21, 1972.
23 UST 2813; TIAS 7470
Amendment:
February 22, 1984 (35 UST 4426; TIAS 10947)

Agreement relating to the establishment of joint pollution contingency plans for spills of oil and other noxious substances.
Exchange of notes at Ottawa June 19, 1974.
Entered into force June 19, 1974.
25 UST 1280; TIAS 7861

Agreement on Great Lakes water quality, 1978, with annexes and terms of reference.
Signed at Ottawa November 22, 1978.
Entered into force November 22, 1978.
30 UST 1383; TIAS 9257; 1153 UNTS 187
Amendments:
October 16, 1983 (35 UST 2370; TIAS 10798)
November 18, 1987 (TIAS 11551; 2185 UNTS 504)
September 7, 2012 (TIAS 13-212)

Memorandum of intent concerning transboundary air pollution, with annex.
Signed at Washington August 5, 1980.
Entered into force August 5, 1980.
32 UST 2521; TIAS 9856; 1274 UNTS 235

Memorandum of understanding regarding accidental and unauthorized discharges of pollutants along the inland boundary, with appendix.
Signed at Ottawa October 17, 1985.
Entered into force October 17, 1985.
TIAS 11170; 2126 UNTS 161

Agreement concerning the transboundary movement of hazardous waste.
Signed at Ottawa October 28, 1986.
Entered into force November 8, 1986.
TIAS 11099; 2120 UNTS 97
Amendment:
November 4 and 25, 1992

Agreement on air quality, with annexes.
Signed at Ottawa March 13, 1991.
Entered into force March 13, 1991.
TIAS
Amendment:
December 7, 2000

POSTAL MATTERS

Money order agreement.
Signed at Washington September 30 and at Ottawa October 3, 1901.
Operative July 1, 1901.
NP

International express mail agreement, with detailed regulations.
Signed at Ottawa and Washington July 18, 23 and August 14, 1979.
Entered into force August 14, 1979; effective August 1, 1979.
31 UST 5745; TIAS 9684; 1221 UNTS 43

Postal convention, with detailed regulations.
Signed at Ottawa and Washington September 10 and 14, 1981.
Entered into force January 1, 1982.
33 UST 3810; TIAS 10263; 1541 UNTS 135

PROPERTY

Convention between the United States and the United Kingdom relating to tenure and disposition of real and personal property.
Signed at Washington March 2, 1899.
Applicable to Canada June 17, 1922.
31 Stat. 1939; TS 146; 12 Bevans 246

Supplementary convention providing for the accession of the Dominion of Canada to the real and personal property convention of March 2, 1899.
Signed at Washington October 21, 1921.
Entered into force June 17, 1922.
42 Stat. 2147; TS 663; 12 Bevans 390; 12 LNTS 425

Agreement concerning construction of new chanceries in Washington and Ottawa.
Exchange of notes at Washington May 13 and October 2, 1985.
Entered into force October 2, 1985.
TIAS 11328

SCIENTIFIC & TECHNICAL COOPERATION

Agreement relating to the establishment of a cooperative meteorological rocket project at Cold Lake, Alberta.
Exchange of notes at Ottawa September 29 and October 6, 1966.
Entered into force October 6, 1966.
17 UST 1832; TIAS 6128; 675 UNTS 63
Amendment:
February 13 and April 24, 1969 (20 UST 720; TIAS 6682; 714 UNTS 326)

Agreement relating to the exchange of information on weather modification activities.
Signed at Washington March 26, 1975.
Entered into force March 26, 1975.
26 UST 540; TIAS 8056

Memorandum of understanding concerning the furnishing of balloon launching and associated services.
Signed at Washington and Ottawa August 26 and September 12, 1983.
Entered into force September 12, 1983.
35 UST 2392; TIAS 10800

Agreement regarding allocation of intellectual property rights, interests and royalties for intellectual property created or furnished under certain scientific and technological cooperative research activities, with attachment.
Exchange of notes at Ottawa February 4, 1997.
Entered into force February 4, 1997.
TIAS

Agreement concerning the operation of commercial remote sensing satellite systems, with annex.
Signed at Washington June 16, 2000.
Entered into force June 16, 2000.
TIAS

Agreement for cooperation in science and technology for critical infrastructure protection and border security.
Signed at Washington June 1, 2004.
Entered into force June 1, 2004.
TIAS 04-601

SOCIAL SECURITY

Agreement relating to Canada Pension Plan.
Signed at Ottawa May 5, 1967.
Entered into force May 5, 1967; effective January 1, 1967.
18 UST 486; TIAS 6254; 685 UNTS 245
Amendment:
October 12 and December 19, 1983 (35 UST 3521; TIAS 10864)

Agreement with respect to social security, with administrative arrangement.*
Signed at Ottawa March 11, 1981.
Entered into force August 1, 1984.
35 UST 3403; TIAS 10863; 1469 UNTS 249
Note:
* See also understanding and administrative arrangement of March 30, 1983, with the Government of Quebec (TIAS 10863).

Supplementary agreement amending the agreement of March 11, 1981, and the administrative arrangement of May 22, 1981 with respect to social security.
Signed at Ottawa May 10, 1983.
Entered into force August 1, 1984.
35 UST 3403; TIAS 10863; 1469 UNTS 271

Second supplementary agreement amending the agreement of March 11, 1981, as amended, with respect to social security.
Signed at Ottawa May 28, 1996.
Entered into force October 1, 1997.
TIAS 12759; 2030 UNTS 283

SPACE

Memorandum of understanding concerning cooperation in the flight of the Canadian measurements of pollution in the troposphere (MOPITT) instrument on the NASA polar orbiting platform and related support for an international earth observing system, with appendix.
Signed at Washington November 15, 1994.
Entered into force November 15, 1994.
TIAS

Agreement concerning cooperation on the Canadian Microgravity Isolation Mount, with attachment.
Exchange of notes at Ottawa July 31, 1997.
Entered into force July 31, 1997.
TIAS

Framework agreement for cooperation in the exploration and use of outer space for peaceful purposes.
Signed at Washington September 9, 2009.
Entered into force May 11, 2010.
TIAS 10-511.2

TAXATION

Agreement relating to provincial and municipal taxation of United States defense projects in Canada.
Exchange of notes at Ottawa August 6 and 9, 1943.
Entered into force August 9, 1943.
57 Stat. 1065; EAS 339; 6 Bevans 326; 29 UNTS 295

Agreement concerning the administration of income tax in Canada affecting employees within Canada of the United States Government who are subject to such tax.
Exchange of notes at Ottawa August 1 and September 17, 1973.
Entered into force September 17, 1973.
28 UST 1134; TIAS 8499

Convention with respect to taxes on income and capital, with exchange of notes.
Signed at Washington September 26, 1980.
*Entered into force August 16, 1984.**
TIAS 11087; 1469 UNTS 189

Note:

* With respect to estates of persons deceased prior to January 1, 1985, the convention of February 17, 1961, for the avoidance of double taxation and the prevention of fiscal evasion with respect to taxes on estates of deceased persons (13 UST 382; TIAS 4995; 445 UNTS 143) shall continue to have effect.
See also Article XXX of the 1980 Convention for the continued effect of the convention and protocol of March 4, 1942, for the avoidance of double taxation and prevention of fiscal evasion in the case of income taxes (56 Stat. 1399; TS 983; 6 Bevans 244; 124 UNTS 271).

Protocol amending the convention of September 26, 1980, with respect to taxes on income and on capital, with exchange of letters.
Signed at Ottawa June 14, 1983.
Entered into force August 16, 1984.
TIAS 11087; 2121 UNTS 364

Second protocol amending the convention of September 26, 1980, with respect to taxes on income and on capital, as amended by the protocol of June 14, 1983.
Signed at Washington March 28, 1984.
Entered into force August 16, 1984.
TIAS 11087; 2121 UNTS 387

Protocol amending the convention with respect to taxes on income and on capital of September 26, 1980, as amended by protocols of June 14, 1983, and March 28, 1984.
Signed at Washington March 17, 1995.
Entered into force November 9, 1995.
TIAS; 2030 UNTS 236

Protocol amending the convention with respect to taxes on income and on capital of September 26, 1980, as amended.
Signed at Ottawa July 29, 1997.
Entered into force December 16, 1997.
TIAS; 2030 UNTS 276

Protocol amending the convention with respect to taxes on income and on capital of September 26, 1980, as amended.
Signed at Chelsea September 21, 2007.
Entered into force December 15, 2008.
TIAS

Agreement to improve international tax compliance through enhanced exchange of information under the convention with respect to taxes on income and on capital, with annexes.
Signed at Ottawa February 5, 2014.
Entered into force June 27, 2014.
TIAS 14-627

TELECOMMUNICATION

Arrangement governing radio communications between private experimental stations.
Exchanges of notes at Washington October 2 and December 29, 1928, and January 12, 1929.
Operative January 1, 1929.
TS 767-A; 6 Bevans 26; 102 LNTS 143
Amendment:
April 23 and May 2 and 4, 1934 (48 Stat. 1876; EAS 62; 147 LNTS 338)

Convention relating to the operation by citizens of either country of certain radio equipment or stations in the other country.
Signed at Ottawa February 8, 1951.
Entered into force May 15, 1952.
3 UST 3787; TIAS 2508; 207 UNTS 17

Agreement concerning the coordination and use of radio frequencies above thirty megacycles per second, with annex.
Exchange of notes at Ottawa October 24, 1962.
Entered into force October 24, 1962.
13 UST 2418; TIAS 5205; 462 UNTS 68
Amendments:
June 16 and 24, 1965 (16 UST 923; TIAS 5833; 549 UNTS 300)
February 26 and April 7, 1982 (TIAS 10646)
November 2, 1993, and January 4, 1994 (TIAS 12529)
June 15 and 20, 2005 (TIAS 05-620)

Agreement on cooperation in intercontinental testing in connection with experimental communications satellites.
Exchange of notes at Washington August 13 and 23, 1963.
Entered into force August 23, 1963.
14 UST 1701; TIAS 5474; 494 UNTS 13

Agreement regarding an experimental communications technology satellite project with memorandum of understanding.
Exchange of notes at Washington April 21 and 27, 1971.
Entered into force April 27, 1971.
22 UST 713; TIAS 7131

Agreement for promotion of safety on the Great Lakes by means of radio, with technical regulations and exchange of notes of
May 6, 1974.
Signed at Ottawa February 26, 1973.
Entered into force May 6, 1975.
25 UST 935; TIAS 7837
Amendments:
December 29, 1978 (30 UST 2523; TIAS 9352; 1170 UNTS 339)
December 22, 1987, August 10 and October 24, 1988

Agreement relating to the AM broadcasting service in the medium frequency band, with annexes.
Signed at Ottawa January 17, 1984.
Entered into force January 17, 1984.
TIAS 11263

Agreement concerning the use of the 88 to 108 megahertz frequency band for frequency modulation broadcasting (FM), with attachment.
Exchange of notes at Washington November 26, 1990 and February 25, 1991.
Entered into force February 25, 1991.
TIAS

Agreement concerning the allotment and assignment of television broadcasting channels in areas adjacent to the border of the United States and Canada, with working arrangement.
Exchange of notes at Washington November 3, 1993, and January 5, 1994.
Entered into force January 5, 1994.
TIAS 12530

TRADE & INVESTMENT

Agreement relating to importation privileges for government officials and employees.
Exchanges of notes at Ottawa July 21, October 29 and November 9, 1942.
Entered into force November 9, 1942.
57 Stat. 1379; EAS 383; 6 Bevans 289; 101 UNTS 233

Agreement relating to the establishment of a Joint United States-Canadian Committee on Trade and Economic Affairs.
Exchange of notes at Washington November 12, 1953.
Entered into force November 12, 1953.
5 UST 314; TIAS 2922; 223 UNTS 139
Amendments:
October 2, 1961 (14 UST 1496; TIAS 5448; 470 UNTS 394)
September 17, 1963 (14 UST 1496; TIAS 5448)

Agreement concerning automotive products, with annexes and exchange of notes.
Signed at Johnson City, Texas January 16, 1965.
Entered into force provisionally January 16, 1965; definitively September 16, 1966.
17 UST 1372; TIAS 6093

Arrangement regarding levels of Canadian oil exports and the proposed looping of the Interprovincial Pipeline via Chicago.
Exchange of notes at Washington September 25, 1967.
Entered into force September 25, 1967.
20 UST 4108; TIAS 6806; 730 UNTS 317

Memorandum of understanding on the exchange of import data, with annexes.
Signed at Montreal July 29, 1987.
Entered into force July 29, 1987.
TIAS

Free-trade agreement, with exchanges of letters.*
Signed at Ottawa, Washington and Palm Springs December 22 and 23, 1987, and January 2, 1988.
Entered into force January 1, 1989.
TIAS
Note:
* This agreement is suspended, subject to certain transition arrangements with respect to dispute settlement proceedings under Chapters 18 and 19, for such time as the United States and Canada are parties to the North American Free Trade Agreement signed at Washington, Ottawa, and Mexico City December 8, 11, 14, and 17, 1992.

Agreement regarding the application of their competition and deceptive marketing practices laws.
Signed at Washington and Ottawa August 1 and 3, 1995.
Entered into force August 3, 1995.
TIAS; 2028 UNTS 135

Agreement on the application of positive comity principles to the enforcement of their competition laws.
Signed at Washington October 5, 2004.
Entered into force October 5, 2004.
TIAS 04-1005.1

Agreement on government procurement, with appendices.
Signed at Mississauga and Washington February 11 and 12, 2010.
Entered into force February 16, 2010.
TIAS 10-216

TRANSPORTATION

Arrangement relating to the issuance of certificates of competency or licenses for the piloting of civil aircraft.
Exchange of notes at Washington July 28, 1938.
Entered into force August 1, 1938.
53 Stat. 1937; EAS 130; 6 Bevans 108; 192 LNTS 115

Agreement providing for the construction of a military highway to Alaska.
Exchange of notes at Ottawa March 17 and 18, 1942.
Entered into force March 18, 1942.
56 Stat. 1458; EAS 246; 6 Bevans 261; 101 UNTS 205

Agreement relating to access to the Alaska Highway.
Exchange of notes at Ottawa April 10, 1943.
Entered into force April 10, 1943.
57 Stat. 1274; EAS 362; 6 Bevans 319; 21 UNTS 237

Agreement relating to the designation of the highway from Dawson Creek, British Columbia, to Fairbanks, Alaska, as the "Alaska Highway".
Exchange of notes at Washington July 19, 1943.
Entered into force July 19, 1943.
57 Stat. 1023; EAS 331; 6 Bevans 324; 29 UNTS 289

Agreement relating to the use by civil aircraft of Stephenville and Argentia military air bases in Newfoundland.
Exchange of notes at Ottawa June 4, 1949.
Entered into force June 4, 1949.
63 Stat. 2486; TIAS 1933; 6 Bevans 488; 200 UNTS 201

Agreement concerning air traffic control.
Exchange of notes at Ottawa December 20 and 27, 1963.
Entered into force December 27, 1963.
14 UST 1737; TIAS 5480; 494 UNTS 21

Memorandum of understanding concerning research and development in transportation.
Signed June 18, 1970.
Entered into force June 18, 1970.
NP

Agreement relating to cooperation in reconstruction of Canadian portions of the Alaska Highway.
Exchange of notes at Ottawa January 11 and February 11, 1977.
Entered into force February 11, 1977.
28 UST 5303; TIAS 8631; 1087 UNTS 3

Memorandum of agreement relating to the provision of flight inspection services.
Signed at Washington and Koblenz March 10 and April 1, 1978.
Entered into force April 1, 1978.
30 UST 278; TIAS 9198
Amendment:
February 4 and 24, 1982 (TIAS 10565; 1871 UNTS 516)

Agreement concerning the airworthiness and environmental certification of imported civil aeronautical products.
Exchange of letters at Ottawa August 31, 1984.
Entered into force August 31, 1984.
TIAS 11023; 1469 UNTS 339

Memorandum of cooperation for mutual cooperation in the area of civil aviation research, engineering and development, with annex.
Signed at Washington and Ottawa May 6 and July 9, 1996.
Entered into force July 9, 1996.
TIAS

Agreement for promotion of aviation safety.
Signed at Toronto June 12, 2000.
Entered into force June 12, 2000.
TIAS 13118

Agreement on air transport preclearance, with annexes and agreed minute.
Signed at Toronto January 18, 2001.
Entered into force May 2, 2003.
TIAS 13136

Air transport agreement, with annexes.
Signed at Washington March 12, 2007.
Entered into force March 12, 2007.
TIAS 07-312

CENTRAL AFRICAN REPUBLIC

CULTURAL EXCHANGES, PROPERTY & COOPERATION

Agreement relating to the establishment of a Peace Corps program in the Central African Republic.
Exchange of notes at Bangui September 9 and November 24, 1966.
Entered into force November 24, 1966.
17 UST 2205; TIAS 6157; 681 UNTS 21

DEFENSE

Agreement regarding grants under the Foreign Assistance Act of 1961, as amended, or successor legislation, and the furnishing of defense articles, defense services and related training, including pursuant to the United States International Military Education and Training (IMET) Program.
Exchange of notes at Bangui December 12, 2008, and December 4, 2009.
Entered into force December 4, 2009.
NP

Agreement regarding the status of United States personnel who may be temporarily present in Central African Republic.
Effected by exchange of notes at Bangui December 10, 2009 and June 3, 2010.
Entered into force June 3, 2010.
TIAS 10-603

FINANCE

Agreement relating to investment guaranties.
Exchange of notes at Bangui December 31, 1964.
Entered into force January 1, 1965.
15 UST 2556; TIAS 5747; 542 UNTS 29

Agreement regarding the consolidation and rescheduling of certain debts owed to, or guaranteed by the United States Government through the Export-Import Bank, with annexes.
Signed at Washington April 29, 1983.
Entered into force June 13, 1983.
TIAS 10721; 1578 UNTS 55

Agreement regarding the consolidation and rescheduling of certain debts owed to, or guaranteed by the United States Government through the Export-Import Bank, with annexes.
Signed at Bangui February 16, 1984.
Entered into force April 16, 1984.
35 UST 4813; TIAS 10967

Agreement regarding the consolidation and rescheduling of certain debts owed to or guaranteed by the United States Government through the Export-Import Bank of the United States.
Signed at Washington May 23, 1986.
Entered into force August 1, 1986.
NP

Agreement regarding the consolidation and rescheduling of certain debts owed to, guaranteed by or insured by the United States Government and its agencies, with annexes.
Signed at Bangui March 22, 1990.
Entered into force May 3, 1990.
NP

Agreement regarding the consolidation, reduction and rescheduling of certain debts owed to, guaranteed by or insured by the United States Government and its agencies, with annexes.
Signed at Bangui September 6, 1994.
Entered into force October 11, 1994.
NP

Agreement regarding the consolidation, reduction and rescheduling of certain debts owed to, guaranteed by, or insured by the United States Government and its Agency, with annexes.
Signed at Bangui September 1, 1999.
Entered into force December 15, 1999.
NP

Agreement regarding the consolidation, reduction, and rescheduling of certain debts owed to, guaranteed by, or insured by the United States Government and its Agency, with annexes.
Signed at Bangui February 20, 2008.
Entered into force April 1, 2008.
NP

Agreement regarding the reduction of certain debts owed to, guaranteed by, or insured by the United States Government and its Agency, with annexes.
Signed at Bangui August 22, 2008.
Entered into force October 7, 2008.
NP

Agreement regarding the reduction of certain debts owed to, guaranteed by, or insured by the United States Government and its Agency, with annexes.
Signed at Bangui March 18, 2010.
Entered into force May 13, 2010.
NP

FOREIGN ASSISTANCE

Agreement relating to economic, technical and related assistance.
Exchange of notes at Bangui February 10, 1963.
Entered into force February 10, 1963.
14 UST 185; TIAS 5294; 473 UNTS 83

INTERNATIONAL CRIMINAL COURT

Agreement regarding the surrender of persons to the International Criminal Court.
Signed at Washington and Bangui January 13 and 19, 2004.
Entered into force January 19, 2004.
TIAS 04-119

POSTAL MATTERS

International express mail agreement, with detailed regulations.
Signed at Bangui and Washington June 22 and September 21, 1988.
Entered into force November 1, 1988.
TIAS 11636

CHAD

CULTURAL EXCHANGES, PROPERTY & COOPERATION

Agreement for the establishment of a Peace Corps program in Chad.
Exchange of notes at Fort Lamy August 31, 1966.
Entered into force August 31, 1966.
17 UST 1384; TIAS 6094

DEFENSE

Agreement regarding the status of personnel of the United States in Chad.
Signed at N'Djamena July 5, 2005.
Entered into force July 5, 2005.
TIAS

Agreement regarding grants under the Foreign Assistance Act of 1961, as amended, or successor legislation, and the furnishing of defense articles, defense services and related training, including pursuant to the United States International Military Education and Training (IMET) Program.
Exchange of notes at N'Djamena July 19, 2006, and May 9, 2007.
Entered into force May 9, 2007.
NP

Acquisition and cross-servicing agreement.
Signed at Stuttgart September 19, 2014.
Entered into force September 19, 2014.
NP

Aviation leadership program agreement.
Signed November 12 and December 15, 2015.
Entered into force December 15, 2015.
NP

EDUCATION

Agreement concerning the creation of the American International School of N'Djamena.
Signed at N'Djamena March 5, 2007.
Entered into force April 6, 2007.
TIAS

EMPLOYMENT

Agreement relating to the employment of dependents of official government employees.
Exchange of notes at N'Djamena April 19, 1991, and June 23, 1992.
Entered into force June 23, 1992.
TIAS

ENVIRONMENT & CONSERVATION

Agreement for cooperation in the Global Learning and Observations to Benefit the Environment (GLOBE) Program, with appendices.
Signed at N'Djamena and Washington September 27 and November 28, 1995.
Entered into force November 28, 1995.
TIAS

FINANCE

Agreement relating to investment guaranties.
Exchange of notes at Fort Lamy May 12, 1965.
Entered into force May 12, 1965.
16 UST 789; TIAS 5812; 546 UNTS 183.

FOREIGN ASSISTANCE

Agreement on economic, technical and related assistance.
Signed at N'Djamena September 22, 1986.
Entered into force September 22, 1986.
TIAS

INTERNATIONAL CRIMINAL COURT

Agreement regarding the surrender of persons to the International Criminal Court.
Exchange of notes at N'Djamena March 26 and June 30, 2003.
Entered into force June 30, 2003.
TIAS

POSTAL MATTERS

International express mail agreement, with detailed regulations.
Signed at N'Djamena and Washington July 19 and 23 and August 6, 1987.
Entered into force August 17, 1987.
TIAS 11553

CHILE

AGRICULTURE

Memorandum of understanding for scientific and technical cooperation in agricultural research and development.
Signed at Santiago August 28, 1981.
Entered into force August 28, 1981.
33 UST 3742; TIAS 10256; 1541 UNTS 113

ATOMIC ENERGY

Agreement providing for a grant for the acquisition of certain nuclear research and training equipment and materials.
Exchange of notes at Santiago July 23, 1959, and February 19, 1960.
Entered into force February 19, 1960.
11 UST 395; TIAS 4457; 371 UNTS 255

CLAIMS & DISPUTE RESOLUTION

Treaty for the advancement of peace and the settlement of disputes that may occur between the United States of America and Chile.
Signed at Washington July 24, 1914.
Entered into force January 19, 1916.
39 Stat. 1645; TS 621; 6 Bevans 550

CONSULAR AFFAIRS

Agreement relating to passport visas for nonimmigrants.*
Exchange of notes at Santiago August 29, 1950.
Effective September 1, 1950.
1 UST 719; TIAS 2137; 122 UNTS 43

Note:

* The status of this agreement is under review.

DEFENSE

Agreement relating to the transfer to Chile of certain United States naval vessels.
Exchange of notes at Washington January 4, 1951, with memorandum of understanding dated January 9, 1951.
Entered into force January 4, 1951.
3 UST 2741; TIAS 2444; 165 UNTS 105

Military assistance agreement.
Signed at Santiago April 9, 1952.
Entered into force July 11, 1952.
3 UST 5123; TIAS 2703; 186 UNTS 53

Agreement for disposition of equipment and materials furnished by the United States under the military assistance agreement of April 9, 1952, and no longer required by Chile.
Exchange of notes at Santiago November 30 and December 28, 1956.
Entered into force December 28, 1956.
8 UST 13; TIAS 3730; 266 UNTS 421

Agreement relating to the deposit by Chile of ten percent of the value of grant military assistance and excess defense articles.
Exchange of notes at Santiago March 28 and April 11, 1972.
Entered into force April 11, 1972; effective February 7, 1972.
23 UST 930; TIAS 7361

Memorandum of understanding on the exchange of officers between the U.S. Marine Corps and the Chilean Navy's Marine Corps.
Signed at Washington October 30, 1989.
Entered into force October 30, 1989.
NP

Memorandum of understanding on the exchange of staff noncommissioned officers between the U.S. Marine Corps and the Chilean Navy's Marine Corps.
Signed at Washington and Santiago February 7 and 26, 1992.
Entered into force February 26, 1992.
NP

Agreement governing the protection of classified military information or material.
Exchange of notes at Santiago August 13 and September 1, 1992.
Entered into force September 1, 1992.
TIAS 12281.

Agreement concerning the exchange and reimbursement of marine aviation and propulsion fuels, with annexes.
Signed at Fort Belvoir and Valparaiso June 28 and July 13, 2005.
Entered into force July 13, 2005.
TIAS 05-713

Agreement regarding the exchange of military personnel, with annexes.
Signed at Santiago December 2, 2005.
Entered into force December 2, 2005.
NP

Amendment and Extension:

December 9 and 30, 2015

Agreement regarding the exchange of administrative and professional personnel in financial management headquarters organizations, with annexes and appendices.
Signed at Valparaiso December 31, 2005.
Entered into force December 31, 2005.
TIAS

Agreement regarding grants under the Foreign Assistance Act of 1961, as amended, and the furnishing of defense articles, defense services, and related training, including pursuant to the United States International Military Education and Training Program (IMET), from the United States to the Government of Chile.
Exchange of notes at Santiago December 6, 2005, and July 5, 2006.
Entered into force July 5, 2006.
NP

Memorandum of understanding concerning the Inter-American Naval Telecommunications Network.
Signed October 18 and November 14, 2006.
Entered into force November 14, 2006.
TIAS 06-1114

Memorandum of agreement establishing a midshipmen/cadet exchange program (MCEP), with appendix.
Signed at Annapolis and Valparaiso May 11, 2007.
Entered into force May 11, 2007.
NP
Extension:
September 8, 2016

Agreement regarding the exchange of engineers and scientists, with annexes and appendices.
Signed at Washington June 13, 2007.
Entered into force June 13, 2007.
NP

Memorandum of understanding regarding the assignment of foreign liaison officers, with annexes.
Signed at Washington September 19 and 26, 2007.
Entered into force September 26, 2007.
NP

Agreement concerning exchange of research and development information, with appendix.
Signed at Washington April 8, 2008.
Entered into force April 8, 2008.
TIAS 08-408

Acquisition and cross-servicing agreement, with annexes.
Signed at Santiago September 2, 2011.
Entered into force September 2, 2011.
NP

EDUCATION

Agreement for educational cooperation.
Signed at Washington February 26, 1997.
Entered into force November 9, 1998.
TIAS 12837

Agreement on the equal opportunities scholarship program.
Signed at Washington August 8, 2007.
Entered into force August 8, 2007.
TIAS 07-808.1

ENVIRONMENT & CONSERVATION

Agreement for cooperation in the Global Learning and Observations to Benefit the Environment (GLOBE) Program, with appendices.
Signed at Santiago April 16, 1998.
Entered into force April 16, 1998.
TIAS 12942

Agreement on environmental cooperation.
Signed at Santiago June 17, 2003.
Entered into force April 30, 2004.
TIAS 04-430

FINANCE

Agreement regarding the consolidation and rescheduling of certain debts owed to, guaranteed or insured by the United States Government and its agencies, with annexes.
Signed at Washington February 6, 1974.
Entered into force February 6, 1974.
25 UST 1712; TIAS 7908

Agreement regarding the consolidation and rescheduling of certain debts owed to the Agency for International Development pursuant to certain loan agreements, with schedules.
Signed at Washington February 6, 1974.
Entered into force February 6, 1974.
25 UST 1714; TIAS 7908

Memorandum of understanding regarding the consolidation and rescheduling of certain Chilean debts owed to, guaranteed or insured by the United States Government and its agencies.
Signed at Washington June 17, 1974.
Entered into force June 17, 1974; effective May 15, 1974.
25 UST 2683; TIAS 7940

Agreement regarding the consolidation and rescheduling of certain debts owed to the Agency for International Development pursuant to certain loan agreements, with schedules.
Signed at Washington July 1, 1974.
Entered into force July 1, 1974.
25 UST 2691; TIAS 7940

Agreement regarding the consolidation and rescheduling of payments under PL 480 Title I agricultural commodity agreements, with annexes.
Signed at Washington October 22, 1974.
Entered into force October 22, 1974.
25 UST 2704; TIAS 7940

Agreement regarding the consolidation and rescheduling of certain debts owed to, guaranteed or insured by the United States Government and its agencies, with annexes and statement.
Signed at Washington July 3, 1975.
Entered into force September 8, 1975.
28 UST 5587; TIAS 8649

Agreement regarding the consolidation and rescheduling of payments under PL 480 Title I agricultural commodity agreements.
Signed at Washington April 5, 1976.
Entered into force April 5, 1976.
28 UST 5587; TIAS 8649

Agreement regarding the consolidation and rescheduling of certain debts owed to the Agency for International Development pursuant to certain loan agreements, with schedules.
Signed at Washington May 26, 1976.
Entered into force May 26, 1976.
28 UST 5609; TIAS 8649

Investment incentive agreement.
Exchange of notes at Santiago September 22, 1983.
Entered into force February 14, 1984.
35 UST 2958; TIAS 10832; 2014 UNTS 537

Agreement regarding the consolidation and rescheduling of certain debts owed to, guaranteed by or insured by the United States Government and its agencies, with annexes.
Signed at Washington February 6, 1986.
Entered into force March 17, 1986.
NP

Agreement regarding the consolidation and rescheduling or refinancing of certain debts owed to, guaranteed by or insured by the United States Government and its agencies, with annexes.
Signed at Washington August 13, 1987.
Entered into force September 21, 1987.
NP

Agreement regarding the reduction of certain debts owed to the United States Government and its agencies, with appendices.
Signed at Washington June 27, 1991.
Entered into force August 8, 1991.
NP

Agreement regarding the reduction of certain debts related to foreign assistance owed to the Government of the United States and its agencies, with appendices.
Signed at Washington and Santiago December 11 and 15, 1992.
Entered into force January 14, 1993.
NP

FOREIGN ASSISTANCE

Basic agreement for technical cooperation.
Signed at Santiago January 16, 1951.
Entered into force July 27, 1951.
3 UST 390; TIAS 2403; 151 UNTS 147
Amendments:
January 8, 1952 (3 UST 4697; TIAS 2627; 179 UNTS 265)
October 17, 1952 (3 UST 5136; TIAS 2704; 184 UNTS 376)

Agreement relating to an informational media guaranty program in Chile.
Exchange of notes at Santiago January 14, 1955.
Entered into force January 14, 1955.
6 UST 41; TIAS 3166; 238 UNTS 191

Agreement granting duty-free entry, exemption from internal taxation, and free transportation within Chile to ultimate beneficiary for certain relief supplies and equipment for U.S. rehabilitation and relief agencies.
Exchange of notes at Santiago April 5, 1955.
Entered into force April 5, 1955.
6 UST 717; TIAS 3210; 250 UNTS 253

Agreement providing for a loan to Chile for reconstruction and rehabilitation as a consequence of the May 1960 earthquakes.
Exchange of notes at Santiago August 3, 1961.
Entered into force August 3, 1961.
12 UST 1390; TIAS 4862; 433 UNTS 21

Agreement concerning the establishment of an Americas Fund and Administering Board.
Signed at Santiago June 30, 1993.
Entered into force June 30, 1993.
TIAS 12504

LAW ENFORCEMENT

Treaty providing for the extradition of fugitives from justice.
Signed at Santiago April 17, 1900.
Entered into force June 26, 1902.
32 Stat. 1850; TS 407; 6 Bevans 543

Agreement concerning cooperation to suppress the processing, trafficking, consumption and export of narcotic drugs.
Signed at Santiago August 5, 1994.
Entered into force August 5, 1994.
TIAS 12561; 2379 UNTS 83

Agreement regarding mutual assistance between their customs administrations.
Signed at Washington June 30, 2014.
Entered into force August 14, 2014.
TIAS 14-814

Extradition treaty.
Signed at Washington June 5, 2013.
Entered into force December 14, 2016.
TIAS 16-1214

MARITIME MATTERS

Agreement regarding the marine scientific research activities of the research vessel Hero.
Signed at Santiago June 1, 1983.
Entered into force June 1, 1983.
35 UST 2892; TIAS 10825; 2014 UNTS 535

PEACE

Treaty of peace, amity, commerce, and navigation, with additional and explanatory convention signed at Santiago September 1, 1833.*
Signed at Santiago May 16, 1832.
Entered into force April 29, 1834.
8 Stat. 434; TS 40; 6 Bevans 518
Note:
* Articles relating to commerce and navigation terminated January 20, 1850.

POSTAL MATTERS

International express mail agreement with detailed regulations.
Signed at Montevideo September 8, 1986.
Entered into force September 26, 1986.
TIAS 11392

PUBLICATIONS

Agreement relating to the exchange of official publications.
Exchange of notes at Santiago October 22 and 27, 1937.
Entered into force October 27, 1937.
51 Stat. 331; EAS 112; 6 Bevans 566

SCIENTIFIC & TECHNICAL COOPERATION

Agreement relating to a cooperative meteorological observation program in Chile.
Exchange of notes at Santiago February 23, June 2 and September 7, 1977.
Entered into force February 15, 1978; effective January 1, 1977.
29 UST 1969; TIAS 8912

Memorandum of understanding for scientific cooperation in the earth sciences.
Signed at Reston and Santiago August 2 and 26, 1982.
Entered into force August 26, 1982.
34 UST 1791; TIAS 10457; 1751 UNTS 47
Amendment and Extension:
April 30 and August 27, 1993 (TIAS 12161)

Basic agreement relating to scientific and technological cooperation, with annexes.
Signed at Washington May 14, 1992.
Entered into force January 19, 1994.
TIAS 12453; 1792 UNTS 321
Extensions:
May 5 and June 22, 1999 (TIAS 99-622)
January 4 and 28, 2005 (TIAS 99-622)
June 27 and 28, 2006 (TIAS 99-622)
June 15 and 29, 2011 (TIAS 99-622)

Memorandum of understanding concerning scientific and technical cooperation in the earth sciences, with annexes.
Signed at Reston and Santiago September 30 and November 17, 1994.
Entered into force November 17, 1994.
TIAS

Memorandum of understanding concerning scientific and technical cooperation in the earth sciences.
Signed at Washington January 16 and 20, 2004.
Entered into force January 20, 2004.
TIAS 04-120

SOCIAL SECURITY

Agreement on social security, with administrative arrangement.
Signed at Santiago February 16, 2000.
Entered into force December 1, 2001.
TIAS 01-1201

SPACE

Agreement concerning a cooperative program for tracking and receiving radio signals from earth satellites and space vehicles.
Exchange of notes at Santiago February 16 and 19, 1959.
Entered into force February 19, 1959; operative December 31, 1958.
10 UST 783; TIAS 4216; 343 UNTS 17

Agreement concerning the use of Mataveri Airport, Isla de Pascua, as a space shuttle emergency landing and rescue site.
Signed at Santiago August 2, 1985.
Entered into force November 6, 1985.
TIAS 11248

TAXATION

Agreement concerning the reciprocal exemption from income tax of income derived from the international operation of aircraft.
Exchange of notes at Washington and Santiago August 6 and December 4, 1990.
Entered into force December 4, 1990.
TIAS 11764; 2202 UNTS 297

TELECOMMUNICATION

Agreement relating to radio communications between amateur stations on behalf of third parties.
Exchange of notes at Santiago August 2 and 17, 1934.
Entered into force August 17, 1934.
49 Stat. 3667; EAS 72; 6 Bevans 564; 157 LNTS 15

Agreement relating to the reciprocal granting of authorizations to permit licensed amateur radio operators of either country to operate their stations in the other country.
Exchange of notes at Washington November 30, 1967.
Entered into force December 30, 1967.
18 UST 2882; TIAS 6380; 701 UNTS 175

TRADE & INVESTMENT

Provisional commercial agreement.
Exchange of notes at Santiago January 6 and February 1, 1938.
Entered into force January 5, 1940.
52 Stat. 1479; EAS 119; 6 Bevans 584; 190 LNTS 9

Reciprocal agreement relating to free importation privileges for consular officers.
Exchange of notes at Washington March 12, April 16, and May 12, 1952.
Entered into force May 12, 1952.
3 UST 4293; TIAS 2577; 177 UNTS 103

United States–Chile free trade agreement, with annexes and related exchanges of letters.
Signed at Miami June 6, 2003.
Entered into force January 1, 2004.
TIAS

Agreement regarding certification of U.S. beef grading.
Exchange of letters at Washington and Santiago March 26, 2009.
Entered into force March 26, 2009.
TIAS

Antitrust cooperation agreement.
Signed at Washington March 31, 2011.
Entered into force March 31, 2011.
TIAS 11-331

TRANSPORTATION

Air transport agreement with exchanges of notes.*
Signed at Santiago May 10, 1947.
Entered into force December 30, 1948.
62 Stat. 3755; TIAS 1905; 6 Bevans 626; 55 UNTS 21
*This agreement is suspended so long as the Multilateral Agreement on
the Liberalization of International Air Transportation, signed May 1, 2001, remains in force between the United States and Chile.

Memorandum of cooperation in the promotion and development of civil aviation, with annex.
Signed at Washington and Santiago July 11, 1997.
Entered into force July 11, 1997.
TIAS 12875

CHINA

NOTE: See also note under TAIWAN at the end of Section 1.

AGRICULTURE

Agreement on agricultural cooperation, with addenda.
Signed at Washington April 10, 1999.
Entered into force April 10, 1999.
TIAS

ATOMIC ENERGY

Agreement on cooperation concerning peaceful uses of nuclear technologies, with annex.
Signed at Beijing June 29, 1998.
Entered into force June 29, 1998.
TIAS 12968

Protocol on cooperation in nuclear safety matters, with addendum and annex.
Signed at Washington July 11, 2013.
Entered into force July 11, 2013.
TIAS 13-711

Agreement for cooperation concerning peaceful uses of nuclear energy, with agreed minute.
Signed at Beijing April 13, 2015.
Entered into force October 29, 2015.
TIAS 15-1029

CLAIMS & DISPUTE RESOLUTION

Agreement concerning the settlement of claims.
Signed at Beijing May 11, 1979.
Entered into force May 11, 1979.
30 UST 1957; TIAS 9306; 1153 UNTS 289
Amendment:
September 28, 1979 (31 UST 5596; TIAS 9675)

Memorandum of understanding concerning settlement of claims relating to deaths, injuries or losses suffered by Chinese personnel as a result of the U.S. bombing of the Chinese Embassy in the Federal Republic of Yugoslavia, with annex.
Signed at Beijing July 30, 1999.
Entered into force July 30, 1999.
TIAS

Memorandum of understanding concerning the settlement of U.S. claims for property loss and damage after the U.S. bombing of the Chinese Embassy in the Federal Republic of Yugoslavia.
Signed at Beijing December 16, 1999.
Entered into force December 16, 1999.
TIAS

Agreement concerning the settlement of Chinese claims for property loss and damage as a result of the U.S. bombing of the Chinese Embassy in the Federal Republic of Yugoslavia.
Signed at Beijing December 16, 1999.
Entered into force December 16, 1999.
TIAS

CONSULAR AFFAIRS

Agreement relating to the reciprocal issuance of visas to crew members of aircraft and vessels.*
Exchange of notes at Beijing January 7, 1981.
Entered into force January 7, 1981.
32 UST 4533; TIAS 9965; 1267 UNTS 335

Agreement relating to reciprocal facilitation of visa issuance.
Exchange of notes at Beijing December 2, 1985.
Entered into force January 2, 1986.
TIAS

Agreement relating to the reciprocal facilitation of visa issuance.*
Exchange of notes at Beijing April 14, 1993.
Entered into force May 14, 1993.
TIAS 12495
Note:
* The status of this agreement is under review.

CULTURAL EXCHANGES, PROPERTY & COOPERATION

Cultural agreement.
Signed at Washington January 31, 1979.
Entered into force January 31, 1979.
TIAS 9178

Memorandum of understanding on the development of bilateral tourism relations.
Signed at Beijing August 5, 1982.
Entered into force August 5, 1982.
34 UST 1418; TIAS 10426

Agreement concerning the United States volunteer program in China.
Signed at Beijing June 29, 1998.
Entered into force June 29, 1998.
TIAS 12969

Memorandum of understanding concerning the imposition of import restrictions on categories of archaeological material from the Paleolithic period through the Tang Dynasty and monumental sculpture and wall art at least 250 years old.
Signed at Washington January 14, 2009.
Entered into force January 14, 2009.
TIAS 09-114
Amendment and Extension:
January 6 and 8, 2014

Implementing accord for cultural exchange for the period of 2014 through 2018 under the cultural agreement of January 31, 1979.
Signed at Beijing July 10, 2014.
Entered into force July 10, 2014.
TIAS

DIPLOMATIC & CONSULAR RELATIONS

Agreement on the mutual establishment of consular relations and the opening of consulates general, with annex.
Signed at Washington January 31, 1979.
Entered into force January 31, 1979.
30 UST 17; TIAS 9177

Agreement concerning the establishment of consulates general.
Exchange of notes at Beijing August 24, 1979.
Entered into force August 24, 1979.
TIAS

Consular convention, with exchange of notes.
Signed at Washington September 17, 1980.
Entered into force February 19, 1982.
33 UST 2973; TIAS 10209; 1529 UNTS 199

Agreement concerning the establishment of additional consulates general.
Exchange of notes at Washington September 17, 1980.
Entered into force September 17, 1980.
TIAS 12007

Agreement relating to privileges and immunities for the respective diplomatic missions in Washington and Beijing.
Exchange of notes at Washington January 5, 1981.
Entered into force January 5, 1981.
TIAS 13079

Agreement modifying the consular convention of September 17, 1980.
Exchange of notes at Beijing January 17, 1981.
Entered into force February 19, 1982.
33 UST 3048; TIAS 10209

Agreement concerning the establishment of additional consulates general, with annex and related letter.
Exchange of notes at Beijing June 16, 1981.
Entered into force June 16, 1981.
TIAS 12007

Agreement concerning the enlargement of existing consular districts.
Exchange of notes at June 16, 1981.
Entered into force June 16, 1981.
TIAS

Agreement regarding the maintenance of the U.S. consulate general in the Hong Kong Special Administrative Region.
Signed at Beijing March 25, 1997.
Entered into force July 1, 1997.
TIAS 12845

EDUCATION

Agreement for cooperation in educational exchanges.
Signed at Beijing July 10, 2014.
Entered into force July 10, 2014.
TIAS

ENVIRONMENT & CONSERVATION

Agreement for cooperation in the Global Learning and Observations to Benefit the Environment (GLOBE) Program, with appendices.
Signed at Beijing October 18, 1995.
Entered into force October 18, 1995.
TIAS 12698

FINANCE

Agreement relating to investment guaranties, with related notes and statement.
Exchange of notes at Beijing October 30, 1980.
Entered into force October 30, 1980.
32 UST 4010; TIAS 9924; 1267 UNTS 315

FISHERIES

Memorandum of understanding on effective cooperation and implementation of United Nations General Assembly Resolution 46/215 of December 20, 1991.
Signed at Washington December 3, 1993.
Entered into force December 3, 1993.
TIAS
Extensions:
November 14 and December 20, 1994
October 22 and December 27, 1996
August 24 and December 2, 1998
August 30 and December 31, 2001

HEALTH & MEDICAL COOPERATION

Agreement on the safety of drugs and medical devices.
Signed at Beijing December 11, 2007.
Entered into force December 11, 2007.
TIAS 07-1211

Agreement of the safety of food and feed, with annex.
Signed at Beijing December 11, 2007.
Entered into force December 11, 2007.
TIAS 07-1211.1

INTELLECTUAL PROPERTY

Memorandum of understanding on the protection of intellectual property.
Signed at Washington January 17, 1992.
Entered into force January 17, 1992.
TIAS 12036

LABOR

Memorandum of understanding on prohibiting import and export trade in prison labor products.
Signed at Washington August 7, 1992.
Entered into force August 7, 1992.
TIAS

Statement of cooperation on the implementation of the memorandum of understanding on prohibiting import and export trade in prison labor products.
Signed at Beijing March 14, 1994.
Entered into force March 14, 1994.
TIAS

LAW ENFORCEMENT

Agreement regarding mutual assistance in customs matters.
Signed at Washington April 9, 1999.
Entered into force April 10, 2003.
TIAS 13029

Agreement on mutual legal assistance in criminal matters.
Signed at Beijing June 19, 2000.
Entered into force March 8, 2001.
TIAS 13102

MARITIME MATTERS

Agreement concerning maritime search and rescue cooperation.
Signed at Washington January 20, 1987.
Entered into force January 20, 1987.
TIAS 12013; 2244 UNTS 71

Agreement on establishing a consultation mechanism to strengthen military maritime safety.
Signed at Beijing January 19, 1998.
Entered into force January 19, 1998.
TIAS 12924

Agreement on maritime transport, with annex.
Signed at Washington December 8, 2003.
Entered into force April 24, 2004.
TIAS

NONPROLIFERATION

Memorandum of agreement on satellite technology safeguards.
Signed at Beijing February 11, 1993.
Entered into force February 11, 1993.
TIAS 12486

POSTAL MATTERS

Memorandum of understanding concerning the operation of the INTELPOST field trial, with details of implementation.
Signed at Beijing and Washington January 17 and February 5, 1987.
Entered into force March 1, 1987.
NP

PROPERTY

Agreement concerning the mutual provision of properties for use of the two countries, with appendices.
Signed at Beijing March 23, 1991.
Entered into force April 22, 1991.
TIAS

Memorandum of understanding concerning the provision of properties in Washington, D.C., Beijing, and Guangzhou.
Signed at Beijing November 1, 2000.
Entered into force November 1, 2000.
TIAS

Agreement on the conditions of construction of new embassy complexes in Washington and Beijing, with appendices.
Signed at Washington November 17, 2003.
Entered into force November 17, 2003.
TIAS 03-1117

Agreement on the conditions of construction of diplomatic and consular complexes in the People's Republic of China and the United States of America, with annex.
Signed at Washington August 20, 2009.
Entered into force August 20, 2009.
TIAS 09-820

SCIENTIFIC & TECHNICAL COOPERATION

Agreement on cooperation in science and technology, with exchange of letters.
Signed at Washington January 31, 1979.
Entered into force January 31, 1979.
30 UST 35; TIAS 9179; 1150 UNTS 349
Amendments and Extensions:
January 12, 1984 (TIAS 12921)
January 25 and 27, 1989
May 22, 1991
April 24 and 25, 2001
April 18, 2006
January 19, 2011
November 20, 2013 (TIAS 13-1120)
April 18 and 21, 2016 (TIAS 16-421)

Protocol on science and technology of transportation.
Signed at Beijing May 11, 1983.
Entered into force May 11, 1983.
TIAS
Amendment:
October 25, 1996

Memorandum of understanding on cooperation in the basic biomedical sciences.
Signed at Beijing May 11, 1983.
Entered into force May 11, 1983.
TIAS
Amendment:
December 20, 2005

Protocol on cooperation in the basic sciences.
Signed at Beijing January 16, 1995.
Entered into force January 16, 1995.
TIAS
Amendment and Extension:
March 27, 2006

Protocol concerning scientific and technical cooperation in the mineral and earth sciences.
Signed at Reston and Beijing July 27, 2006.
Entered into force July 27, 2006.
TIAS 06-727

Protocol concerning scientific and technical cooperation in the earthquake and volcano sciences.
Signed at Washington October 15 and 16, 2009.
Entered into force October 16, 2009.
TIAS 09-1016

Protocol for cooperation on a clean energy research center, with annex.
Signed at Beijing November 17, 2009.
Entered into force November 17, 2009.
TIAS 09-1117.1
Extension:
July 1, 2016 (TIAS 16-701)

Protocol concerning earth observation and related data activities.
Signed at Beijing November 2, 2010.
Entered into force November 2, 2010.
TIAS 10-1102.2

Protocol on cooperation in energy sciences.
Signed at Washington January 18, 2011.
Entered into force January 18, 2011.
TIAS 11-118

Memorandum of understanding on scientific and technical cooperation in the field of environmental protection, with annex.
Signed at Cincinnati June 25, 2012.
Entered into force June 25, 2012.
TIAS 12-0625

Memorandum of understanding for cooperation in the use of U.S. land remote sensing satellite data, with annexes.
Signed at Reston and Beijing October 10 and 20, 2012.
Entered into force October 20, 2012.
TIAS 12-1020

Memorandum of understanding on cooperation in agriculture and related fields, with annex.
Signed at Washington September 24, 2015.
Entered into force September 24, 2015.
TIAS 15-924

Memorandum of understanding on environmental cooperation, with annexes.
Signed at Washington November 19, 2015.
Entered into force November 19, 2015.
TIAS 15-1119

SPACE

Memorandum of agreement on liability for satellite launches.
Signed at Washington December 17, 1988.
Entered into force March 16, 1989.
TIAS

TAXATION

Agreement with respect to mutual exemption from taxation of transportation income of shipping and air transport enterprises.
Signed at Beijing March 5, 1982.
Entered into force September 23, 1983; effective January 1, 1981.
35 UST 3819; TIAS 10884; 2014 UNTS 419

Agreement for the avoidance of double taxation and the prevention of tax evasion with respect to taxes on income, with protocol and exchange of notes.
Signed at Beijing April 30, 1984.
Entered into force November 21, 1986.
TIAS 12065

Protocol concerning the interpretation of paragraph 7 of the protocol to the agreement for the avoidance of double taxation and the prevention of tax evasion with respect to taxes on income of April 30, 1984.
Signed at Beijing May 10, 1986.
Entered into force November 21, 1986.
TIAS 12065

TELECOMMUNICATION

Agreement on the establishment of the direct secure telephone link.
Signed at Beijing April 29, 1998.
Entered into force April 29, 1998.
NP

Agreement on the establishment of a secure defense telephone link.
Signed at Shanghai February 29, 2008.
Entered into force February 29, 2008.
TIAS 08-229

TRADE & INVESTMENT

Agreement on trade exhibitions.
Signed at Beijing May 10, 1979.
Entered into force May 10, 1979.
30 UST 4472; TIAS 9470; 1171 UNTS 305

Agreement on trade relations.
Signed at Beijing July 7, 1979.
Entered into force February 1, 1980.
31 UST 4651; TIAS 9630; 1202 UNTS 179

Accord on industrial and technological cooperation.
Signed at Washington January 12, 1984.
Entered into force January 12, 1984.
35 UST 4233; TIAS 10920

Agreement for orderly trade in ammonium paratungstate and tungstic acid, with annexes.
Signed at Washington September 28, 1987.
Entered into force September 28, 1987;effective October 1, 1987.
TIAS

Memorandum of understanding regarding certain measures granting refunds, reductions or exemptions from taxes or other payments.
Signed at Geneva November 29, 2007.
Entered into force November 29, 2007.
TIAS 07-1129

Agreement on intellectual property rights cooperation.
Signed at Chengdu November 21, 2011.
Entered into force November 21, 2011.
TIAS

Memorandum of understanding regarding films for theatrical release, with annex.
Signed at Geneva April 25, 2012.
Entered into force April 25, 2012.
TIAS 12-425

TRANSPORTATION

Agreement relating to civil air transport, with annexes and exchanges of letters.
Signed at Washington September 17, 1980.
Entered into force September 17, 1980.
33 UST 4559; TIAS 10326

Amendments:
February 10, 1992 (TIAS 12448)
February 16 and March 27, 1996 (TIAS 96-327)
April 8, 1999 (TIAS 96-327)
July 24, 2004 (TIAS 96-327)
July 9, 2007 (TIAS 96-327)

Memorandum of cooperation in the field of civil aviation, with annexes.
Signed at Washington March 14, 1986.
Entered into force March 14, 1986.
TIAS

Amendments and Extensions:
November 23, 1990 and January 26, 1991
November 16, 1994

Agreement concerning the airworthiness certification of imported civil aeronautical products.
Exchange of notes at Beijing October 8 and 14, 1991.
Entered into force October 14, 1991.
TIAS 12437

Agreement for promotion of aviation safety.
Signed at Washington October 20, 2005.
Entered into force October 20, 2005.
TIAS

CHINA (HONG KONG)

In connection with Hong Kong, the People's Republic of China submitted to the Secretary General of the United Nations a note, dated June 20, 1997, which reads in pertinent part as follows:

In accordance with the Joint Declaration of the Government of the United Kingdom of Great Britain and North Ireland and the Government of the People's Republic of China on the Question of Hong Kong signed on 19 December 1984 (hereinafter referred to as the Joint Declaration), the People's Republic of China will resume the exercise of sovereignty over Hong Kong with effect from 1 July 1997. Hong Kong will, with effect from that date, become a Special Administrative Region of the People's Republic of China.

It is provided in Section I of Annex I to the Joint Declaration, "Elaboration by the Government of the People's Republic of China of its Basic Policies Regarding Hong Kong", and in Articles 12, 13 and 14 of the Basic Law of the Hong Kong Special Administrative Region of the People's Republic of China, which was adopted on 4 April 1990 by the National People's Congress of the People's Republic of China (hereinafter referred to as the Basic law), that the Hong Kong Special Administrative Region will enjoy a high degree of autonomy, except in foreign and defence affairs which are the responsibility of the Central People's Government of the People's Republic of China. Furthermore, it is provided both in Section XI of Annex I to the Joint Declaration and Article 153 of the Basic Law that international agreements to which the People's Republic of China is not a party but which are implemented in Hong Kong may continue to be implemented in the Hong Kong Special Administrative Region.

In this connection, on behalf of the Government of the People's Republic of China, I would like to inform Your Excellency as follows:

I. The treaties listed in Annex I [not printed herein] to this Note, to which the People's Republic of China is a party, will be applied to the Hong Kong Special Administrative Region with effect from 1 July 1997 as they:

(i) are applied to Hong Kong before 1 July 1997; or

(ii) fall within the category of foreign affairs or defence or, owing to their nature and provisions, must apply to the entire territory of a State; or

(iii) are not applied to Hong Kong before 1 July 1997 but with respect to which it has been decided to apply them to the Hong Kong Special Administrative Region with effect from that date (denoted by an asterisk in Annex I.)

II. The treaties listed in Annex II [not printed herein] to this Note, to which the People's Republic of China is not yet a party and which apply to Hong Kong before 1 July 1997, will continue to apply to the Hong Kong Special Administrative Region with effect from 1 July 1997.

The provisions of the International Covenant on Civil and Political Rights and the International Covenant on Economic, Social and Cultural Rights as applied to Hong Kong shall remain in force beginning from 1 July 1997....

III. The Government of the People's Republic of China has already carried out separately the formalities required for the application of the treaties listed in the aforesaid Annexes, including all the related amendments, protocols, reservations and declarations, to the Hong Kong Special Administrative Region with effect from 1 July 1997.

IV. With respect to any other treaty not listed in the Annexes to this Note, to which the People's Republic of China is or will become a party, in the event that it is decided to apply such treaty to the Hong Kong Special Administrative Region, the Government of the People's Republic of China will carry out separately the formalities for such application. For the avoidance of doubt, no separate formalities will need to be carried out by the Government of the People's Republic of China with respect to treaties which fall within the category of foreign affairs or defence or which, owing to their nature and provisions, must apply to the entire territory of a State.

LAW ENFORCEMENT

Agreement for the surrender of fugitive offenders.
Signed at Hong Kong December 20, 1996.
Entered into force January 21, 1998.
TIAS 98-121

Agreement for the transfer of sentenced persons.
Signed at Hong Kong April 15, 1997.
Entered into force April 18, 1999.
TIAS

Agreement on mutual legal assistance in criminal matters, with annex.
Signed at Hong Kong April 15, 1997.
Entered into force January 21, 2000.
TIAS

POSTAL MATTERS

Parcel post agreement and regulations of execution.
Signed at Hong Kong January 18 and at Washington February 2, 1961.
Entered into force July 1, 1961.
12 UST 328; TIAS 4721

International express mail agreement, with detailed regulations.
Signed at Hong Kong and Washington January 2 and February 6, 1979.
Entered into force March 15, 1979; effective February 1, 1979.
30 UST 3427; TIAS 9398; 1180 UNTS 25

SCIENTIFIC & TECHNICAL COOPERATION

Protocol concerning scientific and technical cooperation in earth sciences.
Signed at Hong Kong November 9, 2009.
Entered into force November 9, 2009.
TIAS 09-1109

TAXATION

Agreement for the reciprocal exemption with respect to taxes on income from the international operation of ships.
Exchange of notes at Hong Kong August 1, 1989.
Entered into force August 1, 1989.
TIAS 11892; 1549 UNTS 91

TRANSPORTATION

Agreement concerning air services, with annex.
Signed at Hong Kong April 7, 1997.
Entered into force April 7, 1997.
TIAS 12849; 1981 UNTS 231

CHINA (MACAO)

In connection with Macao, the People's Republic of China submitted to the Secretary General of the United Nations a note, dated December 13, 1999, which reads in pertinent part as follows:

In accordance with the Joint Declaration of the Government of the People's Republic of China and the Government of the Republic of Portugal on the Question of Macao signed on 13 April 1987 (hereinafter referred to as the Joint Declaration), the Government of the People's Republic of China will resume the exercise of sovereignty over Macao with effect from 20 December 1999. Macao will, from that date, become a Special Administrative Region of the People's Republic of China.

It is provided in Section I of Elaboration by the Government of the People's Republic of China of its Basic Policies Regarding Macao, which is Annex I to the Joint Declaration, and in Article 12, 13 and 14 of the Basic Law of the Macao Special Administrative Region of the People's Republic of China (hereinafter referred to as the Basic Law),which was adopted by the National People's Congress of the People's Republic of China on 31 March 1993, that the Macao Special Administrative Region will enjoy a high degree of autonomy, except in foreign and defence affairs which are the responsibilities of the Central People's Government of the People's Republic of China. Furthermore, it is provided both in Section VIII of Annex I to the Joint Declaration and Article 138 of the Basic Law that international agreements to which the People's Republic of China is not yet a party but which are implemented in Macao may continue to be implemented in the Macao Special Administrative Region.

In this connection, on behalf of the Government of the People's Republic of China, I have the honour to inform your Excellency that:

I. The Treaties listed in Annex I [not printed herein] to this Note, to which the People's Republic of China is a Party, will be applied to the Macao Special Administrative Region with effect from 20 December 1999 so long as they are one of the following categories:

(i) Treaties that apply to Macao before 20 December 1999;

(ii) Treaties that must apply to the entire territory of a state as they concern foreign affairs or defence or their nature or provisions so require.

II. The Treaties listed in Annex II [not printed herein] to this Note, to which the People's Republic of China is not yet a Party and which apply to Macao before 20 December 1999, will continue to apply to the Macao Special Administrative Region with effect from 20 December 1999.

III. The Government of the People's Republic of China has notified the treaty depositories concerned of the application of the treaties including their amendments and protocols as listed in the aforesaid Annexes as well as reservations and declarations made thereto by the Chinese Government to the Macao Special Administrative Region with effect from 20 December 1999.

IV. With respect to other treaties that are not listed in the Annexes to this Note, to which the People's Republic of China is or will become a Party, the Government of the People's Republic of China will go through separately the necessary formalities for their application to the Macao Special Administrative Region if it is so decided.

POSTAL MATTERS

Parcel post agreement with detailed regulations for execution.
Signed at Macao February 23 and at Washington June 8, 1973.
Entered into force August 1, 1974.
25 UST 2982; TIAS 7961

International express mail agreement, with detailed regulations.
Signed at Macao and Washington May 3 and June 14, 1983.
Entered into force October 1, 1983.
35 UST 1403; TIAS 10736; 2006 UNTS 333

Memorandum of understanding concerning the operation of the INTELPOST field trial, with details of implementation.
Signed at Macao and Washington April 29 and May 21, 1985.
Entered into force May 21, 1985.
TIAS 11246

TRANSPORTATION

Air transport agreement, with annexes.
Signed at Macao July 3, 1996.
Entered into force July 3, 1996.
TIAS 12777

COLOMBIA

AGRICULTURE

Agreement for the eradication of foot-and-mouth disease in the areas adjacent to the Colombian-Panamanian border, with annex.
Signed at Bogota August 8, 1979.
Entered into force October 10, 1979.
33 UST 1643; TIAS 10138

ATOMIC ENERGY

Agreement providing for a grant for the acquisition of nuclear training and research equipment and materials.
Exchange of notes at Bogota July 31, 1959, and January 11, 1960.
Entered into force January 11, 1960.
11 UST 138; TIAS 4421; 371 UNTS 37

CONSULAR AFFAIRS

Agreement relating to the extension of the validity of nonimmigrant visas.*
Exchange of notes at Bogota June 13 and 26, 1956, and May 22, 1957.
Entered into force June 21, 1957.
10 UST 1250; TIAS 4263; 354 UNTS 21

Amendment:
June 5 and 11, 1957 (10 UST 1250; TIAS 4263; 354 UNTS 29)

Note:
* The status of this agreement is under review.

CULTURAL EXCHANGES, PROPERTY & COOPERATION

Agreement for using volunteers to carry out social and economic development projects in Colombia.
Signed at Bogota April 2, 1963.
Entered into force July 12, 1963.
26 UST 1764; TIAS 8134; 1006 UNTS 7

Related Agreement:
May 11, 2010 (TIAS 10-511)

Memorandum of understanding concerning the imposition restrictions on archaeological material from the Pre-Columbian cultures and certain ecclesiastical ethnological material from the colonial period in Colombia.
Signed at Bogota March 15, 2006.
Entered into force March 15, 2006.
TIAS 06-315
Amendment and Extension:
February 25 and March 11, 2011 (TIAS 06-315)
March 9 and 10, 2016 (TIAS 16-310.1)

DEFENSE

Agreement relating to the procurement of strategic materials.
Exchange of notes at Bogota March 29, 1943.
Entered into force March 29, 1943.
58 Stat. 1546; EAS 442; 6 Bevans 954; 124 UNTS 139

Military assistance agreement.
Exchange of notes at Bogota April 17, 1952.
Entered into force April 17, 1952.
3 UST 3690; TIAS 2496; 174 UNTS 15

Agreement for performance by members of Army, Navy, and Air Force missions of duties of military assistance advisory group specified in article V of the military assistance agreement of
April 17, 1952.
Exchange of notes at Bogota July 13 and September 16, 1955.
Entered into force September 20, 1955.
6 UST 3904; TIAS 3393; 256 UNTS 221

Agreement providing for disposition of equipment and materials furnished by the United States under the military assistance agreement of April 17, 1952.
Exchange of notes at Bogota February 22 and March 14, 1956.
Entered into force March 14, 1956.
7 UST 475; TIAS 3531; 270 UNTS 392

Agreement relating to the furnishing of military equipment, materials, and services.
Exchange of notes at Bogota April 3, 1961.
Entered into force April 3, 1961.
12 UST 492; TIAS 4740; 407 UNTS 3

Agreement relating to the deposit of ten percent of the grants of military assistance and excess defense articles given by the United States with related aide memoire.
Exchange of notes at Bogota August 25, 1972.
Entered into force August 25, 1972; effective February 7, 1972.
23 UST 3149; TIAS 7492; 898 UNTS 171

Agreement concerning an army mission, a naval mission, and an air force mission of the United States armed forces in Colombia.
Signed at Bogota October 7, 1974.
Entered into force April 16, 1975.
TIAS 8986; 29 UST 2901; 1148 UNTS 75

Agreement concerning general security of military information.
Exchange of notes at Bogota December 16, 1981.
Entered into force December 16, 1981.
33 UST 4444; TIAS 10315

Memorandum of agreement on the exchange of naval personnel.
Signed at Bogota and Washington March 8 and April 30, 1985.
Entered into force April 30, 1985.
TIAS 11255

Basic exchange and cooperative agreement concerning geospatial information and services cooperation, with annexes.
Signed at Bogota and Washington April 11 and 23, 2002.
Entered into force April 23, 2002.
NP

Agreement regarding the exchange of military personnel (MPEP), with annex.
Signed at Washington and Bogota August 2 and September 10, 2002.
Entered into force September 10, 2002.
NP
Extension:
December 21, 2012 and January 10, 2013

Aviation leadership program agreement.
Signed at Washington and Bogota August 4, 2004, and February 2, 2005.
Entered into force February 2, 2005.
NP

Agreement regarding the assignment of liaison officers, with annex.
Signed at Washington and Bogota July 15 and October 22, 2005.
Entered into force October 22, 2005.
NP
Amendment and Extension:
December 11 and March 9, 2016

Agreement concerning exchange of research and development information, with appendix.
Signed at Bogota and Washington May 22 and July 21, 2009.
Entered into force July 21, 2009.
TIAS 09-721

Agreement for cooperation and technical assistance in defense and security.
Signed at Bogota October 30, 2009.
Entered into force October 30, 2009.
TIAS 09-1030

Agreement regarding grants under the Foreign Assistance Act of 1961, as amended, or successor legislation, and the furnishing of defense articles, related training, and other defense services, including pursuant to the Global Peace Operations Initiative (GPOI) Program, from the United States of America to the Government of Colombia.
Exchange of notes at Bogota December 27, 2010.
Entered into force December 27, 2010.
NP

Acquisition and cross-servicing agreement, with annexes.
Signed at Bogota and Miami June 27 and 30, 2012.
Entered into force June 30, 2012.
NP

DIPLOMATIC & CONSULAR

Consular convention.*
Signed at Washington May 4, 1850.
Entered into force October 30, 1851.
10 Stat. 900; TS 55; 6 Bevans 882

Note:

* Article III, paragraphs 8 and 11, terminated by the United States as of July 1, 1916, in accordance with the Seamen's Act (38 Stat. 1164).

Agreement relating to reciprocal customs privileges for consular officers.
Exchange of notes at Washington May 9 and 10, 1968.
Entered into force May 10, 1968.
19 UST 4864; TIAS 6491; 698 UNTS 237

EDUCATION

Agreement for financing certain educational exchange programs.
Exchange of notes at Bogota June 12, 1967, and March 8, 1971.
Entered into force March 11, 1971.
22 UST 1705; TIAS 7198; 808 UNTS 368

EMPLOYMENT

Agreement relating to the employment of dependents of official government employees.
Exchange of notes at Bogota March 30 and May 25, 1982.
Entered into force May 25, 1982.
35 UST 1301; TIAS 10729; 1607 UNTS 95

ENVIRONMENT & CONSERVATION

Agreement for cooperation in the Global Learning and Observations to Benefit the Environment (GLOBE) Program, with appendices.
Signed at Washington October 28, 1998.
Entered into force October 28, 1998.
TIAS 12989

Agreement on environmental cooperation.
Signed at Washington April 19, 2013.
Entered into force June 28, 2013.
TIAS 13-628

FINANCE

Agreement relating to investment guaranties.
Exchange of letters at Bogota October 5, 1962.
Entered into force October 5, 1962.
13 UST 2465; TIAS 5210; 459 UNTS 191

Investment incentive agreement.
Exchange of notes at Washington April 3, 1985.
Entered into force April 3, 1985.
TIAS 12043

Amendment:

July 18 and August 19, 1985 (TIAS 12043)

Agreement regarding the reduction of certain debts related to foreign assistance owed to the Government of the United States and its agencies, with appendices.
Signed at Washington December 15, 1992.
Entered into force January 14, 1993.
NP

Amendments:

June 1 and 30, 1993 (NP)
July 2 and 19, 1993 (NP)

Agreement regarding a debt-for-nature swap to prepay and cancel certain debt owed by the Government of the Republic of Colombia to the Government of the United States of America, with attachments.
Signed at Bogota March 30, 2004.
Entered into force April 29, 2004.
TIAS 04-429

FISHERIES

Agreement on certain fishing rights in implementation of the treaty and exchange of notes of September 8, 1972 (TIAS 10120).
Exchange of notes at Bogota October 24 and December 6, 1983.
Entered into force December 6, 1983; effective March 1, 1984.
35 UST 3105; TIAS 10842; 2015 UNTS 3

FOREIGN ASSISTANCE

Agreement for a cooperative program of agriculture and natural resources in Colombia.
Exchange of notes at Bogota May 25 and June 9, 1953.
Entered into force June 9, 1953.
4 UST 1601; TIAS 2827; 213 UNTS 3

General agreement for economic, technical and related assistance.
Signed at Bogota July 23, 1962.
Entered into force July 23, 1962.
13 UST 1778; TIAS 5123; 458 UNTS 123

Related Agreements:

September 27, 2000
August 30, 2004
June 19, 2008

Agreement concerning the establishment of an Americas Account and Administering Council.
Signed at Bogota June 18, 1993.
Entered into force June 18, 1993.
TIAS 12502

Amendment:

March 27, 2000

AGENCY FOR INTERNATIONAL DEVELOPMENT

Strategic objective grant agreement to reduce illicit crop production in selected areas of Colombia.
Signed at Bogota August 30, 1999.
Entered into force August 30, 1999.
NP
Amendments:
September 27, 2000 (NP)
June 30, 2005 (NP)
July 19, 2006 (NP)
September 30, 2008 (NP)

Strategic objective grant agreement to promote more responsive, participatory and accountable democracy, with annexes.
Signed at Bogota September 27, 2000.
Entered into force September 27, 2000.
NP
Amendments:
July 1, 2005 (NP)
June 16, 2006 (NP)
September 30, 2008 (NP)

Strategic objective grant for improved environment for demobilization and reintegration, with annexes.
Signed at Bogota August 30, 2006.
Entered into force August 30, 2006.
NP
Amendment:
September 30, 2008 (NP)

Country assistance agreement, with annexes.
Signed April 8, 2009.
Entered into force April 8, 2009.
NP
Amendments:
September 30, 2009 (NP)
May 20, 2010 (NP)
September 29, 2011 (NP)
September 6, 2012 (NP)

Cooperative agreement, with attachments.
Signed July 31, 2012.
Entered into force July 31, 2012.
TIAS

Development objectives grant agreement for expanded state presence, reconciliation, rural economic growth and environmental resiliency.
Signed at Bogota June 12, 2015.
Entered into force June 12, 2015.
NP

INTERNATIONAL CRIMINAL COURT

Agreement regarding the surrender of persons of the United States of America to the International Criminal Court.
Signed at Bogota September 17, 2003.
Entered into force September 17, 2003.
TIAS 03-917

LAW ENFORCEMENT

Procedures for mutual assistance in the administration of justice in connection with the Lockheed Aircraft Corporation matter.
Signed at Washington April 22, 1976.
Entered into force April 22, 1976.
27 UST 1059; TIAS 8244
Related Agreements:
July 7 and 15, 1980 (32 UST 1921; TIAS 9809; 1234 UNTS 423)
August 28 and September 10, 1980 (32 UST 2599; TIAS 9860; 1274 UNTS 261)

Extradition treaty, with annex.
Signed at Washington September 14, 1979.
Entered into force March 4, 1982.
TIAS

Agreement relating to cooperation to curb the illegal traffic in narcotics.
Exchange of notes at Bogota July 21 and August 6, 1980.
Entered into force August 6, 1980.
32 UST 2301; TIAS 9838; 1274 UNTS 255

Mutual cooperation agreement to combat, prevent and control money laundering arising from illicit activities.
Signed at San Antonio February 27, 1992.
Entered into force February 27, 1992.
TIAS 12450

Supplemental memorandum through which mechanisms are established for implementing the July 24, 1990 memorandum of understanding concerning the transfer of forfeited assets.
Signed at Washington October 28, 1998.
Entered into force October 28, 1998.
TIAS 12990

Agreement regarding mutual assistance.
Signed at Miami September 21, 1999.
Entered into force September 21, 1999.
TIAS 13062

Agreement regarding the provision of articles, services and associated training by the Government of the United States for counter-narcotics purposes.
Exchange of notes at Bogota February 28 and 29, 2000.
Entered into force February 29, 2000.
TIAS

Agreement regarding the Cooperating Nation Information Exchange System.
Exchange of notes at Bogota July 18, 2006, January 10, 2007, and January 17, 2007.
Entered into force January 17, 2007.
TIAS

Agreement regarding property title transfer.
Signed at Bogota December 7, 2007.
Entered into force December 7, 2007.
NP

Property title transfer agreement for Grand Caravan aircraft.
Signed at Bogota March 25, 2008.
Entered into force April 14, 2008.
NP

Property title transfer agreement for Schweizer aircraft.
Signed at Bogota April 4, 2008.
Entered into force April 14, 2008.
TIAS 08-414

Agreement concerning the program for the suppression of illicit aerial traffic in narcotic drugs and psychotropic substances (Air Bridge Denial), with annexes.
Signed at Bogota December 30, 2009.
Entered into force December 30, 2009.
NP

Amendment:
August 25, 2012

Title transfer agreement for five UH-60 helicopters.
Signed at Bogota December 29, 2010.
Entered into force December 30, 2010.
NP

Agreement concerning the sharing of forfeited proceeds and instrumentalities of crime.
Signed at Cartagena November 21, 2016.
Entered into force November 21, 2016.
TIAS 16-1121

MARITIME MATTERS

Agreement to suppress illicit traffic by sea.
Signed at Bogota February 20, 1997.
Entered into force February 20, 1997.
TIAS

PEACE

Treaty for the settlement of differences arising out of the events which took place on the Isthmus of Panama in November 1903.
Signed at Bogota April 6, 1914.
Entered into force March 1, 1922.
42 Stat. 2122; TS 661; 6 Bevans 900; 9 LNTS 301

POSTAL MATTERS

Parcel post agreement.
Signed at Bogota January 31 and at Washington February 7, 1939.
Operative April 1, 1939.
53 Stat. 2136; Post Office Department print; 196 LNTS 53

International express mail agreement, with detailed regulations.
Signed at Washington and Bogota June 13 and July 7, 1983.
Entered into force September 3, 1983.
35 UST 1459; TIAS 10738; 2006 UNTS 361

PUBLICATIONS

Agreement relating to the exchange of official publications.
Exchange of notes at Washington July 15 and 26, 1949.
Entered into force July 26, 1949.
63 Stat. 2799; TIAS 2048; 6 Bevans 998; 73 UNTS 105

SCIENTIFIC & TECHNICAL COOPERATION

Agreement relating to the reestablishment, operation, and maintenance of the rawinsonde observation stations at Bogota and on San Andres Island, with memorandum of arrangement.
Exchange of letters at Bogota April 28 and September 8, 1981.
Entered into force September 8, 1981.
TIAS 12377

Memorandum of understanding concerning scientific and technical cooperation in the earth sciences, with annexes, and exchange of rectifying notes.
Signed at Reston and Bogota April 24 and May 9, 2008.
Entered into force May 9, 2008.
TIAS 08-509

Supplemental agreement regarding the strengthening of technical and related assistance for scientific, technical, and technological cooperation and innovation, with annexes.
Signed at Bogota June 9, 2010.
Entered into force September 15, 2010.
TIAS 10-915

Memorandum of understanding concerning scientific and technical cooperation in the earth sciences.
Signed at Reston and Bogota January 10 and February 20, 2013.
Entered into force February 20, 2013.
TIAS 13-220.1

TAXATION

Agreement for relief from double taxation on earnings from operations of ships and aircraft.
Exchange of notes at Washington August 1, 1961.
Entered into force December 11, 1961.
12 UST 3141; TIAS 4916; 433 UNTS 123

Amendment:
October 16, 1987 (TIAS 11563; 2185 UNTS 464)

Agreement for the exchange of tax information.
Signed at Bogota March 30, 2001.
Entered into force April 30, 2014.
TIAS 14-430

TELECOMMUNICATION

Agreement relating to radio communications between amateur stations on behalf of third parties.
Exchange of notes at Bogota November 16 and 29, 1963.
Entered into force December 29, 1963.
14 UST 1754; TIAS 5483; 494 UNTS 49

Agreement relating to the reciprocal granting of authorizations to permit licensed amateur radio operators of either country to operate their stations in the other country.
Exchange of notes at Bogota October 19 and 28, 1965.
Entered into force November 28, 1965.
16 UST 1742; TIAS 5899; 574 UNTS 109

TERRITORIAL ISSUES

Treaty concerning the status of Quita Sueno, Roncador and Serrana, with exchange of notes.
Signed at Bogota September 8, 1972.
*Entered into force September 17, 1981.**
33 UST 1405; TIAS 10120; 1307 UNTS 379
Note:
* With understanding.

TRADE & INVESTMENT

Treaty of peace, amity, navigation, and commerce, with additional article.*
Signed at Bogota December 12, 1846.
Entered into force June 10, 1848.
9 Stat. 881; TS 54; 6 Bevans 868
Note:
* Article 33 terminated by the United States effective July 1, 1916, in accordance with the Seamen's Act (38 Stat. 1164).

Agreement regarding sanitary and phytosanitary measures and technical barriers to trade.
Exchange of letters at Bogota and Washington February 26, 2006.
Entered into force February 26, 2006.
TIAS 06-226

Agreement regarding trade in beef and beef products of the United States, with annex.
Exchange of letters at Bogota and Washington August 21, 2006.
Entered into force August 21, 2006.
TIAS 06-821

Agreement on control measures on salmonella in poultry and poultry products.
Exchange of letters April 15, 2012.
Entered into force April 15, 2012.
TIAS 12-415

Agreement on control measures on avian influenza.
Exchange of letters April 15, 2012.
Entered into force April 15, 2012.
TIAS 12-415.1

Agreement on phytosanitary measures for importation of U.S. paddy rice.
Exchange of letters April 15, 2012.
Entered into force April 15, 2012.
TIAS 12-415.2

Agreement on antitrust cooperation.
Signed at Washington and Montevideo September 5 and 16, 2014.
Entered into force September 16, 2014.
TIAS 14-916

TRANSPORTATION

Agreement for cooperation in the construction of the Colombia segment of the Darien Gap Highway.
Signed at Washington May 6, 1971.
Entered into force May 6, 1971.
22 UST 617; TIAS 7112; 793 UNTS 3

Agreement relating to the sale of six C 47 aircraft to Colombia for civilian cargo and passenger service.
Signed at Bogota April 21, 1976.
Entered into force April 21, 1976.
27 UST 4317; TIAS 8453; 1071 UNTS 73

Memorandum of agreement for the provision of assistance in developing and modernizing Colombia's civil aviation infrastructure.
Signed August 2 and 4, 1994.
Entered into force August 4, 1994.
NP
Amendment:
March 1, 2005 (NP)

Air transport agreement.
Signed at Bogota May 10, 2011.
Entered into force May 6, 2014.
TIAS

COMMISSION OF THE CARTAGENA AGREEMENT (ANDEAN GROUP)

NOTE: Representatives of Bolivia, Colombia, Ecuador, Peru, and Venezuela signed for the Commission.

FOREIGN ASSISTANCE

Memorandum of understanding concerning trade, financing, science and technology, development of industry, agriculture and infrastructure.
Signed at Washington November 21, 1979.
Entered into force November 21, 1979.
32 UST 4399; TIAS 9953; 1266 UNTS 293

SCIENTIFIC & TECHNICAL COOPERATION

Memorandum of understanding on science and technology cooperation.
Signed at Washington November 21, 1979.
Entered into force November 21, 1979.
32 UST 4327; TIAS 9949; 1266 UNTS 285

COMOROS

CULTURAL EXCHANGES, PROPERTY & COOPERATION

Agreement relating to the establishment of a Peace Corps program in Comoros.
Signed at Moroni September 5, 2014.
Entered into force September 5, 2014.
TIAS 14-905

DEFENSE

Agreement concerning the provision of training related to defense articles under the United States International Military Education and Training (IMET) Program.
Exchange of notes at Moroni August 5, 1986, and September 22, 1987.
Entered into force September 22, 1987.
TIAS 11403

Acquisition and cross-servicing agreement.
Signed at Kadani July 6, 2014.
Entered into force July 6, 2014.
NP

Agreement regarding the status of United States personnel in the Union of the Comoros.
Signed at Moroni June 7, 2013.
Entered into force September 24, 2014.
TIAS 14-924.4

EMPLOYMENT

Agreement concerning employment on a reciprocal basis of dependents of members of diplomatic missions and consular posts assigned to official duty in the United States of America or the Union of the Comoros.
Exchange of notes at Washington and New York City April 14 and June 6, 2016.
Entered into force June 6, 2016.
TIAS 16-606

FINANCE

Investment incentive agreement.
Signed at Moroni December 8, 2008.
Entered into force December 8, 2008.
TIAS 08-1208

INTERNATIONAL CRIMINAL COURT

Agreement regarding the surrender of persons to the International Criminal Court.
Signed at Moroni June 30, 2004.
Entered into force June 30, 2004.
TIAS 04-630

TELECOMMUNICATION

Agreement relating to radio communications between amateur stations on behalf of third parties.
Exchange of notes at Moroni March 8 and September 8, 1989.
Entered into force October 8, 1989.
TIAS 11699

CONGO

CONSULAR AFFAIRS

Reciprocal agreement between the United States and France relating to visa fees for nonimmigrants.*
Exchanges of notes at Washington August 19 and September 4, 5, and 16, 1947.
Entered into force September 16, 1947; operative October 1, 1947.
61 Stat. 3776; TIAS 1721; 7 Bevans 1210; 84 UNTS 19
Note:
* The status of this agreement is under review.

CULTURAL EXCHANGES, PROPERTY & COOPERATION

Agreement concerning the establishment of a Peace Corps program in the Congo.
Exchange of notes at Brazzaville April 21, 1990.
Entered into force April 21, 1990.
TIAS

DEFENSE

Agreement regarding the end use of defense articles, relating training, including training material or other defense services.
Signed at Brazzaville March 18 2014.
Entered into force March 18, 2014.
NP

EMPLOYMENT

Agreement relating to the employment of dependents of official government employees.
Exchange of notes at Washington April 11 and May 23, 1997.
Entered into force May 23, 1997.
TIAS 12859

ENVIRONMENT & CONSERVATION

Agreement for cooperation in the Global Learning and Observations to Benefit the Environment (GLOBE) Program.
Signed at Brazzaville June 28, 2005.
Entered into force June 28, 2005.
TIAS 05-628

FINANCE

Agreement regarding the consolidation and rescheduling of certain debts owed to, guaranteed by or insured by the United States Government and its agencies, with annexes.
Signed at Brazzaville June 26, 1987.
Entered into force August 7, 1987.
NP

Agreement regarding the consolidation and rescheduling or refinancing of certain debts owed to, guaranteed by, or insured by the United States Government and its agency, with annexes.
Signed at Brazzaville May 6, 1994.
Entered into force June 30, 1994.
NP

Agreement regarding the consolidation and rescheduling or refinancing of certain debts owed to, guaranteed by or insured by the United States Government and its agency, with annexes.
Signed at Brazzaville November 21, 1994.
Entered into force January 19, 1995.
NP

Investment incentive agreement.
Signed at Washington September 12, 2002.
Entered into force September 12, 2002.
TIAS 02-912

Agreement regarding the consolidation and rescheduling of certain debts owed to, guaranteed by, or insured by the United States Government and its agencies.
Signed at Brazzaville May 6, 2005.
Entered into force June 13, 2005.
NP

Agreement regarding the consolidation and rescheduling of certain debts owed to, guaranteed by, or insured by the United States Government and its agencies, with annexes.
Signed at Brazzaville July 8, 2005.
Entered into force August 22, 2005.
NP

Agreement regarding the reduction of debts owed to, guaranteed by, or insured by the United States Government and its agencies, with annexes.
Signed at Brazzaville January 31, 2007.
Entered into force June 30, 2007.
NP

Agreement regarding the reduction of certain debts owed to, guaranteed by, or insured by the United States Government and its agencies, with annexes.
Signed at Brazzaville June 12, 2009.
Entered into force August 24, 2009.
NP

Agreement regarding the reduction of certain debts owed to, guaranteed by, or insured by the United States Government and its agencies, with annexes.
Signed at Brazzaville July 15, 2010.
Entered into force September 6, 2010.
NP

INTERNATIONAL CRIMINAL COURT

Agreement regarding the surrender of persons to the International Criminal Court.
Signed at Brazzaville June 2, 2004.
Entered into force June 2, 2004.
TIAS 04-602

LAW ENFORCEMENT

Extradition convention between the United States and France.
Signed at Paris January 6, 1909.
Entered into force July 27, 1911.
37 Stat. 1526; TS 561; 7 Bevans 872

Supplementary extradition convention between the United States and France.
Signed at Paris January 15, 1929.
Entered into force May 19, 1929.
46 Stat. 2276; TS 787; 7 Bevans 972; 92 LNTS 259

Supplementary extradition convention between the United States and France.
Signed at Paris April 23, 1936.
Entered into force September 24, 1936.
50 Stat. 1117; TS 909; 7 Bevans 995; 172 LNTS 197

POSTAL MATTERS

International express mail agreement, with detailed regulations.
Signed at Brazzaville and Washington July 15 and August 12, 1988.
Entered into force September 15, 1988.
TIAS 11659

Memorandum of understanding concerning the operation of the INTELPOST service, with details of implementation.
Signed at Brazzaville and Washington March 20, 1990, and May 13, 1991.
Entered into force May 28, 1991.
TIAS 11835

TRADE & INVESTMENT

Treaty concerning the reciprocal encouragement and protection of investment, with annex.
Signed at Washington February 12, 1990.
Entered into force August 13, 1994.
TIAS

TRANSPORTATION

Air transport services agreement between the United States and France.
Signed at Paris March 27, 1946.
Entered into force March 27, 1946.
61 Stat. 3445; TIAS 1679; 7 Bevans 1109; 139 UNTS 114
Extensions and Amendments:
June 23 and July 11, 1950 (1 UST 593; TIAS 2106; 139 UNTS 142)
March 19, 1951 (2 UST 1033; TIAS 2257; 139 UNTS 151)
March 19, 1951 (2 UST 1037; TIAS 2258; 139 UNTS 146)
August 27, 1959 (10 UST 1791; TIAS 4336; 358 UNTS 277)

TREATY LAW

Treaty obligations assumed by the Congo upon its independence.
Exchange of notes at Brazzaville May 12 and August 5, 1961.
Entered into force August 5, 1961.
13 UST 2065; TIAS 5161; 603 UNTS 19

CONGO, DEMOCRATIC REPUBLIC OF THE

CULTURAL EXCHANGES, PROPERTY & COOPERATION

Agreement relating to the establishment of a Peace Corps program in the Democratic Republic of the Congo.
Exchange of notes at Kinshasa May 8 and October 12, 1970.
Entered into force October 12, 1970.
23 UST 268; TIAS 7304

DEFENSE

Agreement relating to military assistance and provision for a military mission to Congo (Leopoldville).
Exchange of notes at Leopoldville June 24 and July 19, 1963.
Entered into force July 19, 1963.
15 UST 142; TIAS 5530; 511 UNTS 47

Agreement relating to the deposit by Zaire of ten percent of the value of grant military assistance and excess defense articles furnished by the United States.
Exchange of notes at Kinshasa April 18 and May 16, 1972.
Entered into force May 16, 1972; effective February 7, 1972.
23 UST 1442; TIAS 7422

Agreement regarding the status of U.S. military personnel and civilian employees of the Department of Defense who may be present in Zaire in connection with humanitarian efforts.
Exchange of notes at Kinshasa July 21 and 22, 1994.
Entered into force July 22, 1994.
TIAS

Acquisition and cross-servicing agreement, with annexes.
Signed at Stuttgart and Kinshasa July 14 and September 29, 2006.
Entered into force September 29, 2006.
NP

Agreement regarding grants under the Foreign Assistance Act of 1961, as amended, or successor legislation, and the furnishing of defense articles, defense services and related training, including pursuant to the United States International Military Education and Training (IMET) Program and the Peacekeeping Operation (PKO) Program.
Exchange of notes at Kinshasa June 5, 2006, and August 9, 2007.
Entered into force August 9, 2007.
NP

Agreement regarding the status of United States personnel who may be temporarily present in the Democratic Republic of the Congo.
Exchange of notes at Kinshasa August 28 and 30, 2008.
Entered into force August 30, 2008.
TIAS 08-830

EDUCATION

Agreement concerning the status of the American School of Kinshasa.
Signed at Kinshasa April 24, 2013.
Entered into force September 14, 2016.
TIAS 16-914

EMPLOYMENT

Agreement concerning the employment of dependents of official government employees, with attachment.
Exchange of notes at Kinshasa January 12, 2002, and October 8, 2003.
Entered into force October 8, 2003.
TIAS 03-1008

FINANCE

Agreement regarding the consolidation and rescheduling of certain debts owed to, guaranteed or insured by the United States government and its agencies.
Signed at Washington June 17, 1977.
Entered into force August 30, 1977.
28 UST 7593; TIAS 8731

Agreement regarding the consolidation and rescheduling of payments due under PL 480 Title I agricultural commodity agreements, with annexes.
Signed at Washington July 19, 1978.
Entered into force July 19, 1978.
30 UST 3511; TIAS 9405; 1179 UNTS 37

Agreement regarding the consolidation and rescheduling of certain debts owed to, guaranteed or insured by the United States Government and its agencies, with annexes.
Signed at Washington February 7, 1979.
Entered into force April 4, 1979.
30 UST 3601; TIAS 9416; 1171 UNTS 135

Agreement regarding the consolidation and rescheduling of payments due under PL 480 Title I agricultural commodities agreements, with annexes.
Signed at Washington August 1, 1979.
Entered into force August 1, 1979.
30 UST 6279; TIAS 9553; 1179 UNTS 49

Agreement regarding the consolidation and rescheduling of certain debts owed to, guaranteed or insured by the United States Government and its agencies, with annexes.
Signed at Kinshasa July 28, 1980.
Entered into force October 20, 1980.
32 UST 3631; TIAS 9907

Agreement regarding the consolidation and rescheduling of payments due under PL 480 Title I agricultural commodity agreements, with annexes.
Signed at Kinshasa March 10, 1981.
Entered into force March 10, 1981.
33 UST 1249; TIAS 10108; 1285 UNTS 3

Implementation agreement regarding the consolidation and rescheduling of repayments due under Agency for International Development loans.
Signed at Kinshasa April 8, 1981.
Entered into force April 8, 1981.
33 UST 1725; TIAS 10141

Agreement regarding the consolidation and rescheduling of certain debts owed to, guaranteed or insured by the United States Government and its agencies, with annexes.
Signed at Kinshasa July 23, 1982.
Entered into force August 30, 1982.
NP

Agreement regarding the consolidation and rescheduling of certain debts owed to, guaranteed or insured by the United States Government and its agencies, with annexes.
Signed at Kinshasa May 3, 1984.
Entered into force June 11, 1984.
NP

Agreement regarding the consolidation and rescheduling of certain debts owed to, guaranteed by or insured by the United States Government and its agencies, with annexes.
Signed at Kinshasa December 3, 1985.
Entered into force January 9, 1986.
NP

Agreement regarding the consolidation and rescheduling of certain debts owed to, guaranteed by or insured by the United States Government and its agencies, with annexes.
Signed at Kinshasa April 9, 1987.
Entered into force May 18, 1987.
NP

Agreement regarding the consolidation and rescheduling of certain debts owed to, guaranteed by or insured by the United States Government and its agencies, with annexes.
Signed at Kinshasa February 20, 1988.
Entered into force April 18, 1988.
NP

Agreement regarding the consolidation and rescheduling of certain debts owed to, guaranteed by, or insured by the United States Government and its agencies, with annexes.
Signed at Kinshasa December 23, 1989.
Entered into force February 5, 1990.
NP

Agreement regarding the reduction and consolidation of debts owed to, guaranteed by, or insured by the United States Government and its agencies, with annexes.
Signed at Kinshasa April 10, 2003.
Entered into force June 5, 2003.
NP

Agreement regarding the reduction and consolidation of debts owed to, guaranteed by, or insured by the United States Government and its agencies, with annexes.
Signed at Kinshasa September 14, 2005.
Entered into force October 20, 2005.
NP

Investment incentive agreement.
Signed at Kinshasa December 23, 2005.
Entered into force December 23, 2005.
TIAS 05-1223

Agreement regarding the reduction of debts owed to, guaranteed by, or insured by the United States Government and its agencies, with annexes.
Signed at Kinshasa April 26, 2011.
Entered into force June 10, 2011.
NP

FOREIGN ASSISTANCE

Economic cooperation agreement between the United States and Belgium.*
Signed at Brussels July 2, 1948.
Entered into force July 29, 1948.
62 Stat. 2173; TIAS 1781; 5 Bevans 678; 19 UNTS 127
Note:
* Only article III is applicable to Congo (Leopoldville).

Agreement for economic and technical cooperation.
Signed at Kinshasa September 11, 2008.
Entered into force September 11, 2008.
TIAS 08-911

INTERNATIONAL CRIMINAL COURT

Agreement regarding the surrender of persons to the International Criminal Court.
Signed at Washington March 19, 2003.
Entered into force July 22, 2003.
TIAS 03-722.2

POSTAL MATTERS

International express mail agreement, with detailed regulations.
Signed at Kinshasa and Washington June 29 and July 20, 1990.
Entered into force August 30, 1990.
TIAS 11736

TRADE & INVESTMENT

Treaty concerning the reciprocal encouragement and protection of investment, with protocol.
Signed at Washington August 3, 1984.
Entered into force July 28, 1989.
TIAS

TRANSPORTATION

Air transport agreement.
Signed at New York August 14, 1970.
Entered into force August 14, 1970.
21 UST 1932; TIAS 6935; 763 UNTS 71

COOK ISLANDS

BOUNDARIES & BOUNDARY WATERS

Treaty on friendship and delimitation of the maritime boundary between the United States and the Cook Islands.
Signed at Rarotonga June 11, 1980.
Entered into force September 8, 1983.
35 UST 2061; TIAS 10774; 1676 UNTS 223

CULTURAL EXCHANGES, PROPERTY & COOPERATION

Agreement relating to the establishment of a Peace Corps program in the Cook Islands.
Exchange of notes at Wellington and Rarotonga April 28, 1981.
Entered into force April 28, 1981.
33 UST 1080; TIAS 10093; 1285 UNTS 113

FINANCE

Investment incentive agreement.
Exchange of notes at Wellington and Rarotonga September 2 and October 10, 1983.
Entered into force April 16, 1984.
35 UST 3116; TIAS 10843; 1676 UNTS 235

MARITIME MATTERS

Agreement concerning cooperation to suppress illicit traffic in narcotic drugs and psychotropic substances by sea.
Signed at Rarotonga November 8, 2007.
Entered into force November 8, 2007.
TIAS 07-1108

Agreement concerning cooperation in joint maritime surveillance operations.
Signed at Apia July 25, 2008.
Entered into force July 25, 2008.
TIAS 08-725

COSTA RICA

AGRICULTURE

Agreement relating to cooperative rubber investigations in Costa Rica.
Exchange of notes at San Jose April 19 and June 16, 1941.
Entered into force June 16, 1941.
55 Stat. 1368; EAS 222; 6 Bevans 1056; 103 LNTS 173

Extensions and Amendments:
April 3, 1943 (57 Stat. 944; EAS 318; 6 Bevans 1074; 13 UNTS 463)
June 21 and July 1, 1943 (57 Stat. 1048; EAS 335)

Agreement confirming the cooperative agreement for the prevention of foot-and-mouth disease and rinderpest in Costa Rica.
Exchange of notes at San Jose April 5 and June 6, 1972.
Entered into force June 6, 1972.
23 UST 1122; TIAS 7372

CONSULAR AFFAIRS

Agreement for the waiver of passport visa fees for nonimmigrants.*
Exchange of notes at San Jose June 29, 1925.
Operative July 25, 1925.
6 Bevans 1046

Note:
* The status of this agreement is under review.

CULTURAL EXCHANGES, PROPERTY & COOPERATION

Agreement relating to the establishment of a Peace Corps program in Costa Rica.
Exchange of notes at San Jose November 21 and 23, 1962.
Entered into force August 11, 1964.
15 UST 2317; TIAS 5719; 541 UNTS 67

DEFENSE

Agreement relating to photomapping project.
Exchange of notes at San Jose August 6 and October 2, 1946.
Entered into force October 2, 1946.
NP

Amendment:
December 3 and 7, 1953 (NP)

Agreement relating to the free movement of the military aircraft of each country into and through the airspace of the other.
Exchange of notes at San Jose February 19 and 25, 1952.
Entered into force February 25, 1952.
3 UST 3882; TIAS 2518; 174 UNTS 233

Agreement relating to privileges and immunities for United States personnel providing assistance to the drought stricken provinces in northern Costa Rica.
Exchange of notes at San Jose March 30, 1983.
Entered into force March 30, 1983.
NP

Basic exchange and cooperative agreement for topographic mapping, nautical and aeronautical charting and information, geodesy and geophysics, digital data and related mapping, charting and geodesy materials, with glossary.
Signed at San Jose and Fairfax June 14 and July 2, 1996.
Entered into force July 2, 1996.
NP

Memorandum of understanding concerning communications equipment installed in Cerro Azul, Nandayure, Nicoya, province of Guanacaste.
Signed at San Jose August 27, 2008.
Entered into force August 27, 2008.
TIAS 08-827

Agreement regarding grants under the Foreign Assistance Act of 1961, as amended, or successor legislation, and the furnishing of defense articles, related training, and other defense services, including pursuant to the United States International Military Education and Training (IMET) Program, from the Government of the United States of America to the Government of Costa Rica
Effected by exchange of notes at San Jose March 4 and 18, 2016. Entered into force March 18, 2016.
NP

Memorandum of agreement regarding the assignment of liaison officers, with annexes.
Signed at Miami April 1, 2016.
Entered into force April 1, 2016.
NP

DIPLOMATIC & CONSULAR RELATIONS

Consular convention.*
Signed at San Jose January 12, 1948.
Entered into force March 19, 1950.
1 UST 247; TIAS 2045; 70 UNTS 27
Note:
* Applicable to all areas of land and water subject to the sovereignty or authority of either state.

EMPLOYMENT

Agreement relating to the employment of dependents of official government employees.
Exchange of notes at San Jose June 8, 1992.
Entered into force June 8, 1992.
TIAS 12455

ENVIRONMENT & CONSERVATION

Agreement for cooperation in the Global Learning and Observations to Benefit the Environment (GLOBE) Program, with appendices.
Signed at San Jose April 22, 1996.
Entered into force April 22, 1996.
TIAS 12743

FINANCE

Agreement relating to investment guaranties.
Signed at San Jose November 22, 1968.
Entered into force October 24, 1969.
20 UST 3001; TIAS 6776; 726 UNTS 157

Agreement regarding the consolidation and rescheduling of certain debts owed to, guaranteed or insured by the United States Government and its agencies, with annexes.
Signed at Washington May 18, 1984.
Entered into force June 22, 1984.
NP

Agreement regarding the consolidation and rescheduling of certain debts owed to, guaranteed by or insured by the United States Government and its agencies.
Signed at San Jose February 22, 1990.
Entered into force April 9, 1990.
NP

Swap agreement among the United States Treasury and the Central Bank of Costa Rica/Government of Costa Rica.
Signed at Washington and San Jose May 18, 1990.
Entered into force May 18, 1990.
TIAS

Agreement regarding the consolidation and rescheduling or refinancing of certain debts owed to, guaranteed by, or insured by the United States Government and its agencies, with annexes.
Signed at San Jose February 19, 1992.
Entered into force April 20, 1992.
NP

Agreement regarding the consolidation and rescheduling or refinancing of certain debts owed to, guaranteed by or insured by the United States Government and its agencies, with annexes.
Signed at San Jose November 22, 1993.
Entered into force August 10, 1994.
NP

Agreement regarding a debt-for-nature swap program under the U.S. Tropical Forest Conservation Act.
Signed at San Jose September 13, 2007.
Entered into force September 13, 2007.
TIAS 07-913
Amendment:
September 25 and 26, 2007 (TIAS 07-913)

Agreement regarding a debt-for-nature swap with respect to certain debt owed by the Central Bank of Costa Rica to the Government of the United States, with schedules.
Signed at San Jose September 13, 2007.
Entered into force September 13, 2007.
TIAS 07-913.1.
Amendment:
September 25 and 27, 2007 (TIAS 07-913.1).

Agreement regarding a debt-for-nature swap program under the U.S. Tropical Forest Conservation Act, with schedules.
Signed at San Jose September 24, 2010.
Entered into force September 24, 2010.
TIAS 10-924

Agreement regarding a debt-for-nature swap with respect to certain debt owed by the Central Bank of Costa Rica to the Government of the United States of America, with schedule.
Signed at San Jose September 24, 2010.
Entered into force September 24, 2010.
TIAS 10-924.1

FOREIGN ASSISTANCE

General agreement for economic, technical and related assistance.
Signed at San Jose December 22, 1961.
Entered into force September 7, 1962.
13 UST 1978; TIAS 5155; 460 UNTS 277

LAW ENFORCEMENT

Agreement relating to the provision of assistance to curb the production and traffic in illegal narcotics.
Exchange of notes at San Jose May 29 and June 2, 1975.
Entered into force June 2, 1975.
26 UST 3868; TIAS 8220; 1045 UNTS 17

Agreement relating to the provision of additional assistance to support cooperative efforts to curb illegal narcotics production and traffic.
Exchange of notes at San Jose June 21 and 24, 1976.
Entered into force June 24, 1976.
28 UST 2924; TIAS 8574; 1068 UNTS 189

Extradition treaty, with exchange of notes.
Signed at San Jose December 4, 1982.
Entered into force October 11, 1991.
TIAS

MARITIME MATTERS

Agreement concerning cooperation to suppress illicit traffic.
Signed at San Jose December 1, 1998.
Entered into force November 19, 1999.
TIAS 13005
Amendment:
July 2, 1999 (TIAS 13005)

POLLUTION

Agreement concerning the transboundary movement of hazardous wastes from Costa Rica to the United States.
Exchange of notes at San Jose September 30 and November 17, 1997.
Entered into force November 17, 1997.
TIAS 97-1117
Amendment:
July 12 and September 13, 2002 (TIAS 97-1117)

POSTAL MATTERS

International express mail agreement, with detailed regulations.
Signed at San Jose and Washington August 19 and September 14, 1989.
Entered into force September 15, 1989.
TIAS 11690

Postal money order agreement.
Signed at Mexico August 16, 1991.
Entered into force October 1, 1991.
TIAS 11799

PUBLICATIONS

Agreement relating to the exchange of official publications.
Exchange of notes at San Jose November 30 and December 2, 1950.
Entered into force December 2, 1950.
2 UST 405; TIAS 2180; 133 UNTS 61

SCIENTIFIC & TECHNICAL COOPERATION

Agreement relating to the operation and maintenance of a rawinsonde observation station at San Jose, with memorandum of arrangement.
Exchange of notes at San Jose April 29 and June 8, 1976.
Entered into force June 8, 1976; effective January 1, 1976.
28 UST 6075; TIAS 8669

TAXATION

Agreement for the exchange of information with respect to taxes, with exchange of notes.
Signed at San Jose March 15, 1989.
Entered into force February 12, 1991.
TIAS 12059

TELECOMMUNICATION

Agreement relating to radio communications between amateur stations on behalf of third parties.
Exchange of notes at Washington August 13 and October 19, 1956.
Entered into force October 19, 1956.
7 UST 2839; TIAS 3665; 278 UNTS 65

Agreement relating to the reciprocal granting of authorizations to permit licensed amateur radio operators of either country to operate their stations in the other country.
Exchange of notes at San Jose August 17 and 24, 1964.
Entered into force August 24, 1964.
15 UST 1787; TIAS 5649; 531 UNTS 107

Agreement concerning the establishment and operation of a Voice of America radio broadcast station in Costa Rica.
Exchange of notes at San Jose July 17 and August 7, 1984.
Entered into force August 7, 1984.
TIAS 11236; 2143 UNTS 437

TRADE & INVESTMENT

Treaty of friendship, commerce and navigation.
Signed at Washington July 10, 1851.
Entered into force May 26, 1852.
10 Stat. 916; TS 62; 6 Bevans 1013

Convention concerning commercial travelers and protocol.
Signed at San Jose March 31, 1924.
Entered into force June 24, 1924.
43 Stat. 1765; TS 688; 6 Bevans 1041

Agreement relating to the Dominican Republic-Central America-United States free trade agreement of August 5, 2004.
Exchange of letters at San Jose and Washington December 1, 2006.
Entered into force December 1, 2006.
TIAS

TRANSPORTATION

Air transport agreement, with annexes.
Signed at San Jose May 8, 1997.
Entered into force October 15, 1999.
TIAS 12854

Memorandum of agreement relating to technical assistance in developing and modernizing Costa Rica's civil aviation infrastructure.
Signed December 10, 1999 and January 14, 2000.
Entered into force January 14, 2000.
NP
Amendment:
November 9, 2006 and January 12, 2007 (NP)

COTE D'IVOIRE

CULTURAL EXCHANGES, PROPERTY & COOPERATION

Agreement relating to the establishment of a Peace Corps program in Ivory Coast.
Exchange of notes at Abidjan April 5 and 21, 1962.
Entered into force April 21, 1962.
15 UST 345; TIAS 5561; 526 UNTS 39

DEFENSE

Agreement concerning the provision of training related to defense articles under the United States International Military Education and Training (IMET) Program.
Exchange of notes at Abidjan March 21 and April 21, 1983.
Entered into force April 21, 1983.
TIAS 10700; 2005 UNTS 153

Agreement relating to United States military personnel and civilian employees of the United States Department of Defense who may be temporarily present in Cote d'Ivoire in connection with the African Crisis Response Initiative and other activities as may be agreed upon by the two governments, with amendment and correction effected by exchange of notes at Abidjan March 16 and April 30, 2015.
Exchange of notes at Abidjan July 20 and November 2, 1998.
Entered into force November 2, 1998.
TIAS 15-430

FINANCE

Agreement relating to investment guaranties.
Exchange of notes at Abidjan December 1, 1961.
Entered into force December 1, 1961.
13 UST 2711; TIAS 5242; 462 UNTS 221

Agreement regarding the consolidation and rescheduling of certain debts owed to, guaranteed by or insured by the United States Government and its agencies, with annexes.
Signed at Abidjan February 27, 1985.
Entered into force April 10, 1985.
NP

Agreement regarding the consolidation and rescheduling of certain debts owed to, guaranteed by or insured by the United States Government and its agencies, with annexes.
Signed at Abidjan January 31, 1986.
Entered into force March 10, 1986.
NP

Agreement regarding the consolidation and rescheduling of certain debts owed to, guaranteed by or insured by the United States Government and its agencies, with annexes.
Signed at Abidjan March 31, 1987.
Entered into force May 21, 1987.
NP

Agreement regarding the consolidation and rescheduling of certain debts owed to, guaranteed by or insured by the United States Government and its agencies, with annexes.
Signed at Abidjan July 14, 1988.
Entered into force August 26, 1988.
NP

Agreement regarding the consolidation and rescheduling of certain debts owed to, guaranteed by or insured by the United States Government and its agencies, with annexes.
Signed at Abidjan September 29, 1990.
Entered into force November 16, 1990.
NP

Agreement regarding the consolidation and rescheduling or refinancing of certain debts owed to, guaranteed by, or insured by the United States Government and its agencies, with annexes.
Signed at Abidjan May 29, 1992.
Entered into force July 20, 1992.
NP

Agreement regarding the consolidation and rescheduling or refinancing of certain debts owed to, guaranteed by or insured by the United States Government and its agencies, with annexes.
Signed at Abidjan August 26, 1994.
Entered into force October 7, 1994.
NP

Agreement regarding the consolidation, reduction and rescheduling of certain debts owed to, guaranteed by, or insured by the United States Government and its Agencies, with annexes.
Signed at Washington July 29, 1998.
Entered into force September 10, 1998.
NP

Agreement regarding the reduction, consolidation and rescheduling of certain debts owed to, guaranteed by, or insured by the United States Government and its agencies, with annexes.
Signed at Washington July 29, 2002.
Entered into force October 8, 2002.
NP

Agreement regarding the partial reduction and rescheduling of certain debts owed to, guaranteed by, or insured by the United States Government and its agencies, with annexes.
Signed at Abidjan September 24, 2009.
Entered into force November 17, 2009.
NP

Agreement regarding the partial reduction and rescheduling of certain debts owed to, guaranteed by, or insured by the United States Government and its agencies. With annexes.
Signed at Abidjan February 1, 2013.
Entered into force March 25, 2013.
NP

FOREIGN ASSISTANCE

Agreement providing for economic, technical and related assistance.
Exchange of notes at Abidjan May 17, 1961.
Entered into force May 17, 1961.
12 UST 652; TIAS 4765; 409 UNTS 241

INTERNATIONAL CRIMINAL COURT

Agreement regarding the surrender of persons to the International Criminal Court.
Signed at Abidjan June 30, 2003.
Entered into force October 16, 2003.
TIAS 03-1016

POSTAL MATTERS

International express mail agreement, with detailed regulations.
Signed at Abidjan and Washington May 5 and 27, 1987.
Entered into force June 15, 1987.
NP

TRANSPORTATION

Air transport agreement.
Signed at Abidjan August 16, 2016.
Entered into force August 16, 2016.
TIAS 16-816

COUNCIL OF EUROPE DEVELOPMENT BANK

FOREIGN ASSISTANCE

Adherence agreement with respect to the regional housing programme fund, with annexes.
Signed at Washington and Paris September 24 and 26, 2012.
Entered into force September 26, 2012.
TIAS 12-926

CROATIA

On June 25, 1991, Croatia became an independent state. For agreements prior to the independence of Croatia, see YUGOSLAVIA.

ATOMIC ENERGY

Arrangement for the exchange of technical information and cooperation in nuclear safety matters. With addenda and annex.
Signed at Vienna September 18, 2013.
Entered into force September 18, 2013.
TIAS 13-918.1

CULTURAL EXCHANGES, PROPERTY & COOPERATION

Agreement on the protection and preservation of certain cultural properties.
Signed at Washington February 9, 2005.
Entered into force January 8, 2007.
TIAS 07-108

DEFENSE

Basic exchange and cooperative agreement concerning geospatial information and services cooperation, with annex.
Signed at Washington and Zagreb May 31 and June 15, 2001.
Entered into force June 15, 2001.
NP

Memorandum of understanding concerning the use of airspace, ranges, airports, seaports, and training facilities by the United States forces in Europe.
Signed at Ramstein AB July 15, 2004.
Entered into force January 11, 2006.
TIAS 06-111

Agreement regarding grants under the Foreign Assistance Act of 1961, as amended, or successor legislation, and the furnishing of defense articles, defense services and related training.
Exchange of notes at Zagreb July 24 and August 2, 2007.
Entered into force August 2, 2007.
NP

Agreement on the status of United States forces in the Republic of Croatia.
Signed at Washington April 3, 2008.
Entered into force August 20, 2008.
TIAS 08-820

Agreement on acquisition and cross-servicing. With annexes.
Signed at Zagreb and Stuttgart July 31 and August 1, 2012.
Entered into force January 30, 2013.
NP

EDUCATION

Agreement on the status of the American International School of Zagreb.
Signed at Zagreb June 27, 2001.
Entered into force November 14, 2002.
TIAS 13156

EMPLOYMENT

Agreement relating to the employment of dependents of official government employees.
Exchange of notes at Washington May 24 and June 20, 1995.
Entered into force June 20, 1995.
TIAS 12669

ENVIRONMENT & CONSERVATION

Agreement for cooperation in the Global Learning and Observations to Benefit the Environment (GLOBE) Program, with appendices.
Signed at Zagreb April 12, 1995.
Entered into force April 12, 1995.
TIAS 12628

FINANCE

Investment incentive agreement.
Signed at Washington January 15, 1993.
Entered into force January 15, 1993.
TIAS 12141

Agreement regarding the consolidation and rescheduling of certain debts owed to, guaranteed by or insured by the United States Government and its agencies, with annexes.
Signed at Zagreb February 1, 1996.
Entered into force July 23, 1996.
NP

FOREIGN ASSISTANCE

Agreement concerning economic, technical and related assistance.
Signed at Zagreb May 6, 1994.
Entered into force May 1, 1995.
TIAS

LAW ENFORCEMENT

Agreement on enhancing cooperation in preventing and combating serious crime.
Signed at Washington February 16, 2011.
Entered into force August 19, 2011, with the exception of Articles 8 through 10.
TIAS 11-819

NONPROLIFERATION

Agreement concerning cooperation to suppress the proliferation of weapons of mass destruction, their delivery systems, and related materials by sea.
Signed at Washington June 1, 2005.
Entered into force March 6, 2007.
TIAS

POSTAL MATTERS

International express mail agreement.
Signed at Zagreb and Washington September 14 and 30, 1992.
Entered into force December 14, 1992.
TIAS 11908

TAXATION

Agreement to improve international tax compliance and to implement the Foreign Account Tax Compliance Act, with annexes and related exchange of notes.
Signed at Zagreb March 20, 2015.
Entered into force December 27, 2016.
TIAS

TRADE & INVESTMENT

Treaty concerning the encouragement and reciprocal protection of investment, with annex and protocol.
Done at Zagreb July 13, 1996.
Entered into force June 20, 2001.
TIAS 01-620

TRANSPORTATION

Air transport agreement, with annexes.
Signed at Washington February 3, 2011.
Entered into force September 7, 2011.
TIAS 11-907

CUBA

BOUNDARIES & BOUNDARY WATERS

Maritime boundary agreement.
Signed at Washington December 16, 1977.
Entered into force provisionally January 1, 1978.
TIAS

Agreement extending provisional application of the maritime boundary agreement of December 16, 1977.
Effected by Exchange of Notes at Havana and Washington November 24 and December 31, 2015.
Entered into force December 31, 2015.
TIAS 15-1231

DEFENSE

Agreement for the lease to the United States of lands in Cuba for coaling and naval stations.
Signed at Habana February 16, 1903, and at Washington February 23, 1903.
Entered into force February 23, 1903.
TS 418; 6 Bevans 1113

Agreement providing conditions for the lease of coaling or naval stations.
Signed at Habana July 2, 1903.
Entered into force October 6, 1903.
TS 426; 6 Bevans 1120

Agreement providing for the informal visits of warships.
Exchange of notes at Habana February 11 and 21, 1949.
Entered into force March 4, 1949.
5 UST 762; TIAS 2965; 231 UNTS 108
Extension and Amendments:
February 13 and 28 and March 3, 1950 (5 UST 762; TIAS 2965; 231 UNTS 113)
February 21 and 26, 1951 (5 UST 762; TIAS 2965; 231 UNTS 118)
February 8 and 21, 1952 (5 UST 773; TIAS 2965)
February 18 and 25, 1953 (5 UST 776; TIAS 2965)
November 23, 1953, and January 20, 1954 (5 UST 778; TIAS 2965; 231 UNTS 127)

Agreement providing for the services of a United States Air Force mission to Cuba.
Signed at Washington December 22, 1950.
Entered into force December 22, 1950.
1 UST 887; TIAS 2166; 122 UNTS 97
Extension:
May 3 and 17, 1955 (6 UST 2266; TIAS 3295; 264 UNTS 351)

Agreement providing for the services of a United States Army mission to Cuba.
Signed at Washington August 28, 1951.
Entered into force August 28, 1951.
2 UST 1677; TIAS 2309; 134 UNTS 225
Extension:
May 3 and 17, 1955 (6 UST 2263; TIAS 3294; 264 UNTS 355)

Agreement providing for the services of a United States Naval mission to Cuba.
Signed at Washington August 28, 1951.
Entered into force August 28, 1951.
2 UST 1689; TIAS 2310; 140 UNTS 239
Extension:
May 3 and 17, 1955 (6 UST 784; TIAS 3222; 253 UNTS 360)

Agreement relating to the control of electro-magnetic radiations in the event of attack.
Exchange of notes at Habana December 10 and 18, 1951.
Entered into force December 18, 1951.
3 UST 2860; TIAS 2459; 165 UNTS 3

Military assistance agreement.
Signed at Habana March 7, 1952.
Entered into force March 7, 1952.
3 UST 2901; TIAS 2467; 165 UNTS 11

Agreement providing for disposition of equipment and materials furnished by the United States under the agreement of March 7, 1952.
Exchange of notes at Habana March 18 and May 3, 1955.
Entered into force May 3, 1955.
6 UST 2059; TIAS 3272; 258 UNTS 408

Agreement providing for performance by members of Army, Navy, and Air Force missions of duties of military assistance advisory group specified in article V of the military assistance agreement of March 7, 1952.
Exchange of notes at Habana June 24 and August 3, 1955.
Entered into force August 10, 1955.
6 UST 2955; TIAS 3343; 265 UNTS 41

Agreement concerning financial arrangements for the furnishing of certain supplies and services to naval vessels of both countries.
Signed at Habana January 10, 1956.
Entered into force April 9, 1956.
7 UST 63; TIAS 3479; 240 UNTS 101

DIPLOMATIC & CONSULAR RELATIONS

Consular convention.
Signed at Habana April 22, 1926.
Entered into force December 1, 1926.
44 Stat. 2471; TS 75; 6 Bevans 1149; 60 LNTS 371

Agreement relating to free-entry privileges for noncommissioned personnel.
Exchange of notes at Habana March 23 and May 16, 1932.
Entered into force May 16, 1932.
5 UST 1638; TIAS 3040; 234 UNTS 283

Treaty of relations.
Signed at Washington May 29, 1934.
Entered into force June 9, 1934.
48 Stat. 1682; TS 866; 6 Bevans 1161

Agreement concerning the termination of the agreement of May 30, 1977, relating to the establishment of interests sections of the United States and Cuba.
Exchange of notes at Havana July 20, 2015.
Entered into force July 20, 2015.
TIAS 15-720

FINANCE

Agreement relating to investment guaranties under section 413 (b)(4) of the Mutual Security Act of 1954, as amended.
Exchange of notes at Habana February 4, 1957.
Entered into force November 29, 1957.
8 UST 2375; TIAS 3953; 302 UNTS 273

LAW ENFORCEMENT

Treaty providing for the mutual extradition of fugitives from justice.
Signed at Washington April 6, 1904.
*Entered into force March 2, 1905.**
33 Stat. 2265; TS 440; 6 Bevans 1128

Note:
* For amendment to the Spanish text, see 33 Stat. 2273; TS 441; 6 Bevans 1134.

Additional extradition treaty.
Signed at Habana January 14, 1926.
Entered into force June 18, 1926.
44 Stat. 2392; TS 737; 6 Bevans 1136; 61 LNTS 363

Convention between the United States of America and the Republic of Cuba for the suppression of smuggling operations between their respective territories.
Signed at Habana March 11, 1926.
Entered into force June 28, 1926.
44 Stat. 2402; TS 739; 6 Bevans 1144; 61 LNTS 383

Arrangement for the direct exchange of certain information regarding the traffic in narcotic drugs.
Exchange of notes at Habana February 12 and March 7, 1930.
Entered into force March 7, 1930.
6 Bevans 1157

MARITIME MATTERS

Arrangement relating to the reciprocal exemption of the pleasure yachts of the two countries from navigation dues and from usual requirements of entry and clearance.
Exchange of notes at Washington December 12 and 17, 1951.
Entered into force December 17, 1951.
3 UST 52; TIAS 2391; 152 UNTS 87

MIGRATION & REFUGEES

Memorandum of understanding between the Embassy of Switzerland in Habana representing the interests of the United States in Cuba and the Foreign Ministry of the Government of Cuba concerning the movement to the United States of Cubans wishing to live in the United States, with related notes.
Exchange of notes at Habana November 6, 1965.
Entered into force November 6, 1965.
17 UST 1045; TIAS 6063; 601 UNTS 81

Joint communique on immigration matters, with minute on implementation.
Signed at New York December 14, 1984.
Entered into force December 14, 1984.
TIAS 11057; 2034 UNTS 193

Joint communique concerning normalizing migration procedures.
Signed at New York September 9, 1994.
Entered into force September 9, 1994.
TIAS

Joint statement further normalizing migration procedures.
Signed at Washington May 2, 1995.
Entered into force May 2, 1995.
TIAS

POSTAL MATTERS

Parcel post convention.
Signed at Washington July 24, 1930.
Entered into force September 1, 1930.
46 Stat. 2844; Post Office Department print

PUBLICATIONS

Agreement for the exchange of official publications.
Exchange of notes at Habana May 4 and 12, 1938.
Entered into force May 12, 1938.
52 Stat. 1497; EAS 123; 6 Bevans 1173; 191 LNTS 19

TELECOMMUNICATION

Agreement relating to the exchange of third-party messages between radio amateurs.
Exchange of notes at Habana September 17, 1951, and February 27, 1952.
Entered into force February 27, 1952.
3 UST 3892; TIAS 2520; 168 UNTS 3

TERRITORIAL ISSUES

Treaty for the adjustment of title to the ownership of the Isle of Pines.
Signed at Washington March 2, 1904.
Entered into force March 23, 1925.
44 Stat. 1997; TS 709; 6 Bevans 1124; 127 LNTS 143

TRANSPORTATION

Agreement to facilitate notification of private flights between Cuba and the United States.
Exchange of notes at Habana January 19 and February 26, 1953.
Entered into force February 26, 1953.
4 UST 210; TIAS 2779; 205 UNTS 213

Air transport agreement, with annex.
Signed at Habana May 26, 1953.
Entered into force June 30, 1953.
4 UST 2837; TIAS 2892; 224 UNTS 75

Amendment:
May 21 and July 30, 1957 (8 UST 1407; TIAS 3891; 289 UNTS 322)

CYPRUS

A treaty concerning the establishment of the Republic of Cyprus was signed August 16, 1960, by the Governments of the United Kingdom, Greece, Turkey and Cyprus (British Treaty Series No. 4 (1691)). Article 8 of the treaty provides that the Republic of Cyprus assumes, from August 16, 1960, all international obligations and responsibilities of the United Kingdom in so far as they may be held to have application to the Republic of Cyprus. Also, the international rights and benefits enjoyed by the Government of the United Kingdom by virtue of their application to the territory of the Republic of Cyprus are from August 16, 1960, enjoyed by the Government of the Republic of Cyprus.

CONSULAR AFFAIRS

Agreement relating to the reciprocal waiver of fingerprinting requirements for nonimmigrants.
Exchange of notes at Nicosia July 11, 1962, and January 11, 1963.
Entered into force January 11, 1963.
14 UST 6; TIAS 5271; 471 UNTS 127

CULTURAL EXCHANGES, PROPERTY & COOPERATION

Agreement relating to the establishment of a Peace Corps program in Cyprus.
Exchange of notes at Nicosia August 23, 1962.
Entered into force August 23, 1962.
13 UST 2089; TIAS 5166; 461 UNTS 147

Memorandum of understanding concerning the imposition of import restrictions on Pre-Classical and Classical archaeological objects and Byzantine and Post-Byzantine period ecclesiastical and ritual ethnological materials.
Signed at Washington July 16, 2002.
Entered into force July 16, 2002.
TIAS 02-716.1

Extension and Amendments:
August 17, 2006 (TIAS 02-716.1)
July 3 and 6, 2007 (TIAS 02-716.1)
July 10, 2012 (TIAS 12-710)

DEFENSE

Agreement between the United States and the United Kingdom relating to the assurances required under the Mutual Security Act of 1951.
Exchange of notes at London January 8, 1952.
Applicable to Cyprus January 8, 1952.
3 UST 4665; TIAS 2622; 126 UNTS 307

Agreement regarding the status of United States personnel who may be present in Cyprus.
Exchange of notes at Nicosia October 21 and December 5, 2002.
Entered into force December 5, 2002.
TIAS

DIPLOMATIC & CONSULAR RELATIONS

Consular convention between the United States and the United Kingdom.
Signed at Washington June 6, 1951.
Entered into force September 7, 1952.
3 UST 3426; TIAS 2494; 165 UNTS 121

EMPLOYMENT

Agreement relating to the employment of dependents of official government employees.
Exchange of notes at Nicosia July 2 and August 2, 2007.
Entered into force August 2, 2007.
TIAS 07-802

ENVIRONMENT & CONSERVATION

Agreement for cooperation in the Global Learning and Observations to Benefit the Environment (GLOBE) Program, with appendices.
Signed at Nicosia November 24, 1998.
Entered into force November 24, 1998.
TIAS 13000

FINANCE

Agreement relating to investment guaranties.
Exchange of notes at Nicosia May 29, 1963.
Entered into force May 29, 1963.
14 UST 843; TIAS 5364; 487 UNTS 283

FOREIGN ASSISTANCE

Economic cooperation agreement between the United States and the United Kingdom.
Signed at London July 6, 1948.
Applicable to Cyprus July 6, 1948.
62 Stat. 2596; TIAS 1795; 12 Bevans 874; 22 UNTS 263

Amendments:
January 3, 1950 (1 UST 184; TIAS 2036; 86 UNTS 304)
May 25, 1951 (2 UST 1292; TIAS 2277; 99 UNTS 308)
February 25, 1953 (4 UST 1528; TIAS 2815; 172 UNTS 332)

General agreement for technical cooperation.
Signed at Nicosia June 29, 1961.
Entered into force June 29, 1961.
12 UST 890; TIAS 4792; 411 UNTS 55

INTELLECTUAL PROPERTY

Declaration by the United States and the United Kingdom relating to reciprocal protection to trade-marks.
Signed at London October 24, 1877.
Entered into force October 24, 1877.
20 Stat. 703; TS 138; 12 Bevans 198

LAW ENFORCEMENT

Agreement regarding mutual assistance between customs services.
Signed at Washington June 2, 1987.
Entered into force August 21, 1987.
TIAS 12113

Extradition treaty.
Signed at Washington June 17, 1996.
Entered into force September 14, 1999.
TIAS 99-914

Treaty on mutual legal assistance in criminal matters.
Signed at Nicosia December 20, 1999.
Entered into force September 18, 2002.
TIAS 13078

Instrument as contemplated by Article 3(2) of the agreement on extradition between the United States of America and the European Union signed June 25, 2003, as to the application of the extradition treaty of June 17, 1996, with annex.
Signed at Nicosia January 20, 2006.
Entered into force February 1, 2010.
TIAS 10-201.4

Instrument as contemplated by Article 3(2) of the agreement on mutual legal assistance between the United States of America and the European Union signed June 25, 2003, as to the application of the treaty of December 20, 1999, with annex.
Signed at Nicosia January 20, 2006.
Entered into force February 1, 2010.
TIAS 10-201.27

MARITIME MATTERS

Agreement relating to jurisdiction over vessels utilizing the Louisiana Offshore Oil Port.
Exchange of notes at Nicosia August 3 and September 7, 1983.
Entered into force September 7, 1983.
35 UST 2170; TIAS 10782; 2011 UNTS 121

NONPROLIFERATION

Agreement concerning cooperation to suppress the proliferation of weapons of mass destruction, their delivery systems, and related materials by sea, with appendix.
Signed at Washington July 25, 2005.
Entered into force January 12, 2006.
TIAS 06-112

POSTAL MATTERS

Parcel post agreement with detailed regulations for execution.
Signed at Nicosia May 7 and at Washington June 8, 1973.
Entered into force September 1, 1974.
25 UST 3015; TIAS 7962

International express mail/datapost special express memorandum of understanding, with detailed regulations.
Signed at Nicosia and Washington September 13 and October 18, 1985.
Entered into force November 1, 1985.
TIAS 11159; 2126 UNTS 281

Memorandum of understanding concerning the operation of the INTELPOST service, with details of implementation.
Signed at Nicosia and Washington March 12 and April 3, 1987.
Entered into force May 6, 1987.
TIAS 11298

PROPERTY

Convention between the United States and the United Kingdom relating to the tenure and disposition of real and personal property.
Signed at Washington March 2, 1899.
Applicable to Cyprus February 9, 1901.
31 Stat. 1939; TS 146; 12 Bevans 246

SCIENTIFIC & TECHNICAL COOPERATION

Agreement on science and technology cooperation, with annexes.
Signed at Nicosia February 5, 2009.
Entered into force October 29, 2009.
TIAS 09-1029

TAXATION

Convention for the avoidance of double taxation and the prevention of fiscal evasion with respect to taxes on income, with related notes.
Signed at Nicosia March 19, 1984.
Entered into force December 31, 1985.
35 UST 4737; TIAS 10965; 2019 UNTS 79

Agreement concerning reciprocal exemption from income tax of income derived from the international operation of ships and aircraft.
Exchange of notes at Nicosia June 21 and July 8, 1988.
Entered into force July 8, 1988.
TIAS 11595; 2192 UNTS 167

TELECOMMUNICATION

Agreement relating to the reciprocal granting of authorizations to permit licensed amateur radio operators of either country to operate their stations in the other country.
Exchange of notes at Nicosia March 4 and 10, 1987.
Entered into force March 10, 1987.
TIAS 11521

TRANSPORTATION

Arrangement between the United States and the United Kingdom relating to pilot licenses to operate civil aircraft.
Exchange of notes at Washington March 28 and April 5, 1935.
Entered into force May 5, 1935.
49 Stat. 3731; EAS 77; 12 Bevans 501; 162 LNTS 59

Agreement between the United States and the United Kingdom relating to air services.
Signed at Bermuda February 11, 1946.
Entered into force February 11, 1946.
60 Stat. 1499; TIAS 1507; 12 Bevans 726; 3 UNTS 253

CZECH REPUBLIC

For agreements prior to the independence of the Czech Republic on January 1, 1993, see CZECHOSLOVAKIA.

ATOMIC ENERGY

Agreement regarding the transfer of fresh and spent nuclear fuel in the Nuclear Research Institute at Rez to the Russian Federation for management and storage.
Exchange of notes at Prague April 26 and May 3, 2007
Entered into force May 3, 2007.
TIAS 07-503

Agreement for cooperation in civilian nuclear energy research and development.
Signed at Prague March 26, 2014.
Entered into force March 26, 2014.
TIAS 14-326

Arrangement for the exchange of technical information and cooperation in nuclear safety matters, with addenda and annex.
Signed at Vienna September 24, 2014.
Entered into force September 24, 2014.
TIAS 14-924.1

DEFENSE

Security agreement concerning security measures for the protection of classified military information.
Signed at Prague September 19, 1995.
Entered into force September 19, 1995.
TIAS 12245

Amendment:
March 8 and August 30, 2007 (TIAS 07-831)

Acquisition and cross-servicing agreement, with annex and implementing arrangement.
Signed at Prague November 19, 1996.
Entered into force November 19, 1996.
TIAS 12815

Agreement concerning exchange and cooperation in the field of geospatial information and services.
Signed at Dobruska September 16, 2002.
Entered into force September 16, 2002.
NP

Agreement concerning the provision of assistance for counterterrorism, military and stability operations.
Signed at Prague August 8, 2007.
Entered into force August 8, 2007.
TIAS 07-808.2

Agreement concerning exchange of research and development information, with appendix.
Signed at Prague February 22, 2008.
Entered into force February 22, 2008.
TIAS 08-222

Agreement concerning the exchange of engineers and scientists, with annexes.
Signed at Prague November 6, 2009.
Entered into force November 6, 2009.
NP

Memorandum of agreement regarding assignment of liaison officers.
Signed at Norfolk March 22, 2010.
Entered into force March 22, 2010.
NP

Amendments and Extensions:
March 20, 2015
December 21, 2015

Agreement for research, development, testing, and evaluation activities, with annexes.
Signed at Brussels June 10, 2010.
Entered into force June 10, 2010.
TIAS 10-610

EMPLOYMENT

Agreement relating to the employment of dependents of official government employees.
Exchange of notes at Prague February 18 and October 1, 1993.
Entered into force October 1, 1993.
TIAS

ENVIRONMENT & CONSERVATION

Agreement for cooperation in the Global Learning and Observations to Benefit the Environment (GLOBE) Program, with appendices.
Signed at Prague April 20, 1995.
Entered into force April 20, 1995.
TIAS 12632

LAW ENFORCEMENT

Treaty on mutual legal assistance in criminal matters.
Signed at Washington February 4, 1998.
Entered into force May 7, 2000.
TIAS 12928

Second supplementary treaty on extradition.
Signed at Prague May 16, 2006.
Entered into force February 1, 2010.
TIAS 10-201.5

Supplementary treaty on mutual legal assistance in criminal matters.
Signed at Prague May 16, 2006.
Entered into force February 1, 2010.
TIAS 10-201.28

Agreement on enhancing cooperation in preventing and combating serious crime.
Signed at Prague November 12, 2008.
Entered into force May 1, 2010.
TIAS 10-501

NONPROLIFERATION

Agreement concerning cooperation in the area of countering the proliferation of nuclear materials and technologies.
Signed at Prague September 17, 2007.
Entered into force September 17, 2007.
TIAS 07-917

POSTAL MATTERS

International express mail agreement, with detailed regulations.
Signed at Prague and Washington June 29 and September 1, 1993.
Entered into force September 1, 1993.
NP

SCIENTIFIC & TECHNICAL COOPERATION

Memorandum of understanding on science and engineering cooperation, with annexes.
Signed at Prague July 13, 1994.
Entered into force July 13, 1994.
TIAS 12556

Agreement for scientific and technological cooperation, with annexes.
Signed at Prague September 6, 2007.
Entered into force May 2, 2008.
TIAS

SOCIAL SECURITY

Agreement on social security, with administrative arrangement.
Signed at Prague September 7, 2007.
Entered into force January 1, 2009.
TIAS 09-101.2

Amendment:
September 23, 2013 (TIAS 16-501)

TAXATION

Convention for the avoidance of double taxation and the prevention of fiscal evasion with respect to taxes on income and capital.
Signed at Prague September 16, 1993.
Entered into force December 23, 1993.
TIAS

Agreement to improve international tax compliance and with respect to the United States information and reporting provisions commonly known as the Foreign Account Tax Compliance Act, with annexes.
Signed at Prague August 4, 2014.
Entered into force December 18, 2014.
TIAS 14-1218.1

TRADE & INVESTMENT

Additional protocol to the treaty between the United States of America and the Czech and Slovak Federal Republic concerning the reciprocal encouragement and protection of investment of October 22, 1991.
Signed at Brussels December 10, 2003.
Entered into force August 10, 2004.
TIAS

TRANSPORTATION

Air transport agreement, with annexes.*
Signed at Prague September 10, 1996.
Entered into force September 10, 1996.
TIAS 12799

Amendment:
June 4, 2001, and February 14, 2002 (TIAS 02-214)

Note:
* This agreement is suspended for the duration of provisional application of the U.S. – E.U. Air Transport Agreement signed April 25 and 30, 2007.

WEAPONS

Agreement concerning ballistic missile defense cooperation.
Signed at Prague October 31, 2008.
Entered into force November 29, 2009.
TIAS 09-1129

CZECHOSLOVAKIA

On December 31, 1992, at midnight, Czechoslovakia ceased to exist and was succeeded by two separate and independent states, the Czech Republic and the Slovak Republic.

CLAIMS & DISPUTE RESOLUTION

Treaty of arbitration.
Signed at Washington August 16, 1928.
Entered into force April 11, 1929.
46 Stat. 2254; TS 781; 6 Bevans 1268; 89 LNTS 225

Treaty of conciliation.
Signed at Washington August 16, 1928.
Entered into force April 11, 1929.
46 Stat. 2257; TS 782; 6 Bevans 1271; 89 LNTS 219

Agreement regarding settlement for certain war accounts and claims incident to the operations of the United States Army in Europe, and accompanying notes.
Signed at Praha July 25, 1947.
Entered into force July 25, 1947.
61 Stat. 3410; TIAS 1675; 6 Bevans 1320; 90 UNTS 19

Agreement on the settlement of certain outstanding claims and financial issues, with annexes and related exchange of letters.
Signed at Prague January 29, 1982.
Entered into force February 2, 1982.
TIAS 11264
Amendments:
February 2, 1982 (TIAS 11264; 2177 UNTS 417)
February 12, 1982 (TIAS 11264; 2177 UNTS 433)

CONSULAR AFFAIRS

Agreement relating to multiple entry visas for diplomatic personnel.
Exchange of notes at Prague December 18 and 21, 1962.
Entered into force December 21, 1962.
13 UST 3842; TIAS 5258; 469 UNTS 115

Agreement relating to issuance of nonimmigrant visas on a facilitated basis to certain holders of diplomatic or official passports.
Exchange of notes at Prague June 20, 1978.
Entered into force June 20, 1978; effective July 1, 1978.
30 UST 1593; TIAS 9266; 1150 UNTS 107

CULTURAL EXCHANGES, PROPERTY & COOPERATION

Agreement on cooperation in culture, education, science, technology and other fields, with annex.
Signed at Prague April 15, 1986.
Entered into force April 15, 1986.
TIAS

Agreement on the program of the United States Peace Corps in Czechoslovakia.
Signed at Prague June 25, 1990.
Entered into force June 25, 1990.
TIAS 12076

Agreement for the protection and preservation of cultural properties, with annex.
Signed at Washington March 17, 1992.
Entered into force March 17, 1992.
TIAS 11399; 2190 UNTS 209

DEFENSE

Basic exchange and cooperative agreement for topographic mapping, nautical and aeronautical charting, geodesy and geophysics, digital data and related MC & G materials.
Signed at Prague December 10, 1991.
Entered into force December 10, 1991.
NP
Note:
This agreement was superseded as pertains to the Czech Republic by the agreement of September 16, 2002.

DIPLOMATIC & CONSULAR RELATIONS

Consular convention, with agreed memorandum and related notes.
Signed at Prague July 9, 1973.
Entered into force November 6, 1987.
TIAS 11083

FINANCE

Agreement relating to the funding of the indebtedness of Czechoslovakia to the United States.
Signed at Washington October 13, 1925.
Operative June 15, 1925.
Treasury Department print; 6 Bevans 1253

Agreement modifying the debt funding agreement of October 13, 1925.
Signed at Washington June 10, 1932.
Operative July 1, 1931.
Treasury Department print; 6 Bevans 1277

Investment incentive agreement.
Signed at Prague October 18, 1990.
Entered into force October 18, 1990.
TIAS

LAW ENFORCEMENT

Treaty concerning the mutual extradition of fugitive criminals.
Signed at Prague July 2, 1925.
Entered into force March 29, 1926.
44 Stat. 2367; TS 734; 6 Bevans 1247; 50 LNTS 143

Arrangement for the direct exchange of certain information regarding the traffic in narcotic drugs.
Exchange of notes at Prague February 9 and June 15, 1928.
Entered into force June 15, 1928.
6 Bevans 1263

Supplementary extradition treaty.
Signed at Washington April 29, 1935.
Entered into force August 28, 1935.
49 Stat. 3253; TS 895; 6 Bevans 1283; 162 LNTS 83

Agreement regarding mutual assistance between customs services.
Signed at Prague May 7, 1991.
Entered into force February 21, 1997.
TIAS

POSTAL MATTERS

Agreement concerning exchange of parcel post, and regulations of execution.
Signed at Washington September 15, and at Praha September 29, 1950.
Entered into force October 1, 1950.
8 UST 997; TIAS 3865; 290 UNTS 3

International express mail agreement, with detailed regulations.
Signed at Prague and Washington July 25 and August 17, 1988.
Entered into force September 30, 1988.
TIAS 11645

PROPERTY

Preliminary agreement regarding principles applying to mutual aid in the prosecution of the war against aggression.
Signed at Washington July 11, 1942.
Entered into force July 11, 1942.
56 Stat. 1562; EAS 261; 6 Bevans 1300; 90 UNTS 257

Agreement on settlement for lend-lease and certain claims.
Signed at Praha September 16, 1948.
Entered into force September 16, 1948.
62 Stat. 2850; TIAS 1818; 6 Bevans 1326; 90 UNTS 35

TRADE & INVESTMENT

Agreement relating to commercial policy.
Exchange of notes at Washington November 14, 1946.
Entered into force November 14, 1946.
61 Stat. 2431; TIAS 1569; 6 Bevans 1314; 7 UNTS 119

Agreement relating to the establishment of a New York branch of the commercial section of the Czechoslovak Embassy.
Exchange of notes at Washington August 8 and 28, 1967.
Entered into force August 28, 1967.
20 UST 2979; TIAS 6771; 726 UNTS 139

Agreement providing for consultations should textile or apparel exports from Czechoslovakia cause market disruptions in the United States.
Exchange of notes at Prague March 22 and 28, 1977.
Entered into force March 28, 1977.
28 UST 5463; TIAS 8645; 1087 UNTS 283

Treaty concerning the reciprocal encouragement and protection of investment, with annex, protocol and exchanges of letters.
Signed at Washington October 22, 1991.
Entered into force December 19, 1992.
TIAS

TRANSPORTATION

Agreement for the reciprocal acceptance of certificates of airworthiness for imported aircraft.
Exchange of notes at Prague October 1 and 21, 1970.
Entered into force October 21, 1970.
21 UST 2468; TIAS 6987; 776 UNTS 67

D

DENMARK

CLAIMS & DISPUTE RESOLUTION

Treaty for the advancement of peace.
Signed at Washington April 17, 1914.
Entered into force January 19, 1915.
38 Stat. 1883; TS 608; 7 Bevans 53

Arbitration treaty.
Signed at Washington June 14, 1928.
Entered into force April 17, 1929.
46 Stat. 2265; TS 784; 7 Bevans 80; 88 LNTS 173

CONSULAR AFFAIRS

Arrangement relating to the waiver of passport visa fees for nonimmigrants.*
Exchange of notes at Copenhagen July 2 and September 29, 1925.
Operative August 6, 1925.
7 Bevans 76

Agreement for the waiver of visa requirements for American citizens entering Denmark for a temporary period, and the granting of gratis visas valid for twenty-four months to Danish subjects coming to the United States for temporary visits.*
Exchanges of notes at Copenhagen June 9 and 21 and July 7 and 8, 1947.
Entered into force July 8, 1947.
62 Stat. 4068; TIAS 2110; 7 Bevans 128; 132 UNTS 145

Amendment:
April 30 and May 1, 1958

Note:
* The status of these agreements is under review.

DEFENSE

Mutual defense assistance agreement.
Signed at Washington January 27, 1950.
Entered into force January 27, 1950.
1 UST 19; TIAS 2011; 48 UNTS 115

Agreement concerning the defense of Greenland.
Signed at Copenhagen April 27, 1951.
Entered into force June 8, 1951.
2 UST 1485; TIAS 2292; 94 UNTS 35

Amendment:
August 6, 2004 (TIAS 04-806)

Related Agreements:
December 2, 1960 (11 UST 2642; TIAS 4657; 402 UNTS 245)
September 30, 1986 (TIAS 12284)

Agreement relating to the assurances required by the Mutual Security Act of 1951.
Exchange of notes at Copenhagen January 8, 1952.
Entered into force January 8, 1952.
3 UST 4554; TIAS 2605; 179 UNTS 65

Agreement relating to the disposition of equipment and material no longer required by Denmark in the furtherance of its mutual defense assistance program.
Exchange of notes at Copenhagen November 16, 1951, and April 28, 1952.
Entered into force April 28, 1952.
3 UST 5278; TIAS 2726; 180 UNTS 275

Amendment:
September 12, 1960 (11 UST 2116; TIAS 4570; 388 UNTS 356)

Agreement relating to the offshore procurement program in Denmark with model contract attached.
Exchange of notes at Copenhagen June 8, 1954.
Entered into force June 8, 1954.
9 UST 141; TIAS 3987; 307 UNTS 133

Agreement relating to the status of the personnel of the U.S. Military Assistance Advisory Group and of the personnel of the offshore procurement program.
Exchange of notes at Copenhagen December 12, 1956.
Entered into force December 12, 1956.
9 UST 271; TIAS 4002; 304 UNTS 311

Agreement relating to a weapons production program.*
Exchange of notes at Copenhagen April 12, 1960.
Entered into force April 12, 1960.
11 UST 1440; TIAS 4484

Note:
* For amendment of paragraph 4.a.(4) of the agreement, see exchange of letters of May 11 and 18, 1960 (11 UST 1447; TIAS 4484).

Memorandum of understanding concerning the principles governing mutual cooperation in the research, development, production, procurement and logistic support of defense equipment.
Signed at Copenhagen and Washington January 2 and 30, 1980.
Entered into force January 30, 1980.
33 UST 3128; TIAS 10216

Agreement on general security of military information.
Exchange of notes at Copenhagen January 23 and February 27, 1981.
Entered into force February 27, 1981.
33 UST 1264; TIAS 10109; 1264 UNTS 475

Mutual logistical support agreement, with annex.
Signed at Vedbaek and Stuttgart-Vaihingen June 1 and 14, 1982.
Entered into force June 14, 1982.
34 UST 1235; TIAS 10411

Memorandum of understanding concerning use of Sondrestrom Aviation Facility, Kulusuk Airfield and other matters related to U.S. military activities in Greenland.
Signed at Copenhagen March 13, 1991.
Entered into force March 13, 1991.
TIAS 12285; 1653 UNTS 389

Amendment:
July 16, 2008 and January 27, 2009

Agreement concerning the closure of the long-range radio aid to navigation transmitting station at Angissoq, Greenland, with annex.
Signed at Copenhagen December 12, 1994.
Entered into force December 12, 1994.
TIAS

Agreement for the transfer of ownership of long-range radio aid to navigation transmitting station at Ejde, Faroe Islands, Denmark, with annex.
Signed at Copenhagen December 12, 1994.
Entered into force December 12, 1994.
TIAS

Basic exchange and cooperative agreement concerning mapping, charting and geodesy cooperation, with glossary.
Signed at Fairfax and Vedbaek December 20, 1995, and February 7, 1996.
Entered into force February 7, 1996.
NP

Acquisition and cross-servicing agreement, with annexes.
Signed at Vedbaek and Patch Barracks January 5 and 8, 1998.
Entered into force January 8, 1998.
TIAS 12915

Memorandum of understanding concerning the Dundas area, with related exchange of notes.
Signed at Nuuk February 20, 2003.
Entered into force February 20, 2003.
TIAS 03-220

Agreement concerning ballistic missile defense technology.
Signed at Washington October 25, 2005.
Entered into force October 25, 2005.
TIAS

Memorandum of understanding regarding the assignment of a foreign liaison officer to the headquarters, United States Strategic Command, with annex.
Signed at Omaha and Vedbaek May 21 and June 2, 2006.
Entered into force June 2, 2006.
NP

Memorandum of agreement regarding the military reserve exchange program.
Signed at Copenhagen December 11, 2012.
Entered into force December 11, 2012.
NP

Memorandum of agreement regarding the assignment of liaison officers to U.S. European Command, with annexes.
Signed at Stuttgart June 2, 2016.
Entered into force June 2, 2016.
NP

EDUCATION

Agreement for financing certain educational exchange programs.
Exchange of notes at Copenhagen May 28, 1962.
Entered into force May 28, 1962.
13 UST 1154; TIAS 5060; 450 UNTS 215

Amendments:
February 18 and 25, 1965 (16 UST 154; TIAS 5775; 542 UNTS 386)
November 2, 1971, and April 27, 1972 (23 UST 2683; TIAS 7462)

EMPLOYMENT

Agreement relating to the employment of dependents of official government employees, with addendum.
Exchange of notes at Washington May 16 and 20, 1983.
Entered into force May 20, 1983.
TIAS 10694; 2005 UNTS 187

FINANCE

Agreement relating to guaranties authorized under Section 111(b)(3) of the Economic Cooperation Act of 1948, as amended.
Exchange of notes at Washington July 30 and August 8, 1952.
Entered into force August 9, 1952.
3 UST 5056; TIAS 2689; 181 UNTS 249

FOREIGN ASSISTANCE

Economic cooperation agreement.*
Signed at Copenhagen June 29, 1948.
Entered into force July 2, 1948.
62 Stat. 2199; TIAS 1782; 7 Bevans 141; 22 UNTS 217

Amendments:
November 4 and 18, 1948 (62 Stat. 3753; TIAS 1904; 7 Bevans 157; 55 UNTS 322)
February 7, 1950 (1 UST 148; TIAS 2022; 79 UNTS 294)
February 2 and 9, 1951 (2 UST 647; TIAS 2218; 132 UNTS 380)
November 24, 1952 (3 UST 5181; TIAS 2713; 184 UNTS 327)

Note:
* Applicable to Greenland.

Agreement concerning a Danish-American Fund for the exchange of technology, with appendix.
Signed at Copenhagen March 25, 1985.
Entered into force March 25, 1985.
TIAS 11179

Amendment:
May 2, 1988 (TIAS 11580)

INTELLECTUAL PROPERTY

Convention for the reciprocal protection of trademarks and trade labels.
Signed at Copenhagen June 15, 1892.
Entered into force September 28, 1892.
27 Stat. 963; TS 72; 7 Bevans 30

Agreement with respect to the protection of industrial designs or models.
Exchange of notes at Washington and Bar Harbor June 22 and 26, 1906.
Entered into force June 26, 1906.
TS 483; 7 Bevans 45

Understanding granting persons domiciled in the United States engaged in gainful occupation the access by registration to the exclusive right of utilization of trademarks in Denmark.
Exchange of notes at Washington June 26 and October 15, 1953.
Entered into force October 15, 1953.
4 UST 2040; TIAS 2860; 215 UNTS 111

Agreement to facilitate the interchange of patent rights and technical information for defense purposes.
Signed at Copenhagen February 19, 1960.
Entered into force February 19, 1960.
11 UST 148; TIAS 4423; 354 UNTS 151

Agreement approving the procedures for the reciprocal filing of classified patent applications in the United States and Denmark.
Exchange of notes at Copenhagen June 13 and 20, 1960.
Entered into force June 20, 1960.
11 UST 1788; TIAS 4521; 378 UNTS 400

LAW ENFORCEMENT

Convention for prevention of smuggling of intoxicating liquors.
Signed at Washington May 29, 1924.
Entered into force July 25, 1924.
43 Stat. 1809; TS 693; 7 Bevans 72; 27 LNTS 361

Arrangement for the direct exchange of certain information regarding the traffic in narcotic drugs.
Exchange of notes at Copenhagen February 3 and April 23, 1928.
Entered into force April 23, 1928.
7 Bevans 78

Treaty on extradition.
Signed at Copenhagen June 22, 1972.
Entered into force July 31, 1974.
25 UST 1293; TIAS 7864

Agreement on mutual assistance in customs matters.
Signed at Nyborg Castle June 20, 1991.
Entered into force July 16, 1991.
TIAS

Instrument as contemplated by Article 3(2) of the agreement on extradition between the United States of America and the European Union signed June 25, 2003, as to the application of the extradition treaty of June 22, 1972, with annex.
Signed at Copenhagen June 23, 2005.
Entered into force February 1, 2010.
TIAS 10-201.6

Instrument as contemplated by Article 3(3) of the agreement on mutual legal assistance between the United States of America and the European Union signed June 25, 2003, with annex.
Signed at Copenhagen June 23, 2005.
Entered into force February 1, 2010.
TIAS 10-201.29

Agreement on enhancing cooperation in preventing and combating serious crime.
Signed at Copenhagen October 14, 2010.
Entered into force May 5, 2011.
TIAS 11-505

MARITIME MATTERS

Agreement for mutual exemption of vessels from readmeasurement in the ports of their respective countries.
Signed at Washington February 26, 1886.
Entered into force April 1, 1886.
TS 70; 7 Bevans 27
Amendment:
October 2 and 28, 1895 (7 Bevans 32)

Agreement relating to jurisdiction over vessels utilizing the Louisiana Offshore Oil Port.
Exchange of notes at Washington August 17 and 22, 1978.
Entered into force August 22, 1978.
30 UST 1702; TIAS 9278; 1153 UNTS 139

POSTAL MATTERS

Agreement concerning the exchange of parcel post, and detailed regulations of execution.*
Signed at Copenhagen December 9 and at Washington December 28, 1932.
Entered into force provisionally July 1, 1932; definitively August 18, 1933.
47 Stat. 2402; Post Office Department print; 140 LNTS 453

Agreement for collect-on-delivery service.*
Signed at Copenhagen October 13, and at Washington November 11, 1933.
Operative November 1, 1933.
48 Stat. 1671; Post Office Department print; 145 LNTS 113
Note:
* Applicable to Puerto Rico, the Virgin Islands, Guam, Samoa, Faroe Islands and Greenland.

International express mail agreement, with detailed regulations.
Signed at Copenhagen and Washington October 19 and November 19, 1984.
Entered into force January 2, 1985.
TIAS 11011; 2021 UNTS 353

PUBLICATIONS

Agreement for the exchange of official publications.
Exchange of notes at Copenhagen July 27 and August 1, 1949.
Entered into force August 1, 1949.
63 Stat. 2680; TIAS 1971; 7 Bevans 159; 79 UNTS 147

SCIENTIFIC & TECHNICAL COOPERATION

Memorandum of understanding concerning the furnishing of balloon launching and associated services.
Signed at Copenhagen and Washington September 14 and 20, 1983.
Entered into force September 20, 1983.
35 UST 2399; TIAS 10801

Memorandum of understanding concerning scientific and technical cooperation in the earth sciences as related to Greenland, with annexes.
Signed at Copenhagen May 31, 2006.
Entered into force May 31, 2006.
TIAS 06-531

Scientific and technological cooperation agreement, with annexes.
Signed at Copenhagen September 15, 2009.
Entered into force September 15, 2009.
TIAS 09-915

SOCIAL SECURITY

Agreement on social security, with administrative arrangement.
Signed at Copenhagen June 13, 2007.
Entered into force October 1, 2008.
TIAS 08-1001.1

TAXATION

Agreement relating to relief from double income tax on shipping profits.
Exchanges of notes at Washington May 22, August 9 and 18, October 24, 25, and 28, and December 5 and 6, 1922.
Entered into force December 6, 1922; operative January 1, 1921.
47 Stat. 2612; EAS 14; 7 Bevans 65; 113 LNTS 381
Amendment:
July 6, 1987 (TIAS 11278)

Agreement relating to relief from taxation of United States expenditures in Denmark for common defense.
Exchange of notes at Copenhagen April 7 and 9, 1952.
Entered into force April 9, 1952; operative April 7, 1952.
3 UST 4041; TIAS 2546; 177 UNTS 257

Convention for the avoidance of double taxation and the prevention of fiscal evasion with respect to taxes on estates.
Signed at Washington April 27, 1983.
Entered into force November 7, 1984.
TIAS 11089; 2120 UNTS 247

Convention for the avoidance of double taxation and the prevention of fiscal evasion with respect to taxes on income, with protocol.
Signed at Washington August 19, 1999.
Entered into force March 31, 2000.
TIAS 13056

Protocol amending the convention of August 19, 1999 for the avoidance of double taxation and the prevention of fiscal evasion with respect to taxes on income, with a related exchange of notes.
Signed at Copenhagen May 2, 2006.
Entered into force December 28, 2007.
TIAS 07-1228

Agreement to improve international tax compliance and to implement the Foreign Account Tax Compliance Act, with attachments.
Exchange of notes at Washington September 25 and 30, 2015.
Entered into force September 30, 2015.
TIAS 15-930

TELECOMMUNICATION

Agreement relating to the registration with the International Telecommunication Union of frequencies used by United States authorities in Greenland.
Exchange of notes at Washington March 25 and April 4, 1952.
Entered into force April 4, 1952.
3 UST 4047; TIAS 2548; 177 UNTS 13

Agreement relating to the reciprocal granting of authorizations to permit licensed amateur radio operators of either country to operate their stations in the other country.
Exchange of notes at Copenhagen October 11, 1973.
Entered into force October 11, 1973.
24 UST 2156; TIAS 7730; 938 UNTS 327

TERRITORIAL ISSUES

Convention for the cession to the United States of the Danish West Indies, and declaration by the United States.
Signed at New York August 4, 1916.
Entered into force January 17, 1917.
39 Stat. 1706; TS 629; 7 Bevans 56

TRADE & INVESTMENT

General convention of friendship, commerce, and navigation.*
Signed at Washington April 26, 1826.
Entered into force August 10, 1826; operative April 26, 1826.
8 Stat. 340; TS 65; 7 Bevans 1
Note:
* Does not apply to Greenland and Iceland (article 6). This convention was abrogated April 15, 1856, and renewed, with the exception of article 5, by the convention of April 11, 1857 (TS 67), and terminated, with the exception of articles 8, 9 and 10 relating to consular matters, by the treaty of October 1, 1951 (TIAS 4797).

Convention for discontinuance of the sound dues.
Signed at Washington April 11, 1857.
Entered into force January 12, 1858.
11 Stat. 719; TS 67; 7 Bevans 11

Treaty of friendship, commerce and navigation, with protocol and minutes of interpretation.
Signed at Copenhagen October 1, 1951.
Entered into force July 30, 1961.
12 UST 908; TIAS 4797; 421 UNTS 105

Protocol to the treaty of friendship, commerce and navigation of October 1, 1951.
Signed at Copenhagen May 2, 2001.
Entered into force December 10, 2008.
TIAS 13149

TRANSPORTATION

Agreement relating to reciprocal treatment of passenger motor vehicles.
Exchange of notes at Bar Harbor and Washington September 4 and October 27, 1928, and February 2, 1929.
Entered into force February 2, 1929; operative February 1, 1929.
48 Stat. 1871; EAS 61; 7 Bevans 83

Arrangement relating to pilot licenses to operate civil aircraft.
Exchange of notes at Copenhagen March 14 and 24, 1934.
Entered into force April 16, 1934.
48 Stat. 1865; EAS 59; 7 Bevans 99; 149 LNTS 485

Agreement relating to air transport services.*
Exchange of notes at Washington December 16, 1944.
Entered into force provisionally January 1, 1945; definitively September 29, 1945.
58 Stat. 1458; EAS 430; 7 Bevans 114; 10 UNTS 213

Amendments:
August 6, 1954 (5 UST 1422; TIAS 3014; 222 UNTS 366)
June 16, 1995 (TIAS 12663)

Note:
* This agreement is suspended for the duration of provisional application of the U.S. – E.U. Air Transport Agreement signed April 25 and 30, 2007 ("Air Transport Agreement") except in respect of the application of this agreement to those areas that are not encompassed within the definition of "territory" in Article 1 of the Air Transport Agreement.

Air service agreement relating to facilities at Kastrup Airport in Denmark.
Exchange of notes at Copenhagen September 26 and October 1, 1946.
Entered into force October 1, 1946.
61 Stat. 3851; TIAS 1734; 7 Bevans 125; 42 UNTS 219

Agreement concerning establishment and operation of certain aeronautical facilities and services in Greenland, with appendix.
Signed at Copenhagen July 7, 1960.
Entered into force July 7, 1960.
11 UST 1861; TIAS 4531; 380 UNTS 39

Amendment:
March 26 and September 6, 1976 (28 UST 3654; TIAS 8593)

Agreement relating to the reciprocal acceptance of airworthiness certifications.
Exchange of notes at Washington January 6, 1982.
Entered into force January 6, 1982.
34 UST 27; TIAS 10335

Agreement for promotion of aviation safety.
Signed at Copenhagen November 6, 1998.
Entered into force November 6, 1998.
TIAS 12992

DENMARK (GREENLAND)

TAXATION

Agreement for reciprocal exemption from taxes on income from the international operation of a ship or ships or aircraft.
Signed at Copenhagen December 9, 2008.
Entered into force June 26, 2010.
TIAS 10-626

DJIBOUTI

DEFENSE

Agreement concerning the provision of training related to defense articles under the United States International Military Education and Training (IMET) Program.
Exchange of notes at Djibouti October 9, 1983, and June 3, 1984.
Entered into force June 3, 1984.
TIAS 10983

Agreement regarding grants under the Foreign Assistance Act of 1961, as amended, and the furnishing of defense articles, related training and other defense services from the United States to Djibouti.
Exchange of notes at Djibouti June 3 and 13, 1992.
Entered into force June 13, 1992.
TIAS 12286

Agreement on access to and use of facilities in the Republic of Djibouti, with annex.
Signed at Djibouti February 19, 2003.
Entered into force February 19, 2003.
TIAS 03-219

Acquisition and cross-servicing agreement, with annexes.
Signed at Djibouti February 1, 2012.
Entered into force February 1, 2012.
NP

EMPLOYMENT

Agreement relating to the employment of dependents of official government employees.
Exchange of notes at Djibouti November 21 and December 24, 1991.
Entered into force December 24, 1991.
TIAS 11843

FINANCE

Investment incentive agreement.
Exchange of notes at Djibouti May 11, 1983.
Entered into force May 11, 1983.
TIAS

INTERNATIONAL CRIMINAL COURT

Agreement regarding the surrender of persons to the International Criminal Court.
Signed at Washington January 24, 2003.
Entered into force July 2, 2003.
TIAS 03-702

POSTAL MATTERS

International express mail agreement, with detailed regulations.
Signed at Djibouti and Washington June 25, July 28 and August 11, 1987.
Entered into force August 17, 1987.
TIAS 11554

SCIENTIFIC & TECHNICAL COOPERATION

Memorandum of understanding concerning scientific and technical cooperation in the earth and mapping sciences, with annexes.
Signed at Reston and Djibouti March 9 and 21, 2001.
Entered into force March 21, 2001.
TIAS 13146

TELECOMMUNICATION

Agreement for the establishment of U.S. radio transmitting facilities in Djibouti, with annexes.
Signed at Djibouti June 18, 2002.
Entered into force June 18, 2002.
TIAS 02-618.1

TRANSPORTATION

Memorandum of agreement for the provision of assistance in developing and modernizing the civil aviation infrastructure in Djibouti
Signed February 3 and 14, 2005.
Entered into force February 14, 2005.
NP

DOMINICA

On November 8, 1978, Dominica became an independent state. In a note dated December 23, 1982, to the Secretary-General of the United Nations, the Prime Minister made a statement reading in part as follows:

The Government of the Commonwealth of Dominica hereby declares that, with regard to multilateral treaties applied or extended to the former British associated state of Dominica, it will continue to apply the terms of each such treaty provisionally and on the basis of reciprocity until such time as it notifies the depository authority of its decision in respect thereof.

As regards bilateral treaties applied or extended to, or entered into on behalf of the former British associated state of Dominica, the Government of the Commonwealth of Dominica declares that it will examine each such treaty and communicate its views to the other state party concerned. In the mean-time, the Government of the Commonwealth of Dominica will continue to observe the terms of each such treaty, which validly so applies and is not inconsistent with its independent sovereign status, provisionally and on the basis of reciprocity.

CULTURAL EXCHANGES, PROPERTY & COOPERATION

Agreement relating to the establishment of a Peace Corps program in Dominica.
Exchange of letters at Bridgetown and Roseau May 15 and 22, 1980.
Entered into force May 22, 1980.
32 UST 5811; TIAS 10016; 1267 UNTS 87

DEFENSE

Agreement concerning the provision of training related to defense articles under the United States International Military Education and Training (IMET) Program.
Exchange of notes at Bridgetown and Roseau December 11, 1980, and February 4, 1981.
Entered into force February 4, 1981.
33 UST 856; TIAS 10069; 1267 UNTS 95

Agreement regarding the provision of articles, services and associated training by the Government of the United States for anti-narcotics purposes.
Exchange of notes at Bridgetown and Roseau November 13 and 30, 1998.
Entered into force November 30, 1998.
TIAS

Agreement regarding the Caribbean Basin Security Initiative (Technical Assistance Field Team).
Effected by exchange of notes at Bridgetown and St. Michael June 29, 2012 and February 7, 2013.
Entered into force February 7, 2013.
TIAS 13-207

DIPLOMATIC & CONSULAR RELATIONS

Consular convention between the United States and the United Kingdom.
Signed at Washington June 6, 1951.
Entered into force September 7, 1952.
3 UST 3426; TIAS 2494; 165 UNTS 121

FINANCE

Agreement relating to investment guaranties.
Signed at Roseau October 11, 1968.
Entered into force October 11, 1968.
19 UST 6063; TIAS 6568; 702 UNTS 263

FOREIGN ASSISTANCE

General agreement for economic, technical, and related assistance.
Signed at Dominica September 16, 1983.
Entered into force September 16, 1983.
35 UST 2948; TIAS 10830; 2014 UNTS 587

INTELLECTUAL PROPERTY

Declaration by the United States and the United Kingdom affording reciprocal protection to trademarks.
Signed at London October 24, 1877.
Entered into force October 24, 1877.
20 Stat. 703; TS 138; 12 Bevans 198

INTERNATIONAL CRIMINAL COURT

Agreement regarding the surrender of persons to the International Criminal Court.
Exchange of notes at Washington and Roseau May 10, 2004.
Entered into force May 10, 2004.
TIAS 04-510

LAW ENFORCEMENT

Treaty on extradition.
Signed at Roseau October 10, 1996.
Entered into force May 25, 2000.
TIAS 00-525

Treaty on mutual legal assistance in criminal matters.
Signed at Roseau October 10, 1996.
Entered into force May 25, 2000.
TIAS

Arial intercept assistance agreement.
Exchange of notes at Washington and Roseau October 7, 2011 and April 19, 2012.
Entered into force April 19, 2012.
TIAS 12-419.1

MARITIME MATTERS

Agreement concerning maritime counter-drug operations.
Signed at Roseau April 19, 1995.
Entered into force April 19, 1995.
TIAS 12630

MIGRATION & REFUGEES

Memorandum of understanding for the establishment within the territory of Dominica of facilities to provide temporary protection under the auspices of the United Nations High Commissioner for Refugees for nationals of Haiti fleeing their country, with related letter.
Signed at Dominica July 10, 1994.
Entered into force July 10, 1994.
TIAS

OCCUPATION & PEACEKEEPING

Agreement for the furnishing of commodities and services in connection with the peacekeeping force for Grenada.
Exchange of notes at Bridgetown and Roseau November 25, 1983, and January 13, 1984.
Entered into force January 13, 1984.
35 UST 4249; TIAS 10923; 2014 UNTS 595

POSTAL MATTERS

International express mail agreement.
Signed at Roseau and Washington September 24, 1997, and December 30, 1999.
Entered into force February 15, 2000.
NP

TAXATION

Agreement for the exchange of information with respect to taxes.
Signed at Washington October 1, 1987.
Entered into force May 9, 1988.
TIAS 11543; 2191 UNTS 203

TELECOMMUNICATION

Agreement between the United States and the United Kingdom relating to the reciprocal granting of authorizations to permit licensed amateur radio operators of either country to operate their stations in the other country.
Exchange of notes at London November 26, 1965.
Applicable to Dominica December 11, 1969.
16 UST 2047; TIAS 5941; 561 UNTS 193

Agreement between the United States and the United Kingdom extending to certain territories the application of the agreement of November 26, 1965, relating to the reciprocal granting of authorizations to permit licensed amateur radio operators of either country to operate their stations in the other country.
Exchange of notes at London December 11, 1969.
Entered into force December 11, 1969.
20 UST 4089; TIAS 6800; 732 UNTS 334

Agreement relating to radio communications between amateur stations on behalf of third parties.
Exchange of telexes at Bridgetown and Roseau December 8, 1983, and February 9, 1984.
Entered into force March 10, 1984.
TIAS 11145; 2126 UNTS 183

TRANSPORTATION

Agreement between the United States and the United Kingdom concerning air services, with annexes and exchange of letters.
Signed at Bermuda July 23, 1977.
Entered into force July 23, 1977.
28 UST 5367; TIAS 8641
Amendment:
April 25, 1978 (29 UST 2680; TIAS 8965)

DOMINICAN REPUBLIC

CONSULAR AFFAIRS

Agreement concerning period of validity of and fees for nonimmigrant visas.*
Exchange of notes at Ciudad Trujillo December 14 and 16, 1955.
Entered into force February 1, 1956.
7 UST 135; TIAS 3484; 241 UNTS 101
Note:
* The status of this agreement is under review.

CULTURAL EXCHANGES, PROPERTY & COOPERATION

Agreement relating to the establishment of a Peace Corps program in the Dominican Republic.
Signed at Washington May 2, 1962.
Entered into force May 2, 1962.
13 UST 447; TIAS 5007; 442 UNTS 107

DEFENSE

Convention entered into in accordance with the "modus operandi" of evacuation, signed June 30, 1922, for the purpose of rectifying certain orders, resolutions, and contracts.
Signed at Santo Domingo June 12, 1924.
Entered into force December 4, 1925.
44 Stat. 2193; TS 729; 7 Bevans 206; 48 LNTS 91

Agreement relating to the transit of military aircraft.
Exchange of notes at Ciudad Trujillo August 11, 1950.
Entered into force August 11, 1950.
1 UST 747; TIAS 2143; 92 UNTS 329

Military assistance agreement.*
Signed at Washington March 6, 1953.
Entered into force June 10, 1953.
4 UST 184; TIAS 2777; 199 UNTS 267
Note:
* Terminated June 20, 1961, except that the provisions of paragraphs 2, 3, 4, 5 and 6 of article 1 continue in force.

Agreement providing for disposition of equipment and materials furnished by the United States under the military assistance agreement of March 6, 1953.
Exchange of notes at Ciudad Trujillo March 23 and April 22, 1955.
Entered into force April 22, 1955.
6 UST 1185; TIAS 3263; 239 UNTS 325

Military assistance agreement.
Signed at Santo Domingo March 8, 1962.
Entered into force June 10, 1964.
15 UST 699; TIAS 5590; 527 UNTS 29

Agreement relating to the deposit by the Dominican Republic of ten percent of the value of military grant assistance and excess defense articles furnished by the United States.
Exchange of notes at Santo Domingo March 23 and April 17, 1972.
Entered into force April 17, 1972; effective February 7, 1972.
23 UST 1094; TIAS 7366; 852 UNTS 235

Agreement concerning payment to the United States of net proceeds from the sale of defense articles furnished under the military assistance program.
Exchange of notes at Santo Domingo May 30 and August 8, 1974.
Entered into force August 8, 1974; effective July 1, 1974.
25 UST 2433; TIAS 7924
Amendment:
February 10 and October 21, 2005

Agreement concerning the status of United States Government personnel temporarily present in the Dominican Republic in connection with their official duties.
Exchange of notes at Santo Domingo July 20 and August 4, 1988.
Entered into force August 4, 1988.
NP

Basic exchange and cooperative agreement for topographic mapping, nautical and aeronautical charting and information, geodesy and geophysics, digital data and related mapping, charting and geodesy materials, with glossary.
Signed at Santo Domingo and Fairfax September 18 and 25, 1995.
Entered into force September 25, 1995.
NP

Memorandum of understanding concerning the Inter-American Naval Telecommunications Network.
Signed August 7, 2006.
Entered into force August 7, 2006.
TIAS 06-807.1

Agreement regarding grants under the Foreign Assistance Act of 1961, as amended, or successor legislation, and the furnishing of defense articles, defense services and related training including pursuant to the United States International Military Education and Training Program.
Exchange of notes at Santo Domingo May 17 and June 28, 2007.
Entered into force June 28, 2007.
NP

Acquisition and cross-servicing agreement, with annexes.
Signed at Santo Domingo and Miami November 27, 2012 and March 5, 2013.
Entered into force March 5, 2013.
NP

Agreement regarding the Caribbean Basin Security Initiative (Technical Assistance Field Team).
Effected by exchange of notes at Santo Domingo April 4 and 8, 2013.
Entered into force April 8, 2013.
TIAS 13-408

Agreement concerning health care for military members and their dependents.
Signed June 11 and 29, 2015.
Entered into force June 29, 2015.
NP

DIPLOMATIC & CONSULAR RELATIONS

Agreement providing free entry upon arrival for Embassy employees, and certain duty-free importations, including new and used automobiles, for six months thereafter.
Exchange of notes at Washington January 12 and 23, 1950.
Entered into force January 23, 1950.
5 UST 1064; TIAS 2989; 236 UNTS 3

ENVIRONMENT & CONSERVATION

Agreement concerning cooperation in the Global Learning and Observations to Benefit the Environment (GLOBE) Program, with appendices.
Signed at Santo Domingo June 20, 1997.
Entered into force June 20, 1997.
TIAS

FINANCE

Agreement relating to investment guaranties.
Signed at Washington May 2, 1962.
Entered into force May 2, 1962.
13 UST 440; TIAS 5005; 442 UNTS 99

Agreement regarding the consolidation and rescheduling of certain debts owed to, guaranteed by or insured by the United States Government and its agencies, with annexes.
Signed at Santo Domingo March 6, 1986.
Entered into force September 9, 1986.
NP

Agreement regarding the consolidation and rescheduling or refinancing of certain debts owed to, guaranteed by, or insured by the United States Government and its agencies, with annexes.
Signed at Santo Domingo October 30, 1992.
Entered into force November 9, 1993.
NP

Agreement regarding the consolidation and rescheduling of certain debts owed to, guaranteed by, or insured by the United States Government and its agencies, with annexes.
Signed at Santo Domingo September 9, 2005.
Entered into force April 28, 2006.
NP

Agreement regarding the consolidation and rescheduling of certain debts owed to, guaranteed by, or insured by the United States Government or its agencies, with annexes.
Signed at Santo Domingo August 29, 2006.
Entered into force November 22, 2006.
NP

FOREIGN ASSISTANCE

General agreement for economic, technical and related assistance.
Signed at Santo Domingo January 11, 1962.
Entered into force January 11, 1962.
13 UST 60; TIAS 4936; 433 UNTS 133

AGENCY FOR INTERNATIONAL DEVELOPMENT

Foreign assistance agreement.
Signed September 4, 2007.
Entered into force September 4, 2007.
NP

Amendments:
September 11, 2008 (NP)
September 16 and 18, 2009 (NP)
March 4, 2010 (NP)
September 17 and 21, 2010 (NP)
May 10, 2011 (NP)
September 27 and 29, 2011 (NP)

INTERNATIONAL CRIMINAL COURT

Agreement regarding the surrender of persons to the International Criminal Court.
Signed at Santo Domingo September 13, 2002.
Entered into force August 12, 2004.
TIAS 04-812

LABOR

Agreement relating to workmens' compensation in connection with certain projects under construction or operation in the Dominican Republic.
Exchange of notes at Ciudad Trujillo October 14 and 19, 1943.
Entered into force October 19, 1943.
57 Stat. 1180; EAS 353; 7 Bevans 268; 21 UNTS 295

LAW ENFORCEMENT

Convention for the mutual extradition of fugitives from justice.
Signed at Santo Domingo June 19, 1909.
Entered into force August 2, 1910.
36 Stat. 2468; TS 550; 7 Bevans 200

Agreement on international narcotics control cooperation.
Signed at Santo Domingo November 18, 1985.
Entered into force November 18, 1985.
TIAS 11350; 2192 UNTS 329

Treaty for the return of stolen or embezzled vehicles, with annexes.
Signed at Santo Domingo April 30, 1996.
Entered into force August 3, 2001.
TIAS

Agreement regarding mutual assistance between their customs administrations.
Signed at Santo Domingo October 31, 2005.
Entered into force October 31, 2005.
TIAS 05-1031

Agreement regarding the Cooperating Nation Information Exchange System.
Exchange of notes at Kingston November 9, 2005, and August 25, 2006.
Entered into force August 25, 2006.
TIAS 06-825

Letter of agreement on sovereign skies aviation support, with annex.
Signed at Santo Domingo February 26, 2010.
Entered into force February 26, 2010.
NP

Agreement concerning the sharing of confiscated proceeds and instrumentalities of crimes.
Signed at Washington April 19, 2012.
Entered into force April 19, 2012.
TIAS 12-419

Extradition treaty.*
Signed at Santo Domingo January 12, 2015.
Entered into force December 15, 2016.
TIAS 16-1215

Note:
* Upon entry into force of this Treaty, the 1909 Treaty shall cease to have any effect as between the Parties, except that the requests pending upon entry into force shall continue under the procedures of the 1909 Treaty supplemented by Article 6 of this Treaty (Article 21, paragraph 3).

MARITIME MATTERS

Agreement concerning maritime counter-drug operations.
Signed at Santo Domingo March 23, 1995.
Entered into force March 23, 1995.
TIAS 12620

Protocol to the agreement of March 23, 1995 concerning maritime counter-drug operations.
Signed at Washington May 20, 2003.
Entered into force May 20, 2003.
TIAS 03-520.1

Search and rescue agreement.
Signed at Washington May 21, 2003.
Entered into force May 21, 2003.
TIAS 03-521

MIGRATION & REFUGEES

Agreement concerning cooperation in maritime migration law enforcement.
Signed at Washington May 20, 2003.
Entered into force May 20, 2003.
TIAS 03-520

POSTAL MATTERS

International express mail agreement, with detailed regulations.
Signed at Santo Domingo and Washington December 3, 1990, and January 8, 1991.
Entered into force February 18, 1991.
TIAS 11782

Postal money order agreement.
Signed at Washington and Santo Domingo August 6 and 14, 1995.
Entered into force September 1, 1995.
NP

PUBLICATIONS

Agreement relating to the exchange of official publications.
Exchange of notes at Ciudad Trujillo December 9 and 10, 1942.
Entered into force December 10, 1942.
56 Stat. 1851; EAS 297; 7 Bevans 248; 24 UNTS 257

SCIENTIFIC & TECHNICAL COOPERATION

Agreement for the continuation of a cooperative program for meteorological observations.
Exchange of notes at Santo Domingo April 7 and 11, 1969.
Entered into force April 11, 1969; effective July 1, 1968.
20 UST 647; TIAS 6670; 707 UNTS 243

TAXATION

Agreement for the exchange of information with respect to taxes.
Signed at Santo Domingo August 7, 1989.
Entered into force October 12, 1989.
TIAS 11694; 2190 UNTS 247

TELECOMMUNICATION

Agreement relating to radio communications between amateur stations on behalf of third parties.
Exchange of notes at Santo Domingo April 18 and 22, 1963.
Entered into force May 22, 1963.
14 UST 817; TIAS 5360; 487 UNTS 169

Agreement relating to the reciprocal granting of authorizations to permit licensed amateur radio operators of either country to operate their stations in the other country.
Exchange of notes at Santo Domingo January 28 and February 2, 1965.
Entered into force February 2, 1965.
16 UST 93; TIAS 5766; 542 UNTS 117

TRADE & INVESTMENT

Agreement on trade in textile and apparel goods.
Exchange of letters at Santo Domingo and Washington October 19 and 24, 2006.
Entered into force October 24, 2006.
NP

TRANSPORTATION

Air transport agreement and exchange of notes.
Signed at Ciudad Trujillo July 19, 1949.
Entered into force July 19, 1949.
63 Stat. 2615; TIAS 1955; 7 Bevans 289; 51 UNTS 145
Amendment:
October 19, 1971 (22 UST 1732; TIAS 7202)

Memorandum of agreement relating to the provision of flight inspection services.
Signed at Washington and Santo Domingo August 16, 1978, and June 22, 1979.
Entered into force June 22, 1979; effective October 1, 1978.
TIAS
Amendment:
May 19 and July 13, 1998

Memorandum of agreement concerning assistance in developing and modernizing the Dominican Republic's civil aviation system, with annex.
Signed at Santo Domingo March 11 and 17, 1988.
Entered into force March 17, 1988.
TIAS 11777; 2202 UNTS 335

E

EAST AFRICAN COMMUNITY

TRADE & INVESTMENT

Trade and investment framework agreement.
Signed at Washington July 16, 2008.
Entered into force July 16, 2008.
TIAS 08-716.1

ECONOMIC COMMUNITY OF CENTRAL AFRICAN STATES

DEFENSE

Agreement regarding grants under the Foreign Assistance Act of 1961, as amended, or successor legislation, and the furnishing of defense articles, related training and other defense services.
Effected by exchange of notes at Libreville October 18, 2012 and January 15, 2013.
Entered into force January 15, 2013.
NP

ECONOMIC COMMUNITY OF WEST AFRICAN STATES (ECOWAS)

DEFENSE

Agreement regarding grants under the Foreign Assistance Act of 1961, as amended, and the furnishing of defense articles, related training and other defense services from the United States of America to ECOWAS in support of the ECOFORCE peacekeeping operation in Côte d'Ivoire.
Exchange of notes at Abuja January 24 and February 14, 2003.
Entered into force February 14, 2003.
NP

FOREIGN ASSISTANCE

AGENCY FOR INTERNATIONAL DEVELOPMENT.

Agreement for promoting regional stability.
Signed September 13, 2006.
Entered into force September 13, 2006.
NP

Amendments and Extensions:
September 29, 2009 (NP)
September 30, 2010 (NP)
August 16, 2011 (NP)
September 20, 2011 (NP)

ECUADOR

CLAIMS & DISPUTE RESOLUTION

Arbitration convention.
Signed at Washington January 7, 1909.
Entered into force June 22, 1910.
36 Stat. 2456; TS 549; 7 Bevans 328

Treaty for the advancement of peace.
Signed at Washington October 13, 1914.
Entered into force January 22, 1916.
39 Stat. 1650; TS 622; 7 Bevans 330

CONSULAR AFFAIRS

Agreement relating to the reciprocal issuance of nonimmigrant visas.*
Exchange of notes at Quito December 11, 1962, and January 7, 1963.
Entered into force January 7, 1963; operative February 7, 1963.
14 UST 757; TIAS 5354; 477 UNTS 101

Note:
* The status of this agreement is under review.

CULTURAL EXCHANGES, PROPERTY & COOPERATION

Agreement relating to the establishment of a Peace Corps program in Ecuador.
Exchange of notes at Quito August 3, 1962.
Entered into force August 3, 1962.
13 UST 1903; TIAS 5145; 460 UNTS 133

Agreement for the recovery and return of stolen archaeological, historical and cultural properties.
Signed at Washington November 17, 1983.
Entered into force January 14, 1987.
TIAS 11075; 2039 UNTS 253

DEFENSE

Agreement relating to transit and technical stop rights for U.S. military planes in Ecuador.
Exchange of notes at Quito June 7 and 11, 1946.
Entered into force June 11, 1946.
3 UST 536; TIAS 2411; 167 UNTS 135

Agreement concerning financial arrangements for the furnishing of certain supplies and services to naval vessels of both countries.
Signed at Quito July 8, 1955.
Entered into force October 6, 1955.
6 UST 2959; TIAS 3344; 265 UNTS 49

Agreement for the return of equipment and materials furnished Ecuador under the military assistance agreement.
Exchange of notes at Quito June 20 and July 19, 1956.
Entered into force July 19, 1956.
11 UST 246; TIAS 4439; 372 UNTS 149

Agreement on mapping, charting and geodesy.
Signed at Quito February 19, 1976.
Entered into force February 19, 1976.
27 UST 1943; TIAS 8290

Agreement relating to eligibility for United States military assistance and training pursuant to the International Security Assistance and Arms Export Control Act of 1976.
Exchange of notes at Quito August 17 and September 3, 1976.
Entered into force September 3, 1976.
27 UST 4009; TIAS 8420; 1059 UNTS 143

General security of military information agreement.
Exchange of notes at Quito July 12, 1985.
Entered into force July 12, 1985.
TIAS 11257; 2174 UNTS 281

Cooperative arrangement for the production of topographic maps of Ecuador, with annexes.
Signed at Washington and Quito April 21 and June 12, 1986.
Entered into force June 12, 1986.
TIAS 11374

Agreement regarding the furnishing of defense articles and services on a grant basis to Ecuador from the United States.
Exchange of notes at Quito January 30 and March 4, 1992.
Entered into force March 4, 1992.
NP

Memorandum of understanding concerning the Inter-American Naval Telecommunications Network.
Signed September 25 and November 8, 2006.
Entered into force November 8, 2006.
TIAS 06-1108.1.

Agreement concerning health care for military members and their dependents.
Signed at Washington and Quito September 27 and October 5, 2012.
Entered into force October 5, 2012.
NP
Extension:
August 24 and October 2, 2015 (NP)

DIPLOMATIC & CONSULAR RELATIONS

Agreement providing for certain customs courtesies and free entry privileges for consular officers and administrative personnel on a reciprocal basis.
Exchange of notes at Quito October 22 and November 6, 1957, and related note of November 11, 1957.
Entered into force November 6, 1957.
8 UST 2469; TIAS 3967; 307 UNTS 49

Agreement on immunities and privileges for the United States Inter-American Geodetic Survey mission.
Signed at Quito November 23, 1973.
Entered into force November 23, 1973.
24 UST 2304; TIAS 7755; 938 UNTS 403

EDUCATION

Agreement for financing certain educational exchange programs.
Signed at Quito September 20, 1963.
Entered into force September 20, 1963.
14 UST 1418; TIAS 5439; 488 UNTS 147

ENVIRONMENT & CONSERVATION

Agreement for cooperation in the Global Learning and Observations to Benefit the Environment (GLOBE) Program, with appendices.
Signed at Quito April 22, 1996.
Entered into force April 22, 1996.
TIAS 12744

FINANCE

Agreement relating to investment guaranties under section 413(b)(4) of the Mutual Security Act of 1954.
Exchange of notes at Washington March 28 and 29, 1955.
Entered into force March 29, 1955.
6 UST 843; TIAS 3230; 261 UNTS 343
Amendments:
September 4, 1963 (14 UST 1251; TIAS 5426; 488 UNTS 262)
July 9, 1993 (TIAS 12156)

Related Agreement:
November 28, 1984 (TIAS 11001; 2024 UNTS 11)

Agreement regarding the consolidation and rescheduling of debts owed to, guaranteed by or insured by the United States Government and its agencies, with annexes.
Signed at Quito March 19, 1984.
Entered into force May 4, 1984.
35 UST 4793; TIAS 10966

Agreement regarding the consolidation and rescheduling of certain debts owed to, guaranteed by or insured by the United States Government and its agencies, with annexes.
Signed at Washington January 14, 1986.
Entered into force March 10, 1986.
NP

Swap agreement between the United States Treasury and the Central Bank of Ecuador/Republic of Ecuador, with related letter.
Signed at Washington and Quito December 3, 1987.
Entered into force December 3, 1987.
TIAS

Agreement regarding the consolidation and rescheduling of certain debts owed to, guaranteed by or insured by the United States Government and its agencies, with annexes.
Signed at Quito July 8, 1988.
Entered into force August 22, 1988.
NP

Agreement regarding the consolidation and rescheduling or refinancing of certain debts owed to, guaranteed by or insured by the United States Government and its agencies, with annexes.
Signed at Washington July 30, 1990.
Entered into force September 12, 1990.
NP

Agreement regarding the consolidation and rescheduling or refinancing of certain debts owed to, guaranteed by, or insured by the United States Government and its agencies, with annexes.
Signed at Quito July 30, 1992.
Entered into force September 11, 1992.
NP

Agreement regarding the consolidation and rescheduling or refinancing of certain debts owed to, guaranteed by or insured by the United States Government and its agencies, with annexes.
Signed at Washington January 19, 1995.
Entered into force March 1, 1995.
NP

Agreement regarding the consolidation and rescheduling of certain debts owed to, guaranteed by, or insured by the United States Government and its agencies, with annexes.
Signed at Washington February 7, 2002.
Entered into force March 28, 2002.
NP

Agreement regarding the reduction of certain debts owed to, guaranteed by, or insured by the United States Government, with annexes.
Signed at Quito April 7, 2005.
Entered into force May 31, 2005.
NP

FOREIGN ASSISTANCE

Agreement granting duty-free entry, exemption from internal taxation, and free transportation within Ecuador to ultimate beneficiary for certain relief supplies and equipment for American voluntary relief and rehabilitation agencies.
Exchange of notes at Quito September 6, 1955.
Entered into force September 6, 1955.
6 UST 3871; TIAS 3388; 256 UNTS 185
Amendment:
August 3, 1970 (21 UST 2502; TIAS 6992; 772 UNTS 450)

General agreement for economic, technical and related assistance.
Signed at Quito April 17, 1962.
Entered into force April 17, 1962.
13 UST 425; TIAS 5003; 442 UNTS 69

AGENCY FOR INTERNATIONAL DEVELOPMENT.

Country assistance agreement, with annexes.
Signed at Quito September 7, 2007.
Entered into force September 7, 2007.
NP

INTELLECTUAL PROPERTY

Agreement concerning the protection and enforcement of intellectual property rights.
Signed at Washington October 15, 1993.
Entered into force October 15, 1993.
TIAS 12679
Amendment:
July 28, 1995 (TIAS 12679)

LAW ENFORCEMENT

Extradition treaty.
Signed at Quito June 28, 1872.
Entered into force November 12, 1873.
18 Stat. 199; TS 79; 7 Bevans 321

Supplementary extradition treaty.
Signed at Quito September 22, 1939.
Entered into force May 29, 1941.
55 Stat. 1196; TS 972; 7 Bevans 346

Agreement concerning cooperation in the control of the illicit traffic in narcotic drugs.
Exchange of notes at Quito November 5 and 20, 1971.
Entered into force November 10, 1971.
22 UST 2109; TIAS 7255

Memorandum of understanding on measures to prevent the diversion of chemical substances.
Signed at Quito June 17, 1991.
Entered into force June 17, 1991.
TIAS 12129

Agreement for the prevention and control of narcotic related money laundering.
Signed at Quito August 7, 1992.
Entered into force February 4, 1993.
TIAS 12471

Agreement to implement the United Nations convention against illicit trafficking in narcotic drugs and psychotropic substances of December 20, 1988, as it relates to the transfer of confiscated property, securities and instrumentalities.
Signed at Quito June 27, 1994.
Entered into force July 15, 1994.
TIAS

Agreement regarding mutual assistance between customs administrations.
Signed at Quito November 6, 2002.
Entered into force November 6, 2002.
TIAS 02-1106

PEACE

Treaty of peace, friendship, navigation and commerce.*
Signed at Quito June 13, 1839.
Entered into force April 9, 1842.
8 Stat. 534; TS 76; 7 Bevans 296
Note:
* Articles with respect to commerce and navigation terminated August 25, 1892.

POSTAL MATTERS

Agreement for the exchange of registered and insured parcel post packages.
Signed at Quito and Washington July 11 and August 6, 1929.
Operative July 1, 1929.
46 Stat. 2378; Post Office Department print

International express mail agreement, with detailed regulations.
Signed at Quito and Washington March 20 and April 11, 1990.
Entered into force March 30, 1990.
TIAS 11900

Postal money order agreement.
Signed at Quito and Washington August 1 and 8, 1990.
Entered into force October 15, 1990.
TIAS 11741

PUBLICATIONS

Agreement relating to the exchange of official publications.
Exchange of notes at Quito October 21 and 29, 1947.
Entered into force October 29, 1947.
61 Stat. 3322; TIAS 1668; 7 Bevans 427; 21 UNTS 21

TELECOMMUNICATION

Agreement relating to radio communications between amateur stations on behalf of third parties.
Exchange of notes at Quito March 16 and 17, 1950.
Entered into force March 17, 1950.
3 UST 2672; TIAS 2433; 177 UNTS 115

Agreement relating to the reciprocal granting of authorizations to permit licensed amateur radio operators of either country to operate their stations in the other country.
Exchange of notes at Quito March 26, 1965.
Entered into force March 26, 1965.
16 UST 181; TIAS 5779; 542 UNTS 237

TRADE & INVESTMENT

Treaty concerning the encouragement and reciprocal protection of investment, with protocol.
Signed at Washington August 27, 1993.
Entered into force May 11, 1997.
TIAS

TRANSPORTATION

Commercial air transport services agreement.
Signed at Quito January 8, 1947.
Entered into force April 24, 1947.
61 Stat. 2773; TIAS 1606; 7 Bevans 409; 22 UNTS 119
Amendment:
January 3 and 10, 1951 (2 UST 482; TIAS 2196; 133 UNTS 312)

Agreement relating to a civil aviation mission to Ecuador.
Exchange of notes at Quito October 24 and 27, 1947.
Entered into force October 27, 1947.
61 Stat. 4013; TIAS 1774; 7 Bevans 422; 44 UNTS 45
Amendment:
June 30 and October 13, 1949 (7 Bevans 460)

Memorandum of agreement concerning assistance in developing and modernizing Ecuador's civil aviation system.
Signed at Washington and Quito October 9 and November 6, 1985.
Entered into force November 6, 1985.
TIAS 11313; 2174 UNTS 357

Memorandum of agreement concerning assistance in developing and modernizing Ecuador's civil aviation infrastructure.
Signed at Washington and Quito March 5 and 23, 1998.
Entered into force March 23, 1998.
NP
Amendment:
November 21, 2005 and November 16, 2006

Protocol to modify the annexes of the air transport agreement of September 26, 1986.*
Signed at Quito July 21, 2010.
Entered into force January 24, 2011.
TIAS 11-124

Extension to Annex I of the air transport agreement of September 26, 1986.*
Exchange of Notes at Quito November 6 and 13, 2015.
Entered into force November 13, 2015.
TIAS 11-124
Extension:
June 21 and 27, 2016 (TIAS 16-627)

Note:
* Not yet in force.

EGYPT

ATOMIC ENERGY

Agreement for cooperation concerning peaceful uses of nuclear energy, with annex and agreed minute.
Signed at Washington June 29, 1981.
Entered into force December 29, 1981.
33 UST 2915; TIAS 10208; 1529 UNTS 143

CANALS

Arrangement relating to assistance by the United States in the salvage and/or removal from the Suez Canal of sunken vessels and certain other hazards to navigation, with annex.
Exchange of notes at Cairo June 11, 1974.
Entered into force June 11, 1974.
25 UST 1273; TIAS 7859

CLAIMS & DISPUTE RESOLUTION

Treaty of arbitration.
Signed at Washington August 27, 1929.
Entered into force August 24, 1932.
47 Stat. 2130; TS 850; 11 Bevans 1325; 142 LNTS 323

Treaty of conciliation.
Signed at Washington August 27, 1929.
Entered into force August 24, 1932.
47 Stat. 2132; TS 851; 11 Bevans 1327; 142 LNTS 317

Agreement concerning claims of nationals of the United States, with agreed minute and related notes.
Signed at Cairo May 1, 1976.
Entered into force October 27, 1976.
27 UST 4214; TIAS 8446

Agreement concerning United States Government and other claims, with exchange of notes.
Signed at Cairo May 19, 1979.
Entered into force November 5, 1979.
30 UST 7303; TIAS 9589; 1182 UNTS 51

CONSULAR AFFAIRS

Agreement providing for the abolition of nonimmigrant visa fees.*
Exchange of notes at Cairo June 3 and August 1, 1963.
Entered into force August 1, 1963; operative September 1, 1963.
14 UST 1191; TIAS 5416; 488 UNTS 189
Note:
* The status of this agreement is under review.

CULTURAL EXCHANGES, PROPERTY & COOPERATION

Cultural agreement.
Signed at Cairo May 21, 1962.
Entered into force May 21, 1962.
13 UST 1253; TIAS 5072; 458 UNTS 197

Agreement on the development and facilitation of tourism.
Signed at Cairo February 21, 1983.
Entered into force August 16, 1983.
TIAS 10680; 2005 UNTS 119

Memorandum of understanding concerning the imposition of import restrictions on categories of archaeological material of the Arab Republic of Egypt.
Signed at Washington November 30, 2016.
Entered into force November 30, 2016.
TIAS 16-1130

DEFENSE

Agreement relating to mutual defense assistance.
Exchange of notes at Cairo April 29, 1952.
Entered into force April 29, 1952.
7 UST 841; TIAS 3564; 241 UNTS 3
Amendment:
December 9 and 10, 1952 (7 UST 844; TIAS 3565; 241 UNTS 8)

Mapping, charting and geodesy cooperative and exchange agreement, with annexes.
Signed at Washington June 25, 1981.
Entered into force June 25, 1981.
NP

Agreement concerning privileges and immunities of United States military and related personnel in Egypt, with related letter and agreed minute.
Exchange of notes at Cairo July 26, 1981.
Entered into force December 5, 1981.
33 UST 3353; TIAS 10238

General security of military information agreement.
Signed at Cairo February 10, 1982.
Entered into force February 10, 1982.
34 UST 203; TIAS 10349

DIPLOMATIC & CONSULAR RELATIONS

Arrangement providing for reciprocal privileges for consular officers to import articles for their personal use free of duty.
Exchange of notes at Washington March 16 and April 7, 1932.
Entered into force April 7, 1932.
11 Bevans 1337

Agreement concerning principles of relations and cooperation.
Signed at Cairo June 14, 1974.
Entered into force June 14, 1974.
25 UST 2359; TIAS 7913

EDUCATION

Agreement for financing certain educational exchange programs.
Exchange of notes at Cairo January 5 and February 21, 1967.
Entered into force February 21, 1967.
TIAS 6234; 18 UST 307; 688 UNTS 229

ENVIRONMENT & CONSERVATION

Agreement for cooperation in the Global Learning and Observations to Benefit the Environment (GLOBE) Program, with appendices.
Signed at Cairo March 20, 1995.
Entered into force March 20, 1995.
TIAS 12616

FINANCE

Agreement regarding the consolidation and rescheduling of past due debts owed to United States Government agencies with annexes.
Signed at Cairo December 6, 1971.
Entered into force August 28, 1972.
23 UST 1457; TIAS 7424; 852 UNTS 3

Agreement regarding the consolidation and rescheduling of certain debts owed to, guaranteed by, or insured by the United States Government and its agencies, with annexes and related letter.
Signed at Cairo November 14, 1987.
Entered into force February 22, 1988.
NP

Agreement regarding the reorganization of certain debts owed to, guaranteed by, or insured by the United States Government and its agencies, with annexes.
Signed at Washington July 18, 1991.
Entered into force September 3, 1991.
NP

Investment incentive agreement.
Signed at Washington July 1, 1999.
Entered into force July 1, 1999.
TIAS 13051

FOREIGN ASSISTANCE

Agreement relating to duty-free entry and defrayment of inland transportation charges on relief supplies and packages.
Exchange of notes at Cairo October 30, 1954.
Entered into force October 30, 1954.
5 UST 2551; TIAS 3119; 234 UNTS 139

Agreement relating to an informational media guaranty program.
Exchange of notes at Washington March 3 and 7, 1955.
Entered into force March 7, 1955.
6 UST 691; TIAS 3206; 252 UNTS 159

Economic, technical, and related assistance agreement, with exchanges of notes.
Signed at Cairo August 16, 1978.
Entered into force October 15, 1978.
30 UST 4609; TIAS 9481; 1169 UNTS 271

Statement relating to greater support to economic progress in Egypt.
Released at Washington February 4, 1982.
Entered into force February 4, 1982.
34 UST 165; TIAS 10346; 1556 UNTS 327.

AGENCY FOR INTERNATIONAL DEVELOPMENT

Agreement for Egypt utilities management.
Signed September 29, 1997.
Entered into force September 29, 1997.
NP

Amendment
September 30, 2007

Assistance agreement for development support program II, with annex.
Signed September 30, 2001.
Entered into force September 30, 2001.
NP

Amendments:
March 20, 2005 (NP)
October 23, 2008 (NP)
September 29, 2009 (NP)
June 22, 2010 (NP)

Agreement for healthier, planned families, with annex.
Signed September 30, 2002.
Entered into force September 30 2002.
NP

Amendment
September 30, 2007

Assistance agreement for basic education, with annexes.
Signed September 30, 2002.
Entered into force September 30 2002.
NP

Signed:
September 30, 2007 (NP)
September 30, 2008 (NP)
September 30, 2009 (NP)
June 27, 2010 (NP)
September 2, 2010 (NP)

Agreement for cash transfer program assistance for human resources and economic sector development.
Signed September 30, 2007.
Entered into force September 20, 2007.

Amendment:
September 29, 2009 (NP)

Assistance agreement for the North Sinai Initiative, with annexes.
Signed September 16, 2010.
Entered into force September 16, 2010.
NP

Agreement for cash transfer program assistance in support of the homegrown economic and fiscal stabilization, recovery and reform program for the economy of Egypt.
Signed March 7, 2013.
Entered into force March 7, 2013.
NP

Assistance grant agreement for the U. S.-Egypt Higher Education Initiative, with annexes.
Signed September 30, 2014.
Entered into force September 30, 2014.
NP

Assistance grant agreement for basic education II, with annexes.
Signed September 30, 2014.
Entered into force September 30, 2014.
NP

Assistance grant agreement for trade and investment promotion in Egypt, with annexes.
Signed September 30, 2014.
Entered into force September 30, 2014.
NP

LAW ENFORCEMENT

Convention between the United States and the Ottoman Empire relating to extradition.
Signed at Constantinople August 11, 1874.
Entered into force April 22, 1875.
19 Stat. 572; TS 270; 10 Bevans 642

Arrangement for the direct exchange of certain information regarding the traffic in narcotic drugs.
Exchange of notes at Alexandria and Cairo June 20 and August 26, 1930.
Entered into force August 26, 1930.
11 Bevans 1331

Agreement on procedures for mutual assistance in connection with matters relating to the Westinghouse Electric Corporation.
Signed at Washington November 29, 1978.
Entered into force November 29, 1978.
30 UST 3996; TIAS 9441; 1169 UNTS 328
Related Agreements:
December 21, 1978, and January 3, 1979 (30 UST 4005; TIAS 9442; 1169 UNTS 335)
March 19 and April 17, 1979 (30 UST 4007; TIAS 9443; 1169 UNTS 337)

Agreement regarding the transfer of forfeited assets.
Signed at Cairo May 20, 1993.
Entered into force May 20, 1993.
TIAS 12499

Agreement on procedures for mutual assistance in connection with matters relating to the General Electric Company.
Signed at Washington September 17, 1993.
Entered into force September 17, 1993.
NP
Amendment:
November 18, 1994 (NP)

Treaty on mutual legal assistance in criminal matters.
Signed at Cairo May 3, 1998.
Entered into force November 29, 2001.
TIAS 12948

MARITIME MATTERS

Agreement for the establishment and operation of an OMEGA navigation system monitoring station.
Signed at Alexandria June 14, 1980.
Entered into force June 14, 1980.
TIAS 12375

OCCUPATION & PEACEKEEPING

Agreement relating to implementation of the Egyptian-Israeli peace treaty of March 26, 1979.*
Letter signed at Washington March 26, 1979.
Entered into force March 26, 1979.
32 UST 2148; TIAS 9827
Note:
* See also MULTINATIONAL FORCE AND OBSERVERS in bilateral section and OCCUPATION & PEACEKEEPING in multilateral section.

Agreement to transfer title of the United States Field Mission base camp at Umm Khusheib from the United States Sinai Support Mission to the Government of the Arab Republic of Egypt.
Signed at Umm Khusheib April 22, 1982.
Entered into force April 22, 1982.
34 UST 1229; TIAS 10410

POSTAL MATTERS

Agreement concerning the exchange of parcel post and regulations of execution.
Signed at Cairo and Washington December 30, 1958, and January 13, 1959.
Entered into force October 1, 1959.
10 UST 1664; TIAS 4315; 358 UNTS 3

International express mail agreement with detailed regulations.
Signed at Cairo and Washington December 3 and 22, 1983.
Entered into force February 1, 1984.
35 UST 3249; TIAS 10854; 2015 UNTS 69

Memorandum of understanding concerning the operation of the INTELPOST field trial, with details of implementation.
Signed at Cairo and Washington August 18 and September 13, 1985.
Entered into force September 13, 1985.
TIAS 11157

SCIENTIFIC & TECHNICAL COOPERATION

Agreement on science and technology cooperation, with annexes.
Signed at Cairo January 29, 2001.
Entered into force December 31, 2001.
TIAS
Extensions:
May 5 and August 27, 2006
March 7 and September 18, 2011
August 31, 2015

TAXATION

Convention for the avoidance of double taxation and the prevention of fiscal evasion with respect to taxes on income.*
Signed at Cairo August 24, 1980.
Entered into force December 31, 1981.
33 UST 1809; TIAS 10149; 1529 UNTS 41
Note:
* With an understanding and a reservation.

TRADE & INVESTMENT

Provisional commercial agreement relating to most-favored-nation treatment in customs matters.
Exchange of notes at Cairo May 24, 1930.
Entered into force May 24, 1930.
47 Stat. 2582; EAS 5; 11 Bevans 1329; 117 LNTS 419

Treaty concerning the reciprocal encouragement and protection of investments, with annex and protocol.
Signed at Washington September 29, 1982.
Entered into force June 27, 1992.
TIAS
Related Agreements:
March 11, 1985
March 11, 1986

TRANSPORTATION

Agreement relating to the use of Payne Field for international civil air traffic.
Exchange of notes at Cairo June 15, 1946.
Entered into force June 15, 1946.
3 UST 363; TIAS 2397; 151 UNTS 135

Air transport agreement.
Signed at Cairo May 5, 1964.
Entered into force provisionally May 5, 1964; definitively April 7, 1965.
15 UST 2202; TIAS 5706; 531 UNTS 229

Memorandum of agreement concerning assistance in evaluating Egypt's civil aviation infrastructure.
Signed at Cairo July 24, 1995.
Entered into force July 24, 1995.
NP

Memorandum of agreement concerning the provision of civil aviation assistance.
Signed at Washington and Cairo September 12 and 14, 1997.
Entered into force September 14, 1997.
TIAS 12881

EL SALVADOR

AGRICULTURE

Agreement confirming the cooperative agreement for the prevention of foot-and-mouth disease and rinderpest in El Salvador.
Exchange of notes at San Salvador February 28 and March 2, 1973.
Entered into force March 2, 1973.
24 UST 1931; TIAS 7701

CONSULAR AFFAIRS

Agreement providing for the reciprocal abolishment of certain visa fees and tourist and immigration charges.*
Exchange of notes at San Salvador December 7 and 15, 1953.
Entered into force January 14, 1954.
5 UST 859; TIAS 2977; 236 UNTS 25

Note:
* The status of this agreement is under review.

CULTURAL EXCHANGES, PROPERTY & COOPERATION

Agreement relating to the establishment of a Peace Corps program in El Salvador.
Exchange of notes at San Salvador August 11, November 13 and 20, 1961.
Entered into force November 13, 1961.
12 UST 2983; TIAS 4899; 433 UNTS 221

Memorandum of understanding concerning the imposition of import restrictions on certain categories of archaeological material from the pre-Hispanic cultures of the Republic of El Salvador, with appendix.
Signed at Washington March 8, 1995.
Entered into force March 8, 1995.
TIAS 12609

Amendments and Extensions:
March 7, 2000 (TIAS 00-307)
March 3 and 4, 2005 (TIAS 00-307)
February 24 and 25, 2010 (TIAS 00-307)
March 6, 2015 (TIAS 15-306)

DEFENSE

Agreement providing for a United States Army mission to El Salvador.
Signed at San Salvador September 23, 1954.
Entered into force November 17, 1954.
5 UST 2870; TIAS 3144; 237 UNTS 91

Extensions and Amendments:
March 16 and 31, 1959 (10 UST 730; TIAS 4206; 342 UNTS 351)
March 27 and May 3, 1963 (14 UST 484; TIAS 5345; 476 UNTS 333)

Air Force mission agreement.
Signed at San Salvador November 21, 1957.
Entered into force November 21, 1957.
8 UST 2356; TIAS 3951; 303 UNTS 19

Extension and Amendments:
March 16 and 31, 1959 (10 UST 730; TIAS 4206; 342 UNTS 361)
January 15 and 22, 1960 (11 UST 76; TIAS 4410; 371 UNTS 324)

Agreement relating to the furnishing of defense articles and services to El Salvador for the purpose of contributing to its internal security.
Exchange of notes at San Salvador April 10 and 13, 1962.
Entered into force April 13, 1962.
13 UST 985; TIAS 5040; 451 UNTS 307

Agreement relating to the deposit by El Salvador of ten percent of the value of grant military assistance and excess defense articles furnished by the United States.
Exchange of notes at San Salvador April 25 and June 15, 1972.
Entered into force June 15, 1972; effective February 1, 1972.
23 UST 1331; TIAS 7416

Agreement concerning payment to the United States of net proceeds from the sale of defense articles furnished under the military assistance program.
Exchange of notes at San Salvador October 24 and December 6, 1974.
Entered into force December 6, 1974; effective July 1, 1974.
25 UST 3155; TIAS 7979

Basic exchange and cooperative agreement for topographic mapping, nautical and aeronautical charting and information, geodesy and geophysics, digital data and related mapping, charting and geodesy materials, with glossary.
Signed at Delgado (San Salvador) and Fairfax May 10 and 22, 1996.
Entered into force May 22, 1996.
NP

Agreement concerning security measures for the protection of classified military information.
Signed at Antiguo Cuscatlan February 1, 2007.
Entered into force February 1, 2007.
TIAS 07-201

Agreement concerning the status of military and civilian personnel of the United States Department of Defense and United States contractors who may be temporarily present in El Salvador in connection with ship visits, training, exercises, humanitarian activities and other activities as mutually agreed.
Exchange of notes at San Salvador February 15, 2007.
Entered into force May 22, 2007.
TIAS 07-522

Acquisition and cross-servicing agreement, with annexes.
Signed at San Salvador and Miami May 22 and June 8, 2012.
Entered into force June 8, 2012.
NP

Agreement concerning health care for military members and their dependents.
Signed April 2 and May 17, 2014.
Entered into force May 17, 2014.
NP

DIPLOMATIC & CONSULAR RELATIONS

Agreement granting reciprocal customs privileges for Foreign Service personnel.
Exchange of notes at Washington March 18 and May 9, 1958.
Entered into force May 9, 1958.
9 UST 617; TIAS 4043; 316 UNTS 29

EMPLOYMENT

Agreement relating to employment of dependents of official government employees.
Exchange of notes at San Salvador January 19 and March 11, 1983.
Entered into force March 11, 1983.
TIAS 12380

FINANCE

Agreement relating to the guaranty of private investments.
Signed at San Salvador January 29, 1960.
Entered into force April 8, 1960.
11 UST 405; TIAS 4459; 372 UNTS 3

Agreement regarding the consolidation and rescheduling or refinancing of certain debts owed to, guaranteed by, or insured by the United States Government and its agencies, with annexes.
Signed at Washington November 13, 1990.
Entered into force January 4, 1991.
NP

Agreement regarding the reduction of certain debts related to agriculture owed to the Government of the United States and its agencies, with appendices.
Signed at San Salvador December 15, 1992.
Entered into force January 14, 1993.
NP

Agreement regarding the reduction of certain debts related to foreign assistance owed to the Government of the United States and its agencies, with appendices.
Signed at San Salvador December 15, 1992.
Entered into force January 14, 1993.
NP

Agreement regarding the reduction of a certain debt related to agricultural trade owed to the Government of the United States and its agencies, with appendix.
Signed at San Salvador July 12, 2001.
Entered into force July 12, 2001.
NP

FOREIGN ASSISTANCE

General agreement for economic, technical and related assistance.
Signed at San Salvador December 19, 1961.
Entered into force January 16, 1962.
13 UST 266; TIAS 4971; 445 UNTS 175

Agreement concerning the establishment of an Americas Fund and Administering Commission.
Signed at Washington June 18, 1993.
Entered into force July 5, 1994.
TIAS

Amendment:
April 2, 2009

Millennium Challenge Compact, with annexes.
Signed at El Salvador September 30, 2014.
Entered into force September 9, 2015.
TIAS 15-909

AGENCY FOR INTERNATIONAL DEVELOPMENT

Grant Agreement for the mitigating the effects of the Global Financial Crisis Project, with annexes.
Signed March 16, 2010
Entered into force March 16, 2010.
NP

Agreement for the tropical storm Ida reconstruction project, with annexes.
Signed March 17, 2011
Entered into force March 17, 2011.
NP

INTERNATIONAL CRIMINAL COURT

Agreement regarding the transfer of persons to the International Criminal Court.
Signed at San Salvador October 25, 2002.
Entered into force June 21, 2004.
TIAS 04-621

LABOR

Arrangement relating to workmen's compensation and unemployment insurance for American citizens employed on projects in El Salvador.
Exchange of notes at San Salvador September 24, 28, and 29, 1943.
Entered into force September 29, 1943.
7 Bevans 586

LAW ENFORCEMENT

Agreement of cooperation concerning United States access to and use of facilities at the International Airport of El Salvador for aerial counter-narcotics activities.
Signed at San Salvador March 31, 2000.
Entered into force August 23, 2000.
TIAS 00-823
Extensions:
July 2, 2008 and April 2, 2009 (TIAS 00-823)
August 20 and 21, 2014 (TIAS 14-821)

Treaty of extradition.
Signed at San Salvador April 18, 1911.
Entered into force July 10, 1911.
37 Stat. 1516; TS 560; 7 Bevans 507

Agreement of cooperation concerning United States access to and use of facilities at the International Airport of El Salvador for aerial counter-narcotics activities.
Signed at San Salvador March 31, 2000.
Entered into force August 23, 2000.
TIAS 00-823
Extensions
July 2, 2008 and April 2, 2009 (TIAS 00-823)
August 20 and 21, 2014 (TIAS 14-821)

Agreement regarding the cooperating nation information exchange system.
Exchange of notes at San Salvador November 29 and December 17, 2004.
Entered into force December 17, 2004.
TIAS

Agreement concerning the establishment of an International Law Enforcement Academy (ILEA).
Signed at San Salvador September 20, 2005.
Entered into force March 1, 2006.
TIAS 06-301

POSTAL MATTERS

International express mail agreement, with detailed regulations.
Signed at San Salvador and Washington August 29 and October 6, 1989.
Entered into force October 30, 1989.
TIAS 11689

Postal money order agreement.
Signed at Mexico August 16, 1991.
Entered into force October 1, 1991.
TIAS 11800

PRIVATE INTERNATIONAL LAW

Agreement for the enforcement of maintenance support obligations.
Signed at San Salvador May 30, 2006.
Entered into force June 21, 2007.
TIAS 07-621

PUBLICATIONS

Agreement relating to the exchange of official publications.
Exchange of notes at San Salvador November 21 and 27, 1941.
Entered into force November 27, 1941.
55 Stat. 1478; EAS 230; 7 Bevans 551; 120 UNTS 161

TAXATION

Agreement concerning relief from double taxation on income derived from operation of aircraft.
Exchange of notes at San Salvador December 17, 1987.
Entered into force December 17, 1987.
TIAS 11557; 2185 UNTS 343

TELECOMMUNICATION

Arrangement relating to radio communications between amateur stations on behalf of third parties.
Exchange of notes at San Salvador April 5, 1962.
Entered into force May 5, 1962.
13 UST 411; TIAS 5001; 442 UNTS 41

Agreement relating to the granting of authorizations to permit licensed amateur radio operators of either country to operate their stations in the other country.
Exchange of notes at San Salvador May 24 and June 5, 1967.
Entered into force June 5, 1967.
18 UST 1661; TIAS 6309; 692 UNTS 221

TRADE & INVESTMENT

Convention facilitating the work of traveling salesmen.
Signed at Washington January 28, 1919.
Entered into force January 18, 1921.
41 Stat. 1725; TS 651; 7 Bevans 514

Trade agreement.
Signed at San Salvador February 19, 1937.
Entered into force May 31, 1937.
50 Stat. 1564; EAS 101; 7 Bevans 536; 179 LNTS 219

Agreement terminating certain provisions of the reciprocal trade agreement of February 19, 1937.
Exchange of notes at San Salvador June 29, 1962.
Entered into force June 29, 1962.
13 UST 1358; TIAS 5095

Agreement regarding the treatment of certain textile and apparel goods under the Dominican Republic-Central America-United States free trade agreement.
Exchange of letters at Washington and San Salvador January 27, 2006.
Entered into force January 27, 2006.
TIAS

TRANSPORTATION

Agreement relating to the construction of the Inter-American highway.
Exchange of notes at Washington January 30 and February 13, 1942.
Entered into force February 13, 1942.
56 Stat. 1842; EAS 294; 7 Bevans 558; 23 UNTS 293
Amendment:
February 19 and March 19, 1951 (2 UST 1840; TIAS 2318; 134 UNTS 245)

Air transport agreement, with annexes.
Signed at San Jose May 8, 1997.
Entered into force January 3, 2000.
TIAS 12861

EQUATORIAL GUINEA

CULTURAL EXCHANGES, PROPERTY & COOPERATION

Agreement relating to the establishment of a Peace Corps program in Equatorial Guinea.
Exchange of notes at Malabo November 18, 1987.
Entered into force November 18, 1987.
TIAS

DEFENSE

Agreement concerning the provision of training related to defense articles under the United States International Military Education and Training (IMET) Program.
Exchange of notes at Malabo March 9 and 30, 1983.
Entered into force March 30, 1983.
35 UST 3889; TIAS 10891

FINANCE

Investment incentive agreement.
Signed at Washington June 11, 1998.
Entered into force June 11, 1998.
TIAS 12963

INTERNATIONAL CRIMINAL COURT

Agreement regarding the surrender of persons to the International Criminal Court.
Signed at New York September 25, 2003.
Entered into force May 6, 2004.
TIAS 04-506

POSTAL MATTERS

International express mail agreement, with detailed regulations.
Signed at Malabo and Washington April 9 and May 21, 1991.
Entered into force July 1, 1991.
TIAS 11810

TRANSPORTATION

Air transport agreement.
Signed at Washington August 7, 2014.
Entered into force August 7, 2014.
TIAS 14-807

ERITREA

On April 27, 1993, Eritrea declared independence from Ethiopia. For agreements prior to the independence of Eritrea, see ETHIOPIA.

CULTURAL EXCHANGES, PROPERTY & COOPERATION

Agreement relating to the establishment of a Peace Corps Program in Eritrea.
Exchange of notes at Asmara May 20, 1994.
Entered into force May 20, 1994.
TIAS 12103

DEFENSE

Agreement concerning the provision of training under the United States International Military Education and Training (IMET) Program.
Exchange of notes at Asmara December 28 and 31, 1993.
Entered into force December 31, 1993.
NP

Agreement regarding grants under the Foreign Assistance Act of 1961, as amended, and the furnishing of defense articles, related training and other services from the United States to Eritrea.
Exchange of notes at Asmara August 31 and September 30, 1995.
Entered into force September 30, 1995.
NP

FINANCE

Investment incentive agreement.
Signed at Washington May 4, 1994.
Entered into force July 7, 1994.
TIAS 12179

INTERNATIONAL CRIMINAL COURT

Agreement regarding the surrender of persons to the International Criminal Court.
Signed at Washington July 8, 2004.
Entered into force July 8, 2004.
TIAS 04-708

POSTAL MATTERS

International express mail agreement, with detailed regulations.
Signed at Asmara and Washington July 4 and 18, 1994.
Entered into force November 1, 1994.
NP

ESTONIA

CLAIMS & DISPUTE RESOLUTION

Treaty of arbitration.
Signed at Tallinn August 27, 1929.
Entered into force June 18, 1930.
46 Stat. 2757; TS 816; 7 Bevans 637; 102 LNTS 233

Treaty of conciliation.
Signed at Tallinn August 27, 1929.
Entered into force June 18, 1930.
46 Stat. 2760; TS 817; 7 Bevans 639; 102 LNTS 239

CULTURAL EXCHANGES, PROPERTY & COOPERATION

Agreement concerning the program of the Peace Corps of the United States in Estonia.
Signed at Tallinn February 6, 1992.
Entered into force February 6, 1992.
TIAS; 1939 UNTS 113

Agreement on the protection and preservation of certain cultural properties.
Signed at Tallinn January 16, 2003.
Entered into force July 22, 2003.
TIAS 03-722

DEFENSE

Agreement concerning the provision of training related to defense articles under the United States International Military, Education and Training (IMET) Program.
Exchange of notes at Tallinn May 18 and 25, 1992.
Entered into force May 25, 1992.
NP

Agreement regarding grants under the Foreign Assistance Act of 1961, as amended, and the furnishing of defense articles, related training or other defense services from the United States to the Republic of Estonia.
Exchange of notes at Tallinn February 11 and 12, 1993.
Entered into force February 12, 1993.
TIAS 12288

Basic exchange and cooperative agreement for topographic mapping, nautical and aeronautical charting, geodesy and geophysics, digital data and related mapping, charting and geodesy materials.
Signed at Tallinn December 7, 1993.
Entered into force December 7, 1993.
NP

Agreement concerning security measures for the protection of classified military information.
Signed at Tallinn February 23, 2000.
Entered into force February 23, 2000.
TIAS 13082; 2109 UNTS 3

Acquisition and cross-servicing agreement, with annexes.
Signed at Tallinn July 1, 2008.
Entered into force July 1, 2008.
NP

Memorandum of agreement regarding the assignment of Estonian defense personnel to the United States army, with annexes.
Signed at Washington and Tallinn July 3 and 9, 2012.
Entered into force July 9, 2012.
NP

Agreement regarding access to and use of facilities and areas located within Estonia.
Exchange of notes at Tallinn May 11 and June 9, 2015.
Entered into force June 9, 2015.
TIAS 15-609

Agreement for research, development, test, and evaluation projects, with annexes.
Signed at Washington June 22, 2016.
Entered into force June 22, 2016.
TIAS 16-622

Reciprocal defense procurement agreement.
Signed at Washington September 23, 2016.
Entered into force September 23, 2016.
TIAS 16-923

DIPLOMATIC & CONSULAR RELATIONS

Memorandum of understanding concerning diplomatic relations.
Signed at Tallinn September 4, 1991.
Entered into force September 4, 1991.
TIAS 12131; 1939 UNTS 93

EMPLOYMENT

Agreement relating to the employment on a reciprocal basis of dependents of official government employees.
Exchange of notes at Tallinn May 28 and June 19, 2012.
Entered into force June 19, 2012.
TIAS

FINANCE

Debt funding agreement.
Signed at Washington October 28, 1925; operative December 15, 1922.
Treasury Department print; 7 Bevans 613

Agreement modifying the debt funding agreement of October 28, 1925.
Signed at Washington June 11, 1932; operative July 1, 1931.
Treasury Department print; 7 Bevans 642

Investment incentive agreement.
Signed at Indianapolis October 28, 1991.
Entered into force October 28, 1991.
TIAS 12099; 1939 UNTS 101

LAW ENFORCEMENT

Treaty on mutual legal assistance in criminal matters.
Signed at Washington April 2, 1998.
Entered into force October 20, 2000.
TIAS 12940

Agreement on enhancing cooperation in preventing and combating serious crime.
Signed at Washington September 29, 2008.
Entered into force November 5, 2008.
TIAS 08-1105

Extradition treaty.
Signed at Tallinn February 8, 2006.
Entered into force April 7, 2009.
TIAS 09-407

Instrument as contemplated by Article 3(2) of the agreement on mutual legal assistance between the United States of America and the European Union signed June 25, 2003, as to the application of the treaty on mutual legal assistance in criminal matters of April 2, 1998, with annex.
Signed at Tallinn February 8, 2006.
Entered into force February 1, 2010.
TIAS 10-201.30

MARITIME MATTERS

Agreement relating to mutual recognition of ship measurement certificates.
Exchange of notes at Washington August 21, 1926, and at New York November 30, 1926.
Entered into force November 30, 1926.
47 Stat. 2597; EAS 9; 7 Bevans 635; 62 LNTS 313

POSTAL MATTERS

International express mail agreement, with detailed regulations.
Signed at Tallinn and Washington December 31, 1991, and February 10, 1992.
Entered into force March 7, 1992.
TIAS 11852

PUBLICATIONS

Agreement relating to the exchange of official publications.
Exchange of notes at Tallinn December 6, 1938.
Entered into force July 15, 1939.
53 Stat. 2059; EAS 138; 7 Bevans 647

SCIENTIFIC & TECHNICAL COOPERATION

Agreement for scientific and technological cooperation, with annexes.
Signed at Tallinn December 11, 2008.
Entered into force October 26, 2009.
TIAS 09-1026

TAXATION

Convention for the avoidance of double taxation and the prevention of fiscal evasion with respect to taxes on income.
Signed at Washington January 15, 1998.
Entered into force December 30, 1999.
TIAS 12919

Agreement to improve international tax compliance and to implement the Foreign Account Tax Compliance Act, with annexes.
Signed at Tallinn April 11, 2014.
Entered into force July 9, 2014.
TIAS 14-709

TRADE & INVESTMENT

Agreement according mutual unconditional most-favored-nation treatment in customs matters.
Exchange of notes at Washington March 2, 1925.
Entered into force August 1, 1925.
TS 722; 7 Bevans 608; 43 LNTS 289

Treaty of friendship, commerce, and consular rights, and protocol.
Signed at Washington December 23, 1925.
Entered into force May 22, 1926.
44 Stat. 2379; TS 736; 7 Bevans 620; 50 LNTS 13

Treaty for the encouragement and reciprocal protection of investment, with annex.
Signed at Washington April 19, 1994.
Entered into force February 16, 1997.
TIAS 97-216; 1987 UNTS 131

Protocol to the treaty for the encouragement and reciprocal protection of investment.
Signed at Brussels October 24, 2003.
Entered into force August 10, 2004.
TIAS 04-810

ETHIOPIA

On April 27, 1993, Eritrea announced its independence from Ethiopia. The status of the agreements listed below is under review.

CLAIMS & DISPUTE RESOLUTION

Treaty of arbitration.
Signed at Addis Ababa January 26, 1929.
Entered into force August 5, 1929.
46 Stat. 2357; TS 799; 7 Bevans 662; 101 LNTS 517

Treaty of conciliation.
Signed at Addis Ababa January 26, 1929.
Entered into force August 5, 1929.
46 Stat. 2368; TS 800; 7 Bevans 665; 101 LNTS 529

Compensation agreement, with agreed minutes.
Signed at Addis Ababa December 19, 1985.
Entered into force December 19, 1985.
TIAS 11193

CULTURAL EXCHANGES, PROPERTY & COOPERATION

Agreement concerning the program of the Peace Corps in Ethiopia.
Signed at Addis Ababa October 2, 2007.
Entered into force October 2, 2007.
TIAS 07-1002

DEFENSE

Agreement relating to mutual defense assistance.
Exchange of notes at Addis Ababa June 12 and 13, 1952.
Entered into force June 13, 1952.
3 UST 5498; TIAS 2751; 205 UNTS 17

Agreement relating to a special program of facilities assistance.
Exchange of notes at Addis Ababa December 26, 1957.
Entered into force December 26, 1957.
8 UST 2483; TIAS 3969; 307 UNTS 71.

Agreement relating to the disposition of equipment and materials no longer needed in the furtherance of the mutual defense assistance program.
Exchange of notes at Addis Ababa January 2 and 6, 1958.
Entered into force January 6, 1958.
9 UST 339; TIAS 4013; 303 UNTS 342

Agreement concerning payment to the United States of net proceeds from the sale of defense articles furnished under the military assistance program.
Exchange of notes at Addis Ababa May 13 and June 26, 1974.
Entered into force July 1, 1974.
25 UST 1437; TIAS 7872

Agreement regarding the furnishing of commodities, services and related training to assist Ethiopia's forces participating in the African Crisis Response Initiative, with attachment.
Exchange of notes at Addis Ababa February 2 and 6, 1998.
Entered into force February 6, 1998.
TIAS

Agreement relating to United States military and civilian personnel of the United States Department of Defense who may be temporarily present in Ethiopia in connection with humanitarian relief, joint exercises and training, and other agreed activities.
Exchange of notes at Addis Ababa February 21 and 27, 2002.
Entered into force February 27, 2002.
TIAS 02-227

Basic exchange and cooperation agreement concerning geospatial information, with annexes.
Signed at Springfield May 13, 2015.
Entered into force May 13, 2015.
NP

Acquisition and cross-servicing agreement, with annexes.
Signed at Stuttgart and Addis Ababa March 24 and 29, 2016.
Entered into force March 29, 2016.
NP

EDUCATION

Agreement for financing certain educational programs, with exchange of notes.
Signed at Addis Ababa December 6, 1961.
Entered into force December 6, 1961.
TIAS 4905; 12 UST 3057; 433 UNTS 231

EMPLOYMENT

Agreement relating to the employment of dependents of official government employees.
Exchange of notes at Addis Ababa August 31 and September 2, 1999.
Entered into force September 2, 1999.
TIAS 13058

ENVIRONMENT & CONSERVATION

Agreement for cooperation in the Global Learning and Observations to Benefit the Environment (GLOBE) Program.
Signed at Addis Ababa August 24, 2005.
Entered into force August 24, 2005.
TIAS 05-824

FINANCE

Agreement relating to investment guaranties.
Exchange of notes at Addis Ababa August 3, 1962.
Entered into force August 3, 1962.
13 UST 1856; TIAS 5134; 459 UNTS 79
Amendment:
March 17, 1967, and March 8, 1968 (19 UST 4725; TIAS 6469; 697 UNTS 280)

Agreement regarding the consolidation and rescheduling or refinancing of certain debts owed to, guaranteed by or insured by the United States Government and its agencies, with annexes.
Signed at Washington May 3, 1993.
Entered into force June 18, 1993.
NP

Agreement regarding the consolidation and rescheduling of certain debts owed to the United States Government and its agency, with annexes.
Signed at Addis Ababa October 9, 1997.
Entered into force December 3, 1997.
NP

Agreement regarding the consolidation and rescheduling of certain debts owed to the United States Government, with annexes.
Signed at Addis Ababa December 17, 2001.
Entered into force January 22, 2002.
NP

Agreement regarding the consolidation and reduction of certain debts owed to the United States Government, with annexes.
Signed at Addis Ababa January 28, 2003.
Entered into force March 12, 2003.
NP

Agreement regarding the cancellation of certain debts owed to, guaranteed by, or insured by the United States Government, with annexes.
Signed at Addis Ababa December 30, 2004.
Entered into force March 4, 2005.
NP

FOREIGN ASSISTANCE

Agreement for economic and technical cooperation.
Signed at Addis Ababa November 15, 1993.
Entered into force November 15, 1993.
TIAS 12167

AGENCY FOR INTERNATIONAL DEVELOPMENT

Strategic objective grant agreement for human capacity and social resiliency increased health, aids, population and nutrition program, with annex.
Signed September 10, 2004.
Entered into force September 10, 2004.
NP
Amendment:
August 8, 2006

POSTAL MATTERS

Parcel post agreement, with regulations of execution.
Signed at Addis Ababa and Washington June 3 and 15, 1967.
Entered into force September 1, 1967.
18 UST 1622; TIAS 6305; 692 UNTS 263

International express mail agreement, with detailed regulations.
Signed at Addis Ababa and Washington August 3 and September 1, 1989.
Entered into force September 15, 1989.
TIAS 11954

Memorandum of understanding concerning the operation of the INTELPOST service, with details of implementation.
Signed at Addis Ababa and Washington March 26 and July 16, 1990.
Entered into force August 15, 1990.
TIAS 11955

PROPERTY

Agreement on the principles applying to mutual aid in the prosecution of the war against aggression, and exchange of notes.
Signed at Washington August 9, 1943.
Entered into force August 9, 1943.
57 Stat. 1043; EAS 334; 7 Bevans 668; 29 UNTS 303

Agreement on lend-lease settlement.
Signed at Addis Ababa May 20, 1949.
Entered into force May 20, 1949.
63 Stat. 2446; TIAS 1931; 7 Bevans 678; 89 UNTS 99

PUBLICATIONS

Agreement relating to the exchange of official publications.
Exchange of notes at Addis Ababa November 25, 1964.
Entered into force November 25, 1964.
15 UST 2150; TIAS 5698; 532 UNTS 125

SCIENTIFIC & TECHNOLGICAL COOPERATION

Memorandum of understanding concerning scientific and technical cooperation in the earth sciences, with annexes.
Signed at Reston and Addis Ababa December 9, 2002, and August 28, 2003.
Entered into force August 28, 2003.
TIAS 03-828.1

TAXATION

Agreement to exempt from income tax, on a reciprocal basis, income derived from the international operation of aircraft and ships.
Exchange of notes at Addis Ababa October 30 and November 12, 1998.
Entered into force November 12, 1998; effective January 1, 1998.
TIAS 12996

TRADE & INVESTMENT

Treaty of amity and economic relations, and related notes.
Signed at Addis Ababa September 7, 1951.
Entered into force October 8, 1953.
4 UST 2134; TIAS 2864; 206 UNTS 41

Agreement amending the treaty of amity and economic relations of September 7, 1951, to terminate notes concerning administration of justice.
Exchange of notes at Addis Ababa September 16, 1965, and October 20, 1972.
Entered into force May 3, 1973.
24 UST 2136; TIAS 7726

TRANSPORTATION

Memorandum of agreement for the provision of assistance in developing and modernizing the civil aviation infrastructure of Ethiopia
Signed September 21 and November 24, 2005.
Entered into force November 24, 2005.
NP
Amendment:
February 3 and 10, 2011 (NP)

Air transport agreement, with annexes.
Signed at Washington May 17, 2005.
Entered into force July 21, 2006.
TIAS 06-721.1

EUROPEAN ATOMIC ENERGY COMMUNITY (EURATOM)

ATOMIC ENERGY

Agreement for cooperation in the peaceful uses of nuclear energy, with annexes, agreed minute and declaration.
Signed at Brussels November 7, 1995, and March 29, 1996.
Entered into force April 12, 1996.
TIAS

Technical exchange and cooperation arrangement in the field of nuclear-related technology research and development, with annexes.
Signed at Brussels March 6, 2003.
Entered into force March 6, 2003.
TIAS 03-306

Agreement in the field of nuclear material safeguards and security research and development, with annexes.
Signed at Vienna November 2, 2010.
Entered into force November 2, 2010.
TIAS 10-1102

Arrangement for the exchange of technical information and cooperation in the field of nuclear safety matters, with addenda and annex.
Signed at Vienna September15, 2015.
Entered into force September 15, 2015.
TIAS 15-915.4

EUROPEAN COMMUNITY

See EUROPEAN UNION

EUROPEAN ORGANIZATION FOR THE EXPLOITATION OF METEOROLOGICAL SATELLITES (EUMETSAT)

SCIENTIFIC & TECHNICAL COOPERATION

Agreement on an initial joint polar-orbiting operational satellite system, with annex.
Signed at Washington November 19, 1998.
Entered into force November 19, 1998.
TIAS 12998

Agreement on access to images and meteorological data distribution material from the EUMETSAT geostationary meteorological satellites.
Signed at Darmstadt July 19, 2000.
Entered into force July 19, 2000.
TIAS 13105

Agreement on joint transition activities regarding polar-orbiting operational environmental satellite systems, with annex.
Signed at Darmstadt June 24, 2003.
Entered into force June 24, 2003.
TIAS 03-624

Amendment:
January 7 and 20, 2005 (TIAS 03-624)

Agreement on access to images and meteorological data distribution material from the EUMETSAT METEOSAT satellites.
Signed at Darmstadt July 1, 2008.
Entered into force July 1, 2008.
TIAS 08-701

Memorandum of understanding for cooperation on the Global Precipitation Measurement Mission.
Signed at Darmstadt and Washington June 28 and July 26, 2013.
Entered into force July 26, 2013.
TIAS 13-726

EUROPEAN ORGANIZATION FOR NUCLEAR RESEARCH (CERN)

ATOMIC ENERGY

Agreement concerning scientific and technical cooperation on Large Hadron Collider activities.
Signed at Washington December 8, 1997.
Entered into force December 8, 1997.
TIAS

Experiments Protocol relating to the agreement of December 8, 1997, concerning scientific and technical cooperation on Large Hadron Collider activities.
Signed at Geneva December 19, 1997.
Entered into force December 19, 1997.
TIAS

Accelerator Protocol relating to the agreement of December 8, 1997, concerning scientific and technical cooperation on Large Hadron Collider activities.
Signed at Geneva December 19, 1997.
Entered into force December 19, 1997.
TIAS

Agreement concerning scientific and technical cooperation in nuclear and particle physics.
Signed at Washington May 7, 2015.
Entered into force May 7, 2015.
TIAS 15-507

Neutrino Protocol I to agreement of May 7, 2015 concerning scientific and technical cooperation in nuclear and particle physics.
Signed at Geneva December 18, 2015.
Entered into force December 18, 2015.
TIAS 15-1218

Nuclear Physics Experiments Protocol I to agreement of May 7, 2015 concerning scientific and technical cooperation in nuclear and particle physics.
Signed at Geneva December 18, 2015.
Entered into force December 18, 2015.
TIAS 15-1218.1

Experiments Protocol II to agreement of May 7, 2015 concerning scientific and technical cooperation in nuclear and particle physics.
Signed at Geneva December 18, 2015.
Entered into force December 18, 2015.
TIAS 15-1218.2

Accelerator Protocol III to agreement of May 7, 2015 concerning scientific and technical cooperation in nuclear and particle physics.
Signed at Geneva December 18, 2015.
Entered into force December 18, 2015.
TIAS 15-1218.3

EUROPEAN POLICE OFFICE

LAW ENFORCEMENT

Agreement to enhance cooperation in preventing, detecting, suppressing, and investigating serious forms of international crime, with annex.
Signed at Brussels December 6, 2001.
Entered into force December 7, 2001.
TIAS 01-1207

Supplemental agreement on the exchange of personal data and related information, with exchange of letters.
Signed at Copenhagen December 20, 2002.
Entered into force December 21, 2002.
TIAS 01-1207

EUROPEAN SOUTHERN OBSERVATORY

SPACE

Agreement concerning the joint construction and operation of the Atacama Large Millimeter Array (ALMA), with annexes.
Signed at Arlington February 7 and 25, 2003.
Entered into force February 25, 2003.
TIAS 03-225

EUROPEAN SPACE AGENCY

SCIENTIFIC & TECHNICAL COOPERATION

Memorandum of understanding for cooperation in the use of U.S. Landsat data, with annexes.
Signed at Reston and Paris June 18 and July 17, 2012.
Entered into force July 17, 2012.
TIAS 12-717

SPACE

Memorandum of understanding for a cooperative program concerning design (Phase B) of a permanently manned space station.
Signed at Paris June 3, 1985.
Entered into force June 3, 1985.
TIAS 11351

Memorandum of understanding concerning the Solar Terrestrial Science Program, with related exchange of letters.
Signed at Washington November 30, 1989.
Entered into force November 30, 1989.
TIAS 12216

Memorandum of understanding concerning cooperation on the civil international space station.
Signed at Washington January 29, 1998.
Entered into force November 27, 2007.
TIAS

Agreement concerning network and operations cross-support.
Signed at Washington March 21, 2007.
Entered into force March 21, 2007.
TIAS 07-321

Memorandum of understanding concerning the James Webb space telescope.
Signed at Paris June 18, 2007.
Entered into force June 18, 2007.
TIAS 07-618.1

Agreement concerning cooperation on the robotic exploration of Mars.
Effected by exchange of letters at Paris and Washington June 22 and 28, 2010.
Entered into force June 28, 2010.
TIAS 10-628

Memorandum of understanding concerning the solar orbiter mission.
Signed at Paris and Washington February 23 and March 6, 2012.
Entered into force March 6, 2012.
TIAS 12-306

Memorandum of understanding concerning the 2016 Exomars Mission.
Signed at Paris and Washington April 14 and 29, 2014.
Entered into force April 29, 2014.
TIAS 14-429

EUROPEAN UNION

In a Verbal Note dated November 27, 2009, that was transmitted to the Government of the United States of America, the Council of the European Union and the Commission of the European Communities stated in part:

The Treaty of Lisbon amending the Treaty on European Union and the Treaty establishing the European Community will enter into force on 1 December 2009. …[A]s from that date all agreements between your country and the European Community/European Union, and all commitments made by the European Community/European Union to your country and made by your country to the European Community/European Union, will be assumed by the European Union.

CIVIL AFFAIRS, EMERGENCIES & DEFENSE

Agreement on the participation of the United States of America in the European Union rule of law mission in Kosovo, EULEX Kosovo, with annex.
Signed at Brussels October 22, 2008.
Entered into force October 22, 2008.
TIAS 08-1022

Agreement on the participation of the United States of America in the European Union crisis management operations.
Signed at Washington May 17, 2011.
Entered into force June 1, 2011.
TIAS 11-601

DEFENSE

Agreement on the security of classified information.
Signed at Washington April 30, 2007.
Entered into force April 30, 2007.
TIAS 07-430.1

Acquisition and cross-servicing agreement, with annexes.
Signed at Brussels December 6, 2016.
Entered into force December 6, 2016.
NP

ENERGY

Agreement on the coordination of energy-efficiency labeling programs for office equipment.
Signed at Brussels and Washington December 10, 2012 and January 18, 2013.
Entered into force February 20, 2013.
TIAS 13-220

LAW ENFORCEMENT

Agreement on precursors and chemical substances frequently used in the illicit manufacture of narcotic drugs or psychotropic substances, with annexes and exchange of letters.
Signed at The Hague May 28, 1997.
Entered into force July 1, 1997.
TIAS

Agreement on customs cooperation and mutual assistance in customs matters.
Done at The Hague May 28, 1997.
Entered into force August 1, 1997.
TIAS 12862

Agreement on mutual legal assistance, with explanatory note.
Signed at Washington June 25, 2003.
Entered into force February 1, 2010.
TIAS 10-201.1

Agreement on extradition, with explanatory note.
Signed at Washington June 25, 2003.
Entered into force February 1, 2010.
TIAS 10-201

Agreement on intensifying and broadening the agreement on customs cooperation and mutual assistance in customs matters to include cooperation on container security and related matters, with annex.
Signed at Washington April 22, 2004.
Entered into force April 22, 2004.
TIAS 04-422

Agreement on the processing and transfer of financial messaging data from the European Union to the United States for the purposes of the terrorist finance tracking program.
Signed at Brussels June 28, 2010.
Entered into force August 1, 2010.
TIAS 10-801

Agreement on the processing and transfer of passenger name record (PNR) to the United States Department of Homeland Security, with annex.
Signed at Brussels December 14, 2011.
Entered into force July 1, 2012.
TIAS 12-701

MARITIME MATTERS

Agreement on the promotion, provision and use of Galileo and GPS satellite-based navigation systems and related applications.
Signed at Newmarket-on-Fergus June 26, 2004.
Entered into force December 12, 2011.
TIAS

SCIENTIFIC & TECHNICAL COOPERATION

Agreement for scientific and technological cooperation, with annex.
Signed at Washington December 5, 1997.
Entered into force October 14, 1998.
TIAS 12910

Amendments and Extensions:
October 8, 2004 (TIAS 04-1008)
May 15 and July 6, 2009 (TIAS 04-1008)
April 28, 2014 and June 12, 2014 (TIAS 14-613)

TRADE & INVESTMENT

Joint declaration on commercial relations.
Signed at Geneva March 7, 1962.
Entered into force March 7, 1962.
13 UST 958; TIAS 5033; 445 UNTS 195

Agreement regulating certain trade in cheese.
Exchange of letters at Brussels December 20, 1974, and January 14, 1975.
Entered into force January 14, 1975.
26 UST 1773; TIAS 8135; 1006 UNTS 85

Agreement concerning exports of pasta, with settlement, annex and related letter.
Exchange of letters at Brussels and Washington August 12 and September 15, 1987.
Entered into force September 15, 1987.
TIAS

Agreement regarding the application of competition laws.
Signed at Washington September 23, 1991.
Entered into force September 23, 1991.
TIAS

Agreement on the mutual recognition of certain distilled spirits/spirit drinks, with related exchange of letters.
Exchange of letters at Brussels and Washington March 15 and 25, 1994.
Entered into force March 25, 1994.
TIAS

Agreement for the conclusion of negotiations between the European Community and the United States under Article XXIV.6, with annexes and exchanges of letters.
Signed at Geneva July 22, 1996.
Entered into force July 22, 1996; effective December 30, 1995.
NP

Agreement on mutual recognition, with annexes.
Signed at London May 18, 1998.
Entered into force December 1, 1998.
TIAS

Agreement on the application of positive comity principles in the enforcement of their competition laws.
Signed at Brussels and Washington June 3 and 4, 1998.
Entered into force June 4, 1998.
TIAS 12958

Agreement on sanitary measures to protect public and animal health in trade in live animals and animal products.
Signed at Brussels July 20, 1999.
Entered into force August 1, 1999.
TIAS

Proces-verbal amending the proces-verbal of July 15, 1997, on rules of origin for certain textile products.
Signed at Geneva August 16, 1999.
Entered into force August 16, 1999.
NP

Agreement on the mutual recognition of certificates of conformity for marine equipment.
Signed at Washington February 27, 2004.
Entered into force July 1, 2004.
TIAS

Agreement on matters related to trade in wine.
Exchange of letters at Brussels November 23, 2005.
Entered into force November 23, 2005.
TIAS

Agreement on trade in wine, with annexes.
Signed at London March 10, 2006.
Entered into force March 10, 2006.
TIAS 06-310

Agreement pursuant to Article XXIV.6 and Article XXVIII of the General Agreement on Tariffs and Trade (GATT), 1994 relating to the modification of concessions in the schedules of the Czech Republic, Estonia, Cyprus, Latvia, Lithuania, Hungary, Malta, Poland, Slovenia and Slovakia in the course of their accession to the European Union, with annex.
Effected by exchange of letters at Geneva March 22, 2006.
Entered into force March 22, 2006.
NP

Memorandum of understanding regarding the importation of beef from animals not treated with certain growth-promoting hormones and increased duties applied by the United States to certain products of the European Communities.
Signed May 13, 2009.
Entered into force May 13, 2009.
TIAS 09-513

TRANSPORTATION

Agreement on cooperation in the regulation of civil aviation safety, with annexes.
Signed at Brussels June 30, 2008.
Entered into force May 1, 2011.
TIAS 11-501

Memorandum of cooperation relating to technical assistance in developing and modernizing civil aviation security infrastructure, with annex.
Signed at Budapest March 3, 2011.
Entered into force October 21, 2011.
NP

EUROPEAN UNION'S JUDICIAL COOPERATION UNIT (EUROJUST)

LAW ENFORCEMENT

Agreement regarding terrorism and transnational crime.
Signed at Washington November 6, 2006.
Entered into force December 19, 2006.
TIAS 06-1219

F

FIJI

On October 10, 1970, Fiji became an independent state. In a note dated October 10, 1970, to the Secretary-General of the United Nations, the Prime Minister of Fiji made a statement reading in part as follows:

[M]any treaty rights and obligations of the Government of the United Kingdom in respect to Fiji were succeeded to by Fiji upon independence by virtue of customary international law.... It is desired that it be presumed that each treaty has been legally succeeded to by Fiji and that action be based on this presumption until a decision is reached that it should be regarded as having lapsed. Should the Government of Fiji be of the opinion that it has legally succeeded to a treaty, and wishes to terminate the operation of the treaty, it will in due course give notice of termination in the terms thereof.

CULTURAL EXCHANGES, PROPERTY & COOPERATION

Agreement relating to the establishment of a Peace Corps program in Fiji.
Exchange of notes at Suva June 25, 1968.
Entered into force June 25, 1968.
19 UST 5208; TIAS 6515; 648 UNTS 65

Agreement continuing in force the agreement of June 25, 1968, relating to the establishment of a Peace Corps program in Fiji.
Exchange of notes at Suva and Washington April 25 and June 27, 1972.
Entered into force June 27, 1972.
23 UST 1156; TIAS 7377

DEFENSE

Agreement concerning the provision of training related to defense articles under the United States International Military Education and Training (IMET) Program.
Exchange of notes at Suva November 18, 1985, and February 14, 1986.
Entered into force February 14, 1986.
TIAS 11105

DIPLOMATIC & CONSULAR RELATIONS

Consular convention between the United States and the United Kingdom.
Signed at Washington June 6, 1951.
Entered into force September 7, 1952.
3 UST 3426; TIAS 2494; 165 UNTS 121

Agreement continuing in force between the United States and Fiji the consular convention of June 6, 1951 (3 UST 3426) between the United States and the United Kingdom.
Exchange of notes at Suva and Washington October 16 and December 12, 1972.
Entered into force December 12, 1972.
23 UST 3770; TIAS 7525

EMPLOYMENT

Agreement concerning the employment of dependents of official government employees.
Exchange of notes at Suva June 20 and November 25, 2003.
Entered into force November 25, 2003.
TIAS 03-1125

ENVIRONMENT & CONSERVATION

Agreement for cooperation in the Global Learning and Observations to Benefit the Environment (GLOBE) Program, with appendices.
Signed at Suva January 28, 1997.
Entered into force January 28, 1997.
TIAS 12827

FINANCE

Agreement relating to investment guaranties.
Exchange of notes at Suva December 30, 1975, and January 9, 1976.
Entered into force January 9, 1976.
27 UST 1826; TIAS 8281

INTELLECTUAL PROPERTY

Declaration affording reciprocal protection to trade-marks.
Signed at London October 24, 1877.
Entered into force October 24, 1877.
20 Stat. 703; TS 138; 12 Bevans 198

Agreement continuing in force between the United States and Fiji the declaration affording reciprocal protection to trade-marks of October 24, 1877 (20 Stat. 703) by the United States and the United Kingdom.
Exchange of notes at Suva and at Washington August 30 and November 4, 1971.
Entered into force November 4, 1971.
22 UST 1891; TIAS 7232

INTERNATIONAL CRIMINAL COURT

Agreement regarding the surrender of persons to the International Criminal Court.
Signed at Suva December 17, 2003.
Entered into force December 17, 2003.
TIAS 03-1217

LAW ENFORCEMENT

Extradition treaty between the United States and the United Kingdom.
Signed at London December 22, 1931.
Entered into force June 24, 1935.
47 Stat. 2122; TS 849; 12 Bevans 482; 163 LNTS 59

Agreement continuing in force between the United States and Fiji the extradition treaty of December 22, 1931 (47 Stat. 2122) between the United States and the United Kingdom.
Exchange of notes at Suva and Washington July 14, 1972, and August 17, 1973.
Entered into force August 17, 1973.
24 UST 1965; TIAS 7707

POSTAL MATTERS

Parcel post agreement, with detailed regulations of execution.
Signed at Washington November 15, 1938, and at Suva January 10, 1939.
Operative January 2, 1939.
53 Stat. 2031; Post Office Department print; 196 LNTS 185

Agreement providing for parcel post insurance.
Signed at Suva April 12 and at Washington April 22, 1965.
Entered into force July 1, 1965.
16 UST 850; TIAS 5822; 685 UNTS 23

Express mail service agreement, with detailed regulations.
Signed at Suva and Arlington August 3 and December 21, 2001.
Entered into force March 1, 2002.
NP

PROPERTY

Convention between the United States and the United Kingdom relating to tenure and disposition of real and personal property.
Signed at Washington March 2, 1899.
Entered into force August 7, 1900; applicable to Fiji February 9, 1901.
31 Stat. 1939; TS 146; 12 Bevans 246

Supplementary convention relating to the tenure and disposition of real and personal property of March 2, 1899.
Signed at Washington May 27, 1936.
Entered into force March 10, 1941.
55 Stat. 1101; TS 964; 5 Bevans 140; 203 LNTS 367

Agreement continuing in force between the United States and Fiji the conventions of March 2, 1899, and May 27, 1936, between the United States and the United Kingdom relating to tenure and disposition of real and personal property.
Exchange of notes at Suva and at Washington November 2 and December 9, 1971.
Entered into force December 9, 1971.
22 UST 1806; TIAS 7222

TAXATION

Agreement for the reciprocal exemption with respect to taxes on income from the international operation of ships and aircraft.
Exchange of notes at Suva June 19 and August 12, 1996.
Entered into force August 12, 1996; effective January 1, 1996.
TIAS

TELECOMMUNICATION

Agreement relating to the reciprocal granting of authorizations to permit licensed amateur radio operators of either country to operate their stations in the other country.
Exchange of notes at London November 26, 1965.
Entered into force November 26, 1965; applicable to Fiji December 11, 1969.
16 UST 2047; TIAS 5941; 561 UNTS 193

Agreement extending to certain territories the application of the agreement of November 26, 1965, relating to the reciprocal granting of authorizations to permit licensed amateur radio operators of either country to operate their stations in the other country.
Exchange of notes at London December 11, 1969.
Entered into force December 11, 1969.
20 UST 4089; TIAS 6800; 732 UNTS 334

Agreement continuing in force between the United States and Fiji the agreement of November 25, 1965, between the United States and the United Kingdom relating to the reciprocal granting of authorizations to permit licensed amateur radio operators of either country to operate their stations in the other country.
Exchange of notes at Suva and Washington July 10 and August 14, 1972.
Entered into force August 14, 1972.
23 UST 1334; TIAS 7417

TRANSPORTATION

Air transport agreement.
Signed at Suva October 1, 1979.
Entered into force provisionally October 1, 1979; definitively October 11, 1979.
32 UST 3747; TIAS 9917
Amendment:
October 25, 1985 (TIAS 11143)
July 10 and August 19, 1996 (TIAS 12792)

FINLAND

ATOMIC ENERGY

Arrangement for the exchange of technical information and cooperation in nuclear safety matters.
Signed at Vienna September 28, 2016.
Entered into force September 28, 2016.
TIAS 16-928

CLAIMS & DISPUTE RESOLUTION

Treaty of arbitration.
Signed at Washington June 7, 1928.
Entered into force January 14, 1929.
45 Stat. 2724; TS 768; 7 Bevans 711; 87 LNTS 9

Treaty of conciliation.
Signed at Washington June 7, 1928.
Entered into force January 14, 1929.
45 Stat. 2726; TS 769; 7 Bevans 713; 87 LNTS 15

CONSULAR AFFAIRS

Agreement relating to the maximum validity of visas for four years and the abolition of visa fees for certain classes of nonimmigrant visas.*
Exchange of notes at Helsinki July 7, August 26, and December 14, 1955.
Entered into force December 14, 1955; operative January 1, 1956.
9 UST 1175; TIAS 4102; 335 UNTS 263

Amendment:
February 15 and 20, 1956 (9 UST 1179; TIAS 4102; 335 UNTS 272)

Note:
* The status of this agreement is under review.

Agreement relating to the waiver of visa requirements for nonimmigrants.
Exchange of notes at Washington August 15, 1958.
Entered into force August 15, 1958; operative September 15, 1958.
9 UST 1183; TIAS 4103; 314 UNTS 43

DEFENSE

Convention regulating military obligations of persons having dual nationality.
Signed at Helsinki January 27, 1939.
Entered into force October 3, 1939.
54 Stat. 1712; TS 953; 7 Bevans 747; 201 LNTS 197

Agreement concerning exchange of research and development information, with appendix.
Signed at Washington and Helsinki September 11 and October 5, 1995.
Entered into force October 5, 1995.
TIAS 12289

Amendment:
May 7 and 25, 2010 (TIAS 10-1004)

Basic exchange and cooperative agreement concerning geospatial information and services cooperation.
Signed at Helsinki August 30, 2000.
Entered into force August 30, 2000.
NP

Memorandum of agreement regarding foreign liaison officers.
Signed at Helsinki and Norfolk February 8 and 13, 2004.
Entered into force February 13, 2004.
NP

Amendments:
February 12, 2009
January 15 and 23, 2014

Memorandum of understanding concerning air force exercises and activities in Finland.
Signed March 31 and April 21, 2005.
Entered into force April 21, 2005.
TIAS

Acquisition and cross-servicing agreement, with annexes.
Signed at Helsinki and Stuttgart June 18 and July 9, 2008.
Entered into force October 16, 2008.
NP

Memorandum of understanding concerning reciprocal defense procurement.
Signed at Helsinki and Washington June 13 and August 5, 2008.
Entered into force October 3, 2009.
TIAS 09-1003

Agreement for research, development, testing, and evaluation projects, with annexes.
Signed at Washington and Helsinki May 2 and August 26, 2011.
Entered into force May 27, 2012.
TIAS

Agreement concerning security measures for the protection of classified information, with appendix.
Signed at Helsinki June 27, 2012.
Entered into force May 1, 2013.
TIAS 13-501

Memorandum of agreement regarding the assignment of Finnish Defense Forces liaison officers, with annexes.
Signed at Mons and Stuttgart January 11 and 22, 2016.
Entered into force January 22, 2016.
NP

EDUCATION

Agreement for financing certain educational exchange programs.
Signed at Helsinki July 2, 1952.
Entered into force July 2, 1952.
3 UST 4126; TIAS 2555; 165 UNTS 203

Amendments:
November 30, 1956 (7 UST 3255; TIAS 3704; 263 UNTS 418)
May 30, 1959 (10 UST 1043; TIAS 4241; 346 UNTS 334)
November 14, 1960 (11 UST 2351; TIAS 4614; 400 UNTS 382)
October 29, 1975 (26 UST 2898; TIAS 8196)

EMPLOYMENT

Agreement relating to the employment of dependents of official government employees.
Exchange of notes at Helsinki March 1 and 12, 1996.
Entered into force April 11, 1996.
TIAS 12734; 1927 UNTS 77

ENVIRONMENT & CONSERVATION

Agreement for cooperation in the Global Learning and Observations to Benefit the Environment (GLOBE) Program, with appendices.
Signed at Helsinki March 23, 1995.
Entered into force March 23, 1995.
TIAS 12621

FINANCE

Debt funding agreement.
Signed at Washington May 1, 1923.
Operative December 15, 1922.
Treasury Department print; 7 Bevans 688

Agreement modifying the debt funding agreement of May 1, 1923.
Signed at Washington May 23, 1932.
Operative July 1, 1931.
Treasury Department print; 7 Bevans 716

Agreement relating to investment guaranties under section 413(b)(4) of the Mutual Security Act of 1954, as amended.
Exchange of notes at Helsinki July 22, 1959.
Entered into force July 22, 1959.
10 UST 1317; TIAS 4275; 354 UNTS 39

LAW ENFORCEMENT

Extradition treaty.
Signed at Helsinki June 11, 1976.
Entered into force May 11, 1980.
31 UST 944; TIAS 9626; 1203 UNTS 165

Agreement regarding mutual assistance in customs matters.
Signed at Washington January 5, 1988.
Entered into force July 13, 1989.
TIAS 12116; 1557 UNTS 155

Protocol to the extradition treaty of June 11, 1976, with annex.
Signed at Brussels December 16, 2004.
Entered into force February 1, 2010.
TIAS 10-201.7

Treaty on certain aspects of mutual legal assistance in criminal matters, with annex.
Signed at Brussels December 16, 2004.
Entered into force February 1, 2010.
TIAS 10-201.31

Agreement on enhancing cooperation in preventing and combating crime.
Signed at Washington March 17, 2010.
Entered into force August 1, 2012, with the exception of Articles 7 through 9, that may enter into force in the future under conditions specified in Article 24.
TIAS 12-801

MARITIME MATTERS

Agreement relating to jurisdiction over vessels utilizing the Louisiana Offshore Oil Port.
Exchange of notes at Washington December 1, 1982.
Entered into force December 1, 1982.
TIAS 10615; 2000 UNTS 451

POSTAL MATTERS

Parcel post convention.
Signed at Helsingfors and Washington September 1 and 23, 1932.
Operative August 1, 1932.
47 Stat. 2169; Post Office Department print

International express mail agreement, with detailed regulations.
Signed at Washington November 19, 1984.
Entered into force February 7, 1985.
TIAS 11010; 2022 UNTS 9

Memorandum of understanding concerning the operation of the INTELPOST field trial, with details of implementation.
Signed at Helsinki and Washington August 23 and September 23, 1985.
Entered into force September 23, 1985.
TIAS 11158

PRIVATE INTERNATIONAL LAW

Agreement for the enforcement of maintenance support obligations.
Signed at Helsinki April 3, 2006.
Entered into force September 29, 2007.
TIAS 07-929

PUBLICATIONS

Agreement relating to the exchange of official publications.
Exchange of notes at Washington December 28 and 30, 1938.
Entered into force December 30, 1938; operative January 1, 1939.
53 Stat. 2071; EAS 139; 7 Bevans 744; 195 LNTS 419

SCIENTIFIC AND TECHNICAL COOPERATION

Agreement relating to scientific and technological cooperation, with annexes.
Signed at Washington May 16, 1995.
Entered into force August 27, 1995.
TIAS 12647
Amendment:
October 16, 2012 (TIAS 14-421)

Memorandum of understanding concerning scientific and technical cooperation in the earth sciences.
Signed at Reston and Espoo March 30 and May 3, 2000.
Entered into force May 3, 2000.
TIAS

SOCIAL SECURITY

Agreement on social security, with administrative arrangement.
Signed at Helsinki June 3, 1991.
Entered into force November 1, 1992.
TIAS 12105; 1705 UNTS 153

TAXATION

Convention for the avoidance of double taxation and the prevention of fiscal evasion with respect to taxes on estates and inheritances.
Signed at Washington March 3, 1952.
Entered into force December 18, 1952.
3 UST 4464; TIAS 2595; 177 UNTS 141

Agreement for relief from double taxation on earnings from operation of ships and aircraft.
Exchange of notes at Helsinki April 8 and 22, 1988.
Entered into force April 22, 1988.
TIAS 11576

Convention for the avoidance of double taxation and the prevention of fiscal evasion with respect to taxes on income and on capital.*
Signed at Helsinki September 21, 1989.
Entered into force December 30, 1990.
TIAS 12101
Note:
* With an understanding.

Protocol amending the convention of September 21, 1989, for the avoidance of double taxation and the prevention of fiscal evasion with respect to taxes on income and on capital.
Signed at Helsinki May 31, 2006.
Entered into force December 28, 2007.
TIAS 07-1228.1

Agreement to improve international tax compliance and to implement the Foreign Account Tax Compliance Act, with annexes.
Signed at Helsinki March 5, 2014.
Entered into force February 20, 2015.
TIAS 15-220

TELECOMMUNICATION

Agreement relating to the reciprocal granting of authorizations to permit licensed amateur radio operators of either country to operate their stations in the other country.
Exchange of notes at Helsinki December 15 and 27, 1967.
Entered into force December 27, 1967.
18 UST 3153; TIAS 6406; 697 UNTS 55

TRADE & INVESTMENT

Treaty of friendship, commerce, and consular rights, and protocol.
Signed at Washington February 13, 1934.
Entered into force August 10, 1934.
49 Stat. 2659; TS 868; 7 Bevans 718; 152 LNTS 45

Protocol modifying article IV of the treaty of friendship, commerce, and consular rights of February 13, 1934.
Signed at Washington December 4, 1952.
Entered into force September 24, 1953.
4 UST 2047; TIAS 2861; 205 UNTS 149

Protocol to the treaty of friendship, commerce and consular rights of February 13, 1934, as modified.
Signed at Washington July 1, 1991.
Entered into force December 1, 1992.
TIAS

TRANSPORTATION

Air transport agreement.*
Signed at Helsinki March 29, 1949.
Entered into force April 28, 1949.
63 Stat. 2550; TIAS 1945; 7 Bevans 752; 55 UNTS 59
Amendment:
June 9, 1995 (TIAS 12657; 2142 UNTS 23)

Related Agreement:
May 12, 1980 (32 UST 2368; TIAS 9845)

Note:
* This agreement is suspended for the duration of provisional application of the U.S. – E.U. Air Transport Agreement signed April 25 and 30, 2007.

Agreement relating to the reciprocal acceptance of certificates of airworthiness for imported civil glider aircraft and civil aircraft appliances.
Exchange of notes at Washington March 7, 1974.
Entered into force March 7, 1974.
25 UST 262; TIAS 7795; 944 UNTS 165

Memorandum of understanding concerning cooperation in the field of transportation.
Signed at Washington July 23, 1981.
Entered into force July 23, 1981.
33 UST 3258; TIAS 10222

Project agreement for cooperation in the field of icebreaking technology.
Signed at Washington July 23, 1981.
Entered into force July 23, 1981.
33 UST 3261; TIAS 10223
Extension:
May 9 and June 13, 1983 (35 UST 1320; TIAS 10731; 1607 UNTS 540)

Memorandum of understanding on highway transportation technology exchange.
Signed at Madrid May 19, 1993.
Entered into force May 19, 1993.
TIAS 12498

Agreement for promotion of air safety.
Signed at Helsinki November 2, 2000.
Entered into force July 8, 2001.
TIAS 13124; 2160 UNTS 195

FOOD AND AGRICULTURE ORGANIZATION

AGRICULTURE

Framework agreement regarding the development of a viable and sustainable global agricultural system.
Signed at Washington March 14, 2007.
Entered into force March 14, 2007.
TIAS 07-314

CULTURAL EXCHANGES, PROPERTY & COOPERATION

Agreement concerning the Peace Corps.
Exchange of notes at Rome March 23 and 29, 1962.
Entered into force March 29, 1962.
13 UST 1391; TIAS 5101; 454 UNTS 13

FOREIGN ASSISTANCE

Agreement relating to a Fund-in-Trust grant to the FAO to supplement activities under the Off-Shore Fishery Development Project for Viet Nam.
Exchange of notes at Washington and Rome May 26, 1967.
Entered into force May 26, 1967.
18 UST 1618; TIAS 6304

FRANCE

ATOMIC ENERGY

Agreement for cooperation in the operation of atomic weapons systems for mutual defense purposes.
Signed at Paris July 27, 1961.
Entered into force October 9, 1961.
12 UST 1423; TIAS 4867; 433 UNTS 29
Amendment:
July 22, 1985 (TIAS 11208; 2145 UNTS 20)

Agreement concerning the retransfer of nuclear power light water reactor technology, with annexes and exchange of notes.
Signed at Washington January 22, 1981.
Entered into force March 13, 1981.
33 UST 968; TIAS 10080

Agreement concerning cooperation on the application of non-proliferation assurances to material, nuclear material, equipment and facilities transferred from France to Taiwan for use in Taiwan's nuclear research and light water nuclear power reactor programs, with annex and related exchanges of notes.
Exchange of notes at Washington January 19, 1993.
Entered into force January 19, 1993.
TIAS

Agreement for cooperation in advanced nuclear reactor science and technology, with annex.
Signed at Vienna September 18, 2000.
Entered into force September 18, 2000.
TIAS 00-918
Amendment:
January 24, 2006 (TIAS 00-918)

Agreement for the exchange of classified information relating to civil nuclear facilities and materials.
Signed at Washington and Paris September 17 and October 16, 2008.
Entered into force October 16, 2008.
TIAS 08-1016

Arrangement for the exchange of technical information and cooperation in nuclear safety matters. With addenda and annex.
Signed at Vienna September 16, 2013.
Entered into force September 16, 2013.
TIAS 13-916

CLAIMS & DISPUTE RESOLUTION

Treaty to facilitate the settlement of disputes.
Signed at Washington September 15, 1914.
Entered into force January 22, 1915.
38 Stat. 1887; TS 609; 7 Bevans 883

Treaty of arbitration and exchange of notes dated March 1 and 5, 1928.
Signed at Washington February 6, 1928.
Entered into force April 22, 1929.
46 Stat. 2269; TS 785; 7 Bevans 968; 91 LNTS 323

Agreement respecting maritime claims and litigation.
Signed at Washington March 14, 1949.
Entered into force March 14, 1949.
63 Stat. 2499; TIAS 1935; 7 Bevans 1300; 84 UNTS 225

Agreement relating to the procedure for the settlement of claims of French nationals who were prisoners of war of United States forces during World War II.
Exchange of notes at Paris June 4, October 15 and December 6, 1951; and January 17 and February 2, 1952.
Entered into force February 2, 1952.
5 UST 622; TIAS 2951; 247 UNTS 223

Agreement concerning payments for certain losses suffered during World War II, with annexes.
Signed at Washington January 18, 2001.
Entered into force February 5, 2001.
TIAS 01-205; 2156 UNTS 281
Amendments:
May 30 and 31, 2002 (TIAS 01-205)
February 21, 2006 (TIAS 01-205)

Agreement on compensation for certain victims of Holocaust-related deportation from France who are not covered by French programs, with annex and exchange of rectifying notes.
Signed at Washington December 8, 2014.
Entered into force November 1, 2015.
TIAS 15-1101

CONSULAR AFFAIRS

Reciprocal agreement relating to visa fees for nonimmigrants.*
Exchanges of notes at Washington August 19 and September 4, 5, and 16, 1947.
Entered into force September 16, 1947; operative October 1, 1947.
61 Stat. 3776; TIAS 1721; 7 Bevans 1210; 84 UNTS 19
Note:
* The status of this agreement is under review. Applicable to all territories.

Arrangement for the waiver by France of visa requirements for United States citizens visiting Metropolitan France and certain French territories, and for the granting by the United States of gratis passport visas to French citizens as nonimmigrants.*
Exchange of notes at Paris March 16 and 31, 1949.
Entered into force March 31, 1949.
63 Stat. 2737; TIAS 1987; 7 Bevans 1311; 84 UNTS 283
Note:
* The status of this agreement is under review.

Agreement relating to the reciprocal issuance of nonimmigrant visas for treaty traders and treaty investors.
Exchange of notes at Paris September 1 and 21, 1961.
Entered into force September 21, 1961; operative October 21, 1961.
12 UST 3197; TIAS 4924; 433 UNTS 243

CULTURAL EXCHANGES, PROPERTY & COOPERATION

Agreement relating to the erection of war memorials in national cemeteries by American citizens.
Exchange of notes at Paris May 24, July 11 and July 12, 1924.
Entered into force July 12, 1924.
7 Bevans 942
Extension:
August 7 and October 19, 1946

Agreement concerning the interment in France and in territories of the French Union, or removal to the United States, of the bodies of American soldiers killed in the war of 1939–1945.
Signed at Paris October 1, 1947.
Entered into force October 1, 1947.
61 Stat. 3767; TIAS 1720; 7 Bevans 1215; 148 UNTS 303

Agreement relating to the grant of plots of land located in France for the creation of permanent military cemeteries or the construction of war memorials, with annexes.
Signed at Paris March 19, 1956.
Entered into force March 19, 1956.
7 UST 561; TIAS 3537; 275 UNTS 37

DEFENSE

Agreement relating to the fulfillment of military obligations during the wars of 1914–1918 and 1939–1945 by persons with dual nationality.
Exchange of notes at Paris December 22, 1948.
Entered into force December 22, 1948.
62 Stat. 3621; TIAS 1876; 7 Bevans 1294; 67 UNTS 38
Amendment:
November 18 and December 31, 1952 (3 UST 5345; TIAS 2741; 185 UNTS 396)

Mutual defense assistance agreement.
Signed at Washington January 27, 1950.
Entered into force January 27, 1950.
1 UST 34; TIAS 2012; 80 UNTS 171

Agreement regarding the establishment of an air depot at Deols-La Martinerie.
Signed at Paris February 27, 1951.
Entered into force February 27, 1951.
17 UST 1865; TIAS 6130; 674 UNTS 55

Agreement relating to the assurances required by the Mutual Security Act of 1951.
Exchange of notes at Paris January 5, 1952.
Entered into force January 5, 1952.
3 UST 4559; TIAS 2606; 181 UNTS 177

Agreement regarding certain air bases and facilities in Metropolitan France placed at the disposition of the United States Air Force.
Signed at Paris October 4, 1952.
Entered into force October 4, 1952.
17 UST 1873; TIAS 6131; 674 UNTS 65

Agreement relating to the transfer to Paris of the headquarters of the Deputy Commander of the Allied Forces in Europe.
Exchange of notes at Paris June 17, 1953.
Entered into force June 17, 1953.
17 UST 1906; TIAS 6134; 674 UNTS 83

Agreement regarding the transport, burial, and embalming of bodies of members of United States forces dying in France.
Signed at Paris July 1, 1955.
Entered into force July 1, 1955.
6 UST 3787; TIAS 3380; 270 UNTS 19

Agreement relating to the disposition of equipment and material no longer required in the furtherance of the mutual defense assistance program, and related notes.
Exchange of notes at Paris September 23, 1955.
Entered into force September 23, 1955.
6 UST 5971; TIAS 3440; 270 UNTS 341

Memorandum of understanding relating to sales to France of military equipment, materials, and services under the mutual defense assistance agreement of January 27, 1950, and exchange of letters.
Signed at Washington January 30, 1958.
Entered into force January 30, 1958.
9 UST 71; TIAS 3980; 304 UNTS 349

Agreement for the transfer of special tools to France under the mutual defense assistance agreement of January 27, 1950.
Exchange of notes at Paris October 28, 1958.
Entered into force October 28, 1958.
9 UST 1450; TIAS 4140; 337 UNTS 397

Agreement concerning system of communications and depots.
Signed at Paris December 8, 1958.
Entered into force December 8, 1958.
17 UST 1890; TIAS 6132; 674 UNTS 99

Agreement for cooperation on uses of atomic energy for mutual defense purposes.
Signed at Washington May 7, 1959.
Entered into force July 20, 1959.
10 UST 1279; TIAS 4268; 354 UNTS 83

Agreement relating to a weapons production program.
Exchange of notes at Paris September 19, 1960.
Entered into force September 19, 1960.
11 UST 2333; TIAS 4611; 400 UNTS 21

Memorandum of understanding relating to military procurement, with an exchange of letters.
Signed at Washington December 20, 1961.
Entered into force December 20, 1961.
12 UST 3132; TIAS 4914; 433 UNTS 340

Agreement regarding the operation, maintenance and security of the Donges-Metz pipeline system, with protocol and exchange of letters.
Signed at Paris March 24, 1967.
Entered into force April 1, 1967.
18 UST 352; TIAS 6242; 688 UNTS 357

Memorandum of understanding relating to a cooperative research project in titanium alloys, with annex.
Signed at Washington and Paris June 23 and August 26, 1977.
Entered into force August 26, 1977.
TIAS 12290

General security of information agreement.
Signed at Paris September 7, 1977.
Entered into force September 7, 1977.
29 UST 1985; TIAS 8914

Memorandum of agreement concerning the use of Diane Range, Solenzara, Corsica.
Signed at Paris March 27, 1986.
Entered into force March 27, 1986.
TIAS 11402; 2190 UNTS 279

Memorandum of understanding for a cooperative deep submergence rescue system program, with annexes.
Signed at Washington and Paris January 27 and February 21, 1989.
Entered into force February 21, 1989.
TIAS 12291

Agreement regarding the exchange of scientists and engineers, with annexes.
Signed at Washington and Paris January 14 and 28, 1994.
Entered into force January 28, 1994.
NP

Amendments:
March 18 and 28, 2004 (NP)
July 12 and August 22, 2005 (NP)
January 15 and 29, 2008 (NP)
January 25 and 29, 2010 (NP)
January 27 and 28, 2011 (NP)
September 13 and October 11, 2013 (NP)

Agreement concerning the application of Article VIII of the agreement between the parties to the North Atlantic Treaty regarding the status of their forces of June 19, 1951.
Exchange of notes at Paris April 15 and May 2, 2002.
Entered into force May 2, 2002.
TIAS 02-502; 2212 UNTS 383

Agreement for test and evaluation program (TEP) cooperation, with annexes.
Signed at Paris January 22 and 23, 2003.
Entered into force January 23, 2003.
TIAS 03-123

Agreement concerning the exchange and reimbursement of marine aviation and propulsion fuels, with annexes.
Signed at Paris and Ft. Belvoir March 6 and May 2, 2006.
Entered into force May 2, 2006.
TIAS 06-502

Memorandum of agreement establishing a midshipmen/cadet exchange program (MCEP), with appendix and annex.
Signed at Annapolis and Brest November 20, 2006.
Entered into force November 20, 2006.
NP

Extension:
September 20, 2011
September 1, 2016

Agreement concerning geospatial-intelligence exchange and cooperation, with annexes and appendices.
Signed at Bethesda December 18 and 19, 2006.
Entered into force December 19, 2006.
TIAS

Agreement for research, development, testing, and evaluation projects, with annexes.
Signed at Washington and Paris March 19 and 30, 2007.
Entered into force March 30, 2007.
TIAS 07-330

Memorandum of agreement establishing a midshipmen/cadet exchange program (MCEP).
Signed at Annapolis and Saint Cyr July 25, 2007.
Entered into force July 25, 2007.
NP

Extension:
June 27, 2012

Arrangement regarding the exchange of military personnel, with annex.
Signed at Arlington November 30, 2009.
Entered into force November 30, 2009.
NP

Agreement concerning health care for military members and their dependents.
Signed June 21, 2011.
Entered into force June 21, 2011.
NP

Extension:
June 17 and 20, 2014

Acquisition and cross-servicing agreement.
Signed at Paris and Stuttgart September 9 and 13, 2013.
Entered into force December 3, 2013.
NP

Memorandum of agreement regarding the assignment of liaison officers, with annexes.
Signed at Paris and Washington January 12 and 27, 2015.
Entered into force January 27, 2015.
NP

Technical arrangement regarding the assignment of liaison officers, with annexes.
Signed at Washington February 27, 2015.
Entered into force February 27, 2015.
NP

DIPLOMATIC & CONSULAR RELATIONS

Consular convention, with protocol and exchange of notes.
Signed at Paris July 18, 1966.
Entered into force January 7, 1968.
18 UST 2939; TIAS 6389; 700 UNTS 257

EDUCATION

Agreement relating to certain academic and cultural exchanges and programs in the field of education.
Signed at Paris May 7, 1965.
Entered into force May 28, 1965.
16 UST 1659; TIAS 5889; 573 UNTS 183

ENERGY

Agreement for cooperation in low carbon energy technologies, with annexes.
Signed at Washington June 19, 2012.
Entered into force June 19, 2012.
TIAS 12-619

ENVIRONMENT & CONSERVATION

Implementing arrangement for cooperation in the Global Learning and Observations to Benefit the Environment (GLOBE) program.
Signed at Washington September 16, 2010.
Entered into force September 16, 2010.
TIAS 10-916

FINANCE

Debt funding agreement.
Signed at Washington April 29, 1926.
Operative June 15, 1925.
100 LNTS 27; Treasury Department print; 7 Bevans 949

Agreement modifying the debt funding agreement of April 29, 1926.
Signed at Washington June 10, 1932.
Operative July 1, 1931.
Treasury Department print; 7 Bevans 987

Agreement relating to guaranties authorized by Section 111(b)(3) of the Economic Cooperation Act of 1948, as amended.
Exchange of notes at Washington July 9 and 22, 1952.
Entered into force July 24, 1952.
3 UST 5048; TIAS 2687; 181 UNTS 319

FISHERIES

Agreement on matters relating to fishing in the economic zones of the French overseas territories of New Caledonia and Wallis and Futuna Islands.
Signed at Washington March 1, 1991.
Entered into force November 1, 1991.
TIAS 11781; 2202 UNTS 277

FOREIGN ASSISTANCE

Economic cooperation agreement.*
Signed at Paris June 28, 1948.
Entered into force July 10, 1948.
62 Stat. 2223; TIAS 1783; 7 Bevans 1257; 19 UNTS 9

Amendments:

September 21 and October 8, 1948 (62 Stat. 3720; TIAS 1897; 7 Bevans 1278; 34 UNTS 418)
November 17 and 20, 1948 (62 Stat. 3720; TIAS 1897; 7 Bevans 1288; 34 UNTS 421)
January 9, 1950 (1 UST 151; TIAS 2023; 79 UNTS 270)
May 22, 1951 (2 UST 1173; TIAS 2264; 141 UNTS 358)
September 25 and 27, 1951 (2 UST 2376; TIAS 2359; 174 UNTS 284)
September 11, 1953 (4 UST 2036; TIAS 2859; 214 UNTS 350)

Note:

* Applicable to Reunion, New Caledonia, Tuamotu Archipelago, including Society Islands, Austral Islands, Marquesas Archipelago, St. Pierre and Miquelon, Martinique, Guadeloupe, French Guiana.

Agreement for free entry and free inland transportation of relief supplies and packages.
Signed at Paris December 23, 1948.
Entered into force December 23, 1948.
62 Stat. 3587; TIAS 1873; 7 Bevans 1296; 67 UNTS 171

Amendments:

January 31, 1950 (1 UST 224; TIAS 2043; 67 UNTS 171)
August 3, 1950 (1 UST 597; TIAS 2107; 93 UNTS 367)
July 2 and August 5, 1952 (3 UST 5039; TIAS 2684; 181 UNTS 345)

INTELLECTUAL PROPERTY

Agreement relating to industrial property rights affected by World War II.
Signed at Washington April 4, 1947.
Entered into force November 10, 1947.
61 Stat. 3316; TIAS 1667; 7 Bevans 1202; 24 UNTS 133

Amendment:

October 28, 1947 (62 Stat. 1876; TIAS 1725; 7 Bevans 1222; 77 UNTS 348)

Agreement to facilitate interchange of patent rights and technical information for defense purposes.
Signed at Paris March 12, 1957.
Entered into force March 12, 1957.
8 UST 353; TIAS 3782; 279 UNTS 275

Agreement approving the procedures for reciprocal filing of classified patent application in the United States and France.
Exchange of notes at Paris May 28 and July 10, 1959.
Entered into force July 10, 1959.
10 UST 2151; TIAS 4386; 367 UNTS 336

LAW ENFORCEMENT

Convention for prevention of smuggling of intoxicating liquors.
Signed at Washington June 30, 1924.
Entered into force March 12, 1927.
45 Stat. 2403; TS 755; 7 Bevans 938; 61 LNTS 415

Arrangement for the direct exchange of certain information regarding the traffic in narcotic drugs.
Exchange of notes at Paris December 27, 1927, and January 30, 1928.
Entered into force January 30, 1928.
7 Bevans 966

Convention on the transfer of sentenced persons.
Signed at Washington January 25, 1983.
Entered into force February 1, 1985.
35 UST 2847; TIAS 10823

Agreement for cooperation with respect to the operation of distribution license systems.
Exchange of notes at Paris September 5, 1986.
Entered into force September 5, 1986.
TIAS 12389

Convention regarding mutual administration assistance in customs matters.
Signed at Paris December 3, 1993.
Entered into force July 1, 1994.
TIAS; 2084 UNTS 13

Treaty on mutual legal assistance in criminal matters.
Signed at Paris December 10, 1998.
Entered into force December 1, 2001.
TIAS 13010 ; 2172 UNTS 69

Extradition treaty, with agreed minute.
Signed at Paris April 23, 1996.
Entered into force February 1, 2002.
TIAS 02-201; 2179 UNTS 341

Instrument as contemplated by Article 3, paragraph 2, of the agreement on extradition between the United States of America and the European Union signed June 25, 2003, as to the application of the extradition treaty of April 23, 1996.
Signed at The Hague September 30, 2004.
Entered into force February 1, 2010.
TIAS 10-201.8

Instrument as contemplated by Article 3, paragraph 2, of the agreement on mutual legal assistance between the United States of America and the European Union signed June 25, 2003, as to the application of the treaty on mutual legal assistance in criminal matters of December 10, 1998.
Signed at The Hague September 30, 2004.
Entered into force February 1, 2010.
TIAS 10-201.32

Agreement on enhancing cooperation in criminal investigations with a view to preventing and combating terrorism and serious crime, with annex.
Exchange of letters at Paris and Washington May 3 and 11, 2012. Entered into force April 1, 2016.
TIAS 16-401.1

MARITIME MATTERS

Memorandum of understanding concerning the operation and maintenance of OMEGA station Le Reunion, with appendices.
Signed at Washington June 24, 1981.
Entered into force June 24, 1981.
33 UST 2109; TIAS 10176; 1530 UNTS 13

Agreement relating to jurisdiction over vessels utilizing the Louisiana Offshore Oil Port, with annex.
Exchange of notes at Washington March 24 and April 6, 1983.
Entered into force April 6, 1983.
TIAS 10682

Agreement concerning the wreck of the CSS Alabama.
Signed at Paris October 3, 1989.
Entered into force October 3, 1989.
TIAS 11687

Agreement regarding the wreck of La Belle.
Signed at Washington March 31, 2003.
Entered into force March 31, 2003.
TIAS 03-331

PEACE

Agreement relating to the allocation of the proceeds of German assets to be received from Sweden as a result of Swedish-Allied negotiations of July 18, 1946.
Exchange of notes at Washington July 18, 1946.
Entered into force July 18, 1946.
61 Stat. 3840; TIAS 1731; 7 Bevans 1176; 125 UNTS 165

POSTAL MATTERS

Convention relative to the exchange of parcel post.
Signed at Paris and Washington December 7 and 30, 1935.
Operative August 1, 1935.
49 Stat. 3322; Post Office Department print; 171 LNTS 117

International express mail agreement, with detailed regulations.
Signed at Washington and Paris March 17 and April 13, 1981.
Entered into force May 18, 1981.
33 UST 1305; TIAS 10113; 1285 UNTS 75

PROPERTY

Agreement relating to principles applying to mutual aid in the prosecution of the war against aggression.
Signed at Washington February 28, 1945.
Entered into force February 28, 1945.
59 Stat. 1304; EAS 455; 7 Bevans 1075; 76 UNTS 193

Agreement relating to supplies and services.
Signed at Washington February 28, 1945.
Entered into force February 28, 1945.
59 Stat. 1307; EAS 455; 7 Bevans 1081; 76 UNTS 223

Agreement, with accompanying memorandum and exchanges of letters, relating to principles applying to the provision of aid to the armed forces of the United States.
Exchange of notes at Washington February 28, 1945.
Entered into force February 28, 1945; operative June 6, 1944.
59 Stat. 1313; EAS 455; 7 Bevans 1078; 76 UNTS 213

Understanding relating to article VII of the lend-lease agreement signed February 28, 1945.
Exchange of notes at Washington November 8, 1945.
Entered into force November 8, 1945.
7 Bevans 1098; 76 UNTS 151

Agreement relating to the transfer of surplus United States property and installations in France and certain French overseas territories, with related documents.
Signed at Washington May 28, 1946.
Entered into force May 28, 1946.
61 Stat. 4179; TIAS 1928; 7 Bevans 1130; 84 UNTS 80

Memorandum of understanding regarding settlement for lend-lease, reciprocal aid, surplus war property, and claims, with related documents.
Signed at Washington May 28, 1946.
Entered into force May 28, 1946.
61 Stat. 4175; TIAS 1928; 7 Bevans 1126; 84 UNTS 59

Memorandum of agreement regarding expenditures of the United States armed forces in France and French overseas territories, with related documents.
Signed at Washington May 28, 1946.
Entered into force May 28, 1946.
61 Stat. 4206; TIAS 1928; 7 Bevans 1155; 84 UNTS 141

Agreement relating to expenditures of the United States armed forces in France and French overseas territories, implementing the agreement of May 28, 1946.
Exchange of notes at Washington February 27, 1948.
Entered into force February 27, 1948.
62 Stat. 3826; TIAS 1930; 7 Bevans 1245; 84 UNTS 207

Agreement regarding settlement of certain residual financial claims and accounts.
Signed at Washington March 14, 1949.
Entered into force March 14, 1949.
63 Stat. 2507; TIAS 1936; 7 Bevans 1304; 84 UNTS 237

Agreement on postponement of installations pursuant to paragraph 3 of the lend-lease agreement of May 28, 1946, and paragraph 2 of the surplus property agreement of December 6, 1947.
Signed at Washington January 30, 1958.
Entered into force January 30, 1958.
9 UST 67; TIAS 3979; 304 UNTS 9

PUBLICATIONS

Agreement relating to exchange of official publications.
Exchange of notes at Paris August 14, 1945.
Entered into force January 1, 1946.
60 Stat. 1944; TIAS 1579; 7 Bevans 1095; 73 UNTS 237

SCIENTIFIC & TECHNICAL COOPERATION

Agreement concerning development of satellite and balloon techniques and instrumentation for the study of meteorological phenomena (Project EOLE).
Exchange of notes at Washington June 16 and 17, 1966.
Entered into force June 17, 1966.
17 UST 1123; TIAS 6069; 601 UNTS 113

Memorandum of understanding concerning the furnishing of balloon launching and associated services.
Signed at Washington and Paris August 26 and November 11, 1983.
Entered into force November 11, 1983.
35 UST 2410; TIAS 10803

Agreement incorporating an intellectual property article into cooperative agreements between scientific and technical agencies of the United States and France.
Exchange of notes at Paris July 27, 1994, and June 6, 1997.
Entered into force June 6, 1997.
TIAS

Memorandum of understanding concerning scientific and technical cooperation in the earth sciences, with annexes.
Signed at Antony February 13, 2008.
Entered into force February 13, 2008.
TIAS 08-213

Agreement on science and technology cooperation, with annexes.
Signed at Paris October 22 , 2008.
Entered into force November 13, 2010.
TIAS 10-1113

SOCIAL SECURITY

Agreement on social security, with administrative arrangement.
Signed at Paris March 2, 1987.
Entered into force July 1, 1988.
TIAS 12106

SPACE

Framework agreement for cooperation in the exploration and use of outer space for peaceful purposes.
Signed at Paris January 23, 2007.
Entered into force April 2, 2008.
TIAS 08-402

TAXATION

Agreement relating to relief from taxation of United States Government expenditures in France in the interests of common defense.
Exchange of notes at Paris June 13, 1952.
Entered into force June 13, 1952.
3 UST 4828; TIAS 2655; 181 UNTS 3
Amendment:
November 27, 1956 (7 UST 3405; TIAS 3712; 265 UNTS 356)

Agreement relating to the payment by the United States of taxes on electricity provided the surplus commodity housing units in France.
Exchange of notes at Paris August 1, 1963.
Entered into force August 1, 1963.
15 UST 727; TIAS 5595; 527 UNTS 89

Convention for the avoidance of double taxation and the prevention of fiscal evasion with respect to taxes on estates, inheritances and gifts.
Signed at Washington November 24, 1978.
Entered into force October 1, 1980.
32 UST 1935; TIAS 9812; 1234 UNTS 187

Convention for the avoidance of double taxation and the prevention of fiscal evasion with respect to taxes on income and capital, with exchanges of notes.
Signed at Paris August 31, 1994.
Entered into force December 30, 1995.
TIAS; 1963 UNTS 67

Agreement for cooperation in research, development and applications of high energy laser-matter interaction physics.
Signed August 9, 1994.
Entered into force August 9, 1994.
TIAS 16-909
Amendments and Extensions:
April 24 and May 5, 2006 (TIAS 16-909)
August 31 and September 9, 2016 (TIAS 16-909)

Protocol amending the convention of November 24, 1978 for the avoidance of double taxation and the prevention of fiscal evasion with respect to taxes on estates, inheritances, and gifts.
Signed at Washington December 8, 2004.
Entered into force December 21, 2006.
TIAS 06-1221

Protocol amending the convention of August 31, 1994 for the avoidance of double taxation and the prevention of fiscal evasion with respect to taxes on income and capital.
Signed at Washington December 8, 2004.
Entered into force December 21, 2006.
TIAS 06-1221.1

Protocol amending the convention of August 31, 1994, as amended, for the avoidance of double taxation and the prevention of fiscal evasion with respect to taxes on income and capital, with memorandum of understanding.
Signed at Paris January 13, 2009.
Entered into force December 23, 2009.
TIAS 09-1223

Agreement to improve international tax compliance and to implement the Foreign Account Tax Compliance Act, with annexes.
Signed at Paris November 14, 2013.
Entered into force October 14, 2014.
TIAS 14-1014

TELECOMMUNICATION

Agreement relating to the reciprocal granting of authorizations to permit licensed amateur radio operators of either country to operate their stations in the other country.*
Exchange of notes at Paris May 5, 1966.
Entered into force July 1, 1966.
17 UST 719; TIAS 6022; 593 UNTS 279
Amendment:
October 3, 1969 (20 UST 2398; TIAS 6711)

Note:
* Applicable to all territories.

Agreement on cooperation in intercontinental testing in connection with experimental communications satellites.
Exchange of notes at Paris March 31, 1961.
Entered into force March 31, 1961.
12 UST 483; TIAS 4738; 409 UNTS 135

TERRITORIAL ISSUES

Treaty for the cession of Louisiana.
Signed at Paris April 30, 1803.
Entered into force October 21, 1803.
8 Stat. 200; TS 86; 7 Bevans 812

TRADE & INVESTMENT

Convention of navigation and commerce, with separate article.*
Signed at Washington June 24, 1822.
Entered into force February 12, 1823; operative October 1, 1822.
8 Stat. 278; TS 87; 7 Bevans 822
Note:
* Article VI terminated by the United States July 1, 1916, in accordance with the Seamen's Act (38 Stat. 1164).

Agreement modifying the provisions of article VII of the convention of navigation and commerce of June 24, 1822.
Signed at Washington July 17, 1919.
Entered into force January 10, 1921.
41 Stat. 1723; TS 650; 7 Bevans 899

Convention of establishment, protocol, and declaration.*
Signed at Paris November 25, 1959.
Entered into force December 21, 1960.
11 UST 2398; TIAS 4625; 401 UNTS 75
Note:
* Applicable to Martinique, Guadeloupe, French Guiana and Reunion.

Agreement providing for the recognition and protection by France of the appellation of origin of Bourbon Whiskey and continued protection by the United States of appellations of origin of the French brandies, Cognac, Armagnac and Calvados.
Exchange of notes at Paris December 2, 1970, and January 18, 1971.
Entered into force March 20, 1971.
22 UST 36; TIAS 7041; 777 UNTS 77

TRANSPORTATION

Agreement relating to cooperation with respect to research and development activities in the field of civil aviation.
Signed at Washington and Paris July 10, 1980.
Entered into force July 10, 1980.
32 UST 2873; TIAS 9881; 1274 UNTS 201

Agreement for promotion of aviation safety.
Signed at Paris May 14, 1996.
Entered into force May 14, 1996.
TIAS 12754

Air transport agreement, with annexes.*
Signed at Washington June 18, 1998.
Entered into force June 18, 1998.
TIAS 12965; 2088 UNTS 489

Amendments:
October 10, 2000 (TIAS 12965; 2155 UNTS 233)
January 22, 2002(TIAS 12965)

Note:
* This agreement is suspended for the duration of provisional application of the U.S. – E.U. Air Transport Agreement signed April 25 and 30, 2007 ("Air Transport Agreement") except in respect of the application of this agreement to those areas that are not encompassed within the definition of "territory" in Article 1 of the Air Transport Agreement.

FRANCE (FRENCH GUIANA)

POSTAL MATTERS

Parcel post convention.
Signed at Washington August 21, 1914.
Operative November 1, 1914.
38 Stat. 1829; Post Office Department print

FRANCE (FRENCH POLYNESIA)

POSTAL MATTERS

International express mail agreement, with detailed regulations.
Signed at Papeete and Washington November 30, 1995, and April 5, 1996.
Entered into force June 15, 1996.
NP

FRANCE (GUADELOUPE)

POSTAL MATTERS

Parcel post convention.
Signed at Washington February 20, 1913.
Operative April 1, 1913.
38 Stat. 1633; Post Office Department print

FRANCE (MARTINIQUE)

POSTAL MATTERS

Money order agreement.
Signed at Washington November 16, 1911.
Operative January 1, 1912.
NP

Parcel post convention.
Signed at Washington February 20, 1913.
Operative April 1, 1913.
38 Stat. 1623; Post Office Department print

FRANCE (NEW CALEDONIA)

POSTAL MATTERS

International express mail agreement, with detailed regulations.
Signed at Noumea and Washington April 9 and May 28, 1991.
Entered into force July 1, 1991.
TIAS 11809

FRANCE (SOCIETY ISLANDS)

POSTAL MATTERS

Parcel post convention.
Signed at Washington April 30, 1918.
Operative June 1, 1918.
41 Stat. 1645; Post Office Department print

GABON

DEFENSE

Agreement regarding the status of United States military and civilian personnel of the U.S. Department of Defense temporarily present in Gabon in connection with "Gabon 2000" and other activities.
Exchange of notes at Libreville November 26 and December 1, 1999.
Entered into force December 1, 1999.
NP

Acquisition and cross service agreement, with annexes.
Signed at Libreville July 19, 2006.
Entered into force July 19, 2006.
NP

EDUCATION

Agreement concerning the American International School of Libreville (AISL).
Signed at Libreville June 21, 2011.
Entered into force January 30, 2012.
TIAS

EMPLOYMENT

Agreement relating to the employment of dependents of official government employees.
Exchange of notes at Libreville November 26, 2007, and March 7, 2008.
Entered into force March 7, 2008.
TIAS 08-307

ENVIRONMENT & CONSERVATION

Agreement for cooperation in the Global Learning and Observations to Benefit the Environment (GLOBE) Program.
Signed at Libreville August 11, 2003.
Entered into force August 11, 2003.
TIAS 03-811

FINANCE

Agreement relating to investment guaranties.
Exchange of notes at Libreville April 10, 1963.
Entered into force April 10, 1963.
14 UST 380; TIAS 5328; 474 UNTS 113

Agreement regarding the consolidation and rescheduling of certain debts owed to, guaranteed by or insured by the United States Government and its agencies, with annexes.
Signed at Libreville February 11, 1988.
Entered into force March 21, 1988.
NP

Agreement regarding the consolidation and rescheduling of certain debts owed to, guaranteed by or insured by the United States Government and its agencies, with annexes.
Signed at Libreville February 16, 1989.
Entered into force March 30, 1989.
NP

Agreement regarding the consolidation and rescheduling or refinancing of certain debts owed to, guaranteed by or insured by the United States Government and its agencies, with annexes.
Signed at Libreville March 5, 1990.
Entered into force April 9, 1990.
NP

Agreement regarding the consolidation and rescheduling or refinancing of certain debts owed to, guaranteed by or insured by the United States Government and its agencies, with annexes.
Signed at Libreville September 2, 1994.
Entered into force November 28, 1994.
NP

Agreement regarding the consolidation and rescheduling of certain debts owed to, guaranteed by or insured by the United States Government and its agencies, with annexes.
Signed at Libreville June 17, 1996.
Entered into force August 12, 1996.
NP

Agreement regarding the consolidation and rescheduling of certain debts owed to, guaranteed by, or insured by the United States Government and its agencies, with annexes.
Signed at Libreville November 9, 2001.
Entered into force December 26, 2001.
NP

Agreement regarding the consolidation and rescheduling of certain debts owed to, guaranteed by, or insured by the United States government and its agencies, with annexes.
Signed at Libreville May 13, 2005.
Entered into force June 20, 2005.
NP

INTERNATIONAL CRIMINAL COURT

Agreement regarding the surrender of persons to the International Criminal Court.
Exchange of notes at Libreville February 26 and April 15, 2003.
Entered into force April 15, 2003.
TIAS 03-415

LAW ENFORCEMENT

Agreement regarding mutual assistance between their customs administrations.
Signed at Libreville August 27, 2015.
Entered into force August 27, 2015.
TIAS 15-827

MARITIME MATTERS

Agreement relating to jurisdiction over vessels utilizing the Louisiana Offshore Oil Port.
Exchange of notes at Libreville July 25 and August 2, 1984.
Entered into force August 2, 1984.
TIAS 11215

POSTAL MATTERS

International express mail agreement, with detailed regulations.
Signed at Libreville and Washington January 23 and March 8, 1989.
Entered into force April 17, 1989.
TIAS 11616

SCIENTIFIC & TECHNICAL COOPERATION

Agreement concerning scientific and technical cooperation in the earth sciences, with annexes.
Signed at Reston and Libreville September 26, 2001, and April 22 and 23, 2003.
Entered into force April 23, 2003.
TIAS 03-423.1

Memorandum of understanding for cooperation in the use of U.S. land remote sensing satellite data, with annexes.
Signed at Buellton February 11, 2013.
Entered into force February 11, 2013.
TIAS 13-211

SOCIAL SECURITY

Agreement to provide certain social security benefits for certain employees of the United States in Gabon.
Signed at Libreville August 25, 1970.
Entered into force August 25, 1970; effective January 1, 1968.
21 UST 2570; TIAS 6999; 175 UNTS 205

TRANSPORTATION

Air transport agreement, with annexes.
Signed at Washington May 26, 2004.
Entered into force May 26, 2004.
TIAS 04-526

THE GAMBIA

On February 18, 1965, The Gambia became an independent state. By an exchange of letters on June 20, 1966, between the High Commissioner for the United Kingdom in The Gambia and the Prime Minister of The Gambia, the Government of The Gambia agreed "that all obligations and responsibilities of the Government of the United Kingdom which arose from any valid international instrument applying to The Gambia immediately before the 18th of February, 1965 continued to apply to The Gambia and were assumed by the Government of The Gambia as from that date; and (ii) that the rights and benefits enjoyed by the Government of the United Kingdom by virtue of the application of any such international instrument to The Gambia continued to be enjoyed by the Government of The Gambia."

CULTURAL EXCHANGES, PROPERTY & COOPERATION

Agreement relating to the establishment of a Peace Corps program in The Gambia.
Exchange of notes at Bathurst November 26 and December 5, 1966.
Entered into force December 5, 1966.
17 UST 2346; TIAS 6181; 681 UNTS 49

DEFENSE

Agreement between the United States and the United Kingdom relating to the assurances required under the Mutual Security Act of 1951.
Exchange of notes at London January 8, 1952.
Entered into force January 8, 1952.
3 UST 4665; TIAS 2622; 126 UNTS 307

Agreement concerning the provision of training related to defense articles under the United States International Military Education and Training (IMET) Program.
Exchange of notes at Banjul December 27, 1983, and January 5, 1984.
Entered into force January 5, 1984.
35 UST 4183; TIAS 10916; 2015 UNTS 81

Agreement regarding grants under the Foreign Assistance Act of 1961, as amended, and the furnishing of defense articles, related training and other defense services from the United States to The Gambia.
Exchange of notes at Banjul August 14 and 18, 2003.
Entered into force August 18, 2003.
TIAS 03-818

DIPLOMATIC & CONSULAR RELATIONS

Consular convention between the United States and the United Kingdom.
Signed at Washington June 6, 1951.
Entered into force September 7, 1952.
3 UST 3426; TIAS 2494; 165 UNTS 121

EMPLOYMENT

Agreement relating to the employment of dependents of official government employees.
Exchange of notes at Banjul June 7 and August 13, 2002.
Entered into force August 13, 2002.
TIAS 02-813

ENVIRONMENT & CONSERVATION

Agreement concerning cooperation in the Global Learning and Observations to Benefit the Environment (GLOBE) Program.
Signed at Banjul July 12, 1996.
Entered into force July 12, 1996.
TIAS

FINANCE

Agreement relating to investment guaranties.
Exchange of notes at Bathurst July 24 and November 4, 1967.
Entered into force November 4, 1967.
18 UST 2997; TIAS 6392; 701 UNTS 139

FOREIGN ASSISTANCE

Economic cooperation agreement between the United States and the United Kingdom.
Signed at London July 6, 1948.
Applicable to The Gambia July 6, 1948.
62 Stat. 2596; TIAS 1795; 12 Bevans 874; 22 UNTS 263

Amendments:
January 3, 1950 (1 UST 184; TIAS 2036; 86 UNTS 304)
May 25, 1951 (2 UST 1292; TIAS 2277; 99 UNTS 308)
February 25, 1953 (4 UST 1528; TIAS 2815; 172 UNTS 332)
June 26 and August 20, 1959 (11 UST 2680; TIAS 4664; 405 UNTS 288)

INTELLECTUAL PROPERTY

Declaration by the United States and the United Kingdom affording reciprocal protection to trademarks.
Signed at London October 24, 1877.
Entered into force October 24, 1877.
20 Stat. 703; TS 138; 12 Bevans 198

INTERNATIONAL CRIMINAL COURT

Agreement regarding the surrender of persons to the International Criminal Court.
Signed at Banjul October 5, 2002.
Entered into force June 27, 2003.
TIAS 03-627

LAW ENFORCEMENT

Extradition treaty between the United States and the United Kingdom.
Signed at London December 22, 1931.
Entered into force June 24, 1935.
47 Stat. 2122; TS 849; 12 Bevans 482; 163 LNTS 59

MARITIME MATTERS

Agreement concerning cooperation to suppress illicit transnational maritime activity.
Signed at Banjul October 10, 2011.
Entered into force October 10, 2011.
TIAS 11-1010

PROPERTY

Convention between the United States and the United Kingdom relating to the tenure and disposition of real and personal property.
Signed at Washington March 2, 1899.
Applicable to The Gambia February 9, 1901.
31 Stat. 1939; TS 146; 12 Bevans 246

Supplementary convention relating to the tenure and disposition
of real and personal property.
Signed at Washington May 27, 1936.
Entered into force March 10, 1941.
55 Stat. 1101; TS 964; 5 Bevans 140; 203 LNTS 367

TELECOMMUNICATION

Agreement relating to radio communications between amateur stations on behalf of third parties.
Exchange of notes at Banjul March 17, 1981.
Entered into force April 16, 1981.
33 UST 1401; TIAS 10119

TRANSPORTATION

Arrangement between the United States and the United Kingdom relating to pilot licenses to operate civil aircraft.
Exchange of notes at Washington March 28 and April 5, 1935.
Entered into force May 5, 1935.
49 Stat. 3731; EAS 77; 12 Bevans 513; 162 UNTS 59

Agreement between the United States and the United Kingdom relating to air services.
Signed at Bermuda February 11, 1946.
Entered into force February 11, 1946.
60 Stat. 1499; TIAS 1507; 12 Bevans 726; 3 UNTS 253

Amendment:
May 27, 1966 (17 UST 683; TIAS 6019; 573 UNTS 274)

Air transport agreement, with annexes.
Signed at Washington May 2, 2000.
Entered into force January 18, 2001.
TIAS 13099

Agreement concerning the provision of assistance in developing and modernizing the civil aviation infrastructure of The Gambia
Signed May 20 and 30, 2004.
Entered into force May 30, 2004.
NP

Amendment
January 31 and February 2, 2005

GEORGIA

For agreements prior to December 31, 1991, see UNION OF SOVIET SOCIALIST REPUBLICS.

CULTURAL EXCHANGES, PROPERTY & COOPERATION

Agreement on the Peace Corps program.
Signed at Tbilisi April 24, 2001.
Entered into force August 14, 2003.
TIAS 13147

DEFENSE

Agreement concerning the provision of training under the United States International Military Education and Training (IMET) Program.
Exchange of notes at Tbilisi December 30, 1993.
Entered into force December 30, 1993.
NP

Agreement regarding grants under the Foreign Assistance Act of 1961, as amended, and the furnishing of defense articles, related training, and other defense services from the United States of America to the Government of Georgia.
Exchange of notes at Tbilisi June 4 and July 15, 1999.
Entered into force July 15, 1999.
TIAS 13052

Agreement on defense cooperation, with annex.
Signed at Tbilisi November 10, 2002.
Entered into force March 25, 2003.
TIAS 03-325

Agreement concerning geospatial-intelligence exchange and cooperation, with annex.
Signed at Bethesda and Tbilisi July 5 and 17, 2006.
Entered into force July 17, 2006.
NP

Acquisition and cross-servicing agreement.
Signed at Tbilisi and Stuttgart April 26, 2013 and June 6, 2013.
Entered into force August 2, 2013.
NP

Agreement concerning health care for military members and their dependents.
Signed January 7 and February 19, 2014.
Entered into force February 19, 2014.
NP

EMPLOYMENT

Agreement relating to the employment of dependents of official government employees.
Exchange of notes at Washington December 5, 1994, and June 20, 1995.
Entered into force June 20, 1995.
TIAS 12667

ENVIRONMENT & CONSERVATION

Agreement concerning the Regional Environmental Centre for the Caucasus
Signed November 8, 2000.
Entered into force November 8, 2000.
TIAS

FINANCE

Investment incentive agreement.
Signed at Tbilisi June 27, 1992.
Entered into force June 27, 1992.
TIAS 12463

Agreement regarding the consolidation and rescheduling of certain debts owed to the United States Government, with annexes.
Signed at Tbilisi March 6, 2002.
Entered into force January 28, 2003.
NP

Agreement regarding the rescheduling of certain debts owed to, guaranteed by, or insured by the United States Government, with annexes.
Signed at Tbilisi November 18, 2005.
Entered into force June 2, 2006.
NP

FOREIGN ASSISTANCE

Agreement regarding cooperation to facilitate humanitarian and technical economic assistance.
Signed at Tbilisi July 31, 1992.
Entered into force July 31, 1992.
TIAS 12468

Millennium Challenge Compact, with annexes.
Signed at Tbilisi July 26, 2013.
Entered into force July 1, 2014.
TIAS 14-701.1

AGENCY FOR INTERNATIONAL DEVELOPMENT

Cash transfer grant agreement.
Signed October 22, 2008.
Entered into force October 22, 2008.
NP

INTERNATIONAL CRIMINAL COURT

Agreement regarding the surrender of persons to the International Criminal Court.
Signed at Tbilisi February 10, 2003.
Entered into force June 26, 2003.
TIAS 03-626

LAW ENFORCEMENT

Agreement on cooperation in the field of law enforcement, with annex.
Signed at Tbilisi June 18, 2001.
Entered into force June 18, 2001.
TIAS

POSTAL MATTERS

Express mail agreement, with detailed regulations.
Signed at Tbilisi and Washington August 16 and September 3, 1996.
Entered into force November 1, 1996.
NP

SCIENTIFIC & TECHNICAL COOPERATION

Memorandum of understanding concerning scientific and technical cooperation in the earth sciences, with annexes.
Signed at Reston July 21 and August 9, 2006.
Entered into force August 9, 2006.
TIAS 06-809

TRADE & INVESTMENT

Agreement on trade relations, with exchanges of letters.
Signed at Tbilisi March 1, 1993.
Entered into force August 13, 1993.
TIAS 12489

Treaty concerning the encouragement and reciprocal protection
of investment, with annex.
Signed at Washington March 7, 1994.
Entered into force August 17, 1997.
TIAS

Trade and investment framework agreement.
Signed at Washington June 20, 2007.
Entered into force June 20, 2007.
TIAS

TRANSPORTATION

Air transport agreement, with annexes.
Signed at Washington June 21, 2007.
Entered into force December 6, 2007.
TIAS 07-1206

WEAPONS

Agreement concerning cooperation in the area of the prevention
of proliferation of weapons of mass destruction and the promotion of defense and military relations.
Signed at Washington July 17, 1997.
Entered into force November 10, 1997.
TIAS 97-1110

Amendment and Extensions:
May 16 and 17, 2002 (TIAS 97-1110)
March 20 and October 13, 2009 (TIAS 97-1110)

Agreement concerning cooperation in the area of prevention of proliferation of technology, pathogens and expertise related to the development of biological weapons.
Signed at Washington December 30, 2002.
Entered into force June 3, 2003.
TIAS

Amendments:
March 19 and 23, 2004
August 30, 2004
October 25 and November 3, 2005
June 21 and 23, 2006
February 26 and March 6, 2007
February 22 and March 5, 2008
July 19 and August 8, 2011

GERMANY

The Federal Republic of Germany provided a note to the Department dated October 15, 1990, which reads in pertinent part as follows:

The Embassy of the Federal Republic of Germany presents its compliments to the Department of State and has the honor to inform the Department that, with regard to the continued application of treaties of the Federal Republic of Germany and the treatment of treaties of the German Democratic Republic following its accession to the Federal Republic of Germany with effect from 3 October 1990, the Treaty of 31 August 1990 between the Federal Republic of Germany and the German Democratic Republic on the Establishment of German Unity (Unification Treaty) contains the following relevant provisions.

1. Article 11

Treaties of the Federal Republic of Germany

The Contracting Parties proceed on the understanding that international treaties and agreements to which the Federal Republic of Germany is a Contracting Party, including treaties establishing its membership of international organizations or institutions, shall retain their validity and that the rights and obligations arising therefrom, with the exception of the treaties named in Article I (not included herein), shall also relate to the territory specified in Article 3. Where adjustments become necessary in individual cases, the all-German Government shall consult with the respective Contracting Parties.

...

2. Article 12

Treaties of the German Democratic Republic

(1) The Contracting Parties are agreed that, in connection with the establishment of German unity, international treaties of the German Democratic Republic shall be discussed with the Contracting Parties concerned with a view to regulating or confirming their continued application, adjustment or expiry, taking into account protection of confidence, the interests of the states concerned, the treaty obligations of the Federal Republic of Germany as well as the principles of a free, democratic basic order governed by the rule of law, and respecting the competence of the European Communities.

(2) The United Germany shall determine its position with regard to the adoption of international treaties of the German Democratic Republic following consultations with the respective Contracting Parties and with the European Communities where the latter's competence is affected.

...

The Federal Republic of Germany will proceed in accordance with these provisions."

AGRICULTURE

Agreement on cooperation in the field of agricultural science and technology.
Signed at Bonn June 1, 1981.
Entered into force June 1, 1981.
34 UST 958; TIAS 10381; 1560 UNTS 423

ATOMIC ENERGY

Agreement for cooperation in the field of nuclear materials safeguards and physical security research and development, with annex.
Exchange of notes at Bonn and Washington September 29, 1977.
Entered into force September 29, 1977.
29 UST 4709; TIAS 9076
Extension:
April 23 and July 22, 1985 (TIAS 12386)

Agreement for the exchange of classified information, with related exchange of letters.
Signed at Washington July 6, 1981.
Entered into force July 6, 1981.
35 UST 3615; TIAS 10872

Agreement concerning the listing of reactors supplied from the Federal Republic of Germany to the Taiwan Power Company on the inventory of the IAEA safeguards agreement of December 6, 1971 (TIAS 7228).
Exchange of letters at Washington November 5, 1981.
Entered into force November 5, 1981.
33 UST 4505; TIAS 10321

Arrangement for the exchange of technical information and cooperation in nuclear safety matters in the field of reactor safety research and development.
Signed at Vienna September 27, 2016.
Entered into force September 27, 2016.
TIAS 16-927

CLAIMS & DISPUTE RESOLUTION

Treaty of arbitration.
Signed at Washington May 5, 1928.
Entered into force February 25, 1929.
45 Stat. 2744; TS 774; 8 Bevans 192; 90 LNTS 177

Treaty of conciliation.
Signed at Washington May 5, 1928.
Entered into force February 25, 1929.
45 Stat. 2748; TS 775; 8 Bevans 194; 90 LNTS 171

Agreement concerning the settlement of claims against United States forces and authorities which arose during the period of August 1, 1945, to June 30, 1947.
Exchange of letters at Bonn March 24 and 30, 1953.
Entered into force March 30, 1953.
5 UST 2149; TIAS 3076; 235 UNTS 285

Agreement regarding the settlement of the claim of the United States for postwar economic assistance (other than surplus property) to Germany.
Signed at London February 27, 1953.
Entered into force September 16, 1953.
4 UST 893; TIAS 2795; 224 UNTS 13

Agreement relating to the indebtedness of Germany for awards made by the Mixed Claims Commission, United States and Germany.
Signed at London February 27, 1953.
Entered into force September 16, 1953.
4 UST 908; TIAS 2796; 224 UNTS 31

Agreement relating to an advance payment by Germany on its indebtedness to the United States for postwar economic assistance.
Exchange of notes at Bonn March 20, 1959.
Entered into force March 20, 1959.
10 UST 401; TIAS 4200; 341 UNTS 15

Agreement relating to partial settlement of German postwar debt to the United States resulting from postwar economic assistance (other than surplus property).
Exchange of notes at Bonn April 25, 1961.
Entered into force April 25, 1961.
12 UST 477; TIAS 4737; 410 UNTS 340

Agreement concerning the settlement of claims which have arisen through the non-duty use of private motor vehicles of members of the United States Forces insured by the Brandaris insurance company.*
Exchange of letters at Bonn February 28 and March 14, 1963.
Entered into force March 14, 1963.
14 UST 342; TIAS 5318; 474 UNTS 71

Note:

* Applicable also in respect of incidents which occurred in West Berlin.

Agreement relating to prepayment of the remaining German debt to the United States resulting from postwar economic assistance (excluding surplus property).
Exchange of notes at Bonn December 29, 1966.
Entered into force December 29, 1966.
18 UST 101; TIAS 6204; 688 UNTS 63

Agreement concerning the settlement of certain property claims, with annex.
Signed at Bonn May 13, 1992.
Entered into force December 28, 1992.
TIAS 11959; 1911 UNTS 27

Agreement concerning final benefits to certain United States nationals who were victims of National Socialist measures of persecution, with exchange of notes.
Signed at Bonn September 19, 1995.
Entered into force September 19, 1995.
TIAS

Supplementary agreement to the agreement of September 19, 1995, concerning final benefits to certain United States nationals who were victims of National Socialist measures of persecution.
Exchange of notes at Bonn January 25, 1999.
Entered into force January 25, 1999.
TIAS 13019

Agreement concerning the Foundation "Remembrance, Responsibility and the Future", with annexes.
Signed at Berlin July 17, 2000.
Entered into force October 19, 2000.
TIAS 13104; 2130 UNTS 249

CULTURAL EXCHANGES, PROPERTY & COOPERATION

Agreement concerning cultural relations.
Exchange of notes at Washington April 9, 1953.
Entered into force April 9, 1953.
4 UST 939; TIAS 2798; 204 UNTS 79

Agreement with respect to the transfer of certain works of art seized in Germany by the United States Army at the end of World War II, with annex.
Exchange of notes at Washington January 28, 1986.
Entered into force January 28, 1986.
TIAS 11977; 2244 UNTS 101

DEFENSE

Agreement relating to the assurances required under the Mutual Security Act of 1951.
Exchange of letters at Bonn December 19 and 28, 1951.
Entered into force December 28, 1951.
3 UST 4564; TIAS 2607; 181 UNTS 45

Agreement relating to the return to the Federal Republic of Germany of Tripartite Naval Commission vessels.
Signed at Bonn August 20, 1953.
Entered into force August 20, 1953.
4 UST 2815; TIAS 2891; 224 UNTS 49

Agreement relating to the purchase by the Federal Republic of Germany from the United States of certain equipment for police use.
Exchange of notes at Washington November 23, 1953.
Entered into force November 23, 1953.
5 UST 170; TIAS 2911; 224 UNTS 107

Mutual defense assistance agreement.
Signed at Bonn June 30, 1955.
Entered into force December 27, 1955.
6 UST 5999; TIAS 3443; 240 UNTS 47

Agreement for the return of equipment pursuant to the mutual defense assistance agreement.
Exchange of notes at Bonn June 30, 1955.
Entered into force December 27, 1955.
6 UST 6005; TIAS 3444; 240 UNTS 69

Amendment:

March 9, 1961 (12 UST 243; TIAS 4703; 405 UNTS 323)

Agreement relating to the sale to the Federal Republic of certain military equipment, materials, and services pursuant to sec. 106 of the Mutual Security Act of 1954, as amended.
Exchange of notes at Washington October 8, 1956.
Entered into force October 8, 1956.
7 UST 2787; TIAS 3660; 278 UNTS 9

Extensions and Amendments:

June 15 and October 24, 1960 (11 UST 2242; TIAS 4599; 393 UNTS 332)
November 24, 1961 (12 UST 3045; TIAS 4903; 434 UNTS 328)

Agreement relating to the training of German army personnel pursuant to the mutual defense assistance agreement.
Exchange of notes at Bonn December 12, 1956.
Entered into force December 12, 1956.
8 UST 149; TIAS 3753; 280 UNTS 63

Agreement relating to the training of German navy personnel pursuant to the mutual defense assistance agreement.
Exchange of notes at Bonn December 12, 1956.
Entered into force December 12, 1956.
8 UST 153; TIAS 3754; 280 UNTS 71

Agreement relating to offshore procurement.
Signed at Bonn April 4, 1955.
Entered into force February 7, 1957.
8 UST 157; TIAS 3755; 279 UNTS 73

Agreement on the model contract containing standard contract clauses referred to in article 16 of the agreement of April 4, 1955, relating to offshore procurement.
Exchange of notes at Bonn April 4, 1955.
Entered into force February 7, 1957.
8 UST 497; TIAS 3804; 289 UNTS 326

Agreement relating to the training of German air force and the transfer to the Federal Republic of the air bases at Landsberg, Kaufbeuren and Fuerstenfeldbruck and the air depot at Erding.
Exchange of notes at Bonn December 10, 1957.
Entered into force December 10, 1957.
8 UST 2475; TIAS 3968; 307 UNTS 59

Agreement for cooperation on uses of atomic energy for mutual defense purposes.
Signed at Bonn May 5, 1959.
Entered into force July 27, 1959.
10 UST 1322; TIAS 4276; 355 UNTS 307

Agreement relating to the use of the International Airport Frankfurt/Main and related papers.
Exchange of letters at Bonn November 10 and 18, 1959.
Entered into force November 18, 1959; effective April 1, 1959.
TIAS

Agreement relating to a weapons production program.
Exchange of notes at Bonn May 27, 1960.
Entered into force May 27, 1960.
11 UST 1606; TIAS 4504; 377 UNTS 45

Agreement relating to the safeguarding of classified information.
Exchange of notes at Washington December 23, 1960.
Entered into force December 23, 1960.
TIAS
Amendment:
July 23, 1982

Agreement relating to the disposition of equipment and materials furnished to the Federal Republic on a grant basis under the mutual defense assistance agreement of June 30, 1955.
Exchange of notes at Bonn May 25, 1962.
Entered into force May 25, 1962.
13 UST 1341; TIAS 5092; 458 UNTS 259

Agreements implementing the NATO status of forces agreement of August 3, 1959 (TIAS 5351).
Signed at Bonn August 3, 1959.
Entered into force July 1, 1963.
14 UST 689; TIAS 5352; 490 UNTS 30

Agreement to support personnel from the Federal Republic of Germany stationed in the United States during emergencies.
Signed at Bonn and Washington October 21 and December 18, 1965.
Entered into force December 18, 1965.
16 UST 1912; TIAS 5922; 579 UNTS 193

Agreement relating to the AIM 9L Sidewinder air-to-air missile.
Signed at Washington February 14, 1975.
Entered into force February 14, 1975.
29 UST 2924; TIAS 8987; 1120 UNTS 23

Memorandum of understanding relating to cooperative tests for the ROLAND 2 all-weather short range air defense system, with annexes.
Signed at Bonn and Washington February 18 and 28, 1975.
Entered into force February 28, 1975.
31 UST 4754; TIAS 9636

Agreement concerning the transfer of the U.S. bridge and ferry equipment to the Federal Republic of Germany, with annex.
Signed at Heidelberg and Bonn May 26 and June 1, 1976.
Entered into force June 1, 1976.
29 UST 1497; TIAS 8893; 1115 UNTS 45

Memorandum of understanding concerning cooperative development of an advanced surface-to-air missile system.
Signed at Washington and Bonn July 16 and 22, 1976.
Entered into force July 22, 1976.
28 UST 5771; TIAS 8658

Agreement on the release and testing of strebo submunitions and on the exchange of information.
Signed at Washington and Bonn August 4 and November 4, 1976.
Entered into force November 4, 1976.
TIAS 12298

Agreement relating to the security of information on the JT-10D aircraft engine.
Exchange of notes at Washington February 24 and March 18, 1977.
Entered into force March 18, 1977.
28 UST 7146; TIAS 8708

Agreement on the provision of United States Army training to the German Air Force in the United States, with annexes.
Signed at Bonn and Washington May 24 and July 6, 1977.
Entered into force July 6, 1977.
29 UST 4859; TIAS 9081; 1148 UNTS 107

Agreement on the stationing of training components of the Federal Minister of Defense in the United States, with annexes.
Signed at Bonn and Washington May 24 and July 6, 1977.
Entered into force July 6, 1977.
30 UST 2671; TIAS 9358

Memorandum of understanding for coproduction and sale of the sidewinder AIM-9L missile system.
Signed at Washington October 7, 1977.
Entered into force October 14, 1977.
30 UST 298; TIAS 9202; 1148 UNTS 117
Amendment:
March 17 and April 21, 1978 (30 UST 315; TIAS 9202; 1148 UNTS 125)

Memorandum of understanding for coproduction and sale of modular thermal imaging systems (MOD FLIR) and their components, with annexes.*
Signed at Washington and Bonn February 27 and March 3, 1978.
Entered into force April 20, 1978.
35 UST 3651; TIAS 10876; 2014 UNTS 359

Related Agreement and Amendment:
March 26, 1979 (35 UST 3651; TIAS 10876; 2016 UNTS 311)
May 9 and June 24, 1997

Note:
* Articles IE, VIIIA, and XII superseded by agreement of February 12, May 21, and December 22, 1981; see NORTH ATLANTIC TREATY ORGANIZATION — COOPERATIVE AGREEMENTS in multilateral section.

Memorandum of understanding for cooperation within the area of army tactical data systems for the purpose of standardization and interoperability.
Signed at Washington and Bonn January 6 and April 14, 1980.
Entered into force April 14, 1980.
32 UST 1003; TIAS 9751; 1221 UNTS 3

Administrative agreement relating to addition of an educational program under paragraph 4, article 71 of the supplementary agreement of August 3, 1959 (TIAS 5351).
Exchange of notes at Bonn November 23 and December 28, 1979.
Entered into force January 1, 1980.
32 UST 783; TIAS 9729; 1220 UNTS 307

Agreement concerning the support of USAFE A-10 aircraft at Forward Operating Locations (FOLS) in the territory of the Federal Republic of Germany, with related letter.
Signed at Bonn and Ramstein November 5 and 9, 1981.
Entered into force November 9, 1981; effective October 1, 1979.
33 UST 4170; TIAS 10293

Agreement concerning host nation support during crisis or war, with annexes.
Signed at Bonn April 15, 1982.
Entered into force April 15, 1982.
34 UST 557; TIAS 10376

Agreement concerning mutual support in Europe and adjacent waters, with annex.
Signed at Bonn January 21, 1983.
Entered into force January 21, 1983.
TIAS 12299

Amendments:
December 21, 1987 (TIAS 12299)
January 21 and 26, 1994 (TIAS 12299)
December 7, 2001

Memorandum of understanding for the dual production and sale of the stinger weapon system, with agreed minute and annexes.
Signed at Washington April 27, 1983.
Entered into force April 27, 1983.
TIAS 12795

Amendments:
March 20 and 26, 1986 (TIAS 12795)
March 23 and April 24, 1995 (TIAS 12795)
April 24 and May 14, 1996 (TIAS 12795)
July 10 and August 22, 1996 (TIAS 12795)

Memorandum of understanding concerning a cooperative project of research in the field of powder metallurgy of titanium alloys.
Signed at Washington January 8, 1985.
Entered into force January 8, 1985.
TIAS 11140; 2126 UNTS 283

Memorandum of understanding concerning the exchange of Air Force officers.
Signed at Bonn and Washington January 15 and February 20, 1986.
Entered into force February 20, 1986.
NP

Memorandum of understanding on the mutual exchange of documents.
Signed at Bonn and Washington January 18, 1989, and February 9, 1990.
Entered into force February 9, 1990.
TIAS 12305

Memorandum of understanding for cooperative projects of research and development in the field of modular avionics, with supplement.
Signed at Bonn and Washington June 26 and July 3, 1990.
Entered into force July 3, 1990.
TIAS 12307

Memorandum of understanding concerning a cooperative program on biological effects of ionizing radiation.
Signed at Bonn and Washington August 2 and 23, 1993.
Entered into force August 23, 1993.
TIAS 12310

Memorandum of understanding for cooperative research in the field of helicopter aeromechanics, with annex.
Signed at Alexandria and Bonn September 2 and 16, 1994.
Entered into force September 16, 1994.
TIAS

Amendment and Extension:
August 13 and September 15, 2003 (TIAS)

Memorandum of agreement concerning German participation in the George C. Marshall European Center for Security Studies at Garmisch-Partenkirchen, with annexes.
Signed at Stuttgart December 2, 1994.
Entered into force December 2, 1994.
TIAS 12312

Agreement concerning collaborative logistics support measures for the Nuclear, Biological, Chemical Reconnaissance System (NBCRS).
Signed at Alexandria and Bonn March 30 and April 18, 1995.
Entered into force April 18, 1995.
TIAS 12629

Amendment and Extension:
October 12 and 26, 2005 (TIAS 05-1026)

Arrangement regarding the application of Article 73 of the Supplementary Agreement of August 3, 1959, to the NATO Status of Forces Agreement.
Exchange of notes at Bonn March 27, 1998.
Entered into force March 27, 1998.
TIAS 12938; 2574 UNTS 17

Agreement regarding the exchange of engineers and scientists, with annexes.
Signed on November 6, 1998.
Entered into force November 6, 1998.
NP
Amendment and Extension:
October 24 and November 12, 2008

Agreement regarding the exchange of administrative and professional personnel, with annexes.
Signed February 17 and March 20, 2000.
Entered into force March 20, 2000.
NP
Amendment and Extension:
March 19, 2010
January 24 and February 27, 2012

Agreement concerning in-service support of the rolling airframe missile MK-31 guided missile weapon system.
Signed January 16 and February 9, 2001.
Entered into force February 9, 2001.
TIAS 01-209
Amendment and Extension:
April 22 and May 18, 2010 (TIAS 01-209)
July 23 and 30, 2014 (TIAS 14-730)

Agreement regarding liaison personnel.
Signed at Bonn and Washington October 20 and December 6, 2001.
Entered into force December 6, 2001.
NP

Basic exchange and cooperative agreement concerning global geospatial information and services cooperation.
Signed at Euskirchen January 25, 2002.
Entered into force January 25, 2002.
NP

Agreement on the reception and use of meteorological data and products which are distributed via the satellite broadcast system DWDSAT in cooperation with EUMETSAT/EUMETCast.
Signed at Offenbach and Ramstein May 11, 2005, and June 12, 2006.
Entered into force June 12, 2006.
TIAS

Memorandum of arrangement on the exchange of students.
Signed April 3 and 23, 2007.
Entered into force April 23, 2007.
NP

Memorandum of understanding concerning cooperation on information assurance (IA) and computer network defense (CND).
Signed at Washington and Berlin May 16 and 26, 2008.
Entered into force May 26, 2008.
TIAS 08-526

Memorandum of agreement regarding the exchange of military personnel of the United States Navy and the German Air Force, with annex.
Signed at Bonn November 27, 2008.
Entered into force November 27, 2008.
NP

Memorandum of agreement for research, development, test, and evaluation projects, with annex.
Signed at Washington and Bonn March 5 and 24, 2009.
Entered into force March 24, 2009.
TIAS 09-324

Memorandum of agreement concerning logistics and administrative support at Ramstein Air Base, Germany, with annex.
Signed at Ramstein May 5 and June 1, 2011.
Entered into force June 1, 2011.

Agreement regarding the exchange of military personnel, with annexes.
Signed at Washington July 12, 2011.
Entered into force July 12, 2011.
NP
Amendments:
May 2, 2013
August 26 and 30, 2013

Memorandum of agreement on the exchange of students, with annex.
Signed at Hamburg and Annapolis April 27 and May 22, 2012.
Entered into force May 22, 2012.
NP

Agreement concerning health care for military members and their dependents.
Signed March 5 and April 7, 2014.
Entered into force April 7, 2014.
NP

Memorandum of agreement regarding the assignment of German Defense Personnel to the Army of the United States of America, with annexes.
Signed at Washington July 30, 2014.
Entered into force July 30, 2014.
NP

DIPLOMATIC & CONSULAR RELATIONS

Treaty establishing friendly relations.
Signed at Berlin August 25, 1921.
Entered into force November 11, 1921.
42 Stat. 1939; TS 658; 8 Bevans 145; 12 LNTS 192

EDUCATION

Agreement for conducting certain educational exchange programs.
Signed at Bonn November 20, 1962.
Entered into force January 24, 1964.
15 UST 78; TIAS 5518; 505 UNTS 263
Amendment:
January 11, 1974 (25 UST 169; TIAS 7778)

EMPLOYMENT

Agreement concerning the pursuit of gainful employment by dependents of employees of diplomatic missions, consular posts or missions to international organizations.
Signed at Washington November 30, 2011.
Entered into force November 30, 2011.
TIAS 11-1130

ENERGY

Agreement on cooperation in energy research, science and technology, and development.
Signed at Washington February 20, 1998.
Entered into force February 20, 1998.
TIAS

ENVIRONMENT & CONSERVATION

Agreement on cooperation in environmental affairs.
Signed at Bonn May 9, 1974.
Entered into force March 26, 1975.
26 UST 840; TIAS 8069
Amendment and Extension:
March 22, 1985 (TIAS 11251; 2177 UNTS 184)

FINANCE

Agreement regarding the validation of dollar bonds of German issue.
Signed at Bonn February 27, 1953.
Entered into force February 27, 1953.
4 UST 797; TIAS 2793; 223 UNTS 167

Agreement regarding certain matters arising from the validation of German dollar bonds.
Signed at Bonn April 1, 1953.
Entered into force September 16, 1953.
4 UST 885; TIAS 2794; 224 UNTS 3

Confirmation of effectiveness in Berlin of agreements relating to the validation of certain German dollar bonds (TIAS 2793 and 2794).
Exchange of notes at Washington February 25 and April 9, 1954.
5 UST 1; 223 UNTS 167

Second agreement regarding certain matters arising from the validation of German dollar bonds.
Signed at Bonn August 16, 1960.
Entered into force June 30, 1961.
12 UST 943; TIAS 4798; 418 UNTS 235

Investment incentive agreement.
Signed at Berlin September 14, 1990.
Entered into force August 9, 1991.
TIAS 12130; 2049 UNTS 291

Agreement relating to and bringing into force the investment incentive agreement of September 14, 1990.
Exchange of notes at Washington August 9, 1991.
Entered into force August 9, 1991.
TIAS 12130; 2052 UNTS 195

FOREIGN ASSISTANCE

Economic cooperation agreement.
Signed at Bonn December 15, 1949.
Entered into force provisionally December 29, 1949; definitively February 6, 1950.
64 Stat. B81; TIAS 2024; 8 Bevans 286; 92 UNTS 269
Amendments:
February 27 and March 28, 1951 (2 UST 1295; TIAS 2278; 141 UNTS 390)
November 14 and December 30, 1952 (3 UST 5323; TIAS 2736; 212 UNTS 329)

Agreement relating to duty-free entry into the Federal Republic of Germany of relief shipments and the defrayment of transportation costs of such shipments, with memorandum attached.
Exchange of notes at Bonn April 10, May 25, and June 7, 1951.
Entered into force May 29, 1951; operative December 29, 1949.
5 UST 2820; TIAS 3135; 238 UNTS 161
Extension and Amendment:
July 8 and September 6, 1952 (5 UST 2835; TIAS 3137; 238 UNTS 167)

INTELLECTUAL PROPERTY

Copyright agreement.
Signed at Washington January 15, 1892.
Entered into force May 6, 1892.
TS 100; 8 Bevans 129

Patent agreement.
Signed at Washington February 23, 1909.
Entered into force August 1, 1909.
36 Stat. 2178; TS 531; 8 Bevans 143

Agreement to facilitate interchange of patent rights and technical information for defense purposes, and exchange of notes.
Signed at Bonn January 4, 1956.
Entered into force January 4, 1956.
7 UST 45; TIAS 3478; 268 UNTS 143

Agreement approving the procedures for reciprocal filing of classified patent applications in the United States and the Federal Republic of Germany.
Exchange of notes at Bonn March 9 and May 23, 1959, and related note of July 31, 1959.
Entered into force May 26, 1959.
10 UST 2001; TIAS 4369; 361 UNTS 337
Amendment:
January 14 and May 28, 1964 (15 UST 765; TIAS 5601; 529 UNTS 350)

Agreement relating to the extension of time for fulfilling the conditions and formalities of the copyright laws of the United States.
Exchange of notes at Washington November 20, 1964, and July 12, 1967.
Entered into force July 12, 1967.
18 UST 2366; TIAS 6341; 692 UNTS 331

LAW ENFORCEMENT

Arrangement concerning the exchange of information relating to the illicit traffic in narcotics.
Exchange of notes at Washington January 17 and August 24, 1955, and March 7, 1956.
Entered into force March 7, 1956.
7 UST 371; TIAS 3514; 271 UNTS 361

Agreement relating to the taking of evidence.
Exchange of notes at Bad Godesberg and Bonn February 11, 1955, January 13 and October 8, 1956.
Entered into force October 8, 1956.
32 UST 4181; TIAS 9938; 1265 UNTS 41

Agreement relating to reciprocal legal assistance in penal matters and information from penal register.
Exchange of notes at Bonn November 7 and December 28, 1960, and January 3, 1961.
Entered into force January 3, 1961.
12 UST 1156; TIAS 4826; 416 UNTS 93

Agreement regarding mutual assistance between the customs services of the United States and the Federal Republic of Germany.
Signed at Washington August 23, 1973.
Entered into force June 13, 1975.
26 UST 1092; TIAS 8098

Agreement concerning mutual assistance in the administration of justice in connection with the Lockheed Aircraft Corporation matter, with agreed minutes.
Signed at Washington September 24, 1976.
Entered into force September 24, 1976.
27 UST 3429; TIAS 8373

Related Agreement:

January 10 and February 1, 1979 (30 UST 3533; TIAS 9407; 1169 UNTS 3)

Agreement concerning cooperation in the field of control of drug and narcotics abuse.
Exchange of notes at Bonn and Bonn-Bad Godesberg June 9, 1978.
Entered into force June 9, 1978.
30 UST 4434; TIAS 9467; 1177 UNTS 317

Agreement relating to the taking of evidence.
Exchange of notes at Bonn October 17, 1979, and February 1, 1980.
Entered into force February 1, 1980.
32 UST 4189; TIAS 9938; 1265 UNTS 46

Extradition treaty, with protocol.
Signed at Bonn June 20, 1978.
Entered into force August 29, 1980.
32 UST 1485; TIAS 9785; 1220 UNTS 269

Supplementary treaty to the treaty concerning extradition of June 20, 1978.
Signed at Washington October 21, 1986.
Entered into force March 11, 1993.
TIAS; 1909 UNTS 441

Treaty on mutual legal assistance in criminal matters, with related exchange of notes.
Signed at Washington October 14, 2003.
Entered into force October 18, 2009.
TIAS 09-1018

Supplementary treaty to the treaty of October 14, 2003 on mutual legal assistance in criminal matters.
Signed at Washington April 18, 2006.
Entered into force October 18, 2009.
TIAS 09-1018.1

Second supplementary treaty to the treaty concerning extradition of June 20, 1978.
Signed at Washington April 18, 2006.
Entered into force February 1, 2010.
TIAS 10-201.9

Agreement on enhancing cooperation in preventing and combating serious crime.
Signed at Washington October 1, 2008.
Entered into force April 19, 2011.
TIAS 11-419.1

MARITIME MATTERS

Agreement relating to jurisdiction over vessels utilizing the Louisiana Offshore Oil Port.
Exchange of notes at Washington July 2, September 4 and 15, 1981.
Entered into force September 15, 1981.
33 UST 3278; TIAS 10225

MIGRATION & REFUGEES

Agreement relating to the continuation of the operations of the International Tracing Service by transferring the Service to the International Committee of the Red Cross.
Effected by exchange of notes at Bonn and Bonn-Bad Godesberg June 6, 1966.
Entered into force June 6, 1966.
6 UST 6169; 315 UNTS 155; TIAS 3471

Amendment and Extensions:

April 28 and May 5, 1960 (TIAS 4736)
May 24, 1968 (NP)

POSTAL MATTERS

Agreement concerning the exchange of parcel post together with regulations of execution.
Signed at Berlin February 6 and at Washington March 16, 1939.
Entered into force March 16, 1939; operative January 2, 1939.
53 Stat. 2183; Post Office Department print; 198 LNTS 237

International express mail/datapost agreement, with detailed regulation.
Signed at Bonn and Washington December 15, 1978, and January 22, 1979.
Entered into force August 8, 1979; effective February 1, 1979.
30 UST 3789; TIAS 9426

PROPERTY

Agreement concerning the transfer of the Berlin Document Center to the Federal Republic of Germany, with exchanges of notes.
Signed at Berlin October 18, 1993.
Entered into force October 18, 1993.
TIAS; 2033 UNTS 387

Agreement concerning real property exchange, with attachments.
Signed at Bonn September 23, 1994.
Entered into force September 23, 1994.
TIAS

PUBLICATIONS

Agreement relating to the exchange of official publications.
Exchange of notes at Washington October 27, 1954.
Entered into force October 27, 1954.
5 UST 2563; TIAS 3121; 234 UNTS 131

SCIENTIFIC & TECHNICAL COOPERATION

Agreement incorporating an intellectual property article into cooperative agreements between US-FRG scientific and technical agencies.
Exchange of notes at Washington March 4 and 7, 1994.
Entered into force March 7, 1994.
TIAS 12176

Agreement on cooperation in research in the geosciences, with annex.
Signed at Bonn March 7, 1994.
Entered into force March 7, 1994.
TIAS 12535

Agreement on cooperation in science and technology concerning homeland/civil security matters, with annex.
Signed at Berlin March 16, 2009.
Entered into force March 16, 2009.
TIAS 09-316.2

Agreement on science and technology cooperation, with annexes.
Signed at Washington February 18, 2010.
Entered into force February 18, 2010.
TIAS 10-218

Memorandum of understanding concerning cooperation in earth observation.
Signed at Washington November 30, 2012.
Entered into force November 30, 2012.
TIAS 12-1130

SOCIAL SECURITY

Agreement on the pension insurance of certain employees of the United States Army.
Signed at Bonn September 11, 1970.
Entered into force June 1, 1972; retroactive to November 1, 1950.
23 UST 638; TIAS 7326

Agreement on social security, with final protocol and administrative agreement.
Signed at Washington January 7, 1976.
Entered into force December 1, 1979.
30 UST 6099; TIAS 9542; 1177 UNTS 257

Amendments:
October 2, 1986 (TIAS 12115)
March 6, 1995

SPACE

Memorandum of understanding on the project of active magnetospheric particle tracer explorers.
Signed at Washington October 15, 1981.
Entered into force October 15, 1981.
33 UST 4088; TIAS 10286; 1549 UNTS 339

Memorandum of understanding on the Roentgensatellit program.
Signed at Vienna August 8, 1982.
Entered into force August 8, 1982.
TIAS 10669; 2000 UNTS 445

Framework agreement on cooperation in aeronautics and the exploration and use of outer space for peaceful purposes.
Signed at Washington and Bonn December 8 and 13, 2010.
Entered into force December 13, 2010.
TIAS 10-1213

TAXATION

Agreement concerning tax relief to be accorded by the Federal Republic of Germany to United States expenditures in interest of the common defense, with annex and exchange of letters.
Signed at Bonn October 15, 1954.
Entered into force November 8, 1955.
6 UST 3081; TIAS 3360; 239 UNTS 135

Convention for the avoidance of double taxation with respect to taxes on estates, inheritances and gifts.
Signed at Bonn December 3, 1980.
Entered into force June 27, 1986.
TIAS 11082; 2120 UNTS 283

Convention for the avoidance of double taxation and the prevention of fiscal evasion with respect to taxes on income and capital and to certain other taxes, with a related protocol, exchanges of notes and memorandum of understanding.
Signed at Bonn August 29, 1989.
Entered into force August 21, 1991.
TIAS; 1708 UNTS 3

Protocol amending the convention of December 3, 1980 for the avoidance of double taxation with respect to taxes on estates, inheritances and gifts.
Signed at Washington December 14, 1998.
Entered into force December 14, 2000.
TIAS 13012

Protocol amending the convention of August 29, 1989 for the avoidance of double taxation and the prevention of fiscal evasion with respect to taxes on income and capital and to certain other taxes, with a related joint declaration.
Signed at Berlin June 1, 2006.
Entered into force December 28, 2007.
TIAS

Agreement to improve international tax compliance and with respect to the United States information and reporting provisions commonly known as the Foreign Account Tax Compliance Act, with Annexes.
Signed at Berlin May 31, 2013.
Entered into force December 11, 2013.
TIAS 13-1211

TELECOMMUNICATION

Agreement regarding the operation of certain radio installations from within the Federal Republic.
Signed at Bonn June 11, 1952.
Entered into force May 5, 1955.
7 UST 789; TIAS 3559; 273 UNTS 105

Agreement relating to the return of the Emden-Cherbourg-Horta submarine telegraph cable to German ownership.*
Exchange of notes at Washington November 4, 1959, and March 16, 1960.
Entered into force March 16, 1960.
11 UST 254; TIAS 4441; 371 UNTS 101

Note:
* The U.S. signed in its own behalf and in behalf of the United Kingdom and France.

Agreement on cooperation in intercontinental testing in connection with experimental communications satellites.
Exchange of notes at Bonn September 5 and 29, 1961.
Entered into force September 29, 1961.
12 UST 1682; TIAS 4885; 424 UNTS 113

Agreement relating to the reciprocal granting of authorizations to permit licensed amateur radio operators of either country to operate their station in the other country.
Exchange of notes at Bonn June 23 and 30, 1966.
Entered into force June 30, 1966.
17 UST 1120; TIAS 6068; 601 UNTS 107

Agreement regarding operation of the radio installation at Erching.
Signed at Bonn January 22 and 26, 1979.
Entered into force January 26, 1979.
30 UST 3540; TIAS 9408

TRADE & INVESTMENT

Treaty of friendship, commerce, and consular rights.*
Signed at Washington December 8, 1923.
Entered into force October 14, 1925.
44 Stat. 2132; TS 725; 8 Bevans 153; 52 LNTS 133

Agreement concerning the treaty of friendship, commerce, and consular rights of December 8, 1923, as amended.*
Signed at Bonn June 3, 1953.
Entered into force October 22, 1954.
5 UST 1939; TIAS 3062; 253 UNTS 89

Treaty of friendship, commerce and navigation with protocol and exchanges of notes.
Signed at Washington October 29, 1954.
Entered into force July 14, 1956.
7 UST 1839; TIAS 3593; 273 UNTS 3

Note:
* Articles I-V, VII-XVI, and XXIX-XXXII of the 1923 treaty as amended and as applied by the agreement of June 3, 1953 (TIAS 3062), were replaced and terminated by the treaty of October
29, 1954 (TIAS 3593). Article VI of the 1923 treaty terminated June
2, 1954 (see 5 UST 827; TIAS 2972).

Agreement relating to mutual cooperation regarding restrictive business practices.
Signed at Bonn June 23, 1976.
Entered into force September 11, 1976.
27 UST 1956; TIAS 8291

TRANSPORTATION

Air transport agreement and exchanges of notes.*
Signed at Washington July 7, 1955.
Entered into force April 16, 1956.
7 UST 527; TIAS 3536; 275 UNTS 3

Amendments:
November 1, 1978 (30 UST 7323; TIAS 9591; 1203 UNTS 280)
April 25, 1989 (TIAS 11942)
May 23, 1996
October 10, 2000

Related Agreements:
November 1, 1978
May 24, 1994

Note:
* This agreement, its amendment and protocols, and related agreements are suspended for the duration of provisional application of the U.S. – E.U. Air Transport Agreement signed April 25 and 30, 2007.

Memorandum of understanding regarding cooperation on the development of advanced ground transportation.
Signed at Bonn June 12, 1973.
Entered into force June 12, 1973.
27 UST 3831; TIAS 8402; 1059 UNTS 3

Extension and Amendments:
March 23 and June 9 and 15, 1976 (27 UST 3836; TIAS 8402; 1059 UNTS 8)
July 12 and August 30, 1978 (30 UST 4100; TIAS 9449; 1228 UNTS 472)

Memorandum of understanding concerning cooperation in the field of transportation.
Signed at Washington September 3, 1975.
Entered into force September 3, 1975.
28 UST 8024; TIAS 8736

Memorandum of understanding relating to cooperation in the development of national airspace systems, with annex.
Signed at Washington and Bonn October 3 and November 6, 1984.
Entered into force November 6, 1984.
TIAS 11025; 2022 UNTS 97

Memorandum of understanding concerning air navigation services in Berlin, with related exchange of letters.
Signed at Bonn October 23, 1990.
Entered into force October 23, 1990.
TIAS 11746; 2202 UNTS 73

Agreement for promotion of aviation safety.
Signed at Milwaukee May 23, 1996.
Entered into force July 18, 1997.
TIAS 12758

GHANA

On March 6, 1957, Ghana became an independent state. In an exchange of letters dated November 25, 1957, between the Government of the United Kingdom and the Government of Ghana it was agreed that all obligations and responsibilities of the Government of the United Kingdom which arise from any valid international instrument shall henceforth in so far as such instrument may be held to have application to Ghana be assumed by the Government of Ghana. The rights and benefits heretofore enjoyed by the Government of the United Kingdom by virtue of the application of any such international instrument to the Gold Coast shall as from March 6, 1957, be enjoyed by the Government of Ghana.

CULTURAL EXCHANGES, PROPERTY & COOPERATION

Agreement relating to the establishment and operation of a Peace Corps program in Ghana.
Exchange of notes at Accra July 19, 1961.
Entered into force July 19, 1961.
12 UST 1066; TIAS 4811; 416 UNTS 167

DEFENSE

Mutual defense assistance agreement between the United States and the United Kingdom.
*Signed at Washington January 27, 1950; made applicable to the Gold Coast July 19, 1952.**
1 UST 126; TIAS 2017; 80 UNTS 261
Note:
* Only article IV is applicable to Ghana.

Agreement relating to the deposit by Ghana of ten percent of the value of grant military assistance furnished by the United States.
Exchange of notes at Accra April 13 and May 29, 1972.
Entered into force May 29, 1972; effective February 7, 1972.
23 UST 1310; TIAS 7410

Agreement concerning the provision of training related to defense articles under the United States International Military Education and Training (IMET) Program.
Exchange of notes at Accra December 4, 1985, and February 28, 1986.
Entered into force February 28, 1986.
TIAS 11102

Agreement concerning assistance under the Foreign Assistance Act of 1961, as amended, and the furnishing of defense articles, related training and other defense services from the United States to Ghana.
Exchange of notes at Accra March 2 and 7, 1995.
Entered into force March 7, 1995.
TIAS

Agreement regarding the provision of commodities, services and associated military education and training to Ghanaian forces participating in ECOMOG peacekeeping operations.
Exchange of notes at Accra October 28 and November 19, 1996.
Entered into force November 19, 1996.
TIAS 12817

Agreement regarding the provision of commodities, services and related training to assist the Republic of Ghana's forces participating in the African Crisis Response Initiative.
Exchange of notes at Accra November 24, 1997, and January 8, 1998.
Entered into force January 8, 1998.
NP

Agreement regarding the status of U.S. military personnel and civilian employees of the U.S. Department of Defense temporarily present in Ghana in connection with the African Crisis Response Initiative and other activities.
Exchange of notes at Accra November 24, 1997, and February 24, 1998.
Entered into force February 24, 1998.
TIAS

Agreement regarding the status of U.S. military and civilian personnel of the U.S. Department of Defense temporarily present in Ghana in connection with humanitarian relief operations in Southern Africa.
Exchange of notes at Accra March 22 and April 7, 2000.
Entered into force April 7, 2000.
NP

Acquisition and cross-servicing agreement.
Signed at Stuttgart and Accra April 13 and 28, 2015.
Entered into force April 28, 2015.
NP

DIPLOMATIC & CONSULAR RELATIONS

Consular convention and protocol of signature between the United States and the United Kingdom.*
Signed at Washington June 6, 1951.
Entered into force September 7, 1952.
3 UST 3426; TIAS 2494; 165 UNTS 121
Note:
* Paragraph 1 of article 7 not in force for Ghana.

EDUCATION

Agreement for financing certain educational exchange programs.
Signed at Accra January 24, 1962.
Entered into force January 24, 1962.
TIAS 4942; 13 UST 87; 435 UNTS 23

EMPLOYMENT

Agreement relating to the employment of dependents of official government employees.
Exchange of notes at Accra July 28, 1989, and April 17, 1991.
Entered into force April 17, 1991.
TIAS

ENVIRONMENT & CONSERVATION

Agreement for cooperation in the Global Learning and Observations to Benefit the Environment (GLOBE) Program, with appendices.
Signed at Accra March 20, 1998.
Entered into force March 20, 1998.
TIAS 12935

FINANCE

Agreement relating to investment guaranties under section 413(b)(4) of the Mutual Security Act of 1954, as amended.
Exchange of notes at Accra September 30, 1958.
Entered into force September 30, 1958.
9 UST 1321; TIAS 4121; 336 UNTS 169
Amendment:
March 3, 1967 (18 UST 231; TIAS 6222; 688 UNTS 376)

Agreement regarding the consolidation and rescheduling of certain debts owed to, guaranteed by, or insured by the United States Government, with annexes.
Signed at Accra March 28, 2002.
Entered into force May 10, 2002.
NP

Investment incentive agreement.
Signed at Washington February 26, 1999.
Entered into force November 24, 2004.
TIAS 13023

Agreement regarding the reduction of certain debts owed to, guaranteed by, or insured by the United States Government, with annexes.
Signed at Accra March 31, 2005.
Entered into force May 16, 2005.
NP

FOREIGN ASSISTANCE

Economic cooperation agreement between the United States and the United Kingdom.
Signed at London July 6, 1948.
Applicable to the Gold Coast July 6, 1948.
62 Stat. 2596; TIAS 1795; 12 Bevans 874; 22 UNTS 263
Amendments:
January 3, 1950 (1 UST 184; TIAS 2036; 86 UNTS 304)
May 25, 1951 (2 UST 1292; TIAS 2277; 99 UNTS 308)
February 25, 1953 (4 UST 1528; TIAS 2815; 172 UNTS 332)

General agreement for technical cooperation.
Signed at Accra June 3, 1957.
Entered into force June 3, 1957.
8 UST 793; TIAS 3838; 284 UNTS 63

Agreement providing for duty-free entry into Ghana and exemption from internal taxation of relief supplies and packages.
Exchange of notes at Accra April 9, 1959.
Entered into force April 9, 1959.
10 UST 720; TIAS 4203; 342 UNTS 21
Amendment:
April 8 and May 3, 1971 (22 UST 575; TIAS 7104; 791 UNTS 376)

Millennium Challenge Compact, with annexes.
Signed at Washington August 5, 2014.
Entered into force September 6, 2016.
TIAS 16-906

AGENCY FOR INTERNATIONAL DEVELOPMENT

Agreement for investing in people: health.
Signed September 28, 2010.
Entered into force September 30, 2010.
Amendments
March 30, 2011 (NP)
September 30, 2011 (NP)

Assistance agreement for economic growth.
Signed September 28, 2010.
Entered into force September 30, 2010
NP

Agreement for competitiveness of Ghanaian private sector in world markets increased.
Signed September 28, 2010.
Entered into force September 30, 2010.
Signed
March 30, 2011 (NP)
September 30, 2011 (NP)

Development agreement for improved reading performance in primary school.
Signed December 26, 2012.
Entered into force December 26, 2012.
TIAS

Development agreement for equitable improvements in health status.
Signed December 26, 2012.
Entered into force December 26, 2012.
TIAS

Development agreement for sustainable and broadly shared economic growth.
Signed December 26, 2012.
Entered into force December 26, 2012.
TIAS

INTELLECTUAL PROPERTY

Declaration by the United States and the United Kingdom relating to reciprocal protection to trademarks.
Signed at London October 24, 1877.
Entered into force October 24, 1877.
20 Stat. 703; TS 138; 12 Bevans 198

INTERNATIONAL CRIMINAL COURT

Agreement regarding the surrender of persons to the International Criminal Court.
Signed at Accra April 17, 2003.
Entered into force October 31, 2003.
TIAS 03-1031

LAW ENFORCEMENT

Extradition treaty between the United States and the United Kingdom.
Signed at London December 22, 1931.
Applicable to the Gold Coast June 24, 1935.
47 Stat. 2122; TS 849; 12 Bevans 482; 163 LNTS 59

POSTAL MATTERS

Parcel post agreement and detailed regulations.
Signed at Accra June 3 and at Washington June 14, 1951.
Entered into force August 1, 1951.
2 UST 1859; TIAS 2322; 137 UNTS 81

International express mail agreement, with detailed regulations.
Signed at Accra and Washington February 9 and March 1, 1990.
Entered into force April 16, 1990.
TIAS 11714

PROPERTY

Convention between the United States and the United Kingdom relating to tenure and disposition of real and personal property.
Signed at Washington March 2, 1899.
Applicable to the Gold Coast July 6, 1901.
31 Stat. 1939; TS 146; 12 Bevans 246

SOCIAL SECURITY

Agreement concerning United States participation on a voluntary, limited basis in the Ghanaian social security system.
Exchange of notes at Accra May 16, September 10 and October 30, 1973.
Entered into force October 30, 1973.
24 UST 2202; TIAS 7734; 938 UNTS 353

TAXATION

Agreement to exempt from income tax, on a reciprocal basis, certain income derived from the international operation of a ship or ships and aircraft.
Exchange of notes at Accra April 24 and November 12, 2001.
Entered into force November 12, 2001.
TIAS 13171

TELECOMMUNICATION

Agreement relating to radio communications between amateur stations on behalf of third parties.
Exchange of notes at Accra October 13 and 27, 1977.
Entered into force November 26, 1977.
29 UST 2787; TIAS 8975

TRANSPORTATION

Arrangement between the United States and the United Kingdom relating to pilot licenses to operate civil aircraft.
Exchange of notes at Washington March 28 and April 5, 1935.
Entered into force May 5, 1935.
49 Stat. 3731; EAS 77; 12 Bevans 513; 162 LNTS 59

Air transport agreement, with annexes.
Signed at Washington October 11, 2000.
Entered into force August 17, 2001.
TIAS 13119

TREATY LAW

Agreement relating to treaty rights and obligations assumed by Ghana upon its independence.
Exchange of notes at Accra September 4 and December 21, 1957, and February 12, 1958.
Entered into force February 12, 1958.
13 UST 240; TIAS 4966; 442 UNTS 175

GREECE

ATOMIC ENERGY

Arrangement for the exchange of technical information and cooperation in nuclear safety matters. With addenda and annex.
Signed at Vienna September 17, 2013.
Entered into force September 17, 2013.
TIAS 13-917.1

CLAIMS & DISPUTE RESOLUTION

Treaty of arbitration.
Signed at Washington June 19, 1930.
Entered into force September 23, 1932.
47 Stat. 2161; TS 853; 8 Bevans 349; 136 LNTS 393

Treaty of conciliation.
Signed at Washington June 19, 1930.
Entered into force September 23, 1932.
47 Stat. 2165; TS 854; 8 Bevans 351; 136 LNTS 399

CONSULAR AFFAIRS

Arrangement for the reciprocal reduction of nonimmigrant passport visa fees.*
Exchange of notes at Athens January 7 and 29, 1949.
Entered into force January 29, 1949.
63 Stat. 2905; TIAS 2144; 8 Bevans 447; 88 UNTS 35

Agreement concerning the reciprocal waiver of visas for non-immigrants.
Exchange of notes at Athens December 28, 1999, and January 24, 2000.
Entered into force January 24, 2000.
TIAS 13080
Note:
* The status of this agreement is under review.

CULTURAL EXCHANGES, PROPERTY & COOPERATION

Memorandum of understanding concerning the imposition of import restrictions on categories of archaeological and Byzantine ecclesiastical ethnological material through the 15th century A.D. of the Hellenic Republic.
Signed at Athens July 17, 2011.
Entered into force November 21, 2011.
TIAS 11-1121

DEFENSE

Agreement relating to the use of certain Greek Islands for training exercises by Marine units of the United States fleet in the Mediterranean.
Exchange of notes at Athens February 11 and 21, 1949.
Entered into force February 21, 1949.
63 Stat. 2683; TIAS 1972; 8 Bevans 455; 88 UNTS 29

Agreement relating to the disposition of equipment and material furnished by the United States under the Act to Provide Assistance to Greece and Turkey, as amended, found surplus to the needs of the armed forces of Greece.
Exchange of notes at Athens December 21, 1951, and January 7, 1952.
Entered into force January 7, 1952.
3 UST 3997; TIAS 2537; 177 UNTS 249
Amendment:
April 17 and 18, 1961 (12 UST 496; TIAS 4741; 407 UNTS 238)

Agreement relating to the assurances required under the Mutual Security Act of 1951.
Exchange of notes at Athens December 21, 1951, and January 7, 1952.
Entered into force January 7, 1952.
3 UST 4569; TIAS 2608; 180 UNTS 171

Agreement concerning the inspection and acceptance testing, security, and storage of military items produced by Greek industries under the offshore procurement program, with memoranda of understanding.
Exchange of notes at Athens December 17 and 24, 1952.
Entered into force December 24, 1952.
3 UST 5330; TIAS 2738; 185 UNTS 193

Agreement concerning military facilities.*
Signed at Athens October 12, 1953.
Entered into force October 12, 1953.
4 UST 2189; TIAS 2868; 191 UNTS 319
Note:
* Article III, Paragraph 1, abrogated by agreement of September 7, 1956 (TIAS 3649), except for reference to memorandum of understanding of Feb. 4, 1953 (TIAS 2775), which continues in effect.

Agreement concerning the status of United States forces in Greece.
Signed at Athens September 7, 1956.
Entered into force September 7, 1956.
7 UST 2555; TIAS 3649; 278 UNTS 141

Agreement for cooperation on the uses of atomic energy for mutual defense purposes.
Exchange of notes at Athens May 6, 1959.
Entered into force August 11, 1959.
10 UST 1429; TIAS 4292; 357 UNTS 163

Agreement relating to the deposit by Greece of ten percent of the value of grant military assistance and excess defense articles furnished by the United States.
Exchange of notes at Athens January 11 and 12, 1973.
Entered into force January 12, 1973; effective February 7, 1972.
24 UST 225; TIAS 7543; 938 UNTS 155

Agreement relating to payment to the United States of net proceeds from the sale of defense articles and eligibility for United States military assistance and training under the military assistance program.
Exchange of notes at Athens August 31, 1976.
Entered into force August 31, 1976.
27 UST 3999; TIAS 8418; 1059 UNTS 137
Amendment:
December 27, 2004 and April 13, 2006

Agreement concerning the grant of defense articles and services under the military assistance program.
Exchange of notes at Athens August 30, 1979.
Entered into force August 30, 1979.
30 UST 7267; TIAS 9583; 1182 UNTS 147
Amendment:
August 13 and 26, 1982 (34 UST 1841; TIAS 10464; 1751 UNTS 498)

General security of military information agreement, with annex on industrial security procedures.
Exchange of notes at Athens January 7, 1986.
Entered into force January 7, 1986.
TIAS 11980

Defense industrial cooperation agreement, with annexes and exchange of letters.
Signed at Athens November 10, 1986.
Entered into force November 10, 1986.
TIAS 12320
Amendment:
March 17 and April 4, 1997 (TIAS 12848)

Mutual defense cooperation agreement, with annex.
Signed at Athens July 8, 1990.
Entered into force November 6, 1990.
TIAS 12321

Extensions:
January 19 and February 19, 1998 (TIAS 98-219)
May 4 and 5, 1999 (TIAS 98-219)
April 20 and May 5, 2000 (TIAS 98-219)
March 13 and April 27, 2001 (TIAS 98-219)
April 11 and 29, 2002 (TIAS 98-219)
April 11 and May 5, 2003 (TIAS 98-219)
April 16 and May 6, 2004 (TIAS 04-506.2)
March 16 and May 5, 2005 (TIAS 04-506.2)
April 25 and May 5, 2006 (TIAS 04-506.2)
May 5 and 6, 2007 (TIAS 04-506.2)
April 16 and May 6, 2008 (TIAS 04-506.2)
August 6 and September 11, 2009 (TIAS 04-506.2)
April 14 and May 21, 2010 (TIAS 10-521)
August 1 and October 11, 2011 (TIAS 10-521)
May 19 and June 25, 2014 (TIAS 14-625.1)
June 12 and September 9, 2015 (TIAS 14-625.1)
May 31 and July 29, 2016 (TIAS 16-729)

Memorandum of understanding concerning the joint use of Hellenic Air Force bases by United States Air Force operational units, with annex.
Signed at Athens and Ramstein AB May 6 and June 8, 1992.
Entered into force June 8, 1992.
TIAS 12322

Agreement concerning the transfer of U.S. Government-origin defense articles or related training or other defense services to the Government of the Hellenic Republic.
Exchange of notes at Athens January 22 and 27, 1993.
Entered into force January 27, 1993.
TIAS 12323

Basic exchange and cooperative agreement for topographic mapping, nautical and aeronautical charting, digital data, geodesy and geophysics and related materials.
Signed at Athens May 25, 1993.
Entered into force May 25, 1993.
NP

Agreement concerning mutual logistic support, with annexes.
Signed at Papagos Camp, Greece, and Patch Barracks, Germany, June 28 and August 5, 1996.
Entered into force August 5, 1996.
TIAS

Amendment and Extension:
December 10, 1999, and January 31, 2000

Agreement regarding grants under the Foreign Assistance Act of 1961, as amended, and the furnishing of defense articles, related training and other defense services from the United States to Greece.
Exchange of notes at Athens August 9 and September 11, 2002.
Entered into force September 11, 2002.
TIAS 02-911

Comprehensive technical agreement.
Signed at Brussels June 13, 2001.
Entered into force April 8, 2003.
TIAS

Agreement concerning the exchange and reimbursement of aviation and ground fuel, with annexes.
Signed at Athens and Ft. Belvoir May 25 and July 26, 2007.
Entered into force July 26, 2007.
TIAS 07-726

Amendment:
February 23 and July 5, 2011 (TIAS 07-726)

Memorandum of agreement regarding the exchange of military personnel, with annexes.
Signed at Arlington March 11, 2015.
Entered into force March 11, 2015.
NP

DIPLOMATIC & CONSULAR RELATIONS

Convention concerning the rights and privileges of consuls,* and protocol of amendment signed March 5 and 18, 1903.
Signed at Athens November 19 and December 2, 1902.
Entered into force July 9, 1903.
33 Stat. 2122; TS 424; 8 Bevans 313

Note:
* Notice of termination was given by the United States of articles XII and XIII, effective July 1, 1916, in accordance with the Seamen's Act (38 Stat. 1164). The notice was accepted by the Greek Government with the understanding that only such provisions of these articles as were in conflict with the Act should be abrogated, and all other provisions, especially those concerning the arrest, detention, and imprisonment of deserters from war vessels, should continue in force.

Agreement regarding reciprocal free entry privileges of consular officers and clerks.
Exchange of notes at Athens October 10, 1940.
Entered into force October 10, 1940.
8 Bevans 373

Agreement relating to the importation of goods by American personnel in Greece under the military facilities agreement.
Exchange of notes at Athens June 27, 1955.
Entered into force June 27, 1955.
6 UST 3711; TIAS 3368

EDUCATION

Agreement for financing educational exchange programs.
Signed at Athens December 13, 1963.
Entered into force December 13, 1963.
14 UST 1770; TIAS 5486; 494 UNTS 55

EMPLOYMENT

Agreement relating to employment of dependents of official government employees.
Exchange of notes at Athens January 30 and February 17, 1995.
Entered into force July 7, 1995.
TIAS 12605

ENVIRONMENT & CONSERVATION

Agreement for cooperation in the Global Learning and Observations to Benefit the Environment (GLOBE) Program, with appendices.
Signed at Athens December 12, 1995.
Entered into force December 12, 1995.
TIAS 12709

FINANCE

Debt funding agreement.
Signed at Washington May 10, 1929.
Operative January 1, 1928.
Treasury Department print; 8 Bevans 333

Agreement modifying the debt funding agreement of May 10, 1929.
Signed at Washington May 24, 1932.
Operative July 1, 1931.
Treasury Department print; 8 Bevans 361

Agreement relating to guaranties authorized by Section 111(b)(3) of the Economic Cooperation Act of 1948, as amended.
Exchange of notes at Washington April 21 and 23, 1952.
Entered into force April 29, 1952.
3 UST 4250; TIAS 2568; 177 UNTS 283
Amendment:
April 19, 1963 (14 UST 397; TIAS 5331; 476 UNTS 250)

Agreement providing for the refunding of certain indebtedness due from Greece to the United States and amortization schedule.
Signed at Athens May 28, 1964.
Entered into force November 5, 1966.
17 UST 2331; TIAS 6178; 680 UNTS 143

FOREIGN ASSISTANCE

Agreement on aid to Greece, and exchanges of notes of May 26 and June 15 and 18, 1947.
Signed at Athens June 20, 1947.
Entered into force June 20, 1947.
61 Stat. 2907; TIAS 1625; 8 Bevans 403; 7 UNTS 267

Economic cooperation agreement.
Signed at Athens July 2, 1948.
Entered into force July 3, 1948.
62 Stat. 2293; TIAS 1786; 8 Bevans 431; 23 UNTS 43
Amendments:
December 15 and 24, 1949 (64 Stat. B104; TIAS 2025; 8 Bevans 459; 79 UNTS 298)
March 6 and 30, 1951 (2 UST 843; TIAS 2238; 132 UNTS 384)
October 14, 1952, and December 2, 1953 (5 UST 2844; TIAS 3139; 225 UNTS 250)
April 19, 1963 (14 UST 397; TIAS 5331; 476 UNTS 250)

Agreement relating to duty-free entry and free inland transportation of relief supplies and packages.
Signed at Athens February 9, 1949.
Entered into force February 9, 1949.
63 Stat. 2359; TIAS 1898; 8 Bevans 450; 79 UNTS 95
Amendments:
December 19, 1951, and May 7, 1952 (3 UST 4282; TIAS 2574; 179 UNTS 216)
July 18 and December 22, 1952 (3 UST 5327; TIAS 2737; 185 UNTS 400)

Agreement for cooperation in the economic, scientific, technological, and educational and cultural fields.
Signed at Athens April 22, 1980.
Entered into force April 22, 1980.
32 UST 1034; TIAS 9754; 1234 UNTS 327

INTELLECTUAL PROPERTY

Agreement to facilitate interchange of patent rights and technical information for defense purposes.
Signed at Athens June 16, 1955.
Entered into force June 16, 1955.
6 UST 2173; TIAS 3286; 262 UNTS 137

Agreement approving the procedures for the reciprocal filing of classified patent applications.
Exchange of notes at Athens April 26, 1960.
Entered into force April 26, 1960.
11 UST 1389; TIAS 4476; 372 UNTS 299.

LAW ENFORCEMENT

Arrangement for the direct exchange of certain information regarding the traffic in narcotic drugs.
Exchange of notes at Athens February 7 and October 15, 1928.
Entered into force October 15, 1928.
8 Bevans 331

Convention for prevention of smuggling of alcoholic beverages.
Signed at Washington April 25, 1928.
Entered into force February 18, 1929.
45 Stat. 2736; TS 772; 8 Bevans 327; 91 LNTS 231

Treaty of extradition, and exchange of notes.
Signed at Athens May 6, 1931.
Entered into force November 1, 1932.
47 Stat. 2185; TS 855; 8 Bevans 353; 138 LNTS 293

Protocol interpreting article I of the treaty of extradition signed at Athens May 6, 1931.
Signed at Athens September 2, 1937.
Entered into force September 2, 1937.
51 Stat. 357; EAS 114; 8 Bevans 366; 185 LNTS 408

Procedures for mutual assistance in the administration of justice in connection with the Lockheed Aircraft Corporation matter.
Signed at Washington May 20, 1976.
Entered into force May 20, 1976.
27 UST 2006; TIAS 8300; 1052 UNTS 349

Agreement regarding mutual assistance between customs administrations.
Signed at Athens July 31, 1991.
Entered into force January 17, 1993.
TIAS 12078

Treaty on mutual legal assistance in criminal matters.
Signed at Washington May 26, 1999.
Entered into force November 20, 2001.
TIAS 13036

Protocol to the treaty on extradition of May 6, 1931, and the protocol of September 2, 1937, as contemplated by Article 3(2) of the agreement on extradition between the United States of America and the European Union, signed June 25, 2003.
Signed at Washington January 18, 2006.
Entered into force February 1, 2010.
TIAS 10-201.10

Protocol to the treaty on mutual legal assistance in criminal matters of May 26, 1999, as contemplated by Article 3(2) of the agreement on mutual legal assistance between the United States of America and the European Union, signed June 25, 2003.
Signed at Washington January 18, 2006.
Entered into force February 1, 2010.
TIAS 10-201.33

Agreement on enhancing cooperation in preventing and combating serious crime .
Signed at Corfu June 28, 2009.
Entered into force September 17, 2010.
TIAS 10-917

MARITIME MATTERS

Agreement relating to jurisdiction over vessels utilizing the Louisiana Offshore Oil Port.
Exchange of notes at Athens May 7 and 12, 1982.
Entered into force May 12, 1982.
34 UST 1747; TIAS 10453; 1750 UNTS 417

POSTAL MATTERS

Agreement concerning the exchange of parcel post, and regulations of execution.
Signed at Athens July 14 and at Washington August 1, 1933.
Operative June 1, 1933.
48 Stat. 1594; Post Office Department print

International express mail agreement, with detailed regulations.
Signed at Athens and Washington June 5 and 21, 1985.
Entered into force July 1, 1985.
TIAS 11152

Memorandum of understanding concerning the operation of the INTELPOST field trial, with details of implementation.
Signed at Athens and Washington July 25 and August 15, 1985.
Entered into force August 19, 1985.
TIAS 11247

PROPERTY

Preliminary agreement regarding principles applying to mutual aid in the prosecution of the war against aggression.
Signed at Washington July 10, 1942.
Entered into force July 10, 1942.
56 Stat. 1559; EAS 260; 8 Bevans 381; 103 UNTS 289

PUBLICATIONS

Agreement relating to the exchange of official publications.
Exchange of notes at Athens September 26 and October 24, 1950.
Entered into force October 24, 1950.
2 UST 473; TIAS 2193; 133 UNTS 41

SOCIAL SECURITY

Agreement on social security, with administrative arrangement.
Signed at Athens June 22, 1993.
Entered into force September 1, 1994.
TIAS

TAXATION

Agreement regarding privileges, immunities, and exemptions from taxes or other levies and charges accorded by Greece in implementation of the common defense program and any and all foreign aid programs of the United States.
Exchange of notes at Athens February 4, 1953.
Entered into force February 4, 1953.
4 UST 166; TIAS 2775; 189 UNTS 3

Convention and protocol for the avoidance of double taxation and the prevention of fiscal evasion with respect to taxes on the estates of deceased persons.*
Signed at Athens February 20, 1950;
Protocol of amendment signed at Athens July 18, 1953.
Entered into force December 30, 1953.
5 UST 12; TIAS 2901; 196 UNTS 269

Note

* For understanding regarding certain errors in the English text, see exchange of notes of August 3 and 19, 1954 (5 UST 1543; TIAS 3032; 222 UNTS 423).

Convention and protocol for the avoidance of double taxation and prevention of fiscal evasion with respect to taxes on income.*
Signed at Athens February 20, 1950;
Protocol of amendment signed at Athens April 20, 1953.
Entered into force December 30, 1953.
5 UST 47; TIAS 2902; 196 UNTS 291

Note:

* For understanding regarding certain errors in the Greek text, see exchange of notes of November 29 and December 19, 1961 (13 UST 151; TIAS 4951; 435 UNTS 334).

Protocol modifying and supplementing the convention of February 20, 1950, for the avoidance of double taxation and the prevention of fiscal evasion with respect to taxes on the estates of deceased persons.
Signed at Athens February 12, 1964.
Entered into force October 27, 1967.
18 UST 2853; TIAS 6375; 632 UNTS 315

Agreement concerning relief from double taxation on earnings derived from the operation of ships and aircraft.
Exchange of notes at Washington June 10, 1988.
Entered into force June 10, 1988.
TIAS 11585; 2191 UNTS 249

TELECOMMUNICATION

Agreement concerning the transfer of community radios to the Government of Greece, with three schedules attached.
Signed at Athens August 18, 1954.
Entered into force August 18, 1954.
5 UST 1725; TIAS 3050; 234 UNTS 161

Agreement relating to the reciprocal granting of authorizations to permit licensed amateur radio operators of either country to operate their stations in the other country.
Exchanges of notes at Athens June 20 and July 5, 1978.
Entered into force July 5, 1978.
30 UST 1648; TIAS 9272; 1153 UNTS 81

TRADE & INVESTMENT

Agreement regarding commercial relations.
Exchange of notes at Washington January 2 and 11, 1946.
Entered into force January 11, 1946.
60 Stat. 1483; TIAS 1505; 8 Bevans 396; 3 UNTS 203

Treaty of friendship, commerce, and navigation.
Signed at Athens August 3, 1951.
Entered into force October 13, 1954.
5 UST 1829; TIAS 3057; 224 UNTS 279

Agreement providing for consultations should cotton textile or cotton textile product exports from Greece cause market disruption in the United States.
Exchange of notes at Athens December 29, 1975, and January 5, 1976.
Entered into force January 5, 1976.
27 UST 1632; TIAS 8273

TRANSPORTATION

Air service agreement.
Exchange of notes at Athens March 11 and June 16 and 25, 1952.
Entered into force June 25, 1952.
3 UST 4856; TIAS 2658; 181 UNTS 53

GRENADA

On February 7, 1974, Grenada became an independent state. In a note dated August 19, 1974, to the Secretary-General of the United Nations, the Prime Minister made a statement reading in part as follows:

I have the honour to inform you that the Government of Grenada, having attained Independence on the 7th February, 1974, and being conscious of the desirability of continuing and maintaining existing International Agreements which applied before Independence and being willing to accept its obligations under International Law to honour its treaty commitments, acknowledges that the many treaty rights and obligations entered into by the Government of the United Kingdom in respect of the Government of Grenada, were succeeded to by the Government of Grenada upon the attainment of Independence and in accordance with customary International Law and Practice.

2. It is desirous, therefore, that it be accepted that each treaty has been legally succeeded to by the Government of Grenada and that actions relating to all treaties be based on this succession until a decision is otherwise taken and due notification communicated to the United Nations and to the states signatories thereto in respect of any such particular treaty.

3. The Government of Grenada reserves the right to terminate the operation of any such treaty succeeded to if it is desirable to do so. In such circumstances due notice will be given of any such termination and in the terms thereof.

CULTURAL EXCHANGES, PROPERTY & COOPERATION

Agreement relating to the establishment of a Peace Corps program in Grenada.
Exchange of notes at Bridgetown and Grenada December 19, 1966, and December 16, 1967.
Entered into force December 16, 1967.
18 UST 3073; TIAS 6398; 701 UNTS 277

DEFENSE

Agreement concerning the status of United States forces in Grenada.
Exchange of notes at St. George's March 12 and 13, 1984.
Entered into force March 13, 1984.
TIAS

Agreement concerning the provision of training related to defense articles under the United States International Military Education and Training (IMET) Program.
Exchange of notes at St. George's May 18 and 24, 1984.
Entered into force May 24, 1984.
NP

Agreement concerning the status of United States Armed Forces personnel in Grenada.
Exchange of notes at St. George's December 7, 1992, and October 11, 1993.
Entered into force October 11, 1993.
NP

Agreement regarding the provision of articles, services and associated training by the Government of the United States for anti-narcotics purposes.
Exchange of notes at St. George's November 18 and December 3, 1998.
Entered into force December 3, 1998.
TIAS

Agreement regarding the Caribbean Basin Security Initiative and the provision of technical support for maritime security forces.
Effected by exchange of notes at St. George's March 18 and April 26, 2013.
Entered into force April 26, 2013.
TIAS 13-426

DIPLOMATIC & CONSULAR RELATIONS

Consular convention between the United States and the United Kingdom.
Signed at Washington June 6, 1951.
Entered into force September 7, 1972.
3 UST 3426; TIAS 2494; 165 UNTS 121

EMPLOYMENT

Agreement relating to employment of dependents of official government employees, with addendum.
Exchange of notes at St. George's September 14 and 15, 1987.
Entered into force September 15, 1987.
TIAS 11539.

FINANCE

Agreement relating to investment guaranties.
Signed at St. Georges June 27, 1968.
Entered into force June 27, 1968.
19 UST 5211; TIAS 6516; 730 UNTS 217

Agreement regarding the consolidation and rescheduling of certain debts owed to, guaranteed by or insured by the United States Government or its agency, with annexes.
Signed at St. Georges July 11, 2007.
Entered into force September 18, 2007.
NP

Amendment:
August 13 and October 2, 2009 (NP)

Agreement regarding the consolidation and rescheduling of certain debts owed to, guaranteed by, or insured by the United States Government or its agency, with Annexes.
Signed at St George's May 21, 2016.
Entered into force July 18, 2016.
NP

FOREIGN ASSISTANCE

General agreement for economic, technical and related assistance.
Signed at Grenada May 7, 1984.
Entered into force May 7, 1984.
TIAS 11132; 2120 UNTS 123

INTELLECTUAL PROPERTY

Declaration by the United States and the United Kingdom affording reciprocal protection to trademarks.
Signed at London October 24, 1877.
Entered into force October 24, 1877.
20 Stat. 703; TS 138; 12 Bevans 198

INTERNATIONAL CRIMINAL COURT

Agreement regarding the surrender of persons to the International Criminal Court.
Exchange of notes at Washington and New York March 11, 2004.
Entered into force March 11, 2004.
TIAS 04-311

LAW ENFORCEMENT

Agreement regarding the provision of articles, services and associated military education and training by the United States Government for anti-narcotics purposes.
Exchange of notes at St. George's December 23, 1996, and March 14, 1997.
Entered into force March 14, 1997.
TIAS 12843

Treaty on mutual legal assistance in criminal matters, with forms.
Done at St. George's May 30, 1996.
Entered into force September 14, 1999.
TIAS

Extradition treaty.
Done at St. George's May 30, 1996.
Entered into force September 14, 1999.
TIAS 99-914.1

MARITIME MATTERS

Agreement concerning maritime counter-drug operations.
Signed at St. George's May 16, 1995.
Entered into force May 16, 1995.
TIAS 12648

POSTAL MATTERS

Money order agreement.
Signed at Washington July 29 and at Grenada August 29, 1904.
Operative October 1, 1904.
NP

Agreement for the direct exchange of parcels by parcel post.
Signed at Grenada May 20 and at Washington June 21, 1935.
Operative July 1, 1935.
49 Stat. 3229; Post Office Department print; 162 LNTS 157

International express mail agreement.
Signed at St. George's and Washington January 4 and April 4, 1995.
Entered into force May 1, 1995.
NP

PROPERTY

Convention between the United States and the United Kingdom relating to tenure and disposition of real and personal property.
Signed at Washington March 2, 1899.
Applicable to Grenada February 9, 1901.
31 Stat. 1939; TS 146; 12 Bevans 246

Supplementary convention relating to the tenure and disposition of real and personal property.
Signed at Washington May 27, 1936.
Entered into force March 10, 1941.
55 Stat. 1101; TS 964; 203 LNTS 367

SCIENTIFIC & TECHNICAL COOPERATION

Memorandum of understanding concerning scientific and technical cooperation in earth sciences, with annexes.
Signed at Reston and St. George's December 9, 2005.
Entered into force December 9, 2005.
TIAS 05-1209

TAXATION

Agreement for the exchange of information with respect to taxes.
Signed at Washington December 18, 1986.
Entered into force July 13, 1987.
TIAS 11410; 2191 UNTS 43

TELECOMMUNICATION

Agreement between the United States and the United Kingdom relating to the reciprocal granting of authorizations to permit licensed amateur radio operators of either country to operate their stations in the other country.
Exchange of notes at London November 26, 1965.
Applicable to Grenada December 11, 1979.
16 UST 2047; TIAS 5941; 561 UNTS 193

Agreement between the United States and the United Kingdom extending to certain territories the application of the agreement of November 26, 1965, relating to the reciprocal granting of authorizations to permit licensed amateur radio operators of either country to operate their stations in the other country.
Exchange of notes at London December 11, 1969.
Entered into force December 11, 1969.
20 UST 4089; TIAS 6800; 732 UNTS 334

Arrangement relating to radio communications between amateur stations on behalf of third parties.
Exchange of notes at St. George's December 5 and 8, 1983.
Entered into force December 8, 1983.
35 UST 3275; TIAS 10855; 2015 UNTS 17

Agreement concerning establishment of a radio relay station of the United States Information Agency (VOA) on the Island of Grenada.
Signed at St. George's September 29, 1987.
Entered into force March 23, 1988.
TIAS 12394

TRADE & INVESTMENT

Treaty concerning the reciprocal encouragement and protection of investment.
Signed at Washington May 2, 1986.
Entered into force March 3, 1989.
TIAS

TRANSPORTATION

Agreement between the United States and the United Kingdom relating to air services.
Signed at Bermuda February 11, 1946.
Entered into force February 11, 1946.
60 Stat. 1499; TIAS 1507; 3 UNTS 253
Amendment:
May 27, 1966 (17 UST 683; TIAS 6019; 573 UNTS 274)

Agreement modifying the agreement of February 11, 1946, as amended, as applied to air services between the United States and Grenada.
Exchange of notes at St. George's March 19 and May 11, 1987.
Entered into force May 11, 1987.
TIAS 11279

GUATEMALA

AGRICULTURE

Memorandum of understanding relating to cooperative efforts to protect crops from pest damage and diseases.
Signed at Guatemala February 21, 1977.
Entered into force February 21, 1977.
29 UST 228; TIAS 8807

Agreement relating to a cooperative program for the prevention of foot-and-mouth disease, rinderpest, and other exotic diseases in Guatemala.
Signed at Guatemala March 3, 1977.
Entered into force March 3, 1977.
29 UST 242; TIAS 8808

ATOMIC ENERGY

Agreement providing for a grant to assist in the acquisition of certain nuclear research and training equipment and materials.
Exchange of notes at Guatemala April 7 and 23, 1960.
Entered into force April 23, 1960.
11 UST 1449; TIAS 4485

CONSULAR AFFAIRS

Agreement providing reciprocally for gratis nonimmigrant visas valid for multiple entries.*
Exchange of notes at Guatemala May 30, 1956.
Entered into force May 30, 1956.
7 UST 1075; TIAS 3589; 275 UNTS 271
Note:
* The status of this agreement is under review.

CULTURAL EXCHANGES, PROPERTY & COOPERATION

Agreement relating to the establishment of a Peace Corps program in Guatemala.
Exchange of notes at Guatemala City December 28 and 29, 1962.
Entered into force December 29, 1962.
14 UST 280; TIAS 5307; 474 UNTS 31

Agreement for the recovery and return of stolen archaeological, historical and cultural properties.
Signed at Washington May 21, 1984.
Entered into force August 22, 1984.
TIAS 11077; 2039 UNTS 241

Memorandum of understanding concerning the imposition of import restrictions on archaeological materials from the pre-Columbian cultures and ecclesiastical ethnological material from the conquest and colonial periods of Guatemala, with appendix.
Signed at Washington September 29, 1997.
Entered into force September 29, 1997.
TIAS 97-929
Amendments and Extensions:
September 20 and 23, 2002 (TIAS 97-929)
August 23 and 24, 2007 (TIAS 97-929)
September 13 and 25, 2012 (TIAS 12-925)

DEFENSE

Military air transit agreement.
Exchange of notes at Guatemala December 20, 1949.
Entered into force December 20, 1949.
64 Stat. B122; TIAS 2042; 8 Bevans 610; 70 UNTS 71

Agreement providing for the transfer of equipment and material to the Government of Guatemala subject to certain understandings.
Exchange of notes at Guatemala July 27 and 30, 1954.
Entered into force July 30, 1954.
5 UST 1926; TIAS 3059; 234 UNTS 235

Military assistance agreement.
Signed at Guatemala June 18, 1955.
Entered into force June 18, 1955.
6 UST 2107; TIAS 3283; 262 UNTS 105

Agreement relating to the disposition of equipment and materials no longer required in furtherance of the mutual defense assistance program.
Exchange of notes at Guatemala December 16, 1957.
Entered into force December 16, 1957.
8 UST 2463; TIAS 3966; 307 UNTS 306

Agreement relating to the furnishing of defense articles and services to Guatemala for the purpose of contributing to its internal security.
Exchange of notes at Guatemala May 25 and August 2, 1962.
Entered into force August 2, 1962.
13 UST 2128; TIAS 5173; 461 UNTS 199

Agreement relating to the status of the Army and Air Force missions to Guatemala.
Exchange of notes at Guatemala April 29 and May 4, 1965.
Entered into force May 4, 1965.
16 UST 742; TIAS 5802; 545 UNTS 163

Agreement concerning payment to the United States of net proceeds from the sale of defense articles furnished under the military assistance program.
Exchange of notes at Guatemala September 20 and 27, 1974.
Entered into force September 27, 1974; effective July 1, 1974.
25 UST 2489; TIAS 7932
Amendment:
January 20 and April 20, 2005 (TIAS 05-420.1)

Basic exchange and cooperative agreement for topographic mapping, nautical and aeronautical charting and information, geodesy and geophysics, digital data and related mapping, charting and geodesy materials, with glossary.
Signed at Guatemala and Fairfax June 7 and July 2, 1996.
Entered into force July 2, 1996.
NP

Agreement regarding the furnishing of articles and services from the United States of America to the Government of the Republic of Guatemala pursuant to the global peacekeeping operations initiative.
Exchange of notes at Guatemala December 1, 2005, and January 3, 2006.
Entered into force March 14, 2006.
TIAS 06-314

Agreement regarding the status of United States personnel who may be temporarily present in Guatemala in connection with Special Operation Training.
Exchange of notes at Guatemala City December 21 and 27, 2010.
Entered into force December 27, 2010.
TIAS
Extensions:
December 26 and 28, 2012
November 26, 2014
November 2 and December 20, 2016

Agreement regarding the status of United States personnel who may be temporarily present in Guatemala in connection with projects under the U.S. Southern Command Humanitarian Assistance Program (HAP).
Exchange of notes at Guatemala City December 17 and 27, 2010.
Entered into force December 27, 2010.
TIAS
Extensions:
December 26 and 28, 2012
November 26 and December 14, 2014
November 2 and December 22, 2016

Agreement concerning the U.S. Army Corps of Engineers.
Effected by exchange of notes at Guatemala City August 24 and 31, 2011.
Entered into force October 11, 2011.
TIAS
Extension:
October 10, 2013 and February 21, 2014

Agreement concerning health care for military members and their dependents.
Signed at Washington April 17, 2013.
Entered into force April 17, 2013.
NP
Extension:
February 17 and March 28, 2016

Memorandum of agreement regarding the assignment of liaison officers, with annexes.
Signed at Guatemala and Doral September 30 and December 13, 2016.
Entered into force December 13, 2016.
NP

EMPLOYMENT

Agreement relating to the employment of dependents of official government employees, with agreement and addendum.
Exchange of notes at Washington March 22 and 23, 1990.
Entered into force March 23, 1990.
TIAS

Agreement on reciprocity in the free exercise of remunerated activities for dependent family members of diplomatic, consular and administrative and technical staff and members of the support staff assigned to diplomatic missions, consular offices and permanent missions to international organizations.
Signed at Guatemala City April 25, 2007.
Entered into force June 14, 2007.
TIAS 07-614

ENVIRONMENT & CONSERVATION

Agreement for cooperation in the Global Learning and Observations to Benefit the Environment (GLOBE) Program, with appendices.
Signed at Guatemala December 5, 1997.
Entered into force December 5, 1997.
TIAS 12909

FINANCE

Agreement relating to investment guaranties.*
Exchange of notes at Guatemala August 9, 1960.
Entered into force August 29, 1962.
13 UST 2008; TIAS 5158; 461 UNTS 15

Note:
* For corrections in the Spanish text, see exchange of notes of August 23 and 27, 1962 (13 UST 2008; TIAS 5158; 461 UNTS 15).

Agreement regarding a debt-for-nature swap to prepay and cancel certain debt owed.
Signed at Guatemala September 8, 2006.
Entered into force September 8, 2006.
TIAS

FOREIGN ASSISTANCE

General agreement for technical cooperation.
Signed at Guatemala September 1, 1954.
Entered into force September 1, 1954.
5 UST 2010; TIAS 3068; 199 UNTS 51

Development assistance agreement.
Signed at Washington December 13, 1954.
Entered into force December 13, 1954.
5 UST 2972; TIAS 3155; 237 UNTS 169

AGENCY FOR INTERNATIONAL DEVELOPMENT

Strategic objective grant agreement for the ruling justly, economic freedom and investing in people.
Signed September 14, 2004.
Entered into force September 14, 2004.
NP

Amendment:
September 28, 2009 (NP)

INTELLECTUAL PROPERTY

Convention for the reciprocal protection of trademarks and trade labels.
Signed at Guatemala April 15, 1901.
Entered into force April 7, 1902.
32 Stat. 1866; TS 404; 8 Bevans 478

Convention for the reciprocal protection of patents.
Signed at Guatemala November 10, 1906.
Entered into force July 9, 1907.
35 Stat. 1878; TS 463; 8 Bevans 489

LAW ENFORCEMENT

Treaty for the mutual extradition of fugitives from justice.
Signed at Washington February 27, 1903.
Entered into force August 15, 1903.
33 Stat. 2147; TS 425; 8 Bevans 482

Supplementary extradition convention.
Signed at Guatemala City February 20, 1940.
Entered into force March 13, 1941.
55 Stat. 1097; TS 963; 8 Bevans 528

Treaty for the return of stolen, robbed, embezzled or appropriated vehicles and aircraft, with annexes and a related exchange of notes.
Signed at Guatemala City on October 6, 1997.
Entered into force April 25, 2007.
TIAS 07-425

Agreement concerning security assistance matters and the provision of articles, services and associated military education and training by the United States Government for anti-narcotics purposes.
Exchange of notes at Guatemala January 12 and February 1, 1999.
Entered into force February 1, 1999.
NP

Agreement regarding the Cooperating Nation Information Exchange System.
Exchange of notes at Guatemala November 30, 2004.
Entered into force November 30, 2004.
TIAS 04-1130

MARITIME MATTERS

Agreement concerning cooperation to suppress illicit traffic in narcotic drugs and psychotropic substances by sea and air.
Signed at Guatemala June 19, 2003.
Entered into force October 10, 2003.
TIAS

PEACE

Treaty of peace, amity, commerce, and navigation.*
Signed at Guatemala March 3, 1849.
Entered into force May 13, 1852.
10 Stat. 875; TS 149; 8 Bevans 461

Note:

* Articles relating to commerce and navigation terminated November 4, 1874.

POSTAL MATTERS

Parcel post agreement.
Signed at Guatemala October 25, and at Washington November 30, 1945.
Operative August 1, 1945.
59 Stat. 1827; EAS 499; 139 UNTS 45

International express mail agreement, with detailed regulations.
Signed at Guatemala and Washington November 7 and December 19, 1989.
Entered into force February 15, 1990.
TIAS 11717

PROPERTY

Convention relating to tenure and disposition of real and personal property.
Signed at Guatemala August 27, 1901.
Entered into force September 26, 1902.
32 Stat. 1944; TS 412; 8 Bevans 480

PUBLICATIONS

Agreement relating to the exchange of official publications.
Exchange of notes at Guatemala March 23 and April 13, 1944.
Entered into force March 23, 1944.
58 Stat. 1362; EAS 412; 8 Bevans 555; 106 UNTS 213

TELECOMMUNICATION

Agreement relating to the reciprocal granting of authorizations to permit licensed amateur radio operators of either country to operate their stations in the other country.
Exchange of notes at Guatemala November 30 and December 11, 1967.
Entered into force October 2, 1969.
20 UST 2883; TIAS 6766; 726 UNTS 147

Arrangement relating to radio communications between amateur stations on behalf of third parties.
Exchange of notes at Guatemala October 21 and November 19, 1971.
Entered into force May 26, 1973.
24 UST 1120; TIAS 7636

TRADE & INVESTMENT

Convention for the development of commerce and to increase the exchange of commodities by facilitating the work of traveling salesmen.
Signed at Washington December 3, 1918.
Entered into force August 25, 1919.
41 Stat. 1669; TS 642; 8 Bevans 498

Agreement on trade in textile and apparel goods.
Exchange of letters at Guatemala and Washington June 23, 2006.
Entered into force June 23, 2006.
NP

TRANSPORTATION

Agreement relating to the construction of the inter-American highway.
Exchange of notes at Guatemala May 19, 1943.
Entered into force May 19, 1943.
57 Stat. 1111; EAS 345; 8 Bevans 545; 28 UNTS 377

Amendments:

May 18, 1948 (62 Stat. 3923; TIAS 2001; 8 Bevans 596; 67 UNTS 161)
July 28 and August 28, 1954 (5 UST 2244; TIAS 3084; 237 UNTS 294)

Agreement providing for cooperation in the construction of the inter-American Highway in Guatemala.
Exchange of notes at Guatemala September 25 and October 3, 1963.
Entered into force October 3, 1963.
14 UST 1591; TIAS 5463; 493 UNTS 45

Air transport agreement, with annexes.
Signed at San Jose May 8, 1997.
Entered into force September 3, 2001.
TIAS

Memorandum of cooperation for mutual cooperation in the promotion and development of civil aviation.
Signed at Washington and Guatemala May 26 and June 11, 1999.
Entered into force June 11, 1999.
TIAS 13041

GUINEA

CULTURAL EXCHANGES, PROPERTY & COOPERATION

Cultural relations agreement.
Exchange of notes at Washington October 28, 1959.
Entered into force October 28, 1959.
10 UST 1829; TIAS 4342; 358 UNTS 169

Agreement relating to the establishment of a Peace Corps program in Guinea.
Exchange of notes at Conakry December 11 and 14, 1962.
Entered into force December 14, 1962.
13 UST 2729; TIAS 5246; 462 UNTS 247

DEFENSE

Agreement relating to military assistance.
Exchange of notes at Conakry June 29, 1965.
Entered into force June 29, 1965.
16 UST 1073; TIAS 5848; 549 UNTS 139

Agreement concerning the provision of training related to defense articles under the United States International Military Education and Training (IMET) Program.
Exchange of notes at Conakry March 29, 1983, and February 13, 1984.
Entered into force February 13, 1984.
35 UST 4412; TIAS 10944

Agreement regarding grants under the Foreign Assistance Act of 1961, as amended, and the furnishing of defense articles, related training, and other defense services from the United States of America to the Government of the Republic of Guinea.
Exchange of notes at Conakry July 13 and December 22, 2000.
Entered into force December 22, 2000.
TIAS 13132

Agreement on the status of United States forces in Guinea.
Signed at Washington December 19, 2014.
Entered into force December 19, 2014.
TIAS 14-1219

ENVIRONMENT & CONSERVATION

Agreement for cooperation in the Global Learning and Observations to Benefit the Environment (GLOBE) Program, with Appendices.
Signed at Conakry May 14, 1998.
Entered into force May 14, 1998.
TIAS 12952

FINANCE

Agreement relating to investment guaranties.
Exchange of notes at Washington May 9, 1962.
Entered into force May 9, 1962.
13 UST 1091; TIAS 5052; 451 UNTS 197

Agreement regarding the consolidation and rescheduling of certain debts owed to or guaranteed by the United States Government and its agencies, with annexes.
Signed at Conakry February 27, 1987.
Entered into force April 8, 1987.
NP

Agreement regarding the consolidation and rescheduling of certain debts owed to, guaranteed by or insured by the United States Government and its agencies, with annexes.
Signed at Conakry November 22, 1989.
Entered into force January 22, 1990.
NP

Agreement regarding the consolidation and rescheduling or refinancing of certain debts owed to, guaranteed by or insured by the United States Government and its agencies, with annexes.
Signed at Conakry June 24, 1993.
Entered into force September 13, 1993.
NP

Agreement regarding the consolidation, reduction and rescheduling of certain debts owed to, guaranteed by, or insured by the United States Government and its agencies.
Signed at Conakry November 18, 1996.
Entered into force April 9, 1997.
NP

Agreement regarding the consolidation, reduction and rescheduling of certain debts owed to, guaranteed by, or insured by the United States Government and its agencies, with annexes.
Signed at Conakry October 29, 1997.
Entered into force December 17, 1997.
NP

Agreement regarding the consolidation and reduction of certain debts owed to, guaranteed by, or insured by the United States Government and its agencies, with annexes.
Signed at Conakry April 8, 2002.
Entered into force May 22, 2002.
NP

Agreement regarding the reduction of certain debts owed to, guaranteed by, or insured by the United States Government and its agencies, with annexes.
Signed at Conakry May 9, 2008.
Entered into force June 16, 2008.
NP

Agreement regarding the partial reduction and rescheduling of certain debts owed to, guaranteed by, or insured by the United States Government and its agencies, with annexes.
Signed at Conakry January 18, 2013.
Entered into force March 8, 2013.
NP

FOREIGN ASSISTANCE

Agreement providing for the furnishing of economic, technical and related assistance.
Exchange of notes at Conakry September 30, 1960.
Entered into force September 30, 1960.
11 UST 2258; TIAS 4603; 394 UNTS 103

Agreement relating to an informational media guaranty program in Guinea.
Exchange of notes at Conakry October 31 and November 3, 1962.
Entered into force November 3, 1962.
13 UST 2508; TIAS 5217; 459 UNTS 259

INTERNATIONAL CRIMINAL COURT

Agreement regarding the surrender of persons to the International Criminal Court.
Signed at Conakry August 23, 2003.
Entered into force March 25, 2004.
TIAS 04-325

POSTAL MATTERS

International express mail agreement, with detailed regulations.
Signed at Conakry and Washington December 31, 1987, and February 2, 1988.
Entered into force March 15, 1988.
TIAS 11562

Postal money order agreement.
Signed at Washington February 23, 1999.
Entered into force February 23, 1999.
NP

TELECOMMUNICATION

Agreement relating to radio communication facilities at or near Embassy sites for transmission of official messages.
Exchange of notes at Conakry February 19 and April 23, 1963.
Entered into force April 23, 1963.
14 UST 847; TIAS 5365; 487 UNTS 291

GUINEA-BISSAU

CULTURAL EXCHANGES, PROPERTY & COOPERATION

Agreement relating to the establishment of a Peace Corps program in Guinea-Bissau.
Exchange of notes at Bissau January 12 and 15, 1988.
Entered into force January 15, 1988.
TIAS 12104

DEFENSE

Agreement concerning the provision of training related to defense articles under the United States International Military Education and Training (IMET) Program.
Exchange of notes at Bissau September 10 and October 16, 1986.
Entered into force October 16, 1986.
TIAS 11378

EMPLOYMENT

Agreement relating to the employment of dependents of official government employees.
Exchange of notes at Bissau July 23, 1997, and February 16, 1998.
Entered into force February 16, 1998.
TIAS 12932

FINANCE

Investment incentive agreement.
Exchange of notes at Bissau August 14 and 15, 1985.
Entered into force August 20, 1986.
TIAS 12088

INTERNATIONAL CRIMINAL COURT

Agreement regarding the surrender of persons to international tribunals.
Exchange of notes at Dakar and Bissau January 28, February 2, and March 14, 2005.
Entered into force February 8, 2005.
TIAS 05-208

POSTAL MATTERS

International express mail agreement, with detailed regulations.
Signed at Bissau and Washington July 17 and August 28, 1991.
Entered into force September 30, 1991.
TIAS 11797

GUYANA

On May 26, 1966, Guyana (former British Guiana) became an independent state. In a letter dated June 30, 1966, to the Secretary General of the United Nations, the Prime Minister of Guyana made a statement reading in part as follows:

I have the honour to inform you that the Government of Guyana, conscious of the desirability of maintaining existing legal relationships, and conscious of its obligations under international law to honour its treaty commitments, acknowledges that many treaty rights and obligations of the Government of the United Kingdom in respect to British Guiana were succeeded to by Guyana upon independence by virtue of customary international law.

2. Since, however, it is likely that by virtue of customary international law certain treaties may have lapsed at the date of independence of Guyana, it seems essential that each treaty should be subjected to legal examination. It is proposed after this examination has been completed, to indicate which, if any, of the treaties which may have lapsed by customary international law the Government of Guyana wishes to treat as having lapsed.

3. As a result, the manner in which British Guiana was acquired by the British Crown, and its history previous to that date, consideration will have to be given to the question which, if any, treaties contracted previous to 1804 remain in force by virtue of customary international law.

4. It is desired that it be presumed that each treaty has been legally succeeded to by Guyana and that action be based on this presumption until a decision is reached that it should be regarded as having lapsed. Should the Government of Guyana be of the opinion that it has legally succeeded to a treaty and wishes to terminate the operation of the treaty, it will in due course give notice of termination in the terms thereof.

CONSULAR AFFAIRS

Agreement relating to extended validity of passports issued by Guyana.
Exchange of notes at Georgetown May 20 and July 18, 1970.
Entered into force January 18, 1971.
22 UST 233; TIAS 7056; 781 UNTS 159

CULTURAL EXCHANGES, PROPERTY & COOPERATION

Agreement relating to the establishment of a Peace Corps program in Guyana.
Exchange of notes at Georgetown May 31 and June 7, 1967.
Entered into force June 7, 1967.
18 UST 1259; TIAS 6277; 686 UNTS 25

DEFENSE

Agreement concerning the provision of training related to defense articles under the United States International Military Education and Training (IMET) Program.
Exchange of notes at Georgetown January 13 and 22, 1981.
Entered into force January 22, 1981.
33 UST 850; TIAS 10068

Agreement regarding grants under the Foreign Assistance Act of 1961, as amended, and the furnishing of defense articles, related training and other defense services from the United States to Guyana.
Exchange of notes at Georgetown March 31 and June 8, 1994.
Entered into force June 8, 1994.
TIAS 12253

Agreement regarding the status of military and civilian personnel of the United States Department of Defense temporarily present in Guyana in connection with military exercises and training, counter-drug related activities, United States security assistance programs, or other agreed purposes.
Exchange of notes at Georgetown December 28 and 29, 2000.
Entered into force December 29, 2000.
NP
Amendment:
April 4 and May 10, 2006

Agreement regarding the Caribbean Basin Security Initiative (Technical Assistance Field Team).
Effected by exchange of notes at Georgetown June 28, 2012 and January 30, 2013.
Entered into force January 30, 2013.
TIAS 13-130

DIPLOMATIC & CONSULAR RELATIONS

Consular convention between the United States and the United Kingdom.
Signed at Washington June 6, 1951.
Entered into force September 7, 1952.
3 UST 3426; TIAS 2494; 165 UNTS 121

EMPLOYMENT

Agreement concerning the employment on a reciprocal basis of dependents of official employees.
Exchange of notes at Georgetown August 16 and 21, 2001.
Entered into force August 21, 2001.
TIAS 13162

FINANCE

Agreement relating to investment guaranties.
Signed at Georgetown May 29, 1965.
Entered into force August 18, 1965.
16 UST 2050; TIAS 5942; 605 UNTS 87

Agreement regarding the consolidation and rescheduling or refinancing of certain debts owed to, guaranteed by, or insured by the United States Government and its agencies, with annexes.
Signed at Georgetown September 8, 1989.
Entered into force October 13, 1989.
NP

Swap agreement among the United States Treasury and the Bank of Guyana/Republic of Guyana, with memorandum of understanding.
Signed at Georgetown and Washington June 19 and 20, 1990.
Entered into force June 20, 1990.
TIAS

Agreement regarding the consolidation and rescheduling of certain debts owed to, guaranteed by, or insured by the United States Government and its agencies, with annexes.
Signed at Georgetown March 28, 1991.
Entered into force May 13, 1991.
NP

Agreement regarding the discharge of certain debts owed to the Government of the United States, with annex.
Signed at Georgetown September 30, 1991.
Entered into force September 30, 1991.
NP

Agreement regarding the consolidation and rescheduling or refinancing of certain debts owed to, guaranteed by or insured by the United States Government and its agencies, with annexes.
Signed at Washington April 5, 1994.
Entered into force May 23, 1994.
NP

Agreement regarding the reduction and reorganization of certain debts owed to, guaranteed by, or insured by the United States Government and its agencies, with annexes.
Signed at Georgetown March 27, 1997.
Entered into force June 6, 1997.
NP

Agreement regarding the reduction and reorganization of certain debts owed to, guaranteed by, or insured by the United States Government and its agencies, with annexes and side letter.
Signed at Georgetown December 20, 2000.
Entered into force March 1, 2001.
NP

Agreement regarding the cancellation of debt owed to, guaranteed by, or insured by the United States Government.
Signed at Georgetown June 24, 2004.
Entered into force September 2, 2004.
NP

FOREIGN ASSISTANCE

General agreement for economic, technical and related assistance.
Signed at Georgetown November 8, 1979.
Entered into force November 8, 1979.
31 UST 4826; TIAS 9644

INTELLECTUAL PROPERTY

Declaration by the United States and the United Kingdom affording reciprocal protection to trade-marks.
Signed at London October 24, 1877.
Entered into force October 24, 1877.
20 Stat. 703; TS 138; 12 Bevans 198

INTERNATIONAL CRIMINAL COURT

Agreement regarding the surrender of persons to the International Criminal Court.
Signed at Georgetown December 11, 2003.
Entered into force May 18, 2004.
TIAS 04-518

LAW ENFORCEMENT

Extradition treaty between the United States and the United Kingdom.
Signed at London December 22, 1931.
Entered into force June 24, 1935.
47 Stat. 2122; TS 849; 12 Bevans 482; 163 LNTS 59

POSTAL MATTERS

Parcel post agreement with detailed regulations of execution.
Signed at Georgetown August 13 and at Washington September 6, 1938.
Entered into force October 1, 1938.
53 Stat. 1989; Post Office Department print; 193 LNTS 117

International express mail agreement with detailed regulations.
Signed at Georgetown and Washington February 25 and March 31, 1986.
Entered into force July 1, 1986.
TIAS 11406

Postal money order agreement.
Signed at Georgetown and Washington September 23 and October 10, 1991.
Entered into force November 15, 1991.
TIAS 11792

International express mail agreement, with detailed regulations.
Signed at Georgetown and Washington June 22 and July 16, 1994.
Entered into force November 1, 1994.
NP

PROPERTY

Convention between the United States and the United Kingdom relating to the tenure and disposition of real and personal property.
Signed at Washington March 2, 1899.
Applicable to British Guiana June 17, 1901.
31 Stat. 1939; TS 146; 12 Bevans 246

Supplementary convention relating to the tenure and disposition of real and personal property of March 2, 1899.
Signed at Washington May 27, 1936.
Entered into force March 10, 1941.
55 Stat. 1101; TS 964; 5 Bevans 140; 203 UNTS 367

SCIENTIFIC & TECHNICAL COOPERATION

Memorandum of understanding concerning scientific and technical cooperation in the earth and mapping sciences, with annexes.
Signed at Georgetown July 21, 1993.
Entered into force July 21, 1993.
TIAS 12158

TAXATION

Agreement for the exchange of information with respect to taxes.
Signed at Georgetown July 22, 1992.
Entered into force August 27, 1992.
TIAS 12137

TELECOMMUNICATION

Agreement relating to the reciprocal granting of authorizations to permit licensed amateur radio operators of either country to operate their stations in the other country.
Exchange of notes at Georgetown May 6 and 13, 1968.
Entered into force May 13, 1968.
19 UST 4892; TIAS 6494; 698 UNTS 243

Arrangement relating to radio communications between the amateur stations on behalf of third parties.
Exchange of notes at Georgetown May 30 and June 6, 1972.
Entered into force July 6, 1972.
23 UST 906; TIAS 7355

TRANSPORTATION

Arrangement between the United States and the United Kingdom relating to pilot licenses to operate civil aircraft.
Exchange of notes at Washington March 28, and April 5, 1935.
Entered into force May 5, 1935.
49 Stat. 3731; EAS 77; 12 Bevans 513; 162 LNTS 59

Air transport agreement.
Signed at Georgetown March 25, 2013.
Entered into force March 25, 2013.
TIAS 13-325

H

HAGUE CONFERENCE ON PRIVATE INTERNATIONAL LAW

TAXATION

Tax reimbursement agreement, with annex.
Signed at The Hague January 27, 1993.
Entered into force January 27, 1993.
TIAS 12142

HAITI

CLAIMS & DISPUTE RESOLUTION

Arbitration convention.
Signed at Washington January 7, 1909.
Entered into force November 15, 1909.
36 Stat. 2193; TS 535; 8 Bevans 658

CULTURAL EXCHANGES, PROPERTY & COOPERATION

Agreement relating to the establishment of a Peace Corps program in Haiti.
Exchange of notes at Port au Prince August 12 and 13, 1982.
Entered into force August 13, 1982.
34 UST 1694; TIAS 10445

DEFENSE

Agreement for disposition of equipment and materials furnished by the United States under the military assistance agreement of January 28, 1955, and no longer required by Haiti.
Exchange of notes at Port au Prince March 21 and April 5, 1955.
Entered into force April 5, 1955.
6 UST 3867; TIAS 3387; 270 UNTS 97

Military assistance agreement.
Signed at Washington January 28, 1955.
Entered into force September 12, 1955.
6 UST 3847; TIAS 3386; 270 UNTS 83

Agreement relating to the transfer of military equipment, materials and services to Haiti.
Exchange of notes at Port au Prince September 1, 1960.
Entered into force September 1, 1960.
11 UST 2097; TIAS 4567; 388 UNTS 249

Agreement between the governments participating in the multinational force (MNF) authorized pursuant to security council resolution 940 and the Republic of Haiti on the status of MNF forces in Haiti, with related letter.
Signed at Miami and Washington December 8 and 22, 1994.
Entered into force December 22, 1994.
NP

Agreement regarding the status of U.S. military personnel and civilian employees of the Department of Defense temporarily in Haiti in connection with their official duties.
Exchange of notes at Port au Prince May 10 and 11, 1995.
Entered into force May 11, 1995.
NP

DIPLOMATIC & CONSULAR RELATIONS

Agreement relating to reciprocal customs privileges for consular officers and clerks.
Exchange of notes at Port au Prince August 14 and 24, 1945.
Entered into force August 24, 1945.
59 Stat. 1868; EAS 503; 8 Bevans 791; 139 UNTS 311

FINANCE

Agreement regarding the consolidation, reduction and rescheduling of certain debts owed to, guaranteed by or insured by the United States Government and its agencies, with annexes.
Signed at Port au Prince August 7, 1995.
Entered into force September 7, 1995.
NP

Investment incentive agreement.
Signed at Port au Prince June 29, 1998.
Entered into force June 29, 1998.
TIAS 12970

Agreement regarding the reduction of debts owed to, guaranteed by, or insured by the United States Government and its agencies, with annexes.
Signed at Port au Prince April 16, 2007.
Entered into force May 29, 2007.
NP

Agreement regarding the reduction of debts owed to, guaranteed by, or insured by the United States Government and its agencies, with annexes.
Signed at Port-au-Prince September 18, 2009.
Entered into force November 17, 2009.
NP

FOREIGN ASSISTANCE

General agreement for technical cooperation.
Exchange of notes at Port au Prince May 2, 1951.
Entered into force May 2, 1951.
3 UST 545; TIAS 2414; 151 UNTS 191

Amendment:
December 15, 1951, and January 8, 1952 (3 UST 4731; TIAS 2635; 180 UNTS 372)

Agreement providing for emergency assistance to Haiti in connection with hurricane disaster.
Exchange of notes at Port au Prince March 22 and April 1, 1955.
Entered into force April 1, 1955; operative October 15, 1954.
6 UST 855; TIAS 3232; 261 UNTS 361

Agreement providing for duty-free entry into Haiti and exemption from internal taxation of relief supplies and packages.
Exchange of notes at Port au Prince September 8 and 9, 1958.
Entered into force September 9, 1958.
9 UST 1170; TIAS 4101; 335 UNTS 257

Agreement for the furnishing of commodities to Haiti on a reimbursable basis, with annex.
Signed at Washington September 28, 1993.
Entered into force September 28, 1993.
TIAS
Amendment and Extension:
October 7, 1994

AGENCY FOR INTERNATIONAL DEVELOPMENT

Haiti reconstruction grant agreement.
Signed May 13, 2011.
Entered into force May 13, 2011.
TIAS
Amendments:
September 16, 2011 (NP)
September 27, 2011 (NP)
September 30, 2011 (NP)
March 27, 2012 (NP)
September 26, 2012 (NP)
September 28, 2012 (NP)

HEALTH & MEDICAL COOPERATION

Agreement for cooperation in health programs, and preventing and controlling diseases, including through provision of surge emergency epidemiology and related services.
Signed at Port-au-Prince January 15, 2010.
Entered into force January 15, 2010.
TIAS 10-115

INTERNATIONAL CRIMINAL COURT

Agreement regarding the surrender of persons to the International Criminal Court.
Signed at Monterrey January 12, 2004.
Entered into force January 12, 2004.
TIAS 04-112

LAW ENFORCEMENT

Treaty for the mutual extradition of fugitives from justice.
Signed at Washington August 9, 1904.
Entered into force June 28, 1905.
TS 447; 34 Stat. 2858; 8 Bevans 653

Agreement on procedures for mutual assistance in law enforcement matters.
Signed at Port au Prince August 15, 1986.
Entered into force August 15, 1986.
TIAS 11389; 2191 UNTS 265

Memorandum of understanding for the interdiction of narcotics trafficking.
Signed at Port au Prince August 31, 1988.
Entered into force August 31, 1988.
TIAS

MARITIME MATTERS

Agreement concerning cooperation to suppress illicit maritime drug traffic.
Signed at Port au Prince October 17, 1997.
Entered into force September 5, 2002.
TIAS

POSTAL MATTERS

International express mail agreement, with detailed regulations.
Signed at Port au Prince and Washington January 22 and March 13, 1997.
Entered into force July 1, 1997.
NP

PROPERTY

Agreement relating to exchange of lands in Haiti.
Signed at Port au Prince October 19, 1942.
Entered into force October 19, 1942.
56 Stat. 1784; EAS 283; 8 Bevans 764; 120 LNTS 171

PUBLICATIONS

Agreement relating to the exchange of official publications.
Exchange of notes at Port au Prince May 29, and June 5, 1941.
Entered into force May 29, 1941.
55 Stat. 1278; EAS 210; 8 Bevans 734; 101 LNTS 125

TELECOMMUNICATION

Agreement for the exchange of third party messages between radio amateurs of the United States and Haiti.
Exchange of notes at Port au Prince January 4 and 6, 1960.
Entered into force February 5, 1960.
11 UST 1; TIAS 4399; 367 UNTS 75

Agreement relating to the reciprocal granting of authorizations to permit licensed amateur radio operators of either country to operate their stations in the other country.
Exchange of notes at Port au Prince April 17 and May 17, 1979.
Entered into force May 17, 1979.
30 UST 4245; TIAS 9456

Agreement regarding terms of reference for the operation of the Radio Democracy project.
Exchange of letters at Washington July 1 and 7, 1994.
Entered into force July 7, 1994.
TIAS 12555

TRANSPORTATION

Memorandum of agreement concerning the provision of civil aviation assistance.
Signed at Washington and Port au Prince August 27 and September 3, 1997.
Entered into force September 3, 1997.
TIAS 12880

Memorandum of agreement relating to assistance in developing and modernizing Haiti's civil aviation infrastructure .
Signed July 2 and 4, 2002.
Entered into force July 4, 2002.
NP

HOLY SEE

TAXATION

Agreement to improve international tax compliance and to implement the Foreign Account Tax Compliance Act, with annexes.
Signed at Vatican City June 10, 2015.
Entered into force June 10, 2015.
TIAS 15-610

HONDURAS

AGRICULTURE

Agreement confirming the cooperative agreement for the prevention of foot-and-mouth disease and rinderpest in Honduras.
Exchange of notes at Tegucigalpa November 17 and December 20, 1972.
Entered into force December 20, 1972.
24 UST 942; TIAS 7604; 938 UNTS 139

Memorandum of understanding relating to cooperative efforts to protect crops from plant pest damage and plant diseases.
Signed at Washington and Tegucigalpa March 4 and April 18, 1977.
Entered into force April 18, 1977.
29 UST 319; TIAS 8816

CONSULAR AFFAIRS

Exchange of notes for the waiver of passport visa fees for nonimmigrants.
Exchange of notes at Tegucigalpa May 20 and 27, 1925.
Entered into force June 1, 1925.
8 Bevans 900

CULTURAL EXCHANGES, PROPERTY & COOPERATION

Agreement relating to the establishment of a Peace Corps program in Honduras.
Exchange of notes at Tegucigalpa July 16 and 20, 1962.
Entered into force July 20, 1962.
13 UST 1892; TIAS 5142; 460 UNTS 125

Memorandum of understanding concerning the imposition of import restrictions on archaeological material from the pre-Columbian cultures and ecclesiastical ethnological material from the Colonial period of Honduras.
Signed at Tegucigalpa March 12, 2004.
Entered into force March 12, 2004.
TIAS 04-312

Amendments and Extensions:
February 2 and 17, 2009 (TIAS 04-312)
March 7, 2014 (TIAS 14-307)

DEFENSE

Agreement establishing a United States Army mission to the Republic of Honduras.
Signed at Washington March 6, 1950.
Entered into force March 6, 1950.
1 UST 212; TIAS 2041; 80 UNTS 71

Extension and Amendment
October 5 and November 23, 1953 (4 UST 2215; TIAS 2873)
April 22 and May 20, 1960 (11 UST 1507; TIAS 4494; 376 UNTS 408)

Agreement establishing a United States Air Force mission to the Republic of Honduras.
Signed at Washington March 6, 1950.
Entered into force March 6, 1950.
1 UST 199; TIAS 2040; 80 UNTS 51

Extension and Amendment
October 5 and November 23, 1953 (4 UST 2212; TIAS 2872)
April 22 and May 20, 1960 (11 UST 1507; TIAS 4494; 376 UNTS 408)

Military air transit agreement.
Exchange of notes at Tegucigalpa January 22, March 20, and April 23, 1952.
Entered into force April 23, 1952.
3 UST 3734; TIAS 2502; 198 UNTS 251

Military assistance agreement.
Signed at Tegucigalpa May 20, 1954.
*Entered into force May 20, 1954.**
5 UST 843; TIAS 2975; 222 UNTS 87

Note:
* See also agreements of May 6 and 7, 1982, and May 20, 1985 (TIAS 11202).

Agreement relating to the disposition of equipment and materials furnished by the United States under the military assistance agreement of May 20, 1954.
Exchange of notes at Tegucigalpa May 20 and 24, 1954.
Entered into force May 24, 1954.
13 UST 78; TIAS 4940; 433 UNTS 155

Agreement for performance by members of Army and Air Force missions of duties of military assistance advisory group specified in article V of military assistance agreement.
Exchange of notes at Tegucigalpa April 17 and 25, 1956.
Entered into force April 26, 1956.
7 UST 929; TIAS 3576; 269 UNTS 25

Agreement relating to military assistance.
Exchange of notes at Tegucigalpa October 24, 1962.
Entered into force October 24, 1962.
13 UST 2474; TIAS 5213; 459 UNTS 211

Agreement relating to the deposit by Honduras of ten percent of the value of grant military assistance and excess defense articles furnished by the United States.
Exchange of notes at Tegucigalpa April 4 and June 26, 1972.
Entered into force June 26, 1972; effective February 7, 1972.
23 UST 1235; TIAS 7393

Arrangement for hydrographic and nautical cartography.
Signed at Tegucigalpa August 30, 1976.
Entered into force August 30, 1976.
30 UST 3453; TIAS 9399; 1178 UNTS 5

Agreement relating to the military assistance agreement of May 20, 1954, concerning the use of certain facilities in Honduras by the United States, with annex.
Exchange of notes at Tegucigalpa May 6 and 7, 1982.
Entered into force May 7, 1982.
TIAS 10578; 1871 UNTS 456

Agreement relating to privileges and immunities for U.S. armed forces personnel participating in combined military exercises in Honduras.
Exchange of notes at Tegucigalpa December 8, 1982.
Entered into force December 8, 1982.
35 UST 3884; TIAS 10890; 2014 UNTS 459

Protocol I to the military assistance agreement of May 20, 1954 concerning the exercise of criminal jurisdiction over United States personnel present in Honduras, with annex.
Signed at Washington May 20, 1985.
Entered into force April 9, 1987.
TIAS 11256; 2177 UNTS 50

Protocol II to the military assistance agreement of May 20, 1954, concerning the conduct of combined military exercises and maneuvers, with annex.
Signed at Tegucigalpa November 14, 1988.
Entered into force May 10, 1989.
TIAS 12254

Basic exchange and cooperative agreement for topographic mapping, nautical and aeronautical charting and information, geodesy and geophysics, digital data and related mapping, charting and geodesy materials, with glossary.
Signed at Comayaguela and Fairfax August 24 and September 5, 1995.
Entered into force September 5, 1995.
NP

Agreement regarding grants under the Foreign Assistance Act of 1961, as amended, and the furnishing of defense articles, defense services, and related training, including pursuant to the United States International Military and Education Training Program (IMET), from the United States to the Government of the Republic of Honduras.
Exchange of notes at Tegucigalpa January 13 and March 28, 2006.
Entered into force March 28, 2006.
NP

Memorandum of understanding concerning the Inter-American Naval Telecommunications Network.
Signed July 28, 2006.
Entered into force July 28, 2006.
TIAS 06-728

Agreement regarding the status of United States personnel who may be temporarily present in Honduras.
Exchange of notes at Tegucigalpa January 25, 2008.
Entered into force January 25, 2008.
TIAS 08-125
Extension:
October 17 and November 19, 2012 (TIAS 08-125)

Agreement concerning health care for military members and their dependents.
Signed January 22 and 30, 2012.
Entered into force January 30, 2012.
NP
Extension:
March 27 and July 9, 2015 (NP)

Acquisition and cross-servicing agreement, with annexes.
Signed at Tegucigalpa and Miami December 14, 2012 and March 5, 2013.
Entered into force March 5, 2013.
NP

Memorandum of agreement regarding the assignment of liaison officers, with annexes.
Signed at U. S. Southern Command, Doral November 14, 2014.
Entered into force November 14, 2014.
NP

EMPLOYMENT

Agreement relating to the employment of dependents of official government employees.
Exchange of notes at Tegucigalpa June 11 and November 27, 1985.
Entered into force November 27, 1985.
TIAS 11340

ENVIRONMENT & CONSERVATION

Agreement for cooperation in the Global Learning and Observations to Benefit the Environment (GLOBE) Program, with appendices.
Signed at Tegucigalpa November 13, 1997.
Entered into force November 13, 1997.
TIAS 12896

FINANCE

Agreement relating to investment guaranties under section 413(b)(4) of the Mutual Security Act of 1954.
Exchange of notes at Tegucigalpa April 22 and June 10, 1955.
Entered into force June 10, 1955.
6 UST 2049; TIAS 3270; 258 UNTS 51

Swap agreement among the United States Treasury and the Central Bank of Honduras/ Government of Honduras, with memorandum of understanding.
Signed at Tegucigalpa and Washington June 27 and 28, 1990.
Entered into force June 28, 1990.
TIAS
Amendment and Extension:
November 30 and December 13, 1990

Agreement regarding the consolidation and rescheduling or refinancing of certain debts owed to, guaranteed by, or insured by the United States Government and its agencies, with annexes.
Signed at Tegucigalpa December 20, 1990.
Entered into force February 1, 1991.
NP

Amendment:
February 25 and 28, 1992 (NP)

Agreement regarding the discharge of certain debts owed to the Government of the United States, with annex.
Signed at Washington September 26, 1991.
Entered into force September 26, 1991.
NP

Agreement regarding the consolidation and rescheduling or refinancing of certain debts owed to, guaranteed by or insured by the United States Government and its agencies, with annexes.
Signed at Tegucigalpa February 2, 1993.
Entered into force March 29, 1993.
NP

Agreement regarding the consolidation, reduction and rescheduling of certain debts owed to, guaranteed by, or insured by the United States Government and its agencies.
Signed at Tegucigalpa December 4, 1996.
Entered into force April 10, 1997.
NP

Agreement regarding the reduction, consolidation, and rescheduling of certain debts owed to, guaranteed by, or insured by the United States Government and its agencies, with annexes.
Signed at Tegucigalpa August 23, 1999.
Entered into force September 27, 1999.
NP

Agreement regarding the reduction of certain debts owed to, guaranteed by, or insured by the United States Government, with annexes.
Signed at Tegucigalpa June 1, 2004.
Entered into force July 8, 2004.
NP

Investment incentive agreement.
Signed at Tegucigalpa July 21, 2004.
Entered into force July 21, 2004.
TIAS 04-721.

Agreement regarding the reduction of certain debts owed to, guaranteed by, or insured by the United States Government and its agencies, with annexes.
Signed at Tegucigalpa October 7, 2005.
Entered into force November 28, 2005.
NP

FOREIGN ASSISTANCE

Agreement providing duty-free entry into Honduras, exemption from internal taxation and transportation within Honduras to ultimate beneficiary, for certain relief supplies and equipment.
Exchange of notes at Tegucigalpa March 21, 1955.
Entered into force March 21, 1955.
6 UST 795; TIAS 3225; 253 UNTS 3

General agreement for economic and technical cooperation.
Signed at Tegucigalpa April 12, 1961.
Entered into force May 27, 1961.
12 UST 959; TIAS 4800; 413 UNTS 181

Millennium challenge account threshold program grant agreement, with annexes.
Signed at Tegucigalpa August 28, 2013.
Entered into force August 28, 2013.
TIAS 13-828

INTERNATIONAL CRIMINAL COURT

Agreement regarding the surrender of persons to the International Criminal Court.
Signed at New York September 19, 2002.
Entered into force June 30, 2003.
TIAS 03-630

LAW ENFORCEMENT

Treaty for the extradition of fugitives from justice.
Signed at Washington January 15, 1909.
Entered into force July 10, 1912.
37 Stat. 1616; TS 569; 8 Bevans 892

Supplementary extradition convention.
Signed at Tegucigalpa February 21, 1927.
Entered into force June 5, 1928.
45 Stat. 2489; TS 761; 8 Bevans 903; 85 LNTS 491

Agreement on mutual cooperation to combat the production of and illicit trafficking in drugs.
Signed at Tegucigalpa November 14, 1988.
Entered into force May 15, 1989.
TIAS 11632; 2191 UNTS 133

Agreement concerning security assistance matters and the provision of articles, services and associated military education and training by the United States Government for anti-narcotics purposes.
Exchange of notes at Tegucigalpa October 16 and 22, 1998.
Entered into force October 22, 1998.
NP

Treaty for return of stolen, robbed, and embezzled vehicles and aircraft, with annexes and exchange of notes.
Signed at Tegucigalpa November 23, 2001.
Entered into force September 30, 2004.
TIAS

Agreement regarding the Cooperating Nation Information Exchange System.
Exchange of notes at Tegucigalpa October 19 and November 30, 2004.
Entered into force November 30, 2004.
TIAS

MARITIME MATTERS

Agreement concerning cooperation for the suppression of illicit maritime traffic in narcotic drugs and psychotropic substances, with implementing agreement.
Signed at Tegucigalpa March 29, 2000.
Entered into force January 30, 2001.
TIAS 13088

POSTAL MATTERS

International express mail agreement, with detailed regulations.
Signed at Buenos Aires September 11, 1990.
Entered into force November 15, 1990.
TIAS 11748

Postal money order agreement.
Signed at Montevideo March 14, 1991.
Entered into force May 1, 1991.
TIAS 11926

PUBLICATIONS

Agreement relating to the exchange of official publications.
Exchange of notes at Tegucigalpa March 1 and 24, 1950.
Entered into force March 24, 1950.
1 UST 391; TIAS 2057; 93 UNTS 11

SCIENTIFIC & TECHNICAL COOPERATION

Memorandum of understanding concerning scientific, technical and policy cooperation in the earth and mapping sciences, with annexes.
Signed at Tegucigalpa June 10, 1991.
Entered into force June 10, 1991.
TIAS 12432

TAXATION

Agreement for the exchange of information with respect to taxes.
Signed at Washington September 27, 1990.
Entered into force October 11, 1991.
TIAS 11745; 2202 UNTS 47

Agreement to improve international tax compliance and to implement the Foreign Account Tax Compliance Act, with annexes.
Signed at Tegucigalpa March 31, 2014.
Entered into force February 19, 2015.
TIAS 15-219

TELECOMMUNICATION

Agreement relating to radio communications between amateur radio stations on behalf of third parties.
Exchange of notes at Tegucigalpa October 26, 1959, and February 17, 1960, and related note of February 19, 1960.
Entered into force March 17, 1960.
11 UST 257; TIAS 4442; 371 UNTS 109

Agreement relating to the reciprocal granting of authorizations to permit licensed amateur radio operators of either country to operate their stations in the other country.
Exchange of notes at Tegucigalpa December 29, 1966, January 24 and April 17, 1967.
Entered into force April 17, 1967.
18 UST 525; TIAS 6259; 685 UNTS 165

TERRITORIAL ISSUES

Treaty on the Swan Islands with related notes.
Signed at San Pedro Sula November 22, 1971.
Entered into force September 1, 1972.
23 UST 2630; TIAS 7453

TRADE & INVESTMENT

Treaty of friendship, commerce and consular rights.*
Signed at Tegucigalpa December 7, 1927.
Entered into force July 19, 1928.
45 Stat. 2618; TS 764; 8 Bevans 905; 87 LNTS 421

Note:

* Provisions which are inconsistent with the trade agreement of December 18, 1935 (49 Stat. 3851; EAS 86), are replaced by that agreement.

Trade agreement.*
Signed at Tegucigalpa December 18, 1935.
Entered into force March 2, 1936.
49 Stat. 3851; EAS 86; 8 Bevans 919; 167 LNTS 313

Note:

* The schedules, articles I, II, IV and V, together with references to article V contained in article XVI, terminated February 28, 1961 (12 UST 84; TIAS 4677; 402 UNTS 169).

Treaty concerning the encouragement and reciprocal protection of investment, with annex and protocol.
Signed at Denver July 1, 1995.
Entered into force July 11, 2001.
TIAS

Agreement on trade in textile and apparel goods under the Dominican Republic-Central America-United States Free Trade Agreement.
Exchange of letters at Tegucigalpa and Washington March 7, 2006.
Entered into force March 7, 2006.
NP

TRANSPORTATION

Agreement relating to the inter-American highway.
Exchange of notes at Washington September 9 and October 26, 1942.
Entered into force October 26, 1942.
56 Stat. 1848; EAS 296; 8 Bevans 945; 24 UNTS 209
Amendment:
May 10 and 12, 1955 (6 UST 3763; TIAS 3376; 270 UNTS 3)

Civil aviation security agreement.
Signed at Tegucigalpa August 5, 1991.
Entered into force August 5, 1991.
TIAS 11804; 2207 UNTS 381

Memorandum of agreement concerning assistance in developing and modernizing Honduras' civil aviation infrastructure.
Signed at Washington and Tegucigalpa July 24 and August 23, 1996.
Entered into force August 23, 1996.
TIAS 12796

Memorandum of agreement concerning the deployment of air marshals on board aircraft.
Signed at Tegucigalpa July 18 and 28, 2013.
Entered into force July 28, 2013.
TIAS 13-728

HUNGARY

ATOMIC ENERGY

Agreement concerning the transfer of Russian-origin spent nuclear fuel from the research reactor at the KFKI Atomic Energy Research Institute in Budapest to the Russian Federation.
Exchange of notes at Budapest July 3, 2008.
Entered into force July 7, 2008.
TIAS 08-707

Arrangement for the exchange of technical information and cooperation in nuclear safety matters, with addenda.
Signed at Rockville March 14, 2012.
Entered into force March 14, 2012.
TIAS 12-314

CLAIMS & DISPUTE RESOLUTION

Arbitration treaty.
Signed at Washington January 26, 1929.
Entered into force July 24, 1929.
46 Stat. 2349; TS 797; 8 Bevans 1134; 96 LNTS 173

Conciliation treaty.
Signed at Washington January 26, 1929.
Entered into force July 24, 1929.
46 Stat. 2353; TS 798; 8 Bevans 1137; 96 LNTS 207

Agreement regarding the settlement of claims, with exchanges of letters and negotiating records.
Signed at Washington March 6, 1973.
Entered into force March 6, 1973.
24 UST 522; TIAS 7569; 938 UNTS 167

CONSULAR AFFAIRS

Agreement relating to issuance of nonimmigrant visas on a facilitated basis to certain holders of diplomatic or official passports.
Exchange of notes at Budapest March 29 and April 7, 1976.
Entered into force April 7, 1976.
28 UST 1311; TIAS 8513

Agreement relating to reciprocal facilitation of visas for diplomatic and official passport holders.
Exchange of notes at Budapest February 10, 1978.
Entered into force February 10, 1978.
30 UST 248; TIAS 9193

Agreement relating to reciprocal facilitation of transit or temporary duty visas for diplomatic and official passport holders.
Exchange of notes at Budapest February 10, 1978.
Entered into force April 11, 1978.
30 UST 255; TIAS 9194

CULTURAL EXCHANGES, PROPERTY & COOPERATION

Agreement relating to interment of American military personnel in Hungary.
Exchange of notes at Budapest June 18, July 15, and August 9, 1946.
Entered into force August 9, 1946.
61 Stat. 3898; TIAS 1748; 8 Bevans 1145; 148 UNTS 313

Agreement on cooperation in culture, education, science and technology.
Signed at Budapest April 6, 1977.
Entered into force May 21, 1979.
30 UST 1502; TIAS 9259

Agreement concerning the operation of the United States Peace Corps in Hungary.
Signed at Budapest February 14, 1990.
Entered into force July 12, 1990.
TIAS 12072

Agreement on the protection and preservation of certain cultural properties.
Signed at Budapest April 15, 2004.
Entered into force June 30, 2004.
TIAS 04-630.1

DEFENSE

Exchange and cooperative agreement for military, topographic mapping, aeronautical charting, digital data and related MC & G materials.
Signed at Budapest December 9, 1991.
Entered into force December 9, 1991.
NP

Agreement regarding grants under the Foreign Assistance Act of 1961, as amended, or successor legislation, and the furnishing of defense articles, related training, or other defense services from the United States to Hungary.
Exchange of notes at Budapest February 12 and August 31, 1993.
Entered into force August 31, 1993.
NP

Agreement concerning security measures for the protection of classified military information.
Signed at Washington May 16, 1995.
Entered into force June 4, 1996.
TIAS 12649; 2044 UNTS 67

Agreement concerning the activities of United States Forces in the territory of the Republic of Hungary.
Signed at Budapest May 14, 1997.
Entered into force June 23, 1997.
TIAS 12857

Memorandum of understanding regarding assignment of liaison officers, with annex.
Signed at Budapest and Norfolk September 22 and October 23, 2006.
Entered into force October 23, 2006.
NP

Amendment:
August 23 and October 20, 2011
August 1 and September 5, 2016

Agreement concerning exchange of research and development information, with appendix.
Signed at Washington and Budapest August 9 and September 6, 2012.
Entered into force September 6, 2012.
TIAS 12-906

Acquisition and cross-servicing agreement.
Signed at Budapest and Stuttgart November 26 and December 10, 2014.
Entered into force December 10, 2014.
NP

DIPLOMATIC & CONSULAR RELATIONS

Treaty establishing friendly relations.
Signed at Budapest August 29, 1921.
Entered into force December 17, 1921.
42 Stat. 1951; TS 660; 8 Bevans 982; 48 LNTS 191

Consular convention.
Signed at Budapest July 7, 1972.
Entered into force July 6, 1973.
24 UST 1141; TIAS 7641

EDUCATION

Agreement regarding the status of the American International School of Budapest.
Exchange of notes at Budapest November 30, 1998.
Entered into force November 30, 1998.
TIAS 13003

Agreement concerning the Hungarian-American Commission for educational exchange.
Signed at Washington March 8, 2007.
Entered into force March 16, 2009.
TIAS 09-316

EMPLOYMENT

Agreement relating to employment of dependents of official government employees.
Exchange of notes at Budapest November 18, 1991, and January 16, 1992.
Entered into force January 16, 1992.
TIAS 11841

ENVIRONMENT & CONSERVATION

Agreement for cooperation in the Global Learning and Observations to Benefit the Environment (GLOBE) Program, with appendices.
Signed at Washington March 10, 1999.
Entered into force March 10, 1999.
TIAS 13024

FINANCE

Debt funding agreement.
Signed at Washington April 25, 1924.
Operative December 15, 1923.
Treasury Department print; 8 Bevans 1108

Agreement modifying the debt funding agreement of April 25, 1924.
Signed at Washington May 27, 1932.
Operative July 1, 1931.
Treasury Department print; 8 Bevans 1140

Investment guaranty agreement.
Signed at Budapest October 9, 1989.
Entered into force December 27, 1989.
TIAS 12040

Swap agreement among the United States Treasury and the National Bank of Hungary/Government of Hungary, with memorandum of understanding.
Signed at Washington and Budapest June 19, 1990.
Entered into force June 19, 1990.
TIAS

FOREIGN ASSISTANCE

Agreement concerning economic, technical and related assistance, with related letter.
Signed at Budapest December 22, 1995.
Entered into force December 22, 1995.
TIAS; 2044 UNTS 31

INTELLECTUAL PROPERTY

Agreement on intellectual property, with protocol and exchanges of letters.
Signed at Washington September 24, 1993.
Entered into force November 9, 1994.
TIAS 12138

LAW ENFORCEMENT

Agreement regarding cooperation and mutual assistance between customs services.
Signed at Budapest May 8, 1991.
Entered into force October 7, 1993.
TIAS

Treaty on mutual legal assistance in criminal matters, with attachments.
Signed at Budapest December 1, 1994.
Entered into force March 18, 1997.
TIAS; 2181 UNTS 271

Treaty on extradition.
Signed at Budapest December 1, 1994.
Entered into force March 18, 1997.
TIAS 97-318.

Agreement on establishing an International Law Enforcement Academy, with implementing agreement.
Signed at Budapest April 24, 1995.
Entered into force November 3, 1995.
TIAS 12637

Agreement for the exchange of screening information concerning known or suspected terrorists.
Signed at Budapest May 20, 2008.
Entered into force July 2, 2008.
TIAS

Agreement on enhancing cooperation in preventing and combating serious crime.
Signed at Budapest October 1, 2008.
Entered into force December 11, 2008.
TIAS

Protocol to the treaty on mutual legal assistance in criminal matters of December 1, 1994, as contemplated by Article 3(2) of the agreement on mutual legal assistance between the United States of America and the European Union signed June 25, 2003.
Signed at Budapest November 15, 2005.
Entered into force February 1, 2010.
TIAS 10-201.34

Protocol to the treaty on extradition of December 1, 1994, as contemplated by Article 3(2) of the agreement on extradition between the United States of America and the European Union signed June 25, 2003.
Signed at Budapest November 15, 2005.
Entered into force February 1, 2010.
TIAS 10-201-11

NONPROLIFERATION

Agreement concerning cooperation in the area of countering the proliferation of nuclear materials and technologies.
Signed at Budapest July 8, 2008.
Entered into force July 8, 2008.
TIAS 08-708

POSTAL MATTERS

Agreement for collect-on-delivery service.
Signed at Budapest December 15, 1930, and at Washington January 15, 1931.
Operative February 1, 1931.
46 Stat. 2894; Post Office Department print

Parcel post agreement, with detailed regulations.
Signed at Washington May 11, 1979.
Entered into force provisionally May 11, 1979; definitively August 8, 1979.
32 UST 1695; TIAS 9797; 1734 UNTS 165

International express mail agreement, with detailed regulations.
Signed at Budapest and Washington June 24 and July 10, 1987.
Entered into force September 1, 1987.
TIAS 11306

PROPERTY

Agreement regarding new chancery facilities in Budapest, with associated agreement on purchase of lots.
Signed at Budapest September 29, 1989.
Entered into force September 29, 1989.
TIAS

SCIENTIFIC & TECHNICAL COOPERATION

Memorandum of understanding concerning scientific and technical cooperation in the earth sciences.
Signed at Budapest and Reston November 22, 2000.
Entered into force November 22, 2000.
TIAS 13129

Agreement for scientific and technological cooperation, with annexes.
Signed at Budapest February 4, 2010.
Entered into force April 7, 2010.
TIAS 10-407

SOCIAL SECURITY

Agreement on social security, with administrative arrangement.
Signed at Budapest February 3, 2015.
Entered into force September 1, 2016.
TIAS 16-901

TAXATION

Convention for the avoidance of double taxation and the prevention of fiscal evasion with respect to taxes on income, with exchange of notes.
Signed at Washington February 12, 1979.
Entered into force September 18, 1979.
30 UST 6357; TIAS 9560; 1180 UNTS 205

Agreement to improve international tax compliance and to implement the Foreign Account Tax Compliance Act, with annexes.
Signed at Budapest February 4, 2014.
Entered into force July 16, 2014.
TIAS 14-716

TRADE & INVESTMENT

Agreement relating to the establishment in New York of a branch office of the commercial section of the Hungarian Embassy.
Exchange of notes at Washington September 19, 1969.
Entered into force September 19, 1969.
20 UST 2982; TIAS 6772; 726 UNTS 177

Agreement providing for consultations should exports of cotton, wool, and man-made fiber textiles and apparel products from Hungary cause market disruption in the United States.
Exchange of notes at Budapest February 12 and 18, 1976.
Entered into force February 18, 1976.
27 UST 1619; TIAS 8270

Agreed minutes on a comprehensive trade package, with annex and related letters.
Signed at Budapest January 30, 2002.
Entered into force March 26, 2002.
TIAS

TRANSPORTATION

Understanding concerning research cooperation in the field of transportation.
Signed at Budapest October 11, 1978.
Entered into force October 11, 1978.
30 UST 743; TIAS 9216

Air transport agreement, with annex and memorandum of understanding.*
Signed at Budapest July 12, 1989.
Entered into force definitively February 8, 1990.
TIAS 11260; 2174 UNTS 297

Extension:

June 25, August 1 and September 5, 2007 (TIAS 07-905)

Note:

* This agreement is suspended for the duration of provisional application of the U.S.–E.U. Air Transport Agreement signed April 25 and 30, 2007.

I

ICELAND

CLAIMS & DISPUTE RESOLUTION

Treaty between the United States and Denmark looking to the advancement of the cause of general peace.
Signed at Washington April 17, 1914.
Entered into force January 19, 1915.
38 Stat. 1883; TS 608; 7 Bevans 53

Treaty of arbitration.
Signed at Washington May 15, 1930.
Entered into force October 2, 1930.
46 Stat. 2841; TS 828; 8 Bevans 1154; 108 LNTS 109

CONSULAR AFFAIRS

Arrangement relating to the waiver of passport visa fees for nonimmigrants.*
Exchange of notes at Copenhagen November 3 and December 21, 1925; and June 11, 19, and 21, 1926.
Entered into force June 21, 1926; operative August 6, 1925.
8 Bevans 1150

Agreement relating to the reciprocal extension of the validity period of visas for certain nonimmigrants.*
Exchange of notes at Reykjavik June 4, 1956.
Entered into force June 4, 1956; operative August 1, 1956.
7 UST 1017; TIAS 3584; 275 UNTS 189

Note:
* The status of this agreement is under review.

DEFENSE

Defense agreement pursuant to the North Atlantic Treaty.
Signed at Reykjavik May 5, 1951.
Entered into force May 5, 1951.
2 UST 1195; TIAS 2266; 205 UNTS 173

Annex on the status of United States personnel and property.
Signed at Reykjavik May 8, 1951.
Entered into force May 8, 1951.
2 UST 1533; TIAS 2295; 205 UNTS 180

Agreement relating to the assurances required under the Mutual Security Act of 1951.
Exchange of notes at Reykjavik January 7 and 8, 1952.
Entered into force January 8, 1952.
3 UST 4577; TIAS 2609; 180 UNTS 183

Agreement concerning the sale to Iceland of certain military equipment, materials, and services.
Exchange of notes at Reykjavik October 4 and December 10, 1954.
Entered into force December 10, 1954.
5 UST 2991; TIAS 3157; 237 UNTS 191

Agreement relating to the presence of defense forces in Iceland, discontinuing the discussions for revision of the 1951 defense agreement and setting up an Iceland Defense Standing Group.
Exchanges of notes at Reykjavik December 6, 1956.
Entered into force December 6, 1956.
7 UST 3437; TIAS 3716; 265 UNTS 261

Agreement relating to the continuation of the defense agreement of May 5, 1951, with memorandum of understanding and agreed minute.
Exchange of notes at Reykjavik October 22, 1974.
Entered into force October 22, 1974.
25 UST 3079; TIAS 7969

Agreement concerning the provision of training related to defense articles under the United States International Military Education and Training (IMET) Program.
Exchange of notes at Reykjavik January 7 and February 12, 1986.
Entered into force February 12, 1986.
TIAS 11107

Treaty to facilitate defense relationship, with related memorandum of understandings.
Signed at New York September 24, 1986.
Entered into force October 31, 1986.
TIAS 11098; 2120 UNTS 109

Memorandum of understanding regarding the resolution of certain groundwater contamination.
Signed at Reykjavik July 17, 1989.
Entered into force August 30, 1989.
TIAS 12315

Basic exchange and cooperative agreement concerning global geospatial information and services cooperation, with annexes.
Signed at Bethesda and Reykjavik June 7 and July 1, 1999.
Entered into force July 1, 1999.
NP

Agreement regarding the withdrawal of United States forces from and the return to Iceland of certain agreed areas and facilities in Iceland, with attachments.
Signed at Washington and Reykjavik September 27 and 29, 2006.
Entered into force September 29, 2006.
TIAS 06-929

Acquisition and cross-servicing agreement, with annexes.
Signed at Washington and Reykjavik January 24 and February 1, 2013.
Entered into force February 1, 2013.
NP

Agreement regarding grants under the Foreign Assistance Act of 1961, as amended, or successor legislation, and the furnishings of defense articles, defense services and related training.
Effected by exchange of notes at Reykjavik September 4, 2013 and September 13, 2013.
Entered into force September 13, 2013.
NP

EDUCATION

Agreement for financing certain educational exchange programs.
Signed at Reykjavik February 13, 1964.
Entered into force February 13, 1964.
15 UST 226; TIAS 5542; 524 UNTS 235

FOREIGN ASSISTANCE

Economic cooperation agreement.
Signed at Reykjavik July 3, 1948.
Entered into force July 3, 1948.
62 Stat. 2363; TIAS 1787; 8 Bevans 1193; 20 UNTS 141

Amendments:
February 7, 1950 (1 UST 154; TIAS 2026; 79 UNTS 280)
February 23, 1951 (2 UST 1317; TIAS 2284; 148 UNTS 398)
October 9, 1952, and October 1, 1953 (5 UST 166; TIAS 2910; 223 UNTS 316)

Agreement concerning special economic assistance to Iceland on a loan basis.
Exchange of notes at Reykjavik June 23, 1959.
Entered into force June 23, 1959.
10 UST 1237; TIAS 4260; 354 UNTS 3

Agreement providing for an assistance grant in support of Iceland's economic stabilization program.
Exchange of notes at Washington December 30, 1960.
Entered into force December 30, 1960.
11 UST 2574; TIAS 4647; 401 UNTS 43

HEALTH & MEDICAL COOPERATION

Memorandum of understanding concerning cooperation to assure the sanitary quality of bivalve mollusca exported to the United States.
Signed at Reykjavik and Washington October 25 and December 28, 1978.
Entered into force December 28, 1978.
30 UST 2873; TIAS 9368; 1180 UNTS 89

LAW ENFORCEMENT

Conventions between the United States and Denmark applicable to Iceland treaty for the extradition of fugitives from justice.
Signed at Washington January 6, 1902.
Effective May 16, 1902.
TS 405; 32 Stat. 1096; 7 Bevans 38

Supplementary treaty between the United States and Denmark for the extradition of criminals.
Signed at Washington November 6, 1905.
Entered into force for Iceland February 19, 1906.
TS 449; 34 Stat. 2887; 7 Bevans 43

Agreement on enhancing cooperation in preventing and combating serious crime.
Signed at Reykjavik May 14, 2012.
Entered into force February 24, 2014, with the exception of Articles 8 through 10.
TIAS 14-224

MARITIME MATTERS

Agreement concerning Icelandic whaling for scientific purposes, with summary of discussions.
Exchange of letters at Washington September 14 and 15, 1987.
Entered into force September 15, 1987.
TIAS 11541; 2192 UNTS 19

POSTAL MATTERS

Agreement concerning the exchange of parcel post and detailed regulations of execution.
Signed at Reykjavik October 11 and at Washington October 31, 1938.
Operative September 1, 1938.
53 Stat. 2006; Post Office Department print

International express mail agreement, with detailed regulations.
Signed at Reykjavik and Washington July 10 and August 8, 1985.
Entered into force November 7, 1985.
TIAS 11155; 2126 UNTS 265

Memorandum of understanding concerning the operation of the INTELPOST service, with details of implementation.
Signed at Reykjavik and Washington March 5 and April 3, 1987.
Entered into force May 6, 1987.
TIAS 11299

PROPERTY

Agreement relating to aid for defense, with note.
Signed at Washington November 21, 1941.
Entered into force November 21, 1941.
58 Stat. 1455; EAS 429; 8 Bevans 1163; 124 UNTS 179

PUBLICATIONS

Agreement relating to the exchange of official publications.
Exchange of notes at Reykjavik August 17, 1942.
Entered into force August 17, 1942.
56 Stat. 1600; EAS 269; 8 Bevans 1166; 24 UNTS 163

SCIENTIFIC & TECHNICAL COOPERATION

Memorandum of understanding for scientific and technical cooperation in earth sciences.
Signed at Reykjavik and Reston January 28 and April 9, 1982.
Entered into force April 9, 1982.
34 UST 1223; TIAS 10409

Amendments and Extensions:
March 5 and August 9, 1991 (TIAS 11801)
June 9 and July 8, 1999 (TIAS 99-708)
March 25 and April 12, 2007 (TIAS 99-708)
March 18, 2014 (TIAS 14-318.1)

Memorandum of understanding on cooperation in science and engineering research, with annexes.
Signed at Reykjavik September 30, 2000.
Entered into force September 30, 2000.
TIAS 13117

Agreement for scientific and technology cooperation on geothermal research and development, with annex.
Signed at Reykjavik October 6, 2010.
Entered into force October 6, 2010.
TIAS 10-1006

TAXATION

Agreement relating to relief from taxation of United States expenditures in Iceland for common defense.
Exchange of notes at Reykjavik March 5 and 18, 1952.
Entered into force March 18, 1952.
3 UST 4150; TIAS 2557; 177 UNTS 263

Convention for the avoidance of double taxation and the prevention of fiscal evasion with respect to taxes on income, with protocol.
Signed at Washington October 23, 2007.
Entered into force December 15, 2008.
TIAS 08-1215

Agreement to improve international tax compliance and to implement the Foreign Account Tax Compliance Act, with annexes.
Signed at Reykjavik May 26, 2015.
Entered into force September 22, 2015.
TIAS 15-922

TELECOMMUNICATION

Agreement relating to the registration with the International Frequency Registration Board of radio frequencies for the use of the Iceland defense force.
Exchange of notes at Reykjavik July 11 and 20, 1955.
Entered into force July 20, 1955.
6 UST 3910; TIAS 3395; 256 UNTS 245

Agreement relating to the reciprocal granting of authorizations to permit licensed amateur radio operators of either country to operate their stations in the other country.
Exchange of notes at Reykjavik April 26, 1978.
Entered into force April 26, 1978.
30 UST 1516; TIAS 9260; 1150 UNTS 41

TRANSPORTATION

Air transport agreement, with annexes.
Signed at Washington June 14, 1995.
Entered into force October 12, 1995.
TIAS 12661

Amendments:
March 1, 2002 (TIAS 02-301.1)
August 14, 2006, and March 9, 2007 (TIAS 02-301.1)

Memorandum of agreement relating to the loan of aviation-related equipment to the Civil Aviation Administration of Iceland.
Signed at Washington December 8, 1997.
Entered into force December 8, 1997.
NP

Memorandum of agreement on the purchase of aviation-related equipment on behalf of Keflavik Airport.
Signed April 27 and 28, 2010.
Entered into force April 28, 2010.
NP

Agreement for the promotion of aviation safety.
Signed at Montreal September 27, 2004.
Entered into force February 11, 2009.
TIAS 09-211

INDIA

The Schedule to the Indian Independence (International Arrangements) Order, 1947, provides that (1) membership of all international organizations together with the rights and obligations attached to such membership devolves solely upon India; (2) rights and obligations under all international agreements to which India is a party immediately before the appointed day [August 15, 1947] devolve upon India and Pakistan and will, if necessary, be apportioned between them, except that rights and obligations under international agreements having an exclusive application to an area comprised in the Dominion of India devolve upon it.

The Dominion of India, which came into being August 15, 1947, became the Republic of India on January 26, 1950, but remains a member of the British Commonwealth of Nations. This change is understood not to have affected any agreements listed below in their application between the United States and India.

ATOMIC ENERGY

Agreement providing for a grant of nuclear research equipment in the field of agriculture.
Exchange of notes at New Delhi April 22 and June 13, 1960.
Entered into force June 13, 1960.
11 UST 1619; TIAS 4505; 377 UNTS 37

Agreement providing for a grant for assistance in obtaining materials and equipment for establishing a Radiation Medicine Centre at Tata Memorial Hospital, Bombay.
Exchange of notes at New Delhi January 4 and February 1, 1963.
Entered into force February 1, 1963.
14 UST 156; TIAS 5288; 473 UNTS 37

Agreement for cooperation concerning the peaceful uses of nuclear energy, with agreed minute.
Signed at Washington October 10, 2008.
Entered into force December 6, 2008.
TIAS 08-1206

Arrangement for the exchange of technical information and cooperation in nuclear safety matters, with addenda and annex.
Signed at Rockville and Mumbai September 26 and October 9, 2013.
Entered into force October 9, 2013.
TIAS 13-1009

CONSULAR AFFAIRS

Arrangement for the continuance, on a reciprocal basis, of the existing practice of levying a fee of $2.00 for a nonimmigrant visa.*
Exchange of notes at New Delhi July 19 and August 11, 1948.
Entered into force August 11, 1948.
5 UST 193; TIAS 2913; 224 UNTS 115
Note:
* The status of this agreement is under review.

CULTURAL EXCHANGES, PROPERTY & COOPERATION

Agreement relating to the establishment of a Peace Corps program in India.
Exchange of notes at New Delhi November 13 and 21, 1962.
Entered into force November 21, 1962; operative December 20, 1961.
13 UST 2735; TIAS 5247; 462 UNTS 255

DEFENSE

Agreement relating to transit privileges for military aircraft.
Exchange of notes at New Delhi July 2 and 4, 1949.
Entered into force July 5, 1949.
3 UST 575; TIAS 2417; 200 UNTS 181
Amendments:
June 9 and 15, 1955 (14 UST 1449; TIAS 5442; 488 UNTS 242)
March 5 and July 22, 1963 (14 UST 1449; TIAS 5442; 488 UNTS 246)
March 5 and August 29, 1963 (14 UST 1449; TIAS 5442; 488 UNTS 250)

Agreement relating to the transfer by the Government of the United States to the Government of India of certain military supplies and equipment (military sales agreement).
Exchange of notes at Washington March 7 and 16, 1951.
Entered into force March 16, 1951.
2 UST 872; TIAS 2241; 14 UNTS 47

Understanding that the assurances contained in the agreement of March 7 and 16, 1951, are applicable to equipment, materials, information, and services furnished under the Mutual Security Act of 1954, as amended, and such other applicable U.S. laws as may come into effect.
Exchange of notes at New Delhi April 16 and December 17, 1958.
Entered into force December 17, 1958.
10 UST 1713; TIAS 4322; 358 UNTS 77

Agreement supplementing the 1951 military sales agreement.
Exchange of notes at Washington November 14, 1962.
Entered into force November 14, 1962.
13 UST 2449; TIAS 5206; 461 UNTS 224

Agreement relating to military assistance.
Exchange of notes at New Delhi January 13, 1965.
Entered into force January 13, 1965.
16 UST 33; TIAS 5753; 541 UNTS 107

Agreement concerning security measures for the protection of classified military information.
Signed at Washington January 17, 2002.
Entered into force January 17, 2002.
TIAS 02-117

Agreement concerning exchange of research and development information, with appendix.
Signed at Washington and New Delhi September 9, 2003 and February 7, 2004.
Entered into force February 7, 2004.
TIAS 04-207

Memorandum of agreement for research, development, testing and evaluation projects, with annexes.
Signed at Washington and New Delhi December 6, 2005, and January 9, 2006.
Entered into force January 9, 2006.
TIAS 06-109
Amendment:
January 22, 2015 (TIAS 15-122)

EDUCATION

Agreement for financing certain educational exchange programs.
Signed at New Delhi July 4, 2008.
Entered into force July 4, 2008.
TIAS 08-704

EMPLOYMENT

Arrangement on employment for family members of a diplomatic mission or consular post.
Signed at New Delhi April 10, 2000.
Entered into force April 10, 2000.
TIAS 13090

ENVIRONMENT & CONSERVATION

Agreement for cooperation in the Global Learning and Observations to Benefit the Environment (GLOBE) Program, with appendices.
Signed at New Delhi August 25, 2000.
Entered into force August 25, 2000.
TIAS 13113

FINANCE

Agreement regarding the consolidation and rescheduling of certain debts owed to the United States Government and its agencies, with annexes.
Signed at Washington March 30, 1973.
Entered into force March 30, 1973.
24 UST 907; TIAS 7601

Agreement on Public Law 480 and other funds, with annexes.
Signed at New Delhi February 18, 1974.
Entered into force February 18, 1974.
25 UST 866; TIAS 7831

Agreements regarding the consolidation and rescheduling of certain debts owed to the United States Government and its agencies, with annexes.
Signed at Washington June 7, 1974.
Entered into force June 7, 1974.
25 UST 1547; TIAS 7890

Agreement regarding the consolidation and rescheduling of certain debts owed to the United States Government and its agencies, with annexes.
Signed at Washington May 2, 1975.
Entered into force June 13, 1975.
26 UST 951; TIAS 8082

Investment incentive agreement.
Signed at New Delhi November 19, 1997.
Entered into force April 16, 1998.
TIAS 12904

FOREIGN ASSISTANCE

General agreement for technical cooperation.
Signed at New Delhi December 28, 1950.
Entered into force December 28, 1950.
2 UST 425; TIAS 2185; 99 UNTS 39

Agreement relating to the technical cooperation program.
Signed at New Delhi January 5, 1952.
Entered into force January 5, 1952.
3 UST 2921; TIAS 2470; 157 UNTS 39
Extension:
June 29, 1957 (8 UST 732; TIAS 3828; 288 UNTS 368)

Agreement for duty-free entry and defrayment of inland transportation charges of voluntary agency supplies and equipment.
Signed at New Delhi December 5, 1968.
Entered into force December 5, 1968.
19 UST 7836; TIAS 6617; 713 UNTS 351

Agreement to establish a Joint Commission on Economic, Commercial, Scientific, Technological, Educational and Cultural Cooperation.
Signed at New Delhi October 28, 1974.
Entered into force October 28, 1974.
25 UST 2807; TIAS 7947

Agreed minutes of the second session of the United States-India Joint Commission on Economic, Commercial, Scientific, Technological, Educational and Cultural Cooperation.
Signed at Washington October 7, 1975.
Entered into force October 7, 1975.
26 UST 2590; TIAS 8176; 1028 UNTS 23

AGENCY FOR INTERNATIONAL DEVELOPMENT

Agreement for health, with addendum and attachment.
Signed September 30, 2010.
Entered into force September 30, 2010.
Amendment:
September 28 and October 1, 2012 (NP)

INTELLECTUAL PROPERTY

Declaration by the United States and the United Kingdom affording reciprocal protection to trade-marks.
Signed at London October 24, 1877.
Entered into force October 24, 1877.
20 Stat. 703; TS 138; 12 Bevans 198

Agreement relating to copyright relations.
Exchange of notes at Washington October 21, 1954.
Entered into force October 21, 1954; operative August 15, 1947.
5 UST 2525; TIAS 3114; 234 UNTS 119

INTERNATIONAL CRIMINAL COURT

Agreement regarding the surrender of persons to international tribunals.
Signed at New Delhi December 26, 2002.
Entered into force December 3, 2003.
TIAS 03-1203

LABOR

Joint statement on enhanced Indo-U.S. cooperation on eliminating child labor, with annex.
Signed April 25, 2000.
Entered into force August 31, 2000.
TIAS

LAW ENFORCEMENT

Agreement on procedures for mutual assistance in connection with matters relating to the Boeing Company.
Signed at Washington August 19, 1977.
Entered into force August 19, 1977.
28 UST 7497; TIAS 8726; 1087 UNTS 209
Related Agreements:
March 28 and April 17, 1979 (35 UST 3721; TIAS 10878; 2016 UNTS 58)
November 18 and December 10, 1981 (35 UST 3721; TIAS 10878; 2016 UNTS 62)

Mutual cooperation agreement for reducing demand, preventing illicit use of and traffic in drugs, and for matters relating to licit trade in opiates.
Signed at New Delhi March 29, 1990.
Entered into force March 29, 1990.
TIAS 12412; 2357 UNTS 35

Extradition treaty, with exchange of letters.
Signed at Washington June 25, 1997.
Entered into force July 21, 1999.
TIAS 12873

Agreement regarding mutual assistance between their customs administrations.
Signed at New Delhi December 15, 2004.
Entered into force July 11, 2005.
TIAS 05-711

Treaty on mutual legal assistance in criminal matters.
Signed at New Delhi October 17, 2001.
Entered into force October 3, 2005.
TIAS

NONPROLIFERATION

Agreement on technology safeguards at all facilities under the jurisdiction and/or control of the Government of the Republic of India associated with the launch of U.S. licensed spacecraft, with exchange of letters.
Signed at New Delhi July 20, 2009.
Entered into force July 20, 2009.
TIAS 09-720
Extension:
September 22 and 23, 2015 (TIAS 15-923)

POSTAL MATTERS

Parcel post agreement with detailed regulations.
Signed at New Delhi July 29 and at Washington September 17, 1954.
Entered into force January 1, 1955.
6 UST 819; TIAS 3229; 239 UNTS 69

International express mail agreement, with detailed regulations.
Signed at New Delhi and Washington November 20 and December 11, 1986.
Entered into force January 17, 1987.
TIAS 11415

PROPERTY

Convention relating to tenure and disposition of real and personal property.
Signed at Washington March 2, 1899.
31 Stat. 1939; TS 146; 12 Bevans 246
Notes:
Applicable to India from June 30, 1902.

Supplementary convention extending the time within which notifications may be given of the accession of British colonies or foreign possessions to the convention of March 2, 1899.
Signed at Washington January 13, 1902.
32 Stat. 1914; TS 402; 12 Bevans 261
Notes:
Applicable to India from June 30, 1902.

Agreement on settlement for lend-lease, reciprocal aid, surplus war property, and claims.
Signed at Washington May 16, 1946.
Entered into force May 16, 1946.
60 Stat. 1753; TIAS 1532; 8 Bevans 1226; 4 UNTS 183
Amendment:
June 24 and 26, 1946 (8 Bevans 1233)

Related Agreement:
January 24, 1975 (26 UST 305; TIAS 8035; 992 UNTS 111)

PUBLICATIONS

Agreement for the exchange of official publications.
Exchange of notes at New Delhi November 8, 1950, and January 11, 1951.
Entered into force January 11, 1951.
2 UST 1563; TIAS 2297; 148 UNTS 49

SCIENTIFIC & TECHNICAL COOPERATION

Agreement on cooperation in the conduct of the monsoon experiment (MONEX-79), with annexes.
Signed at New Delhi May 24, 1979.
Entered into force May 24, 1979.
30 UST 5877; TIAS 9524; 1180 UNTS 355

Agreement on the Indo-U.S. Science and Technology Forum.
Signed at New Delhi March 21, 2000.
Entered into force March 21, 2000.
TIAS 13087

Agreement on science and technology cooperation, with annexes.
Signed at Washington October 17, 2005.
Entered into force March 14, 2006.
TIAS 06-314.1
Extension:
March 8 and 10, 2016 (TIAS 16-310)

Memorandum of understanding concerning scientific and technical cooperation in the field of gas hydrates research.
Signed at Washington December 16, 2008.
Entered into force December 16, 2008.
TIAS 08-1216

Agreement to establish a board and an endowment for joint research and development, innovation, entrepreneurial and commercialization activities in science and technology.
Signed at New Delhi July 20, 2009.
Entered into force July 20, 2009.
TIAS 09-720.1

Memorandum of understanding for technical cooperation in earth observations and earth sciences.
Signed at Washington and New Delhi April 16, 2008.
Entered into force November 4, 2010.
TIAS 10-1104

Agreement for cooperation on a joint clean energy research and development center.
Signed at New Delhi November 4, 2010.
Entered into force November 4, 2010.
TIAS 10-1104.1

Implementing agreement for cooperation in the area of accelerator and particle detector research and development for discovery science.
Signed at New Delhi July 19, 2011.
Entered into force July 19, 2011.
TIAS 11-719

Memorandum of understanding for cooperation in the exchange and use of United States land remote sensing satellite data, with annexes.
Signed at Reston and Bangalore June 4 and July 9, 2016.
Entered into force July 9, 2016.
TIAS 16-709

SPACE

Memorandum of understanding on cooperation concerning NASA's moon mineralogy mapper (M3) instrument on ISRO's Chandrayaan 1 Mission.
Signed at Bangalore May 9, 2006.
Entered into force May 9, 2006.
TIAS 06-509.1

Memorandum of understanding on cooperation concerning NASA's miniature synthetic aperture radar instrument on ISRO's Chandrayaan 1 Mission.
Signed at Bangalore May 9, 2006.
Entered into force May 9, 2006.
TIAS 06-509

Agreement for cooperation in the exploration and use of outer space for peaceful purposes.
Signed at Cape Canaveral February 1, 2008.
Entered into force February 1, 2008.
TIAS 08-201

Implementing arrangement for collaboration on Oceansat-2 activities.
Signed at Ahmedabad and Washington March 20 and 26, 2012.
Entered into force March 26, 2012.
TIAS 12-326

Implementing arrangement for cooperation on Global Precipitation Measurement and Megha-Tropiques.
Signed at Ahmedabad and Washington March 20 and 26, 2012.
Entered into force March 26, 2012.
TIAS 12-326.1

TAXATION

Agreement concerning the reciprocal exemption from income tax of income derived from the international operation of ships and aircraft.
Exchange of notes at New Delhi April 12, 1989.
Entered into force April 12, 1989.
TIAS 11771; 2204 UNTS 529

Convention for the avoidance of double taxation and the prevention of fiscal evasion with respect to taxes on income, together with a related protocol.
Signed at New Delhi September 12, 1989.
Entered into force December 18, 1990.
TIAS

Agreement to improve international tax compliance and to implement the Foreign Account Tax Compliance Act, with annexes.
Signed at New Delhi July 9, 2015.
Entered into force August 31, 2015.
TIAS 15-831

TELECOMMUNICATION

Agreement relating to the reciprocal granting of authorizations to permit licensed amateur radio operators of either country to operate their stations in the other country.
Exchange of notes at New Delhi May 16 and 25, 1966.
Entered into force May 25, 1966.
17 UST 813; TIAS 6038; 593 UNTS 157

TRADE & INVESTMENT

Convention to regulate commerce (article III) between the United States and the United Kingdom.
Signed at London July 3, 1815.
Entered into force July 3, 1815.
8 Stat. 228; TS 110; 12 Bevans 49

Convention to regulate commerce (article IV) between the United States and the United Kingdom.
Signed at London July 3, 1815.
Effective July 3, 1815.
8 Stat. 228; TS 110; 12 Bevans 49

TRANSPORTATION

Memorandum of cooperation for the promotion and development of technical cooperation in civil aviation
Signed December 7, 1993, and January 3, 1994.
Entered into force January 3, 1994.
TIAS

Air transport agreement, with annexes.
Signed at New Delhi April 14, 2005.
Entered into force June 21, 2005.
TIAS 05-621.1

Memorandum of agreement for assistance in developing and modernizing the civil aviation infrastructure of India.
Signed November 13, 2006.
Entered into force November 13, 2006.
NP

Agreement for the promotion of aviation safety.
Signed at New Delhi July 18, 2011.
Entered into force July 18, 2011.
TIAS 11-718.1

Memorandum of agreement regarding the sharing of United States' sensitive security information and protected aviation security information of India.
Signed at New Delhi December 16, 2013.
Entered into force December 16, 2013.
TIAS 13-1216.1

INDONESIA

Sovereignty over Indonesia was transferred on December 27, 1949, by the Kingdom of the Netherlands to the Republic of Indonesia in accordance with the Charter of the Transfer of Sovereignty signed on that date.

The Agreement on Transitional Measures adopted by the Round Table Conference at The Hague on November 2, 1949, provides that the treaty obligations of the Republic of Indonesia arising out of treaties and other international agreements concluded by the Netherlands are considered "as the rights and obligations of the Republic of the United States of Indonesia only where and inasmuch as such treaties and agreements are applicable to the jurisdiction of the Republic of the United States of Indonesia and with the exception of rights and duties arising out of treaties and agreements to which the Republic of the United States of Indonesia cannot become a party on the ground of the provisions of such treaties and agreements."

ATOMIC ENERGY

Agreement for cooperation concerning peaceful uses of atomic energy, with annex and agreed minute.
Signed at Washington June 30, 1980.
Entered into force December 30, 1981.
33 UST 3194; TIAS 10219

Amendment and Extension:
August 23, 1991
February 20, 2004 (TIAS 04-1014)

Arrangement for the exchange of technical information and cooperation in nuclear safety matters, with addenda and annex.
Signed at Vienna September 16, 2015.
Entered into force September 16, 2015.
TIAS

CULTURAL EXCHANGES, PROPERTY & COOPERATION

Memorandum of understanding concerning the program of the Peace Corps in Indonesia.
Signed at Jakarta December 11, 2009.
Entered into force December 11, 2009.
TIAS 09-1211

DEFENSE

Agreement for a program of military assistance in the form of constabulary equipment to be supplied by the United States to the Republic of Indonesia.
Exchange of notes at Djakarta August 15, 1950.
Entered into force August 15, 1950.
2 UST 1619; TIAS 2306; 134 UNTS 255

Agreement for the transfer from a grant to an aid on a reimbursable basis of the undelivered balance of constabulary equipment authorized under the agreement of August 15, 1950.
Exchange of notes at Washington January 5, and at Djakarta January 12, 1953.
Entered into force January 12, 1953.
4 UST 113; TIAS 2768; 198 UNTS 400

Agreement relating to the sale to Indonesia of military equipment, materials, and services.
Exchange of notes at Djakarta August 13, 1958.
Entered into force August 13, 1958.
9 UST 1149; TIAS 4095; 335 UNTS 187

Agreement relating to the furnishing of military equipment, materials, and services for a program of civic action.
Exchange of notes at Djakarta April 14, 1967.
Entered into force April 14, 1967.
18 UST 384; TIAS 6247; 689 UNTS 3

Agreement relating to the provision by the United States of basic pilot training aircraft.
Exchange of notes at Djakarta April 9 and 17, 1969.
Entered into force April 17, 1969.
20 UST 702; TIAS 6678; 719 UNTS 121

Agreement relating to the furnishing of combat equipment to Indonesia as additional military assistance.
Exchange of notes at Djakarta August 18 and 19, 1970.
Entered into force August 19, 1970.
21 UST 2140; TIAS 6959; 764 UNTS 219

Agreement concerning payment to the United States of net proceeds from the sale of defense articles furnished under the military assistance program.
Exchange of notes at Jakarta June 12 and 29, 1974.
Entered into force July 1, 1974.
25 UST 2609; TIAS 7938

Agreement relating to eligibility for United States military assistance and training pursuant to the International Security Assistance and Arms Export Control Act of 1976.
Exchange of notes at Jakarta August 3 and 24, 1976.
Entered into force August 24, 1976.
27 UST 4006; TIAS 8419; 1059 UNTS 131

Memorandum of understanding concerning mapping, charting, and geodesy cooperation.
Signed at Jakarta October 21, 1977.
Entered into force October 21, 1977.
29 UST 4810; TIAS 9079; 1134 UNTS 339

Agreement relating to payment to the United States of the net proceeds from the sale of defense articles by Indonesia.
Exchange of notes at Jakarta June 29 and September 6, 2006.
Entered into force September 6, 2006.
TIAS

Acquisition and cross-servicing agreement, with annexes.
Signed at Jakarta December 9, 2009.
Entered into force May 14, 2010.
NP

DIPLOMATIC & CONSULAR RELATIONS

Agreement granting reciprocal customs privileges to diplomatic and consular officers and personnel.
Exchange of notes at Washington March 23 and 31, 1961.
Entered into force March 31, 1961.
12 UST 251; TIAS 4706; 405 UNTS 119

EDUCATION

Memorandum of understanding concerning the establishment of the American-Indonesian Exchange Foundation (AMINEF).
Signed at Jakarta February 16, 2009.
Entered into force February 16, 2009.
TIAS 09-216
Extension and Amendment:
January 15 and February 6, 2014 (TIAS 14-206)

FINANCE

Memorandum of agreement regarding the rescheduling of payments under the agricultural commodities agreements of April 18, 1966, as amended, and June 28, 1966, as amended; the surplus property agreement of May 28, 1947, as amended and certain loan and credit agreements.
Signed at Djakarta March 16, 1971.
Entered into force March 16, 1971.
22 UST 514; TIAS 7092; 792 UNTS 170

Agreement regarding the consolidation and rescheduling of certain debts owed to, guaranteed by, or insured by the United States Government and its agencies, with annexes.
Signed at Washington September 1, 1999.
Entered into force October 22, 1999.
NP

Agreement regarding the consolidation and rescheduling of certain debts owed to, guaranteed by, or insured by the United States Government and its agencies, with annexes.
Signed at Jakarta December 8, 2000.
Entered into force January 16, 2001.
NP

Agreement regarding the consolidation and rescheduling of certain debts owed to, guaranteed by, or insured by the United States Government and its agencies, with annexes.
Signed at Jakarta October 1, 2002.
Entered into force November 12, 2002.
NP

Agreement regarding the consolidation and rescheduling of certain debts owed to, guaranteed by, or insured by the United States Government or its agencies, with annexes.
Signed at Jakarta June 14, 2005.
Entered into force July 19, 2005.
NP

Agreement regarding debt-for-nature swap with respect to certain debt owed by the Government of the Republic of Indonesia to the Government of the United States of America, with schedules.
Signed at Jakarta June 30, 2009.
Entered into force July 1, 2009.
TIAS 09-701.1
Amendment:
August 27, 2009 (TIAS 09-701.1)

Investment support agreement.
Signed at Washington April 13, 2010.
Entered into force August 5, 2010.
TIAS 10-805

Agreement regarding debt-for-nature swap with respect to certain debt owed by the Government of the Republic of Indonesia to the Government of the United States of America, with schedules.
Signed at Jakarta September 29, 2011.
Entered into force September 29, 2011.
TIAS 11-929

Third agreement regarding a debt-for-nature swap with respect to certain debt owed by the Government of the Republic of Indonesia to the Government of the United States of America.
Signed at Jakarta September 29, 2014.
Entered into force September 29, 2014.
TIAS 14-929
Amendment
December 12, 2014 (TIAS 14-1212.1)

FOREIGN ASSISTANCE

Economic cooperation agreement.
Signed at Djakarta October 16, 1950.
Entered into force provisionally October 16, 1950 (recognized by the Republic of Indonesia as a binding obligation pending Parliamentary action).
7 UST 2241; TIAS 3624; 281 UNTS 105

Agreement relating to continuation of economic and technical cooperation under the agreement of October 16, 1950.
Exchange of notes at Washington January 5 and at Djakarta January 12, 1953.
Entered into force January 12, 1953.
4 UST 18, TIAS 2762; 215 UNTS 121

Agreement relating to an informational media guaranty program pursuant to Section 1011 of the U.S. Information and Educational Exchange Act of 1948, as amended.
Exchange of notes at Djakarta September 15, 1955.
Entered into force September 15, 1955.
6 UST 3957; TIAS 3406; 256 UNTS 293

Millennium Challenge Compact, with annexes.
Signed at Bali November 19, 2011.
Entered into force April 2, 2013.
TIAS 13-402

AGENCY FOR INTERNATIONAL DEVELOPMENT

Strategic objective grant agreement to support improved quality of decentralized basic education, with annexes.
Signed August 30, 2004.
Entered into force August 30, 2004.
NP
Signed
July 8, 2005
August 29, 2006
September 26, 2007
August 22, 2008

Strategic objective grant agreement to support higher quality basic human services utilized in Indonesia, with annex.
Signed August 30, 2004.
Entered into force August 30, 2004.
NP
Signed
July 8, 2005
August 29, 2006
September 26, 2007
August 22, 2008

Strategic objective grant agreement for economic growth and job creation in Indonesia, with attachment.
Signed at Jakarta May 7, 2005.
Entered into force May 7, 2005.
NP
Amendment
August 22, 2008

Strategic objective grant agreement to support tsunami recovery and reconstruction in Indonesia, with annexes.
Signed at Jakarta July 7, 2005.
Entered into force July 7, 2005.
NP

Strategic objective grant agreement to support effective democratic and decentralized governance in Indonesia, with annexes.
Signed at Jakarta July 11, 2005.
Entered into force July 11, 2005.
NP
Amendments
November 16, 2005
August 15, 2006
September 28, 2007
August 22, 2008

Strategic objective grant agreement to strengthen anti-corruption efforts and promote immunization coverage, with annexes.
Signed at Jakarta November 17, 2006.
Entered into force November 17, 2006.
NP

Assistance agreement for the achievement of a stronger Indonesia advancing national and global development, with annexes.
Signed September 29, 2014.
Entered into force September 29, 2014.
NP

INTELLECTUAL PROPERTY

Agreement on copyright protection.
Signed at Washington March 22, 1989.
Entered into force August 1, 1989.
TIAS 11608; 2192 UNTS 101

LAW ENFORCEMENT

Understandings concerning the assignment of a Drug Enforcement Administration representative to the American Embassy in Jakarta to advance the U.S.-Indonesian common interest in preventing illegal traffic in narcotic drugs, with annex.
Exchange of letters at Jakarta April 1, 1975.
Entered into force April 1, 1975.
27 UST 2001; TIAS 8299; 1052 UNTS 227

Memorandum of understanding regarding mutual assistance between customs administrations.
Signed at Jakarta November 17, 2006.
Entered into force November 17, 2006.
TIAS 06-1117

MARITIME MATTERS

Agreement on maritime search and rescue.
Signed at Jakarta July 5, 1988.
Entered into force July 5, 1988.
TIAS 11655; 2202 UNTS 23

POSTAL MATTERS

Agreement concerning the exchange of parcel post, and detailed regulations of execution.
Signed at Bandoeng June 14 and at Washington October 4, 1934.
Operative October 4, 1933.
49 Stat. 2967; Post Office Department print; 158 LNTS 395

International express mail agreement, with detailed regulations.
Signed at Jakarta and Washington January 23 and February 26, 1987.
Entered into force April 1, 1987.
TIAS 11300

PUBLICATIONS

Agreement relating to the exchange of official publications.
Exchange of notes at Djakarta May 17 and June 7, 1950.
Entered into force June 7, 1950.
1 UST 649; TIAS 2122; 98 UNTS 167

SCIENTIFIC & TECHNICAL COOPERATION

Memorandum of understanding on general cooperation in science and technology for natural hazard assessment, analysis, warning, preparedness and mitigation, with annexes.
Signed at Jakarta November 20, 2006.
Entered into force November 20, 2006.
TIAS 06-1120
Extension:
November 15, 2011 (TIAS 06-1120)

Agreement scientific and technological cooperation, with annex.
Signed at Jakarta March 29, 2010.
Entered into force February 16, 2011.
TIAS 11-216

Implementing arrangement for cooperation in the use of U.S. land remote sensing satellite data, with annexes.
Signed at Reston and Jakarta October 10 and November 2, 2012.
Entered into force November 2, 2012.
TIAS 12-1102

SPACE

Agreement concerning the furnishing of launching and associated services by the National Aeronautics and Space Administration for Indonesian satellites, with annexes.
Exchange of notes at Washington March 26, 1975.
Entered into force March 26, 1975.
26 UST 524; TIAS 8054; 992 UNTS 308

Agreement for cooperation on the southeast Asia composition, cloud, climate coupling regional study.
Signed at Washington and Jakarta May 31 and June 19, 2012.
Entered into force June 19, 2012.
TIAS 12-619.1

TAXATION

Convention for the avoidance of double taxation and the prevention of fiscal evasion with respect to taxes on income, with protocol and exchange of notes.
Signed at Jakarta July 11, 1988.
Entered into force December 30, 1990.
TIAS 11593; 2190 UNTS 287

Protocol amending the convention of July 11, 1988, for the avoidance of double taxation and the prevention of fiscal evasion with respect to taxes on income.
Signed at Jakarta July 24, 1996.
Entered into force December 23, 1996.
TIAS

TELECOMMUNICATION

Agreement relating to the reciprocal granting of authorizations to permit licensed amateur radio operators of either country to operate their stations in the other country.
Exchange of notes at Djakarta December 10, 1968.
Entered into force December 10, 1968.
20 UST 490; TIAS 6654; 707 UNTS 149

TRADE AND INVESTMENT

Memorandum of understanding on combating illegal logging and associated trade.
Signed at Hanoi November 17, 2006.
Entered into force November 17, 2006.
TIAS 06-1117.1

TRANSPORTATION

Air transport agreement with schedule.
Signed at Djakarta January 15, 1968.
Entered into force January 15, 1968.
19 UST 4496; TIAS 6441; 697 UNTS 209
Amendments:
May 2, 1986 (TIAS 11371; 2194 UNTS 181)
April 12 and June 19, 1990 (TIAS 11760)

Agreement concerning the airworthiness and environmental certification of imported civil aeronautical products.
Exchange of notes at Jakarta January 23, 1987.
Entered into force January 23, 1987.
TIAS 11320

Memorandum of agreement concerning assistance in developing and modernizing the Indonesian civil aviation infrastructure, with annexes.
Signed at Washington and Jakarta August 23 and October 19, 1990.
Entered into force October 19, 1990.
TIAS 11749; 2202 UNTS 149

Memorandum of agreement concerning assistance in the development of Indonesia's civil aeronautics and air commerce, with annex.
Signed at Washington and Jakarta April 3 and May 3, 1996.
Entered into force May 3, 1996.
TIAS 12748

INTER–AMERICAN DEVELOPMENT BANK

FINANCE

Social progress trust fund agreement with exchange of letters.
Signed at Washington June 19, 1961.
Entered into force June 19, 1961.
12 UST 632; TIAS 4763; 410 UNTS 33
Related Agreements:
February 17, 1964 (15 UST 104; TIAS 5522; 511 UNTS 296)
September 7, 1966 (17 UST 1200; TIAS 6081)
April 28, 1972 (23 UST 1497; TIAS 7430)
October 3, 1975 (27 UST 2627; TIAS 8333; 1054 UNTS 338)

INTER–AMERICAN INSTITUTE FOR COOPERATION ON AGRICULTURE

TAXATION

Tax reimbursement agreement.
Signed at Washington December 30, 1994.
Entered into force December 30, 1994.
TIAS 12594

INTERNATIONAL ATOMIC ENERGY AGENCY

NOTE: For agreements between the IAEA, the United States, and other countries, see under ATOMIC ENERGY in multilateral section.

ATOMIC ENERGY

Agreement for cooperation in the civil uses of atomic energy.
Signed at Vienna May 11, 1959.
Entered into force August 7, 1959.
10 UST 1424; TIAS 4291; 339 UNTS 359
Extension and Amendments:
February 12, 1974 (25 UST 1199; TIAS 7852)
January 14, 1980 (32 UST 1143; TIAS 9762; 1220 UNTS 316)
January 21, 2014 (TIAS 14-606)

Agreement for the application of safeguards in the United States, with protocol.
Done at Vienna November 18, 1977.
Entered into force December 9, 1980.
32 UST 3059; TIAS 9889
Amendment:
June 12, 1998

Agreement relating to provision by the United States Nuclear Regulatory Commission to the International Atomic Energy Agency of experts in the various fields of the peaceful applications of atomic energy.
Signed at Vienna and Bethesda May 29 and September 16, 1981.
Entered into force September 16, 1981.
33 UST 3849; TIAS 10264; 1543 UNTS 111

Agreement for the application of safeguards in connection with the treaty of February 14, 1967, for the prohibition of nuclear weapons in Latin America, with protocol.
Signed at Vienna February 17, 1989.
Entered into force April 6, 1989.
TIAS 12398

TAXATION

Tax reimbursement agreement, with annex.
Signed at Vienna April 5, 1989.
Entered into force April 5, 1989.
TIAS 11774

INTERNATIONAL CENTRE FOR THE STUDY OF THE PRESERVATION AND RESTORATION OF CULTURAL PROPERTY (ICCROM)

TAXATION

Agreement relating to a procedure for United States income tax reimbursement.
Exchange of letters at Rome April 1 and May 4, 1981.
Entered into force May 4, 1981; effective January 1981.
33 UST 1922; TIAS 10155

Tax reimbursement agreement, with annex.
Signed at Rome March 3, 2014.
Entered into force March 3, 2014.
TIAS 14-303.1

INTERNATIONAL CIVIL AVIATION ORGANIZATION

TAXATION

Tax reimbursement agreement, with annex.
Signed at Montreal July 14, 1992.
Entered into force July 14, 1992.
TIAS 12465

TRANSPORTATION

Memorandum of cooperation for the provision of technical expertise in the field of civil aviation security.
Signed at Washington and Montreal September 7 and 18, 1989.
Entered into force September 18, 1989.
TIAS
Amendments and Extensions:
January 31 and February 14, 1992 (NP)
October 7 and November 18, 1994 (NP)
September 3 and 12, 1997 (NP)
August 8 and 29, 2000 (NP)
October 6, 2003 (NP)
October 2 and 6, 2003 (NP)

Memorandum of agreement regarding the detail of Federal Aviation Administration personnel to the International Civil Aviation Organization.
Signed February 19, 1999.
Entered into force February 19, 1999.
NP

Memorandum of understanding concerning technical assistance.
Signed September 23, 2003.
Entered into force September 23, 2003.
NP

Memorandum of understanding concerning the provision of civil aviation technical assistance.
Signed September 29, 2004.
Entered into force September 29, 2004.
NP

INTERNATIONAL COTTON ADVISORY COMMITTEE

TAXATION

Agreement relating to a procedure for United States income tax reimbursement.
Exchange of notes at Washington November 17 and 19, 1981.
Entered into force January 1, 1982.
33 UST 4242; TIAS 10299

INTERNATIONAL HYDROGRAPHIC BUREAU

TAXATION

Agreement relating to a procedure for United States income tax reimbursement.
Exchange of letters at Marseilles December 7 and 13, 1982.
Entered into force January 1, 1983.
TIAS 12058

INTERNATIONAL INSTITUTE FOR THE UNIFICATION OF PRIVATE LAW

TAXATION

Tax Reimbursement Agreement, with annex.
Signed at Rome September 17, 2013.
Entered into force September 17, 2013.
TIAS 13-917

INTERNATIONAL LABOR ORGANIZATION

CULTURAL EXCHANGES, PROPERTY & COOPERATION

Agreement concerning the Peace Corps program.
Exchange of notes at Geneva February 21 and 22, 1963.
Entered into force February 22, 1963.
14 UST 1554; TIAS 5458; 489 UNTS 347

TAXATION

Agreement relating to a procedure for United States income tax reimbursement, with annex.
Signed at Washington May 18, 1984.
Entered into force May 18, 1984; effective January 1, 1984.
TIAS 11076; 2039 UNTS 267

INTERNATIONAL MARITIME ORGANIZATION

TAXATION

Tax reimbursement agreement, with annex.
Signed at London January 12, 1995.
Entered into force January 12, 1995.
TIAS 12597

INTERNATIONAL MONETARY FUND

FINANCE

Agreement relating to provision of financing by the United States in connection with the establishment of the Supplementary Financing Facility.
Exchange of letters at Washington January 5 and 12, 1979.
Entered into force January 16, 1979.
30 UST 3526; TIAS 9406; 1180 UNTS 131

INTERNATIONAL NATURAL RUBBER ORGANIZATION

TAXATION

Tax reimbursement agreement, with annex.
Signed at Kuala Lumpur October 5, 1988.
Entered into force October 5, 1988.
TIAS 11627; 2191 UNTS 169

INTERNATIONAL ORGANIZATION OF LEGAL METROLOGY

TAXATION

Tax reimbursement agreement, with annex.
Signed at Paris December 9, 2011.
Entered into force December 9, 2011.
TIAS 11-1209

INTERNATIONAL ORGANIZATION FOR MIGRATION

TAXATION

Tax reimbursement agreement, with annex.
Signed at Washington September 17, 1997.
Entered into force September 17, 1997.
TIAS 12883

INTERNATIONAL RENEWABLE ENERGY AGENCY

TAXATION

Tax reimbursement agreement, with annex.
Signed at Abu Dhabi December 3, 2013.
Entered into force December 3, 2013.
TIAS 13-1203

INTERNATIONAL TELECOMMUNICATION UNION

TAXATION

Tax reimbursement agreement, with annex.
Signed at Geneva January 19, 1990.
Entered into force January 19, 1990.
TIAS 11710; 2207 UNTS 371

TELECOMMUNICATION

Special arrangement permitting third party exchanges between the International Telecommunications Union amateur radio station and amateur radio stations under United States jurisdiction.
Exchange of letters at Geneva and Washington April 28 and June 7, 1976.
Entered into force June 7, 1976.
28 UST 5019; TIAS 8608

INTERNATIONAL TELECOMMUNICATIONS SATELLITE ORGANIZATION

TELECOMMUNICATION

Headquarters agreement.
Signed at Washington November 22 and 24, 1976.
Entered into force November 24, 1976.
28 UST 2248; TIAS 8542

Memorandum of agreement with respect to the Pan American Satellite Corporation consultation, with related letter.
Signed at Washington November 10, 1986.
Entered into force November 10, 1986.
TIAS 12390

INTERNATIONAL THERMONUCLEAR EXPERIMENTAL REACTOR (ITER) INTERNATIONAL FUSION ENERGY ORGANIZATION

TAXATION

Tax reimbursement agreement, with annex.
Signed at Cadarache November 29, 2010.
Entered into force November 29, 2010.
TIAS 10-1129

INTERNATIONAL TRIBUNAL FOR THE PROSECUTION OF PERSONS RESPONSIBLE FOR GENOCIDE AND OTHER SERIOUS VIOLATIONS OF INTERNATIONAL HUMANITARIAN LAW COMMITTED IN THE TERRITORY OF RWANDA

RULES OF WAR

Agreement on surrender of persons, with statement of understanding.
Signed at The Hague January 24, 1995.
Entered into force February 14, 1996.
TIAS 12601

INTERNATIONAL TRIBUNAL FOR THE PROSECUTION OF PERSONS RESPONSIBLE FOR SERIOUS VIOLATIONS OF INTERNATIONAL HUMANITARIAN LAW IN THE TERRITORY OF THE FORMER YUGOSLAVIA

RULES OF WAR

Agreement on surrender of persons.
Signed at The Hague October 5, 1994.
Entered into force February 14, 1996.
TIAS 12570; 1911 UNTS 223

INTERNATIONAL TROPICAL TIMBER ORGANIZATION

TAXATION

Tax reimbursement agreement, with annex.
Signed at Tokyo December 27, 1988.
Entered into force December 27, 1988.
TIAS 11629; 2191 UNTS 189

IRAN

CIVIL AFFAIRS, EMERGENCIES & DEFENSE

Memorandum of understanding relating to the provision of advisory technical assistance to Iran in organizing its civil emergency preparedness capability
Signed January 26, 1977.
Entered into force January 26, 1977.
30 UST 4354; TIAS 9461

CLAIMS & DISPUTE RESOLUTION

Declarations of the Government of the Democratic and Popular Republic of Algeria concerning commitments and settlement of claims by the United States and Iran with respect to resolution of the crisis arising out of the detention of 52 United States nationals in Iran, with Undertakings and Escrow Agreement.*
Initialed at Algiers January 19, 1981.
Entered into force January 19, 1981.
TIAS
Note:
* For technical agreements concerning the security account, see NETHERLANDS — CLAIMS.

Settlement agreement regarding certain claims before the Iran-U.S. Claims Tribunal, with annex.
Signed at The Hague February 9, 1996.
Entered into force February 9, 1996.
TIAS

Settlement agreement on the case concerning the aerial incident of July 3, 1988 before the International Court of Justice, with annexes.
Signed at The Hague February 9, 1996.
Entered into force February 9, 1996.
TIAS

General agreement on the settlement of certain I.C.J. and Tribunal cases, with related statement.
Signed at The Hague February 9, 1996.
Entered into force February 9, 1996.
TIAS

CONSULAR AFFAIRS

Agreement relating to the reciprocal waiver of passport visa fees for nonimmigrants.*
Exchange of notes at Tehran March 27 and April 20 and 21, 1926.
Entered into force April 21, 1926; operative May 15, 1926.
8 Bevans 1260

Agreement relating to the reciprocal issuance of multiple-entry nonimmigrant visas.*
Exchange of letters at Tehran December 13 and 16, 1976.
Entered into force December 16, 1976; effective January 1, 1977.
28 UST 8161; TIAS 8751
Note:
* The status of this agreement is under review.

CULTURAL EXCHANGES, PROPERTY & COOPERATION

Agreement relating to the establishment of a Peace Corps program in Iran.
Exchange of notes at Tehran September 5 and 16, 1962.
Entered into force September 16, 1962.
22 UST 434; TIAS 7078; 791 UNTS 19

DEFENSE

Mutual defense assistance agreement.
Exchange of notes at Washington May 23, 1950.
Entered into force May 23, 1950.
1 UST 420; TIAS 2071; 81 UNTS 3

Agreement relating to the continuation of military assistance to Iran.
Exchange of notes at Tehran April 24, 1952.
Entered into force April 24, 1952.
5 UST 788; TIAS 2967

Agreement relating to the disposition of equipment and materials no longer required in the furtherance of the mutual defense assistance program.
Exchange of notes at Tehran July 12 and October 31, 1957.
Entered into force October 31, 1957.
8 UST 2369; TIAS 3952; 303 UNTS 320

Agreement relating to the privileges and immunities granted American military and non-military technicians assisting in the modernization program of the Imperial Iranian Armed Forces.
Exchange of notes at Tehran May 24 and 30, 1973.
Entered into force May 30, 1973.
25 UST 3048; TIAS 7963

Agreement relating to the safeguarding of classified information, with annex.
Exchange of notes at Tehran May 28 and June 6, 1974.
Entered into force June 6, 1974.
25 UST 1266; TIAS 7857

Agreement relating to the furnishing of certain federal catalog data and cataloging services to Iran.
Signed at Washington December 5, 1974, and at Tehran January 25, 1975.
Entered into force January 25, 1975.
26 UST 302; TIAS 8034; 991 UNTS 401

Agreement concerning management, disposal, and utilization of funds derived from the sale of military assistance program property.
Signed at Tehran October 6, 1975.
Entered into force October 6, 1975.
TIAS

Agreement concerning management, disposal, and utilization of funds derived from sale of military assistance program property.
Signed at Tehran October 19, 1976.
Entered into force October 19, 1976.
TIAS

Memorandum of understanding concerning revisions of Foreign Military Sales letters of offer and acceptance in force between the United States and Iran.
Signed at Tehran February 3, 1979.
Entered into force February 3, 1979.
30 UST 3597; TIAS 9415

EDUCATION

Agreement for financing certain educational exchange programs.
Signed at Tehran October 24, 1963.
Entered into force October 24, 1963.
14 UST 1510; TIAS 5451; 489 UNTS 303

FINANCE

Agreement relating to investment guaranties under section 413(b)(4) of the Mutual Security Act of 1954, as amended.
Exchange of notes at Tehran September 17 and 21, 1957.
Entered into force September 24, 1957.
8 UST 1599; TIAS 3913; 293 UNTS 287

Agreement supplementing the agreement of September 17 and 21, 1957, relating to investment guaranties.
Exchange of notes at Tehran March 12, 1970.
Entered into force March 12, 1970.
22 UST 1030; TIAS 7146; 797 UNTS 396

FOREIGN ASSISTANCE

Agreement relating to duty-free entry and defrayment of inland transportation charges for relief supplies to Iran.
Exchange of notes at Tehran September 22 and October 5 and 13, 1953.
Entered into force October 13, 1953.
4 UST 2809; TIAS 2890; 222 UNTS 67

General agreement for economic cooperation.
Signed at Tehran December 21, 1961.
Entered into force December 21, 1961.
12 UST 3229; TIAS 4930; 433 UNTS 269

Joint communique concerning United States-Iran relations and establishment of a Joint Commission for cooperation in various fields.
Issued at Tehran November 2, 1974.
Entered into force November 2, 1974.
25 UST 3073; TIAS 7967

Agreed minutes of the Joint Commission:
March 4, 1975 (26 UST 420; TIAS 8042)
August 7, 1976 (27 UST 4329; TIAS 8455)
February 28, 1978 (30 UST 1027; TIAS 9238; 1152 UNTS 103)

LAW ENFORCEMENT

Agreement on procedures for mutual assistance in connection with matters relating to the Lockheed Aircraft Corporation, Grumman Corporation and Northrop Corporation.
Signed at Washington June 14, 1977.
Entered into force June 14, 1977.
28 UST 5205; TIAS 8621

POSTAL MATTERS

Parcel post agreement with detailed regulations for execution.
Signed at Tehran July 15 and at Washington August 28, 1969.
Entered into force January 1, 1971.
21 UST 2605; TIAS 7002; 775 UNTS 17

PUBLICATIONS

Agreement relating to the exchange of official publications.
Exchange of notes at Tehran August 21, 1943.
Entered into force August 21, 1943.
57 Stat. 1133; EAS 349; 8 Bevans 1280; 101 UNTS 189

SCIENTIFIC & TECHNICAL COOPERATION

Agreement relating to a cooperative program to improve and modernize the Iranian meteorological services, with annexes.
Signed at Tehran November 26, 1977.
Entered into force November 26, 1977.
29 UST 5546; TIAS 9127; 1134 UNTS 359

TRADE & INVESTMENT

Treaty of amity, economic relations, and consular rights.
Signed at Tehran August 15, 1955.
Entered into force June 16, 1957.
8 UST 899; TIAS 3853; 284 UNTS 93

TRANSPORTATION

Air transport agreement, with exchange of notes.
Signed at Tehran February 1, 1973.
Entered into force January 9, 1974.
26 UST 1929; TIAS 8149; 1027 UNTS 129

Memorandum of agreement relating to the provision of technical assistance to the Iranian Civil Aviation Organization, with annex.
Signed at Washington and Tehran May 12 and June 9, 1977.
Entered into force June 9, 1977.
29 UST 5319; TIAS 9111

IRAQ

CLAIMS & DISPUTE RESOLUTION

Agreement concerning claims resulting from attack on the U.S.S. Stark.
Exchange of notes at Baghdad March 27 and 28, 1989.
Entered into force March 28, 1989.
TIAS 12030

Claims settlement agreement, with annex.
Signed at Baghdad September 2, 2010.
Entered into force May 22, 2011.
TIAS 11-522

CULTURAL EXCHANGES, PROPERTY & COOPERATION

Cultural agreement.
Signed at Baghdad January 23, 1961.
Entered into force August 13, 1963.
14 UST 1168; TIAS 5411; 488 UNTS 163

DEFENSE

Agreement regarding grants under the Foreign Assistance Act of 1961, as amended, and the provision of defense articles, defense services, and related training, including under the United States International Military Education and Training Program.
Exchange of notes at Baghdad July 24 and August 14, 2004.
Entered into force August 14, 2004.
NP

Strategic framework agreement for a relationship of friendship and cooperation.
Signed at Baghdad November 17, 2008.
Entered into force January 1, 2009.
TIAS 09-101.1

DIPLOMATIC & CONSULAR RELATIONS

Agreement relating to the privilege, on a reciprocal basis, of free entry to all articles imported for the personal use of consular officers.
Exchange of notes at Washington March 14, May 15, June 19, and August 8, 1951.
Entered into force August 8, 1951.
5 UST 657; TIAS 2956; 229 UNTS 185.

EDUCATION

Agreement providing for the United States education foundation in Iraq.
Signed at Baghdad August 16, 1951.
Entered into force August 16, 1951.
2 UST 1908; TIAS 2327; 147 UNTS 65

FINANCE

Agreement regarding the cancellation of certain debts owed to, guaranteed by, or insured by the United States Government, with annex.
Signed at Washington December 17, 2004.
Entered into force March 7, 2005.
TIAS

Investment incentive agreement.
Signed at Amman July 11, 2005.
Entered into force June 24, 2013.
TIAS 13-624

FOREIGN ASSISTANCE

General agreement for technical cooperation.
Signed at Baghdad April 10, 1951.
Entered into force June 2, 1951.
3 UST 541; TIAS 2413; 151 UNTS 179
Amendment:
December 18, 1951, and February 21, 1952 (3 UST 4748; TIAS 2638; 198 UNTS 225)

Commercial, economic and technical cooperation agreement.
Signed at Washington August 26, 1987.
Entered into force October 27, 1987.
TIAS 12020

Agreement for economic and technical cooperation.
Signed at Amman July 11, 2005.
Entered into force December 18, 2013.
TIAS 13-1218

LAW ENFORCEMENT

Extradition treaty.
Signed at Baghdad June 7, 1934.
Entered into force April 23, 1936.
49 Stat. 3380; TS 907; 9 Bevans 1; 170 LNTS 267

POSTAL MATTERS

International express mail agreement, with detailed regulations.
Signed at Baghdad and Washington April 6 and May 5, 1989.
Entered into force June 15, 1989.
TIAS 11609.

PROPERTY

Agreement on the principles applying to aid for defense, and exchange of notes.
Signed at Washington July 31, 1945.
Entered into force July 31, 1945.
59 Stat. 1535; EAS 470; 9 Bevans 22; 121 UNTS 239

Agreement on diplomatic and consular property.
Signed at Baghdad October 31, 2004.
Entered into force October 31, 2004.
TIAS 04-1031

PUBLICATIONS

Agreement relating to the exchange of official publications.
Exchange of notes at Baghdad February 16, 1944.
Entered into force February 16, 1944.
58 Stat. 1253; EAS 403; 9 Bevans 14; 109 UNTS 223

SCIENTIFIC & TECHNICAL COOPERATION

Memorandum of understanding concerning scientific and technical cooperation in the earth sciences, with annexes.
Signed at Baghdad and Reston November 14 and December 23, 2010.
Entered into force December 23, 2010.
TIAS 10-1223

TRADE & INVESTMENT

See also FOREIGN ASSISTANCE

Treaty of commerce and navigation.
Signed at Baghdad December 3, 1938.
Entered into force June 19, 1940.
54 Stat. 1790; TS 960; 9 Bevans 7; 203 LNTS 107

Trade and investment framework agreement.
Signed at Amman July 11, 2005.
Entered into force May 31, 2013.
NP

IRELAND

ATOMIC ENERGY

Agreement providing for a grant to assist in the acquisition of certain nuclear research and training equipment and materials.
Exchange of notes at Dublin March 24, 1960.
Entered into force April 7, 1960.
11 UST 376; TIAS 4453; 371 UNTS 237

CONSULAR AFFAIRS

Agreement relating to the relaxation of visa requirements for American citizens entering Ireland and the granting of gratis nonimmigrant passport visas to Irish citizens entering the United States.*
Exchange of notes at Dublin August 1, 1949.
Entered into force August 1, 1949.
63 Stat. 2807; TIAS 2050; 9 Bevans 66; 82 UNTS 37.
Note:
* The status of this agreement is under review.

DEFENSE

Agreement concerning security measures for the protection of classified military information.
Signed at Dublin January 31, 2003.
Entered into force January 31, 2003.
TIAS 03-131

Acquisition and cross-servicing agreement, with annexes.
Signed at Stuttgart and Newbridge June 17, 2014.
Entered into force June 17, 2014.
NP

DIPLOMATIC & CONSULAR RELATIONS

Consular convention.*
Signed at Dublin May 1, 1950.
Entered into force June 12, 1954.
5 UST 949; TIAS 2984; 222 UNTS 107
Amendment:
June 16, 1998 (TIAS 12964)

Supplementary protocol to the consular convention of May 1, 1950.
Signed at Dublin March 3, 1952.
Entered into force June 12, 1954.
5 UST 949; TIAS 2984; 222 UNTS 107
Note:
* Applicable to all territories.

EMPLOYMENT

Agreement relating to the employment of dependents of official government employees.
Exchange of notes at Washington September 17, 1996, and August 1, 1997.
Entered into force August 1, 1997.
TIAS 12877; 2080 UNTS 83

ENVIRONMENT & CONSERVATION

Agreement for cooperation in the Global Learning and Observations to Benefit the Environment (GLOBE) Program, with appendices.
Signed at Dublin June 12, 1995.
Entered into force June 12, 1995.
TIAS 12659

FINANCE

NOTE: For International Fund for Ireland, see under FINANCE in multilateral section.

Agreement relating to investment guaranties under section 413(b)(4) of the Mutual Security Act of 1954, as amended.
Exchange of notes at Dublin October 5, 1955.
Entered into force October 5, 1955.
6 UST 3953; TIAS 3405; 256 UNTS 285

LAW ENFORCEMENT

Treaty on extradition.
Signed at Washington July 13, 1983.
Entered into force December 15, 1984.
TIAS 10813

Agreement regarding mutual assistance between their customs administrations.
Signed at Dublin September 16, 1996.
Entered into force May 21, 1998.
TIAS 12800; 2141 UNTS 51

Treaty on mutual legal assistance in criminal matters.
Signed at Washington January 18, 2001.
Entered into force August 11, 2009.
TIAS 13137

Instrument as contemplated by Article 3(2) of the agreement on mutual legal assistance between the United States of America and the European Union signed June 25, 2003, as to the application of the treaty on mutual legal assistance in criminal matters of January 18, 2001, with annex.
Signed at Dublin July 14, 2005.
Entered into force February 1, 2010.
TIAS 10-201.35

Instrument as contemplated by Article 3(2) of the agreement on extradition between the United States of America and the European Union signed June 25, 2003, as to the application of the treaty on extradition of July 13, 1983, with annex.
Signed at Dublin July 14, 2005.
Entered into force February 1, 2010.
TIAS 10-201.12

Agreement on enhancing cooperation in preventing and combating serious crime.
Signed at Dublin July 21, 2011.
Entered into force October 19, 2012, with the exception of Articles 8 through 10.
TIAS 12-1019.1

POSTAL MATTERS

Parcel post convention.
Signed at Dublin April 23 and at Washington May 6, 1926.
Operative May 1, 1926.
44 Stat. 2412; Post Office Department print; 56 LNTS 433

International express mail agreement with detailed regulations.
Signed at Dublin and Washington February 29 and March 20, 1984.
Entered into force May 19, 1984.
35 UST 4856; TIAS 10971; 1566 UNTS 169

PROPERTY

Convention between the United States and the United Kingdom relating to tenure and disposition of real and personal property.*
Signed at Washington March 2, 1899.
Entered into force August 7, 1900.
31 Stat. 1939; TS 146; 12 Bevans 246

Note:
* Only Article III is in force for Ireland.

SOCIAL SECURITY

Agreement on social security, with administrative arrangement.
Signed at Washington April 14, 1992.
Entered into force September 1, 1993.
TIAS 12117

TAXATION

Convention for the avoidance of double taxation and the prevention of fiscal evasion with respect to taxes on the estates of deceased persons.
Signed at Dublin September 13, 1949.
Entered into force December 20, 1951.
2 UST 2294; TIAS 2355; 127 UNTS 119

Convention for the avoidance of double taxation and the prevention of fiscal evasion with respect to taxes on income and capital gains, with protocol and related agreement.*
Signed at Dublin July 28, 1997.
Entered into force December 17, 1997.
TIAS; 2141 UNTS 167

Note:
* With understanding.

Convention amending the convention of July 28, 1997 for the avoidance of double taxation and the prevention of fiscal evasion with respect to taxes on income and capital gains.
Signed at Washington September 24, 1999.
Entered into force July 13, 2000.
TIAS; 2142 UNTS 330

Agreement to improve international tax compliance and to implement the Foreign Account Tax Compliance Act, with Annexes.
Signed at Dublin December 21, 2012.
Entered into force April 2, 2014.
TIAS 14-402

TELECOMMUNICATION

Agreement relating to the reciprocal granting of authorizations to permit licensed amateur radio operators of either country to operate their stations in the other country.
Exchange of notes at Dublin October 10, 1968.
Entered into force October 10, 1968.
19 UST 6057; TIAS 6566; 694 UNTS 103

TRADE & INVESTMENT

Treaty of friendship, commerce and navigation, with protocol.
Signed at Dublin January 21, 1950.
Entered into force September 14, 1950.
1 UST 785; TIAS 2155; 206 UNTS 269

Protocol to the treaty of friendship, commerce and navigation of January 21, 1950.
Signed at Washington June 24, 1992.
Entered into force November 18, 1992.
TIAS

TRANSPORTATION

Arrangement relating to air navigation.
Exchange of notes at Dublin September 29 and November 4, 1937.
Entered into force November 4, 1937; operative December 4, 1937.
51 Stat. 319; EAS 110; 9 Bevans 36; 185 LNTS 71

Agreement relating to air transport services.*
Exchange of notes at Washington February 3, 1945.
Entered into force February 3, 1945; operative February 15, 1945.
59 Stat. 1402; EAS 460; 9 Bevans 43; 122 UNTS 305

Amendments:
January 25, 1988, and September 29, 1989 (TIAS 11692)
July 25 and September 6, 1990 (TIAS 11739)

Note:
* This agreement is suspended for the duration of provisional application of the U.S. – E.U. Air Transport Agreement signed April 25 and 30, 2007.

Memorandum of agreement relating to flight inspection services.
Signed at Washington and Dublin March 10 and August 4, 1978.
Entered into force August 4, 1978; effective September 1, 1978.
30 UST 230; TIAS 9190; 1150 UNTS 141

Agreement for promotion of aviation safety.
Signed at Dublin February 5, 1997.
Entered into force February 5, 1997.
TIAS 12831; 2141 UNTS 293

Agreement on technical cooperation in civil aviation matters.
Signed at Dublin June 11, 1999.
Entered into force June 11, 1999.
TIAS 13042

Agreement on air transport preclearance, with annex.
Signed at Washington November 17, 2008.
Entered into force August 4, 2009.
TIAS 09-804

ISRAEL

ATOMIC ENERGY

Agreement providing for a grant to assist in the acquisition of certain nuclear research and training equipment and materials.
Exchange of notes at Tel Aviv October 19, 1960,and at Jerusalem December 19, 1960.
Entered into force December 19, 1960.
11 UST 2631; TIAS 4655; 401 UNTS 195

Agreement continuing in effect safeguards and guarantee provisions of the agreement of July 12, 1955 (6 UST 2641; TIAS 3311), as amended, for cooperation concerning civil uses of atomic energy.
Exchange of notes at Washington April 7 and 8, 1977.
Entered into force April 8, 1977.
28 UST 2407; TIAS 8557

Arrangement for the exchange of technical information and cooperation in nuclear safety and research matters, with addenda.
Signed at Rockville and Tel Aviv, August 18 and October 13, 2016.
Entered into force October 13, 2016.
TIAS 16-1013

CLAIMS & DISPUTE RESOLUTION

Agreement concerning claims arising from damage to the United States ship "Liberty".
Exchange of notes at Washington December 15 and 17, 1980.
Entered into force December 17, 1980.
32 UST 4434; TIAS 9957; 1268 UNTS 33

CONSULAR AFFAIRS

Agreement relating to the issue of visas to authorized crew members of aircraft operated by air carriers designated by Israel and the United States.*
Exchange of notes at Tel Aviv March 27 and June 1, 1951.
Entered into force June 1, 1951.
3 UST 4796; TIAS 2650; 212 UNTS 129

Agreement providing for the reciprocal waiver of nonimmigrant passport visa fees.*
Exchanges of notes at Jerusalem and Tel Aviv February 14 and 28 and March 2, 1955.
Entered into force March 2, 1955.
7 UST 2125; TIAS 3614; 220 UNTS 113

Note:
* The status of this agreement is under review.

DEFENSE

Agreement relating to assurances and economic assistance as authorized in the Mutual Security Act of 1951.
Exchange of notes at Washington December 7, 1951.
Entered into force December 7, 1951.
3 UST 2874; TIAS 2462; 157 UNTS 53

Agreement relating to mutual defense assistance.
Exchange of notes at Tel Aviv July 1 and 23, 1952.
Entered into force July 23, 1952.
3 UST 4985; TIAS 2675; 179 UNTS 139

Agreement relating to general procurement arrangements for goods and services.
Exchange of notes at Washington July 15 and 20, 1965.
Entered into force July 20, 1965.
16 UST 983; TIAS 5839; 549 UNTS 55

Agreement relating to the purchase of various goods from Israel for sale in United States Navy ships stores overseas.
Exchange of notes at Washington July 20 and 26, 1965.
Entered into force July 26, 1965.
16 UST 981; TIAS 5838; 549 UNTS 49

General security of information agreement.
Exchange of notes at Tel Aviv and Jerusalem July 30 and December 10, 1982.
Entered into force December 10, 1982.
TIAS 10617; 2001 UNTS 3

Memorandum of understanding concerning the principles governing mutual cooperation in research and development, scientist and engineer exchange, and procurement and logistic support of defense equipment, with annexes and attachment.
Signed at Washington December 14, 1987.
Entered into force December 14, 1987.
TIAS
Amendment:
December 19, 1997 and January 8, 1998

Mutual logistics support agreement, with annexes.
Signed at Stuttgart-Vaihingen and Tel Aviv May 10 and 24, 1988.
Entered into force May 24, 1988.
TIAS 12325
Amendment:
June 22, 1990 and October 9, 1991 (TIAS 12325)

Agreement on the status of United States personnel, with annexes and related letter.
Signed at Jerusalem January 22, 1991.
Entered into force January 12, 1994.
TIAS

Agreement on the status of Israeli personnel.
Signed at Jerusalem January 22, 1991.
Entered into force January 12, 1994.
TIAS

Memorandum of agreement concerning combating terrorism research and development, with annex.
Signed at Washington and Tel Aviv February 7 and March 24, 2005.
Entered into force March 24, 2005.
TIAS 05-324
Amendment:
September 16 and 17, 2014 (TIAS 14-917)

Memorandum of agreement regarding the assignment of individuals at government facilities to serve as liaison officers.
Signed at Washington September 6 and 7, 2005.
Entered into force September 7, 2005.
NP

Agreement for research, development, test and evaluation projects, with annex.
Signed at Washington July 16 and September 13, 2006.
Entered into force September 13, 2006.
TIAS

DIPLOMATIC & CONSULAR RELATIONS

Memorandum of agreement regarding joint political, security and economic cooperation.
Signed at Washington and Jerusalem April 21 and 28, 1988.
Entered into force April 21, 1988.
TIAS 11578

EDUCATION

Agreement for financing certain educational exchange programs, with memorandum of understanding.
Exchange of notes at Tel Aviv and Jerusalem June 18 and 22, 1962.
Entered into force June 22, 1962.
TIAS 5097; 13 UST 1364; 448 UNTS 273
Amendments:
March 21 and 23, 1967 (TIAS 6240; 18 UST 346; 630 UNTS 404)
January 10 and 30, 1985 (TIAS 11223)

EMPLOYMENT

Agreement relating to the employment of dependents of official government employees.
Exchange of notes at Tel Aviv and Jerusalem September 23 and October 3, 1985.
Entered into force October 3, 1985.
TIAS 11171; 2126 UNTS 227
Amendment:
July 1 and 21, 2011 (TIAS 11-721)

ENERGY

Memorandum of agreement concerning an oil supply arrangement, with related understanding.
Signed at Washington June 22, 1979.
Entered into force November 25, 1979.
30 UST 5994; TIAS 9533; 1234 UNTS 224
Amendment and Extensions:
October 19 and November 13, 1994 (TIAS 12580)
November 23, 2004

Contingency implementing arrangements for the memorandum of agreement of June 22, 1979, concerning an oil supply arrangement, with related letter.
Signed at Washington October 17, 1980.
Entered into force October 17, 1980.
32 UST 3667; TIAS 9908; 1266 UNTS 370
Amendment:
June 21 and 27, 1995 (TIAS 12670)

Agreement concerning energy cooperation, with annexes.
Signed at Jerusalem February 22, 2000.
Entered into force May 1, 2001.
TIAS 01-501.1
Amendment:
April 28, 2011 (TIAS 01-501.1)

Related Agreement:
August 10, 2011

ENVIRONMENT & CONSERVATION

Memorandum of understanding concerning cooperation in the field of environmental protection, with annexes.
Signed at Jerusalem February 20, 1991.
Entered into force February 20, 1991.
TIAS 11832

Agreement for cooperation in the Global Learning and Observations to Benefit the Environment (GLOBE) Program, with appendices.
Signed at Jerusalem March 24, 1995.
Entered into force March 24, 1995.
TIAS 12622

FINANCE

Agreement relating to the industrial investment guaranty program pursuant to Section 111(b)(3) of the Economic Cooperation Act of 1948, as amended.
Exchange of notes at Tel Aviv August 7 and 8, 1952.
Entered into force August 8, 1952.
3 UST 5045; TIAS 2686; 181 UNTS 37
Amendments:
July 31 and August 11, 1957 (8 UST 1410; TIAS 3892; 289 UNTS 318)
February 5 and 20, 1963 (14 UST 337; TIAS 5316; 474 UNTS 332)

Agreement on encouragement of investment.
Signed at Washington September 12, 1994.
Entered into force September 12, 1994.
TIAS 12190

FOREIGN ASSISTANCE

General agreement for technical cooperation.
Signed at Tel Aviv February 26, 1951.
Entered into force February 26, 1951.
3 UST 379; TIAS 2401; 137 UNTS 57
Amendment:
June 21, 1954 (5 UST 1401; TIAS 3010; 219 UNTS 348)

Agreement relating to emergency economic assistance.
Exchange of notes at Washington May 1, 1952.
Entered into force May 1, 1952.
3 UST 4266; TIAS 2571; 177 UNTS 89

Agreement relating to the informational media guaranty program pursuant to Section 111(b)(3) of the Economic Cooperation Act of 1948, as amended.
Exchange of notes at Tel Aviv June 9, 1952.
Entered into force June 9, 1952.
3 UST 4398; TIAS 2588; 178 UNTS 297

Agreement relating to special economic assistance.
Exchange of notes at Tel Aviv and Jerusalem November 25, 1953.
Entered into force November 25, 1953.
4 UST 2308; TIAS 2884; 219 UNTS 205
Amendment:
January 31, 1955 (6 UST 561; TIAS 3189; 241 UNTS 520)

Joint statement of the U.S.-Israel Joint Committee for Investment and Trade relating to expansion of economic cooperation.
Signed at Washington May 13, 1975.
Entered into force May 13, 1975.
26 UST 1674; TIAS 8127; 1006 UNTS 153

Agreement establishing the Israel-United States Binational Industrial Research and Development Foundation, with annexes.
Signed at Jerusalem March 3, 1976.
Entered into force May 18, 1977.
28 UST 5129; TIAS 8615

AGENCY FOR INTERNATIONAL DEVELOPMENT

Agreement for cash transfer assistance.
Signed at Washington December 14, 2005.
Entered into force December 14, 2005.
NP

INTELLECTUAL PROPERTY

Agreement relating to reciprocal copyright relations.
Exchange of notes at Washington May 4, 1950.
Entered into force May 4, 1950; operative May 15, 1948.
1 UST 645; TIAS 2121; 132 UNTS 189

INTERNATIONAL CRIMINAL COURT

Agreement regarding the surrender of persons to the International Criminal Court.
Signed at Jerusalem August 4, 2002.
Entered into force November 27, 2003.
TIAS 03-1127

LAW ENFORCEMENT

Convention relating to extradition.
Signed at Washington December 10, 1962.
*Entered into force December 5, 1963.**
14 UST 1707; TIAS 5476; 484 UNTS 283

Counterterrorism cooperation accord.
Signed at Washington April 30, 1996.
Entered into force July 29, 1996.
TIAS 12747; 1966 UNTS 3

Agreement regarding mutual assistance in customs matters.
Signed at Washington May 16, 1996.
Entered into force September 24, 1997.
TIAS 12755; 2017 UNTS 213

Treaty on mutual legal assistance in criminal matters, with related exchange of notes.
Signed at Jerusalem January 26, 1998.
Entered into force May 25, 1999.
TIAS 12925; 2094 UNTS 17

Protocol amending the convention of December 10, 1962 on extradition.
Signed at Jerusalem July 6, 2005.
Entered into force January 10, 2007.
TIAS 07-110
Note:
* For understanding regarding certain errors in the translation of the Hebrew text, see exchange of notes of April 4 and 11, 1967 (18 UST 382; TIAS 6246).

OCCUPATION & PEACEKEEPING

Memorandum of agreement concerning assurances, consultations, and United States policy on matters related to Middle East peace.
Initialed at Jerusalem September 1, 1975; signed at Washington and Jerusalem February 27, 1976.
*Entered into force February 27, 1976.**
32 UST 2150; TIAS 9828

Memorandum of agreement concerning the United States role at any future Geneva peace conference.
Initialed at Jerusalem September 1, 1975; signed at Washington and Jerusalem February 27, 1976.
*Entered into force February 27, 1976.**
32 UST 2160; TIAS 9829

Agreement relating to implementation of the Egyptian-Israeli peace treaty of March 26, 1979.†
Letter signed at Washington March 26, 1979.
Entered into force March 26, 1979.
32 UST 2146; TIAS 9826

Memorandum of agreement relating to assurances concerning Middle East peace.
Signed at Washington March 26, 1979.
Entered into force March 26, 1979.
32 UST 2141; TIAS 9825; 1252 UNTS 77

Agreement relating to privileges and immunities for United States military members and civilian observers of the Multinational Force and Observers on leave in Israel.
Exchange of notes at Jerusalem and Tel Aviv September 28 and October 1, 1982.
Entered into force October 1, 1982.
TIAS 10558; 1871 UNTS 323

Memorandum of agreement concerning ballistic missile threats.
Signed at Jerusalem and Washington October 31 and November 12, 1998.
Entered into force November 12, 1998.
TIAS 12997

Notes:
* Some provisions are no longer in force.
† See also MULTINATIONAL FORCE AND OBSERVERS in bilateral section and PEACEKEEPING in multilateral section.

POSTAL MATTERS

International express mail agreement, with detailed regulations.
Signed at Washington and Jerusalem September 8 and October 24, 1982.
Entered into force January 24, 1983.
TIAS 10548; 1777 UNTS 397

Memorandum of understanding concerning the operation of the INTELPOST service, with details of implementation.
Signed at Jerusalem and Washington July 20 and November 5, 1987.
Entered into force November 5, 1987; effective September 1, 1987.
TIAS 11568

PROPERTY

Land lease and purchase agreement for construction of diplomatic facilities, with annexes.
Signed at Jerusalem January 18, 1989.
Entered into force January 18, 1989.
TIAS

Amendments:
March 21 and April 10, 1989
July 14 and 23, 1989
January 22 and 30, 1990
January 21 and March 8, 1992 (TIAS 11858)
February 9 and December 13, 2000
December 3, 2001, and January 15, 2002
January 2 and 14, 2003

PUBLICATIONS

Agreement relating to the exchange of official publications.
Exchange of notes at Tel Aviv February 13 and 19, 1950.
Entered into force February 19, 1950.
1 UST 912; TIAS 2169; 122 UNTS 117

SCIENTIFIC & TECHNICAL COOPERATION

Agreement relating to a cooperative meteorological program in support of the rawinsonde observation station at Bet Dagan.
Exchange of notes at Tel Aviv and Jerusalem April 29 and May 22, 1968.
Entered into force May 22, 1968; effective January 1, 1968.
19 UST 5180; TIAS 6510; 653 UNTS 143

Agreement on the United States-Israel binational science foundation with exchange of letters.
Signed at New York September 27, 1972.
Entered into force September 27, 1972.
23 UST 2669; TIAS 7460

Memorandum of understanding concerning the installation, operation and maintenance of a seismic station.
Signed at Tel Aviv May 1, 1985.
Entered into force May 1, 1985.
TIAS 11176; 2130 UNTS 3

Agreement on cooperation in science and technology for homeland security matters, with annex.
Signed at Jerusalem May 29, 2008.
Entered into force November 30, 2010.
TIAS 10-1130

SPACE

Agreement for cooperation in aeronautics and the exploration and use of airspace and outer space for peaceful purposes.
Signed at Jerusalem October 13, 2015.
Entered into force October 13, 2015.
TIAS 15-1013

TAXATION

Convention with respect to taxes on income.
Signed at Washington November 20, 1975.
Entered into force December 30, 1994.
TIAS

Protocol amending the convention with respect to taxes on income of November 20, 1975, with exchanges of notes.
Signed at Washington May 30, 1980.
Entered into force December 30, 1994.
TIAS

Second protocol amending the convention with respect to taxes on income of November 20, 1975, as amended, with exchange of notes.
Signed at Jerusalem January 26, 1993.
Entered into force December 30, 1994.
TIAS

Agreement to improve international tax compliance and to implement the Foreign Account Tax Compliance Act, with related exchange of notes.
Signed at Jerusalem June 30, 2014.
Entered into force August 29, 2016.
TIAS 16-829

TELECOMMUNICATION

Agreement relating to radio communication facilities at or near Embassy sites for transmission of official messages.
Exchange of notes at Tel Aviv and Jerusalem May 10 and 21, 1963.
Entered into force May 21, 1963.
14 UST 866; TIAS 5367; 487 UNTS 319

Agreement relating to radio communications between amateur stations on behalf of third parties.
Exchange of notes at Washington July 7, 1965.
Entered into force August 6, 1965.
16 UST 883; TIAS 5827; 549 UNTS 281

Agreement relating to the reciprocal granting of authorizations to permit licensed amateur radio operators of either country to operate their stations in the other country.
Exchange of notes at Washington June 15, 1966.
Entered into force June 15, 1966.
17 UST 760; TIAS 6028; 578 UNTS 159

TRADE & INVESTMENT

Treaty of friendship, commerce, and navigation, with protocol and exchange of notes.
Signed at Washington August 23, 1951.
Entered into force April 3, 1954.
5 UST 550; TIAS 2948; 219 UNTS 237

Agreement on the establishment of a free trade area, with annexes, exchange of letters and related letter.
Signed at Washington April 22, 1985.
Entered into force August 19, 1985.
TIAS

Agreement regarding the application of their competition laws.
Signed at Washington March 15, 1999.
Entered into force November 7, 2000.
TIAS 13025

Agreement concerning certain aspects of trade in agricultural products, with attachment and annexes.
Exchange of letters at Washington and Jerusalem July 27, 2004.
Entered into force September 10, 2004; effective January 1, 2004.
TIAS 04-910

Amendment and Extensions:
December 10, 2008 (TIAS 04-910)
December 6, 2009 (TIAS 04-910)
November 19, 2012 (TIAS 04-910)

TRANSPORTATION

Agreement relating to the reciprocal acceptance of certificates of airworthiness for imported aircraft.
Exchange of notes at Washington July 23, 1968.
Entered into force July 23, 1968.
19 UST 5459; TIAS 6530; 653 UNTS 159

Amendment:
September 4, 1974 (25 UST 2445; TIAS 7926)

Memorandum of agreement relating to technical assistance in developing and improving air traffic operation in the Ben Gurion Airport.
Signed at Washington January 27, 1983.
Entered into force January 27, 1983.
35 UST 3061; TIAS 10838; 1590 UNTS 73

Memorandum of cooperation concerning technical cooperation in civil aviation security with annex.
Signed at Washington and Tel Aviv July 6 and September 30, 1990.
Entered into force September 30, 1990.
TIAS 11970; 2244 UNTS 283

Memorandum of cooperation concerning civil aviation.
Signed November 14 and December 27, 1990.
Entered into force December 27, 1990.
TIAS

Agreement for promotion of aviation safety.
Signed December 19, 2000.
Entered into force December 19, 2000.
TIAS

Memorandum of cooperation relating to developing and modernizing the civil aviation security infrastructure in Israel.
Signed at Washington November 24, 2010.
Entered into force November 24, 2010.
NP

Air transport agreement.
Signed at Jerusalem December 1, 2010.
Entered into force March 29, 2011.
TIAS 11-329

ITALY

ATOMIC ENERGY

Agreement for cooperation in civilian nuclear energy research and development.
Signed at Washington September 29, 2009.
Entered into force September 29, 2009.
TIAS 09-929

Arrangement for the exchange of technical information and cooperation in nuclear safety matters, with addenda and annex.
Signed at Vienna September 17, 2015.
Entered into force September 17, 2015.
TIAS 15-917.2

CLAIMS & DISPUTE RESOLUTION

Treaty for the advancement of peace.
Signed at Washington May 5, 1914.
Entered into force March 19, 1915.
39 Stat. 1618; TS 615; 9 Bevans 126

Treaty of arbitration.
Signed at Washington April 19, 1928.
Entered into force January 20, 1931.
46 Stat. 2890; TS 831; 9 Bevans 153; 113 LNTS 183

Treaty modifying the terms of article II of the treaty for the advancement of peace.
Signed at Washington September 23, 1931.
Entered into force July 30, 1932.
47 Stat. 2102; TS 848; 9 Bevans 164; 134 LNTS 191

Memorandum of understanding regarding settlement of certain wartime claims and related matters; memorandum of understanding regarding Italian assets in the United States and certain claims of United States nationals, and supplementary exchanges of notes.
Signed at Washington August 14, 1947.
*Entered into force August 14, 1947.**
61 Stat. 3962; TIAS 1757; 9 Bevans 215; 36 UNTS 53

Note:

* For agreed interpretation of the agreement signed August 14, 1947, see exchange of notes verbales of February 24, 1949 (63 Stat. 2415; TIAS 1919; 9 Bevans 342; 80 UNTS 319).

Agreement relating to procedure for final settlement of claims of Italian prisoners of war.
Exchange of letters at Rome February 14, 1948.
Entered into force February 14, 1948.
62 Stat. 3853; TIAS 1948; 9 Bevans 299; 67 UNTS 115

Amendment:

January 14, 1949 (63 Stat. 2602; TIAS 1950; 9 Bevans 338; 67 UNTS 115)

Agreement relating to the disposal of currencies, securities and articles of value taken in Italy from the German forces.
Exchange of notes at Rome May 16, 1951.
Entered into force May 16, 1951.
3 UST 2950; TIAS 2476; 206 UNTS 325

Memorandum of understanding regarding war damage claims.
Signed at Rome March 29, 1957.
Entered into force October 22, 1957.
8 UST 1725; TIAS 3924; 299 UNTS 157

Agreement supplementing the memorandum of understanding of March 29, 1957, regarding war damage claims.
Exchange of notes at Rome July 12, 1960.
Entered into force June 15, 1961.
12 UST 904; TIAS 4796; 411 UNTS 312

CONSULAR AFFAIRS

Agreement relating to the waiver of passport visa fees for nonimmigrants.*
Exchange of notes at Rome February 11, 21, and 26, 1929.
Operative March 1, 1929.
9 Bevans 158

Arrangement relating to the waiver of passport visas and passport visa fees.*
Exchange of notes verbales dated at Rome September 28 and 29, 1948.
Entered into force September 29, 1948; operative November 1, 1948.
62 Stat. 3480; TIAS 1867; 9 Bevans 323; 84 UNTS 43

Note:

* The status of this agreement is under review.

CULTURAL EXCHANGES, PROPERTY & COOPERATION

Agreement relating to interment of American military personnel in Italy.
Exchange of notes verbales at Rome September 13 and 24, 1946.
Entered into force September 24, 1946.
61 Stat. 3750; TIAS 1713; 9 Bevans 194; 148 UNTS 323.

Amendments:

December 18, 1947 and January 21(62 Stat. 1889; TIAS 1743; 9 Bevans 258; 148 UNTS 332)
March 24, and April 19, 1948 (62 Stat. 1889; TIAS 1743; 9 Bevans 304; 148 UNTS 332)

Memorandum of understanding concerning the imposition of import restrictions on categories of archaeological material representing the pre-Classical, Classical and Imperial Roman periods of Italy.
Signed at Washington January 19, 2001.
Entered into force January 19, 2001.
TIAS 13141

Amendments and Extensions:

January 13, 2006 (TIAS 13141)
January 11, 2011 (TIAS 11-119)
January 12, 2016 (TIAS 16-112)

Agreement concerning the protection and preservation of places of commemoration.
Signed at Rome December 18, 2008.
Entered into force August 21, 2009.
TIAS 09-821

DEFENSE

Mutual defense assistance agreement.
Exchange of notes at Washington January 27, 1950.
Entered into force January 27, 1950.
1 UST 50; TIAS 2013; 80 UNTS 145

Agreement relating to the disposition of equipment and material furnished Italy and no longer required in the furtherance of its mutual defense assistance program.
Exchange of notes at Rome November 20 and December 14, 1951.
Entered into force December 14, 1951.
5 UST 2829; TIAS 3136; 238 UNTS 310
Amendment:
September 7, 1960 (11 UST 2129; TIAS 4573; 389 UNTS 307)

Agreement relating to the assurances required by the Mutual Security Act of 1951.
Exchange of notes at Rome January 7, 1952.
Entered into force January 7, 1952.
3 UST 4613; TIAS 2611; 179 UNTS 165

Agreement relating to offshore procurement program with memorandum of understanding and model contract attached.
Exchange of notes at Rome March 31, 1954.
Entered into force March 31, 1954.
5 UST 2185; TIAS 3083; 235 UNTS 293

Agreement concerning facilities for overhaul and repair of jet engines in Torino, Italy.
Signed at Rome July 8, 1955.
Entered into force July 8, 1955.
6 UST 3797; TIAS 3381; 270 UNTS 29

Agreement relating to a weapons production program.
Exchange of notes at Rome July 7, 1960.
Entered into force July 7, 1960.
11 UST 1912; TIAS 4538; 380 UNTS 143

Agreement for cooperation on uses of atomic energy for mutual defense purposes.
Signed at Rome December 3, 1960.
Entered into force May 24, 1961.
12 UST 641; TIAS 4764; 410 UNTS 3

Agreement relating to the safeguarding of classified information with annex.
Exchange of notes at Washington August 4, 1964.
Entered into force August 4, 1964.
15 UST 1494; TIAS 5629; 529 UNTS 205
Amendment:
April 15 and September 2, 1982 (TIAS 10632; 1935 UNTS 420)

Memorandum of understanding concerning the principles governing mutual cooperation in the research, development, production and procurement of defense equipment.
Signed at Washington September 11, 1978.
Entered into force September 11, 1978.
TIAS
Amendments and Extensions:
February 10 and April 8, 1988
May 30 and June 27, 1989
November 19, 1990

Mutual logistical support agreement, with annexes.
Signed at Stuttgart February 23, 1983.
Entered into force February 23, 1983.
TIAS 11165; 2126 UNTS 201

Memorandum of understanding on the exchange of officers between the United States Air Force and the Italian Air Force.
Signed at Rome and Washington May 30 and August 12, 1988.
Entered into force August 12, 1988.
NP

Technical arrangement concerning the installation and maintenance of a U.S. interface with the Italian MRCS 403 radar at Capo Frasca, Sardinia.
Signed at Rome and Ramstein Air Base August 1 and 23, 1988.
Entered into force August 23, 1988.
TIAS 12343

Memorandum of agreement on the exchange of officers between the United States Marine Corps and the Italian Navy.
Signed at Rome and Washington June 7 and July 26, 1993.
Entered into force July 26, 1993.
NP

Memorandum of understanding concerning use of installations/infrastructure by U.S. forces in Italy, with annexes.
Signed at Rome February 2, 1995.
Entered into force February 2, 1995.
TIAS 12317

Acquisition and cross-servicing agreement, with annexes.
Signed at Rome and Stuttgart April 4 and 15, 2001.
Entered into force April 15, 2001.
NP

Agreement regarding the cooperative framework for system development and demonstration of the joint strike fighter, with annexes.
Signed at Washington June 24, 2002.
Entered into force July 17, 2002.
TIAS 02-717.1

Basic exchange and cooperative agreement concerning global geospatial information and services cooperation, with annexes.
Signed at Rome October 28, 2002.
Entered into force October 28, 2002.
NP

Agreement concerning loan of U.S. Government equipment and the provision of logistic support services for use in South Eastern European Brigade (SEEBRIG).
Exchange of notes at Rome October 11, and December 18, 2002.
Entered into force December 18, 2002.
TIAS 02-1218

Technical arrangement regarding the installations/infrastructure in use by the U.S. forces in Sigonella, Italy, with annexes.
Signed at Rome April 6, 2006.
Entered into force April 6, 2006.
TIAS

Agreement regarding the participation of Italy and other member nations of the South Eastern European Brigade in peacekeeping operations and the furnishing of articles and services from the United States of America to the Government of Italy pursuant to the Global Peace Operations Initiative.
Exchange of notes at Rome April 6 and 12, 2006.
Entered into force April 12, 2006.
TIAS 06-412

Agreement concerning the exchange and reimbursement of aviation and ground fuels, with annexes and attachment.
Signed at Ft. Belvoir and Rome June 2 and July 10, 2006.
Entered into force July 10, 2006.
TIAS 06-710
Amendment:
October 2 and 9, 2014 (TIAS 14-1009)

Memorandum of understanding regarding exchange of engineers and scientists, with annexes.
Signed July 21 and August 1, 2006.
Entered into force August 1, 2006.
NP

Memorandum of agreement for research, development, test and evaluation projects, with annex and appendix.
Signed at Washington and Rome September 15 and 26, 2006.
Entered into force September 26, 2006.
TIAS 06-926

Memorandum of understanding concerning the mutual exchange of military satellite communications services and support, with annex.
Signed at Offutt AFB and Rome July 20 and November 6, 2006.
Entered into force November 6, 2006.
TIAS 06-1106
Extension:
September 27 and November 2, 2011 (TIAS 06-1106)

Memorandum of understanding regarding the assignment of a liaison officer, with annexes.
Signed March 19, 2007.
Entered into force March 19, 2007.
NP
Amendment:
March 13 and 14, 2012

Memorandum of agreement regarding the reciprocal exchange of military personnel (MPEP), with annexes.
Signed at Fort Myer April 19, 2007.
Entered into force April 19, 2007.
NP

Technical arrangement regarding the installations/infrastructure in use by U.S. forces in San Vito Dei Normanni, Italy, with annexes.
Signed at La Maddalena September 12, 2007.
Entered into force September 12, 2007.
TIAS

Technical arrangement regarding the installations/infrastructure in use by the U.S. forces in Vicenza, Italy, with annexes and attachments.
Signed at Pisa April 16, 2008.
Entered into force April 16, 2008.
TIAS

Memorandum of understanding concerning reciprocal defense procurement, with annex.
Signed at Washington October 20, 2008.
Entered into force May 3, 2009
TIAS 09-503

Agreement regarding the exchange of military personnel, with annexes.
Signed at Washington and Rome January 17 and June 11, 2009.
Entered into force June 11, 2009.
NP

Agreement concerning cooperative production, sustainment, and follow-on development of the AGM-88E Advanced Anti-Radiation Guided Missile (AARGM), with annexes.
Signed at Washington and Rome November 19 and 23, 2009.
Entered into force November 23, 2009.
TIAS

Memorandum of understanding regarding the assignment of a coordination officer to Commander, Submarine Force Atlantic, with annex.
Signed at Norfolk and Rome February 16 and March 8, 2012.
Entered into force March 8, 2012.
NP

Memorandum of agreement regarding the assignment of Italian Navy personnel to the U. S. Navy, with annexes.
Signed at Rome and Washington October 12 and November 2, 2015.
Entered into force November 2, 2015.
NP

Memorandum of agreement regarding the assignment of liaison officers, with annexes.
Signed at Rome and Washington October 12 and November 2, 2015.
Entered into force November 2, 2015.
NP

DIPLOMATIC & CONSULAR RELATIONS

Consular convention.*
Signed at Washington May 8, 1878.
Entered into force September 18, 1878.
20 Stat. 725; TS 178; 9 Bevans 91
Note
* Article XI replaced by convention of February 24, 1881 (22 Stat. 831; TS 179); articles XI and XIII abrogated by the United States, effective July 1, 1916, in accordance with the Seamen's Act (38 Stat. 1164).

EDUCATION

Agreement for exchanges in the fields of education and culture.
Signed at Rome December 15, 1975.
Entered into force July 28, 1980.
32 UST 1981; TIAS 9813; 1228 UNTS 145

Memorandum of understanding relating to exchanges and cooperation in the field of education, with annex.
Signed at Rome May 4, 1978.
Entered into force May 4, 1978.
30 UST 116; TIAS 9182; 1150 UNTS 67

EMPLOYMENT

Agreement relating to the employment of dependents of diplomatic agents, consular personnel and administrative and technical staff.
Exchange of notes at Rome June 9, 1997.
Entered into force April 30, 1999.
TIAS 12863

ENVIRONMENT & CONSERVATION

Memorandum of understanding concerning cooperation in the field of environmental protection.
Signed at Rome March 3, 1987.
Entered into force March 3, 1987.
TIAS 11283

FINANCE

Agreement relating to the funding of the indebtedness of Italy to the United States.
Signed at Washington November 14, 1925.
Operative June 15, 1925.
Treasury Department print; 9 Bevans 145

Agreement modifying the agreement of November 14, 1925.
Signed at Washington June 3, 1932.
Operative July 1, 1931.
Treasury Department print; 9 Bevans 176

Agreement relating to guaranties authorized by Section 111(b)(3) of the Economic Cooperation Act of 1948, as amended.
Exchange of notes at Rome December 28, 1951.
Entered into force December 28, 1951.
3 UST 2877; TIAS 2463; 157 UNTS 63
Amendment:
October 18, 1957 (8 UST 1881; TIAS 3934; 291 UNTS 309)

Agreement relating to the establishment of a revolving industrial loan fund for Southern Italy.
Exchange of notes at Rome June 16, 1954.
Entered into force June 16, 1954.
5 UST 2116; TIAS 3073; 236 UNTS 149

FISHERIES

Agreement concerning large-scale driftnet fishing on the high seas.
Exchange of notes at Washington July 22 and 26, 1996.
Entered into force July 26, 1996.
TIAS 12787

FOREIGN ASSISTANCE

Economic cooperation agreement.
Signed at Rome June 28, 1948.
Entered into force June 28, 1948.
62 Stat. 2421; TIAS 1789; 9 Bevans 306; 20 UNTS 43
Amendments:
September 28 and October 2, 1948 (62 Stat. 3815; TIAS 1917; 9 Bevans 326; 55 UNTS 318)
February 7, 1950 (1 UST 160; TIAS 2028; 79 UNTS 274)
May 21, 1951 (2 UST 1169; TIAS 2263; 141 UNTS 362)
January 13, 1953 (4 UST 116; TIAS 2769; 200 UNTS 264)

Agreement providing for duty-free entry of relief supplies and packages and for the payment of transportation charges.
Exchange of notes at Rome November 26, 1948.
Entered into force November 26, 1948.
62 Stat. 3809; TIAS 1914; 9 Bevans 328; 79 UNTS 71
Amendments:
November 26, 1948 (62 Stat. 3809; TIAS 1914; 9 Bevans 331; 79 UNTS 71)
July 19, 1952 (3 UST 5078; TIAS 2694; 181 UNTS 353)

Agreement relating to the use of counterpart funds derived from United States economic aid to Trieste.
Exchange of notes at Rome February 11, 1955.
Entered into force February 11, 1955.
6 UST 593; TIAS 3195; 241 UNTS 91

Agreement relating to the provision of assistance to earthquake victims of Italy.
Exchange of notes at Rome June 9, 1976.
Entered into force June 9, 1976.
27 UST 3988; TIAS 8416; 1059 UNTS 73

HEALTH & MEDICAL COOPERATION

Memorandum of understanding for cooperation in the field of health and medicine, with annex.
Signed at Rome November 21, 1977.
Entered into force November 21, 1977.
29 UST 5897; TIAS 9159

INTELLECTUAL PROPERTY

Declaration for the reciprocal protection of marks of manufacture and trade.
Signed at Washington June 1, 1882.
Entered into force June 1, 1882.
23 Stat. 726; TS 180; 9 Bevans 101

Reciprocal copyright arrangement.
Exchange of notes at Washington October 28, 1892.
Entered into force October 28, 1892.
9 Bevans 104

Reciprocal copyright arrangement.
Exchanges of notes at Manchester, Massachusetts, September 2, 1914; and at Washington February 12 and March 4 and 11, 1915.
Entered into force March 11, 1915; operative May 1, 1915.
9 Bevans 129

Agreement on arrangements respecting patents and technical information in defense programs.
Signed at Rome October 3, 1952.
Entered into force provisionally October 3, 1952; definitively December 16, 1960.
12 UST 189; TIAS 4693

Agreement approving the procedures for reciprocal filing of classified patent applications in the United States and Italy.
Exchange of notes at Rome March 9 and October 27, 1959.
Entered into force provisionally October 27, 1959; definitively December 16, 1960.
12 UST 189; TIAS 4693
Amendment:
April 29 and August 2, 1960 (12 UST 208; TIAS 4693)

LAW ENFORCEMENT

Arrangement for the direct exchange of certain information regarding the traffic in narcotic drugs.
Exchange of notes at Rome January 5 and April 27, 1928.
Entered into force April 27, 1928.
9 Bevans 156

Procedures for mutual assistance in the administration of justice in connection with the Lockheed Aircraft Corporation matter.
Signed at Washington March 29, 1976.
Entered into force April 12, 1976.
27 UST 3437; TIAS 8374

Treaty on mutual assistance in criminal matters, with memorandum of understanding.
Signed at Rome November 9, 1982.
*Entered into force November 13, 1985.**
TIAS
Note:
* Except for the application of Article 18, paragraph 2.

Extradition treaty.
Signed at Rome October 13, 1983.
Entered into force September 24, 1984.
35 UST 3023; TIAS 10837; 1590 UNTS 161

Instrument as contemplated by Article 3(2) of the agreement on mutual legal assistance between the United States of America and the European Union, as to the application of the treaty on mutual assistance in criminal matters of November 9, 1982, with annex.
Signed at Rome May 3, 2006.
Entered into force February 1, 2010.
TIAS 10-201.36

Instrument as contemplated by Article 3(2) of the agreement on extradition between the United States of America and the European Union signed June 25, 2003, as to the application of the extradition treaty of October 13, 1983, with annex.
Signed at Rome May 3, 2006.
Entered into force February 1, 2010.
TIAS 10-201.13

Agreement on enhancing cooperation in preventing and combating serious crime.
Signed at Rome May 28, 2009.
Entered into force, with the exception of Articles 7 and 9, on October 3, 2014.
TIAS 14-1003.1

MARITIME MATTERS

Agreement relating to jurisdiction over vessels utilizing the Louisiana Offshore Oil Port.
Exchange of notes at Washington January 12 and 19, 1982.
Entered into force January 19, 1982.
TIAS 10598; 1871 UNTS 195

Memorandum of understanding concerning the installation and management of U.S. navigational aids.
Signed at Rome and Ramstein October 8 and 11, 1985.
Entered into force October 11, 1985.
TIAS 11191; 2129 UNTS 431

Agreement relating to the agreement of August 14, 1987, on the resolution of practical problems with respect to deep seabed mining areas.*
Exchange of notes at Rome August 14, 1987.
Entered into force August 14, 1987.
TIAS 11438
Note:
* Parties to the multilateral agreement of August 14, 1987, are Belgium, Canada, Italy, Netherlands and Union of Soviet Socialist Republics.

PEACE

Agreement concerning the designation of a permanent third member of the United States-Italian Conciliation Commission established pursuant to article 83 of the treaty of peace with Italy (TIAS 1648; 4 Bevans 311; 49 and 50 UNTS).
Exchange of notes at Rome February 12 and 13, 1951.
Entered into force February 13, 1951.
2 UST 807; TIAS 2232; 148 UNTS 57

Agreement regarding the release of Italy from certain of its obligations to the United States under the treaty of peace with Italy (TIAS 1648; 4 Bevans 311; 49 and 50 UNTS).
Exchange of notes at Washington December 8 and 21, 1951.
Entered into force December 21, 1951.
3 UST 2869; TIAS 2461; 167 UNTS 163

POSTAL MATTERS

Parcel post convention.
Signed at Washington October 11, 1929.
Entered into force December 1, 1929.
46 Stat. 2397; Post Office Department print

International express mail agreement with detailed regulations.
Signed at Rome and Washington November 21 and December 9, 1983.
Entered into force February 18, 1984.
35 UST 3167; TIAS 10848; 2014 UNTS 603

PRIVATE INTERNATIONAL LAW

Agreement relating to documentary requirements for marriage of American citizens in Italy.
Exchange of notes at Rome July 29 and August 18, 1964.
Entered into force March 26, 1966.
18 UST 342; TIAS 6239; 688 UNTS 37

SCIENTIFIC & TECHNICAL COOPERATION

Memorandum of understanding concerning the furnishing of balloon launching and associated services.
Signed at Washington and Rome September 2 and 30, 1983.
Entered into force September 30, 1983.
35 UST 2335; TIAS 10794; 2011 UNTS 179

Agreement for scientific and technological cooperation.
Signed at Rome April 1, 1988.
Entered into force April 1, 1988.
TIAS 11574; 2185 UNTS 305
Amendment and Extension:
October 4, 1993 (TIAS 12165)

Memorandum of understanding for scientific and technical cooperation in the earth sciences.
Signed at Rome April 14, 2000.
Entered into force April 14, 2000.
TIAS 00-414

Memorandum of understanding concerning scientific and technical cooperation in the earth sciences.
Signed at Reston and Rome February 7 and July 11, 2002.
Entered into force July 11, 2002.
TIAS 02-711

Agreement in the field of energy research and development.
Signed at Rome November 13, 2007.
Entered into force November 13, 2007.
TIAS 07-1113

Arrangement for cooperation in high energy, astroparticle, and nuclear physics research and related fields and technologies.
Signed at Washington July 17, 2015.
Entered into force July 17, 2015.
TIAS 15-717

SOCIAL SECURITY

Agreement on social security, with administrative protocol.
Signed at Washington May 23, 1973.
Entered into force November 1, 1978.
29 UST 4263; TIAS 9058; 1228 UNTS 81

Supplemental agreement to the agreement of May 23, 1973 on the matter of social security.
Signed at Rome April 17, 1984.
Entered into force January 1, 1986.
TIAS 11173

SPACE

Agreement confirming a memorandum of understanding concerning the furnishing of certain services by NASA for Italian satellites.
Exchange of notes at Rome June 15 and 20, 1970.
Entered into force June 20, 1970.
21 UST 1465; TIAS 6903; 753 UNTS 259

Agreement for the design, development, operation and utilization of three mini pressurized logistics modules for the International Space Station, with memorandum of understanding.
Exchange of notes at Rome April 18, 2001, and January 11, 2005.
Entered into force January 11, 2005.
TIAS 05-111

Agreement concerning the Dawn Mission, with memorandum of understanding.
Exchange of notes at Rome July 2 and 6, 2007.
Entered into force July 6, 2007.
TIAS 07-706

Agreement concerning the Juno Mission, with memorandum of understanding.
Exchange of notes at Washington June 29 and August 3, 2011.
Entered into force August 3, 2011.
TIAS 11-803

Agreement for cooperation on the European Space Agency-led Bepi Colombo Mission, with memorandum of understanding.
Effected by exchange of notes at Washington August 20 and September 27, 2013.
Entered into force September 27, 2013.
TIAS 13-927

Framework agreement for cooperation in the exploration and use of outer space for peaceful purposes.
Signed at Washington March 19, 2013.
Entered into force February 11, 2016.
TIAS 16-211

TAXATION

Agreement relating to relief from taxation of United States expenditures in Italy for the common defense.
Exchange of notes at Rome March 5, 1952.
Entered into force March 5, 1952.
3 UST 4234; TIAS 2566; 179 UNTS 3

Convention for the avoidance of double taxation and the prevention of fiscal evasion with respect to taxes on estates and inheritances.
Signed at Washington March 30, 1955.
Entered into force October 26, 1956.
7 UST 2977; TIAS 3678; 257 UNTS 199

Agreement concerning taxation of income of some U.S. Navy employees in Italy.
Exchange of notes at Rome July 24, 1982.
Entered into force September 28, 1984; effective January 1, 1982.
TIAS 11499

Convention for the avoidance of double taxation with respect to taxes on income and the prevention of fraud or fiscal evasion, with protocol and related exchange of notes.
Signed at Washington August 25, 1999.
Entered into force December 16, 2009.
TIAS

Agreement to improve international tax compliance and to implement the Foreign Account Tax Compliance Act, with annexes.
Signed at Rome January 10, 2014.
Entered into force August 17, 2015.
TIAS 15-817

TELECOMMUNICATION

Agreement relating to the reciprocal granting of authorizations to permit licensed amateur radio operators of either country to operate their stations in the other country.
Exchange of notes at Rome July 28 and August 28, 1981.
Entered into force August 28, 1981.
33 UST 4393; TIAS 10308; 1549 UNTS 309

TRADE & INVESTMENT

Agreement relating to the resumption of normal commercial relations.
Exchange of notes at Washington December 6, 1945.
Entered into force December 6, 1945.
59 Stat. 1731; EAS 492; 9 Bevans 190; 3 UNTS 131

Treaty of friendship, commerce, and navigation, protocol, additional protocol, and exchange of notes.
Signed at Rome February 2, 1948.
Entered into force July 26, 1949.
63 Stat. 2255; TIAS 1965; 9 Bevans 261; 79 UNTS 171

Agreement supplementing the treaty of friendship, commerce and navigation of February 2, 1948.
Signed at Washington September 26, 1951.
Entered into force March 2, 1961.
12 UST 131; TIAS 4685; 404 UNTS 326

TRANSPORTATION

Air navigation arrangement.*
Exchange of notes at Washington October 13 and 14, 1931.
Entered into force October 31, 1931.
47 Stat. 2668; EAS 24; 9 Bevans 167; 137 LNTS 209

Note:
* Article 9 terminated January 26, 1955 (see 6 UST 25; TIAS 3164).

Agreement relating to air service facilities in Italy, with annex.
Exchange of notes at Rome June 9, 1947.
Entered into force June 9, 1947.
62 Stat. 4074; TIAS 2127; 9 Bevans 200; 104 UNTS 157

Air transport agreement with memorandum and exchange of notes.*
Signed at Rome June 22, 1970.
Entered into force provisionally June 22, 1970; definitively August 9, 1973.
21 UST 2096; TIAS 6957; 764 UNTS 161

Amendments:
October 25, 1988 (TIAS 11634; 2204 UNTS 508)
December 30, 1998, and February 2, 1999

Note:
* This agreement is suspended for the duration of provisional application of the U.S. – E.U. Air Transport Agreement signed April 25 and 30, 2007.

Agreement relating to reciprocal acceptance of airworthiness certifications.
Exchange of notes at Rome June 30 and August 3, 1973.
Entered into force August 3, 1973.
25 UST 1565; TIAS 7895

Memorandum of understanding relating to the air transport services agreement of June 22, 1970, as amended, with related exchange of letters.*
Signed at Rome September 27, 1990.
Entered into force September 27, 1990.†
TIAS 11767

Note:
* This agreement is suspended for the duration of provisional application of the U.S. – E.U. Air Transport Agreement signed April 25 and 30, 2007.
† Amendment to Article 10 not yet in force.

Agreement amending and supplementing the air transport services agreement of June 22, 1970, as amended, and amending the memorandum of understanding of September 27, 1990, with memorandum of understanding.*
Exchange of notes at Rome November 22 and December 23, 1991.
Entered into force December 23, 1991.
TIAS 11845

Note:
* This agreement is suspended for the duration of provisional application of the U.S. – E.U. Air Transport Agreement signed April 25 and 30, 2007.

Agreement amending and supplementing the air transport agreement of June 22, 1970, as amended, and amending the memorandum of understanding of September 27, 1990, as amended.*
Exchange of notes at Rome May 30 and October 21, 1997.
Entered into force October 21, 1997.
TIAS

Note:
* This agreement is suspended for the duration of provisional application of the U.S. – E.U. Air Transport Agreement signed April 25 and 30, 2007.

Agreement for promotion of aviation safety.
Signed at Rome October 27, 1999.
Entered into force October 27, 1999.
TIAS 13069

J

JAMAICA

On August 6, 1962, Jamaica attained fully responsible status within the British Commonwealth. By an exchange of notes on August 7, 1962, between the High Commissioner for the United Kingdom in Jamaica and the Prime Minister and Minister of External Affairs and Defense of Jamaica, the Government of Jamaica agreed to assume, from August 6, 1962, all obligations and responsibilities of the United Kingdom which arise from any valid instrument (including any instrument made by the Government of the Federation of The West Indies by virtue of the authority entrusted by the Government of the United Kingdom). The rights and benefits heretofore enjoyed by the Government of the United Kingdom by virtue of application of any such international instrument to Jamaica are from August 6, 1962, enjoyed by the Government of Jamaica.

CULTURAL EXCHANGES, PROPERTY & COOPERATION

Agreement relating to the establishment of a Peace Corps program in Jamaica.
Exchange of notes at Kingston February 15 and 22, 1962.
Entered into force February 22, 1962.
13 UST 166; TIAS 4954; 435 UNTS 127

DEFENSE

Agreement relating to the furnishing of defense articles and services to Jamaica.
Exchange of notes at Kingston June 6, 1963.
Entered into force June 6, 1963.
14 UST 821; TIAS 5361; 477 UNTS 29

Agreement regarding grants under the Foreign Assistance Act of 1961, as amended, or successor legislation, and the furnishing of defense articles, defense services and related training, including pursuant to the United States International Military Education and Training (IMET) Program.
Exchange of notes at Kingston February 5 and July 30, 2007.
Entered into force July 30, 2007.
NP

Agreement regarding the Caribbean Basin Security Initiative and the provision of technical support for maritime security forces.
Exchange of notes at Kingston September 24 and November 6, 2012.
Entered into force November 6, 2012.
TIAS 12-1106

Acquisition and cross-servicing agreement, with annexes.
Signed at Kingston and Miami January 27 and March 6, 2014.
Entered into force March 6, 2014.
NP

DIPLOMATIC & CONSULAR RELATIONS

Consular convention between the United States and the United Kingdom.
Signed at Washington June 6, 1951.
Entered into force September 7, 1952.
3 UST 3426; TIAS 2494; 165 UNTS 121

EMPLOYMENT

Agreement relating to the employment of dependents of official government employees.
Exchange of notes at Kingston May 3 and October 11, 1982.
Entered into force October 11, 1982.
TIAS 10886; 35 UST 3834; 1577 UNTS 417

ENVIRONMENT & CONSERVATION

Agreement concerning the establishment of an Enterprise for the Americas Environmental Foundation.
Signed at Kingston June 29, 2015.
Entered into force June 29, 2015.
TIAS 15-629

FINANCE

Agreement relating to investment guaranties.
Exchange of notes at Kingston December 11, 1962, and January 4, 1963.
Entered into force January 4, 1963.
14 UST 1; TIAS 5270; 471 UNTS 119

Agreement regarding the consolidation and rescheduling of certain debts owed to, guaranteed or insured by the United States Government and its agencies, with annexes.
Signed at Washington November 8, 1984.
Entered into force December 13, 1984.
TIAS 10999; 2022 UNTS 83

Agreement regarding the consolidation and rescheduling of certain debts owed to, guaranteed by or insured by the United States Government and its agencies, with annexes.
Signed at Washington September 26, 1985.
Entered into force November 18, 1985.
NP

Agreement regarding the consolidation and rescheduling of certain debts owed to, guaranteed by, or insured by the United States Government and its agencies, with annexes.
Signed at Kingston November 12, 1987.
Entered into force January 7, 1988.
NP
Amendment:
February 2 and March 15, 1989 (NP)

Agreement regarding the consolidation and rescheduling of certain debts owed to, guaranteed by, or insured by the United States Government and its agencies, with annexes.
Signed at Kingston July 6, 1989.
Entered into force August 24, 1989.
NP
Amendment:
November 27, 1989, and January 18, 1990 (NP)

Agreement regarding the consolidation and rescheduling or refinancing of certain debts owed to, guaranteed by, or insured by the United States Government and its agencies, with annexes.
Signed at Kingston December 20, 1990.
Entered into force February 8, 1991.
NP

Agreement regarding the reduction of certain debts owed to the United States Government and its agencies.
Signed at Washington August 23, 1991.
NP

Agreement regarding the consolidation and rescheduling or refinancing of certain debts owed to, guaranteed by, or insured by the United States Government and its agencies, with annexes.
Signed at Kingston January 14, 1992.
Entered into force March 2, 1992.
NP
Amendment:
August 28 and September 11, 1992 (NP)

Agreement regarding the reduction of certain debts related to foreign assistance owed to the Government of the United States and its agencies, with appendices.
Signed at Washington and Kingston January 13 and 15, 1993.
Entered into force February 14, 1993.
NP

Agreement regarding the consolidation and rescheduling or refinancing of certain debts owed to, guaranteed by or insured by the United States Government and its agencies, with annexes.
Signed at Kingston October 22, 1993.
Entered into force January 3, 1994.
NP

Agreement regarding a debt-for-nature swap to prepay and cancel certain debt owed by the Government of Jamaica to the Government of the United States of America, with attachments.
Signed at Kingston September 21, 2004.
Entered into force September 21, 2004.
TIAS 04-921

FOREIGN ASSISTANCE

General agreement for economic, technical and related assistance.
Signed at Kingston October 24, 1963.
Entered into force October 24, 1963.
14 UST 1550; TIAS 5457; 489 UNTS 337

INTELLECTUAL PROPERTY

Declaration by the United States and the United Kingdom affording reciprocal protection to trade-marks.
Signed at London October 24, 1877.
Entered into force October 24, 1877.
20 Stat. 703; TS 138; 12 Bevans 198

LAW ENFORCEMENT

Procedures for mutual assistance in connection with matters relating to the Jamaica Nutrition Holdings Ltd., its holding company, State Trading Corporation and its associated companies.
Signed at Washington March 30, 1979.
Entered into force March 30, 1979.
30 UST 3868; TIAS 9430; 1170 UNTS 59

Extradition treaty.
Signed at Kingston June 14, 1983.
Entered into force July 7, 1991.
TIAS

Treaty on mutual legal assistance in criminal matters, with attachments.
Signed at Kingston July 7, 1989.
Entered into force July 25, 1995.
TIAS

Agreement regarding the sharing of forfeited assets or the proceeds of disposition of such assets, with exchange of letters.
Signed at Kingston August 22, 2001.
Entered into force August 22, 2001.
TIAS 01-822

Agreement regarding the Cooperating Nation Information Exchange System.
Exchange of notes at Kingston August 26 and September 23, 2005.
Entered into force September 23, 2005.
TIAS 05-923

MARITIME MATTERS

Agreement concerning cooperation in suppressing illicit maritime drug trafficking.
Signed at Kingston May 6, 1997.
Entered into force March 10, 1998.
TIAS 98-310

Protocol to the agreement of May 6, 1997 concerning cooperation in suppressing illicit maritime drug trafficking.
Signed at Kingston February 6, 2004.
Entered into force February 6, 2004.
TIAS 98-310

OCCUPATION & PEACEKEEPING

Agreement for the furnishing of commodities and services in connection with the peacekeeping force for Grenada.
Exchange of notes at Kingston November 29 and December 6, 1983.
Entered into force December 6, 1983.
35 UST 3192; TIAS 10849; 2015 UNTS 15

Agreement concerning the disposition of commodities and services furnished in connection with peacekeeping operations for Grenada.
Exchange of notes at Kingston February 2 and April 21, 1987.
Entered into force April 21, 1987.
TIAS 11270

POSTAL MATTERS

Postal convention.
Signed at Washington July 22 and at Kingston September 3, 1887.
Operative October 1, 1887.
25 Stat. 1393

Money order agreement.
Signed at Washington September 20 and at Kingston October 6, 1922.
Operative November 1, 1922.

International express mail agreement, with detailed regulations.
Signed at Kingston and Washington January 9 and February 11, 1991.
Entered into force March 18, 1991.
TIAS 11812

PROPERTY

Convention between the United States and the United Kingdom relating to the tenure and disposition of real and personal property.
Signed at Washington March 2, 1899.
Applicable to Jamaica February 9, 1901.
31 Stat. 1939; TS 146; 12 Bevans 246

Supplementary convention relating to the tenure and disposition of real and personal property.
Signed at Washington May 27, 1936.
Applicable to Jamaica March 10, 1941.
55 Stat. 1101; TS 964; 5 Bevans 140; 203 LNTS 367

PUBLICATIONS

Agreement for the exchange of official publications.
Exchange of notes at Kingston December 20, 1966.
Entered into force December 20, 1966.
17 UST 2409; TIAS 6187; 681 UNTS 115

SCIENTIFIC & TECHNICAL COOPERATION

Agreement for a cooperative meteorological program in Jamaica, with memorandum of arrangement.
Exchange of notes at Kingston August 27 and 29, 1985.
Entered into force August 29, 1985.
TIAS 11324

TAXATION

Convention for the avoidance of double taxation and the prevention of fiscal evasion with respect to taxes on income, with exchange of notes.*
Signed at Kingston May 21, 1980.
Entered into force December 29, 1981.
33 UST 2865; TIAS 10206
Note:
* With reservation and understanding.

Protocol amending the convention for the avoidance of double taxation and the prevention of fiscal evasion with respect to taxes on income, with exchange of notes.*
Signed at Kingston July 17, 1981.
Entered into force December 29, 1981.
33 UST 2903; TIAS 10207
Note:
* With reservation and understanding.

Agreement concerning administration of income tax affecting Jamaican citizens employed by the U.S. Government.
Exchange of notes at Kingston April 3 and May 1, 1986.
Entered into force May 1, 1986.
TIAS 11362

Agreement for the exchange of information with respect to taxes.
Signed at Washington December 18, 1986.
Entered into force December 18, 1986.
TIAS 11411; 2191 UNTS 79

TELECOMMUNICATION

Agreement relating to the reciprocal granting of authorizations to permit licensed amateur radio operators of either country to operate their stations in the other country.
Exchange of notes at Kingston March 4 and April 28, 1971.
Entered into force April 28, 1971.
22 UST 694; TIAS 7127; 792 UNTS 337

Agreement relating to radio communications between amateur stations on behalf of third parties.
Exchange of notes at Kingston February 24 and May 12, 1977.
Entered into force June 11, 1977.
29 UST 1888; TIAS 8908

TRADE & INVESTMENT

Treaty concerning the reciprocal encouragement and protection of investment, with annex and protocol.
Signed at Washington February 4, 1994.
Entered into force March 7, 1997.
TIAS

TRANSPORTATION

Arrangement between the United States and the United Kingdom relating to pilot licenses to operate civil aircraft.
Exchange of notes at Washington March 28 and April 5, 1935.
Entered into force May 5, 1935.
49 Stat. 3731; EAS 77; 12 Bevans 513; 162 UNTS 59

Agreement concerning conversion and remittance of Jamaica dollar earnings by U.S. airlines.
Exchange of notes at Kingston March 22 and 30, 1984.
Entered into force March 30, 1984.
35 UST 4896; TIAS 10975; 1658 UNTS 309

Air transport agreement, with annexes.
Signed at Kingston October 30, 2008.
Entered into force October 30, 2008.
TIAS 08-1030.1

JAPAN

ATOMIC ENERGY

Agreement for cooperation concerning peaceful uses of nuclear energy, with annexes, agreed minutes, implementing agreement and exchanges of notes.
Signed at Tokyo November 4, 1987.
Entered into force July 17, 1988.
TIAS; 1574 UNTS 287

Agreement regarding cooperation in the field of nuclear energy-related research and development.
Exchange of notes March 9, 2012.
Entered into force March 9, 2012.
TIAS 12-309

Arrangement for the exchange of technical information and cooperation in nuclear safety matters, with annex.
Signed at Tokyo and Vienna September 10 and 14, 2015.
Entered into force September 14, 2015.
TIAS 15-914

CLAIMS & DISPUTE RESOLUTION

Agreement for settlement for the AWA MARU claim.
Signed at Tokyo April 14, 1949.
Entered into force April 14, 1949.
63 Stat. 2397; TIAS 1911; 9 Bevans 467; 89 UNTS 141

Agreement relating to compensation for personal and property damage as a result of nuclear tests in the Marshall (Bikini) Islands.
Exchange of notes at Tokyo January 4, 1955.
Entered into force January 4, 1955.
6 UST 1; TIAS 3160; 237 UNTS 197

Agreement relating to settlement of claims of Japanese nationals formerly resident in certain Japanese Islands arising from measures taken by the United States in connection with the exercise of its rights under article 3 of the peace treaty.
Exchange of notes at Tokyo June 8, 1961.
Entered into force June 8, 1961.
12 UST 830; TIAS 4781; 410 UNTS 183

Agreement concerning the trust territory of the Pacific Islands with exchanges of notes.
Signed at Tokyo April 18, 1969.
Entered into force July 7, 1969.
20 UST 2654; TIAS 6724; 719 UNTS 127

Agreement implementing the agreement of April 18, 1969, concerning the trust territory of the Pacific Islands.
Exchange of notes at Washington March 13, 1973.
Entered into force March 13, 1973.
24 UST 767; TIAS 7581

Agreement relating to the use of interest accrued in connection with payments made under the agreement of April 18, 1969, concerning the trust territory of the Pacific Islands.
Exchange of notes at Tokyo April 18, 1975.
Entered into force April 18, 1975.
26 UST 671; TIAS 8064; 992 UNTS 340

Agreement extending the period for provision of products and services by Japan under the agreement of April 18, 1969, concerning the trust territory of the Pacific Islands.
Exchange of notes at Tokyo April 18, 1975.
Entered into force April 18, 1975.
26 UST 666; TIAS 8063; 992 UNTS 336

CONSULAR AFFAIRS

Agreement relating to the reciprocal waiver of nonimmigrant visa fees.*
Exchange of notes at Tokyo May 21, August 12, August 26, and September 18, 1952.
Entered into force September 18, 1952; operative October 1, 1952.
5 UST 363; TIAS 2930; 227 UNTS 85

Agreement relating to the reciprocal issuance of nonimmigrant visas.*
Exchange of notes at Tokyo August 9 and 23, 1966.
Entered into force September 22, 1966.
17 UST 1228; TIAS 6087

Note:

* The status of these agreements is under review.

CULTURAL EXCHANGES, PROPERTY & COOPERATION

Agreement establishing the Joint Committee on United States-Japan Cultural and Educational Cooperation.
Exchange of notes at Tokyo November 8, 1968.
Entered into force November 8, 1968.
19 UST 7549; TIAS 6597; 702 UNTS 277

Amendment:

February 25, 1977 (28 UST 5326; TIAS 8635)

DEFENSE

Agreement relating to the sending of technical missions by Japan to the United States to study the production of defense equipment and supplies.
Exchange of notes at Washington January 21, 1954.
Entered into force January 21, 1954.
5 UST 317; TIAS 2923; 223 UNTS 145

Agreement for return of equipment under article I of the mutual defense assistance agreement.
Signed at Tokyo March 8, 1954.
Entered into force May 1, 1954.
5 UST 708; TIAS 2958; 232 UNTS 215

Mutual defense assistance agreement, with annexes.*
Signed at Tokyo March 8, 1954.
Entered into force May 1, 1954.
5 UST 661; TIAS 2957; 232 UNTS 169

Note:

* For the revision of references in the agreement consequent to the mutual security treaty (TIAS 4509), see exchange of notes of January 19, 1960 (11 UST 1758; TIAS 4511). See also agreement of July 4, 1969 (TIAS 6715).

Agreement relating to the transfer of military equipment and supplies to Japan.
Exchange of notes at Tokyo November 19, 1954.
Entered into force November 19, 1954.
5 UST 2404; TIAS 3101; 238 UNTS 207

Arrangement relating to the furnishing of military equipment pursuant to article I of the mutual defense assistance agreement.*
Exchange of notes at Tokyo January 7, 1955.
Entered into force January 7, 1955.
6 UST 9; TIAS 3161; 251 UNTS 404
Note:
* For agreement on the clarification of terms, see exchange of notes of November 25, 1957 (8 UST 2413; TIAS 3958; 303 UNTS 348).

Agreement relating to a program of aircraft assembly or manufacture in Japan.
Exchange of notes at Tokyo June 3, 1955.
Entered into force June 3, 1955.
6 UST 3817; TIAS 3383; 270 UNTS 51

Agreement setting forth understandings with respect to the program of aircraft assembly or manufacture in Japan pursuant to the agreement of June 3, 1955.
Exchange of notes at Tokyo April 13, 1956.
Entered into force April 13, 1956.
7 UST 649; TIAS 3547; 273 UNTS 223

Treaty of mutual cooperation and security, with agreed minute and exchanges of notes.
Signed at Washington January 19, 1960.
Entered into force June 23, 1960.
11 UST 1632; TIAS 4509; 373 UNTS 186
Amendment:
December 26, 1990 (TIAS 12335)

Agreement under article VI of the treaty of mutual cooperation and security regarding facilities and areas and the status of United States armed forces in Japan, with agreed minutes and exchange of notes.*
Signed at Washington January 19, 1960.
Entered into force June 23, 1960.
11 UST 1652; TIAS 4510; 373 UNTS 248
Note:
* For the understanding concerning the application of the agreement to small maritime claims, see exchange of notes of August 22, 1960
(11 UST 2160; TIAS 4580; 394 UNTS 310). For special measures under Article XXIV, see agreement of January 30, 1987.

Understanding revising references to the mutual security treaty (TIAS 4509) and the administrative agreement in the mutual defense assistance agreement of March 8, 1954 (TIAS 2957).
Exchange of notes at Washington January 19, 1960.
Entered into force June 23, 1960.
11 UST 1758; TIAS 4511

Agreement relating to a program for the acquisition and production in Japan of the F 4EJ aircraft and related equipment and material.
Exchange of notes at Tokyo April 4, 1969.
Entered into force April 4, 1969.
20 UST 545; TIAS 6664; 707 UNTS 207
Related Agreements:
November 21, 1972 (23 UST 3794; TIAS 7529)
July 12, 1977 (29 UST 1901; TIAS 8910)

Agreement relating to the change in designation of organization of its personnel from Military Assistance Advisory Group to the Mutual Defense Assistance Office pursuant to the mutual defense assistance agreement of March 8, 1954 (TIAS 2957).
Exchange of notes at Tokyo July 4, 1969.
Entered into force July 4, 1969.
20 UST 2525; TIAS 6715; 719 UNTS 294

Agreement relating to the production and acquisition in Japan of the Sparrow missile for ship-to-air application.
Exchange of notes at Tokyo July 12, 1977.
Entered into force October 7, 1977.
29 UST 1513; TIAS 8896

Agreement relating to acquisition and production in Japan of F 15 aircraft and related equipment and materials.
Exchange of notes at Tokyo June 20, 1978.
Entered into force June 20, 1978.
30 UST 1599; TIAS 9267
Related Agreements:
December 28, 1984 (TIAS 11978)
February 14, 1989 (TIAS 12331)
March 31, 1992 (TIAS 12331)

Agreement relating to acquisition and production in Japan of P 3C aircraft and related equipment and materials.
Exchange of notes at Tokyo June 20, 1978.
Entered into force June 20, 1978.
30 UST 1608; TIAS 9268; 1150 UNTS 123
Related Agreements:
September 10, 1985 (TIAS 12017)
March 24, 1989 (TIAS 12017)
March 24, 1995 (TIAS 12341)

Agreement for the transfer of defense-related technologies, with annex.
Exchange of notes at Tokyo November 8, 1983.
Entered into force November 8, 1983.
35 UST 2981; TIAS 10835; 2014 UNTS 563
Amendments:
January 8, 1988 (TIAS 12329)
December 22, 1994 (TIAS 12329)
February 6, 1998

Agreement relating to the acquisition and production in Japan of the Patriot weapon system.
Exchange of notes at Tokyo October 4, 1985.
Entered into force October 4, 1985.
TIAS 11979

Agreement relating to the furnishing of assistance in the field of training for defense services personnel and defense-related civilian personnel.
Exchange of notes at Tokyo January 21, 1986.
Entered into force January 21, 1986.
TIAS 12005

Agreement relating to a program for the development of the XSH-60J weapon system.
Exchange of notes at Tokyo January 20, 1987.
Entered into force January 20, 1987.
TIAS 12014; 2244 UNTS 91

Agreement concerning the acquisition and production of the EP 3 aircraft in Japan.
Exchange of notes at Tokyo March 29, 1988.
Entered into force March 29, 1988.
TIAS

Amendments:
March 31, 1992
March 26, 1993
March 29, 1994
March 31, 1995
March 29, 1996
March 28, 1997
March 27, 1998

Memorandum of understanding concerning joint use of facilities and areas at Kasuga Air Base.
Signed at Kasuga-shi July 19, 1988.
Entered into force July 19, 1988.
TIAS

Agreement concerning the acquisition and production in Japan of the SH 60J and UH 60J aircraft.
Exchange of notes at Tokyo March 31, 1989.
Entered into force March 31, 1989.
TIAS

Amendments:
March 30, 1990
March 29, 1991
March 31, 1992
January 8, 1993
March 22, 1994
March 10, 1995
March 29, 1996
March 28, 1997
March 27, 1998
March 23, 1999

Agreement concerning the acquisition and production in Japan of the HYDRA 70 Rocket System.
Exchange of notes at Tokyo March 31, 1989.
Entered into force March 31, 1989.
TIAS 12332

Agreement concerning the acquisition and production in Japan of the Sparrow Missile System (AIM 7M).
Exchange of notes at Tokyo March 27, 1990.
Entered into force March 27, 1990.
TIAS 12333

Amendment:
March 29, 1991 (TIAS 12333)

Agreement for the assembly and repair in Japan of the AN/ALQ 131 System (Electronic Countermeasures Pod) and related equipment and materials, with exchange of letters.
Exchange of notes at Tokyo March 12, 1993.
Entered into force March 12, 1993.
TIAS 12338

Agreement concerning cooperative research of fighting vehicle propulsion technology using ceramic materials.
Exchange of notes at Tokyo October 31, 1995.
Entered into force October 31, 1995.
TIAS 12701

Agreement concerning cooperative research of advanced steel technology.
Exchange of notes at Tokyo October 31, 1995.
Entered into force October 31, 1995.
TIAS 12344

Agreement relating to the production of the Support Fighter (F 2) Weapon system.
Exchange of notes at Tokyo July 30, 1996.
Entered into force July 30, 1996.
TIAS 12788

Agreement concerning a program for the cooperative research of eyesafe laser radar.
Exchange of notes at Washington September 20, 1996.
Entered into force September 20, 1996.
TIAS 12802

Agreement concerning reciprocal provision of logistic support, supplies and services between the Armed Forces of the United States of America and the Self-Defense Forces of Japan, with annex.
Signed at Tokyo April 15, 1996.
Entered into force October 22, 1996.
TIAS 12742

Amendments:
April 28, 1998
February 27, 2004
January 9, 2007

Agreement concerning a cooperative modification program for the ACES II Ejection Seat.
Exchange of notes at Tokyo March 27, 1998.
Entered into force March 27, 1998.
TIAS

Agreement concerning a program for the cooperative research of Advanced Hybrid Propulsion Technologies.
Exchange of notes at Tokyo May 26, 1998.
Entered into force May 26, 1998.
TIAS

Agreement concerning a program for the cooperative research of Shallow Water Acoustic Technology (SWAT).
Exchange of notes at Tokyo June 18, 1999.
Entered into force June 18, 1999.
TIAS 13047

Agreement concerning a program for the cooperative research on ballistic missile defense technologies.
Exchange of notes at Tokyo August 16, 1999.
Entered into force August 16, 1999.
TIAS 13055

Agreement concerning the acquisition and production in Japan of the UH 60J and UH 60JA aircraft and related equipment and material.
Exchange of notes at Tokyo March 10, 2000.
Entered into force March 10, 2000.
TIAS

Agreement concerning a program for the cooperative research of Low Vulnerability Gun Propellant for Artillery.
Exchange of notes at Tokyo March 24, 2000.
Entered into force March 24, 2000.
TIAS

Agreement concerning the acquisition and production in Japan of the UH 60J and UH 60JA aircraft and related equipment and materials.
Exchange of notes at Tokyo March 23, 2001.
Entered into force March 23, 2001.
TIAS

Agreement concerning the acquisition and production in Japan of the UP-3C aircraft and related equipment and materials.
Exchange of notes at Tokyo March 23, 2001.
Entered into force March 23, 2001.
TIAS

Agreement concerning logistic support, supplies and services contributed by Japan to the armed forces or other similar entities of the United States of America.
Exchange of notes at Tokyo November 16, 2001.
Entered into force November 16, 2001.
TIAS 13173

Agreement concerning the acquisition and production in Japan of the OP 3C Aircraft and related equipment and materials.
Exchange of notes at Tokyo March 26, 2002.
Entered into force March 26, 2002.
TIAS

Agreement concerning the acquisition and production in Japan of the SH 60J/UH 60J/ UH 60JA Aircraft and related equipment and materials and the SH 60JMOD Aircraft.
Exchange of notes at Tokyo March 26, 2002.
Entered into force March 26, 2002.
TIAS

Agreement concerning a program for the cooperative research of Software Radio.
Exchange of notes at Tokyo March 26, 2002.
Entered into force March 26, 2002.
TIAS

Agreement concerning a program for the Cooperative Avionics and Missions Systems Study for Maritime Patrol Aircraft of Japan and Multi-Mission Maritime Aircraft of the United States of America.
Exchange of notes at Tokyo March 26, 2002.
Entered into force March 26, 2002.
TIAS

Agreement concerning the acquisition and production in Japan of the Multiple Launch Rocket Systems and related equipment and materials.
Exchange of notes at Tokyo March 26, 2002.
Entered into force March 26, 2002.
TIAS

Agreement concerning the program for the acquisition and production in Japan of the SH 60J/UH 60J/UH 60JA/SH 60JMOD Aircraft, and related equipment and materials.
Exchange of notes at Tokyo March 18, 2003.
Entered into force March 18, 2003.
TIAS

Agreement concerning the program for the acquisition and production in Japan of the AH 64 Helicopter System and related equipment and materials.
Exchange of notes at Tokyo March 18, 2003.
Entered into force March 18, 2003.
TIAS

Agreement concerning an engineers and scientists exchange program arising from implementation of the mutual defense assistance agreement of March 8, 1954.
Exchange of notes at Tokyo May 9, 2003.
Entered into force May 9, 2003.
NP

Agreement concerning the acquisition and production in Japan of the EP-3, UP 3C, UP 3D and OP 3C aircraft and related equipment and materials.
Exchange of notes at Tokyo March 30, 2004.
Entered into force March 30, 2004.
TIAS

Agreement concerning the Advance Hull Materials & Structures Technology (AHM&ST) cooperative research project.
Exchange of notes at Tokyo April 14, 2005.
Entered into force April 14, 2005.
NP

Memorandum of understanding international defining responsibilities for the Government of Japan's use of the Kadena munitions storage area, with enclosures.
Signed at Okinawa February 8 and 10, 2006.
Entered into force February 10, 2006.
TIAS

Agreement for cooperation on ballistic missile defense.
Exchange of notes at Tokyo June 23, 2006.
Entered into force June 23, 2006.
TIAS

Agreement concerning cooperation in the field of geospatial information.
Exchange of notes at Tokyo December 22, 2006.
Entered into force December 22, 2006.
NP

Agreement concerning security measures for the protection of classified military information.
Signed at Tokyo August 10, 2007.
Entered into force August 10, 2007.
TIAS 07-810

Memorandum of understanding concerning airborne intercept/electronic warfare (A/EW) exercises, with addendums and attachment.
Signed September 20 and 26, 2008
Entered into force September 26, 2008.
TIAS

Agreement concerning the implementation of the relocation of III Marine Expeditionary Force personnel and their dependents from Okinawa to Guam.
Signed at Tokyo February 17, 2009.
Entered into force May 9, 2009.
TIAS 09-519
Amendment:
October 3, 2013 (TIAS 09-519)

Agreement for the cooperative research on Image Gyro for airborne applications.
Exchange of notes at Tokyo February 17, 2010.
Entered into force February 17, 2010.
TIAS 10-217

Memorandum of agreement regarding the exchange of military personnel, with annexes.
Signed at Arlington February 23, 2010.
Entered into force February 23, 2010.
NP

Agreement concerning security measures for the protection of classified military information relating to the Joint Strike Fighter (JSF) F-35 air system and associated ancillary mission equipment.
Exchange of notes at Tokyo January 18, 2011.
Entered into force January 18, 2011.
TIAS 11-118.1

Agreement for the cooperative research on hybrid electric propulsion program.
Exchange of notes at Tokyo November 2, 2012.
Entered into force November 2, 2012.
TIAS 12-1102.1

Memorandum of agreement regarding the assignment of Japan maritime self-defense force personnel to the U.S. Navy, with annexes.
Signed at Washington and Tokyo August 7 and 15, 2013.
Entered into force August 15, 2013.
NP

Agreement regarding the assignment of Japan ground self-defense force personnel to the U.S. Army, with annexes.
Signed at Washington and Tokyo July 18 and August 22, 2013.
Entered into force August 22, 2013.
NP

Agreement for the cooperative research on high-speed multi-hull vessel optimization.
Exchange of notes at Tokyo March 4, 2014.
Entered into force March 4, 2014.
TIAS 14-304

Memorandum of agreement regarding the assignment of liaison officers to Headquarters, PACAF, with annexes.
Signed at Pearl Harbor-Hickam and Tokyo July 3 and 22, 2014.
Entered into force July 22, 2014.
NP

Agreement on cooperation in the field of environmental stewardship relating to the United States Forces in Japan.
Signed at Washington September 28, 2015.
Entered into force September 28, 2015.
TIAS 15-928

Agreement concerning new special measures relating to Article XXIV of the Agreement under Article VI of the Treaty of mutual cooperation and security regarding facilities and areas and the status of United States armed forces in Japan, with agreed minutes.
Signed at Tokyo January 22, 2016.
Entered into force April 1, 2016.
TIAS

Agreement concerning reciprocal defense procurement.
Exchange of notes at Tokyo June 3, 2016.
Entered into force June 3, 2016.
TIAS 16-603

DIPLOMATIC & CONSULAR RELATIONS

Consular convention and protocol.
Signed at Tokyo March 22, 1963.
Entered into force August 1, 1964.
15 UST 768; TIAS 5602; 518 UNTS 179

EDUCATION

Agreement on educational exchange programs.
Signed at Tokyo February 15, 1979.
Entered into force December 24, 1979.
31 UST 381; TIAS 9615; 1202 UNTS 149

Agreement concerning the Mike Mansfield Fellowship Program.
Exchange of notes at Tokyo August 21, 1996.
Entered into force August 21, 1996.
TIAS 12794

ENVIRONMENT & CONSERVATION

Convention for the protection of migratory birds and birds in danger of extinction, and their environment, with annex.
Signed at Tokyo March 4, 1972.
Entered into force September 19, 1974.
25 UST 3329; TIAS 7990
Amendment:
September 19, 1974 (25 UST 3329; TIAS 7990)

Agreement on cooperation in the field of environmental protection, with agreed minutes.
Signed at Washington August 5, 1975.
Entered into force August 5, 1975.
26 UST 2534; TIAS 8172; 1027 UNTS 371
Amendment and Extensions:
August 5, 1980 (32 UST 2468; TIAS 9853; 1274 UNTS 336)
July 31, 1985 (TIAS 12387)

Agreement concerning cooperation in the Global Learning and Observations to Benefit the Environment (GLOBE) Program.
Exchange of notes at Washington August 29, 1995.
Entered into force August 29, 1995.
TIAS 12686

FINANCE

Agreement regarding guaranty of investments in Japan, with a related exchange of notes.
Signed at Tokyo March 8, 1954.
Entered into force May 1, 1954.
5 UST 791; TIAS 2968; 232 UNTS 251

Agreement concerning payments from Japanese utility companies for uranium enrichment services.
Exchange of notes at Washington September 1, 1978.
Entered into force September 1, 1978.
30 UST 1850; TIAS 9295; 1153 UNTS 151

FOREIGN ASSISTANCE

Productivity agreement.
Signed at Tokyo April 7, 1955.
Entered into force April 7, 1955.
6 UST 1007; TIAS 3241; 263 UNTS 285

Agreement providing for a third-country technical assistance training program in Japan.
Exchange of notes at Tokyo March 23, 1960.
Entered into force March 23, 1960.
11 UST 1382; TIAS 4475; 372 UNTS 289

HEALTH & MEDICAL COOPERATION

Agreement providing for cooperative efforts to be directed toward sanitary control of the shellfish industry.
Exchange of notes at Washington October 24, 1962.
Entered into force October 24, 1962.
13 UST 2452; TIAS 5207; 462 UNTS 119

Agreement relating to the establishment of the Radiation Effects Research Foundation.
Exchange of notes at Tokyo December 27, 1974.
Entered into force December 27, 1974.
26 UST 7; TIAS 8001

INTELLECTUAL PROPERTY

Agreement to facilitate the interchange of patent rights and technical information for purposes of defense, and protocol.
Signed at Tokyo March 22, 1956.
Entered into force June 6, 1956.
7 UST 1021; TIAS 3585; 275 UNTS 195

Agreement implementing the agreement of March 22, 1956, to facilitate interchange of patent rights and technical information for purposes of defense, with memorandum of understanding, procedures, related notes and letters.
Exchange of notes at Tokyo April 12, 1988.
Entered into force April 12, 1988.
TIAS

LAW ENFORCEMENT

Arrangement for the direct exchange of certain information regarding the traffic in narcotic drugs.
Exchange of notes at Tokyo February 16 and July 6, 1928.
Entered into force July 6, 1928.
9 Bevans 452

Arrangement for the exchange of information relating to the seizure of illicit narcotic drugs and to persons engaged in the illicit traffic.
Exchange of notes at Tokyo April 23 and September 6, 1929.
Entered into force September 6, 1929.
9 Bevans 455

Convention for prevention of smuggling of intoxicating liquors.
Signed at Washington May 31, 1928.
Entered into force January 16, 1930.
46 Stat. 2446; TS 807; 9 Bevans 446; 101 LNTS 63

Procedures for mutual assistance in the administration of justice in connection with the Lockheed Aircraft Corporation matter.
Signed at Washington March 23, 1976.
Entered into force March 23, 1976.
27 UST 946; TIAS 8233
Related Agreement:
January 20 and 22, 1979 (30 UST 3473; TIAS 9400; 1180 UNTS 157)

Treaty on extradition, with exchange of notes.
Signed at Tokyo March 3, 1978.
Entered into force March 26, 1980.
31 UST 892; TIAS 9625; 1203 UNTS 225

Agreement regarding mutual assistance between customs administrations, with exchange of notes.
Signed at Washington June 17, 1997.
Entered into force June 17, 1997.
TIAS 12869

Treaty on mutual legal assistance in criminal matters, with attachment and related exchange of notes.
Signed at Washington on August 5, 2003.
Entered into force July 21, 2006.
TIAS 06-721.3

MARITIME MATTERS

Agreement relating to the establishment, operation, and maintenance of an OMEGA navigational aid station in Japan.
Exchange of notes at Tokyo August 15, 1972.
Entered into force August 15, 1972.
23 UST 1480; TIAS 7428; 898 UNTS 55

Agreement on maritime search and rescue.
Signed at Tokyo December 12, 1986.
Entered into force December 12, 1986.
TIAS 11413; 2191 UNTS 57
Amendment:
September 30, 1998 (TIAS 12986)

NONPROLIFERATION

Agreement for cooperation in research and development concerning nuclear material control and accounting measures for safeguards and non-proliferation, with annex.
Signed at Washington July 21, 2006.
Entered into force July 21, 2006.
TIAS 06-721.2

PEACE

Agreement concerning the Amami Islands, and exchange of notes.
Signed at Tokyo December 24, 1953.
Entered into force December 25, 1953.
4 UST 2912; TIAS 2895; 222 UNTS 193

Agreement concerning Nanpo Shoto and other islands with exchange of notes.
Signed at Tokyo April 5, 1968.
Entered into force June 26, 1968.
19 UST 4895; TIAS 6495; 683 UNTS 285

Agreement concerning the Ryukyu Islands and the Daito Islands with related arrangements.
Signed at Washington and Tokyo June 17, 1971.
Entered into force May 15, 1972.
23 UST 446; TIAS 7314

POSTAL MATTERS

Memorandum of understanding relating to the initiation of accelerated mail service.
Signed at Tokyo and Washington May 8 and 27, 1975.
Entered into force May 27, 1975; effective June 16, 1975.
29 UST 90; TIAS 8794

Memorandum of understanding relating to the exchange of postal money orders.
Signed at Tokyo and Washington August 31 and December 24, 1984.
Effective January 1, 1985.
NP

Amendment:
June 21 and July 12, 1985

PROPERTY

Arrangement relating to perpetual leaseholds.
Exchange of notes at Tokyo March 25, 1937.
Entered into force March 25, 1937.
50 Stat. 1611; EAS 104; 9 Bevans 464; 181 LNTS 217

Agreement relating to the payment of damages caused by United States aircraft to property of Japanese nationals.
Exchange of notes at Tokyo August 24, 1955.
Entered into force August 24, 1955.
6 UST 4064; TIAS 3418; 257 UNTS 297

PUBLICATIONS

Agreement relating to the exchange of official publications.
Exchange of notes at Tokyo September 5, 1956.
Entered into force September 5, 1956.
7 UST 2497; TIAS 3638; 277 UNTS 267

SCIENTIFIC & TECHNICAL COOPERATION

Agreement on cooperation in research and development in science and technology, with annexes and exchanges of letters.
Signed at Toronto June 20, 1988.
Entered into force June 20, 1988.
TIAS 12025; 2250 UNTS 117

Amendment and Extensions:
June 16, 1998 (TIAS 98-620)
March 19, 1999 (TIAS 98-620)
May 19, 1999 (TIAS 98-620)
July 16, 1999 (TIAS 98-620)
July 19, 2004 (TIAS 98-620)
April 23, 2014 (TIAS 14-720)

Agreement concerning cooperation in joint scientific balloon launchings, with memorandum of understanding.
Exchange of notes at Washington June 2, 1993.
Entered into force June 2, 1993.
TIAS

Agreement concerning the acquisition by the Government of Japan of remote sensing parts and components and related information for the indigenous development of an Information Gathering Satellite System.
Exchange of notes at Tokyo September 29, 1999.
Entered into force September 29, 1999.
TIAS

Agreement on cooperation to maintain meteorological satellite observation over the Pacific region through the mutual back-up of geostationary meteorological satellites, with implementing arrangement.
Exchange of notes at Washington February 18, 2005.
Entered into force February 18, 2005.
TIAS 05-218

Agreement for cooperation on the formulation activity of the global precipitation measurement program, with memorandum of understanding.
Exchange of notes at Washington June 10, 2005.
Entered into force June 10, 2005.
TIAS 05-610.2

Memorandum of understanding for cooperation in the use of U.S. land remote sensing satellite data, with annexes.
Signed at Reston and Tsukuba November 13 and 21, 2013.
Entered into force November 21, 2013.
TIAS 13-1121.1

SOCIAL SECURITY

Agreement concerning enrollment of Japanese employees of the Okinawa office of the Voice of America in the employment insurance scheme of Japan.
Exchange of notes at Tokyo September 30 and October 15, 1976.
Entered into force October 15, 1976; effective April 1, 1976.
27 UST 4312; TIAS 8452; 1066 UNTS 291

Agreement on social security, with administrative arrangement.
Signed at Washington February 19, 2004.
Entered into force October 1, 2005.
TIAS 05-1001

SPACE

Agreement relating to the establishment by Japan of a satellite tracking station in Okinawa.
Exchange of notes at Tokyo September 2, 1968.
Entered into force September 2, 1968.
19 UST 6011; TIAS 6558; 702 UNTS 151
Amendment:
September 25, 1969 (20 UST 3017; TIAS 6778; 727 UNTS 429)

Agreement concerning cooperation in space activities for peaceful purposes.
Exchange of notes at Tokyo July 31, 1969.
Entered into force July 31, 1969.
20 UST 2720; TIAS 6735; 720 UNTS 79

Agreement concerning the furnishing of launching and associated services by NASA for Japanese satellites, with memorandum of understanding.
Exchange of notes at Washington May 23, 1975.
Entered into force May 23, 1975.
26 UST 1029; TIAS 8090

Agreement relating to space launch assistance, with exchange of letters.
Exchange of notes at Washington December 3, 1980.
Entered into force December 3, 1980.
32 UST 4197; TIAS 9940; 1266 UNTS 143

Memorandum of understanding for a cooperative program concerning design (Phase B) of a permanently manned space station.
Signed at Tokyo May 9, 1985.
Entered into force May 9, 1985.
TIAS 11327

Agreement concerning cooperation regarding the Geotail Scientific Satellite Program.
Exchange of notes at Tokyo September 25, 1989.
Entered into force September 25, 1989.
TIAS 12203

Agreement concerning cross-waiver of liability for cooperation in the exploration and use of space for peaceful purposes, with annex and exchanges of notes.
Signed at Washington April 24, 1995.
Entered into force July 20, 1995.
TIAS 12638
Amendment:
December 1, 2008 (TIAS 08-1201.1)

Agreement concerning cooperation on the Advanced Spaceborne Thermal Emission and Reflection Radiometer Program, with memorandum of understanding.
Exchange of notes at Washington October 24, 1996.
Entered into force October 24, 1996.
TIAS 12809
Extension:
October 19, 2012 (TIAS 12-1019)

Agreement concerning cooperation on the Tropical Rainfall Measuring Mission Program, with memorandum of understanding of October 20, 1995, and its amendment.
Exchange of notes at Washington May 30, 1997.
Entered into force May 30, 1997.
TIAS 97-530
Extensions:
June 2, 1997 (TIAS 97-530)
May 28, 2002 (TIAS 97-530)
May 22, 2008 (TIAS 97-530)

Agreement concerning cooperation on the Advanced Microwave Scanning Radiometer E (AMSR E) Program.
Exchange of notes at Washington November 30, 1998.
Entered into force November 30, 1998.
TIAS 13004
Extension
May 22, 2008 (TIAS 08-522)

Agreement for cooperation on the MU Space Engineering Spacecraft-C (MUSES-C) Program, with memorandum of understanding.
Exchange of notes at Washington April 25, 2003.
Entered into force April 25, 2003.
TIAS 03-425
Extension:
April 22, 2011 (TIAS 03-425)

Agreement for the x ray astronomy satellite (ASTRO EII) project, with memorandum of understanding.
Exchange of notes at Washington June 10, 2005.
Entered into force June 10, 2005.
TIAS 05-610
Extension:
June 6, 2012 (TIAS 05-610)

Agreement concerning activities related to the solar physics satellite (Solar B) project, with memorandum of understanding.
Exchange of notes at Washington June 10, 2005.
Entered into force June 10, 2005.
TIAS 05-610.1
Extension:
June 5, 2013 (TIAS 13-605)

Agreement concerning cooperation on the Joint Program between the Greenhouse Gases Observing Satellite (GOSAT) and the Orbiting Carbon Observatory (OCO) satellite.
Exchange of notes at Washington December 1, 2008.
Entered into force December 1, 2008.
TIAS 08-1201

Agreement for cooperation on the development and operations activity of a Global Precipitation Measurement (GPM) mission, with memorandum of understanding.
Exchange of notes at Washington December 19, 2008.
Entered into force December 19, 2008.
TIAS 08-1219 and 08-1219A

Agreement concerning the space situational awareness services and information sharing for the safety of space, with memorandum of understanding.
Effected by exchange of notes at Tokyo May 28, 2013.
Entered into force May 28, 2013.
TIAS 13-528

Agreement for cooperation on the X-ray Astronomy Satellite (Astro-H) Project, with memorandum of understanding.
Effected by exchange of notes at Washington October 8, 2013.
Entered into force October 8, 2013.
TIAS 13-1008

TAXATION

Agreement relating to tax relief for expenditures made by the United States in Japan under mutual security programs.
Exchange of notes at Tokyo July 14 and 25, 1952.
Entered into force July 25, 1952.
3 UST 2955; TIAS 2477; 198 UNTS 281

Convention for the avoidance of double taxation and the prevention of fiscal evasion with respect to taxes on estates, inheritances, and gifts.
Signed at Washington April 16, 1954.
Entered into force April 1, 1955.
6 UST 113; TIAS 3175; 238 UNTS 3

Agreement concerning reciprocal exemption from taxation of income accruing from the business of shipping.
Exchange of notes at Washington August 29, 1989.
Entered into force August 29, 1989.
TIAS 11697; 2207 UNTS 401

Convention for the avoidance of double taxation and the prevention of fiscal evasion with respect to taxes on income, with protocol and related exchange of notes.
Signed at Washington November 6, 2003.
Entered into force March 30, 2004.
TIAS 04-330

TELECOMMUNICATION

Agreement providing for a program of cooperation in the testing of experimental communications satellites.
Exchange of notes at Tokyo November 6, 1962.
Entered into force November 6, 1962.
13 UST 2470; TIAS 5212; 459 UNTS 203

Agreement relating to the reciprocal granting of authorizations to permit licensed amateur radio operators of either country to operate their stations in the other country.
Exchange of notes at Tokyo August 8, 1985.
Entered into force September 7, 1985.
TIAS 12004

TRADE & INVESTMENT

Treaty of friendship, commerce, and navigation, protocol, and exchange of notes of August 29, 1953.*
Signed at Tokyo April 2, 1953.
Entered into force October 30, 1953.
4 UST 2063; TIAS 2863; 206 UNTS 143

Note:

* Applicable to Bonin Islands and Ryukyu Islands.

Agreement for the establishment of a Joint United States-Japan Committee on Trade and Economic Affairs.
Exchange of notes at Washington June 22, 1961.
Entered into force June 22, 1961.
12 UST 731; TIAS 4776; 410 UNTS 53

Agreement to accelerate tariff reductions.
Exchange of letters at Washington September 30, 1981.
Entered into force September 30, 1981.
33 UST 4490; TIAS 10318

Agreement concerning market access for beef, fresh oranges, orange juice and other products, with annex.
Exchange of letters at Washington July 5, 1988.
Entered into force July 5, 1988.
TIAS

Agreement concerning market access for various agricultural products, with annexes.
Exchange of letters at Washington August 2, 1988.
Entered into force August 2, 1988.
TIAS

Agreement concerning trade in certain machine tools, with arrangement, agreed minutes, exchanges of notes and related letters.
Exchange of letters at Washington June 30, 1992.
Entered into force June 30, 1992.
TIAS

Agreement concerning cooperation on anticompetitive activities.
Signed at Washington October 7, 1999.
Entered into force October 7, 1999.
TIAS

Agreement on mutual recognition of results of conformity assessment procedures, with annex.
Signed at Washington February 16, 2007.
Entered into force January 1, 2008.
TIAS

TRANSPORTATION

Civil air transport agreement and exchange of notes relating to provisional application.
Signed at Tokyo August 11, 1952.
Entered into force provisionally August 11, 1952; definitively September 15, 1953.
4 UST 1948; TIAS 2854; 212 UNTS 27
Amendments:
May 9, 1972 (23 UST 677; TIAS 7333)
July 26, 1977 (29 UST 1375; TIAS 8882)
August 21, 1996 (TIAS 12793)
April 20, 1998 (TIAS 12945)
November 13, 2010 (TIAS 10-1113.1)
April 26, 2016 (TIAS 16-1030)

Interim agreement relating to the civil air transport agreement of August 11, 1952, as amended (TIAS 2854, 7333, 8882), with record of consultations, memorandum of understanding and exchange of letters.
Exchange of letters at Washington September 7, 1982.
*Entered into force September 7, 1982.**
34 UST 1541; TIAS 10434; 1736 UNTS 284
Note:
* Provisions relating to Guam, Saipan and Micronesia have been superseded by the 1985 memorandum of understanding.

Interim agreement relating to the civil air transport agreement of August 11, 1952, as amended, with memorandum of understanding, exchange of letters and related letter.
Exchange of notes at Bonn May 1, 1985.
Entered into force May 1, 1985.
TIAS 11999; 2246 UNTS 88

Interim agreement relating to the civil air transport agreement of August 11, 1952, as amended, with memorandum of understanding.
Exchange of notes at Washington December 27, 1989.
Entered into force December 27, 1989.
TIAS 12406; 2361 UNTS 3

Interim arrangement relating to the civil air transport agreement of August 11, 1952, as amended, with attachment.
Exchange of notes at Washington February 26, 1996.
Entered into force February 26, 1996.
TIAS 12728; 2478 UNTS 52

Agreement for the provision of technical assistance in developing and modernizing the civil aviation infrastructure of Japan, with letter of understanding.
Signed July 5 and 17, 2002.
Entered into force July 17, 2002.
NP
Amendments:
January 22 and 26, 2010 (NP)
July 16 and 30, 2010 (NP)

Agreement for the promotion of aviation safety.
Signed at Tokyo April 27, 2009.
Entered into force April 27, 2009.
TIAS 09-427.1

JORDAN

ATOMIC ENERGY

Arrangement for the exchange of technical information and cooperation in nuclear safety matters, with addenda.
Signed at Vienna September 20, 2012.
Entered into force September 20, 2012.
TIAS 12-920

CULTURAL EXCHANGES, PROPERTY & COOPERATION

Agreement concerning the program of the Peace Corps in Jordan.
Signed at Amman October 28, 1996.
Entered into force October 28, 1996.
TIAS 12810

DEFENSE

Agreement concerning payment to the United States of net proceeds from the sale of defense articles furnished under the military assistance program.
Exchange of letters at Amman May 20 and August 24, 1974.
Entered into force August 24, 1974; effective July 1, 1974.
25 UST 2422; TIAS 7921
Amendment:
November 10, 2004, and February 7, 2005

Agreement relating to the furnishing of defense articles and services to Jordan.
Exchange of notes at Amman October 20, 1976, and February 23, 1977.
Entered into force February 23, 1977.
28 UST 4494; TIAS 8602

Agreement concerning the grant of defense articles and services under the military assistance program.
Exchange of notes at Amman August 27, 1979.
Entered into force August 28, 1979.
30 UST 7537; TIAS 9597; 1205 UNTS 9
Amendment:
August 18 and September 20, 1982 (TIAS 10501)

Agreement concerning the grant of defense articles and services under the military assistance program.
Exchange of notes at Amman August 14 and 30, 1980.
Entered into force August 30, 1980; effective August 28, 1980.
32 UST 2412; TIAS 9850
Amendment:
August 18 and September 20, 1982 (TIAS 10501)

Agreement regarding the status of United States military personnel and civilian employees of the Department of Defense who may be in Jordan temporarily in connection with their official duties.
Exchange of notes at Amman April 4 and 10, 1996.
Entered into force April 10, 1996.
TIAS

Agreement concerning the transfer of United States Government granted or sold defense articles or related training or other defense services to the Government of Jordan.
Exchange of notes at Amman August 13 and 27, 2000.
Entered into force August 27, 2000.
TIAS 13114

Aviation leadership program agreement.
Signed at Washington and Amman April 21 and 29, 2004.
Entered into force April 29, 2004.
NP

Acquisition and cross-servicing agreement, with annexes.
Signed at Tampa and Amman March 21 and 29, 2006.
Entered into force March 29, 2006.
TIAS 06-329

Memorandum of arrangement regarding assignment of liaison officers.
Signed at Norfolk and Washington July 12, 2006.
Entered into force July 12, 2006.
NP
Extensions:
April 4, 2011
April 19 and July 12, 2016

Agreement concerning geospatial intelligence exchange and cooperation, with annexes.
Signed at Springfield September 7, 2011.
Entered into force September 7, 2011.
NP

Agreement regarding grants under the Foreign Assistance Act of 1961, as amended, or successor legislation, and the furnishing of defense articles, related training, and other defense services, including pursuant to the U.S.C. Title 10, Section 2282, by the United States of America to the Government of the Kingdom of Jordan.
Exchange of notes at Amman July 28 and August 16, 2015.
Entered into force August 16, 2015.
TIAS 15-816

DIPLOMATIC & CONSULAR RELATIONS

Joint statement on United States-Jordan relations.
Issued at Amman June 18, 1974.
Entered into force June 18, 1974.
25 UST 1510; TIAS 7885

ENVIRONMENT & CONSERVATION

Agreement concerning cooperation in the Global Learning and Observations to Benefit the Environment (GLOBE) Program, with appendices.
Signed at Amman October 31, 1996.
Entered into force October 31, 1996.
TIAS 12812

FINANCE

Agreement regarding the consolidation and rescheduling or refinancing of certain debts owed to, guaranteed by, or insured by the United States Government and its agencies, with annexes.
Signed at Amman October 31, 1989.
Entered into force December 6, 1989.
NP

Agreement regarding the consolidation and rescheduling or refinancing of certain debts owed to, guaranteed by, or insured by the United States Government and its agencies, with annexes.
Signed at Amman May 10, 1992.
Entered into force June 22, 1992.
NP
Amendment:
October 7 and November 1, 1993 (NP)

Agreement regarding the consolidation and rescheduling or refinancing of certain debts owed to, guaranteed by or insured by the United States Government and its agencies, with annexes.
Signed at Amman August 18, 1994.
Entered into force September 19, 1994.
NP

Agreement regarding the reduction of certain debts related to foreign assistance owed to the Government of the United States, with annexes.
Signed at Amman September 29, 1994.
Entered into force September 29, 1994.
NP

Agreement regarding the consolidation and rescheduling of certain debts owed to, guaranteed by, or insured by the United States Government and its agencies, with annexes.
Signed at Amman August 25, 1997.
Entered into force September 25, 1997.
NP

Agreement regarding the reduction of certain debts owed to the Government of the United States, with annex.
Signed at Amman September 25, 1997.
Entered into force September 25, 1997.
NP

Agreement regarding the reduction of certain debts owed to, guaranteed by or insured by the Government of the United States and its agencies, with annexes.
Signed at Amman September 25, 1995.
Entered into force September 30, 1995.
NP

Agreement regarding the consolidation and rescheduling of certain debts owed to, guaranteed by, or insured by the United States Government and its agencies, with annexes.
Signed at Amman October 17, 1999.
Entered into force December 13, 1999.
NP

Agreement regarding the consolidation of certain debts owed to, guaranteed or insured by the United States Government and its agencies, with annexes.
Signed at Amman March 23, 2003.
Entered into force April 28, 2003.
NP

Investment incentive agreement.
Signed at Amman February 7, 2007.
Entered into force March 26, 2007.
TIAS 07-326

Agreement regarding the early repayment of certain debts owed to, guaranteed by, or insured by the United States Government and its agencies, with annexes.
Signed at Amman March 30, 2008.
Entered into force March 30, 2008.
NP

FOREIGN ASSISTANCE

Agreement relating to duty-free entry and defrayment of inland transportation charges for relief supplies of United States voluntary agencies.
Exchange of notes at Amman May 1 and June 29, 1954.
Entered into force June 29, 1954.
5 UST 2896; TIAS 3145; 237 UNTS 111
Amendment:
July 6, September 28, and October 15, 1955
(8 UST 369; TIAS 3784; 279 UNTS 324)

General agreement providing for economic, technical, and related assistance to Jordan.
Exchange of notes at Amman June 25 and 27, 1957.
Entered into force July 1, 1957.
8 UST 1073; TIAS 3870; 288 UNTS 269

Agreement relating to economic assistance.
Exchange of notes at Amman June 29, 1957.
Entered into force June 29, 1957.
8 UST 1069; TIAS 3869; 288 UNTS 263

Loan guarantee agreement, with declaration, with annexes.
Signed at Amman August 14, 2013.
Entered into force October 26, 2013.
TIAS 13-1026

Loan guarantee agreement, with declaration, with annexes.
Signed at Amman May 5, 2014.
Entered into force June 21, 2014.
TIAS 14-621

Loan guarantee agreement, with annexes.
Signed at Amman May 31, 2015.
Entered into force June 24, 2015.
TIAS 15-624

AGENCY FOR INTERNATIONAL DEVELOPMENT

Strategic object grant agreement for the improved economic opportunities for Jordanians strategic objective, with attachment.
Signed February 23, 2004.
Entered into force February 23, 2004.
NP
Amendments:
July 20, 2005 (NP)
August 10, 2006 (NP)

Special objective grant agreement for the cash transfer special objective, with attachment.
Signed March 23, 2004.
Entered into force March 23, 2004.
NP
Amendments:
July 20, 2005 (NP)
August 10, 2006 (NP)

Strategic object grant agreement for the improved social sector development and governance strategic objective, with annex.
Signed June 2, 2004.
Entered into force June 2, 2004.
NP
Amendments:
July 20, 2005 (NP)
August 10, 2006 (NP)

Strategic object grant agreement for the enhanced integrated water strategic objective resources, with annex.
Signed June 2, 2004.
Entered into force June 2, 2004.
NP
Amendments:
July 20, 2005 (NP)
August 10, 2006 (NP)

Agreement for investing in people/economic growth, with annex.
Signed September 17, 2007.
Entered into force September 17, 2007.
Amendments:
September 28, 2011 (NP)
October 4, 2011 (NP)
September 30, 2012 (NP)

Agreement for governing justly and democratically, with annex.
Signed September 19, 2007.
Entered into force September 19, 2007.
Amendments:
September 28, 2011 (NP)
September 30, 2012 (NP)

Agreement for investing in people, with annex.
Signed September 24, 2007.
Entered into force September 24, 2007.
Amendments:
September 28, 2011 (NP)
October 20, 2011 (NP)
September 30, 2012 (NP)

Agreement for economic growth, with annex.
Signed September 24, 2007.
Entered into force September 24, 2007.

Amendments:
September 28, 2011 (NP)
October 20, 2011 (NP)
September 4, 2012 (NP)
September 30, 2012 (NP)

LAW ENFORCEMENT

Extradition treaty.
Signed at Washington March 28, 1995.
Entered into force July 29, 1995.
TIAS

Agreement regarding mutual assistance between their customs administrations.
Signed at Amman December 8, 2004.
Entered into force December 8, 2004.
TIAS 04-1208.2

Agreement concerning the training of Iraqi police in Jordan.
Signed at Amman and Washington September 24, 2004.
Entered into force September 6, 2005.
TIAS

POSTAL MATTERS

International express mail agreement, with detailed regulations.
Signed at Amman and Washington December 31, 1986, and January 30, 1987.
Entered into force March 27, 1987.
TIAS 11308

SCIENTIFIC & TECHNICAL COOPERATION

Agreement on science and technology cooperation, with annexes.
Signed at Amman April 5, 2007.
Entered into force June 12, 2007.
TIAS 07-612

TAXATION

Agreement concerning the reciprocal exemption from income tax of income derived from the international operation of ships and aircraft.
Exchange of notes at Amman April 7, 1988.
Entered into force April 7, 1988.
TIAS 11888

TELECOMMUNICATION

Agreement relating to radio communications between amateur stations on behalf of third parties.
Exchange of notes at Washington November 13 and 30, 1972.
Entered into force December 30, 1972.
23 UST 3492; TIAS 7508

Agreement relating to the reciprocal granting of authorizations to permit licensed amateur radio operators of either country to operate their stations in the other country.
Exchange of letters at Amman February 6 and March 11, 1979.
Entered into force March 11, 1979.
30 UST 3783; TIAS 9425; 1170 UNTS 9

TRADE & INVESTMENT

Agreement on the establishment of a free trade area, with annexes, schedules, memoranda of understanding, joint statements and exchanges of letters.
Signed at Washington October 24, 2000.
Entered into force December 17, 2001.
TIAS

Treaty concerning the encouragement and reciprocal protection of investment, with annex and protocol.
Signed at Amman July 2, 1997.
Entered into force June 12, 2003.
TIAS

TRANSPORTATION

Agreement relating to the provision of technical assistance and services to the Civil Aviation Department of Jordan.
Signed at Amman and Washington April 1 and May 3, 1980.
Entered into force June 1, 1980.
32 UST 1360; TIAS 9777; 1267 UNTS 77

Extension:
May 31 and June 25, 1990 (TIAS 11738; 2204 UNTS 565)

Air transport agreement, with annexes.
Signed at Amman November 10, 1996.
Entered into force November 10, 1996.
TIAS 12813

Amendment:
August 21 and November 7, 2006 (TIAS 06-1107)

Memorandum of agreement for the provision of technical assistance in developing, modernizing, operating or maintaining the civil aviation infrastructure in Jordan
Signed May 24 and June 20, 2005.
Entered into force June 20, 2005.
NP

Amendment:
May 12 and 27, 2010

KAZAKHSTAN

NOTE: For agreements prior to December 31, 1991, see UNION OF SOVIET SOCIALIST REPUBLICS.

ARMS CONTROL

Agreement concerning the establishment and operation of nuclear test seismic monitoring stations in Kazakhstan.
Signed at Washington November 18, 1997.
Entered into force November 18, 1997.
TIAS 12901

ATOMIC ENERGY

Agreement for cooperation concerning peaceful uses of nuclear energy, with annex and agreed minute.
Signed at Washington November 18, 1997.
Entered into force November 5, 1999.
TIAS 12900

Implementing arrangement concerning the decommissioning of the BN-350 Reactor.
Signed at Washington December 19, 1999.
Entered into force December 19, 1999.
TIAS

Arrangement for the exchange of technical information and cooperation in nuclear safety matters, with annex.
Signed at Vienna September 24, 2014.
Entered into force September 24, 2014.
TIAS 14-924.2

CULTURAL EXCHANGES, PROPERTY & COOPERATION

Agreement concerning the activity of the Peace Corps of the United States in the Republic of Kazakhstan.
Signed at Washington December 22, 1992.
Entered into force December 22, 1992.
TIAS 12084

DEFENSE

Agreement regarding grants under the Foreign Assistance Act of 1961, as amended, or successor legislation, and the furnishing of defense articles, defense services and related training, including pursuant to the United States International Military Education and Training (IMET) Program.
Exchange of notes at Astana July 5 and August 2, 2007.
Entered into force August 2, 2007.
NP

Agreement on support for commercial rail transit of special cargo through the territory of the Republic of Kazakhstan in connection with the participation of the United States of America in efforts for the stabilization and reconstruction of the Islamic Republic of Afghanistan.
Signed at Astana June 20, 2010.
Entered into force July 14, 2010.
TIAS 10-714

Amendment:
July 8, 2011(TIAS 11-1122)

Agreement on the air transit of cargo and personnel through the territory of the Republic of Kazakhstan in connection with the participation of the United States of America in efforts for ensuring the security, stabilization, and reconstruction of the Islamic Republic of Afghanistan, with annex.
Signed at Washington November 12, 2010.
Entered into force November 19, 2010.
TIAS

EMPLOYMENT

Agreement relating to the employment of dependents of official government employees.
Exchange of notes at Washington May 23 and June 3, 1996.
Entered into force June 3, 1996.
TIAS 11496

ENVIRONMENT & CONSERVATION

Agreement on cooperation in the fields of protection of the environment and natural resources, with annex.
Signed at Washington March 27, 1995.
Entered into force March 27, 1995.
TIAS 12623

Agreement for cooperation in the Global Learning and Observations to Benefit the Environment (GLOBE) Program, with appendices.
Signed at Washington March 27, 1995.
Entered into force March 27, 1995.
TIAS 12624

Memorandum of understanding concerning the Regional Environmental Center for Central Asia.
Signed at Almaty March 1, 2002.
Entered into force March 1, 2002.
TIAS 02-301

FINANCE

Investment incentive agreement.
Signed at Washington May 19, 1992.
Entered into force May 19, 1992.
TIAS

FOREIGN ASSISTANCE

Agreement regarding cooperation to facilitate the provision of assistance.
Signed at Washington May 20, 1992.
Entered into force May 20, 1992.
TIAS 11474

AGENCY FOR INTERNATIONAL DEVELOPMENT

Agreement on the Kazakhstan-U.S. program for economic development.
Signed May 5, 2006.
Entered into force May 6, 2006.
Amendment:
February 22, 2010 (NP)

Memorandum of understanding regarding gender equity in Kazakhstan.
Signed November 23, 2010.
Entered into force November 23, 2010.

INTERNATIONAL CRIMINAL COURT

Agreement regarding the surrender of persons to the International Criminal Court.
Signed at New York September 22, 2003.
Entered into force October 7, 2004.
TIAS 04-1007

LAW ENFORCEMENT

Agreement regarding cooperation and mutual assistance between their customs services.
Signed at Washington November 18, 1997.
Entered into force August 21, 2000.
TIAS

Treaty on mutual legal assistance in criminal matters.
Signed at Washington February 20, 2015.
Entered into force December 6, 2016.
TIAS 16-1206

NONPROLIFERATION

Agreement concerning control, accounting and physical protection of nuclear material to promote the prevention of nuclear weapons proliferation.
Signed at Almaty December 13, 1993.
Entered into force December 13, 1993.
TIAS
Amendments:
June 30, 1995
November 17, 1997
November 17 and 26, 2003

Implementing arrangements concerning long-term disposition of BN–350 nuclear material.
Signed at Washington November 18, 1997.
Entered into force November 18, 1997.
TIAS

Implementing arrangement for cooperation in the prevention of illicit trafficking in nuclear material.
Signed at Astana May 5, 2006.
Entered into force May 5, 2006.
TIAS

Implementing arrangement for cooperation in the field of nuclear material safeguards and security, with annex.
Signed at Washington and Astana November 10 and 23, 2011.
Entered into force September 23, 2011.
TIAS 11-1123

PROPERTY

Memorandum of understanding on providing a land plot to the Government of the United States of America for the construction of new diplomatic mission facilities of the United States of America, with exhibits.
Signed at Almaty October 3, 2002.
Entered into force June 26, 2003.
TIAS 03-626.3

SCIENTIFIC & TECHNICAL COOPERATION

Agreement on science and technology cooperation, with annexes.
Signed at Washington April 11, 2010.
Entered into force July 13, 2011.
TIAS 11-713

Agreement concerning scientific and technical cooperation in the earth sciences.
Signed at Reston and Astana June 6 and 16, 2014.
Entered into force June 16, 2014.
TIAS 14-616

TAXATION

Convention for the avoidance of double taxation and the prevention of fiscal evasion with respect to taxes on income and capital, with protocol.
Signed at Almaty October 24, 1993.
Entered into force December 30, 1996.
TIAS

Agreement concerning the relationship between the taxation convention of October 24, 1993, and the General Agreement on Trade in Services with regard to the consultation, most-favored-nation and national treatment provisions.
Exchange of notes at Washington July 10, 1995.
Entered into force December 30, 1996.
TIAS

TRADE & INVESTMENT

Agreement on trade relations, with related exchanges of letters.
Signed at Washington May 19, 1992.
Entered into force February 18, 1993.
TIAS

Treaty concerning the reciprocal encouragement and protection of investment, with annex.
Signed at Washington May 19, 1992.
Entered into force January 12, 1994.
TIAS

WEAPONS

Agreement concerning the destruction of silo launchers of intercontinental ballistic missiles, emergency response and the prevention of proliferation of nuclear weapons.
Signed at Almaty December 13, 1993.
Entered into force December 13, 1993.
TIAS

Amendment and Extension:
December 1 and 5, 2000
December 13, 2007

Agreement concerning the provision of material, services and related training to Kazakhstan in connection with the destruction of silo launchers of intercontinental ballistic missiles and associated equipment and components.
Signed at Almaty December 13, 1993.
Entered into force December 13, 1993.
TIAS

Amendment:
July 1, 1995

Agreement concerning the elimination of nuclear weapons infrastructure.
Signed at Almaty September 22 and October 3, 1995.
Entered into force October 3, 1995.
TIAS

Amendments and Extensions:
June 10, 1996
September 9, 1998
December 17, 1999
July 29, 2000
May 13 and 31, 2002
March 11 and April 2, 2003
June 25 and 28, 2004
November 29 and December 7, 2004
August 15 and 23, 2005
April 28 and May 2, 2006
July 7 and August 13, 2009
April 7, 2015

KENYA

CULTURAL EXCHANGES, PROPERTY & COOPERATION

Agreement relating to the establishment of a peace corps program in Kenya.
Exchange of notes at Nairobi August 26, 1964.
Entered into force August 26, 1964.
15 UST 1906; TIAS 5666; 531 UNTS 51

DEFENSE

Agreement relating to eligibility for United States military assistance and training pursuant to the International Security Assistance and Arms Export Control Act of 1976.
Exchange of notes at Nairobi August 10 and 24, 1976.
Entered into force August 24, 1976.
28 UST 2468; TIAS 8568

Agreement regarding Kenya's participation in the African Crisis Response Initiative and the furnishing of commodities, services, and related training by the Government of the United States of America for peacekeeping and humanitarian response purposes.
Exchange of notes at Nairobi March 10 and August 23, 2000.
Entered into force August 23, 2000.
NP

Agreement regarding grants under the Foreign Assistance Act of 1961, as amended, and the furnishing of defense articles, related training, and other defense services from the United States of America to the Government of Kenya.
Exchange of notes at Nairobi July 28 and August 23, 2000.
Entered into force August 23, 2000.
TIAS 13112

Agreement concerning geospatial-intelligence exchange and cooperation, with annexes.
Signed at Bethesda and Nairobi March 6 and 18, 2008.
Entered into force March 18, 2008.
NP

ENVIRONMENT & CONSERVATION

Agreement for cooperation in the Global Learning and Observations to Benefit the Environment (GLOBE) Program.
Signed at Nairobi June 9, 1997.
Entered into force June 9, 1997.
TIAS 12864

FINANCE

Agreement regarding the consolidation and rescheduling of certain debts owed to, guaranteed by or insured by the United States Government and its agency, with annexes.
Signed at Nairobi July 1, 1994.
Entered into force August 26, 1994.
NP

Investment incentive agreement.
Signed at Nairobi December 3, 1998.
Entered into force December 3, 1998.
TIAS

Agreement regarding the consolidation and rescheduling of certain debts owed to, guaranteed by, or insured by the United States Government and its agencies, with annexes.
Signed at Nairobi February 24, 2001.
Entered into force March 30, 2001.
NP

Agreement regarding the consolidation and rescheduling of certain debts owed to, guaranteed by, or insured by the United States Government and its agencies, with annexes.
Signed at Nairobi May 11, 2004.
Entered into force June 21, 2004.
NP

FOREIGN ASSISTANCE

Economic cooperation agreement between the United States and the United Kingdom.
Signed at London July 6, 1948.
Applicable to Kenya July 6, 1948.
62 Stat. 2596; TIAS 1795; 22 UNTS 263

Amendments:
January 3, 1950 (1 UST 184; TIAS 2036; 86 UNTS 304)
May 25, 1951 (2 UST 1292; TIAS 2277; 99 UNTS 308)
February 25, 1953 (4 UST 1528; TIAS 2815; 172 UNTS 332)

Agreement between the United States and the United Kingdom for technical cooperation in respect of the territories for the international relations of which the Government of the United Kingdom are responsible.
Signed at London July 13, 1951.
Applicable to Kenya July 14, 1961.
2 UST 1307; TIAS 2281; 105 UNTS 71

Agreement regarding the non-taxation of the United States Trade and Development Agency's development assistance activities in Kenya.
Signed at Nairobi July 20, 2015.
Entered into force July 20, 2015.
TIAS 15-720.1

AGENCY FOR INTERNATIONAL DEVELOPMENT

Amendments to the Agreement of August 19, 2002, as amended, for increased rural household income.

Signed:
September 17, 2010 (NP)
September 20, 2011 (NP)
September 28, 2012 (NP)
December 27, 2012 (NP)

Amendments to the development assistance grant agreement of August 19, 2003, as amended, for reduced fertility and the risk of HIV/AIDS transmission through sustainable, integrated family planning and health services, with attachment.

Signed:
June 25, 2007 (NP)
September 27, 2007 (NP)
September 26, 2008 (NP)
September 12, 2009 (NP)
September 17, 2010 (NP)
September 20, 2011 (NP)
September 28, 2012 (NP)
December 27, 2012 (NP)

Development assistance grant agreement for strengthening and sustaining Kenya's post-election recovery, with attachment.
Signed September 12, 2009.
Entered into force September 12, 2009.

Amendments:
September 12, 2009 (NP)
September 24 and 28, 2009 (NP)

LAW ENFORCEMENT

Extradition treaty between the United States and the United Kingdom.
Signed at London December 22, 1931.
Applicable to Kenya June 24, 1935.
47 Stat. 2122; TS 849; 12 Bevans 482; 163 LNTS 59

Agreement to continue in force between the United States and Kenya the extradition treaty of December 22, 1931, between the United States and the United Kingdom.
Exchange of notes at Nairobi May 14 and August 19, 1965.
Entered into force August 19, 1965.
16 UST 1866; TIAS 5916; 574 UNTS 153

POSTAL MATTERS

International express mail agreement.
Signed at Washington December 11, 1989.
Entered into force January 30, 1990.
NP

SOCIAL SECURITY

Agreement concerning United States participation on a limited voluntary basis in the National Social Security Fund of Kenya.
Exchange of notes at Nairobi January 31 and March 21, 1977.
Entered into force March 25, 1977.
29 UST 678; TIAS 8847

TRANSPORTATION

Memorandum of agreement for the provision of technical assistance in developing and modernizing the civil aviation infrastructure of Kenya.
Signed at Washington and Nairobi November 2, 2001.
Entered into force November 2, 2001.
NP

Amendment:
March 15 and 19, 2004
August 18 and 26, 2009

Air transport agreement, with annex.
Signed at Washington June 18, 2008.
Entered into force June 18, 2008.
TIAS 08-618

KIRIBATI

On July 12, 1979, the Gilbert Islands became the independent state of Kiribati. Referring to the status of conventions, treaties and other international instruments applied to, or entered into on behalf of the Gilbert Islands by the United Kingdom prior to independence, the Beretitenti (President) of Kiribati, in a note dated September 11, 1979, to the Secretary-General of the United Nations, made a statement reading in part as follows:

The Government of the Republic of Kiribati desires that questions of succession to such conventions, treaties and other international instruments be governed by accepted rules of international law and by the relevant principles contained in the Convention on Succession of States in respect of Treaties, done at Vienna on 23 August 1978. Accordingly, the Government of the Republic of Kiribati declares that, with regard to multi-lateral treaties applied or extended to the former Gilbert Islands it will continue to apply the terms of each such treaty provisionally and on the basis of reciprocity until such time as it notifies the depositary authority of its decision with respect thereto. With regard to bilateral treaties applied or extended to, or entered into on behalf of, the former Gilbert Islands, the Government of the Republic of Kiribati declares that it will examine each such treaty and communicate its views to the other State Party concerned. In the meantime the Government of the Republic of Kiribati will continue to observe the terms of each such treaty, which validly so applies and is not inconsistent with its advent to independence, provisionally and on a basis of reciprocity.

CULTURAL EXCHANGES, PROPERTY & COOPERATION

Agreement relating to the establishment of a Peace Corps program in the Gilbert and Ellice Islands.
Exchange of notes at Suva and Tarawa November 12 and 20, 1974.
Entered into force November 20, 1974.
25 UST 3383; TIAS 7991

DIPLOMATIC & CONSULAR RELATIONS

Consular convention between the United States and the United Kingdom.
Signed at Washington June 6, 1951.
Entered into force September 7, 1952.
3 UST 3426; TIAS 2494; 165 UNTS 121

Treaty of friendship, with agreed minute.
Signed at Tarawa September 20, 1979.
Entered into force September 23, 1983.
35 UST 2095; TIAS 10777

FINANCE

Investment incentive agreement.
Exchange of notes at Suva and Tarawa January 22, 1990.
Entered into force January 22, 1990.
TIAS 12095

INTELLECTUAL PROPERTY

Declaration by the United States and the United Kingdom affording reciprocal protection to trade-marks.
Signed at London October 24, 1877.
Entered into force October 24, 1877.
20 Stat. 703; TS 138; 12 Bevans 198

INTERNATIONAL CRIMINAL COURT

Agreement regarding the surrender of persons to the International Criminal Court.
Signed at Tarawa March 4, 2004.
Entered into force March 4, 2004.
TIAS 04-304

LAW ENFORCEMENT

Extradition treaty between the United States and the United Kingdom with protocol of signature and exchange of notes.
Signed at London June 8, 1972.
Entered into force January 21, 1977.
28 UST 227; TIAS 8468

MARITIME MATTERS

Agreement concerning cooperation in joint maritime surveillance operations.
Signed at Tarawa November 24, 2008.
Entered into force November 24, 2008.
TIAS 08-1124

SCIENTIFIC & TECHNICAL COOPERATION

Memorandum of understanding concerning scientific and technical cooperation in the earth sciences on global seismic data acquisition, with annexes.
Signed at Suva February 23, 2006.
Entered into force February 23, 2006.
TIAS 06-223

TELECOMMUNICATION

Agreement between the United States and the United Kingdom relating to the reciprocal granting of authorizations to permit licensed amateur radio operators of either country to operate their stations in the other country.
Exchange of notes at London November 26, 1965.
Applicable to Kiribati December 11, 1969.
16 UST 2047; TIAS 5941; 561 UNTS 193

Agreement between the United States and the United Kingdom extending to certain territories the application of the agreement of November 26, 1965, relating to the reciprocal granting of authorizations to permit licensed amateur radio operators of either country to operate their stations in the other country.
Exchange of notes at London December 11, 1969.
Entered into force December 11, 1969.
20 UST 4089; TIAS 6800; 732 UNTS 334

TRANSPORTATION

Agreement between the United States and the United Kingdom concerning air services, with annexes and exchange of letters.
Signed at Bermuda July 23, 1977.
Entered into force July 23, 1977.
28 UST 5367; TIAS 8641
Amendment:
April 25, 1978 (29 UST 2680; TIAS 8965)

KOREA

ATOMIC ENERGY

Agreement providing for a grant to the Government of Korea to assist in the acquisition of certain nuclear research and training equipment and materials.
Exchange of notes at Seoul October 14 and November 18, 1960.
Entered into force November 18, 1960.
11 UST 2364; TIAS 4617; 400 UNTS 49

Arrangement for the exchange of technical information and cooperation in nuclear safety matters, with addenda.
Signed at Vienna September 18, 2012.
Entered into force September 18, 2012.
TIAS 12-918

Agreement with respect to the transfer of certain nuclear technologies in the course of the joint fuel cycle study.
Exchange of notes at Washington July 19 and 22, 2013
Entered into force July 25, 2013.
TIAS

Agreement for cooperation concerning peaceful uses of nuclear energy, with agreed minute.
Signed at Washington June 15, 2015.
Entered into force November 25, 2015.
TIAS 15-1125

CLAIMS & DISPUTE RESOLUTION

Utilities claims settlement agreement between the Unified Command and Korea.
Signed at Seoul December 18, 1958.
Entered into force December 18, 1958.
10 UST 41; TIAS 4168; 325 UNTS 233

CONSULAR AFFAIRS

Agreement relating to the issuance of nonimmigrant visas and the reciprocal waiver of fees.*
Exchange of notes at Seoul March 28, 1968.
Entered into force April 27, 1968.
19 UST 4789; TIAS 6479; 693 UNTS 199
Note:
* The status of this agreement is under review.

CULTURAL EXCHANGES, PROPERTY & COOPERATION

Agreement establishing the Korean-American Cultural Exchange Committee.
Exchange of notes at Seoul April 17, 1981.
Entered into force April 17, 1981.
33 UST 1773; TIAS 10145; 1529 UNTS 359

DEFENSE

Mutual defense assistance agreement.
Signed at Seoul January 26, 1950.
Entered into force January 26, 1950.
1 UST 137; TIAS 2019; 80 UNTS 205

Agreement relating to the assurances required by the Mutual Security Act of 1951.
Exchange of notes at Pusan January 4 and 7, 1952.
Entered into force January 7, 1952.
3 UST 4619; TIAS 2612; 179 UNTS 105

Mutual defense treaty.
Signed at Washington October 1, 1953.
Entered into force November 17, 1954.
5 UST 2368; TIAS 3097; 238 UNTS 199

Agreed minute relating to continued cooperation in economic and military matters.
Initialed at Seoul November 17, 1954.
Entered into force November 17, 1954.
6 UST 3913; TIAS 3396; 256 UNTS 251
Amendment:
January 30, 1962 (13 UST 244; TIAS 4967; 442 UNTS 323)

Agreement relating to the establishment of minimum facilities for an arsenal and the reworking of ammunition.
Exchange of notes at Seoul May 29, 1955.
Entered into force May 29, 1955.
6 UST 3919; TIAS 3397; 256 UNTS 263

Agreement providing for the disposition of equipment and materials furnished to Korea under the mutual defense assistance agreement.
Exchange of notes at Seoul May 28 and July 2, 1956.
Entered into force July 2, 1956.
7 UST 2174; TIAS 3616; 281 UNTS 41

Agreement under Article IV of the mutual defense treaty of October 1, 1953, regarding facilities and areas and the status of United States armed forces in Korea, with agreed minutes and exchange of notes.
Signed at Seoul July 9, 1966.
Entered into force February 9, 1967.
17 UST 1677; TIAS 6127; 674 UNTS 163
Amendments:
January 18, 2001 (TIAS 13138)
January 18, 2001 (TIAS 13138)

Agreement regarding the status of the Korean Service Corps with agreed understandings.
Signed at Seoul February 23, 1967.
Entered into force March 10, 1967.
18 UST 249; TIAS 6226; 688 UNTS 245

Memorandum of understanding relating to the establishment of an M 16 rifle production program in Korea, with annexes.
Signed at Seoul and Washington March 31 and April 22, 1971.
Entered into force April 22, 1971.
29 UST 3537; TIAS 9026
Amendments:
July 30, 1976 (29 UST 3547; TIAS 9026)
October 14, 1977 (29 UST 3550; TIAS 9026)

Agreement concerning payment to the United States of net proceeds from the sale of defense articles furnished under the military assistance program.
Exchange of notes at Seoul June 25 and 27, 1974.
Entered into force July 1, 1974.
25 UST 1434; TIAS 7871

Memorandum of agreement concerning conventional ammunition logistics, with protocol.
Signed at Seoul November 25, 1974.
Entered into force November 25, 1974.
27 UST 2817; TIAS 8351

Agreement relating to eligibility for United States military assistance and training pursuant to the International Security Assistance and Arms Export Control Act of 1976.
Exchange of notes at Seoul February 14 and 25, 1977.
Entered into force February 25, 1977.
TIAS 10559; 1577 UNTS 289

Memorandum of agreement regarding the construction of facilities at 2nd ID USA to improve combined defense capabilities.
Signed at Seoul February 2, 1982.
Entered into force February 2, 1982.
34 UST 125; TIAS 10343

Memorandum of understanding for fuel exchange between the United States Navy and the Korean Air Force, with appendix.
Signed at Seoul October 31, 1986.
Entered into force October 31, 1986.
TIAS

Mutual logistics support agreement, with annexes.
Signed at Seoul June 8, 1988.
Entered into force June 8, 1988.
TIAS 12024
Amendments:
February 5, 1991
February 23, 2004
June 30, 2010

Memorandum of understanding on defense technological and industrial cooperation.
Signed at Seoul June 8, 1988.
Entered into force June 8, 1988.
TIAS

Memorandum of understanding on royalty fees for U.S. origin defense articles.
Signed at Washington July 18, 1989.
Entered into force July 18, 1989.
TIAS 12032
Amendment:
August 2, 1993 (TIAS 12505)

Agreement for the establishment of the Joint United States Military Affairs Group to the Republic of Korea.
Signed at Seoul January 25, 1991.
Entered into force February 27, 1991.
TIAS 12035

Agreement terminating the agreed understandings and exchange of letters related to the agreement of July 9, 1966, under Article IV of the mutual defense treaty regarding facilities and areas and the status of United States Armed Forces in Korea.
Exchange of letters at Seoul February 1, 1991.
Entered into force February 1, 1991.
TIAS

Agreement concerning wartime host nation support, with annexes and agreed minute.
Signed at Seoul November 21, 1991.
Entered into force December 23, 1992.
TIAS; 1738 UNTS 265

Memorandum of understanding concerning technology research and development projects, with annex.
Signed at Washington and Seoul May 29, 1996.
Entered into force May 29, 1996.
TIAS 12761

Memorandum of agreement concerning construction, operation and maintenance of a munitions demilitarization facility (DEFAC) in the Republic of Korea.
Signed at Seoul April 21, 1999.
Entered into force April 21, 1999.
TIAS 13032

Agreement regarding the exchange of engineers and scientists, with annexes.
Signed at Washington June 30, 2000.
Entered into force June 30, 2000.
NP
Amendments and Extension:
May 17 and 27, 2010
February 3 and April 5, 2012
April 10, 2014

Understandings to the agreement under Article IV of the mutual defense treaty regarding facilities and areas and the status of United States armed forces in the Republic of Korea and related agreed minutes, as amended.
Signed at Seoul January 18, 2001.
Entered into force April 2, 2001.
TIAS 13139

Memorandum of understanding on preferential hiring of Korean employees and employment of family members.
Signed at Seoul January 18, 2001.
Entered into force April 2, 2001.
TIAS 13140

Agreement for the land partnership plan, with appendices, annexes, and agreed recommendation.
Signed at Seoul March 29, 2002.
Entered into force March 29, 2002.
TIAS
Amendment:
October 26, 2004

Basic exchange and cooperative agreement concerning geospatial information and services cooperation, with annexes.
Signed at Seoul September 26, 2002.
Entered into force September 26, 2002.
NP

Agreement concerning mutual airlift support utilizing aircraft operated by/for the military forces of the parties in case of military hostilities in the Republic of Korea, with annexes.
Signed at Daejeon and Belleville June 25 and July 6, 2004.
Entered into force August 18, 2004.
TIAS 04-818
Extensions:
August 18, 2009 (TIAS 04-818)
August 18, 2010 (TIAS 04-818)

Memorandum of agreement for mutual aid in fire protection.
Signed at Daegu City September 21 and October 5, 2004.
Entered into force October 5, 2004.
TIAS 04-1005

Memorandum of understanding concerning liquid oxygen support.
Signed at Seoul November 12 and December 6, 2004.
Entered into force December 6, 2004.
TIAS 04-1206

Agreement on the relocation of United States forces from the Seoul metropolitan area.
Signed at Seoul October 26, 2004.
Entered into force December 13, 2004.
TIAS 04-1213

Memorandum of agreement regarding the agreed recommendation for implementation of the agreement on the relocation of United States forces from the Seoul metropolitan area, with annex.
Signed at Seoul October 26, 2004.
Entered into force December 13, 2004.
TIAS 04-1213

Memorandum of understanding international concerning the reduced vertical separation minimum in the Republic of Korea.
Signed at Osan September 29, 2005.
Entered into force September 29, 2005.
TIAS 05-929

Memorandum of understanding regarding assignment of liaison officers.
Signed at Seoul and Norfolk August 29 and November 21, 2005.
Entered into force November 21, 2005.
NP
Amendments and Extensions:
November 11, 2010 (NP)
August 30 and September 12, 2013 (NP)

Memorandum of understanding international concerning combined disaster management, with annexes.
Signed June 7, 2006.
Entered into force June 7, 2006.
TIAS 06-607

Agreement regarding the exchange of naval personnel, with annexes.
Signed March 12 and 30, 2007.
Entered into force March 30, 2007.
NP

Memorandum of agreement concerning the transfer of munitions, equipment, and materiel from United States War Reserve Stockpile for Allies, Korea, with appendices.
Signed at Washington October 17, 2008.
Entered into force November 26, 2008.
TIAS 08.1126.1

Memorandum of agreement concerning communications interoperability and security, with annexes.
Signed October 27, 2008.
Entered into force October 27, 2008.
TIAS 08-1027

Memorandum of understanding concerning cooperation on information assurance (IA) and computer network defense (CND).
Signed at Washington and Seoul April 30, 2009.
Entered into force April 30, 2009.
TIAS 09-430

Agreement regarding the exchange of military personnel.
Signed at Washington July 16 and August 24, 2009.
Entered into force August 24, 2009.
NP

Agreement concerning exchange of research and development information, with appendix.
Signed at Seoul and Washington September 3 and October 13, 2009.
Entered into force October 13, 2009.
TIAS 09-1013

Agreement for research, development, test, and evaluation (RDT&E) projects, with annex.
Signed at Washington November 5, 2009.
Entered into force November 5, 2009.
TIAS 09-1105

Memorandum of agreement regarding the assignment of liaison officers, with annex.
Signed at Seoul and Scott AFB March 5 and April 6, 2010.
Entered into force April 6, 2010.
NP

Basic exchange and cooperation agreement concerning geospatial intelligence.
Signed at Bethesda and Washington November 19, 2010.
Entered into force November 19, 2010.
NP

Agreement regarding the exchange of military personnel for professional military education (PME).
Signed November 3, 2010 and at Seoul December 7, 2010.
Entered into force December 7, 2010.
NP

Agreement concerning special measures relating to Article V of the Agreement under Article IV of the Mutual defense treaty regarding facilities and areas and the status of United States armed forces in the Republic of Korea with implementation arrangement, exchanges of notes and correcting notes.
Signed at Seoul February 2, 2014.
Entered into force June 18, 2014.
TIAS 14-618

Memorandum of agreement regarding the assignment of the Republic of Korea Navy personnel to the U. S. Navy, with annexes.
Signed at Washington September 8 and 11, 2015.
Entered into force September 11, 2015.
NP

Memorandum of agreement regarding the assignment of liaison officers, with annexes.
Signed at Seoul and Stuttgart October 5 and December 3, 2015.
Entered into force December 3, 2015.
NP

DIPLOMATIC & CONSULAR RELATIONS

Consular convention.
Signed at Seoul January 8, 1963.
Entered into force December 19, 1963.
14 UST 1637; TIAS 5469; 493 UNTS 105

EDUCATION

Agreement for financing certain educational exchange programs.
Signed at Seoul June 18, 1963.
Entered into force June 18, 1963.
14 UST 850; TIAS 5366; 487 UNTS 297
Amendments:
June 10 and November 2, 1965 (17 UST 71; TIAS 5960; 586 UNTS 282)
September 24 and November 26, 1971 (22 UST 2056; TIAS 7240)
June 1 and July 10, 1972 (23 UST 1328; TIAS 7415; 852 UNTS 282)

ENERGY

Petroleum agreement of 1964, with agreed minutes.
Signed at Seoul May 12, 1964.
Entered into force September 3, 1964.
15 UST 1412; TIAS 5614; 529 UNTS 299

ENVIRONMENT & CONSERVATION

Agreement for cooperation in the Global Learning and Observations to Benefit the Environment (GLOBE) Program, with appendices.
Signed at Seoul April 21, 1995.
Entered into force April 21, 1995.
TIAS 12635

Agreement on environmental cooperation.
Signed at Washington January 23, 2012.
Entered into force March 15, 2012.
TIAS 12-315

FINANCE

Initial financial and property settlement.*
Signed at Seoul September 11, 1948.
Entered into force September 20, 1948.
62 Stat. 3422; TIAS 1851; 9 Bevans 481; 89 UNTS 155
Amendment:
September 11, 1948 (62 Stat. 3443; TIAS 1851; 9 Bevans 489; 89 UNTS 186)

Note:
* Article VII superseded by electric power agreement of June 13, 1949
(9 UST 509; TIAS 4026; 316 UNTS 278). Agreement superseded in part by article II of agreement on facilities and areas and the status of United States armed forces in Korea of July 9, 1966 (17 UST 1677; TIAS 6127).

Electric power agreement.
Signed at Seoul June 13, 1949.
Entered into force December 28, 1949.
9 UST 509; TIAS 4026; 316 UNTS 278

Agreement regarding expenditures by forces under command of the Commanding General of the Armed Forces of Member States of the United Nations, and exchange of notes of September 5 and 6, 1950.
Signed at Taegu July 28, 1950.
Entered into force July 28, 1950.
1 UST 705; TIAS 2135; 140 UNTS 57

Agreement relating to investment guaranties under section 413(b)(4) of the Mutual Security Act of 1954, as amended.
Exchange of notes at Seoul February 19, 1960.
Entered into force February 19, 1960.
11 UST 202; TIAS 4431; 372 UNTS 109
Amendment:
April 16, 1965 (16 UST 655; TIAS 5790; 546 UNTS 372)

Investment incentive agreement.
Signed at Washington July 30, 1998.
Entered into force July 30, 1998.
TIAS 12980

FISHERIES

Agreement concerning the improvement and standardization of shellfish sanitation practices and exchanges of information on sanitary controls applied to the production and handling of fresh or frozen oysters, clams and mussels, with related notes.
Exchange of notes at Washington November 24, 1972.
Entered into force November 24, 1972.
23 UST 3696; TIAS 7516; 898 UNTS 91

Agreement regarding the collection and exchange of data on fisheries harvests in the international waters of the Bering Sea.
Exchange of notes at Washington April 25 and July 14, 1988.
Entered into force July 14, 1988.
TIAS 11596; 2190 UNTS 239

FOREIGN ASSISTANCE

Agreement on economic coordination between the Republic of Korea and the United States acting as the Unified Command, with exchange of notes and minutes.*
Signed at Pusan May 24, 1952.
Entered into force May 24, 1952.
3 UST 4420; TIAS 2593; 179 UNTS 23

Note:

* Superseded February 28, 1961, with exception of paragraph 13, article III, by agreement of February 8, 1961 (TIAS 4710).

Agreement relating to duty-free entry and defrayment of inland transportation charges on relief supplies and packages, with memorandum of interpretation.
Exchange of notes at Seoul April 22 and May 2, 1955.
Entered into force May 2, 1955.
6 UST 1189; TIAS 3264; 258 UNTS 3

Amendments:

November 9 and December 28, 1962 (13 UST 3838; TIAS 5257; 469 UNTS 428)
May 19, 1971 (22 UST 698; TIAS 7128; 791 UNTS 360)

Agreement for an informational media guaranty program.
Exchange of notes at Seoul April 4, 1958, and September 25, 1959.
Entered into force September 25, 1959.
10 UST 1826; TIAS 4341; 358 UNTS 163

Agreements relating to exemptions from Korean income and social security taxes in connection with economic and technical programs in Korea.
Exchanges of notes at Seoul February 8, 1961.
Entered into force February 8, 1961.
12 UST 976; TIAS 4802; 413 UNTS 392

Agreement providing for economic, technical and related assistance, with agreed minute and related exchange of notes.
Exchange of notes at Seoul February 8, 1961.
Entered into force February 28, 1961.
12 UST 268; TIAS 4710; 405 UNTS 37

Agreement concerning supplemental economic assistance.
Letter of October 16, 1971.
Entered into force October 16, 1971.
28 UST 7591; TIAS 8730

HEALTH & MEDICAL COOPERATION

Agreement relating to the provision of medical treatment to Korean veterans of the Korean and Vietnam conflicts in Veterans Administration hospitals in the United States.
Exchange of notes at Seoul February 3, 1978.
Entered into force February 3, 1978.
30 UST 4479; TIAS 9471; 1170 UNTS 17

INTELLECTUAL PROPERTY

Agreement relating to the reciprocal granting and protection of the right of priority on patents.
Exchange of notes at Seoul October 30, 1978.
Entered into force October 30, 1978.
30 UST 2183; TIAS 9324; 1170 UNTS 23

Record of understanding on intellectual property rights, with related letter.
Signed at Washington August 28, 1986.
Entered into force August 28, 1986.
TIAS 11948

Agreement for the safeguarding of secrecy of inventions relating to defense and for which applications for patents have been made.
Signed at Seoul January 6, 1992.
Entered into force July 29, 1993.
TIAS 12445; 1751 UNTS 153

LAW ENFORCEMENT

Agreement on mutual customs service assistance.
Signed at Washington November 3, 1986.
Entered into force March 10, 1987.
TIAS 12010

Treaty on mutual legal assistance in criminal matters, with annex and exchange of notes.
Signed at Washington November 23, 1993.
Entered into force May 23, 1997.
TIAS

Extradition treaty.
Signed at Washington June 9, 1998.
Entered into force December 20, 1999.
TIAS 12962

Agreement on enhancing cooperation to prevent and combat crime, with annex.
Signed at Washington November 7, 2008.
Entered into force December 29, 2008.
TIAS 08-1229

NONPROLIFERATION

Agreement with respect to the transfer of technologies regarding nuclear safety on technical, economic, and nonproliferation aspects of spent fuel management technologies.
Effected by Exchange of Notes at Washington July 19 and 22, 2013.
Entered into force July 25, 2013.
TIAS 13-725

OCCUPATION & PEACEKEEPING

Arrangement relating to the transfer of authority to the Government of the Republic of Korea and the withdrawal of United States occupation forces.
Exchange of letters at Seoul August 9 and 11, 1948.
Entered into force August 11, 1948.

Agreement concerning interim military and security matters during the transitional period.
Signed at Seoul August 24, 1948.
Entered into force August 24, 1948.
62 Stat. 3817; TIAS 1918; 9 Bevans 477; 79 UNTS 57

POSTAL MATTERS

Parcel post agreement and detailed regulations.
Signed at Seoul and Washington February 17 and April 13, 1949.
Entered into force December 1, 1949.
64 Stat. (3) B46; TIAS 2002; 9 Bevans 500; 74 UNTS 167

Insured parcel post agreement.
Signed at Seoul July 15 and at Washington August 17, 1960.
Entered into force January 1, 1961.
11 UST 2456; TIAS 4630; 400 UNTS 339

International express mail agreement, with detailed regulations.
Signed at Seoul and Washington December 27, 1979, and January 14, 1980.
Entered into force March 1, 1980.
32 UST 4343; TIAS 9951; 1274 UNTS 3

Memorandum of understanding concerning the operation of the INTELPOST field trial, with details of implementation.
Signed at Seoul and Washington February 19 and March 4, 1985.
Entered into force March 4, 1985.
TIAS 11244

PUBLICATIONS

Agreement for the exchange of official publications.
Exchange of notes at Seoul April 18 and September 24, 1966.
Entered into force September 24, 1966.
17 UST 1552; TIAS 6110; 607 UNTS 157

RULES OF WAR

Memorandum of agreement on the transfer of prisoners of war/civilian internees.
Signed at Seoul February 12, 1982.
Entered into force February 12, 1982.
34 UST 1173; TIAS 10406; 1734 UNTS 295

SCIENTIFIC & TECHNICAL COOPERATION

Agreement relating to scientific and technical cooperation, with annexes.
Signed at Washington July 2, 1999.
Entered into force July 2, 1999; effective April 29, 1999.
TIAS 99-702

Extensions:
June 24 and 25, 2004 (TIAS 99-702)
July 1 and 7, 2009 (TIAS 99-702)
July 31, 2015 (TIAS 15-731)
February 1 and 22, 2016 (TIAS 16-222)

Memorandum of understanding concerning scientific and technical cooperation in the earth sciences.
Signed at Seoul and Reston February 14 and March 5, 2002.
Entered into force March 5, 2002.
TIAS 02-305

Amendments and Extension:
May 15 and 19, 2006 (TIAS 02-305)
October 4, 2011 (TIAS 11-1004)

Memorandum of understanding concerning scientific and technical cooperation in the earth and marine sciences.
Signed at Ansan and Reston November 4, 2005, and January 5, 2006.
Entered into force January 5, 2006.
TIAS 06-105

Agreement concerning the Korean seismic research station Wonju, Republic of Korea, with appendices.
Signed at Seoul December 22, 2006.
Entered into force December 27, 2006.
TIAS 06-1227

Arrangement for cooperation in the area of high-energy and nuclear physics research and related fields.
Signed at Washington May 12, 2011.
Entered into force May 12, 2011.
TIAS 11-512

SOCIAL SECURITY

Agreement on social security, with administrative arrangement.
Signed at Washington March 13, 2000.
Entered into force April 1, 2001.
TIAS

SPACE

Agreement for cooperation in aeronautics and the exploration and use of airspace and outer space for civil and peaceful purposes.
Signed at Seoul April 27, 2016.
Entered into force November 3, 2016.
TIAS 16-1103

TAXATION

Convention for the avoidance of double taxation and the prevention of fiscal evasion with respect to taxes on income and the encouragement of international trade and investment, with related notes.
Signed at Seoul June 4, 1976.
Entered into force October 20, 1979.
30 UST 5253; TIAS 9506; 1178 UNTS 3

Agreement to improve international tax compliance, with annexes.
Signed at Seoul June 10, 2015.
Entered into force September 8, 2016.
TIAS 16-908

TRADE & INVESTMENT

Treaty of friendship, commerce, and navigation, with protocol.
Signed at Seoul November 28, 1956.
Entered into force November 7, 1957.
8 UST 2217; TIAS 3947; 302 UNTS 281

Agreement on access of United States firms to Korea's insurance markets.
Exchange of letters at Washington August 28, 1986.
Entered into force August 28, 1986.
TIAS
Related Agreement:
September 10, 1987

Agreement relating to limitation of imports of specialty steel from Korea, with annexes and agreed minutes.
Exchange of letters at Washington October 20, 1987.
Entered into force October 20, 1987.
TIAS

Record of understanding concerning market access for cigarettes.
Signed at Washington May 27, 1988.
Entered into force May 27, 1988.
TIAS

Agreement concerning market access for wine and wine products in Korea, with annexes.
Exchange of letters at Washington January 18, 1989.
Entered into force January 18, 1989.
TIAS

Framework agreement for agreements on steel trade liberalization, with appendices and exchange of letters.
Signed at Washington April 20, 1990.
Entered into force April 20, 1990.
TIAS

TRANSPORTATION

Air transport agreement, with annexes.
Signed at Washington June 9, 1998.
Entered into force June 9, 1998.
TIAS 12961
Amendment:
February 27 and March 13, 2007 (TIAS 07-313)

Memorandum of agreement for assistance in developing the civil aviation infrastructure of the Republic of Korea.
Signed May 7, 2002.
Entered into force May 7, 2002.
NP
Amendment:
May 14, 2010

Agreement for the promotion of aviation safety.
Signed at Singapore February 19, 2008.
Entered into force February 19, 2008.
TIAS 08-219

KOSOVO

On February 17, 2008, the Republic of Kosovo declared its independence. For agreements prior to February 17, 2008, see YUGOSLAVIA.

CULTURAL EXCHANGES, PROPERTY & COOPERATION

Agreement on the protection and preservation of certain cultural properties.
Signed at Washington December 14, 2011.
Entered into force December 14, 2011.
TIAS 11-1214

Agreement concerning the program of the Peace Corps in Kosovo.
Signed at Pristina September 9, 2013.
Entered into force September 9, 2013.
TIAS 13-909

DEFENSE

Agreement regarding grants under the Foreign Assistance Act of 1961, as amended, or successor legislation, and the furnishing of defense articles, defense services and related training, including pursuant to the United States International Military Education and Training (IMET) Program.
Exchange of notes at Pristina June 16 and 17, 2008.
Entered into force June 17, 2008.
NP

Agreement on the status of armed forces of the United States of America in the territory of the Republic of Kosovo.
Exchange of notes at Pristina February 18, 2012.
Entered into force June 27, 2012.
TIAS 12-627

Acquisition and cross-servicing agreement, with annexes.
Signed at Pristina and Stuttgart January 10 and 27, 2014.
Entered into force January 27, 2014.
NP

EMPLOYMENT

Agreement relating to the employment of dependents of official government employees.
Exchange of notes at Washington April 3 and 17, 2009.
Entered into force April 17, 2009.
TIAS

FINANCE

Investment incentive agreement.
Signed at Washington June 30, 2009.
Entered into force October 5, 2009.
TIAS 09-1005

FOREIGN ASSISTANCE

Agreement for economic and technical cooperation.
Signed at Pristina March 29, 2012.
Entered into force March 29, 2012.
TIAS 12-329

TAXATION

Agreement to improve international tax compliance and to implement the Foreign Account Tax Compliance Act.
Signed at Pristina February 26, 2015.
Entered into force November 4, 2015.
TIAS 15-1104

WEAPONS

Agreement concerning cooperation in the area of the prevention of proliferation of weapons of mass destruction.
Signed at Pristina May 23, 2012.
Entered into force June 28, 2012.
TIAS 12-628

KUWAIT

CLAIMS & DISPUTE RESOLUTION

Adherence by the United States to the "Guidelines for the work of bilateral committees to be formed to resolve certain issues involving the State of Kuwait and other states relating to overlapping claims and stand-alone claims at the United Nations Compensation Commission", with attachment.
Signed at Geneva November 19, 2002.
Entered into force November 19, 2002.
TIAS 02-1119

CONSULAR AFFAIRS

Agreement relating to the reciprocal granting of nonimmigrant passport visas.*
Exchange of notes at Kuwait December 11 and 27, 1960.
Entered into force December 27, 1960; operative January 26, 1961.
11 UST 2650; TIAS 4659; 401 UNTS 185
Note:
* The status of this agreement is under review.

DEFENSE

Agreement concerning the procurement of defense articles and defense services by Kuwait and the establishment of a U.S. Liaison Office in Kuwait.
Exchange of notes at Kuwait February 24 and April 15, 1975.
Entered into force April 15, 1975.
26 UST 682; TIAS 8066; 992 UNTS 199

Technical security arrangement.
Signed at Kuwait January 18, 1976.
Entered into force January 18, 1976.
27 UST 4177; TIAS 8444; 1071 UNTS 377
Amendment:
June 26, 1977 (29 UST 1874; TIAS 8905)

Basic exchange and cooperative agreement for geospatial information and services.
Signed at Washington and Kuwait August 7, 1998.
Entered into force August 7, 1998.
NP

Acquisition and cross-servicing agreement.
Signed at Camp Arifjan November 1, 2013.
Entered into force November 1, 2013.
NP

DIPLOMATIC & CONSULAR RELATIONS

Consular convention between the United States and the United Kingdom.
Signed at Washington June 6, 1951.
Entered into force September 7, 1952.
3 UST 3426; TIAS 2494; 165 UNTS 121

FINANCE

Agreement on investment guaranties.
Signed at Kuwait April 24, 1989.
Entered into force October 24, 1989.
TIAS 12071

LAW ENFORCEMENT

Agreement on procedures for mutual assistance in connection with matters relating to the Boeing Company.
Signed at Washington October 6, 1978.
Entered into force October 6, 1978.
NP
Related Agreement:
December 21, 1978, and January 2, 1979 (NP)

POSTAL MATTERS

Agreement concerning the exchange of parcel post and regulations of execution.
Signed at Kuwait October 9, 1963, and at Washington October 21, 1963.
Entered into force September 16, 1964.
15 UST 1841; TIAS 5658; 530 UNTS 281

International express mail agreement with detailed regulations.
Signed at Kuwait and Washington February 28 and March 11, 1981.
Entered into force April 1, 1981.
33 UST 1353; TIAS 10114; 1285 UNTS 29

SCIENTIFIC & TECHNICAL COOPERATION

Memorandum of understanding concerning scientific and technical cooperation in the earth sciences, with annexes.
Signed at Reston February 17, 2011.
Entered into force February 17, 2011.
TIAS 11-217

TAXATION

Memorandum of understanding for the reciprocal tax exemption on income derived from the operation of aircraft.
Signed at Kuwait March 28, 2011.
Entered into force March 12, 2014.
TIAS 14-312

Agreement to improve international tax compliance and to implement the Foreign Account Tax Compliance Act, with annexes.
Signed at Kuwait April 29, 2015.
Entered into force January 28, 2016.
TIAS 16-128

TELECOMMUNICATION

Agreement relating to the reciprocal granting of authorizations to permit licensed amateur radio operators of either country to operate their stations in the other country.
Exchange of notes at Kuwait July 19 and 24, 1966.
Entered into force July 19, 1966.
17 UST 1039; TIAS 6061; 593 UNTS 289

Agreement for the establishment and operation of a United States radio relay station in the State of Kuwait.
Signed at Kuwait August 2, 1992.
Entered into force August 29, 1992.
TIAS 12469

TRANSPORTATION

Agreement on aviation security.
Exchange of notes at Kuwait November 22, 1987, and January 11, 1988.
Entered into force July 5, 1988.
TIAS 12023

Air transport agreement, with annexes.
Signed at Kuwait August 30, 2006.
Entered into force May 27, 2007.
TIAS 07-527

KYRGYZ REPUBLIC

NOTE: For agreements prior to December 31, 1991, see UNION OF SOVIET SOCIALIST REPUBLICS.

CULTURAL EXCHANGES, PROPERTY & COOPERATION

Agreement concerning the activity of the Peace Corps in Kyrgyzstan.
Signed at Washington November 5, 1992.
Entered into force November 5, 1992.
TIAS 11502

DEFENSE

Agreement regarding grants under the Foreign Assistance Act of 1961, as amended, or successor legislation, and the furnishing of defense articles, defense services and related training, including pursuant to the United States International Military Education and Training (IMET) Program.
Exchange of notes at Bishkek April 11 and November 13, 2008.
Entered into force November 13, 2008.
NP

Agreement regarding acquisition of fuel for operations at the transit center.
Signed at Bishkek February 8, 2011.
Entered into force April 22, 2011.
TIAS 11-422

EMPLOYMENT

Agreement relating to the employment of dependents of official government employees.
Exchange of notes at Washington December 6 and 22, 1993.
Entered into force December 22, 1993.
TIAS 12170

ENVIRONMENT & CONSERVATION

Agreement for cooperation in the Global Learning and Observations to Benefit the Environment (GLOBE) Program, with appendices.
Signed at Washington June 9, 1995.
Entered into force June 9, 1995.
TIAS 12658

FINANCE

Investment incentive agreement.
Signed at Washington May 8, 1992.
Entered into force May 8, 1992.
TIAS 12452

FOREIGN ASSISTANCE

Agreement regarding cooperation to facilitate the provision of assistance.
Signed at Washington May 19, 1993.
Entered into force May 19, 1993.
TIAS 12152

NONPROLIFERATION

Memorandum of understanding concerning prevention of illicit trafficking in nuclear and other radioactive material.
Signed at Bishkek August 15, 2008.
Entered into force August 15, 2008.
TIAS 08-815.1

TRADE & INVESTMENT

Agreement on trade relations, with related exchanges of letters.
Signed at Washington May 8, 1992.
Entered into force August 21, 1992.
TIAS

Treaty concerning the encouragement and reciprocal protection of investment, with annex.
Signed at Washington January 19, 1993.
Entered into force January 12, 1994.
TIAS

L

LAOS

DEFENSE

Agreement relating to the assurances required by the Mutual Security Act of 1951.
Exchange of notes at Vientiane December 18 and 31, 1951.
Entered into force December 31, 1951.
3 UST 4622; TIAS 2613; 198 UNTS 243

Memorandum of understanding concerning payment to the United States of the net proceeds from the sale of defense articles furnished under the military assistance program.
Signed at Vientiane May 31, 1974.
Entered into force May 31, 1974; effective July 1, 1974.
27 UST 2989; TIAS 8357; 1066 UNTS 115

Agreement regarding the furnishing of defense articles, related training and other defense services from the United States to Laos.
Exchange of notes at Vientiane December 7, 1992, and September 29, 1993.
Entered into force September 29, 1993.
TIAS 12346

FINANCE

Investment incentive agreement.
Signed at Washington March 8, 1996.
Entered into force March 26, 1996.
TIAS 12733; 2473 UNTS 273

FOREIGN ASSISTANCE

Economic cooperation agreement, with annex and exchange of notes.
Signed at Vientiane September 9, 1951.
Entered into force September 9, 1951.
2 UST 2177; TIAS 2344; 174 UNTS 141

Agreement providing for additional direct economic assistance.
Exchange of notes at Vientiane July 6 and 8, 1955.
Entered into force July 8, 1955; operative January 1, 1955.
7 UST 2833; TIAS 3664; 278 UNTS 59

Memorandum of understanding concerning prosthetics and rehabilitation assistance.
Signed at Vientiane May 15, 1990.
Entered into force May 15, 1990.
TIAS 11721; 2207 UNTS 291

INTERNATIONAL CRIMINAL COURT

Agreement regarding the surrender of persons to international tribunals.
Signed at Vientiane December 24, 2003.
Entered into force December 24, 2003.
TIAS 03-1224

LAW ENFORCEMENT

Memorandum of understanding concerning cooperation on narcotics issues.
Signed at Vientiane January 9, 1990.
Entered into force January 9, 1990.
TIAS 12407

POSTAL MATTERS

International express mail agreement.
Signed at Vientiane and Washington September 10 and October 16, 1991.
Entered into force November 16, 1991.
NP

TRANSPORTATION

Air transport agreement, with annex.
Signed at Washington July 13, 2010.
Entered into force July 13, 2010.
TIAS 10-713

LATVIA

CLAIMS & DISPUTE RESOLUTION

Treaty of conciliation.
Signed at Riga January 14, 1930.
Entered into force July 10, 1930.
46 Stat. 2766; TS 819; 9 Bevans 548; 105 LNTS 301

Treaty of arbitration.
Signed at Riga January 14, 1930.
Entered into force July 10, 1930.
46 Stat. 2763; TS 818; 9 Bevans 546; 105 LNTS 307

CONSULAR AFFAIRS

Agreement for the reciprocal waiver of passport visa fees for nonimmigrants.*
Exchange of notes at Riga February 18 and March 27, 1935.
Entered into force March 27, 1935; operative April 1, 1935.
9 Bevans 556

Note:

* The status of this agreement is under review.

CULTURAL EXCHANGES, PROPERTY & COOPERATION

Agreement concerning the program of the Peace Corps of the United States in Latvia.
Signed at Riga February 6, 1992.
Entered into force February 6, 1992.
TIAS 12081

Agreement on the protection and preservation of certain cultural properties.
Signed at Riga October 7, 2002.
Entered into force November 12, 2004.
TIAS 04-1112

DEFENSE

Agreement concerning the provision of training related to defense articles under the United States International Military Education and Training (IMET) Program.
Exchange of notes at Riga February 21 and March 4, 1992.
Entered into force March 4, 1992.
NP

Agreement regarding grants under the Foreign Assistance Act of 1961, as amended, or successor legislation, and the furnishing of defense articles, related training, or other defense services from the United States to Latvia.
Exchange of notes at Riga February19 and April 12, 1993.
Entered into force April 12, 1993.
NP

Basic exchange and cooperative agreement for topographic mapping, nautical and aeronautical charting, geodesy and geophysics, digital data and related mapping, charting and geodesy materials, with attachment.
Signed at Riga August 24, 1993.
Entered into force August 24, 1993.
NP

Agreement concerning security measures for the protection of classified military information.
Signed at Washington January 15, 1998.
Entered into force January 15, 1998.
TIAS 12922

Agreement regarding U.S. government equipment and provision of logistic support services to Polish-led multinational division and its members in support of Peacekeeping Operations (PKO) in Iraq.
Exchange of notes at Riga August 22 and September 18, 2003.
Entered into force September 18, 2003.
TIAS

Basic exchange and cooperative agreement concerning global geospatial information and services cooperation, with annexes.
Signed at Riga May 18, 2004.
Entered into force May 18, 2004.
NP

Acquisition and cross-servicing agreement, with annexes.
Signed at Riga and Stuttgart October 1 and 15, 2008.
Entered into force October 15, 2008.
NP

Agreement regarding access to and use of facilities and areas located within the Republic of Latvia.
Exchange of notes at Riga June 19 and July 15, 2015.
Entered into force July 15, 2015.
TIAS 15-715.1

DIPLOMATIC & CONSULAR RELATIONS

Memorandum of understanding concerning diplomatic relations.
Signed at Riga September 5, 1991.
Entered into force September 5, 1991.
TIAS 12132

EDUCATION

Agreement concerning the status of private educational institution "The International School of Latvia".
Signed at Riga March 12, 2003.
Entered into force August 29, 2006.
TIAS 06-829

EMPLOYMENT

Agreement relating to the employment of dependents of official government employees.
Exchange of notes at Riga April 24 and July 16, 1996.
Entered into force July 16, 1996.
TIAS 12781

ENVIRONMENT & CONSERVATION

Agreement for cooperation in the Global Learning and Observations to Benefit the Environment (GLOBE) Program, with appendices.
Signed at Riga January 27, 1999.
Entered into force January 27, 1999.
TIAS 13021

FINANCE

Agreement relating to the funding of the indebtedness of Latvia to the United States.
Signed at Washington September 24, 1925.
Operative December 15, 1922.
Treasury Department print; 9 Bevans 521

Debt funding agreement of September 24, 1925.
Signed at Washington June 11, 1932.
Operative July 1, 1931.
Treasury Department print; 9 Bevans 551

Investment incentive agreement.
Signed at Indianapolis October 28, 1991.
Entered into force October 28, 1991.
TIAS 12440

FOREIGN ASSISTANCE

Agreement concerning economic, technical and related assistance.
Signed at Riga December 20, 1995.
Entered into force February 7, 1996.
TIAS 12713; 2060 UNTS 103

AGENCY FOR INTERNATIONAL DEVELOPMENT

Memorandum of Understanding on assistance through USAID, in the field of justice sector reform.
Signed June 28, 2012.
Entered into force June 28, 2012.
NP

LAW ENFORCEMENT

Memorandum of understanding concerning cooperation in the pursuit of Nazi war criminals.
Signed at Riga September 11, 1992.
Entered into force September 11, 1992.
TIAS 12477

Treaty on mutual legal assistance in criminal matters, with exchange of notes.
Signed at Washington June 13, 1997.
Entered into force September 17, 1999.
TIAS 12867

Agreement regarding mutual assistance between their customs administrations.
Signed at Washington April 17, 1998.
Entered into force July 23, 1999.
TIAS 12944

Extradition treaty.
Signed at Riga December 7, 2005.
Entered into force April 15, 2009.
TIAS 09-415

Protocol to the treaty on mutual legal assistance in criminal matters of June 13, 1997.
Signed at Riga December 7, 2005.
Entered into force February 1, 2010.
TIAS 10-201.37

Agreement on enhancing cooperation in preventing and combating serious crime .
Signed at Riga September 29, 2008.
Entered into force July 20, 2010.
TIAS 10-720.1

NONPROLIFERATION

Agreement concerning cooperation in the area of countering the proliferation of nuclear materials and technologies.
Signed at Washington April 25, 2005.
Entered into force April 25, 2005.
TIAS 05-425.1

Agreement for cooperation in the prevention of illicit trafficking in nuclear and other radioactive material.
Signed at Riga December 3, 2007.
Entered into force December 3, 2007.
TIAS 07-1203

POSTAL MATTERS

International express mail agreement, with detailed regulations.
Signed at Washington April 17, 1992.
Entered into force April 17, 1992.
TIAS 11860

SCIENTIFIC & TECHNICAL COOPERATION

Agreement on science and technology cooperation, with annex.
Signed at Riga July 6, 1994.
Entered into force July 6, 1994.
TIAS 12187

Extension:

May 24 and September 7, 2000

TAXATION

Convention for the avoidance of double taxation and the prevention of fiscal evasion with respect to taxes on income.
Signed at Washington January 15, 1998.
Entered into force December 30, 1999.
TIAS 12920

Agreement to improve international tax compliance and to implement the Foreign Account Tax Compliance Act, with annexes.
Signed at Riga June 27, 2014.
Entered into force December 15, 2014.
TIAS 14-1215

TRADE & INVESTMENT

Provisional commercial agreement according mutual unconditional most-favored-nation treatment in customs matters.
Signed at Riga February 1, 1926.
Entered into force April 30, 1926.
TS 740; 9 Bevans 528; 55 LNTS 33

Treaty of friendship, commerce, and consular rights.
Signed at Riga April 20, 1928.
Entered into force July 25, 1928.
45 Stat. 2641; TS 765; 9 Bevans 531; 80 LNTS 35

Agreement on trade relations and intellectual property rights protection.
Signed at Riga July 6, 1994.
Entered into force January 20, 1995.
TIAS

Treaty concerning the encouragement and reciprocal protection of investment, with annex and protocol.
Signed at Washington January 13, 1995.
Entered into force December 26, 1996.
TIAS 96-1226

Additional protocol to the treaty between the United States of America and the Republic of Latvia for the encouragement and reciprocal protection of investment of January 13, 1995.
Signed at Brussels September 22, 2003.
Entered into force July 14, 2004.
TIAS 04-714.1

WEAPONS

Agreement concerning technical assistance related to the elimination of conventional weapons systems and facilities formerly controlled by the Russian Federation Armed Forces stationed in the territory of the Republic of Latvia.
Signed at Riga August 12, 1994.
Entered into force August 12, 1994.
TIAS

Agreement concerning cooperation in the area of the prevention of proliferation of weapons of mass destruction.
Signed at Washington December 11, 2001.
Entered into force May 5, 2003.
TIAS 03-505
Extension:
May 4, 2010 (TIAS 03-505)

LEBANON

ATOMIC ENERGY

Agreement providing for a grant to the Government of Lebanon to assist in the acquisition of nuclear research and training equipment and supplies.
Exchange of notes at Beirut September 16, 1959.
Entered into force September 16, 1959.
10 UST 1834; TIAS 4343; 358 UNTS 175

DEFENSE

Agreement relating to reimbursable military aid.
Exchange of notes at Beirut March 6 and 23, 1953.
Entered into force March 23, 1953.
5 UST 2908; TIAS 3147; 239 UNTS 45

Military assistance agreement.
Exchange of notes at Beirut June 3 and 6, 1957.
Entered into force June 6, 1957.
8 UST 943; TIAS 3855; 284 UNTS 155
Amendment:
June 9 and 12, 1958 (9 UST 927; TIAS 4055; 317 UNTS 350)

Agreement relating to the deposit by Lebanon of ten percent of the value of grant military assistance furnished by the United States.
Exchange of notes at Beirut April 12 and May 8, 1972.
Entered into force May 8, 1972; effective February 7, 1972.
23 UST 687; TIAS 7334

Agreement regarding grants under the Foreign Assistance Act of 1961, as amended, and the furnishing of defense articles, related training and other defense services from the United States to Lebanon.
Exchange of notes at Beirut June 21 and July 18, 1994.
Entered into force July 18, 1994.
TIAS 12347

Acquisition and cross-servicing agreement.
Signed at Beirut May 3 and 20, 2006.
Entered into force September 30, 2006.
NP

DIPLOMATIC & CONSULAR RELATIONS

Convention between the United States and France relating to rights in Syria and Lebanon.
Signed at Paris April 4, 1924.
Entered into force July 13, 1924.
43 Stat. 1821; TS 695; 7 Bevans 925

Agreement between the United States and France relating to customs privileges for educational, religious, and philanthropic institutions in Syria and Lebanon.
Exchange of notes at Paris February 18, 1937.
Entered into force February 18, 1937.
51 Stat. 279; EAS 107; 7 Bevans 1017; 184 LNTS 479

Agreement relating to rights of American nationals.
Exchange of notes at Beirut September 7 and 8, 1944.
Entered into force September 8, 1944.
58 Stat. 1493; EAS 435; 9 Bevans 562; 124 UNTS 187

ENVIRONMENT & CONSERVATION

Agreement for cooperation in the Global Learning and Observations to Benefit the Environment (GLOBE) Program, with appendices.
Signed at Antelias December 23, 1998.
Entered into force December 23, 1998.
TIAS

FINANCE

Investment incentive agreement.
Exchange of notes at Beirut September 17, 1980, and February 10, 1981.
Entered into force April 30, 1981.
33 UST 861; TIAS 10070; 1280 UNTS 471

FOREIGN ASSISTANCE

General agreement for technical cooperation.
Signed at Beirut May 29, 1951.
Entered into force December 13, 1951.
3 UST 2843; TIAS 2457; 160 UNTS 49

Agreement relating to the assurances required under section 511(b) of the Mutual Security Act of 1951.
Exchange of notes at Beirut December 26, 1951, and January 5, 1952.
Entered into force January 5, 1952.
3 UST 4751; TIAS 2639; 180 UNTS 199

Technical cooperation program agreement.
Signed at Beirut June 26, 1952.
Entered into force June 26, 1952.
3 UST 4860; TIAS 2659; 181 UNTS 187
Amendments:
April 14, 1953 (4 UST 1563; TIAS 2821; 212 UNTS 360)
April 30, 1954 (5 UST 1078; TIAS 2991; 247 UNTS 442)

Agreement relating to special economic assistance.
Exchange of notes at Beirut June 11 and 18, 1954.
Entered into force June 18, 1954.
5 UST 1392; TIAS 3009; 233 UNTS 177

Agreement granting special assistance to Lebanon for budgetary support.
Exchange of notes at Beirut September 2 and 3, 1958.
Entered into force September 3, 1958.
9 UST 1260; TIAS 4113; 336 UNTS 91

AGENCY FOR INTERNATIONAL DEVELOPMENT

Grant agreement for post-conflict cash transfer assistance.
Signed December 17, 2007.
Entered into force December 17, 2007.
NP

Amendment:
April 8, 2009 (NP)

LAW ENFORCEMENT

Grant agreement for a cooperative program to curtail illicit traffic in narcotics and dangerous drugs.
Signed at Beirut June 29, 1973.
Entered into force June 29, 1973.
24 UST 1672; TIAS 7673

Letter of agreement on law enforcement, with annex.
Signed at Beirut October 5, 2007.
Entered into force October 5, 2007.
NP

OCCUPATION & PEACEKEEPING

Agreement on United States participation in a multinational force in Beirut.
Exchange of notes at Beirut August 18 and 20, 1982.
Entered into force August 20, 1982.
34 UST 1833; TIAS 10463; 1751 UNTS 3

Agreement on United States participation in a multinational force in Beirut.
Exchange of notes at Beirut September 25, 1982.
Entered into force September 25, 1982.
TIAS 10509; 1777 UNTS 363

TRANSPORTATION

Air transport agreement, with exchange of notes.
Signed at Beirut September 1, 1972.
Entered into force provisionally September 1, 1972; definitively June 5, 1974.
24 UST 245; TIAS 7546

Agreement relating to air transport route rights.
Exchange of notes at Beirut September 24 and October 13, 1977.
Entered into force October 13, 1977.
28 UST 7479; TIAS 8722; 1087 UNTS 313

Agreement relating to air transport route rights.
Exchange of notes at Washington December 22, 1982.
Entered into force December 22, 1982.
34 UST 2358; TIAS 10489; 1751 UNTS 17

Amendment:
April 29, 1983 (TIAS 10701; 2005 UNTS 536)

LESOTHO

In a note dated September 7, 1971, to the Secretary General of the United Nations, the Minister of Foreign Affairs of Lesotho made a Declaration reading in part as follows:

Reference is made to the Declarations of the Government of the Kingdom of Lesotho in relation to its treaty relationships dated 22 March 1967 and 5 March 1969.

As regards bilateral treaties validly concluded by the Government of the United Kingdom on behalf of the country formerly known as Basutoland, or validly applied or extended by the said Government to the country known as Basutoland, the Government of the Kingdom of Lesotho, it will be recalled, willingly undertook to apply within its territory, on a basis of reciprocity, the terms of all such treaties from the date of Independence until October 4, 1970, unless abrogated or modified earlier by mutual consent. That time has now expired before it has been possible to evaluate all the treaties.

The Government of the Kingdom of Lesotho, mindful of the desirability of the continuity of treaty relationships consistent with its independent status, and desirous of continuing negotiations with the various States concerned in relation to the possible continuation, modification or termination of such treaties, has decided that the period during which it will apply, on a basis of reciprocity, the terms of such bilateral treaties shall be extended without limit of time, pending the reaching of a satisfactory accord with each State concerned.

Nothing in this Declaration shall, however, be held to constitute a succession to treaties which are not consistent with the accession to full sovereign status by the Kingdom of Lesotho, nor shall it be held to constitute an extension or renewal of treaties which, by virtue of their termination clauses, have already expired or have been terminated before the date of this Declaration.

Under the terms of the Declaration of the Government of the Kingdom of Lesotho of 22 March 1967 it is not necessary to extend the period in relation to multilateral treaties. As represented in that Declaration, the Government of the Kingdom of Lesotho will review each of the multilateral treaties which has been applied or extended to the country formerly known as Basutoland and indicate to the depositary concerned what steps it desires to take in relation to such instrument.

During this period of review, as stated in the Declaration of 22 March 1967, any party to a multilateral treaty which has, prior to independence, been applied or extended to the country known as Basutoland, may, on a basis of reciprocity, rely as against Lesotho on the terms of such treaty, the Government of the Kingdom of Lesotho wishes it to be understood, as stated in its Declaration of 5 March 1969, that this is merely a transitional arrangement. Under no circumstances should it be implied that by these Declarations of Lesotho has either acceded to any particular treaty or indicated continuity of any particular treaty by way of succession.

CULTURAL EXCHANGES, PROPERTY & COOPERATION

Agreement concerning the program of the Peace Corps in the Kingdom of Lesotho.
Signed at Maseru on April 13, 2016.
Entered into force April 13, 2016.
TIAS 16-413

FINANCE

Agreement relating to investment guaranties.
Signed at Maseru February 24, 1967.
Entered into force March 7, 1967.
18 UST 273; TIAS 6227; 688 UNTS 275

FOREIGN ASSISTANCE

Agreement for economic, technical and related assistance.
Signed at Maseru October 17, 1984.
Entered into force October 17, 1984.
TIAS 11167; 2126 UNTS 145

INTELLECTUAL PROPERTY

Declaration by the United States and the United Kingdom affording reciprocal protection to trade-marks.
Signed at London October 24, 1877.
Entered into force October 24, 1877.
20 Stat. 703; TS 138; 12 Bevans 198

INTERNATIONAL CRIMINAL COURT

Agreement regarding the surrender of persons to the international criminal court.
Signed at Maseru June 21, 2006.
Entered into force June 21, 2006.
TIAS 06-621

LAW ENFORCEMENT

Extradition treaty between the United States and the United Kingdom.
Signed at London December 22, 1931.
Entered into force June 24, 1935.
47 Stat. 2122; TS 849; 12 Bevans 482; 163 LNTS 59

POSTAL MATTERS

International express mail agreement, with detailed regulations.
Signed at Maseru and Washington June 19 and July 20, 1990.
Entered into force August 30, 1990.
TIAS 11737

PROPERTY

Convention between the United States and the United Kingdom relating to the tenure and disposition of real and personal property.
Signed at Washington March 2, 1899.
Applicable to Basutoland July 24, 1902.
31 Stat. 1939; TS 146; 12 Bevans 246

Supplementary convention relating to the tenure and disposition of real and personal property of March 2, 1899.
Signed at Washington May 27, 1936.
Entered into force March 10, 1941.
55 Stat. 1101; TS 964; 5 Bevans 140; 203 LNTS 367

LIBERIA

CLAIMS & DISPUTE RESOLUTION

Arbitration convention with exchange of notes.
Signed at Monrovia February 10, 1926.
Entered into force September 27, 1926.
44 Stat. 2438; TS 747; 9 Bevans 585; 88 LNTS 346

Treaty of conciliation.
Signed at Monrovia August 21, 1939.
Entered into force March 13, 1941.
55 Stat. 1137; TS 968; 9 Bevans 618; 204 LNTS 165

CONSULAR AFFAIRS

Agreement relating to the waiver of passport visa fees for nonimmigrants.*
Signed at Monrovia August 31, 1925.
Entered into force August 31, 1925; operative September 1, 1925.
9 Bevans 584

Arrangement relating to the period of validity of temporary visitors' visas.*
Exchange of notes at Monrovia October 27 and 28, 1947.
Entered into force October 28, 1947; operative December 1, 1947.
62 Stat. 3930; TIAS 2021; 9 Bevans 641; 82 UNTS 23

Note:
* The status of this agreement is under review.

CULTURAL EXCHANGES, PROPERTY & COOPERATION

Agreement concerning the program of the Peace Corps in Liberia.
Signed at Monrovia August 15, 2008.
Entered into force August 15, 2008.
TIAS 08-815

DEFENSE

Agreement relating to mutual defense assistance.
Exchange of notes at Washington November 16 and 19, 1951.
Entered into force November 19, 1951.
3 UST 2805; TIAS 2450; 167 UNTS 141

Agreement relating to the use of Roberts Field by the United Stated Government during an national emergency.
Exchange of notes at Washington May 10, June 29, July 6 and July 13, 1954.
Entered into force July 13, 1954.
TIAS

Agreement relating to the transfer to Liberia of certain property located at Roberts Field, Liberia.
Exchange of notes at Washington April 19, 1955, and August 21 and September 22, 1956.
Entered into force January 4, 1957.
8 UST 141; TIAS 3751; 278 UNTS 109

Understanding that the assurances contained in the agreement of November 16 and 19, 1951, are applicable to equipment, materials, information, and services furnished under the Mutual Security Act of 1954, as amended, and such other applicable U.S. laws as may come into effect.
Exchange of notes at Monrovia April 10 and July 19, 1958.
Entered into force July 19, 1958.
10 UST 1995; TIAS 4367; 361 UNTS 316

Agreement of cooperation.
Signed at Washington July 8, 1959.
Entered into force July 8, 1959.
10 UST 1598; TIAS 4303; 357 UNTS 93

Agreement concerning the furnishing of military equipment and materials to Liberia.
Exchange of notes at Monrovia May 23 and June 17, 1961.
Entered into force June 17, 1961.
12 UST 876; TIAS 4788; 410 UNTS 233
Amendment:
January 18 and 23, 1962 (13 UST 58; TIAS 4935; 433 UNTS 390)

Agreement relating to the transfer of the Port of Monrovia to Liberia.
Exchange of notes at Monrovia April 13 and 14, 1964.
Entered into force April 14, 1964.
15 UST 641; TIAS 5583; 526 UNTS 221

Agreement relating to the deposit by Liberia of ten percent of the value of grant military assistance and excess defense articles furnished by the United States.
Exchange of notes at Monrovia April 27 and May 10, 1972.
Entered into force May 10, 1972; effective February 7, 1972.
23 UST 886; TIAS 7350

Agreement on construction of additional facilities at Roberts International Airport.
Signed at Monrovia February 3, 1983.
Entered into force February 3, 1983.
TIAS 10677
Amendment:
March 25 and April 4, 1983 (TIAS 10677)

Agreement regarding the status of United States personnel who may be temporarily present in Liberia.
Exchange of notes at Monrovia April 15 and 20, 2005.
Entered into force April 20, 2005.
TIAS 05-420.2

Acquisition and cross-servicing agreement, with annexes.
Signed at Monrovia April 18, 2007.
Entered into force April 18, 2007.
TIAS 07-418

Agreement regarding the provision of articles and services pursuant to Section 1206 of the National Defense Authorization Act for fiscal year 2007, as modified and extended, or successor legislation.
Exchange of notes at Monrovia July 30 and August 1, 2007.
Entered into force August 1, 2007.
NP

Agreement regarding grants under the Foreign Assistance Act of 1961, as amended, or successor legislation, and the furnishing of defense articles, defense services and related training, including pursuant to the United States International Military Education and Training (IMET) Program.
Effected by exchange of notes at Monrovia June 2 and September 22, 2010.
Entered into force September 22, 2010.
NP

DIPLOMATIC & CONSULAR RELATIONS

Consular convention.
Signed at Monrovia October 7, 1938.
Entered into force December 21, 1939.
54 Stat. 1751; TS 957; 9 Bevans 607; 201 LNTS 183

Agreement relating to privileges, on a reciprocal basis, of free entry to all articles imported for the personal use of diplomatic and consular personnel.
Exchange of notes at Washington May 2 and July 22, 1949.
Entered into force July 22, 1949.
5 UST 734; TIAS 2961; 232 UNTS 283

EDUCATION

Agreement for financing certain educational exchange programs.
Signed at Monrovia May 8, 1964.
Entered into force May 8, 1964.
15 UST 660; TIAS 5586; 526 UNTS 239

EMPLOYMENT

Agreement relating to the employment of dependents of official government employees.
Exchange of notes at Washington October 2 and 16, 1984.
Entered into force October 16, 1984.
TIAS

FINANCE

Agreement relating to investment guaranties under section 413(b)(4) of the Mutual Security Act of 1954, as amended.*
Exchange of notes at Monrovia September 6 and 12, 1960.
Entered into force September 12, 1960.
11 UST 2119; TIAS 4571; 389 UNTS 245
Amendment:
September 26 and 29, 1964 (15 UST 2064; TIAS 5686; 533 UNTS 348)
December 15, 2006

Note:
* Subparagraphs (d) and (e) of paragraph 3 terminated September 29, 1964.

Agreement regarding the consolidation and rescheduling of certain debts owed to, or guaranteed by the United States Government and its agencies, with annexes.
Signed at Monrovia May 7, 1981.
Entered into force June 29, 1981.
33 UST 1929; TIAS 10156

Agreement regarding the consolidation and rescheduling of payments due under P.L. 480 Title I agricultural commodity agreement, with annexes.
Signed at Monrovia October 15, 1981.
Entered into force October 15, 1981.
33 UST 1945; TIAS 10157

Agreements regarding the consolidation and rescheduling of certain debts owed to, or guaranteed by the United States Government and its agencies, with annexes.
Signed at Monrovia October 19, 1982.
Entered into force December 22, 1982.
TIAS 10528; 1777 UNTS 393

Agreement regarding the consolidation and rescheduling of certain debts owed to or guaranteed by the United States Government and its agencies, with annexes and implementing agreement regarding payments due under P.L. 480 agricultural commodity agreements, with annexes.
Signed at Monrovia June 22, 1984.
Entered into force July 27, 1984.
TIAS 10995; 2022 UNTS 85

Agreement regarding the consolidation and rescheduling of certain debts owed to, guaranteed by or insured by the United States Government and its agencies, with annexes and implementing agreement regarding payments due under P.L. 480 agricultural commodity agreements.
Signed at Monrovia May 3, 1985.
Entered into force June 24, 1985.
NP

Agreement regarding the reduction of certain debts owed to, guaranteed by, or insured by the United States Government and its agencies, with annexes.
Signed at Monrovia June 12, 2008.
Entered into force August 12, 2008.
NP

Agreement regarding the reduction of certain debts owed to, guaranteed by, or insured by the United States Government and its agencies, with annexes.
Signed at Monrovia November 30, 2010.
Entered into force February 22, 2011.
NP

FOREIGN ASSISTANCE

Memorandum of understanding on the Joint Liberian-United States Commission for Economic Development.
Signed at Monrovia October 6, 1955.
Entered into force October 6, 1955; operative February 3, 1956.
7 UST 600; TIAS 3541; 275 UNTS 87

General agreement for technical assistance and cooperation.
Signed at Monrovia October 6, 1955.
Entered into force February 3, 1956.
7 UST 603; TIAS 3542; 275 UNTS 93

AGENCY FOR INTERNATIONAL DEVELOPMENT

Agreement for economic growth, with attachments.
Signed September 28, 2007.
Entered into force September 28, 2007.
NP

Amendments:
September 12, 2008 (NP)
January 12 and 26, 2009 (NP)
August 21, 2009 (NP)
September 30, 2009 (NP)
December 3, 2009 (NP)
July 17 and September 17, 2010 (NP)
September 30, 2011 (NP)

Agreement for investing in people: health, with attachments.
Signed September 28, 2007.
Entered into force September 28, 2007.
NP

Amendments:
September 12, 2008 (NP)
September 25 and 26, 2008 (NP)
August 21, 2009 (NP)
September 30, 2009 (NP)
December 3, 2009 (NP)
September 17, 2010 (NP)
September 30, 2011 (NP)

Agreement for investing in people: education.
Signed September 28, 2007.
Entered into force September 28, 2007.
NP

Amendments:
September 12, 2008 (NP)
August 21, 2009 (NP)
December 3, 2009 (NP)
September 17, 2010 (NP)
September 30, 2011 (NP)

Agreement for governing justly and democratically.
Signed September 28, 2007.
Entered into force September 28, 2007.
NP

Signed:
September 12, 2008 (NP)
August 21, 2009 (NP)
December 3, 2009 (NP)
September 17, 2010 (NP)
December 29, 2010 and January 3, 2011 (NP)
September 30, 2011 (NP)

Development objective agreement for USAID Development Objective 1: more effective, accountable and inclusive governance, with annexes.
Signed September 29, 2012.
Entered into force September 29, 2012.
NP

Development objective agreement for USAID Development Objective 2: sustained, market-driven economic growth to reduce poverty, with annexes.
Signed September 29, 2012.
Entered into force September 29, 2012.
NP

Development objective agreement of September 29, 2012, as amended, for improved health status of Liberians, with attachments.
Signed September 29, 2012.
Entered into force September 29, 2012.
NP
Amendment:
September 27 and October 16, 2013 (NP)

Development objective agreement for USAID Development Objective 4: better-educated Liberians, with annexes.
Signed September 29, 2012.
Entered into force September 29, 2012.
NP
Amendment:
September 27 and October 16, 2013 (NP)

HEALTH & MEDICAL COOPERATION

Agreement for cooperation and provision of assistance to respond to Ebola.
Signed at Monrovia November 19, 2014.
Entered into force November 19, 2014.
TIAS 14-1119

INTERNATIONAL CRIMINAL COURT

Agreement regarding the surrender of persons to the International Criminal Court.
Signed at Washington October 8, 2003.
Entered into force November 3, 2003.
TIAS 03-1103

LAW ENFORCEMENT

Treaty of extradition.
Signed at Monrovia November 1, 1937.
Entered into force November 21, 1939.
54 Stat. 1733; TS 955; 9 Bevans 589; 201 LNTS 151

MARITIME MATTERS

Agreement relating to jurisdiction over vessels utilizing the Louisiana Offshore Oil Port.
Exchange of notes at Washington October 27, 1978, and January 15, 1979.
Entered into force January 15, 1979.
30 UST 1706; TIAS 9279; 1153 UNTS 283

NONPROLIFERATION

Agreement concerning cooperation to suppress the proliferation of weapons of mass destruction, their delivery systems, and related materials by sea.
Signed at Washington February 11, 2004.
Entered into force December 8, 2004.
TIAS 04-1208

POSTAL MATTERS

Agreement concerning the exchange of parcel post, and regulations of execution.
Signed at Monrovia March 16, and at Washington May 9, 1957.
Entered into force August 1, 1957.
8 UST 1035; TIAS 3866; 290 UNTS 59

International express mail agreement, with detailed regulations.
Signed at Monrovia and Washington November 15, 1988, and January 6, 1989.
Entered into force January 30, 1989.
TIAS 11620

PROPERTY

Preliminary agreement regarding principles applying to mutual aid for defense and exchange of notes.
Signed at New York June 8, 1943.
Entered into force June 8, 1943.
57 Stat. 978; EAS 324; 9 Bevans 630; 117 UNTS 241

PUBLICATIONS

Agreement relating to the exchange of official publications.
Exchange of notes at Monrovia January 15, 1942.
Entered into force January 15, 1942.
56 Stat. 1419; EAS 239; 9 Bevans 621; 117 UNTS 227

TAXATION

Agreement for reciprocal relief from double taxation on earnings from operation of ships and aircraft.
Exchange of notes at Monrovia July 1 and August 11, 1982.
Entered into force August 11, 1982.
34 UST 1553; TIAS 10435
Amendment:
October 7 and 23, 1987 (TIAS 11921)

TELECOMMUNICATION

Agreement relating to radio communications between amateur stations on behalf of third parties.
Exchange of notes at Monrovia November 9, 1950, and January 8, 9, and 10, 1951.
Entered into force January 11, 1951.
2 UST 683; TIAS 2223; 132 UNTS 255

Agreement supplementing articles III and VII of the agreement of August 13, 1959, relating to radio relay facilities in Liberia.
Exchange of notes at Monrovia August 8 and 15, 1960.
Entered into force August 15, 1960.
12 UST 1367; TIAS 4858; 421 UNTS 332
Amendment:
July 11 and 24, 1961 (12 UST 1367; TIAS 4858; 421 UNTS 340)

Agreement relating to the reciprocal granting of authorizations to permit licensed amateur radio operators of either country to operate their stations in the other country.
Exchange of notes at Monrovia March 20, 1974, and July 22, 1977.
Entered into force July 22, 1977.
29 UST 1494; TIAS 8892

TRADE & INVESTMENT

Treaty of friendship, commerce and navigation.
Signed at Monrovia August 8, 1938.
Entered into force November 21, 1939.
54 Stat. 1739; TS 956; 9 Bevans 595; 201 LNTS 163

Trade and investment framework agreement.
Signed at Washington February 15, 2007.
Entered into force February 15, 2007.
TIAS

TRANSPORTATION

Air navigation agreement.
Exchange of notes at Monrovia June 14, 1939.
Entered into force June 15, 1939.
54 Stat. 2018; EAS 166; 9 Bevans 615; 202 LNTS 93

Air transport agreement, with annexes.
Signed at Washington February 15, 2007.
Entered into force February 15, 2007.
TIAS 07-215.1

LIBYA

ATOMIC ENERGY

Agreement to facilitate the provision of assistance for the transfer of spent high-enriched uranium nuclear fuel to the Russian Federation.
Signed at Tripoli October 28, 2009.
Entered into force October 28, 2009.
TIAS 09-1028

CLAIMS & DISPUTE RESOLUTION

Claims settlement agreement, with annex.
Signed at Tripoli August 14, 2008.
Entered into force August 14, 2008.
TIAS 08-814

DEFENSE

Arrangement for return of equipment and material no longer needed in the furtherance of the mutual defense assistance program.
Signed at Tripoli June 30, 1957.
Entered into force June 30, 1957.
8 UST 963; TIAS 3858; 284 UNTS 188

Military assistance agreement.*
Signed at Tripoli June 30, 1957.
Entered into force June 30, 1957.
8 UST 957; TIAS 3857; 284 UNTS 177
Note:
* Terminated February 5, 1972, except that Article I, paragraphs 2 and 4, arrangements under Article I, paragraphs 3, 5, and 7, and under Article II remain in force.

Agreement relating to the termination of outstanding agreements with Libya.
Exchange of notes at Tripoli February 5, 1972.
Entered into force February 5, 1972.
23 UST 82; TIAS 7275

Agreement regarding grants under the Foreign Assistance Act of 1961, as amended, or successor legislation, and the furnishing of defense articles, defense services and related training, including pursuant to the United States International Military Education and Training (IMET) Program.
Exchange of notes at Tripoli May 2 and December 8, 2009.
Entered into force December 8, 2009.
NP

SCIENTIFIC & TECHNICAL COOPERATION

Agreement on science and technology cooperation, with annexes.
Signed at Washington January 3, 2008.
Entered into force April 4, 2008.
TIAS 08-404

WEAPONS

Memorandum of understanding regarding elimination of the remaining stock of chemical weapons in Libya.
Signed at Tripoli September 8, 2013.
Entered into force September 8, 2013.
TIAS 13-908

LIECHTENSTEIN

CONSULAR AFFAIRS

Arrangement for the waiver of passport visa fees for nonimmigrants.*
Exchange of notes at Bern April 22 and June 18 and 30, 1926.
Entered into force June 30, 1926; operative June 1, 1925.
9 Bevans 644

Arrangement relating to the waiver of passport visa fees for nonimmigrants.*
Exchanges of notes at Washington October 22 and 31 and November 4 and 13, 1947.
Entered into force November 13, 1947.
6 UST 93; TIAS 3172; 251 UNTS 79
Note
* The status of these agreements is under review.

EMPLOYMENT

Agreement relating to employment of dependents of official government employees.
Exchange of notes at Bern and Vaduz September 18 and November 14, 1997.
Entered into force November 14, 1997.
TIAS 12899

ENVIRONMENT & CONSERVATION

Agreement for cooperation in the Global Learning and Observations to Benefit the Environment (GLOBE) Program.
Signed at Vaduz March 26, 2003.
Entered into force March 26, 2003.
TIAS 03-326

LAW ENFORCEMENT

Extradition treaty.
Signed at Bern May 20, 1936.
Entered into force June 28, 1937.
50 Stat. 1337; TS 915; 9 Bevans 648; 183 LNTS 181

Treaty on mutual legal assistance in criminal matters, with exchange of notes.
Signed at Vaduz July 8, 2002.
Entered into force August 1, 2003.
TIAS 03-801

SOCIAL SECURITY

Agreement concerning reciprocity of payment of certain social security benefits.
Exchange of notes at Bern April 13, 1972.
Entered into force April 13, 1972; effective July 1, 1968.
23 UST 2896; TIAS 7476

TAXATION

Agreement on tax cooperation and the exchange of information relating to taxes, with appendix.
Signed at Vaduz December 8, 2008.
Entered into force December 4, 2009.
TIAS 09-1204

Protocol amending agreement on tax cooperation and the exchange of information relating to taxes.
Signed at Vaduz May 16, 2014.
Entered into force January 22, 2015.
TIAS 15-122.1

Agreement to improve international tax compliance and to implement the Foreign Account Tax Compliance Act, with annexes.
Signed at Vaduz May 16, 2014.
Entered into force January 22, 2015.
TIAS 15-122.2

LITHUANIA

ATOMIC ENERGY

Arrangement for the exchange of technical information and cooperation in nuclear safety matters, with addenda and annex.
Signed at Vienna September 14, 2015.
Entered into force September 22, 2015.
TIAS 15-922.1

CLAIMS & DISPUTE RESOLUTION

Arbitration treaty.
Signed at Washington November 14, 1928.
Entered into force January 20, 1930.
46 Stat. 2457; TS 809; 9 Bevans 671; 100 LNTS 111

Treaty of conciliation.
Signed at Washington November 14, 1928.
Entered into force January 20, 1930.
46 Stat. 2459; TS 810; 9 Bevans 673; 100 LNTS 117

CONSULAR AFFAIRS

Arrangement for the reciprocal waiver of passport visa fees for nonimmigrants.*
Exchange of notes at Washington April 17, 1937.
Entered into force April 17, 1937; operative May 1, 1937.
9 Bevans 688

Note:

* The status of this agreement is under review.

CULTURAL EXCHANGES, PROPERTY & COOPERATION

Agreement concerning the program of the Peace Corps of the United States in Lithuania.
Signed at Vilnius February 7, 1992.
Entered into force February 7, 1992.
TIAS 12447

Agreement on the protection and preservation of certain cultural properties.
Signed at Vilnius October 15, 2002.
Entered into force August 3, 2006.
TIAS 06-803

DEFENSE

Agreement concerning the provision of training related to defense articles under the United States International Military Education and Training (IMET) Program.
Exchange of notes at Vilnius March 31 and June 10, 1992.
Entered into force June 10, 1992.
NP

Agreement regarding grants under the Foreign Assistance Act of 1961, as amended, and the furnishing of defense articles, related training or other defense services from the United States to Lithuania.
Exchange of notes at Vilnius February 11 and March 26, 1993.
Entered into force March 26, 1993.
TIAS 12348

Basic exchange and cooperative agreement for topographic mapping, nautical and aeronautical charting, geodesy and geophysics, digital data and related mapping, charting and geodesy materials.
Signed at Vilnius January 21, 1994.
Entered into force February 15, 1994.
NP

Security agreement concerning security measures for the protection of classified military information.
Signed at Vilnius November 21, 1995.
Entered into force November 21, 1995.
TIAS 12243

Agreement concerning exchange of research and development information, with appendix.
Signed at Washington October 16, 1997.
Entered into force October 16, 1997.
TIAS

Basic exchange and cooperative agreement concerning global geospatial information and services cooperation, with annexes.
Signed at Vilnius June 11, 1999.
Entered into force June 11, 1999.
NP

Agreement regarding logistic support, supplies and services, with annexes.
Signed at Stuttgart and Vilnius May 22 and 31, 2006.
Entered into force May 31, 2006.
NP

Agreement regarding access to and use of facilities and areas located within the Republic of Lithuania..
Exchange of notes at Vilnius June 15 and 18, 2015.
Entered into force June 18, 2015.
TIAS 15-618

DIPLOMATIC & CONSULAR RELATIONS

Memorandum of understanding concerning diplomatic relations.
Signed at Vilnius September 6, 1991.
Entered into force September 6, 1991.
TIAS 12133

EMPLOYMENT

Agreement relating to the employment of dependents of official government employees.
Exchange of notes at Washington November 21 and December 8, 1994.
Entered into force December 8, 1994.
TIAS 12197

ENVIRONMENT & CONSERVATION

Agreement for cooperation in the Global Learning and Observations to Benefit the Environment (GLOBE) Program, with appendices.
Signed at Vilnius October 3, 2002.
Entered into force October 3, 2002.
TIAS 02-1003

FINANCE

Agreement for the funding of the debt of Lithuania to the United States.
Signed at Washington September 22, 1924.
Operative June 15, 1924.
Treasury Department print; 9 Bevans 661
Amendment:
June 9, 1932 (Treasury Department print; 9 Bevans 681)

Investment incentive agreement.
Signed at Indianapolis October 28, 1991.
Entered into force February 7, 1992.
TIAS 12640; 1775 UNTS 291

INTELLECTUAL PROPERTY

Agreement relating to the registration of trademarks.
Exchange of notes at Riga September 14, 1929, and at Kaunas October 11, 1929.
Entered into force October 11, 1929.
9 Bevans 675

LAW ENFORCEMENT

Memorandum of understanding concerning cooperation in the pursuit of war criminals, with related note.
Signed at Vilnius August 3, 1992.
Entered into force August 3, 1992.
TIAS 12470

Treaty on mutual legal assistance in criminal matters.
Signed at Washington January 16, 1998.
Entered into force August 26, 1999.
TIAS 12923

Extradition treaty.
Signed at Vilnius October 23, 2001.
Entered into force March 31, 2003.
TIAS 13166

Protocol on the application of the agreement on extradition between the United States of America and the European Union to the extradition treaty of October 23, 2001, with annex.
Signed at Brussels June 15, 2005.
Entered into force February 1, 2010.
TIAS 10-201.14

Protocol on the application of the agreement on mutual legal assistance between the United States of America and the European Union to the treaty on mutual legal assistance in criminal matters of January 16, 1998, with annex.
Signed at Brussels June 15, 2005.
Entered into force February 1, 2010.
TIAS 10-201.38

Agreement on enhancing cooperation in preventing and combating crime .
Signed at Vilnius October 29, 2008.
Entered into force July 20, 2010.
TIAS 10-720

NONPROLIFERATION

Agreement on cooperation in preventing illicit trafficking of nuclear and other radioactive material.
Signed at Vilnius February 22, 2011.
Entered into force February 22, 2011.
TIAS 11-222

POSTAL MATTERS

Parcel post agreement.
Signed at Kaunas December 4 and at Washington December 28, 1939.
Operative February 1, 1940.
54 Stat. 2021; Post Office Department print; 202 LNTS 381

International express mail agreement, with detailed regulations.
Signed at Vilnius and Washington September 21 and October 29, 1992.
Entered into force December 14, 1992.
TIAS 11905

TAXATION

Convention for the avoidance of double taxation and the prevention of fiscal evasion with respect to taxes on income.
Signed at Washington January 15, 1998.
Entered into force December 30, 1999.
TIAS 12921

Agreement to improve international tax compliance and to implement the Foreign Account Tax Compliance Act, with annexes.
Signed at Vilnius August 26, 2014.
Entered into force October 7, 2014.
TIAS 14-1007.1

TRADE & INVESTMENT

Agreement according mutual unconditional most-favored-nation treatment in customs matters.
Exchange of notes at Washington December 23, 1925.
Entered into force July 10, 1926.
TS 742; 9 Bevans 668; 54 LNTS 377

Arrangement regarding reciprocal privileges for consular officers to import articles free of duty for their personal use.
Exchanges of notes at Washington July 28, September 17 and 19, and October 4, 1934.
Entered into force October 4, 1934; operative October 15, 1934.
9 Bevans 685

Treaty for the encouragement and reciprocal protection of investment, with annex and protocol.
Signed at Washington January 14, 1998.
Entered into force November 22, 2001.
TIAS 12918

Additional protocol to the treaty for the encouragement and reciprocal protection of investment of January 14, 1998.
Signed at Brussels September 22, 2003.
Entered into force July 13, 2004.
TIAS 04-713

WEAPONS

Agreement concerning cooperation in the area of the prevention of proliferation of weapons of mass destruction and the promotion of defense and military relations.
Signed at Vilnius October 10, 2002.
Entered into force April 24, 2003.
TIAS 03-424
Amendment and Extension:
November 30, 2009 (TIAS 03-424)

LUXEMBOURG

CLAIMS & DISPUTE RESOLUTION

Treaty of conciliation.
Signed at Luxembourg April 6, 1929.
Entered into force September 2, 1930.
46 Stat. 2813; TS 826; 9 Bevans 704; 106 LNTS 469

Treaty of arbitration.
Signed at Luxembourg April 6, 1929.
Entered into force September 2, 1930.
46 Stat. 2809; TS 825; 9 Bevans 701; 106 LNTS 475

Memorandum of understanding regarding claims between the two Governments arising out of the conduct of the war.
Signed at Luxembourg September 12, 1946.
Entered into force September 12, 1946.
62 Stat. 4006; TIAS 2067; 9 Bevans 721; 149 UNTS 19

Agreement relating to war damage to private property.
Exchange of notes at Luxembourg June 15, 1955.
Entered into force June 15, 1955.
6 UST 2577; TIAS 3302; 264 UNTS 279

CONSULAR AFFAIRS

Agreement relating to the waiver of visas and visa fees for nonimmigrants.*
Exchange of notes at Luxembourg April 25 and May 22 and 26, 1936.
Entered into force May 26, 1936; operative June 15, 1936.
9 Bevans 710
Note:
* The status of this agreement is under review.

CULTURAL EXCHANGES, PROPERTY & COOPERATION

Agreement concerning the establishment of a permanent World War II cemetery in Luxembourg with exchange of notes.
Signed at Luxembourg March 20, 1951.
Entered into force June 11, 1952.
3 UST 2745; TIAS 2445; 180 UNTS 283

Agreement concerning concessions granted to United States in establishing a permanent World War II cemetery in Luxembourg.
Exchange of notes at Luxembourg March 20, 1951.
Entered into force March 20, 1951.
3 UST 2750; TIAS 2446; 180 UNTS 289

DEFENSE

Mutual defense assistance agreement.
Signed at Washington January 27, 1950.
Entered into force March 28, 1950.
1 UST 69; TIAS 2014; 80 UNTS 187

Agreement relating to the assurances required under the Mutual Security Act of 1951.
Exchange of notes at Luxembourg January 8, 1952.
Entered into force January 8, 1952.
3 UST 4627; TIAS 2614; 180 UNTS 191

Agreement relating to the offshore procurement program.
Signed at Luxembourg April 17, 1954.
Entered into force September 30, 1955.
6 UST 3989; TIAS 3415; 257 UNTS 255

Agreement approving the offshore procurement contract with Luxembourg.
Exchange of notes at Luxembourg April 17, 1954.
Entered into force September 30, 1955.
6 UST 4009; TIAS 3416; 257 UNTS 270
Amendment:
May 10 and July 16, 1954 (6 UST 4009; TIAS 3416; 257 UNTS 292)

Memorandum of understanding relating to the disposal of redistributable and excess property furnished in connection with the mutual defense assistance program, with related notes.
Signed at Luxembourg July 7, 1954.
Entered into force July 7, 1954.
5 UST 1524; TIAS 3029; 233 UNTS 23
Amendment:
March 4 and June 10, 1960 (11 UST 2169; TIAS 4583; 393 UNTS 328)

Agreement concerning general security of military information.
Signed at Luxembourg September 17, 1981.
Entered into force September 17, 1981.
33 UST 3922; TIAS 10270; 1543 UNTS 117

Agreement concerning NATO civil air augmentation.
Signed at Scott AFB and Luxembourg March 11 and May 17, 1985.
Entered into force May 17, 1985.
TIAS 11108; 2120 UNTS 345

Memorandum of understanding concerning reciprocal defense procurement.
Signed at Brussels October 14, 2010.
Entered into force October 14, 2010.
TIAS 10-1014

Acquisition and cross-servicing agreement, with annexes.
Signed at Stuttgart and Luxembourg April 23 and May 15, 2015. Entered into force May 15, 2015.
NP

EDUCATION

Agreement for the financing of certain academic and cultural exchanges and programs in the field of education.
Signed at Brussels December 12, 1968.
Entered into force May 13, 1971.
22 UST 1538; TIAS 7175; 806 UNTS 231

ENVIRONMENT & CONSERVATION

Agreement concerning cooperation in the Global Learning and Observations to Benefit the Environment (GLOBE) Program, with appendices.
Signed at Luxembourg October 10, 1996.
Entered into force October 10, 1996.
TIAS 12807

FINANCE

Agreement relating to investment guaranties under section 413(b)(4) of the Mutual Security Act of 1954, as amended.
Exchange of notes at Luxembourg November 26 and December 7, 1956.
Entered into force December 7, 1956.
7 UST 3432; TIAS 3715; 265 UNTS 255

FOREIGN ASSISTANCE

Economic cooperation agreement.
Signed at Luxembourg July 3, 1948.
Entered into force July 3, 1948.
62 Stat. 2451; TIAS 1790; 9 Bevans 722; 24 UNTS 35
Amendments:
November 17 and December 22, 1948 (62 Stat. 3750; TIAS 1903; 9 Bevans 740; 55 UNTS 324)
January 17 and 19, 1950 (1 UST 163; TIAS 2030; 79 UNTS 306)
August 30 and October 17, 1951 (2 UST 2149; TIAS 2342; 137 UNTS 280)
December 31, 1952, and February 26, 1953 (4 UST 226; TIAS 2780; 212 UNTS 286)

LAW ENFORCEMENT

Extradition treaty.
Signed at Washington October 1, 1996.
Entered into force February 1, 2002.
TIAS 12804

Treaty on mutual legal assistance in criminal matters, with exchange of notes.
Signed at Luxembourg March 13, 1997.
Entered into force February 1, 2001.
TIAS 12842; 2147 UNTS 391

Instrument as contemplated by Article 3, paragraph 2(a), of the agreement on mutual legal assistance between the United States of America and the European Union signed June 25, 2003, as to the application of the treaty on mutual legal assistance in criminal matters of March 13, 1997.
Signed at Washington February 1, 2005.
Entered into force February 1, 2010.
TIAS 10-201.39

Instrument as contemplated by Article 3, paragraph 2(a), of the agreement on extradition between the United States of America and the European Union signed June 25, 2003 as to the application of the extradition treaty of October 1, 1996.
Signed at Washington February 1, 2005.
Entered into force February 1, 2010.
TIAS 10-201.15

Agreement concerning the sharing of 601,654.34 Euros (equivalent to US$842,917.73) of confiscated property.
Signed at February 10 and 27, 2012.
Entered into force February 27, 2012.
TIAS

POSTAL MATTERS

International express mail agreement, with detailed regulations.
Signed at Luxembourg and Washington April 21 and June 14, 1983.
Entered into force October 1, 1983.
35 UST 1431; TIAS 10737; 2006 UNTS 331

Memorandum of understanding concerning the operation of the INTELPOST field trial, with details of implementation.
Signed at Luxembourg and Washington April 29 and May 28, 1985.
Entered into force June 3, 1985.
TIAS 11245

PROPERTY

Mutual aid settlement.
Exchange of memorandums at Luxembourg August 29, 1946.
Entered into force August 29, 1946.
62 Stat. 4003; TIAS 2065; 9 Bevans 718; 140 UNTS 101

SOCIAL SECURITY

Agreement on social security, with administrative arrangement.
Signed at Luxembourg February 12, 1992.
Entered into force November 1, 1993.
TIAS 12119

TAXATION

Agreement relating to relief from taxation of United States expenditures in Luxembourg for common defense.
Exchange of notes at Luxembourg March 10 and 13, 1952.
Entered into force March 13, 1952.
3 UST 4001; TIAS 2538; 168 UNTS 57

Agreement concerning the reciprocal exemption from income tax of income derived from the international operation of ships and aircraft.
Exchange of notes at Luxembourg April 11 and June 22, 1989.
Entered into force January 8, 1993.
TIAS 12056

Convention for the avoidance of double taxation and the prevention of fiscal evasion with respect to taxes on income and capital, with related exchange of notes.
Signed at Luxembourg April 3, 1996.
Entered into force December 20, 2000.
TIAS; 2148 UNTS 81

Agreement to improve international tax compliance and with respect to the United States information reporting provisions commonly known as the Foreign Account Tax Compliance Act, with annexes and exchange of modifying notes.
Signed at Luxembourg March 28, 2014.
Entered into force July 29, 2015.
TIAS 15-729.1

TELECOMMUNICATION

Agreement relating to the establishment of a radio range station in Luxembourg.
Exchange of notes at Luxembourg July 22 and August 17, 1953.
Entered into force August 17, 1953.
5 UST 1823; TIAS 3056; 234 UNTS 219.

Agreement relating to reciprocal granting of authorizations to permit licensed amateur radio operators of either country to operate their stations in the other country.
Exchange of notes at Luxembourg July 7 and 29, 1965.
Entered into force July 29, 1965.
16 UST 1746; TIAS 5900; 573 UNTS 197

TRADE & INVESTMENT

Treaty of friendship, establishment and navigation, and protocol.
Signed at Luxembourg February 23, 1962.
Entered into force March 28, 1963.
14 UST 251; TIAS 5306; 474 UNTS 3

TRANSPORTATION

Air transport agreement, with annex.*
Signed at Luxembourg August 19, 1986.
Entered into force August 3, 1988.
TIAS 11249; 2174 UNTS 239

Amendment:
June 6, 1995 (TIAS 12656)
July 13 and 21, 1998 (TIAS 12977)

Note:
* This agreement is suspended for the duration of provisional application of the U.S. – E.U. Air Transport Agreement signed April 25 and 30, 2007.

M

MACEDONIA

On September 8, 1991, Macedonia became an independent state. For agreements prior to the independence of Macedonia, see YUGOSLAVIA.

CULTURAL EXCHANGES, PROPERTY & COOPERATION

Agreement concerning the protection and preservation of certain cultural properties, with annex.
Exchange of notes at Washington December 10, 2002.
Entered into force July 12, 2010.
TIAS 10-712

DEFENSE

Agreement regarding grants under the Foreign Assistance Act of 1961, as amended, or successor legislation, and the furnishing of defense articles, related training, and other defense services from the United States of America to the Former Yugoslav Republic of Macedonia.
Exchange of notes at Skopje June 5, 1997.
Entered into force June 5, 1997.
NP

Acquisition and cross-servicing agreement, with annexes.
Signed at Skopje and Stuttgart September 16 and 22, 2008.
Entered into force September 22, 2008.
NP

ENVIRONMENT AND CONSERVATION

Agreement concerning cooperation in the Global Learning and Observations to Benefits the Environment (GLOBE) Program.
Effected by exchange of notes at Skopje July 27 and August 24, 1998.
Entered into force August 24, 1998.
TIAS

EMPLOYMENT

Agreement concerning the reciprocal employment of dependents of official government employees, with attachment.
Exchange of notes at Washington December 10, 1998.
Entered into force December 10, 1998.
TIAS 13011

FINANCE

Investment incentive agreement, with attachment.
Exchange of notes at Skopje April 5, 1996.
Entered into force April 5, 1996.
TIAS

Agreement on the consolidation of the debt of the borrower, with attachment.
Exchange of letters at Skopje September 17, 1997.
Entered into force December 3, 1997.
NP

Agreement regarding the reorganization of certain debts owed to the United States Government and its agencies, with attachment.
Exchange of notes at Skopje January 15 and 30, 2003.
Entered into force March 17, 2003.
NP

FOREIGN ASSISTANCE

Agreement concerning economic, technical and related assistance, with attachment.
Exchange of letters at Skopje September 9, 2001.
Entered into force September 9, 2001.
TIAS

INTERNATIONAL CRIMINAL COURT

Agreement regarding the surrender of persons to the International Criminal Court.
Signed at Skopje June 30, 2003.
Entered into force November 12, 2003.
TIAS 03-1112

SCIENTIFIC & TECHNICAL COOPERATION

Agreement for scientific and technical cooperation, with annexes.
Signed at Skopje January 25, 2006.
Entered into force July 14, 2008.
TIAS 08-714

TRADE & INVESTMENT

Bilateral textile agreement.
Signed at Skopje November 7, 1997.
Entered into force November 7, 1997.
NP

Amendments:
September 17, 1999
June 2, 2000

TRANSPORTATION

Air Transport Agreement.
Signed at Skopje August 23, 2012.
Entered into force July 5, 2013.
TIAS 13-705

MADAGASCAR

By a note dated December 4, 1962, the Minister of Foreign Affairs of the Malagasy Republic informed the American Ambassador of the following (translation):

No official act specifies, in the agreements with the French Republic, the juridical position of the Malagasy Republic with regard to the rights and obligations contracted for Madagascar in the treaties, agreements, and conventions signed by France prior to Madagascar's accession to international sovereignty. In accordance with usage, the Malagasy Republic considers itself implicitly bound by such texts unless it explicitly denounces them. The Ministry of Foreign Affairs informs the Embassy of the United States of America that, in order to avoid any ambiguity, the Malagasy Republic transmits, as soon as it is in a position to reach an affirmative decision on each of the texts in question, a formal declaration in which it declares itself bound by the Treaty, the Agreement or the Convention under consideration.

CONSULAR AFFAIRS

Reciprocal agreement between the United States and France relating to visa fees for nonimmigrants.*

Exchanges of notes at Washington August 19 and September 4, 5, and 16, 1947.

Entered into force September 16, 1947; operative October 1, 1947.

61 Stat. 3776; TIAS 1721; 7 Bevans 1210; 84 UNTS 19

Note:

* The status of this agreement is under review.

CULTURAL EXCHANGES, PROPERTY & COOPERATION

Agreement relating to the establishment of a Peace Corps program in Madagascar.

Exchange of notes at Antananarivo June 11, 1992.

Entered into force June 11, 1992.

TIAS 12107

DEFENSE

Agreement relating to the status of United States military and civilian personnel of the United States Department of Defense temporarily present in Madagascar in connection with humanitarian relief operations.

Exchange of notes at Antananarivo March 11 and 13, 2000.

Entered into force March 13, 2000.

TIAS

Agreement concerning the provision of defense articles, related training and other defense services pursuant to the International Military Education and Training (IMET) Program, the Africa Military Education Program (AMEP), the Africa Military Education Program (AMEP) and peacekeeping operations under Section 551 of the Foreign Assistance Act.

Exchange of notes at Antananarivo June 21 and September 1, 2015.

Entered into force September 1, 2015.

NP

EMPLOYMENT

Agreement relating to the employment of dependents of official government employees.

Exchange of notes at Antananarivo April 12, 2001, and September 3, 2004.

Entered into force September 3, 2004.

TIAS 04-903

ENVIRONMENT & CONSERVATION

Agreement concerning cooperation in the Global Learning and Observations to Benefit the Environment (GLOBE) Program, with appendices.

Signed at Antananarivo June 11, 1997.

Entered into force June 11, 1997

TIAS

FINANCE

Agreement regarding the consolidation and rescheduling of certain debts owed to, guaranteed by or insured by the United States Government, with annexes.

Signed at Washington September 28, 1984.

Entered into force November 19, 1984.

TIAS 10998; 2022 UNTS 79

Agreement regarding the consolidation and rescheduling of certain debts owed to, guaranteed by or insured by the United States Government and its agencies, with annex.

Signed at Antananarivo October 8, 1985.

Entered into force November 12, 1985.

NP

Agreement regarding the consolidation and rescheduling of certain debts owed to, guaranteed by or insured by the United States Government and its agencies, with annexes.

Signed at Antananarivo May 7, 1987.

Entered into force June 15, 1987.

NP

Agreement regarding the consolidation and rescheduling of certain debts owed to, guaranteed by, or insured by the United States Government and its agencies, with annexes.

Signed at Antananarivo August 9, 1989.

Entered into force September 14, 1989.

NP

Amendment:

March 23 and May 2, 1990 (NP)

Agreement regarding the consolidation and rescheduling of certain debts owed to, guaranteed by, or insured by the United States Government and its agencies, with annexes.

Signed at Antananarivo June 19, 1991.

Entered into force August 9, 1991.

NP

Agreement regarding the consolidation, reduction and rescheduling of certain debts owed to, guaranteed by, or insured by the United States Government and its Agency, with annexes.

Signed at Washington December 16, 1997.
Entered into force March 4, 1998.
NP

Amendment:
February 14 and May 20, 2003

Investment incentive agreement.

Signed at Washington March 31, 1998.
Entered into force February 7, 2000.
TIAS 12939

Agreement regarding the reduction of certain debts owed to, guaranteed by, or insured by the United States Government and its agency.

Signed at Antananarivo January 7, 2004.
Entered into force March 10, 2004.
NP

Agreement regarding the reduction of certain debts owed to, guaranteed by, or insured by the United States Government, with annexes.

Signed at Antananarivo March 18, 2005.
Entered into force May 19, 2005.
NP

FOREIGN ASSISTANCE

Agreement providing for the furnishing of economic, technical and related assistance.

Exchange of notes at Tananarive June 22, 1961.
Entered into force June 22, 1961.
12 UST 1049; TIAS 4808; 413 UNTS 219

INTERNATIONAL CRIMINAL COURT

Agreement regarding the surrender of persons to the International Criminal Court.

Signed at Antananarivo April 23, 2003.
Entered into force August 4, 2003.
TIAS 03-804

POSTAL MATTERS

International express mail agreement, with detailed regulations.

Signed at Antananarivo and Washington April 28 and May 26, 1988.
Entered into force July 15, 1988.
TIAS 11597

TRADE & INVESTMENT

Convention of navigation and commerce between the United States and France, with separate article.*

Signed at Washington June 24, 1822; extended to Madagascar in 1896.
8 Stat. 278; TS 87; 7 Bevans 822

Note:
* Article VI abrogated by the United States July 1, 1916, in accordance with the Seamen's Act (38 Stat. 1164).

Agreement modifying the provisions of article VII of the convention of navigation and commerce of June 24, 1822.

Signed at Washington July 17, 1919.
Entered into force January 10, 1921.
41 Stat. 1723; TS 650; 7 Bevans 899

TRANSPORTATION

Air transport services agreement between the United States and France.

Signed at Paris March 27, 1946.
Entered into force March 27, 1946.
61 Stat. 3445; TIAS 1679; 7 Bevans 1109; 139 UNTS 114

Amendments and Extensions:
June 23 and July 11, 1950 (1 UST 593; TIAS 2106; 139 UNTS 142)
March 19, 1951 (2 UST 1033; TIAS 2257; 139 UNTS 151)
March 19, 1951 (2 UST 1037; TIAS 2258; 139 UNTS 146)
August 27, 1959 (10 UST 1791; TIAS 4336; 358 UNTS 277)

MALAWI

CULTURAL EXCHANGES, PROPERTY & COOPERATION

Agreement relating to the establishment of a Peace Corps program in Malawi.

Exchange of notes at Blantyre and Zomba September 14, 1971.
Entered into force September 14, 1971.
22 UST 1633; TIAS 7191

DEFENSE

Agreement concerning the provision of training related to defense articles under the United States International Military Education and Training (IMET) Program.

Exchange of notes at Lilongwe March 20 and May 1, 1980.
Entered into force May 1, 1980.
32 UST 965; TIAS 9744; 1222 UNTS 331

Agreement regarding grants under the Foreign Assistance Act of 1961, as amended, and the furnishing of defense articles, related training and other defense services from the United States to Malawi.

Exchange of notes at Lilongwe May 28 and July 24, 1992.
Entered into force July 24, 1992.
TIAS 12525

Agreement regarding the provision of commodities, services and associated military education and training to assist the Republic of Malawi's forces participating in the African Crisis Response Initiative.
Exchange of notes at Lilongwe July 28 and August 27, 1997.
Entered into force August 27, 1997.
NP

Acquisition and cross-servicing agreement, with annexes.
Signed at Stuttgart and Blantyre February 11 and March 7, 2013.
Entered into force March 7, 2013.
NP

Agreement regarding military cooperation.
Signed at Lilongwe February 24, 2016.
Entered into force February 24, 2016.
TIAS 16-224

EMPLOYMENT

Agreement concerning the employment of dependents of official government employees.
Exchange of notes at Washington October 29, 1998, and April 16, 1999.
Entered into force April 16, 1999.
TIAS 13030

FINANCE

Agreement relating to investment guaranties.
Exchange of notes at Blantyre May 1 and July 21, 1967.
Entered into force July 21, 1967.
18 UST 2335; TIAS 6334; 693 UNTS 3

Agreement regarding the consolidation and rescheduling of certain debts owed to, guaranteed or insured by the United States Government and its agencies, with annexes.
Signed at Lilongwe March 10, 1983.
Entered into force May 16, 1983.
TIAS 10684; 2005 UNTS 133

Agreement regarding the consolidation and rescheduling of certain debts owed to, guaranteed or insured by the United States Government and its agencies with annexes and implementing agreement regarding repayments due under A.I.D. loans, with annexes.
Signed at Lilongwe April 30, 1984.
Entered into force June 11, 1984.
TIAS 10993; 2022 UNTS 81

Agreement regarding the consolidation and rescheduling of certain debts owed to, guaranteed by or insured by the United States Government and its agencies, with annexes.
Signed at Lilongwe February 21, 1989.
Entered into force April 6, 1989.
NP

FOREIGN ASSISTANCE

Millennium Challenge Compact, with annexes.
Signed at Lilongwe April 7, 2011.
Entered into force September 20, 2013.
TIAS 13-920
Amendment:
July 26 and 31, 2013 (TIAS 13-920)

INTERNATIONAL CRIMINAL COURT

Agreement regarding the surrender of persons to the International Criminal Court.
Signed at Lilongwe September 23, 2003.
Entered into force September 23, 2003.
TIAS 03-923

LAW ENFORCEMENT

Extradition treaty between the United States and the United Kingdom.
Signed at London December 22, 1931.
Applicable to Nyasaland June 24, 1935.
47 Stat. 2122; TS 849; 12 Bevans 482; 163 LNTS 59

POSTAL MATTERS

International express mail agreement, with detailed regulations.
Signed at Lilongwe and Washington April 26 and June 21, 1988.
Entered into force July 15, 1988.
TIAS 11582

TREATY LAW

Agreement continuing in force between the United States and Malawi the extradition treaty and the double taxation convention* between the United States and the United Kingdom.
Exchange of notes at Zomba and Blantyre December 17, 1966, January 6 and April 4, 1967.
Entered into force April 4, 1967.
18 UST 1822; TIAS 6328; 692 UNTS 191
Note:
* Notification of termination of the 1945 taxation convention as applicable to Malawi given by the United States June 28, 1983, effective January 1, 1984.

MALAYSIA

On August 31, 1957, the Federation of Malaya attained fully responsible status within the British Commonwealth (Federation of Malaya Independence Act, 1957). By an exchange of notes dated September 12, 1957, between the United Kingdom and the Federation of Malaya there were formally transferred to the Federation, as of August 31, 1957, the rights and obligations of treaties and agreements entered into between the United Kingdom and any other government in so far as such instruments may be held to have application to or in respect of the Federation of Malaya. The British Colonies of North Borneo and Sarawak and the State of Singapore were federated with the existing States of the Federation of Malaya under the provisions of a general agreement between them and the United Kingdom, signed at London July 9, 1963. On September 16, 1963, the Federation of Malaya changed its name to Malaysia. The Constitution of the Federation of Malaya was amended by the Malaysia Act of 1963 to provide for the Government of Malaysia's assumption of rights and obligations of treaties and agreements entered into between the United Kingdom and any other government on behalf of the Borneo States and Singapore. On August 9, 1965, Singapore became an independent and sovereign state.

CONSULAR AFFAIRS

Agreement between the United States and the United Kingdom relating to visas.*
Exchange of notes at London October 15 and 22, 1954.

Agreement continuing in force the 1954 agreement with respect to the Federation of Malaya.*
Exchange of letters at Kuala Lumpur March 5 and 12, 1958.

Note:
* The status of this agreement is under review.

CULTURAL EXCHANGES, PROPERTY & COOPERATION

Agreement relating to the establishment of a Peace Corps program in the Federation of Malaya.
Exchange of notes at Kuala Lumpur September 4, 1961.
Entered into force September 4, 1961.
12 UST 1236; TIAS 4843; 421 UNTS 215

Agreement between the United States and the United Kingdom relating to the establishment of a Peace Corps program in Sarawak.
Exchange of notes at London October 25, 1962.
Entered into force October 25, 1962.
13 UST 2394; TIAS 5202; 457 UNTS 129

Agreement between the United States and the United Kingdom relating to the establishment of a Peace Corps program in North Borneo.
Exchange of notes at London October 25, 1962.
Entered into force October 25, 1962.
13 UST 2389; TIAS 5201; 457 UNTS 137

DEFENSE

Agreement relating to the purchase by Malaya of military equipment, materials, and services from the United States.
Exchange of notes at Washington June 30 and July 9, 1958.
Entered into force July 9, 1958.
9 UST 1235; TIAS 4108; 336 UNTS 79

Agreement relating to the deposit by Malaysia of ten percent of the value of grant military assistance furnished by the United States.
Exchange of notes at Kuala Lumpur March 8 and April 4, 1972.
Entered into force April 4, 1972; effective February 7, 1972.
23 UST 294; TIAS 7309

Agreement relating to eligibility for United States military assistance and training pursuant to the International Security Assistance and Arms Export Control Act of 1976.
Exchange of notes at Kuala Lumpur February 11 and March 14, 1977.
Entered into force March 14, 1977.
29 UST 663; TIAS 8845

Agreement concerning a military education exchange program.
Exchange of letters at Washington and Kuala Lumpur May 16 and 29, 1991.
Entered into force May 29, 1991.
NP

Acquisition and cross-servicing agreement, with annexes
Signed May 9, 2005.
Entered into force May 9, 2005.
TIAS 05-509

Agreement regarding grants under the Foreign Assistance Act of 1961, as amended, or successor legislation, and the furnishing of defense articles, defense services and related training, including pursuant to the United States International Military and Education Training Program (IMET).
Exchange of notes at Kuala Lumpur March 3 and September 18, 2006.
Entered into force September 18, 2006.
NP

DIPLOMATIC & CONSULAR RELATIONS

Consular convention and protocol of signature between the United States and the United Kingdom.
Signed at Washington June 6, 1951.
Entered into force September 7, 1952.
3 UST 3426; TIAS 2494; 165 UNTS 121

EDUCATION

Agreement concerning the establishment of the Malaysian-American Commission on Educational Exchange.
Signed at Kuala Lumpur September 20, 2010.
Entered into force September 20, 2010 with effect from August 3, 2005.
TIAS 10-920.1

Memorandum of understanding on the Fulbright English Teaching Assistant Program, with appendix.
Signed at Kuala Lumpur August 8, 2012.
Entered into force August 8, 2012 with effect from May 3, 2011.
TIAS 12-808
Extension:
April 8 and 11, 2014 (TIAS 14-411)

EMPLOYMENT

Agreement concerning employment on a reciprocal basis of dependents of official Government employees.
Exchange of notes at Kuala Lumpur April 23 and 24, 2014.
Entered into force April 24, 2014.
TIAS 14-424

FINANCE

Agreement relating to investment guaranties under section 413(b)(4) of the Mutual Security Act of 1954, as amended.
Exchange of notes at Kuala Lumpur April 21, 1959.
Entered into force April 21, 1959.
10 UST 776; TIAS 4214; 343 UNTS 3
Amendment:
June 24, 1965 (16 UST 1086; TIAS 5850; 564 UNTS 230)

FOREIGN ASSISTANCE

Economic cooperation agreement between the United States and the United Kingdom.
Signed at London July 6, 1948.
Applicable to the Federation of Malaya July 20, 1948.
62 Stat. 2596; TIAS 1795; 12 Bevans 874; 22 UNTS 263
Amendments:
January 3, 1950 (1 UST 184; TIAS 2036; 86 UNTS 304)
May 25, 1951 (2 UST 1292; TIAS 2277; 99 UNTS 308)
February 25, 1953 (4 UST 1528; TIAS 2815; 172 UNTS 332)

INTELLECTUAL PROPERTY

Declaration by the United States and the United Kingdom relating to reciprocal protection to trademarks.
Signed at London October 24, 1877.
Entered into force October 24, 1877.
20 Stat. 703; TS 138; 12 Bevans 198

LAW ENFORCEMENT

Agreement relating to a cooperative program to combat the spread of heroin addiction and other forms of drug abuse in Malaysia.
Exchange of notes at Kuala Lumpur November 16 and December 8, 1978.
Entered into force December 8, 1978.
30 UST 7183; TIAS 9577; 1182 UNTS 101
Amendment:
April 9 and May 18, 1979 (30 UST 7192; TIAS 9577; 1182 UNTS 105)

Memorandum of understanding for reducing demand, preventing illicit use and combatting illicit production and traffic of drugs, including precursor chemicals.
Signed at Kuala Lumpur April 20, 1989.
Entered into force April 20, 1989.
TIAS 12399

Extradition treaty, with exchange of notes.
Signed at Kuala Lumpur August 3, 1995.
Entered into force June 2, 1997.
TIAS 97-602

Treaty on mutual legal assistance in criminal matters, with annex.
Signed at Kuala Lumpur July 28, 2006.
Entered into force January 21, 2009.
TIAS 09-121

Memorandum of understanding regarding mutual assistance on customs matters.
Signed at Sepang December 9, 2014.
Entered into force December 9, 2014.
TIAS 14-1209.1

Agreement on enhancing co-operation in preventing and combating serious crime.
Signed at Kuala Lumpur November 19, 2015.
Entered into force April 25, 2016.
TIAS 16-425

NONPROLIFERATION

Agreement concerning cooperation to prevent the illicit trafficking in nuclear and other radioactive material, with agreed minute.
Signed at Selangor February 27, 2008.
Entered into force February 27, 2008.
TIAS 08-227

POLLUTION

Agreement concerning the transboundary movement of hazardous wastes from Malaysia to the United States.
Signed at Kuala Lumpur March 10, 1995.
Entered into force March 10, 1995.
TIAS 12612

POSTAL MATTERS

Parcel post convention.
Signed at Kuala Lumpur January 21 and at Washington March 22, 1935.
Entered into force April 1, 1935.
49 Stat. 3133; Post Office Department print; 161 LNTS 41

International express mail agreement, with detailed regulations.
Signed at Washington and Kuala Lumpur February 14 and March 14, 1983.
Entered into force June 1, 1983.
TIAS 10671; 2001 UNTS 47

PROPERTY

Convention between the United States and the United Kingdom relating to tenure and disposition of real and personal property.*
Signed at Washington March 2, 1899.
Entered into force August 7, 1900.
31 Stat. 1939; TS 146; 12 Bevans 246
Note:
* Notification given on February 9, 1901, of application to the Straits Settlements.

SCIENTIFIC & TECHNICAL COOPERATION

Memorandum of understanding on science and technology cooperation, with annex.
Signed at Putrajaya November 2, 2010.
Entered into force November 2, 2010.
TIAS 10-1102.1

TAXATION

Agreement concerning reciprocal exemption with respect to taxes on income of shipping and air transport enterprises.
Signed at Kuala Lumpur April 18, 1989.
Entered into force March 12, 1990.
TIAS 11618; 2191 UNTS 143

TRANSPORTATION

Arrangement between the United States and the United Kingdom relating to pilot licenses to operate civil aircraft.
Exchange of notes at Washington March 28 and April 5, 1935.
Entered into force May 5, 1935.
49 Stat. 3731; EAS 77; 12 Bevans 513; 162 LNTS 59

Agreement concerning assistance in developing and modernizing Malaysia's civil aviation infrastructure.
Signed at Washington and Kuala Lumpur July 22 and August 6, 1994.
Entered into force August 6, 1994
NP

Agreement for promotion of aviation safety.
Signed at Kuala Lumpur May 28, 1996.
Entered into force May 28, 1996.
TIAS 12760

Air transport agreement, with annexes.
Signed at San Francisco June 21, 1997.
Entered into force June 21, 1997.
TIAS 12871
Amendment:
August 7 and October 20, 2006 (TIAS 06-1020)

MALDIVES

DEFENSE

Agreement regarding military and Department of Defense civilian personnel.
Exchange of notes at Colombo December 31, 2004.
Entered into force December 31, 2004.
TIAS 04-1231

Agreement regarding grants under the Foreign Assistance Act of 1961, as amended, or successor legislation, and the furnishing of defense articles, defense services and related training, including pursuant to the United States International Military Education and Training (IMET) Program.
Exchange of notes at Colombo June 10 and September 9, 2010.
Entered into force September 9, 2010.
NP

Acquisition and cross-servicing agreement, with annexes
Signed at Kurumba September 22, 2010.
Entered into force September 22, 2010.
NP

ENVIRONMENT & CONSERVATION

Agreement for cooperation in the Global Learning and Observations to Benefit the Environment (GLOBE) Program.
Signed at Male December 8, 2003.
Entered into force December 8, 2003.
TIAS

FINANCE

Investment incentive agreement.
Signed at Male March 15, 2010.
Entered into force March 15, 2010.
TIAS 10-315

INTERNATIONAL CRIMINAL COURT

Agreement regarding the surrender of persons to international tribunals.
Signed at Male and Colombo April 8 and 10, 2003.
Entered into force July 8, 2003.
TIAS 03-708

LAW ENFORCEMENT

Agreement regarding mutual assistance between their customs administrations.
Signed at Brussels June 25, 2005.
Entered into force June 25, 2005.
TIAS 05-625

POSTAL MATTERS

International express mail agreement, with detailed regulations.
Signed at Male and Washington October 20 and November 8, 1990.
Entered into force December 5, 1990.
TIAS 11766

TRADE & INVESTMENT

Trade and investment framework agreement.
Signed at Male October 17, 2009.
Entered into force October 17, 2009.
TIAS 09-1017

TRANSPORTATION

Memorandum of agreement concerning assistance in developing and modernizing Maldives's civil aviation infrastructure, with annex.
Signed at Washington and Male February 12 and 17, 1997.
Entered into force February 17, 1997.
TIAS 12833

Air transport agreement, with annexes.
Signed at Washington May 5, 2005.
Entered into force May 5, 2005.
TIAS 05-505

MALI

CULTURAL EXCHANGES, PROPERTY & COOPERATION

Agreement relating to the establishment of a Peace Corps program in Mali.
Exchange of notes at Bamako December 23, 1969, and April 17, 1971.
Entered into force April 17, 1971.
26 UST 2611; TIAS 8178; 1027 UNTS 121

Agreement concerning the imposition of import restrictions on archaeological material from the Paleolithic Era (Stone Age) to approximately the Colonial Era of Mali, with appendix.
Signed at Washington September 19, 1997.
Entered into force September 19, 1997.
TIAS 97-919

Amendment and Extensions:
September 11 and 17, 2002 (TIAS 97-919)
September 11 and 17, 2007 (TIAS 97-919)
August 15 and September 5, 2012 (TIAS 12-905)

DEFENSE

Military assistance agreement.
Exchange of notes at Bamako May 20, 1961.
Entered into force May 20, 1961.
12 UST 1030; TIAS 4805; 413 UNTS 205

Understanding regarding delivery of two C 47 aircraft and related articles and services.
Exchange of notes at Bamako January 5, 1967.
Entered into force January 5, 1967.
18 UST 338; TIAS 6238

Geodetic survey agreement.
Signed at Bamako January 17, 1968.
Entered into force January 17, 1968.
19 UST 4568; TIAS 6446; 697 UNTS 231

Agreement relating to the deposit by Mali of ten percent of the value of grant military assistance and excess defense articles furnished by the United States.
Exchange of notes at Bamako April 18 and June 6, 1972.
Entered into force June 6, 1972; effective February 7, 1972.
23 UST 1106; TIAS 7368

Agreement concerning the provision of training related to defense articles under the United States International Military Education and Training (IMET) Program.
Exchange of notes at Bamako November 4, 1983, and March 23, 1984.
Entered into force March 23, 1984.
NP

Agreement regarding the status of U.S. military personnel and civilian employees of the Department of Defense who may be temporarily present in Mali in connection with the African Crisis Response Initiative.
Exchange of notes at Bamako July 30 and September 30, 1997.
Entered into force September 30, 1997.
NP

Agreement regarding grants under the Foreign Assistance Act of 1961, as amended, and the furnishing of defense articles, related training, and other defense services from the United States of America to the Government of Mali for purposes of participation in peacekeeping operations (PKO) in Liberia under Economic Community of West African States (ECOWAS) or other ECOWAS PKO.
Exchange of notes at Bamako August 18 and 22, 2003.
Entered into force August 22, 2003.
TIAS

Acquisition and cross-servicing agreement, with annexes.
Signed at Bamako September 20, 2006.
Entered into force September 20, 2006.
NP

EMPLOYMENT

Agreement relating to the employment of dependents of official government employees.
Exchange of notes at Washington March 6 and June 20, 1995.
Entered into force June 20, 1995.
TIAS 12668

ENVIRONMENT & CONSERVATION

Agreement for cooperation in the Global Learning and Observations to Benefit the Environment (GLOBE) Program, with appendices.
Signed at Washington November 19, 1997.
Entered into force November 19, 1997.
TIAS 12905

FINANCE

Agreement relating to investment guaranties.
Exchange of notes at Bamako June 4 and 9, 1964.
Entered into force June 9, 1964.
15 UST 1533; TIAS 5636; 530 UNTS 133

Agreement regarding the consolidation and rescheduling of certain debts owed to, guaranteed by, or insured by the United States Government and its agencies, with annexes.
Signed at Bamako June 3, 1989.
Entered into force July 21, 1989.
NP

Agreement regarding the consolidation of debt owed to, guaranteed by, or insured by the United States Government, with annexes.
Signed at Bamako September 10 and October 29, 2004.
Entered into force January 18, 2005.
NP

FOREIGN ASSISTANCE

Agreement providing for the furnishing of economic, technical and related assistance.
Exchange of notes at Bamako January 4, 1961.
Entered into force January 4, 1961.
12 UST 1; TIAS 4668; 405 UNTS 165

POSTAL MATTERS

International express mail agreement, with detailed regulations.
Signed at Bamako and Washington April 2 and 16, 1987.
Entered into force June 1, 1987.
TIAS 11304

Postal money order agreement.
Signed at Bamako and Washington February 10 and April 7, 1994.
Entered into force May 1, 1994.
NP

SOCIAL SECURITY

Agreement to provide social security benefits for certain employees of the United States in Mali.
Signed at Bamako December 2, 1969.
Entered into force January 1, 1970.
21 UST 2145; TIAS 6961; 764 UNTS 151

TRANSPORTATION

Civil aviation security agreement.
Signed at Bamako June 25, 1993.
Entered into force June 25, 1993.
TIAS 12155

Air transport agreement, with annexes.
Signed at Washington October 17, 2005.
Entered into force October 17, 2005.
TIAS 05-1017

MALTA

On September 21, 1964, Malta attained fully responsible status within the British Commonwealth (Malta Independence Act, 1964). By an exchange of letters dated December 31, 1964, between the Government of the United Kingdom and the Government of Malta, it was agreed that all obligations and responsibilities of the Government of the United Kingdom which arise from any valid international instrument shall, as from September 21, 1964, be assumed by the Government of Malta insofar as such instruments may be held to have application to Malta. Also, rights and benefits heretofore enjoyed by the Government of the United Kingdom in virtue of the application of any such international instrument to Malta shall, as from September 21, 1964, be enjoyed by the Government of Malta.

CONSULAR AFFAIRS

Arrangement between the United States and the United Kingdom providing for waiver of the visa requirement for United States citizens visiting Malta and for waiver of visa fees for British subjects residents of Malta visiting the United States.
Exchange of notes at Washington October 31 and December 12, 1949.
Entered into force December 12, 1949; operative December 1, 1949.
64 Stat. B137; TIAS 2069; 12 Bevans 950; 92 UNTS 191

CULTURAL EXCHANGES, PROPERTY & COOPERATION

Agreement relating to the establishment of a Peace Corps program in Malta.
Exchange of notes at Valletta April 29 and June 24, 1970.
Entered into force June 24, 1970.
21 UST 1486; TIAS 6907; 753 UNTS 281

DEFENSE

Agreement regarding grants under the Foreign Assistance Act of 1961, as amended, or successor legislation, and the furnishing of defense articles, related training and other defense services, including pursuant to the United States International Military Education and Training (IMET) Program.
Exchange of notes at Valletta November 30 and December 15, 2011.
Entered into force December 15, 2011.
NP

DIPLOMATIC & CONSULAR RELATIONS

Consular convention between the United States and the United Kingdom.
Signed at Washington June 6, 1951.
Entered into force September 7, 1952.
3 UST 3426; TIAS 2494; 165 UNTS 121

EMPLOYMENT

Agreement relating to employment of dependents of official government employees.
Exchange of notes at Floriana September 25 and October 3, 1991.
Entered into force October 3, 1991.
TIAS 11795

FINANCE

Agreement relating to investment guaranties.
Signed at Washington November 16, 1966.
Entered into force January 26, 1967.
18 UST 106; TIAS 6205; 688 UNTS 45

FOREIGN ASSISTANCE

Economic cooperation agreement between the United States and the United Kingdom.
Signed at London July 6, 1948.
Applicable to Malta July 6, 1948.
62 Stat. 2596; TIAS 1795; 12 Bevans 874; 22 UNTS 263

Amendments:
January 3, 1950 (1 UST 184; TIAS 2036; 86 UNTS 304)
May 25, 1951 (2 UST 1292; TIAS 2277; 99 UNTS 308)
February 25, 1953 (4 UST 1528; TIAS 2815; 172 UNTS 332)

INTELLECTUAL PROPERTY

Declaration by the United States and the United Kingdom affording reciprocal protection to trade-marks.
Signed at London October 24, 1877.
Entered into force October 24, 1877.
20 Stat. 703; TS 138; 12 Bevans 198

LAW ENFORCEMENT

Agreement regarding mutual assistance between customs administrations.
Signed at Valletta March 6, 2001.
Entered into force March 6, 2001.
TIAS 13144

Extradition treaty, with exchange of letters.
Signed at Valletta May 18, 2006.
Entered into force July 1, 2009.
TIAS 09-701

Treaty on certain aspects of mutual legal assistance in criminal matters, with annex.
Signed at Valletta May 18, 2006.
Entered into force February 1, 2010.
TIAS 10-201.40

Agreement enhancing cooperation in preventing and combating serious crime.
Signed at Washington October 3, 2008.
Entered into force October 11, 2011.
TIAS 11-1011

MARITIME MATTERS

Agreement concerning cooperation to suppress illicit traffic in narcotic drugs and psychotropic substances by sea.
Signed at Valletta June 16, 2004.
Entered into force January 10, 2008.
TIAS 08-110

NONPROLIFERATION

Agreement concerning cooperation to suppress the proliferation of weapons of mass destruction, their delivery systems, and related materials by sea, with appendix.
Signed at Washington March 15, 2007.
Entered into force December 19, 2007.
TIAS 07-1219

POSTAL MATTERS

International express mail agreement.
Signed at Valletta August 20 and October 29, 1991.
Entered into force December 2, 1991.
TIAS 11789

PROPERTY

Convention between the United States and the United Kingdom relating to the tenure and disposition of real and personal property.
Signed at Washington March 2, 1899.
Applicable to Malta May 29, 1947.
31 Stat. 1939; TS 146; 12 Bevans 246

Supplementary convention between the United States and the United Kingdom relating to the tenure and disposition of real and personal property.
Signed at Washington May 27, 1936.
Applicable to Malta May 29, 1947.
55 Stat. 1101; TS 964; 5 Bevans 140; 203 LNTS 367

TAXATION

Agreement on reciprocal exemption from taxes on earnings derived from the operation of ships and aircraft.
Exchange of notes at Washington December 26, 1996, and March 11, 1997.
Entered into force March 11, 1997.
TIAS 12841

Convention for the avoidance of double taxation and the prevention of fiscal evasion with respect to taxes on income, with exchange of notes.
Signed at Valletta August 8, 2008.
Entered into force November 23, 2010.
TIAS 10-1123

Agreement to improve international tax compliance and to implement the Foreign Account Tax Compliance Act, with annexes.
Signed at Valletta December 16, 2013.
Entered into force June 26, 2014.
TIAS 14-626

TRADE & INVESTMENT

Convention to regulate the commerce between the United States and the United Kingdom.*
Signed at London July 3, 1815.
Entered into force July 3, 1815.
8 Stat. 228; TS 110; 12 Bevans 49

Convention continuing in force indefinitely the convention of July 3, 1815 between the United States and the United Kingdom.
Signed at London August 6, 1827.
Entered into force April 2, 1828.
8 Stat. 361; TS 117; 12 Bevans 76

Note:

* Article IV superseded from September 7, 1952, by consular convention of June 6, 1951 (3 UST 3426; TIAS 2494).

TRANSPORTATION

Arrangement between the United States and the United Kingdom relating to pilot licenses to operate civil aircraft.
Exchange of notes at Washington March 28 and April 5, 1935.
Applicable to Malta May 5, 1935.
49 Stat. 3731; EAS 77; 12 Bevans 513; 162 LNTS 59

Air transport agreement, with annexes.*
Signed at Washington October 12, 2000.
Entered into force October 12, 2000.
TIAS 13120.

Note:

* This agreement is suspended for the duration of provisional application of the U.S. – E.U. Air Transport Agreement signed April 25 and 30, 2007.

MARSHALL ISLANDS

DEFENSE

Agreement regarding the provision of services of a military civic action team to the Marshall Islands.
Signed at Honolulu July 26, 1988.
Entered into force October 24, 1988.
TIAS 11657

DIPLOMATIC & CONSULAR RELATIONS

Agreement relating to diplomatic relations, with related notes.
Exchange of notes at Washington August 23 and September 6, 1989.
Entered into force September 6, 1989.
TIAS 11890

EDUCATION

Agreement regarding augmentation of educational assistance.
Signed at Washington September 7, 1988.
Entered into force September 7, 1988.
TIAS 11639

ENVIRONMENT & CONSERVATION

Agreement for cooperation in the Global Learning and Observations to Benefit the Environment (GLOBE) Program, with appendices.
Signed at Majuro October 17, 1996.
Entered into force October 17, 1996.
TIAS 12808

FINANCE

Investment incentive agreement.
Exchange of notes at Majuro January 20, 1988, and January 25, 1989.
Entered into force January 25, 1989.
TIAS 12092

INTERNATIONAL CRIMINAL COURT

Agreement regarding the surrender of persons to the International Criminal Court.
Signed at Majuro September 10, 2002.
Entered into force June 26, 2003.
TIAS 03-626.1

LAW ENFORCEMENT

Agreement regarding customs laws and regulations governing the arrival and departure of yachts.
Exchange of notes at Washington July 9, 2002.
Entered into force July 9, 2002.
TIAS

MARITIME MATTERS

Agreement concerning cooperation in maritime surveillance and interdiction activities.
Signed at Majuro August 5, 2008.
Entered into force August 5, 2008.
TIAS 08-805

Protocol to the agreement of August 5, 2008 concerning cooperation in maritime surveillance and interdiction activities.
Signed at Majuro March 19, 2013.
Entered into force March 19, 2013.
TIAS 13-319

NONPROLIFERATION

Agreement concerning cooperation to suppress the proliferation of weapons of mass destruction, their delivery systems, and related materials by sea.
Signed at Honolulu August 13, 2004.
Entered into force November 24, 2004.
TIAS 04-1124

REGIONAL ISSUES

Agreement for the implementation of the Compact of Free Association between the Government of the United States and the Government of the Republic of the Marshall Islands (Title II, PL 99-239), with related agreements.
Signed at Majuro October 10, 1986.
Entered into force October 15, 1986; effective October 21, 1986.
TIAS

Amendments
October 20, 1986
March 18, 1988 (TIAS 11661)

Agreement amending the agreement of June 25, 1983 concerning the Compact of Free Association, as amended.
Signed at Majuro April 30, 2003.
Entered into force May 1, 2004.
TIAS 04-501

Agreement on extradition, mutual assistance in law enforcement matters and penal sanctions, with agreed minute.
Signed at Majuro April 30, 2003.
Entered into force May 1, 2004; effective October 21, 1986.
TIAS 04-501.2

Agreement regarding protections for citizens of the Republic of the Marshall Islands seeking to engage in employment in the United States pursuant to recruitment or other placement services.
Signed at Majuro April 30, 2003.
Entered into force May 1, 2004.
TIAS 04-501.1

Agreement implementing section 216 and section 217 of the Compact, as amended, regarding a trust fund.
Signed at Majuro April 30, 2003.
Entered into force May 1, 2004.
TIAS 04-501.5

Agreement regarding the military use and operating rights of the Government of the United States in the Republic of the Marshall Islands, with agreed minutes and annexes.
Signed at Majuro April 30, 2003.
Entered into force May 1, 2004.
TIAS 04-501.3

Related Agreement:
March 23, 2004 (TIAS 04-501.3)

Status of forces agreement, with agreed minutes.
Signed at Majuro April 30, 2003.
Entered into force May 1, 2004.
TIAS 04-501.4

Agreement concerning procedures for the implementation of United States economic assistance provided in the Compact of Free Association, as amended.
Signed at Majuro March 23, 2004.
Entered into force May 1, 2004.
TIAS 04-501.7

Federal programs and services agreement, with annex and agreed minute.
Signed at Majuro March 23, 2004.
Entered into force May 1, 2004.
TIAS 04-501.6

TAXATION

Agreement concerning the reciprocal exemption from income tax of income derived from the international operation of ships and aircraft.
Exchange of notes at Majuro December 5, 1989.
Entered into force December 5, 1989.
TIAS 11728

Agreement for the exchange of information with respect to taxes, with attachment and exchange of notes.
Signed at Majuro March 14, 1991.
Entered into force March 14, 1991.
TIAS 11830; 2211 UNTS 401

TELECOMMUNICATION

Agreement relating to radio communications between amateur radio stations on behalf of third parties.
Exchange of notes at Majuro October 8 and 15, 1991.
Entered into force November 14, 1991.
TIAS 12439

Agreement relating to the reciprocal granting of authorizations to permit licensed amateur radio operators of either country to operate their stations in the other country.
Exchange of notes at Majuro October 15 and 18, 1993.
Entered into force October 18, 1993.
TIAS 12512

TRANSPORTATION

Memorandum of agreement concerning assistance in developing and modernizing the Marshall Islands' civil aviation system.
Signed at Washington and Majuro May 23 and June 15, 1989.
Entered into force June 15, 1989.
TIAS 11665

MAURITANIA

CULTURAL EXCHANGES, PROPERTY & COOPERATION

Agreement relating to the establishment of a Peace Corps program in Mauritania.
Exchange of notes at Nouakchott September 19 and October 17, 1966.
Entered into force October 17, 1966.
17 UST 2046; TIAS 6143; 676 UNTS 3

DEFENSE

Agreement concerning the provision of training related to defense articles under the United States International Military Education and Training (IMET) Program.
Exchange of notes at Nouakchott May 21, 1982, and August 26, 1984.
Entered into force August 26, 1984.
TIAS 10987; 2022 UNTS 117

Agreement of cooperation regarding the Pan-Sahel initiative project.
Signed at Nouakchott June 3, 2005.
Entered into force June 3, 2005.
TIAS

Acquisition and cross-servicing agreement, with annexes.
Signed at Nouakchott June 22, 2005.
Entered into force June 22, 2005.
NP

Agreement regarding grants under the Foreign Assistance Act of 1961, amended, or successor legislation, and the furnishing of defense articles, defense services and related training, including pursuant to the United States International Military and Education Training (IMET) Program.
Effected by exchange of notes at Nouakchott June 9, 2005 and July 31, 2007.
Entered into force July 31, 2007.
NP

ENVIRONMENT & CONSERVATION

Agreement for cooperation in the GLOBE Program.
Signed at Nouakchott July 6, 2004.
Entered into force July 6, 2004.
TIAS 04-706

FINANCE

Agreement relating to investment guaranties.
Exchange of Notes at Nouakchott May 4 and July 3, 1964.
Entered into force July 3, 1964.
15 UST 2385; TIAS 5727; 532 UNTS 307

Agreement regarding the consolidation and rescheduling of certain debts owed to, guaranteed by or insured by the United States Government and its agencies, with annex.
Signed at Washington August 14, 1985.
Entered into force September 23, 1985.
NP

Agreement regarding the consolidation and rescheduling of certain debts owed to, guaranteed by, or insured by the United States Government and its agency, with annexes.
Signed at Nouakchott February 4, 1990.
Entered into force March 12, 1990.
NP

Agreement regarding the consolidation and rescheduling of certain debts owed to, guaranteed by or insured by the United States Government and its agencies, with annexes.
Signed at Washington July 29, 1993.
Entered into force September 13, 1993.
NP

Agreement regarding the consolidation and reduction of certain debts owed to, guaranteed by, or insured by the United States Government and its agency, with annexes.
Signed at Nouakchott November 9, 2000.
Entered into force February 15, 2001.
NP

Agreement regarding the consolidation of debt owed to, guaranteed by, or insured by the United States Government, with annexes.
Signed at Nouakchott April 1, 2003.
Entered into force June 30, 2003.
NP

FOREIGN ASSISTANCE

General agreement for special development assistance.
Signed at Nouakchott March 23, 1971.
Entered into force March 23, 1971.
22 UST 667; TIAS 7121; 792 UNTS 205

INTERNATIONAL CRIMINAL COURT

Agreement regarding the surrender of persons to the International Criminal Court.
Signed at New York September 17, 2002.
Entered into force July 6, 2003.
TIAS 03-706

POSTAL MATTERS

International express mail agreement, with detailed regulations.
Signed at Nouakchott and Washington June 28 and July 17, 1992.
Entered into force September 21, 1992.
TIAS 11872

MAURITIUS

On March 12, 1968, Mauritius became an independent state. In a note dated March 12, 1968, to the Secretary-General of the United Nations, the Prime Minister and Minister of External Affairs made a statement reading in part as follows:

I have the honour to inform you that the Government of Mauritius, conscious of the desirability of maintaining existing legal relationships, and conscious of its obligation under international law to honour its treaty commitments, acknowledges that many treaty rights and obligations of the Government of the United Kingdom in respect of Mauritius were succeeded to by Mauritius upon independence by virtue of customary international law.

Since, however, it is likely that by virtue of customary international law certain treaties may have lapsed at the date of independence of Mauritius, it seems essential that each treaty should be subjected to legal examination. It is proposed after this examination has been completed, to indicate which, if any, of the treaties which may have lapsed by customary international law the Government of Mauritius wish to treat as having lapsed.

It is desired that it be presumed that each treaty has been legally succeeded to by Mauritius and that action be based upon this presumption until a decision is reached that it should be regarded as having lapsed. Should the Government of Mauritius be of the opinion that they have legally succeeded to a treaty but subsequently wish to terminate its operation, they will in due course give notice of termination in the terms thereof.

CULTURAL EXCHANGES, PROPERTY & COOPERATION

Agreement relating to the establishment of a Peace Corps program in Mauritius.
Exchange of notes at Port Louis March 18, 1971.
Entered into force March 18, 1971.
22 UST 453; TIAS 7080; 792 UNTS 197

DEFENSE

Agreement regarding grants under the Foreign Assistance Act of 1961, as amended, or successor legislation, and the furnishing of defense articles, defense services and related training, including pursuant to the United States International Military Education and Training (IMET) Program.
Exchange of notes at Port Louis June 8 and July 8, 2009.
Entered into force July 8, 2009.
NP

DIPLOMATIC & CONSULAR RELATIONS

Consular convention between the United States and the United Kingdom.
Signed at Washington June 6, 1951.
Entered into force September 7, 1952.
3 UST 3426; TIAS 2494; 165 UNTS 121

EMPLOYMENT

Agreement relating to the employment of dependents of official government employees.
Exchange of notes at Port Louis March 17 and June 13, 1997.
Entered into force June 13, 1997.
TIAS 12868

FINANCE

Investment incentive agreement.
Signed at Port Louis December 15, 1997.
Entered into force May 26, 1998.
TIAS 12912

FOREIGN ASSISTANCE

Economic cooperation agreement between the United States and the United Kingdom.
Signed at London July 6, 1948.
Applicable to Mauritius July 6, 1948.
62 Stat. 2596; TIAS 1795; 12 Bevans 874; 22 UNTS 263

Amendments:
January 3, 1950 (1 UST 184; TIAS 2036; 86 UNTS 304)
May 25, 1951 (2 UST 1292; TIAS 2277; 99 UNTS 308)
February 25, 1953 (4 UST 1528; TIAS 2815; 172 UNTS 332)

INTELLECTUAL PROPERTY

Declaration by the United States and the United Kingdom relating to reciprocal protection to trade-marks.
Signed at London October 24, 1877.
Entered into force October 24, 1877.
20 Stat. 703; TS 138; 12 Bevans 198

INTERNATIONAL CRIMINAL COURT

Agreement regarding the surrender of persons to the International Criminal Court.
Signed at Washington June 25, 2003.
Entered into force June 30, 2003.
TIAS 03-630.2

LAW ENFORCEMENT

Extradition treaty between the United States and the United Kingdom.
Signed at London December 22, 1931.
Entered into force June 24, 1935.
47 Stat. 2122; TS 849; 12 Bevans 482; 163 LNTS 59

Agreement regarding mutual assistance between their customs administrations.
Signed at Washington October 25, 2007.
Entered into force October 25, 2007.
TIAS 07-1025

POSTAL MATTERS

International express mail agreement.
Signed at Port Louis and Washington September 9 and October 2, 1992.
Entered into force December 14, 1992.
TIAS 11909

PROPERTY

Convention between the United States and the United Kingdom relating to the tenure and disposition of real and personal property.
Signed at Washington March 2, 1899.
Applicable to Mauritius June 10, 1901.
31 Stat. 1939; TS 146; 12 Bevans 246

Supplementary convention relating to the tenure and disposition of real and personal property of March 2, 1899.
Signed at Washington May 27, 1936.
Entered into force March 10, 1941.
55 Stat. 1101; TS 964; 5 Bevans 140; 203 LNTS 367

TAXATION

Agreement to improve international tax compliance and to implement the Foreign Account Tax Compliance Act, with annexes.
Signed at Port Louis December 27, 2013.
Entered into force August 29, 2014.
TIAS 14-829

Agreement for the exchange of information relating to taxes.
Signed at Port Louis December 27, 2013.
Entered into force August 29, 2014.
TIAS 14-829.1

TRANSPORTATION

Agreement between the United States and the United Kingdom relating to air services.
Signed at Bermuda February 11, 1946.
Entered into force February 11, 1946.
60 Stat. 1499; TIAS 1507; 12 Bevans 726; 3 UNTS 253
Amendment
May 27, 1966 (17 UST 683; TIAS 6019)

Agreement relating to the installation, operation and use of distance measuring equipment at Plaisance Airfield.
Exchange of notes at Port Louis November 4 and December 29, 1969.
Entered into force December 29, 1969.
21 UST 434; TIAS 6829; 740 UNTS 135

MEXICO

AGRICULTURE

Convention safeguarding livestock interests through the prevention of infectious and contagious diseases.
Signed at Washington March 16, 1928.
Entered into force January 18, 1930.
46 Stat. 2451; TS 808; 9 Bevans 959; 106 LNTS 481

Agreement relating to the establishment of an agricultural commission.
Exchange of notes at Mexico January 6 and 27, 1944.
Entered into force January 27, 1944.
58 Stat. 1425; EAS 421; 9 Bevans 1162; 106 UNTS 275

Agreement establishing the Mexican-United States Commission for the Prevention of Foot-and-Mouth Disease.
Exchange of notes at Washington August 26, 1952.
Entered into force August 26, 1952.
6 UST 2543; TIAS 3300; 264 UNTS 269
Amendment:
December 12, 1953, and July 30, 1954 (7 UST 937; TIAS 3578)

Memorandum of understanding concerning cooperative efforts to protect crops from plant pest damage and diseases.
Signed at Mexico February 8, 1973.
Entered into force February 8, 1973.
28 UST 7004; TIAS 8701
Amendments
September 10 and October 9, 1973 (28 UST 7013; TIAS 8701)
July 15 and 24, 1976 (28 UST 7015; TIAS 8701)

Agreement relating to the termination of the 1972 agreement to eradicate screwworms.
Signed at Mexico City and Washington September 24 and 25, 2012.
Entered into force September 25, 2012.
TIAS 12-925.1

Wildfire protection agreement.
Signed at Washington and Boquillas April 8 and 10, 2015.
Entered into force April 10, 2015.
TIAS 15-410

ATOMIC ENERGY

Arrangement for the exchange of technical information and cooperation in nuclear safety matters, with addenda.
Signed at Vienna September 18, 2012.
Entered into force September 18, 2012.
TIAS 12-918.2

BOUNDARIES & BOUNDARY WATERS

Treaty relating to the boundary line, transit of persons, etc., across the Isthmus of Tehuantepec (Gadsden Treaty).*
Signed at Mexico December 30, 1853.
Entered into force June 30, 1854.
10 Stat. 1031; TS 208; 9 Bevans 812
Note:
* Article VIII terminated December 21, 1937.

Convention to avoid the difficulties occasioned by reason of the changes which take place in the beds of the Rio Grande and Colorado River.*
Signed at Washington March 1, 1889.
Entered into force December 24, 1890.
26 Stat. 1512; TS 232; 9 Bevans 877
Note:
* Extended indefinitely by Article 2 of treaty signed February 3, 1944 (59 Stat. 1219; TS 994). This convention established the International Boundary Commission, subsequently the International Boundary and Water Commission.

Convention providing for the equitable distribution of the waters of the Rio Grande for irrigation purposes.
Signed at Washington May 21, 1906.
Entered into force January 16, 1907.
34 Stat. 2953; TS 455; 9 Bevans 924

Convention for the rectification of the Rio Grande (Rio Bravo del Norte) in the El Paso-Juarez Valley, and exchanges of notes of February 1 and September 8, 1933.
Signed at Mexico February 1, 1933.
Entered into force November 10, 1933.
48 Stat. 1621; TS 864; 9 Bevans 976

Treaty terminating article VIII of the boundary treaty of December 30, 1853.
Signed at Washington April 13, 1937.
Entered into force December 21, 1937.
52 Stat. 1457; TS 932; 9 Bevans 1023

Treaty relating to the utilization of waters of the Colorado and Tijuana Rivers and of the Rio Grande, and supplementary protocol signed November 14, 1944.
Signed at Washington February 3, 1944.
Entered into force November 8, 1945.
59 Stat. 1219; TS 994; 9 Bevans 1166; 3 UNTS 313

Agreement to proceed with the construction of Amistad Dam on the Rio Grande to form part of the system of international storage dams provided for by the water treaty of February 3, 1944.
Signed at Ciudad Acuna October 24, 1960.
Entered into force October 24, 1960.
11 UST 2396; TIAS 4624; 401 UNTS 137

Convention for the solution of the problem of the Chamizal.
Signed at Mexico August 29, 1963.
Entered into force January 14, 1964.
15 UST 21; TIAS 5515; 505 UNTS 185

Act approving minute no. 228 of the International Boundary and Water Commission concerning demarcation of new international boundary between the United States and Mexico.
Signed at Washington October 27, 1967.
Entered into force October 28, 1967.
18 UST 2836; TIAS 6372; 724 UNTS 308

Minute 234 of the International Boundary and Water Commission: Waters of the Rio Grande allotted to the United States from the Conchos, San Diego, San Rodrigo, Escondido and Salado Rivers and the Las Vacas Arroyo.
Signed at Ciudad Juarez December 2, 1969.
Entered into force December 19, 1969.
TIAS

Treaty to resolve pending boundary differences and maintain the Rio Grande and Colorado River as the international boundary between the United States and Mexico, with maps.
Signed at Mexico November 23, 1970.
Entered into force April 18, 1972.
23 UST 371; TIAS 7313

Agreement approving Minute 242 of the International Boundary and Water Commission setting forth a permanent and definitive solution to the international problem of the salinity of the Colorado River.
Exchange of notes at Mexico August 30, 1973.
Entered into force August 30, 1973.
24 UST 1968; TIAS 7708

Act approving Minute 257 of the International Boundary and Water Commission confirming relocation of the channel of the Rio Grande.
Signed at Washington May 26, 1977.
Entered into force May 26, 1977.
28 UST 5256; TIAS 8625

Minute 261 of the International Boundary and Water Commission concerning recommendations for the solution to the border sanitation problems.
Signed at El Paso September 24, 1979.
Entered into force October 2, 1979.
31 UST 5099; TIAS 9658; 1221 UNTS 189

Minute 264 of the International Boundary and Water Commission: Recommendations for solution of the New River border sanitation problem at Calexico, California Mexicali, Baja California Norte.
Signed at Ciudad Juarez August 26, 1980.
Entered into force December 4, 1980.
32 UST 3764; TIAS 9918; 1267 UNTS 163

Minute 270 of the International Boundary and Water Commission: Recommendations concerning border sanitation problem at San Diego, California-Tijuana, Baja California.
Signed at Ciudad Juarez April 30, 1985.
Entered into force July 16, 1985.
TIAS 11267

Minute 273 of the International Boundary and Water Commission: Recommendations for the solution of the border sanitation problem at Naco, Arizona-Naco, Sonora.
Signed at El Paso March 19, 1987.
Entered into force April 15, 1987.
TIAS 11292

Amendment:
September 19, 1996

Minute 274 of the International Boundary and Water Commission: Joint project for improvement of the quality of waters of the New River at Calexico, California-Mexicali, Baja California, with joint report.
Signed at Ciudad Juarez April 15, 1987.
Entered into force May 13, 1987.
TIAS 11316

Agreement concerning rediversion of Rio Grande waters allocated to Mexico under the convention of 1906.
Exchange of notes at Mexico June 24 and November 10, 1987.
Entered into force November 10, 1987.
TIAS 11549

Minute 276 of the International Boundary and Water Commission: Conveyance, treatment and disposal of sewage from Nogales, Arizona and Nogales, Sonora exceeding the capacities allocated to the United States and Mexico at the Nogales international sewage treatment plant under Minute 227, with joint report.
Signed at Ciudad Juarez July 26, 1988.
Entered into force August 19, 1988.
TIAS 12396

Minute 279 of the International Boundary and Water Commission: Joint measures to improve the quality of the waters of the Rio Grande at Laredo, Texas/Nuevo Laredo, Tamaulipas, with joint report.
Signed at Laredo and Nuevo Laredo August 28, 1989.
Entered into force August 28, 1989.
TIAS 11701

Minute 283 of the International Boundary and Water Commission: Conceptual plan for the international solution to the border sanitation problem in San Diego, California/Tijuana, Baja California.
Signed at El Paso July 2, 1990.
Entered into force August 8, 1990.
TIAS 11735

Minute 290 of the International Boundary and Water Commission: Replacement of the International Cordova-Bridge of the Americas over the Rio Grande at El Paso, Texas-Ciudad Juarez, Chihuahua, Mexico.
Signed at Ciudad Juarez September 21, 1993.
Entered into force September 24, 1993.
TIAS

Minute 291 of the International Boundary and Water Commission: Improvements to the conveying capacity of the international boundary segment of the Colorado River.
Signed at San Diego July 16, 1994.
Entered into force August 16, 1994.
TIAS

Treaty on maritime boundaries.
Signed at Mexico City May 4, 1978.
Entered into force November 13, 1997.
TIAS; 2143 UNTS 405

Minute 298 of the International Boundary and Water Commission: Recommendations for construction of works parallel to the city of Tijuana, B.C. wastewater pumping and disposal system and rehabilitation of the San Antonio de los Buenos treatment plant.
Signed at El Paso December 2, 1997.
Entered into force January 23, 1998.
TIAS 12907

Treaty on the delimitation of the continental shelf in the western Gulf of Mexico beyond 200 nautical miles, with annexes.
Signed at Washington June 9, 2000.
Entered into force January 17, 2001.
TIAS 01-117; 2143 UNTS 417
Extension:
June 22, 2010 (TIAS 10-622.1)

Minute 306 of the International Boundary and Water Commission: Conceptual framework for United States-Mexico studies for future recommendations concerning the riparian and estuarine ecology of the limitrophe section of the Colorado River and its associated delta.
Signed at El Paso December 12, 2000.
Entered into force December 13, 2000.
TIAS 13157

Minute 307 of the International Boundary and Water Commission: Partial coverage of allocation of the Rio Grande Treaty tributary water deficit from Fort Quitman to Falcon Dam.
Signed at Washington March 16, 2001.
Entered into force March 16, 2001.
TIAS 13158

Minute 308 of the International Boundary and Water Commission: United States allocation of Rio Grande waters during the last year of the current cycle.
Signed at Ciudad Juarez June 28, 2002.
Entered into force June 28, 2002.
TIAS 02-628

Minute 309 of the International Boundary and Water Commission: Volumes of water saved with the modernization and improved technology projects for the irrigation districts in the Rio Conchos Basin and measures for their conveyance to the Rio Grande.
Signed at El Paso July 3, 2003.
Entered into force July 7, 2003.
TIAS 03-707

Minute 310 of the International Boundary and Water Commission: Emergency delivery of Colorado River water for use in Tijuana, Baja California.
Signed at Ciudad Juarez July 28, 2003.
Entered into force October 1, 2003.
TIAS 03-1001.1

Minute 311 of the International Boundary and Water Commission: Recommendations for secondary treatment in Mexico of the sewage emanating from the Tijuana River area in Baja California, Mexico, with related letter.
Signed at El Paso February 20, 2004.
Entered into force March 5, 2004.
TIAS 04-305.1

Minute 313 of the International Boundary and Water Commission: Maintenance in the rectified channel of the Rio Grande.
Signed at El Paso February 5, 2008.
Entered into force March 6, 2008.
TIAS 08-306

Minute 314 of the International Boundary and Water Commission: Extension of IBWC Minute 310 for the temporary emergency delivery of Colorado River water for use in Tijuana, Baja California.
Signed at Ciudad Juarez November 14, 2008.
Entered into force November 26, 2008.
TIAS 08-1126
Extension:
October 16 and November 2, 2009 (TIAS 08-1126)

Minute 316 of the International Boundary and Water Commission: Utilization of the Wellton-Mohawk Bypass drain and necessary infrastructure in the United States for the conveyance of water by Mexico and non-governmental organizations of both countries to the Santa Clara Wetland during the Yuma Desalting Plant pilot run.
Signed at Yuma April 16, 2010.
Entered into force May 14, 2010.
TIAS 10-514

Minute 317 of the International Boundary and Water Commission: Adoption of a conceptual framework for U.S.-Mexico discussions on Colorado River cooperative actions.
Signed at Ciudad Juarez June 17, 2010.
Entered into force June 29, 2010.
TIAS 10-630

Minute 318 of the International Boundary and Water Commission: Adjustment of delivery schedules for water allotted to Mexico for the years 2010 through 2013 as a result of infrastructure damage in Irrigation District 014, Rio Colorado, caused by the April 2010 earthquake in the Mexicali Valley, Baja California.
Signed at El Paso December 17, 2010.
Entered into force December 20, 2010.
TIAS 10-1220

Minute 319 of the International Boundary and Water Commission: Interim international cooperative measures in the Colorado River Basin through 2017 and extension of Minute 318 cooperative measures to address the continued effects of the April 2010 earthquake in the Mexicali Valley, Baja California.
Signed at Coronado, California November 20, 2012.
Entered into force November 27, 2012.
TIAS 12-1127

Agreement concerning transboundary hydrocarbon reservoirs in the Gulf of Mexico.
Signed at Los Cabos February 20, 2012.
Entered into force July 18, 2014.
TIAS 14-718

CIVIL AFFAIRS, EMERGENCIES & DEFENSE

Agreement on emergency management cooperation in cases of natural disasters and accidents.
Signed at Puerto Vallarta October 23, 2008.
Entered into force March 20, 2011.
TIAS 11-320

CLAIMS & DISPUTE RESOLUTION

Convention for the adjustment and settlement of certain outstanding claims.
Signed at Washington November 19, 1941.
Entered into force April 2, 1942.
56 Stat. 1347; TS 980; 9 Bevans 1059; 125 UNTS 287

CONSULAR AFFAIRS

Agreement on documentation for nonimmigrants traveling between the United States and Mexico.
Exchange of notes at Mexico October 28 and November 10 and 12, 1953.
Entered into force November 12, 1953.
5 UST 174; TIAS 2912; 224 UNTS 187
Amendment:
May 29, 1974 (25 UST 1172; TIAS 7847)

CULTURAL EXCHANGES, PROPERTY & COOPERATION

Agreement establishing a United States-Mexican Commission on Cultural Cooperation.
Exchange of notes at Mexico December 28, 1948, and August 30, 1949.
Entered into force August 30, 1949.
63 Stat. 2842; TIAS 2086; 9 Bevans 1264; 98 UNTS 183
Amendments:
June 15, 1972 (23 UST 925; TIAS 7360)
October 30, 1978, and January 23, 1979 (30 UST 2932; TIAS 9374; 1177 UNTS 338)

Treaty of cooperation providing for the recovery and return of stolen archaeological, historical and cultural properties.
Signed at Mexico July 17, 1970.
Entered into force March 24, 1971.
22 UST 494; TIAS 7088; 791 UNTS 313

Agreement on the development and facilitation of tourism.
Signed at Washington October 3, 1989.
Entered into force August 22, 1990.
TIAS 12403

Agreement to establish a program of the Peace Corps in Mexico.
Signed at Washington November 12, 2003.
Entered into force November 12, 2003.
TIAS 03-1112.1

Agreement to promote science and technology of the United Mexican States in the areas of environment and natural resources.
Signed at Mexico City June 13, 2006.
Entered into force June 13, 2006.
TIAS 06-613

DEFENSE

Agreement to facilitate the reciprocal transit of military aircraft.
Signed at Washington April 1, 1941.
Entered into force April 25, 1941.
55 Stat. 1191; TS 971; 9 Bevans 1049

Agreement relating to the deposit by Mexico of ten percent of the value of military training scholarships provided by the United States.
Exchange of notes at Mexico April 4 and July 12, 1972.
Entered into force July 12, 1972; effective February 7, 1972.
23 UST 2809; TIAS 7469

Agreement concerning the provision of training related to defense articles under the United States International Military Education and Training (IMET) Program.
Exchange of notes at Mexico August 21 and September 24, 1987.
Entered into force September 24, 1987.
NP

Agreement regarding grants of defense articles, related training, or other defense services to Mexico from the U.S. With the related letter.
Effected by exchange of notes at Mexico September 21, 1990.
Entered into force September 21,1990.

Agreement regarding the exchange of naval personnel.
Signed at Washington January 26, 2004.
Entered into force January 26, 2004.
NP

Agreement regarding the assignment of a liaison officer, with annex.
Signed at Washington and Mexico August 17 and September 11, 2004.
Entered into force September 11, 2004.
NP

Agreement regarding the assignment of a liaison officer.
Signed at Mexico City and Peterson AFB, October 20, 2006 and January 25, 2007.
Entered into force January 25, 2007.

Agreement concerning security measures with the Department of the Navy of the United Mexican States for the protection of classified information.
Signed September 15, 2008.
Entered into force September 15, 2008.
TIAS 08-915

Agreement concerning security measures with the National Defense of the United Mexican States for the protection of classified information.
Signed March 16, 2010.
Entered into force March 16, 2010.
TIAS 10-316

Agreement regarding the exchange of military personnel, with annexes.
Signed at Washington September 4 and 9, 2013.
Entered into force September 9, 2013.
NP

Agreement concerning health care for military members and their dependents.
Signed May 1,21 & 22, 2014
Entered into force May 22, 2014
NP

Basic exchange and cooperation agreement concerning geospatial information.
Signed at Springfield, Aguascalientes and Mexico City February 3, March 18 and 19, 2015.
Entered into force March 19, 2015.
NP

DIPLOMATIC & CONSULAR RELATIONS

Consular convention.
Signed at Mexico August 12, 1942.
Entered into force July 1, 1943. Exchanges of notes dated August 12 and December 11 and 12, 1942.
57 Stat. 800; TS 985; 9 Bevans 1076; 125 UNTS 301

EDUCATION

Agreement relating to creation of a joint commission to review operation of the Abraham Lincoln and Benito Juarez scholarship funds.
Exchange of notes at Mexico September 30 and October 25, 1966.
Entered into force October 25, 1966.
17 UST 2023; TIAS 6140; 676 UNTS 11

Agreement for the establishment of the U.S.-Mexico commission for educational and cultural exchange, with memorandum of understanding.
Signed at Monterrey November 27, 1990.
Entered into force November 27, 1990.
TIAS 11769; 2001 UNTS 143

Amendments and Extensions:
March 30 and May 10, 1995
May 5, 1997 (2001 UNTS 143)
May 18, 2000
November 17 and 24, 2010

ENERGY

Agreement on natural gas.
Announced September 21, 1979.
Entered into force September 21, 1979.
31 UST 5097; TIAS 9657; 1221 UNTS 185

ENVIRONMENT & CONSERVATION

Convention for the protection of migratory birds and game mammals.
Signed at Mexico February 7, 1936.
Entered into force March 15, 1937.
50 Stat. 1311; TS 912; 9 Bevans 1017; 178 LNTS 309

Amendment
May 5, 1997

Agreement supplementing the convention of February 7, 1936, for the protection of migratory birds and game mammals.
Exchange of notes at Mexico and Tlatelolco March 10, 1972.
Entered into force March 10, 1972.
23 UST 260; TIAS 7302

Agreement on cooperation for the protection and improvement of the environment in the border area.
Signed at La Paz August 14, 1983.
Entered into force February 16, 1984.
35 UST 2916; TIAS 10827; 1352 UNTS 67

Annex I to the agreement of August 14, 1983 concerning cooperation for solution of the border sanitation problem at San Diego, California-Tijuana, Baja California.
Signed at San Diego July 18, 1985.
Entered into force July 18, 1985.
TIAS 11269

Annex II to the agreement of August 14, 1983 concerning cooperation regarding pollution of the environment along the inland international boundary by discharges of hazardous substances, with appendices.
Signed at San Diego July 18, 1985.
Entered into force November 29, 1985.
TIAS 11269
Amendment:
June 4, 1999

Annex III to the agreement of August 14, 1983 concerning cooperation regarding the transboundary shipments of hazardous wastes and hazardous substances.
Signed at Washington November 12, 1986.
Entered into force January 29, 1987.
TIAS 11269
Amendment:
September 6 and November 28, 2012 (TIAS 12-1128)

Annex IV to the agreement of August 14, 1983 concerning cooperation regarding transboundary air pollution caused by copper smelters along their common border.
Signed at Washington January 29, 1987.
Entered into force January 29, 1987.
TIAS 11269

Annex V to the agreement of August 14, 1983 concerning cooperation regarding international transport of urban air pollution, with appendix.
Signed at Washington October 3, 1989.
Entered into force August 22, 1990.
TIAS 11269
Amendment:
May 7, 1996

Agreement on cooperation for the protection and improvement of the environment in the metropolitan area of Mexico City.
Signed at Washington October 3, 1989.
Entered into force August 22, 1990.
TIAS 11688; 2191 UNTS 269

Agreement concerning the establishment of a border environment cooperation commission and a North American development bank, with annex.
Signed at Washington and Mexico November 16 and 18, 1993.
Entered into force January 1, 1994.
TIAS 12516
Amendment:
November 25 and 26, 2002 (TIAS 04-806.1)

Agreement for cooperation in the Global Learning and Observations to Benefit the Environment (GLOBE) Program, with appendices.
Signed at Mexico November 15, 1996.
Entered into force November 15, 1996.
TIAS 12814

Memorandum of understanding on cooperation for the protection, management, sustainable use and conservation of the environment and natural resources.
Signed at Mexico City February 25, 2016.
Entered into force February 25, 2016.
TIAS 16-225

FINANCE

Agreement regarding the consolidation and rescheduling of certain debts owed to, guaranteed or insured by the United States through the Export-Import Bank of the United States.
Signed at Mexico March 7, 1984.
Entered into force May 2, 1984.
35 UST 4609; TIAS 10961

Agreement regarding the consolidation and rescheduling of certain debts owed to, guaranteed by, or insured by the United States Government and its agencies, with annexes.
Signed at Washington April 9, 1987.
Entered into force May 21, 1987.
NP

Swap agreement between the United States Treasury and the Banco de Mexico/Government of Mexico, with memorandum of understanding.
Signed at Washington and Mexico September 14, 1989.
Entered into force September 14, 1989.
TIAS

Swap agreement among the United States Treasury and the Banco de Mexico/Government of Mexico, with memorandum of understanding.
Signed at Washington and Mexico March 23, 1990.
Entered into force March 23, 1990.
TIAS

Agreement regarding the consolidation and rescheduling or refinancing of certain debts owed to, guaranteed by, or insured by the United States Government and its agencies, with annexes.
Signed at Mexico March 14, 1990.
Entered into force April 23, 1990.
NP

Investment incentive agreement.
Signed at San Francisco June 9, 2003.
Entered into force June 14, 2004.
TIAS 04-614

FOREIGN ASSISTANCE

General agreement for technical cooperation.
Exchange of notes at Mexico June 27, 1951.
Entered into force June 27, 1951.
2 UST 1243; TIAS 2273; 141 UNTS 211
Amendments:
January 21 and 22, 1952 (3 UST 4781; TIAS 2646; 200 UNTS 312)
April 13, 1954 (5 UST 1373; TIAS 3006; 233 UNTS 306)

Agreement relating to a program of industrial productivity in Mexico.
Exchange of notes at Mexico February 21 and November 15, 1961.
Entered into force November 15, 1961.
13 UST 1882; TIAS 5140; 460 UNTS 113

Agreement providing for the designation of officials to maintain contact between Mexico and the United States in matters relating to economic and social development of the border area.
Exchange of notes at Mexico June 23, 1970.
Entered into force June 23, 1970.
21 UST 1475; TIAS 6905; 753 UNTS 275

Agreement for cooperation in the field of housing and urban development.
Signed at Mexico February 16, 1979.
Entered into force February 16, 1979.
30 UST 5865; TIAS 9523; 1180 UNTS 255

Agreement on cooperation in cases of natural disasters.
Signed at Mexico January 15, 1980.
Entered into force provisionally January 15, 1980; definitively March 18, 1981.
32 UST 5714; TIAS 10013; 1241 UNTS 207

HEALTH & MEDICAL COOPERATION

Agreement to establish a United States-Mexico Border Health Commission.
Signed at Washington and Mexico July 14 and 24, 2000.
Entered into force November 24, 2000.
TIAS 13107

LAW ENFORCEMENT

Arrangement for the direct exchange of certain information regarding the traffic in narcotic drugs.
Exchange of notes at Mexico August 5 and October 2, 1930.
Entered into force October 2, 1930.
9 Bevans 967

Agreement relating to the opening of a border inspection station for the international traffic of persons and goods between the United States and Mexico.
Exchange of notes at Washington July 31 and August 5, 1959.
Entered into force August 5, 1959.
10 UST 1398; TIAS 4285; 356 UNTS 3

Agreement relating to the transfer of equipment for the use of the national police force of Mexico.
Exchange of notes at Washington June 26, 1961.
Entered into force June 26, 1961.
12 UST 1063; TIAS 4810; 413 UNTS 229

Agreement concerning a grant to Mexico of reference books in the field of narcotics abuse.
Exchange of letters at Mexico June 26 and 27, 1973.
Entered into force June 27, 1973.
24 UST 1805; TIAS 7694

Agreement relating to the provision by the United States of communications equipment to combat contraband and especially the illegal flow of narcotics across the border.
Exchange of notes at Mexico and Tlatelolco August 31, 1973.
Entered into force August 31, 1973.
24 UST 1978; TIAS 7709

Agreement concerning the provision of four helicopters and related assistance by the United States to help Mexico in curbing traffic in illegal narcotics.
Exchange of letters at Mexico December 3, 1973.
Entered into force December 3, 1973.
25 UST 1694; TIAS 7906
Amendments:
December 21, 1973 (25 UST 1698; TIAS 7906)
June 24, 1974 (25 UST 1700; TIAS 7906)

Agreement providing additional helicopters and related assistance to Mexico in support of its efforts to curb production and traffic in illegal narcotics.
Exchange of letters at Mexico February 1, 1974.
Entered into force February 1, 1974.
25 UST 1704; TIAS 7907
Amendments:
June 24, 1974 (25 UST 1708; TIAS 7907)
December 4, 1974 (25 UST 3172; TIAS 7983)

Agreement relating to the provision of support by the United States for a multi-spectral aerial photographic system capable of detecting opium poppy cultivation, with annexes.
Exchange of letters at Mexico June 10 and 24, 1974.
Entered into force June 24, 1974.
25 UST 1286; TIAS 7863
Amendment:
September 19, 1974 (25 UST 2963; TIAS 7956)

Agreement relating to a training program for Mexican helicopter pilots and mechanics as part of U.S.-Mexican cooperative efforts to reduce traffic in illegal narcotics.
Exchange of letters at Mexico September 30, 1974.
Entered into force September 30, 1974.
25 UST 3166; TIAS 7982; 991 UNTS 367

Agreement providing additional helicopters and related assistance to Mexico in support of its efforts to curb illegal production and traffic in narcotics.
Exchange of letters at Mexico November 1, 1974.
Entered into force November 1, 1974.
25 UST 2956; TIAS 7955

Agreement relating to the provision of assistance to Mexico in narcotics enforcement training activities.
Exchange of letters at Mexico December 4, 1974.
Entered into force December 4, 1974.
25 UST 3176; TIAS 7984; 991 UNTS 373

Agreement relating to cooperative arrangements to support Mexican efforts to curb the illegal traffic in narcotics.
Exchange of letters at Mexico December 11, 1974.
Entered into force December 11, 1974.
26 UST 1274; TIAS 8108
Amendments:
February 24, 1975 (26 UST 1285; TIAS 8108)
March 20, 1975 (26 UST 1289; TIAS 8108)
May 18, 1976 (27 UST 1977; TIAS 8295)

Agreement concerning the provision by the United States of four mobile interdiction systems for use in curbing the illicit flow of narcotic substances through Mexico.
Exchange of letters at Mexico February 24, 1975.
Entered into force February 24, 1975.
26 UST 414; TIAS 8041; 991 UNTS 379

Agreement relating to the provision of equipment and training by the United States to support U.S.-Mexican efforts to curb illegal narcotics traffic.
Exchange of letters at Mexico May 29, 1975.
Entered into force May 29, 1975.
26 UST 1633; TIAS 8123; 1006 UNTS 37

Agreement relating to the provision of equipment and training by the United States to support U.S.-Mexican efforts to curb illegal narcotics traffic.
Exchange of letters at Mexico June 25, 1975.
Entered into force June 25, 1975.
26 UST 1659; TIAS 8125; 1006 UNTS 43

Agreement to indemnify and safeguard the United States Government, its personnel and contractors for liability arising out of aircraft operations training in support of the cooperative program to curb illegal narcotics traffic.
Exchange of letters at Mexico September 12, 1975.
Entered into force September 12, 1975.
27 UST 1985; TIAS 8296
Amendment:
August 13, 1976 (28 UST 8241; TIAS 8758)

Agreement relating to the provision of two helicopters by the United States to support U.S.-Mexican efforts to curb the production and traffic in illegal narcotics.
Exchange of letters at Mexico October 24 and 29, 1975.
Entered into force October 29, 1975.
27 UST 1996; TIAS 8298

Agreement relating to the provision of aircraft by the United States to support U.S.-Mexican efforts to curb the illegal production and traffic in narcotics.
Exchange of letters at Mexico January 29, 1976.
Entered into force January 29, 1976.
27 UST 4261; TIAS 8449

Agreement relating to the provision of supplies, equipment, and services by the United States to support U.S.-Mexican efforts to curb the illegal production and traffic in narcotics.
Exchange of letters at Mexico February 4, 1976.
Entered into force February 4, 1976.
27 UST 1973; TIAS 8294
Amendment:
May 18, 1976 (27 UST 1977; TIAS 8295)

Procedures for mutual assistance in the administration of justice in connection with the General Tire and Rubber Company and the Firestone Tire and Rubber Company matters.
Signed at Washington June 23, 1976.
Entered into force June 23, 1976.
28 UST 2083; TIAS 8533
Related Agreements:
February 23 and March 6, 1978 (29 UST 2153; TIAS 8930)
May 31 and June 1, 1978 (29 UST 3200; TIAS 9005; 1124 UNTS 433)
November 17 and December 5, 1978 (30 UST 2177; TIAS 9322)
August 25 and November 9, 1981 (33 UST 4353; TIAS 10305)
November 1 and 25, 1981 (33 UST 4353; TIAS 10305)

Agreement relating to additional cooperative arrangements to curb illegal traffic in narcotics.
Exchange of letters at Mexico June 30, 1976.
Entered into force June 30, 1976.
27 UST 1990; TIAS 8297

Agreement relating to the provision of additional equipment, material and technical sup-port by the United States to curb illegal traffic in narcotics.
Exchange of letters at Mexico August 9, 1976.
Entered into force August 9, 1976.
27 UST 3937; TIAS 8411; 1059 UNTS 123

Agreement relating to additional cooperative arrangements to curb the illegal traffic in narcotics.
Exchange of letters at Mexico March 8, 1977.
Entered into force March 8, 1977.
29 UST 268; TIAS 8810

Agreement relating to additional cooperative arrangements to curb the illegal traffic in narcotics, with annexes.
Exchange of notes at Mexico June 2, 1977.
Entered into force June 2, 1977.
29 UST 2483; TIAS 8952
Amendments:
September 28, 1977 (29 UST 2496; TIAS 8952)
July 20 and 26, 1978 (30 UST 1285; TIAS 9251; 1153 UNTS 454)
August 24, 1978 (30 UST 1289; TIAS 9251; 1153 UNTS 457)
January 15, 1979 (30 UST 1294; TIAS 9251; 1153 UNTS 460)
September 27 and 28, 1979 (31 UST 4760; TIAS 9637; 1202 UNTS 416)
December 5, 1979 (31 UST 5913; TIAS 9695; 1221 UNTS 376)
April 11, 1980 (32 UST 992; TIAS 9749; 1221 UNTS 379)
November 6, 1980 (32 UST 4157; TIAS 9933; 1266 UNTS 326)
January 2, 1981 (32 UST 4525; TIAS 9963; 1266 UNTS 329)
August 19, 1981 (33 UST 3683; TIAS 10249; 1541 UNTS 433)
October 14, 1981 (33 UST 4081; TIAS 10285; 1549 UNTS 463)
December 4, 1981 (33 UST 4406; TIAS 10310; 1549 UNTS 466)
January 6 and 8, 1982 (34 UST 35; TIAS 10336)
March 15 and 17, 1982 (34 UST 350; TIAS 10360; 1556 UNTS 386)
August 6, 1982 (34 UST 1449; TIAS 10430; 1736 UNTS 365)
November 8, 1982 (TIAS 10582; 1871 UNTS 502)
February 9, 1983 (TIAS 10657; 2001 UNTS 417)
May 12 and 27, 1983 (TIAS 10657; 2001 UNTS 422)
November 10, 1983 (35 UST 4104; TIAS 10907; 2016 UNTS 67)
January 4, 1984 (TIAS 11124)
May 29, 1984 (TIAS 11124)
October 29, 1984 (TIAS 11124)
February 4, 1985
April 3, 1985
September 13 and 25, 1985
November 13 and 29, 1985
November 29 and December 2, 1985
January 13 and March 12, 1986 (TIAS 11517)
March 13 and April 7, 1986 (TIAS 11517)
June 3 and July 1, 1986 (TIAS 11517)
November 3 and December 18, 1986 (TIAS 11517)
July 14 and 28, 1987 (TIAS 11561)
August 7 and 28, 1987 (TIAS 11561)
August 10 and 28, 1987 (TIAS 11561)
December 22, 1987, and February 11, 1988 (TIAS 11652; 2204 UNTS 535)

Agreement relating to additional cooperative arrangements to curb the illegal traffic in narcotics.
Exchange of letters at Mexico July 29, 1977.
Entered into force July 29, 1977.
29 UST 1509; TIAS 8895

Agreement relating to additional cooperative arrangements to curb the illegal traffic in narcotics.
Exchange of letters at Mexico August 5, 1977.
Entered into force August 5, 1977.
29 UST 2500; TIAS 8953
Amendment:
September 29, 1977 (29 UST 2505; TIAS 8953)

Agreement relating to computerization of information in support of programs against illegal narcotics production and traffic.
Exchange of letters at Mexico September 6, 1977.
Entered into force September 6, 1977.
29 UST 2551; TIAS 8955

Agreement relating to the development of telecommunications capability to support the narcotics control effort.
Exchange of letters at Mexico September 7, 1977.
Entered into force September 7, 1977.
29 UST 1994; TIAS 8915

Treaty on the execution of penal sentences.
Signed at Mexico November 25, 1976.
Entered into force November 30, 1977.
28 UST 7399; TIAS 8718

Agreement concerning training for helicopter pilots as part of the cooperative effort to reduce illegal narcotics traffic.
Exchange of letters at Mexico April 3, 1978.
Entered into force April 3, 1978.
30 UST 1007; TIAS 9234; 1152 UNTS 235

Agreement relating to additional cooperative arrangements to curb the illegal production and traffic in narcotics.
Exchange of letters at Mexico May 15, 1978.
Entered into force May 15, 1978.
30 UST 1270; TIAS 9250; 1152 UNTS 241
Amendments:
January 5, 1979 (30 UST 1276; TIAS 9250; 1152 UNTS 245)
February 7, 1979 (30 UST 1280; TIAS 9250; 1152 UNTS 248)
July 23, 1979 (30 UST 6186; TIAS 9544; 1179 UNTS 414)

Agreement relating to additional cooperative arrangements to curb the illegal traffic in narcotics.
Exchange of letters at Mexico May 16, 1978.
Entered into force May 16, 1978.
30 UST 1299; TIAS 9252; 1152 UNTS 257
Amendments:
January 8, 1979 (30 UST 1305; TIAS 9252; 1152 UNTS 261)
July 24, 1979 (30 UST 6197; TIAS 9546; 1179 UNTS 419)

Agreement concerning an illicit crop detection system to be used in curbing the illegal traffic in narcotics.
Exchange of letters at Mexico May 22, 1978.
Entered into force May 22, 1978.
30 UST 1237; TIAS 9248; 1152 UNTS 269
Amendments:
September 26, 1978 (30 UST 1247; TIAS 9248; 1152 UNTS 275)
January 12, 1979 (30 UST 1251; TIAS 9248; 1152 UNTS 278)
December 6, 1979 (31 UST 5904; TIAS 9693; 1221 UNTS 449)
January 27, 1981 (33 UST 990; TIAS 10082; 1274 UNTS 411)

Agreement relating to additional cooperative arrangements to curb the illegal traffic in narcotics.
Exchange of letters at Mexico May 23, 1978.
Entered into force May 23, 1978.
30 UST 1255; TIAS 9249; 1152 UNTS 289
Amendments:
July 11 and 13, 1978 (30 UST 1262; TIAS 9249; 1152 UNTS 293)
January 11, 1979 (30 UST 1266; TIAS 9249; 1152 UNTS 296)

Agreement relating to additional cooperative arrangements to curb the illegal traffic in narcotics.
Exchange of letters at Mexico May 24, 1978.
Entered into force May 24, 1978.
30 UST 1488; TIAS 9258; 1148 UNTS 26
Amendments:
January 9, 1979 (30 UST 1494; TIAS 9258; 1148 UNTS 31)
April 20, 1979 (30 UST 1498; TIAS 9258; 1148 UNTS 34)

Agreement relating to the provision and utilization of aircraft to curb the illegal traffic in narcotics.
Exchange of letters at Mexico August 23, 1978.
Entered into force August 23, 1978.
30 UST 1319; TIAS 9254; 1152 UNTS 305
Amendment:
July 26, 1979 (30 UST 6191; TIAS 9545; 1179 UNTS 424)

Agreement relating to computerization of information in support of programs against illegal narcotics production and traffic.
Exchange of letters at Mexico August 25, 1978.
Entered into force August 25, 1978.
30 UST 1309; TIAS 9253; 1152 UNTS 311
Amendment:
January 10, 1979 (30 UST 1315; TIAS 9253; 1152 UNTS 315)

Agreement relating to salary supplements to personnel dedicated to opium poppy eradication and narcotics interdiction.
Exchange of letters at Mexico December 3, 1979.
Entered into force December 3, 1979.
31 UST 5918; TIAS 9696; 1221 UNTS 199
Amendments
April 25, 1980 (32 UST 1324; TIAS 9772; 1221 UNTS 203)
October 10, 1980 (32 UST 2901; TIAS 9884; 1274 UNTS 436)
December 29, 1981 (33 UST 4679; TIAS 10329)

Extradition treaty, with appendix.
Signed at Mexico May 4, 1978.
Entered into force January 25, 1980.
31 UST 5059; TIAS 9656

Agreement relating to additional cooperative arrangements to curb the illegal traffic in narcotics.
Exchange of letters at Mexico April 7, 1980.
Entered into force April 7, 1980.
32 UST 997; TIAS 9750

Agreement relating to additional cooperative arrangements to curb the illegal traffic in narcotics.
Exchange of letters at Mexico July 25, 1980.
Entered into force July 25, 1980.
32 UST 2105; TIAS 9822

Amendments:
December 2, 1980 (33 UST 1217; TIAS 10106; 1285 UNTS 347)
March 31, 1981 (33 UST 1535; TIAS 10129)
April 2, 1982 (TIAS 10519)
May 17, 1984 (TIAS 11122)
September 25 and October 10, 1984 (TIAS 11122)
April 2, 1985 (TIAS 11346; 2194 UNTS 483)
July 24 and August 20, 1985 (TIAS 11347; 2194 UNTS 490)

Agreement relating to additional cooperative arrangements to curb the illegal traffic in narcotics.
Exchange of letters at Mexico January 3, 1981.
Entered into force January 3, 1981.
33 UST 823; TIAS 10064; 1267 UNTS 181

Convention for the recovery and return of stolen or embezzled vehicles and aircraft.
Signed at Washington January 15, 1981.
Entered into force June 28, 1983.
TIAS 10653

Agreement relating to additional cooperative arrangements to curb the illegal traffic in narcotics.
Exchange of letters at Mexico April 8, 1981.
Entered into force April 8, 1981.
33 UST 1757; TIAS 10142

Agreement relating to additional cooperative arrangements to curb the illegal traffic in narcotics.
Exchange of letters at Mexico March 29, 1983.
Entered into force March 29, 1983.
TIAS 10675; 2005 UNTS 155

Amendments:
April 25, 1985 (TIAS 11348)
November 25 and 29, 1985 (TIAS 11349)
January 29 and March 12, 1986 (TIAS 11348)
August 25 and September 29, 1986 (TIAS 11349)
September 27 and 30, 1986 (TIAS 12090)
March 16 and April 14, 1987 (TIAS 11548)

Agreement relating to additional cooperative arrangements to curb the illegal traffic in narcotics.
Exchange of letters at Mexico November 5, 1984.
Entered into force November 5, 1984.
TIAS 11125

Agreement on cooperation in combatting narcotics trafficking and drug dependency.
Signed at Mexico February 23, 1989.
Entered into force July 30, 1990.
TIAS 11604; 2192 UNTS 107

Treaty on cooperation for mutual legal assistance.
Signed at Mexico December 9, 1987.
Entered into force May 3, 1991.
TIAS

Mutual cooperation agreement for the exchange of information in respect to transactions in currency through financial institutions in order to combat illicit activities.
Signed at Washington October 28, 1994.
Entered into force February 3, 1995.
TIAS; 1901 UNTS 3

Amendment:
May 5, 1997

Agreement regarding mutual assistance between their customs administrations.
Signed at Washington June 20, 2000.
Entered into force June 20, 2000.
TIAS 13103

Protocol to the extradition treaty of May 4, 1978.
Signed at Washington November 13, 1997.
Entered into force May 21, 2001.
TIAS 12897

Agreement regarding the sharing of forfeited assets.
Signed at Washington September 4, 2001.
Entered into force September 4, 2001.
TIAS 13163

Letter of agreement on the Merida Initiative.
Signed at Mexico City December 3, 2008.
Entered into force December 3, 2008.
NP

MARITIME MATTERS

Treaty for the sending of vessels for purposes of assistance and salvage.
Signed at Mexico June 13, 1935.
Entered into force March 7, 1936.
49 Stat. 3359; TS 905; 9 Bevans 1015; 168 LNTS 135

Agreement on maritime search and rescue.
Signed at Mexico August 7, 1989.
Entered into force June 25, 1990.
TIAS 11700; 1580 UNTS 385

MIGRATION & REFUGEES

Joint statement relating to the problem of illegal entry into the United States by Mexican migratory workers, with annexes.
Signed at Washington July 18, 1973.
Entered into force July 18, 1973.
26 UST 1724; TIAS 8131; 1006 UNTS 25

PEACE

Treaty of peace, friendship, limits, and settlement.*
Signed at Guadalupe Hidalgo February 2, 1848.
Entered into force May 30, 1848.
9 Stat. 922; TS 207; 9 Bevans 791

Note

* Articles V, VI and VII were amended and article XI was abrogated by the Gadsden treaty, signed December 30, 1853 (10 Stat. 1031; TS 208). Articles II IV, XII XV, and XVII XX have been executed.

POLLUTION

Agreement of cooperation regarding pollution of the marine environment by discharges of hydrocarbons and other hazardous substances, with annexes.
Signed at Mexico July 24, 1980.
Entered into force provisionally July 24, 1980; definitively March 30, 1981.
32 UST 5899; TIAS 10021; 1241 UNTS 225

POSTAL MATTERS

International express mail agreement, with detailed regulations, as amended.
Signed at Mexico February 13, 1981.
Entered into force September 1, 1987.
TIAS 11005; 2023 UNTS 321

Amendment:
July 28, 1987

Postal money order agreement.
Signed at Mexico and Washington May 31 and June 17, 1988.
Entered into force August 1, 1988.
TIAS 11584

PUBLICATIONS

Agreement relating to the exchange of official journals and parliamentary papers.
Exchange of notes at Mexico September 9 and 24, 1937.
Entered into force September 24, 1937.
51 Stat. 311; EAS 108; 9 Bevans 1025; 185 LNTS 23

Agreement relating to the exchange of official publications.
Exchange of notes at Washington June 3 and August 29, 1938.
Entered into force September 1, 1938.
53 Stat. 1977; EAS 134; 9 Bevans 1028; 195 LNTS 359

SCIENTIFIC & TECHNICAL COOPERATION

Agreement for scientific and technical cooperation.
Exchange of notes at Washington June 15, 1972.
Entered into force June 15, 1972.
23 UST 934; TIAS 7362

Amendment:
August 10 and September 22, 1994 (TIAS 12566)

Memorandum of understanding on scientific and technical cooperation in the mapping and earth sciences, with annex.
Signed at Washington August 12, 1992.
Entered into force August 12, 1992.
TIAS 11961

Memorandum of understanding concerning scientific and technical cooperation in the earth and mapping sciences, with annexes.
Signed at Mexico May 9, 1994.
Entered into force May 9, 1994.
TIAS 12180

Memorandum of understanding concerning scientific and technical cooperation in the earth and mapping sciences.
Signed at Mexico November 29, 1994.
Entered into force November 29, 1994.
TIAS 12583

Memorandum of understanding concerning scientific and technical cooperation on biological data and information, with annex.
Signed at Washington May 16, 1995.
Entered into force May 16, 1995.
TIAS 12650

Memorandum of understanding concerning scientific and technical cooperation in the earth and mapping sciences, with annex.
Signed at Mexico May 7, 1996.
Entered into force May 7, 1996.
TIAS 12751

Memorandum of understanding concerning scientific and technical cooperation in the earth sciences.
Signed at Reston and Mexico April 24 and May 2, 2007.
Entered into force May 2, 2007.
TIAS 07-502.1

Agreement on cooperation in science and technology for homeland security matters, with annexes.
Signed at New Orleans April 21, 2008.
Entered into force April 21, 2008.
TIAS 08-421

SOCIAL SECURITY

Agreement relating to the payment of social security benefits.
Exchange of notes at Mexico and Tlatelolco March 27, 1968.
Entered into force March 27, 1968.
24 UST 1045; TIAS 7620

SPACE

Agreement for participation by Mexican scientists in certain programs of space research by the National Aeronautics and Space Administration.
Exchange of notes at Mexico February 27, 1965.
Entered into force February 27, 1965.
16 UST 620; TIAS 5783; 546 UNTS 135

TAXATION

Agreement for the exchange of information with respect to taxes.
Signed at Washington November 9, 1989.
Entered into force January 18, 1990.
TIAS 12404

Convention for the avoidance of double taxation and the prevention of fiscal evasion with respect to taxes on income, with protocol.*
Signed at Washington September 18, 1992.
Entered into force December 28, 1993.
TIAS
Note:
* With understandings.

Additional protocol that modifies the convention of September 18, 1992, for the avoidance of double taxation and the prevention of fiscal evasion with respect to taxes on income.
Signed at Mexico September 8, 1994.
Entered into force October 26, 1995.
TIAS

Protocol that modifies the agreement of November 9, 1989, for the exchange of information with respect to taxes.
Signed at Mexico September 8, 1994.
Entered into force October 26, 1995.
TIAS 12404

Second additional protocol that modifies the convention of September 18, 1992, as amended, for the avoidance of double taxation and the prevention of fiscal evasion with respect to taxes on income.
Signed at Mexico City November 26, 2002.
Entered into force July 3, 2003.
TIAS

Agreement to improve international tax compliance including with respect to the Foreign Account Tax Compliance Act, with Annexes.
Signed at Mexico City April 9, 2014.
Entered into force April 10, 2014.
TIAS 14-410

TELECOMMUNICATION

Arrangement for radio communications between amateur stations on behalf of third parties.
Exchange of notes at Mexico July 31, 1959.
Entered into force August 30, 1959.
10 UST 1449; TIAS 4295; 357 UNTS 187

Agreement relating to the assignment and use of television channels along the United States-Mexican border.
Exchange of notes at Mexico April 18, 1962.
Entered into force April 18, 1962.
13 UST 997; TIAS 5043; 452 UNTS 3
Amendments:
August 20, 1975 (26 UST 2700; TIAS 8185; 1052 UNTS 374)
August 23 and September 4, 1979 (31 UST 4810; TIAS 9641)
January 22 and April 7, 1980 (32 UST 975; TIAS 9746; 1220 UNTS 327)
December 22, 1981, and August 17, 1982 (34 UST 1708; TIAS 10447; 1736 UNTS 316)
October 12, November 13, 1984, April 8 and 25, 1985
September 14 and 26, 1988 (1540 UNTS 404)

Agreement relating to assignments and usage of television broadcasting channels in the frequency range 470–806 MHz (channels 14–69) along the United States-Mexico border.
Signed at Mexico June 18, 1982.
Entered into force January 17, 1983.
TIAS 10535
Amendments:
October 31, 1984, and April 8, 1985 (TIAS 11237)
June 22 and October 19, 1988 (TIAS 12426)
September 12, 1988 (1540 UNTS 277)

Agreement relating to the AM broadcasting service in the medium frequency band, with annexes.
Signed at Mexico August 28, 1986.
Entered into force April 27, 1987.
TIAS

Agreement regarding an earth station coordination procedure, with annex.
Signed at Chestertown July 2, 1991.
Entered into force February 25, 1993.
TIAS 12434; 1733 UNTS 215

Administrative arrangement concerning frequencies used by the International Boundary and Water Commission, with annex.
Signed at Queretaro August 11, 1992.
Entered into force August 11, 1992.
TIAS 12472

Agreement relating to the FM broadcasting service in the band 88–108 MHz, with annexes.
Signed at Queretaro August 11, 1992.
Entered into force June 2, 1995.
TIAS 12474

Agreement for the use of the band 1605–1705 KHz in the AM broadcasting service, with annexes.
Signed at Queretaro August 11, 1992.
Entered into force May 30, 1995.
TIAS 12473

Agreement on the use of the 17.7–17.8 GHz band.
Signed at Washington June 21, 1993.
Entered into force March 8, 1994.
TIAS; 1792 UNTS 303

Agreement concerning the allocation and use of frequency bands by terrestrial non-broadcasting radio communication services along the common border, with annexes.
Signed at Williamsburg June 16, 1994.
Entered into force June 2, 1995.
TIAS 12548

Protocol concerning the use of bands allocated to the aeronautical radio navigation and aeronautical communications services along the common border, with appendices.
Signed at Morelia, Michoacan April 26, 1996.
Entered into force April 26, 1996.
TIAS 12745

Agreement concerning the transmission and reception of signals from satellites for the provision of satellite services to users in the United States and Mexico.
Signed at Mexico April 28, 1996.
Entered into force November 6, 1996.
TIAS

Protocol concerning the transmission and reception of signals from satellites for the provision of direct-to-home satellite services in the United States and Mexico, with exchange of letters.
Signed at Washington November 8, 1996.
Entered into force November 11, 1996.
TIAS

Protocol concerning use of the 929–930 MHz and 931–932 MHz bands for paging services along the common border, with appendices and letter of understanding.
Signed at Washington February 27, 1997.
Entered into force February 27, 1997.
TIAS 12838

Memorandum of understanding for the use of radio frequencies, coordination and cooperation for emergency purposes, with annexes.
Signed at Washington and Mexico City December 9, 1998.
Entered into force December 9, 1998.
TIAS 13009

Protocol concerning the transmission and reception of signals from satellites for the provision of mobile-satellite services and associated feeder links in the United States of America and the United Mexican States, with appendix.
Signed at Mexico City December 21, 1998.
Entered into force December 21, 1998.
TIAS 13014

Agreement concerning the use of the 2310–2360 MHz band, with appendices.
Signed at Mexico City July 24, 2000.
Entered into force January 25, 2001.
TIAS

Protocol concerning the allotment and use of the 406.1–420 MHz band for fixed and mobile services along the common border, with appendices.
Signed at Mexico City July 27, 2005.
Entered into force July 27, 2005.
TIAS 05-727

Protocol concerning the allotment and use of the 380–399.9 MHz band for fixed and mobile terrestrial non-broadcasting services along the common border, with appendices.
Signed at Mexico City July 27, 2005.
Entered into force July 27, 2005.
TIAS 05-727.2
Amendment:
July 17, 2006 (TIAS 05-727.2)

Protocol concerning the allotment and use of the 698–806 MHz band for terrestrial non-broadcasting radio communication services along the common border, with appendices.
Signed at Mexico City and Antalya November 1 and 8, 2006.
Entered into force November 8, 2006.
TIAS 06-1108.2
Amendment:
July 19 and 28, 2011(TIAS 11-728)

Protocol concerning the allotment and use of the 138–144 MHz band for terrestrial non-broadcasting radio communication services along the common border, with appendices.
Signed at Mexico City August 3, 2007.
Entered into force August 3, 2007.
TIAS 07-803
Note:
This agreement of August 3, 2007 supersedes agreement of December 9, 1998 to extent that the MOU's provisions pertain to the two frequencies 139.150 MHz and 142.725 MHz (Art. III.1.).

Protocol concerning the use of the 1710–1755 MHz and 2110–2155 MHz bands for terrestrial non-broadcasting radio communication services along the common border, with appendices.
Signed at Washington and Mexico City December 16 and 19, 2008.
Entered into force December 19, 2008.
TIAS 08-1219.1

Protocol concerning the use of radio frequencies by certain fixed terrestrial links constituting a cross border public security communications network along the common border.
Signed at Washington and Mexico City August 31 and September 1, 2009.
Entered into force September 1, 2009.
TIAS 09-901

Protocol concerning the use of the 4940–4990 MHz band for terrestrial non-broadcasting radio communication services along the common border, with appendices.
Signed at Washington December 1, 2009.
Entered into force December 1, 2009.
TIAS 09-1201

Protocol concerning the use of the 806–824/851–869 MHz and 896–901/935–940 MHz bands for terrestrial non-broadcasting radio communication services along the common border, with appendices.
Signed at Washington June 8, 2012.
Entered into force June 8, 2012.
TIAS 12-608

Protocol concerning the use of the 1850–1915 MHz and 1930–1995 MHz bands for personal communications services along the common border.
Signed at Washington June 8, 2012.
Entered into force June 8, 2012.
TIAS 12-608.1

Protocol concerning the allotment and use of channels in the 220-222 MHz band for land mobile services along the common border, with annexes.
Signed at Washington and Mexico City November 4 and 22, 2016.
Entered into force November 22, 2016.
TIAS 16-1122

TRADE & INVESTMENT

Agreement on steel trade liberalization, with appendices.
Signed at Washington October 3, 1989.
Entered into force October 3, 1989.
TIAS

Agreement regarding the application of their competition laws.
Signed at Mexico July 11, 2000.
Entered into force July 11, 2000.
TIAS

Agreement on the application by Mexico of a North American Free Trade Agreement safeguard measure on certain poultry products.
Exchange of letters at Mexico City and Washington July 24 and 25, 2003.
Entered into force July 25, 2003.
TIAS 03-725

Agreement on trade on tequila, with annex.
Signed at Washington January 17, 2006.
Entered into force January 17, 2006.
TIAS 06-117

Agreement on customs cooperation regarding claims of origin under cumulation provisions of certain free trade agreements.
Signed at Davos January 26, 2007.
Entered into force August 15, 2008.
TIAS 08-815.2

Mutual recognition agreement for conformity assessment of telecommunications equipment, with appendices and annexes.
Signed at Paris May 26, 2011.
Entered into force June 10, 2011.
TIAS 11-610

TRANSPORTATION

Agreement to facilitate flight notifications on non-scheduled, private, commercial or industrial flights between Mexico and the United States in both directions across the border.
Exchange of notes at Washington July 15, 1952.
Entered into force August 1, 1952.
3 UST 4943; TIAS 2667; 181 UNTS 263

Agreement for acceptance by the United States of certificates of airworthiness for aircraft manufactured by Lockheed Azcarate, S.A.
Exchange of notes at Washington June 26 and July 19, 1961.
Entered into force July 19, 1961.
12 UST 1384; TIAS 4861; 433 UNTS 43

Amendment
January 19 and 30, 1962 (13 UST 199; TIAS 4961; 442 UNTS 343)

Memorandum of understanding concerning research cooperation in the field of transportation.
Signed at Merida November 16, 1972.
Entered into force November 16, 1972.
30 UST 823; TIAS 9221

Memorandum of agreement relating to technical assistance in reviewing air traffic operations in Mexico City terminal area.
Signed at Washington February 19, 1981.
Entered into force February 19, 1981.
35 UST 3599; TIAS 10870; 1577 UNTS 345

Memorandum of understanding on additional services (double designation), with annex.
Signed at Mexico September 23, 1988.
Entered into force September 23, 1988.
TIAS

Agreement on reduced air fares.
Exchange of letters at Mexico September 23, 1988.
Entered into force September 23, 1988.
TIAS

Agreement concerning assistance in developing and modernizing Mexico's civil aviation infrastructure in the managerial, operational and technical areas, with annex.
Signed at Washington and Mexico June 4 and July 4, 1991.
Entered into force July 4, 1991.
NP

Memorandum of understanding relating to the recognition and validity of commercial driver's licenses and licencias federales de conductor, with annex.
Signed at Washington November 21, 1991.
Entered into force November 21, 1991.
TIAS 12442

Memorandum of cooperation for Research and Development of the Global Navigation Satellite System (GNSS).
Signed at Mexico July 11, 15 and 26, 1996.
Entered into force July 26, 1996.
TIAS

Memorandum of cooperation in the promotion and development of civil aviation, with letter of understanding.
Signed at Washington and Mexico September 17, October 14 and 16, 1997.
Entered into force October 16, 1997.
TIAS 12891

Memorandum of agreement for the provision of assistance in developing and modernizing Mexico's civil aviation infrastructure.
Signed at Mexico City and Washington October 14 and 20, 1997.
Entered into force October 20, 1997.
NP
Amendment:
May 17, 2010

Agreement for the promotion of aviation safety.
Signed at Montreal September 18, 2007.
Entered into force February 24, 2010.
TIAS

Air transport agreement.
Signed at Washington December 18, 2015.
Entered into force August 21, 2016.
TIAS 16-821

MICRONESIA

A letter of November 2, 1995, from the Government of the Federated States of Micronesia to the Secretary-General of the United Nations refers to a letter of May 22, 1992,

... containing a declaration setting out the position of the Government of the Federated States of Micronesia (FSM) with regard to international agreements entered into by the United States of America and made applicable to the FSM pursuant to the United Nations Trusteeship Agreement for the former Japanese Mandated Islands.

The Declaration stated that as to bilateral treaties validly concluded by the United States on behalf of the FSM, or validly applied or extended by the former to the latter before 3 November 1986, the Government of the FSM would examine each such treaty and communicate its views to the other State Party concerned. The Declaration also stated that the Government of the FSM would continue to observe the terms of each treaty which validly so applied and was not inconsistent with the letter or the spirit of the Constitution of the FSM, provisionally and on a basis of reciprocity. The period of examination was to extend until 3 November 1995, except in the case of any treaty in respect of which an earlier statement of views was or had been made. At the expiration of this period, the Government of the FSM would consider such of these treaties that could not by the application of the rules of customary international law be regarded as otherwise surviving, as having terminated.

The letter of November 2, 1995, extends

... the period of examination of the bilateral treaties indicated above for two additional years, or until 3 November 1997.

With regard to multilateral treaties previously applied, the Declaration of 22 May 1992 stated that the Government of the FSM intends to review each of them individually and to communicate to the depositary in each case what steps it would take, whether by way of confirmation of termination or confirmation of succession or accession. During such period of review, any party to a multilateral treaty that had been validly applied or extended to the Federated States of Micronesia prior to 3 November 1986, and was not inconsistent with the letter or spirit of the Constitution of the FSM, may, on the basis of reciprocity, rely as against the FSM on the terms of such treaty."

AGRICULTURE

Agreement concerning technical assistance in soil and water conservation.
Signed at Palikir April 20, 1990.
Entered into force April 20, 1990.
TIAS 12221

DEFENSE

Agreement regarding grants under the Foreign Assistance Act of 1961, as amended, and the furnishing of defense articles, related training, and other defense services from the United States of America to the Government of the Federated States of Micronesia.
Exchange of notes at Kolonia and Pohnpei November 6, 2001, and March 14, 2002.
Entered into force March 14, 2002.
NP

Agreement concerning operational cooperation to suppress illicit transnational maritime activity.
Signed at Palikir March 3, 2014.
Entered into force March 3, 2014.
TIAS 14-303

DIPLOMATIC & CONSULAR RELATIONS

Agreement relating to diplomatic relations, with related notes.
Exchange of notes at Washington August 23 and 24, 1989.
Entered into force August 24, 1989.
TIAS 11891

EDUCATION

Agreement regarding augmentation of educational assistance.
Signed at Washington August 19, 1987.
Entered into force August 19, 1987.
TIAS 11277

ENVIRONMENT & CONSERVATION

Agreement for cooperation in the Global Learning and Observations to Benefit the Environment (GLOBE) Program, with appendices.
Signed at Kolonia November 7, 1997.
Entered into force November 7, 1997.
TIAS 12895

FINANCE

Agreement relating to investment guaranties.
Exchange of notes at Kolonia February 13 and March 3, 1988.
Entered into force March 3, 1988.
TIAS 12047

INTERNATIONAL CRIMINAL COURT

Agreement regarding the surrender of persons to the International Criminal Court.
Signed at Washington September 24, 2002.
Entered into force June 30, 2003.
TIAS 03-630.1

MARITIME MATTERS

Maritime search and rescue agreement.
Signed at Honolulu June 10, 1988.
Entered into force June 10, 1988.
TIAS 11586; 2192 UNTS 195.

Agreement concerning operational cooperation to suppress illicit transnational maritime activity.
Signed at Palikir March 3, 2014.
Entered in to force March 3, 2014.
TIAS 14-303

REGIONAL ISSUES

Agreement for the implementation of the Compact of Free Association between the Government of the United States and the Government of the Federated States of Micronesia (Title II, PL 99 239), with related agreements.
Signed at Washington October 24, 1986.
Entered into force October 24, 1986; effective November 3, 1986.
TIAS
Amendment:
March 9, 1988 (TIAS 11660)

Agreement on extradition, mutual assistance in law enforcement matters and penal sanctions, with agreed minute.
Signed at Palikir May 14, 2003.
Entered into force June 25, 2004; effective November 3, 1986.
TIAS 04-625.4

Federal programs and services agreement, with annex.
Signed at Palikir May 14, 2003.
Entered into force June 25, 2004.
TIAS 04-625.1

Agreement regarding protections for citizens of the Republic of the Federated States of Micronesia seeking to engage in employment in the United States pursuant to recruitment or other placement services.
Signed at Palikir May 14, 2003.
Entered into force June 25, 2004.
TIAS 04-625.3

Agreement concerning procedures for the implementation of United States economic assistance provided in the Compact of Free Association, as amended, with annex.
Signed at Palikir May 14, 2003.
Entered into force June 25, 2004.
TIAS 04-625.2

Agreement implementing section 215 and section 216 of the Compact, as amended, regarding a trust fund.
Signed at Palikir May 14, 2003.
Entered into force June 25, 2004.
TIAS 04-625.7

Status of forces agreement, with agreed minutes.
Signed at Palikir May 14, 2003.
Entered into force June 25, 2004.
TIAS 04-625.6

Agreement regarding the military use and operating rights of the Government of the United States in the Federated States of Micronesia, with annex.
Signed at Palikir May 14, 2003.
Entered into force June 25, 2004.
TIAS 04-625.5

Agreement amending the Compact of Free Association of October 1, 1982, as amended.
Signed at Palikir May 14, 2003.
Entered into force June 25, 2004.
TIAS 04-625

TELECOMMUNICATION

Agreement relating to radio communications between amateur stations on behalf of third parties.
Exchange of notes at Kolonia April 4 and September 12, 1989.
Entered into force October 12, 1989.
TIAS 12401

Agreement terminating the agreement of June 25, 1983, regarding the provision of telecommunication services.
Exchange of notes at Kolonia and Palikir May 28 and June 7, 1993.
Entered into force June 7, 1993.
TIAS 12501

TRANSPORTATION

Memorandum of agreement concerning assistance in developing and modernizing Micronesia's civil aviation infrastructure.
Signed at Washington and Kolonia October 30, 1989, and January 10, 1990.
Entered into force January 10, 1990.
TIAS 12408
Amendments:
March 20 and September 30, 1999 (NP)
May 29 and June 10, 2009 (NP)
March 7 and April 4, 2011 (NP)

MOLDOVA

For agreements prior to December 31, 1991, see UNION OF SOVIET SOCIALIST REPUBLICS.

CULTURAL EXCHANGES, PROPERTY & COOPERATION

Agreement concerning the program of the Peace Corps of the United States in the Republic of Moldova.
Signed at Chisinau February 2, 1993.
Entered into force February 2, 1993.
TIAS 12485

Agreement on the protection and preservation of certain cultural properties.
Signed at Washington June 20, 2001.
Entered into force July 19, 2010.
TIAS 10-719

DEFENSE

Agreement regarding grants under the Foreign Assistance Act of 1961, as amended, and the furnishing of defense articles, related training and other defense services from the United States to Moldova.
Exchange of notes at Chisinau October 9 and 10, 1997.
Entered into force October 10, 1997.
NP

Basic exchange and cooperative agreement concerning global geospatial information and services cooperation, with annexes.
Signed at Brussels June 24, 2002.
Entered into force February 3, 2003.
NP

EMPLOYMENT

Agreement relating to the employment of dependents of official government employees, with attachment.
Exchange of notes at Chisinau September 8 and 13, 1994.
Entered into force September 13, 1994.
TIAS 12191

ENVIRONMENT & CONSERVATION

Agreement for cooperation in the Global Learning and Observations to Benefit the Environment (GLOBE) Program, with appendices.
Signed at Washington January 30, 1995.
Entered into force January 30, 1995.
TIAS 12603

FINANCE

Investment incentive agreement.
Signed at Washington June 19, 1992.
Entered into force December 2, 1992.
TIAS 12459

Agreement regarding the rescheduling of certain debts owed to, guaranteed by, or insured by the United States Government and its agency, with annexes.
Signed at Chisinau October 31, 2006.
Entered into force February 14, 2007.
NP

FOREIGN ASSISTANCE

Agreement regarding cooperation to facilitate the provision of assistance.
Signed at Chisinau March 21, 1994.
Entered into force March 21, 1994.
TIAS

TRADE & INVESTMENT

Agreement on trade relations, with exchanges of letters.
Signed at Washington June 19, 1992.
Entered into force July 2, 1992.
TIAS

Treaty concerning the encouragement and reciprocal protection of investment, with annex, protocol and exchange of letters.
Signed at Washington April 21, 1993.
Entered into force November 25, 1994.
TIAS

WEAPONS

See also Foreign Assistance

Implementing agreement to the agreement of March 21, 1994 concerning cooperation in border security assistance and preventing the proliferation of weapons of mass destruction with the Border Police.
Signed at Chisinau December 21, 2012.
Entered into force December 21, 2012.
TIAS 12-1221

Implementing agreement to the agreement of March 21, 1994 concerning cooperation in border security assistance and preventing the proliferation of weapons of mass destruction with the Customs Service.
Signed at Chisinau December 21, 2012.
Entered into force December 21, 2012.
TIAS 12-1221.1

MONACO

CONSULAR AFFAIRS

Agreement relating to the reciprocal waiver of passport visa fees for nonimmigrants.*
Exchange of notes at Monaco and Nice March 31, 1952.
Entered into force March 31, 1952; operative May 1, 1952.
3 UST 3942; TIAS 2528; 177 UNTS 195

Note:
* The status of this agreement is under review.

EMPLOYMENT

Agreement concerning the employment of dependents of members of diplomatic missions and consular posts assigned to official duty in the respective countries.
Exchange of notes at Washington July 9, 2015.
Entered into force July 9, 2015.
TIAS 15-709

INTELLECTUAL PROPERTY

Agreement relating to reciprocal copyright relations.
Exchange of notes at Monaco and Nice September 24, 1952.
Entered into force September 24, 1952; operative October 15, 1952.
3 UST 5112; TIAS 2702; 186 UNTS 43

LAW ENFORCEMENT

Extradition treaty.
Signed at Monaco February 15, 1939.
Entered into force March 28, 1940.
54 Stat. 1780; TS 959; 9 Bevans 1272; 202 LNTS 61

Agreement regarding the sharing of confiscated proceeds of crime or property.
Signed at Monaco March 24, 2007.
Entered into force July 1, 2007.
TIAS 07-701

TAXATION

Agreement for the exchange of information relating to tax matters.
Signed at Washington September 8, 2009.
Entered into force March 11, 2010.
TIAS 10-311

TELECOMMUNICATION

Agreement relating to the reciprocal granting of authorizations to permit licensed amateur radio operators of either country to operate their stations in the other country.
Exchange of notes at Monaco March 29 and at Paris October 16, 1968.
Entered into force December 1, 1968.
19 UST 7852; TIAS 6622; 719 UNTS 115

MONGOLIA

CONSULAR AFFAIRS

Agreement concerning the reciprocal issuance of visas to government officials.
Exchange of notes at Ulaanbaatar August 2, 1990.
Entered into force August 2, 1990.
TIAS 12418

CULTURAL EXCHANGES, PROPERTY & COOPERATION

Agreement on cooperation through the United States Peace Corps in Mongolia.
Signed at Ulaanbaatar August 2, 1990.
Entered into force August 2, 1990.
TIAS 11505

DEFENSE

Agreement on military exchanges and visits, with annex.
Signed at Ulaanbaatar June 26, 1996.
Entered into force April 3, 1998.
NP

Basic exchange and cooperative agreement concerning geospatial information and services cooperation, with annexes.
Signed at Bethesda March 22, 2004.
Entered into force March 22, 2004.
NP

Agreement concerning the provision of equipment, training and related services under the United States International Military Education and Training (IMET) Program.
Exchange of notes at Ulaanbaatar August 11, 2003, and July 27, 2005.
Entered into force July 27, 2005.
NP

Acquisition and cross-servicing agreement, with annexes.
Signed at Ulaanbaatar August 2, 2013.
Entered into force August 2, 2013.
NP

DIPLOMATIC & CONSULAR RELATIONS

Memorandum of understanding concerning facilitation of the work of diplomatic missions.
Signed at Washington January 27, 1987.
Entered into force January 27, 1987.
TIAS 11457

Consular convention.
Signed at Ulaanbaatar August 2, 1990.
Entered into force April 5, 2007.
TIAS

EDUCATION

Agreement concerning the international school of Ulaanbaatar.
Signed at Ulaanbaatar May 26, 2004.
Entered into force November 19, 2005.
TIAS 05-1119

EMPLOYMENT

Agreement concerning the employment of dependents of official government employees.
Exchange of notes at Ulaanbaatar March 24 and April 5, 1999.
Entered into force April 5, 1999.
TIAS 13028

ENVIRONMENT & CONSERVATION

Agreement for cooperation in the Global Learning and Observations to Benefit the Environment (GLOBE) Program, with appendices.
Signed at Ulaanbaatar May 6, 1997.
Entered into force May 6, 1997.
TIAS 12853

FINANCE

Investment incentive agreement.
Signed at New York September 29, 1990.
Entered into force January 4, 1991.
TIAS 11501

FOREIGN ASSISTANCE

Agreement concerning economic, technical and related assistance with protocol and memorandum of understanding.
Signed at Ulaanbaatar September 8, 1992.
Entered into force September 8, 1992.
TIAS 12476

INTERNATIONAL CRIMINAL COURT

Agreement regarding the surrender of U.S. persons to third parties.
Exchange of notes at Washington June 6, 2003.
Entered into force June 27, 2003.
TIAS 03-627.2

LAW ENFORCEMENT

Agreement regarding cooperation and mutual assistance in customs matters.
Signed at Hong Kong June 19, 1996.
Entered into force June 19, 1996.
TIAS 12769

NONPROLIFERATION

Agreement concerning cooperation to suppress the proliferation of weapons of mass destruction, their delivery systems, and related materials by sea.
Signed at Washington October 23, 2007.
Entered into force February 20, 2008.
TIAS 08-220

POSTAL MATTERS

Express mail agreement, with detailed regulations.
Signed at Ulaanbaatar and Washington June 5 and July 1, 1996.
Entered into force September 1, 1996.
NP

PROPERTY

Memorandum of understanding concerning facilitation of the work of diplomatic missions, with attachments.
Signed at Washington March 27, 1992.
Entered into force March 27, 1992.
TIAS

SCIENTIFIC & TECHNICAL COOPERATION

Memorandum of understanding concerning scientific and technical cooperation in the earth sciences, with annexes.
Signed at Reston and Ulaanbaatar April 2 and June 26, 2003.
Entered into force June 26, 2003.
TIAS 03-626.2

TRADE & INVESTMENT

Agreement on trade relations, with exchange of letters.
Signed at Washington January 23, 1991.
Entered into force November 27, 1991.
TIAS

Treaty concerning the encouragement and reciprocal protection of investment, with annex and protocol.
Signed at Washington October 6, 1994.
Entered into force January 1, 1997.
TIAS

TRANSPORTATION

Memorandum of agreement relating to technical assistance in developing, modernizing, operating, or maintaining Mongolia's civil aviation infrastructure.
Signed at Washington June 16, 2011.
Entered into force June 16, 2011.
NP

MONTENEGRO

On June 3, 2006, Montenegro declared independence from the state of Serbia and Montenegro. For agreements prior to June 3, 2006, see SERBIA AND MONTENEGRO and YUGOSLAVIA.

DEFENSE

Agreement on status protections and access to and use of military infrastructure in Montenegro.
Signed at Washington May 1, 2007.
Entered into force May 1, 2007.
TIAS 07-501

Agreement regarding grants under the Foreign Assistance Act of 1961, as amended, or successor legislation, and the furnishing of defense articles, defense services and related training including pursuant to the United States International Military Education and Training (IMET) Program.
Exchange of notes at Podgorica May 4 and 18, 2007.
Entered into force May 18, 2007.
NP

Acquisition and cross-servicing agreement.
Signed at Podgorica September 25, 2007.
Entered into force September 25, 2007.
NP

FINANCE

Investment incentive agreement.
Signed at Washington and Brussels March 23 and 29, 2000.
Entered into force March 29, 2000.
TIAS 00-329

Agreement regarding certain debts owed to, guaranteed by, or insured by the United States Government and its agencies.
Signed at Podgorica February 26, 2008.
Entered into force April 14, 2008.
NP

INTERNATIONAL CRIMINAL COURT

Agreement regarding the surrender of persons to the International Criminal Court.
Exchange of notes at Podgorica April 17 and 19, 2007.
Entered into force April 19, 2007.
TIAS 07-419

TRANSPORTATION

Air transport agreement.
Signed at Podgorica March 2, 2012.
Entered into force March 2, 2012.
TIAS 12-302

MOROCCO

The independence of Morocco was recognized in a joint declaration signed March 2, 1956, on behalf of the Government of France and the Sultan of Morocco.

A diplomatic agreement on general relations between France and Morocco signed at Paris May 28, 1956, provided inter alia (1) that none of the provisions of that agreement must be interpreted as affecting the obligations which result either from the Charter of the United Nations or from agreements, treaties, or conventions in force between one of the High Contracting Parties and third powers (article 6), and (2) that Morocco assumes the obligations resulting from international treaties passed by France in the name of Morocco as well as those resulting from international acts relating to Morocco which have not been subject to observations on its part (article 11).

ARMS CONTROL

Agreement regarding the development and operation of a seismic monitoring station in the Kingdom of Morocco.
Signed at Rabat December 31, 2008.
Entered into force December 31, 2008.
TIAS 08-1231

ATOMIC ENERGY

Agreement for cooperation concerning peaceful uses of nuclear energy, with annex and agreed minute.
Signed at Washington May 30, 1980.
Entered into force May 16, 1981.
32 UST 5823; TIAS 10018; 1267 UNTS 101
Amendment
September 20, 2001 (TIAS 13168)

CONSULAR AFFAIRS

Arrangement between the United States and France for the waiver by France of visa requirements for United States citizens visiting Metropolitan France and certain French territories, and for the granting by the United States of gratis passport visas to French citizens resident in those territories who enter the United States as nonimmigrants.*
Exchange of notes at Paris March 16 and 31, 1949.
Entered into force March 31, 1949.
63 Stat. 2737; TIAS 1987; 7 Bevans 1311; 84 UNTS 283
Note:
* The status of this agreement is under review.

CULTURAL EXCHANGES, PROPERTY & COOPERATION

Agreement relating to the establishment of a Peace Corps program in Morocco.
Exchange of notes at Rabat February 8 and 9, 1963.
Entered into force February 9, 1963.
23 UST 209; TIAS 7297
Amendment:
March 10, 1972 (23 UST 209; TIAS 7297)

Cultural agreement.
Signed at Washington February 10, 1967.
Entered into force February 10, 1967.
18 UST 174; TIAS 6215; 688 UNTS 149

Agreement on the development and facilitation of tourism.
Signed at Washington July 22, 1985.
Entered into force July 22, 1985.
TIAS 12001

DEFENSE

Agreement concerning mapping, charting and geodesy cooperation.
Signed at Rabat April 29, 1982.
Entered into force April 29, 1982.
34 UST 987; TIAS 10386

Agreement concerning the use of certain facilities in Morocco by the United States.
Exchange of notes at Washington May 27, 1982.
Entered into force May 27, 1982.
34 UST 1127; TIAS 10399; 1566 UNTS 139

Memorandum of agreement concerning hydrographic surveys and nautical charting.
Signed at Rabat November 20, 1985.
Entered into force November 20, 1985.
TIAS 11210

Agreement regarding grants under the Foreign Assistance Act of 1961, as amended, or successor legislation, and the furnishing of defense articles, defense services and related training, including pursuant to the United States International Military Education and Training (IMET) Program.
Exchange of notes at Rabat July 21 and November 24, 2006.
Entered into force November 24, 2006.
NP

Acquisition and cross-servicing agreement, with annexes.
Signed at Stuttgart and Rabat April 27 and May 6, 2015.
Entered into force May 6, 2015.
NP

Agreement concerning health care for military members and their dependents.
Signed June 7 and July 4, 2016.
Entered into force July 4, 2016.
NP

EDUCATION

Agreement establishing a Binational Commission for Educational and Cultural Exchange.
Signed at Marrakech February 12, 1982.
Entered into force May 20, 1982.
TIAS 10407; 34 UST 1180

EMPLOYMENT

Agreement relating to the employment of dependents of official government employees.
Exchange of notes at Rabat February 27 and April 2, 1992.
Entered into force April 2, 1992.
TIAS

ENVIRONMENT & CONSERVATION

Agreement for cooperation in the Global Learning and Observations to Benefit the Environment (GLOBE) Program, with appendices.
Signed at Rabat March 27, 1996.
Entered into force March 27, 1996.
TIAS 12739

FINANCE

Agreement regarding the consolidation and rescheduling of certain debts owed to, guaranteed by or insured by the United States Government and its agencies, with annexes.
Signed at Rabat December 30, 1983.
Entered into force February 10, 1984.
TIAS 11015; 2022 UNTS 73

Agreement regarding the consolidation and rescheduling of certain debts owed to, guaranteed by or insured by the United States Government and its agencies, with annexes.
Signed at Rabat December 23, 1985, and February 13, 1986.
Entered into force January 21, 1986.
NP

Agreement regarding the consolidation and rescheduling of certain debts owed to, guaranteed by, or insured by the United States Government and its agencies, with annexes.
Signed at Rabat March 1, 1988.
Entered into force April 11, 1988.
NP

Agreement regarding the consolidation and rescheduling of certain debts owed to, guaranteed by, or insured by the United States Government and its agencies, with annexes.
Signed at Rabat August 21, 1989.
Entered into force September 25, 1989.
NP

Agreement regarding the consolidation and rescheduling or refinancing of certain debts owed to, guaranteed by, or insured by the United States Government and its agencies, with annexes.
Signed at Rabat February 14, 1991.
Entered into force March 29, 1991.
NP

Agreement regarding the consolidation and rescheduling or refinancing of certain debts owed to, guaranteed by, or insured by the United States Government and its agencies, with annexes.
Signed at Rabat August 24, 1992.
Entered into force October 12, 1992.
NP

Investment incentive agreement.
Signed at Washington March 15, 1995.
Entered into force September 22, 1999.
TIAS

FOREIGN ASSISTANCE

Agreement providing for economic, technical, and related assistance.
Exchange of notes at Rabat April 2, 1957.
Entered into force April 2, 1957.
8 UST 459; TIAS 3799; 288 UNTS 157.
Amendment:
May 19, 1958 (9 UST 923; TIAS 4054; 317 UNTS 354).

INTERNATIONAL CRIMINAL COURT

Agreement regarding the surrender of persons to the International Criminal Court.
Signed at New York September 24, 2003.
Entered into force November 19, 2003.
TIAS 03-1119

LAW ENFORCEMENT

Convention on mutual assistance in criminal matters.
Signed at Rabat October 17, 1983.
Entered into force June 23, 1993.
TIAS

Agreement regarding joint cooperation in fighting against international terrorism, organized crime, and the illicit production, trafficking and abuse of narcotics.
Signed at Rabat February 10, 1989.
Entered into force February 10, 1989.
TIAS 12029

Agreement regarding mutual assistance between customs administrations.
Signed at Washington November 21, 2013.
Entered into force February 1, 2016.
TIAS 16-201

PEACE

Treaty of peace.*
Signed at Meccanez September 16, 1836.
Entered into force January 28, 1837.
8 Stat. 484; TS 244-2; 9 Bevans 1286
Note:
* Extraterritorial jurisdiction in Morocco relinquished by the United States October 6, 1956.

POSTAL MATTERS

International express mail agreement, with detailed regulations.
Signed at Rabat and Washington March 18 and May 11, 1988.
Entered into force June 1, 1988.
TIAS 11588

SCIENTIFIC & TECHNICAL COOPERATION

Agreement on science and technology cooperation, with annexes.
Signed at Rabat November 14, 2006.
Entered into force February 8, 2012.
TIAS 12-208

SPACE

Agreement concerning the use of Ben Guerir Air Base as a space shuttle emergency landing site.
Signed at Rabat and Washington January 21 and 28, 1987.
Entered into force January 28, 1987.
TIAS 12209

TAXATION

Convention for the avoidance of double taxation and the prevention of fiscal evasion with respect to taxes on income, with related notes.*
Signed at Rabat August 1, 1977.
Entered into force December 30, 1981.
33 UST 2545; TIAS 10194

Agreement interpreting certain articles of the convention of August 1, 1977 (TIAS 10194).
Signed at Washington and Rabat October 25, 1979, and at Rabat April 17, 1981.
Entered into force December 30, 1981.
33 UST 2672; TIAS 10195

Note:
* With reservation and understanding.

TRADE & INVESTMENT

Treaty concerning the encouragement and reciprocal protection of investments, with protocol.
Signed at Washington July 22, 1985.
Entered into force May 29, 1991.
TIAS

The United States-Morocco free trade agreement, with annexes.
Signed at Washington June 15, 2004.
Entered into force January 1, 2006.
TIAS

TRANSPORTATION

Memorandum of agreement on technical assistance with the Federal Aviation Administration, with annex.
Signed at Rabat April 18, 1983.
Entered into force April 18, 1983.
TIAS 10702; 2005 UNTS 175

Air transport agreement, with annexes.
Signed at Rabat October 10, 2001.
Entered into force August 19, 2002.
TIAS 13165

MOZAMBIQUE

CULTURAL EXCHANGES, PROPERTY & COOPERATION

Agreement concerning the program of the Peace Corps in Mozambique.
Signed at Maputo December 27, 1991.
Entered into force December 27, 1991.
TIAS

DEFENSE

Agreement concerning the provision of training related to defense articles under the United States International Military Education and Training (IMET) Program.
Exchange of notes at Maputo November 7, 1984, and April 12, 1985.
Entered into force April 12, 1985.
TIAS 11338

Agreement regarding grants under the Foreign Assistance Act of 1961, as amended, and the furnishing of defense articles, related training and other defense services from the United States to Mozambique.
Exchange of notes at Maputo March 30 and May 13, 1994.
Entered into force May 13, 1994.
NP

Amendment:
June 23 and August 23, 2004

Agreement concerning the status of United States military and civilian personnel of the U.S. Department of Defense temporarily present in Mozambique in connection with humanitarian relief operations.
Exchange of notes at Maputo March 3 and 7, 2000.
Entered into force March 7, 2000.
TIAS

Acquisition and cross-servicing agreement, with annexes.
Signed at Maputo May 2, 2007.
Entered into force May 2, 2007.
NP

EDUCATION

Agreement regarding the establishment and functioning of the American International School of Mozambique.
Signed at Maputo October 20, 2014.
Entered into force March 29, 2016.
TIAS 16-329

EMPLOYMENT

Agreement relating to the employment of dependents of official government employees.
Exchange of notes at Washington June 29 and July 14, 1998.
Entered into force July 14, 1998.
TIAS 12972

FINANCE

Agreement regarding the consolidation and rescheduling of certain debts owed to, guaranteed by or insured by the United States Government and its agencies, with annex.
Signed at Maputo February 12, 1987.
Entered into force March 27, 1987.
NP

Agreement regarding the consolidation and rescheduling of certain debts owed to, guaranteed by, or insured by the United States Government and its agencies, with annexes.
Signed at Maputo March 6, 1990.
Entered into force April 23, 1990.
NP

Agreement regarding the consolidation and rescheduling of certain debts owed to, guaranteed by, or insured by the United States Government and its agencies, with annexes.
Signed at Maputo August 27, 1991.
Entered into force September 30, 1991.
NP

Agreement regarding the consolidation and rescheduling of certain debts owed to, guaranteed by or insured by the United States Government and its agency, with annexes.
Signed at Maputo August 13, 1993.
Entered into force September 27, 1993.
NP
Amendment:
July 13 and August 31, 1995 (NP)

Agreement regarding the consolidation, reduction and rescheduling of certain debts owed to, guaranteed by, or insured by the United States Government and its Agency, with annexes.
Signed at Maputo August 13, 1997.
Entered into force September 29, 1997.
NP
Amendment:
September 30 and October 27, 1998

Investment incentive agreement.
Signed at Maputo September 23, 1999.
Entered into force September 23, 1999.
TIAS 13063

Agreement regarding the consolidation and reduction of debt owed to, guaranteed by, or insured by the United States Government and its agency, with annexes.
Signed at Maputo May 28, 2002.
Entered into force July 11, 2002.
NP

FOREIGN ASSISTANCE

Agreement for economic and technical cooperation.
Signed at Maputo December 9, 2015.
Entered into force April 20, 2016.
TIAS 16-420

AGENCY FOR INTERNATIONAL DEVELOPMENT

Strategic objective grant agreement for the HIV/AIDS program, with attachments.
Signed September 11, 2003.
Entered into force September 11, 2003.
NP
Amendments:
July 31, 2006
August 13, 2007

Assistance agreement for the health program, with attachment and annexes.
Signed September 30, 2009.
Entered into force September 30, 2009.
NP
Amendment:
September 28, 2010 (NP)

INTERNATIONAL CRIMINAL COURT

Agreement regarding the surrender of persons to international tribunals.
Signed at Maputo June 24, 2003.
Entered into force March 2, 2004.
TIAS 04-302

POSTAL MATTERS

International express mail agreement, with detailed regulations.
Signed at Maputo and Washington July 9 and 23, 1990.
Entered into force August 30, 1990.
TIAS 11758

PROPERTY

Agreement concerning reciprocal and property ownership rights for the diplomatic and consular missions of the United States and the Republic of Mozambique.
Exchange of notes at Maputo September 21 and October 7, 2005.
Entered into force October 7, 2005.
TIAS 05-1007

TRADE & INVESTMENT

Treaty concerning the encouragement and reciprocal protection of investment, with annex, protocol and exchange of letters.
Signed at Washington December 1, 1998.
Entered into force March 3, 2005.
TIAS

Trade and investment framework agreement.
Signed at Washington June 21, 2005.
Entered into force June 21, 2005.
TIAS

MULTINATIONAL FORCE AND OBSERVERS

CLAIMS & DISPUTE RESOLUTION

Agreement concerning the settlement of claims by the United States against the Multinational Force and Observers (MFO).
Exchange of notes at Rome May 3, 1990.
Entered into force May 3, 1990.
TIAS 11899

OCCUPATION & PEACEKEEPING

Agreement relating to participation of United States military and civilian personnel in the Multinational Force and Observers established by Egypt and Israel, with annexes and agreed minute, and related exchange of letters.*
Exchange of letters at Washington March 26, 1982.
Entered into force March 26, 1982.
TIAS 10557

Note:

* See also PEACEKEEPING in multilateral section and in bilateral section under EGYPT and ISRAEL.

N

NAMIBIA

CULTURAL EXCHANGES, PROPERTY & COOPERATION

Peace corps agreement.
Signed at Windhoek August 28 and September 19, 1990.
Entered into force September 19, 1990.
TIAS

DEFENSE

Agreement regarding grants under the Foreign Assistance Act of 1961, as amended, and the furnishing of defense articles, related training and other defense services from the United States Government to the Republic of Namibia.
Exchange of notes at Windhoek May 21, 1992, and February 19, 1998.
Entered into force February 19, 1998.
NP

EMPLOYMENT

Agreement relating to the employment of dependents of official government employees.
Exchange of notes at Windhoek January 24 and June 8, 1994.
Entered into force June 8, 1994.
TIAS 12184

ENVIRONMENT & CONSERVATION

Agreement for cooperation in the Global Learning and Observations to Benefit the Environment (GLOBE) Program, with appendices.
Signed at Windhoek October 8, 1997.
Entered into force October 8, 1997.
TIAS 12886

FINANCE

Investment incentive agreement.
Signed at Washington June 20, 1990.
Entered into force June 5, 1991.
TIAS 12096

FOREIGN ASSISTANCE

General agreement for special development assistance.
Signed at New York September 28, 1990.
Entered into force September 28, 1990.
TIAS 11901

Agreement for special development assistance.
Signed at Windhoek May 27, 1992.
Entered into force May 27, 1992.
TIAS 11863

POSTAL MATTERS

International express mail agreement, with detailed regulations.
Signed at Windhoek and Washington September 30 and October 24, 1994.
Entered into force December 1, 1994.
NP

NAURU

On January 31, 1968, Nauru became an independent state. In a note dated May 28, 1968, to the Secretary-General of the United Nations, the Chief Secretary made a statement reading in part as follows:

Prior to Nauru attaining independence on 31st January, 1968, treaty relationships were entered into, on its behalf, by the Government of the Commonwealth of Australia. The Government of Nauru now wishes to make clear its position in regard to obligations arising from those treaties entered into prior to 31st January, 1968 by the Government of the Commonwealth of Australia, and accordingly makes the following declarations.

In respect of all bilateral treaties validly concluded by Australia on behalf of Nauru, or validly applied or extended by Australia to Nauru, before 31st January, 1968, the Government of Nauru will continue, on a basis of reciprocity, to apply the terms of such treaties for a period of twenty-four months unless such treaties are abrogated or modified earlier by agreement with the other contracting parties. At the expiration of this period the Government of Nauru will regard each such treaty as having terminated unless it has earlier agreed with the other contracting party to continue that treaty in existence.

It is the earnest hope of the Government of Nauru that during the aforementioned period of twenty-four months, the normal processes of diplomatic negotiations will enable it to reach satisfactory accord with the States concerned upon the possibility of the continuance or modification or termination of such treaties. In respect of multilateral treaties, the Government of Nauru intends to review each of them individually and to indicate to the depositary in each case what steps it wishes to take, whether by way of confirmation of succession, confirmation of termination or accession, in relation to each such instrument. During such period of review, any party to a multilateral treaty which was, prior to independence, validly applied or extended to Nauru may, on a basis of reciprocity, rely as against Nauru on the terms of the treaty." In subsequent notes to the Secretary-General of the United Nations this period of review has been extended indefinitely.

EMPLOYMENT

Agreement relating to the employment of dependents of official government employees.
Exchange of notes at Washington and New York August 22 and September 11, 2007.
Entered into force September 11, 2007.
TIAS 07-911

INTERNATIONAL CRIMINAL COURT

Agreement regarding the surrender of persons to the International Criminal Court.
Signed at Washington February 26, 2003.
Entered into force December 4, 2003.
TIAS 03-1204

LAW ENFORCEMENT

Extradition treaty between the United States and the United Kingdom.
Signed at London December 22, 1931; applicable to Australia (including Papua, Norfolk Island, and the mandated territories of New Guinea and Nauru), in accordance with article 14, from August 30, 1935.
47 Stat. 2122; TS 849; 12 Bevans 482; 163 LNTS 59

MARITIME MATTERS

Agreement concerning operational cooperation to suppress illicit transnational maritime activity.
Signed at Auckland September 8, 2011.
Entered into force September 8, 2011.
TIAS 11-908

POSTAL MATTERS

International express mail agreement, with detailed regulations.
Signed at Washington and Nauru October 8, 1993, and January 17, 1994.
Entered into force April 4, 1994.
NP

SCIENTIFIC & TECHNICAL COOPERATION

Agreement providing for the construction and operation of a weather station on Nauru Island.
Exchange of notes at Canberra February 19 and 25, 1958.
Entered into force February 25, 1958.
9 UST 266; TIAS 4001; 317 UNTS 153

NEPAL

CULTURAL EXCHANGES, PROPERTY & COOPERATION

Agreement relating to the establishment of a Peace Corps program in Nepal.
Exchange of notes at Kathmandu August 24, 1962.
Entered into force August 24, 1962.
13 UST 1909; TIAS 5146; 460 UNTS 143

DEFENSE

Agreement regarding military assistance under the Foreign Assistance Act of 1961, as amended, and the furnishing of defense articles, related training and other defense services from the United States to Nepal.
Exchange of notes at Kathmandu September 19, 1994, and January 25, 1995.
Entered into force January 25, 1995.
TIAS 12350

Agreement concerning the status of United States military and civilian personnel of the U.S. Department of Defense temporarily present in the Kingdom of Nepal in connection with the Multi-Platoon Training Event.
Exchange of notes at Kathmandu January 12 and 13, 2000.
Entered into force January 13, 2000.
NP

EDUCATION

Agreement for financing certain educational exchange programs.
Signed at Kathmandu June 9, 1961.
Entered into force June 9, 1961.
TIAS 4845; 12 UST 1253; 421 UNTS 223

Amendment:
July 10, 1974, December 13, 1974, and May 18, 1975 (TIAS 8352; 27 UST 2831)

EMPLOYMENT

Agreement relating to the employment of dependents of official government employees.
Exchange of notes at Washington December 19, 1996, and May 13, 1997.
Entered into force May 13, 1997.
TIAS 12856

ENVIRONMENT & CONSERVATION

Agreement for cooperation in the Global Learning and Observations to Benefit the Environment (GLOBE) Program, with appendices.
Signed at Kathmandu March 3, 2000.
Entered into force March 3, 2000.
TIAS 13084

FINANCE

Agreement relating to investment guaranties authorized by section 413(b)(4) of the Mutual Security Act of 1954, as amended.
Exchange of notes at Washington May 17, 1960.
Entered into force May 17, 1960.
11 UST 1396; TIAS 4477; 372 UNTS 313

Amendment:
June 4, 1963 (14 UST 994; TIAS 5391; 487 UNTS 376)

FOREIGN ASSISTANCE

Point four general agreement for technical cooperation between the United States of America and Nepal.
Signed at New Delhi January 23, 1951.
Entered into force January 23, 1951.
2 UST 489; TIAS 2198; 184 UNTS 65

Amendment:
January 2 and 8, 1952 (3 UST 4760; TIAS 2642; 184 UNTS 74)

AGENCY FOR INTERNATIONAL DEVELOPMENT

Agreement for USAID foreign assistance programs, with annexes.
Signed September 22, 2009.
Entered into force September 22, 2009.

Amendments:
September 21, 2010 (NP)
September 29, 2011 (NP)
September 21 and 24, 2012 (NP)
January 8 and February 2, 2014 (NP)
September 23, 2014 (NP)

INTERNATIONAL CRIMINAL COURT

Agreement regarding the surrender of persons to the International Criminal Court.
Signed at Kathmandu December 31, 2002.
Entered into force July 22, 2003.
TIAS 03-722.1

LAW ENFORCEMENT

Procedures for mutual assistance in connection with matters relating to the Boeing Company.
Signed at Washington January 5, 1979.
Entered into force January 5, 1979.
30 UST 2495; TIAS 9347; 1171 UNTS 111

POSTAL MATTERS

Express mail agreement, with detailed regulations.
Signed at Nepal and Washington July 9 and October 25, 1996.
Entered into force January 1, 1997.
NP

TRADE & INVESTMENT

Agreement relating to friendship and commerce.
Exchange of notes at Kathmandu April 25, 1947.
Entered into force April 25, 1947.
61 Stat. 2566; TIAS 1585; 10 Bevans 1; 16 UNTS 97

NETHERLANDS

ATOMIC ENERGY

Arrangement for the exchange of technical information and cooperation in nuclear safety matters, with addenda and annex.
Signed at Vienna September 18, 2013.
Entered into force September 18, 2013.
TIAS 13-918

Amendment and Extension:
September 15, 2015 (TIAS 15-915.3)
September 9 and 15, 2016

CLAIMS & DISPUTE RESOLUTION

Treaty for the advancement of peace.*
Signed at Washington December 18, 1913.
Entered into force March 10, 1928.
45 Stat. 2462; TS 760; 10 Bevans 64

Note:
* Declaration interpretative of article I signed at Washington February 13, 1928. Entered into force February 27, 1928.

Treaty of arbitration.
Signed at Washington January 13, 1930.
Entered into force July 17, 1930.
46 Stat. 2769; TS 820; 10 Bevans 100; 107 LNTS 69

Memorandum of understanding regarding claims by the Netherlands to looted securities, with annex and related note.
Signed at Washington January 19, 1951.
Entered into force January 19, 1951.
2 UST 1262; TIAS 2275; 141 UNTS 221

Agreement relating to selection of De Nederlandsche Bank of Amsterdam by the United States, Iran, and Algeria as the mutually agreeable central bank to manage the depositary of funds in the security account established by the January 19, 1981, Declaration of the Government of the Democratic and Popular Republic of Algeria,* with related technical agreements signed
August 17, 1981.
Exchange of notes at The Hague July 10, 1981.
Entered into force July 10, 1981.
TIAS

Note:
* See IRAN — CLAIMS & DISPUTE RESOLUTION.

CONSULAR AFFAIRS

Agreement relating to the reciprocal waiver of passport visa fees for nonimmigrants.*
Exchanges of notes at The Hague January 21, February 11, and March 5 and 13, 1946.
Entered into force April 15, 1946.
61 Stat. 3834; TIAS 1728; 10 Bevans 178; 84 UNTS 3

Note:
* The status of this agreement is under review.

Agreement relating to visa requirements.*
Exchange of notes at The Hague July 30 and August 20, 1947.
Entered into force August 20, 1947.
61 Stat. 3838; TIAS 1729; 10 Bevans 220; 84 UNTS 11

Note:
* The status of this agreement is under review.

CULTURAL EXCHANGES, PROPERTY & COOPERATION

Agreement concerning American military cemeteries, with annex.
Signed at The Hague May 4, 1970.
Entered into force November 18, 1970.
21 UST 2416; TIAS 6978; 775 UNTS 77

DEFENSE

Mutual defense assistance agreement.
Signed at Washington January 27, 1950.
Entered into force January 27, 1950.
1 UST 88; TIAS 2015; 80 UNTS 219

Agreement relating to the assurances required by the Mutual Security Act of 1951.
Exchange of notes at The Hague January 8, 1952.
Entered into force January 8, 1952.
3 UST 4633; TIAS 2615; 173 UNTS 372

Agreement relating to the disposition of equipment and materials furnished by the United States under the mutual defense assistance agreement and no longer required for the purposes for which originally made available.
Exchange of notes at The Hague November 12 and 26, 1953.
Entered into force November 26, 1953.
11 UST 2017; TIAS 4556; 388 UNTS 303
Amendment:
August 10 and 13, 1960 (11 UST 2017; TIAS 4556; 388 UNTS 303)

Agreement relating to a memorandum of understanding and a model contract for the offshore procurement program.
Exchange of notes at The Hague April 15 and May 7, 1954.
Entered into force July 30, 1954.
5 UST 2027; TIAS 3069; 213 UNTS 325

Agreement relating to the stationing of United States armed forces in the Netherlands, with annex.
Exchange of notes at The Hague August 13, 1954.
Entered into force November 16, 1954.
6 UST 103; TIAS 3174; 251 UNTS 91

Agreement establishing an air defense technical center with cost reimbursement contract attached.
Exchange of notes at The Hague December 14, 1954.
Entered into force December 14, 1954.
6 UST 915; TIAS 3236; 262 UNTS 35

Agreement for cooperation on uses of atomic energy for mutual defense purposes.
Signed at The Hague May 6, 1959.
Entered into force July 27, 1959.
10 UST 1334; TIAS 4277; 355 UNTS 327

Agreement relating to a weapons production program.
Exchange of notes at The Hague March 24, 1960.
Entered into force provisionally March 24, 1960; definitively January 2, 1962.
12 UST 180; TIAS 4692; 406 UNTS 165

Agreement relating to the safeguarding of classified information.
Exchange of notes at Washington August 18, 1960.
Entered into force August 18, 1960.
TIAS
Amendment:
March 4 and April 6, 1981

General arrangement relating to the cooperative production of the M109 vehicle and its components.
Signed at The Hague May 3, 1966.
Entered into force May 3, 1966.
29 UST 5713; TIAS 9144
Amendments:
March 17, 1969 (29 UST 5721; TIAS 9144)
December 30, 1974, and June 5, 1975 (29 UST 5722; TIAS 9144)
March 2 and April 14, 1979 (TIAS 10641)
January 31, 1983 (TIAS 10641)

Administrative arrangements pertaining to pre-financed NATO common infrastructure projects.
Exchange of letters at The Hague and Heidelberg May 30 and July 24, 1975.
Entered into force July 24, 1975.
30 UST 2885; TIAS 9369; 1177 UNTS 247

Memorandum of understanding concerning principles governing mutual cooperation in research and development, production and procurement of conventional defense equipment.
Signed at Washington and The Hague July 25 and August 24, 1978.
Entered into force August 24, 1978.
33 UST 3105; TIAS 10214

Agreement relating to storage of prepositioned war readiness materials by United States forces.
Exchange of notes at The Hague January 15, 1981.
Entered into force August 20, 1981.
33 UST 891; TIAS 10073; 1268 UNTS 77

Arrangement concerning the installation and support of a USAFE Loran C/D transmitter site, with annex.
Signed at Ramstein and The Hague May 17 and July 12, 1982.
Entered into force July 12, 1982.
TIAS 12379

Agreement establishing a television transmitter at Soesterberg Airfield.
Exchange of notes at The Hague December 7, 1981, and March 4, 1982.
Entered into force July 19, 1983.
35 UST 3814; TIAS 10883; 1359 UNTS 249

Mutual logistical support agreement, with annexes.
Signed at Stuttgart February 22, 1983.
Entered into force February 22, 1983.
TIAS 10663; 1359 UNTS 257
Amendment:
February 27 and March 20, 1992 (TIAS 12353)

Memorandum of understanding regarding the exchange of Air Force officers.
Signed at The Hague and Washington May 22, 1984, and May 7, 1985.
Entered into force May 7, 1985.
TIAS 11233

Agreement on termination of agreement of November 4, 1985, concerning the stationing, support and operation of the Ground Launched Cruise Missile (GLCM) system in the territory of the Netherlands.
Exchange of notes at The Hague December 18, 1987.
Entered into force June 1, 1988.
TIAS

Memorandum of understanding between the United States Air Forces in Europe and the Royal Netherlands Air Force concerning the logistical support/services for the Soviet inspection(s) under the INF Treaty at Woensdrecht AB, Netherlands, with annexes.
Signed at Royal Netherlands Air Force Headquarters and Ramstein Air Base, Germany, July 13 and August 10, 1989.
Entered into force August 10, 1989.
TIAS 12351

Memorandum of understanding regarding the joint training of Royal Netherlands Air Force and United States Air Force aircrews on the F 16 weapons system in the United States.
Signed at The Hague October 30, 1989.
Entered into force October 30, 1989.
NP

Memorandum of understanding concerning the residual value of the U.S. funded facilities for the Ground Launched Cruise Missile (GLCM) at Woensdrecht Air Base, the Netherlands, with annexes.
Signed at The Hague December 6, 1989.
Entered into force December 6, 1989.
TIAS 12352

Memorandum of understanding for the dynamic behavior of composite ship structures (DYCOSS) project, with annexes.
Signed at The Hague and Washington July 18 and August 11, 1994.
Entered into force August 11, 1994.
TIAS 12355

Basic exchange and cooperative agreement concerning mapping, charting and geodesy cooperation, with glossary.
Signed at Fairfax April 26, 1995.
Entered into force April 26, 1995.
NP

Memorandum of understanding concerning technology research and development projects, with annex.
Signed at Washington May 14, 1998.
Entered into force May 14, 1998.
TIAS 98-514
Amendments:
August 21 and September 26, 2007 (TIAS 98-514)
December 7, 2012 and February 5, 2013 (TIAS 13-205)

Agreement regarding the exchange of military personnel (MPEP), with annexes.
Signed at Washington and The Hague July 16 and 30, 1999.
Entered into force July 30, 1999.
NP
Amendment:
January 28, 2008

Agreement supplementing the cooperative framework for system development and demonstration of the joint strike fighter, with annexes.
Signed at Soesterberg Airbase and Washington June 5 and 10, 2002.
Entered into force July 10, 2002.
TIAS 02-710.1

Memorandum of understanding for test and evaluation program cooperation, with annexes.
Signed at The Hague and Washington January 26 and February 12, 2004.
Entered into force February 12, 2004.
TIAS 04-212
Amendment:
June 28 and July 5, 2013 (NP)

Memorandum of agreement for information exchange and research, development, testing and evaluation projects.
Signed at The Hague May 25, 2004.
Entered into force May 25, 2004.
TIAS 04-525

Memorandum of understanding concerning operations and support of the advanced extremely high frequency military satellite communications system, with annexes.
Signed at Washington and The Hague August 21 and 26, 2010.
Entered into force August 26, 2010.
TIAS 10-826

Agreement on the status of United States personnel in the Caribbean part of the Kingdom of the Netherlands.
Signed at Washington October 19, 2012.
Entered into force September 1, 2013.
TIAS 13-901

DIPLOMATIC & CONSULAR RELATIONS

Arrangement regarding reciprocal free entry privileges for consular officers.
Exchange of notes at The Hague and at Washington April 7, June 17, August 20, and September 19, 1930.
Entered into force September 19, 1930.
Foreign Relations, 1931, Vol. II, p. 771; 10 Bevans 105
Amendment:
February 1, 1947, and August 20, 1948

Reciprocal arrangement providing that trade commissioners may import, free of duty, articles for their personal use during their official residence.
Exchange of notes at The Hague July 2 and November 10, 1936.
Entered into force November 10, 1936.
TIAS

EDUCATION

Agreement for the financing of certain education exchange programs.
Signed at The Hague October 16, 1972.
Entered into force August 8, 1973.
24 UST 1924; TIAS 7700

EMPLOYMENT

Agreement relating to the employment of dependents of official government employees.
Exchange of notes at The Hague June 23, 1986.
Entered into force May 13, 1987.
TIAS 11359

ENVIRONMENT & CONSERVATION

Memorandum of understanding concerning cooperation in the field of environmental protection.
Signed at Paris June 17, 1985.
Entered into force June 17, 1985.
TIAS 11161; 2126 UNTS 267

Memorandum of understanding for cooperation in the GLOBE program.
Signed at Washington February 28, 1995.
Entered into force February 28, 1995.
TIAS 12607

FINANCE

Agreement relating to the guaranties authorized by Section 111(b)(3) of the Economic Cooperation Act of 1948, as amended.
Exchange of notes at Washington September 24 and October 7, 1952.
Entered into force October 8, 1952.
3 UST 5060; TIAS 2690; 173 UNTS 378

FOREIGN ASSISTANCE

Economic cooperation agreement.
Signed at The Hague July 2, 1948.
Entered into force July 2, 1948.
62 Stat. 2477; TIAS 1791; 10 Bevans 240; 20 UNTS 91

Amendments:

January 16 and February 2, 1950 (1 UST 665; TIAS 2126; 93 UNTS 361)
March 7 and April 3, 1951 (2 UST 1319; TIAS 2285; 141 UNTS 368)
November 28, 1952 (3 UST 5260; TIAS 2721; 173 UNTS 382)

Agreement relating to duty-free entry of relief goods, relief packages, and standard packs and to the defrayment of transportation charges thereon.
Exchange of notes at The Hague January 17, 1949.
Entered into force January 17, 1949.
63 Stat. 2322; TIAS 1881; 10 Bevans 259; 32 UNTS 241

Agreement relating to the assumption by Indonesia of all responsibilities and obligations of the Netherlands incurred under the economic cooperation agreements of July 2, 1948, as amended, and April 26, 1949, as amended, and the loan agreements of October 28, 1948, and December 22, 1949, and memorandum of understanding.
Signed at Washington February 11, 1952, by the United States, Indonesia, and the Netherlands.
Entered into force February 11, 1952.
3 UST 2989; TIAS 2484; 165 UNTS 77

General agreement for technical cooperation for Suriname and Netherlands Antilles.*
Signed at The Hague January 22, 1954.
Entered into force April 21, 1954.
5 UST 919; TIAS 2982; 190 UNTS 207

Note:

* Also applicable to Aruba.

INTELLECTUAL PROPERTY

Agreement to facilitate the interchange of patent rights and technical information for defense purposes with exchange of notes.
Signed at The Hague April 29, 1955.
Entered into force provisionally April 29, 1955; definitively July 13, 1955.
6 UST 2187; TIAS 3287; 219 UNTS 105

Agreement approving the procedures for reciprocal filing of classified patent applications in the United States and the Netherlands.
Exchange of notes at The Hague October 8, 1959.
Entered into force October 8, 1959.
10 UST 1774; TIAS 4332; 358 UNTS 286

LAW ENFORCEMENT

Convention for the prevention of smuggling of alcoholic liquors.
Signed at Washington August 21, 1924.
Entered into force April 8, 1925.
44 Stat. 2013; TS 712; 10 Bevans 76; 33 LNTS 434

Procedures for mutual assistance in the administration of justice in connection with the Lockheed Aircraft Corporation matter.
Signed at Washington March 29, 1976.
Entered into force March 29, 1976.
27 UST 1064; TIAS 8245

Related Agreement:

March 21, 1979 (30 UST 2500; TIAS 9348; 1171 UNTS 215)

Extradition treaty, with appendix.
Signed at The Hague June 24, 1980.
Entered into force September 15, 1983.
35 UST 1334; TIAS 10733

Treaty on mutual assistance in criminal matters, with exchange of notes.
Signed at The Hague June 12, 1981.
Entered into force September 15, 1983.
35 UST 1361; TIAS 10734; 1359 UNTS 209

Agreement on mutual administrative assistance in the exchange of information in securities matters.
Signed at The Hague December 11, 1989.
Entered into force July 1, 1992.
TIAS 12405; 1921 UNTS 163

Agreement regarding mutual cooperation in the tracing, freezing, seizure and forfeiture of proceeds and instrumentalities of crime and the sharing of forfeited assets.
Signed at Washington November 20, 1992.
Entered into force August 4, 1994.
TIAS 12482; 2029 UNTS 189

Agreement on mutual administrative assistance in the exchange of information in futures matters.
Signed at Washington April 29, 1993.
Entered into force February 1, 1994.
TIAS 12151

Agreement on mutual administrative assistance for the proper application of customs law and for the prevention, investigation and combating of customs offences, with annex.
Signed at Washington October 28, 1996.
Entered into force May 1, 1998.
TIAS 12811; 2015 UNTS 411

Agreement of cooperation concerning access to and use of the facilities in the Netherlands Antilles and Aruba for aerial counter-narcotics activities.
Signed at Oranjestad March 2, 2000.
Entered into force November 2, 2001.
TIAS 13083
Extensions:
May 28, 2010 and February 15, 2011 (TIAS 16-1102.1)
December 16, 2015 and November 2, 2016 (TIAS 16-1102.1)

Agreement extending to the Netherlands Antilles and Aruba the application of the agreement of October 28, 1996, on mutual administrative assistance for the proper application of customs law and for the prevention, investigation and combating of customs offenses.
Exchange of notes at Washington April 27 and November 28, 2001.
Entered into force December 13, 2002.
TIAS 13176

Agreement comprising the instrument as contemplated by Article 3(2) of the agreement on extradition between the United States of America and the European Union signed June 25, 2003, as to the application of the extradition treaty of June 24, 1980, with annex and exchange of notes.
Signed at The Hague September 29, 2004.
Entered into force February 1, 2010.
TIAS 10-201.16

Agreement comprising the instrument as contemplated by Article 3(2) of the agreement on mutual legal assistance between the United States of America and the European Union signed June 25, 2003, as to the application of the treaty on mutual legal assistance in criminal matters of June 12, 1981, with annex and exchange of notes.
Signed at The Hague September 29, 2004.
Entered into force February 1, 2010.
TIAS 10-201.41

MARITIME MATTERS

Agreement relating to jurisdiction over vessels utilizing the Louisiana Offshore Oil Port.
Exchange of notes at Washington March 9 and 16, 1981.
Entered into force November 2, 1981.
33 UST 1555; TIAS 10132; 1307 UNTS 409

Agreement relating to the agreement of August 14, 1987, on the resolution of practical problems with respect to deep seabed mining areas.*
Exchange of notes at The Hague August 14, 1987.
Entered into force October 14, 1988.
TIAS 11438; 1649 UNTS 117
Note
* Parties to the multilateral agreement of August 14, 1987, are Belgium, Canada, Italy, Netherlands and Union of Soviet Socialist Republics.

NONPROLIFERATION

Memorandum of understanding concerning measures to be taken for the transfer, security and safeguarding of technical information, software and equipment to the Ministry of Defense to enable industry to establish North Sea ACMI range display and debriefing system facilities in the Netherlands.
Signed at Washington July 6, 1992.
Entered into force July 6, 1992.
TIAS 12354

OCCUPATION & PEACEKEEPING

Agreement concerning the participation of the Netherlands forces in the United Nations operations in Korea.
Signed at Washington May 15, 1952.
Entered into force May 15, 1952.
3 UST 3987; TIAS 2534; 177 UNTS 233

POSTAL MATTERS

Parcel post agreement and detailed regulations.
Signed at Washington September 5 and at The Hague September 20, 1937.
Entered into force November 1, 1937.
51 Stat. 295; Post Office Department print; 184 LNTS 319

Parcel post agreement and detailed regulations for execution.
Signed at Willemstad May 10 and at Washington May 17, 1951.
Operative February 1, 1951.
TIAS 2294; 2 UST 1509

International express mail agreement, with detailed regulations.
Signed at The Hague and Washington May 19 and June 10, 1980.
Entered into force September 1, 1980.
32 UST 2033; TIAS 9816; 1252 UNTS 153

International express mail agreement, with detailed regulations.
Signed at Willemstad and Washington June 10 and 22, 1987.
Entered into force August 3, 1987.
TIAS 11305

International express mail agreement, with detailed regulations.
Signed at Oranjestad and Washington August 15 and September 14, 1989.
Entered into force October 16, 1989.
TIAS 11695

PRIVATE INTERNATIONAL LAW

Agreement for the enforcement of maintenance (support) obligations.
Signed at Washington May 30, 2001.
Entered into force May 1, 2002.
TIAS 13152

PROPERTY

Preliminary agreement regarding principles applying to mutual aid in the prosecution of the war against aggression, and exchange of notes.
Signed at Washington July 8, 1942.
Entered into force July 8, 1942.
56 Stat. 1554; EAS 259; 10 Bevans 142; 103 UNTS 277

Mutual aid agreement relating to supplies and services, with accompanying memorandum and exchange of notes.
Signed at Washington April 30, 1945.
Entered into force April 30, 1945.
59 Stat. 1627; EAS 480; 10 Bevans 158; 139 UNTS 341

Agreement relating to principles applying to the provision of aid to the armed forces of the United States, and exchange of notes.
Exchange of notes at Washington April 30, 1945.
Operative from July 8, 1942.
59 Stat. 1635; EAS 480; 10 Bevans 167; 139 UNTS 319

Related agreement settlement for lend-lease, reciprocal aid, surplus property, military relief, and claims, and exchanges of notes with memorandum of arrangement between the United States, the United Kingdom, and the Netherlands.
Signed at Washington May 28, 1947.
Entered into force May 28, 1947.
61 Stat. 3924; TIAS 1750; 8 Bevans 1250; 10 Bevans 188 and 213; 17 UNTS 29

Amendment:
June 1 and 8, 1950 (1 UST 638; TIAS 2119; 81 UNTS 320)

SCIENTIFIC & TECHNICAL COOPERATION

Agreement providing for lending ultra-high frequency radio equipment for installation on Netherlands ocean weather ships stationed along the North Atlantic route.
Exchange of notes at Washington March 16 and 21, 1955.
Entered into force March 21, 1955.
9 UST 1302; TIAS 4119; 289 UNTS 129

Agreement relating to continuation of the cooperative meteorological observation program in the Netherlands Antilles.*
Exchange of notes at The Hague June 15, 1970.
Entered into force provisionally June 15, 1970; definitively December 11, 1970.
21 UST 2643; TIAS 7005; 772 UNTS 147

Note:
* Also applicable to Aruba.

Agreement on cooperation in science and technology concerning homeland and civil security matters.
Signed at Washington November 29, 2012.
Entered into force April 1, 2016.
TIAS 16-401

SOCIAL SECURITY

Agreement on social security, with administrative arrangement.
Signed at The Hague December 8, 1987.
Entered into force November 1, 1990.
TIAS

Protocol to the agreement on social security and administrative arrangement of December 8, 1987.
Signed at The Hague December 7, 1989.
Entered into force November 1, 1990.
TIAS

Second protocol to the agreement on social security of December 8, 1987.
Signed at The Hague August 30, 2001.
Entered into force May 1, 2003.
TIAS

TAXATION

Convention with respect to taxes on income and certain other taxes.*
Signed at Washington April 29, 1948.
Entered into force December 1, 1948.
62 Stat. 1757; TIAS 1855; 10 Bevans 225; 32 UNTS 167

Note:
* The convention was supplemented by a protocol, signed at Washington June 15, 1955, for the purpose of facilitating the extension of the convention to the Netherlands Antilles (TIAS 3366; 6 UST 3696; 239 UNTS 342). This was effectuated in accordance with exchanges of notes at Washington June 24 and August 7, 1952, and September 15 and November 4 and 10, 1955 (TIAS 3367; 6 UST 3703; 239 UNTS 346).
A further protocol modifying and supplementing the extension of the convention to the Netherlands Antilles was signed at The Hague October 23, 1963 (TIAS 5665; 15 UST 1900; 521 UNTS 377). The convention became applicable to Aruba as a separate entity as of January 1, 1986.
In accordance with notifications given by the United States on June 29 and July 10, 1987, the convention ceased to apply to Aruba and the Netherlands Antilles as of January 1, 1988, with the exception of Article VIII of the convention and such ancillary provisions as apply to effectuate, modify, or limit that article.

Agreement relating to relief from taxation on United States Government expenditures in the Netherlands for the common defense, with memorandum.
Exchange of notes at The Hague March 7, 1952.
Entered into force March 7, 1952.
3 UST 4183; TIAS 2563; 135 UNTS 199

Agreement concerning the tax relief techniques and procedures pursuant to the agreement of March 7, 1952.
Exchange of notes at The Hague May 29 and June 22, 1953.
Entered into force June 22, 1953.
5 UST 2556; TIAS 3120; 234 UNTS 320

Convention modifying and supplementing the convention of April 29, 1948, as amended, for avoidance of double taxation with respect to taxes on income and certain other taxes.
Signed at Washington December 30, 1965.
Entered into force July 8, 1966.
17 UST 896; TIAS 6051; 577 UNTS 295

Convention for the avoidance of double taxation and the prevention of fiscal evasion with respect to taxes on estates and inheritances, with protocol.
Signed at Washington July 15, 1969.
Entered into force February 3, 1971.
22 UST 247; TIAS 7061; 791 UNTS 201

Convention for the avoidance of double taxation and the prevention of fiscal evasion with respect to taxes on income, with understanding and exchange of notes.
Signed at Washington December 18, 1992.
Entered into force December 31, 1993.
TIAS; 2291 UNTS 3

Protocol amending the convention of December 18, 1992, for the avoidance of double taxation and the prevention of fiscal evasion with respect to taxes on income, with exchange of notes.
Signed at Washington October 13, 1993.
Entered into force December 30, 1993.
TIAS; 2339 UNTS 556

Protocol amending Article VIII of the convention of April 29, 1948, with respect to taxes on income and certain other taxes as applicable to the Netherlands Antilles.
Signed at Washington October 10, 1995.
Entered into force December 30, 1996.
TIAS

Agreement in respect of the Netherlands Antilles for the exchange of information with respect to taxes.
Signed at Washington April 17, 2002.
Entered into force March 22, 2007.
TIAS 07-322

Agreement in respect of Aruba for the exchange of information with respect to taxes.
Signed at Washington November 21, 2003.
Entered into force September 13, 2004.
TIAS 04-913

Protocol amending the convention of December 18, 1992, as amended, for the avoidance of double taxation and the prevention of fiscal evasion with respect to taxes on income, with exchange of notes.
Signed at Washington March 8, 2004.
Entered into force December 28, 2004.
TIAS 04-1228; 2339 UNTS 557

Agreement to improve tax compliance and to implement the Foreign Account Tax Compliance Act, with annexes.
Signed at The Hague December 18, 2013.
Entered into force April 9, 2015.
TIAS 15-409

Agreement in respect of Curaçao to improve international tax compliance and to implement the Foreign Account Tax Compliance Act, with annexes and related exchange of notes.
Signed at Willemstad December 16, 2014.
Entered into force August 3, 2016.
TIAS 16-803

TELECOMMUNICATION

Agreement relating to the reciprocal granting of authorizations to permit licensed amateur radio operators of either country to operate their stations in the other country.
Exchange of notes at The Hague June 22, 1966.
Entered into force December 21, 1966.
17 UST 2426; TIAS 6189; 590 UNTS 109

TRADE & INVESTMENT

Treaty of friendship, commerce and navigation, with protocol and exchange of notes.
Signed at The Hague March 27, 1956.
Entered into force December 5, 1957.
8 UST 2043; TIAS 3942; 285 UNTS 231

TRANSPORTATION

Agreement providing for non-assertion of sovereign immunity from suit of air transport enterprises.
Exchange of notes at Washington June 19, 1953.
Entered into force June 19, 1953.
4 UST 1610; TIAS 2828; 212 UNTS 249

Air transport agreement.*
Signed at Washington April 3, 1957.
Entered into force provisionally April 3, 1957; definitively May 31, 1957.
12 UST 837; TIAS 4782; 410 UNTS 193

Amendments:
March 31, 1978 (29 UST 3088; TIAS 8998; 1123 UNTS 345)*
June 11, 1986 (TIAS 11365; 2194 UNTS 122)
October 13 and December 22, 1987 (TIAS 11927)
January 29 and March 13, 1992 (TIAS 11929)
October 14, 1992 (TIAS 11976)

Notes:
* This agreement is suspended for the duration of provisional application of the U.S. – E.U. Air Transport Agreement signed April 25 and 30, 2007.
* Articles 3, 4, 6 and 9 have been superseded by subsequent amendments.

Memorandum of understanding concerning cooperation in the field of transportation.
Signed at Washington and The Hague September 28 and October 6, 1977.
Entered into force October 6, 1977.
29 UST 3577; TIAS 9029; 1134 UNTS 327

Memorandum of agreement relating to the provision of flight inspection services.
Signed at Washington and The Hague March 10 and June 15, 1978.
Entered into force June 15, 1978; effective April 1, 1978.
30 UST 283; TIAS 9199
Amendment:
February 19 and May 4, 1982 (TIAS 10546)

Agreement in respect of Aruba on preclearance. With annex
Signed at Washington December 2, 1994.
Entered into force March 4, 1996
TIAS
Amendment:
May 2, 2009

Agreement for the promotion of aviation safety.
Signed at The Hague September 13, 1995.
Entered into force December 1, 1996.
TIAS 12691; 1999 UNTS 31

Agreement relating to air transportation between the United States and Aruba, with annexes.
Signed at Washington September 18, 1997.
Entered into force June 11, 1998.
TIAS 12885; 2032 UNTS 359
Amendment:
July 27 and November 27, 2007 (TIAS 08-428)

Agreement relating to air transport between the Netherlands Antilles and the United States of America, with annexes.
Signed at Washington July 14, 1998.
Entered into force February 16, 1999.
TIAS 12973; 2066 UNTS 437
Amendment:
July 27 and November 27, 2007 (TIAS 12973)

Agreement concerning cooperation in civil aviation safety.
Signed at Washington May 23, 2013
Entered into force February 1, 2014.
TIAS 14-201

NEW ZEALAND

ANTARCTICA & ARCTIC

Agreement relating to cooperation in scientific and logistical operations in Antarctica, with memorandum of understanding.
Exchange of notes at Wellington December 24, 1958.
Entered into force December 24, 1958.
9 UST 1502; TIAS 4151; 324 UNTS 111
Extension:
October 18, 1960 (11 UST 2205; TIAS 4591; 447 UNTS 356)

ATOMIC ENERGY

Agreement providing for a grant to assist in the acquisition of nuclear research and training equipment and materials.
Exchange of notes at Wellington March 23, 1960.
Entered into force March 23, 1960.
11 UST 277; TIAS 4445; 371 UNTS 147

BOUNDARIES & BOUNDARY WATERS

Treaty on the delimitation of the maritime boundary between Tokelau and the United States of America.
Signed at Atafu December 2, 1980.
Entered into force September 3, 1983.
35 UST 2073; TIAS 10775

CLAIMS & DISPUTE RESOLUTION

Treaty amending in their application to New Zealand certain provisions of the treaty for the advancement of peace between the United States and the United Kingdom signed at Washington September 15, 1914.
Signed at Washington September 6, 1940.
Entered into force August 13, 1941.
55 Stat. 1217; TS 976; 10 Bevans 282

CONSULAR AFFAIRS

Agreement relating to the reciprocal reduction of nonimmigrant passport visa fees and the extension of validity of temporary visitors' visas.*
Exchange of notes at Wellington March 14, 1949.
Entered into force March 14, 1949; operative April 1, 1949.
63 Stat. 2538; TIAS 1940; 10 Bevans 331; 32 UNTS 369
Note:
* Applicable to all territories.
* The status of this agreement is under review.

Agreement relating to the abolition of visa fees and the extension of the period of validity for certain types of nonimmigrant visas.*
Exchange of notes at Wellington December 16, 1957, and May 2 and 5, 1958.
Entered into force May 5, 1958; operative June 1, 1958.
9 UST 913; TIAS 4053; 317 UNTS 59
Amendment:
May 13, 1958 (9 UST 919; TIAS 4053; 317 UNTS 70)

Note:
* The status of this agreement is under review.

DEFENSE

Agreement relating to mutual defense assistance.
Exchange of notes at Washington June 19, 1952.
Entered into force June 19, 1952.
3 UST 4408; TIAS 2590; 178 UNTS 315

Agreement relating to an aerial photographic survey of the New Zealand coastline.
Exchange of notes at Washington October 30, 1959.
Entered into force October 30, 1959.
10 UST 1983; TIAS 4364; 361 UNTS 21

Understanding that the assurances contained in the mutual defense assistance agreement of June 19, 1952, are applicable to equipment, materials, information and services furnished under the Mutual Security Act of 1954, as amended, and such other applicable United States laws as may come into effect.
Exchange of notes at Wellington March 25, 1960.
Entered into force March 25, 1960.
11 UST 315; TIAS 4450; 380 UNTS 424

Agreement relating to a reciprocal arrangement under which, in certain circumstances, either of the respective armed forces would advance funds to units or personnel of the other for their temporary support, with annex.
Exchange of notes at Wellington September 3, 1969.
Entered into force September 3, 1969.
20 UST 2839; TIAS 6755; 723 UNTS 233

Agreement concerning defense communications services, with annexes.
Signed at Wellington and Arlington August 12 and November 18, 1992.
Entered into force November 18, 1992.
TIAS 12357; 1937 UNTS 283

Agreement concerning certain mutual defense commitments.
Exchange of notes at Washington July 16, 1996.
Entered into force July 16, 1996.
TIAS 12782; 1950 UNTS 15

Acquisition and cross-servicing agreement, with annexes.
Signed at Sydney November 6, 2012.
Entered into force November 6, 2012.
NP

EDUCATION

Agreement for the financing of certain educational and cultural exchange programs.
Signed at Wellington February 3, 1970.
Entered into force March 3, 1970.
21 UST 421; TIAS 6827; 240 UNTS 217
Amendment:
June 21, 1995

EMPLOYMENT

Agreement relating to the employment of dependents of official government employees.
Exchange of notes at Washington May 18 and 21, 1999.
Entered into force May 21, 1999.
TIAS 13034

FISHERIES

Memorandum of understanding concerning cooperation to assure the sanitary quality of bivalve molluscs exported to the United States.
Signed at Washington and Wellington October 14 and 30, 1980.
Entered into force October 30, 1980.
32 UST 4545; TIAS 9968; 1266 UNTS 35

HEALTH & MEDICAL COOPERATION

Memorandum of understanding relative to exporting dry milk products to the United States.
Signed at Wellington and at Washington October 23 and November 11, 1975.
Entered into force November 11, 1975.
28 UST 345; TIAS 8472

LAW ENFORCEMENT

Treaty on extradition.*
Signed at Washington January 12, 1970.
Entered into force December 8, 1970.
22 UST 1; TIAS 7035; 791 UNTS 253
Note:
* Applicable to all territories.

Agreement regarding mutual assistance between their customs services.
Signed at Hong Kong June 13, 1996.
Entered into force June 13, 1996.
TIAS 12767; 1950 UNTS 3

NONPROLIFERATION

Agreement on technology safeguards associated with United States participation in space launches from New Zealand.
Signed at Washington June 16, 2016.
Entered into force December 12, 2016.
TIAS 16-1212

POSTAL MATTERS

Agreement concerning the exchange of parcel post.
Signed at Wellington March 3 and at Washington April 24, 1933.
Operative October 1, 1932.
48 Stat. 1491; Post Office Department print

Memorandum of understanding concerning international express mail service, with detailed regulations.
Signed at Wellington and Washington August 1 and 20, 1984.
Entered into force October 28, 1984.
TIAS 11003; 2022 UNTS 51

Memorandum of understanding concerning the operation of the INTELPOST service, with details of implementation.
Signed at Berne April 28, 1989.
Entered into force May 1, 1989.
TIAS 11610

PROPERTY

Convention between the United States and the United Kingdom relating to tenure and disposition of real and personal property.
Signed at Washington March 2, 1899.
Entered into force for New Zealand June 10, 1901.
31 Stat. 1939; TS 146; I Malloy 774

Supplementary convention relating to the tenure and disposition of real and personal property.
Signed at Washington May 27, 1936, by the United States, United Kingdom, Australia, and New Zealand.
Entered into force March 10, 1941.
55 Stat. 1101; TS 964; 5 Bevans 140; 203 LNTS 367

Agreement relating to the principles applying to the provision of aid in the prosecution of war.
Exchange of notes at Washington September 3, 1942.
Entered into force September 3, 1942.
56 Stat. 1611; EAS 272; 10 Bevans 285; 24 UNTS 185

Agreement on settlement for lend-lease and reciprocal aid, surplus war property, and claims.
Signed at Washington July 10, 1946.
Entered into force July 10, 1946.
60 Stat. 1791; TIAS 1536; 10 Bevans 296; 6 UNTS 341

SCIENTIFIC & TECHNICAL COOPERATION

Agreement concerning a program of research on aerospace disturbances, with memorandum of understanding.
Exchange of notes at Wellington May 15, 1963.
Entered into force May 15, 1963.
14 UST 524; TIAS 5350; 477 UNTS 55

Agreement concerning the establishment of an astronomical observatory at Blackbirch Ridge, with memorandum of understandings and agreed minute.
Exchange of notes at Wellington November 11, 1982.
Entered into force November 11, 1982.
TIAS 10604; 1675 UNTS 247

Agreement for scientific and technological cooperation, with annex and exchange of letters.
Signed at Washington May 21, 1991.
Entered into force May 21, 1991.
TIAS 11829; 1937 UNTS 235

Agreement concerning the installation, operation and maintenance in New Zealand of Global Sea Level Data Collection (GSL) Stations, with arrangements.
Exchange of notes at Wellington November 18, 1992.
Entered into force November 18, 1992.
TIAS 11973; 1937 UNTS 271

Agreement on science and technology cooperation contributing to domestic and external security capabilities, with annex.
Signed at Washington January 8, 2010.
Entered into force September 9, 2010.
TIAS 10-909

SPACE

Agreement for a space vehicle tracking program.
Exchange of notes at Wellington July 9, 1968.
Entered into force July 9, 1968.
19 UST 5836; TIAS 6539; 644 UNTS 99

TAXATION

Convention for the avoidance of double taxation and the prevention of fiscal evasion with respect to taxes on income, with protocol.*
Signed at Wellington July 23, 1982.
Entered into force November 2, 1983.
35 UST 1949; TIAS 10772

Note:
* Does not include Tokelau or the Associated Self Governing States of the Cook Islands and Niue.

Protocol amending the convention for the avoidance of double taxation and the prevention of fiscal evasion with respect to taxes on income of July 23, 1982.
Signed at Washington December 1, 2008.
Entered into force November 12, 2010.
TIAS 10-1112

Agreement to improve international tax compliance and to implement the Foreign Account Tax Compliance Act.
Signed at Wellington June 12, 2014.
Entered into force July 3, 2014.
TIAS 14-703

TELECOMMUNICATION

Agreement relating to the reciprocal granting of authorizations to permit licensed amateur radio operators of either country to operate their stations in the other country.
Exchange of notes at Wellington June 21, 1967.
Entered into force June 21, 1967.
18 UST 1272; TIAS 6281; 644 UNTS 77

TRADE & INVESTMENT

Convention to regulate commerce (article IV) between the United States and the United Kingdom.
Signed at London July 3, 1815.
Entered into force July 3, 1815.
8 Stat. 228; TS 110; 12 Bevans 49

TRANSPORTATION

Air transport agreement, with annexes.*
Signed at Washington June 18, 1997.
Entered into force June 18, 1997.
TIAS 12860; 2049 UNTS 379
*This agreement is suspended so long as the Multilateral agreement on the liberalization of international air transportation, signed May 1, 2001, remains in force between the United States and New Zealand.

NICARAGUA

AGRICULTURE

Agreement confirming the cooperative agreement for the prevention of foot-and-mouth disease and rinderpest in Nicaragua.
Exchange of notes at Managua March 24 and April 13, 1972.
Entered into force April 13, 1972.
23 UST 1228; TIAS 7392; 852 UNTS 201

Cooperative agreement for the eradication of screwworms.
Signed at Washington November 26, 1991.
Entered into force January 11, 1993.
TIAS 12444

CONSULAR AFFAIRS

Agreement relating to the reciprocal granting of nonimmigrant visas, without fee, for maximum validity for four years.*
Exchange of notes at Managua July 6, September 30 and October 22, 1955.
Entered into force October 22, 1955.
10 UST 1696; TIAS 4319; 358 UNTS 51

Note:
* The status of this agreement is under review.

CULTURAL EXCHANGES, PROPERTY & COOPERATION

Agreement relating to the establishment of a Peace Corps program in Nicaragua.
Exchange of notes at Managua May 23 and 25, 1968.
Entered into force May 25, 1968.
19 UST 5073; TIAS 6507; 707 UNTS 61

Agreement concerning the imposition of import restrictions on archaeological material from the pre-Hispanic cultures of the Republic of Nicaragua.
Signed at Managua June 16, 1999.
Entered into force October 20, 2000.
TIAS 13044

Amendments and Extensions:
October 6 and 18, 2005 (TIAS 13044)
October 4 and 13, 2010 (TIAS 10-1020)
September 8 and 15, 2015 (TIAS 15-915.1)

DEFENSE

NOTE: The Air Force and Army missions were consolidated September 10, 1965.

Agreement relating to an air force mission to Nicaragua.
Signed at Managua November 19, 1952.
Entered into force November 19, 1952.
3 UST 5027; TIAS 2683; 186 UNTS 2

Extensions and Amendments:
August 21 and 27, 1956 (7 UST 2465; TIAS 3634; 277 UNTS 352)
March 25 and May 22, 1959 (10 UST 1446; TIAS 4294; 357 UNTS 369)

Agreement providing for a United States Army mission to Nicaragua.
Signed at Managua November 19, 1953.
Entered into force November 19, 1953.
4 UST 2238; TIAS 2876; 206 UNTS 117

Amendment:
March 25 and May 22, 1959 (10 UST 1446; TIAS 4294; 357 UNTS 369)

Military assistance agreement.
Signed at Managua April 23, 1954.
Entered into force April 23, 1954.
5 UST 453; TIAS 2940; 229 UNTS 37

Agreement relating to the disposition of equipment and materials furnished by the United States under the military assistance agreement of April 23, 1954.
Exchange of notes at Managua April 23, 1954.
Entered into force April 23, 1954.
13 UST 116; TIAS 4946; 435 UNTS 340

Agreement for performance by members of army and air force missions of duties of military assistance advisory group specified in article V of military assistance agreement.
Exchange of notes at Managua January 17 and February 9, 1957.
Entered into force February 9, 1957.
8 UST 285; TIAS 3773; 279 UNTS 191

Agreement relating to deposit by Nicaragua of ten percent of the value of grant military assistance and excess defense articles furnished by the United States.
Exchange of notes at Managua March 6 and April 10, 1972.
Entered into force April 10, 1972; effective February 7, 1972.
23 UST 671; TIAS 7332

Basic exchange and cooperative agreement for topographic mapping, nautical and aeronautical charting and information, geodesy and geophysics, digital data and related mapping, charting and geodesy materials.
Signed at Managua and Fairfax November 28 and December 1, 1994.
Entered into force December 1, 1994.
NP

Agreement regarding the status of U.S. military and civilian personnel of the Department of Defense present in Nicaragua in connection with the disaster relief/assistance effort and mutually agreed follow-on activities.
Exchange of notes at Managua November 7 and 25, 1998.
Entered into force November 25, 1998.
TIAS

Agreement regarding loan of military equipment.
Exchange of notes at Managua August 26 and September 4, 2003.
Entered into force September 4, 2003.
TIAS

Agreement regarding grants under the Foreign Assistance Act of 1961, as amended, and the furnishing of defense articles, defense services, and related training, including pursuant to the United States International Military and Education Training Program (IMET), from the United States to the Government of the Republic of Nicaragua.
Exchange of notes at Managua December 5, 2005, and April 19, 2006.
Entered into force April 19, 2006.
NP

Acquisition and cross-servicing agreement, with annexes.
Signed at Managua November 20, 2009.
Entered into force November 20, 2009.
NP

DIPLOMATIC & CONSULAR RELATIONS

Interim agreement relating to customs exemptions of diplomatic and consular officials.
Exchange of notes at Washington December 3, 1951, and October 9, 1952.
Entered into force October 9, 1952.
3 UST 5154; TIAS 2708; 184 UNTS 105

EMPLOYMENT

Agreement relating to the employment of dependents of official government employees.
Exchange of notes at Managua January 26 and February 2, 1994.
Entered into force February 2, 1994.
TIAS 12173

FINANCE

Agreement regarding the discharge of certain debts owed to the Government of the United States, with annex.
Signed at Managua September 25, 1991.
Entered into force September 25, 1991.
NP

Agreement regarding the consolidation and rescheduling or refinancing of certain debts owed to, guaranteed by, or insured by the United States Government and its agencies, with annexes.
Signed at Managua May 13, 1992.
Entered into force July 10, 1992.
NP
Amendment:
July 21 and September 26, 1997 (NP)

Agreement among the United States and the Government of Nicaragua/Central American Business Administration Institute regarding the assumption, payment and discharge of certain debts.
Exchange of notes at Managua August 28, 1995.
Entered into force August 28, 1995.
NP

Agreement regarding the consolidation and rescheduling of certain debts owed to, guaranteed by or insured by the United States Government and its agencies, with annexes.
Signed at Managua August 28, 1995.
Entered into force November 1, 1995.
NP

Agreement regarding the consolidation, reduction and rescheduling of certain debts owed to, guaranteed by, or insured
by the United States Government and its agencies, with annexes.
Signed at Managua October 20, 1998.
Entered into force December 21, 1998.
NP
Amendment:
April 9 and May 19, 1999 (NP)

Agreement regarding the reduction of certain debts owed to, guaranteed by, or insured by the United States Government, with annexes.
Signed at Managua April 25, 2003.
Entered into force June 9, 2003.
NP

Investment incentive agreement.
Signed at Managua July 20, 2004.
Entered into force July 20, 2004.
TIAS

Agreement regarding the cancellation of certain debts owed to, guaranteed by, or insured by the United States Government, with annexes.
Signed at Managua August 17, 2004.
Entered into force December 27, 2004.
NP

FOREIGN ASSISTANCE

General agreement for economic, technical and related assistance.
Exchange of notes at Managua March 30, 1962.
Entered into force May 14, 1962.
13 UST 1208; TIAS 5065; 456 UNTS 241

INTERNATIONAL CRIMINAL COURT

Agreement regarding the surrender of persons to the International Criminal Court.
Signed at Managua June 4, 2003.
Entered into force September 12, 2003.
TIAS 03-912

LAW ENFORCEMENT

Treaty on extradition.
Signed at Washington March 1, 1905.
Entered into force July 14, 1907.
35 Stat. 1869; TS 462; 10 Bevans 356

Agreement concerning Cooperating Nation Information Exchange System (CNIES).
Exchange of notes at Managua October 18 and November 23, 2004.
Entered into force November 23, 2004.
TIAS 04-1123

MARITIME MATTERS

Agreement concerning cooperation to suppress illicit traffic by sea and air.
Signed at Managua June 1, 2001.
Entered into force November 15, 2001.
TIAS 13153

POSTAL MATTERS

Agreement for parcel post service.
Signed at Managua March 19 and at Washington April 4, 1956.
Entered into force July 1, 1956.
7 UST 1051; TIAS 3586; 275 UNTS 231

International express mail agreement, with detailed regulations.
Signed at Managua and Washington July 24 and August 16, 1991.
Entered into force September 30, 1991.
TIAS 11798

PUBLICATIONS

Agreement relating to the exchange of official publications.
Exchange of notes at Managua February 14 and 19, 1940.
Entered into force February 14, 1940.
54 Stat. 2294; EAS 171; 10 Bevans 411; 203 LNTS 47

SCIENTIFIC & TECHNICAL COOPERATION

Memorandum of understanding concerning scientific cooperation in the earth and mapping sciences, with annexes.
Signed at Reston and Managua March 4 and 10, 1999.
Entered into force March 10, 1999.
TIAS 99-310
Amendment and Extension:
May 24 and June 25, 2004 (TIAS 99-310)

TELECOMMUNICATION

Agreement relating to radio communications between amateur stations on behalf of third parties.
Exchange of notes at Managua October 8 and 16, 1956.
Entered into force October 16, 1956.
7 UST 3159; TIAS 3694; 282 UNTS 29

Agreement relating to the reciprocal granting of authorizations to permit licensed amateur radio operators of either country to operate their stations in the other country.
Exchange of notes at Managua September 3 and 20, 1966.
Entered into force September 20, 1966.
17 UST 1560; TIAS 6112; 607 UNTS 167

TRADE & INVESTMENT

Agreement terminating the agreement of September 5, 1972, relating to trade in cotton textiles and providing for consultations on problems of market disruption as defined in the arrangement regarding international trade in textiles of December 20, 1973.
Exchange of notes at Managua December 26, 1974, and January 3, 1975.
Entered into force January 3, 1975.
26 UST 41; TIAS 8007

Agreement on trade in textile and apparel goods under the Dominican Republic-Central America-United States Free Trade Agreement.
Exchange of letters at Managua and Washington March 24 and 27, 2006.
Entered into force March 27, 2006.
NP

TRANSPORTATION

Agreement relating to the construction of the inter-American highway.
Exchange of notes at Washington April 8, 1942.
Entered into force April 8, 1942.
56 Stat. 1845; EAS 295; 10 Bevans 424; 24 UNTS 145
Amendment:
April 4 and 20, 1951 (2 UST 1848; TIAS 2320; 138 UNTS 57)

Agreement relating to the construction of the Rama Road.
Exchange of notes at Washington April 8 and 18, 1942.
Entered into force April 18, 1942.
2 UST 722; TIAS 2229; 132 UNTS 343
Amendments:
September 2, 1953 (4 UST 1944; TIAS 2853; 215 UNTS 69)
March 13 and August 2, 1956 (7 UST 2237; TIAS 3623; 281 UNTS 99)

Air transport agreement, with annexes.
Signed at San Jose May 8, 1997.
Entered into force December 5, 1997.
TIAS 12855

Memorandum of agreement for the provision of assistance in developing and modernizing Nicaragua's civil aviation infrastructure.
Signed at Washington and Managua April 29 and August 30, 1999.
Entered into force August 30, 1999.
NP

NIGER

CULTURAL EXCHANGES, PROPERTY & COOPERATION

Agreement relating to the establishment of a Peace Corps program in Niger.
Exchange of notes at Niamey July 23, 1962.
Entered into force July 23, 1962.
14 UST 868; TIAS 5368; 487 UNTS 325

DEFENSE

Agreement relating to the furnishing of military equipment, materials and services to Niger to help assure its security and independence.
Exchange of notes at Niamey May 22 and June 14, 1962.
Entered into force June 14, 1962.
13 UST 1301; TIAS 5083; 458 UNTS 233

Agreement concerning the provision of training related to defense articles under the United States International Military Education and Training (IMET) Program.
Exchange of notes at Niamey March 11 and June 9, 1980.
Entered into force June 9, 1980.
33 UST 576; TIAS 10049; 1267 UNTS 123

Agreement regarding the terms and conditions relating to the furnishing of defense articles and services on a grant basis to the Government of Niger by the United States.
Exchange of notes at Niamey July 18 and September 24, 1992.
Entered into force September 24, 1992.
TIAS 12359
Amendment:
January 13 and February 18, 2005

Agreement regarding grants under the Foreign Assistance Act of 1961, as amended, and the furnishing of defense articles, related training to include training related to defense articles under the United States International Military Education and Training (IMET) Program, and other defense services from the United States of America to the Government of Niger.
Exchange of notes at Niamey January 22 and March 12, 2004.
Entered into force March 12, 2004.
NP

Agreement regarding the status of United States personnel who may be temporarily present in Niger.
Effected by exchange of notes at Niamey July 6, 2012 and January 28, 2013.
Entered into force January 28, 2013.
TIAS 13-128

Acquisition and cross-servicing agreement, with annexes.
Signed at Stuttgart and Niamey June 17 and August 13, 2013.
Entered into force August 13, 2013.
NP

Agreement concerning United States access to and use of facilities in the Republic of Niger.
Effected by Exchange of Notes at Niamey August 22, 2014.
Entered into force August 22, 2014.
NP

ENVIRONMENT & CONSERVATION

Agreement for cooperation in the GLOBE program.
Signed at Niamey August 11, 2005.
Entered into force August 11, 2005.
TIAS 05-811

FINANCE

Agreement relating to investment guaranties.
Exchange of notes at Niamey February 28 and April 26, 1962.
Entered into force April 26, 1962.
13 UST 2203; TIAS 5187; 459 UNTS 129

Agreement regarding the consolidation and rescheduling of certain debts owed to, guaranteed by or insured by the United States Government and its agencies, with annexes.
Signed at Niamey June 11, 1984.
Entered into force July 24, 1984.
TIAS 10994; 2022 UNTS 77

Agreement regarding the consolidation and rescheduling of certain debts owed to, guaranteed by or insured by the United States Government and its agencies, with annexes.
Signed at Niamey April 9, 1985.
Entered into force May 28, 1985.
NP

Agreement regarding the consolidation and rescheduling of certain debts owed to, guaranteed by, or insured by the United States Government and its agencies, with annexes.
Signed at Niamey April 11, 1986.
Entered into force May 19, 1986.
NP

Agreement regarding the consolidation and rescheduling of certain debts owed to, guaranteed by or insured by the United States Government and its agencies, with annexes.
Signed at Niamey February 10, 1988.
Entered into force March 17, 1988.
NP

Agreement regarding the consolidation and rescheduling of certain debts owed to, guaranteed by or insured by the United States Government and its agencies, with annexes.
Signed at Niamey February 21, 1989.
Entered into force March 30, 1989.
NP

Agreement regarding the consolidation and rescheduling of certain debts owed to, guaranteed by, or insured by the United States Government and its agencies, with annexes.
Signed at Washington June 29, 1989.
Entered into force August 24, 1989.
NP

Agreement regarding the consolidation and rescheduling of certain debts owed to, guaranteed by, or insured by the United States Government and its agencies, with annexes.
Signed at Washington February 12, 1991.
Entered into force March 28, 1991.
NP

Agreement regarding the consolidation, reduction and rescheduling of certain debts owed to, guaranteed by or insured by the United States Government and its agencies, with annexes.
Signed at Niamey July 29, 1994.
Entered into force August 29, 1994.
NP

Agreement regarding the consolidation, reduction and rescheduling of certain debts owed to, guaranteed by, or insured by the United States Government and its agencies, with annexes.
Signed at Niamey January 14, 1998.
Entered into force March 27, 1998.
NP

Agreement regarding the consolidation, reduction, and rescheduling of certain debts owed to, guaranteed by, or insured by the United States Government and its agencies, with annexes.
Signed at Niamey August 1, 2001.
Entered into force September 4, 2001.
NP
Amendment:
January 29 and 30, 2003

Agreement regarding the reduction of certain debts owed to, guaranteed by, or insured by the United States Government, with annexes.
Signed at Niamey January 31, 2005.
Entered into force March 10, 2005.
NP

FOREIGN ASSISTANCE

Agreement providing for the furnishing of economic, technical and related assistance.
Exchange of notes at Niamey May 26, 1961.
Entered into force May 26, 1961.
12 UST 858; TIAS 4786; 410 UNTS 213

POSTAL MATTERS

International express mail agreement, with detailed regulations.
Signed at Niamey and Washington May 6 and 29, 1987.
Entered into force June 15, 1987.
TIAS 11302

SOCIAL SECURITY

Agreement to provide certain social security benefits for certain employees of the United States in Niger.
Signed at Niamey July 21, 1975.
Entered into force July 21, 1975; effective January 1, 1974.
26 UST 2758; TIAS 8194; 1045 UNTS 65

NIGERIA

On October 1, 1960, the territories formerly comprising the British Colony and Protectorate of Nigeria attained fully responsible status within the British Commonwealth under the name of the Federation of Nigeria (Federation of Nigeria Independence Act, 1960). By an exchange of notes, dated October 1, 1960, between the High Commissioner for the United Kingdom in the Federation of Nigeria and the Prime Minister of the Federation of Nigeria, Nigeria agreed to assume, from October 1, 1960, all obligations and responsibilities of the United Kingdom which arise from any valid international instrument insofar as such instruments may be held to have application to or in respect of Nigeria are from October 1, 1960, enjoyed by the Federation of Nigeria.

CULTURAL EXCHANGES, PROPERTY & COOPERATION

Agreement establishing a Peace Corps program in Nigeria.
Exchange of notes at Lagos August 19 and 22, 1991.
Entered into force August 22, 1991.
TIAS 12108

DEFENSE

Agreement between the United States and the United Kingdom relating to the assurances required under the Mutual Security Act of 1951.
Exchange of notes at London January 8, 1952.
Applicable to Nigeria January 8, 1952.
3 UST 4665; TIAS 2622; 126 UNTS 307

Agreement relating to the deposit by Nigeria of ten percent of the value of grant military assistance furnished by the United States.
Exchange of notes at Lagos April 12 and 20, 1972.
Entered into force April 20, 1972; effective February 7, 1972.
23 UST 773; TIAS 7338

Agreement concerning the provision of training related to defense articles under the United States International Military Education and Training (IMET) Program.
Exchange of notes at Lagos November 19, 1985, and February 26, 1986.
Entered into force February 26, 1986.
TIAS 11106

Agreement regarding the provision of commodities and services to Nigerian forces participating in ECOMOG peacekeeping operations.
Exchange of notes at Abuja November 9, 1996.
Entered into force November 9, 1996.
TIAS 12778

Agreement regarding grants under the Foreign Assistance Act of 1961, as amended, and the furnishing of defense articles, related training, and other defense services from the United States of America to the Government of the Federal Republic of Nigeria.
Exchange of notes at Abuja July 27 and August 17, 2000.
Entered into force August 17, 2000.
TIAS 13111

Agreement concerning the status of United States military and civilian personnel of the U.S. Department of Defense temporarily present in Nigeria in connection with military training and other activities as may be agreed upon by the two governments.
Exchange of notes at Abuja August 24 and September 7, 2000.
Entered into force September 7, 2000.
NP

Agreement concerning end-use, retransfer and security assurances regarding AKM rifles and related equipment provided to the Government of Nigeria for use in connection with regional efforts concerning Sierra Leone and Operation Focus Relief and other purposes related to self-defense and regional security, with attachment.
Exchange of notes at Abuja January 29 and March 6, 2002.
Entered into force March 6, 2002.
TIAS 02-306

Acquisition and cross-servicing agreement, with annexes.
Signed at Abuja November 9, 2016.
Entered into force November 9, 2016.
NP

DIPLOMATIC & CONSULAR RELATIONS

Consular convention between the United States and the United Kingdom.
Signed at Washington June 6, 1951.
Entered into force September 7, 1952.
3 UST 3426; TIAS 2494; 165 UNTS 121

EDUCATION

Agreement on the training of Nigerian technical educators, with annexes.
Signed at Washington September 9, 1981.
Entered into force September 9, 1981.
TIAS 10261; 33 UST 3783; 1541 UNTS 181

EMPLOYMENT

Bilateral employment agreement.
Signed at Abuja May 12, 2005.
Entered into force May 12, 2005.
TIAS 05-512

FINANCE

Agreement regarding the consolidation and rescheduling of certain debts owed to, guaranteed by or insured by the United States Government and its agencies, with annexes.
Signed at Lagos December 23, 1987.
Entered into force February 16, 1988.
NP

Agreement regarding the consolidation and rescheduling of certain debts owed to, guaranteed by, or insured by the United States Government and its agencies.
Signed at Lagos December 4, 1989.
Entered into force January 22, 1990.
NP

Agreement regarding the consolidation and rescheduling or refinancing of certain debts owed to, guaranteed by, or insured by the United States Government and its agencies, with annexes.
Signed at Lagos August 2, 1991.
Entered into force September 18, 1991.
NP

Investment incentive agreement.
Signed at Abuja December 6, 1999.
Entered into force January 20, 2003.
TIAS

Agreement regarding the reduction of certain debts owed to, guaranteed by, or insured by the United States Government and its agency, with annexes.
Signed at Abuja December 17, 2005.
Entered into force January 20, 2006.
NP

FOREIGN ASSISTANCE

Economic cooperation agreement between the United States and the United Kingdom.
Signed at London July 6, 1948.
Applicable to Nigeria July 6, 1948.
62 Stat. 2596; TIAS 1795; 12 Bevans 874; 22 UNTS 263

Amendments:
January 3, 1950 (1 UST 184; TIAS 2036; 86 UNTS 304)
May 25, 1951 (2 UST 1292; TIAS 2277; 99 UNTS 308)
February 25, 1953 (4 UST 1528; TIAS 2815; 172 UNTS 332)

AGENCY FOR INTERNATIONAL DEVELOPMENT

Development objectives assistance agreement for reduced extreme poverty in a more stable, democratic Nigeria through the development objectives: broadened and inclusive growth, a healthier, more educated population in targeted states, strengthened good governance.
Signed at Abuja September 29, 2015.
Entered into force September 29, 2015.
TIAS

INTELLECTUAL PROPERTY

Declaration by the United States and the United Kingdom relating to reciprocal protection to trade-marks.
Signed at London October 24, 1877.
Entered into force October 24, 1877.
20 Stat. 703; TS 138; 12 Bevans 198

INTERNATIONAL CRIMINAL COURT

Agreement regarding the surrender of persons to the International Criminal Court.
Signed at Abuja June 30, 2003.
Entered into force October 6, 2003.
TIAS 03-1006

LAW ENFORCEMENT

Extradition treaty between the United States and the United Kingdom.
Signed at London December 22, 1931.
Applicable to Nigeria June 24, 1935.
47 Stat. 2122; TS 849; 12 Bevans 482; 163 LNTS 59

Procedures for mutual assistance in the administration of justice in connection with the Lockheed Aircraft Corporation matter.
Signed at Washington April 20, 1976.
Entered into force April 20, 1976.
27 UST 1054; TIAS 8243
Related Agreement:
March 8 and 26, 1979 (NP)

Mutual cooperation agreement for reducing demand, preventing illicit use and combatting illicit production and trafficking in drugs.
Exchange of notes at Lagos January 13 and 24, 1989.
Entered into force January 24, 1989.
TIAS 11598; 2190 UNTS 333

Treaty on mutual legal assistance in criminal matters, with attachments.
Signed at Washington September 13, 1989.
Entered into force January 14, 2003.
TIAS

Agreement regarding mutual assistance between their customs administrations.
Signed at Washington April 23, 2013.
Entered into force April 23, 2013.
TIAS 13-423

POSTAL MATTERS

International express mail agreement, with detailed regulations.
Signed at Lagos and Washington March 7 and April 21, 1986.
Entered into force July 1, 1986.
TIAS 11407

Postal money order agreement, with attachments.
Signed at Lagos and Washington June 14 and 28, 1990.
Entered into force September 1, 1990.
TIAS 11759

PROPERTY

Convention between the United States and the United Kingdom relating to the tenure and disposition of real and personal property.*
Signed at Washington March 2, 1899.
Entered into force August 7, 1900.
31 Stat. 1939; TS 146; 12 Bevans 246
Note:
* Notification given on July 22, 1901, of application to Northern Nigeria, and on July 27, 1901, of application to Southern Nigeria.

TELECOMMUNICATION

Agreement relating to the installation and operation of a radio transmitter by the Embassy of Nigeria.
Exchange of notes at Washington November 19, 1974, November 22, 1974, and June 4, 1975.
Entered into force June 4, 1975.
27 UST 3297; TIAS 8364; 1068 UNTS 457

TRANSPORTATION

Arrangement between the United States and the United Kingdom relating to pilot licenses to operate civil aircraft.
Exchange of notes at Washington March 28 and April 5, 1935.
Entered into force May 5, 1935.
49 Stat. 3731; EAS 77; 12 Bevans 513; 162 LNTS 59

Air transport agreement, with memorandum of understanding.
Signed at Lagos April 27, 1978.
Entered into force provisionally April 27, 1978; definitively June 16, 1978.
29 UST 3102; TIAS 8999; 1124 UNTS 255

Agreement, regarding the provision of technical assistance for developing and modernizing civil aviation infrastructure in Nigeria.
Signed April 12 and May 31, 2002.
Entered into force May 31, 2002.
NP
Amendments:
July 9 and August 9, 2002
March 13 and April 15, 2009

NIUE

BOUNDARIES & BOUNDARY WATERS

Treaty on the delimitation of a maritime boundary. With annex.
Signed at Wellington May 13, 1997.
Entered into force October 7, 2014.
TIAS 14-1007

CULTURAL EXCHANGES, PROPERTY & COOPERATION

Agreement concerning the program of the Peace Corps in Niue.
Signed at Alofi September 23, 1994.
Entered into force September 23, 1994.
TIAS 12109

NORTH ATLANTIC TREATY ORGANIZATION (NATO)

DEFENSE

Agreement between the United States and the Headquarters of the Supreme Allied Commander Atlantic regarding the headquarters, with exchange of letters.
Signed at Washington October 22, 1954.
Entered into force October 22, 1954; operative April 10, 1954.
5 UST 2519; TIAS 3113; 249 UNTS 175

Agreement concerning the North Atlantic Treaty Organization satellite communications earth terminal in the United States.
Signed at Washington July 10 and at Mons, Belgium August 20, 1970.
Entered into force August 20, 1970.
21 UST 2089; TIAS 6955; 764 UNTS 225

Memorandum of agreement concerning the interconnection of the Initial Voice Switched Network (IVSN) of the NATO Integrated Communications System and the Defense Switched Network (DSN) of the U.S. Defense Information Infrastructure, with annex.
Signed at Brussels and Arlington February 16 and April 21, 1995.
Entered into force April 21, 1995.
TIAS 12633

Agreement regarding U.S. approval for retransfer of U.S. defense articles and services to NATO for purposes of supporting the NATO–led Implementation Force (IFOR).
Exchange of letters at Brussels December 18, 1995.
Entered into force December 18, 1995.
TIAS

Memorandum of agreement concerning the interconnection of the NATO Core Network (NCN) and the U.S. Defense Switched Network (DSN) via gateways, with annexes.
Signed September 3 and October 28, 2007.
Entered into force October 28, 2007.
TIAS 07-1028

Memorandum of agreement for the continuation of a national expert office at NC3A, with annex.
Signed at Brussels November 5, 2007.
Entered into force November 5, 2007.
TIAS 07-1105

Memorandum of agreement concerning cooperation on projects, with annexes.
Signed February 24 and March 20, 2015.
Entered into force March 20, 2015.
TIAS 15-320

DIPLOMATIC & CONSULAR RELATIONS

Agreement concerning the application of part IV of the agreement on the status of the North Atlantic Treaty Organization, national representatives and international staff, September 20, 1951 (TIAS 2992) to the officials of NATO civilian bodies located on the territory of the United States of America.
Signed at Brussels March 3, 1981.
Entered into force March 3, 1981.
33 UST 1272; TIAS 10110; 1307 UNTS 423

EMPLOYMENT

Arrangement concerning the employment by the North Atlantic Treaty Organization of United States nationals.
Signed at London September 29, 1951.
Entered into force September 29, 1951.
5 UST 1112; TIAS 2992

Agreement concerning the employment by the International Military Headquarters of United States nationals.
Signed at Paris February 25, 1953.
Entered into force February 25, 1953.
5 UST 890; TIAS 2978

Supplemental arrangement concerning the employment by NATO bodies of United States nationals.
Signed at Brussels June 3, 1983.
Entered into force June 3, 1983.
TIAS 10695; 2005 UNTS 189

TAXATION

Tax reimbursement agreement, with annex.
Signed at Brussels July 18, 1990.
Entered into force July 18, 1990.
TIAS 11947

NATO AEW&C PROGRAMME MANAGEMENT ORGANIZATION (NAPMO)

DEFENSE

Memorandum of agreement concerning the cooperative production of radar system improvements for the E-3 aircraft.
Signed at Hanscom AFB and Washington August 3 and 11, 1995.
Entered into force August 11, 1995.
TIAS 12682

Memorandum of agreement concerning cooperative projects for the E 3 aircraft, with annex.
Signed at Washington and Brunssum August 10 and 30, 1999.
Entered into force August 30, 1999.
TIAS 13057

NATO COMMUNICATIONS AND INFORMATION ORGANIZATION

DEFENSE

Memorandum of agreement concerning cooperation on projects, with annexes.
Signed February 24 and March 20, 2015.
Entered into force March 20, 2015.
TIAS 15-320

NATO CONSULTATION, COMMAND AND CONTROL ORGANIZATION (NC3O)

DEFENSE

Memorandum of agreement concerning air command, control, communications and intelligence capabilities.
Signed at Washington and Brussels April 23 and May 7, 2002.
Entered into force May 7, 2002.
TIAS 02-507
Amendment and Extension:
September 5 and October 19, 2007 (TIAS 02-507)

Acquisition and cross-servicing agreement, with annexes.
Signed May 27, 2011.
Entered into force May 27, 2011.
NP

NATO HAWK PRODUCTION AND LOGISTICS ORGANIZATION

DEFENSE

Amendment one to the agreement for the fire direction operation center project.
Signed at Biloxi March 12, 2002.
Entered into force March 12, 2002.
TIAS

NATO MAINTENANCE AND SUPPORT ORGANIZATION

DEFENSE

Acquisition and cross-servicing agreement with the NATO Support Organization (NSPO), with annexes.
Signed at Capellen and Stuttgart February 21 and 25, 2013.
Entered into force February 25, 2013.
NP

NATO MAINTENANCE AND SUPPLY ORGANIZATION (NAMSO)

DEFENSE

Agreement for credit sales of military equipment, materials, and services.
Signed at Paris June 22, 1959.
Entered into force June 22, 1959.
10 UST 1156; TIAS 4252

Agreement regarding consolidated procurement of munitions.
Signed at Washington and Capellen April 5 and 12, 1988.
Entered into force April 12, 1988.
TIAS

Agreement regarding the transfer of USG-origin spare parts and components maintained and serviced by NAMSO.
Exchange of notes at Brussels and Capellen November 16, 1992, and March 5, 1993.
Entered into force March 5, 1993.
TIAS

NORWAY

CLAIMS & DISPUTE RESOLUTION

Treaty for the advancement of peace.
Signed at Washington June 24, 1914.
Entered into force October 21, 1914.
38 Stat. 1843; TS 599; 10 Bevans 456

Treaty of arbitration.
Signed at Washington February 20, 1929.
Entered into force June 7, 1929.
46 Stat. 2278; TS 788; 10 Bevans 498; 91 LNTS 413

Memorandum of understanding on conflicting claims to enemy property.
Signed at Washington June 21, 1952.
Entered into force April 27, 1954.
5 UST 907; TIAS 2980; 236 UNTS 9

CONSULAR AFFAIRS

Agreement for the waiver by Norway of visa requirements for United States citizens entering continental Norway and of the visa fee for United States citizens entering Norwegian territory outside continental Norway, and for the waiver by the United States of the visa fee for Norwegian citizens entering the United States and possessions as nonimmigrants.*
Exchange of notes at Washington July 7 and 29, 1947.
Entered into force July 29, 1947; operative August 1, 1947.
61 Stat. 3101; TIAS 1644; 10 Bevans 563; 87 UNTS 343
Amendment:
April 25, 1958

Note:
* The status of this agreement is under review.

Agreement relating to the waiver of visas for American citizens proceeding to Svalbard (Spitzbergen) and the temporary suspension of visa requirements for American citizens proceeding to certain Norwegian possessions.
Exchange of notes at Washington September 10 and October 19, 1948.
Entered into force October 19, 1948.
62 Stat. 3649; TIAS 1884; 10 Bevans 596; 87 UNTS 348

DEFENSE

Treaty relating to exemption from military service or other act of allegiance of persons having dual nationality.
Signed at Oslo November 1, 1930.
Entered into force February 11, 1931.
46 Stat. 2904; TS 832; 10 Bevans 503; 112 LNTS 399

Mutual defense assistance agreement.
Signed at Washington January 27, 1950.
Entered into force February 24, 1950.
1 UST 106; TIAS 2016; 80 UNTS 241

Agreement relating to the disposition of excess equipment and materials furnished by the United States under the mutual defense assistance agreement.
Exchange of notes at Oslo December 12 and 28, 1950.
Entered into force December 28, 1950.
6 UST 6151; TIAS 3467; 240 UNTS 391

Agreement relating to the assurances required under the Mutual Security Act of 1951.
Exchange of notes at Oslo January 8, 1952.
Entered into force January 8, 1952.
3 UST 4639; TIAS 2616; 179 UNTS 185

Agreement relating to the disposition of equipment and materials furnished by the United States under the mutual defense assistance agreement and found surplus to the needs of the armed forces of Norway.
Exchange of notes at Oslo May 15 and June 26, 1953.
Entered into force June 26, 1953.
6 UST 6153; TIAS 3468; 240 UNTS 396
Amendment:
September 1, 1960, and January 14, 1961 (12 UST 214; TIAS 4695; 406 UNTS 312)

Agreement concerning the status of military assistance advisory group under article I, paragraph 1(a), of the NATO status of forces agreement (TIAS 2846).
Exchange of notes at Oslo April 13, 1954.
Entered into force April 13, 1954.
5 UST 619; TIAS 2950; 229 UNTS 223

Agreement relating to a weapons production program.
Exchange of notes at Oslo February 13, 1960.
Entered into force February 13, 1960.
11 UST 2105; TIAS 4569; 388 UNTS 255
Amendment:
April 26 and September 16, 1960 (11 UST 2105; TIAS 4569; 388 UNTS 255)

Agreement relating to a shipbuilding program for the Norwegian Navy.
Exchange of notes at Oslo July 6, 1960.
Entered into force July 6, 1960.
11 UST 1796; TIAS 4522; 378 UNTS 25

Agreement relating to a shipbuilding program of the Norwegian Navy.
Exchange of notes at Oslo November 29, 1960.
Entered into force January 31, 1961.
12 UST 101; TIAS 4681; 404 UNTS 251

Agreement relating to the coproduction of the M109G vehicles.
Signed at Oslo December 30, 1966.
Entered into force December 30, 1966.
TIAS 12360
Amendment:
February 6, 1976 (TIAS 12360)

Agreement relating to the safeguarding of classified information with annex.
Exchange of notes at Oslo February 26, 1970.
Entered into force February 26, 1970.
21 UST 462; TIAS 6836; 240 UNTS 251
Amendment:
September 27, 1984 (TIAS 11136)

Mutual logistical support agreement, with annex.
Signed at Stuttgart-Vaihingen and Oslo January 29 and August 20, 1982.
Entered into force August 20, 1982.
34 UST 1721; TIAS 10449
Amendment:
November 14, 1992, and January 15, 1993 (TIAS 12361)

Memorandum of understanding on the exchange of officers between the United States and Royal Norwegian Air Forces.
Signed at Oslo and Washington November 14, 1983, and January 5, 1984.
Entered into force January 5, 1984.
35 UST 4173; TIAS 10915; 2014 UNTS 529

Memorandum of understanding on the exchange of officers between the United States Marine Corps and the Norwegian Army.
Signed at Oslo and Washington May 21 and July 3, 1986.
Entered into force July 3, 1986.
NP

Memorandum of understanding concerning the provision of United States hospital prepositioned storage to support Allied Forces during operations in the Norwegian Sea and in Norway.
Signed at London and Oslo February 17 and April 10, 1987.
Entered into force April 10, 1987.
TIAS 11662

Memorandum of agreement concerning the exchange of engineers and scientists, with annexes.
Signed at Washington and Oslo September 2 and 24, 1992.
Entered into force September 24, 1992.
NP

Agreement concerning the transfer of U.S. Government-origin defense articles or related training or other defense services to the Government of Norway.
Exchange of notes at Oslo September 18 and October 1, 1992.
Entered into force October 1, 1992.
TIAS 12362

Memorandum of understanding for the dynamic analysis support system project, with annexes.
Signed at Washington and Haakonsvern August 12 and November 14, 1994.
Entered into force November 14, 1994.
TIAS 12364

Agreement for the transfer of ownership of the long-range radio aid to navigation transmitting stations at Bo and Jan Mayen Island, Norway, with annex.
Signed at Oslo December 15, 1994.
Entered into force December 15, 1994.
TIAS

Agreement regarding the exchange of engineers and scientists, with annexes.
Signed at Oslo and Washington January 11 and April 15, 1999.
Entered into force April 15, 1999.
NP
Amendment:
May 27 and June 3, 2009

Memorandum of agreement concerning an arrangement to exchange operational information, with appendix and annex.
Signed at Washington and Oslo August 30 and September 21, 2006.
Entered into force September 21, 2006.
TIAS 06-921
Related Agreement:
July 9 and August 27, 2010

Memorandum of understanding on reciprocal exchange of units.
Signed at Washington and Oslo October 23 and 26, 2006.
Entered into force October 26, 2006.
NP
Amendment:
May 2 and 16, 2016

Memorandum of understanding governing prestockage and reinforcement of Norway.
Signed at Stavanger June 8, 2005.
Entered into force February 27, 2007.
TIAS 07-227.1

Basic exchange and cooperation agreement concerning geospatial information .
Signed at Oslo October 6, 2008.
Entered into force October 6, 2008.
NP
Supplement
October 5, 2010

Acquisition and cross-servicing agreement, with annexes.
Signed at Oslo and Stuttgart July 8 and August 5, 2009.
Entered into force August 5, 2009.
NP

Agreement for research, development, testing, and evaluation projects, with annexes.
Signed at Washington and Oslo July 8 and 18, 2011.
Entered into force July 18, 2011.
TIAS 11-718

Memorandum of agreement regarding the assignment of Royal Norwegian Navy defense personnel to the United States Navy, with annexes.
Signed at Washington and Oslo May 7 and June 27, 2013.
Entered into force June 27, 2013.
NP

Memorandum of understanding concerning test and evaluation program cooperation.
Signed at Washington and Oslo December 22, 2014 and January 19, 2015.
Entered into force January 19, 2015.
TIAS 15-119

Memorandum of agreement regarding the assignment of liaison officers to U.S. European Command, with annexes.
Signed at Oslo and Mons January 19 and 22, 2016.
Entered into force January 22, 2016.
NP

DIPLOMATIC & CONSULAR RELATIONS

Arrangement relating to customs treatment of importations for consular offices and officers.
Exchange of notes at Washington January 20, 1932.
Entered into force January 20, 1932; operative February 1, 1932.
47 Stat. 2698; EAS 32; 10 Bevans 505; 126 LNTS 393

EDUCATION

Agreement relating to the United States Educational Foundation in Norway, and exchange of notes.
Signed at Oslo May 25, 1949.
Entered into force May 25, 1949.
63 Stat. 2764; TIAS 2000; 10 Bevans 598; 32 UNTS 345
Amendments:
August 12 and October 30, 1954 (5 UST 2545; TIAS 3118; 234 UNTS 298)
June 15, 1955 (6 UST 2103; TIAS 3282; 261 UNTS 380)
June 21, 1960 (11 UST 1602; TIAS 4503; 377 UNTS 390)
March 16, 1964 (15 UST 241; TIAS 5545; 524 UNTS 294)

EMPLOYMENT

Agreement relating to the employment of dependents of official government employees.
Exchange of notes at Oslo April 15 and July 21, 1981.
Entered into force July 21, 1981.
35 UST 3810; TIAS 10882; 2015 UNTS 711

ENVIRONMENT & CONSERVATION

Agreement regarding cooperation on environmental protection in defense matters.
Signed at Baltimore May 19, 1994.
Entered into force May 19, 1994.
TIAS 12363

Agreement for cooperation in the Global Learning and Observations to Benefit the Environment (GLOBE) Program.
Signed at Washington April 5, 1995.
Entered into force April 5, 1995.
TIAS 12627

FINANCE

Agreement relating to guaranties authorized by Section 111(b)(3) of the Economic Cooperation Act of 1948, as amended.
Exchange of notes at Washington March 28 and April 1, 1952.
Entered into force April 3, 1952.
3 UST 4246; TIAS 2567; 177 UNTS 291

FOREIGN ASSISTANCE

Economic cooperation agreement.
Signed at Oslo July 3, 1948.
Entered into force July 3, 1948.
62 Stat. 2514; TIAS 1792; 10 Bevans 580; 20 UNTS 185
Amendments:
January 17, 1950 (1 UST 166; TIAS 2032; 79 UNTS 284)
July 5, 1951 (2 UST 1289; TIAS 2276; 148 UNTS 402)
January 8, 1953 (4 UST 109; TIAS 2767; 198 UNTS 366)

Agreement for free entry and free inland transportation of relief supplies and packages.
Exchange of notes at Oslo October 31, 1949.
Entered into force October 31, 1949.
64 Stat. (3) B71; TIAS 2006; 10 Bevans 607; 68 UNTS 3

INTELLECTUAL PROPERTY

Agreement to facilitate interchange of patent rights and technical information for defense purposes, with agreed minutes.
Signed at Oslo April 6, 1955.
Entered into force April 6, 1955.
6 UST 799; TIAS 3226; 269 UNTS 65

Agreement approving procedures for reciprocal filing of classified patent applications in the United States and Norway.
Exchange of notes at Oslo December 5, 1958, and January 6 and 17, 1959.
Entered into force January 17, 1959.
10 UST 302; TIAS 4187; 341 UNTS 410
Amendment:
April 25 and August 12, 1960 (11 UST 2002; TIAS 4552; 388 UNTS 374)

LAW ENFORCEMENT

Convention for prevention of smuggling of intoxicating liquors.
Signed at Washington May 24, 1924.
Entered into force July 2, 1924.
43 Stat. 1772; TS 689; 10 Bevans 473; 26 LNTS 44

Extradition treaty.
Signed at Oslo June 9, 1977.
Entered into force March 7, 1980.
31 UST 5619; TIAS 9679; 1220 UNTS 221

Agreement regarding mutual assistance between customs authorities.
Signed at Oslo May 17, 1989.
Entered into force August 30, 1989.
TIAS 12118

MARITIME MATTERS

Agreement relating to jurisdiction over vessels utilizing the Louisiana Offshore Oil Port.
Exchange of notes at Washington July 11, 1978.
Entered into force July 11, 1978.
30 UST 1671; TIAS 9275; 1153 UNTS 89

Memorandum of agreement to enhance communication and cooperation.
Signed at Oslo December 3, 2005.
Entered into force December 3, 2005.
TIAS

OCCUPATION & PEACEKEEPING

Agreement concerning participation of a Norwegian mobile surgical hospital in the United Nations operations in Korea.
Signed at Washington September 17, 1951.
Entered into force September 17, 1951.
2 UST 1903; TIAS 2325; 140 UNTS 313

POSTAL MATTERS

Parcel post convention.
Signed at Oslo October 6 and at Washington November 9, 1934.
Operative November 1, 1934.
49 Stat. 3042; Post Office Department print; 156 LNTS 33.

International express mail agreement, with detailed regulations.
Signed at Oslo and Washington July 5 and August 10, 1984.
Entered into force October 15, 1984.
TIAS 11007; 2022 UNTS 91.

Memorandum of understanding concerning the operation of the INTELPOST field trial, with details of implementation.
Signed at Oslo and Washington July 9 and 25, 1985.
Entered into force July 25, 1985.
TIAS 11154.

PRIVATE INTERNATIONAL LAW

Agreement for the enforcement of maintenance obligations.
Signed at Washington June 10, 2002.
Entered into force June 10, 2002.
TIAS 02-610

PROPERTY

Preliminary agreement regarding principles applying to mutual aid in the prosecution of the war against aggression, and exchange of notes.
Signed at Washington July 11, 1942.
Entered into force July 11, 1942.
56 Stat. 1565; EAS 262; 10 Bevans 531

Agreement regarding settlement for lend-lease, military relief, and claims, and exchanges of notes.
Signed at Washington February 24, 1948.
Entered into force February 24, 1948.
62 Stat. 1848; TIAS 1716; 10 Bevans 566; 34 UNTS 155

PUBLICATIONS

Agreement for the exchange of official publications.
Exchange of notes at Oslo June 20, 1947, and March 15, 1948.
Entered into force March 15, 1948.
62 Stat. 1954; TIAS 1758; 10 Bevans 577; 73 UNTS 81
Amendment:
August 10 and 11, 1964 (15 UST 1502; TIAS 5630; 530 UNTS 334)

SCIENTIFIC & TECHNICAL COOPERATION

Agreement relating to the installation, operation and management of a seismic array facility in Norway.
Exchange of notes at Oslo June 15, 1968.
Entered into force June 15, 1968.
19 UST 5439; TIAS 6526; 707 UNTS 79

Memorandum of understanding concerning scientific and technical cooperation in the earth sciences, with annexes.
Signed at Reston November 25, 2003.
Entered into force November 25, 2003.
TIAS 03-1125.1

Agreement on science and technology cooperation, with annexes.
Signed at Washington December 9, 2005.
Entered into force March 26, 2006.
TIAS 06-326

Implementing Agreement for cooperation in the use of U.S. land remote sensing satellite data.
Signed at Reston and Oslo March 12 and 22, 2013.
Entered into force March 22, 2013.

SOCIAL SECURITY

Agreement on social security, with administrative agreement.
Signed at Oslo November 30, 2001.
Entered into force September 1, 2003.
TIAS 13177

SPACE

Agreement for cooperation in the civil uses of outer space, with annex
Signed October 20, 2000, and November 14, 2001.
Entered into force November 14, 2001.
TIAS 13172
Extension:
October 23, 2006 (TIAS 13172)

Implementing agreement on cooperation in satellite tracking and environmental data acquisition and utilization.
Signed March 26 and April 2, 2002.
Entered into force April 2, 2002.
TIAS 02-402

Arrangement on the interface region imaging spectrograph (IRIS) mission.
Signed at Washington and Oslo December 14, 2010 and January 10, 2011.
Entered into force January 10, 2011.
TIAS 11-110

Implementing arrangement on the use of analogue sites within the United States and Norway .
Signed at Washington and Oslo May 3 and 10, 2011.
Entered into force May 10, 2011.
TIAS 11-510

TAXATION

Convention for the avoidance of double taxation and the prevention of fiscal evasion with respect to taxes on estates and inheritances.
Signed at Washington June 13, 1949.
Entered into force December 11, 1951.
2 UST 2353; TIAS 2358; 127 UNTS 163

Agreement relating to relief from taxation of United States Government expenditures in Norway for common defense.
Exchange of notes at Oslo June 27, 1952.
Entered into force June 27, 1952.
3 UST 5253; TIAS 2720; 184 UNTS 271

Convention for the avoidance of double taxation and the prevention of fiscal evasion with respect to taxes on income and property with related notes.
Signed at Oslo December 3, 1971.
Entered into force November 29, 1972.
23 UST 2832; TIAS 7474

Protocol amending the convention of December 3, 1971 (TIAS 7474) for the avoidance of double taxation and the prevention of fiscal evasion with respect to taxes on income and property.
Signed at Oslo September 19, 1980.
Entered into force December 15, 1981.
33 UST 2828; TIAS 10205
Note:
* With understanding.

Agreement concerning the reciprocal exemption from income tax of income derived from the international operation of ships and aircraft.
Exchange of notes at Washington May 24, 1990.
Entered into force May 24, 1990.
TIAS 11715; 2207 UNTS 205

Agreement to improve international tax compliance and implement the Foreign Account Tax Compliance Act, with annexes.
Signed at Oslo April 15, 2013.
Entered into force January 27, 2014.
TIAS 14-127

TELECOMMUNICATION

Agreement relating to the reciprocal granting of authorizations to permit licensed amateur radio operators of either country to operate their stations in the other country.
Exchange of notes at Oslo May 27 and June 1, 1967.
Entered into force June 1, 1967.
18 UST 1241; TIAS 6273; 631 UNTS 119

TRADE & INVESTMENT

Treaty of commerce and navigation, with separate article.*
Signed at Stockholm July 4, 1827.
Entered into force January 18, 1828.
8 Stat. 346; TS 348; 11 Bevans 876

Note:

* Articles 13 and 14 were abrogated effective July 1, 1916; the entire treaty, with the exception of that part of article 1 concerning entry and residence of nationals of one country in territories of the other for purposes of trade, was terminated September 13, 1932, by the treaty of friendship, commerce, and consular rights signed June 5, 1928, and the additional article thereto signed February 25, 1929 (TS 852).

Treaty of friendship, commerce, and consular right with exchange of notes and additional article signed February 25, 1929.
Signed at Washington June 5, 1928.
Entered into force September 13, 1932.
47 Stat. 2135; TS 852; 10 Bevans 481; 134 LNTS 81

TRANSPORTATION

Arrangement relating to pilot licenses to operate civil aircraft.
Exchange of notes at Washington October 16, 1933.
Entered into force November 15, 1933.
48 Stat. 1818; EAS 51; 10 Bevans 514; 145 LNTS 31

Agreement relating to air transport services.
Exchange of notes at Washington October 6, 1945.
Entered into force October 6, 1945; operative October 15, 1945.
59 Stat. 1658; EAS 482; 10 Bevans 553; 122 UNTS 319

Amendments:

August 6, 1954 (5 UST 1433; TIAS 3015; 222 UNTS 269)
June 16, 1995 (TIAS 12664)

Agreement relating to air service facilities at Gardermoen Airfield.
Signed at Oslo November 12, 1946.
Entered into force November 12, 1946.
61 Stat. 3861; TIAS 1737; 10 Bevans 560; 42 UNTS 227

Agreement relating to certificates of airworthiness for imported aircraft.
Exchange of notes at Oslo February 5, 1957.
Entered into force February 5, 1957.
8 UST 265; TIAS 3769; 279 UNTS 169

Amendment:

January 24, 1978 (29 UST 5660; TIAS 9141)

Agreement for promotion of aviation safety.
Signed at Oslo June 27, 2001.
Entered into force June 27, 2001.
TIAS 13159

O

OMAN

CULTURAL EXCHANGES, PROPERTY & COOPERATION

Agreement relating to the establishment of a Peace Corps program in Oman.
Exchange of notes at Muscat November 15 and 28, 1972.
Entered into force November 28, 1972.
24 UST 1013; TIAS 7614
Amendment:
May 4 and August 25, 1977 (29 UST 5358; TIAS 9116; 1148 UNTS 366)

DEFENSE

Agreement concerning the provision of training related to defense articles under the United States International Military Education and Training (IMET) Program.
Exchange of notes at Muscat January 4 and April 28, 1986.
Entered into force April 28, 1986.
TIAS 11981

Agreement regarding grants under the Foreign Assistance Act of 1961, as amended, and the furnishing of defense articles, related training and other defense services from the United States to Oman.
Exchange of notes at Muscat May 5 and June 1, 1992.
Entered into force June 1, 1992.
TIAS

Agreement concerning the provision of petroleum products and related services, with annexes.
Signed at Muscat and Ft. Belvoir August 18 and September 19, 2008.
Entered into force September 19, 2008.
TIAS 08-919
Amendments:
July 20 and August 12, 2012 (TIAS 12-812)
January 9 and February 11, 2014 (TIAS 12-812)
August 10 and September 15, 2015 (TIAS 15-915.2)
March 11 and 28, 2016 (TIAS 16-328)
October 25 and November 8, 2016 (TIAS 16-1108)

Memorandum of understanding regarding cooperation in acquisition and cross-servicing, with annexes.
Signed February 6 and 20, 2014.
Entered into force February 20, 2014.
NP

Basic exchange and cooperation agreement concerning geospatial intelligence.
Signed at Springfield June 12, 2014.
Entered into force June 12, 2014.
NP

ENVIRONMENT & CONSERVATION

Memorandum of understanding for cooperation in the Global Learning and Observations to Benefit the Environment (GLOBE) program.
Signed at Muscat December 8, 2009.
Entered into force December 8, 2009.
TIAS 09-1208

FINANCE

Agreement relating to investment guaranties.
Exchange of notes at Muscat September 9, 1976.
Entered into force September 9, 1976.
28 UST 5670; TIAS 8651; 1087 UNTS 11

FOREIGN ASSISTANCE

Agreement to establish a joint commission on economic and technical cooperation.
Signed at Muscat August 19, 1980.
Entered into force August 19, 1980.
33 UST 2428; TIAS 10189; 1529 UNTS 13
Amendment and Extension:
December 1, 1990

Agreement on economic and technical cooperation.
Signed at Muscat December 1, 1990.
Entered into force December 1, 1990.
TIAS

INTERNATIONAL CRIMINAL COURT

Agreement regarding the surrender of persons to the International Criminal Court, with understanding.
Exchange of letters at Muscat July 26 and August 1, 2004.
Entered into force August 1, 2004.
TIAS

POSTAL MATTERS

International express mail agreement.
Signed at Muscat and Washington February 12 and March 27, 1986.
Entered into force May 1, 1986.
NP

SCIENTIFIC & TECHNICAL COOPERATION

Agreement on science and technology cooperation, with annexes.
Signed at Davos January 22, 2016.
Entered into force March 31, 2016.
TIAS 16-331

TRADE & INVESTMENT

Treaty of amity, economic relations and consular rights and protocol.
Signed at Salalah December 20, 1958.
Entered into force June 11, 1960.
11 UST 1835; TIAS 4530; 380 UNTS 181

Free trade agreement, with annexes.
Signed at Washington January 19, 2006.
Entered into force January 1, 2009.
TIAS

TRANSPORTATION

Agreement on aviation security.
Exchange of notes at Muscat June 28 and 30, 1994.
Entered into force June 30, 1994.
TIAS 12554

Air transport agreement, with annexes.
Signed at Muscat December 19, 2013.
Entered into force January 16, 2015.
TIAS 15-116

ORGANIZATION FOR ECONOMIC COOPERATION AND DEVELOPMENT (OECD)

ATOMIC ENERGY

Arrangement for cooperation in the field of nuclear data and computer programs.
Signed at Washington April 10, 2006.
Entered into force April 10, 2006.
TIAS 06-410

TAXATION

Tax reimbursement agreement, with annex.
Signed at Paris October 15, 1987.
Entered into force October 15, 1987.
TIAS

ORGANIZATION FOR THE PROHIBITION OF CHEMICAL WEAPONS

TAXATION

Tax reimbursement agreement, with annex.
Signed at The Hague February 25, 1999.
Entered into force February 25, 1999.
TIAS 13022

ORGANIZATION OF AMERICAN STATES

FOREIGN ASSISTANCE

Understanding relating to the establishment and operation of training centers and other services under the program of technical cooperation of the Organization of American States.
Exchange of notes at Washington February 12 and March 3, 1952.
Entered into force March 3, 1952.
3 UST 2995; TIAS 2485; 165 UNTS 67

DIPLOMATIC & CONSULAR RELATIONS

Agreement relating to privileges and immunities.
Signed at Washington March 20, 1975.
Entered into force March 20, 1975.
26 UST 1025; TIAS 8089

REGIONAL ISSUES

Headquarters agreement, with annexes.
Signed at Washington May 14, 1992.
Entered into force November 17, 1994.
TIAS
Amendments:
May 24 and 29, 1996
September 27, 2000, and March 19, 2001

TAXATION

Agreement relating to a procedure for United States income tax reimbursement, with addenda.
Signed at Washington January 10, 1984.
Entered into force January 10, 1984; effective January 1, 1984.
35 UST 4224; TIAS 10919; 2015 UNTS 101

P

PAKISTAN

The Schedule to the Independence (International Arrangements) Order, 1947, provides that rights and obligations under all international agreements to which India is a party immediately before the appointed day [August 15, 1947] devolve upon India and Pakistan and will, if necessary, be apportioned between them; except that (1) Pakistan will take such steps as may be necessary to apply for membership of such international organizations as it chooses to join, and (2) rights and obligations under international agreements having an exclusive application to an area comprised in the Dominion of Pakistan will devolve upon it.

CONSULAR AFFAIRS

Agreement relating to the reciprocal reduction of visa fees.*
Exchange of notes at Karachi October 10 and 18, 1949.
Entered into force October 18, 1949; operative November 15, 1949.
3 UST 365; TIAS 2398; 141 UNTS 333

Amendments:
August 16, October 11, November 19, and December 16 and 29, 1952, and March 19 and April 8, 1953 (4 UST 11; TIAS 2761; 204 UNTS 378)
August 4, October 20, and November 25 and 29, 1955 (6 UST 6107; TIAS 3463; 240 UNTS 438)

Note:
* The status of this agreement is under review.

Agreement relating to the reciprocal issuance of nonimmigrant visas, and related notes of July 28, 1959, September 6 and 29, 1961.
Exchange of notes at Karachi March 16 and June 27, 1959.
Entered into force June 27, 1959; operative August 1, 1959.
12 UST 1685; TIAS 4886; 360 UNTS 327

CULTURAL EXCHANGES, PROPERTY & COOPERATION

Agreement relating to the establishment of a Peace Corps program in Pakistan.
Exchange of notes at Karachi May 31, 1962.
Entered into force May 31, 1962; operative from October 28, 1961.
13 UST 1563; TIAS 5113; 460 UNTS 75

DEFENSE

Agreement relating to transfer of military supplies and equipment to Pakistan.
Exchange of notes at Washington November 29 and December 15, 1950.
Entered into force December 15, 1950.
1 UST 884; TIAS 2165; 122 UNTS 89

Mutual defense assistance agreement.
Signed at Karachi May 19, 1954.
Entered into force May 19, 1954.
5 UST 852; TIAS 2976; 202 UNTS 301

Defense support assistance agreement.
Signed at Karachi January 11, 1955.
Entered into force January 11, 1955.
6 UST 501; TIAS 3183; 251 UNTS 111

Amendment:
March 11, 1961 (12 UST 226; TIAS 4698; 406 UNTS 318)

Agreement providing for the disposition of equipment and materials furnished to Pakistan under the mutual defense assistance agreement of May 19, 1954.
Signed at Karachi March 15 and May 15, 1956.
Entered into force May 15, 1956.
7 UST 2389; TIAS 3627; 280 UNTS 368

Construction agreement pursuant to article I, paragraph 1, of the mutual defense assistance agreement of May 19, 1954.
Signed at Karachi May 28, 1956.
Entered into force May 28, 1956.
7 UST 923; TIAS 3575

Agreement concerning financial arrangements for the furnishing of certain supplies and services to naval vessels.
Signed at Karachi September 10, 1956.
Entered into force December 9, 1956.
7 UST 2493; TIAS 3637; 277 UNTS 259

Agreement of cooperation.
Signed at Ankara March 5, 1959.
Entered into force March 5, 1959.
10 UST 317; TIAS 4190; 327 UNTS 285

Agreement concerning general security of military information.
Exchange of notes at Islamabad April 6, June 21 and 24, 1982.
Entered into force June 24, 1982.
34 UST 1765; TIAS 10455; 1750 UNTS 443

Agreement concerning the provision of training related to defense articles under the United States International Military Education and Training (IMET) Program.
Exchange of notes at Islamabad December 10, 1985, and July 30, 1986.
Entered into force July 30, 1986.
NP

Memorandum of understanding on coassembly and coproduction of AN/UAS 12A night sight equipment, with appendix.
Signed at Rawalpindi January 27, 1990.
Entered into force January 27, 1990.
TIAS 12365

Agreement regarding grants under the Foreign Assistance Act of 1961, as amended, and the furnishing of defense articles, related training and other defense services from the United States to Pakistan.
Exchange of notes at Islamabad June 27, 2003.
Entered into force June 27, 2003.
TIAS 03-627.1

DIPLOMATIC & CONSULAR RELATIONS

Arrangement relating to reciprocal concessions and privileges accorded to diplomatic and consular officers.
Exchange of notes at Washington October 27, 1948, and February 4, 1949.
Entered into force February 4, 1949.
10 Bevans 646

EDUCATION

Agreement for financing certain educational exchange programs.
Signed at Islamabad October 18, 1972.
Entered into force October 18, 1972.
TIAS 7483; 23 UST 3115; 938 UNTS 11

EMPLOYMENT

Agreement relating to the employment of dependents of official government employees.
Exchange of notes at Washington January 21 and February 13, 2004.
Entered into force February 13, 2004.
TIAS 04-213

ENVIRONMENT & CONSERVATION

Agreement for co-operation in the Global Learning and Observations to Benefit the Environment (GLOBE) Program, with appendices.
Signed at Islamabad November 18, 1997.
Entered into force November 18, 1997.
TIAS 12902

FINANCE

Agreements regarding the consolidation and rescheduling of certain debts owed to the United States Government and its agencies with annexes and related letter.
Signed at Washington September 20, 1972.
Entered into force September 20, 1972.
23 UST 2601; TIAS 7449

Agreement regarding the consolidation and rescheduling of certain debts owed to the United States Government, with annexes.
Signed at Washington March 4, 1976.
Entered into force May 12, 1976.
27 UST 4231; TIAS 8447
Amendment:
April 13 and June 5, 1979 (30 UST 5985; TIAS 9532; 1177 UNTS 391)

Agreement regarding the consolidation and rescheduling of certain debts owed to the United States Government and the Agency for International Development, with annexes.
Signed at Islamabad May 10, 1981.
Entered into force July 13, 1981.
33 UST 3628; TIAS 10246; 1541 UNTS 3

Implementing agreement regarding the consolidation and rescheduling of certain debts owed to the Agency for International Development.
Signed at Islamabad August 18, 1981.
Entered into force September 7, 1981.
33 UST 3628; TIAS 10246; 1541 UNTS 21

Agreement regarding the consolidation and rescheduling of payments due under P.L. 480 Title I agricultural commodity agreements, with annexes.
Signed at Islamabad September 27, 1981.
Entered into force September 27, 1981.
33 UST 3628; TIAS 10246

Investment incentive agreement.
Signed at Islamabad November 18, 1997.
Entered into force January 28, 1998.
TIAS 12903

Agreement regarding the consolidation and rescheduling of certain debts owed to, guaranteed by, or insured by the United States Government and its agencies, with annexes.
Signed at Islamabad November 26, 1999.
Entered into force February 23, 2000.
NP

Agreement regarding the consolidation and rescheduling of certain debts owed to, guaranteed by, or insured by the United States Government and its agencies, with annexes.
Signed at Islamabad September 24, 2001.
Entered into force October 26, 2001.
NP

Agreement regarding the consolidation of debt owed to, guaranteed by, or insured by the United States Government and its agencies, with annexes.
Signed at Islamabad August 23, 2002.
Entered into force October 21, 2002.
NP

Agreement regarding the reduction of certain debts owed to, guaranteed or insured by the United States Government, with annexes.
Signed at Islamabad April 5, 2003.
Entered into force June 5, 2003.
NP

Agreement regarding the reduction of certain debts owed to, guaranteed or insured by the United States Government.
Signed at Islamabad July 16, 2004.
Entered into force September 2, 2004.
NP

FOREIGN ASSISTANCE

Agreement for technical cooperation.
Signed at Karachi February 9, 1951.
Entered into force February 9, 1951.
2 UST 1008; TIAS 2254; 100 UNTS 67
Amendment:
January 8, 1952 (3 UST 2616; TIAS 2427; 157 UNTS 370)

Supplementary agreement for technical cooperation.
Signed at Karachi February 2, 1952.
Entered into force February 2, 1952.
3 UST 3767; TIAS 2506; 131 UNTS 346
Amendments:
March 27, 1953 (4 UST 1478; TIAS 2811; 172 UNTS 350)
December 28, 1953 (4 UST 2805; TIAS 2889; 222 UNTS 410)
June 24, 1954 (5 UST 1361; TIAS 3004; 233 UNTS 302)
January 18, 1955 (6 UST 511; TIAS 3185; 239 UNTS 358)

Agreement relating to an informational media guaranty program pursuant to Section 111 (b)(3) of the Economic Cooperation Act of 1948, as amended.
Exchange of notes at Karachi February 12 and May 1, 1954.
Entered into force May 1, 1954.
5 UST 2272; TIAS 3088; 237 UNTS 231
Amendments:
January 1 and 8, 1957 (8 UST 1757; TIAS 3928; 299 UNTS 420)
August 10, 1962, and April 15, 1963 (15 UST 167; TIAS 5535; 510 UNTS 318)

Agreement relating to emergency flood assistance for East Pakistan.
Exchange of notes at Washington August 23, 1954.
Entered into force August 23, 1954.
5 UST 1779; TIAS 3052; 234 UNTS 243
Amendment:
November 29 and December 16, 1954 (5 UST 2182; TIAS 3082; 234 UNTS 250)

Agreement relating to duty-free entry and defrayment of inland transportation charges on relief supplies and packages for Pakistan.
Exchange of notes at Karachi June 18, 1953, and October 2, 1954.
Entered into force October 2, 1954.
5 UST 1983; TIAS 3065; 236 UNTS 187

Joint commission on economic, commercial, scientific, technological, educational, and cultural cooperation.
Signed at Washington December 6, 1982.
Entered into force December 6, 1982.
TIAS 10623; 2000 UNTS 457

AGENCY FOR INTERNATIONAL DEVELOPMENT

Strategic objective grant agreement for education sector reform support program, with annex.
Signed August 9, 2002.
Entered into force August 9, 2002.
NP
Amendments and extensions:
May 26, 2005 (NP)
September 24, 2007 (NP)
September 22, 2008 (NP)

Strategic objective grant agreement for economic growth.
Signed August 5, 2003.
Entered into force August 5, 2003.
NP
Amendments and extensions:
September 24, 2007 (NP)
August 19, 2008 (NP)
September 22, 2008 (NP)

Strategic objective grant agreement of for health and population welfare, with annex.
Signed August 18, 2003.
Entered into force August 18, 2003.
NP
Amendments and extensions:
May 26, 2005 (NP)
August 8, 2006 (NP)
September 24, 2007 (NP)
August 19, 2008 (NP)
September 22, 2008 (NP)

Strategic objective grant agreement for governance, with annex.
Signed August 21, 2003.
Entered into force August 21, 2003.
NP
Amendments and Extensions:
September 24, 2007 (NP)
September 22, 2008 (NP)

Program assistance grant agreement, with appendix and attachment.
Signed at Islamabad June 10, 2005.
Entered into force June 10, 2005.
NP

Special objective grant agreement for earthquake reconstruction, with annexes.
Signed at Islamabad January 21, 2006.
Entered into force January 21, 2006.
NP
Amendments and extensions:
July 1, 2006 (NP)
September 24, 2007 (NP)
September 22, 2008 (NP)

Program assistance grant agreement, with annexes.
Signed at Islamabad June 15, 2006.
Entered into force June 15, 2006.
NP

Program assistance grant agreement, with appendices and attachment.
Signed at Islamabad June 15, 2007.
Entered into force June 15, 2007.
NP

Agreement for the federally administrated tribal areas development program, with attachment.
Signed September 30, 2007.
Entered into force September 30, 2007.
NP
Amendments:
September 22, 2008 (NP)
May 25, 2009 (NP)

Pakistan enhanced partnership agreement.
Signed September 30, 2010.
Entered into force September 30, 2010.
NP

Amendments:
June 27, 2012 (NP)
July 19, 2012 (NP)
September 20 and 25, 2012 (NP)
September 4 and 5, 2013 (NP)
September 20 and 24, 2013 (NP)

Activity agreement for the Peshawar-Torkham road, with attachments.
Signed September 18, 2012.
Entered into force September 18, 2012.
NP

INTELLECTUAL PROPERTY

Declaration by the United States and the United Kingdom affording reciprocal protection to trademarks.
Signed at London October 24, 1877.
Entered into force October 24, 1877.
20 Stat. 703; TS 138; I Malloy 737

INTERNATIONAL CRIMINAL COURT

Agreement regarding the surrender of persons to international tribunals.
Signed at Washington July 21, 2003.
Entered into force November 6, 2003.
TIAS 03-1106

LAW ENFORCEMENT

Extradition treaty between the United States and the United Kingdom, signed at London December 22, 1931, made applicable to India, in accordance with the provisions of article 14, from March 9, 1942.
47 Stat. 2122; TS 849; 12 Bevans 482; 163 LNTS 59

Agreement on procedures for mutual assistance in connection with matters relating to the Lockheed Aircraft Corporation and the Boeing Company.
Signed at Washington September 9, 1977.
Entered into force September 9, 1977.
28 UST 7488; TIAS 8724

Related Agreement:
January 6 and 10, 1978 (29 UST 492; TIAS 8827; 1115 UNTS 177)

Agreement regarding mutual assistance between their customs administrations.
Signed at Port Qasim April 30, 2007.
Entered into force April 30, 2007.
TIAS 07-430

MIGRATION & REFUGEES

Agreement for assistance in the transport of relief commodities to Afghan refugee camps in Pakistan.
Signed at Islamabad September 30, 1981.
Entered into force September 30, 1981.
33 UST 3932; TIAS 10272

POSTAL MATTERS

Agreement for the exchange of parcels by parcel post, and detailed regulations of execution.
Signed at Karachi July 20 and at Washington October 7, 1955.
Entered into force January 1, 1956.
7 UST 1; TIAS 3475; 241 UNTS 255

International express mail agreement, with detailed regulations.
Signed at Islamabad and Washington March 11 and 30, 1987.
Entered into force May 1, 1987.
TIAS 11315

INTELPOST memorandum of understanding, with detailed regulations.
Signed at Islamabad and Washington February 23 and March 11, 1993.
Entered into force March 15, 1993.
TIAS 11917

PROPERTY

Convention relating to tenure and disposition of real and personal property.
Signed at Washington March 2, 1899.
TS 146; 31 Stat. 1939; 12 Bevans 246

Note:
Signed between the United States and the United Kingdom, applicable to Pakistan.

Supplementary convention extending the time within which notifications may be given of the accession of British colonies or foreign possessions to the convention of March 2, 1899.
Signed at Washington January 13, 1902.
TS 402; 32 Stat. 1914; 12 Bevans 261

Note:
Signed between the United States and the United Kingdom, applicable to Pakistan.

Agreement on settlement for lend-lease, reciprocal aid, surplus war property, and claims.
Signed at Washington May 16, 1946.
Entered into force May 16, 1946.
60 Stat. 1753; TIAS 1532

Note:
In a note of June 12, 1948, to the American Ambassador at Karachi, the
Minister of Foreign Affairs gave assurance that: "the terms of the United
States Settlement Agreement with India of May 16, 1946 [60 Stat. 1753;
TIAS 1532], would continue to devolve on the Government of Pakistan to
the extent to which they are applicable and have to be fulfilled in Pakistan."

PUBLICATIONS

Agreement for the exchange of official publications.
Exchange of notes at Karachi April 25 and May 23, 1951.
Entered into force May 23, 1951.
2 UST 1701; TIAS 2311; 134 UNTS 265
Amendment:
April 22 and December 29, 1953 (5 UST 2850; TIAS 3141; 237 UNTS 312)

SCIENTIFIC & TECHNICAL COOPERATION

Agreement on science and technology cooperation, with annexes.
Signed at Washington June 25, 2003.
Entered into force October 16, 2003.
TIAS 03-1016.1
Extension:
August 21 and September 8, 2008 (TIAS 03-1016.1)

Protocol extending the agreement on science and technology cooperation.
Signed at Washington October 23, 2013.
Entered into force October 23, 2013.
TIAS 03-1016.1

TAXATION

Convention for the avoidance of double taxation and the prevention of fiscal evasion with respect to taxes on income.
Signed at Washington July 1, 1957.
Entered into force May 21, 1959.
10 UST 984; TIAS 4232; 344 UNTS 203

Agreement for the reciprocal exemption with respect to taxes on income from the international operation of ships.
Exchange of notes at Islamabad July 26 and 27, 1989.
Entered into force July 27, 1989.
TIAS 11679; 2190 UNTS 411

TRADE & INVESTMENT

Convention to regulate commerce (article IV) between the United States and the United Kingdom.
Signed at London July 3, 1815.
Effective July 3, 1815.
8 Stat. 228; TS 110; 12 Bevans 49

Treaty of friendship and commerce, and protocol.
Signed at Washington November 12, 1959.
Entered into force February 12, 1961.
12 UST 110; TIAS 4683; 404 UNTS 259

Memorandum of understanding relating to concessions and contributions to be made to the multilateral trade negotiations, with related letters, and related letter of January 28, 1980.
Done at Geneva April 2 and 11, and August 2 and 30, 1979.
Entered into force August 30, 1979.
32 UST 5471; TIAS 9999; 1265 UNTS 213

TRANSPORTATION

Air transport agreement, with annexes.
Signed at Rawalpindi April 10, 1997.
Entered into force April 10, 1997.
TIAS 12851
Amendments:
April 12 and 29, 1999. (TIAS 12851)
February 23 and March 19, 2007 (TIAS 07-319)

PALAU

CULTURAL EXCHANGES, PROPERTY & COOPERATION

Agreement concerning the program of the Peace Corps in Palau.
Signed at Koror March 8, 1995.
Entered into force March 8, 1995.
TIAS 12610

DIPLOMATIC & CONSULAR RELATIONS

Agreement concerning relations under the Vienna convention on diplomatic relations.
Signed at Washington December 14, 1994.
Entered into force March 2, 1995.
TIAS 12587

ENVIRONMENT & CONSERVATION

Agreement concerning cooperation in the Global Learning and Observations to Benefit the Environment (GLOBE) Program, with appendices.
Signed at Koror January 30, 1997.
Entered into force January 30, 1997.
TIAS 12828

FINANCE

Investment incentive agreement.
Signed at Washington March 15, 2002.
Entered into force March 15, 2002.
TIAS 02-315

INTERNATIONAL CRIMINAL COURT

Agreement regarding the surrender of persons to the International Criminal Court.
Signed at Koror September 13, 2002.
Entered into force July 7, 2003.
TIAS 03-707.1

LAW ENFORCEMENT

Agreement on extradition, mutual assistance in law enforcement matters and panel sanctions concluded pursuant to Section 175 of the Compact of Free Association.
Signed at Palau January 10, 1986.
Entered into force October 1, 1994.
TIAS

MARITIME MATTERS

Agreement concerning operational cooperation to suppress illicit transnational maritime activity.
Signed at Koror August 15, 2013.
Entered into force August 15, 2013.
TIAS 13-815

REGIONAL ISSUES

Agreement for the implementation of the Compact of Free Association between the Government of the United States and the Government of Palau.
Signed January 10, 1986.
Entered into force October 1, 1994.

TRANSPORTATION

Memorandum of agreement concerning assistance in developing and modernizing Palau's civil aviation infrastructure.
Signed at Washington and Koror December 11, 1995, and January 17 and February 8, 1996.
Entered into force February 8, 1996.
TIAS 12722

PALESTINE AUTHORITY

FOREIGN ASSISTANCE

AGENCY FOR INTERNATIONAL DEVELOPMENT

Cash transfer grant agreement.
Signed March 19, 2008.
Entered into force March 19, 2008.
NP

Cash transfer grant agreement.
Signed October 10, 2008.
Entered into force October 10, 2008.
NP

Cash transfer grant agreement.
Signed July 15, 2009.
Entered into force July 15, 2009.
NP

Cash transfer grant agreement.
Signed December 8, 2009.
Entered into force December 8, 2009.
NP

Cash transfer grant agreement.
Signed April 24, 2010.
Entered into force April 24, 2010.
NP

Cash transfer grant agreement.
Signed October 25, 2010.
Entered into force October 25, 2010.
NP

Cash transfer grant agreement.
Signed September 9, 2011.
Entered into force September 9, 2011.
NP

Cash transfer grant agreement.
Signed August 13, 2013.
Entered into force August 13, 2013.
NP

PALESTINE LIBERATION ORGANIZATION

FINANCE

Agreement on encouragement of investment.
Signed at Gaza and Washington August 11 and September 12, 1994.
Entered into force September 12, 1994.
TIAS 12564

PANAMA

AGRICULTURE

Agreement confirming the cooperative agreement for the prevention of foot-and-mouth disease and rinderpest in Panama.
Exchange of notes at Panama June 21 and October 5, 1972.
Entered into force October 5, 1972.
23 UST 3108; TIAS 7482
Amendment:
May 28 and June 12, 1974 (25 UST 1522; TIAS 7888)

Agreement on cooperation in agricultural products.
Signed at Washington and Panama City December 20, 2006.
Entered into force December 20, 2006.
TIAS

CANALS

Agreement for enlargement and use by Canal Zone of sewerage facilities in Colon Free Zone Area.
Exchange of notes at Panama March 8 and 25, 1954.
Entered into force March 25, 1954.
5 UST 782; TIAS 2966; 232 UNTS 289

Treaty concerning the permanent neutrality and operation of the Panama Canal, with annexes and protocol.
Signed at Washington September 7, 1977.
Entered into force October 1, 1979, subject to amendments, conditions, reservations, and understandings.
33 UST 1; TIAS 10029; 1161 UNTS 177
Depositary for the Protocol :Organization of American States

Agreement relating to the status of the Cardenas (FAA housing) area under the agreement in implementation of Article III of the Panama Canal Treaty.
Signed at Panama August 29, 1980.
Entered into force August 29, 1980.
33 UST 570; TIAS 10048; 1280 UNTS 415

Agreement concerning disposition of the Mount Hope warehouse and transportation areas.
Exchange of notes at Panama February 12 and May 7, 1982.
Entered into force May 7, 1982.
34 UST 1972; TIAS 10474; 1750 UNTS 287

Agreement concerning transfer of the Ancon District Court (Building 310) from the United States to Panama.
Exchange of notes at Panama July 13, 1982.
Entered into force July 13, 1982.
TIAS 10544; 1777 UNTS 333

Agreement concerning transfer of Mindi and Coco Solo housing units from the United States to Panama.
Exchange of notes at Panama August 9 and 11, 1982.
Entered into force August 11, 1982.
TIAS

Agreement concerning creation of a preparatory committee to study alternatives to the Panama Canal.
Exchange of notes at Washington September 30, 1982.
Entered into force September 30, 1982.
TIAS

Agreement regarding housing civilian and military personnel of U.S. Forces stationed in Panama.
Exchange of notes November 29, 1984.
Effective October 1, 1984.
TIAS

Agreement concerning establishment of the commission for the study of alternatives to the Panama Canal, with annex and related notes.
Exchange of notes at New York September 26, 1985.
*Entered into force September 26, 1985.**
TIAS 11935

Extension:
September 25, 1990

Note:
* See also exchanges of notes of the same date concerning Japanese participation.

CONSULAR AFFAIRS

Reciprocal agreement for gratis nonimmigrant visas.*
Exchange of notes at Panama March 27 and May 22 and 25, 1956.
Entered into force June 1, 1956.
7 UST 905; TIAS 3573; 268 UNTS 333

Agreement modifying the agreement of March 27 and May 22 and 25, 1956, for gratis nonimmigrant visas.*
Exchange of notes at Panama June 14 and 17, 1971.
Entered into force June 17, 1971.
22 UST 815; TIAS 7142; 796 UNTS 353

Note:
* The status of these agreements is under review.

CULTURAL EXCHANGES, PROPERTY & COOPERATION

Agreement authorizing the United States to construct a custodian's house in the Corozal Cemetery.
Exchange of notes at Panama September 29 and 30, 1982.
Entered into force September 29, 1982.
TIAS 10518; 1777 UNTS 343

Agreement concerning the use of Corozal Cemetery.
Signed at Panama City June 11, 1999.
Entered into force June 27, 2000.
TIAS 13043

Agreement relating to the establishment of a Peace Corps program in Panama.
Exchange of notes at Washington May 1, 1990.
Entered into force November 23, 1990.
TIAS

DEFENSE

Agreement relating to the detail of a military officer to serve as adviser to the Minister of Foreign Affairs of Panama.
Signed at Washington July 7, 1942.
Entered into force July 7, 1942.
56 Stat. 1545; EAS 258; 10 Bevans 817; 9 UNTS 289

Extension and amendments:
February 17, March 23, September 22, and November 6, 1959 (12 UST 718; TIAS 4773; 409 UNTS 307)
March 26 and July 6, 1962 (13 UST 2598; TIAS 5226; 460 UNTS 360)
September 20 and October 8, 1962 (13 UST 2600; TIAS 5226; 460 UNTS 362)

Agreement relating to the sale of military equipment, materials, and services to Panama.
Exchange of notes at Panama May 20, 1959.
Entered into force May 20, 1959; operative from April 27, 1959.
10 UST 1000; TIAS 4234; 346 UNTS 235

Agreement relating to the furnishing of defense articles and services to Panama for the purpose of contributing to its internal security.
Exchange of notes at Panama March 26 and May 23, 1962.
Entered into force May 23, 1962.
13 UST 1294; TIAS 5081; 458 UNTS 225

Agreement relating to the deposit by Panama of ten percent of the value of grant military assistance and excess defense articles furnished by the United States.
Exchange of notes at Panama April 4 and May 9, 1972.
Entered into force May 9, 1972; effective February 7, 1972.
23 UST 897; TIAS 7353

Agreement concerning payment to the United States of net proceeds from the sale of defense articles furnished under the military assistance program.
Exchange of notes at Panama May 20 and December 6, 1974.
Entered into force December 6, 1974; effective July 1, 1974.
25 UST 3135; TIAS 7977; 991 UNTS 317

Agreement concerning general security of military information.
Signed at Panama August 17, 1984.
Entered into force August 17, 1984.
TIAS 11196; 2129 UNTS 265

Cooperative arrangement for the production of topographic maps of Panama, with annexes.
Signed at Washington and Panama January 29, 1986.
Entered into force January 29, 1986.
TIAS 11212

Agreement regarding the status of United States personnel who may be temporarily present in Panama.
Exchange of notes at Panama July 3 and 10, 2001.
Entered into force July 10, 2001.
TIAS 13160

Agreement regarding grants under the Foreign Assistance Act of 1961, as amended, or successor legislation, and the furnishing of defense articles, defense services and related training, including pursuant to the United States International Military and Education Training (IMET) Program.
Exchange of notes at Panama July 24 and August 23, 2007.
Entered into force August 23, 2007.
NP

DIPLOMATIC & CONSULAR RELATIONS

Agreement relating to customs privileges for consular officers.
Exchange of notes at Panama January 7 and 31, 1935.
Entered into force January 31, 1935.
5 UST 1520; TIAS 3028; 234 UNTS 277

Joint declaration re-establishing diplomatic relations, with friendly declaration of the Presidents of both countries annexed there to.
Signed at Washington April 3, 1964.
Entered into force April 3, 1964.
Department Bulletin April 27, 1964, p. 655.

EDUCATION

Memorandum of understanding on the Fulbright Exchange Program.
Signed at Panama City December 10, 2008.
Entered into force December 10, 2008.
TIAS 08-1210

EMPLOYMENT

Agreements relating to the employment of dependents of official government employees.
Exchange of notes at Panama November 26, 1993.
Entered into force November 26, 1993.
TIAS 12517

ENERGY

Agreement relating to electric power.
Exchange of notes at Panama October 1, 1979.
Entered into force October 1, 1979.
TIAS 10600; 1581 UNTS 3

ENVIRONMENT & CONSERVATION

Agreement pursuant to article VI of the convention on nature protection and wildlife preservation in the Western Hemisphere of October 12, 1940 (56 Stat. 1354; TS 981), with related notes.
Signed at Washington September 7, 1977.
Entered into force October 1, 1979.
33 UST 446; TIAS 10035; 1280 UNTS 311

Agreement relating to custodianship of the Barro Colorado Nature Monument by the Smithsonian Tropical Research Institute.
Exchange of notes at Washington September 7, 1977.
Entered into force October 1, 1979.
33 UST 457; TIAS 10036; 1280 UNTS 319

Agreement concerning cooperation in the Global Learning and Observations to Benefit the Environment (GLOBE) Program.
Signed at Panama City March 2, 2000.
Entered into force March 2, 2000.

Agreement regarding assistance with respect to certain environmental pollution incidents in the Panama Canal area.
Signed at Panama City April 1, 2002.
Entered into force April 1, 2002.
TIAS 02-401

Agreement on environmental cooperation.
Signed at Panama City May 2, 2012.
Entered into force December 7, 2013.
TIAS 13-1207

Agreement establishing a secretariat for environmental enforcement matters under the United States-Panama trade promotion agreement.
Signed December 21, 2015.
Entered into force August 27, 2016.
TIAS 16-827

FINANCE

Agreement relating to legal tender and fractional silver coinage by Panama.
Exchange of notes at Washington and New York June 20, 1904.
Entered into force June 20, 1904.
10 Bevans 681

Amendments:
March 26 and April 2, 1930 (10 Bevans 731)
May 28 and June 6, 1931 (10 Bevans 734)
March 2, 1936 (53 Stat. 1807; TS 945)
June 17, 1946 (10 Bevans 834)
May 9 and 24, 1950
September 11 and October 22, 1953
August 23 and October 25, 1961
September 26 and October 23, 1962

Agreement relating to payments to be made by the Panama Canal Commission to Panama pursuant to articles III(5) and XIII(4) of the Panama Canal Treaty, with agreed minute.
Exchange of notes at Panama March 25, 1980.
Entered into force March 25, 1980.
TIAS 10601; 1590 UNTS 17

Agreement relating to payment to be made by Panama to the Panama Canal Company and the Canal Zone Government for goods and services, with agreed minute.
Exchange of notes at Panama March 25, 1980.
Entered into force March 25, 1980.
TIAS 10601; 1590 UNTS 3

Agreement regarding the consolidation and rescheduling of certain debts owed to, guaranteed by or insured by the United States Government and its agencies, with annexes.
Signed at Washington July 2, 1986.
Entered into force August 18, 1986.
NP

Agreement regarding the consolidation and rescheduling of certain debts owed to, guaranteed by, or insured by the United States Government and its agencies, with annexes.
Signed at Panama August 21, 1991.
Entered into force September 27, 1991.
NP

Swap agreement among the United States Treasury and the Government of Panama/Banco Nacional de Panama, with letter of understandings.
Signed at Washington and Panama January 29 and 30, 1992.
Entered into force January 30, 1992.
TIAS

Investment incentive agreement.
Signed at Panama City April 19, 2000.
Entered into force July 12, 2000.
TIAS 13091

Agreement regarding a debt-for-nature swap, with attachments.
Signed at Panama City July 10, 2003.
Entered into force July 30, 2003.
TIAS 03-730

Agreement regarding a debt-for-nature swap, with attachments.
Signed at Panama City August 19, 2004.
Entered into force August 19, 2004.
TIAS 04-819.1

FOREIGN ASSISTANCE

Agreement relating to the establishment of headquarters in Panama for a civil aviation technical assistance group for the Latin American area.
Exchange of notes at Panama August 8, 1952.
Entered into force August 8, 1952.
3 UST 5064; TIAS 2691; 181 UNTS 257

General agreement for technical and economic cooperation.
Signed at Panama December 11, 1961.
Entered into force March 5, 1962.
13 UST 274; TIAS 4972; 445 UNTS 161

INTERNATIONAL CRIMINAL COURT

Agreement regarding the surrender of persons to the International Criminal Court.
Signed at Panama City June 23, 2003.
Entered into force November 6, 2003.
TIAS 03-1106.1

LAW ENFORCEMENT

Treaty providing for the extradition of criminals.
Signed at Panama May 25, 1904.
Entered into force May 8, 1905.
34 Stat. 2851; TS 445; 10 Bevans 673

Convention for prevention of smuggling of intoxicating liquors.
Signed at Washington June 6, 1924.
Entered into force January 19, 1925.
43 Stat. 1875; TS 707; 10 Bevans 717; 138 LNTS 397

Informal arrangement relating to cooperation between the American Embassy, or Consulate, and Panamanian authorities when American merchant seamen or tourists are brought before a magistrate's court.
Exchange of notes at Panama September 18 and October 15, 1947.
Effective October 15, 1947.
10 Bevans 841

Treaty on the execution of penal sentences.
Signed at Panama January 11, 1979.
Entered into force June 27, 1980.
32 UST 1565; TIAS 9787; 1280 UNTS 363

Mutual cooperation for reducing demand, preventing illicit use and combating illicit production and traffic of drugs.
Signed at Panama January 10, 1990.
Entered into force January 10, 1990.
TIAS 12409

Arrangement concerning assistance in the development of civilian law enforcement institutions.
Signed at Panama December 28, 1990.
Entered into force December 28, 1990.
TIAS 12425

Treaty on mutual assistance in criminal matters, with annex and appendix.
Signed at Panama April 11, 1991.
Entered into force September 6, 1995.
TIAS

Treaty for the return of stolen, robbed, or converted vehicles and aircraft, with annexes and related exchange of notes.
Signed at Panama June 6, 2000.
Entered into force September 13, 2001.
TIAS 13098

Agreement regarding the Cooperating Nation Information Exchange System.
Exchange of notes at Panama City February 2 and 10, 2005.
Entered into force February 10, 2005.
TIAS 05-210

Agreement regarding the transfer of forfeited assets.
Signed October 11, 2011 and May 16, 2012.
Entered into force May 16, 2012.
TIAS

MARITIME MATTERS

Agreement relating to the mutual recognition of ship measurement certificates.
Exchange of notes at Washington August 17, 1937.
Entered into force August 17, 1937.
50 Stat. 1626; EAS 106; 10 Bevans 781; 182 LNTS 159

Agreement relating to jurisdiction over vessels utilizing the Louisiana Offshore Oil Port.
Exchange of notes at Washington August 15 and October 10, 1980.
Entered into force October 10, 1980.
32 UST 2906; TIAS 9885; 1275 UNTS 97

Arrangement for support and assistance from the United States Coast Guard for the National Maritime Service of the Ministry of Government and Justice.
Signed at Panama March 18, 1991.
Entered into force March 18, 1991.
TIAS 11833; 2212 UNTS 7

Supplementary arrangement to the arrangement of March 18, 1991 for support and assistance from the United States Coast Guard for the National Maritime Service of the Ministry of Government and Justice.
Signed at Panama February 5, 2002.
Entered into force February 5, 2002.
TIAS 02-205.1

POSTAL MATTERS

International express mail agreement, with detailed regulations.
Signed at Panama and Washington March 29 and May 21, 1985.
Entered into force July 1, 1985.
TIAS 11151; 2126 UNTS 179

PRIVATE INTERNATIONAL LAW

Agreement concerning enforcement of alimony and child support obligations of Panama Canal Commission employees, with annexes.
Exchange of notes at Panama February 22, 1988.
Entered into force February 22, 1988.
TIAS

PUBLICATIONS

Agreement relating to the exchange of official publications.
Exchange of notes at Panama November 27, 1941, and March 7, 1942.
Entered into force November 27, 1941.
56 Stat. 1444; EAS 243; 10 Bevans 805; 101 UNTS 157

SCIENTIFIC & TECHNICAL COOPERATION

Agreement relating to the operation in Panama of the Smithsonian Tropical Research Institute, with annex.
Exchange of notes at Washington September 7, 1977.
Entered into force September 7, 1977; effective October 1, 1979.
33 UST 465; TIAS 10037; 1280 UNTS 327

Agreement relating to the Port Meteorological Office.
Exchange of notes at Panama October 1, 1979.
Entered into force October 1, 1979.
TIAS 10599; 1871 UNTS 33

SOCIAL SECURITY

Agreement concerning participation by members of the Panama Canal Commission and United States forces in the Panamanian social security system.
Exchange of notes at Panama March 9, 1982.
Entered into force March 9, 1982.
TIAS 10492; 1750 UNTS 273

TAXATION

Arrangement providing for relief from double income tax on shipping profits.
Exchange of notes at Washington January 15, February 8, and March 28, 1941.
Entered into force March 28, 1941; operative January 1, 1936.
55 Stat. 1363; EAS 221; 10 Bevans 801; 103 UNTS 163
Amendment:
July 30 and December 30, 1987 (TIAS 11555; 2185 UNTS 333)

Agreement for withholding of Panamanian income tax from compensation paid to Panamanians employed within Canal Zone by the canal, railroad, or auxiliary works.
Exchange of notes at Panama August 12 and 30, 1963.
Entered into force August 30, 1963.
14 UST 1478; TIAS 5445; 488 UNTS 11

Agreement relating to the withholding of contributions for educational insurance from salaries paid to certain Canal Zone employees.
Exchange of notes at Panama September 8 and October 13, 1972.
Entered into force October 13, 1972.
23 UST 3495; TIAS 7509; 898 UNTS 189

Agreement relating to the agreements in implementation of articles III and IV of the Panama Canal Treaty with respect to tax on moveable property.
Exchange of notes at Panama October 1, 1979.
Entered into force October 1, 1979.
33 UST 565; TIAS 10047; 1280 UNTS 409

Agreement concerning taxation of income of United States contractors and subcontractors of the Panama Canal Commission or United States Forces, with attachments and related note.
Exchange of notes at Panama September 11, 1986.
Entered into force September 11, 1986.
TIAS

Agreement for tax cooperation and the exchange of information relating to taxes.
Signed at Washington November 30, 2010.
Entered into force April 18, 2011.
TIAS 11-418.1

TELECOMMUNICATION

Agreement for radio communications between amateur stations on behalf of third parties.
Exchange of notes at Panama July 19 and August 1, 1956.
Entered into force September 1, 1956.
7 UST 2179; TIAS 3617; 281 UNTS 49

Agreement relating to the granting of reciprocal authorizations to permit licensed amateur radio operators of either country to operate their stations in the other country.
Exchange of notes at Panama November 16, 1966.
Entered into force November 16, 1966.
17 UST 2215; TIAS 6159; 680 UNTS 303

TRADE & INVESTMENT

Declaration permitting consuls to take note in person, or by authorized representatives, of declarations of values of exports made by shippers before customs officers.
Exchange of notes at Washington April 17, 1913.
Entered into force June 1, 1913.
TS 578; 10 Bevans 699

Convention facilitating the work of traveling salesmen.
Signed at Washington February 8, 1919.
Entered into force December 8, 1919.
41 Stat. 1696; TS 646; 10 Bevans 714

Treaty concerning the treatment and protection of investments, with memoranda of understanding, annex and agreed minutes.
Signed at Washington October 27, 1982.
Entered into force May 30, 1991.
TIAS
Amendment
June 1, 2000

Understanding relating to Article X of the treaty concerning the treatment and protection of investments of October 27, 1982.
Exchange of notes at Panama July 1 and 12, 1985.
Entered into force May 30, 1991.
TIAS

Agreement on SPS issues for United States-Panama trade in agricultural products, with annex.
Signed at Washington and Panama City December 20, 2006.
Entered into force December 20, 2006.
TIAS 06-1220.1

Agreement on cooperation in agricultural trade.
Signed at Washington and Panama City December 20, 2006.
Entered into force December 20, 2006.
TIAS 06-1220

TRANSPORTATION

Agreement concerning the regulation of commercial aviation in the Republic of Panama.
Exchange of notes at Panama April 22, 1929.
Entered into force April 22, 1929.
Foreign Relations, 1929, Vol. III, p. 729; 10 Bevans 729

Agreement relating to the construction of the inter-American highway.
Exchange of notes at Panama May 15 and June 7, 1943.
Entered into force June 7, 1943.
57 Stat. 1298; EAS 365; 10 Bevans 826; 21 UNTS 269
Amendment:
January 16 and 26, 1951 (2 UST 1852; TIAS 2321; 137 UNTS 69)

Agreement relating to the furnishing by the Federal Aviation Agency of certain services and materials for air navigation aids.
Exchange of notes at Panama December 5, 1967, and February 22, 1968.
Entered into force February 22, 1968.
19 UST 4731; TIAS 6471; 698 UNTS 79

Agreement for cooperation in the construction of the Panama segment of the Darien Gap highway.
Signed at Washington May 6, 1971.
Entered into force May 6, 1971.
22 UST 602; TIAS 7111; 793 UNTS 31
Amendments:
May 15, 1974 (33 UST 3622; TIAS 10245; 1540 UNTS 420)
September 13, 1979 (33 UST 3622; TIAS 10245; 1540 UNTS 421)
July 18, 1980 (33 UST 3622; TIAS 10245; 1540 UNTS 422)

Memorandum of agreement relating to the provision of flight inspection services.
Signed at Washington and Panama August 16 and September 1, 1978.
Entered into force September 1, 1978; effective October 1, 1978.
30 UST 268; TIAS 9196; 1150 UNTS 231

Memorandum of agreement concerning assistance in developing and modernizing Panama's civil aviation infrastructure, with annexes.
Signed at Panama and Washington January 24 and February 15, 1990.
Entered into force February 15, 1990.
TIAS 11707; 2208 UNTS 223

Air transport agreement, with annexes.
Signed at Panama May 8, 1997.
Entered into force December 28, 1998.
TIAS 98-1228
Amendments:
May 27 and June 29, 1998 (TIAS 98-1228)
August 7 and September 27, 2006 (TIAS 98-1228)

Memorandum of cooperation for the promotion and development of civil aviation.
Signed at Washington and Panama February 17 and March 3, 1998.
Entered into force March 3, 1998.
NP

Memorandum of agreement concerning assistance in developing and modernizing Panama's civil aviation infrastructure.
Signed June 22 and 24, 2009.
Entered into force June 24, 2009.
NP

PAN AMERICAN UNION

(See ORGANIZATION OF AMERICAN STATES)

PAPUA NEW GUINEA

On September 16, 1975, Papua New Guinea became an independent state. In a note dated September 16, 1975, to the Secretary-General of the United Nations, the Governor-General made a statement reading in part as follows:

1. The Government of Papua New Guinea will make an examination of all treaties applying to its territory before independence, both bilateral and multilateral, with a view to making a statement of intention in respect of each of them. The statement will declare the Government's view as to whether the treaty continues or should be continued in force (on the basis of either succession or mutual consent, and with or without modification), or should be treated as having lapsed, or should be terminated. The statement will be forwarded to the other party or parties or to the depository, as may be appropriate.

2. During the period of examination, the Government will, on a basis of reciprocity, accept all treaty rights and obligations accruing and arising under treaties previously applicable. The period of examination will extend for five years from the date of Independence, that is, until 15th September, 1980, except in the case of any treaty in respect of which an earlier statement of intention is made.

CULTURAL EXCHANGES, PROPERTY & COOPERATION

Agreement relating to the establishment of a Peace Corps program in Papua New Guinea, with related note.
Exchange of notes at Washington October 6, 1980.
Entered into force October 6, 1980.
32 UST 2984; TIAS 9882; 1275 UNTS 89

DEFENSE

Status of forces agreement.
Signed at Port Moresby February 28, 1989.
Entered into force February 28, 1989.
TIAS 11612

Memorandum of understanding concerning an exchange of officers.
Signed at Port Moresby and Honolulu May 17 and June 13, 1989.
Entered into force June 13, 1989.
TIAS 11667

Memorandum of understanding concerning joint and combined military activities by Papua New Guinea defense forces and United States military forces in independent Papua New Guinea, with appendices.
Signed at Port Moresby March 26, 1990.
Entered into force March 26, 1990.
TIAS 12366

Acquisition and cross-servicing agreement, with annexes.
Signed at Papua New Guinea April 15, 2014.
Entered into force March 11, 2016.
NP

FINANCE

Agreement relating to investment guaranties.
Exchange of notes at Port Moresby and Waigani November 28, 1977, and April 4, 1978.
Entered into force April 13, 1978.
29 UST 3190; TIAS 9004; 1124 UNTS 237

FISHERIES

Agreement concerning fishing by United States vessels in Papua New Guinea's archipelagic waters pursuant to the treaty on fisheries between the United States and certain Pacific Island states.
Exchange of notes at Waigani and Port Moresby March 4, 5 and 25, 1987.
Entered into force March 25, 1987.
TIAS 11290

FOREIGN ASSISTANCE

Development cooperation agreement.
Signed at Port Moresby May 7, 1990.
Entered into force May 7, 1990.
TIAS 11722; 2207 UNTS 261

INTERNATIONAL CRIMINAL COURT

Agreement regarding the surrender of persons to the International Criminal Court.
Signed at Washington September 30, 2004.
Entered into force September 30, 2004.
TIAS 04-930

LAW ENFORCEMENT

Extradition treaty between the United States and the United Kingdom.
Signed at London December 22, 1931, applicable to Australia (including Papua, Norfolk Island, and the mandated territories
of New Guinea and Nauru), in accordance with article 14, from August 30, 1935.
47 Stat. 2122; TS 849; 12 Bevans 482; 163 LNTS 59

Agreement continuing in force between the United States and Papua New Guinea the extradition treaty of December 22, 1931, between the United States and the United Kingdom, with enclosures.
Exchange of notes at Port Moresby and Waigani February 2 and 23, 1988.
Entered into force February 23, 1988.
TIAS

POSTAL MATTERS

Agreement for exchange of postal parcels between the United States and the Territory of Papua and the Trust Territory of New Guinea, and detailed regulations of execution.
Signed at Canberra May 22 and at Washington June 20, 1958.
Entered into force October 1, 1958.
9 UST 1266; TIAS 4115; 336 UNTS 97

Memorandum of understanding concerning the operation of the INTELPOST field trial, with details of implementation.
Signed at Boroko and Washington June 30 and November 23, 1987.
Entered into force January 1, 1988.
TIAS 11301

International express mail agreement with detailed regulations.
Signed at Boroko and Washington August 4 and 19, 1988.
Entered into force September 30, 1988.
TIAS 11644

TELECOMMUNICATION

Agreement relating to the reciprocal granting of authorizations to permit licensed amateur radio operators of either country to operate their stations in the other country.
Exchange of notes at Port Moresby and Waigani August 17, 1989, and April 26, 1990.
Entered into force April 26, 1990.
TIAS

TRADE & INVESTMENT

Convention to regulate commerce (article IV) between the United States and the United Kingdom.
Signed at London July 3, 1815.
Entered into force July 3, 1815.
8 Stat. 228; TS 110; 12 Bevans 49

PARAGUAY

ARMS CONTROL

Memorandum of understanding concerning the operation of a seismic monitoring station in Paraguay.
Signed at Asuncion September 13, 1999.
Entered into force September 13, 1999.
TIAS 99-913

CLAIMS & DISPUTE RESOLUTION

Treaty for the advancement of peace.
Signed at Asuncion August 29, 1914.
Entered into force March 9, 1915.
39 Stat. 1615; TS 614; 10 Bevans 902

CULTURAL EXCHANGES, PROPERTY & COOPERATION

Agreement relating to the establishment of a Peace Corps program in Paraguay.
Exchange of notes at Asuncion November 4, 1966.
Entered into force November 4, 1966.
17 UST 2050; TIAS 6144; 676 UNTS 17

DEFENSE

Cooperative mapping agreement.
Signed at Asuncion January 16, 1962.
Entered into force January 16, 1962.
13 UST 52; TIAS 4934; 433 UNTS 169

Agreement concerning the furnishing of assistance to Paraguay for the purpose of increasing the air transport capability of the Paraguayan Air Force.
Exchange of notes at Asuncion August 25, 1962.
Entered into force August 25, 1962.
13 UST 2132; TIAS 5174; 461 UNTS 207

Agreement providing for assistance to increase the road construction and maintenance capability of the Paraguayan Army.
Exchange of notes at Asuncion February 10, 1964.
Entered into force February 10, 1964.
15 UST 149; TIAS 5532; 511 UNTS 53

Agreement relating to the furnishing of additional military assistance to Paraguay.
Exchange of notes at Asuncion April 11, 1966.
Entered into force April 11, 1966.
17 UST 661; TIAS 6014; 578 UNTS 99

Agreement concerning payment to the United States of net proceeds from the sale of defense articles furnished under the military assistance program.
Exchange of notes at Asuncion June 27, 1974.
Entered into force July 1, 1974.
25 UST 1440; TIAS 7873

Agreement concerning United States Armed Forces technical personnel deployments to Paraguay.
Exchange of notes at Asuncion February 28, 1995.
Entered into force February 28, 1995.
NP

Agreement regarding grants under the Foreign Assistance Act of 1961, as amended, or successor legislation, and the furnishing of defense articles, defense services and related training, including pursuant to the United States International Military and Education Training (IMET) Program.
Exchange of notes at Asuncion April 12, 2007.
Entered into force April 12, 2007.
NP

Memorandum of agreement regarding the assignment of liaison officers, with annexes.
Signed at Asuncion and Miami March 20 and April 14, 2015.
Entered into force April 14, 2015.
NP

DIPLOMATIC & CONSULAR RELATIONS

Agreement for reciprocal import privileges for non-diplomatic personnel.
Exchange of notes at Asuncion May 9 and 11, 1956.
Entered into force May 11, 1956.
7 UST 933; TIAS 3577

EDUCATION

Agreement for financing certain educational exchange programs.
Signed at Asuncion August 20, 1963.
Entered into force October 1, 1964.
TIAS 5675; 15 UST 1982; 531 UNTS 197

ENVIRONMENT & CONSERVATION

Agreement for cooperation in the Global Learning and Observations to Benefit the Environment Program, with appendices.
Signed at Asuncion October 27, 2000.
Entered into force October 27, 2000.
TIAS 13123

FINANCE

Investment incentive agreement.
Signed at Asuncion September 24, 1992.
Entered into force May 19, 1993.
TIAS 12478.

Agreement concerning the establishment of a Tropical Forest Conservation Fund and a Tropical Forest Conservation Board.
Signed at Asuncion June 7, 2006.
Entered into force July 17, 2006.
TIAS 06-717

Agreement regarding the reduction of certain debts owed to the Government of the United States and its agencies, with attachment.
Signed at Asuncion June 7, 2006.
Entered into force July 17, 2006.
NP

FOREIGN ASSISTANCE

Agreement providing for duty-free entry into Paraguay and exemption from internal taxation of relief supplies and packages.
Signed at Asuncion April 4, 1957.
Entered into force April 4, 1957.
8 UST 617; TIAS 3811; 283 UNTS 193
Amendments:
December 27, 1960, and March 7, 1961 (12 UST 240; TIAS 4702; 405 UNTS 328)
September 25 and October 26, 1970 (21 UST 2507; TIAS 6993; 772 UNTS 462)

General agreement for economic, technical and related assistance.
Signed at Asuncion September 26, 1961.
Entered into force September 26, 1961.
13 UST 2287; TIAS 5196; 461 UNTS 91

AGENCY FOR INTERNATIONAL DEVELOPMENT

Agreement regarding strategic objective grant to fight corruption, with annex.
Signed at Asuncion May 8, 2006.
Entered into force May 8, 2006.
NP

LAW ENFORCEMENT

Agreement on the control of the unlawful use of and illicit trafficking in narcotics and other dangerous drugs.
Signed at Asuncion October 26, 1972.
Entered into force provisionally October 26, 1972; definitively January 11, 1973.
24 UST 1008; TIAS 7613

Mutual cooperation agreement for reducing demand, illicit production and traffic of drugs.
Signed at Asuncion September 22, 1988.
Entered into force September 22, 1988.
TIAS 12397

Agreement to cooperate in the prevention and control of money laundering arising from illegal trafficking in narcotics and psychotropic substances.
Signed at Asuncion November 30, 1993.
Entered into force August 17, 1994.
TIAS

Extradition treaty.
Signed at Washington November 9, 1998.
Entered into force March 9, 2001.
TIAS 12995

Agreement regarding mutual assistance between their customs administrations.
Signed at Asuncion December 19, 2002.
Entered into force December 19, 2002.
TIAS 02-1219

POSTAL MATTERS

International express mail agreement, with detailed regulations.
Signed at Asuncion and Washington July 13 and August 22, 1988.
Entered into force September 30, 1988.
TIAS 11643

PUBLICATIONS

Agreement relating to the exchange of official publications.
Exchange of notes at Asuncion November 26 and 28, 1942.
Entered into force November 28, 1942; operative August 5, 1942.
56 Stat. 1868; EAS 301; 10 Bevans 916; 101 UNTS 173

TELECOMMUNICATION

Agreement relating to radio communications between amateur stations on behalf of third parties.
Exchange of notes at Asuncion August 31 and October 6, 1960.
Entered into force November 5, 1960.
11 UST 2229; TIAS 4596; 393 UNTS 281

Agreement relating to the reciprocal granting of authorizations to permit licensed amateur radio operators of either country to operate their stations in the other country.
Exchange of notes at Asuncion March 18, 1966.
Entered into force March 18, 1966.
17 UST 328; TIAS 5978; 586 UNTS 189

Agreement relating to establishing and maintaining monitoring premises and installations of the Foreign Broadcast Information Service (FBIS).
Exchange of notes at Asuncion May 24, 1973.
Entered into force May 24, 1973.
24 UST 1132; TIAS 7639

TRADE & INVESTMENT

Treaty of friendship, commerce, and navigation.
Signed at Asuncion February 4, 1859.
Entered into force March 7, 1860.
12 Stat. 1091; TS 272; 10 Bevans 888

Convention facilitating the work of traveling salesmen.
Signed at Washington October 20, 1919.
Entered into force March 22, 1922.
42 Stat. 2128; TS 662; 10 Bevans 906

Reciprocal trade agreement and supplemental exchanges of notes.
Signed at Asuncion September 12, 1946.
Entered into force April 9, 1947.
61 Stat. 2688; TIAS 1601; 10 Bevans 933; 125 UNTS 179
Related Agreement:
April 2, 1962 (13 UST 407; TIAS 5000; 442 UNTS 315)

Agreement terminating parts and amending and continuing parts of the agreement of September 12, 1946.
Exchange of notes at Asuncion June 26, 1963.
Entered into force June 26, 1963.
14 UST 1021; TIAS 5396; 487 UNTS 334

TRANSPORTATION

Memorandum of agreement concerning assistance in developing and modernizing the Paraguay civil aviation infrastructure, with annex.
Signed at Washington May 27, 1992.
Entered into force May 27, 1992.
TIAS 11862

Air transport agreement, with annexes.
Signed at Asuncion May 2, 2005.
Entered into force August 1, 2006.
TIAS 06-801; 2429 UNTS 301

PERMANENT COURT OF ARBITRATION

TAXATION

Tax reimbursement agreement, with annex.
Signed at The Hague June 26, 2007.
Entered into force June 26, 2007.
TIAS 07-626

PERU

AGRICULTURE

Memorandum of understanding relating to cooperative efforts to protect crops from plant pest damage and plant diseases.
Signed at Lima November 30, 1981.
Entered into force November 30, 1981.
33 UST 4360; TIAS 10306

ATOMIC ENERGY

Agreement providing for a grant to the Government of Peru to assist in the acquisition of nuclear research and training equipment and materials.
Exchange of notes at Lima July 12 and August 22, 1959.
Entered into force August 22, 1959.
10 UST 1600; TIAS 4304; 357 UNTS 99

CLAIMS & DISPUTE RESOLUTION

Arbitration convention.
Signed at Washington December 5, 1908.
Entered into force June 29, 1909.
36 Stat. 2169; TS 528; 10 Bevans 1081

Treaty for the advancement of peace.
Signed at Lima July 14, 1914.
Entered into force March 4, 1915.
39 Stat. 1611; TS 613; 10 Bevans 1083

CONSULAR AFFAIRS

Agreement relating to the waiver of nonimmigrant passport visas and visa fees, with related note.*
Exchange of notes at Lima April 6 and September 26, 1956.
Entered into force September 26, 1956; operative January 1, 1957.
8 UST 468; TIAS 3800; 288 UNTS 165
Amendment:
January 4 and 7, 1957 (8 UST 468; TIAS 3800; 288 UNTS 170)

Agreement relating to the reciprocal liberalization of nonimmigrant visa regulations.*
Exchange of notes at Lima March 18 and April 23, 1970.
Entered into force April 23, 1970.
21 UST 1317; TIAS 6885; 751 UNTS 355
Note:
* The status of these agreements is under review.

CULTURAL EXCHANGES, PROPERTY & COOPERATION

Agreement for the recovery and return of stolen archaeological, historical and cultural properties.
Signed at Lima September 15, 1981.
Entered into force September 15, 1981.
33 UST 1607; TIAS 10136

Memorandum of understanding concerning the imposition of import restrictions on archaeological material from the pre-Hispanic cultures and certain ethnological material from the colonial period of Peru.
Signed at Washington June 9, 1997.
Entered into force June 9, 1997.
TIAS 97-609
Amendments and Extensions:
March 22, 2002 (TIAS 97-609)
May 23 and 28, 2007 (TIAS 97-609)
May 30 and June 6, 2012 (TIAS 97-609)

Agreement concerning the program of the Peace Corps in the Republic of Peru.
Signed at Lima March 23, 2002.
Entered into force March 23, 2002.
TIAS 02-323

DEFENSE

Agreement relating to the making of aeronautical charts for air navigation.
Exchange of notes at Lima March 7 and April 23, 1942.
Entered into force April 23, 1942.
10 Bevans 1138

Agreement relating to a program of aerial and topographic cartography of Peru and exchanges of notes.
Signed at Lima February 5, 1948.
Entered into force February 5, 1948.
10 Bevans 1269

Military assistance agreement.
Signed at Lima February 22, 1952.
Entered into force April 26, 1952.
3 UST 2890; TIAS 2466; 165 UNTS 31

Agreement concerning financial arrangements for the furnishing of certain supplies and services to naval vessels of both countries.
Signed at Lima January 7, 1955.
Entered into force April 7, 1955.
6 UST 806; TIAS 3227; 261 UNTS 321

Agreement providing for disposition of equipment and materials furnished by the United States under the military assistance agreement of February 22, 1952.
Exchange of notes at Lima March 22 and April 30, 1955.
Entered into force April 30, 1955.
6 UST 2064; TIAS 3273; 258 UNTS 415

Agreement for performance by members of Army, Navy, and military aviation missions of duties specified in article V of the military assistance agreement of February 22, 1952.
Exchanges of notes at Lima June 28, July 18, and October 20 and 28, 1955.
Entered into force October 26, 1955.
6 UST 3771; TIAS 3377; 239 UNTS 181

Agreement relating to the furnishing of defense articles and services to Peru.
Exchange of notes at Lima December 17 and 20, 1962.
Entered into force December 20, 1962.
13 UST 3896; TIAS 5265; 471 UNTS 75

Agreement relating to the deposit by Peru of ten percent of the value of grant military assistance furnished by the United States.
Exchange of notes at Lima May 3, 1972.
Entered into force May 3, 1972; effective February 7, 1972.
23 UST 877; TIAS 7348

Cooperative arrangement for the production of topographic maps of Peru.
Signed at Washington and Lima April 25 and May 22, 1986.
Entered into force May 22, 1986.
TIAS 11372

Memorandum of understanding on exchange of officers between United States and Peruvian Marine Corps.
Signed at Lima and Washington August 20 and September 22, 1986.
Entered into force September 22, 1986.
TIAS 11383

Memorandum of understanding on maritime trade.
Signed at Washington May 1, 1987.
Entered into force May 1, 1987.
TIAS 11273

Agreement concerning the status of certain United States military personnel who may serve for a period of less than ninety days at the ground-based radar site at Yurimaguas, and at other locations as agreed by the Peruvian Air Force.
Exchange of notes at Lima November 7, 1995.
Entered into force November 7, 1995.
NP

Agreement concerning security assistance matters and the provision of articles, services and associated military educational training by the United States Government for antinarcotics purposes.
Exchange of notes at Lima October 14, 1999, and January 14, 2000.
Entered into force January 14, 2000.
NP

Agreement regarding grants under the Foreign Assistance Act of 1961, as amended, or successor legislation, and the furnishing of defense articles, related training and other defense services.
Exchange of notes at Lima May 24 and July 13, 2007.
Entered into force July 13, 2007.
NP

Agreement regarding the assignment of foreign liaison officers, with annex.
Signed at Washington and Lima October 31 and November 23, 2007.
Entered into force November 23, 2007.
NP

Acquisition and cross-servicing agreement, with annexes.
Signed at Lima and Miami January 17 and March 20, 2012.
Entered into force March 20, 2012.
NP

Agreement concerning health care for military members and their dependents.
Signed August 21 and 29, 2012.
Entered into force August 31, 2012.
NP
Extension:
August 11 and 27, 2015

Memorandum of agreement regarding the assignment of defense personnel of the Navy of Peru to the United States Navy, with annexes.
Signed at Washington April 28 and 30, 2015.
Entered into force April 30, 2015.
NP

DIPLOMATIC & CONSULAR RELATIONS

Agreement granting reciprocal customs privileges to diplomatic and consular officers and personnel.
Exchange of notes at Lima November 7 and December 28, 1960, and February 4 and 13, 1961.
Entered into force February 13, 1961.
12 UST 217; TIAS 4696; 406 UNTS 177

EDUCATION

Agreement for financing certain educational exchange programs.
Signed at Lima January 28, 1965.
Entered into force August 25, 1965.
TIAS 5858; 16 UST 1149; 587 UNTS 273
Amendment:
November 23, 1981 and January 19, 1982 (TIAS 10332; 34 UST 15)

EMPLOYMENT

Agreement relating to employment of dependents of official government employees.
Exchange of notes at Lima August 27, 1987, and February 17, 1988.
Entered into force February 17, 1988.
TIAS 11650

ENVIRONMENT & CONSERVATION

Agreement for cooperation in the Global Learning and Observations to Benefit the Environment (GLOBE) Program, with appendices.
Signed at Lima July 10, 1997.
Entered into force July 10, 1997.
TIAS 12874

Environmental cooperation agreement.
Signed at Lima July 24, 2006.
Entered into force August 23, 2009.
TIAS

FINANCE

Agreement relating to investment guaranties under section 413 (b)(4)(B)(i) of the Mutual Security Act of 1954.
Exchange of notes at Lima March 14 and 16, 1955.
Entered into force March 16, 1955.
6 UST 678; TIAS 3203; 252 UNTS 151

Agreement regarding the consolidation and rescheduling of certain debts owed to, guaranteed or insured by the United States Government and its agencies, with annexes.
Signed at Lima July 5, 1979.
Entered into force August 22, 1979.
32 UST 1; TIAS 9698; 1221 UNTS 159

Agreement regarding the consolidation and rescheduling of certain debts owed to, guaranteed by or insured by the United States Government and its agencies, with implementing agreement.
Signed at Lima November 29, 1983.
Entered into force March 9, 1984.
35 UST 4944; TIAS 10978

Agreement regarding the consolidation and rescheduling or refinancing of certain debts owed to, guaranteed by, or insured by the United States Government and its agencies, with annexes.
Signed at Washington August 27, 1992.
Entered into force September 30, 1992.
NP

Investment incentive and financial agreement.
Signed at Washington December 16, 1992.
Entered into force December 16, 1992.
TIAS 12542

SWAP agreement between the United States Treasury and the Government of Peru/Central Bank of Peru, with memorandum of understanding.
Signed at Washington March 9, 1993.
Entered into force March 9, 1993.
TIAS

Agreement regarding the consolidation and rescheduling or refinancing of certain debts owed to, guaranteed by or insured by the United States Government and its agencies, with annexes.
Signed at Washington August 30, 1993.
Entered into force September 30, 1993.
NP

Agreement supplementing the investment incentive and financial agreement of December 16, 1992, relating to the Export-Import Bank.
Signed at Washington May 20, 1994.
Entered into force May 20, 1994.
TIAS 12542

Agreement regarding the rescheduling and reorganization of certain debts owed to or guaranteed by the United States Government and its agencies.
Signed at Lima December 31, 1996.
Entered into force February 18, 1997.
NP

Agreement regarding a debt-for-nature swap, with attachments.
Signed at Washington June 26, 2002.
Entered into force July 16, 2002.
TIAS 02-716

Agreement regarding the prepayment of certain debts owed to, guaranteed by, or insured by the United States Government and its Agencies, with annexes.
Signed at Lima September 25, 2007.
Entered into force September 25, 2007.
NP

Agreement concerning the establishment of a tropical forest conservation fund and administering board, with annex.
Signed at Washington September 18, 2008.
Entered into force September 18, 2008.
TIAS

Agreement regarding the reduction of certain debts owed to the Government of the United States of America and its agencies, with annexes.
Signed at Washington September 18, 2008.
Entered into force September 18, 2008.
NP

FOREIGN ASSISTANCE

General agreement for technical cooperation.
Signed at Lima January 25, 1951.
Entered into force January 15, 1953.
4 UST 132; TIAS 2772

Amendments:
January 7, 1952 (4 UST 139; TIAS 2772)
February 21 and 28, 1952 (4 UST 143; TIAS 2772)
January 15, 1953 (4 UST 146; TIAS 2772)

Agreement granting duty-free entry, exemption from internal taxation, and free transportation within Peru for supplies for U.S. rehabilitation and relief agencies distributing surplus agricultural food products in Peru.
Exchange of notes at Lima October 21 and 25, 1954.
Entered into force October 29, 1954.
5 UST 2725; TIAS 3128; 238 UNTS 247

Amendment:
June 23 and August 3, 1955 (7 UST 781; TIAS 3557; 273 UNTS 295)

Agreement concerning the establishment of an Americas Fund and Administering Board.
Signed at Lima December 24, 1997.
Entered into force December 24, 1997.
TIAS 12914

Amendment:
September 18, 2008 (TIAS 08-918.1)

Agreement concerning Millennium Challenge Account Threshold Program to combat corruption and increase immunization rates, with annexes.
Signed at Lima June 9, 2008.
Entered into force June 9, 2008.
TIAS

AGENCY FOR INTERNATIONAL DEVELOPMENT

Strategic objective grant agreement for sustained reduction of illicit coca crops through alternative development in target areas of Peru, with attachment.
Signed September 12, 2002.
Entered into force September 12, 2002.
NP

Amendments and Extensions:
September 30, 2003 (NP)
February 9, 2004 (NP)
July 27, 2004 (NP)
July 19, 2005 (NP)
July 6, 2006 (NP)
September 26, 2007 (NP)

Assistance agreement.
Signed September 29, 2008.
Entered into force September 29, 2008.
NP

Amendments and Extensions:
September 29, 2010 (NP)
September 26, 2011 (NP)
September 20, 2012 (NP)
January 21, 2015 (NP)

HEALTH & MEDICAL COOPERATION

Agreement for the establishment and operation of the Naval Medical Research Institute (NAMRID) in Lima.
Signed at Lima October 21, 1983.
Entered into force October 21, 1983.
35 UST 3003; TIAS 10836; 2014 UNTS 617

LAW ENFORCEMENT

Treaty on the execution of penal sentences.
Signed at Washington July 6, 1979.
Entered into force July 21, 1980.
32 UST 1471; TIAS 9784; 1233 UNTS 139

Procedures for mutual assistance in connection with matters relating to the Lockheed Aircraft Corporation.
Signed at Washington August 8, 1979.
Entered into force August 8, 1979.
NP

Agreement regarding cooperation in the prevention and control of money laundering arising from illicit trafficking in narcotic drugs and psychotropic substances, with attachment.
Signed at Lima October 14, 1991.
Entered into force October 14, 1991.
TIAS 12438

Extradition treaty.
Signed at Lima July 26, 2001.
Entered into force August 25, 2003.
TIAS 03-825

Agreement regarding the Cooperating Nation Information Exchange System, with annex.
Exchange of notes at Lima August 16, 2005.
Entered into force October 6, 2005.
TIAS 05-1006.1

Agreement regarding mutual assistance between their customs administrations.
Signed at Washington March 1, 2006.
Entered into force March 1, 2006.
TIAS 06-301.1

POSTAL MATTERS

International express mail agreement, with detailed regulations.
Signed at Lima and Washington October 29 and November 30, 1990.
Entered into force January 14, 1991.
TIAS 11787

Agreement for the transmission and payment of postal money orders.
Signed at Washington and Lima August 21 and September 8, 1995.
Entered into force December 1, 1995.
NP

PUBLICATIONS

Agreement relating to the exchange of official publications.
Exchange of notes at Lima October 16 and 20, 1936.
Entered into force October 20, 1936.
50 Stat. 1601; EAS 103; 10 Bevans 1106; 181 LNTS 161

RULES OF WAR

Convention regarding the rights of neutrals at sea.
Signed at Lima July 22, 1856.
Entered into force October 31, 1857.
11 Stat. 695; TS 277; 10 Bevans 1019

SCIENTIFIC & TECHNICAL COOPERATION

Agreement for the continuation of the cooperative meteorological program in Peru.
Exchange of notes at Lima July 7, 1964.
Entered into force July 7, 1964; operative January 1, 1963.
15 UST 1523; TIAS 5634; 530 UNTS 113

Agreement concerning scientific and technical cooperation in the earth and mapping sciences, with annexes.
Signed at Lima July 19, 1990.
Entered into force July 19, 1990.
TIAS 12416

TAXATION

Agreement concerning the reciprocal exemption from income tax of income derived from the international operation of ships.
Exchange of notes at Lima December 15, 1988.
Entered into force December 15, 1988.
TIAS 11621

Agreement for the exchange of tax information.
Signed at Cartagena February 15, 1990.
Entered into force March 31, 1993.
TIAS 12060

TELECOMMUNICATION

Arrangement concerning radio communications between amateur stations on behalf of third parties.
Exchange of notes at Lima February 16 and May 23, 1934.
Entered into force May 23, 1934.
49 Stat. 3555; EAS 66; 10 Bevans 1103

Agreement relating to the reciprocal granting of authorizations to permit licensed amateur radio operators of either country to operate their stations in the other country.
Exchange of notes at Lima June 28 and August 11, 1965.
Entered into force August 11, 1965.
16 UST 1160; TIAS 5860; 564 UNTS 135

TRADE & INVESTMENT

Convention concerning commercial travelers, and protocol.
Signed at Lima January 19, 1923.
Entered into force July 8, 1924.
43 Stat. 1802; TS 692; 10 Bevans 1091

Agreement terminating the agreement of November 23, 1971, relating to trade in cotton textiles and providing for consultation on problems of market disruption caused by exports of textiles or textile products from Peru.
Exchange of notes at Lima June 13 and September 10, 1975.
Entered into force September 10, 1975.
26 UST 2125; TIAS 8153

Agreement regarding sanitary and phytosanitary measures and technical barriers to trade, with annexes.
Exchange of letters January 5, 2006.
Entered into force January 5, 2006.
TIAS 06.105.1

Agreement additional to the agreement of January 5, 2006, regarding sanitary and phytosanitary measures and technical barriers to trade, with annex.
Exchange of letters at Lima and Washington April 10, 2006.
Entered into force April 10, 2006.
TIAS

Agreement regarding trade in beef and beef products of the United States, with annex.
Exchange of letters at Lima and Washington October 6 and 25, 2006.
Entered into force October 25, 2006.
TIAS 06-1025.1

United States-Peru trade promotion agreement, with annexes, understandings, and related exchange of letters.
Signed at Washington April 12, 2006.
Entered into force February 1, 2009.
TIAS

Protocol of amendment to the United States-Peru trade promotion agreement.
Signed at Washington and Lima June 24 and 25, 2007.
Entered into force February 1, 2009.
TIAS

TRANSPORTATION

Memorandum of agreement concerning the provision of assistance in developing and modernizing Peru's civil aviation infrastructure.
Signed at Washington and Lima August 17 and 23, 1995.
Entered into force August 23, 1995.
NP

Air transport agreement, with annexes.
Signed at Lima June 10, 1998.
Entered into force February 8, 1999.
TIAS

Memorandum of cooperation concerning mutual cooperation in the promotion and development of civil aviation.
Signed at Washington and Lima March 16 and 27, 2000.
Entered into force March 27, 2000.
NP

PHILIPPINES

CLAIMS & DISPUTE RESOLUTION

Agreement relating to settlement of claims for damages arising from maneuvers at Laur Training Area.
Exchange of aide memoire at Manila February 6, 1957.
Entered into force February 6, 1957.
9 UST 313; TIAS 4009; 303 UNTS 237

Agreement relating to settlement of claims for damages arising from SEATO maneuvers and ground field training exercises.
Exchange of aide memoire at Manila November 1, 1957.
Entered into force November 1, 1957.
8 UST 2456; TIAS 3965; 307 UNTS 39

Agreement relating to settlement of claims for damages arising from maneuvers in Laur-Dingalan Bay area.
Exchange of aide memoire at Manila February 20, 1958.
Entered into force February 20, 1958.
9 UST 327; TIAS 4011; 303 UNTS 261

Agreement relating to settlement of claims arising from maneuvers at Laur Training Area during January and February 1959.
Exchange of aide memoire at Manila January 21, 1959.
Entered into force January 21, 1959.
10 UST 204; TIAS 4184; 341 UNTS 255

Agreement on the settlement of claims for pay and allowances of recognized Philippine guerillas not previously paid in full and for erroneous deductions of advanced salary from the backpay of eligible Philippine veterans.
Signed at Manila June 29, 1967.
Entered into force June 29, 1967.
18 UST 1392; TIAS 6295; 686 UNTS 71

Agreement for compensation for damage to the Tubbataha Reef caused by the grounding of the USS Guardian.
Effected by Exchange of Notes at Manila and Pasay City November 13 and December 18, 2014.
Entered into force December 18, 2014.
TIAS 14-1218

CONSULAR AFFAIRS

Agreement relating to waiver of nonimmigrant passport visa fees.*
Exchange of notes at Manila November 24, 1952.
Entered into force November 24, 1952; operative December 24, 1952.
3 UST 5196; TIAS 2715; 181 UNTS 155
Note:
* The status of this agreement is under review.

CULTURAL EXCHANGES, PROPERTY & COOPERATION

Agreement relating to the establishment of a Peace Corps program in the Republic of the Philippines.
Exchange of notes at Manila October 11 and 31, 1961.
Entered into force October 31, 1961.
12 UST 1699; TIAS 4889; 424 UNTS 129

Agreement relating to cooperation in consecrating Corregidor Island as a World War II memorial site, with annex.
Exchange of notes at Manila December 22, 1965.
Entered into force December 22, 1965.
16 UST 1925; TIAS 5925; 579 UNTS 203

Agreement on the development and facilitation of reciprocal tourism.
Signed at Washington September 17, 1982.
Entered into force September 17, 1982.
TIAS 10498

DEFENSE

Mutual defense treaty.
Signed at Washington August 30, 1951.
Entered into force August 27, 1952.
3 UST 3947; TIAS 2529; 177 UNTS 133

Agreement relating to the assurances required under the Mutual Security Act of 1951.
Exchange of notes at Manila January 4 and 7, 1952.
Entered into force January 7, 1952.
3 UST 4644; TIAS 2617; 179 UNTS 193

Agreement relating to military assistance.
Exchange of notes at Manila June 26, 1953.
Entered into force July 5, 1953.
4 UST 1682; TIAS 2834; 213 UNTS 77

Agreement relating to military assistance.
Exchange of notes at Manila April 27, 1955.
Entered into force April 27, 1955.
6 UST 847; TIAS 3231; 261 UNTS 351
Amendments:
April 20, 1956 (7 UST 727; TIAS 3551; 273 UNTS 316)
June 14, 1957 (8 UST 859; TIAS 3845; 291 UNTS 342)
April 14, 1958 (9 UST 397; TIAS 4019; 308 UNTS 324)

Agreement providing for disposition of equipment and material furnished by the United States.
Exchange of notes at Manila July 27, 1953, and March 3, 1956.
Entered into force March 3, 1956.
7 UST 425; TIAS 3523; 270 UNTS 400

Interim arrangement to permit the exploitation of mineral resources located on specific sites within the U.S. Military Reservation, Fort Stotsenberg, Tarlac.
Exchange of notes at Manila April 8, 1957.
Entered into force April 8, 1957.
9 UST 309; TIAS 4008; 303 UNTS 227

Agreement for the establishment of a Mutual Defense Board and the assignment of Philippine military liaison officers to United States military bases in the Philippines.
Exchange of notes at Manila May 15, 1958.
Entered into force May 15, 1958.
9 UST 547; TIAS 4033; 316 UNTS 163
Amendment:
April 2 and May 10, 1993 (TIAS 12496)

Agreement relating to the installation of a submarine cable with a terminal facility at San Miguel Communications Station.
Exchange of notes at Manila August 12, 1965.
Entered into force August 12, 1965.
16 UST 1127; TIAS 5855; 579 UNTS 47

Agreement relating to the installation and operation of a petroleum products pipeline from Subic Bay Naval Reservation through Basa Air Base to Clark Air Base.
Exchange of notes at Manila August 26, 1966.
Entered into force August 26, 1966.
17 UST 1206; TIAS 6083

Agreement relating to the exploitation of natural resources within United States bases in the Philippines.
Exchange of notes at Manila August 24, 1967.
Entered into force August 24, 1967.
18 UST 2340; TIAS 6335; 693 UNTS 53

Agreement relating to the employment of Philippine nationals in the United States military bases in the Philippines.
Signed at Manila May 27, 1968.
Entered into force May 27, 1968.
19 UST 5892; TIAS 6542; 658 UNTS 347
Amendments:
September 5, 1985
July 19, 1989

Agreement relating to the recruitment and employment of Filipino citizens by the United States military forces and contractors of military and civilian agencies of the United States in certain areas of the Pacific and Southeast Asia.
Signed at Manila December 28, 1968.
Entered into force December 28, 1968.
19 UST 7560; TIAS 6598; 658 UNTS 365.

Agreement concerning payment to the United States of net proceeds from the sale of defense articles furnished under the military assistance program.
Exchange of notes at Manila May 16 and July 16, 1974.
Entered into force July 16, 1974; effective July 1, 1974.
25 UST 1447; TIAS 7875
Amendment:
March 8, 2005 and May 2, 2006 (TIAS 06-502.1)

Memorandum of understanding for the exchange of individual personnel between the United States Army Western Command and the Armed Forces of the Philippines.
Signed at Manila March 25, 1981.
Entered into force March 25, 1981.
35 UST 3606; TIAS 10871; 1577 UNTS 355

Agreement concerning mapping, charting and geodesy cooperation, with annexes.
Signed at Makati and Fairfax June 27 and September 9, 1991.
Entered into force September 9, 1991.
NP

Agreement regarding the status of U.S. military and civilian personnel.
Exchange of notes at Manila April 2, June 11 and 21, 1993.
Entered into force June 21, 1993.
TIAS
Extensions:
September 19, 1994
April 28, 1995
November 29, December 1 and 8, 1995

Agreement regarding the treatment of United States armed forces visiting the Philippines.
Signed at Manila February 10, 1998.
Entered into force June 1, 1999.
TIAS 12931.

Agreement regarding the treatment of Republic of Philippines personnel visiting the United States of America.
Signed at Manila October 9, 1998.
Entered into force June 1, 1999.
TIAS 12931

Agreement to establish a Security Engagement Board.
Exchange of notes at Manila April 11 and 12, 2006.
Entered into force April 12, 2006.
TIAS 06-412.1

Agreement regarding grants under the Global Peace Operations Initiative (GPOI).
Exchange of notes at Manila December 18, 2007, and January 3, 2008.
Entered into force January 3, 2008.
NP

Mutual logistics support agreement, with annexes.
Signed at Quezon City November 8, 2007.
Entered into force January 14, 2009.
NP
Extension:
November 6, 2012

Agreement regarding grants under the Global Security Contingency Fund (GSCF).
Effected by Exchange of Notes at Manila and Pasay City October 16 and December 16, 2013.
Entered into force December 16, 2013.
NP

Agreement on enhanced defense cooperation.
Signed at Quezon City April 28, 2014.
Entered into force June 25, 2014.
TIAS 14-625
Amendment:
April 12 and 13, 2016 (TIAS 16-413.1)

DIPLOMATIC & CONSULAR RELATIONS

Provisional agreement concerning friendly relations and diplomatic and consular representation.
Signed at Manila July 4, 1946.
Entered into force July 4, 1946.
60 Stat. 1800; TIAS 1539; 11 Bevans 1; 6 UNTS 335

Treaty of general relations, and protocol.
Signed at Manila July 4, 1946.
Entered into force October 22, 1946.
61 Stat. 1174; TIAS 1568; 11 Bevans 3; 7 UNTS 3

Consular convention.
Signed at Manila March 14, 1947.
Entered into force November 18, 1948.
62 Stat. 1593; TIAS 1741; 11 Bevans 74; 45 UNTS 23

Agreement relating to entry of nationals of either country into the territories of the other for purposes of trade, investment, and related activities.
Exchange of notes at Washington September 6, 1955.
Entered into force September 6, 1955.
6 UST 3030; TIAS 3349; 238 UNTS 109

EDUCATION

Agreement for financing certain educational exchange programs.
Signed at Manila March 23, 1963.
Entered into force March 23, 1963.
14 UST 352; TIAS 5321; 474 UNTS 81
Amendment:
December 11, 1968, January 31 and March 19, 1969 (20 UST 508; TIAS 6657; 719 UNTS 354)

Agreement concerning the Special Fund for Education.
Exchange of notes at Manila April 26, 1966.
*Entered into force April 26, 1966.**
19 UST 5079; TIAS 6508; 706 UNTS 110
Note:
* For implementing agreements, see 19 UST 5082; TIAS 6508; 706 UNTS 57 (May 18, 1967, June 26, 1967, August 11, 1967, and June 11, 1968); 20 UST 2845; TIAS 6756; 723 UNTS 243 (September 5, 1969); 22 UST 501; TIAS 7089; 792 UNTS 261 (March 30, 1971); 23 UST 251; TIAS 7300 (March 21, 1972).

EMPLOYMENT

Agreement relating to the employment of dependents of official government employees.
Exchange of notes at Washington September 20 and October 19, 1983.
Entered into force October 19, 1983.
35 UST 2428; TIAS 10805

ENVIRONMENT & CONSERVATION

Agreement for cooperation in the Global Learning and Observations to Benefit the Environment (GLOBE) Program, with appendices.
Signed at Manila January 14, 1999.
Entered into force January 14, 1999.
TIAS 13018

FINANCE

Agreement establishing a joint American-Philippine financial commission.
Exchange of notes at Manila September 13 and 17, 1946.
Entered into force September 17, 1946.
61 Stat. 2840; TIAS 1612; 11 Bevans 34; 15 UNTS 249

Agreement relating to the repayment of funds advanced to the National Defense Forces, Republic of the Philippines, by the United States Philippines-Ryukyus Command.
Signed at Washington November 6, 1950.
Entered into force November 6, 1950.
1 UST 765; TIAS 2151; 122 UNTS 63

Agreement for adjustment of the amount and final settlement of obligations under the agreement of November 6, 1950, relating to the repayment of funds advanced to Philippine National Defense Forces.
Exchange of notes at Washington March 27, 1961.
Entered into force March 27, 1961.
12 UST 297; TIAS 4715; 405 UNTS 304

Agreement regarding the consolidation and rescheduling of certain debts owed to, guaranteed by or insured by the United States Government and its agencies, with annexes.
Signed at Manila July 29, 1985.
Entered into force August 30, 1985.
NP

Agreement regarding the consolidation and rescheduling of certain debts owed to, guaranteed by, or insured by the United States Government and its agencies, with annexes.
Signed at Manila May 16, 1988.
Entered into force June 17, 1988.
NP
Amendment:
April 25, 1989 (NP)

Agreement regarding the consolidation and rescheduling or refinancing of certain debts owed to, guaranteed by, or insured by the United States Government and its agencies, with annexes.
Signed at Manila November 3, 1989.
Entered into force December 13, 1989.
NP

Agreement regarding the consolidation and rescheduling or refinancing of certain debts owed to, guaranteed by, or insured by the United States Government and its agencies with annexes.
Signed at Washington December 11, 1991.
Entered into force March 2, 1992.
NP
Amendment:
March 4 and 9, 1993 (NP)

Agreement relating to investments supported by the Overseas Private Investment Corporation.
Signed at Manila October 22, 1998.
Entered into force February 15, 2000.
TIAS 12988

Agreement concerning the establishment of a Tropical Forest Conservation Fund and a Tropical Forest Conservation Board.
Signed at Manila September 19, 2002.
Entered into force November 1, 2002.
TIAS 02-1101

Agreement regarding the reduction of a certain debt owed to the Government of the United States and its agencies, with attachments.
Signed at Manila September 19, 2002.
Entered into force November 1, 2002.
NP

Agreement concerning the establishment of a second Tropical Forest Conservation Fund.
Signed at Manila July 18, 2013.
Entered into force September 3, 2013.
TIAS 13-903

Second agreement regarding the reduction of certain debts owed to the Government of the United States of America and its agencies.
Signed at Manila July 18, 2013.
Entered into force September 3, 2013.
NP

FOREIGN ASSISTANCE

Economic and technical cooperation agreement.
Signed at Manila April 27, 1951.
Entered into force May 21, 1951.
3 UST 3707; TIAS 2498; 174 UNTS 251

Agreement providing for duty-free entry into the Philippines and exemption from internal taxation of relief supplies and packages.
Exchange of notes at Manila April 29, 1954, and October 18, 1956.
Entered into force October 18, 1956.
8 UST 144; TIAS 3752; 280 UNTS 55
Amendment
August 6 and September 19, 1970 (21 UST 2510; TIAS 6994; 772 UNTS 458)

AGENCY FOR INTERNATIONAL DEVELOPMENT

Agreement for strategic objective 3: improved family health sustainable achieved, with attachment.
Signed September 27, 2006.
Entered into force September 27, 2006.
NP
Amendment:
September 22, 2010 (NP)
September 14, 2011 (NP)

Agreement for Mindanao Peace and Development.
Signed September 19, 2007.
Entered into force September 19, 2007.
NP
Amendment:
September 17, 2010 (NP)

Agreement for economic growth and democracy and governance, with annex.
Signed September 30, 2011.
Entered into force September 30, 2011.
NP
Amendments:
May 5, 2012 (NP)
September 30, 2013 (NP)
September 16, 2014 (NP)

Development objective agreement for "Family Health Improved," with attachment.
Signed September 28, 2012.
Entered into force September 28, 2012.
NP
Amendment:
September 24, 2013 (NP)
September 26, 2014 (NP)

HEALTH AND MEDICAL COOPERATION

Agreement permanently locating the United States Naval Medical Research Unit-Two (NAMRU 2) in the Philippines.
Exchange of notes at Manila February 26, 1979, and June 5, 1981.
Entered into force June 5, 1981.
33 UST 2093; TIAS 10174; 1529 UNTS 469

Agreement on employees' compensation and medical care programs [for Philippine employees of U.S. Forces], with annex.
Signed at Manila March 10, 1982.
Entered into force March 10, 1982.
34 UST 312; TIAS 10358; 1557 UNTS 21
Amendment:
July 19, 1989

INTELLECTUAL PROPERTY

Agreement relating to the reciprocal application of certain rights of priority in the filing of patent applications.
Exchange of notes at Washington February 12 and August 4 and 23, 1948.
Entered into force August 23, 1948.
62 Stat. 3461; TIAS 1861; 11 Bevans 149; 82 UNTS 11

Arrangement relating to reciprocal copyright relations between the United States and the Philippines.
Exchange of notes at Washington October 21, 1948.
Entered into force October 21, 1948.
62 Stat. 2996; TIAS 1840; 11 Bevans 160; 77 UNTS 197

Agreement regarding the protection and enforcement of intellectual property rights, with agreed minutes.
Effected by exchange of letters at Manila and Washington April 4, 1993.
Entered into force April 4, 1993.

INTERNATIONAL CRIMINAL COURT

Agreement regarding the surrender of persons to international tribunals.
Exchange of notes at Manila May 9 and 13, 2003.
Entered into force May 13, 2003.
TIAS 03-513

LAW ENFORCEMENT

Agreement concerning the provision of documents to Government of the Republic of the Philippines.
Exchange of notes at Washington March 15, 1986.
Entered into force March 15, 1986.
NP

Agreement on procedures for mutual legal assistance.
Signed at Manila March 31, 1987.
Entered into force March 31, 1987.
NP

Extradition treaty.
Signed at Manila November 13, 1994.
Entered into force November 22, 1996.
TIAS 96-1122; 1994 UNTS 279

Treaty on mutual legal assistance in criminal matters, with attachments.
Signed at Manila November 13, 1994.
Entered into force November 22, 1996.
TIAS; 1994 UNTS 309

MARITIME MATTERS

Agreement relating to naval charter for lease of vessels to the Philippines.
Exchanges of notes at Manila September 26 and December 9, 1947, and May 6 and June 7, 1948.
Entered into force June 7, 1948.
62 Stat. 3870; TIAS 1954; 11 Bevans 137; 70 UNTS 280

POSTAL MATTERS

Parcel post convention.
Signed at Manila September 21 and at Washington November 12, 1964.
Entered into force November 1, 1965.
16 UST 1680; TIAS 5893; 574 UNTS 159

International express mail agreement, with detailed regulations.
Signed at Manila and Washington April 21 and May 22, 1992.
Entered into force September 21, 1992.
TIAS 11861

PUBLICATIONS

Agreement relating to the exchange of official publications.
Exchange of notes at Manila April 12 and June 7, 1948.
Entered into force June 7, 1948.
62 Stat. 2024; TIAS 1767; 11 Bevans 134; 73 UNTS 89
Amendment:
December 2 and 20, 1965 (16 UST 1909; TIAS 5921; 578 UNTS 196)

SCIENTIFIC & TECHNICAL COOPERATION

Memorandum of understanding concerning scientific and technical cooperation in the earth sciences.
Signed at Taguig March 7, 2007.
Entered into force March 7, 2007.
TIAS 07-307

Agreement on scientific and technological cooperation, with annex.
Signed at Washington June 8, 2012.
Entered into force October 15, 2012.
TIAS 12-1015

SOCIAL SECURITY

Agreement providing for social security coverage for non-United States citizen employees of the United States armed forces in the Philippines.
Exchange of notes at Manila April 23, 1962, and August 30, 1963.
Entered into force August 30, 1963.
14 UST 1523; TIAS 5452; 489 UNTS 323

Agreement providing for social security coverage for non-United States citizen employees of the United States Employees Association, JUSMAG Officers Club, JUSMAG NCO Club, and the AID Employees' Recreation Association in the Philippines.
Exchange of notes at Manila August 30 and October 8, 1963.
Entered into force October 8, 1963.
14 UST 1523; TIAS 5452; 489 UNTS 332

Agreement providing for social security coverage for Philippine citizen civilian employees of the Agency for International Development Mission to the Philippines, with annex.
Exchange of notes at Manila November 12, 1964, and March 10, 1965.
Entered into force March 10, 1965.
20 UST 536; TIAS 6663; 706 UNTS 41

Agreement providing for social security coverage for Philippine citizen civilian employees of the Peace Corps and United States Joint Military Advisory Group (JUSMAG), with annex.
Exchange of notes at Manila April 5 and July 15, 1965.
Entered into force July 15, 1965.
20 UST 540; TIAS 6663; 706 UNTS 49

TAXATION

Convention with respect to taxes on income.*
Signed at Manila October 1, 1976.
Entered into force October 16, 1982.
34 UST 1277; TIAS 10417
Note:
* With reservations and understandings.

TELECOMMUNICATION

Agreement regarding radio broadcasting facilities with protocol and exchange of notes.
Signed at Manila May 6, 1963.
Entered into force May 6, 1963.
14 UST 741; TIAS 5353; 477 UNTS 67
Amendment:
September 10, 1965 (16 UST 1186; TIAS 5865; 595 UNTS 368)

Agreement relating to the reciprocal granting of authorizations to permit licensed amateur radio operators of either country to operate their stations in the other country.
Exchange of notes at Manila October 25, 1976.
Entered into force October 25, 1976.
27 UST 3985; TIAS 8415; 1059 UNTS 67

Agreement relating to radio communications between amateur stations on behalf of third parties, with attachment.
Exchange of notes at Manila February 13 and June 4, 1991.
Entered into force June 4, 1991.
TIAS 12431

TRADE & INVESTMENT

Agreement relating to extension of free-entry privileges to dependents of United States Government employees newly assigned to South Viet-Nam who elect to reside in the Philippines.
Exchange of notes at Manila May 14 and 28, 1965.
Entered into force May 28, 1965.
19 UST 7807; TIAS 6612; 713 UNTS 235

Agreement relating to customs regulations governing cargo consigned to United States military authorities or armed forces personnel, with annexes.
Exchange of notes at Manila April 24, 1969.
Entered into force May 4, 1969.
20 UST 2816; TIAS 6752; 723 UNTS 185

Understanding concerning a framework of principles and procedures and the establishment of a consultative mechanism for the expansion of trade and investment flows between the two countries.
Signed at Washington November 9, 1989.
Entered into force November 9, 1989.
NP

Memorandum of understanding concerning cooperation in trade in textile and apparel goods.
Signed at Kuala Lumpur August 23, 2006.
Entered into force August 23, 2006.
NP

Protocol to the November 9,1989 trade and investment framework agreement concerning customs administration and trade facilitation.
Signed at Honolulu November 13, 2011.
Entered into force November 13, 2011.
NP

TRANSPORTATION

Agreement, with memorandum of consultation, concerning air transport services, with exchanges of letters.
Exchange of notes at Washington September 16, 1982.
Entered into force September 16, 1982.
34 UST 1623; TIAS 10443; 2126 UNTS 297
Amendments:
May 29, 1987, and January 13, 1988 (TIAS 11564; 2185 UNTS 597)
November 20, 1995 (TIAS 12702)

WEAPONS

Agreement concerning cooperation in countering the proliferation of weapons of mass destruction, strengthening maritime security, and for other purposes.
Signed at Manila October 15 and 16, 2015.
Entered into force February 5, 2016.
TIAS 16-205

POLAND

ATOMIC ENERGY

Agreement to facilitate the provision of assistance for nuclear non-proliferation purposes.
Exchange of notes at Warsaw August 28 and September 8, 2009.
Entered into force September 8, 2009.
TIAS 09-908

Arrangement for the exchange of technical information and cooperation in nuclear safety matters, with addenda and annex.
Signed at Vienna September 28, 2016.
Entered into force September 28, 2016.
TIAS 16-928.1

CLAIMS & DISPUTE RESOLUTION

Treaty of arbitration.
Signed at Washington August 16, 1928.
Entered into force February 3, 1930.
46 Stat. 2438; TS 805; 11 Bevans 218; 99 LNTS 409

Treaty of conciliation.
Signed at Washington August 16, 1928.
Entered into force February 3, 1930.
46 Stat. 2442; TS 806; 11 Bevans 221; 99 LNTS 403

Agreement relating to settlement of claims of nationals of the United States against Poland and exchange of notes.
Signed at Washington July 16, 1960.
Entered into force July 16, 1960.
11 UST 1953; TIAS 4545; 384 UNTS 169

Protocol to the claims settlement agreement of July 16, 1960.
Signed at Warsaw November 29, 1960.
Entered into force November 29, 1960.
11 UST 2450; TIAS 4629; 401 UNTS 338

CONSULAR AFFAIRS

Agreement relating to the reciprocal waiver of visa fees for performing artists.*
Exchange of notes at Warsaw December 17, 1962, and January 21, 1963.
Entered into force January 21, 1963; operative February 1, 1963.
14 UST 118; TIAS 5279; 471 UNTS 151.

Note:

* The status of this agreement is under review.

CULTURAL EXCHANGES, PROPERTY & COOPERATION

Agreement concerning the program of the United States Peace Corps in Poland.
Signed at Warsaw February 23, 1990.
Entered into force February 23, 1990.
TIAS 12073

Cultural property agreement on the protection of certain cultural properties.
Signed at Washington May 11, 2004.
Entered into force August 3, 2010.
TIAS 10-803

DEFENSE

Agreement concerning provision of training related to defense articles under the United States International Military Education Training (IMET) Program.
Exchange of notes at Warsaw April 25 and June 6, 1991.
Entered into force June 6, 1991.
NP

Basic exchange and cooperative agreement for military topographic mapping, nautical and aeronautical charting, geodesy and geophysics, digital data and related MC&G materials.
Signed at Washington November 10, 1992.
Entered into force November 10, 1992.
NP

Agreement regarding grants under the Foreign Assistance Act of 1961, as amended, or successor legislation, and the furnishing of defense articles, related training, or other defense services from the United States to Hungary.
Exchange of notes at Warsaw February 10 and October 13, 1993.
Entered into force October 13, 1993.
TIAS

Memorandum of understanding on science and engineering cooperation, with annex.
Signed at Washington October 26, 1994.
Entered into force October 26, 1994.
TIAS 12576

Agreement concerning exchange of research and development information, with appendix (Master Information Exchange Agreement).
Signed at Warsaw June 9, 1995.
Entered into force June 9, 1995.
TIAS 12367

Amendment:

October 16 and 27, 2009 (TIAS 09-1027.1)

Agreement regarding the exchange of engineers and scientists.
Signed at Washington and Warsaw July 21 and 31, 2006.
Entered into force July 31, 2006.
NP

Memorandum of arrangement regarding assignment of liaison officers, with annex.
Signed September 22, 2006.
Entered into force September 22, 2006.
NP

Agreement concerning security measures for the protection of classified information in the military sphere.
Signed at Warsaw March 8, 2007.
Entered into force October 9, 2007.
TIAS 07-1009

Memorandum of understanding regarding reciprocal government quality assurance services.
Signed at Warsaw and Washington May 31 and June 22, 2007.
Entered into force June 22, 2007.
TIAS 07-622.1

Agreement on the status of armed forces of the United States of America in the territory of the Republic of Poland.
Signed at Warsaw December 11, 2009.
Entered into force March 31, 2010.
TIAS 10-331

Agreement concerning cooperation on information assurance (IA) and computer network defense (CND).
Signed at Warsaw June 21, 2010.
Entered into force June 21, 2010.
TIAS 10-621.1

Memorandum of understanding regarding the exchange of military personnel, with annexes.
Signed at Warsaw May 30, 2012.
Entered into force May 30, 2012.
NP

Acquisition and cross-servicing agreement, with annexes.
Signed at Warsaw and Stuttgart November 28 and December 3, 2012.
Entered into force December 3, 2012.
TIAS 12-1203.

Agreement concerning cooperation.
Exchange of notes at Warsaw June 22 and July 15, 2015.
Entered into force July 15, 2015.
TIAS 15-715

DIPLOMATIC & CONSULAR RELATIONS

Agreement relating to reciprocal customs privileges for foreign service personnel.
Exchange of notes at Warsaw October 5 and 30, 1945.
Entered into force October 30, 1945.
61 Stat. 2297; TIAS 1544; 11 Bevans 283; 15 UNTS 225

Consular convention, with protocols and exchanges of notes.
Signed at Warsaw May 31, 1972.
Entered into force July 6, 1973.
24 UST 1231; TIAS 7642

EDUCATION

Agreement for the establishment of the U.S.-Polish Fulbright Commission.
Signed at Warsaw October 20, 1995.
Entered into force May 31, 1996.
TIAS 96-531
Extension:
October 28 and November 25, 2005 (TIAS 96-531)

Agreement on cooperation within the framework of the U.S.-Polish Fulbright Commission.
Signed at Washington March 10, 2008.
Entered into force November 13, 2008.
TIAS 08-1113

EMPLOYMENT

Agreement relating to the employment of dependents of official government employees, with annex.
Exchange of notes at Warsaw April 30 and May 16, 1991.
Entered into force May 16, 1991.
TIAS 12430

ENVIRONMENT & CONSERVATION

Agreement for cooperation in the Global Learning and Observations to Benefit the Environment (GLOBE) Program, with appendices.
Signed at Warsaw April 22, 1997.
Entered into force April 22, 1997.
TIAS

FINANCE

Agreement relating to the funding of the indebtedness of Poland to the United States.
Signed at Washington November 14, 1924.
Operative December 15, 1922.
Treasury Department print; 11 Bevans 195; 58 LNTS 97

Agreement modifying the debt funding agreement of November 14, 1924.
Signed at Washington June 10, 1932.
Operative July 1, 1931.
Treasury Department print; 11 Bevans 260

Agreement establishing a procedure for funding international travel and transportation and other travel-related expenses from U.S.-owned zlotys in Poland.
Exchange of notes at Washington October 7, 1972.
Entered into force October 7, 1972; effective January 1, 1973.
24 UST 426; TIAS 7557

Agreement regarding the consolidation and rescheduling of certain debts owed to, guaranteed by or assured by the United States Government and its agencies, with annexes.
Signed at Warsaw August 27, 1981.
Entered into force October 20, 1981.
33 UST 3727; TIAS 10255; 1541 UNTS 85

Agreement regarding the consolidation and rescheduling of certain debts owed to, guaranteed by or insured by the United States Government and its agencies.
Signed at Warsaw July 29, 1986.
Entered into force September 8, 1986.
NP

Agreement regarding the consolidation and rescheduling of certain debts for 1985, owed to, guaranteed by, or insured by the United States Government and its agencies, with annexes.
Signed at Warsaw July 10, 1989.
Entered into force September 6, 1989.
NP

Agreement regarding the consolidation and rescheduling of certain debts for 1987, owed to, guaranteed by, or insured by the United States Government and its agencies, with annexes.
Signed at Warsaw July 10, 1989.
Entered into force September 6, 1989.
NP

Investment guaranty agreement.
Signed at Warsaw October 13, 1989.
Entered into force February 21, 1990.
TIAS 12039

Swap agreement among the United States Treasury and the Narodowy Bank Polski/Government of Poland, with memorandum of understanding.
Signed at Washington and Poland December 22, 1989.
Entered into force December 22, 1989.
TIAS

Agreement regarding the consolidation and rescheduling of certain debts owed to, guaranteed by, or insured by the United States Government and its agencies, with annexes.
Signed at Warsaw August 24, 1990.
Entered into force October 22, 1990.
NP

Agreement regarding the reduction and reorganization of certain debts owed to, guaranteed by, or insured by the Government of the United States and its agencies, with annexes.
Signed at Warsaw July 17, 1991.
Entered into force September 3, 1991.
NP

FOREIGN ASSISTANCE

Agreement providing for an informational media guaranty program.
Exchange of notes at Warsaw February 12, 1958.
Entered into force February 12, 1958.
9 UST 253; TIAS 3999; 304 UNTS 287

HEALTH AND MEDICAL COOPERATION

Agreement on cooperation in the field of health.
Signed at Washington October 8, 1974.
Entered into force October 8, 1974.
25 UST 2750; TIAS 7943

LAW ENFORCEMENT

Convention to aid in the prevention of smuggling of alcoholic beverages into the United States.
Signed at Washington June 19, 1930.
Entered into force August 2, 1930.
46 Stat. 2773; TS 821; 11 Bevans 233; 108 LNTS 323

Arrangement for the direct exchange of certain information regarding the traffic in narcotic drugs.
Exchange of notes at Warsaw August 17 and September 17, 1931.
Entered into force September 17, 1931.
11 Bevans 257

Agreement regarding cooperation and mutual assistance between customs services.
Signed at Warsaw August 8, 1990.
Entered into force May 15, 1991.
TIAS 12077

Extradition treaty.
Signed at Washington July 10, 1996.
Entered into force September 17, 1999.
TIAS 99-917

Treaty on mutual legal assistance in criminal matters, with forms.
Done at Washington July 10, 1996.
Entered into force September 17, 1999.
TIAS 99-917.1

Agreement on the application of the extradition treaty of July 10, 1996, pursuant to Article 3(2) of the agreement on extradition between the United States of America and the European Union signed on June 25, 2003, with annex.
Signed at Warsaw June 9, 2006.
Entered into force February 1, 2010.
TIAS 10-201.17

Agreement on the application of the treaty on mutual legal assistance in criminal matters of July 10, 1996, pursuant to Article 3(2) of the agreement on mutual legal assistance between the United States of America and the European Union signed on June 25, 2003, with annex.
Signed at Warsaw June 9, 2006.
Entered into force February 1, 2010.
TIAS

MARITIME MATTERS

Agreement relating to the mutual recognition of ship measurement certificates.
Exchanges of notes at Washington January 17, March 14, and April 22, 1930, and October 5, 1934.
Operative April 22, 1930.
49 Stat. 3663; EAS 71; 11 Bevans 229; 156 LNTS 91

Agreement relating to jurisdiction over vessels utilizing the Louisiana Offshore Oil Port.
Exchange of notes at Washington March 30 and April 10, 1984.
Entered into force April 10, 1984.
TIAS; 2174 UNTS 199

NONPROLIFERATION

Agreement concerning cooperation in the area of countering the proliferation of nuclear materials and technologies.
Signed at Warsaw September 11, 2009.
Entered into force September 11, 2009.
TIAS 09-911

POSTAL MATTERS

Convention concerning the exchange of parcel post.
Signed at Warsaw February 19 and at Washington April 26, 1923.
Entered into force April 1, 1923.
43 Stat. 1640; Post Office Department print

International express mail agreement, with detailed regulations.
Signed at Washington December 11, 1989.
Entered into force February 1, 1990.
TIAS 11720

PROPERTY

Preliminary agreement regarding principles applying to mutual aid in the prosecution of the war against aggression.
Signed at Washington July 1, 1942.
Entered into force July 1, 1942.
56 Stat. 1542; EAS 257; 11 Bevans 274; 103 UNTS 267

Agreement on the settlement for lend-lease and certain claims.
Signed at Washington June 28, 1956.
Entered into force June 28, 1956.
7 UST 1930; TIAS 3594; 273 UNTS 79

PUBLICATIONS

Agreement relating to the distribution in Poland of a Polish-language magazine on life in the United States.
Exchange of notes at Warsaw May 30, 1958.
Entered into force May 30, 1958.
9 UST 601; TIAS 4040; 315 UNTS 231

SCIENTIFIC & TECHNICAL COOPERATION

Agreement for scientific and technical cooperation, with annexes.
Signed at Washington February 10, 2006.
Entered into force November 22, 2006.
TIAS 06-1122

Memorandum of understanding concerning scientific and technical cooperation in the earth sciences.
Signed at Warsaw March 16, 2016.
Entered into force March 16, 2016.
TIAS 16-316

SOCIAL SECURITY

Agreement concerning the United States Government participation in the Polish social insurance system for Polish national employees of the United States Government in Poland.
Exchange of notes at Warsaw June 15 and September 30, 1971.
Entered into force September 30, 1971.
22 UST 1725; TIAS 7200

Social security agreement, with administrative arrangement.
Signed at Warsaw April 2, 2008.
Entered into force March 1, 2009.
TIAS 09-301

TAXATION

Convention for the avoidance of double taxation and the prevention of fiscal evasion with respect to taxes on income, with related notes.
Signed at Washington October 8, 1974.
Entered into force July 22, 1976.
28 UST 891; TIAS 8486

TRADE & INVESTMENT

Agreement relating to economic and financial cooperation.
Exchange of notes at Washington April 24, 1946.
Entered into force April 24, 1946.
60 Stat. 1609; TIAS 1516; 11 Bevans 286; 4 UNTS 155

Joint statement on the development of agricultural trade.
Signed at Washington October 8, 1974.
Entered into force October 8, 1974.
25 UST 2763; TIAS 7944

Treaty concerning business and economic relations, with annex, protocol and related exchanges of letters.
Signed at Washington March 21, 1990.
Entered into force August 6, 1994.
TIAS

Additional protocol to the treaty concerning business and economic relations done at Washington on March 21, 1990.
Signed at Brussels January 12, 2004.
Entered into force August 20, 2004.
TIAS

TRANSPORTATION

Memorandum of understanding concerning research cooperation in the field of transportation.
Signed at Warsaw November 3, 1971.
Entered into force November 3, 1971.
29 UST 5642; TIAS 9139; 1152 UNTS 19

Extension and Amendments:
October 16, 1978 (29 UST 5649; TIAS 9139; 1152 UNTS 22)
February 28 and June 22, 1979 (30 UST 7287; TIAS 9586; 1182 UNTS 401)

Agreement relating to the acceptance of airworthiness certifications, with annex.
Exchange of notes at Washington November 8, 1976.
Entered into force November 8, 1976.
27 UST 3882; TIAS 8407; 1059 UNTS 179

Amendments:
January 28, 1980 (32 UST 529; TIAS 9723; 1221 UNTS 342)
September 5, 2003, and February 9, 2004 (TIAS 04-209)

Memorandum of agreement concerning assistance in developing and modernizing Poland's civil aviation infrastructure.
Signed at Washington and Warsaw January 5 and 14, 1998.
Entered into force January 14, 1998.
NP

Air transport agreement, with annexes.*
Signed at Warsaw June 16, 2001.
Entered into force September 15, 2003.
TIAS 13155
Note
* This agreement is suspended for the duration of provisional application of the U.S. – E.U. Air Transport Agreement signed April 25 and 30, 2007.

WEAPONS

Agreement concerning the deployment of ground-based ballistic missile defense interceptors in the territory of the Republic of Poland, with annex.
Signed at Warsaw August 20, 2008.
Entered into force September 15, 2011.
TIAS 11-915
Amendment:
July 3, 2010 (TIAS 11-915)

PORTUGAL

CLAIMS & DISPUTE RESOLUTION

Treaty for the advancement of peace.
Signed at Lisbon February 4, 1914.
Entered into force October 24, 1914.
38 Stat. 1847; TS 600; 11 Bevans 331

Arbitration treaty.
Signed at Washington March 1, 1929.
Entered into force October 31, 1929.
46 Stat. 2421; TS 803; 11 Bevans 344; 99 LNTS 375

CONSULAR AFFAIRS

Agreement relating to reciprocal facilitation of visa issuance.*
Exchange of notes at Lisbon June 7, 1983.
Entered into force July 7, 1983.
TIAS 10723; 1607 UNTS 139
Note:
* The status of this agreement is under review.

CULTURAL EXCHANGES, PROPERTY & COOPERATION

Protocol relating to exchanges in the field of physical education and sports.
Signed at Lisbon December 22, 1976.
Entered into force December 22, 1976.
28 UST 5342; TIAS 8637

DEFENSE

Mutual defense assistance agreement.
Signed at Lisbon January 5, 1951.
Entered into force January 5, 1951.
2 UST 438; TIAS 2187; 133 UNTS 75

Agreement relating to the assurances required by the Mutual Security Act of 1951.
Exchange of notes at Lisbon January 8, 1952.
Entered into force January 8, 1952.
3 UST 4648; TIAS 2618; 207 UNTS 51

Agreement relating to the disposition of equipment and material furnished by the United States under the mutual defense assistance agreement of January 5, 1951, found surplus to the needs of the armed forces of Portugal.
Exchange of notes at Lisbon June 16 and July 9, 1952.
Entered into force July 9, 1952.
3 UST 4979; TIAS 2674; 180 UNTS 251
Amendment:
September 15, 1960 (11 UST 2202; TIAS 4590; 393 UNTS 315)

Agreement relating to a weapons production program.
Exchange of notes at Lisbon September 26, 1960.
Entered into force September 26, 1960.
11 UST 2218; TIAS 4594; 393 UNTS 257

Agreement relating to the deposit by Portugal of ten percent of the value of grant military assistance and excess defense articles furnished by the United States.
Exchange of notes at Lisbon March 16 and May 2, 1972.
Entered into force May 2, 1972; effective February 7, 1972.
23 UST 881; TIAS 7349

Agreement relating to payment to the United States of net proceeds from the sale of defense articles furnished under the military assistance program.
Exchange of notes at Lisbon May 30, 1974, and June 30, 1975.
Entered into force June 30, 1975; effective July 1, 1974.
26 UST 1004; TIAS 8087
Amendment:
December 19, 2004, and January 19, 2005

Memorandum of understanding concerning the principles governing mutual cooperation in the research, development, production, procurement and logistic support of defense equipment.
Signed at Lisbon and Washington December 18, 1978, and March 28, 1979.
Entered into force March 28, 1979.
30 UST 3892; TIAS 9433; 1171 UNTS 221

Agreement concerning the grant of defense articles and services under the military assistance program.
Exchange of notes at Lisbon August 14 and 27, 1979.
Entered into force August 27, 1979.
30 UST 7555; TIAS 9599; 1205 UNTS 3
Amendment:
August 16 and September 29, 1982 (TIAS 10503)

Agreement concerning the grant of defense articles and services under the military assistance program.
Exchange of notes at Lisbon August 12 and 28, 1980.
Entered into force August 28, 1980.
32 UST 2388; TIAS 9846; 1275 UNTS 3
Amendment:
August 16 and September 29, 1982 (TIAS 10503)

Agreement concerning the grant of defense articles and services under the military assistance program.
Exchange of notes at Lisbon August 24 and 28, 1981.
Entered into force August 28, 1981.
33 UST 3702; TIAS 10252; 1541 UNTS 105
Amendment:
August 16 and September 29, 1982 (TIAS 10503)

Agreement concerning general security of military information.
Exchange of notes at Lisbon August 19 and September 10, 1982.
Entered into force September 10, 1982.
TIAS 11060; 2039 UNTS 199

Agreement concerning the installation in Portugal of a ground-based electro-optical deep space surveillance (GEODSS) station.
Exchange of notes at Lisbon March 27, 1984.
Entered into force March 27, 1984.
35 UST 4885; TIAS 10973; 2019 UNTS 159

Agreement on cooperation and defense, with supplemental technical and labor agreements and exchange of notes.
Signed at Lisbon June 1, 1995.
Entered into force November 21, 1995.
TIAS

Basic exchange and cooperative agreement concerning mapping, charting and geodesy cooperation, with annexes.
Signed at Fairfax and Lisbon July 30, 1997.
Entered into force July 30, 1997.
NP

Memorandum of understanding regarding assignment of foreign liaison officers, with annex.
Signed April 26 and May 2, 2007.
Entered into force May 2, 2007.
NP
Amendment:
April 20 and May 2, 2012

Acquisition and cross-servicing agreement, with annexes.
Signed at Lisbon and Stuttgart October 30 and December 8, 2009.
Entered into force December 8, 2009.
NP

Technical arrangement regarding the assignment of liaison officers, with annexes.
Signed September 21 and December 3, 2015.
Entered into force December 3, 2015.
NP

Memorandum of agreement establishing a midshipmen/cadet exchange program, with appendix and annex.
Signed at Lisbon and Annapolis February 16 and 24, 2016.
Entered into force February 24, 2016.
NP

EDUCATION

Agreement concerning the continuation of the Commission for Educational Exchange.
Signed at Lisbon February 11, 2015.
Entered into force July 13, 2015.
TIAS 15-713

EMPLOYMENT

Agreement on gainful activities of the dependents of members of diplomatic missions and consular posts assigned to official duty.
Exchange of notes at Lisbon September 23 and October 10, 2013.
Entered into force February 20, 2014.
TIAS 14-220

FINANCE

Agreement relating to guaranties authorized under Section 111 (b)(3) of the Economic Cooperation Act of 1948, as amended.
Exchange of notes at Washington May 22 and 25, 1953.
Entered into force May 26, 1953.
4 UST 1596; TIAS 2826; 212 UNTS 290

Agreement relating to resumption of the investment guaranty program and interpretation of the agreement of May 22 and 25, 1953.
Exchange of notes at Lisbon October 31 and November 10, 1977.
Entered into force November 10, 1977.
29 UST 2792; TIAS 8977

FOREIGN ASSISTANCE

Economic cooperation agreement.*
Signed at Lisbon September 28, 1948.
Entered into force September 28, 1948.
62 Stat. 2856; TIAS 1819; 11 Bevans 370; 29 UNTS 213
Amendments:
February 14, 1950 (1 UST 169; TIAS 2033; 79 UNTS 310)
May 17, 1951 (2 UST 1298; TIAS 2279; 134 UNTS 370)
March 9 and 18, 1953 (4 UST 1437; TIAS 2801; 207 UNTS 320)

Note:
* Applicable to all Portuguese territories.

Agreement relating to the provision of economic assistance to Portugal, with related letter.
Exchange of letters at Brussels December 9, 1971.
Entered into force December 9, 1971.
23 UST 264; TIAS 7303

INTELLECTUAL PROPERTY

Agreement to facilitate interchange of patent rights and technical information for defense purposes.
Signed at Lisbon October 31, 1960.
Entered into force October 31, 1960.
11 UST 2314; TIAS 4608; 394 UNTS 127

LAW ENFORCEMENT

Extradition convention and exchange of notes concerning the death penalty.*
Signed at Washington May 7, 1908.
Entered into force November 14, 1908.
35 Stat. 2071; TS 512; 11 Bevans 314
Note:
* Applicable to all territories.

Arrangement for the direct exchange of certain information regarding the traffic in narcotic drugs.
Exchange of notes at Lisbon February 11, 1928, and February 22, 1929.
Entered into force February 22, 1929.
11 Bevans 341

Agreement regarding mutual assistance between customs services.
Signed at Washington September 15, 1994.
Entered into force June 20, 1996.
TIAS 12565

Instrument as contemplated by Article 3(2) of the agreement on extradition between the United States of America and the European Union signed June 25, 2003, with annex.
Signed at Washington July 14, 2005.
Entered into force February 1, 2010.
TIAS 10-201.18

Instrument as contemplated by Article 3(3) of the agreement on mutual legal assistance between the United States of America and the European Union signed June 25, 2003, with annex.
Signed at Washington July 14, 2005.
Entered into force February 1, 2010.
TIAS 10-201.43.

Agreement on enhancing cooperation in preventing and combating crime.
Signed at Lisbon June 30, 2009.
Entered into force November 29, 2011.
TIAS 11-1129

MARITIME MATTERS

Agreement relating to jurisdiction over vessels utilizing the Louisiana Offshore Oil Port.
Exchange of notes at Washington June 22 and July 11, 1979.
Entered into force July 11, 1979.
30 UST 5931; TIAS 9526; 1179 UNTS 125

POSTAL MATTERS

Parcel post agreement and regulations of execution.*
Signed at Lisbon January 12, 1959, and at Washington February 27, 1959.
Entered into force May 1, 1959.
10 UST 801; TIAS 4220; 343 UNTS 49
Note:
* Applicable to Puerto Rico, the Virgin Islands, Guam, Samoa, the Azores and Madeira Archipelagoes.

International express mail agreement, with detailed regulations.
Signed at Washington and Lisbon November 20 and December 21, 1984.
Entered into force January 15, 1985.
TIAS 11013; 2022 UNTS 93

Memorandum of understanding concerning the operation of the INTELPOST field trial, with details of implementation.
Signed at Lisbon and Washington April 15 and July 3, 1985.
Entered into force August 1, 1985.
TIAS 11243

PRIVATE INTERNATIONAL LAW

Agreement for the recovery of maintenance.
Signed at Lisbon May 30, 2000.
Entered into force March 17, 2001.
TIAS 13096

SOCIAL SECURITY

Agreement on social security, with administrative arrangement.
Signed at Lisbon March 30, 1988.
Entered into force August 1, 1989.
TIAS 12121

TAXATION

Convention for the avoidance of double taxation and the prevention of fiscal evasion with respect to taxes on income, with protocol.
Signed at Washington September 6, 1994.
Entered into force December 18, 1995.
TIAS

Agreement to improve international tax compliance and to implement the Foreign Account Tax Compliance Act, with annexes.
Signed at Lisbon August 6, 2015.
Entered into force August 10, 2016.
TIAS 16-810

TELECOMMUNICATION

Agreement relating to the reciprocal granting of authorizations to permit licensed amateur radio operators of either country to operate their stations in the other country.
Exchange of notes at Lisbon May 17 and 26, 1965.
Entered into force May 26, 1965.
16 UST 817; TIAS 5815; 546 UNTS 189

Agreement relating to the continuation of international broadcast activities carried out in Portugal by RARET.
Exchange of notes at Lisbon February 15, 1977.
Entered into force February 15, 1977.
29 UST 660; TIAS 8844

TRADE & INVESTMENT

Commercial arrangement.
Exchange of notes at Washington June 28, 1910.
Entered into force June 28, 1910.
TS 514 1/2; 11 Bevans 324

Agreement terminating the agreement of November 17, 1970 (TIAS 6980), relating to trade in cotton textiles and providing for consultations on problems of market disruption from exports of cotton, wool and man-made fiber textiles and apparel products from Portugal.
Exchange of notes at Washington August 20, 1975.
Entered into force August 20, 1975.
26 UST 2713; TIAS 8187; 1052 UNTS 291

TRANSPORTATION

Memorandum of agreement concerning provision of site test and commissioning and/or periodic flight checks of Portuguese Civil Aviation Administration air navigation aids.
Signed at Washington and Lisbon March 10 and April 13, 1978.
Entered into force April 13, 1978; effective April 1, 1978.
30 UST 293; TIAS 9201

Memorandum of agreement concerning the provision of assistance in developing and modernizing Portugal's civil aviation infrastructure.
Signed at Washington and Lisbon July 30, 1998.
Entered into force July 30, 1998.
NP

Air transport agreement, with annexes.*
Signed at Lisbon May 30, 2000.
Entered into force May 9, 2002.
TIAS 13101

Note:

* This agreement is suspended for the duration of provisional application of the U.S. – E.U. Air Transport Agreement signed April 25 and 30, 2007.

PREPARATORY COMMISSION FOR THE COMPREHENSIVE NUCLEAR-TEST-BAN TREATY ORGANIZATION

TAXATION

Tax reimbursement agreement, with annex.
Signed at Washington October 21, 1998.
Entered into force October 21, 1998.
TIAS 12987

QATAR

DEFENSE

Agreement concerning security measures for the protection of classified military information, with appendix.
Signed July 17, 2012.
Entered into force August 15, 2012.
TIAS 12-815

Basic exchange and cooperation agreement concerning geospatial intelligence, with implementing annexes.
Signed at Springfield and Doha April 3 and 10, 2013.
Entered into force April 10, 2013.
NP

Acquisition and cross-servicing agreement.
Signed at Doha and Tampa December 9 and 19, 2013.
Entered into force December 19, 2013.
NP

ENVIRONMENT & CONSERVATION

Agreement concerning cooperation in the Global Learning and Observations to Benefits the Environment (GLOBE) Program, with appendices.
Signed at Doha September 27, 2000.
Entered into force September 27, 2000.

FINANCE

Investment incentive agreement.
Exchange of notes at Doha March 28, 1987.
Entered into force April 1, 1987.
TIAS

POSTAL MATTERS

International express mail agreement, with detailed regulations.
Signed at Doha and Washington January 19 and February 14, 1983.
Entered into force June 1, 1983.
TIAS 10661; 2001 UNTS 33

Memorandum of understanding concerning the operation of the INTELPOST field trial, with details of implementation.
Signed at Doha and Washington August 12 and September 13, 1985.
Entered into force September 13, 1985.
TIAS 11156

TAXATION

Agreement to improve international tax compliance and to implement the Foreign Account Tax Compliance Act, with annexes.
Signed at Doha January 7, 2015.
Entered into force June 23, 2015.
TIAS 15-623

TRANSPORTATION

Agreement on the security of civil aviation.
Signed at Doha June 27, 1994.
Entered into force June 30, 1994.
NP

Memorandum of agreement for assistance in developing and modernizing the civil aviation infrastructure of Qatar.
Signed May 10 and August 5, 2004.
Entered into force August 5, 2004.
NP

ROMANIA

AGRICULTURE

Protocol on cooperation in agriculture.
Signed at Washington September 11, 1975.
Entered into force September 11, 1975.
26 UST 2486; TIAS 8166; 1028 UNTS 3

ARMS CONTROL

Agreement concerning the continued operation of a seismic monitoring station in Romania.
Signed at Bucharest February 23, 2012.
Entered into force January 28, 2013.
TIAS 13-128.1

ATOMIC ENERGY

Agreement clarifying certain understandings relating to the supply of enriched uranium to Romania for the TRIGA reactor.
Exchange of notes at Washington February 13, 1978.
Entered into force February 13, 1978.
29 UST 2961; TIAS 8992; 1120 UNTS 97

Agreement for cooperation in the prevention of illicit trafficking in nuclear and other radioactive material.
Signed at Bucharest September 15, 2008.
Entered into force September 15, 2008.
TIAS 08-915.1

Arrangement for the exchange of technical information and cooperation in nuclear safety matters.
Signed at Vienna April 4, 2011.
Entered into force October 19, 2011.
TIAS 11-1019

CLAIMS & DISPUTE RESOLUTION

Treaty of arbitration.
Signed at Washington March 21, 1929.
Entered into force July 22, 1929.
46 Stat. 2336; TS 794; 11 Bevans 408; 105 LNTS 79

Treaty of conciliation.
Signed at Washington March 21, 1929.
Entered into force July 22, 1929.
46 Stat. 2339; TS 795; 11 Bevans 411; 105 LNTS 85

CONSULAR AFFAIRS

Agreement relating to the issuance of visas to diplomatic and non-diplomatic personnel.
Exchange of notes at Bucharest April 20, May 14 and 26, 1962.
Entered into force May 26, 1962; operative June 1, 1962.
13 UST 1192; TIAS 5063; 456 UNTS 265
Amendment:
May 31 and June 17, 1967 (18 UST 1266; TIAS 6279; 685 UNTS 404)

Agreement relating to reciprocal simplification of procedures for issuance of diplomatic and official visas.
Exchange of notes at Bucharest September 12 and October 10, 1977.
Entered into force October 10, 1977.
29 UST 2765; TIAS 8970

Agreement relating to reciprocal facilitation of visa issuance.
Exchange of notes at Bucharest September 1 and October 10, 1977.
Entered into force October 10, 1977.
29 UST 4705; TIAS 9075; 1134 UNTS 209

CULTURAL EXCHANGES, PROPERTY & COOPERATION

Agreement relating to war graves registration and associated matters.
Exchange of notes at Bucharest June 19 and 28, 1946.
Entered into force June 28, 1946.
61 Stat. 4042; TIAS 1796; 11 Bevans 428; 148 UNTS 355

Understanding regarding the establishment and operation in the United States and Romania of an American and a Romanian library, respectively.
Signed at Bucharest August 3, 1969.
Entered into force August 3, 1969.
20 UST 2712; TIAS 6733; 720 UNTS 91

Agreement on cooperation and exchanges in the cultural, educational, scientific and technological fields.
Signed at Bucharest December 13, 1974.
Entered into force January 1, 1975.
26 UST 31; TIAS 8006

Agreement concerning the program of the United States Peace Corps in Romania.
Signed at Washington January 24, 1992.
Entered into force January 24, 1992.
TIAS 12080

Agreement for the protection and preservation of certain cultural properties.
Signed at Bucharest July 8, 1992.
Entered into force provisionally, July 8, 1992; definitively, July 29, 1993.
TIAS 12136

DEFENSE

Agreement concerning the provision of training related to defense articles under the United States International Military Education and Training (IMET) program.
Exchange of notes at Bucharest November 23 and December 7, 1992.
Entered into force December 7, 1992.
NP

Agreement concerning military assistance under the United States Foreign Assistance Act of 1961, as amended, and the furnishing of defense articles, related training, and other defense services from the United States to Romania.
Exchange of notes at Bucharest October 3, 1994, and March 31, 1995.
Entered into force March 31, 1995.
NP

Agreement regarding the status of United States forces in Romania.
Signed at Washington October 30, 2001.
Entered into force June 10, 2002.
TIAS 13170

Memorandum of understanding concerning training conducted in Romania by the United States Marine Corps.
Signed at Stuttgart June 12, 2002.
Entered into force June 12, 2002.
NP

Agreement concerning measures for the protection of classified military information.
Signed at Washington June 21, 1995.
Entered into force September 25, 2003.
TIAS 03-925
Amendment:
December 14, 2011 (TIAS 03-925)

Agreement regarding the activities of United States forces located on the territory of Romania, with annexes.
Signed at Bucharest December 6, 2005.
Entered into force July 21, 2006.
TIAS 06-721

Agreement concerning health care for military members and their dependents.
Signed September 6, 2012.
Entered into force February 22, 2013.
NP
Extension:
March 14 and 17 (NP)

Acquisition and cross-servicing agreement, with annexes.
Signed at Bucharest and Stuttgart November 28 and December 5, 2012.
Entered into force January 23, 2014.
NP

DIPLOMATIC & CONSULAR RELATIONS

Consular convention with protocol.
Signed at Bucharest July 5, 1972.
Entered into force July 6, 1973.
24 UST 1317; TIAS 7643

Joint statement concerning relations between the United States and Romania.
Signed at Washington December 5, 1973.
Entered into force December 5, 1973.
24 UST 2257; TIAS 7746; 938 UNTS 457

EDUCATION

Agreement concerning educational and scholarly exchanges administered by the Romanian-U.S. Fulbright Commission.
Signed at Bucharest October 26, 2000.
Entered into force March 14, 2002.
TIAS 02-314

EMPLOYMENT

Agreement relating to the employment of dependents of official government employees.
Exchange of notes at Washington July 1 and 28, 1993.
Entered into force July 28, 1993.
TIAS 12159

ENVIRONMENT & CONSERVATION

Agreement for cooperation in the Global Learning and Observations to Benefit the Environment (GLOBE) Program, with appendices.
Signed at Bucharest and Washington April 11 and May 22, 1995.
Entered into force May 22, 1995.
TIAS 12653

FINANCE

Agreement relating to the funding of the debt of Romania to the United States.
Signed at Washington December 4, 1925.
Operative June 15, 1925.
Treasury Department print; 11 Bevans 398

Agreement modifying the debt funding agreement of December 4, 1925.
Signed at Washington June 11, 1932.
Operative July 1, 1931.
Treasury Department print; 11 Bevans 420

Agreement relating to investment guaranties.
Exchange of notes at Bucharest April 28, 1973.
Entered into force April 28, 1973.
24 UST 1073; TIAS 7627

Agreement regarding the consolidation and rescheduling of certain debts owed to, guaranteed or insured by the United States Government and its agencies, with annexes.
Signed at Bucharest March 10, 1983.
Entered into force April 22, 1983.
TIAS 10683

Agreement regarding the consolidation and rescheduling of certain debts owed to, guaranteed or insured by the United States Government and its agencies, with annexes.
Signed at Bucharest February 15, 1984.
Entered into force April 16, 1984.
35 UST 4563; TIAS 10957

Swap agreement among the United States Treasury, the National Bank of Romania/ Government of Romania, with memorandum of understanding.
Signed at Washington and Bucharest March 6, 1991.
Entered into force March 6, 1991.
TIAS

Investment incentive agreement.
Signed at Bucharest June 30, 1992.
Entered into force December 4, 1992.
TIAS 12464

FOREIGN ASSISTANCE

Joint statement on economic, industrial and technological cooperation.
Issued at Washington December 5, 1973.
26 UST 2342; TIAS 8159

Long term agreement on economic, industrial and technical cooperation, with annexes.
Signed at Bucharest November 21, 1976.
Entered into force May 5, 1977.
28 UST 5228; TIAS 8624; 1087 UNTS 119

INTELLECTUAL PROPERTY

Convention for the reciprocal protection of trade-marks.
Signed at Bucharest March 18/31, 1906.
Entered into force June 25, 1906.
34 Stat. 2901; TS 451; 11 Bevans 389

LAW ENFORCEMENT

Arrangement for the direct exchange of certain information regarding the traffic in narcotic drugs.
Exchange of notes at Bucharest February 4, 1928, and April 17, 1929.
Entered into force April 17, 1929.
11 Bevans 414

Agreement regarding mutual assistance between their customs administrations.
Signed at Washington July 16, 1998.
Entered into force June 1, 1999.
TIAS 12976

Treaty on mutual legal assistance in criminal matters.
Signed at Washington May 26, 1999.
Entered into force October 17, 2001.
TIAS 13037

Extradition treaty.
Signed at Bucharest September 10, 2007.
Entered into force May 8, 2009.
TIAS 09-508

Protocol to the treaty on mutual legal assistance in criminal matters of May 26, 1999.
Signed at Bucharest September 10, 2007.
Entered into force February 1, 2010.
TIAS 10-201.44

POSTAL MATTERS

Agreement concerning the exchange of parcel post, and regulations of execution.
Signed at Washington August 10, 1937, and at Bucharest March 12, 1937.
Entered into force September 1, 1937.
50 Stat. 1630; Post Office Department print; 183 LNTS 7

Parcel post agreement, with detailed regulations.
Signed at Washington June 19, 1981.
Entered into force July 19, 1981.
NP

International express mail agreement, with detailed regulations.
Signed at Washington December 14, 1989.
Entered into force February 15, 1990.
TIAS 11718

SCIENTIFIC & TECHNICAL COOPERATION

Agreement on cooperation in science and technology, with annexes.
Signed at Washington July 15, 1998.
Entered into force April 5, 2000.
TIAS 12975

TAXATION

Convention with respect to taxes on income.
Signed at Washington December 4, 1973.
Entered into force February 26, 1976; effective January 1, 1974.
27 UST 165; TIAS 8228

Agreement to improve international tax compliance and to implement the Foreign Account Tax Compliance Act, with annexes.
Signed at Bucharest May 28, 2015.
Entered into force November 3, 2015.
TIAS 15-1103

TRADE & INVESTMENT

Agreement on trade relations, with related exchanges of letters.
Signed at Bucharest April 3, 1992.
Entered into force November 8, 1993.
TIAS

Treaty concerning the reciprocal encouragement and protection of investment, with annex, protocol and related letter.
Signed at Bucharest May 28, 1992.
Entered into force January 15, 1994.
TIAS

Additional protocol to the treaty between the United States of America and Romania concerning the reciprocal encouragement and protection of investment of May 28, 1992.
Signed at Brussels September 22, 2003.
Entered into force February 9, 2007.
TIAS

TRANSPORTATION

Air transport agreement, with annexes.*
Signed at Washington July 15, 1998.
Entered into force August 19, 1999.
TIAS 12974

Note:

* This agreement is suspended for the duration of pro-visional application of the U.S. – E.U. Air Transport Agreement signed April 25 and 30, 2007.

Agreement for promotion of aviation safety.
Signed at Bucharest September 10, 2002.
Entered into force October 18, 2004.
TIAS 04-1018

WEAPONS

Agreement concerning cooperation in the area of counterproliferation of weapons of mass destruction, and the promotion of defense and military relations.
Signed at Washington March 30, 1998.
Entered into force July 8, 2003.
TIAS 03-708.1

Amendments and Extensions:
January 16 and June 14, 2004 (TIAS 03-708.1)
July 7 and November 2, 2010 (TIAS 03-708.1)
July 5, 2012 (TIAS 03-708.1)

Agreement concerning cooperation in the area of countering the proliferation of nuclear materials and technologies.
Signed at New York July 19, 2004.
Entered into force July 19, 2004.
TIAS 04-719

Amendment:
December 3, 2008 (TIAS 04-719)

Agreement on the deployment of the United States ballistic missile defense system in Romania, with attachment.
Signed at Washington September 13, 2011.
Entered into force December 23, 2011.
TIAS 11-1223

RUSSIAN FEDERATION

For agreements prior to December 31, 1991, see UNION OF SOVIET SOCIALIST REPUBLICS.

ARMS CONTROL

Treaty on measures for the further reduction and limitation of strategic offensive arms.
Signed at Prague April 8, 2010.
Entered into force February 5, 2011.
TIAS 11-205

ATOMIC ENERGY

Agreement concerning the disposition of highly enriched uranium extracted from nuclear weapons.
Signed at Washington February 18, 1993.
Entered into force February 18, 1993.
TIAS

Memorandum of understanding relating to transparency and additional arrangements concerning the agreement of February 18, 1993 concerning the disposition of highly enriched uranium extracted from nuclear weapons.
Signed at Washington September 1, 1993.
Entered into force September 1, 1993.
TIAS

Agreement on cooperation in research on radiation effects for the purpose of minimizing the consequences of radioactive contamination on health and the environment, with annex.
Signed at Moscow January 14, 1994.
Entered into force January 14, 1994.
TIAS 11481

Amendments and Extensions:
March 10, 2000 (TIAS 00-310)
May 4, 2007 (TIAS 00-310)
July 13, 2011 (TIAS 00-310)

Protocol on highly enriched uranium (HEU) transparency arrangements in furtherance of the memorandum of understanding of September 1, 1993.
Signed at Washington March 18, 1994.
Entered into force March 18, 1994.
TIAS

Agreement for cooperation on enhancing the safety of Russian nuclear fuel cycle facilities and research reactors.
Signed at Moscow June 30, 1995.
Entered into force June 30, 1995.
TIAS 12672

Extension:
January 31 and February 26, 2002 (TIAS 02-226)

Agreement concerning cooperation regarding plutonium production reactors, with memorandum of understanding.
Signed at Moscow September 23, 1997.
Entered into force September 23, 1997.
TIAS 97-923

Amendment:
March 12, 2003 (TIAS 97-923)

Agreement concerning the transfer of source material to the Russian Federation, with annex and administrative arrangement.
Signed at Washington March 24, 1999.
Entered into force March 24, 1999.
TIAS 13026

Agreement regarding assurances concerning the source material transferred from the United States to the Russian Federation, with annex.
Exchange of notes at Washington March 24, 1999.
Entered into force March 24, 1999.
TIAS 13026

Agreement concerning the cessation of plutonium production at the operating ADE 4 and ADE 5 reactors in Seversk (Tomsk Region) and the ADE 2 reactor in Zheleznogorsk (Krasnoyarsk Region).
Signed at Vienna March 12, 2003.
Entered into force March 12, 2003.
TIAS 03-312

Agreement concerning cooperation for the transfer of Russian-produced research reactor nuclear fuel to the Russian Federation.
Signed at Moscow May 27, 2004.
Entered into force May 27, 2004.
TIAS 04-527
Amendment and Extension:
December 17 and 27, 2013 (TIAS 13-1227)

Agreement for cooperation in the field of peaceful uses of nuclear energy.
Signed at Moscow May 6, 2008.
Entered into force January 11, 2011.
TIAS 11-111

Agreement regarding cooperation under the framework agreement on a multilateral nuclear environmental program in the Russian Federation of May 21, 2003 and the June 14, 2013, protocol to the framework agreement on a multilateral nuclear environmental program in the Russian Federation of May 21, 2013.
Signed at Washington June 14, 2013.
Entered into force June 17, 2013.
NP

Agreement on cooperation in nuclear and energy related scientific research and development, with annexes.
Signed at Vienna September 16, 2013.
Entered into force January 24, 2014.
TIAS 14-124

CIVIL AFFAIRS, EMERGENCIES & DEFENSE

Memorandum of understanding on cooperation in emergency management.
Signed at Moscow July 16, 1996.
Entered into force July 16, 1996.
TIAS 12783
Amendment and Extensions:
September 11, 2006
June 26, 2007 (TIAS 07-626.1)

CONSULAR AFFAIRS

Visa agreement.
Exchange of notes at Moscow and Washington November 1 and 19, 2011.
Entered into force September 9, 2012.
TIAS 12-909

DEFENSE

Agreement concerning the provision of training related to defense articles under the United States International Military Education and Training (IMET) Program.
Exchange of notes at Moscow and Washington April 22 and June 17, 1992.
Entered into force June 17, 1992.
NP

Memorandum on cooperation in the field of defense conversion.
Signed at Moscow December 16, 1993.
Entered into force December 16, 1993.
TIAS

Agreement on the establishment of a direct secure communications system between the United States of America and the Russian Federation.
Signed at Washington October 30, 2008.
Entered into force October 30, 2008.
TIAS 08-1030

Agreement on the transit of armaments, military equipment, military property, and personnel through the territory of the Russian Federation in connection with the participation of the United States of America in efforts for ensuring the security, stabilization and reconstruction of the Islamic Republic of Afghanistan, with exchange of notes.
Signed at Moscow July 6, 2009.
Entered into force April 19, 2011.
TIAS 11-419

ENVIRONMENT & CONSERVATION

Memorandum of understanding on cooperation in the field of forestry, with annex.
Signed at Washington May 13, 1994.
Entered into force May 13, 1994.
TIAS 12541

Agreement on cooperation in the field of protection of the environment and natural resources, with annex.
Signed at Washington June 23, 1994.
Entered into force June 23, 1994.
TIAS 12550; 2379 UNTS 51

Agreement for cooperation in the Global Learning and Observations to Benefit the Environment (GLOBE) Program, with appendices.
Signed at Moscow December 16, 1994.
Entered into force December 16, 1994.
TIAS 12590

Agreement on cooperation in the prevention of pollution of the environment in the Arctic.
Signed at Moscow December 16, 1994.
Entered into force December 16, 1994.
TIAS 12589

Agreement on the conservation and management of the Alaska-Chukotka polar bear population.
Signed at Washington October 16, 2000.
Entered into force September 23, 2007.
TIAS

FINANCE

Investment incentive agreement.
Signed at Washington April 3, 1992.
Entered into force June 17, 1992.
TIAS 11471

Agreement regarding the consolidation and rescheduling of certain debts owed to or guaranteed by the United States Government, with annexes.
Signed at Washington September 30, 1993.
Entered into force November 4, 1993.
NP

Agreement regarding the consolidation and rescheduling of certain debts owed to or guaranteed by the United States Government, with annexes.
Signed at Moscow October 25, 1994.
Entered into force December 19, 1994.
NP

Agreement regarding the rescheduling of certain debts owed to or guaranteed by the United States Government, with annexes.
Signed at Washington October 9, 1995.
Entered into force November 29, 1995.
NP
Amendment:
November 28 and December 1, 1995 (NP)

Agreement regarding the rescheduling of certain debts owed to or guaranteed by the United States Government, with annexes.
Signed at Washington February 6, 1997.
Entered into force May 7, 1997.
NP

Agreement regarding the rescheduling of certain debts owed to or guaranteed by the United States Government, with annexes.
Signed at Moscow May 26, 2000.
Entered into force June 29, 2000.
NP

FISHERIES

Agreement concerning Pacific salmon fishing within the respective 200 nautical mile zones of the United States and Russia.
Exchange of notes at Washington August 27 and September 3, 1992.
Entered into force September 3, 1992.
TIAS 11449

Agreement on the conservation of straddling fish stocks in the central part of the Sea of Okhotsk.
Signed at Moscow June 13, 1996.
Entered into force June 13, 1996.
TIAS 12768

Agreement on cooperation for the purposes of preventing, deterring and eliminating illegal, unreported, and unregulated fishing.
Signed at Portland, Oregon September 11, 2015.
Entered into force December 4, 2015.
TIAS 15-1204

FOREIGN ASSISTANCE

Grant agreement for an energy efficiency and environment commodity import program.
Signed at Moscow December 16, 1993.
Entered into force December 16, 1993.
TIAS 11483

Memorandum of understanding for the establishment of the Russian-American oil and gas technology center in Tyumen City, with annex.
Signed at Washington and Tyumen City June 23 and July 26, 1994.
Entered into force July 26, 1994.
TIAS 12558

LAW ENFORCEMENT

Agreement on cooperation and mutual assistance in customs matters.
Signed at Washington September 28, 1994.
Entered into force December 15, 1994.
TIAS

Treaty on mutual legal assistance in criminal matters, with related note.
Signed at Moscow June 17, 1999.
Entered into force January 31, 2002.
TIAS 13046

MARITIME MATTERS

Agreement amending the agreement of May 25, 1972, on the prevention of incidents on and over the high seas.
Exchange of notes at Moscow October 12, 1997, and May 28, 1998.
Entered into force May 28, 1998.
TIAS 12957

Agreement on maritime transport.
Signed at St. Petersburg June 20, 2001.
Entered into force June 20, 2001.
TIAS 01-620.1

NONPROLIFERATION

Agreement on the establishment of nuclear risk reduction centers, with protocols.
Signed at Washington September 15, 1987.
Entered into force September 15, 1987.
NP
Amendment:
October 7, 2013 (NP)

Agreement concerning the future consultation procedure for implementation of the agreement of September 30, 1971, on measures to reduce the risk of outbreak of nuclear war between the United States and the Union of Soviet Socialist Republics.
Exchange of notes at Moscow May 13 and June 25, 2004.
Entered into force June 25, 2004.
TIAS

Agreement on technology safeguards associated with the activities under the "Sea Launch" Program.
Signed at Washington March 21, 2006.
Entered into force July 30, 2007.
TIAS 07-730

Agreement concerning the management and disposition of plutonium designated as no longer required for defense purposes and related cooperation, with annexes and joint statement.
Signed at Moscow and Washington August 29 and September 1, 2000.
Entered into force July 13, 2011.
TIAS 11-713.1
Amendments:
September 15, 2006 (TIAS 11-713.1)
April 13, 2010 (TIAS 11-713.2)

PROPERTY

Memorandum of mutual understanding on settlement of the problem of the new embassy administrative buildings in Washington and Moscow.
Signed at Washington June 17, 1992.
Entered into force June 17, 1992.
TIAS
Amendment:
December 15, 1992

SCIENTIFIC & TECHNICAL COOPERATION

Agreement on science and technology cooperation, with annexes.
Signed at Moscow December 16, 1993.
Entered into force December 16, 1993.
TIAS 12527
Extensions:
October 28 and December 15, 2003 (TIAS 03-1216)
November 23 and December 16, 2004 (TIAS 03-1216)
December 15 and 16, 2005 (TIAS 03-1216)
March 2 and June 24, 2016 (TIAS 16-624)

Memorandum of understanding on cooperation in geoscience, with annexes.
Signed at Washington June 23, 1994.
Entered into force June 23, 1994.
TIAS 12552

Memorandum of understanding on basic scientific research cooperation, with annexes.
Signed at Washington June 23, 1994.
Entered into force June 23, 1994.
TIAS 12551

Memorandum of understanding on basic scientific research cooperation, with annexes.
Signed at Washington February 7, 1997.
Entered into force February 7, 1997.
TIAS 12832

Memorandum of understanding on cooperation in seismology and geodynamics, with appendix.
Signed at Washington March 24, 1999.
Entered into force March 24, 1999.
TIAS
Extension:
December 11, 2009, effective March 24, 2009

Memorandum of understanding concerning scientific and technical cooperation in the earth sciences, with annexes.
Signed at Reston November 14, 2003.
Entered into force November 14, 2003.
TIAS 03-1114

Memorandum of understanding for cooperation in the areas of meteorology, hydrology and oceanography, with annexes.
Signed at Geneva June 23, 2005.
Entered into force June 23, 2005.
TIAS 05-623

Memorandum of understanding on cooperation in the field of research on high energy and nuclear physics.
Signed at Washington April 29, 2010.
Entered into force April 29, 2010.
TIAS 10-429

SPACE

Agreement concerning cooperation in the exploration and use of outer space for peaceful purposes, with annex.
Signed at Washington June 17, 1992.
Entered into force June 17, 1992.
TIAS 12457
Amendments and Extensions:
June 13 and 16, 1997
July 3 and August 9, 2002
December 3 and 26, 2007 and January 25, 2008 (TIAS 07-1227.1)
August 25, 2011 and April 3, 2013 (TIAS 07-1227.1)

Interim agreement for the conduct of activities leading to Russian partnership in the detailed design, development, operation and utilization of the permanently manned civil space station.
Signed at Washington June 23, 1994.
Entered into force June 30, 1995.
TIAS

Implementing agreement on the flight of a U.S. stratospheric aerosol and gas experiment (SAGE) III and a total ozone mapping spectrometer (TOMS) aboard Russian meteor 3M spacecraft, with annexes.
Signed at Moscow December 16, 1994.
Entered into force February 22, 1995.
TIAS 12592

Protocol regarding the balance of their contributions and obligations to the International Space Station, with appendices.
Signed at Moscow June 11, 1996.
Entered into force June 11. 1996.
TIAS 96-611

Implementing agreement on the flight of the Russian High Energy Neutron Detector (HEND) on the United States 2001 Mars Odyssey Orbiter Mission, with annex.
Signed April 6, 2001.
Entered into force April 6, 2001.
TIAS 01-406
Amendment and Extension:
September 12 and 18, 2006 (TIAS 01-406)

Addendum to the protocol of June 11, 1996 regarding the balance of contributions to the International Space Station.
Signed at Moscow September 9, 2004.
Entered into force January 26, 2005.
TIAS 96-611

Second addendum to the protocol of June 11, 1996 regarding the balance of contributions to the International Space Station.
Signed at Cape Canaveral July 1, 2006.
Entered into force July 1, 2006.
TIAS 96-611

TAXATION

Convention for the avoidance of double taxation and the prevention of fiscal evasion with respect to taxes on income and capital, with protocol.
Signed at Washington June 17, 1992.
Entered into force December 16, 1993.
TIAS

TRADE & INVESTMENT

Agreement on trade relations, with related exchanges of letters.
Signed at Washington June 1, 1990.
Entered into force June 17, 1992.
TIAS
Amendment:
September 26 and October 31, 1990

Agreement on the exports of firearms and ammunition from the Russian Federation to the United States, with annexes.
Signed at Washington April 3, 1996.
Entered into force April 3, 1996.
TIAS 96-403
Amendment:
June 25, 2003, and March 4, 2004 (TIAS 96-403)

Agreement on protection and enforcement of intellectual property rights.
Exchange of letters at Hanoi and Washington November 19, 2006.
Entered into force November 19, 2006.
TIAS 06-1119.5

Agreement on tariff treatment of certain combine harvester-threshers and self-propelled forage harvesters.
Exchange of letters at Hanoi and Washington November 19, 2006.
Entered into force November 19, 2006.
TIAS

Agreement on tariff treatment of certain aircraft imported under operational lease.
Exchange of letters at Hanoi and Washington November 19, 2006.
Entered into force November 19, 2006.
TIAS

Agreement on agricultural biotechnology.
Exchange of letters at Hanoi and Washington November 19, 2006.
Entered into force November 19, 2006.
TIAS 06-1119.1

Agreement on importation of pork and pork by products into the Russian Federation.
Exchange of letters at Hanoi and Washington November 19, 2006.
Entered into force November 19, 2006.
TIAS 06-1119.3

Agreement on exporting pork and poultry to the Russian Federation.
Exchange of letters at Hanoi and Washington November 19, 2006.
Entered into force November 19, 2006.
TIAS 06-1119.4

Agreement on market access for beef and beef byproducts.
Exchange of letters at Hanoi and Washington November 19, 2006.
Entered into force November 19, 2006.
TIAS 06-1119.2

Agreement on establishment of import licensing procedures for imports of goods containing encryption technology, with annex.
Exchange of letters at Hanoi and Washington November 19, 2006.
Entered into force November 19, 2006.
TIAS 06-1119.6

Memorandum of understanding concerning certification of seafood products from the United States of America to the Russian Federation, with appendix.
Signed January 27 and February 25, 2010.
Entered into force February 25, 2010.
TIAS 10-225

TRANSPORTATION

Memorandum of understanding on air navigation, airspace use and air traffic control.
Signed at Washington June 17, 1992.
Entered into force June 17, 1992.
TIAS 11477

Air transport agreement, with annexes.
Signed at Moscow January 14, 1994.
Entered into force January 14, 1994.
TIAS

Memorandum of understanding on technical cooperation towards a bilateral airworthiness agreement.
Signed at Moscow June 30, 1995.
Entered into force June 30, 1995.
TIAS 12673

Memorandum of understanding on cooperation in the field of civil aircraft accident/incident investigation and prevention.
Signed at Moscow September 2, 1998.
Entered into force September 2, 1998.
TIAS 12983

Agreement for promotion of aviation safety.
Signed at Moscow September 2, 1998.
Entered into force September 2, 1998.
TIAS 12982

Memorandum of cooperation concerning cooperation in the promotion and development of civil aviation.
Signed at Washington and Moscow February 19 and March 22, 1999.
Entered into force March 22, 1999.
TIAS

Memorandum of agreement providing technical assistance in developing, modernizing, operating or maintaining the civil aviation infrastructure in the Russian Federation.
Signed June 20 and 29, 2007.
Entered into force June 29, 2007.
NP

RWANDA

CULTURAL EXCHANGES, PROPERTY & COOPERATION

Agreement concerning the program of the Peace Corps in Rwanda.
Signed at Kigali July 18, 2008.
Entered into force July 18, 2008.
TIAS 08-718

DEFENSE

Agreement concerning the provision of training related to defense articles under the United States International Military Education and Training (IMET) Program.
Exchange of notes at Kigali March 6 and 11, 1980.
Entered into force March 11, 1980.
33 UST 3064; TIAS 10211; 1529 UNTS 7

Agreement regarding grants under the Foreign Assistance Act of 1961, as amended, and the furnishing of defense articles, related training and other defense services from the United States to Rwanda.
Exchange of notes at Kigali January 26 and February 6, 1998.
Entered into force February 6, 1998.
NP

Agreement regarding the status of United States military and civilian personnel of the United States Department of Defense who may be temporarily present in Rwanda in connection with the military airlift of Rwandan military forces in support of operations in Darfur and future mutually agreed activities.
Exchange of notes at Kigali July 5 and 11, 2005.
Entered into force July 11, 2005.
TIAS

Acquisition and cross-servicing agreement (ACSA).
Signed at Stuttgart and Kigali October 15 and December 15, 2014.
Entered into force December 15, 2014.
NP

EMPLOYMENT

Agreement relating to the employment of dependents of official government employees, with related note.
Exchange of notes at Washington July 15 and October 22, 1992.
Entered into force October 22, 1992.
TIAS 11904

ENVIRONMENT & CONSERVATION

Agreement for cooperation in the Global Learning and Observations to Benefit the Environment (GLOBE) Program.
Signed at Kigali August 21, 2003.
Entered into force August 21, 2003.
TIAS 03-821

FINANCE

Agreement relating to investment guaranties.
Exchange of notes at Kigali July 6 and August 9, 1965.
Entered into force April 27, 1967.
18 UST 2346; TIAS 6337; 692 UNTS 101

Agreement regarding the consolidation, reduction, and rescheduling of certain debts owed to the United States Government and its Agency, with annexes.
Signed at Kigali October 26, 1999.
Entered into force December 13, 1999.
NP

Agreement regarding the reduction of certain debts owed to, guaranteed by, or insured by the United States Government, with annexes.
Signed at Kigali April 22, 2003.
Entered into force June 9, 2003.
NP

Agreement regarding the reduction of certain debts owed to, guaranteed by, or insured by the United States Government, or its agency, with annexes.
Signed at Kigali October 13, 2005.
Entered into force November 30, 2005.
NP

FOREIGN ASSISTANCE

Economic and technical cooperation agreement.
Signed at Kigali June 7, 1989.
Entered into force January 17, 1992.
TIAS 12063

INTERNATIONAL CRIMINAL COURT

Agreement regarding the surrender of persons to international tribunals.
Signed at Washington March 4, 2003.
Entered into force July 11, 2003.
TIAS 03-711

POSTAL MATTERS

International express mail agreement with detailed regulations.
Signed at Kigali and Washington January 15 and February 8, 1988.
Entered into force March 15, 1988.
TIAS 11648

TRADE & INVESTMENT

Trade and investment framework agreement.
Signed at Washington June 7, 2006.
Entered into force June 7, 2006.
TIAS

Treaty concerning the encouragement and reciprocal protection of investment, with annexes.
Signed at Kigali February 19, 2008.
Entered into force January 1, 2012.
TIAS

TRANSPORTATION

Air transport agreement, with annexes.
Signed at Washington October 11, 2000.
Entered into force July 14, 2010.
TIAS

Memorandum of agreement relating to assistance in developing and modernizing Rwanda's civil aviation infrastructure.
Signed November 28 and December 6, 2001.
Entered into force December 6, 2001.
NP

Amendment:
August 20, 2009 and February 3, 2010

SAINT KITTS AND NEVIS

On September 19, 1983, Saint Christopher and Nevis became an independent state. In a note dated November 2, 1983, to the Secretary-General of the United Nations, the Prime Minister and Minister of Foreign Affairs made a statement reading in part as follows:

I have the honor to refer to the attainment of in-dependence by the former British Associated State of St. Christopher and Nevis on 19th September, 1983, as Saint Christopher and Nevis or Saint Kitts and Nevis, and to the question of status of conventions, treaties and other international instruments applied to, or entered into on behalf of Saint Christopher and Nevis by the United Kingdom Government prior to independence.

The Government of Saint Christopher and Nevis considers that questions of succession to such conventions, treaties and other international instruments should be governed by the accepted rules of international law and by the relevant principles contained in the Convention on Succession of States in respect of Treaties done at Vienna on 23rd August, 1978.

The Government of Saint Christopher and Nevis hereby declares that, with regard to multilateral treaties applied or extended to the former British Associated State of Saint Christopher and Nevis, it will continue to apply the terms of each treaty provisionally and on the basis of reciprocity until such time as it notifies the depositary authority of its decision in respect thereof.

As regards bilateral treaties applied or extended to, or entered into on behalf of the former British Associated State of Saint Christopher and Nevis, the Government of Saint Christopher and Nevis declares that it will examine each such treaty and communicate its views to the other State Party concerned. In the mean-time, the Government of Saint Christopher and Nevis will continue to observe the terms of each treaty, which validly so applies and is not inconsistent with its independent sovereign status, provisionally and on basis of reciprocity.

CULTURAL EXCHANGES, PROPERTY & COOPERATION

Agreement relating to the establishment of a Peace Corps program in St. Kitts/Nevis.
Exchange of letters at Bridgetown and Basseterre May 15, 1980, and January 13, 1981.
Entered into force January 13, 1981.
33 UST 846; TIAS 10067; 1275 UNTS 131

DEFENSE

Agreement concerning the provision of training related to defense articles under the United States International Military Education and Training (IMET) Program.
Exchange of notes at St. John's and Basseterre March 19 and 20, 1984.
Entered into force March 20, 1984.
35 UST 4881; TIAS 10972

Agreement concerning the status of United States Armed Forces personnel present in St. Christopher and Nevis.
Exchange of notes at St. John's and Basseterre March 2 and June 9, 1987.
Entered into force June 9, 1987.
TIAS

Agreement regarding the provision of articles, services and associated training by the Government of the United States for anti-narcotics purposes.
Exchange of notes at Bridgetown and Basseterre November 13, 1998, and March 11, 1999.
Entered into force March 11, 1999.
TIAS

Agreement regarding the Caribbean Basin Security Initiative and the provision of technical support for maritime security forces.
Exchange of notes at Bridgetown and Basseterre June 29 and July 10, 2012.
Entered into force July 10, 2012.
TIAS

DIPLOMATIC & CONSULAR RELATIONS

Consular convention between the United States and the United Kingdom.
Signed at Washington June 6, 1951.
Entered into force September 7, 1952.
3 UST 3426; TIAS 2494; 165 UNTS 121

EMPLOYMENT

Agreement relating to the employment of dependents of official government employees.
Exchange of notes at Bridgetown and Basseterre February 26 and April 14, 2003.
Entered into force April 14, 2003.
TIAS 03-414

FINANCE

Agreement relating to investment guaranties.
Signed at Basseterre November 21, 1968.
Entered into force November 21, 1968.
19 UST 7546; TIAS 6596; 702 UNTS 311

Agreement regarding the consolidation and rescheduling of certain debts owed to, guaranteed by, or insured by the United States Government or its agencies.
Signed at Washington January 15, 2013.
Entered into force March 6, 2013.
NP

FOREIGN ASSISTANCE

General agreement for economic, technical and related assistance.
Signed at Basseterre April 24, 1986.
Entered into force April 24, 1986.
TIAS 11514

INTELLECTUAL PROPERTY

Declaration by the United States and the United Kingdom affording reciprocal protection to trademarks.
Signed at London October 24, 1877.
Entered into force October 24, 1877.
20 Stat. 703; TS 138; 12 Bevans 198

INTERNATIONAL CRIMINAL COURT

Agreement regarding the surrender of persons to the International Criminal Court.
Exchange of notes at Washington January 31, 2005.
Entered into force January 31, 2005.
TIAS 05-131

LAW ENFORCEMENT

Extradition treaty.
Signed at Basseterre September 18, 1996.
Entered into force February 23, 2000.
TIAS 12805

Treaty on mutual legal assistance in criminal matters, with related exchange of notes.
Signed at Basseterre September 18, 1997.
Entered into force February 23, 2000.
TIAS 12884.

Aerial intercept assistance agreement.
Effected by exchange of notes at Bridgetown and Basseterre October 7, 2011 and May 18, 2012.
Entered into force May 18, 2012.
TIAS 12-518

MARITIME MATTERS

Agreement concerning maritime counter-drug operations.
Signed at Basseterre April 13, 1995.
Entered into force April 13, 1995.
TIAS 12775
Amendment:
June 27, 1996 (TIAS 12775)

OCCUPATION & PEACEKEEPING

Agreement for the furnishing of commodities and services in connection with the peacekeeping force for Grenada.
Exchange of notes at St. John's and Basseterre January 19 and 20, 1984.
Entered into force January 20, 1984.
35 UST 4276; TIAS 10929; 2015 UNTS 123

POSTAL MATTERS

Convention for the exchange of postal money orders with the British Colony of Saint Christopher, Nevis and Anguilla.
Signed at Basseterre, St. Kitts, June 27 and at Washington September 14, 1959.
Entered into force February 1, 1960.
11 UST 1433; TIAS 4483

International express mail agreement, with detailed regulations.
Signed at St. Kitts and Washington June 16 and August 21, 1997.
Entered into force October 1, 1997.
NP

PROPERTY

Convention between the United States and the United Kingdom relating to tenure and disposition of real and personal property.
Signed at Washington March 2, 1899.
Applicable to St. Christopher-Nevis June 17, 1901.
31 Stat. 1939; TS 146; 12 Bevans 246

Supplementary convention relating to the tenure and disposition of real and personal property.
Signed at Washington May 27, 1936.
Entered into force March 10, 1941.
55 Stat. 1101; TS 964; 5 Bevans 140; 203 LNTS 367

TAXATION

Agreement to improve international tax compliance and to implement the Foreign Account Tax Compliance Act, with annexes.
Signed at Bridgetown August 31, 2015.
Entered into force April 28, 2016.
TIAS 16-428

TELECOMMUNICATION

Agreement relating to radio communications between amateur stations on behalf of third parties.
Exchange of notes at St. John's and St. Kitts July 6 and 9, 1984.
Entered into force August 8, 1984.
TIAS 11147; 2126 UNTS 185

TRANSPORTATION

Air transport agreement.
Signed at Basseterre December 13, 2011.
Entered into force December 13, 2011.
TIAS 11-1213.1

SAINT LUCIA

On February 22, 1979, Saint Lucia became an independent state. In a note dated March 14, 1979, to the Secretary-General of the United Nations, the Prime Minister made a statement reading in part as follows:

Saint Lucia … is now ready to participate with other nations in fulfilling obligations under international law with respect to treaties to which this Government succeeded upon Independence. However, it is necessary to examine in depth such treaties to ascertain whether or not under customary international law any may have lapsed. Until this has been done the Government of Saint Lucia wish:

(a) that it be presumed that each treaty has been legally succeeded to by Saint Lucia; and

(b) that future action be based on the presumption in (a) above.

You will be notified in due course of those treaties this Government regards as having lapsed and those treaties which this Government wishes to terminate."

CULTURAL EXCHANGES, PROPERTY & COOPERATION

Agreement relating to the establishment of a Peace Corps program in St. Lucia.
Exchange of letters at Bridgetown and Castries May 15 and July 8, 1980.
Entered into force July 8, 1980.
32 UST 4408; TIAS 9954; 1267 UNTS 137

DEFENSE

Agreement concerning the provision of training related to defense articles under the United States International Military Education and Training (IMET) Program.
Exchange of notes at Bridgetown and Castries December 11, 1980, and January 27, 1981.
Entered into force January 27, 1981.
33 UST 983; TIAS 10081; 1275 UNTS 185

Agreement regarding the provision of articles, services and associated training by the Government of the United States for anti-narcotics purposes.
Exchange of notes at Bridgetown and Castries November 13, 1998, and April 8, 1999.
Entered into force April 8, 1999.
NP

Agreement regarding the status of members of the armed forces of the United States and civilian personnel of the United States Department of Defense present in St. Lucia in connection with military exercises and training, counter-drug related activities, United States security assistance programs, or other agreed peaceful purposes.
Exchange of notes at Bridgetown and Castries December 28 and 29, 2000.
Entered into force December 29, 2000.
NP

Agreement regarding the status of United States personnel who may be temporarily present in St. Lucia.
Effected by Exchange of Notes at Bridgetown and Saint Lucia April 23, 2013 and April 30, 2013.
Entered into force April 30, 2013.
TIAS 13-430

Agreement regarding the Caribbean Basin Security Initiative and the provision of technical support for maritime security forces.
Effected by Exchange of Notes at Bridgetown and Saint Lucia June 29, 2012 and April 30, 2013.
Entered into force April 30, 2013.
TIAS 13-430.1

DIPLOMATIC & CONSULAR RELATIONS

Consular convention between the United States and the United Kingdom.
Signed at Washington June 6, 1951.
Entered into force September 7, 1952.
3 UST 3426; TIAS 2494; 165 UNTS 121

FINANCE

Agreement relating to investment guaranties.
Signed at Castries August 9, 1968.
Entered into force August 9, 1968.
19 UST 5921; TIAS 6546; 730 UNTS 225

FOREIGN ASSISTANCE

General agreement for economic, technical and related assistance.
Signed at Castries October 20, 1983.
Entered into force October 20, 1983.
35 UST 2953; TIAS 10831; 2014 UNTS 607

INTELLECTUAL PROPERTY

Declaration by the United States and the United Kingdom affording reciprocal protection to trade-marks.
Signed at London October 24, 1877.
Entered into force October 24, 1877.
20 Stat. 703; TS 138; 12 Bevans 198

LAW ENFORCEMENT

Treaty on mutual legal assistance in criminal matters, with forms.
Signed at Castries April 18, 1996.
Entered into force February 2, 2000.
TIAS

Extradition treaty.
Signed at Castries April 18, 1996.
Entered into force February 2, 2000.
TIAS 00-202

MARITIME MATTERS

Agreement concerning maritime counter-drug operations.
Signed at Castries April 20, 1995.
Entered into force April 20, 1995.
TIAS 12764
Amendment:
June 5, 1996 (TIAS 12764)

MIGRATION & REFUGEES

Memorandum of understanding for the establishment within the territory of St. Lucia of facilities to provide temporary protection under the auspices of the United Nations High Commissioner for Refugees for nationals of Haiti fleeing their country.
Signed at St. Lucia July 15, 1994.
Entered into force July 15, 1994.
TIAS

OCCUPATION & PEACEKEEPING

Agreement for the furnishing of commodities and services in connection with the peacekeeping force for Grenada.
Exchange of notes at Bridgetown and Castries November 25, 1983, and January 13, 1984.
Entered into force January 13, 1984.
35 UST 4253; TIAS 10924; 2014 UNTS 615

POSTAL MATTERS

Money order agreement.
Signed at Washington July 29 and at Grenada August 29, 1904.
Operative October 1, 1904.
NP

Agreement for the direct exchange of parcels by parcel post.
Signed at Grenada May 20 and at Washington June 21, 1935.
Operative July 1, 1935.
49 Stat. 3229; 162 LNTS 157

International express mail agreement with detailed regulations.
Signed at Castries and Washington August 11 and September 14, 1989.
Entered into force September 15, 1989.
TIAS 11953

INTELPOST memorandum of understanding, with detailed regulations.
Signed at Castries and Washington September 22 and October 29, 1992.
Entered into force November 23, 1992.
TIAS 11902

PROPERTY

Convention between the United States and the United Kingdom relating to tenure and disposition of real and personal property.
Signed at Washington March 2, 1899.
Applicable to St. Lucia February 9, 1901.
31 Stat. 1939; TS 146; 12 Bevans 246

Supplementary convention relating to the tenure and disposition of real and personal property.
Signed at Washington May 27, 1936.
Entered into force March 10, 1941.
55 Stat. 1101; TS 964; 5 Bevans 140; 203 LNTS 367

TAXATION

Agreement for the exchange of information with respect to taxes, with annex.
Signed at Washington January 30, 1987.
Entered into force April 22, 1991.
TIAS 12057

Agreement to improve international tax compliance and to implement the Foreign Account Tax Compliance Act, with annexes.
Signed at Bridgetown November 19, 2015.
Entered into force September 1, 2016.
TIAS 16-901.1

TELECOMMUNICATION

Agreement between the United States and the United Kingdom relating to the reciprocal granting of authorizations to permit licensed amateur radio operators of either country to operate their stations in the other country.
Exchange of notes at London November 26, 1965.
Applicable to St. Lucia December 11, 1969.
16 UST 2047; TIAS 5941; 561 UNTS 193

Agreement between the United States and the United Kingdom extending to certain territories the application of the agreement of November 26, 1965, relating to the reciprocal granting of authorizations to permit licensed amateur radio operators of either country to operate their stations in the other country.
Exchange of notes at London December 11, 1969.
Entered into force December 11, 1969.
20 UST 4089; TIAS 6800; 732 UNTS 334

Arrangement relating to radio communications between amateur stations on behalf of third parties.
Exchange of notes at Bridgetown and Castries August 10, 1981, and February 17, 1982.
Entered into force March 19, 1982.
34 UST 287; TIAS 10354; 1557 UNTS 3

TRANSPORTATION

Agreement between the United States and the United Kingdom relating to the future status and use of Beane Field, St. Lucia.
Exchange of notes at London August 20, 1964.
Entered into force August 20, 1964.
15 UST 1685; TIAS 5642; 531 UNTS 85

Agreement between the United States and the United Kingdom concerning air services, with annexes and exchange of letters.
Signed at Bermuda July 23, 1977.
Entered into force July 23, 1977.
28 UST 5367; TIAS 8641
Amendment:
April 25, 1978 (29 UST 2680; TIAS 8965)

SAINT VINCENT AND THE GRENADINES

On October 27, 1979, Saint Vincent and the Grenadines became an independent state. In a note dated September 30, 1983, to the Secretary-General of the United Nations, the Prime Minister and Minister of Finance made a statement reading in part as follows:

I have the honour to refer to the attainment of independence by the former British Associated State of St. Vincent on 27th October, 1979, as the State of St. Vincent and the Grenadines, and to the question of status of convention, treaties and other international instruments applied to or entered into on behalf of St. Vincent by the United Kingdom Government prior to independence.

The Government of the State of St. Vincent and the Grenadines considers that questions of succession to such conventions, treaties and other international instruments should be governed by the accepted rules of international law and by the relevant principles contained in the Convention on Succession of States in respect of treaties done at Vienna on 23rd August, 1978.

The Government of the State of St. Vincent and the Grenadines hereby declares that, with regard to multilateral treaties applied or extended to the former British Associated State of St. Vincent, it will continue to apply the terms of each such treaty provisionally and on the basis of reciprocity until such time as it notifies the depository authority of its decision in respect thereof.

As regards bilateral treaties applied or extended to, or entered into on behalf of the former British Associated State of St. Vincent, the Government of the State of St. Vincent and the Grenadines declares that it will examine each such treaty and communicate its views to the other State Party concerned. In the meantime, the Government of the State of St. Vincent and the Grenadines will continue to observe the terms of each such treaty, which validly so applies and is not inconsistent with its independent sovereign status, provisionally and on basis of reciprocity.

CULTURAL EXCHANGES, PROPERTY & COOPERATION

Agreement relating to the establishment of a Peace Corps program in St. Vincent.
Exchange of letters at Bridgetown and St. Vincent May 15 and June 26, 1980.
Entered into force June 26, 1980.
32 UST 5815; TIAS 10017; 1267 UNTS 129

DEFENSE

Agreement concerning the provision of training related to defense articles under the United States International Military Education and Training (IMET) Program.
Exchange of notes at Bridgetown and Kingstown December 11, 1980, and January 20, 1981.
Entered into force January 20, 1981.
33 UST 912; TIAS 10076; 1275 UNTS 149

Agreement regarding articles, services and associated training transferred to the Government of Saint Vincent and the Grenadines for antinarcotics purposes.
Exchange of notes at Bridgetown and Kingstown November 13 and 26, 1998.
Entered into force November 26, 1998.
TIAS

Agreement regarding the Caribbean Basin Security Initiative (Technical Assistance Field Team).
Exchange of notes at Bridgetown and Kingstown June 29 and December 11, 2012.
Entered into force December 11, 2012.
TIAS 12-1211

DIPLOMATIC & CONSULAR RELATIONS

Consular convention between the United States and the United Kingdom.
Signed at Washington June 6, 1951.
Entered into force September 7, 1952.
3 UST 3426; TIAS 2494; 165 UNTS 121

EMPLOYMENT

Agreement relating to the employment of dependents of official government employees.
Exchange of notes at Bridgetown and Kingstown February 26 and June 16, 2003.
Entered into force June 16, 2003.
TIAS 03-616

FINANCE

Agreement relating to investment guaranties.
Exchange of notes at Bridgetown and St. Vincent May 15 and June 14, 1972.
Entered into force June 14, 1972.
23 UST 3802; TIAS 7530

FOREIGN ASSISTANCE

General agreement for economic, technical and related assistance.
Signed at Kingstown September 30, 1983.
Entered into force September 30, 1983.
35 UST 2970; TIAS 10833; 2014 UNTS 441

INTELLECTUAL PROPERTY

Declaration by the United States and the United Kingdom affording reciprocal protection to trade-marks.
Signed at London October 24, 1877.
Entered into force October 24, 1877.
20 Stat. 703; TS 138; 12 Bevans 198

LAW ENFORCEMENT

Extradition treaty.
Signed at Kingstown August 15, 1996.
Entered into force September 8, 1999.
TIAS 99-908

Agreement regarding the provision of articles, services and associated training by the Government of the United States for anti-narcotics purposes.
Exchange of notes at Bridgetown and Kingstown November 13 and 26, 1998.
Entered into force November 26, 1998.
TIAS

Treaty on mutual legal assistance in criminal matters, with a related protocol.
Signed at Kingstown January 8, 1998.
Entered into force September 8, 1999.
TIAS 12917

MARITIME MATTERS

Agreement concerning maritime counter-drug operations.
Signed at Kingstown and Bridgetown June 29 and July 4, 1995.
Entered into force July 4, 1995.
TIAS 12676

NONPROLIFERATION

Agreement concerning cooperation to suppress the proliferation of weapons of mass destruction, their delivery systems, and related materials by sea.
Signed at Kingstown May 11, 2010.
Entered into force May 11, 2010.
TIAS 10-511.1

OCCUPATION & PEACEKEEPING

Agreement for the furnishing of commodities and services in connection with the peacekeeping force for Grenada.
Exchange of notes at Bridgetown and St. Vincent November 25, 1983, and January 13, 1984.
Entered into force January 13, 1984.
35 UST 4257; TIAS 10925; 2014 UNTS 449

POSTAL MATTERS

Money order agreement.
Signed at Washington July 29 and at Grenada August 29, 1904.
Operative October 1, 1904.
NP

Agreement for the direct exchange of parcels by parcel post.
Signed at Grenada May 20 and at Washington June 21, 1935.
Operative July 1, 1935.
49 Stat. 3229; Post Office Department print; 162 LNTS 157

International express mail agreement, with detailed regulations.
Signed at Kingston and Washington January 27 and February 25, 1992.
Entered into force March 7, 1992.
TIAS 11854

PROPERTY

Convention between the United States and the United Kingdom relating to tenure and disposition of real and personal property.
Signed at Washington March 2, 1899.
Applicable to St. Vincent February 9, 1901.
31 Stat. 1939; TS 146; 12 Bevans 246

Supplementary convention relating to the tenure and disposition
of real and personal property.
Signed at Washington May 27, 1936.
Entered into force March 10, 1941.
55 Stat. 1101; TS 964; 5 Bevans 140; 203 LNTS 367

TAXATION

Agreement concerning reciprocal exemption from income tax of income derived from the international operation of ships and aircraft.
Exchange of notes at Bridgetown and Kingston October 11, 1988, and February 15, 1989.
Entered into force February 15, 1989.
TIAS 11601; 2191 UNTS 241

Agreement to improve international tax compliance and to implement the Foreign Account Tax Compliance Act.
Signed at Kingstown August 18, 2015.
Entered into force May 13, 2016.
TIAS 16-513

TELECOMMUNICATION

Agreement between the United States and the United Kingdom relating to the reciprocal granting of authorizations to permit licensed amateur radio operators of either country to operate their stations in the other country.
Exchange of notes at London November 26, 1965.
Applicable to St. Vincent December 11, 1969.
16 UST 2047; TIAS 5941; 561 UNTS 193

Agreement between the United States and the United Kingdom extending to certain territories the application of the agreement of November 26, 1965, relating to the reciprocal granting of authorizations to permit licensed amateur radio operators of either country to operate their stations in the other country.
Exchange of notes at London December 11, 1969.
Entered into force December 11, 1969.
20 UST 4089; TIAS 6800; 732 UNTS 334

Agreement relating to radio communications between amateur stations on behalf of third parties.
Exchange of notes at Bridgetown and St. Vincent April 22 and September 27, 1982.
Entered into force September 27, 1982; effective October 27, 1982.
35 UST 3830; TIAS 10885; 2014 UNTS 439

TRANSPORTATION

Agreement between the United States and the United Kingdom concerning air services, with annexes and exchange of letters.
Signed at Bermuda July 23, 1977.
Entered into force July 23, 1977.
28 UST 5367; TIAS 8641

Amendment:

April 25, 1978 (29 UST 2680; TIAS 8965)

SAMOA

On January 1, 1962, Samoa (then called "Western Samoa") became an independent state. In an exchange of letters dated November 30, 1962, between the Office of the High Commissioner for New Zealand and the Prime Minister of Western Samoa, the Government of Western Samoa agreed that "All obligations and responsibilities of the Government of New Zealand which arise from any valid international instrument are, from January 1, 1962, assumed by the Government of Western Samoa in so far as such instrument may be held to have application to or in respect of Western Samoa."

In 1997, the name "Western Samoa" was changed to "Samoa."

CULTURAL EXCHANGES, PROPERTY & COOPERATION

Agreement relating to the establishment of a Peace Corps program in Western Samoa.
Exchange of notes at Wellington October 1, 1970.
Entered into force October 1, 1970.
21 UST 2186; TIAS 6967; 764 UNTS 281

DEFENSE

Status of forces agreement.
Signed at Apia June 25, 1990.
Entered into force June 25, 1990.
TIAS

Agreement concerning the provision of training related to defense articles under the United States International Military Education and Training (IMET) program.
Exchange of notes at Apia December 1, 1992, and March 8, 1993.
Entered into force March 8, 1993.
NP

EMPLOYMENT

Agreement relating to the employment of dependents of official government employees.
Exchange of notes at New York and Washington February 27 and March 15, 1995.
Entered into force March 15, 1995.
TIAS 12613

FINANCE

Investment guaranty agreement.
Signed at Wellington and Apia June 5 and July 22, 1969.
Entered into force July 22, 1969.
20 UST 2766; TIAS 6745; 720 UNTS 53

MARITIME MATTERS

Agreement concerning operational cooperation to suppress illicit transnational maritime activity.
Signed at Apia June 2, 2012.
Entered into force June 2, 2012.
TIAS 12-602

POSTAL MATTERS

International express mail agreement, with detailed regulations.
Signed at Apia and Washington February 16 and March 18, 1993.
Entered into force May 1, 1993.
NP

SCIENTIFIC & TECHNICAL COOPERATION

Memorandum of understanding concerning scientific and technical cooperation in the earth sciences, with annexes.
Signed at Reston and Apia March 27 and June 4, 2009.
Entered into force June 4, 2009.
TIAS 09-604

SAN MARINO

EMPLOYMENT

Agreement concerning employment on a reciprocal basis of dependents of official government employees.
Exchange of notes at Florence February 25 and September 15, 2004.
Entered into force September 22, 2004.
TIAS 04-922.1

LAW ENFORCEMENT

Treaty for the mutual extradition of fugitive criminals.
Signed at Rome January 10, 1906.
Entered into force July 8, 1908.
35 Stat. 1971; TS 495; 11 Bevans 440

Supplementary extradition convention.
Signed at Washington October 10, 1934.
Entered into force June 28, 1935.
49 Stat. 3198; TS 891; 11 Bevans 446; 161 LNTS 149

TAXATION

Agreement for cooperation to facilitate the implementation of the Foreign Account Tax Compliance Act, with annexes.
Signed at San Marino October 28, 2015.
Entered into force August 30, 2016.
TIAS 16-830

SAO TOME AND PRINCIPE

DEFENSE

Agreement concerning the provision of training related to defense articles under the United States International Military Education and Training (IMET) Program.
Exchange of notes at Libreville and Sao Tome April 2, 1985, and February 26, 1986.
Entered into force February 26, 1986.
NP

Agreement regarding grants under the Foreign Assistance Act of 1961, as amended, and the furnishing of defense articles, related training and other defense services from the United States to the Government of Sao Tome and Principe.
Exchange of notes at Libreville and Sao Tome March 14 and August 19, 2005.
Entered into force August 19, 2005.
NP

FINANCE

Investment incentive agreement.
Signed at Washington September 10, 1998.
Entered into force September 10, 1998.
TIAS 12985

INTERNATIONAL CRIMINAL COURT

Agreement regarding the surrender of persons to the International Criminal Court.
Exchange of notes at Libreville and Sao Tome November 10 and 12, 2003.
Entered into force November 12, 2003.
TIAS 03-1112.2

TELECOMMUNICATION

Agreement for the operation of radio transmission facilities, with addendum.
Signed at Sao Tome May 22, 1992.
Entered into force June 21, 1992.
TIAS 97-214

SAUDI ARABIA

CIVIL AFFAIRS, EMERGENCIES & DEFENSE

Technical cooperation agreement.
Signed at Riyadh May 16, 2008.
Entered into force May 16, 2008.
TIAS
Extension:
January 16, 2013

CULTURAL EXCHANGES, PROPERTY & COOPERATION

Agreement for cultural exchange.
Signed at Jidda July 25, 1968.
Entered into force July 25, 1968.
20 UST 2804; TIAS 6749; 723 UNTS 141

DEFENSE

Agreement relating to the extending of procurement assistance to Saudi Arabia for the transfer of military supplies and equipment.
Exchange of notes at Jidda June 18, 1951.
Entered into force June 18, 1951.
2 UST 1460; TIAS 2289; 141 UNTS 67

Agreement providing for a military assistance advisory group.*
Exchange of notes at Jidda June 27, 1953.
Entered into force June 27, 1953.
4 UST 1482; TIAS 2812; 212 UNTS 335
Note:
* Terminated February 27, 1977, except that the provisions of paragraph 7 remain in force in respect of activities under the agreement of February 8 and 27, 1977 (28 UST 2409; TIAS 8558).

Agreement for the loan of F-86 aircraft to Saudi Arabia.*
Exchange of notes at Jidda November 10 and 13, 1962.
Entered into force November 13, 1962.
14 UST 1181; TIAS 5414; 488 UNTS 175
Amendment:
May 1 and 22, 1963 (14 UST 1184; TIAS 5414; 488 UNTS 180)

Note:
* Paragraph 1, first sentence of paragraph 5, and paragraphs 7 and 8 terminated by agreement of May 16 and November 11, 1965 (17 UST 1390; TIAS 6095).

Agreement relating to the transfer of F-86 aircraft to Saudi Arabia.
Exchange of notes at Jidda May 16 and November 11, 1965.
Entered into force November 11, 1965.
17 UST 1390; TIAS 6095

Agreement on privileges and immunities for United States personnel engaged in the training program for the maintenance and operation of F 5 aircraft in Saudi Arabia.
Exchange of notes at Jidda April 4 and July 5, 1972.
Entered into force July 5, 1972.
23 UST 1469; TIAS 7425

Agreement relating to the deposit by Saudi Arabia of ten percent of the value of grant military assistance provided by the United States.
Exchange of notes at Jidda April 11, April 19, and May 15, 1972.
Entered into force May 15, 1972.
23 UST 2664; TIAS 7459

Memorandum of understanding concerning the Saudi Arabian National Guard modernization program.
Signed at Jidda March 19, 1973.
Entered into force March 19, 1973.
24 UST 1106; TIAS 7634

Agreement relating to a United States military training mission in Saudi Arabia.
Exchange of notes at Jidda February 8 and 27, 1977.
Entered into force February 27, 1977.
28 UST 2409; TIAS 8558

Agreement concerning general security of military information.
Exchange of notes at Jidda February 24, 1981 and July 10, 1982.
Entered into force July 10, 1982.
TIAS

Memorandum of agreement regarding the assignment of Royal Saudi Naval Forces personnel to the U. S. Navy, with annexes.
Signed at Riyadh and Washington September 2, 2015 and February 1, 2016.
Entered into force February 1, 2016.
NP

ENVIRONMENT & CONSERVATION

Agreement for cooperation in the Global Learning and Observations to Benefit the Environment (GLOBE) Program, with appendices.
Signed at Washington September 30, 2002.
Entered into force September 30, 2002.
TIAS 02-930

FINANCE

Agreement on guaranteed private investment.
Signed at Washington February 27, 1975.
Entered into force April 26, 1975.
26 UST 459; TIAS 8045; 992 UNTS 231

FOREIGN ASSISTANCE

Economic assistance agreement for the expansion of the Port of Damman.
Exchange of notes at Jidda March 1 and at Riyadh May 1, 1958.
Entered into force May 1, 1958.
9 UST 589; TIAS 4038; 315 UNTS 221

Agreement on cooperation in the fields of economics, technology, industry and defense.
Signed at Washington June 8, 1974.
Entered into force June 8, 1974.
25 UST 3115; TIAS 7974.

Joint communique on the first session of the U.S.-Saudi Arabian Joint Commission on Economic Cooperation.
Done at Washington February 27, 1975.
Entered into force February 27, 1975.
26 UST 1689; TIAS 8128; 1006 UNTS 121

MARITIME MATTERS

Agreement relating to jurisdiction over vessels utilizing the Louisiana Offshore Oil Port.
Exchange of notes at Jidda March 1, 1981, and October 20, 1982.
Entered into force October 20, 1982.
TIAS 10552; 1871 UNTS 165

POSTAL MATTERS

Memorandum of understanding for the exchange of international express mail, with details of implementation.
Signed at Washington November 2, 1984.
Entered into force February 1, 1985.
TIAS 11009; 2022 UNTS 137

SCIENTIFIC & TECHNICAL COOPERATION

Agreement on science and technology cooperation, with annexes.
Signed at Riyadh December 2, 2008.
Entered into force October 20, 2009.
TIAS 09-1020

Memorandum of understanding for cooperation in the use of U.S. land remote sensing satellite data, with annexes.
Signed at Reston and Riyadh February 19, 2013 and April 27, 2013.
Entered into force April 27, 2013.
TIAS 13-427

TAXATION

Agreement for reciprocal exemption of taxes on income from the international operation of a ship or ships or aircraft.
Signed at Riyadh December 11, 1999.
Entered into force January 31, 2000.
TIAS 13077

TRADE & INVESTMENT

Provisional agreement in regard to diplomatic and consular representation, juridical protection, commerce, and navigation.
Signed at London November 7, 1933.
Entered into force November 7, 1933.
48 Stat. 1826; EAS 53; 11 Bevans 456; 142 LNTS 329

TRANSPORTATION

Memorandum of arrangement relating to technical assistance in developing and modernizing Saudi Arabia's civil aviation system, with annex.
Signed at Washington and Riyadh May 16 and August 3, 1985.
Entered into force August 3, 1985.
TIAS 11397

Memorandum of agreement relating to technical assistance in developing, modernizing, operating, or maintaining Saudi Arabia's civil aviation infrastructure.
Signed at Washington and Oklahoma City March 14 and 17, 2011.
Entered into force March 17, 2011.
NP

Air transport agreement, with annexes.
Signed at Jeddah May 28, 2013.
Entered into force October 22, 2014.
TIAS 14-1022

SENEGAL

CULTURAL EXCHANGES, PROPERTY & COOPERATION

Agreement relating to the establishment of a Peace Corps program in Senegal.
Exchange of notes at Dakar January 10 and 17, 1963.
Entered into force January 17, 1963.
14 UST 1622; TIAS 5467

DEFENSE

Agreement relating to the furnishing of military equipment, materials and services to Senegal for the purpose of assuring its security and supporting its development.
Exchange of notes at Dakar July 20, 1962.
Entered into force July 20, 1962.
13 UST 1803; TIAS 5127; 458 UNTS 137

Agreement concerning the provision of training related to defense articles under the United States International Military Education and Training (IMET) Program.
Exchange of notes at Dakar February 25 and July 15, 1983.
Entered into force July 15, 1983.
35 UST 3070; TIAS 10839; 2014 UNTS 555

Agreement regarding the provision of commodities, services and associated military education and training to assist Senegalese forces participating in the African Crisis Response Initiative.
Exchange of notes at Dakar July 24 and August 29, 1997.
Entered into force August 29, 1997.
NP

Agreement regarding grants under the Foreign Assistance Act of 1961, as amended, and the furnishing of defense articles, related training, and other defense services from the United States of America to the Government of Senegal.
Exchange of notes at Dakar November 22, 2000, and February 2, 2001.
Entered into force February 2, 2001.
NP

Acquisition and cross-servicing (mutual logistic support) agreement, with annexes.
Signed at Dakar and Patch Barracks May 8 and 14, 2001.
Entered into force May 14, 2001.
NP

Agreement on defense cooperation, the status of United States forces, and access to and use of agreed facilities and areas in the Republic of Senegal, with annex and appendices.
Signed at Dakar May 2, 2016.
Entered into force August 12, 2016.
TIAS 16-812

EMPLOYMENT

Agreement relating to employment of dependents of staff members of diplomatic and consular missions.
Signed at Dakar April 28, 1998.
Entered into force April 28, 1998.
TIAS 12947

ENVIRONMENT & CONSERVATION

Agreement for cooperation in the Global Learning and Observations to Benefit the Environment (GLOBE) Program, with appendices.
Signed at Dakar March 17, 1995.
Entered into force March 17, 1995.
TIAS

FINANCE

Agreement relating to investment guaranties.
Signed at Dakar June 12, 1963.
Entered into force provisionally June 12, 1963; definitively March 27, 1970.
18 UST 3197; TIAS 6417

Agreement regarding the consolidation and rescheduling of certain debts owed to or guaranteed by the United States Government and its agencies, with annexes.
Signed at Dakar August 26, 1982.
Entered into force October 25, 1982.
34 UST 1987; TIAS 10475; 1751 UNTS 55

Agreement regarding the consolidation and rescheduling of certain debts owed to or guaranteed by the United States Government and its agencies, with annexes.
Signed at Washington August 11, 1983.
Entered into force September 13, 1983.
35 UST 2444; TIAS 10808; 2011 UNTS 105

Agreement regarding the consolidation and rescheduling of certain debts owed to, guaranteed or insured by the United States Government and its agencies, with annexes.
Signed at Dakar August 22, 1984.
Entered into force September 24, 1984.
NP

Agreement regarding the consolidation and rescheduling of certain debts owed to, guaranteed by or insured by the United States Government and its agencies, with annexes.
Signed at Dakar June 5, 1985.
Entered into force July 15, 1985.
NP

Agreement regarding the consolidation and rescheduling of certain debts owed to, guaranteed by or insured by the United States Government and its agencies, with annexes.
Signed at Washington April 10, 1987.
Entered into force May 18, 1987.
NP

Agreement regarding the consolidation and rescheduling of certain debts owed to, guaranteed by or insured by the United States Government and its agencies, with annexes.
Signed at Dakar June 10, 1988.
Entered into force July 28, 1988.
NP

Agreement regarding the consolidation and rescheduling of certain debts owed to, guaranteed by, or insured by the United States Government and its agencies, with annexes.
Signed at Dakar July 14, 1989.
Entered into force August 24, 1989.
NP

Agreement regarding the consolidation and rescheduling of certain debts owed to, guaranteed by, or insured by the United States Government and its agencies, with annexes.
Signed at Dakar July 13, 1990.
Entered into force September 5, 1990.
NP

Agreement regarding the consolidation and rescheduling of certain debts owed to, guaranteed by, or insured by the United States Government and its agencies, with annexes.
Signed at Dakar November 26, 1991.
Entered into force February 10, 1992.
NP

Agreement regarding the consolidation, reduction and rescheduling of certain debts owed to, guaranteed by or insured by the United States Government and its agencies, with annexes.
Signed at Dakar July 28, 1994.
Entered into force August 29, 1994.
NP

Agreement regarding the consolidation, reduction and rescheduling of certain debts owed to, guaranteed by or insured by the United States Government and its agencies, with annexes.
Signed at Dakar August 28, 1995.
Entered into force November 1, 1995.
NP

Amendment:
November 17, 1997, and May 28, 1998 (NP)

Agreement regarding the reduction and reorganization of certain debts owed to, guaranteed by, or insured by the United States Government and its agencies, with annexes.
Signed at Dakar December 17, 1998.
Entered into force March 17, 1999.
NP

Agreement regarding the consolidation and reduction of certain debts owed to, guaranteed by, or insured by the United States Government and its agencies, with annexes.
Signed at Dakar July 17, 2001.
Entered into force September 6, 2001.
NP

Amendments:
November 26, 2002, and February 24, 2003
March 18 and May 25, 2004

Agreement regarding the reduction of certain debts owed to, guaranteed by, or insured by the United States Government, with annexes.
Signed at Dakar November 19, 2004.
Entered into force January 18, 2005.
NP

FOREIGN ASSISTANCE

Agreement providing for economic, financial, technical and related assistance.
Signed at Washington May 13, 1961.
Entered into force May 13, 1961.
12 UST 566; TIAS 4754; 409 UNTS 231

INTERNATIONAL CRIMINAL COURT

Agreement concerning the surrender of persons to the International Criminal Court.
Signed at Dakar June 19, 2003.
Entered into force June 27, 2003.
TIAS 03-627.3

LAW ENFORCEMENT

Agreement regarding mutual assistance between their customs administrations.
Signed at Dakar April 27, 2015.
Entered into force April 27, 2015.
TIAS 15-427

MARITIME MATTERS

Agreement concerning operational cooperation to suppress illicit transnational maritime activity.
Signed at Dakar April 29, 2011.
Entered into force April 29, 2011.
TIAS 11-429

POSTAL MATTERS

International express mail agreement, with detailed regulations.
Signed at Dakar and Washington June 5 and July 3, 1986.
Entered into force September 1, 1986.
TIAS 11519

TRADE & INVESTMENT

Treaty concerning the reciprocal encouragement and protection of investment, with annex and protocol.
Signed at Washington December 6, 1983.
Entered into force October 25, 1990.
TIAS

TRANSPORTATION

Memorandum of agreement for the provision of assistance in developing and modernizing the civil aviation infrastructure of Senegal
Signed July 28, 2000.
Entered into force July 28, 2000.
NP

Air transport agreement, with annexes.
Signed at Washington January 11, 2001.
Entered into force August 11, 2003.
TIAS 13134

SERBIA

On June 3, 2006, Montenegro declared independence from the state of Serbia and Montenegro. For agreements prior to June 3, 2006, see SERBIA AND MONTENEGRO and YUGOSLAVIA.

DEFENSE

Agreement on status protections and access to and use of military infrastructure.
Signed at Washington September 7, 2006.
Entered into force June 15, 2009.
NP

Acquisition and cross-servicing agreement, with annexes.
Signed at Belgrade November 8, 2006.
Entered into force June 15, 2009.
NP

Agreement regarding grants under the Foreign Assistance Act of 1961, as amended, or successor legislation, and the furnishing of defense articles, related training and defense services, including pursuant to the United States International Military Education and Training (IMET) Program.
Exchange of notes at Belgrade December 2 and 15, 2011.
Entered into force December 15, 2011.
NP

EDUCATION

Agreement on the status of the international school in Belgrade.
Signed at Belgrade June 5, 2006.
Entered into force September 28, 2010.
TIAS 10-928

FINANCE

Agreement regarding certain debts owed to, guaranteed by, or insured by the United States Government and its agencies, with annexes.
Signed at Belgrade January 30, 2009.
Entered into force March 13, 2009.
NP

TRANSPORTATION

Air transport agreement, with annexes.
Signed at Belgrade May 29, 2015.
Entered into force August 5, 2015.
TIAS 15-805

SERBIA AND MONTENEGRO

For agreements prior to April, 1992, see YUGOSLAVIA.
On June 3, 2006, the Republic of Montenegro declared its independence. The United States is reviewing the continued applicability of the agreements listed below.

EMPLOYMENT

Agreement on employment of dependents of members of diplomatic missions and consular posts.
Exchange of notes at Belgrade May 18 and 19, 2006.
Entered into force June 10, 2010.
TIAS 10-610.1

FINANCE

Investment incentive agreement.
Signed at Belgrade July 21, 2001.
Entered into force December 12, 2001.
TIAS

Agreement regarding the consolidation, reduction and rescheduling of certain debts owed to, guaranteed by, or insured by the United States Government and its agencies, with annexes.
Signed at Belgrade October 3, 2002.
Entered into force November 12, 2002.
NP

FOREIGN ASSISTANCE

Agreement concerning economic, technical and related assistance.
Signed at Belgrade March 6, 2001.
Entered into force May 11, 2001.
TIAS

SEYCHELLES

On June 28, 1976, Seychelles became an independent state. By an exchange of notes dated June 29, 1976, between the Government of the United Kingdom and the Government of Seychelles, it was agreed that all obligations and responsibilities of the Government of the United Kingdom which arise from any valid international instrument shall, as from the 29th of June 1976, be assumed by the Government of Seychelles insofar as such instruments may be held to have application to Seychelles. Also, rights and benefits heretofore enjoyed by the Government of the United Kingdom in virtue of the application of any such international instrument to Seychelles shall, as from the 29th of June 1976, be enjoyed by the Government of Seychelles.

CULTURAL EXCHANGES, PROPERTY & COOPERATION

Agreement relating to the establishment of a Peace Corps program in the Seychelles.
Exchange of notes at Victoria May 31 and June 9, 1978.
Entered into force June 9, 1978.
30 UST 1916; TIAS 9300; 1153 UNTS 41

DEFENSE

Agreement between the United States and the United Kingdom relating to the assurances required under the Mutual Security Act of 1951.
Exchange of notes at London January 8, 1952.
Entered into force January 8, 1952.
3 UST 4665; TIAS 2622; 126 UNTS 307

Agreement regarding the status of United States personnel who may be temporarily present in Seychelles.
Exchange of notes at Port Louis and Victoria October 27, 2008 and July 22, 2009.
Entered into force September 9, 2009.
TIAS

Agreement regarding grants under the Foreign Assistance Act of 1961, as amended, or successor legislation, the furnishing of defense articles, defense services and related training, including pursuant to the United States International Military Education and Training (IMET) Program.
Exchange of notes at Port Louis and Victoria August 28 and September 25, 2009.
Entered into force September 25, 2009.
NP

DIPLOMATIC & CONSULAR RELATIONS

Consular convention between the United States and the United Kingdom.
Signed at Washington June 6, 1951.
Entered into force September 7, 1952.
3 UST 3426; TIAS 2494; 165 UNTS 121

FINANCE

Investment incentive agreement.
Signed at Victoria February 3, 2012.
Entered into force October 5, 2012.
TIAS 12-1005

FOREIGN ASSISTANCE

Economic cooperation agreement between the United States and the United Kingdom.
Signed at London July 6, 1948.
Applicable to Seychelles July 6, 1948.
62 Stat. 2596; TIAS 1795; 12 Bevans 874; 22 UNTS 263

Amendments:
January 3, 1950 (1 UST 184; TIAS 2036; 86 UNTS 304)
May 25, 1951 (2 UST 1292; TIAS 2277; 99 UNTS 308)
February 25, 1953 (4 UST 1528; TIAS 2815; 172 UNTS 332)

INTELLECTUAL PROPERTY

Declaration by the United States and the United Kingdom affording reciprocal protection to trade-marks.
Signed at London October 24, 1877.
Entered into force October 24, 1877.
20 Stat. 703; TS 138; 12 Bevans 198

INTERNATIONAL CRIMINAL COURT

Agreement regarding the surrender of persons to the International Criminal Court.
Signed at Victoria June 4, 2003.
Entered into force July 17, 2003.
TIAS 03-717

LAW ENFORCEMENT

Extradition treaty between the United States and the United Kingdom.
Signed at London December 22, 1931.
Entered into force June 24, 1935.
47 Stat. 2122; TS 849; 12 Bevans 482; 163 LNTS 59

POSTAL MATTERS

International express mail agreement, with detailed regulations.
Signed at Victoria and Washington May 13 and June 15, 1992.
Entered into force September 21, 1992.
TIAS 11871

TELECOMMUNICATION

Agreement between the United States and the United Kingdom relating to the reciprocal granting of authorizations to permit licensed amateur radio operators of either country to operate their stations in the other country.
Exchange of notes at London November 26, 1965.
Applicable to Seychelles December 11, 1969.
16 UST 2047; TIAS 5941; 561 UNTS 193

Agreement between the United States and the United Kingdom extending to certain territories the application of the agreement of November 26, 1965, relating to the reciprocal granting of authorizations to permit licensed amateur radio operators of either country to operate their stations in the other country.
Exchange of notes at London December 11, 1969.
Entered into force December 11, 1969.
20 UST 4089; TIAS 6800; 732 UNTS 334

TRANSPORTATION

Air transport agreement.
Signed at Victoria December 7, 2015.
Entered into force January 7, 2016.
TIAS 16-107

SIERRA LEONE

On April 27, 1961, Sierra Leone attained fully responsible status within the British Commonwealth (Sierra Leone Independence Act, 1961). By an exchange of letters, dated May 5, 1961, between the High Commissioner for the United Kingdom in Sierra Leone and the Minister of External Affairs of Sierra Leone, the Government of Sierra Leone agreed to assume, from April 27, 1961, all obligations and responsibilities of the United Kingdom which arise from any valid international instrument insofar as such instrument may be held to have application to Sierra Leone. Also, rights and benefits enjoyed by the Government of the United Kingdom by virtue of the application of any such international instrument to Sierra Leone are from April 27, 1961, enjoyed by the Government of Sierra Leone.

CULTURAL EXCHANGES, PROPERTY & COOPERATION

Agreement concerning the program of the Peace Corps in Sierra Leone.
Signed at Freetown November 2, 2009.
Entered into force November 2, 2009.
TIAS 09-1102

DEFENSE

Agreement concerning the provision of training related to defense articles under the United States International Military Education and Training (IMET) Program.
Exchange of notes at Freetown April 1 and May 26, 1982.
Entered into force May 26, 1982.
34 UST 1115; TIAS 10397; 1566 UNTS 125

Agreement regarding grants under the Foreign Assistance Act of 1961, as amended, and the furnishing of defense articles, related training and other defense services to the Government of Sierra Leone.
Exchange of notes at Freetown May 3 and 19, 1999.
Entered into force May 19, 1999.
NP

DIPLOMATIC & CONSULAR RELATIONS

Consular convention between the United States and the United Kingdom.
Signed at Washington June 6, 1951.
Entered into force September 7, 1952.
3 UST 3426; TIAS 2494; 165 UNTS 121

EMPLOYMENT

Agreement relating to the employment of dependents of official government employees.
Exchange of notes at Freetown January 17 and February 24, 1997.
Entered into force February 24, 1997.
TIAS 12836

FINANCE

Agreement relating to investment guaranties under section 413 (b)(4) of the Mutual Security Act of 1954, as amended.
Exchange of notes at Freetown May 16 and 19, 1961.
Entered into force May 19, 1961.
12 UST 619; TIAS 4759; 409 UNTS 251
Amendment:
December 28, 1962, and November 13, 1963 (14 UST 1667; TIAS 5470; 494 UNTS 324)

Agreement regarding the consolidation and rescheduling of certain debts owed to, guaranteed by or insured by the United States Government and its agencies, with annex.
Signed at Freetown August 28, 1985.
Entered into force October 23, 1985.
NP

Agreement regarding the consolidation and rescheduling of certain debts owed to, guaranteed by or insured by the United States Government and its agencies, with annexes.
Signed at Freetown August 21, 1987.
Entered into force November 5, 1987.
NP

Agreement regarding the consolidation and rescheduling or refinancing of certain debts owed to, guaranteed by, or insured by the United States Government and its agencies, with annexes.
Signed at Freetown April 19, 1993.
Entered into force June 18, 1993.
NP

Agreement regarding the consolidation and rescheduling of certain debts owed to, guaranteed by or insured by the United States Government, with annexes.
Signed at Freetown January 11, 1995.
Entered into force March 1, 1995.
NP

Agreement regarding the consolidation and rescheduling of certain debts owed to, guaranteed by or insured by the United States Government, with annexes.
Signed at Freetown August 7, 1996.
Entered into force October 16, 1996.
NP

Agreement regarding the consolidation and reduction of certain debts owed to, guaranteed by, or insured by the United States Government, with annexes.
Signed at Freetown April 25, 2003.
Entered into force June 9, 2003.
NP

Amendments:
November 2, 2005, and January 12, 2006
September 7, 2006
December 27, 2006, and March 27, 2007

Agreement regarding the reduction of certain debts owed to, guaranteed by, or insured by the United States Government and its Agency.
Signed at Freetown June 7, 2007.
Entered into force January 29, 2008.
NP

FOREIGN ASSISTANCE

General agreement for a program of economic, technical and related assistance.
Signed at Freetown May 5, 1961.
Entered into force May 5, 1961.
12 UST 547; TIAS 4752; 409 UNTS 193

Millennium Challenge Account Threshold Program Grant Agreement.
Signed at Freetown November 17, 2015.
Entered into force February 16, 2016.
TIAS 16-216

INTELLECTUAL PROPERTY

Declaration by the United States and the United Kingdom relating to reciprocal protection to trade-marks.
Signed at London October 24, 1877.
Entered into force October 24, 1877.
20 Stat. 703; TS 138; 12 Bevans 198

INTERNATIONAL CRIMINAL COURT

Agreement regarding the surrender of persons to the International Criminal Court.
Signed at Freetown March 31, 2003.
Entered into force May 20, 2003.
TIAS 03-520.2

LAW ENFORCEMENT

Extradition treaty between the United States and the United Kingdom.
Signed at London December 22, 1931.
Entered into force June 24, 1935.
47 Stat. 2122; TS 849; 12 Bevans 482; 163 LNTS 59

Agreement to facilitate the conduct of litigation with international aspects in either country.
Exchange of notes at Freetown March 31 and May 6, 1966.
Entered into force May 6, 1966.
17 UST 944; TIAS 6056; 594 UNTS 47

POSTAL MATTERS

Parcel post convention.
Signed at Freetown February 27, 1930, and at Washington April 16, 1930.
Operative May 1, 1930.
46 Stat. 2736; Post Office Department print; 109 LNTS 9

International express mail agreement, with detailed regulations.
Signed at Freetown and Washington May 31 and July 26, 1988.
Entered into force August 15, 1988.
TIAS 11591.

Postal money order agreement.
Signed at Freetown and Washington March 29 and July 18, 1989.
Entered into force September 18, 1989.
TIAS 11683

INTELPOST memorandum of understanding, with detailed regulations.
Signed at Freetown and Washington June 5 and 19, 1995.
Entered into force August 1, 1995.
NP

PROPERTY

Convention between the United States and the United Kingdom relating to the tenure and disposition of real and personal property.
Signed at Washington March 2, 1899.
Applicable to Sierra Leone February 9, 1901.
31 Stat. 1939; TS 146; 12 Bevans 246

TELECOMMUNICATION

Agreement relating to the reciprocal granting of authorizations to permit licensed amateur radio operators of either country to operate their stations in the other country.
Exchange of notes at Freetown August 14 and 16, 1965.
Entered into force August 16, 1965.
16 UST 1131; TIAS 5856; 579 UNTS 55

Agreement relating to radio communications between amateur stations on behalf of third parties.
Exchange of notes at Freetown October 23, 1985, and June 18, 1986.
Entered into force July 18, 1986.
TIAS 11358

TRANSPORTATION

Arrangement between the United States and the United Kingdom relating to pilot licenses to operate civil aircraft.
Exchange of notes at Washington March 28 and April 5, 1935.
Entered into force May 5, 1935.
49 Stat. 3731; EAS 77; 12 Bevans 513; 162 LNTS 59

Air transport agreement.
Signed at Washington September 10, 2012.
Entered into force September 10, 2012.
TIAS 12-910

SINGAPORE

On August 9, 1965, Singapore became an independent and sovereign state. Article 13 of the Constitution and Malaysia (Singapore Amendment) Act, 1965, annexed to the Independence of Singapore agreement, 1965, reads in part as follows:

Any treaty, agreement or convention entered into before Singapore Day between the Yang di Pertuan Agong or the Government of Malaysia and another country or countries, including those deemed to be so by Article 169 of the Constitution of Malaysia shall insofar as such instruments have application to Singapore, be deemed to be a treaty, agreement or convention between Singapore and that country or countries, and any decision taken by an international organization and accepted before Singapore Day by the Government of Malaysia shall insofar as that decision has application to Singapore be deemed to be a decision of an international organization of which Singapore is a member.

CONSULAR AFFAIRS

Agreement relating to visas.*
Exchange of notes at London October 15 and 22, 1954.

Agreement continuing in force the 1954 agreement with respect to the Federation of Malaya.*
Exchange of letters at Kuala Lumpur March 5 and 12, 1958.

Note:

* The status of this agreement is under review.

DEFENSE

Agreement relating to the purchase by Malaya of military equipment, materials, and services from the United States.
Exchange of notes at Washington June 30 and July 9, 1958.
Entered into force July 9, 1958.
9 UST 1235; TIAS 4108; 336 UNTS 79

Agreement relating to the establishment of a United States Air Force management training assistance team in Singapore, with appendices.
Exchange of letters at Singapore February 23 and 24, 1977.
Entered into force February 24, 1977.
29 UST 1474; TIAS 8889

Memorandum of understanding for the exchange of individual personnel between the United States Army Western Command and the Republic of Singapore Armed Forces.
Signed at Singapore March 25, 1981.
Entered into force March 25, 1981.
TIAS 10874

Agreement concerning the provision of training related to defense articles under the United States International Military Education and Training (IMET) Program.
Exchange of notes at Singapore May 12 and June 23, 1981.
Entered into force June 23, 1981.
33 UST 2034; TIAS 10166; 1529 UNTS 491

Memorandum of understanding concerning exchange of service personnel between the United States Navy and Republic of Singapore Air Force.
Signed at Singapore and Washington July 19 and September 1, 1982.
Entered into force September 1, 1982.
34 UST 2151; TIAS 10482; 1751 UNTS 115

Agreement concerning general security of military information.
Exchange of notes at Singapore June 25, 1982, and March 9, 1983.
Entered into force March 9, 1983.
35 UST 2796; TIAS 10819; 1590 UNTS 85

Memorandum of understanding concerning configuration management of tactical command, control and communications standards, with annexes.
Signed at Camp Smith, Hawaii February 22, 1991.
Entered into force February 22, 1991.
TIAS 12369

Agreement on the status of Singapore personnel in the United States, with agreed minutes.
Signed at Singapore December 3, 1993.
Entered into force December 3, 1993.
TIAS 12519

Agreement concerning exchange of research and development information, with appendix.
Signed at Washington December 4, 1995.
Entered into force December 4, 1995.
TIAS

Note:

Only the annexes of this agreement remain in force. They are now applicable to the agreement signed December 30, 2009 and January 28, 2010.

Agreement concerning technology research and development projects, with annex.
Signed at Washington May 2, 1998.
Entered into force May 2, 1998.
TIAS

Agreement regarding the exchange of engineers and scientists, with annexes.
Signed at Singapore and Washington March 8 and 22, 2004.
Entered into force March 22, 2004.
NP

Strategic framework agreement for a closer cooperation partnership in defense and security.
Signed at Washington July 12, 2005.
Entered into force July 12, 2005.
TIAS 05-712

Agreement concerning combating terrorism research and development, with annex.
Signed at Washington and Singapore March 14 and 22, 2006.
Entered into force March 22, 2006.
TIAS 06-322

Amendment:

February 26 and March 21, 2016 (TIAS 06-322)

Agreement concerning the cooperation on information assurance (IA) and computer network defense (CND).
Signed at Singapore February 18, 2008.
Entered into force February 18, 2008.
TIAS 08-218

Agreement regarding the exchange of military personnel, with annexes.
Signed at Washington and Singapore May 22 and October 22, 2009.
Entered into force October 22, 2009.
NP

Agreement concerning exchange of research and development information.
Signed at Singapore and Washington December 30, 2009 and January 28, 2010.
Entered into force January 28, 2010.
NP
Amendment:
May 17 and June 5, 2013

Acquisition and cross-servicing agreement, with annexes.
Signed at Camp H.M. Smith, Hawaii and MINDEF, Singapore March 28 and April 4, 2011.
Entered into force April 4, 2011.
NP

Agreement for research, development, testing, and evaluation projects, with annexes.
Signed at Washington April 22 and 28, 2011.
Entered into force April 28, 2011.
TIAS 11-428

Memorandum of agreement on establishing a student exchange program, with appendixes.
Signed August 26, 2015.
Entered into force August 26, 2015.
NP

DIPLOMATIC & CONSULAR RELATIONS

Consular convention between the United States and the United Kingdom.
Signed at Washington June 6, 1951.
Entered into force September 7, 1952.
3 UST 3426; TIAS 2494; 165 UNTS 121

FINANCE

Agreement relating to investment guaranties.
Exchange of notes at Singapore March 25, 1966.
Entered into force March 25, 1966.
17 UST 534; TIAS 5999; 580 UNTS 221

FOREIGN ASSISTANCE

Economic cooperation agreement between the United States and the United Kingdom.
Signed at London July 6, 1948.
Applicable to Singapore July 6, 1948.
62 Stat. 2596; TIAS 1795; 12 Bevans 874; 22 UNTS 263
Amendments:
January 3, 1950 (1 UST 184; TIAS 2036; 86 UNTS 304)
May 25, 1951 (2 UST 1292; TIAS 2277; 99 UNTS 308)
February 25, 1953 (4 UST 1528; TIAS 2815; 172 UNTS 332)

HEALTH & MEDICAL COOPERATION

Agreement establishing the Regional Emergency Diseases Intervention (REDI) Center.
Signed at Singapore November 22, 2005.
Entered into force April 7, 2006.
TIAS 06-407.1

INTELLECTUAL PROPERTY

Declaration by the United States and the United Kingdom relating to reciprocal protection to trade-marks.
Signed at London October 24, 1877.
Entered into force October 24, 1877.
20 Stat. 703; TS 138; 12 Bevans 198

Agreement regarding the establishment of copyright relations, with enclosures.
Exchange of letters at Washington April 16 and 27, 1987.
Entered into force April 27, 1987; effective May 18, 1987.
TIAS 11928

INTERNATIONAL CRIMINAL COURT

Agreement regarding the surrender of persons to international tribunals.
Exchange of notes at Singapore October 17, 2003.
Entered into force October 17, 2003.
TIAS 03-1017

LAW ENFORCEMENT

Extradition treaty between the United States and the United Kingdom.
Signed at London December 22, 1931.
Entered into force June 24, 1935.
47 Stat. 2122; TS 849; 12 Bevans 482; 163 LNTS 59

Agreement confirming the continuance in force between the United States and Singapore of the December 22, 1931, extradition treaty between the United States and the United Kingdom.
Exchange of notes at Singapore April 23 and June 10, 1969.
Entered into force June 10, 1969.
20 UST 2764; TIAS 6744; 723 UNTS 201

Agreement concerning the investigation of drug trafficking offences and the seizure and forfeiture of proceeds and instrumentalities of drug trafficking, with exchange of notes.
Signed at Singapore November 3, 2000.
Entered into force February 12, 2001.
TIAS 13125

Agreement regarding mutual assistance between their customs administrations.
Signed at Singapore December 1, 2014.
Entered into force February 1, 2015.
TIAS 15-201

Agreement on enhancing cooperation in preventing and combating serious crime.
Signed at Singapore July 19, 2012.
Entered into force December 20, 2016.
TIAS

MARITIME MATTERS

Agreement relating to jurisdiction over vessels utilizing the Louisiana Offshore Oil Port.
Exchange of notes at Singapore September 1, 1983, and January 16, 1984.
Entered into force January 17, 1984.
35 UST 4262; TIAS 10926; 2015 UNTS 117

POSTAL MATTERS

Parcel post convention.
Signed at Kuala Lumpur January 21 and at Washington March 22, 1935.
Entered into force April 1, 1935.
49 Stat. 3133; Post Office Department print; 161 LNTS 41

International express mail agreement, with detailed regulations.
Signed at Singapore and Washington January 5 and 10, 1979.
Entered into force February 9, 1979; effective January 1, 1979.
30 UST 3383; TIAS 9396; 1180 UNTS 109.

Memorandum of understanding concerning the operation of the INTELPOST field trial, with details of implementation.
Signed at Singapore and Washington November 26, 1986, and February 5, 1987.
Entered into force February 5, 1987; effective December 1, 1986.
TIAS 11307

PROPERTY

Convention between the United States and the United Kingdom relating to tenure and disposition of real and personal property.*
Signed at Washington March 2, 1899.
Entered into force August 7, 1900.
31 Stat. 1939; TS 146; 12 Bevans 246

Note:
* Notification given on February 9, 1901, of application to the Straits Settlements.

SCIENTIFIC & TECHNICAL COOPERATION

Agreement on cooperation in science and technology for homeland/domestic security matters.
Signed at Washington March 27, 2007.
Entered into force March 27, 2007.
TIAS 07-327

SOCIAL SECURITY

Agreement concerning United States participation on a limited voluntary basis in the Central Provident Fund Act for certain employees of the United States Government in Singapore.
Exchange of notes at Singapore September 8 and 9, 1975.
Entered into force September 9, 1975.
26 UST 2734; TIAS 8190; 1052 UNTS 297

TAXATION

Agreement concerning reciprocal exemption from income tax of income derived from the international operation of ships and aircraft.
Exchange of notes at Singapore July 5 and 28, 1988.
Entered into force July 28, 1988.
TIAS 11658; 2204 UNTS 699

Agreement to improve international tax compliance and to implement the Foreign Account Tax Compliance Act, with annexes.
Signed at Singapore December 9, 2014.
Entered into force March 18, 2015.
TIAS 15-318

TRADE & INVESTMENT

United States-Singapore free trade agreement, with annexes and related exchanges of letters.
Signed at Washington May 6, 2003.
Entered into force January 1, 2004.
TIAS

TRANSPORTATION

Arrangement between the United States and the United Kingdom relating to pilot licenses to operate civil aircraft.
Exchange of notes at Washington March 28, and April 5, 1935.
Entered into force May 5, 1935.
49 Stat. 3731; EAS 77; 12 Bevans 513; 162 LNTS 59

Memorandum of agreement relating to the provision of flight inspection services.
Signed at Washington and Singapore August 16 and October 25, 1978.
Entered into force October 25, 1978; effective October 1, 1978.
30 UST 263; TIAS 9195; 1150 UNTS 263

Air transport agreement, with annexes.*
Signed at Singapore April 8, 1997.
Entered into force April 8, 1997.
TIAS 12850
*This agreement is suspended so long as the Multilateral Agreement on the Liberalization of International Air Transportation, signed May 1, 2001, remains in force between the United States and Singapore.

Agreement for the promotion of aviation safety.
Signed at Singapore February 24, 2004.
Entered into force February 24, 2004.
TIAS 04-224

Memorandum of cooperation in civil aviation security.
Signed at Washington June 2, 2008.
Entered into force June 2, 2008.
TIAS 08-602

WEAPONS

Agreement concerning cooperation on combating nuclear terrorism, the non-proliferation of weapons of mass destruction, and related items and technologies, with annexes.
Signed at Singapore January 18, 2010.
Entered into force January 18, 2010.
TIAS 10-118

SLOVAK REPUBLIC

For agreements prior to the independence of the Slovak Republic on January 1, 1993, see CZECHOSLOVAKIA.

ATOMIC ENERGY

Arrangement for the exchange of technical information and cooperation in nuclear safety matters, with addenda and annex.
Signed at Vienna September 16, 2015.
Entered into force September 16, 2015.
TIAS 15-916.1

CULTURAL EXCHANGES, PROPERTY & COOPERATION

Agreement on protection and preservation of certain cultural sites and monuments.
Signed at Washington March 9, 2001.
Entered into force March 9, 2001.
TIAS 13145

DEFENSE

Agreement regarding grants under the Foreign Assistance Act of 1961 and the furnishing of defense articles, related training, and other defense services from the United States of America to the Slovak Republic.
Exchange of notes at Bratislava December 12, 1994 and January 3, 1995.
Entered into force January 3, 1995.
NP

Agreement concerning security measures for the protection of classified military information.
Signed at Washington April 11, 1995.
Entered into force April 11, 1995.
TIAS 12246

Acquisition and cross-servicing agreement, with annex.
Signed at Bratislava December 15, 1998.
Entered into force December 15, 1998.
NP

EDUCATION

Agreement concerning the J. William Fulbright Commission for Educational Exchange in the Slovak Republic.
Signed at Bratislava March 22, 2005.
Entered into force April 21, 2005; effective September 23, 2004.
TIAS 05-421.2

Memorandum of understanding concerning the Fulbright Exchange Program.
Signed at Ljubljana October 6, 2011. Effected by Exchange of Notes at Ljubljana November 30 and December 2, 2011.
Entered into force December 2, 2011.
TIAS 11-1202

EMPLOYMENT

Agreement relating to the employment of dependents of official government employees.
Exchange of notes at Bratislava April 8, 1994, February 17 and July 12, 1995.
Entered into force July 12, 1995.
TIAS 12677

LAW ENFORCEMENT

Agreement on enhancing cooperation in preventing and combating crime.
Signed at Washington October 8, 2008.
Entered into force April 17, 2009.
TIAS 09-417

Instrument on extradition as contemplated by Article 3(2) of the agreement on extradition between the United States of America and the European Union signed June 25, 2003, with annex.
Signed at Bratislava February 6, 2006.
Entered into force February 1, 2010.
TIAS 10-201.19

Instrument as contemplated by Article 3(3) of the agreement on mutual legal assistance between the United States of America and the European Union signed June 25, 2003, with annex.
Signed at Bratislava February 6, 2006.
Entered into force February 1, 2010.
TIAS 10-201.45

POSTAL MATTERS

International express mail agreement, with detailed regulations.
Signed at Bratislava and Washington June 24 and 27, 1994.
Entered into force August 1, 1994.
NP

SCIENTIFIC & TECHNICAL COOPERATION

Memorandum of understanding on science and engineering cooperation, with annexes.
Signed at Bratislava July 14, 1994.
Entered into force July 14, 1994.
TIAS 12557

Agreement for scientific and technological cooperation, with annexes.
Signed at Washington November 8, 2007.
Entered into force June 12, 2008.
TIAS 08-612

SOCIAL SECURITY

Social security agreement, with administrative arrangement.
Signed at Bratislava December 10, 2012.
Entered into force May 1, 2014.
TIAS 14-501

TAXATION

Convention for the avoidance of double taxation and the prevention of fiscal evasion with respect to taxes on income and capital.*
Signed at Bratislava October 8, 1993.
Entered into force December 30, 1993.
TIAS

Note:

* With understanding.

Agreement to improve international tax compliance and to implement the Foreign Account Tax Compliance Act, with annexes.
Signed at Bratislava July 31, 2015.
Entered into force November 9, 2015.
TIAS 15-1109

TRADE & INVESTMENT

Additional protocol to the treaty between the United States and the Czech and Slovak Federal Republic concerning the reciprocal encouragement and protection of investment of October 22, 1991.
Signed at Brussels September 22, 2003.
Entered into force July 13, 2004.
TIAS

TRANSPORTATION

Air transport agreement, with annexes.*
Signed at Bratislava January 22, 2001.
Entered into force February 7, 2001.
TIAS 13142

Note:

* This agreement is suspended for the duration of provisional application of the U.S. – E.U. Air Transport Agreement signed April 25 and 30, 2007.

SLOVENIA

On June 25, 1991, Slovenia became an independent state. For agreements prior to the independence of Slovenia, see YUGOSLAVIA.

ATOMIC ENERGY

Arrangement for the exchange of technical information and cooperation in nuclear safety matters, with addenda.
Signed at Vienna April 4, 2011.
Entered into force April 24, 2012.
TIAS 12-424.1

CULTURAL EXCHANGES, PROPERTY & COOPERATION

Agreement on the protection and preservation of certain cultural properties.
Signed at Washington May 8, 1996.
Entered into force June 23, 1997.
TIAS 12752

DEFENSE

Agreement concerning the provision of training related to defense articles under the United States International Military Education and Training (IMET) Program.
Exchange of notes at Ljubljana July 29 and August 6, 1993.
Entered into force August 6, 1993.
NP

Security agreement concerning security measures for the protection of classified military information.
Signed at Washington May 8, 1996.
Entered into force June 27, 1997.
TIAS 12753

Agreement concerning the overflight and transit through the territory and airspace of Slovenia by U.S. aircraft, vehicles and personnel for purposes of supporting security, transition and reconstruction operations in Iraq.
Exchange of notes at Ljubljana June 9 and 11, 2003.
Entered into force September 2, 2003.
TIAS 03-902

Agreement concerning geospatial intelligence information exchange and cooperation, with appendix.
Signed at Ljubljana and Bethesda February 25 and March 24, 2009.
Entered into force June 2, 2010.
NP

Agreement concerning the provision of training related to defense articles pursuant to the Global Peace Operations Initiative (GPOI) and the United States International Military Education and Training (IMET) Program.
Effected by exchange of notes at Ljubljana November 16, 2012 and March 1, 2013.
Entered into force March 1, 2013.
NP

Acquisition and cross-servicing agreement, with annexes.
Signed at Ljubljana and Patch Barracks November 27 and December 10, 2014.
Entered into force November 11, 2015.
NP

Reciprocal defense procurement agreement.
Signed at Washington April 8, 2016.
Entered into force June 21, 2016.
TIAS 16-621

EDUCATION

Memorandum of understanding concerning the Fulbright Exchange Program . Effected by exchange of notes at Ljubljana November 30 and December 2, 2011.
Signed at Ljubljana October 6,2011.
Entered into force December 2,2011.
TIAS 11-1202
Amendment:
September 4, 2014 (TIAS 11-1202)

EMPLOYMENT

Agreement relating to the employment of dependents of official government employees.
Exchange of notes at Ljubljana April 30 and May 8, 1998.
Entered into force June 10, 1998.
TIAS 12951

FINANCE

Investment incentive agreement.
Signed at Washington April 26, 1994.
Entered into force September 8, 1994.
TIAS 12178

Agreement regarding the payment by the Republic of Slovenia of the debt incurred by the former Socialist Federal Republic of Yugoslavia and owed to the United States Government including its agencies, with annexes.
Signed at Ljubljana June 9, 2015.
Entered into force July 27, 2015.
TIAS 15-727

LAW ENFORCEMENT

Agreement comprising the instrument as contemplated by Article 3(2) of the agreement on extradition between the United States of America and the European Union signed June 25, 2003, as to the application of the treaty on extradition between the United States and the Kingdom of Serbia of October 25, 1901, with annex.
Signed at Ljubljana October 17, 2005.
Entered into force February 1, 2010.
TIAS 10-201.20

Agreement comprising the instrument as contemplated by Article 3(3) of the agreement on mutual legal assistance between the United States of America and the European Union signed June 25, 2003, with annex.
Signed at Ljubljana October 17, 2005.
Entered into force February 1, 2010.
TIAS 10-201.46

Agreement for the exchange of terrorism screening information.
Signed at Washington February 8, 2011.
Entered into force November 24, 2011.
TIAS 11-1124.1

Agreement on enhancing cooperation in preventing and combating serious crime.
Signed Ljubljana September 13, 2012.
Entered into force May 12, 2013, with the exception of Articles 8 through 10.
TIAS 13-512

POSTAL MATTERS

International express mail agreement, with detailed regulations.
Signed at Ljubljana and Washington January 27 and March 22, 1993.
Entered into force May 1, 1993.
TIAS 11918

SCIENTIFIC & TECHNICAL COOPERATION

Agreement for scientific and technological cooperation, with annexes.
Signed at Ljubljana June 21, 1999.
Entered into force December 17, 1999.
TIAS 13048

TAXATION

Convention for the avoidance of double taxation and the prevention of fiscal evasion with respect to taxes on income and capital.
Signed at Ljubljana June 21, 1999.
Entered into force June 22, 2001.
TIAS

Agreement to improve international tax compliance and to implement the Foreign Account Tax Compliance Act, with annexes.
Signed at Ljubljana June 2, 2014.
Entered into force July 1, 2014.
TIAS 14-701.2

SOLOMON ISLANDS

On July 7, 1978, Solomon Islands became an independent state. In a note dated July 7, 1978, to the Secretary General of the United Nations, the Prime Minister made a statement reading in part as follows:

I have the honour to inform you that Solomon Islands is now an independent nation ready to participate with other nations in fulfilling obligations under international law with respect to treaties to which this Government succeeded upon Independence. However, it is necessary to examine in depth such treaties to ascertain whether or not under customary international law any may have lapsed. Until this has been done the Government of Solomon Islands wish —

(a) that it be presumed that each treaty has been legally succeeded to by Solomon Islands; and

(b) that future action be based on the presumption in (a) above.

You will be notified in due course of those treaties this Government regards as having lapsed and those treaties which this Government wishes to terminate. Notice of lapse or termination in an appropriate form will also be given to the country or countries that is or are party to those treaties.

CULTURAL EXCHANGES, PROPERTY & COOPERATION

Agreement concerning the program of the Peace Corps in the Solomon Islands.
Signed at Honiara November 6, 1998.
Entered into force November 6, 1998.
TIAS 12994

DEFENSE

Agreement between the United States and the United Kingdom relating to the assurances required under the Mutual Security Act of 1951.
Exchange of notes at London January 8, 1952.
Applicable to Solomon Islands January 8, 1952.
3 UST 4665; TIAS 2622; 126 UNTS 307.

Agreement concerning the provision of training related to defense articles under the United States International Military Education and Training (IMET) Program.
Exchange of notes at Port Moresby and Honiara June 7 and August 18, 1983.
Entered into force August 18, 1983.
35 UST 1699; TIAS 10759; 2011 UNTS 107

Agreement concerning the status of members of the United States Forces in Solomon Islands.
Signed at Honiara July 3, 1991.
Entered into force July 3, 1991.
TIAS

FOREIGN ASSISTANCE

Economic cooperation agreement between the United States and the United Kingdom.
Signed at London July 6, 1948.
Applicable to Solomon Islands July 6, 1948.
62 Stat. 2596; TIAS 1795; 12 Bevans 874; 22 UNTS 263

Amendments:
January 3, 1950 (1 UST 184; TIAS 2036; 86 UNTS 304)
May 25, 1951 (2 UST 1292; TIAS 2277; 99 UNTS 308)
February 25, 1953 (4 UST 1528; TIAS 2815; 172 UNTS 332)

INTERNATIONAL CRIMINAL COURT

Agreement regarding the surrender of persons to the International Criminal Court.
Signed at Washington September 19, 2003.
Entered into force March 17, 2004.
TIAS 04-317

POSTAL MATTERS

International express mail agreement, with detailed regulations.
Signed at Honiara and Washington April 19 and June 27, 1991.
Entered into force August 1, 1991.
TIAS 11808

TELECOMMUNICATION

Agreement between the United States and the United Kingdom relating to the reciprocal granting of authorizations to permit licensed amateur radio operators of either country to operate their stations in the other country.
Exchange of notes at London November 26, 1965.
Applicable to the Solomon Islands December 11, 1969.
16 UST 2047; TIAS 5941; 561 UNTS 193

Agreement between the United States and the United Kingdom extending to certain territories the application of the agreement relating to the reciprocal granting of authorizations to permit licensed amateur radio operators of either country to operate their stations in the other country.
Exchange of notes at London December 11, 1969.
Entered into force December 11, 1969.
20 UST 4089; TIAS 6800; 732 UNTS 334

SOMALIA

CULTURAL EXCHANGES, PROPERTY & COOPERATION

Agreement relating to the establishment of a Peace Corps program in the Somali Republic.
Exchange of notes at Mogadishu March 29 and April 17, 1962.
Entered into force April 17, 1962.
13 UST 499; TIAS 5016; 436 UNTS 107

DEFENSE

Agreement concerning mapping, charting and geodesy cooperation, with annex.
Signed at Washington and Mogadishu December 31, 1984.
Entered into force December 31, 1984.
TIAS 11224

Agreement regarding grants under the Foreign Assistance Act of 1961, as amended, or successor legislation, and the furnishing of defense articles, defense services, and related training, including, pursuant to the United States International Military Education and Training (IMET) Program.
Effected by exchange of Notes at Nairobi February 26 and May 30, 2013.
Entered into force May 30, 2013.
NP

EMPLOYMENT

Agreement relating to employment of dependents of members of diplomatic missions and consular posts assigned to official duty.
Exchange of notes at Washington March 11 and April 8, 2015.
Entered into force April 8, 2015.
TIAS 15-408

FINANCE

Agreement relating to investment guaranties.
Exchange of notes at Mogadishu November 27, 1962, and January 8, 1964.
Entered into force January 8, 1964.
15 UST 6; TIAS 5512; 505 UNTS 165

Agreement regarding the consolidation and rescheduling of certain debts owed to, guaranteed by or insured by the United States Government and its agencies, with annexes.
Signed at Washington May 9, 1985.
Entered into force June 12, 1985.
NP

Agreement regarding the consolidation and rescheduling of certain debts owed to, guaranteed by or insured by the United States Government and its agencies, with annexes.
Signed at Mogadishu January 25, 1988.
Entered into force February 26, 1988.
NP

FOREIGN ASSISTANCE

Agreement on economic and technical cooperation.
Exchange of notes at Mogadishu June 14, October 12 and 13, 1981.
Entered into force October 13, 1981.
33 UST 3975; TIAS 10276; 1549 UNTS 325

POSTAL MATTERS

International express mail agreement, with detailed regulations.
Signed at Mogadishu and Washington June 28 and July 26, 1988.
Entered into force August 15, 1988.
TIAS 11592

SOUTH AFRICA

ATOMIC ENERGY

Agreement for cooperation concerning peaceful uses of nuclear energy, with annex and agreed minute.
Signed at Pretoria August 25, 1995.
Entered into force December 4, 1997.
TIAS 12685

Agreement on cooperation in research and development of nuclear energy, with annex.
Signed at Vienna September 14, 2009.
Entered into force September 14, 2009.
TIAS 09-914.1

Arrangement for the exchange of technical information and cooperation in nuclear safety matters, with addenda and annex.
Signed at Vienna September 24, 2014.
Entered into force September 24, 2014.
TIAS 14-924.3

CLAIMS & DISPUTE RESOLUTION

Treaty to amend in their application to the Union of South Africa certain provisions of the treaty for the advancement of peace between the United States and the United Kingdom signed September 15, 1914.
Signed at Washington April 2, 1940.
Entered into force March 11, 1941.
55 Stat. 1130; TS 966; 11 Bevans 476

CONSULAR AFFAIRS

Agreement relating to the reciprocal issuance of passport visas to nonimmigrants.*
Exchange of notes at Cape Town March 28 and April 3, 1956.
Entered into force May 1, 1956.
7 UST 631; TIAS 3544; 249 UNTS 395

Amendment:
March 31, 1958 (9 UST 1023; TIAS 4076; 300 UNTS 382)

Notes:
- * Applied to Namibia.
- * The status of this agreement is under review.

DEFENSE

Agreement relating to mutual defense assistance.
Exchange of notes at Washington November 9, 1951.
Entered into force November 9, 1951.
3 UST 2565; TIAS 2424; 160 UNTS 41

Agreement concerning the provision of training under the United States International Military Education and Training (IMET) Program.
Exchange of notes at Pretoria June 14 and July 11, 1994.
Entered into force July 11, 1994.
NP

Agreement regarding grants under the Foreign Assistance Act of 1961, as amended, and the furnishing of defense articles, related training and other defense services from the United States to South Africa.
Exchange of notes at Pretoria November 8, 1994, and October 24, 1995.
Entered into force October 24, 1995.
NP

Agreement concerning cooperation on defense trade controls.
Signed at Pretoria January 24, 1997.
Entered into force January 24, 1997.
TIAS 12825

Agreement concerning security measures for the protection of classified military information.
Signed at Pretoria November 20, 1998.
Entered into force November 20, 1998.
TIAS 12999

Agreement regarding the status of military personnel and civilian employees of the U.S. Department of Defense who may be present in the Republic of South Africa in connection with mutually agreed exercises and activities.
Exchange of notes at Pretoria April 9 and June 10, 1999.
Entered into force June 10, 1999.
NP

Acquisition and cross-servicing agreement, with annexes.
Signed at Pretoria May 8, 2001.
Entered into force May 8, 2001.
NP

Basic exchange and cooperation agreements.
Signed at Pretoria and Springfield June 17 and August 2, 2013.
Entered into force August 2, 2013.
NP

ENVIRONMENT & CONSERVATION

Terms of reference of the Conservation, Environment and Water Committee of the South Africa-United States Binational Commission.
Signed at Pretoria December 5, 1995.
Entered into force December 5, 1995.
TIAS 12706

Agreement for cooperation in the Global Learning and Observations to Benefit the Environment (GLOBE) Program, with annexes.
Signed at Cape Town February 17, 1997.
Entered into force February 17, 1997.
TIAS 12834

FINANCE

Investment incentive agreement.
Signed at Cape Town November 30, 1993.
Entered into force February 10, 1994.
TIAS 12169

FOREIGN ASSISTANCE

Economic, technical and related assistance agreement.
Signed at Pretoria December 5, 1995.
Entered into force December 5, 1995.
TIAS 12707; 2462 UNTS 179

AGENCY FOR INTERNATIONAL DEVELOPMENT

Strategic objective grant agreement for increased use of HIV/AIDS and other primary health care services, with annexes.
Signed at Pretoria September 21, 2005.
Entered into force September 21, 2005.
NP

LAW ENFORCEMENT

Extradition treaty.
Signed at Washington September 16, 1999.
Entered into force June 25, 2001.
TIAS 13060

Treaty on mutual legal assistance in criminal matters.
Signed at Washington September 16, 1999.
Entered into force June 25, 2001.
TIAS 13061

POSTAL MATTERS

Parcel post convention.
Signed at Cape Town April 17 and at Washington June 20, 1919.
Entered into force April 12, 1919.
41 Stat. 1656; Post Office Department print

International express mail agreement, with detailed regulations.
Signed at Pretoria and Washington May 25 and June 29, 1981.
Entered into force July 1, 1981.
33 UST 2434; TIAS 10190; 1530 UNTS 31

Insured postal parcels agreement.
Signed at Pretoria and Washington June 19 and August 5, 1992.
Entered into force October 1, 1992.
TIAS 11869

PROPERTY

Convention relating to tenure and disposition of real and personal property.
Signed at Washington March 2, 1899.
TS 146; 31 Stat. 1939; 12 Bevans 246

Notes:

The 1899 convention and the 1902 Supplementary Convention between the United States and the United Kingdom may be considered in force with respect to the Republic of South Africa by virtue of the adherence by the United Kingdom for the Cape Colony on February 9, 1901, and for the Orange River Colony and the Transvaal on July 24, 1902, except for Natal and Namibia.

Supplementary convention extending the time within which notifications may be given of the accession of British colonies or foreign possessions to the convention of March 2, 1899.
Signed at Washington January 13, 1902.
TS 402; 32 Stat. 1914; 12 Bevans 261

Agreement placing all forms of mutual aid reciprocally on a cash basis.
Exchange of notes at Washington April 17, 1945.
Entered into force April 17, 1945.
60 Stat. 1576; TIAS 1511; 11 Bevans 486; 90 UNTS 267

Agreement relating to settlement for lend-lease, reciprocal aid, surplus war property and claims.
Exchange of notes at Washington March 21, 1947.
Entered into force March 21, 1947.
61 Stat. 2640; TIAS 1593; 11 Bevans 493; 16 UNTS 47

PUBLICATIONS

Agreement relating to the exchange of official publications.
Exchange of notes at Pretoria November 16, 1949.
Entered into force November 16, 1949.
64 Stat. (3) B109; TIAS 2038; 11 Bevans 513; 73 UNTS 97

SCIENTIFIC & TECHNICAL COOPERATION

Agreement for cooperation regarding an integrated, real-time global seismic data acquisition system.
Signed at Pretoria December 1, 1987.
Entered into force December 1, 1987.
TIAS 11560

Framework agreement concerning cooperation in the scientific, technological and environmental fields, with annex.
Signed at Pretoria December 5, 1995.
Entered into force August 27, 2001.
TIAS 12772

Memorandum of understanding concerning scientific and technical cooperation in the earth sciences.
Signed at Reston and Pretoria March 7, 2005.
Entered into force March 7, 2005.
TIAS 05-307

Memorandum of understanding for cooperation in the use of U.S. land remote sensing satellite data, with annexes.
Signed at Reston and Hartebeesthoek February 19 and May 29, 2013.
Entered into force May 29, 2013.
TIAS 13-529

TAXATION

Convention with respect to taxes on the estates of deceased persons.
Signed at Cape Town April 10, 1947.
Entered into force July 15, 1952.
3 UST 3792; TIAS 2509; 167 UNTS 211

Protocol supplementing the estate tax convention of April 10, 1947.
Signed at Pretoria July 14, 1950.
Entered into force July 15, 1952.
3 UST 3792; TIAS 2509; 167 UNTS 228

Convention for the avoidance of double taxation and the prevention of fiscal evasion with respect to taxes on income and capital gains.
Signed at Cape Town February 17, 1997.
Entered into force December 28, 1997.
TIAS

Agreement to improve international tax compliance and to implement the Foreign Account Tax Compliance Act, with annexes.
Signed at Pretoria June 9, 2014.
Entered into force October 28, 2014.
TIAS 14-1028

TELECOMMUNICATION

Agreement relating to the reciprocal granting of authorizations to permit licensed amateur radio operators of either country to operate their stations in the other country.
Exchange of notes at Pretoria March 28 and May 1, 1985.
Entered into force May 1, 1985.
TIAS 11332

Arrangement relating to radio communications between amateur stations on behalf of third parties.
Exchange of notes at Pretoria September 13 and October 4, 1993.
Entered into force October 4, 1993.
TIAS 12509

TRADE & INVESTMENT

Agreement relating to postwar economic settlements.
Exchange of notes at Washington April 17, 1945.
Entered into force April 17, 1945.
60 Stat. 1579; TIAS 1512; 11 Bevans 489; 90 UNTS 275

Agreement concerning the development of trade and investment.
Signed at Washington June 18, 2012.
Entered into force June 18, 2012.
TIAS

TRANSPORTATION

Arrangement relating to pilot licenses to operate civil aircraft.
Exchange of notes at Pretoria March 17 and September 20, 1933.
Entered into force September 20, 1933.
48 Stat. 1837; EAS 55; 11 Bevans 469; 148 LNTS 203

Air navigation arrangement.
Exchange of notes at Pretoria March 17 and September 20, 1933.
Entered into force September 20, 1933.
48 Stat. 1828; EAS 54; 11 Bevans 462; 148 LNTS 189

Arrangement relating to certificates of airworthiness for imported aircraft.
Exchange of notes at Pretoria October 29, 1954, and February 22, 1955.
Entered into force February 22, 1955.
6 UST 657; TIAS 3200; 247 UNTS 247

Amendment:
June 7 and October 8, 1984 (TIAS 11024; 2024 UNTS 2)

Agreement on aviation security.
Exchanges of notes at Pretoria August 19, October 3, October 11, and October 30, 1991.
Entered into force October 30, 1991.
TIAS 11788; 2202 UNTS 283

Air transport agreement, with annex.
Signed at Washington July 23, 1996.
Entered into force July 23, 1996.
TIAS 12785; 2547 UNTS 267

Memorandum of cooperation concerning mutual cooperation in the area of air navigation and air traffic control.
Signed at Washington and Pretoria May 15 and 20, 1998.
Entered into force May 20, 1998.
TIAS 12955

SOUTH PACIFIC COMMISSION

TAXATION

Agreement relating to a procedure for United States income tax reimbursement.
Exchange of notes at Suva and Noumea December 21, 1981, and April 28, 1982.
Entered into force April 28, 1982; effective January 1, 1982.
34 UST 979; TIAS 10384

SOUTH SUDAN

On July 9, 2011, South Sudan declared its independence from Sudan. For agreements prior to the independence of the South Sudan , see SUDAN.

DEFENSE

Agreement regarding grants under the Foreign Assistance Act of 1961, as amended, or successor legislation, and the furnishing of defense articles, defense services and related training, including pursuant to the United States International Military Education and Training (IMET) Program.
Exchange of notes at Juba August 17 and November 14, 2011.
Entered into force November 14, 2011.
NP

FINANCE

Investment incentive agreement.
Signed at Washington April 17, 2013.
Entered into force June 26, 2013.
TIAS 13-626

FOREIGN ASSISTANCE

Agreement for economic and technical cooperation.
Signed at Juba September 11, 2012.
Entered into force September 11, 2012.
TIAS 12-911

AGENCY FOR INTERNATIONAL DEVELOPMENT

U.S. Foreign Assistance Agreement.
Signed September 30, 2008.
Entered into force September 30, 2008.
NP

Amendments:
January 14, 2009 (NP)
September 17, 2009 (NP)
May 7, 2010 (NP)
August 6, 2010 (NP)
September 17, 2010 (NP)
September 27 and 28, 2011 (NP)
September 27 and 30, 2011 (NP)
December 20, 2012 (NP)

SOUTHEAST EUROPEAN LAW ENFORCEMENT CENTER

LAW ENFORCEMENT

Cooperation agreement.
Signed at Bucharest September 9, 2014.
Entered into force September 10, 2014.
TIAS 14-910

SPAIN

ATOMIC ENERGY

Arrangement for the exchange of technical information and cooperation in nuclear safety matters, with addenda and annex.
Signed at Rockville October 19, 2015.
Entered into force October 19, 2015.
TIAS

CLAIMS & DISPUTE RESOLUTION

Treaty for the settlement of disputes between the two countries.
Signed at Washington September 15, 1914.
Entered into force December 21, 1914.
38 Stat. 1862; TS 605; 11 Bevans 661; 89 LNTS 427

Related agreement:
December 20, 1915

Arrangement relating to claims.
Exchange of notes at Washington August 24, 1927, May 13, 1929, and June 20, 1929.
Entered into force June 20, 1929.
47 Stat. 2641; EAS 18; 11 Bevans 687; 120 LNTS 401

Agreement relating to the restitution of monetary gold looted by Germany.
Exchange of notes at Madrid April 30 and May 3, 1948.
Entered into force May 3, 1948.
62 Stat. 4071; TIAS 2123; 11 Bevans 708; 132 UNTS 155

Agreement regarding claims arising from Exercise CRISEX.
Signed at Madrid November 13, 1979.
Entered into force November 13, 1979.
31 UST 5876; TIAS 9690

CONSULAR AFFAIRS

Agreement relating to the reciprocal waiver of visa fees for nonimmigrants.*
Exchange of notes at Madrid January 21, 1952.
Entered into force January 21, 1952; operative February 21, 1952.
3 UST 2927; TIAS 2471; 160 UNTS 63

Amendment:
May 11 and July 5, 1963 (14 UST 1206; TIAS 5418; 488 UNTS 236)

Note:
* Applicable to all territories.
The status of this agreement is under review.

DEFENSE

Mutual defense assistance agreement with tax relief annex and interpretative note in regard to tax relief annex.
Signed at Madrid September 26, 1953.
Entered into force September 26, 1953.
4 UST 1876; TIAS 2849; 207 UNTS 61

Agreement confirming the bilateral arrangements for a facilities assistance program pursuant to the mutual defense assistance agreement of September 26, 1953.
Exchange of notes at Madrid April 9 and May 11 and 19, 1954.
Entered into force May 19, 1954.
5 UST 2377; TIAS 3098; 235 UNTS 87

Supplementary Agreements:
May 25, 1955 (6 UST 1155; TIAS 3257; 251 UNTS 416)
September 17, 1956 (7 UST 2777; TIAS 3658; 278 UNTS 283)

Agreement relating to offshore procurement in Spain, with memorandum of understanding and standard contract attached.
Exchange of notes at San Sebastian July 30, 1954.
Entered into force July 30, 1954.
5 UST 2328; TIAS 3094; 235 UNTS 45

Amendments:
October 26, 1954 (5 UST 2357; TIAS 3094; 235 UNTS 66)
October 29 and November 11, 1958 (10 UST 344; TIAS 4196; 341 UNTS 400)

Agreement relating to the disposition of military equipment and materials furnished by the United States under the mutual defense assistance agreement.
Exchange of notes at Madrid November 27, 1956.
Entered into force November 27, 1956.
7 UST 3392; TIAS 3710; 265 UNTS 374.

Master data exchange agreement for the mutual development of weapons systems.
Signed at Washington June 19, 1980.
Entered into force June 19, 1980.
TIAS 12376

Cover agreement on the territorial command net, with annexes.
Signed at Madrid July 24, 1980.
Entered into force July 24, 1980.
35 UST 3745; TIAS 10880; 1577 UNTS 297

Agreement on friendship, defense and cooperation, with complementary agreements* and exchanges of notes.
Signed at Madrid July 2, 1982.
Entered into force May 14, 1983.
TIAS 10589

Note:
* Complementary agreement one – United States Spanish Council
* Complementary agreement two – operational and support installations (IDAs) and authorizations.
* Complementary agreement three – cooperation in defense support.
* Complementary agreement four – defense industrial cooperation.
* Complementary agreement five – status of United States forces in Spain
* Complementary agreement six – status of Spanish forces in the United States.
* Complementary agreement seven -- scientific, technological, cultural, educational and economic cooperation.

Memorandum of understanding pertaining to installation of satellite ground terminal at Rota, Spain.
Signed at Rota November 3, 1982.
Entered into force November 3, 1982.
TIAS 10566; 1871 UNTS 381

General security of military information agreement, with protocol on security procedures for industrial operations with appendices.
Signed at Washington March 12, 1984.
Entered into force March 12, 1984.
35 UST 4639; TIAS 10962

Agreement concerning technical cooperation in cartography and geodesy.
Signed at Madrid and Washington September 4 and October 27, 1986.
Entered into force October 27, 1986.
TIAS 11408; 2192 UNTS 181

Agreement on defense cooperation, with annexes and related letters.
Signed at Madrid December 1, 1988.
Entered into force May 4, 1989.
TIAS

Amendments:
April 10, 2002
October 10, 2012
June 17, 2015

Memorandum of understanding on the exchange of service personnel between the United States Navy and the Spanish Air Force and on the general conditions which will apply to the exchange of such personnel.
Signed at Washington and Madrid July 20 and August 13, 1991.
Entered into force August 13, 1991.
NP

Memorandum of understanding on the exchange of service personnel between the United States Navy and the Spanish Navy and on the general conditions which will apply to the exchange of such personnel.
Signed at Washington and Madrid August 5 and September 5, 1991.
Entered into force September 5, 1991.
NP

Basic exchange and technical cooperation agreement for mapping, nautical and aeronautical charting, geodesy and geophysics, digital data and related materials, with appendix and annexes.
Signed at Madrid June 29, 1992.
Entered into force June 29, 1992.
NP

Agreement for research, development, test, evaluation, production and life cycle support activities for technologies and systems for AEGIS-equipped ships, with annex.
Signed at Ferrol February 28, 2002.
Entered into force February 28, 2002.
TIAS 02-228
Amendments and Extension:
June 24 and 27, 2008 (TIAS 02-228)
June 26 and 29, 2009 (TIAS 02-228)
February 7 and 28, 2012 (TIAS 02-228)

Agreement regarding the assignment of liaison officers of its respective Marine Corps, with annex.
Signed at Madrid and Washington July 31 and September 11, 2006.
Entered into force September 11, 2006.
NP

Memorandum of understanding regarding the exchange of engineers and scientists, with annexes.
Signed at Washington and Madrid September 21, 2002 and February 7, 2007.
Entered into force February 7, 2007.
NP

Memorandum of agreement regarding assignment of liaison officers to the U.S. Joint Forces Command, with annex.
Signed at Norfolk June 19 and 20, 2007.
Entered into force June 20, 2007.
NP

Memorandum of agreement establishing a midshipmen/cadet exchange program (MCEP), with appendix.
Signed at Marin and Annapolis October 24 and November 14, 2007.
Entered into force November 14, 2007.
NP
Extension:
November 14, 2012

Agreement regarding the exchange of professional military education (PME).
Signed at Arlington and Madrid April 7 and June 25, 2008.
Entered into force June 25, 2008.
NP
Extension:
June 22, 2012

Acquisition and cross-servicing agreement, with annexes.
Signed at USEUCOM and Madrid April 30 and May 9, 2011.
Entered into force May 9, 2011.
NP

Implementing arrangement concerning the exchange and reimbursement of fuel, with annexes.
Signed at Madrid and Ft. Belvoir December 2, 2011 and March 30, 2012.
Entered into force March 30, 2012.
NP

Agreement for research, development, test, evaluation, and prototyping projects, with Annexes.
Signed at Washington and Madrid August 21 and September 25, 2015.
Entered into force September 25, 2013.
TIAS 15-925.1

Memorandum of agreement regarding the assignment of Spanish Army personnel to the United States Army, with annexes.
Signed at Washington and Madrid April 30, 2013 and May 22, 2013.
Entered into force May 22, 2013.
NP

Memorandum of agreement regarding the assignment of liaison officers, with annexes.
Signed at Madrid and Stuttgart November 15, 2014 and January 8, 2015.
Entered into force January 8, 2015.
NP

EDUCATION

See also complementary agreement seven to the agreement on friendship, defense and cooperation of July 2, 1982 (TIAS 10589).

Agreement for educational, cultural and scientific cooperation.
Signed at Madrid October 27, 1994.
Entered into force April 26, 1995.
TIAS 12577; 1872 UNTS 287
Extension:
January 20 and February 2, 2004 (TIAS 05-107)

EMPLOYMENT

Agreement concerning the free pursuit of gainful employment by dependents of employees of diplomatic missions, consular posts or missions to international organizations, with exchange of notes.
Signed at Madrid July 25, 1990.
Entered into force April 1, 1991.
TIAS

ENVIRONMENT & CONSERVATION

Agreement for cooperation in the Global Learning and Observations to Benefit the Environment (GLOBE) Program, with appendices.
Signed at Madrid May 5, 1998.
Entered into force May 5, 1998.
TIAS 12949

FOREIGN ASSISTANCE

See also complementary agreement seven to the agreement on friendship, defense and cooperation of July 2, 1982 (TIAS 10589).

Economic aid agreement.
Signed at Madrid September 26, 1953.
Entered into force September 26, 1953.
4 UST 1903; TIAS 2851; 207 UNTS 93

Agreement relating to the waiver of the counterpart deposit requirement for certain categories of AID financed commodities.
Exchange of notes at Madrid May 22, 1962.
Entered into force May 22, 1962.
13 UST 1830; TIAS 5131; 458 UNTS 304

INTELLECTUAL PROPERTY

Copyright agreement.*
Exchange of notes at Washington July 6 and 15, 1895.
Entered into force July 10, 1895.
TS 342-A; 11 Bevans 597
Note
* Applicable to all Spanish territories.

Agreement relating to the restoration of the copyright agreement of July 6 and 15, 1895.
Exchange of notes at Madrid January 29, November 18, and November 26, 1902.
Entered into force November 26, 1902.
TS 474; 11 Bevans 639

Agreement to facilitate interchange of patent rights and technical information for defense purposes.
Exchange of notes at Madrid July 13 and 21, 1960.
Entered into force July 21, 1960.
11 UST 2187; TIAS 4588; 393 UNTS 289

LAW ENFORCEMENT

Agreement exempting from authentication signatures attached to letters rotatory exchanged between Puerto Rico, the Philippine Islands, and Spain, with declaration.
Exchange of notes at Washington August 5, 1901, and at Manchester, Massachusetts, August 7, 1901.
Declaration signed at Washington November 7, 1901.
Entered into force November 28, 1901.
TS 395; 11 Bevans 625

Convention for the prevention of smuggling of alcoholic liquors.
Signed at Washington February 10, 1926.
Entered into force November 17, 1926.
44 Stat. 2465; TS 749; 11 Bevans 676; 67 LNTS 131

Arrangement for the direct exchange of certain information regarding the traffic in narcotic drugs.
Exchange of notes at Madrid February 3, March 10, and May 24, 1928.
Entered into force May 24, 1928.
11 Bevans 684

Treaty on extradition.
Signed at Madrid May 29, 1970.
Entered into force June 16, 1971.
22 UST 737; TIAS 7136; 796 UNTS 245

Agreement on procedures for mutual assistance in connection with the Lockheed Aircraft Corporation matter, with annex.
Signed at Washington July 14, 1976.
Entered into force July 14, 1976.
27 UST 3409; TIAS 8370
Related Agreement:
June 7 and July 22, 1977 (28 UST 7494; TIAS 8725)

Supplementary treaty on extradition.
Signed at Madrid January 25, 1975.
Entered into force June 2, 1978.
29 UST 2283; TIAS 8938

Agreement regarding mutual assistance between customs services.
Signed at Madrid July 3, 1990.
Entered into force February 28, 1993.
TIAS 12120; 1717 UNTS 223

Agreement on cooperation to reduce the demand for narcotic drugs.
Signed at Madrid November 25, 1991.
Entered into force May 7, 1993.
TIAS 12443

Treaty on mutual legal assistance in criminal matters, with attachments.
Signed at Washington November 20, 1990.
Entered into force June 30, 1993.
TIAS; 1730 UNTS 113

Second supplementary treaty on extradition.
Signed at Madrid February 9, 1988.
Entered into force July 2, 1993.
TIAS

Third supplementary extradition treaty.
Signed at Madrid March 12, 1996.
Entered into force July 25, 1999.
TIAS

Instrument as contemplated by Article 3(2) of the agreement on extradition between the United States of America and the European Union signed June 25, 2003, as to the application of the treaty on extradition of May 29, 1970, and the supplementary treaties on extradition of January 25, 1975, February 9, 1988, and March 12, 1996, with annex.
Signed at Madrid December 17, 2004.
Entered into force February 1, 2010.
TIAS 10-201.21

Instrument as contemplated by Article 3(2) of the agreement on mutual legal assistance between the United States of America and the European Union signed June 25, 2003, as to the application of the treaty on mutual legal assistance in criminal matters of November 20, 1990, with annex.
Signed at Madrid December 17, 2004.
Entered into force February 1, 2010.
TIAS 10-201.47

Agreement on enhancing cooperation in preventing and combating serious crime.
Signed at Washington June 23, 2009.
Entered into force July 20, 2010.
TIAS

MARITIME MATTERS

Agreement relating to jurisdiction over vessels utilizing the Louisiana Offshore Oil Port.
Exchange of notes at Madrid November 5 and 22, 1983.
Entered into force October 19, 1984.
35 UST 3131; TIAS 10845

PEACE

Treaty of peace.
Signed at Paris December 10, 1898.
Entered into force April 11, 1899.
30 Stat. 1754; TS 343; 11 Bevans 615

POSTAL MATTERS

Parcel post agreement.*
Signed at Madrid July 16 and at Washington August 30, 1955.
Entered into force January 1, 1956.
7 UST 451; TIAS 3530; 270 UNTS 211

Note:

* Applicable to Puerto Rico, Guam, Samoa, the Virgin Islands, Andorra, and Spanish Territories of Africa.

International express mail agreement, with detailed regulations.
Signed at Madrid October 18, 1982.
Entered into force April 1, 1983.
TIAS 10555; 1871 UNTS 341

PUBLICATIONS

Agreement relating to the exchange of official publications.
Exchange of notes at Madrid May 8, 1950.
Entered into force May 8, 1950.
1 UST 466; TIAS 2085; 98 UNTS 175

SCIENTIFIC & TECHNICAL COOPERATION

See also complementary agreement seven to the agreement on friendship, defense and cooperation of July 2, 1982 (TIAS 10589).

Agreement on scientific and technological cooperation, with annex.
Signed at Madrid June 10, 1994.
Entered into force provisionally, June 10, 1994; definitively, January 18, 1996.
TIAS 12547; 1920 UNTS 309

Memorandum of understanding concerning the Senseco Seismographic Station, with annexes.
Signed at Madrid January 18, 1996.
Entered into force January 18, 1996.
TIAS 12719; 1926 UNTS 409

Memorandum of understanding on scientific and technological cooperation in the field of water resources development.
Signed at Madrid May 20, 1997.
Entered into force May 20, 1997.
TIAS 12858

Implementing arrangement on cooperation in research on radiological evaluations.
Signed at Madrid September 15, 1997.
Entered into force September 15, 1997.
TIAS 12882

Memorandum of understanding concerning scientific and technical cooperation in the earth sciences.
Signed at Reston and Madrid February 20 and March 5, 2004.
Entered into force March 5, 2004.
TIAS 04-305

SOCIAL SECURITY

Agreement on social security, with administrative arrangement.
Signed at Madrid September 30, 1986.
Entered into force April 1, 1988.
TIAS 12123

SPACE

Agreement providing for a project in Spain to measure winds and temperatures at high altitudes and for continuing other cooperative space research projects.
Exchange of notes at Washington April 14, 1966.
Entered into force April 14, 1966.
17 UST 493; TIAS 5992; 586 UNTS 79

Agreement on space cooperation.
Exchange of memoranda at Madrid August 31 and September 4, 1984.
Entered into force September 4, 1984.
TIAS 11067; 2039 UNTS 227

Extension:

March 13 and 31, 1989 (TIAS 12208)

Agreement on space cooperation.
Signed at Madrid July 11, 1991.
Entered into force May 9, 1994.
TIAS; 1785 UNTS 393

Agreement concerning cooperation on the Mars Science Laboratory Mission.
Signed at Madrid March 17, 2011.
Entered into force March 17, 2011.
TIAS 11-317
Amendment and Extension:
June 16, 2015 (TIAS 15-616)

TAXATION

Tax relief annex attached to the mutual defense assistance agreement, and interpretative note.
Signed at Madrid September 26, 1953.
Entered into force September 26, 1953.
4 UST 1876; TIAS 2849; 207 UNTS 61

Convention for the avoidance of double taxation and the prevention of fiscal evasion with respect to taxes on income, with protocol.
Signed at Madrid February 22, 1990.
Entered into force November 21, 1990.
TIAS; 1591 UNTS 41

Agreement to improve international tax compliance and to implement FATCA, with annexes.
Signed at Madrid May 14, 2013.
Entered into force December 9, 2013.
TIAS 13-1209

TELECOMMUNICATION

Agreement concerning a program of joint participation in intercontinental testing in connection with experimental communications satellites.
Exchange of notes at Madrid September 18, 1964, and January 26, 1965.
Entered into force January 26, 1965.
16 UST 68; TIAS 5761; 542 UNTS 81

Agreement relating to the reciprocal granting of authorizations to permit licensed amateur radio operators of either country to operate their stations in the other country.
Exchange of notes at Madrid December 11 and 20, 1979.
Entered into force December 20, 1979.
32 UST 517; TIAS 9721

TRADE & INVESTMENT

Treaty of friendship and general relations.*
Signed at Madrid July 3, 1902.
Entered into force April 14, 1903.
33 Stat. 2105; TS 422; 11 Bevans 628
Note:
* Applicable to all territories.
Notice of termination was given by the United States of articles XXIII and XXIV, effective July 1, 1916, in accordance with the Seamen's Act (38 Stat. 1164). The notice was accepted by the Spanish Government with the understanding that only such provisions of these articles as were in conflict with the act should be terminated, and all other provisions, especially those concerning the arrest, detention, and imprisonment of deserters from war vessels, should continue in force; also on the understanding that United States consuls in Spain should not exercise the powers of which Spanish consuls in the United States were deprived by the provisions of the Act.

Agreement providing for consultations should exports of textiles or textile products from Spain cause market disruption in the United States.
Exchange of notes at Madrid September 23, 1976.
Entered into force September 23, 1976.
28 UST 1308; TIAS 8512

Agreement relating to the subsidization of exports in the context of the agreement on interpretation and application of articles VI, XVI, and XXIII (subsidies code) of the General Agreement on Tariffs and Trade (TIAS 9619).
Exchange of letters at Washington April 13 and 14, 1982.
Entered into force April 14, 1982.
TIAS
Amendment:
January 16 and 29, 1985

TRANSPORTATION

Arrangement relating to certificates of airworthiness for imported aircraft.
Exchange of notes at Madrid September 23, 1957.
Entered into force September 23, 1957.
8 UST 1549; TIAS 3906; 290 UNTS 261
Amendment:
September 18 and October 13, 1978 (30 UST 750; TIAS 9217)

Air transport agreement.*
Signed at Madrid February 20, 1973.
Entered into force provisionally February 20, 1973; definitively August 3, 1973.
24 UST 2102; TIAS 7725
Amendments:
May 31, 1989 (TIAS 11672; 1597 UNTS 466)
November 27, 1991 (TIAS 11946; 1722 UNTS 304)

Related Agreement:
February 20, March 31 and April 7, 1987 (TIAS 11297; 2177 UNTS 122)

Note:
* This agreement is suspended for the duration of provisional application of the U.S. – E.U. Air Transport Agreement signed April 25 and 30, 2007.

Memorandum of agreement relating to technical assistance to Spain in civil aviation activities.
Signed at Washington and Madrid June 30 and July 22, 1982.
Entered into force July 22, 1982.
TIAS 10547

Agreement for the promotion of aviation safety.
Signed at Washington September 23, 1999.
Entered into force September 23, 1999.
TIAS 13064; 2084 UNTS 401

SRI LANKA

Article 6 of the External Affairs Agreement between the United Kingdom and Ceylon, signed at Colombo November 11, 1947, which entered into force on February 4, 1948, provides: "All obligations and responsibilities heretofore devolving on the Government of the United Kingdom which arise from any valid international instrument shall henceforth insofar as such instrument may be held to have application to Ceylon devolve upon the Government of Ceylon. The reciprocal rights and benefits heretofore enjoyed by the Government of the United Kingdom in virtue of the application of any such international instrument to Ceylon shall henceforth be enjoyed by the Government of Ceylon.

CLAIMS & DISPUTE RESOLUTION

Agreement concerning a full and final settlement of the investment dispute between Enterprise Development International, Inc., formerly Enterprise Development Inc., and the Sri Lanka State Timber Corporation relating to Charlanka Company Ltd.
Exchange of notes at Washington October 30, 1998.
Entered into force October 30, 1998.
NP

Agreement concerning a full and final settlement of the commercial dispute between Evans International Ltd. Co. and Centrepoint Colombo Ltd. Urban Development Authority of Sri Lanka, and the Government of the Democratic Socialist Republic of Sri Lanka relating to reconstruction of the Colombo financial district.
Exchange of notes at Washington June 7, 1999.
Entered into force June 7, 1999.
NP

CONSULAR AFFAIRS

Agreement providing for the reciprocal reduction of nonimmigrant visa fees and issuance of multiple-entry nonimmigrant visas.*
Exchange of notes at Colombo August 25 and September 7, 1956.
Entered into force September 7, 1956; operative September 15, 1956.
8 UST 83; TIAS 3743; 280 UNTS 35

Note:

* The status of this agreement is under review.

CULTURAL EXCHANGES, PROPERTY & COOPERATION

Agreement relating to the establishment of a Peace Corps program in Sri Lanka.
Exchange of notes at Colombo November 20, 1983.
Entered into force November 20, 1983.
35 UST 3124; TIAS 10844; 2014 UNTS 641

DEFENSE

Agreement relating to the purchase by Ceylon of certain military equipment, materials, and services.
Exchange of notes at Washington October 25 and November 2, 1956.
Entered into force November 2, 1956.
7 UST 3193; TIAS 3698; 282 UNTS 93

Agreement regarding the status of U.S. military personnel and civilian employees of the Department of Defense who may be present in Sri Lanka for exercises or official duties.
Exchange of notes at Colombo February 9 and May 16, 1995.
Entered into force May 16, 1995.
NP

Agreement regarding grants under the Foreign Assistance Act of 1961, as amended, and the furnishing of defense articles, related training, and other defense services from the United States of America to the Government of Sri Lanka.
Exchange of notes at Colombo July 23 and August 4, 1998.
Entered into force August 4, 1998.
NP

Agreement concerning acquisition and cross-servicing, with annexes.
Signed March 5, 2007.
Entered into force March 5, 2007.
NP

DIPLOMATIC & CONSULAR RELATIONS

Convention to regulate commerce (article IV) between the United States and the United Kingdom.
Signed at London July 3, 1815.
Entered into force July 3, 1815.
8 Stat. 228; TS 110; 12 Bevans 49

EDUCATION

Agreement for financing certain educational exchange programs.
Signed at Colombo August 29, 1964.
Entered into force August 29, 1964.
TIAS 5645; 15 UST 1699; 531 UNTS 93

Amendment:

June 23 and August 13, 1998 (TIAS 12981)

EMPLOYMENT

Agreement relating to the employment of dependents of official government employees.
Exchange of notes at Colombo December 12, 1995.
Entered into force December 12, 1995.
TIAS 12710

ENVIRONMENT & CONSERVATION

Agreement for cooperation in the Global Learning and Observations to Benefit the Environment (GLOBE) Program, with appendices.
Signed at Colombo December 20, 1999.
Entered into force December 20, 1999.
TIAS

FINANCE

Investment incentive agreement.
Signed at Washington October 19, 1993.
Entered into force August 8, 2003.
TIAS

Agreement regarding the consolidation and rescheduling of certain debts owed to, guaranteed by, or insured by the United States Government or its agencies, with annexes.
Signed at Colombo September 30, 2005.
Entered into force November 17, 2005.
NP

FOREIGN ASSISTANCE

General agreement for technical cooperation.
Signed at Colombo November 7, 1950.
Entered into force November 7, 1950.
1 UST 723; TIAS 2138; 92 UNTS 125

Agreement relating to a development assistance program in Ceylon.
Exchange of notes at Colombo April 28, 1956.
Entered into force April 28, 1956.
7 UST 751; TIAS 3554; 274 UNTS 35

INTELLECTUAL PROPERTY

Declaration by the United States and the United Kingdom affording reciprocal protection to trade-marks.
Signed at London October 24, 1877.
Entered into force October 24, 1877.
20 Stat. 703; TS 138; 12 Bevans 198

Agreement on the protection and enforcement of intellectual property rights.
Signed at Colombo September 20, 1991.
Entered into force October 20, 1991.
TIAS 12436

INTERNATIONAL CRIMINAL COURT

Agreement regarding the surrender of persons to the International Criminal Court.
Signed at Colombo November 22, 2002.
Entered into force July 4, 2003.
TIAS 03-704

LAW ENFORCEMENT

Extradition treaty.
Signed at Washington September 30, 1999.
Entered into force January 12, 2001.
TIAS 13066

POSTAL MATTERS

Parcel post agreement and detailed regulations.
Signed at Colombo July 18 and at Washington November 25, 1955.
Entered into force July 1, 1956.
7 UST 2871; TIAS 3670; 281 UNTS 295

International express mail agreement, with detailed regulations.
Signed at Colombo and Washington February 1 and 14, 1990.
Entered into force March 30, 1990.
TIAS 11716

PROPERTY

Convention between the United States and the United Kingdom relating to tenure and disposition of real and personal property.
Signed at Washington March 2, 1899.
Applicable to Ceylon February 9, 1901.
31 Stat. 1939; TS 146; 12 Bevans 246

PUBLICATIONS

Agreement relating to the exchange of official publications.
Exchange of notes at Colombo January 4 and 31, 1949.
Entered into force January 31, 1949.
63 Stat. 2356; TIAS 1894; 6 Bevans 515; 88 UNTS 21

TAXATION

Convention for the avoidance of double taxation and the prevention of fiscal evasion with respect to taxes on income.
Signed at Colombo March 14, 1985.
Entered into force July 12, 2004.
TIAS 04-712

Protocol amending the convention for the avoidance of double taxation and the prevention of fiscal evasion with respect to taxes on income of March 14, 1985, with exchange of notes.
Signed at Washington September 20, 2002.
Entered into force July 12, 2004.
TIAS 04-712

TELECOMMUNICATION

Agreement to terminate a 1951 broadcast and 1991 lease agreement.
Exchange of notes at Colombo December 22 and 28, 2016.
Entered into force December 28, 2016.
TIAS 16-1228

TRADE & INVESTMENT

Treaty concerning the encouragement and reciprocal protection of investment, with annex, protocol and exchange of letters.
Signed at Colombo September 20, 1991.
Entered into force May 1, 1993.
TIAS

TRANSPORTATION

Arrangement between the United States and the United Kingdom relating to pilot licenses to operate civil aircraft.
Exchange of notes at Washington March 28 and April 5, 1935.
49 Sat. 3731;EAS 77; 12 Bevans 513; 162 LNTS 59

Air service agreement relating to equipment located at Ratmalana Aerodrome and St. Ives Estate, Ceylon.
Signed at Colombo April 1, 1946
Entered into force April 12, 1946.

Air transport agreement, with annexes.
Signed at Washington June 11, 2002.
Entered into force November 18, 2002.
TIAS 02-1118
Amendment:
September 6 and 12, 2006 (TIAS 02-1118)

SUDAN

DEFENSE

Agreement relating to the deposit by Sudan of ten percent of the value of grant military assistance furnished by the United States.
Exchange of notes at Khartoum April 27 and May 24, 1973.
Entered into force May 24, 1973.
24 UST 1740; TIAS 7677

Mutual defense assistance agreement.
Exchange of notes at Khartoum April 8 and 22, 1981.
Entered into force April 22, 1981.
34 UST 1000; TIAS 10389; 1560 UNTS 415

Agreement concerning the grant of defense articles and services under the military assistance program.
Exchange of notes at Khartoum August 24 and 30, 1981.
Entered into force August 30, 1981.
TIAS 10500; 1750 UNTS 171
Amendment:
August 30 and September 25, 1982 (TIAS 10500; 1750 UNTS 178)

Agreement relating to the status of United States personnel temporarily stationed in Sudan.
Exchange of letters at Khartoum November 12 and December 27, 1981.
Entered into force December 27, 1981.
33 UST 4513; TIAS 10322

FINANCE

Agreement relating to investment guaranties under section 413 (b)(4) of the Mutual Security Act of 1954, as amended.
Exchange of notes at Khartoum March 17, 1959.
Entered into force March 17, 1959.
10 UST 408; TIAS 4201; 342 UNTS 13
Amendment:
March 2, 1964 (15 UST 238; TIAS 5544; 524 UNTS 318)

Agreement regarding the consolidation and rescheduling of certain debts owed to, guaranteed or insured by the United States and its agencies, with annexes.
Signed at Khartoum May 17, 1980.
Entered into force June 19, 1980 and April 14, 1981 for 1979/1980 debt and 1980/1981 debt respectively.
32 UST 4373; TIAS 9952

Agreement regarding the consolidation and rescheduling of payments due under P.L. 480 Title I agricultural commodity agreements.
Signed at Khartoum August 18, 1980.
Entered into force August 18, 1980 and April 14, 1981 for 1979/1980 debt and 1980/1981 debt respectively.
32 UST 4373; TIAS 9952

Agreement regarding the consolidation and rescheduling of certain debts owed to, guaranteed or insured by the United States Government and its agencies, with annexes.
Signed at Khartoum July 20, 1982.
Entered into force August 23, 1982.
34 UST 1567; TIAS 10437

Agreement regarding the consolidation and rescheduling of certain debts owed to, guaranteed or insured by the United States Government and its agencies.
Signed at Khartoum January 21, 1984.
Entered into force March 27, 1984.
TIAS 10981

Agreement regarding the consolidation and rescheduling of certain debts owed to, guaranteed by or insured by the United States Government and its agencies, with annexes.
Signed at Khartoum December 22, 1984.
Entered into force January 25, 1985.
NP

FOREIGN ASSISTANCE

Agreement concerning the privileges and immunities of the International Verification and Investigation Team.
Exchange of notes at Khartoum August 29 and September 23 and 30, 2002.
Entered into force September 30, 2002.
TIAS

LAW ENFORCEMENT

Agreement on procedures for mutual assistance in connection with matters relating to the Boeing Company.
Signed at Washington September 23, 1977.
Entered into force September 23, 1977.
28 UST 7482; TIAS 8723

POSTAL MATTERS

International express mail agreement, with detailed regulations.
Signed at Khartoum and Washington October 22 and November 30, 1990.
Entered into force January 14, 1991.
TIAS 11768

TELECOMMUNICATION

Agreement for the establishment of U.S. radio transmitting facilities.
Signed at Khartoum July 12, 2006.
Entered into force July 12, 2006.
TIAS 06-712

SUPREME ALLIED COMMANDER TRANSFORMATION (SACT)

DEFENSE

Implementing arrangement concerning mutual logistics support, with annexes.
Signed at Norfolk April 30 and May 12, 2005.
Entered into force May 12, 2005.
NP

Acquisition and cross-servicing agreement, with annexes.
Signed at Norfolk April 18, 2008.
Entered into force April 18, 2008.
NP

SUPREME HEADQUARTERS ALLIED POWERS EUROPE (SHAPE)

DEFENSE

Mutual support agreement for telecommunications, with annex.
Signed at Casteau and Vaihingen January 22 and February 25, 1985.
Entered into force February 25, 1985.
TIAS 11187; 2130 UNTS 399

Agreement concerning support of the allied tactical operations center at Sembach Air Base, Germany, with annexes.
Signed at Heidelberg and Sembach Air Base August 28 and November 25, 1987.
Entered into force November 25, 1987; effective May 1, 1983.
TIAS

SURINAME

On November 25, 1975, Suriname became an independent state. In a note dated November 29, 1975, to the Secretary-General of the United Nations, the Prime Minister made a statement reading in part as follows:

The Government of the Republic of Surinam, conscious of the desirability of maintaining existing legal relationship, and conscious of its obligation under International Law to honour its treaty commitments, acknowledges that treaty rights and obligations of the Government of the Kingdom of the Netherlands in respect of Surinam were succeeded by the Republic of Surinam upon Independence by virtue of customary International Law.

Since, however, it is likely that by virtue of customary International Law certain treaties may have lapsed at the date of Independence of Surinam, it seems essential that each treaty should be subjected to legal examination. It is proposed after this examination has been completed, to indicate which, if any, of the treaties which may have lapsed by customary International Law the Government of the Republic of Surinam wish to treat as having lapsed.

It is desired that it be presumed that each treaty has been legally succeeded to by the Republic of Surinam and that action be based upon this presumption until a decision is reached that it should be regarded as having lapsed. Should the Government of the Republic of Surinam be of the opinion it has legally succeeded to a treaty but subsequently wish to terminate its operation, the Government will in due course give notice of termination in the terms thereof.

CONSULAR AFFAIRS

Agreement between the United States and the Netherlands relating to the reciprocal waiver of passport visa fees for nonimmigrants.*
Exchanges of notes at The Hague January 21, February 11, March 5, and March 13, 1946.
Entered into force April 15, 1946.
61 Stat. 3834; TIAS 1728; 10 Bevans 178; 84 UNTS 3
Note:
* The status of this agreement is under review.

CULTURAL EXCHANGES, PROPERTY & COOPERATION

Agreement concerning the establishment of a Peace Corps program in Suriname.
Exchange of notes at Paramaribo October 12, 1994, and January 5, 1995.
Entered into force January 5, 1995.
TIAS 12595

DEFENSE

Agreement between the United States and The Netherlands relating to the assurances required by the Mutual Security Act of 1951.
Exchange of notes at The Hague January 8, 1952.
Entered into force January 8, 1952.
3 UST 4633; TIAS 2615; 173 UNTS 372

Agreement concerning the provision of training related to defense articles under the United States International Military Education and Training (IMET) Program.
Exchange of notes at Paramaribo August 22 and 25, 1980.
Entered into force August 25, 1980.
32 UST 3741; TIAS 9916; 1267 UNTS 155

Agreement regarding the status of U.S. Special Forces Deployment for Training Exercise Mission.
Exchange of notes at Paramaribo January 17 and February 2, 1996.
Entered into force February 2, 1996.
NP

Agreement regarding the status of United States personnel who may be temporarily present in the Republic of Suriname.
Exchange of notes at Paramaribo April 11 and October 20, 2005.
Entered into force October 20, 2005.
TIAS 05-1020

Agreement regarding the Caribbean Basin Security Initiative and the provision of technical support for maritime security forces (Technical Assistance Field Team).
Exchange of notes at Paramaribo November 29, 2012 and February 4, 2015.
Entered into force February 4, 2015.
TIAS 15-204.1

ENVIRONMENT & CONSERVATION

Agreement for cooperation in the Global Learning and Observations to Benefit the Environment (GLOBE) Program, with appendices.
Signed at Paramaribo December 23, 1997.
Entered into force December 23, 1997.
TIAS 12913

FINANCE

Investment incentive agreement.
Signed at Paramaribo May 28, 1993.
Entered into force February 20, 1996.
TIAS 12500

FOREIGN ASSISTANCE

Economic cooperation agreement between the United States and The Netherlands.
Signed at The Hague July 2, 1948.
Entered into force July 2, 1948.
62 Stat. 2477; TIAS 1791; 10 Bevans 240; 20 UNTS 91

Amendments:
January 16 and February 2, 1950 (1 UST 665; TIAS 2126; 93 UNTS 361)
March 7 and April 3, 1951 (2 UST 1319; TIAS 2285; 141 UNTS 368)
November 28, 1952 (3 UST 5260; TIAS 2721; 173 UNTS 382)

General agreement between the United States and The Netherlands for technical cooperation for Suriname and Netherlands Antilles.
Signed at The Hague January 22, 1954.
Entered into force April 21, 1954.
5 UST 819; TIAS 2982; 190 UNTS 207

LAW ENFORCEMENT

Convention between the United Stated and The Netherlands for the extradition of criminals.
Signed at Washington June 2, 1887.
Entered into force July 11, 1889.
26 Stat. 1481; TS 256: 10 Bevans 47

Treaty extending the extradition convention of June 2, 1887 between the United States and The Netherlands to their respective island possessions and colonies.
Signed at Washington January 18, 1904.
Entered into force August 28, 1904.
33 Sat. 2257: TS 436: 10 Bevans 53

Procedures for mutual assistance in connection with matters relating to the Reynolds Metals Company.
Signed at Washington March 14, 1979.
Entered into force March 14, 1979.
30 UST 3864; TIAS 9429; 1171 UNTS 209

MARITIME MATTERS

Agreement concerning cooperation in maritime law enforcement.
Signed at Paramaribo December 31, 1998.
Entered into force August 26, 1999.
TIAS

POSTAL MATTERS

Parcel post convention.
Signed at Paramaribo July 9 and at Washington August 18, 1930.
Operative September 1, 1930.
46 Stat. 2798; Post Office Department print; 125 LNTS 123

SCIENTIFIC & TECHNICAL COOPERATION

Memorandum of understanding concerning scientific and technical cooperation in the earth sciences, with annexes and related agreement.
Signed at Paramaribo March 22, 1995.
Entered into force March 22, 1995.
TIAS 12619

TELECOMMUNICATION

Agreement relating to the reciprocal granting of authorizations to permit licensed amateur radio operators of either country to operate their stations in the other country.
Exchange of notes at Paramaribo October 3 and 12, 1978.
Entered into force October 12, 1978.
30 UST 2107; TIAS 9314

TRADE & INVESTMENT

Treaty of friendship, commerce and navigation, with protocol and exchange of notes between the United States and the Netherlands.
Signed at The Hague March 27, 1956.
Applicable to Suriname February 10, 1963.
8 UST 2043; TIAS 3942; 285 UNTS 231

TRANSPORTATION

Agreement between the United States and the Netherlands providing for no assertion of sovereign immunity from suit of air transport enterprises.
Exchange of notes at Washington June 19, 1953.
Entered into force June 19, 1953.
4 UST 1610; TIAS 2828; 212 UNTS 249

Air transport agreement between the United States and The Netherlands.
Signed at Washington April 3, 1957.
Entered into force provisionally April 3, 1957; definitively May 31, 1957.
12 UST 837; TIAS 4782; 410 UNTS 193
Amendment:
November 25, 1969 (20 UST 4070; TIAS 6797; 732 UNTS 316)

Memorandum of agreement concerning assistance in developing and modernizing the Suriname civil aviation infrastructure, with annexes.
Signed at Washington and Paramaribo June 21 and August 27, 1990.
Entered into force August 27, 1990.
TIAS 11754; 2202 UNTS 171

Air transport agreement.
Signed at Paramaribo July 8, 2013.
Entered into force December 9, 2014.
TIAS 14-1209

SWAZILAND

In a note dated October 22, 1968, to the Secretary General of the United Nations, the Minister of State of Swaziland made a statement reading in part as follows:

[F]or a period of two years with effect from September 6, 1968, the Government of the Kingdom of Swaziland accepts all treaty rights and obligations entered into prior to independence by the British Government on behalf of the Kingdom of Swaziland, during which period the treaties and international agreements in which such rights and obligations are embodied will receive examination with a view to determining, at the expiration of that period of two years, which of those rights and obligations will be adopted, which will be terminated, and which of these will be adopted with reservations in respect of particular matters.

In a further note dated October 30, 1970, it was stated that the Government of the Kingdom of Swaziland shall continue to apply the terms of these treaties within Swaziland, on a basis of reciprocity, for an indefinite period of time. This provisional arrangement should be deemed to continue in each case until the depositary is notified of the decision of the Government of the Kingdom of Swaziland either to accede definitively or to terminate its further adherence to the treaty.

CULTURAL EXCHANGES, PROPERTY & COOPERATION

Agreement relating to the establishment of a Peace Corps program in Swaziland.
Exchange of notes at Mbabane November 11, 1970.
Entered into force November 11, 1970.
21 UST 2487; TIAS 6989; 772 UNTS 173

DEFENSE

Agreement concerning the provision of training related to defense articles under the United States International Military Education and Training (IMET) Program.
Exchange of notes at Mbabane January 10 and February 28, 1984.
Entered into force February 28, 1984.
35 UST 4505; TIAS 10952

Agreement regarding the status of United States personnel who may be temporarily present in Swaziland in connection with mutually agreed activities.
Exchange of notes at Mbabane June 25 and July 24, 2009.
Entered into force July 24, 2009.
TIAS 09-724.1

FINANCE

Agreement relating to investment guaranties.
Signed at Mbabane September 29, 1967.
Entered into force September 29, 1967.
18 UST 2510; TIAS 6350; 693 UNTS 167

Agreement continuing in force the agreement of September 29, 1967 (TIAS 6350), relating to investment guaranties.
Exchange of notes at Mbabane April 3 and July 28, 1970.
Entered into force July 28, 1970.
21 UST 2006; TIAS 6944; 763 UNTS 53

FOREIGN ASSISTANCE

General agreement on special development assistance.
Signed at Mbabane June 3, 1970.
Entered into force June 3, 1970.
21 UST 1412; TIAS 6898; 756 UNTS 95

Agreement for economic, technical and related assistance.
Signed at Mbabane December 5, 1989.
Entered into force December 5, 1989.
TIAS 11733; 2202 UNTS 3

INTERNATIONAL CRIMINAL COURT

Agreement regarding the surrender of persons to the International Criminal Court.
Signed at Mbabane May 10, 2006.
Entered into force September 20, 2006.
TIAS 06-920

LAW ENFORCEMENT

Extradition treaty between the United States and the United Kingdom.
Signed at London December 22, 1931.
Entered into force June 24, 1935.
47 Stat. 2122; TS 849; 12 Bevans 482; 163 LNTS 59

Agreement continuing in force between the United States and Swaziland the extradition treaty of December 22, 1931 (47 Stat. 2122), between the United States and the United Kingdom.
Exchange of notes at Mbabane May 13 and July 28, 1970.
Entered into force July 28, 1970.
21 UST 1930; TIAS 6934; 756 UNTS 103

POSTAL MATTERS

International express mail agreement, with detailed regulations.
Signed at Mbabane and Washington March 3 and April 6, 1988.
Entered into force May 1, 1988.
TIAS 11583

TELECOMMUNICATION

Agreement relating to establishment of a Bureau of Foreign Broadcast Information Service (FBIS) in Swaziland.
Signed at Mbabane August 3, 1981.
Entered into force August 3, 1981.
33 UST 3344; TIAS 10235

Arrangement relating to radio communications between amateur stations on behalf of third parties.
Exchange of notes at Mbabane April 12 and May 27, 1983.
Entered into force June 26, 1983.
TIAS 10718; 1607 UNTS 131

SWEDEN

ATOMIC ENERGY

Agreement regarding participation in the USNRC international piping integrity research group, with appendices.
Signed at Stockholm and Bethesda February 2 and March 3, 1987.
Entered into force March 3, 1987.
TIAS 12218

Arrangement for the exchange of technical information and cooperation in nuclear safety matters, with addenda and annex.
Signed at Vienna September 27, 2016.
Entered into force September 27, 2016.
TIAS 16-927.1

CLAIMS & DISPUTE RESOLUTION

Treaty for the advancement of peace.
Signed at Washington October 13, 1914.
Entered into force January 11, 1915.
38 Stat. 1872; TS 607; 11 Bevans 741

Treaty of arbitration.
Signed at Washington October 27, 1928.
Entered into force April 15, 1929.
46 Stat. 2261; TS 783; 11 Bevans 760; 91 LNTS 225

Agreement concerning compensation for commissioners designated under the treaty for advancement of peace signed October 13, 1914.
Exchange of notes at Stockholm June 30, 1939.
Entered into force June 30, 1939.
53 Stat. 2428; EAS 154; 11 Bevans 821; 199 LNTS 203

CONSULAR AFFAIRS

Agreement relating to passport visa fees for nonimmigrants.*
Exchange of notes at Washington April 10 and 30, 1947.
Entered into force April 30, 1947;operative June 1, 1947.
61 Stat. 4050; TIAS 1798; 11 Bevans 834; 84 UNTS 33

Note:
* The status of this agreement is under review.

DEFENSE

Convention relating to exemption from military service of persons having dual nationality.
Signed at Stockholm January 31, 1933.
Entered into force May 20, 1935.
49 Stat. 3195; TS 890; 11 Bevans 778; 159 LNTS 261

Agreement relating to the procurement of reimbursable military equipment, materials, or services.
Exchange of notes at Stockholm June 30 and July 1, 1952.
Entered into force July 1, 1952.
3 UST 2968; TIAS 2480; 187 UNTS 3

Memorandum of understanding relating to the furnishing by Sweden to the United States of data resulting from the activities carried out under authorized contracts from research, development, modification, improvement or production of weapons or weapons systems.
Signed at Washington July 26, 1961 and Stockholm August 7, 1961. Entered into force August 7, 1961

Agreement concerning general security of military information.
Exchange of notes at Washington December 4 and 23, 1981.
Entered into force December 23, 1981.
33 UST 4400; TIAS 10309

Memorandum of understanding relating to the principles governing mutual cooperation in the defense procurement area, with related exchange of letters.
Signed at Washington and Stockholm June 11 and July 16, 1987.
Entered into force July 16, 1987.
TIAS; 1557 UNTS 313
Amendment:
June 12 and August 11, 2003

Memorandum of agreement concerning the exchange of engineers and scientists, with annexes.
Signed at Washington and Stockholm June 9 and 15, 1992.
Entered into force June 15, 1992.
NP

Agreement for cooperative research and development efforts in the fields of aircrew protection and performance, with annexes.
Signed at Stockholm April 23, 1993.
Entered into force April 23, 1993.
TIAS 12371

Agreement for the bilateral cooperative program in electromagnetic effects measurement and analysis (RF Effects Program).
Signed at Washington June 2 and December 20, 1995.
Entered into force December 20, 1995.
TIAS 12373

Agreement concerning exchange of research and development information.
Signed at Washington and Stockholm May 16 and June 13, 1997.
Entered into force June 13, 1997.
TIAS 97-613
Amendments:
August 13 and September 17, 2008 (TIAS 97-613)
November 16 and December 13, 2012 (TIAS 97-613)

Agreement regarding the exchange of engineers and scientists, with annexes.
Signed at Stockholm and Washington October 7 and December 20, 1999.
Entered into force December 20, 1999.
NP

Acquisition and cross-servicing agreement, with annex.
Signed at Stuttgart and Stockholm August 28 and September 11, 2003.
Entered into force September 11, 2003.
NP

Agreement for cooperation in environmental protection and defense matters.
Signed at Stockholm and Washington November 23 and December 6, 2005.
Entered into force December 6, 2005.
TIAS 05-1206

Agreement concerning cooperation on Information Assurance (IA) and Computer Network Defense (CND).
Signed at Washington and Stockholm April 30 and May 29, 2009.
Entered into force May 29, 2009.
TIAS

Memorandum of agreement concerning research, development, test, and evaluation projects, with annex.
Signed at Stockholm and Washington April 8 and 18, 2011.
Entered into force April 18, 2011.
TIAS 11-418
Related Agreement:
April 16 and June 1, 2012

Basic exchange and cooperation agreement concerning geospatial information, with annexes.
Signed at Stockholm and Washington August 23 and October 20, 2011.
Entered into force October 20, 2011.
NP

Agreement concerning end-use, retransfer and security assurances regarding U.S. sold or granted defense articles, related training or other defense services (including all associated components and technical data).
Exchange of notes at Stockholm February 16 and October 12, 2012.
Entered into force October 12, 2012.
TIAS

Memorandum of agreement regarding the assignment of liaison officers to U. S. European Command, with annexes.
Signed at Stockholm and Stuttgart September 15 and October 25, 2015.
Entered into force October 15, 2015.
NP

Memorandum of agreement regarding the assignment of liaison officers, with annexes.
Signed at Washington November 30 and December 7, 2016. Entered into force December 7, 2016.
NP

DIPLOMATIC & CONSULAR RELATIONS

Consular convention.*
Signed at Washington June 1, 1910.
Entered into force March 18, 1911.
37 Stat. 1479; TS 557; 11 Bevans 730
Note
* Articles XI and XII abrogated as of March 18, 1921.

Arrangement relating to free entry, on a reciprocal basis, for goods imported by career consular representatives.
Exchange of notes at Stockholm June 23 and 29, 1931.
Entered into force July 1, 1931.
11 Bevans 771

Arrangement for the reciprocal exemption from duty of articles imported by diplomatic officers and all other persons belonging to missions, but not including personal servants.
Exchange of notes at Washington January 5 and 17, 1933.
Entered into force January 17, 1933.
11 Bevans 776

EDUCATION

Agreement for financing certain educational exchange programs.
Signed at Stockholm November 20, 1952.
Entered into force November 20, 1952.
3 UST 4812; TIAS 2653; 177 UNTS 203

Amendments:
November 20, 1959 (10 UST 1921; TIAS 4359; 360 UNTS 396)
June 28, 1963 (14 UST 985; TIAS 5389; 479 UNTS 358)
December 7, 1970 (21 UST 2732; TIAS 7018; 776 UNTS 330)

EMPLOYMENT

Arrangement relating to the employment of dependents of official government employees.
Exchange of notes at Washington October 27 and 30, 1981.
Entered into force October 30, 1981.
33 UST 4148; TIAS 10291

ENVIRONMENT & CONSERVATION

Agreement for cooperation on environmental protection in defense matters.
Signed at Stockholm April 24, 1995.
Entered into force April 24, 1995.
TIAS 12372

Agreement for cooperation in the Global Learning and Observations to Benefit the Environment (GLOBE) Program, with appendices.
Signed at Stockholm August 23, 1995.
Entered into force August 23, 1995.
TIAS 12684

FOREIGN ASSISTANCE

Economic cooperation agreement.
Signed at Stockholm July 3, 1948.
Entered into force July 21, 1948.
62 Stat. 2541; TIAS 1793; 11 Bevans 855; 23 UNTS 101

Amendments:
January 5 and 17, 1950 (1 UST 181; TIAS 2034; 76 UNTS 254)
February 8 and 23, 1951 (3 UST 2800; TIAS 2448; 185 UNTS 326)

INTELLECTUAL PROPERTY

Agreement facilitating the interchange of patent rights and technical information for defense purposes.
Exchange of notes at Washington October 4, 1962.
Entered into force October 4, 1962.
13 UST 2161; TIAS 5178; 462 UNTS 31

Agreement approving the procedures for reciprocal filing of classified patent applications in the United States and Sweden.
Exchange of notes at Washington October 20 and November 17, 1964.
Entered into force November 17, 1964.
15 UST 2086; TIAS 5690; 532 UNTS 378

LAW ENFORCEMENT

Convention for the prevention of smuggling of intoxicating liquors.
Signed at Washington May 22, 1924.
Entered into force August 18, 1924.
43 Stat. 1830; TS 698; 11 Bevans 750; 29 LNTS 421

Convention on extradition, with protocol.*
Signed at Washington October 24, 1961.
Entered into force December 3, 1963.
14 UST 1845; TIAS 5496; 494 UNTS 141

Note:
* Protocol terminated January 1, 1965.

Supplementary convention on extradition.
Signed at Stockholm March 14, 1983.
Entered into force September 24, 1984.
35 UST 2501; TIAS 10812

Agreement regarding mutual assistance in customs matters.
Signed at Washington July 8, 1987.
Entered into force May 8, 1988.
TIAS 12122

Treaty on mutual legal assistance in criminal matters.
Signed at Stockholm December 17, 2001.
Entered into force June 1, 2009.
TIAS 09-601

Instrument as contemplated by Article 3(2) of the agreement on extradition between the United States of America and the European Union signed June 25, 2003, as to the application of the convention on extradition of October 24, 1961 and the supplementary convention on extradition of March 14, 1983, with annex.
Signed at Brussels December 16, 2004.
Entered into force February 1, 2010.
TIAS 10-201.22

Instrument as contemplated by Article 3(2) of the agreement on mutual legal assistance between the United States of America and the European Union signed June 25, 2003, as to the application of the treaty on mutual legal assistance in criminal matters of December 17, 2001, with annex.
Signed at Brussels December 16, 2004.
Entered into force February 1, 2010.
TIAS 10-201.48

Agreement on enhancing cooperation in preventing and combating crime.
Signed at Washington December 16, 2011.
Entered into force November 2, 2016.
TIAS 16-1102

MARITIME MATTERS

Arrangement relating to the reciprocal exemption of pleasure yachts from all navigation dues.
Exchange of notes at Stockholm October 22 and 29, 1930.
Entered into force October 29, 1930.
47 Stat. 2655; EAS 21; 11 Bevans 763; 109 LNTS 181

Agreement relating to jurisdiction over vessels utilizing the Louisiana Offshore Oil Port.
Exchange of notes at Washington August 17 and 22, 1978.
Entered into force August 22, 1978.
30 UST 1698; TIAS 9277; 1153 UNTS 145

POSTAL MATTERS

Parcel post convention.
Signed at Stockholm June 28 and at Washington July 11, 1932.
Operative July 1, 1932.
47 Stat. 2106; Post Office Department print

International express mail agreement, with detailed regulations.
Signed at Stockholm and Washington August 26 and 30, 1983.
Entered into force October 1, 1983.
35 UST 2136; TIAS 10780; 2011 UNTS 115

PUBLICATIONS

Agreement relating to exchange of official publications.
Exchange of notes at Stockholm December 16, 1947.
Entered into force December 16, 1947.
61 Stat. 3605; TIAS 1688; 11 Bevans 843; 73 UNTS 65

SCIENTIFIC & TECHNICAL COOPERATION

Agreement on science and technology cooperation, with annexes.
Signed at Stockholm June 29, 2006.
Entered into force June 29, 2006.
TIAS 06-629
Related Agreement:
June 28, 2007 (TIAS 06-629)

Memorandum of understanding concerning scientific and technical cooperation in the earth sciences, with annexes.
Signed at Reston and Stockholm December 7 and 18, 2006.
Entered into force December 18, 2006.
TIAS 06-1218

Agreement on cooperation in science and technology for homeland security matters, with annex.
Signed at Washington April 13, 2007.
Entered into force April 13, 2007.
TIAS 07-413

SOCIAL SECURITY

Agreement on social security, with administrative arrangement.
Signed at Stockholm May 27, 1985.
Entered into force January 1, 1987.
TIAS 11266

Supplementary agreement on social security.
Signed at Stockholm June 22, 2004.
Entered into force November 1, 2007.
TIAS 07-1101

SPACE

Framework agreement for cooperative activities in the exploration and use of outer space for peaceful purposes.
Signed at Stockholm October 14, 2005.
Entered into force October 14, 2005.
TIAS 05-1014
Amendment:
October 6, 2015 (TIAS 15-1006)

Implementing arrangement for cooperation in aeronautic and space research using nanosatellite technologies.
Signed at Washington and Solna May 10 and 19, 2011.
Entered into force May 19, 2011.
TIAS 11-519

TAXATION

Arrangement relating to relief from double income tax on shipping profits.
Exchange of notes at Washington March 31, 1938.
Entered into force March 31, 1938.
52 Stat. 1490; EAS 121; 11 Bevans 806; 189 LNTS 327
Amendment:
June 26 and July 24, 1987 (TIAS 11286; 2174 UNTS 379)

Convention for the avoidance of double taxation and the prevention of fiscal evasion with respect to taxes on income, with exchange of letters.
Signed at Stockholm September 1, 1994.
Entered into force October 26, 1995.
TIAS

Protocol amending the convention of September 1, 1994 for the avoidance of double taxation and the prevention of fiscal evasion with respect to taxes on income.
Signed at Washington September 30, 2005.
Entered into force August 31, 2006.
TIAS

Agreement to improve international tax compliance and to implement the Foreign Account Tax Compliance Act, with annexes.
Signed at Stockholm August 8, 2014.
Entered into force March 11, 2015.
TIAS 15-311

TELECOMMUNICATION

Agreement relating to the reciprocal granting of authorizations to permit licensed amateur radio operators of either country to operate their station in the other country.
Exchange of notes at Stockholm May 27 and June 2, 1969.
Entered into force June 2, 1969.
20 UST 773; TIAS 6690; 715 UNTS 75

TRANSPORTATION

Arrangement relating to pilot licenses to operate civil aircraft.
Exchange of notes at Washington September 8 and 9, 1933.
Entered into force October 9, 1933.
48 Stat. 1799; EAS 48; 11 Bevans 788; 144 LNTS 171

Agreement relating to air transport services.*
Exchange of notes at Washington December 16, 1944.
Entered into force January 1, 1945.
58 Stat. 1466; EAS 431; 11 Bevans 825; 6 UNTS 397

Amendments:
August 6, 1954 (5 UST 1411; TIAS 3013; 222 UNTS 376)
June 16, 1995; (TIAS 12665)

Note:
* This agreement is suspended for the duration of provisional application of the U.S. – E.U. Air Transport Agreement signed April 25 and 30, 2007.

Agreement relating to air service facilities in Sweden.
Signed at Stockholm September 30, 1946.
Entered into force September 30, 1946.
61 Stat. 3893; TIAS 1742; 11 Bevans 832; 42 UNTS 213

Agreement relating to airworthiness certifications.
Exchange of notes at Stockholm April 24 and 26, 1973.
Entered into force April 26, 1973.
24 UST 997; TIAS 7611

Memorandum of understanding on highway management and technology.
Signed at Borlange June 15, 1992.
Entered into force June 15, 1992.
TIAS 11870

Agreement for the promotion of aviation safety.
Signed at Stockholm February 9, 1998.
Entered into force February 9, 1998.
TIAS 12929

SWITZERLAND

ATOMIC ENERGY

Agreement regarding participation in the USNRC international piping integrity research group, with appendices.
Signed at Bern and Bethesda February 3 and March 3, 1987.
Entered into force March 3, 1987.
TIAS 12219

Agreement for cooperation concerning peaceful uses of atomic energy, with agreed minute and annexes.
Signed at Bern October 31, 1997.
Entered into force June 23, 1998.
TIAS 12894

Arrangement for the exchange of technical information and cooperation in nuclear safety matters, with addenda.
Signed at Vienna September 19, 2012.
Entered into force September 19, 2012.
TIAS 12-919

CLAIMS & DISPUTE RESOLUTION

Treaty of arbitration and conciliation.
Signed at Washington February 16, 1931.
Entered into force May 23, 1932.
47 Stat. 1983; TS 844; 11 Bevans 920; 129 LNTS 465

CONSULAR AFFAIRS

Agreement relating to the waiver of passport visa fees for nonimmigrants.*
Exchange of notes at Bern May 11, 1925.
Entered into force May 11, 1925; operative June 1, 1925.
11 Bevans 915

Agreement relating to the waiver of passport visa fees for nonimmigrants.*
Exchanges of notes at Washington October 22, October 31, November 4, and November 13, 1947.
Entered into force November 13, 1947.
6 UST 93; TIAS 3172; 251 UNTS 79

Note
* The status of this agreement is under review.

DEFENSE

Convention relative to military obligations of certain persons having dual nationality.
Signed at Bern November 11, 1937.
Entered into force December 7, 1938.
53 Stat. 1791; TS 943; 11 Bevans 936; 193 LNTS 181

Agreement on the exchange of military personnel between the U.S. Navy and the Swiss Air Force and Anti-Aircraft Command.
Signed at Bern and Washington July 5 and August 17, 1995.
Entered into force August 17, 1995.
NP

Basic exchange and cooperative agreement concerning global geospatial information and services cooperation, with annexes.
Signed at Brussels June 19, 2001.
Entered into force June 19, 2001.
NP

Agreement concerning acquisition and cross-servicing, with annex.
Signed at Stuttgart and Bern March 23 and December 6, 2001.
Entered into force December 6, 2001.
NP

Memorandum of understanding concerning reciprocal defense procurement.
Signed at Bern and Washington November 29, 2006 and February 15, 2007.
Entered into force February 15, 2007.
TIAS 07-215

DIPLOMATIC & CONSULAR RELATIONS

Agreement concerning the status, privileges, and immunities of the SALT (START) delegation in Switzerland with annex.
Exchange of notes at Bern November 21 and 22, 1972.
Entered into force November 22, 1972.
23 UST 3736; TIAS 7523
Related Agreement:
June 9, 1982 (34 UST 1263; TIAS 10414)

Agreement on rights, privileges and immunities of the United States-Union of Soviet Socialist Republics Standing Consultative Commission.
Exchange of notes at Bern February 26 and March 5, 1973.
Entered into force March 5, 1973.
24 UST 772; TIAS 7582; 944 UNTS 95

Agreement establishing rights, privileges and immunities of the delegation to the negotiations concerning theater (intermediate range) nuclear forces.
Exchange of letters at Bern October 17, 1980.
Entered into force October 17, 1980.
33 UST 610; TIAS 10056; 1265 UNTS 177
Related Agreement:
November 11 and 20, 1981 (33 UST 4237; TIAS 10298)

Agreement establishing rights, privileges and immunities of the United States delegation to the negotiations on nuclear and space arms.
Exchange of notes at Bern March 1 and 5, 1985.
Entered into force March 5, 1985.
TIAS 11188; 2129 UNTS 425

ENVIRONMENT & CONSERVATION

Agreement for cooperation in the Global Learning and Observations to Benefit the Environment (GLOBE) Program, with appendices.
Signed at Berne April 22, 1998.
Entered into force April 22, 1998.
TIAS 12946

INTELLECTUAL PROPERTY

Agreement relating to the registration of trade-marks.
Exchange of notes at Washington April 27 and May 14, 1883.
Entered into force May 14, 1883.
TS 471; 11 Bevans 901

Arrangement relating to reciprocal benefits under the patent laws of the two countries.
Exchange of notes at Bern January 17 and 28, 1908.
Entered into force January 28, 1908.
11 Bevans 909

LAW ENFORCEMENT

Arrangement for the direct exchange of certain information regarding the traffic in narcotic drugs.
Exchange of notes at Bern November 15 and 16, 1929.
Entered into force November 16, 1929.
11 Bevans 917

Treaty on mutual assistance in criminal matters with related notes.
Signed at Bern May 25, 1973.
Entered into force January 23, 1977.
27 UST 2019; TIAS 8302; 1052 UNTS 61
Related Agreement:
November 3, 1993 (TIAS 12514)

Extradition treaty.
Signed at Washington November 14, 1990.
Entered into force September 10, 1997.
TIAS 97-910

Agreement on the transfer of passenger name record (PNR).
Exchange of notes at Bern December 23, 2008.
Entered into force December 23, 2008.
TIAS 08-1223

POSTAL MATTERS

Agreement concerning the exchange of parcel post, and regulations of execution.*
Signed at Washington April 1 and at Bern May 18, 1932.
Operative April 1, 1932.
47 Stat. 1997; Post Office Department print
Note:
* Applicable to Liechtenstein.

International express mail agreement, with detailed regulations.
Signed at Bern and Washington December 7, 1978, and January 22, 1979.
Entered into force February 1, 1979.
32 UST 5549; TIAS 10008; 1265 UNTS 131

PRIVATE INTERNATIONAL LAW

Agreement for the enforcement of maintenance (support) obligations.
Signed at Washington August 31, 2004.
Entered into force September 30, 2004.
TIAS 04-930.1

PUBLICATIONS

Agreement relating to the exchange of official publications.
Exchange of notes at Washington January 5 and February 24, 1950.
Entered into force February 24, 1950.
1 UST 396; TIAS 2058; 93 UNTS 3

SCIENTIFIC & TECHNICAL COOPERATION

Agreement for scientific and technological cooperation, with annexes.
Signed at Washington April 1, 2009.
Entered into force July 24, 2009.
TIAS 09-724

SOCIAL SECURITY

Agreement on social security, with administrative arrangement.
Signed at Bern December 3, 2012.
Entered into force August 1, 2014.
TIAS 14-801

TAXATION

Convention for the avoidance of double taxation with respect to taxes on estates and inheritances.
Signed at Washington July 9, 1951.
Entered into force September 17, 1952.
3 UST 3972; TIAS 2533; 165 UNTS 51

Convention for the avoidance of double taxation with respect to taxes on income, with protocol.
Signed at Washington October 2, 1996.
Entered into force December 19, 1997.
TIAS

Agreement for cooperation to facilitate the implementation of the Foreign Account Tax Compliance Act.
Signed at Bern February 14, 2013.
Entered into force June 2, 2014.
TIAS 14-602
Amendment:
September 6 and 13, 2013 (TIAS 14-602)

TELECOMMUNICATION

Agreement relating to the reciprocal granting of authorizations to permit licensed amateur radio operators of either country to operate their stations in the other country.
Exchange of notes at Bern January 12 and May 16, 1967.
Entered into force May 16, 1967.
18 UST 554; TIAS 6264; 685 UNTS 319

TRADE & INVESTMENT

Convention of friendship, commerce and extradition.*
Signed at Bern November 25, 1850.
Entered into force November 8, 1855.
11 Stat. 587; TS 353; 11 Bevans 894
Note
* Articles 8-12 terminated March 23, 1900, as a result of notice given by the United States on March 23, 1899; articles 13-17 relating to extradition were superseded and expressly repealed by the extradition treaty signed May 14, 1900 (31 Stat. 1928; TS 354; 11 Bevans 904).

TRANSPORTATION

Air service agreement relating to equipment at Cointrin Airport.
Signed at Bern April 30, 1947.
Entered into force April 30, 1947.
61 Stat. 3859; TIAS 1736; 11 Bevans 957; 42 UNTS 235

Agreement concerning the reciprocal acceptance of certificates of airworthiness for imported aircraft.
Exchange of notes at Bern October 13, 1961.
Entered into force provisionally October 13, 1961; definitively November 21, 1962.
13 UST 2479; TIAS 5214; 459 UNTS 219
Amendment:
January 7, 1977 (28 UST 2446; TIAS 8563)

Agreement for promotion of aviation safety.
Signed at Washington September 26, 1996.
Entered into force September 26, 1996.
TIAS 12803

Air transport agreement, with annexes.
Signed at Bern June 21, 2010.
Entered into force June 21, 2010.
TIAS 10-621

SYRIAN ARAB REPUBLIC

CULTURAL EXCHANGES, PROPERTY & COOPERATION

Cultural agreement.
Signed at Damascus May 12, 1977.
Entered into force May 12, 1977.
28 UST 5321; TIAS 8634

DIPLOMATIC & CONSULAR RELATIONS

Convention between the United States and France relating to rights in Syria and Lebanon.
Signed at Paris April 4, 1924.
Entered into force July 13, 1924.
43 Stat. 1821; TS 695; 7 Bevans 925

Agreement between the United States and France relating to customs privileges for educational, religious, and philanthropic institutions in Syria and Lebanon.
Exchange of notes at Paris February 18, 1937.
Entered into force February 18, 1937.
51 Stat. 279; EAS 107; 7 Bevans 1017; 184 LNTS 479

Agreement relating to rights of American nationals.
Exchange of notes at Damascus September 7 and 8, 1944.
Entered into force September 8, 1944.
58 Stat. 1491; EAS 434; 11 Bevans 970; 124 UNTS 251

FINANCE

Agreement relating to investment guaranties, with related letter.
Exchange of notes at Damascus August 9, 1976.
Entered into force August 13, 1977.
TIAS 8707; 28 UST 7122

POSTAL MATTERS

Agreement with the United Arab Republic concerning the exchange of parcel post and regulations of execution.
Signed at Cairo December 30, 1958, and at Washington January 13, 1959.
Entered into force October 1, 1959.
10 UST 1664; TIAS 4315; 358 UNTS 3

International express mail agreement, with detailed regulations.
Signed at Damascus and Washington September 26 and November 16, 1993.
Entered into force January 1, 1994.
NP

TELECOMMUNICATION

Agreement relating to reciprocal authorization for each Government to install and operate a low-power radio station in the fixed service at or near its Embassy for transmission of official messages.
Exchange of notes at Washington November 13, 1974, and May 15, 1975.
Entered into force May 15, 1975.
27 UST 3292; TIAS 8363; 1068 UNTS 359

T

TAJIKISTAN

For agreements prior to December 31, 1991, see UNION OF SOVIET SOCIALIST REPUBLICS.

DEFENSE

Agreement regarding the status of United States military and civilian personnel of the United States Department of Defense present in Tajikistan in connection with cooperative efforts in response to terrorism, humanitarian assistance and other agreed activities.
Exchange of notes at Dushanbe November 20 and 23, 2001.
Entered into force November 23, 2001.
TIAS

Agreement on construction of a bridge between the Republic of Tajikistan and the Islamic State of Afghanistan.
Signed at Dushanbe December 31, 2003.
Entered into force December 31, 2003.
TIAS 03-1231

Agreement regarding grants under the Foreign Assistance Act of 1961, as amended, or successor legislation, and the furnishing of defense articles, related training, and other defense services, including pursuant to the United States International Military Education and Training Program, from the United States of America to the Government of the Republic of Tajikistan.
Exchange of notes at Dushanbe July 2, 2007 and March 17, 2008.
Entered into force March 17, 2008.
NP

EMPLOYMENT

Employment agreement concerning dependents of officials serving in both countries.
Exchange of notes at Dushanbe March 11 and August 12, 2003.
Entered into force August 12, 2003.
TIAS 03-812

FINANCE

Investment incentive agreement.
Signed at Dushanbe June 25, 1992.
Entered into force June 25, 1992.
TIAS 12461

FOREIGN ASSISTANCE

Agreement regarding cooperation to facilitate the provision of humanitarian and technical economic assistance.
Signed at Dushanbe September 13, 1993.
Entered into force September 13, 1993
TIAS 12163

Agreement on construction of a bridge between the Republic of Tajikistan and the Islamic State of Afghanistan.
Signed at Dushanbe December 31, 2003.
Entered into force December 31,2003.
TIAS 03-1231

INTERNATIONAL CRIMINAL COURT

Agreement regarding the surrender of persons to the International Criminal Court.
Signed at Dushanbe August 26, 2002.
Entered into force June 23, 2003.
TIAS 03-623
Amendment:
September 27, 2004 (TIAS 03-623)

PROPERTY

Agreement concerning the ownership of property for the diplomatic and consular missions of the United States and Tajikistan.
Exchange of notes at Dushanbe October 5, 2000, and January 2, 2001.
Entered into force January 2, 2001.
TIAS

TAXATION

Agreement concerning the taxation of United States embassy locally employed staff.
Signed at Dushanbe April 29, 2015.
Entered into force July 10, 2015.
TIAS 15-710

TRADE & INVESTMENT

Agreement on trade relations, with exchanges of letters.
Signed at Dushanbe July 1, 1993.
Entered into force November 24, 1993.
TIAS

TANZANIA

On December 9, 1961, Tanganyika attained fully responsible status within the British Commonwealth. In a note dated December 9, 1961, to the Secretary-General of the United Nations from the Prime Minister, the Government of Tanganyika stated that it is willing to continue to apply, on a reciprocal basis, all such treaties validly applied or extended to it as a territory for a period of two years from the date of independence, that is to December 8, 1963, unless abrogated or modified earlier by mutual consent. On April 26, 1964, the Republic of Tanganyika and the People's Republic of Zanzibar were united as one Sovereign State under the name of the United Republic of Tanganyika and Zanzibar. In a note dated May 6, 1964, the United Republic of Tanganyika and Zanzibar informed the Secretary-General of the United Nations that "all international treaties and agreements in force between the Republic of Tanganyika or the People's Republic of Zanzibar and other States or international organizations will, to the extent that their implementation is consistent with the constitutional position established by the Articles of Union, remain in force within the regional limits prescribed on their conclusion and in accordance with the principles of international law." On October 29, 1964, the name of the Republic was changed to the United Republic of Tanzania.

DEFENSE

Agreement regarding grants under the Foreign Assistance Act of 1961, as amended, or successor legislation, and the furnishing of defense articles, defense services and related training, including pursuant to the United States International Military Education and Training (IMET) Program.
Exchange of notes at Dar es Salaam May 24 and June 29, 2006.
Entered into force June 29, 2006.
NP

DIPLOMATIC & CONSULAR RELATIONS

Consular convention and protocol of signature between the United States and the United Kingdom.
Signed at Washington June 6, 1951.
*Entered into force September 7, 1952.**
3 UST 3426; TIAS 2494; 165 UNTS 121

Note:

* Treaty continued in force between the United States and Tanzania by the exchange of notes of November 30 and December 6, 1965 (16 UST 2066; TIAS 5946).
Paragraph 1 of article 7 is not applicable to Tanganyika.

EMPLOYMENT

Agreement for the employment of dependents of employees of consular and diplomatic personnel.
Exchange of notes at Dar es Salaam May 9 and September 6, 2007.
Entered into force September 6, 2007.
TIAS 07-906

ENVIRONMENT & CONSERVATION

Agreement for cooperation in the Global Learning and Observations to Benefit the Environment (GLOBE) Program, with appendices.
Signed at Dar es Salaam April 1, 1997.
Entered into force April 1, 1997.
TIAS 12847

FINANCE

Agreement relating to investment guaranties.
Exchange of notes at Dar es Salaam November 14, 1963.
Entered into force November 14, 1963.
14 UST 1608; TIAS 5465; 493 UNTS 75

Agreement regarding the consolidation and rescheduling of certain debts owed to, guaranteed by or insured by the United States Government, and its agencies, with annexes.
Signed at Dar es Salaam March 18, 1987.
Entered into force April 27, 1987.
NP

Agreement regarding the consolidation and rescheduling of certain debts owed to, guaranteed by or insured by the United States Government and its agencies, with annexes.
Signed at Dar es Salaam May 4, 1989.
Entered into force June 15, 1989.
NP

Agreement regarding the consolidation and rescheduling of certain debts owed to, guaranteed by, or insured by the United States Government and its agencies, with annexes.
Signed at Dar es Salaam October 31, 1990.
Entered into force January 9, 1991.
NP

Agreement regarding the consolidation and rescheduling or refinancing of certain debts owed to, guaranteed by or insured by the United States Government and its agencies, with annexes.
Signed at Dar es Salaam September 11, 1992.
Entered into force December 3, 1992.
NP

Investment incentive agreement.
Signed at Dar es Salaam December 24, 1996.
Entered into force November 26, 1997.
TIAS 12824

Agreement regarding the consolidation, reduction and rescheduling of certain debts owed to, guaranteed by, or insured by the United States Government and its Agency, with annexes.
Signed at Dar es Salaam January 16, 1998.
Entered into force March 27, 1998.
NP

Agreement regarding the consolidation and reduction of certain debts owed to, guaranteed by, or insured by the United States Government and its agencies, with annexes.
Signed at Dar es Salaam June 14, 2001.
Entered into force September 6, 2001.
NP

Agreement regarding the consolidation of debt owed to, guaranteed by, or insured by the United States Government, with annexes.
Signed at Dar es Salaam July 4, 2002.
Entered into force August 26, 2002.
NP

FOREIGN ASSISTANCE

Agreement providing for the furnishing of economic, technical, and related assistance.
Exchange of notes at Dar es Salaam February 8, 1968.
Entered into force February 8, 1968.
19 UST 4614; TIAS 6448; 698 UNTS 67

AGENCY FOR INTERNATIONAL DEVELOPMENT

Strategic objective grant agreement for Strategic Objective No. 10: enhanced multisectoral response to HIV/AIDS, with annex.
Signed June 7, 2005.
Entered into force June 7, 2005.
NP

Amendments:
September 26, 2005 (NP)
June 5, 2006 (NP)
July 11, 2007 (NP)
August 28, 2008 (NP)
September 10, 2009 (NP)
September 28, 2009 (NP)
March 7, 2011 (NP)
September 24, 2010 (NP)
September 13, 2011 (NP)
September 28, 2011 (NP)
April 24, 2013 (NP)

Strategic objective grant agreement for incomes of small farmers increased in selected agricultural commodity sub-sectors, with annex.
Signed July 26, 2005.
Entered into force July 26, 2005.
NP

Amendments:
September 16, 2010 (NP)
September 16 and 19, 2011 (NP)
September 22 and 26, 2012 (NP)

Strategic objective grant agreement for health status of Tanzania families improved, with annex.
Signed August 23, 2005.
Entered into force August 23, 2005.
NP

Amendments:
August 15, 2008 (NP)
September 8 and 10, 2009 (NP)
August 23, 2010 (NP)
September 27 and 28, 2011 (NP)
September 24 and 26, 2012 (NP)

Strategic assistance agreement, with annexes.
Signed at Dar Es Salaam August 1, 2016.
Entered into force August 1, 2016.
NP

LAW ENFORCEMENT

Extradition treaty between the United States and the United Kingdom.*
Signed at London December 22, 1931.
Entered into force June 24, 1935.
47 Stat. 2122; TS 849; 12 Bevans 482; 163 LNTS 59

Note:
* Treaty continued in force between the United States and Tanzania by the exchange of notes of November 30 and December 6, 1965 (16 UST 2066; TIAS 5946).

POSTAL MATTERS

Parcel post agreement and regulations of execution.
Signed at Zanzibar October 20 and at Washington December 30, 1959.
Entered into force May 1, 1960.
11 UST 293; TIAS 4449

International express mail agreement, with detailed regulations.
Signed at Dar es Salaam and Washington December 30, 1987, and January 25, 1988.
Entered into force February 15, 1988.
TIAS 11886

TRANSPORTATION

Memorandum of agreement concerning civil aviation assistance and services.
Signed August 24 and September 19, 2001.
Entered into force September 19, 2001.
NP

TREATY LAW

Agreement continuing in force between the United States and Tanzania the extradition treaty and the consular convention between the United States and the United Kingdom.
Exchange of notes at Dar es Salaam November 30 and December 6, 1965.
Entered into force December 6, 1965; effective December 9, 1963.
16 UST 2066; TIAS 5946; 592 UNTS 53

THAILAND

ATOMIC ENERGY

Arrangement for the exchange of technical information and cooperation in nuclear safety matters, with addenda.
Signed at Rockville March 13, 2012.
Entered into force March 13, 2012.
TIAS 12-313

CONSULAR AFFAIRS

Arrangement relating to the waiver of passport visas and visa fees for nonimmigrants.
Exchange of notes at Bangkok September 19, 1925.
Entered into force September 19, 1925.
11 Bevans 1014

CULTURAL EXCHANGES, PROPERTY & COOPERATION

Agreement relating to the establishment of a Peace Corps program in Thailand.
Exchange of notes at Bangkok November 20 and 28, 1961.
Entered into force November 28, 1961.
12 UST 3225; TIAS 4929; 434 UNTS 77

DEFENSE

Agreement respecting military assistance.
Signed at Bangkok October 17, 1950.
Entered into force October 17, 1950.
3 UST 2675; TIAS 2434; 79 UNTS 41

Agreement relating to the assurances required by the Mutual Security Act of 1951.
Exchange of notes at Bangkok December 27 and 29, 1951.
Entered into force December 29, 1951.
3 UST 4653; TIAS 2619; 179 UNTS 113

Agreement providing for an aerial photographic mapping survey of Thailand.
Exchange of notes at Bangkok November 8 and December 3, 1952.
Entered into force December 3, 1952.
3 UST 5893; TIAS 2759; 213 UNTS 91

Agreement relating to the disposition of military equipment and materials furnished under the military assistance agreement.
Exchange of notes at Bangkok July 6, 1955.
Entered into force July 6, 1955.
6 UST 2067; TIAS 3274; 258 UNTS 386

Memorandum of agreement on integrated communications system, with appendix.
Signed at Bangkok January 10, 1977.
Entered into force January 10, 1977.
29 UST 591; TIAS 8837

Memorandum of agreement relating to the storage of ammunition in Thailand.
Signed at Bangkok March 22, 1977.
Entered into force March 22, 1977.
29 UST 743; TIAS 8850

General security of military information agreement.
Exchange of notes at Bangkok March 30 and April 5, 1983.
Entered into force April 5, 1983.
TIAS 10678; 2005 UNTS 165

Agreement relating to a war reserve stockpile program in Thailand, with annexes.*
Signed at Bangkok January 9, 1987.
Entered into force March 22, 1988.
TIAS 12604

Amendment and Extension:
February 15, 1995 (TIAS 12604)

* This agreement superseded by Memorandum of Agreement of November 26, 2002, except for Annexes I and III to the 1987 Agreement which shall be incorporated and become an integral part of that Memorandum of Agreement.

Memorandum of agreement concerning mapping, charting and geodesy.
Signed at Bangkok and Fairfax February 27 and March 15, 1990.
Entered into force March 15, 1990.
NP

Agreement concerning measures to be taken for the transfer, security and safeguarding of technical information, software and equipment to the Ministry of Defense to enable industry to operate, maintain and expand Royal Thai Air Force air combat maneuvering instrumentation range facilities.
Signed at Washington September 30, 1993.
Entered into force September 30, 1993.
TIAS 11509

Memorandum of agreement concerning the transfer of equipment and munitions from United States war reserve stocks to the Government of the Kingdom of Thailand, with appendices and understanding.
Signed at Bangkok November 26, 2002.
Entered into force November 26, 2002.
TIAS 02-1126

Agreement regarding grants under the Foreign Assistance Act of 1961, as amended, and the furnishing of defense articles, defense services, and related training, including pursuant to the United States International Military and Education Training Program (IMET), from the United States to the Government of the Kingdom of Thailand.
Exchange of notes at Bangkok December 27, 2005, and March 14, 2006.
Entered into force March 14, 2006.
NP

Amendment:
March 28 and April 17, 2006

Acquisition and cross-servicing agreement, with annexes.
Signed at Bangkok and Camp Smith January 6 and 30, 2014.
Entered into force January 30, 2014.
NP

EDUCATION

Agreement for financing certain educational exchange programs.
Signed at Bangkok May 24, 1963.
Entered into force May 24, 1963.
TIAS 5355; 14 UST 770; 477 UNTS 123

Amendment:
June 9 and July 9, 1970 (TIAS 6912; 21 UST 1512; 753 UNTS 392)

FINANCE

Agreement relating to investment guaranties under section 413 (b)(4) of the Mutual Security Act of 1954.
Exchange of notes at Washington August 27 and September 1, 1954.
Entered into force September 1, 1954.
5 UST 2258; TIAS 3086; 237 UNTS 209
Amendment:
December 22, 1965 (16 UST 2041; TIAS 5940; 551 UNTS 292)

Agreement amending the Agreement of August 27, and September 1, 1954; relating to investment guaranties and terminating the agreement of August 27, 1957
Signed at Bangkok, December 22, 1965.
Entered into force December 22, 1965.

Agreement regarding the reduction of a certain debt owed to the Government of the United States and its agencies.
Signed at Bangkok September 19, 2001.
Entered into force September 19, 2001.
NP

FOREIGN ASSISTANCE

Economic and technical cooperation agreement, with exchange of notes.
Signed at Bangkok June 2, 1977.
Entered into force June 2, 1977.
28 UST 5210; TIAS 8622

HEALTH & MEDICAL COOPERATION

Agreement relating to the conversion of the Southeast Asia Treaty Organization cholera research project in Thailand to a SEATO medical research laboratory.
Exchange of notes at Bangkok December 23, 1960.
Entered into force December 23, 1960.
11 UST 2683; TIAS 4665; 405 UNTS 135

Agreement relating to the establishment and operation of a SEATO Clinical Research Center at the School of Graduate Studies of the University of Medical Sciences, with memorandum of understanding.
Exchange of notes at Bangkok April 1 and 25, 1963.
Entered into force April 25, 1963.
14 UST 459; TIAS 5340; 476 UNTS 115

Agreement modifying and continuing the agreements of December 23, 1960, and April 1 and 25, 1963, relating to the SEATO medical research project and the SEATO clinical research centre.
Exchange of notes at Bangkok January 19 and 28, 1977.
Entered into force July 1, 1977.
29 UST 643; TIAS 8840

INTERNATIONAL CRIMINAL COURT

Agreement regarding the surrender of persons to the International Criminal Court.
Exchange of notes at Bangkok June 3, 2003.
Entered into force June 3, 2003.
TIAS 03-603

LAW ENFORCEMENT

Memorandum of understanding on cooperation in the narcotics field.
Signed at Washington September 28, 1971.
Entered into force September 28, 1971.
22 UST 1587; TIAS 7185; 807 UNTS 49

Treaty on cooperation in the execution of penal sentences.
Signed at Bangkok October 29, 1982.
Entered into force December 7, 1988.
TIAS

Treaty relating to extradition.
Signed at Washington December 14, 1983.
Entered into force May 17, 1991.
TIAS

Treaty on mutual assistance in criminal matters, with attachments.
Signed at Bangkok March 19, 1986.
Entered into force June 10, 1993.
TIAS

Agreement concerning an International Law Enforcement Academy.
Signed at Bangkok September 30, 1998.
Entered into force September 30, 1998.
TIAS

POSTAL MATTERS

Parcel post agreement.
Signed at Bangkok May 31 and at Washington June 7, 1962.
Entered into force October 1, 1962.
13 UST 2209; TIAS 5188; 459 UNTS 135

International express mail agreement, with detailed regulations.
Signed at Bangkok and Washington November 14 and December 9, 1983.
Entered into force February 18, 1984.
35 UST 3142; TIAS 10847; 2015 UNTS 25

PUBLICATIONS

Agreement relating to the exchange of official publications.
Exchange of notes at Bangkok September 5, 1947.
Entered into force September 5, 1947.
61 Stat. 3154; TIAS 1654; 11 Bevans 1040; 73 UNTS 57

SCIENTIFIC & TECHNICAL COOPERATION

Memorandum of understanding relating to Chiang Mai seismic research station.
Signed at Bangkok December 29, 1976.
Entered into force December 29, 1976.
28 UST 8866; TIAS 8774; 1095 UNTS 191

Memorandum of understanding concerning scientific and technical cooperation in the earth sciences, with annexes.
Signed at Reston October 28, 2005.
Entered into force October 28, 2005.
TIAS 05-1028

Agreement for cooperation in the use of U.S. land remote sensing satellite data, with annexes.
Signed at South Dakota and Bangkok April 12, 2013 and April 29, 2013.
Entered into force April 29, 2013.
TIAS 13-429

Agreement relating to scientific and technical cooperation, with annexes.
Signed at Bangkok August 6, 2013.
Entered into force August 6, 2013.
TIAS 13-806

Memorandum of understanding concerning scientific and technical cooperation in the earth sciences.
Signed at Reston and Bangkok November 10, 2014 and February 4, 2015.
Entered into force February 4, 2015.
TIAS 15-204

TAXATION

Convention for the avoidance of double taxation and the prevention of fiscal evasion with respect to taxes on income, with exchange of notes.
Signed at Bangkok November 26, 1996.
Entered into force December 15, 1997.
TIAS

TELECOMMUNICATION

Agreement relating to the reciprocal granting of authorizations to permit licensed amateur radio operators of either country to operate their station in the other country.
Exchange of notes at Bangkok October 11 and 30, 1990.
Entered into force December 14, 1990.
TIAS 12421

TRADE & INVESTMENT

Treaty of amity and economic relations with exchanges of notes.
Signed at Bangkok May 29, 1966.
Entered into force June 8, 1968.
19 UST 5843; TIAS 6540; 652 UNTS 253

TRANSPORTATION

Agreement relating to air service facilities at Don Muang Airport and Bangkapi.
Signed at Bangkok May 8, 1947.
Entered into force May 8, 1947.
61 Stat. 3855; TIAS 1735; 11 Bevans 1037; 42 UNTS 241

Air transport agreement, with annexes.
Signed at Washington September 19, 2005.
Entered into force September 19, 2005.
TIAS 05-919

TIMOR-LESTE

CULTURAL EXCHANGES, PROPERTY & COOPERATION

Agreement concerning the program of the Peace Corps in the Democratic Republic of East Timor.
Signed at Dili May 24, 2002.
Entered into force May 24, 2002.
TIAS 02-524

DEFENSE

Agreement regarding grants under the Foreign Assistance Act of 1961, as amended, and the furnishing of defense articles, related training to include training related to defense articles under the International Military and Education Training program, and other defense services from the United States of America to the Government of the Democratic Republic of East Timor.
Exchange of notes at Dili July 8 and 10, 2002.
Entered into force July 10, 2002.
TIAS 02-710

Status of forces agreement.
Signed at Washington October 1, 2002.
Entered into force October 1, 2002.
TIAS 02-1001

EMPLOYMENT

Agreement relating to the employment of dependents of official government employees.
Exchange of notes at Dili July 31 and August 8, 2002.
Entered into force August 8, 2002.
TIAS 02-808

FINANCE

Investment incentive agreement.
Signed at Washington July 25, 2002.
Entered into force July 25, 2002.
TIAS 02-725

FOREIGN ASSISTANCE

Agreement for economic and technical cooperation.
Signed at Dili June 6, 2003.
Entered into force April 25, 2005; effective January 1, 2003.
TIAS 05-425

INTERNATIONAL CRIMINAL COURT

Agreement regarding the surrender of persons to the International Criminal Court.
Signed at Dili August 23, 2002.
Entered into force October 30, 2003.
TIAS 03-1030

TOGO

CULTURAL EXCHANGES, PROPERTY & COOPERATION

Agreement relating to the establishment of a Peace Corps program in Togo.
Exchange of notes at Lome August 1 and September 5, 1962.
Entered into force September 5, 1962.
13 UST 2251; TIAS 5191; 461 UNTS 47

DEFENSE

Agreement concerning the loan of U.S. Government equipment and provision of logistic support services to the Economic Community of West African States (ECOWAS) and its members in support of the ECOFORCE peacekeeping operation in Cote d'Ivoire.
Exchange of notes at Lome January 22 and February 5, 2003.
Entered into force February 5, 2003.
TIAS 03-205

Agreement regarding grants under the Foreign Assistance Act of 1961, as amended, or successor legislation, and the furnishing of defense articles, defense services and related training, including pursuant to the United States International Military Education and Training (IMET) Program.
Exchange of notes at Lome May 22 and October 8, 2008.
Entered into force October 8, 2008.
NP

FINANCE

Agreement relating to investment guaranties.
Signed at Washington March 20, 1962.
Entered into force March 20, 1962.
13 UST 321; TIAS 4983; 445 UNTS 79

Agreement regarding the consolidation and rescheduling of certain debts owed to, guaranteed or insured by the United States Government and the Export-Import Bank of the United States, with annexes.
Signed at Lome March 28, 1980.
Entered into force May 2, 1980.
32 UST 933; TIAS 9740; 1222 UNTS 225

Agreement regarding the consolidation and rescheduling of certain debts owed to, or guaranteed by the United States Government through the Export-Import Bank of the United States, with annexes and agreed minute.
Signed at Lome September 18, 1981.
Entered into force December 7, 1981.
NP

Agreement regarding the consolidation and rescheduling of certain debts owed to, or guaranteed by the United States Government through the Export-Import Bank.
Signed at Lome November 29, 1983.
Entered into force January 31, 1984.
NP

Agreement regarding the reduction of certain debts owed to, guaranteed by, or insured by the United States Government and its agency, with annexes.
Signed at Lome July 23, 2009.
Entered into force September 22, 2009.
NP

FOREIGN ASSISTANCE

Agreement providing for economic, technical and related assistance.
Exchange of notes at Lome December 22, 1960.
Entered into force December 22, 1960.
11 UST 2566; TIAS 4646; 401 UNTS 33

INTERNATIONAL CRIMINAL COURT

Agreement regarding the surrender of persons to the International Criminal Court.
Signed at Lome June 13, 2003.
Entered into force January 15, 2004.
TIAS 04-115

LAW ENFORCEMENT

Procedures for mutual assistance in connection with matters relating to the Gulfstream American Corporation, formerly known as Grumman American Aviation Corporation.
Signed at Washington January 30, 1979.
Entered into force January 30, 1979.
30 UST 3477; TIAS 9401; 1180 UNTS 199

POSTAL MATTERS

International express mail agreement, with detailed regulations.
Signed at Lome and Washington November 28, 1988, and January 6, 1989.
Entered into force January 30, 1989.
NP

SOCIAL SECURITY

Agreement relating to United States participation with respect to its eligible employees in the Togolese social security system.
Exchange of notes at Lome March 17 and 26, 1971.
Entered into force March 26, 1971.
22 UST 526; TIAS 7094; 792 UNTS 223

TRADE & INVESTMENT

Treaty of amity and economic relations.
Signed at Lome February 8, 1966.
Entered into force February 5, 1967.
18 UST 1; TIAS 6193; 680 UNTS 159

TRANSPORTATION

Air transport agreement, with annexes.
Signed at Lome April 7, 2015.
Entered into force April 7, 2015.
TIAS 15-407

TONGA

On June 4, 1970, Tonga became an independent state. In a note dated June 18, 1970, to the Secretary-General of the United Nations, the Prime Minister of Tonga stated that each treaty validly made on behalf of the Kingdom of Tonga by the Government of the United Kingdom pursuant to and within the powers of the United Kingdom derived from certain instruments entered into between the United Kingdom and the Kingdom of Tonga, continues to bind the latter until validly terminated, that it is desired that it be presumed that each treaty continues to create rights and obligations, and that action be based on this presumption until a decision is reached that the treaty should be regarded as not having been validly made for the Kingdom of Tonga or as having lapsed. Should the Government of the Kingdom of Tonga be of the opinion that it continues to be legally bound by the treaty, and wishes to terminate the operation of the treaty, it will in due course give notice of termination in the terms thereof. With respect to duly ratified treaties which were entered into by the Kingdom of Tonga before the United Kingdom undertook the responsibility for the foreign relations thereof, the Government of the Kingdom of Tonga acknowledges that they remain in force to the extent to which their provisions were unaffected in virtue of international law by certain instruments entered into between the United Kingdom and the Kingdom of Tonga or by other events.

CULTURAL EXCHANGES, PROPERTY & COOPERATION

Agreement relating to the establishment of a Peace Corps program in Tonga with exchange of letters.
Exchange of notes at Suva and Nuku'alofa May 17 and 27, 1968.
Entered into force May 27, 1968.
19 UST 5486; TIAS 6534; 707 UNTS 71

DEFENSE

Agreement concerning the provision of training related to defense articles under the United States International Military Education and Training (IMET) Program.
Exchange of notes at Suva and Nuku'alofa November 18 and 25, 1985.
Entered into force November 25, 1985.
TIAS 11101

Agreement concerning the status of members of the United States Armed Forces in the Kingdom of Tonga.
Signed at Suva July 20, 1992.
Entered into force July 20, 1992.
TIAS 12523

Agreement regarding grants under the Foreign Assistance Act of 1961, as amended, or successor legislation, and the furnishing of defense articles, defense services and related training, including pursuant to the United States International Military Education and Training (IMET) Program, from the United States of America to the Kingdom of Tonga.
Exchange of notes at Suva and Nuku'alofa March 16 and August 24, 2006.
Entered into force August 24, 2006.
NP

Acquisition and cross-servicing agreement.
Signed at Camp Smith and Nuku'alofa August 20 and September 11, 2007.
Entered into force September 11, 2007.
NP

DIPLOMATIC & CONSULAR RELATIONS

Consular convention between the United States and the United Kingdom.
Signed at Washington June 6, 1951.
Entered into force September 7, 1952.
3 UST 3426; TIAS 2494; 165 UNTS 121

FINANCE

Investment incentive agreement.
Exchange of notes at Suva and Nuku'alofa August 22, 1983, and November 26, 1984.
Entered into force November 26, 1984.
TIAS 11000; 2022 UNTS 125

INTELLECTUAL PROPERTY

Declaration by the United States and the United Kingdom affording reciprocal protection to trade-marks.
Signed at London October 24, 1877.
Entered into force October 24, 1877.
20 Stat. 703; TS 138; 12 Bevans 198

INTERNATIONAL CRIMINAL COURT

Agreement regarding the surrender of persons to the International Criminal Court.
Signed at Washington March 21, 2003.
Entered into force March 24, 2004.
TIAS 04-324

LAW ENFORCEMENT

Extradition treaty.
Signed at London December 22, 1931.
Entered into force June 24, 1935; applicable to Tonga August 1, 1966.
47 Stat. 2122; TS 849; 12 Bevans 482; 163 LNTS 59

Agreement continuing in force between the United States and Tonga the extradition treaty of December 22, 1931, between the United States and the United Kingdom.
Exchange of notes at Nuku'alofa and Wellington March 14 and April 13, 1977.
Entered into force April 13, 1977.
28 UST 5290; TIAS 8628; 1087 UNTS 289

TRINIDAD AND TOBAGO

On August 31, 1962, Trinidad and Tobago became independent. By an exchange of letters on August 31, 1962, between the High Commissioner for the United Kingdom in Trinidad and Tobago and the Prime Minister of Trinidad and Tobago, the Government of Trinidad and Tobago agreed to assume all obligations and responsibilities of the United Kingdom which arise from any valid inter-national instrument (including any such instrument made by the Government of the Federation of the West Indies by virtue of authority entrusted by the Government of the United Kingdom). The rights and benefits heretofore enjoyed by the Government of the United Kingdom by virtue of application of any such international instrument to Trinidad and Tobago shall henceforth be enjoyed by the Government of Trinidad and Tobago.

CLAIMS & DISPUTE RESOLUTION

Agreement between the United States and the United Kingdom relating to claims for damages resulting from acts of armed forces or civilian personnel.
Exchange of notes at Washington October 23, 1946, and January 23, 1947.
Entered into force January 23, 1947; operative from June 6, 1944.
61 Stat. 2876; TIAS 1622; 12 Bevans 805; 15 UNTS 281

CONSULAR AFFAIRS

Agreement relating to extended validity of passports issued by Trinidad and Tobago.
Exchange of notes at Port-of-Spain October 28 and November 12, 1969.
Entered into force November 12, 1969.
21 UST 1995; TIAS 6942; 763 UNTS 9

DEFENSE

Agreement between the United States and the United Kingdom relating to the assurances required under the Mutual Security Act of 1951.
Exchange of notes at London January 8, 1952.
Entered into force January 8, 1952.
3 UST 4665; TIAS 2622; 126 UNTS 307

Agreement concerning the provision of training related to defense articles under the United States International Military Education and Training (IMET) Program, with aide memoire.
Exchange of notes at Port of Spain December 29, 1983, and November 16, 1984.
Entered into force November 16, 1984.
TIAS 10989; 2022 UNTS 123

Agreement concerning grants under the Foreign Assistance Act of 1961, as amended, and the furnishing of defense articles, related training, and other defense services from the United States to Trinidad and Tobago for counter-narcotics purposes.
Exchange of notes at Port of Spain February 4 and 13, 1998.
Entered into force February 13, 1998.
NP

Agreement regarding the status of United States personnel who may be temporarily present in Trinidad and Tobago in connection with mutually agreed activities.
Exchange of notes at Port of Spain February 20 and May 22, 2013.
Entered into force May 22, 2013.
TIAS 13-522
Extension:
April 22, 2015 and February 17, 2016

DIPLOMATIC & CONSULAR RELATIONS

Consular convention between the United States and the United Kingdom.
Signed at Washington June 6, 1951.
Entered into force September 7, 1952.
3 UST 3426; TIAS 2494; 165 UNTS 121

EMPLOYMENT

Agreement relating to the employment of dependents of official government employees.
Exchange of notes at Port of Spain May 15, 1990, and July 23, 1992.
Entered into force July 23, 1992.
TIAS 11924

ENVIRONMENT & CONSERVATION

Agreement for cooperation in the Global Learning and Observations to Benefit the Environment (GLOBE) Program, with appendices.
Signed at Port of Spain July 16, 1996.
Entered into force July 16, 1996.
TIAS 12784

FINANCE

Agreement relating to investment guaranties.
Exchange of notes at Port-of-Spain January 8 and 15, 1963.
Entered into force January 15, 1963.
14 UST 113; TIAS 5278; 471 UNTS 141

Agreement regarding the consolidation and rescheduling of certain debts owed to, guaranteed by, or insured by the United States Government and its agencies.
Signed at Port-of-Spain July 28, 1989.
Entered into force September 13, 1989.
NP

Agreement regarding the consolidation and rescheduling of certain debts owed to, guaranteed by, or insured by the United States Government and its agencies, with annexes.
Signed at Port-of-Spain November 26, 1990.
Entered into force January 14, 1991.
NP

FOREIGN ASSISTANCE

Economic cooperation agreement between the United States and the United Kingdom.
Signed at London July 6, 1948.
Applicable, with the exception of article IV, to Trinidad and Tobago March 17, 1949.
62 Stat. 2596; TIAS 1795; 12 Bevans 874; 22 UNTS 263

Amendments:
January 3, 1950 (1 UST 184; TIAS 2036; 84 UNTS 304)
May 25, 1951 (2 UST 1292; TIAS 2277; 99 UNTS 308)
February 23, 1953 (4 UST 1528; TIAS 2815; 172 UNTS 332)
June 26 and August 20, 1959 (11 UST 2680; TIAS 4664; 405 UNTS 288)

Agreement between the United States and the United Kingdom for technical cooperation in respect of the territories for the international relations of which the Government of the United Kingdom are responsible.
Signed at London July 13, 1951.
Applicable to Trinidad and Tobago August 14, 1954.
2 UST 1307; TIAS 2281; 105 UNTS 71

INTELLECTUAL PROPERTY

Declaration by the United States and the United Kingdom affording reciprocal protection to trade-marks.
Signed at London October 24, 1877.
Entered into force October 24, 1877.
20 Stat. 703; TS 138; 12 Bevans 198

LAW ENFORCEMENT

Procedures for mutual assistance in the administration of justice in connection with matters relating to the investigation designated as MA 106.
Signed at Washington June 7, 1982.
Entered into force June 7, 1982.
34 UST 1271; TIAS 10416

Extradition treaty.
Signed at Port of Spain March 4, 1996.
Entered into force November 29, 1999.
TIAS 99-1129

Treaty on mutual legal assistance in criminal matters, with forms.
Signed at Port of Spain March 4, 1996.
Entered into force November 29, 1999.
TIAS

Agreement regarding the Cooperating Nation Information Exchange System (CNIES).
Exchange of notes at Port of Spain October 6, 2004, and February 23, 2005.
Entered into force February 23, 2005.
TIAS

Agreement regarding mutual assistance between their customs administrations.
Signed at Port of Spain September 21, 2016.
Entered into force September 21, 2016.
TIAS 16-921

MARITIME MATTERS

Agreement concerning maritime counter-drug operations.
Signed at Port of Spain March 4, 1996.
Entered into force March 4, 1996.
TIAS 12732

POSTAL MATTERS

Money order agreement.
Signed at Port-of-Spain September 18 and at Washington October 23, 1891.
Operative January 1, 1891.
NP

Parcel post agreement with regulations of execution.
Signed at Port-of-Spain and Washington March 9 and 18, 1968.
Entered into force May 1, 1968.
19 UST 4735; TIAS 6472; 698 UNTS 121

International express mail agreement, with detailed regulations.
Signed at Port of Spain and Washington November 3 and December 7, 1987.
Entered into force July 1, 1988.
TIAS 11558

PROPERTY

Convention between the United States and the United Kingdom relating to the tenure and disposition of real and personal property.
Signed at Washington March 2, 1899.
Applicable to Trinidad and Tobago February 9, 1901.
31 Stat. 1939; TS 146; 12 Bevans 246

Supplementary convention relating to the tenure and disposition of real and personal property.
Signed at Washington May 27, 1936.
Entered into force March 10, 1941.
55 Stat. 1101; TS 964; 5 Bevans 140; 203 LNTS 367

SCIENTIFIC & TECHNICAL COOPERATION

Agreement for a cooperative meteorological observation program in Trinidad.
Exchange of notes at Port-of-Spain October 7, 1970.
Entered into force October 7, 1970; effective January 1, 1968.
21 UST 2495; TIAS 6991; 772 UNTS 163

TAXATION

Convention for the avoidance of double taxation, the prevention
of fiscal evasion with respect to taxes on income, and the encouragement of international trade and investment, with related notes.*
Signed at Port-of-Spain January 9, 1970.
Entered into force December 30, 1970.
22 UST 164; TIAS 7047; 781 UNTS 99

Note:
* With reservation.

Agreement for the exchange of information with respect to taxes.
Signed at Port of Spain January 11, 1989.
Entered into force February 9, 1990.
TIAS 11607; 2192 UNTS 89

TELECOMMUNICATION

Agreement relating to the reciprocal granting of authorizations to permit licensed amateur radio operators of either country to operate their stations in the other country.
Exchange of notes at Port-of-Spain January 14 and March 16, 1967.
Entered into force March 16, 1967.
18 UST 543; TIAS 6261; 685 UNTS 93

Arrangement relating to radio communications between amateur stations on behalf of third parties.
Exchange of notes at Port-of-Spain October 26 and November 18, 1971.
Entered into force December 18, 1971.
22 UST 2053; TIAS 7239

TRADE & INVESTMENT

Agreement on removal of trade distorting practices in steel trade, with appendices and exchange of letters.
Exchange of letters at Washington and Port-of-Spain March 29 and April 12, 1990.
Entered into force April 12, 1990.
TIAS

Treaty concerning the encouragement and reciprocal protection of investment, with annex and protocol.
Signed at Washington September 26, 1994.
Entered into force December 26, 1996.
TIAS

TRANSPORTATION

Arrangement between the United States and the United Kingdom relating to pilot licenses to operate civil aircraft.
Exchange of notes at Washington March 28 and April 5, 1935.
Entered into force May 5, 1935.
49 Stat. 3731; EAS 77; 12 Bevans 513; 162 LNTS 59

Air transport agreement.
Signed at Port of Spain May 22, 2010.
Entered into force November 1, 2010.
TIAS 10-1101

TUNISIA

A general convention between France and Tunisia signed June 3, 1955, provided inter alia (1) for recognition of the primacy of international conventions and treaties over internal law (article 3) and (2) that Tunisia would take, within the framework of its internal autonomy, measures necessary for rendering applicable treaties concerning Tunisia and for assuring their execution (article 8).

The independence of Tunisia was recognized in a protocol between France and Tunisia signed March 20, 1956, recognizing Tunisia's exercise of its responsibilities in foreign affairs and providing for organization of interdependent cooperation in external relations.

CONSULAR AFFAIRS

Arrangement between the United States and France for the waiver by France of visa requirements for United States citizens visiting Metropolitan France and certain French territories, and for the granting by the United States of gratis passport visas to French citizens resident in those territories who enter the United States as nonimmigrants.*
Exchange of notes at Paris March 16 and 31, 1949.
Entered into force March 31, 1949.
63 Stat. 2737; TIAS 1987; 7 Bevans 1311; 84 UNTS 283

Note:
* The status of this agreement is under review.

CULTURAL EXCHANGES, PROPERTY & COOPERATION

Agreement relating to the establishment of a Peace Corps program in Tunisia.
Exchange of notes at Tunis February 7 and 13, 1962.
Entered into force February 13, 1962.
13 UST 249; TIAS 4968; 442 UNTS 155

Agreement on cultural cooperation.
Signed at Tunis September 28,1979.
Entered into Force September 28,1979.
31 UST 5027; TIAS 9653

DEFENSE

Agreement concerning payment to the United States of net proceeds from the sale of defense articles furnished under the military assistance program.
Exchange of notes at Tunis May 21 and June 29, 1974.
Entered into force July 1, 1974.
25 UST 1554; TIAS 7892

Agreement relating to a program of grants of military equipment and material to Tunisia.
Exchange of notes at Tunis September 12 and October 25, 1974.
Entered into force October 25, 1974; effective July 1, 1974.
25 UST 3051; TIAS 7964

Mapping, charting and geodesy cooperative and exchange agreement, with annexes.
Signed at Tunis December 8, 1980.
Entered into force December 8, 1980.
TIAS 10698; 2005 UNTS 97
Amendment
July 14 and August 31, 1982 (TIAS 10698; 2005 UNTS 107)

Agreement concerning the security of military information.
Exchange of notes at Washington April 4,1984 & 4,25,1984
Entered into Force April 25,1984

Memorandum of understanding for cooperation in the field of military medicine.
Signed at Tunis August 14, 1985.
Entered into force August 14, 1985.
TIAS 12008

Memorandum of understanding on the exchange of officers.
Signed at Tunis and Washington February 14 and March 12, 1992.
Entered into force March 12, 1992.
NP

Agreement concerning mutual logistic support, with annexes.
Signed at Tunis and Stuttgart-Vaihingen March 29 and April 29, 1994.
Entered into force April 29, 1994.
TIAS 12374

Agreement regarding grants under the Foreign Assistance Act of 1961, as amended, or successor legislation, and the furnishing of defense articles, defense services and related training, including pursuant to the United States International Military Education and Training (IMET) Program.
Exchange of notes at Tunis November 23, 2007, and February 13, 2008.
Entered into force February 13, 2008.
NP

Agreement regarding grants under the Foreign Assistance Act of 1961, as amended, or successor legislation, and the furnishing of defense articles, defense services and related training, including pursuant to the United States International Military Education and Training (IMET) Program.
Exchange of notes at Tunis April 25 and May 20, 2008.
Entered into force May 20, 2008.
NP

Agreement concerning health care for military members and their dependents.
Signed February 4 and March 5, 2013.
Entered into force March 5, 2013.
NP
Extension:
March 17 and June 2, 2016.

Basic exchange and cooperation agreement concerning geospatial information, with annexes.
Signed at Springfield and Tunis March 10 and 25, 2013.
Entered into force March 25, 2013.
NP

DIPLOMATIC & CONSULAR RELATIONS

Treaty between the United States and France for the determination of their relations in Tunis.
Signed at Washington March 15, 1904.
Entered into force May 7, 1904.
33 Stat. 2263; TS 434; 7 Bevans 862

Consular convention.
Signed at Tunis May 12, 1988.
Entered into force January 15, 1994.
TIAS

EDUCATION

Agreement for financing certain educational exchange programs.
Signed at Tunis November 18, 1963.
Entered into force November 18, 1963.
TIAS 5499; 14 UST 1881; 494 UNTS 193

ENVIRONMENT & CONSERVATION

Agreement for cooperation in the Global Learning and Observations to Benefit the Environment (GLOBE) Program, with appendices.
Signed at Washington July 27, 1995.
Entered into force July 27, 1995.
TIAS 12678

FINANCE

Investment incentive agreement.
Signed at Washington February 17, 2004.
Entered into force April 20, 2005.
TIAS 05-420

FOREIGN ASSISTANCE

Agreement providing for economic, technical and related assistance.
Exchange of notes at Tunis March 26, 1957.
Entered into force March 26, 1957.
8 UST 427; TIAS 3794; 283 UNTS 117

Agreement regarding certain assurances by Tunisia supplementing the economic, technical, and related assistance agreement of
March 26, 1957.
Exchange of notes at Tunis October 8, 1958.
Entered into force October 8, 1958.
9 UST 1324; TIAS 4122; 336 UNTS 389

Agreement relating to the commitment by the United States to Tunisia's three-year plan.
Exchange of notes at Tunis September 28 and October 29, 1962.
Entered into force October 29, 1962.
13 UST 2667; TIAS 5239; 462 UNTS 201

Loan guarantee agreement, with annexes.
Signed at Washington June 8, 2012.
Entered into force July 10, 2012.
TIAS 12-710.1

Loan guarantee agreement, with annexes.
Signed at Washington June 3, 2014.
Entered into force July 18, 2014.
TIAS 14-718.1

Loan guarantee agreement, with annex.
Signed at Tunis and Washington June 3 and 6, 2016.
Entered into force August 2, 2016.
TIAS 16-802

INTERNATIONAL CRIMINAL COURT

Agreement regarding the surrender of persons to the International Criminal Court.
Exchange of notes at Tunis June 5, 2003.
Entered into force December 22, 2003.
TIAS 03-605

SCIENTIFIC & TECHNICAL COOPERATION

Agreement on science and technology cooperation, with annexes.
Signed at Tunis August 15, 2014.
Entered into force December 9, 2014.
TIAS 14-1209.2

TRADE & INVESTMENT

Treaty concerning the reciprocal encouragement and protection of investment, with protocol.
Signed at Washington May 15, 1990.
Entered into force February 7, 1993.
NP

POSTAL MATTERS

International express mail agreement, with detailed regulations.
Signed at Tunis and Washington November 12, 1982, and January 4, 1983.
Entered into force April 1, 1983.
TIAS 10640; 1935 UNTS 321

Memorandum of understanding concerning the operation of the INTELPOST service, with details of implementation.
Signed at Tunis and Washington December 19, 1989, and October 3, 1991.
Entered into force February 1, 1993.
TIAS 11903

SCIENTIFIC & TECHNICAL COOPERATION

Agreement relating to the establishment and operation of a Mediterranean Marine Sorting Center in Tunisia.
Exchange of notes at Tunis September 26, 1966.
Entered into force September 26, 1966.
17 UST 1412; TIAS 6101; 616 UNTS 259

Agreement establishing principles for cooperation between American institutions conducting basic scientific research in Tunisia under Smithsonian Institution sponsorship and appropriate Tunisian institutions, organizations or governmental agencies.
Exchange of notes at Tunis July 17, 1968.
Entered into force July 17, 1968.
19 UST 5900; TIAS 6543; 707 UNTS 127

TAXATION

Convention for the avoidance of double taxation and the prevention of fiscal evasion with respect to taxes on income, with exchange of notes.
Signed at Washington June 17, 1985.
Entered into force December 26, 1990.
TIAS

Supplementary protocol to the convention for the avoidance of double taxation and the prevention of fiscal evasion with respect to taxes on income of June 17, 1985.
Signed at Tunis October 4, 1989.
Entered into force December 26, 1990.
TIAS

TELECOMMUNICATION

Agreement relating to the installation and operation of a radio transmitter by the Embassy of Tunisia.
Exchange of notes at Washington May 28, 1975, and May 13, 1976.
Entered into force May 13, 1976.
28 UST 2437; TIAS 8561

TURKEY

ATOMIC ENERGY

Agreement continuing in effect safeguards and guarantee provisions of the agreement of June 10, 1955, as amended, for cooperation concerning civil uses of atomic energy (TIAS 3320, 4748, 5828, 6040, 7122).
Exchange of notes at Ankara April 15 and June 9, 1981.
Entered into force June 9, 1981.
TIAS 10560; 1577 UNTS 403

Agreement for cooperation concerning peaceful uses of nuclear energy, with agreed minute.
Signed at Ankara July 26, 2000.
Entered into force June 2, 2008.
TIAS

Arrangement for the exchange of technical information and cooperation in nuclear safety matters, with addenda.
Signed at Vienna September 18, 2012.
Entered into force September 18, 2012.
TIAS 12-918.1

CONSULAR AFFAIRS

Agreement relating to passport visas and visa fees.*
Exchange of notes at Washington June 27, August 8, September 27, and October 11, 1955.
Entered into force October 11, 1955; operative December 1, 1955.
7 UST 337; TIAS 3508; 272 UNTS 145

Note:

* The status of this agreement is under review.

CULTURAL EXCHANGES, PROPERTY & COOPERATION

Agreement relating to the establishment of a Peace Corps program in Turkey.
Exchange of notes at Ankara August 27, 1962.
Entered into force August 27, 1962.
13 UST 2263; TIAS 5193; 461 UNTS 55

DEFENSE

Agreement relating to the assurances required by the Mutual Security Act of 1951.
Exchange of notes at Ankara January 7, 1952.
Entered into force January 7, 1952.
3 UST 4660; TIAS 2621; 179 UNTS 121

Agreement relating to implementation of the agreement between the parties to the North Atlantic Treaty regarding the status of their forces of June 19, 1951 (4 UST 1792; TIAS 2846), with two minutes of understanding.
Signed at Ankara June 23, 1954.
Entered into force June 23, 1954.
5 UST 1465; TIAS 3020; 233 UNTS 189

Agreement relating to redistributable and excess equipment and materials furnished pursuant to the mutual defense assistance program.
Exchange of notes at Ankara May 26, 1955.
Entered into force May 26, 1955.
6 UST 2071; TIAS 3275; 262 UNTS 97

Amendment:

August 10, 1962 (13 UST 2628; TIAS 5232; 462 UNTS 350)

Agreement relating to a program of offshore procurement, with memorandum of understanding and model contract attached, and exchange of notes.
Exchange of notes at Ankara June 29, 1955.
Entered into force June 29, 1955.
6 UST 3729; TIAS 3372

Agreement amending the minute of understanding on paragraph 7 of the agreement of June 23, 1954.
Exchange of notes at Ankara April 22 and July 21, 1955.
Entered into force July 21, 1955.
6 UST 2917; TIAS 3337; 265 UNTS 418

Agreement of cooperation.
Signed at Ankara March 5, 1959.
Entered into force March 5, 1959.
10 UST 320; TIAS 4191; 327 UNTS 293

Agreement for cooperation on uses of atomic energy for mutual defense purposes.
Exchange of notes at Ankara May 5, 1959.
Entered into force July 27, 1959.
10 UST 1340; TIAS 4278; 355 UNTS 341

Agreement relating to the introduction of modern weapons into NATO defense forces in Turkey.
Exchange of notes at Ankara September 18 and October 28, 1959.
Entered into force October 28, 1959.
10 UST 1866; TIAS 4350; 360 UNTS 265

Agreement for the establishment of a facility for repairing and rebuilding M-12 range finders in Turkey.
Exchange of notes at Ankara November 30, 1959.
Entered into force November 30, 1959.
10 UST 2027; TIAS 4372; 361 UNTS 107

Agreement relating to a weapons production program.
Exchange of notes at Ankara March 2, 1960.
Entered into force March 2, 1960.
11 UST 1322; TIAS 4465; 372 UNTS 37

Agreement concerning duty certificates in implementation of article VII of the agreement between the parties to the North Atlantic Treaty regarding the status of their forces.
Exchange of notes at Ankara September 24, 1968.
Entered into force September 24, 1968.
19 UST 6317; TIAS 6582; 702 UNTS 235

Agreement concerning payment to the United States of net proceeds from the sale of defense articles furnished under the military assistance program.
Exchange of notes at Ankara October 9 and 10, 1974.
Entered into force October 10, 1974; effective July 1, 1974.
25 UST 2494; TIAS 7933

Agreement concerning the grant of defense articles and services under the military assistance program.
Exchange of notes at Ankara August 15 and 31, 1979.
Entered into force August 31, 1979.
30 UST 7299; TIAS 9588; 1182 UNTS 93

Amendment:

August 13 and September 24, 1982 (TIAS 10502)

Agreement for cooperation on defense and economy in accordance with articles II and III of the North Atlantic Treaty, with related note; supplementary agreement number 1 on defense support; supplementary agreement number 2 on defense industrial cooperation; and supplementary agreement number 3 on installations, with implementing agreements (annexes).
Signed at Ankara March 29, 1980.
Entered into force December 18, 1980.
32 UST 3323; TIAS 9901

Memorandum of understanding on co-operative measures for enhancing air defense capabilities of selected COBs in Turkey.
Signed at Washington and Ankara November 14 and December 26, 1984.
Entered into force December 26, 1984.
TIAS

Agreement supplementing and extending the agreement of March 29, 1980, for cooperation on defense and economy.
Exchange of letters at Washington March 16, 1987.
Entered into force March 16, 1987.
TIAS

Acquisition and cross-servicing agreement, with annexes.
Signed at Ankara and Stuttgart July 26 and August 12, 1996.
Entered into force August 12, 1996.
TIAS 12789

Support and procedures arrangement.
Signed at Ankara December 1, 2000.
Entered into force December 1, 2000.
TIAS

Memorandum of understanding for a bilateral missile defense architecture analysis.
Signed at Washington and Ankara May 31 and June 6, 2001.
Entered into force June 6, 2001.
TIAS

Agreement supplementing the cooperative framework for system development and demonstration of the Joint Strike Fighter.
Signed at Washington July 11, 2002.
Entered into force August 10, 2002.
TIAS 02-810

Letter of agreement concerning the use of the Turkish NATO Pipeline System (TNPS), with annexes
Signed December 30 and 31, 2004.
Entered into force December 31, 2004.
TIAS
Amendment:
July 11 and 17, 2008

Administrative arrangement concerning accommodation, facilities, services and assistance made available to personnel of the Armed Forces of the United States of America at Headquarters NATO Rapid Deployable Corps-Turkey (NRDC-T), with annex
Signed January 5 and February 10, 2005.
Entered into force February 10, 2005.
TIAS

DIPLOMATIC & CONSULAR RELATIONS

Agreement for the regularization of relations between the United States and Turkey.
Exchange of notes at Ankara February 17, 1927.
Entered into force February 17, 1927.
Foreign Relations, 1927, Vol. III, p. 794 ff.; 11 Bevans 1109

EDUCATION

Agreement for the establishment of the United States Educational Commission in Turkey, and exchanges of notes.
Signed at Ankara December 27, 1949.
Entered into force March 21, 1950.
TIAS 2111; 1 UST 603; 98 UNTS 141
Amendments:
January 8, 1957 (TIAS 3737; 8 UST 41; 266 UNTS 404)
February 1, 1960 (TIAS 4458; 11 UST 399; 371 UNTS 282)
April 21 and May 30, 1961 (TIAS 4766; 12 UST 661; 409 UNTS 302)
April 26 and May 2, 1967 (TIAS 6307; 18 UST 1654; 692 UNTS 400)

EMPLOYMENT

Agreement relating to the employment of dependents of official government employees.
Exchange of notes at Ankara November 23, 1999.
Entered into force February 3, 2000.
TIAS 13072

ENVIRONMENT & CONSERVATION

Agreement for cooperation in the Global Learning and Observations to Benefit the Environment (GLOBE) Program, with appendices.
Signed at Ankara May 5, 1995.
Entered into force May 5, 1995.
TIAS 12643

FINANCE

Agreement relating to assurances by the Government of Turkey with respect to guaranties to investors pursuant to article III of the economic cooperation agreement, as amended.
Exchange of notes at Ankara November 15, 1951.
Entered into force November 15, 1951.
3 UST 3720; TIAS 2500; 177 UNTS 315
Amendments:
January 15, 1957 (8 UST 202; TIAS 3761; 280 UNTS 79)
November 27, 1964 (15 UST 2197; TIAS 5704; 531 UNTS 322)

Agreement regarding ownership and use of local currency repayments made by Turkey to the Development Loan Fund.
Exchange of notes at Ankara September 6, 1958.
Entered into force September 6, 1958.
9 UST 1251; TIAS 4111; 336 UNTS 85

Agreements regarding the consolidation and rescheduling of certain debts owed to, guaranteed or insured by the United States Government and its agencies, with annexes.
Signed at Washington and Ankara September 21 and December 5, 1978.
Entered into force December 7, 1978.
30 UST 2723; TIAS 9361; 1171 UNTS 3

Agreement regarding the consolidation and rescheduling of certain debts owed to, guaranteed or insured by the United States Government and its agencies, with annexes.
Signed at Ankara December 11, 1979.
Entered into force January 14, 1980.
32 UST 1461; TIAS 9783; 1234 UNTS 273

Implementing agreement regarding the consolidation and rescheduling of certain debts owed to the Agency for International Development.
Signed at Ankara April 22, 1980.
Entered into force April 22, 1980; effective January 14, 1980.
32 UST 1549; TIAS 9786; 1234 UNTS 293

Agreement regarding the consolidation and rescheduling of certain debts owed to, guaranteed or insured by the United States Government and its agencies, with agreed minute and annexes.
Signed at Ankara October 24, 1980.
Entered into force November 28, 1980.
32 UST 3674; TIAS 9909; 1267 UNTS 347

Implementing agreement regarding the consolidation and rescheduling of certain debts owed to the Agency for International Development.
Signed at Ankara February 7, 1981.
Entered into force February 7, 1981.
33 UST 1057; TIAS 10091; 1280 UNTS 437

Agreement regarding the consolidation and rescheduling of payments due under P. L. 480 Title I agricultural commodity agreements, with annexes.
Signed at Ankara March 27, 1981.
Entered into force March 27, 1981.
33 UST 1545; TIAS 10131

Agreement regarding the consolidation and rescheduling of certain debts owed to, guaranteed or insured by the United States Government and its agencies, with annexes and agreed minute.
Signed at Ankara September 24, 1981.
Entered into force November 2, 1981.
34 UST 1469; TIAS 10432

Agreement regarding the consolidation and rescheduling of payments due under P.L. 480 Title I agricultural commodity agreements, with annexes.
Signed at Ankara November 25, 1981.
Entered into force November 25, 1981.
34 UST 1469; TIAS 10432

Implementing agreement regarding the consolidation and rescheduling of certain debts owed to the Agency for International Development.
Signed at Ankara January 22, 1982.
Entered into force January 22, 1982.
34 UST 1469; TIAS 10432

FOREIGN ASSISTANCE

Agreement on aid to Turkey.
Signed at Ankara July 12, 1947.
Entered into force July 12, 1947.
61 Stat. 2953; TIAS 1629; 11 Bevans 1163; 7 UNTS 309

Economic cooperation agreement.
Signed at Ankara July 4, 1948.
Entered into force July 13, 1948.
62 Stat. 2566; TIAS 1794; 11 Bevans 1166; 24 UNTS 67
Amendments:
January 31, 1950 (1 UST 188; TIAS 2037; 76 UNTS 258)
August 16, 1951 (3 UST 54; TIAS 2392; 152 UNTS 276)
December 30, 1952 (3 UST 5348; TIAS 2742; 185 UNTS 330)

INTELLECTUAL PROPERTY

Agreement to facilitate interchange of patent rights and technical information for purposes of defense.
Signed at Ankara May 18, 1956.
Entered into force April 2, 1957.
8 UST 597; TIAS 3809; 283 UNTS 167

Agreement approving the procedures for reciprocal filing of classified patent applications in the United States and Turkey.
Exchange of notes at Ankara March 17 and September 16, 1959.
Entered into force September 16, 1959.
11 UST 388; TIAS 4456; 371 UNTS 314

LAW ENFORCEMENT

Arrangement for the direct exchange of certain information regarding the traffic in narcotic drugs.
Exchange of notes at Constantinople and Angora February 18 and October 3, 1928.
Entered into force October 3, 1928.
11 Bevans 1117

Treaty on extradition and mutual assistance in criminal matters.
Signed at Ankara June 7, 1979.
Entered into force January 1, 1981.
32 UST 3111; TIAS 9891

Treaty on the enforcement of penal judgments.
Signed at Ankara June 7, 1979.
Entered into force January 1, 1981.
32 UST 3187; TIAS 9892

Agreement regarding mutual assistance between customs administrations.
Signed at Washington March 28, 1996.
Entered into force October 15, 2002.
TIAS 12773

MARITIME MATTERS

Agreement relating to jurisdiction over vessels utilizing the Louisiana Offshore Oil Port.
Exchange of notes at Washington April 9 and 10, 1984.
Entered into force April 10, 1984.
TIAS 11239; 2174 UNTS 187

MIGRATION & REFUGEES

Agreement concerning the reimbursement of costs arising from the transit of United States Government employees and their families.
Done at Ankara September 13, 1996.
Entered into force September 13, 1996.
TIAS

POSTAL MATTERS

Agreement concerning the exchange of parcel post, and regulations of execution.
Signed at Washington July 2 and at Ankara May 25, 1935.
Entered into force August 1, 1935.
49 Stat. 3201; 164 LNTS 125

International express mail agreement, with detailed regulations.
Signed at Ankara and Washington October 16 and November 29, 1984.
Entered into force March 21, 1985.
TIAS 11012; 2022 UNTS 87

Memorandum of understanding concerning the operation of the BUREAUFAX service.
Signed at Ankara and Washington February 14 and March 14, 1990.
Entered into force March 15, 1990.
TIAS 11712

PROPERTY

Agreement on the principles applying to aid under the Act of March 11, 1941, and exchanges of notes.
Signed at Ankara February 23, 1945.
Entered into force February 23, 1945.
59 Stat. 1476; EAS 465; 11 Bevans 1147; 121 UNTS 165

Agreement on lend-lease and claims.
Signed at Ankara May 7, 1946.
Entered into force May 25, 1946.
60 Stat. 1809; TIAS 1541; 11 Bevans 1158; 6 UNTS 293

SCIENTIFIC & TECHNICAL COOPERATION

Agreement concerning the closure of Belbasi installation and the activation of a new seismic research station.
Signed at Ankara February 8, 2000.
Entered into force March 30, 2004.
TIAS 04-330.1

Memorandum of understanding concerning scientific and technical cooperation in the earth sciences, with annexes.
Signed at Reston and Ankara February 7 and April 10, 2002.
Entered into force April 10, 2002.
TIAS 02-410

Agreement on scientific and technological cooperation, with annexes.
Signed at Washington October 20, 2010.
Entered into force July 8, 2013.
TIAS 13-708

Memorandum of understanding concerning scientific and technical cooperation in the earth sciences, with annexes.
Signed at Ankara and Reston January 26 and February 18, 2011.
Entered into force February 18, 2011.
TIAS 11-218

TAXATION

Agreement relating to relief from Turkish taxation on expenditures made by or on behalf of the United States for common defense, with annex and minute.
Signed at Ankara June 23, 1954.
Entered into force June 23, 1954.
5 UST 1258; TIAS 2996; 222 UNTS 161

Agreement for the avoidance of double taxation and the prevention of fiscal evasion with respect to taxes on income, with protocol.
Signed at Washington March 28, 1996.
Entered into force December 19, 1997.
TIAS

TELECOMMUNICATION

Arrangement relating to radio communications between amateur stations on behalf of third parties.
Exchange of notes at Ankara November 27, 1996.
Entered into force November 27, 1996.
TIAS 12818

Agreement relating to the reciprocal granting of authorizations to permit licensed amateur radio operators of either country to operate their stations in the other country.
Exchange of notes at Ankara November 27, 1996.
Entered into force November 27, 1996.
TIAS 12819

TRADE & INVESTMENT

Treaty of commerce and navigation.
Signed at Ankara October 1, 1929.
Entered into force April 22, 1930.
46 Stat. 2743; TS 813; 11 Bevans 1122; 114 LNTS 499

Treaty of establishment and sojourn.
Signed at Ankara October 28, 1931.
Entered into force February 15, 1933.
47 Stat. 2432; TS 859; 11 Bevans 1127; 138 LNTS 345

Treaty concerning the reciprocal encouragement and protection of investments, with protocol.
Signed at Washington December 3, 1985.
Entered into force May 18, 1990.
TIAS

TRANSPORTATION

Air transport agreement, with annexes.
Signed at New York May 2, 2000.
Entered into force August 13, 2001.
TIAS 13100

WEAPONS

Agreement regarding cooperation to facilitate the provision of assistance for preventing the proliferation of weapons of mass destruction, with exchange of notes.
Signed at Ankara June 14, 2005.
Entered into force June 9, 2008.
TIAS 08-609

TURKMENISTAN

For agreements prior to December 31, 1991, see UNION OF SOVIET SOCIALIST REPUBLICS.

CULTURAL EXCHANGES, PROPERTY & COOPERATION

Agreement concerning the program of the Peace Corps of the United States in Turkmenistan.
Signed at Ashgabat February 26, 1993.
Entered into force February 26, 1993.
TIAS 11467

DEFENSE

Agreement concerning the provision of training related to defense articles under the United States International Military Education and Training (IMET) Program.
Exchange of notes at Ashgabat November 29, 1993, and January 3, 1994.
Entered into force January 3, 1994.
NP

Agreement regarding grants under the Foreign Assistance Act of 1961, as amended, and the furnishing of defense articles, related training, and other defense services from the United States of America to the Government of Turkmenistan.
Exchange of notes April 5 and 24, 1999.
Entered into force April 24, 1999.
NP

EMPLOYMENT

Agreement relating to the employment of dependents of official government employees.
Exchange of notes at Ashgabat July 15 and 20, 1999.
Entered into force July 20, 1999.
TIAS 13053

FINANCE

Investment incentive agreement.
Signed at Ashgabat June 26, 1992.
Entered into force June 26, 1992.
TIAS 12462

FOREIGN ASSISTANCE

Agreement regarding cooperation to facilitate the provision of assistance.
Signed at Ashgabat November 30, 1993.
Entered into force November 30, 1993.
TIAS 12518

INTERNATIONAL CRIMINAL COURT

Agreement regarding the surrender of persons to the International Criminal Court.
Signed at Ashgabat December 25, 2003.
Entered into force January 30, 2004.
TIAS 04-130

TRADE & INVESTMENT

Agreement on trade relations, with exchanges of letters.
Signed at Washington March 23, 1993.
Entered into force October 25, 1993.
TIAS 12491

TUVALU

On October 1, 1978, Tuvalu became an independent state. In a note dated December 19, 1978, to the Secretary-General of the United Nations, the Prime Minister of Tuvalu made a statement reading in part as follows:

2 The Government of Tuvalu, conscious of the desirability of maintaining existing international legal relationships, and conscious of its obligations under international law to honour its treaty commitments, acknowledges that many treaty rights and obligations of the Government of the United Kingdom in respect of the Gilbert and Ellice Islands Protectorate, the Gilbert and Ellice Islands Colony and Tuvalu were succeeded to by Tuvalu upon Independence by virtue of customary international law. Since, however, it is likely that by virtue of that law certain of such treaties may be said to have lapsed at the date of Tuvalu's Independence, it seems essential that each treaty purporting or deemed to bind Tuvalu before that date should be subjected to legal examination. The Government of Tuvalu proposes after such examination has been completed to indicate which, if any, of the treaties which may be said to have lapsed by virtue of customary international law it proposes to treat as having lapsed.

3 The Government of Tuvalu desires that it should be presumed that each treaty purporting or deemed to bind Tuvalu before Independence has been legally succeeded to by Tuvalu and that action should be based on such presumption unless and until the Government of Tuvalu decides that any particular treaty should be treated as having lapsed. Should the Government of Tuvalu be of opinion that it has legally succeeded to any treaty, and wish to terminate the operation of such treaty, it will in due course give notice of termination in the terms thereof.

4 For the avoidance of doubt, the Government of Tuvalu further declares that it does not regard itself as bound by the terms of any convention creating an international organisation to the extent that such convention requires the payment of any sum by any State, by virtue only of the accession of the Government of the United Kingdom to such convention."

CULTURAL EXCHANGES, PROPERTY & COOPERATION

Agreement relating to the establishment of a Peace Corps program in Tuvalu.
Exchange of notes at Suva August 25, 1977.
Entered into force August 25, 1977.
29 UST 5428; TIAS 9119

DIPLOMATIC & CONSULAR RELATIONS

Consular convention between the United States and the United Kingdom.
Signed at Washington June 6, 1951.
Entered into force September 7, 1952.
3 UST 3426; TIAS 2494; 165 UNTS 121

Treaty of friendship.
Signed at Funafuti February 7, 1979.
Entered into force September 23, 1983.
35 UST 2087; TIAS 10776; 2011 UNTS 79

INTELLECTUAL PROPERTY

Declaration by the United States and the United Kingdom affording reciprocal protection to trade-marks.
Signed at London October 24, 1877.
Entered into force October 24, 1877.
20 Stat. 703; TS 138; 12 Bevans 198

INTERNATIONAL CRIMINAL COURT

Agreement on the surrender of persons to the International Criminal Court.
Exchange of notes at Suva and Funafuti September 19, 2002, and January 9, 2003.
Entered into force February 3, 2003.
TIAS 03-203

LAW ENFORCEMENT

Extradition treaty between the United States and the United Kingdom, with protocol of signature and exchange of notes.
Signed at London June 8, 1972.
Entered into force January 21, 1977.
28 UST 227; TIAS 8468

MARITIME MATTERS

Agreement concerning operational cooperation to suppress illicit transnational maritime activity.
Signed at Auckland September 9, 2011.
Entered into force September 9, 2011.
TIAS 11-909

SCIENTIFIC & TECHNICAL COOPERATION

Memorandum of understanding concerning scientific and technical cooperation in the earth sciences, with annexes.
Signed at Reston and Funafuti August 3 and October 26, 2001.
Entered into force October 26, 2001.
TIAS 13167

TELECOMMUNICATION

Agreement between the United States and the United Kingdom relating to the reciprocal granting of authorizations to permit licensed amateur radio operators of either country to operate their stations in the other country.
Exchange of notes at London November 26, 1965.
Applicable to Tuvalu December 11, 1969.
16 UST 2047; TIAS 5941; 561 UNTS 193

Agreement between the United States and the United Kingdom extending to certain territories the application of the agreement of November 26, 1965, relating to the reciprocal granting of authorizations to permit licensed amateur radio operators of either country to operate their stations in the other country.
Exchange of notes at London December 11, 1969.
Entered into force December 11, 1969.
20 UST 4089; TIAS 6800; 732 UNTS 334

TRANSPORTATION

Agreement between the United States and the United Kingdom concerning air services with annexes and exchange of letters.
Signed at Bermuda July 23, 1977.
Entered into force July 23, 1977.
28 UST 5367; TIAS 8641
Amendment:
April 25, 1978 (29 UST 2680; TIAS 8965)

TREATY LAW

Agreement relating to treaty obligations assumed by Tuvalu upon its independence.
Exchange of notes at Suva and Funafuti January 29 and April 25, 1980.
Entered into force April 25, 1980.
32 UST 1310; TIAS 9770; 1222 UNTS 293

U

UGANDA

CULTURAL EXCHANGES, PROPERTY & COOPERATION

Agreement concerning the program of the Peace Corps in the Republic of Uganda.
Signed at Kampala December 10, 2007.
Entered into force December 10, 2007.
TIAS 07-1210

DEFENSE

Agreement concerning the provision of training related to defense articles under the United States International Military Education and Training (IMET) Program.
Exchange of notes at Kampala April 6, 1981, and June 15, 1984.
Entered into force June 15, 1984.
TIAS 10984; 2022 UNTS 121

Agreement regarding grants under the Foreign Assistance Act of 1961, as amended, and the furnishing of defense articles, related training and other defense services from the United States to Uganda.
Exchange of notes at Kampala January 31 and March 25, 1994.
Entered into force March 25, 1994.
TIAS 11476

Agreement regarding the status of U.S. personnel and civilian employees of the Department of Defense who may be temporarily present in Uganda in connection with the African Crisis Response Initiative mobile training team visit and other activities as may be agreed upon by the two governments.
Exchange of notes at Kampala July 15 and September 1, 1997.
Entered into force September 1, 1997.
TIAS 97-901.1

Acquisition and cross-servicing agreement.
Signed at Stuttgart and Kampala December 18 and 22, 2014.
Entered into force December 22, 2014.
NP

EMPLOYMENT

Agreement relating to the employment of dependents of official government employees.
Exchange of notes at Kampala October 8, 1998, and June 18, 1999.
Entered into force June 18, 1999.
TIAS

Agreement concerning the employment on a reciprocal basis of dependents of official government employees.
Effected by Exchange of Notes at Kampala August 20 and 21, 2013.
Entered into force October 17, 2013.
TIAS 13-1017

ENVIRONMENT & CONSERVATION

Agreement for cooperation on the Global Learning and Observations to Benefit the Environment (GLOBE) Program, with appendices.
Signed at Kampala November 26, 1998.
Entered into force November 26, 1998.
TIAS 13001

FINANCE

Agreement relating to investment guaranties.
Exchange of notes at Kampala May 29, 1965.
Entered into force May 29, 1965.
16 UST 827; TIAS 5818; 546 UNTS 209

Agreement regarding the consolidation and rescheduling of certain debts owed to, guaranteed or insured by the United States Government and its agencies, with annexes.
Signed at Kampala May 10, 1982.
Entered into force June 21, 1982.
NP

Agreements regarding the consolidation and rescheduling of certain debts owed to, or guaranteed by the United States Government and its agencies, with annexes, and implementing agreements regarding AID loans and agricultural commodity agreements.
Signed at Kampala March 31, 1983.
Entered into force May 23, 1983.
NP

Agreement regarding the consolidation and rescheduling of certain debts owed to, guaranteed by, or insured by the United States Government and its agencies, with annexes.
Signed at Kampala January 13, 1988.
Entered into force February 22, 1988.
NP

Agreement regarding the consolidation and rescheduling of certain debts owed to, guaranteed by, or insured by the United States Government and its agencies, with annexes.
Signed at Kampala December 19, 1989.
Entered into force January 26, 1990.
NP

Agreement regarding the reduction and reorganization of certain debts owed to, guaranteed by, or insured by the United States Government and its Agency, with annexes.
Signed at Kampala June 22, 1999.
Entered into force August 19, 1999.
NP

Agreement regarding the reduction of certain debts owed to, guaranteed by, or insured by the United States Government and its Agency, with annexes.
Signed at Kampala May 28, 2002.
Entered into force August 19, 2002.
NP

FOREIGN ASSISTANCE

Agreement relating to economic, technical and related assistance.
Exchange of notes at Kampala December 3 and 11, 1971.
Entered into force December 11, 1971.
22 UST 1848; TIAS 7229

INTERNATIONAL CRIMINAL COURT

Agreement regarding the surrender of persons to the International Criminal Court.
Signed at Washington June 12, 2003.
Entered into force October 23, 2003.
TIAS 03-1023

POSTAL MATTERS

International express mail agreement, with detailed regulations.
Signed at Kampala and Washington October 4 and November 3, 1988.
Entered into force December 15, 1988.
TIAS 11628

TRANSPORTATION

Memorandum of agreement for the provision of assistance in developing and modernizing the civil aviation infrastructure of Uganda.
Signed at Washington and Kampala November 10 and 11, 2003.
Entered into force November 11, 2003.
NP
Amendment:
August 16 and September 5, 2005

Air transport agreement, with annexes.
Signed at Atlanta October 27, 2009.
Entered into force October 27, 2009.
TIAS 09-1027

UKRAINE

The following agreements include those between the United States and Ukraine, as well as those between the United States and the former Union of Soviet Socialist Republics that the United States and Ukraine have agreed remain in force between them. Bilateral arms limitation and related agreements between the United States and the former Union of Soviet Socialist Republics remain under review. No conclusion can be drawn from their absence from the following list.

ATOMIC ENERGY

Agreement concerning operational safety enhancements, risk reduction measures and nuclear safety regulation for civilian nuclear facilities in Ukraine, with exchange of notes.
Signed at Kiev October 25, 1993.
Entered into force October 25, 1993.
TIAS 12513
Amendment and Extensions:
July 22, 1998 (TIAS 98-722)
April 5 and 23, 2004 (TIAS 98-722)
February 6, May 6 and May 8, 2009 (TIAS 98-722)
September 24 and October 24, 2013 (TIAS 13-1024)

Agreement for cooperation concerning peaceful uses of nuclear energy, with annex and agreed minute.
Signed at Kiev May 6, 1998.
Entered into force May 28, 1999.
TIAS 12950

Implementing agreement concerning the Ukraine Nuclear Fuel Qualification Project, with annex.
Signed at Kiev June 5, 2000.
Entered into force June 5, 2000.
TIAS 00-605
Extensions:
April 14 and June 4, 2005 (TIAS 00-605)
August 25, 2010 and February 4, 2011 (TIAS 00-605)

Arrangement for the exchange of technical information and cooperation in nuclear safety matters, with addenda.
Signed at Rockville April 10, 2006.
Entered into force February 10, 2012.
TIAS 12-210
Amendment:
September 21, 2011 (TIAS 12-210)

CLAIMS & DISPUTE RESOLUTION

Declaration between the United States and the Union of Soviet Socialist Republics on international guarantees (Afghanistan Settlement Agreement).
Signed at Geneva April 14, 1988.
Entered into force May 15, 1988.
TIAS

CONSULAR AFFAIRS

Agreement between the United States and the Union of Soviet Socialist Republics relating to the reciprocal issuance of multiple entry and exit visas to American and Soviet correspondents.
Exchange of notes at Moscow September 29, 1975.
Entered into force September 29, 1975.
27 UST 4258; TIAS 8448

CULTURAL EXCHANGES, PROPERTY & COOPERATION

Agreement concerning the program of the Peace Corps of the United States in Ukraine.
Signed at Washington May 6, 1992.
Entered into force May 6, 1992.
TIAS 11510

Agreement on the protection and preservation of cultural heritage.
Signed at Washington March 4, 1994.
Entered into force March 4, 1994.
TIAS 11480

DEFENSE

Agreement between the United States and the Union of Soviet Socialist Republics on the prevention of dangerous military activities, with annexes and agreed statements.
Signed at Moscow June 12, 1989.
Entered into force January 1, 1990.
TIAS

Memorandum of understanding between the United States and the Union of Soviet Socialist Republics on cooperation in the mapping sciences, with annexes.
Signed at Moscow May 14, 1991.
Entered into force May 14, 1991.
NP

Acquisition and cross-servicing agreement, with annexes.
Signed at Stuttgart and Kiev November 17 and 19, 1999.
Entered into force November 19, 1999.
NP

Implementing arrangement concerning mutual logistic support, with annexes.
Signed at Kiev and Stuttgart November 19 and December 7, 1999.
Entered into force December 7, 1999.
NP

Agreement concerning exchange of research and development information in the sphere of military technical cooperation, with appendix.
Signed at Washington March 31, 2000.
Entered into force July 27, 2001.
TIAS

Agreement on protection of classified defense information.
Signed at Kiev August 4, 2003.
Entered into force July 14, 2004.
TIAS 04-714

Agreement concerning the provision of equipment, training and related services under the United States International Military Education and Training (IMET) Program.
Exchange of notes at Kiev August 18, 2003, and May 5, 2004.
Entered into force May 5, 2004.
NP

Agreement concerning health care for military members and their dependents.
Signed December 23 and 30, 2009.
Entered into force December 30, 2009.
NP

Extensions:
January 21 and February 25, 2013
December 23, 2015 and January 21, 2016

DIPLOMATIC & CONSULAR RELATIONS

Arrangements between the United States and the Union of Soviet Socialist Republics relating to the establishment of diplomatic relations, nonintervention, freedom of conscience and religious liberty, legal protection, and claims.
Exchanges of notes at Washington November 16, 1933.
Entered into force November 16, 1933.
Department of State Publication 528; European and British Commonwealth Series 2 [new series]; Eastern European Series No. 1 [old series]; 11 Bevans 1248

Consular convention between the United States and the Union of Soviet Socialist Republics.
Signed at Moscow June 1, 1964.
Entered into force July 13, 1968.
19 UST 5018; TIAS 6503; 655 UNTS 213

Agreement between the United States and the Union of Soviet Socialist Republics relating to privileges and immunities of all members of the Soviet and American embassies and their families, with agreed minute.
Exchange of notes at Washington December 14, 1978.
Entered into force December 14, 1978; effective December 29, 1978.
30 UST 2341; TIAS 9340; 1171 UNTS 73

Agreement between the United States and the Union of Soviet Socialist Republics relating to immunity of family members of consular officers and employees from criminal jurisdiction.
Exchange of notes at Washington October 31, 1986.
Entered into force October 31, 1986.
TIAS 11432

EDUCATION

Agreement between the United States and the Union of Soviet Socialist Republics on expansion of undergraduate exchanges.
Signed at Washington June 1, 1990.
Entered into force June 1, 1990.
TIAS

EMPLOYMENT

Agreement relating to the employment of dependents of official government employees.
Exchange of notes at Washington November 21, 1994.
Entered into force November 21, 1994.
TIAS 12196

ENVIRONMENT & CONSERVATION

Agreement on cooperation in the field of environmental protection.
Signed at Washington May 7, 1992.
Entered into force May 7, 1992.
TIAS 11466

Agreement concerning a regional environmental center in Ukraine.
Signed at Washington December 8, 1999.
Entered into force December 8, 1999.
TIAS 13074

FINANCE

Investment incentive agreement.
Signed at Washington May 6, 1992.
Entered into force May 6, 1992.
TIAS 11475

Agreement regarding the consolidation and rescheduling of certain debts owed to, guaranteed by, or insured by the United States Government and its agency, with annexes.
Signed at Kiev June 10, 2002.
Entered into force July 19, 2002.
NP

FOREIGN ASSISTANCE

Agreement regarding humanitarian and technical economic cooperation.
Signed at Washington May 7, 1992.
Entered into force May 7, 1992.
TIAS 11472

Loan guarantee agreement.
Signed at Washington April 14, 2014.
Entered into force May 13, 2014.
TIAS 14-513

Loan guarantee agreement.
Signed at Kyiv May 18, 2015.
Entered into force May 26, 2015.
TIAS 15-526

Loan guarantee agreement, with annexes.
Signed at Kyiv June 3, 2016.
Entered into force September 27, 2016.
TIAS 16-927.2

HEALTH AND MEDICAL COOPERATION

Agreement between the United States and the Union of Soviet Socialist Republics on cooperation in artificial heart research and development.
Signed at Moscow June 28, 1974.
Entered into force June 28, 1974.
25 UST 1331; TIAS 7867

Agreement between the United States and the Union of Soviet Socialist Republics on emergency medical supplies and related assistance.
Signed at Moscow July 30, 1991.
Entered into force July 30, 1991.
TIAS

LAW ENFORCEMENT

Agreement between the United States and the Union of Soviet Socialist Republics relating to the procedure to be followed in the execution of letters rogatory.
Exchange of notes at Moscow November 22, 1935.
Entered into force November 22, 1935.
49 Stat. 3840; EAS 83; 11 Bevans 1262; 167 LNTS 303

Memorandum of understanding between the United States and the Union of Soviet Socialist Republics on cooperation to combat illegal narcotics trafficking.
Signed at Paris January 8, 1989.
Entered into force January 8, 1989.
TIAS 11436

Agreement between the United States and the Union of Soviet Socialist Republics on a mutual understanding on cooperation in the struggle against the illicit traffic in narcotics.
Signed at Washington January 31, 1990.
Entered into force January 31, 1990.
TIAS

Memorandum of understanding concerning cooperation in the pursuit of Nazi war criminals.
Signed at Washington August 26, 1993.
Entered into force August 26, 1993.
TIAS

Treaty on mutual legal assistance in criminal matters, with annex.
Signed at Kiev July 22, 1998.
Entered into force February 27, 2001.
TIAS 12978

Agreement regarding mutual assistance between their customs administrations.
Signed at Kyiv May 23, 2016.
Entered into force December 13, 2016.
TIAS 16-1213

MARITIME MATTERS

Agreement between the United States and the Union of Soviet Socialist Republics on the prevention of incidents on and over the high seas.
Signed at Moscow May 25, 1972.
Entered into force May 25, 1972.
23 UST 1168; TIAS 7379; 852 UNTS 151

Protocol between the United States and the Union of Soviet Socialist Republics to the agreement of May 25, 1972 (TIAS 7379) on the prevention of incidents on and over the high seas.
Signed at Washington May 22, 1973.
Entered into force May 22, 1973.
24 UST 1063; TIAS 7624

Memorandum of understanding between the United States and the Union of Soviet Socialist Republics regarding marine cargo insurance.
Signed at London April 5, 1979.
Entered into force April 5, 1979.
30 UST 2194; TIAS 9326; 1171 UNTS 93

Agreement between the United States and the Union of Soviet Socialist Republics concerning the confidentiality of data on deep seabed areas, with related exchange of letters.
Exchange of notes at Moscow December 5, 1986.
Entered into force December 5, 1986.
TIAS

Agreement between the United States and the Union of Soviet Socialist Republics relating to the agreement of August 14, 1987, on the resolution of practical problems with respect to deep seabed mining areas.*
Exchange of notes at Moscow August 14, 1987.
Entered into force August 14, 1987.
TIAS 11438

Note

* Parties to the multilateral agreement of August 14, 1987, are Belgium, Canada, Italy, Netherlands and Union of Soviet Socialist Republics.

NONPROLIFERATION

Agreement concerning development of state systems of control, accounting and physical protection of nuclear materials to promote the prevention of nuclear weapons proliferation from Ukraine.
Signed at Washington December 18, 1993.
Entered into force December 31, 1993.
TIAS

Amendments and Extensions:
March 21, 1994
June 27, 1995
July 7, 1999
February 18 and March 23, 2004

Agreement concerning development of state systems of control, accounting and physical protection of nuclear materials to promote the prevention of nuclear weapons proliferation from Ukraine.
Signed at Kiev June 27, 1995.
Entered into force June 27, 1995.
TIAS

Agreement on the establishment of a secure communications link between the Nuclear Risk Reduction Center of the United States of America and the Military Cooperation and Verification Center of the General Staff of the Armed Forces of Ukraine, with annexes.
Signed at Kiev September 20, 2001.
Entered into force September 20, 2001.
TIAS

Implementing arrangement for cooperation in the area of prevention of illicit trafficking in nuclear and other radioactive material.
Signed at Washington and Kiev April 8 and 20, 2005.
Entered into force April 20, 2005.
TIAS 05-420.3

Implementing arrangement concerning cooperation to enhance the security of Ukraine's usable sources of ionizing radiation, with appendix.
Signed at Washington and Kiev June 16 and 23, 2006.
Entered into force June 23, 2006.
TIAS 06-623

POSTAL MATTERS

International express mail agreement, with detailed regulations.
Signed at Kiev and Washington June 1 and November 8, 1993.
Entered into force January 1, 1994.
NP

PROPERTY

Preliminary agreement between the United States and the Union of Soviet Socialist Republics relating to principles applying to mutual aid in the prosecution of the war against aggression, and exchange of notes.
Signed at Washington June 11, 1942.
Entered into force June 11, 1942.
56 Stat. 1500; EAS 253; 11 Bevans 1281; 105 UNTS 285

Agreement between the United States and the Union of Soviet Socialist Republics regarding settlement of lend-lease, reciprocal aid and claims.
Signed at Washington October 18, 1972.
Entered into force October 18, 1972.
23 UST 2910; TIAS 7478; 898 UNTS 297

Agreement between the United States and the Union of Soviet Socialist Republics regarding settlement of lend-lease accounts.
Exchange of letters at Washington June 1, 1990.
Entered into force June 1, 1990.
TIAS

RULES OF WAR

Convention relating to the rights of neutrals at sea.*
Signed at Washington July 22, 1854.
Entered into force October 31, 1854.
10 Stat. 1105; TS 300; 11 Bevans 1214

Note:
* Declaration of accession by Nicaragua signed at Granada June 9, 1855 (7 Miller 139).

Agreement between the United States and the Union of Soviet Socialist Republics relating to prisoners of war and civilians liberated by forces operating under Soviet command and forces operating under United States of America command.
Signed at Yalta February 11, 1945.
Entered into force February 11, 1945;
59 Stat. 1874; EAS 505; 11 Bevans 1286; 68 UNTS 175

SCIENTIFIC & TECHNICAL COOPERATION

Agreement on scientific and technological cooperation, with annexes.
Signed at Washington December 4, 2006.
Entered into force May 26, 2009.
TIAS 09-526

SPACE

Framework agreement for cooperation in the exploration and use of outer space for peaceful purposes.
Signed at Kiev March 31, 2008.
Entered into force January 22, 2009.
TIAS 09-122

TAXATION

Convention for the avoidance of double taxation and the prevention of fiscal evasion with respect to taxes on income and capital, with protocol.
Signed at Washington March 4, 1994.
Entered into force June 5, 2000.
TIAS

Agreement concerning the relationship between the taxation convention of March 4, 1994, and the General Agreement on Trade in Services with regard to the consultation, most-favored-nation and national treatment provisions.
Exchange of notes at Washington May 26 and June 6, 1995.
Entered into force June 5, 2000.
TIAS

TRADE & INVESTMENT

Agreement regulating the position of corporations and other commercial associations.
Signed at St. Petersburg June 25, 1904.
Entered into force June 25, 1904.
36 Stat. 2163; TS 526; 11 Bevans 1235

Agreement on trade relations, with related exchanges of letters.
Signed at Washington May 6, 1992.
Entered into force June 23, 1992.
TIAS

Treaty concerning the encouragement and reciprocal protection of investment, with annex and exchange of letters.
Signed at Washington March 4, 1994.
Entered into force November 16, 1996.
TIAS

Agreement on export duties on ferrous and nonferrous scrap metal.
Exchange of letters at Kiev and Washington February 22, 2006.
Entered into force February 22, 2006.
TIAS 06-222

Agreement on sanitary and phyto-sanitary measures.
Exchange of letters at Kiev and Washington February 21 and 22, 2006.
Entered into force February 22, 2006.
TIAS 06-222.1

TRANSPORTATION

Air transport agreement, with annexes.
Signed at Washington July 14, 2015.
Entered into force January 14, 2016.
TIAS 16-114

TREATY LAW

Agreement concerning the succession of Ukraine to bilateral treaties between the United States and the former Union of Soviet Socialist Republics, with annex.
Exchange of notes at Kiev May 10, 1995.
Entered into force May 15, 1995.
TIAS

WEAPONS

Agreement concerning assistance to Ukraine in the elimination of strategic nuclear arms and the prevention of proliferation of weapons of mass destruction.
Signed at Kiev October 25, 1993.
Entered into force December 31, 1993.
TIAS

Amendment and Extensions:
June 30 and July 29, 1999
July 24 and September 18, 2003
July 19, December 8 and 15, 2006
December 24 and 27, 2013

Agreement concerning the provision of material, services and related training to Ukraine in connection with the elimination of strategic nuclear arms, with annexes.
Signed at Kiev December 5, 1993.
Entered into force December 31, 1993.
TIAS

Amendments and Extensions:
December 18, 1993
December 18, 1993
March 21, 1994
April 1, 1995
June 27, 1995
June 4, 1996
May 1, 1997
June 12, 1998
July 10, 1999
July 24 and 28, 2000
December 1 and 4, 2000
January 24 and 31, 2001
August 30 and September 9, 2002
July 24 and September 18, 2003
December 26, 2006, and January 5, 2007
September 19 and October 27, 2008
June 11 and July 9, 2009

Agreement on the provision of assistance to Ukraine in establishing an export control system in order to prevent the proliferation from Ukraine of weapons of mass destruction.
Signed at Kiev October 22, 2001.
Entered into force October 22, 2001; effective December 31, 1999.
TIAS 01-1022

Amendments:
March 15 and 26, 2004 (TIAS 01-1022)
June 27, 2005 (TIAS 01-1022)
August 31 and September 12, 2006 (TIAS 01-1022)
July 30 and August 17, 2007 (TIAS 01-1022)
April 4 and 16, 2008 (TIAS 01-1022)
April 9 and 29, 2009 (TIAS 01-1022)

Agreement concerning cooperation in the area of prevention of proliferation of technology, pathogens and expertise that could be used in the development of biological weapons.
Signed at Kiev August 29, 2005.
Entered into force August 29, 2005.
TIAS 05-829

UNION OF SOVIET SOCIALIST REPUBLICS

The Union of Soviet Socialist Republics dissolved December 25, 1991. As stated in the Alma-Ata Declaration of December 21, 1991, "… The States participating in the Commonwealth guarantee in accordance with their constitutional procedures the discharge of the international obligations deriving from treaties and agreements concluded by the former Union of Soviet Socialist Republics…."

In addition, the Russian Federation has informed the United States Government by a note dated January 13, 1992, that it "… continues to perform the rights and fulfil the obligations following from the international agreements signed by the Union of the Soviet Socialist Republics…."

Section 2 of Treaties in Force covers multilateral treaties and agreements. Where a multilateral treaty action was taken prior to dissolution, "Union of Soviet Socialist Republics" is retained; where a successor state has taken action it is listed separately.

The United States is reviewing the continued applicability of the agreements listed below. Bilateral agreements subsequent to December 31, 1991, are listed under individual country headings.

ARMS CONTROL

Basic principles of negotiation on the further limitation of strategic offensive arms.
Signed at Washington June 21, 1973.
Entered into force June 21, 1973.
24 UST 1472; TIAS 7653; 944 UNTS 41

Treaty on the limitation of underground nuclear weapon tests.
Signed at Moscow July 3, 1974.
Entered into force December 11, 1990.
TIAS

Treaty on underground nuclear explosions for peaceful purposes, with agreed minute.
Signed at Washington and Moscow May 28, 1976.
Entered into force December 11, 1990.
TIAS; 1714 UNTS 387

Treaty on the elimination of their intermediate-range and shorter-range missiles, with memorandum of understanding and protocols.
Signed at Washington December 8, 1987.
Entered into force June 1, 1988.
TIAS; 1657 UNTS 2

Protocol to the treaty of May 28, 1976, on underground nuclear explosions for peaceful purposes.
Signed at Washington June 1, 1990.
Entered into force December 11, 1990.
TIAS; 1714 UNTS 440

Protocol to the treaty of July 3, 1974, on the limitation of underground nuclear weapon tests.
Signed at Washington June 1, 1990.
Entered into force December 11, 1990.
TIAS

BOUNDARIES & BOUNDARY WATERS

Agreement to abide by terms of maritime boundary agreement of June 1, 1990, pending entry into force.
Exchange of notes at Washington June 1, 1990.
Entered into force June 1, 1990; effective June 15, 1990.
TIAS 11451

CLAIMS & DISPUTE RESOLUTION

Treaty for the settlement of disputes.
Signed at Washington October 1, 1914.
Entered into force March 22, 1915.
39 Stat. 1622; TS 616; 11 Bevans 1239

Declaration on international guarantees (Afghanistan Settlement Agreement).
Signed at Geneva April 14, 1988.
Entered into force May 15, 1988.
TIAS

CONSULAR AFFAIRS

Agreement relating to the reciprocal waiver of visa fees to nonimmigrants.*
Exchange of notes at Moscow March 26, August 11, and August 20, 1958.
Entered into force August 20, 1958.
9 UST 1413; TIAS 4134; 336 UNTS 269

Agreement relating to the reciprocal issuance of multiple entry and exit visas to American and Soviet correspondents.
Exchange of notes at Moscow September 29, 1975.
Entered into force September 29, 1975.
27 UST 4258; TIAS 8448

Agreement concerning diplomatic and other visas, with agreed minute and oral understanding.
Exchange of notes at Moscow July 30, 1984.
Entered into force July 30, 1984.
TIAS

Agreement modifying the agreement of July 30, 1984, concerning diplomatic and other visas.
Exchange of notes at Washington October 31, 1986.
Entered into force October 31, 1986.
TIAS

Note:
* The status of this agreement is under review.

Agreement concerning mutual visits by inhabitants of the Bering Straits Region.
Signed at Jackson Hole, Wyoming September 23, 1989.
Entered into force July 10, 1991.
TIAS 11455

CULTURAL EXCHANGES, PROPERTY & COOPERATION

Agreement on cooperation in the exchange of archival records regarding the Nazi invasion of the occupied territory of the Soviet Union during World War II.
Signed at Moscow July 29, 1988.
Entered into force July 29, 1988.
TIAS

DEFENSE

Agreement on the prevention of dangerous military activities, with annexes and agreed statements.
Signed at Moscow June 12, 1989.
Entered into force January 1, 1990.
TIAS 11485; 1566 UNTS 309

Memorandum of understanding on cooperation in the mapping sciences, with annexes.
Signed at Moscow May 14, 1991.
Entered into force May 14, 1991.
NP

DIPLOMATIC & CONSULAR RELATIONS

Arrangements relating to the establishment of diplomatic relations, nonintervention, freedom of conscience and religious liberty, legal protection, and claims.
Exchanges of notes at Washington November 16, 1933.
Entered into force November 16, 1933.
Department of State Publication 528; European and British Commonwealth Series 2 [new series]; Eastern European Series No. 1 [old series]; 11 Bevans 1248

Consular convention.
Signed at Moscow June 1, 1964.
Entered into force July 13, 1968.
19 UST 5018; TIAS 6503; 655 UNTS 213

Agreement relating to privileges and immunities of all members of the Soviet and American embassies and their families, with agreed minute.
Exchange of notes at Washington December 14, 1978.
Entered into force December 14, 1978; effective December 29, 1978.
30 UST 2341; TIAS 9340; 1171 UNTS 73

Agreement relating to immunity of family members of consular officers and employees from criminal jurisdiction.
Exchange of notes at Washington October 31, 1986.
Entered into force October 31, 1986.
TIAS 11432

ENVIRONMENT & CONSERVATION

Convention concerning the conservation of migratory birds and their environment.
Signed at Moscow November 19, 1976.
Entered into force October 13, 1978.
29 UST 4647; TIAS 9073; 1134 UNTS 97

FISHERIES

Agreement relating to the consideration of claims resulting from damage to fishing vessels or gear and measures to prevent fishing conflicts, with annex and protocol.
Signed at Moscow February 21, 1973.
Entered into force February 21, 1973.
24 UST 669; TIAS 7575; 938 UNTS 38
Amendment:
February 26, 1975 (26 UST 167; TIAS 8022)

Protocol to the agreement of February 21, 1973 (TIAS 7575), relating to the consideration of claims resulting from damage to fishing vessels or gear and measures to prevent fishing conflicts, with annex.
Signed at Copenhagen June 21, 1973.
Entered into force June 21, 1973.
24 UST 1588; TIAS 7663; 938 UNTS 49

Agreement on mutual fisheries relations, with annexes.
Signed at Moscow May 31, 1988.
Entered into force October 28, 1988.
TIAS 11442; 2191 UNTS 3
Amendments and Extensions:
March 11 and September 15, 1993
December 22, 1993 and January 5, 1994
July 28 and November 23, 1998
March 3, 2003, and January 30, 2004
June 15, 2005
April 1 and September 19, 2008

HEALTH AND MEDICAL COOPERATION

Agreement relating to the exchange of medical films.
Exchange of notes at Washington March 17 and September 5, 1955.
Entered into force September 5, 1955.
6 UST 3969; TIAS 3409; 256 UNTS 307

Agreement on cooperation in the field of medical science and public health.
Signed at Moscow May 23, 1972.
Entered into force May 23, 1972.
23 UST 836; TIAS 7344

Agreement on cooperation in artificial heart research and development.
Signed at Moscow June 28, 1974.
Entered into force June 28, 1974.
25 UST 1331; TIAS 7867

Agreement on emergency medical supplies and related assistance.
Signed at Moscow July 30, 1991.
Entered into force July 30, 1991.
TIAS 11468

LAW ENFORCEMENT

Agreement relating to the procedure to be followed in the execution of letters rogatory.
Exchange of notes at Moscow November 22, 1935.
Entered into force November 22, 1935.
49 Stat. 3840; EAS 83; 11 Bevans 1262; 167 LNTS 303

Memorandum of understanding on cooperation to combat illegal narcotics trafficking.
Signed at Paris January 8, 1989.
Entered into force January 8, 1989.
TIAS 11436; 2191 UNTS 35

Memorandum of understanding concerning cooperation in the pursuit of Nazi war criminals.
Signed at Moscow October 19, 1989.
Entered into force October 19, 1989.
TIAS 11462

Agreement on a mutual understanding on cooperation in the struggle against the illicit traffic in narcotics.
Signed at Washington January 31, 1990.
Entered into force January 31, 1990.
TIAS

MARITIME MATTERS

Agreement on the prevention of incidents on and over the high seas.
Signed at Moscow May 25, 1972.
Entered into force May 25, 1972.
23 UST 1168; TIAS 7379; 852 UNTS 151

Protocol to the agreement of May 25, 1972 (TIAS 7379) on the prevention of incidents on and over the high seas.
Signed at Washington May 22, 1973.
Entered into force May 22, 1973.
24 UST 1063; TIAS 7624

Memorandum of understanding regarding marine cargo insurance.
Signed at London April 5, 1979.
Entered into force April 5, 1979.
30 UST 2194; TIAS 9326; 1171 UNTS 93

Agreement concerning the confidentiality of data on deep seabed areas, with related exchange of letters.
Exchange of notes at Moscow December 5, 1986.
Entered into force December 5, 1986.
TIAS

Agreement relating to the agreement of August 14, 1987, on the resolution of practical problems with respect to deep seabed mining areas.*
Exchange of notes at Moscow August 14, 1987.
Entered into force August 14, 1987.
TIAS 11438
Note:
* Parties to the multilateral agreement of August 14, 1987, are Belgium, Canada, Italy, Netherlands and Union of Soviet Socialist Republics.

Agreement on maritime search and rescue, with exchange of letters.
Signed at Moscow May 31, 1988.
Entered into force July 3, 1989.
TIAS 11440; 2191 UNTS 115

NONPROLIFERATION

Agreement on measures to reduce the risk of outbreak of nuclear war.
Signed at Washington September 30, 1971.
Entered into force September 30, 1971.
22 UST 1590; TIAS 7186; 807 UNTS 57

Agreement on the establishment of nuclear risk reduction centers, with protocols.
Signed at Washington September 15, 1987.
Entered into force September 15, 1987.
TIAS
Amendment:
October 7, 2013

Agreement on the conduct of a joint verification experiment, with annex.
Signed at Moscow May 31, 1988.
Entered into force May 31, 1988.
TIAS

Agreement on notifications of launches of intercontinental ballistic missiles and submarine-launched ballistic missiles.
Signed at Moscow May 31, 1988.
Entered into force May 31, 1988.
TIAS

Agreement on reciprocal advance notification of major strategic exercises.
Signed at Jackson Hole, Wyoming, September 23, 1989.
Entered into force January 1, 1990.
TIAS 11458; 2191 UNTS 283

POLLUTION

Agreement concerning cooperation in combatting pollution in the Bering and Chukchi Seas in emergency situations.
Signed at Moscow May 11, 1989.
Entered into force August 17, 1989.
TIAS 11446; 2190 UNTS 179

POSTAL MATTERS

International express mail agreement, with detailed regulations.
Signed at Moscow March 31, 1988.
Entered into force May 1, 1988.
TIAS 11439

Memorandum of understanding concerning the operation of the INTELPOST service, with details of implementation.
Signed at Moscow and Washington February 14 and March 9, 1989.
Entered into force April 3, 1989.
TIAS 11528

PROPERTY

Preliminary agreement relating to principles applying to mutual aid in the prosecution of the war against aggression, and exchange of notes.
Signed at Washington June 11, 1942.
Entered into force June 11, 1942.
56 Stat. 1500; EAS 253; 11 Bevans 1281; 105 UNTS 285

Agreement relating to the disposition of lend-lease supplies in inventory or procurement in the United States.
Signed at Washington October 15, 1945.
Entered into force October 15, 1945.
7 UST 2819; TIAS 3662; 278 UNTS 151 and 315 UNTS 249

Agreement on the reciprocal allocation for use free of charge of plots of land in Moscow and Washington with annexes and exchanges of notes.
Signed at Moscow May 16, 1969.
Entered into force May 16, 1969.
20 UST 789; TIAS 6693; 715 UNTS 33

Agreement regarding settlement of lend-lease, reciprocal aid and claims.
Signed at Washington October 18, 1972.
Entered into force October 18, 1972.
23 UST 2910; TIAS 7478; 898 UNTS 297

Agreement on the conditions of construction of complexes of buildings of the U.S. Embassy in Moscow and the Russian Embassy in Washington with attachment.
Signed at Washington December 4, 1972.
Entered into force December 4, 1972.
23 UST 3544; TIAS 7512

Agreement regarding settlement of lend-lease accounts.
Exchange of letters at Washington June 1, 1990.
Entered into force June 1, 1990.
TIAS

REGIONAL ISSUES

Agreement concerning the Bering Straits Regional Commission.
Signed at Jackson Hole, Wyoming September 23, 1989.
Entered into force July 10, 1991.
TIAS 11448

RULES OF WAR

Convention relating to the rights of neutrals at sea.*
Signed at Washington July 22, 1854.
Entered into force October 31, 1854.
10 Stat. 1105; TS 300; 11 Bevans 1214
Note:
* Declaration of accession by Nicaragua signed at Granada June 9, 1855 (7 Miller 139).

Agreement relating to prisoners of war and civilians liberated by forces operating under Soviet command and forces operating under United States of America command.
Signed at Yalta February 11, 1945.
Entered into force February 11, 1945.
59 Stat. 1874; EAS 505; 11 Bevans 1286; 68 UNTS 175

Agreement on the prevention of nuclear war.
Signed at Washington June 22, 1973.
Entered into force June 22, 1973.
24 UST 1478; TIAS 7654

SPACE

Implementing agreement concerning cooperation in the space flight of a Soviet Meteor 3 satellite employing a U.S. Total Ozone Mapping Spectrometer (TOMS).
Signed at Moscow July 25, 1990.
Entered into force August 24, 1990.
TIAS

TAXATION

Convention on matters of taxation, with related letters.
Signed at Washington June 20, 1973.
Entered into force January 29, 1976; effective January 1, 1976.
27 UST 1; TIAS 8225

TERRITORIAL ISSUES

Convention ceding Alaska.
Signed at Washington March 30, 1867.
Entered into force June 20, 1867.
15 Stat. 539; TS 301; 11 Bevans 1216

TRADE & INVESTMENT

Agreement regulating the position of corporations and other commercial associations.
Signed at St. Petersburg June 25, 1904.
Entered into force June 25, 1904.
36 Stat. 2163; TS 526; 11 Bevans 1235

Agreement on the establishment of a U.S.-U.S.S.R. Commercial Commission.
Communique issued at Moscow May 26, 1972.
Entered into force May 26, 1972.
26 UST 1334; TIAS 8116; 1006 UNTS 17

Protocol relating to the possibility of establishing a U.S.-U.S.S.R. Chamber of Commerce.
Signed at Washington June 22, 1973.
Entered into force June 22, 1973.
24 UST 1498; TIAS 7656

Protocol relating to expansion and improvement of commercial facilities in Washington and Moscow.
Signed at Washington June 22, 1973.
Entered into force June 22, 1973.
24 UST 1501; TIAS 7657; 938 UNTS 127

Protocol relating to a Trade Representation of the U.S.S.R. in Washington and a Commercial Office of the U.S.A. in Moscow.
Signed at Moscow October 3, 1973.
Entered into force October 3, 1973.
24 UST 2222; TIAS 7738; 938 UNTS 135
Amendment:
May 21 and October 7, 1974 (27 UST 2987; TIAS 8356)

Agreement relating to the status of the Commercial Office of the United States in Moscow and the Trade Representation of the Soviet Union in Washington, with annexes.
Exchange of letters at Washington June 1, 1990.
Entered into force June 1, 1990.
TIAS

TRANSPORTATION

Memorandum of cooperation concerning air traffic control, with annexes.
Signed at Washington February 16, 1990.
Entered into force February 16, 1990.
TIAS 11450

Civil air transport agreement, with annexes.
Signed at Washington June 1, 1990.
Entered into force June 1, 1990.
TIAS 11461

UNITED ARAB EMIRATES

ATOMIC ENERGY

Agreement concerning peaceful uses of nuclear energy, with agreed minute.
Signed at Washington May 21, 2009.
Entered into force December 17, 2009.
TIAS 09-1217

Arrangement for the exchange of technical information and cooperation in nuclear safety matters, with addenda.
Signed at Vienna September 15, 2015.
Entered into force September 15, 2015.
TIAS

DEFENSE

Agreement relating to the sale of defense articles and services to the United Arab Emirates.
Exchange of notes at Abu Dhabi June 15 and 21, 1975.
Entered into force June 21, 1975.
26 UST 1789; TIAS 8139; 1006 UNTS 251

General security of military information agreement.
Signed at Abu Dhabi May 23, 1987.
Entered into force May 23, 1987.
TIAS

Acquisition and cross servicing agreement, with annexes.
Signed at Tampa and Abu Dhabi August 18, 2005, and January 22, 2006.
Entered into force February 1, 2006.
NP

ENVIRONMENT & CONSERVATION

Agreement for cooperation in the Global Learning and Observations to Benefit the Environment (GLOBE) Program, with appendices.
Signed at Abu Dhabi June 6, 1999.
Entered into force June 6, 1999.
TIAS 13040

FINANCE

Agreement on investment guaranties.
Signed at Abu Dhabi September 29, 1991.
Entered into force April 22, 1992.
TIAS 12079

INTERNATIONAL CRIMINAL COURT

Agreement regarding the surrender of persons to the International Criminal Court.
Exchange of notes at Abu Dhabi January 27 and February 15, 2004.
Entered into force February 15, 2004.
TIAS 04-215

POSTAL MATTERS

Memorandum of understanding for the exchange of international express mail, with details of implementation.
Signed at Dubai and Washington December 31, 1984, and January 16, 1985.
Entered into force March 21, 1985.
TIAS 11149; 2126 UNTS 181

SCIENTIFIC & TECHNICAL COOPERATION

Memorandum of understanding concerning scientific and technical cooperation in the earth sciences.
Signed at Abu Dhabi February 6, 1988.
Entered into force February 6, 1988.
TIAS

Extensions:
June 26, 1993
February 6, 2003

TAXATION

Agreement regarding taxation of income derived from the international operation of ships or aircraft.
Exchange of notes at Abu Dhabi October 7 and December 1, 1997.
Entered into force December 1, 1997; effective January 1, 1994.
TIAS 12906

Agreement to improve international tax compliance and to implement the Foreign Account Tax Compliance Act, with annexes.
Signed at Abu Dhabi June 17, 2015.
Entered into force February 19, 2016.
TIAS 16-219

TRANSPORTATION

Air transport agreement, with annexes.
Signed at Abu Dhabi March 11, 2002.
Entered into force December 11, 2002.
TIAS 02-1211

Agreement on air transport preclearance, with annex and related exchange of notes.
Signed at Washington April 15, 2013.
Entered into force December 8, 2013.
TIAS 13-1208

UNITED KINGDOM

ARMS CONTROL

Agreement concerning a hydroacoustic monitoring facility on Ascension Island.
Signed at London April 3, 2012.
Entered into force April 3, 2012.
TIAS

ATOMIC ENERGY

Articles of agreement governing collaboration between the authorities of the United States of America and the United Kingdom in the matter of tube alloys.
Signed at Quebec August 19, 1943.
Entered into force August 19, 1943.
5 UST 1114; TIAS 2993; 214 UNTS 341

Agreement in the field of decommissioning nuclear facilities, with appendix.
Signed at Washington March 1, 1985.
Entered into force March 1, 1985.
TIAS 11342

Extension:
February 17 and March 6, 1989

Agreement regarding the technical exchange and cooperation arrangement in the field of reactor safety research and development, with appendices and annex.
Signed at Rockville and Merseyside February 7 and 12, 2007.
Entered into force February 12, 2007.
TIAS 07-212

Arrangement for the exchange of technical information and cooperation in nuclear safety matters, with addenda.
Signed at Rockville March 12, 2008.
Entered into force March 12, 2008.
TIAS 08-312

BOUNDARIES & BOUNDARY WATERS

Convention respecting fisheries, boundary, and the restoration of slaves.
Signed at London October 20, 1818.
Entered into force January 30, 1819.
8 Stat. 248; TS 112; 12 Bevans 57

Treaty to settle and define the boundaries between the territories of the United States and the possessions of Her Britannic Majesty in North America; for the final suppression of the African slave trade, and for the giving up of criminals, fugitive from justice in certain cases (Webster-Ashburton treaty).*
Signed at Washington August 9, 1842.
Entered into force October 13, 1842.
8 Stat. 572; TS 119; 12 Bevans 82
Note:
* Article X terminated June 24, 1935, upon entry into force of extradition convention signed December 22, 1931 (47 Stat. 2122; TS 849).

Treaty establishing the boundary in the territory on the northwest coast of America lying westward of the Rocky Mountains (Oregon Treaty).
Signed at Washington June 15, 1846.
Entered into force July 17, 1846.
9 Stat. 869; TS 120; 12 Bevans 95

Declaration adopting maps of boundary prepared by the Joint Commission of the Northwest Boundary for surveying and marking the boundaries between the United States and British possessions on the forty-ninth parallel of north latitude, under the first article of the treaty of June 15, 1846 between the United States and the United Kingdom.
Signed at Washington February 24, 1870.
Entered into force February 24, 1870.
TS 129; 12 Bevans 157

Protocol of a conference respecting the northwest water boundary.
Signed at Washington March 10, 1873.
Entered into force March 10, 1873.
18 Stat. (Pt. 2, Public Treaties) 369; TS 135; 12 Bevans 190

Convention providing for the settlement of questions between the United States and the United Kingdom with respect to the boundary line between the territory of Alaska and the British possessions in North America.*
Signed at Washington January 24, 1903.
Entered into force March 3, 1903.
32 Stat. 1961; TS 419; 12 Bevans 263
Note:
* Obsolete except for first paragraph of Article VI.

Acceptance of the report of the commissioners to complete the award under the convention of January 24, 1903, respecting the boundary line between Alaska and the British North American possessions.
Exchange of notes at Washington March 25, 1905.
Entered into force March 25, 1905.
TS 476; 12 Bevans 269

Convention providing for the surveying and marking out upon the ground of the 141st degree of west longitude where said meridian forms the boundary line between Alaska and the British possessions in North America.*
Signed at Washington April 21, 1906.
Entered into force August 16, 1906.
34 Stat. 2948; TS 452; 12 Bevans 276
Note:
* Obsolete except for Article II.

Treaty concerning the Canadian international boundary.
Signed at Washington April 11, 1908.
Entered into force June 4, 1908.
35 Stat. 2003; TS 497; 12 Bevans 297

Treaty relating to boundary waters and questions arising along the boundary between the United States and Canada.*
Signed at Washington January 11, 1909.
Entered into force May 5, 1910.
36 Stat. 2448; TS 548; 12 Bevans 319
Note:
* Paragraphs 3, 4, and 5 of Article V terminated October 10, 1950, upon the entry into force of the treaty relating to uses of waters on the Niagara River (see under CANADA — BOUNDARIES & BOUNDARY WATERS).

Treaty concerning the boundary line in Passamaquoddy Bay.
Signed at Washington May 21, 1910.
Entered into force August 20, 1910.
36 Stat. 2477; TS 551; 12 Bevans 341

Treaty in regard to the boundary between the United States and Canada.
Signed at Washington February 24, 1925.
Entered into force July 17, 1925.
44 Stat. 2102; TS 720; 6 Bevans 7; 43 LNTS 239

Treaty on the delimitation in the Caribbean of a maritime boundary relating to Puerto Rico/U.S. Virgin Islands and the British Virgin Islands, with annex.
Signed at London November 5, 1993.
Entered into force June 1, 1995.
TIAS; 1913 UNTS 67

Treaty on the delimitation in the Caribbean of a maritime boundary relating to the U.S. Virgin Islands and Anguilla.
Signed at London November 5, 1993.
Entered into force June 1, 1995.
1913 UNTS 59

CANALS

Treaty to facilitate the construction of a ship canal.
Signed at Washington November 18, 1901.
Entered into force February 21, 1902.
32 Stat. 1903; TS 401; 12 Bevans 258

CLAIMS & DISPUTE RESOLUTION

Treaty for the advancement of peace.
Signed at Washington September 15, 1914.
Entered into force November 10, 1914.
38 Stat. 1853; TS 602; 12 Bevans 370

Arrangement for the disposal of certain pecuniary claims arising out of World War I.
Exchange of notes at Washington May 19, 1927.
Entered into force May 19, 1927.
TS 756; 12 Bevans 462; 64 LNTS 101

Agreement relating to certain problems of marine transportation and litigation, and exchange of notes.
Signed at London December 4, 1942.
Entered into force December 4, 1942.
56 Stat. 1780; EAS 282; 12 Bevans 631; 205 LNTS 33

Amendments:

March 25 and May 7, 1946 (60 Stat. 1958; TIAS 1558; 12 Bevans 792; 6 UNTS 285)

June 17 and 27, 1947 (61 Stat. 3014; TIAS 1636; 12 Bevans 818; 16 UNTS 360)

Agreement relating to claims for damages resulting from acts of armed forces personnel.
Exchange of notes at London February 29 and March 28, 1944.
Entered into force March 28, 1944.
61 Stat. 2728; TIAS 1602; 12 Bevans 660; 15 UNTS 413

Amendment:

March 27, 1946 (60 Stat. 1525; TIAS 1509; 12 Bevans 745; 4 UNTS 2)

Agreement relating to mutual forbearance in claims resulting from acts of armed forces or civilian personnel.
Exchange of notes at Washington October 23, 1946, and January 23, 1947.
Entered into force January 23, 1947; operative June 6, 1944.
61 Stat. 2876; TIAS 1622; 12 Bevans 805; 15 UNTS 281

Agreement relating to the interpretation of paragraph 6 of the agreement on settlement of intergovernmental claims of March 27, 1946 (60 Stat. 1534; TIAS 1509).
Exchange of notes at Washington February 19 and 28, 1947.
Entered into force February 28, 1947.
61 Stat. 3012; TIAS 1635; 12 Bevans 812; 89 UNTS 368

Agreement relating to indemnities on ammunition shipments in the United Kingdom or in British ships traveling to or from the United Kingdom.
Exchange of notes at London October 27, 1966.
Entered into force October 27, 1966.
17 UST 2186; TIAS 6154; 597 UNTS 265

CONSULAR AFFAIRS

Agreement for the waiver of the visa requirements for United States citizens traveling to the United Kingdom and for the granting of gratis passport visas to British subjects entering the United States as nonimmigrants.*
Exchange of notes at London November 9 and 12, 1948.
Entered into force November 12, 1948.
62 Stat. 3824; TIAS 1926; 12 Bevans 917; 84 UNTS 275

Notes:

* Applicable to all territories.

Agreement for the sharing of visa, immigration and nationality information.
Signed at Queenstown, NZ April 18, 2013.
Entered into force November 8, 2013.
TIAS 13-1108

Amendment:

September 28 and 29, 2016 (TIAS 16-929)

CULTURAL EXCHANGES, PROPERTY & COOPERATION

Agreement relating to the use of land at Madingley, near Cambridge, as a United States military cemetery.
Exchange of notes at London June 21, 1954.
Entered into force June 21, 1954.
5 UST 1404; TIAS 3011; 209 UNTS 61

DEFENSE

Arrangement relating to naval and air bases.
Exchange of notes at Washington September 2, 1940.
Entered into force September 2, 1940.
54 Stat. 2405; EAS 181; 12 Bevans 551; 203 LNTS 201

Note:

* Superseded by agreement of February 10, 1961 (12 UST 408; TIAS 4734) between the United States and the Federation of the West Indies, in so far as any provisions relate to any territory in the Federation. Further, the agreement of February 10, 1961 was terminated December 31, 1977.

Protocol concerning the defense of Newfoundland.
Signed at London March 27, 1941.
Entered into force March 27, 1941.
55 Stat. 1599; EAS 235; 12 Bevans 560; 204 LNTS 70

Mutual defense assistance agreement.*
Signed at Washington January 27, 1950.
Entered into force January 27, 1950.
1 UST 126; TIAS 2017; 80 UNTS 261

Note:

* Article IV is applicable to Falkland Islands, Gibraltar, Leeward Islands, St. Helena and Western Pacific Dependencies.

Agreement relating to the assurances required under the Mutual Security Act of 1951.*
Exchange of notes at London January 8, 1952.
Entered into force January 8, 1952.
3 UST 4665; TIAS 2622; 126 UNTS 307

Note:

* Applicable to Falkland Islands, Gibraltar, Leeward Islands, St. Helena, Western Pacific Islands.

Agreement concerning the extension of the Bahamas Long Range Proving Ground by the establishment of additional sites in Ascension Island.
Signed at Washington June 25, 1956.
Entered into force June 25, 1956.
7 UST 1999; TIAS 3603; 249 UNTS 91

Amendment:

July 17, 1967 (18 UST 1657; TIAS 6308; 619 UNTS 330)

Related agreement:

August 24 and 25, 1959 (10 UST 1453; TIAS 4296; 351 UNTS 438)

Agreement relating to the disposition of equipment and material furnished by the United States under the mutual defense assistance program and found surplus to the needs of the armed forces of the United Kingdom.
Exchange of notes at London May 10 and 13, 1957.
Entered into force May 13, 1957.
8 UST 835; TIAS 3843; 291 UNTS 300
Amendments:
December 17 and 30, 1958 (9 UST 1547; TIAS 4156; 340 UNTS 342)
November 7 and 10, 1961 (12 UST 2947; TIAS 4895; 431 UNTS 288)
August 28, 1963 (14 UST 1178; TIAS 5413; 486 UNTS 398)

Agreement for the establishment of oceanographic research stations in the Bahama Islands.*
Signed at Washington November 1, 1957.
Entered into force November 1, 1957.
8 UST 1741; TIAS 3927; 299 UNTS 167
Amendment:
May 12, 1960 (11 UST 1405; TIAS 4479; 372 UNTS 364)

Note:
* See agreement of July 10 and 20, 1973 (TIAS 7688), between the United States and the Bahamas, under BAHAMAS — DEFENSE.

Agreement relating to the supply by the United States to the United Kingdom of intermediate range ballistic missiles, with memorandum.
Exchange of notes at Washington February 22, 1958.
Entered into force February 22, 1958.
9 UST 195; TIAS 3990; 307 UNTS 207

Agreement for cooperation on the uses of atomic energy for mutual defense purposes.
Signed at Washington July 3, 1958.
Entered into force August 4, 1958.
9 UST 1028; TIAS 4078; 326 UNTS 3
Amendments:
May 7, 1959 (10 UST 1274; TIAS 4267; 351 UNTS 458)
September 27, 1968 (20 UST 518; TIAS 6659)
October 16, 1969 (21 UST 1064; TIAS 6861)
July 22, 1974 (26 UST 110; TIAS 8014)
December 5, 1979 (31 UST 5853; TIAS 9688; 1203 UNTS 317)
June 5, 1984 (TIAS 11114)
July 22, 2014 (TIAS 14-1217)

Agreement relating to the establishment and operation of a ballistic missile early warning station at Fylingdales Moor, with memorandum.
Exchange of notes at London February 15, 1960.
Entered into force February 15, 1960.
11 UST 156; TIAS 4425; 371 UNTS 45

Agreement relating to rights of the United Kingdom in connection with the use of oceanographic research stations and parts of the Long Range Proving Ground.*
Exchange of notes at Port-of-Spain February 10, 1961.
Entered into force February 10, 1961.
12 UST 442; TIAS 4735; 409 UNTS 129
Note:
* This agreement relates to an agreement of the same date between the United States and the short-lived Federation of the West Indies (12 UST 408; TIAS 4734).

Agreement relating to the safeguarding of classified information.
Effected by exchange of notes April 4, 1961.
Entered into force April 14, 1961.
NP
Amendment:
December 19, 1983

Agreement on the setting up of a missile defense alarm system station in the United Kingdom, with memorandum.
Exchange of notes at London July 18, 1961.
Entered into force July 18, 1961.
12 UST 1058; TIAS 4809; 404 UNTS 227

Agreement relating to a weapons production program.
Exchange of notes at London June 29, 1962.
Entered into force June 29, 1962.
13 UST 1318; TIAS 5087; 449 UNTS 286

Agreement relating to the use of the airfield at Widewake in Ascension Island by aircraft of the Royal Air Force.
Exchange of notes at Washington August 29, 1962.
Entered into force August 29, 1962.
13 UST 1917; TIAS 5148; 449 UNTS 177

Polaris sales agreement.
Signed at Washington April 6, 1963.
Entered into force April 6, 1963.
14 UST 321; TIAS 5313; 474 UNTS 49

Agreement concerning the availability of certain Indian Ocean Islands for the defense purposes of both governments.*
Exchange of notes at London December 30, 1966.
Entered into force December 30, 1966.
18 UST 28; TIAS 6196; 603 UNTS 273
Amendments:
June 22 and 25, 1976 (27 UST 3448; TIAS 8376)
November 16, 1987 (1576 UNTS 179)

Note:
* See also agreement of February 25, 1976, concerning Diego Garcia, as amended (TIAS 8230, 10616).

Understanding relating to the use by Bahamian organizations of certain land at the United States Navy Base, Georgetown, Great Exuma Island, with map and schedule.*
Exchange of notes at Nassau June 19, September 12 and November 2, 1972.
Entered into force November 2, 1972.
23 UST 3688; TIAS 7514
Note:
* See agreement of July 10 and 20, 1973 (TIAS 7688), between the United States and the Bahamas, under BAHAMAS — DEFENSE.

Agreement relating to the lease of certain land to the United States Navy on the Island of Anegada in the British Virgin Islands for use as a drone launching facility.
Exchange of notes at Washington February 1, 1973.
Entered into force February 1, 1973.
24 UST 482; TIAS 7567

Agreement relating to the expanded use of Ascension Island.
Exchange of notes at London March 30, 1973.
Entered into force March 30, 1973.
24 UST 918; TIAS 7602

Arrangement relating to the status of United States forces engaged in clearance of the Suez Canal which are using British Sovereign Base areas in Cyprus.
Exchange of notes at London June 24 and July 4, 1974.
Entered into force July 4, 1974.
25 UST 2399; TIAS 7917

Agreement concerning a United States naval support facility on Diego Garcia, British Indian Ocean Territory, with plan, related notes, and supplementary arrangement.
Exchange of notes at London February 25, 1976.
Entered into force February 25, 1976.
27 UST 315; TIAS 8230; 1018 UNTS 372
Related Agreement:
December 13, 1982 (TIAS 10616; 2001 UNTS 397)

Memorandum of understanding concerning the transfer of technical data relating to the JT–10D jet engine collaboration agreement to third countries.
Signed at Washington December 30, 1976.
Entered into force December 30, 1976.
27 UST 4385; TIAS 8459; 1068 UNTS 437

Memorandum of agreement on the exchange of personnel between the United States Coast Guard and the Royal Navy.
Signed at Washington August 29, 1980.
Entered into force August 29, 1980.
32 UST 2403; TIAS 9849; 1267 UNTS 187

Agreement extending the Polaris sales agreement of April 6, 1963 (TIAS 5313) to cover the sale of Trident I weapon system.
Exchange of notes at Washington September 30, 1980.
Entered into force September 30, 1980.
TIAS 9879

Memorandum of understanding regarding support to the Royal Air Force detachment at Hickam Air Force Base.
Signed at Honolulu April 21, 1981.
Entered into force April 21, 1981.
33 UST 998; TIAS 10084; 1285 UNTS 97

Memorandum of understanding concerning the shared use of communications facilities in the northern Federal Republic of Germany, with annexes.
Signed May 11 and June 2, 1981.
Entered into force June 2, 1981.
33 UST 2025; TIAS 10165; 1529 UNTS 415

Agreement extending the Polaris sales agreement of April 6, 1963 (TIAS 5313) to cover the sale of Trident II weapon system.
Exchange of notes at Washington October 19, 1982.
Entered into force October 19, 1982.
TIAS 10549

Memorandum of understanding on the exchange of personnel between the U.S. Coast Guard and the Royal Air Force.
Signed at Washington November 14 and 16, 1983.
Entered into force November 16, 1983.
35 UST 4110; TIAS 10908; 2014 UNTS 437

Agreement regarding arrangements for continued United Kingdom access to and use of the Atlantic Undersea Test and Evaluation Centre (AUTEC) facility in The Bahamas.
Exchange of notes at Washington April 5, 1984.
Entered into force April 5, 1984.
TIAS 11059

Agreement concerning certain communications facilities in the defense areas in the Turks and Caicos Islands.
Exchange of notes at Washington December 18, 1984.
Entered into force December 18, 1984.
TIAS 11139

Agreement relating to sharing facility construction costs on Ascension Island, with memoranda of agreement.
Exchange of notes at London March 25, 1985.
Entered into force March 25, 1985.
TIAS 12383; 1443 UNTS 25

Memorandum of understanding concerning the exchange of medical cadets between the British Army Medical Services and the Uniformed Services University of the Health Sciences.
Signed at Washington and London March 25 and June 21, 1985.
Entered into force June 21, 1985.
TIAS 11109

Agreement relating to cooperation in mapping, charting and geodesy.
Signed at Feltham and Washington July 4 and 18, 1985.
Entered into force July 18, 1985.
TIAS 11530

Memorandum of understanding concerning the exchange of medical cadets between the Royal Navy and the Uniformed Services University of the Health Sciences.
Signed at Washington and London March 25 and October 7, 1985.
Entered into force October 7, 1985.
TIAS 11225

Memorandum of understanding for the procurement of an airborne early warning system for the Royal Air Force, with related letter.
Signed at Washington February 25, 1987.
Entered into force February 25, 1987.
TIAS 11281

Memorandum of understanding on the status of certain persons working for United States defense contractors in the United Kingdom, with annex.
Signed at Washington July 7, 1987.
Entered into force July 7, 1987; effective for tax years beginning on or after April 6, 1987.
TIAS 11537

Memorandum of understanding on the exchange of sub units.
Signed at Washington October 5, 1988.
Entered into force October 5, 1988.
TIAS 11630

Memorandum of understanding concerning the exchange of reserve officers.
Signed at Washington September 11, 1989.
Entered into force September 11, 1989.
TIAS 11698; 2207 UNTS 483

Agreement concerning defense cooperation arrangements.
Exchange of notes at Washington May 27, 1993.
Entered into force May 27, 1993.
TIAS 12237; 1792 UNTS 145
Amendment:
March 12 and June 1, 2007 (TIAS 07-601)

Agreement regarding U.S. approval for retransfer of U.S. defense articles and services to NATO for purposes of supporting the NATO-led Implementation Force (IFOR).
Exchange of notes at Brussels December 18 and 19, 1995.
Entered into force December 19, 1995.
TIAS

Agreement concerning the termination of the agreement and related exchanges of notes of March 27, 1941, between the Government of the United States of America and the Government of the United Kingdom of Great Britain and Northern Ireland, as amended and supplemented, relating to the bases leased to the United States of America, with annexes.
Exchange of notes at Washington June 18, 2002.
Entered into force June 18, 2002.
TIAS 02-618; 2207 UNTS 485

Treaty concerning defense trade cooperation.
Signed at Washington and London June 21 and 26, 2007.
Entered into force April 13, 2012.
TIAS

Agreement concerning the use of Wideawake Airfield on Ascension Island by civil aircraft (air links and alternate aerodrome agreement), with attachment and annex.
Exchange of notes at Washington June 6, 2016.
Entered into force June 6, 2016, with effect from September 30, 2014.
TIAS 16-606.1

DIPLOMATIC & CONSULAR RELATIONS

Agreement for the waiver of the visa requirements for United States citizens traveling to the United Kingdom and for the granting of gratis passport visas to British subjects entering the United States as nonimmigrants.*
Exchange of notes at London November 9 and 12, 1948.
Entered into force November 12, 1948.
62 Stat. 3824; TIAS 1926; 12 Bevans 917; 84 UNTS 275
Note:
* Applicable to all territories.
The status of this agreement is under review.

Understanding relating to the importation in bulk, free from customs duties, of certain articles for the use of the diplomatic staff of United States embassy and consular officers and other employees on duty in the United Kingdom.
Exchange of notes at Washington February 16, 1949.
Entered into force February 16, 1949.
12 Bevans 928

Consular convention and protocol of signature.*
Signed at Washington June 6, 1951.
Entered into force September 7, 1952.
3 UST 3426; TIAS 2494; 165 UNTS 121
Note:
* Applicable to all territories over which the United States has jurisdiction or international responsibility and to all British territories.

EDUCATION

Agreement for financing certain educational and cultural exchange programs.*
Signed at London May 10, 1965.
Entered into force May 10, 1965.
16 UST 758; TIAS 5806; 545 UNTS 181
Amendments:
February 16, 1967 (18 UST 297; TIAS 6232; 605 UNTS 394)
June 30, 1971 (22 UST 1629; TIAS 7190)
September 11 and 23, 1992 (1723 UNTS 270)

Note:
* Applicable to Bermuda, British Virgin Islands, Falkland Islands, Gibraltar, Montserrat, Anguilla, St. Helena.

EMPLOYMENT

Arrangement relating to the employment of dependents of official government employees.
Exchange of notes at Washington January 14 and 15, 1981.
Entered into force January 15, 1981.
32 UST 4581; TIAS 9971; 1267 UNTS 209

ENVIRONMENT & CONSERVATION

Memorandum of understanding concerning cooperation in the field of environmental affairs.
Signed at Washington June 2, 1986.
Entered into force June 2, 1986.
TIAS 11364

FINANCE

See also international fund for Ireland under FINANCE in multilateral section.

Debt funding agreement.
Signed at Washington June 18, 1923.
Operative December 15, 1922.
Treasury Department print; 12 Bevans 397

Agreement modifying the debt funding agreement of June 18, 1923.
Signed at Washington June 4, 1932.
Operative July 1, 1931.
Treasury Department print; 12 Bevans 491

Agreement concerning arrangements for the establishment of revolving loan funds in Uganda protectorate and Tanganyika with counterpart funds.
Exchange of letters at London June 24, 1953.
Entered into force June 24, 1953.
5 UST 160; TIAS 2909; 224 UNTS 141

FISHERIES

Agreement adopting, with certain modifications, the rules and method of procedure recommended in the award of September 7, 1910, of the North Atlantic Coast Fisheries Arbitration.
Signed at Washington July 20, 1912.
Entered into force November 15, 1912.
37 Stat. 1634; TS 572; 12 Bevans 357

Reciprocal fisheries agreement, with agreed minute.
Signed at London March 27, 1979.
Entered into force March 10, 1983.
TIAS 10545

FOREIGN ASSISTANCE

Economic cooperation agreement.*
Signed at London July 6, 1948.
Entered into force July 6, 1948.
62 Stat. 2596; TIAS 1795; 12 Bevans 874; 22 UNTS 263

Amendments:
January 3, 1950 (1 UST 184; TIAS 2036; 86 UNTS 304)
May 25, 1951 (2 UST 1292; TIAS 2277; 99 UNTS 308)
February 25, 1953 (4 UST 1528; TIAS 2815; 172 UNTS 332)
June 26 and August 20, 1959 (11 UST 2680; TIAS 4664; 405 UNTS 288)

Note:
* Applicable to Channel Islands, Falkland Islands, Western Pacific High Commission territories, Gibraltar, British Virgin Islands, Isle of Man, St. Helena and Dependencies. Applicable, with the exception of Article IV, to Turks and Caicos Islands and Cayman Islands, Montserrat, and Anguilla.

Agreement for technical cooperation in respect of the territories for the international relations of which the Government of the United Kingdom are responsible.*
Signed at London July 13, 1951.
Entered into force July 13, 1951.
2 UST 1307; TIAS 2281; 105 UNTS 71

Note:
* Applicable to British Virgin Islands, Montserrat, Anguilla, Turks and Caicos Islands and Cayman Islands.

Agreement relating to the use of the counterpart aid funds allotted to the United Kingdom* under Section 115 (k) of the Economic Cooperation Act, as amended.
Exchange of notes at London February 25, 1953.
Entered into force February 25, 1953.
4 UST 1532; TIAS 2816

Note:
* Including Isle of Man.

HEALTH & MEDICAL COOPERATION

Agreement relating to the synthesis of penicillin.
Exchange of notes at Washington January 25, 1946.
Entered into force January 25, 1946; operative December 1, 1943.
60 Stat. 1485; TIAS 1506; 12 Bevans 713; 3 UNTS 209

INTELLECTUAL PROPERTY

Declaration affording reciprocal protection to trade-marks.*
Signed at London October 24, 1877.
Entered into force October 24, 1877.
20 Stat. 703; TS 138; 12 Bevans 198

Note:
* Applicable to all territories.

Agreement to facilitate the interchange of patent and technical information for defense purposes, and exchange of notes.
Signed at London January 19, 1953.
Entered into force January 19, 1953.
4 UST 150; TIAS 2773; 161 UNTS 3

Agreement concerning the annex on intellectual property rights, with attachment.
Exchange of notes at Washington November 29, 1995.
Entered into force November 29, 1995.
TIAS 12703; 1945 UNTS 295

LAW ENFORCEMENT

Convention for the prevention of smuggling of intoxicating liquors.
Signed at Washington January 23, 1924.
Entered into force May 22, 1924.
43 Stat. 1761; TS 685; 12 Bevans 414; 27 LNTS 182

Arrangement for the direct exchange of certain information regarding the traffic in narcotic drugs.
Exchange of notes at London December 23, 1927, January 4, 1928, and January 11, 1928.
Entered into force January 11, 1928.
12 Bevans 467

Treaty concerning the Cayman Islands relating to mutual legal assistance in criminal matters, with attachments, protocol and exchange of notes.
Signed at Grand Cayman July 3, 1986.
Entered into force March 19, 1990.
TIAS; 1648 UNTS 179

Amendment:
September 10, 2004, and February 9, 2005

Agreement extending the application of the treaty of July 3, 1986, concerning the Cayman Islands relating to mutual legal assistance in criminal matters to Anguilla, the British Virgin Islands and the Turks and Caicos Islands.
Exchange of notes at Washington November 9, 1990.
Entered into force November 9, 1990.
TIAS 11765

Agreement extending application of the treaty of July 3, 1986, concerning the Cayman Islands relating to mutual legal assistance in criminal matters to Montserrat.
Exchange of notes at Washington April 26, 1991.
Entered into force April 26, 1991.
TIAS 12429; 1670 UNTS 375

Agreement for mutual assistance in administration of justice in connection with the Bank of Credit and Commerce International.
Signed at London and Washington November 15 and December 4, 1991.
Entered into force December 4, 1991.
TIAS

Treaty on mutual legal assistance in criminal matters, with appendices and related exchange of notes.
Signed at Washington January 6, 1994.
Entered into force December 2, 1996.
TIAS 96-1202

Agreement concerning the application of the treaty on mutual legal assistance in criminal matters of January 6, 1994.
Exchange of notes at Washington April 30 and May 1, 2001.
Entered into force May 1, 2001.
TIAS 01-501; 2189 UNTS 468

Extradition treaty, with related exchanges of letters.
Signed at Washington March 31, 2003.
Entered into force April 26, 2007.
TIAS 07-426

Agreement regarding the sharing of forfeited or confiscated assets or their equivalent funds.
Signed at Washington March 31, 2003.
Entered into force March 31, 2003.
TIAS 03-331.1

Agreement on the application to the Isle of Man of the treaty on mutual legal assistance in criminal matters of January 6, 1994.
Exchange of notes at London June 2 and 5, 2003.
Entered into force June 5, 2003.
TIAS 03-605.1

Instrument as contemplated by Article 3(2) of the agreement on extradition between the United States of America and the European Union signed June 25, 2003, as to the application of the extradition treaty of March 31, 2003, with annex and exchange of notes.
Signed at London December 16, 2004.
Entered into force February 1, 2010.
TIAS 10-201.23

Instrument as contemplated by Article 3(2) of the agreement on mutual legal assistance between the United States of America and the European Union signed June 25, 2003, as to the application of the treaty on mutual legal assistance in criminal matters of January 6, 1994, with annex and exchange of notes.
Signed at London December 16, 2004.
Entered into force February 1, 2010.
TIAS 10-201.49

MARITIME MATTERS

Agreement relating to jurisdiction over vessels utilizing the Louisiana Offshore Oil Port.
Exchange of notes at Washington May 14 and 25, 1979.
Entered into force May 25, 1979.
30 UST 5926; TIAS 9525; 1162 UNTS 351

Agreement to facilitate the interdiction by the United States of vessels of the United Kingdom suspected of trafficking in drugs.
Exchange of notes at London November 13, 1981.
Entered into force November 13, 1981.
33 UST 4224; TIAS 10296; 1285 UNTS 197

Agreement concerning maritime and aerial operations to suppress illicit trafficking by sea in waters of the Caribbean and Bermuda.
Signed at Washington July 13, 1998.
Entered into force October 30, 2000.
TIAS

NONPROLIFERATION

Memorandum of understanding concerning the measures to be taken for the transfer to, and security and safeguarding of MK IV radar instrumentation system technical information, software and equipment in the United Kingdom.
Signed at Washington February 6, 1991.
Entered into force February 6, 1991.
TIAS 11834

PEACE

Definitive treaty of peace.*
Signed at Paris September 3, 1783.
Entered into force May 12, 1784.
8 Stat. 80; TS 104; 12 Bevans 8

Treaty of peace and amity.
Signed at Ghent December 24, 1814.
Entered into force February 17, 1815.
8 Stat. 218; TS 109; 12 Bevans 41

Note:
* Only article 1 is in force.

Treaty for an amicable settlement of all causes of differences between the two countries (Treaty of Washington).*
Signed at Washington May 8, 1871.
Entered into force June 17, 1871.
17 Stat. 863; TS 133; 12 Bevans 170

Note:
* Articles I XVII and XXXIV XLII have been executed; articles XVIII, XXV, XXX, and XXXII terminated July 1, 1885; articles XXVIII and XXIX not considered in force.

POSTAL MATTERS

Agreement for the direct exchange of parcels by parcel post.
Signed at Washington October 1 and at London October 27, 1924.
Operative October 1, 1924.
43 Stat. 1854; Post Office Department print

International express mail agreement, with detailed regulations.
Signed at London and Washington November 6 and December 14, 1978.
Entered into force February 12, 1979; effective January 1, 1979.
30 UST 3357; TIAS 9395; 1180 UNTS 3

PROPERTY

Convention relating to tenure and disposition of real and personal property.*
Signed at Washington March 2, 1899.
Entered into force August 7, 1900.
31 Stat. 1939; TS 146; 12 Bevans 246
Note:
* Applicable to Puerto Rico, Ascension, Bermuda, Falkland Islands, Gibraltar, Leeward Islands, St. Helena.

Supplementary convention relating to the tenure and disposition of real and personal property.
Signed at Washington May 27, 1936, by the United States, the United Kingdom, Australia, and New Zealand.
Entered into force March 10, 1941.
55 Stat. 1101; TS 964; 5 Bevans 140; 203 LNTS 367

Preliminary agreement regarding principles applying to mutual aid in the prosecution of the war against aggression.
Signed at Washington February 23, 1942.
Entered into force February 23, 1942.
56 Stat. 1433; EAS 241; 12 Bevans 603

Agreement relating to principles applying to the provision of aid to the armed forces of the United States.
Exchange of notes at Washington September 3, 1942.
Entered into force September 3, 1942.
56 Stat. 1605; EAS 270; 12 Bevans 617

Joint statement regarding settlement for lend-lease, reciprocal aid, surplus war property, and claims.
Dated at Washington December 6, 1945.
60 Stat. 1525; TIAS 1509; 12 Bevans 700; 4 UNTS 2

Memorandum pursuant to joint statement of December 6, 1945, regarding settlement for lend-lease, reciprocal aid, surplus war property, and claims, with supplementary agreements annexed thereto.
Signed at Washington March 27, 1946.
Entered into force March 27, 1946.
12 Bevans 745

Agreement relating to settlement of the lend-lease interest in future sales of surplus stores in the Middle East.
Signed at London January 7, 1948.
Entered into force January 7, 1948; operative July 15, 1947.
62 Stat. 1836; TIAS 1698; 12 Bevans 843; 89 UNTS 372

Agreement relating to the settlement of the interests of the Government of the United States and the Government of the United Kingdom in joint installations in the Middle East.
Signed at Washington July 12, 1948.
Entered into force July 12, 1948.
62 Stat. 2027; TIAS 1769; 12 Bevans 891; 71 UNTS 199

Agreement relating to settlement of lend-lease and reciprocal aid accounts and intergovernmental claims.
Signed at Washington July 12, 1948.
Entered into force July 12, 1948.
62 Stat. 2034; TIAS 1770; 12 Bevans 897; 71 UNTS 270
Amendment:
April 24 and 25, 1957 (8 UST 771; TIAS 3834; 284 UNTS 362)

PUBLICATIONS

Agreement for the exchange of official publications.
Exchange of notes at Washington July 13 and 30, 1951.
Entered into force July 30, 1951.
2 UST 1745; TIAS 2314; 105 UNTS 81

SCIENTIFIC & TECHNICAL COOPERATION

Agreement for the continuation of a cooperative meteorological program in the Cayman Islands, with memorandum of arrangement.
Exchange of notes at Washington April 6 and 13, 1976.
Entered into force April 13, 1976.
27 UST 1867; TIAS 8285

Agreement on cooperation in science and technology for critical infrastructure protection and other homeland/civil security matters.
Signed at London December 8, 2004.
Entered into force December 8, 2004.
TIAS 04-1208.1

SOCIAL SECURITY

Agreement on social security.
Signed at London February 13, 1984.
Entered into force January 1, 1985, except for Part III, which entered into force January 1, 1988.
TIAS 11086

Administrative agreement for implementation of agreement on social security.
Signed at London February 13, 1984.
Entered into force January 1, 1985.
TIAS 11086

Supplementary agreement amending the agreement on social security of February 13, 1984 and supplementary administrative agreement amending the administrative agreement.
Done at London June 6, 1996.
Entered into force September 1, 1997.
TIAS 12776; 1995 UNTS 489

SPACE

Agreement providing for the establishment of a lunar and planetary spacecraft tracking facility on Ascension Island.
Exchange of notes at London July 7, 1965.
Entered into force July 7, 1965.
16 UST 1183; TIAS 5864; 551 UNTS 221

Agreement providing for the establishment and operation of space vehicle tracking and communications stations in the United Kingdom.
Exchange of notes at London December 28, 1966, and January 1, 1967.
Entered into force January 1, 1967.
18 UST 129; TIAS 6208; 604 UNTS 3

Agreement concerning the establishment and operation of a space vehicle tracking and communications station on Antigua.
Exchange of notes at Washington January 17 and 23, 1967.
Entered into force January 23, 1967.
18 UST 112; TIAS 6207

Agreement confirming a memorandum of understanding concerning the furnishing of launching and associated services by NASA for United Kingdom satellites, with annexes.
Exchange of notes at Washington January 17, 1973.
Entered into force January 17, 1973.
24 UST 228; TIAS 7544; 881 UNTS 3

TAXATION

Agreement relating to relief from taxation of United States Government expenditures in the United Kingdom for the common defense effort.
Exchange of notes at London March 17 and 18, 1952.
Entered into force March 18, 1952.
3 UST 4158; TIAS 2559; 177 UNTS 33

Convention for the avoidance of double taxation and the prevention of fiscal evasion with respect to taxes on estates of deceased persons and on gifts.*
Signed at London October 19, 1978.
Entered into force November 11, 1979.
30 UST 7223; TIAS 9580; 1182 UNTS 83

Notes:

* See article 14 for the circumstances under which the convention for the avoidance of double taxation and the prevention of fiscal evasion with respect to taxes on the estates of deceased persons of April 16, 1945 (60 Stat. 1391; TIAS 1547) would continue to have effect in the United Kingdom.

Convention (on behalf of the Government of Bermuda) relating to the taxation of insurance enterprises and mutual assistance in tax matters, with exchange of notes.
Signed at Washington July 11, 1986.
Entered into force December 2, 1988.
TIAS 11676; 2192 UNTS 139

Agreement (on behalf of the Government of Bermuda) for the exchange of information with respect to taxes.
Signed at Washington December 2, 1988.
Entered into force December 2, 1988.
TIAS 11986

Agreement (on behalf of the Isle of Man) for the reciprocal exemption with respect to taxes on income from the international operation of ships.
Exchange of notes at Washington August 1 and 15, 1989.
Entered into force August 15, 1989.
TIAS 11678

Convention for the avoidance of double taxation and the prevention of fiscal evasion with respect to taxes on income and on capital gains, with exchange of notes.
Signed at London July 24, 2001.
Entered into force March 31, 2003.
TIAS 13161; 2224 UNTS 247

Protocol amending the convention for the avoidance of double taxation and the prevention of fiscal evasion with respect to taxes on income and on capital gains of July 24, 2001.
Signed at Washington July 19, 2002.
Entered into force March 31, 2003.
TIAS 13161

Agreement for the exchange of information relating to taxes, for the Cayman Islands.
Signed at Washington November 27, 2001.
Entered into force March 10, 2006.
TIAS 13175

Agreement to improve international tax compliance and to implement the Foreign Account Tax Compliance Act. With annexes.
Signed at London September 12, 2012.
Entered into force August 11, 2014.
TIAS 14-811

Amendment:

June 13 and 14, 2013 (TIAS 14-811.1)

TELECOMMUNICATION

Agreement on distance measuring equipment.
Signed at Washington October 13, 1947.
Entered into force October 13, 1947.
61 Stat. 3131; TIAS 1652; 12 Bevans 824; 66 UNTS 269

Agreement on cooperation in intercontinental testing in connection with experimental communications satellites.
Exchange of notes at London March 29, 1961.
Entered into force March 29, 1961.
12 UST 246; TIAS 4704; 405 UNTS 107

Agreement relating to the reciprocal granting of authorizations to permit licensed amateur radio operators of either country to operate their stations in the other country.*
Exchange of notes at London November 26, 1965.
Entered into force November 26, 1965.
16 UST 2047; TIAS 5941; 561 UNTS 193

Agreement extending to certain territories the application of the agreement of November 26, 1965, relating to the reciprocal granting of authorizations to permit licensed amateur radio operators of either country to operate their stations in the other country.*
Exchange of notes at London December 11, 1969.
Entered into force December 11, 1969.
20 UST 4089; TIAS 6800; 732 UNTS 334

Note:

* Applicable to all territories, for whose international relations the United States is responsible and the following British territories: Bermuda, British Virgin Islands, Cayman Islands, Falkland Islands, Gibraltar, Montserrat, St. Helena, Turks and Caicos Islands.

TRADE & INVESTMENT

Treaty of amity, commerce, and navigation (Jay Treaty).*
Signed at London November 19, 1794.
Entered into force October 28, 1795.
8 Stat. 116; TS 105; 12 Bevans 13
Note:
* Only articles 9 and 10 appear to remain in force between the United States and the United Kingdom. Article 3, so far as it relates to the right of Indians to pass across the border, appears to remain in force between the United States and Canada. But see Akins v. U.S., 551 F 2d 1222 (1977).

Convention to regulate commerce.*
Signed at London July 3, 1815.
Entered into force July 3, 1815.
8 Stat. 228; TS 110; 12 Bevans 49

Convention continuing in force indefinitely the convention of July 3, 1815.
Signed at London August 6, 1827.
Entered into force April 2, 1828.
8 Stat. 361; TS 117; 12 Bevans 76
Note:
* Article IV superseded from September 7, 1952, by consular convention of June 6, 1951 (3 UST 3426; TIAS 2494), including territories to which consular convention applies.

Declaration exempting commercial travelers' samples from customs inspection.
Signed at Washington December 3 and 8, 1910.
Entered into force January 1, 1911.
TS 552; 12 Bevans 348

TRANSPORTATION

Arrangement relating to pilot licenses to operate civil aircraft.*
Exchange of notes at Washington March 28 and April 5, 1935.
Entered into force May 5, 1935.
49 Stat. 3731; EAS 77; 12 Bevans 513; 162 LNTS 59
Note:
* Applicable to American Samoa, Puerto Rico, Virgin Islands of the U.S., Bermuda, Falkland Islands and Dependencies, Gibraltar, Turks and Caicos Islands, and the Cayman Islands, Leeward Islands, St. Helena and Ascension.

Agreement relating to the transfer and maintenance of radio range and SCS 51 equipment.
Exchange of notes at London May 8 and July 31, 1946.
Entered into force July 31, 1946.
61 Stat. 4008; TIAS 1766; 12 Bevans 795; 42 UNTS 199

Agreement relating to the reciprocal acceptance of airworthiness certifications.
Exchange of notes at London December 28, 1972.
Entered into force December 28, 1972.
23 UST 4309; TIAS 7537

Agreement concerning air services, with annexes and exchange of letters. †
Signed at Bermuda July 23, 1977.
Entered into force July 23, 1977.
28 UST 5367; TIAS 8641.
Amendments:
April 25, 1978 (29 UST 2680; TIAS 8965; 1124 UNTS 437)†
December 4, 1980 (33 UST 655; TIAS 10059)†
February 20, 1985 (TIAS 11396)†
May 25, 1989 (TIAS 11674; 1584 UNTS 445)†
March 27, 1997 (TIAS 12846;1986 UNTS 499)†

Agreement relating to North Atlantic air fares.†
Exchange of letters at Washington March 17, 1978.
Entered into force March 17, 1978.
29 UST 2676; TIAS 8964
Extension and Amendment:
November 2 and 9, 1978 (30 UST 979; TIAS 9231; 1152 UNTS 473)†

Note:
† These agreements are suspended for the duration of provisional application of the U.S. – E.U. Air Transport Agreement signed April 25 and 30, 2007 ("Air Trans-port Agreement") except in respect of the application of this agreement to those areas that are not encompassed within the definition of "territory" in Article 1 of the Air Transport Agreement.

Memorandum of understanding concerning cooperation in the testing and development of anti-misting kerosene and related equipment, with appendix.
Signed at Washington and London June 1 and 14, 1978.
Entered into force June 14, 1978.
30 UST 1369; TIAS 9256; 1153 UNTS 49

Agreement concerning reciprocal recognition of airline fitness and citizenship determinations.
Exchange of notes at Washington May 25, 1989.
Entered into force May 25, 1989.
TIAS 11675

Agreement concerning settlement of the Heathrow Arbitration and the UK Arbitration and amending the air transport agreement of July 23, 1977, as amended.
Exchange of notes at Washington March 11, 1994.
Entered into force March 11, 1994.
TIAS 12536; 1882 UNTS 413

Agreement concerning the facilitation of air navigation services.
Signed at London May 11, 1995.
Entered into force May 11, 1995.
TIAS 12645; 1913 UNTS 77

Agreement for the promotion of aviation safety.
Signed at London December 20, 1995.
Entered into force December 20, 1995.
TIAS; 1921 UNTS 321

WEAPONS

Agreement for cooperation in research and development of weapons detection and protection-related technologies, with annex.
Signed at Washington July 3, 2002.
Entered into force July 3, 2002.
TIAS 02-703

UNITED KINGDOM (ANGUILLA)

CULTURAL EXCHANGES, PROPERTY & COOPERATION

Agreement relating to the establishment of a Peace Corps program in Anguilla.
Exchange of letters at Washington February 19 and June 24, 1981.
Entered into force June 24, 1981; effective May 1, 1981.
33 UST 2053; TIAS 10169; 1529 UNTS 429

POSTAL MATTERS

Convention for the exchange of postal money orders with the British Colony of Saint Christopher, Nevis and Anguilla.
Signed at Basseterre, St. Kitts, June 27 and at Washington September 14, 1959.
Entered into force February 1, 1960.
11 UST 1433; TIAS 4483

Express mail agreement, with detailed regulations.
Signed at Anguilla and Washington May 28, 1998, and January 8, 1999.
Entered into force April 15, 1999.
NP

TRADE & INVESTMENT

Investment incentive agreement on behalf of Anguilla.
Exchange of notes at London November 9, 1987.
Entered into force November 9, 1987.
TIAS 12045; 1556 UNTS 43

UNITED KINGDOM (BERMUDA)

LAW ENFORCEMENT

Treaty relating to mutual legal assistance in criminal matters.
Signed at Hamilton January 12, 2009.
Entered into force April 12, 2012.
TIAS 12-412

POLLUTION

Agreement concerning assistance to be rendered on a reimbursable basis by the United States Coast Guard in the event of major oil spills.
Signed at Hamilton July 13, 1976.
Entered into force July 13, 1976.
27 UST 3788; TIAS 8396

POSTAL MATTERS

Parcel post agreement.
Signed at Washington December 13, 1906, and at Bermuda January 15, 1907.
Operative February 1, 1907.
34 Stat. 2983; Post Office Department print

International express mail agreement, with detailed regulations.
Signed at Hamilton and Washington July 31 and August 13, 1979.
Entered into force September 1, 1979.
30 UST 6493; TIAS 9563; 1180 UNTS 47

TAXATION

Agreement for cooperation to facilitate the implementation of the Foreign Account Tax Compliance Act, with memorandum of understanding and annexes.
Signed at Hamilton December 19, 2013.
Entered into force August 19, 2014.
TIAS 14-819

TRANSPORTATION

Agreement on preclearance for entry into the United States, with annex.
Signed at Hamilton January 15, 1974.
Entered into force January 15, 1974.
25 UST 288; TIAS 7801
Amendment:
August 28 and 29, 1979 (30 UST 7562; TIAS 9600; 1203 UNTS 365)

UNITED KINGDOM (BRITISH VIRGIN ISLANDS)

POLLUTION

Agreement concerning assistance to be rendered during discharge of oil or other hazardous and noxious substances into waters of the British Virgin Islands.
Signed at Tortola August 12, 2004.
Entered into force August 12, 2004.
TIAS 04-812.1

POSTAL MATTERS

Convention for the exchange of postal money orders with the Colony of British Virgin Islands.
Signed at Road Town, Tortola, February 18 and at Washington March 14, 1957.
Entered into force July 1, 1957.
11 UST 1409; TIAS 4480

TAXATION

Agreement for the exchange of information relating to taxes.
Signed at Washington April 3, 2002.
Entered into force March 10, 2006.
TIAS 06-310

UNITED KINGDOM (CAYMAN ISLANDS)

POSTAL MATTERS

International express mail agreement, with detailed regulations.
Signed at Grand Cayman and Washington August 25 and September 9, 1986.
Entered into force November 26, 1986.
TIAS 11390

TAXATION

Agreement for the exchange of information relating to taxes.
Signed at London November 29, 2013.
Entered into force April 14, 2014.
TIAS 14-414

Agreement to improve international tax compliance and to implement the Foreign Account Tax Compliance Act, with annexes.
Signed at London November 29, 2013.
Entered into force July 1, 2014.
TIAS 14-701

UNITED KINGDOM (GIBRALTAR)

POSTAL MATTERS

Agreement for the exchange of parcel post and detailed regulations for the execution thereof.
Signed at Gibraltar December 18, 1936, and at Washington January 5, 1937.
Operative January 1, 1937.
50 Stat. 1488; Post Office Department print; 177 LNTS 21

TAXATION

Agreement for the exchange of information relating to taxes.
Signed at London March 31, 2009.
Entered into force December 22, 2009.
TIAS 09-1222.
Amendment:
May 8, 2014 (TIAS 14-629)

Agreement to improve international tax compliance and to implement the Foreign Account Tax Compliance Act, with annexes.
Signed at London May 8, 2014.
Entered into force September 17, 2015.
TIAS 15-917

UNITED KINGDOM (GUERNSEY)

LAW ENFORCEMENT

Agreement regarding the sharing of confiscated or forfeited assets or their equivalent funds.
Signed at St. Peter Port January 27, 2015.
Entered into force February 24, 2015.
TIAS 15-224

TAXATION

Agreement for the exchange of information relating to taxes.
Signed at Washington September 19, 2002.
Entered into force March 30, 2006.
TIAS 06-330

Protocol amending the agreement for the exchange of information relating to taxes.
Signed at London December 13, 2013.
Entered into force August 26, 2015.
TIAS 15-826.2

Agreement to improve international tax compliance and to Implement the Foreign Account Tax Compliance Act, with annexes.
Signed at London December 13, 2013.
Entered into force August 26, 2015.
TIAS 15-826.3

UNITED KINGDOM (ISLE OF MAN)

TAXATION

Agreement for the exchange of information relating to taxes.
Signed at Washington October 3, 2002.
Entered into force June 26, 2006.
TIAS 06-626
Amendment:
December 13, 2013 (TIAS 15-826)

Agreement to improve international tax compliance and to implement the Foreign Account Tax Compliance Act, with annexes.
Signed at London December 13, 2013.
Entered into force August 26, 2015.
TIAS 15-826.1

UNITED KINGDOM (JERSEY)

LAW ENFORCEMENT

Agreement regarding the sharing of confiscated of forfeited assets or their equivalent funds.
Signed at Saint Helier January 28, 2015.
Entered into force April 24, 2015.
TIAS 15-424

TAXATION

Agreement for the exchange of information relating to taxes.
Signed at Washington November 4, 2002.
Entered into force June 26, 2006.
TIAS 06-626.1

Protocol amending the agreement for the exchange of information relating to taxes.
Signed at London December 13, 2013.
Entered into force October 28, 2015.
TIAS 15-1028

Agreement to improved international tax compliance and to implement the Foreign Account Tax Compliance Act, with annexes.
Signed at London December 13, 2013.
Entered into force October 28, 2015.
TIAS 15-1028.1

UNITED KINGDOM (LEEWARD ISLANDS)

POSTAL MATTERS

Parcel post agreement.
Signed at Antigua May 27 and at Washington July 11, 1929.
Operative September 1, 1929.
46 Stat. 2321; Post Office Department print; 98 LNTS 161

UNITED KINGDOM (MONTSERRAT)

CULTURAL EXCHANGES, PROPERTY & COOPERATION

Agreement relating to the establishment of a Peace Corps program in Montserrat.
Exchange of letters at Bridgetown and Plymouth January 13 and February 9, 1981.
Entered into force February 9, 1981.
33 UST 1075; TIAS 10092; 1307 UNTS 415

POSTAL MATTERS

Convention for the exchange of postal money orders with the British Colony of Montserrat.
Signed at Montserrat March 15 and at Washington June 10, 1957.
Entered into force September 1, 1957.
11 UST 1417; TIAS 4481

UNITED KINGDOM (TURKS AND CAICOS ISLANDS)

CULTURAL EXCHANGES, PROPERTY & COOPERATION

Agreement relating to the establishment of a Peace Corps program in the Turks and Caicos Islands.
Exchange of letters at Washington April 17 and December 5, 1980.
Entered into force December 5, 1980.
32 UST 4235; TIAS 9945; 1267 UNTS 201

DEFENSE

Memorandum of understanding concerning the establishment of a portable radar tracking station in the Turks and Caicos Islands.
Signed at London July 24, 1987.
Entered into force July 24, 1987.
TIAS

FINANCE

Agreement on behalf of the Turks and Caicos Islands relating to investment guaranties.
Signed at Washington April 20, 1999.
Entered into force April 20, 1999.
TIAS 13031; 2076 UNTS 215

MIGRATION & REFUGEES

Memorandum of understanding to establish in the Turks and Caicos Islands a processing facility to determine the refugee status of boat people from Haiti, with related letter.
Signed at Grand Turk June 18, 1994.
Entered into force June 18, 1994.
TIAS
Amendment:
July 13, 1994

UNITED NATIONS

DEFENSE

Agreement regarding the furnishing of defense articles and defense services by the United States to the United Nations for purposes of supporting the Rapid Reactor Force established pursuant to United Nations Security Council Resolution 998.
Exchange of notes at New York July 28, 1995.
Entered into force July 28, 1995.
TIAS 12680

Agreement concerning the establishment of security for the United Nations Assistance Mission for Iraq.
Signed at New York December 8, 2005.
Entered into force December 8, 2005.
TIAS

Agreement concerning the establishment of security for the United Nations presence in Iraq.
Signed at New York December 31, 2008.
Entered into force January 1, 2009.
TIAS

Acquisition and cross-servicing agreement, with annexes.
Signed at New York September 25, 2015.
Entered into force September 25, 2015.
NP

FOREIGN ASSISTANCE

AGENCY FOR INTERNATIONAL DEVELOPMENT

Assistance Agreement on HIV/AIDS.
Signed September 29 and October 12, 2011.
Entered into force October 12, 2011.
NP

POSTAL MATTERS

Postal agreement
Signed March 28, 1951.
Entered into force October 24, 1951.
3 UST 369; TIAS 2399; 108 UNTS 231
Amendments:
November 7 and 17, 1952 (3 UST 5164; TIAS 2711; 149 UNTS 414)
April 15 and 19, 1965 (16 UST 745; TIAS 5803; 531 UNTS 314)
June 20 and August 8, 1994 (1819 UNTS 497)

TAXATION

Agreement relating to a procedure for United States income tax reimbursement.
Exchange of letters at New York June 30 and July 12, 1978.
Entered into force July 12, 1978.
30 UST 124; TIAS 9183; 1095 UNTS 307

TELECOMMUNICATION

Agreement to permit the exchange of third-party messages between amateur stations of the United States and amateur station 4U1VIC of the Vienna International Amateur Radio Club.
Exchange of letters at Vienna November 21 and December 3, 1985.
Entered into force January 2, 1986.
TIAS

UN & RELATED ORGANIZATIONS

Agreement regarding the headquarters of the United Nations.
Signed at Lake Success June 26, 1947.
Entered into force November 21, 1947.
61 Stat. 3416; TIAS 1676; 12 Bevans 956; 11 UNTS 11

Supplemental agreement regarding the headquarters of the United Nations.
Signed at New York February 9, 1966.
Entered into force February 9, 1966.
17 UST 74; TIAS 5961; 554 UNTS 308
Amendment:
December 8, 1966 (17 UST 2319; TIAS 6176; 581 UNTS 362)

Second supplemental agreement regarding the headquarters of the United Nations.
Signed at New York August 28, 1969.
Entered into force August 28, 1969.
20 UST 2810; TIAS 6750; 687 UNTS 408

Third supplemental agreement regarding the headquarters of the United Nations.
Signed at New York December 10, 1980.
Entered into force December 10, 1980.
32 UST 4414; TIAS 9955

Fourth supplemental agreement regarding the headquarters of the United Nations, with annex.
Signed at New York June 18, 2009.
Entered into force June 18, 2009.
TIAS 09-618

UNITED NATIONS EDUCATIONAL, SCIENTIFIC AND CULTURAL ORGANIZATION

ENVIRONMENT & CONSERVATION

Agreement concerning the establishment of the International Centre for Integrated Water Resources Management at the U. S. Army Corps of Engineers Institute for Water Resources as a Category 2 Centre under the auspices of UNESCO.
Signed at Alexandria October 29, 2009.
Entered into force February 10, 2016.
TIAS 16-210

TAXATION

Tax reimbursement agreement, with annex.
Signed at Paris December 14, 2010.
Entered into force December 14, 2010.
TIAS 10-1214

UNITED NATIONS ENVIRONMENT PROGRAMME

ENVIRONMENT & CONSERVATION

Agreement to cooperate on activities and facilities to support the UNEP division of early warning and assessment in North America.
Signed at Washington December 21, 2004.
Entered into force December 21, 2004.
TIAS 04-1221
Amendment:
November 21, 2014 (TIAS 14-1121)

UNITED NATIONS HIGH COMMISSIONER FOR REFUGEES

MIGRATION & REFUGEES

Agreement relating to assistance with Cuban refugees.
Done at Geneva May 16 and 21, 1980.
Entered into force May 21, 1980.
TIAS

Agreement concerning United States and UNHCR cooperation in providing assistance to the Cuban boat people.
Exchange of letters at Washington September 29 and October 5, 1994.
Entered into force October 5, 1994.
TIAS

UNITED NATIONS INTERIM ADMINISTRATION MISSION IN KOSOVO

FINANCE

Agreement for investment support projects in Kosovo.
Signed at Washington and Pristina May 17 and 30, 2002.
Entered into force May 30, 2002.
TIAS

UNIVERSAL POSTAL UNION

TAXATION

Tax reimbursement agreement, with annex.
Signed at Bern January 12, 1995.
Entered into force January 12, 1995.
TIAS 12598

URUGUAY

CLAIMS & DISPUTE RESOLUTION

Arbitration convention.
Signed at Washington January 9, 1909.
Entered into force November 14, 1913.
38 Stat. 1741; TS 583; 12 Bevans 986

Treaty for the advancement of peace.
Signed at Washington July 20, 1914.
Entered into force February 24, 1915.
38 Stat. 1908; TS 611; 12 Bevans 988

CONSULAR AFFAIRS

Agreement relating to passport visas and fees for nonimmigrants.*
Exchange of notes at Montevideo November 3 and 8, 1949.
Entered into force November 10, 1949.
64 Stat. (3) B122; TIAS 2046; 12 Bevans 1035; 82 UNTS 45

Note:

* The status of this agreement is under review.

CULTURAL EXCHANGES, PROPERTY & COOPERATION

Agreement relating to the establishment of a Peace Corps program in Uruguay.
Exchange of notes at Montevideo March 19 and July 31, 1963.
Entered into force July 31, 1963.
14 UST 1455; TIAS 5443; 488 UNTS 3

DEFENSE

Military assistance agreement.
Signed at Montevideo June 30, 1952.
Entered into force June 11, 1953.
4 UST 197; TIAS 2778; 207 UNTS 139

Agreement providing for disposition of equipment and materials furnished by the United States under the military assistance agreement and no longer required by Uruguay.
Exchange of notes at Montevideo June 1 and September 16, 1955, and note of April 20, 1956.
Entered into force September 16, 1955.
7 UST 831; TIAS 3562; 273 UNTS 259

Agreement relating to the deposit by Uruguay of ten percent of the value of grant military assistance and excess defense articles furnished by the United States.
Exchange of notes at Montevideo May 2, 1972.
Entered into force May 2, 1972; effective February 7, 1972.
23 UST 653; TIAS 7329

Agreement relating to payment to the United States of net proceeds from the sale of defense articles furnished under the military assistance program.
Exchange of notes at Montevideo December 11 and 30, 1974.
Entered into force December 30, 1974; effective July 1, 1974.
25 UST 3181; TIAS 7985; 991 UNTS 407

Cooperative mapping, charting and geodesy agreement.
Signed at Montevideo and Fairfax August 27 and October 25, 1991.
Entered into force October 25, 1991.
NP

Memorandum of understanding concerning the inter-American Naval telecommunications network.
Signed September 13, 2006.
Entered into force September 13, 2006.
TIAS 06-913

Agreement regarding grants under the Foreign Assistance Act of 1961, as amended, or successor legislation, and the furnishing of defense articles, defense services and related training, including pursuant to the United States International Military Education and Training (IMET) Program.
Exchange of notes at Montevideo October 29 and November 9, 2009.
Entered into force November 9, 2009.
NP

Agreement concerning health care for military members and their dependents.
Signed at Washington October 10 and December 12, 2012.
Entered into force December 12, 2012.
NP
Extension:
December 7 and December 23, 2015 (NP)

DIPLOMATIC & CONSULAR RELATIONS

Agreement providing more liberal exemptions from customs duties and related taxes for diplomatic and consular personnel.
Exchange of notes at Washington October 31 and November 12, 1952.
Entered into force November 12, 1952.
5 UST 824; TIAS 2971; 231 UNTS 145

EDUCATION

Agreement for financing certain educational exchange programs.
Exchange of notes at Montevideo March 22 and May 17, 1965.
Entered into force May 17, 1965.
16 UST 872; TIAS 5825; 564 UNTS 69

EMPLOYMENT

Agreement relating to the employment of dependents of official government employees.
Exchange of notes at Washington June 26 and July 14, 2008.
Entered into force July 14, 2008.
TIAS 08-714.1

FINANCE

Agreement relating to investment guaranties.
Exchange of notes at Montevideo December 15, 1982.
Entered into force July 21, 1983.
TIAS 12038

Agreement regarding the reduction of certain debts related to foreign assistance owed to the Government of the United States and its agencies, with appendices.
Signed at Washington December 15, 1992.
Entered into force January 14, 1993.
NP

Agreement regarding the reduction of certain debts related to agriculture owed to the Government of the United States and its agencies, with appendices (P.L. 480).
Signed at Washington December 15, 1992.
Entered into force January 14, 1993.
NP

FOREIGN ASSISTANCE

General agreement for a program of technical cooperation.
Signed at Montevideo March 23, 1956.
Entered into force March 22, 1960.
11 UST 1489; TIAS 4491; 376 UNTS 311

Agreement concerning the establishment of an Americas Fund and Administering Commission.
Signed at Montevideo June 25, 1993.
Entered into force June 25, 1993.
TIAS 12503

LAW ENFORCEMENT

Treaty on extradition and cooperation in penal matters.
Signed at Washington April 6, 1973.
Entered into force April 11, 1984.
35 UST 3197; TIAS 10850

Treaty on mutual legal assistance in criminal matters.
Signed at Montevideo May 6, 1991.
Entered into force April 15, 1994.
TIAS

Agreement regarding mutual assistance between their customs administrations.
Signed at Washington 13, 2014.
Entered into force August 18, 2015.
TIAS 15-818

POSTAL MATTERS

International express mail agreement with detailed regulations.
Signed at Washington September 22, 1983.
Entered into force February 15, 1984.
35 UST 3080; TIAS 10841; 2014 UNTS 597

SCIENTIFIC & TECHNICAL COOPERATION

Agreement on science and technology cooperation, with annexes.
Signed at Washington April 29, 2008.
Entered into force October 21, 2010.
TIAS 10-1021

TELECOMMUNICATION

Agreement relating to radio communications between radio amateurs on behalf of third parties.
Exchange of notes at Montevideo September 12, 1961.
Entered into force September 26, 1966.
17 UST 1574; TIAS 6115; 607 UNTS 175

Agreement relating to the reciprocal granting of authorizations to permit licensed amateur radio operators of either country to operate their stations in the other country.
Exchange of notes at Montevideo May 28, 1971.
Entered into force May 28, 1971.
22 UST 701; TIAS 7129; 797 UNTS 23

TRADE & INVESTMENT

Convention facilitating the work of traveling salesmen.
Signed at Washington August 27, 1918.
Entered into force August 2, 1919.
41 Stat. 1663; TS 640; 12 Bevans 991

Treaty concerning the encouragement and reciprocal protection of investment, with annexes.
Signed at Mar del Plata November 4, 2005.
Entered into force November 1, 2006.
TIAS 06-1101

Trade and investment framework agreement, with annex.
Signed at Montevideo January 25, 2007.
Entered into force January 25, 2007.
NP

TRANSPORTATION

Memorandum of agreement relating to provision of Federal Aviation Administration services to the Government of Uruguay.
Signed at Washington and Montevideo March 19 and 20, 1981.
Entered into force March 20, 1981.
33 UST 1461; TIAS 10122

Memorandum of agreement concerning assistance in developing and modernizing Uruguay's civil aviation infrastructure.
Signed at Washington and Montevideo September 25 and 30, 1997.
Entered into force September 30, 1997.
NP

Air transport agreement, with annexes and exchange of notes.
Signed at Montevideo October 20, 2004.
Entered into force June 16, 2006.
TIAS 06-616

UZBEKISTAN

For agreements prior to December 31, 1991, see UNION OF SOVIET SOCIALIST REPUBLICS.

CULTURAL EXCHANGES, PROPERTY & COOPERATION

Agreement concerning the activity of the Peace Corps of the United States in the Republic of Uzbekistan.
Signed at Tashkent November 4, 1992.
Entered into force November 4, 1992.
TIAS 12083

DEFENSE

Agreement concerning the provision of training under the United States International Military Education and Training (IMET) Program.
Exchange of notes at Tashkent January 25 and February 21, 1995.
Entered into force February 21, 1995.
NP

Agreement regarding grants under the Foreign Assistance Act of 1961, as amended, and the furnishing of defense articles, related training, and other defense services to the Government of Uzbekistan.
Exchange of notes at Tashkent March 18 and May 4, 1999.
Entered into force May 4, 1999.
NP

Agreement on procedure for ground transit of cargo shipped from the Islamic Republic of Afghanistan through the territory of the Republic of Uzbekistan in connection with the participation of the United States of America in efforts to ensure the security, stabilization, and reconstruction of the Islamic Republic of Afghanistan with mandatory involvement of the State Joint Stock Railway Company "Uzbekiston Temir Yullari", with annex.
Signed at Tashkent November 17, 2011.
Entered into force December 15, 2011.
TIAS 11-1215

Agreement on procedures for transit through the territory of the Republic of Uzbekistan of motorized wheeled armored vehicles (not fitted with weapons) in connection with the participation of the United States of America in efforts to ensure the security, stabilization, and reconstruction of the Islamic Republic of Afghanistan.
Signed at Tashkent November 17, 2011.
Entered into force December 15, 2011.
TIAS 11-1215.1

Agreement on the air transit of cargo and personnel through the territory of the Republic of Uzbekistan in connection with the participation of the United States of America in efforts for supporting the security, stabilization, and reconstruction of the Islamic Republic of Afghanistan.
Signed at Tashkent March 28, 2012.
Entered into force September 26, 2012.
TIAS 12-926.1

Acquisition and cross-servicing agreement.
Signed at Tampa and Tashkent June 1 and July 7, 2016.
Entered into force July 7, 2016.
NP

FINANCE

Investment incentive agreement.
Signed at Tashkent October 28, 1992.
Entered into force October 28, 1992.
TIAS

FOREIGN ASSISTANCE

Agreement regarding cooperation to facilitate the provision of assistance.
Signed at Tashkent March 1, 1994.
Entered into force March 1, 1994.
TIAS 12534

INTERNATIONAL CRIMINAL COURT

Agreement regarding the surrender of persons to the International Criminal Court.
Signed at Washington September 18, 2002.
Entered into force January 7, 2003.
TIAS 03-107

NONPROLIFERATION

Agreement concerning cooperation in the area of prevention of proliferation of nuclear materials and technologies.
Signed at Washington March 12, 2002.
Entered into force March 12, 2002.
TIAS 02-312

SCIENTIFIC & TECHNICAL COOPERATION

Agreement on science and technology cooperation, with annex.
Signed at Tashkent December 2, 2010.
Entered into force March 17, 2011.
TIAS 11-317.1

TRADE & INVESTMENT

Agreement on trade relations, with exchanges of letters.
Signed at Tashkent November 5, 1993.
Entered into force January 13, 1994.
TIAS 12515

TRANSPORTATION

Air transport agreement, with annexes.
Signed at Washington February 27, 1998.
Entered into force February 27, 1998.
TIAS 12933

WEAPONS

Implementing agreement on border security assistance.
Signed at Tashkent June 2, 2000.
Entered into force June 2, 2000.
NP

Amendments and extensions:
February 6 and 27, 2002
September 10 and October 17, 2003
April 11 and May 23, 2005
September 29 and October 11, 2006
December 14, 2006 and January 5, 2007

Agreement concerning cooperation in the area of the promotion of defense relations and the prevention of proliferation of weapons of mass destruction.
Signed at Washington June 5, 2001.
Entered into force June 5, 2001.
TIAS 01-605

Amendment and Extension:
October 15, 2007, June 4, 2008 and March 25, 2009 (TIAS 01-605)
August 21, 2014, April 9, 2015 and August 10, 2016 (TIAS 01-605)

Agreement concerning cooperation in the area of demilitarization of biological weapons associated facilities and the prevention of proliferation of biological weapons technology.
Signed at Tashkent October 22, 2001.
Entered into force October 22, 2001.
TIAS

Amendments and Extensions:
June 27 and July 29, 2003
May 6 and 17, 2004
August 14 and September 10, 2004
April 12 and December 19, 2005
September 29 and October 11, 2006
December 14, 2006 and January 5, 2007
February 12 and March 3, 2008
May 19 and July 25, 2008
March 7 and 27, 2009

V

VANUATU

NOTE: Treaties and other agreements previously applicable to the New Hebrides are under review.

CULTURAL EXCHANGES, PROPERTY & COOPERATION

Agreement concerning the program of the Peace Corps in Vanuatu.
Signed at Port Vila July 22, 2008.
Entered into force July 22, 2008.
TIAS 08-722

POSTAL MATTERS

International express mail agreement, with detailed regulations.
Signed at Port Vila and Washington May 23 and June 30, 1989.
Entered into force July 31, 1989.
TIAS 11668

VENEZUELA

ATOMIC ENERGY

Agreement continuing in effect safeguards and guarantee provisions of the agreement of October 8, 1958, as amended (TIAS 4416, 6945), for cooperation concerning civil uses of atomic energy.
Exchange of notes at Caracas February 18, 1981.
Entered into force February 18, 1981.
33 UST 1111; TIAS 10097; 1281 UNTS 3

Maritime boundary treaty.
Signed at Caracas March 28, 1978.
Entered into force November 24, 1980.
32 UST 3100; TIAS 9890

CLAIMS & DISPUTE RESOLUTION

Treaty for the advancement of peace.
Signed at Caracas March 21, 1914.
Entered into force February 12, 1921.
42 Stat. 1920; TS 652; 12 Bevans 1122

CULTURAL EXCHANGES, PROPERTY & COOPERATION

Agreement relating to the establishment of a Peace Corps program in Venezuela.
Exchange of notes at Caracas April 14 and May 28, 1962.
Entered into force May 28, 1962.
13 UST 1326; TIAS 5089; 458 UNTS 249

Agreement on the development and facilitation of tourism.
Signed at New York September 27, 1989.
Entered into force September 27, 1989.
TIAS 12402

DEFENSE

Agreement for the appointment of United States naval officers and personnel to constitute a naval mission to Venezuela.
Signed at Washington August 23, 1950.
Entered into force August 23, 1950.
1 UST 573; TIAS 2104; 92 UNTS 341
Extension and Amendment:
March 31 and April 29, 1959 (10 UST 2120; TIAS 4382; 366 UNTS 392)

Agreement for appointment of an Army mission to Venezuela.
Signed at Washington August 10, 1951.
Entered into force August 10, 1951.
2 UST 1570; TIAS 2299; 140 UNTS 345
Extension and Amendment:
March 31 and April 29, 1959 (10 UST 2117; TIAS 4381; 366 UNTS 405)

Agreement relating to an Air Force mission to Venezuela.
Signed at Washington January 16, 1953.
Entered into force January 16, 1953.
4 UST 97; TIAS 2766; 199 UNTS 287
Extension and Amendment:
March 31 and April 29, 1959 (10 UST 2114; TIAS 4380; 361 UNTS 326)

Agreement providing for a joint program of aerial photography in Venezuela.
Exchange of notes at Caracas August 23 and September 24, 1957.
Entered into force September 24, 1957.
8 UST 1614; TIAS 3915; 293 UNTS 307

Agreement relating to the deposit by Venezuela of ten percent of the value of grant military assistance furnished by the United States.
Exchange of notes at Caracas July 19, 1972.
Entered into force July 19, 1972; effective February 7, 1972.
23 UST 1312; TIAS 7411

Agreement relating to eligibility for United States military assistance and training pursuant to the International Security Assistance and Arms Export Control Act of 1976.
Exchange of notes at Caracas June 16 and 30, 1977.
Entered into force June 30, 1977.
29 UST 1884; TIAS 8907

General security of military information agreement.
Signed at Caracas July 15, 1983.
Entered into force July 15, 1983.
35 UST 1570; TIAS 10747; 2006 UNTS 363

Agreement governing cooperation in mapping, charting and geodesy.
Signed at Washington and Caracas June 18 and November 26, 1985.
Entered into force November 26, 1985.
TIAS 11209

Agreement regarding grants under the Foreign Assistance Act of 1961, as amended, and the furnishing of defense articles, related training and other defense services from the United States to Venezuela.
Exchange of letters at Caracas February 26 and 27, 1996.
Entered into force February 27, 1996.
TIAS 12729; 2473 UNTS 297

Basic exchange and cooperative agreement for topographic mapping, nautical and aeronautical charting and information, geodesy and geophysics, digital data and related mapping, charting and geodesy materials.
Signed at Fairfax March 20, 1996.
Entered into force March 20, 1996.
NP

DIPLOMATIC & CONSULAR RELATIONS

Agreement relating to duty-free entry privileges for non-diplomatic personnel.
Exchange of notes at Caracas April 7 and 17, 1959.
Entered into force April 17, 1959.
10 UST 1715; TIAS 4323; 358 UNTS 83

EMPLOYMENT

Agreement concerning employment of dependents of official government employees.
Exchange of notes at Caracas July 18 and 29, 1988.
Entered into force July 29, 1988, except with respect to dependents of employees of permanent missions to international organizations.
TIAS

FINANCE

Agreement relating to investment guaranties.
Exchange of notes at Caracas November 26 and 29, 1962.
Entered into force November 29, 1962.
14 UST 374; TIAS 5326; 474 UNTS 107

Swap agreement between the United States Treasury and the Central Bank of Venezuela/Government of Venezuela, with related letter.
Signed at Washington and Caracas March 10, 1989.
Entered into force March 10, 1989.
TIAS

Swap agreement among the United States Treasury and the Central Bank of Venezuela/Government of Venezuela, with memorandum of understanding.
Signed at Washington and Caracas March 16, 1990.
Entered into force March 16, 1990.
TIAS

Investment incentive agreement.
Signed at Washington June 22, 1990.
Entered into force June 22, 1990.
TIAS 12098

Agreement supplementing the investment incentive agreement of June 22, 1990, relating to the Export-Import Bank.
Signed at Washington April 22, 1992.
Entered into force April 22, 1992.
TIAS 12098

FOREIGN ASSISTANCE

Agreement relating to grants to Venezuelan nationals to facilitate their training in the United States.
Exchange of notes at Caracas May 23 and June 7, 1951.
Entered into force June 7, 1951.
2 UST 1302; TIAS 2280; 141 UNTS 273

Amendment:
December 20, 1951, and January 8 and April 8, 1952 (3 UST 4787; TIAS 2648; 205 UNTS 331)

General agreement on technical cooperation.
Exchange of notes at Caracas September 29, 1952.
Entered into force September 29, 1952.
3 UST 5096; TIAS 2700; 186 UNTS 23

LAW ENFORCEMENT

Treaty of extradition, and additional article.
Signed at Caracas January 19 and 21, 1922.
Entered into force April 14, 1923.
43 Stat. 1698; TS 675; 12 Bevans 1128; 49 LNTS 435

Agreement concerning the establishment and operation of a regional office of the Drug Enforcement Administration in Caracas.
Exchange of notes at Caracas August 26, 1974.
Entered into force August 26, 1974.
25 UST 2440; TIAS 7925

Agreement on procedures for mutual assistance in connection with the Boeing Company matter.
Signed at Washington May 31, 1977.
Entered into force May 31, 1977.
28 UST 5219; TIAS 8623

Related Agreement:
December 6 and 8, 1978 (30 UST 2254; TIAS 9333; 1171 UNTS 105)

Memorandum of understanding concerning cooperation in the narcotics field.
Signed at Caracas March 28, 1978.
Entered into force March 28, 1978.
30 UST 1012; TIAS 9235; 1152 UNTS 203

Agreement regarding cooperation in the prevention and control of money laundering arising from illicit trafficking in narcotic drugs and psychotropic substances, with attachment.
Signed at Washington November 5, 1990.
Entered into force January 1, 1991.
TIAS 12422

Treaty on mutual legal assistance in criminal matters.
Signed at Caracas October 12, 1997.
Entered into force March 1, 2004.
TIAS 12941

MARITIME MATTERS

Agreement for exemption of merchant vessels from requirements of admeasurement by port authorities.
Signed at Caracas February 21, 1957.
Entered into force February 21, 1957.
8 UST 289; TIAS 3774; 279 UNTS 199

Agreement to suppress illicit traffic in narcotic drugs and psychotropic substances by sea.
Signed at Caracas November 9, 1991.
Entered into force November 9, 1991.
TIAS 11827; 2211 UNTS 387

Protocol to the agreement of November 9, 1991 to suppress illicit traffic in narcotic drugs and psychotropic substances by sea.
Signed at Caracas July 23, 1997.
Entered into force July 23, 1997.
TIAS 12876

POSTAL MATTERS

International express mail agreement.
Signed at Washington and Caracas August 10 and 15, 1984.
Entered into force December 1, 1984.
TIAS 11008; 2022 UNTS 89

SCIENTIFIC & TECHNICAL COOPERATION

Memorandum of understanding concerning scientific and technical cooperation in the earth and mapping sciences.
Signed at Caracas January 15, 1992.
Entered into force January 15, 1992.
TIAS 11842

TAXATION

Agreement for the avoidance of double taxation with respect to shipping and air transport.
Signed at Caracas December 29, 1987.
Entered into force August 10, 1988; effective with respect to taxable years beginning on or before January 1, 1987.
TIAS 11556; 2185 UNTS 353

Convention for the avoidance of double taxation and the prevention of fiscal evasion with respect to taxes on income and capital, with protocol.
Signed at Caracas January 25, 1999.
Entered into force December 30, 1999.
TIAS 13020

TELECOMMUNICATION

Arrangement for radio communications between amateur stations on behalf of third parties.
Exchange of notes at Caracas November 12, 1959.
Entered into force December 12, 1959.
10 UST 3019; TIAS 4394; 367 UNTS 81

Agreement relating to the reciprocal granting of authorizations to permit licensed amateur radio operators of either country to operate their stations in the other country.
Exchange of notes at Caracas September 18, 1967.
Entered into force October 3, 1967.
18 UST 2499; TIAS 6348; 693 UNTS 109

TRADE & INVESTMENT

Treaty of peace, friendship, navigation and commerce.*
Signed at Caracas January 20, 1836.
Entered into force May 31, 1836.
8 Stat. 466; TS 366; 12 Bevans 1038

Note

* Articles with respect to commerce and navigation terminated January 3, 1851.

Convention facilitating the work of traveling salesmen.
Signed at Caracas July 3, 1919.
Entered into force August 18, 1920.
41 Stat. 1719; TS 648; 12 Bevans 1125

Reciprocal trade agreement.*
Signed at Caracas November 6, 1939.
Entered into force provisionally December 16, 1939; definitively December 14, 1940.
54 Stat. 2375; EAS 180; 12 Bevans 1141; 203 LNTS 273

Supplementary trade agreement.*
Signed at Caracas August 28, 1952.
Entered into force October 11, 1952.
3 UST 4195; TIAS 2565; 178 UNTS 51

Note:

* Terminated in part June 30, 1972, by exchange of notes dated June 26, 1972.

Agreement relating to effectiveness of the United States revised tariff schedules to the trade agreement of November 6, 1939, as supplemented.*
Exchange of notes at Caracas July 15 and 23, 1963.
Entered into force July 23, 1963.
14 UST 1901; TIAS 5502; 505 UNTS 316

Note:

* Terminated in part June 30, 1972, by exchange of notes dated June 26, 1972.

Agreement terminating in part the reciprocal trade agreement of November 6, 1939, as supplemented.
Exchange of notes at Caracas June 26, 1972.
Entered into force June 26, 1972.
23 UST 1213; TIAS 7387

TRANSPORTATION

Air transport agreement, with exchange of notes.
Signed at Caracas August 14, 1953.
Entered into force August 22, 1953.
4 UST 1493; TIAS 2813; 213 UNTS 99

Amendments:

February 11, 1972 (24 UST 271; TIAS 7549)
September 22, 1976 (27 UST 4111; TIAS 8433)
July 19 and October 10, 1990 (TIAS 11751; 2204 UNTS 214)

Memorandum of agreement concerning the provision of technical assistance to develop and modernize Venezuela's civil aviation infrastructure, with annexes.
Signed at Washington and Caracas February 1 and 4, 1977.
Entered into force February 4, 1977.
29 UST 5300; TIAS 9110

VIETNAM, REPUBLIC OF

NOTE: The agreements listed below were in force between the United States and the Republic of Viet Nam (South Viet Nam). The status of these agreements is under review.

CLAIMS & DISPUTE RESOLUTION

Agreement relating to mutual waiver of government claims for damages to government property and for injury or death of members of armed services.
Exchange of notes at Saigon February 9, 1965.
Entered into force February 9, 1965.
16 UST 140; TIAS 5773; 542 UNTS 175

DEFENSE

Agreement relating to the assurances required by the Mutual Security Act of 1951.
Exchange of notes at Saigon December 18, 1951, January 3, 1952, January 16, 1952, and January 19, 1952.
Entered into force January 3, 1952.
3 UST 4672; TIAS 2623; 205 UNTS 127

Agreement relating to the disposition of equipment and materials furnished by the United States found surplus to the needs of the Vietnamese armed forces.
Exchange of notes at Saigon March 1 and May 10, 1955.
Entered into force May 10, 1955.
7 UST 837; TIAS 3563; 273 UNTS 157

Agreement relating to the transfer of scrap to Viet Nam as supplementary military assistance.
Exchange of notes at Saigon November 8 and December 14, 1972.
Entered into force December 14, 1972.
23 UST 4263; TIAS 7534
Amendment:
September 3 and October 14, 1974 (25 UST 2906; TIAS 7953)

FINANCE

Agreement relating to investment guaranties under section 413 (b)(4) of the Mutual Security Act of 1954, as amended.
Exchange of notes at Washington November 5, 1957.
Entered into force November 5, 1957.
8 UST 1869; TIAS 3932; 300 UNTS 23
Amendment:
August 8, 1963 (14 UST 1210; TIAS 5419; 488 UNTS 270)

Agreement modifying the agreement of November 5, 1957, as amended, relating to investment guaranties.
Exchange of notes at Saigon December 16, 1969, and February 12, 1970.
Entered into force February 12, 1970.
21 UST 1148; TIAS 6869; 745 UNTS 312

FOREIGN ASSISTANCE

Economic cooperation agreement, with exchange of notes.
Signed at Saigon September 7, 1951.
Entered into force September 7, 1951.
2 UST 2205; TIAS 2346; 174 UNTS 165
Amendment:
June 7, 1962 (13 UST 1279; TIAS 5076; 458 UNTS 300)

Agreement relating to duty-free entry and defrayment of inland transportation charges on relief supplies and packages.
Exchange of notes at Saigon August 20 and 26, 1954.
Entered into force August 26, 1954.
5 UST 2531; TIAS 3115; 234 UNTS 111

Agreement providing for additional direct economic assistance pursuant to the economic cooperation agreement of September 7, 1951.
Exchange of notes at Saigon February 21 and March 7, 1955.
Entered into force March 7, 1955; operative January 1, 1955.
7 UST 2507; TIAS 3640; 277 UNTS 285

Agreement providing for an informational media guaranty program pursuant to Section 1011 of the United States Information and Educational Exchange Act of 1948, as amended.
Exchange of notes at Saigon October 11 and November 3, 1955.
Entered into force November 3, 1955.
6 UST 3940; TIAS 3402; 239 UNTS 195

INTELLECTUAL PROPERTY

Declaration respecting the rights of nationals concerning trademark protection, with related note.
Exchange of notes at Washington November 3, 1953, and October 25, 1954; related note dated November 22, 1954.
Entered into force October 25, 1954.
5 UST 2400; TIAS 3100; 235 UNTS 11

PUBLICATIONS

Agreement relating to the exchange of official publications.
Exchange of notes at Saigon April 4, 1961.
Entered into force April 4, 1961.
12 UST 310; TIAS 4717; 405 UNTS 77

TAXATION

Agreement regarding income tax administration.
Exchange of notes at Saigon March 31 and May 3, 1967.
Entered into force May 3, 1967.
18 UST 546; TIAS 6262; 685 UNTS 207

TELECOMMUNICATION

Agreement relating to television broadcasting in Viet Nam.
Exchange of notes at Saigon January 3, 1966.
Entered into force January 3, 1966.
17 UST 44; TIAS 5954; 579 UNTS 99

TRADE & INVESTMENT

Treaty of amity and economic relations.
Signed at Saigon April 3, 1961.
Entered into force November 30, 1961.
12 UST 1703; TIAS 4890; 424 UNTS 137

VIETNAM, SOCIALIST REPUBLIC OF

The United States established diplomatic relations with the Socialist Republic of Vietnam on July 12, 1995.

ATOMIC ENERGY

Arrangement for the exchange of technical information and cooperation in nuclear safety matters, with addenda.
Signed at Washington June 25, 2008.
Entered into force June 25, 2008.
TIAS 08-625.1

Arrangement for the exchange of technical information and cooperation in nuclear safety matters, with addenda and annex.
Signed at Washington May 9, 2013.
Entered into force May 9, 2013.
TIAS 13-509

Agreement for cooperation concerning peaceful uses of nuclear energy, with agreed minute.
Signed at Hanoi May 6, 2014.
Entered into force October 3, 2014.
TIAS 14-1003

CLAIMS & DISPUTE RESOLUTION

Agreement concerning the settlement of certain property claims.
Signed at Hanoi January 28, 1995.
Entered into force January 28, 1995.
TIAS 12602

CULTURAL EXCHANGES, PROPERTY & COOPERATION

Framework agreement concerning the program of the Peace Corps in Viet Nam.
Signed at Hanoi May 24, 2016.
Entered into force May 24, 2016.
TIAS 16-524

DEFENSE

Agreement concerning the provision of equipment, training and related services under the United States International Military Education and Training (IMET) Program.
Exchange of notes at Hanoi June 17, 2005.
Entered into force June 17, 2005.
NP

DIPLOMATIC & CONSULAR AFFAIRS

Agreement concerning the opening of a Vietnam Consulate General in Houston, Texas.
Effected by exchange of notes at Hanoi July 29 and 31, 2009.
Entered into force July 31, 2009.
TIAS 09-731

FINANCE

Agreement regarding the consolidation and rescheduling of certain debts owed to, guaranteed by, or insured by the United States Government and the Agency for International Development, with annexes.
Signed at Hanoi April 7, 1997.
Entered into force June 23, 1997.
NP

Agreement regarding the operations of the Overseas Private Investment Corporation in Vietnam.
Signed at Washington and Hanoi March 19 and 26, 1998.
Entered into force March 26, 1998.
TIAS 12936.

Project incentive agreement regarding the operations of the Export-Import Bank of the United States in Vietnam.
Signed at Hanoi December 9, 1999.
Entered into force December 9, 1999.
TIAS 13076

FOREIGN ASSISTANCE

Agreement for economic and technical cooperation.
Signed at Washington June 22, 2005.
Entered into force July 27, 2005.
TIAS 05-727.1

INTELLECTUAL PROPERTY

Agreement on the establishment of copyright relations.
Signed at Hanoi June 27, 1997.
Entered into force December 23, 1998.
TIAS 13015
Amendment:
December 23, 1998 (TIAS 13015)

MARITIME MATTERS

Agreement on maritime transport.
Signed at Washington March 15, 2007.
Entered into force July 15, 2007.
TIAS 07-715

MIGRATION & REFUGEES

Agreement on the implementation of the special released reeducation center detainees resettlement program, with annex.
Exchange of letters at Washington and Hanoi August 18 and 28, 1989.
Entered into force August 28, 1989.
TIAS

Agreement on the acceptance of the return of Vietnamese citizens, with annexes.
Signed at Hanoi January 22, 2008.
Entered into force March 22, 2008.
TIAS 08-322

POSTAL MATTERS

International express mail agreement, with detailed regulations.
Signed at Seoul September 13, 1994.
Entered into force December 1, 1994.
NP

PROPERTY

Agreement concerning the transfer of diplomatic properties, with appendices and amendment.
Signed at Hanoi January 28, 1995.
Entered into force January 28, 1995.
TIAS

SCIENTIFIC & TECHNICAL COOPERATION

Agreement on scientific and technological cooperation, with annexes.
Signed at Hanoi November 17, 2000.
Entered into force March 26, 2001.
TIAS 13128

Memorandum of understanding concerning scientific and technical cooperation in earth sciences and effective management of natural resources in the context of climate change.
Signed at Hanoi December 10, 2010.
Entered into force December 10, 2010.
TIAS 10-1210

Memorandum of understanding concerning scientific and technical cooperation in the earth sciences.
Signed at Reston and Vietnam November 10 and December 30, 2014.
Entered into force December 30, 2014.
TIAS 14-1230

TAXATION

Agreement to improve international tax compliance and to implement the Foreign Account Tax Compliance Act.
Signed at Hanoi April 1, 2016.
Entered into force July 7, 2016.
TIAS 16-707

TRADE & INVESTMENT

Agreement on trade relations, with annexes, schedules and exchange of letters.
Signed at Washington July 13, 2000.
Entered into force December 10, 2001.
TIAS

Trade and investment framework agreement, with annex.
Signed at Washington June 21, 2007.
Entered into force June 21, 2007.
TIAS

TRANSPORTATION

Air Transport agreement, with annexes.
Signed at Washington December 4, 2003.
Entered into force January 14, 2004.
TIAS 04-114

Amendment:
May 18, 2010 (TIAS 04-114)
December 13, 2012 (TIAS 04-114)

Memorandum of agreement concerning technical assistance in developing, modernizing, operating, or maintaining Vietnam's civil aviation infrastructure.
Signed at Washington and Hanoi May 25 and July 19, 2011.
Entered into force July 19, 2011.
NP

W

WORLD CUSTOMS ORGANIZATION

TAXATION

Tax reimbursement agreement, with annex.
Signed at Brussels January 26, 1990.
Entered into force January 26, 1990.
TIAS 11711; 2208 UNTS 3

WORLD FOOD PROGRAM

FOREIGN ASSISTANCE

AGENCY FOR INTERNATIONAL DEVELOPMENT

Agreement relating to the transfer of agricultural commodities to the World Food Program for its relief efforts in Ethiopia.
Signed May 9, 2011.
Entered into force May 9, 2011.
NP

Agreement relating to the transfer of agricultural commodities to the World Food Program for its relief efforts in Chad.
Signed August 11, 2011.
Entered into force August 11, 2011.
NP

Agreement to provide support for an emergency food security program in Afghanistan.
Signed September 30, 2011.
Entered into force September 30, 2011.
NP

Transfer authorization, World Food Program: Emergency Operation in Sudan, with attachment.
Signed September 9, 2014.
Entered into force September 9, 2014.
NP
Amendment:
March 11 and 12, 2015

WORLD HEALTH ORGANIZATION

HEALTH & MEDICAL COOPERATION

Memorandum of understanding regarding U.S. Environmental Protection Agency collaboration in the international program on chemical safety.
Signed at Washington and Geneva January 19 and March 19, 1981.
Entered into force March 19, 1981.
TIAS

WORLD INTELLECTUAL PROPERTY ORGANIZATION

TAXATION

Tax reimbursement agreement, with annex.
Signed at Geneva December 5, 1988.
Entered into force December 5, 1988.
TIAS 11625; 2191 UNTS 159

WORLD METEOROLOGICAL ORGANIZATION

TAXATION

Agreement relating to a procedure for United States income tax reimbursement, with annex.
Signed at Geneva January 23, 1987.
Entered into force January 23, 1987.
TIAS 11293; 2174 UNTS 207

WORLD TRADE ORGANIZATION

TAXATION

Tax reimbursement agreement, with annex.
Signed at Geneva December 22, 2000.
Entered into force December 22, 2000.
TIAS 13133

YEMEN

The People's Democratic Republic of Yemen and the Yemen Arab Republic merged into a single sovereign State on May 22, 1990, called the Republic of Yemen. In a note dated May 19, 1990, to the Secretary-General of the United Nations, it was stated that

"All treaties and agreements concluded between either the Yemen Arab Republic or the People's Democratic Republic of Yemen and other States and international organizations in accordance with international law which are in force on May 22, 1990 will remain in effect, and international relations existing on May 22, 1990 between the People's Democratic Republic of Yemen and the Yemen Arab Republic and other States will continue."

CULTURAL EXCHANGES, PROPERTY & COOPERATION

Agreement relating to the establishment of a Peace Corps program in the Yemen Arab Republic.
Exchange of notes at Sanaa September 30, 1972, and January 29, 1973.
Entered into force January 29, 1973.
24 UST 853; TIAS 7588

DEFENSE

Agreement concerning the provision of training related to defense articles under the United States International Military Education and Training (IMET) Program.
Exchange of notes at Sanaa September 9, 1986, and May 19, 1987.
Entered into force May 19, 1987.
TIAS 12015

Agreement regarding grants under the Foreign Assistance Act of 1961, as amended, and the furnishing of defense articles, related training and other defense services from the United States to Yemen.
Exchange of notes at Sanaa June 5 and July 20, 1999.
Entered into force July 20, 1999.
NP

FINANCE

Agreement relating to investment guaranties.
Exchange of notes at Sanaa October 22 and December 4, 1972.
Entered into force December 4, 1972.
24 UST 845; TIAS 7586

Agreement regarding the consolidation and rescheduling of certain debts owed to, guaranteed by, or insured by the United States Government and its agencies, with annexes.
Signed at Sanaa April 8, 1997.
Entered into force May 22, 1997.
NP

Agreement regarding consolidation and rescheduling of certain debts owed to, guaranteed by, or insured by the United States Government and its agency, with annexes.
Signed at Sanaa May 19, 1998.
Entered into force August 10, 1998.
NP

Agreement regarding the reduction and reorganization of certain debts owed to, guaranteed by, or insured by the United States Government, with annexes.
Signed at Sanaa July 31, 2002.
Entered into force October 8, 2002.
NP

FOREIGN ASSISTANCE

Economic, technical, and related assistance agreement, with related letter.
Signed at Sanaa April 20, 1974.
Entered into force April 20, 1974.
25 UST 715; TIAS 7820

AGENCY FOR INTERNATIONAL DEVELOPMENT

Assistance agreement, with attachment.
Signed September 16, 2009.
Entered into force September 16, 2009.
NP

Amendments:
September 15, 2010 (NP)
April 12, 2012 (NP)
September 30, 2012 (NP)
September 23, 2014 (NP)

POSTAL MATTERS

International express mail agreement, with detailed regulations.
Signed at Sanaa and Washington June 17 and July 23, 1992.
Entered into force September 21, 1992.
TIAS 11873

TRADE & INVESTMENT

Agreement relating to friendship and commerce.
Exchange of notes at Sanaa May 4, 1946.
Entered into force May 4, 1946.
60 Stat. 1782; TIAS 1535; 12 Bevans 1223; 4 UNTS 165

UN & RELATED ORGANIZATIONS

Arrangement regarding the surrender of persons to international tribunals.
Exchange of notes at Washington and Sanaa December 10 and 17, 2003.
Entered into force December 17, 2003.
TIAS

YUGOSLAVIA

Yugoslavia has dissolved. For agreements prior to dissolution, see below. Subsequent agreements are listed under individual country headings.

Section 2 of Treaties in Force covers multi-lateral treaties and agreements. Where a multilateral treaty action was taken prior to dissolution, "Yugoslavia" is retained; where a successor state has taken action it is listed separately.

ATOMIC ENERGY

Agreement providing for a grant to assist in the acquisition of certain nuclear research and training equipment and materials.
Exchange of notes at Belgrade April 19, 1961.
Entered into force April 19, 1961.
12 UST 398; TIAS 4731; 409 UNTS 163

CLAIMS & DISPUTE RESOLUTION

Treaty of arbitration.
Signed at Washington January 21, 1929.
Entered into force June 22, 1929.
46 Stat. 2293; TS 790; 12 Bevans 1253; 93 LNTS 307

Treaty of conciliation.
Signed at Washington January 21, 1929.
Entered into force June 22, 1929.
46 Stat. 2297; TS 791; 12 Bevans 1256; 93 LNTS 301

Agreement relating to the settlement of pecuniary claims against Yugoslavia, and accompanying aide memoire and notes.
Signed at Washington July 19, 1948.
Entered into force July 19, 1948.
62 Stat. 2658; TIAS 1803; 12 Bevans 1277; 89 UNTS 43

CONSULAR AFFAIRS

Agreement relating to the reduction of passport visa fees for nonimmigrants.*
Exchange of notes at Belgrade December 24 and 29, 1925.
Operative February 1, 1926.
12 Bevans 1243

Understanding relating to entry and exit visas for American citizens visiting Yugoslavia.
Exchange of notes at Belgrade March 23 and 25, 1950.
Entered into force March 25, 1950; operative April 1, 1950.
1 UST 471; TIAS 2087; 98 UNTS 195

Agreement for the abolition of all nonimmigrant visa fees.*
Exchange of notes at Belgrade December 30, 1963, March 27 and April 4, 1964.
Entered into force April 15, 1964.
15 UST 355; TIAS 5564; 526 UNTS 47

Note:

* The status of this agreement is under review.

CULTURAL EXCHANGES, PROPERTY & COOPERATION

Memorandum of understanding relating to the establishment, maintenance, and operation of American reading rooms in Yugoslavia.
Signed at Belgrade June 14, 1961.
Entered into force provisionally June 14, 1961; definitively December 28, 1961.
20 UST 2826; TIAS 6753; 723 UNTS 133

Implementing Agreements:

Ljubljana: June 5, 1970 (22 UST 398; TIAS 7073; 791 UNTS 293)
Skopje: April 13, 1972 (24 UST 457; TIAS 7564)
Sarajevo: July 18, 1973 (24 UST 2316; TIAS 7757)
Titograd: June 25, 1979 (31 UST 301; TIAS 9612; 1202 UNTS 173)

Agreement on cooperation in the field of tourism.
Signed at Washington February 2, 1984.
Entered into force June 18, 1984.
35 UST 4517; TIAS 10954; 2019 UNTS 517

DEFENSE

Memorandum of understanding relating to offshore procurement with standard contract and related notes.
Signed at Belgrade October 18, 1954.
Entered into force October 18, 1954.
7 UST 849; TIAS 3567; 273 UNTS 163

Agreement relating to the termination of military assistance furnished on a grant basis by the United States to Yugoslavia and amending the memorandum of understanding of October 18, 1954 relating to offshore procurement.
Exchange of notes at Belgrade August 25, 1959.
Entered into force August 25, 1959.
10 UST 1468; TIAS 4300; 357 UNTS 77

Agreement relating to the purchase by Yugoslavia of military equipment, materials, and services.
Exchange of notes at Belgrade August 25, 1959.
Entered into force August 25, 1959.
10 UST 1474; TIAS 4301; 357 UNTS 87

DIPLOMATIC & CONSULAR RELATIONS

Consular convention.
Signed at Belgrade October 2 and 14, 1881.
Entered into force November 15, 1882.
22 Stat. 968; TS 320; 12 Bevans 1233

Arrangement providing for the taking of testimony by consular officers.
Exchange of notes at Belgrade October 17 and 24, 1938.
Entered into force October 24, 1938.
12 Bevans 1261

Agreement relating to reciprocal customs privileges for consular officers.
Exchange of notes at Washington May 21, 1956.
Entered into force July 30, 1956.
7 UST 2234; TIAS 3622; 281 UNTS 93

EDUCATION

Agreement for financing certain educational exchange programs.
Signed at Belgrade November 9, 1964.
Entered into force November 9, 1964.
15 UST 2081; TIAS 5689; 533 UNTS 39

Amendment:
January 20, 1984 (TIAS 10980)

FINANCE

Agreement relating to the funding of the indebtedness of Yugoslavia to the United States.
Signed at Washington May 3, 1926.
Operative June 15, 1925.
12 Bevans 1246; Treasury Department print

Counterpart release agreement, with annex.
Signed at Belgrade April 16, 1954.
Entered into force April 16, 1954.
5 UST 2853; TIAS 3142; 237 UNTS 77

Agreement providing for certain economic assistance on a loan basis pursuant to section 402 of the Mutual Security Act of 1954.
Exchange of notes at Belgrade January 19, 1956.
Entered into force January 19, 1956.
7 UST 149; TIAS 3487; 240 UNTS 121

Swap agreement between the U.S. Treasury and the Central Bank of the Federated Republics of Yugoslavia, with related letter.
Signed at Washington and Belgrade June 10, 1988.
Entered into force June 10, 1988.
TIAS

FOREIGN ASSISTANCE

Agreement governing the furnishing of assistance under the Yugoslav Emergency Relief Assistance Act of 1950.
Signed at Belgrade January 6, 1951.
Entered into force January 6, 1951.
2 UST 13; TIAS 2174; 122 UNTS 137

Economic cooperation agreement.
Signed at Belgrade January 8, 1952.
Entered into force January 8, 1952.
3 UST 1; TIAS 2384; 152 UNTS 61

Amendment:
February 25 and March 10, 1953 (4 UST 439; TIAS 2791; 207 UNTS 360)

Agreement for duty-free entry and defrayment of inland transportation and related costs of relief supplies and packages, and note of December 3, 1952.
Signed at Belgrade December 3, 1952.
Entered into force December 3, 1952.
3 UST 5318; TIAS 2735; 185 UNTS 183

LAW ENFORCEMENT

Extradition treaty.
Signed at Belgrade October 25, 1901.
Entered into force June 12, 1902.
32 Stat. 1890; TS 406; 12 Bevans 1238

Arrangement for the direct exchange of certain information regarding traffic in narcotic drugs.
Exchange of notes at Belgrade February 17, 1928, and May 8, 1930.
Entered into force May 8, 1930.
12 Bevans 1259

Agreement regarding mutual assistance between customs administrations.
Signed at Belgrade April 11, 1990.
Entered into force November 18, 1990.
TIAS 12074

MARITIME MATTERS

Agreement concerning the reciprocal recognition of tonnage certificates.
Exchange of notes at Washington June 12 and 16, 1958.
Entered into force June 16, 1958.
9 UST 709; TIAS 4047; 317 UNTS 31

POSTAL MATTERS

Agreement concerning the exchange of parcel post and regulations of execution.
Signed at Belgrade August 14 and at Washington September 1, 1950.
Entered into force January 1, 1950.
2 UST 2079; TIAS 2336; 137 UNTS 131

International express mail agreement, with detailed regulations.
Signed at Belgrade and Washington January 22 and March 1, 1990.
Entered into force March 30, 1990.
TIAS 11713

PROPERTY

Preliminary agreement regarding principles applying to mutual aid in the prosecution of the war against aggression.
Signed at Washington July 24, 1942.
Entered into force July 24, 1942.
56 Stat. 1570; EAS 263; 12 Bevans 1263; 34 UNTS 361

Agreement regarding settlement for lend-lease, military relief, and claims.
Signed at Washington July 19, 1948.
Entered into force July 19, 1948.
62 Stat. 2133; TIAS 1779; 12 Bevans 1273; 34 UNTS 195

PUBLICATIONS

Agreement relating to the exchange of official publications.
Exchange of letters at Belgrade October 4 and 9, 1950.
Entered into force October 9, 1950.
TIAS 2208; 2 UST 573; 133 UNTS 25

TAXATION

Agreement relating to relief from taxation of United States Government expenditures in Yugoslavia for facilities, equipment, materials, or services.
Exchange of letters at Belgrade July 23, 1953.
Entered into force July 23, 1953.
4 UST 2208; TIAS 2871; 221 UNTS 365

TELECOMMUNICATION

Agreement relating to the reciprocal granting of authorization to permit licensed amateur radio operators who are citizens of either country to operate their stations in the other country.
Exchange of notes at Belgrade October 31 and November 11, 1980.
Entered into force November 11, 1980.
32 UST 4173; TIAS 9936; 1267 UNTS 377

TRADE & INVESTMENT

Treaty of commerce.
Signed at Belgrade October 2 and 14, 1881.
Entered into force November 15, 1882.
22 Stat. 963; TS 319; 12 Bevans 1227

TRANSPORTATION

Nonscheduled air services agreement. With annexes, and protocol.
Signed at Belgrade September 27, 1973.
Entered into force April 16, 1974
TIAS 7819

Amendment:
May 14, 1976 (TIAS 8305)
December 15, 1977 (TIAS 9460)

Air transport agreement. With memorandum of understating .
Signed at Washington December 15,1977.
Entered into force May 15, 1979.
TIAS 9364

Nonscheduled air services agreement. With annexes, and protocol.
Exchange of notes at Washington May 17, 1976 and June 30, 1977
Entered into force June 30,1977
TIAS 8972

Agreement amending the nonscheduled air services agreement of September 27, 1973, as amended, the air transport agreement of December 15, 1977 and extending the memoranda of understanding (March 17 and May 19, 1982), as amended and extended.
Effected by exchange of notes at Belgrade January 15 and July 6, 1987.
Entered into force provisionally July 6, 1987.
Entered into force definitively January 11, 1988.
TIAS 11547

ZAMBIA

On October 24, 1964, Zambia (former Northern Rhodesia) became an independent state. In a note dated September 1, 1965, to the Secretary General of the United Nations, the Minister of Foreign Affairs of Zambia made a Declaration reading in part as follows:

I have the honour to inform you that the Government of Zambia, conscious of the desirability of maintaining existing legal relationships, and conscious of its obligations under international law to honour its treaty commitments acknowledges that many treaty rights and obligations of the Government of the United Kingdom in respect of Northern Rhodesia were succeeded to by Zambia upon independence by virtue of customary international law.

Since, however, it is likely that in virtue of customary international law certain treaties may have lapsed at the date of independence of Zambia, it seems essential that each treaty should be subjected to legal examination. It is proposed after this examination has been completed, to indicate which, if any, of the treaties which may have lapsed by customary international law the Government of Zambia wishes to treat as having lapsed.

The question of Zambia's succession to treaties is complicated by legal questions arising from the entrustment of external affairs powers to the former Federation of Rhodesia and Nyasaland. Until these questions have been resolved it will remain unclear to what extent Zambia remains affected by the treaties contracted by the former Federation.

It is desired that it be presumed that each treaty has been legally succeeded to by Zambia and that action be based on this presumption until a decision is reached that it should be regarded as having lapsed. Should the Government of Zambia be of the opinion that it has legally succeeded to a treaty, and wishes to terminate the operation of the treaty, it will in due course give notice of termination in the terms thereof.

DEFENSE

Agreement relating to the assurances required under the Mutual Security Act of 1951.
Exchange of notes at London January 8, 1952.
Entered into force January 8, 1952.
3 UST 4665; TIAS 2622; 126 UNTS 307

Agreement concerning the provision of training related to defense articles under the United States International Military, Education and Training (IMET) Program.
Exchange of notes at Lusaka March 9, 1992.
Entered into force March 9, 1992.
NP

Agreement concerning the provision of equipment, training and related services under the United States International Military Education and Training (IMET) Program.
Exchange of notes at Lusaka February 19, 2004, and February 15, 2005.
Entered into force February 15, 2005.
NP

Agreement concerning the provision of defense articles, related training and other defense services pursuant to the International Military Education and Training (IMET) Program, the Africa Military Education Program (AMEP), and Peacekeeping Operations Under Section 551 of the Foreign Assistance Act.
Exchange of notes at Lusaka August 25, 2014 and February 11, 2015.
Entered into force February 11, 2015.
NP

DIPLOMATIC & CONSULAR RELATIONS

Consular convention between the United States and the United Kingdom.
Signed at Washington June 6, 1951.
Entered into force September 7, 1952.
3 UST 3426; TIAS 2494; 165 UNTS 121

EMPLOYMENT

Agreement relating to the employment of dependents of official government employees.
Exchange of notes at Lusaka June 26, 1989, and January 4, 1990.
Entered into force January 4, 1990.
TIAS

FINANCE

Agreement regarding the consolidation and rescheduling of certain debts owed to, or guaranteed by the United States Government and its agencies, with annexes.
Signed at Lusaka December 19, 1983.
Entered into force February 10, 1984.
35 UST 4387; TIAS 10941

Agreement regarding the consolidation and rescheduling of certain debts owed to, guaranteed by or insured by the United States Government and its agencies, with annexes and implementing agreement.
Signed at Lusaka December 15, 1984.
Entered into force January 22, 1985.
TIAS 11002; 2022 UNTS 75

Agreement regarding the consolidation and rescheduling of certain debts owed to, guaranteed by or insured by the United States Government and its agencies.
Signed at Lusaka July 25, 1986.
Entered into force August 28, 1986.
NP

Agreement regarding the consolidation and rescheduling of certain debts owed to, guaranteed by or insured by the United States Government and its agencies, with annexes.
Signed at Lusaka September 14, 1990.
Entered into force November 5, 1990.
NP

Agreement regarding the consolidation and rescheduling or refinancing of certain debts owed to, guaranteed by or insured by the U.S. Government and its agencies, with annexes and addendum.
Signed at Lusaka March 23, 1993.
Entered into force August 11, 1993.
NP

Agreement regarding the consolidation, reduction, and rescheduling of certain debts owed to, guaranteed by, or insured by the United States Government and its agency, with annexes.
Signed at Lusaka September 26, 1997.
Entered into force December 3, 1997.
NP

Investment incentive agreement.
Signed at Lusaka June 23, 1999.
Entered into force July 2, 1999.
TIAS 13050

Agreement regarding the reduction, consolidation, and rescheduling of certain debts owed to, guaranteed by, or insured by the United States Government and its Agency, with annexes.
Signed at Lusaka November 19, 1999.
Entered into force February 23, 2000.
NP

Agreement regarding the consolidation and reduction of certain debts owed to, guaranteed by, or insured by the United States Government and its agencies, with annexes.
Signed at Lusaka November 3, 2003.
Entered into force December 17, 2003.
NP

Agreement regarding the reduction of certain debts owed to, guaranteed by, or insured by the United States Government and its agencies, with annexes.
Signed at Lusaka December 30, 2005.
Entered into force February 6, 2006.
NP

FOREIGN ASSISTANCE

Economic cooperation agreement between the United States and the United Kingdom.
Signed at London July 6, 1948.
Applicable to Zambia July 20, 1948.
62 Stat. 2596; TIAS 1795; 12 Bevans 874; 22 UNTS 263
Amendments:
January 3, 1950 (1 UST 184; TIAS 2036; 86 UNTS 304)
May 25, 1951 (2 UST 1292; TIAS 2277; 99 UNTS 308)
February 25, 1953 (4 UST 1528; TIAS 2815; 172 UNTS 332)

Agreement for technical cooperation in respect of the territories for the international relations of which the Government of the United Kingdom are responsible.
Signed at London July 13, 1951.
Applicable to Federation of Rhodesia and Nyasaland April 8, 1960.
2 UST 1307; TIAS 2281; 105 UNTS 71

Millennium Challenge Compact, with annexes.
Signed at Lusaka May 10, 2012.
Entered into force November 15, 2013.
TIAS 13-1115

AGENCY FOR INTERNATIONAL DEVELOPMENT

Development Cooperation Agreement.
Signed September 27, 2011.
Entered into force September 27, 2011.
NP

Implementing Letter amending the Development Cooperation Agreement of September 27,2011.
Signed September 25, 2012.
Entered into force September 25, 2012.
NP

INTELLECTUAL PROPERTY

Declaration by the United States and the United Kingdom affording reciprocal protection to trade-marks.
Signed at London October 24, 1877.
Entered into force October 24, 1877.
20 Stat. 703; TS 138; 12 Bevans 198

LAW ENFORCEMENT

Extradition treaty between the United States and the United Kingdom.
Signed at London December 22, 1931.
Entered into force June 24, 1935.
47 Stat. 2122; TS 849; 12 Bevans 482; 163 LNTS 59

POSTAL MATTERS

International express mail agreement, with detailed regulations.
Signed at Ndola and Washington April 25 and May 16, 1988.
Entered into force June 15, 1988.
TIAS 11589

PROPERTY

Convention between the United States and the United Kingdom relating to tenure and disposition of real and personal property.
Signed at Washington March 2, 1899.
Applicable to Zambia May 29, 1947.
31 Stat. 1939; TS 146; 12 Bevans 246

Supplementary convention relating to the tenure and disposition
of real and personal property of March 2, 1899.
Signed at Washington May 27, 1936.
Entered into force March 10, 1941.
55 Stat. 1101; TS 964; 5 Bevans 140; 203 LNTS 367

SCIENTIFIC & TECHNICAL COOPERATION

Memorandum of understanding concerning scientific and technical cooperation in the earth sciences, with annexes.
Signed at Reston and Lusaka September 9 and 23, 2002.
Entered into force September 23, 2002.
TIAS 02-923

TRANSPORTATION

Arrangement between the United States and the United Kingdom relating to pilot licenses to operate civil aircraft.
Exchange of notes at Washington March 28 and April 5, 1935.
Entered into force May 5, 1935.
49 Stat. 3731; EAS 77; 12 Bevans 513; 162 UNTS 59

Agreement on civil aviation security.
Exchange of notes at Lusaka February 16 and March 28, 1988.
Entered into force March 28, 1988.
TIAS 11573; 2185 UNTS 299

Air transport agreement, with annexes.
Signed at Lusaka March 16, 2010.
Entered into force March 16, 2010.
TIAS 10-316.1

UN & RELATED ORGANIZATIONS

Agreement regarding the surrender of persons to international tribunals.
Signed at Lusaka July 1, 2003.
Entered into force July 2, 2003.
TIAS 03-702

ZIMBABWE

On April 18, 1980, Zimbabwe became an independent state. In a note dated February 24, 1981, to the Secretary General of the United Nations, the Prime Minister made a statement reading in part as follows:

My Government will continue to apply within its territory, on the basis of the principles of reciprocity and mutual respect for sovereign independence, all
bilateral treaties validly concluded or recognised by the United Kingdom Government in respect of Southern Rhodesia for a period of three years from the date of independence, i.e. 18th April, 1980, unless such treaties are terminated or modified earlier by mutual consent. It is the intention of my Government during such period to subject all bilateral treaties to full examination for the purpose of determining whether such treaties require termination, revision or renegotiation in the light of Zimbabwe's sovereign status. It is the earnest hope of my Government that during the aforementioned period the normal processes of diplomatic negotiation will enable it to reach satisfactory accord with the States concerned upon the possibility of the continuance, modification or termination of such treaties.

At the end of the three year period referred to above my Government will regard such treaties whose continuance or modification have not been agreed as having terminated.

As regards multilateral treaties validly concluded or recognised by the United Kingdom Government in respect of Southern Rhodesia, my Government pro-poses to review at least some of those treaties during a period of six years from the date of independence, i.e. 18th April, 1980. It will indicate to the depositaries in each case of review whether the Republic of Zimbabwe will confirm, seek to modify or terminate its obligations under the treaty concerned. During such period of review any party to a multilateral treaty which was validly applied or extended to Southern Rhodesia may, on the basis of reciprocity and respect for national independence, rely on the terms of such treaty until it is modified or terminated. At the expiration of the period of review treaties as modified, or which have not been terminated, shall continue fully in force as if they had been concluded by the Republic of Zimbabwe.

By note of April 14, 1983, to the Secretary-General of the United Nations, the Government of Zimbabwe extended the period of review of bilateral treaties to April 18, 1984. This period of review was further extended by a note dated April 11, 1984, in which the Prime Minister notified the Secretary-General that "... my Government will continue to apply within its territory all such bilateral treaties until the 18th April 1985, unless terminated earlier or modified by mutual consent. Thereafter my Government will regard those treaties whose continuance or modification has not been agreed upon as having terminated."

In a further letter to the Secretary-General, received February 20, 1985, the Prime Minister stated in part:

During the past four years my Government has re-viewed all such bilateral treaties as were available to it or were brought to its attention and has also concluded a number of bilateral treaties with other governments with the effect that these instruments have superseded some of the earlier ones. It has become evident to my Government that many contracting parties prefer to enter into new arrangements with my Government rather than revive those treaties whose operations might have been suspended or terminated between 1965 and 1979 or which are now considered to be obsolete in the conduct of present-day international relations.

Whilst it has not been practicable for my Government to re-negotiate and finalise all such agreements on which a willingness to keep and maintain them in force was mutually indicated by my Government and other contracting parties, my Government has reached the stage at which it considers that legal continuity between itself and Other Contracting States has been achieved with an understanding either to revive, modify, renegotiate, terminate or adopt such bilateral treaties and, accordingly, my Government now wishes to inform Your Excellency, and through you all Member States of the United Nations Organisation as follows:

All bilateral treaties that were validly concluded or recognised by the United Kingdom Government in respect of Southern Rhodesia and continued to be applied and respected by my Government pursuant to the declaration aforementioned will now expire on 18 April 1985, UNLESS:

(i) Either my Government has already communicated to the other contracting party its intention to maintain the continuance in force of the treaty or the process of re-negotiating its terms and provisions has been agreed upon; or

(ii) The other contracting party notifies my Government before 18 April 1985 through normal diplomatic channels of its intention either to keep and maintain the continuance in force of the treaty concerned or to renegotiate its terms and provisions, in which case, my Government will consider itself bound by that Treaty.

The United States presented Zimbabwe by diplomatic note of April 17, 1985, a list of international agreements which the Government of the United States intended to maintain in force.

CULTURAL EXCHANGES, PROPERTY & COOPERATION

Agreement relating to the establishment of a Peace Corps in Zimbabwe.
Signed at Harare March 18, 1991.
Entered into force March 18, 1991.
TIAS 12114

DEFENSE

Agreement concerning the provision of training related to defense articles under the United States International Military Education and Training (IMET) Program.
Exchange of notes at Harare September 2 and 17, 1981.
Entered into force September 17, 1981.
35 UST 2319; TIAS 10791

DIPLOMATIC & CONSULAR RELATIONS

Consular convention between the United States and the United Kingdom.
Signed at Washington June 6, 1951.
Entered into force September 7, 1952.
3 UST 3426; TIAS 2494; 165 UNTS 121

EMPLOYMENT

Agreement relating to the employment of dependents of official government employees.
Exchange of notes at Harare February 7, 1991, and March 7, 1992.
Entered into force March 7, 1992.
TIAS 11857

FINANCE

Investment incentive agreement.
Signed at Harare June 20, 1990.
Entered into force June 20, 1990.
TIAS 12097

FOREIGN ASSISTANCE

General agreement for economic, technical, and related assistance.
Exchange of notes at Salisbury February 10 and March 22, 1982.
Entered into force March 22, 1982.
34 UST 194; TIAS 10348; 1557 UNTS 51

INTELLECTUAL PROPERTY

Declaration by the United States and the United Kingdom affording reciprocal protection to trade-marks.
Signed at London October 24, 1877.
Entered into force October 24, 1877.
20 Stat. 703; TS 138; 12 Bevans 198

LAW ENFORCEMENT

Extradition treaty.
Signed at Harare July 25, 1997.
Entered into force April 26, 2000.
TIAS

POSTAL MATTERS

International express mail agreement, with detailed regulations.
Signed at Harare and Washington February 15 and March 9, 1988.
Entered into force April 1, 1988.
TIAS 11569

PROPERTY

Convention relating to tenure and disposition of real and personal property.
Signed at Washington March 2, 1899.
Applicable to Southern Rhodesia July 27, 1901.
31 Stat. 1939; TS 146; 12 Bevans 246

Supplementary convention relating to the tenure and disposition of real and personal property.
Signed at Washington May 27, 1936.
Entered into force March 10, 1941.
55 Stat. 1101; TS 964; 5 Bevans 140; 203 LNTS 367

SCIENTIFIC & TECHNICAL COOPERATION

Agreement for scientific and technical cooperation.
Signed at Salisbury September 25, 1980.
Entered into force September 25, 1980.
32 UST 4543; TIAS 9967; 1267 UNTS 243

TRANSPORTATION

Agreement between the United States and the United Kingdom concerning air services, with annexes and exchange of letters.
Signed at Bermuda July 23, 1977.
Entered into force July 23, 1977.
28 UST 5367; TIAS 8641

Amendments:
April 25, 1978 (29 UST 2680; TIAS 8965)
December 27, 1979 (32 UST 524; TIAS 9722)

TAIWAN

On January 1, 1979, the United States recognized the Government of the People's Republic of China as the sole legal Government of China. Within this context, the people of the United States maintain cultural, commercial and other unofficial relations with the people on Taiwan. The United States acknowledges the Chinese position that there is but one China and Taiwan is part of China. The United States does not recognize the "Republic of China" as a state or government.

Pursuant to the Taiwan Relations Act and Executive Order 12143, 78 F.R. 13906, agreements concluded after January 1, 1979, by the American Institute in Taiwan, 1700 North Moore Street, Rosslyn, Virginia 22209, with its nongovernmental Taiwan counterpart, the Taipei Economic and Cultural Representative Office, are reported to the Congress as in effect under the law of the United States. A list of such agreements appears at 65 F.R. 81898.

Pursuant to Section 6 of the Taiwan Relations Act, (P.L. 96-8, 93 Stat. 14, 22 U.S.C. 3305) and Executive Order 12143, 78 F.R. 13906, the following agreements concluded with the Taiwan authorities prior to January 1, 1979, and any multilateral treaty or agreement relationship listed in Section 2 of this volume, are administered on a nongovernmental basis by the American Institute in Taiwan, a nonprofit District of Columbia corporation, and constitute neither recognition of the Taiwan authorities nor the continuation of any official relationship with Taiwan. The following bilateral agreements are on record as of January 1, 2017:

CLAIMS & DISPUTE RESOLUTION

Treaty of arbitration.
Signed at Washington June 27, 1930.
Entered into force December 15, 1932.
47 Stat. 2213; TS 857; 6 Bevans 724; 140 LNTS 183

CONSULAR AFFAIRS

Agreement prescribing nonimmigrant visa fees and validity of nonimmigrant visas.*
Exchange of notes at Taipei December 20, 1955, and February 20, 1956.
Entered into force February 20, 1956; operative April 1, 1956.
7 UST 585; TIAS 3539; 275 UNTS 73

Amendments:
July 11, October 17 and December 7, 1956 (18 UST 3167; TIAS 6410; 697 UNTS 256)
May 8, June 9 and 15, 1970 (21 UST 2213; TIAS 6972; 776 UNTS 344)

Note:
* The status of this agreement is under review.

EDUCATION

Agreement for financing certain educational and cultural exchange programs.
Signed at Taipei April 23, 1964.
Entered into force April 23, 1964.
15 UST 408; TIAS 5572; 524 UNTS 141

FINANCE

Agreement relating to guaranties for projects in Taiwan proposed by nationals of the United States.
Exchange of notes at Taipei June 25, 1952.
Entered into force June 25, 1952.
3 UST 4846; TIAS 2657; 136 UNTS 229

Amendment:
December 30, 1963 (14 UST 2222; TIAS 5509; 505 UNTS 308)

Agreement regarding the ownership and use of local currency repayments made by China to the Development Loan Fund.
Exchange of notes at Taipei December 24, 1958.
Entered into force December 24, 1958.
10 UST 16; TIAS 4162; 340 UNTS 251

FOREIGN ASSISTANCE

Agreement relating to duty-free entry of relief goods and relief packages and to the defrayment of transportation charges on such shipments.
Exchange of notes at Nanking November 5 and 18, 1948.
Entered into force November 18, 1948.
3 UST 5462; TIAS 2749; 198 UNTS 287

Amendments:
October 20 and December 12, 1952 (3 UST 5462; TIAS 2749; 198 UNTS 294)
July 12 and October 26, 1954 (5 UST 2930; TIAS 3151; 237 UNTS 337)

Agreement on technological advancement in connection with water resources, land utilization and various fields of irrigated agriculture.
Signed at Taipei May 12, 1972.
Entered into force May 12, 1972.
23 UST 1135; TIAS 7374

LAW ENFORCEMENT

Arrangement for the direct exchange of certain information regarding the traffic in narcotic drugs.
Exchanges of notes at Nanking March 12, June 21, July 28, and August 30, 1947.
Entered into force August 30, 1947.
6 Bevans 797

MARITIME MATTERS

Agreement relating to the loan of small naval craft to China.
Exchange of notes at Taipei May 14, 1954.
Entered into force May 14, 1954.
5 UST 892; TIAS 2979; 231 UNTS 165

Extensions and Amendments:
March 22 and 31, 1955 (6 UST 750; TIAS 3215; 251 UNTS 399)
June 18, 1955 (6 UST 2973; TIAS 3346; 265 UNTS 406)
May 16, 1957 (8 UST 787; TIAS 3837; 284 UNTS 380)
October 12, 1960 (11 UST 2233; TIAS 4597; 393 UNTS 320)
August 15, 1962 (13 UST 1924; TIAS 5150; 460 UNTS 237)
February 23, 1965 (16 UST 126; TIAS 5771; 542 UNTS 361)
December 16, 1970, and January 14, 1971 (22 UST 12; TIAS 7037; 776 UNTS 334)

POSTAL MATTERS

Parcel post convention.
Signed at Peking May 29, 1916, and at Washington July 11, 1916.
Entered into force August 1, 1916.
39 Stat. 1665; Post Office Department print

Agreement for exchange of insured parcel post and regulations of execution.
Signed at Taipei July 30 and at Washington August 19, 1957.
Entered into force November 1, 1957.
8 UST 2031; TIAS 3941; 300 UNTS 61

International express mail agreement, with detailed regulations.
Signed at Taipei and Washington September 11 and November 10, 1978.
Entered into force December 30, 1978; effective December 27, 1978.
30 UST 3277; TIAS 9392; 1179 UNTS 291

PROPERTY

Preliminary agreement regarding principles applying to mutual aid in the prosecution of the war against aggression.
Signed at Washington June 2, 1942.
Entered into force June 2, 1942.
56 Stat. 1494; EAS 251; 6 Bevans 735; 14 UNTS 343

Agreement on the disposition of lend-lease supplies in inventory or procurement in the United States.
Signed at Washington June 14, 1946.
Operative September 2, 1945.
60 Stat. 1760; TIAS 1533; 6 Bevans 753; 4 UNTS 253

Agreement under section 3 (c) of the Lend-Lease Act.
Signed at Washington June 28, 1946.
Entered into force June 28, 1946.
61 Stat. 3895; TIAS 1746; 6 Bevans 758; 34 UNTS 121

TRADE & INVESTMENT

Treaty of friendship, commerce, and navigation with accompanying protocol.
Signed at Nanking November 4, 1946.
Entered into force November 30, 1948.
63 Stat. 1299; TIAS 1871; 6 Bevans 761; 25 UNTS 69

Agreement relating to trade in textiles with letter dated April 10, 1974.
Exchange of letters at Washington April 11, 1974.
*Entered into force April 11, 1974.**
25 UST 720; TIAS 7821

Note:

Exchange of letters of April 11, 1974 terminated January 1, 1975. April 10, 1974 letter remain in force.

Agreement on trade matters, with annexes.
Exchange of letters at Washington December 29, 1978.
Entered into force December 29, 1978.
30 UST 6439; TIAS 9561; 1179 UNTS 313

Note:

* Exchange of letters dated April 11, 1974, terminated January 1, 1975. Letter dated April 10, 1974, remains in force.

TRANSPORTATION

Memorandum of agreement relating to the provision of flight inspection services.
Signed at Washington and Taipei August 21 and October 1, 1978.
Entered into force October 1, 1978.
30 UST 273; TIAS 9197; 1150 UNTS 271

SECTION 2:

MULTILATERAL TREATIES AND OTHER AGREEMENTS

This page intentionally left blank.

Contents

Depositary Websites

The multilateral section of this volume lists the parties only for those treaties which have no designated depositary. For treaties with a designated depositary, the most reliable party information can be obtained by consulting the depositary website, or contacting the depositary country or organization directly. Below is a list of several of these depositary websites.

Country/Agency	Website
Australia	http://www.austlii.edu.au/au/other/dfat/treaty_list/depository/
Belgium (French and Dutch only)	http://diplomatie.belgium.be/en/treaties/
Canada	http://www.treaty-accord.gc.ca/search-recherche.aspx?type=10&page=TLA
Caribbean Community Secretariat (CARICOM)	http://caricom.org/treaties#
The Caribbean Environment Programme	http://www.cep.unep.org/
Convention on International Trade in Endangered Species of Wild Fauna and Flora (CITES)	http://www.cites.org/
Council of Europe	http://www.coe.int/en/web/conventions/full-list
European Bank of Reconstruction and Development	http://www.ebrd.com/shareholders-and-board-of-governors.html
European Union	http://ec.europa.eu/world/agreements/searchByType.do?id=2
Food and Agriculture Organization	http://www.fao.org/legal/home/fao-members/en/
France (French only)	http://basedoc.diplomatie.gouv.fr/Traites/Accords_Traites.php?W=+O%20RDER+BY+DATOP/Ascend
Germany	http://www.auswaertiges-amt.de/EN/Aussenpolitik/Themen/InternatRecht/Vertraege/Verwahrer.html
Inter-American Development Bank	http://www.iadb.org/en/about-us/how-the-inter-american-development-bank-is-organized,5998.html?open_accordion=1
International Atomic Energy Agency (IAEA)	https://ola.iaea.org/ola/treaties/multi.html
International Bank for Reconstruction and Development	http://www.worldbank.org/en/about/leadership/members#1
International Centre for the Study of the Preservation and Restoration of Cultural Property (ICCROM)	http://www.iccrom.org/about/member-state/
International Civil Aviation Organization (ICAO)	http://www.icao.int/secretariat/legal/Lists/Current%20lists%20of%20parties/AllItems.aspx
International Committee of the Red Cross	https://ihl-databases.icrc.org/ihl
International Development Law Organization	http://www.idlo.int/about-idlo/governance/assembly-of-parties
International Institute for the Unification of Private Law (UNIDROIT)	http://www.unidroit.org/about-unidroit/membership
International Labour Organization (ILO)	http://www.ilo.org/dyn/normlex/en/f?p=1000:12000:::NO:::
International Maritime Organization	http://www.imo.org/en/About/Conventions/Pages/Home.aspx
International Organization for Migration (IMO or OIM)	http://www.iom.int/members-and-observers
International Organization of Legal Metrology	https://www.oiml.org/en/structure/members
International Science and Technology Center	http://www.istc.int/
International Telecommunication Union (ITU)	http://www.itu.int/en/membership/Pages/member-states.aspx
International Union for the Protection of New Varieties of Plants (UPOV)	http://www.upov.int/portal/index.html.en
Italy (Italian only)	http://www.esteri.it/mae/en (search Legal Affairs)
Netherlands	https://treatydatabase.overheid.nl/en/Verdrag/OverigeDepositaireVerdragen
New Zealand	https://mfat.govt.nz/en/about-us/who-we-are/treaties/#Internationaltreaties
Nuclear Threat Initiative (NTI) (tracks nonproliferation treaties)	http://www.nti.org/treaties-and-regimes/treaties/
Organisation for Economic Co-operation and Development (OECD)	http://www.oecd.org/about/membersandpartners/
Organization of the American States	http://www.oas.org/en/sla/dil/treaties_agreements.asp
NOTE: Trade agreements for which OAS is depositary are tracked through SICE:	http://www.sice.oas.org/agreements_e.asp

Switzerland	https://www.fdfa.admin.ch/eda/en/home/foreign-policy/international-law/internationale-vertraege/depositary.html
United Kingdom	http://treaties.fco.gov.uk/treaties/treaty.htm;jsessionid=A61ECBDB86D700BA50F189EC5B10A7C3 or https://www.gov.uk/government/collections/treaties-for-which-the-uk-is-depositary
United Nations	https://treaties.un.org/pages/participationstatus.aspx
United Nations Educational, Scientific and Cultural Organization (UNESCO)	http://portal.unesco.org/en/ev.php-URL_ID=12025&URL_DO=DO_TOPIC&URL_SECTION=-471.html
Universal Postal Union	http://www.upu.int/en/the-upu/member-countries.html
United States	http://www.state.gov/s/l/treaty/depositary/
World Bank	http://www.worldbank.org/en/about/leadership/members
World Customs Organization	http://www.wcoomd.org/en/about-us/wco-members/membership.aspx
World Health Organization – International Agency for Research on Cancer	https://www.iarc.fr/en/about/membership.php
World Health Organization – International Health Regulations	http://www.who.int/topics/international_health_regulations/en/
World Intellectual Property Organization (WIPO)	http://www.wipo.int/treaties/en/
World Trade Organization	https://www.wto.org/english/thewto_e/whatis_e/tif_e/org6_e.htm

AGRICULTURE

See also Foreign Assistance

International agreement for the creation at Paris of an international office for epizootics, with annex.
Done at Paris January 25, 1924.
Entered into force January 17, 1925;
for the United States July 29, 1975.
26 UST 1840; TIAS 8141; 57 LNTS 135
Depositary: France

Convention placing the International Poplar Commission within the framework of the Food and Agricultural Organization.
Approved at the 10th Session of the Conference of the Food and Agricultural Organization, Rome, November 19, 1959.
Entered into force September 26, 1961;
for the United States August 13, 1970.
UST 2060; TIAS 6952; 410 UNTS 155
Amendments
October 30, 1967 (21 UST 2060; TIAS 6952; 634 UNTS 433)
November 15, 1977 (29 UST 5579; TIAS 9130)

Depositary: Food and Agriculture Organization

Amended constitution of the International Rice Commission.
Approved at the 11th Session of the Conference of the Food and Agriculture Organization, Rome, November 23, 1961.
Entered into force November 23, 1961.
13 UST 2403; TIAS 5204; 418 UNTS 334
Depositary: Food and Agriculture Organization

North American plant protection agreement.
Signed at Yosemite October 13, 1976.
Entered into force October 13, 1976.
28 UST 6223; TIAS 8680
Parties:
Canada
Mexico
United States

Convention on the Inter-American Institute for Cooperation on Agriculture.*
Done at Washington March 6, 1979.
Entered into force December 8, 1979; for the United States December 8, 1980.
32 UST 3779; TIAS 9919
Depositary: Organization of American States

Notes:
* Replaces as between contracting parties the convention on the Inter-American Institute of Agricultural Sciences of January 15, 1944 (58 Stat. 1169; TS 987; 3 Bevans 881; 161 UNTS 281). Cuba is a party to the 1944 convention only.

Cooperative agreement supplementary to the North American plant protection agreement of October 13, 1976.
Signed at Alexandria October 20, 1991.
Entered into force October 20, 1991.
TIAS
Parties:
Canada
Mexico
United States

Revised text of the international plant protection convention, with annex.
Done at Rome November 17, 1997.
Entered into force October 2, 2005.
TIAS
Depositary: Food and Agriculture Organization

Cooperative agreement for the prevention, detection, suppression and eradication of the Mediterranean Fruit Fly and other economically important fruit flies.
Signed at Washington and Mexico City May 13 and May 19, 2014.
Entered into force February 11, 2015.
TIAS 15-211
Parties:
Guatemala
Mexico
United States

ANTARCTICA & ARCTIC

Antarctic treaty.
Signed at Washington December 1, 1959.
Entered into force June 23, 1961.
12 UST 794; TIAS 4780; 402 UNTS 71
Depositary: United States

Protocol on environmental protection to the Antarctic treaty, with schedule and annexes I - IV.
Signed at Madrid October 4, 1991.
Entered into force January 14, 1998.
TIAS
Depositary: United States

Annex V to the Protocol on environmental protection to the Antarctic Treaty.
Adopted at Bonn October 17, 1971.
Entered into force January 14, 1998.
Entered into force for the United States May 24, 2002.
TIAS
Depositary: United States

ARMS CONTROL

(See also Nonproliferation, Rules of War)

Protocol for the prohibition of the use in war of asphyxiating, poisonous or other gases, and of bacteriological methods of warfare.
Done at Geneva June 17, 1925.
Entered into force February 8, 1928;for the United States April 10, 1975.
26 UST 571; TIAS 8061; 94 LNTS 65
Depositary: France

Treaty banning nuclear weapon tests in the atmosphere, in outer space and under water.
Done at Moscow August 5, 1963.
Entered into force October 10, 1963.
14 UST 1313; TIAS 5433; 480 UNTS 43
Depositary: Russia, United Kingdom, United States

Treaty on the prohibition of the emplacement of nuclear weapons and other weapons of mass destruction on the seabed and the ocean floor and in the subsoil thereof.

Done at Washington, London and Moscow February 11, 1971
Entered into force May 18, 1972.
23 UST 701; TIAS 7337; 955 UNTS 115

Depositary: Russia, United Kingdom, United States

Convention on the prohibition of the development, production and stockpiling of bacteriological (biological) and toxin weapons and on their destruction.

Done at Washington, London, and Moscow April 10, 1972.
Entered into force March 26, 1975.
26 UST 583; TIAS 8062; 1015 UNTS 163

Depositary: Russia, United Kingdom, United States

Convention on prohibitions or restrictions on the use of certain conventional weapons which may be deemed to be excessively injurious or to have indiscriminate effects.

Adopted at Geneva October 10, 1980.
Entered into force December 2, 1983; for the United States September 24, 1995.
TIAS

Amendment:
December 21, 2001

Depositary: United Nations

Protocol on non-detectable fragments (Protocol I).

Adopted at Geneva October 10, 1980.
Entered into force December 2, 1983; for the United States September 24, 1995.
TIAS

Depositary: United Nations

Protocol on restrictions on the use of mines, booby-traps and other devices (Protocol II).

Adopted at Geneva October 10, 1980.
Entered into force December 2, 1983; for the United States September 24, 1995.
TIAS

Amendment:
May 3, 1996

Depositary: United Nations

Protocol on prohibitions or restrictions on the use of incendiary weapons (Protocol III).

Adopted at Geneva October 10, 1980.
Entered into force December 2, 1983; for the United States July 21, 2009.
TIAS 09-721.1

Depositary: United Nations

Treaty on conventional armed forces in Europe, with protocols and annexes.

Done at Paris November 19, 1990.
Entered into force November 9, 1992.
TIAS

Depositary: Netherlands

Treaty on open skies, with annexes.

Done at Helsinki March 24, 1992.
Entered into force January 1, 2002.
TIAS

Depositary: Canada

Convention on the prohibition of the development, production, stockpiling and use of chemical weapons and on their destruction, with annexes.

Done at Geneva September 3, 1992.
Entered into force April 29, 1997; for the United States May 25, 1997.
TIAS

Depositary: United Nations

Proces-verbal of rectification of the Spanish original text of the September 3, 1992 convention on the prohibition of the development, production, stockpiling and use of chemical weapons and on their destruction.

Done at New York January 10, 1994.
Entered into force January 10, 1994.
TIAS

Protocol on blinding laser weapons (Protocol IV).

Adopted at Vienna October 13, 1995.
Entered into force July 30, 1998; for the United States July 21, 2009.
TIAS 09-721.2

Depositary: United Nations

Document agreed among the States Parties to the Treaty on Conventional Armed Forces in Europe of November 19, 1990 ("the flank agreement"), with understanding.

Adopted at Vienna May 31, 1996.
Entered into force May 15, 1997.
TIAS

Depositary: Netherlands

Protocol on explosive remnants of war (Protocol V).

Adopted at Geneva November 28, 2003.
Entered into force November 12, 2006; for the United States July 21, 2009.
TIAS 09-721.3

Depositary: United Nations

ATOMIC ENERGY

Agreed declaration on atomic energy by the President of the United States, the Prime Minister of the United Kingdom, and the Prime Minister of Canada.

Signed at Washington November 15, 1945.
Entered into force November 15, 1945.
60 Stat. 1479; TIAS 1504; 3 Bevans 1304; 3 UNTS 123

Agreement as to disposition of rights in atomic energy inventions.

Signed at Washington September 24, 1956.
Entered into force September 24, 1956.
7 UST 2526; TIAS 3644; 253 UNTS 171

Parties:
Canada
United Kingdom
United States

Statute of the International Atomic Energy Agency.
Done at New York October 26, 1956.
Entered into force July 29, 1957.
8 UST 1093; TIAS 3873; 276 UNTS 3

Amendments:
October 4, 1961 (14 UST 135; TIAS 5284; 471 UNTS 334)
September 28, 1970 (24 UST 1637; TIAS 7668)
September 27, 1984

Depositary: United States

Trilateral agreements signed at Vienna between the International Atomic Energy Agency, the United States, and other countries for the application of safeguards by the International Atomic Energy Agency to equipment, devices and materials supplied under the bilateral agreements for cooperation concerning civil uses of atomic energy between the United States and the following countries

---

ARGENTINA
June 13, 1969; entered into force July 25, 1969.
20 UST 2629; TIAS 6722; 694 UNTS 233

AUSTRIA
August 20, 1969; entered into force January 24, 1970. [1]
21 UST 56; TIAS 6816; 798 UNTS 77

BRAZIL
March 10, 1967; entered into force October 31, 1968.
19 UST 6322; TIAS 6583; 670 UNTS 109

Amendment:
July 27, 1972 (23 UST 2526; TIAS 7440)

CHINA (TAIWAN)
December 6, 1971; entered into force December 6, 1971. [2]
22 UST 1837; TIAS 7228

COLOMBIA
December 9, 1970; entered into force December 9, 1970.
21 UST 2677; TIAS 7010; 795 UNTS 93

Extension:
March 28, 1977 (28 UST 2404; TIAS 8556)

IRAN
March 4, 1969; entered into force August 20, 1969. [3]
20 UST 2748; TIAS 6741; 694 UNTS 163

ISRAEL
April 4, 1975; entered into force April 4, 1975.
26 UST 483; TIAS 8051

Extension:
April 7, 1977 (28 UST 2397; TIAS 8554)

KOREA
January 5, 1968; entered into force January 5, 1968.
19 UST 4404; TIAS 6435; 637 UNTS 123

Amendment:
November 30, 1972 (24 UST 829; TIAS 7584)

PHILIPPINES
July 15, 1968; entered into force July 19, 1968. [4]
19 UST 5426; TIAS 6524; 650 UNTS 287

PORTUGAL
July 11, 1969; entered into force July 19, 1969. [5]
20 UST 2564; TIAS 6718; 694 UNTS 315.

SOUTH AFRICA
July 26, 1967; entered into force July 26, 1967.
18 UST 1643; TIAS 6306

Amendment:
June 20, 1974 (25 UST 1175; TIAS 7848)

SPAIN
December 9, 1966; entered into force December 9, 1966.[6]
17 UST 2351; TIAS 6182; 589 UNTS 55

Amendment:
June 28, 1974 (25 UST 1261; TIAS 7856)

SWEDEN
March 1, 1972; entered into force March 1, 1972. [7]
23 UST 195; TIAS 7295

SWITZERLAND
February 28, 1972; entered into force February 28, 1972. [5]
23 UST 184; TIAS 7294

TURKEY
September 30, 1968; entered into force June 5, 1969. [8]
20 UST 780; TIAS 6692; 694 UNTS 139

Extension:
June 30, 1981 (33 UST 2782; TIAS 10201; 1271 UNTS 360)

VENEZUELA
March 27, 1968; entered into force March 27, 1968.[9]
19 UST 4385; TIAS 6433; 650 UNTS 195.

Extension:
February 18, 1981 (33 UST 1106; TIAS 10096)

Notes:
1 Suspended by agreement signed September 21, 1971.
2 See note under CHINA (TAIWAN) in Section 1.
3 Suspended by agreement signed June 19, 1973.
4 Suspended by agreement signed February 21, 1973.
5 Suspended by agreement signed September 23, 1980.
6 Suspended by agreement signed March 23, 1993.
7 Suspended by agreement signed April 14, 1975.
8 Suspended by agreement signed January 15, 1985.
9 Suspended by agreement signed September 27, 1983.

Trilateral agreements signed at Vienna between the International Atomic Energy Agency, the United States, and other countries for the application of safeguards pursuant to the non-proliferation treaty of July 1, 1968 (21 UST 483; TIAS 6839; 729 UNTS 161) have been concluded with the following countries:

AUSTRALIA

July 10, 1974; entered into force July 10, 1974.

25 UST 1325; TIAS 7865

AUSTRIA

September 21, 1971; entered into force July 23, 1972.[1]

23 UST 1308; TIAS 7409

DENMARK

March 1, 1972; entered into force March 1, 1972.

23 UST 167; TIAS 7289; 873 UNTS 155

GREECE

March 1, 1972; entered into force March 1, 1972.

23 UST 169; TIAS 7290

IRAN

June 19, 1973; entered into force May 15, 1974.[1]

25 UST 853; TIAS 7829

NORWAY

September 25, 1973; entered into force July 25, 1973.

24 UST 2046; TIAS 7721

PHILIPPINES

February 21, 1973; entered into force October 16, 1974.[1]

25 UST 2967; TIAS 7957

PORTUGAL

September 23, 1980; entered into force September 23, 1980.[1,2]

32 UST 3311; TIAS 9899; 1266 UNTS 382

SPAIN

March 23, 1993; entered into force October 13, 1993.

SWEDEN

April 14, 1975; entered into force May 6, 1975.[1]

26 UST 478; TIAS 8049

SWITZERLAND

September 23, 1980; entered into force September 23, 1980.[1,2]

32 UST 3317; TIAS 9900

THAILAND

June 27, 1974; entered into force June 27, 1974.

25 UST 1178; TIAS 7849

TURKEY

January 15, 1985; entered into force January 15, 1985.[1, 2]

TIAS 11932

VENEZUELA

September 27, 1983; entered into force September 27, 1983.[1, 2, 3]

35 UST 2329; TIAS 10793

Notes:

1 For suspension of previous agreements on safeguards, see entry above.

2 Also pursuant to the United States–IAEA agreement of November 18, 1977, for the application of safeguards in the United States (32 UST 3059; TIAS 9889).

3 Also pursuant to the treaty for the prohibition of nuclear weapons in Latin America (22 UST 762; TIAS 7137).

Agreements between the International Atomic Energy Agency, the United States, and other countries for the supply of nuclear material or equipment have been concluded with the following countries: [1]

ARGENTINA AND PERU

Vienna, May 9, 1978; entered into force May 9, 1978, with an exchange of notes signed at Buenos Aires and Washington March 31, April 7, May 10 and 22, 1978.

30 UST 1539; TIAS 9263; 1161 UNTS 305

CANADA AND JAMAICA

Vienna, January 25, 1984; entered into force January 25, 1984.

35 UST 4309; TIAS 10933

COLOMBIA

Vienna and Bogota, May 30, June 7 and 17, 1994; entered into force June 17, 1994.

TIAS; 1857 UNTS 105

INDONESIA

New Delhi, December 7, 1979; entered into force December 7, 1979.

32 UST 361; TIAS 9705

JAMAICA

Vienna May 2 and December 16, and Geneva November 25, 2013; entered into force December 16, 2013.

TIAS 13-1216

MALAYSIA

Vienna, September 22, 1980; entered into force September 22, 1980.

32 UST 2610; TIAS 9863

Amendment:

June 12 and July 22, 1981 (33 UST 2785; TIAS 10202)

MEXICO

Vienna, December 18, 1963; entered into force December 18, 1963.

32 UST 3607; TIAS 9906; 490 UNTS 383

Vienna, February 12, 1974; entered into force February 12, 1974.

TIAS 10705

Vienna, June 14, 1974; entered into force June 14, 1974.

TIAS 10705

Vienna, March 6, 1980; entered into force March 6, 1980.

32 UST 3628; TIAS 9906; 1267 UNTS 51

Vienna July 13, 29 and August 1, 2011; entered into force August 1, 2011.

TIAS 11-801

MOROCCO

Vienna, December 2, 1983; entered into force December 2, 1983.

35 UST 3531; TIAS 10866

POLAND

Warsaw and Vienna January 8, 12, and 16, 2007; entered into force January 16, 2007.

TIAS 07-116

THAILAND

Vienna, September 30, 1986; entered into force September 30, 1986.

TIAS

YUGOSLAVIA [2]

Vienna, June 14, 1974; entered into force June 14, 1974.

32 UST 773; TIAS 9728

Vienna, January 16, 1980; entered into force July 14, 1980.

32 UST 1228; TIAS 9767; 1266 UNTS 364

Belgrade and Vienna, February 26, 1980; entered into force February 26, 1980.

32 UST 773; TIAS 9728

Vienna, December 14, 15 and 20, 1982; entered into force December 20, 1982.

TIAS 10621

Vienna, February 23, 1983; entered into force February 23, 1983.

TIAS 10664

Notes:

1 Similar supply agreements, which have not been printed in the United States treaty series but are on file in the Office of Treaty Affairs, were concluded during the 1960's and early 1970's with the following countries: Argentina, Chile, Finland, Greece, India, Iran, Iraq, Norway, Pakistan, Philippines, Romania, Spain, Turkey, Venezuela, Yugoslavia, and Zaire.

2 See note under YUGOSLAVIA in Section 1.

Agreement concerning a joint project for planning, design, experiment preparation, performance and reporting of reactor safety experiments concerning containment response, with appendices

Dated January 24, 1975.

Entered into force for the United States February 20, 1975.

28 UST 629; TIAS 8479

Parties:

Denmark
Finland
France
Germany, Federal Republic of [1]
Japan [2]
Norway
Sweden
United States

Notes

1 See note under GERMANY in Section 1.

2 Subject to approval of funds.

Agreement concerning a joint project for planning, design, experiment preparation, performance and reporting of reactor safety experiments concerning critical flow, with appendices

Dated April 14, 1977.

Entered into force June 17, 1977.

30 UST 129; TIAS 9184

Parties:

Denmark
Finland
France
Netherlands
Norway
Sweden
United States

Implementing agreement for a program of research and development on superconducting magnets for fusion power, with annex.

Done at Paris October 6, 1977.

Entered into force October 6, 1977.

33 UST 2201; TIAS 10180

Depositary: International Energy Agency

Agreement on research participation and technical exchange in the in-pile CABRI and Annular Core Pulsed Reactor (ACPR) research programs related to fast reactor safety, with memorandum of understanding and appendices

Signed May 2, June 7 and 22, 1978.

Entered into force June 22, 1978.

30 UST 7545; TIAS 9603

Parties:

France
Germany, Federal Republic of [1]
United States

Note:

1 See note under GERMANY in Section 1.

Implementing agreement for a program of research and development on radiation damage in fusion materials, with annexes.

Done at Paris October 21, 1980.
Entered into force October 21, 1980.

TIAS

Parties:

Canada
European Atomic Energy Community
Japan
Switzerland
United States

Depositary: International Energy Agency

Agreement regarding protection of information transferred into the United States in connection with the initial phase of a project for the establishment of a uranium enrichment installation in the United States based upon the gas centrifuge process developed within the three European countries.

Signed at Washington April 11, 1990.
Entered into force April 11, 1990.

TIAS; 1640 UNTS 369

Extension:

April 5 and 9, 1991

Parties:

Germany, Federal Republic of [1]
Netherlands
United Kingdom
United States

Note:

1 See note under GERMANY in Section 1.

Agreement regarding the establishment, construction and operation of a uranium enrichment installation in the United States, with annex and agreed minute.

Signed at Washington July 24, 1992.
Entered into force February 1, 1995.

TIAS

Parties:

Germany
Netherlands
United Kingdom
United States

Convention on nuclear safety.

Signed at Vienna September 20, 1994.
Entered into force October 24, 1996. for the United States July 10, 1999.

TIAS

Depositary: International Atomic Energy Agency

Agreement on the establishment of the Korean Peninsula Energy Development Organization.

Done at New York March 9, 1995.
Entered into force March 9, 1995.

TIAS

Amendment:

September 19, 1997 (2035 UNTS 280)

Parties:

European Atomic Energy Community
Japan
Korea
United States

Joint convention on the safety of spent fuel management and on the safety of radioactive waste management.

Done at Vienna September 5, 1997.
Entered into force June 18, 2001; for the United States July 14, 2003.

TIAS

Depositary: International Atomic Energy Agency

Agreement on cooperation among the original members of the Korean Peninsula Energy Development Organization.

Signed at Washington September 19, 1997.
Entered into force September 19, 1997.

TIAS; 2032 UNTS 235

Parties:

Japan
Korea
United States

Agreement concerning cooperation on the application of non-proliferation assurances to low enriched uranium transferred to the United States for fabrication into fuel and retransfer to Taiwan, with annex and related side letter.

Exchanges of notes at Washington July 21, 1999.
Entered into force May 1, 2000.

TIAS 13054

Parties:

Germany
Netherlands
United Kingdom
United States

Framework agreement on a multilateral nuclear environmental programme in the Russian Federation.

Signed at Stockholm May 21, 2003.
Entered into force April 14, 2004; for the United States June 14, 2013.

TIAS 13-614

Depositary: Organization for Economic Cooperation and Development, Russian Federation

Framework agreement for international collaboration on research and development of generation IV nuclear energy systems.

Signed at Washington February 28, 2005.
Entered into force February 28, 2005.

TIAS 05-228

Parties:

Canada
France
Japan
United Kingdom
United States

Agreement on the establishment of the ITER International Fusion Energy Organization for the Joint Implementation of the ITER project, with annexes.

Signed at Paris November 21, 2006.
Entered into force October 24, 2007.

TIAS 07-1024

Depositary: International Atomic Energy Agency

Agreement regarding the establishment, construction and operation of uranium enrichment installations using gas centrifuge technology in the United States of America, with agreed minute.

Signed at Paris February 24, 2011.
Entered into force January 31, 2012.
TIAS 12-131

Parties:

France
Germany
Netherlands
United Kingdom
United States

Convention on supplementary compensation for nuclear damage, with annex.

Done at Vienna September 12, 1997.
Entered into force April 15, 2015.
TIAS

Depositary: International Atomic Energy Agency

BOUNDARY & BOUNDARY WATERS

Convention on the continental shelf.

Done at Geneva April 29, 1958.
Entered into force June 10, 1964.
15 UST 471; TIAS 5578; 499 UNTS 311

Depositary: United Nations

CANALS

(see Panama in the Bilaterals section)

CIVIL AFFAIRS, EMERGENCIES & DEFENSE

Act of Habana concerning the provisional administration of European colonies and possessions in the Americas contained in the Final Act of the Second Meeting of Ministers of Foreign Affairs of the American Republics.

Signed at Havana July 30, 1940.
Entered into force July 30, 1940.
54 Stat..2491; 3 Bevans 619

Depositary: Cuba, Organization of American States

Convention on the provisional administration of European colonies and possessions in the Americas.

Signed at Havana July 30, 1940.
Entered into force January 8, 1942.
TS 977; 3 Bevans 623; 161 UNTS 253

Depositary: Cuba, Organization of American States

CLAIMS & DISPUTE RESOLUTION

HAGUE CONVENTIONS

Convention for the pacific settlement of international disputes.*

Signed at The Hague July 29, 1899.
Entered into force September 4, 1900.
32 Stat. 1779; TS 392; 1 Bevans 230

Depositary: Netherlands

Notes:

* Replaced by convention of October 18, 1907, as between contracting parties to the later convention. The parties to the 1899 and/or 1907 conventions comprise the members of the Permanent Court of Arbitration.

Convention for the pacific settlement of international disputes.

Signed at The Hague October 18, 1907.
Entered into force January 26, 1910.
36 Stat. 2199; TS 536; 1 Bevans 577

Depositary: Netherlands

Convention for the establishment of International Commissions of Inquiry.

Signed at Washington February 7, 1923.
Entered into force June 13, 1925.
44 Stat. 2070; TS 717; 2 Bevans 387

Depositary: United States

INTER-AMERICAN CONVENTIONS

Convention for the arbitration of pecuniary claims.

Signed at Buenos Aires August 11, 1910.
Entered into force January 1, 1913.
38 Stat. 1799; TS 594; 1 Bevans 763

Depositary: Argentina

General treaty of inter-American arbitration and protocol of progressive arbitration.

Signed at Washington January 5, 1929.
Entered into force October 28, 1929; for the United States April 16, 1935.
49 Stat. 3153; TS 886; 2 Bevans 737; 130 LNTS 135

Depositary: United States

General convention of inter-American conciliation.

Signed at Washington January 5, 1929.
Entered into force November 15, 1929.
46 Stat. 2209; TS 780; 2 Bevans 745; 100 LNTS 401

Depositary: Chile

Anti-war treaty of nonaggression and conciliation.*

Signed at Rio de Janeiro October 10, 1933.
Entered into force November 13, 1935.
49 Stat. 3363; TS 906; 3 Bevans 135; 163 LNTS 395

Depositary: Argentina

Notes:

* The treaty was "open to the adherence of all states."

Additional protocol to the general convention of inter-American conciliation.
Signed at Montevideo December 26, 1933.
Entered into force March 10, 1935.
49 Stat. 3185; TS 887; 3 Bevans 161
Depositary: Chile

Inter-American treaty on good offices and mediation.
Signed at Buenos Aires December 23, 1936.
Entered into force July 29, 1937.
51 Stat. 90; TS 925; 3 Bevans 362; 188 LNTS 75
Depositaries: Argentina, Organization of American States

Inter-American convention on international commercial arbitration.
Done at Panama January 30, 1975.
Entered into force June 16, 1976;
for the United States October 27, 1990.
TIAS
Depositary: Organization of American States

WORLD WAR II RELATED AGREEMENTS

Protocol on the talks between the Heads of the three governments at the Crimea Conference on the question of the German reparation in kind.
Signed at Yalta February 11, 1945.
Entered into force February 11, 1945.
Foreign Relations of the United States: "The Conferences at Malta and Yalta, 1945," pp. 968-975. 3 Bevans 1020

Parties:
Union of Soviet Socialist Republics [1]
United Kingdom
United States

Note:
1 See note under UNION OF SOVIET SOCIALIST REPUBLICS in Section 1.

Agreement on reparation from Germany, on the establishment of an inter-Allied reparation agency and on the restitution of monetary gold.
Concluded at Paris January 14, 1946.
Entered into force January 24, 1946.
61 Stat. 3157; TIAS 1655; 4 Bevans 5; 555 UNTS 69
Depositary: France

Agreement on a plan for allocation of a reparation share to nonrepatriable victims of German action, with annex.
Signed at Paris June 14, 1946.
Entered into force June 14, 1946.
61 Stat. 2649; TIAS 1594; 4 Bevans 75
Depositary: France

Protocol relating to Austrian participation in the restitution of monetary gold looted by Germany, as provided in the reparation agreement of January 14, 1946.
Signed at London November 4, 1947.
Entered into force November 4, 1947.
61 Stat. 3571; TIAS 1683; 4 Bevans 689; 93 UNTS 61
Depositary: United Kingdom

Protocol relating to participation by Italy in the restitution of monetary gold looted by Germany, as provided in the reparation agreement of January 14, 1946.
Signed at London December 16, 1947; effective September 15, 1947.
61 Stat. 3729; TIAS 1707; 4 Bevans 692; 82 UNTS 237
Depositary: United Kingdom

Agreement relating to the restitution of gold looted by Germany and transferred to the Bank for International Settlements.
Effected by exchanges of letters at Washington May 13, 1948, between the Chairman of the Bank for International Settlements and representatives of the United States, United Kingdom, and France.
Entered into force May 13, 1948.
62 Stat. 2672; TIAS 1805; 4 Bevans 754; 140 UNTS 187

Agreement for the submission to an arbitrator of certain claims with respect to gold looted by the Germans from Rome in 1943.
Signed at Washington April 25, 1951.
Entered into force April 25, 1951.
2 UST 991; TIAS 2252; 91 UNTS 21; 100 UNTS 304

Parties:
France
United Kingdom
United States

Agreement relating to certain Marechal Joffre claims, with memorandum of understanding.
Signed at Washington October 19, 1948.
Entered into force October 19, 1948.
62 Stat. 2841; TIAS 1816; 4 Bevans 783; 84 UNTS 201

Parties:
Australia
France
United States

Protocol relating to participation by Poland in the restitution of monetary gold looted by Germany, as provided in the reparation agreement signed at Paris January 14, 1946.
Signed at London July 6, 1949.
Entered into force July 6, 1949.
63 Stat. 2677; TIAS 1970; 4 Bevans 850
Depositary: United Kingdom

Administrative agreement concerning the Arbitration Tribunal and the Arbitral Commission on property, rights, and interests in Germany.
Signed at Bonn July 13, 1956.
Entered into force July 13, 1956; operative from May 5, 1955.
7 UST 2129; TIAS 3615; 281 UNTS 3

Parties:
France
Germany, Federal Republic of [1]
United Kingdom
United States

Note:
1 See note under GERMANY in Section 1.

Agreement relating to the waiver of immunity from legal process of members of the Arbitration Tribunal and the Arbitral Commission on property, rights and interests in Germany under the administrative agreement of July 13, 1956.

*Exchange of notes between the United States and the Federal Republic of Germany at Bonn July 24 and 27, 1956.**

Entered into force July 27, 1956.

7 UST 2773; TIAS 3657; 278 UNTS 3

Note:

* Notes were exchanged mutatis mutandis between the Federal Republic of Germany and France and the United Kingdom.

COMMODITIES

Terms of reference of the International Copper Study Group.

Done at Geneva February 24, 1989.

Entered into force January 23, 1992.

TIAS

Amendment:

June 26, 1992

Depositary: United Nations

International tropical timber agreement, 2006, with annexes.

Done at Geneva January 27, 2006.

Entered into force December 7, 2011.

TIAS

Depositary: United Nations

International coffee agreement 2007, with annex.

Done at London September 28, 2007.

Entered into force February 2, 2011.

TIAS 11-202

Depositary: United Nations

CONSULAR AFFAIRS

Protocol relating to military obligations in certain cases of double nationality

Concluded at The Hague April 12, 1930.

Entered into force May 25, 1937.

50 Stat. 1317; TS 913; 2 Bevans 1049; 178 LNTS 227

Depositary: United Nations

Convention on the nationality of women.

Signed at Montevideo December 26, 1933.

Entered into force August 29, 1934.

49 Stat. 2957; TS 875; 3 Bevans 141

Depositary: Organization of American States, Uruguay

Convention on protection of children and cooperation in respect of intercountry adoption.

Done at The Hague May 29, 1993.

Entered into force May 1, 1995; for the United States April 1, 2008.

TIAS

Depositary: Netherlands

CULTURAL EXCHANGES, PROPERTY & COOPERATION

Treaty on the protection of artistic and scientific institutions and historic monuments.

Signed at Washington April 15, 1935.

Entered into force August 26, 1935.

49 Stat. 3267; TS 899; 3 Bevans 254; 167 LNTS 279

Depositaries: Organization of American States, International Committee of the Red Cross

Convention concerning artistic exhibitions.

Signed at Buenos Aires December 23, 1936.

Entered into force December 7, 1937.

51 Stat. 206; TS 929; 3 Bevans 383; 188 LNTS 151

Depositary: Organization of American States

Constitution of the United Nations Educational, Scientific and Cultural Organization concluded at London November 16, 1945.

*Entered into force November 4, 1946; re-entered into force for the United States October 1, 2003.**

61 Stat. 2495; TIAS 1580; 3 Bevans 1311; 4 UNTS 275

Depositary: United Kingdom

Notes:

* The Constitution entered into force for the United States November 4, 1946. By a letter dated December 28, 1983, the United States informed the Director General of UNESCO of its intention to withdraw from the organization, effective December 31, 1984. By deposit of instrument of acceptance, the United States resumed membership in UNESCO, effective October 1, 2003.

Agreement for facilitating the international circulation of visual and auditory materials of an educational, scientific and cultural character, with protocol. (Beirut agreement)

Done at Lake Success July 15, 1949.

Entered into force August 12, 1954; for the United States January 12, 1967.

17 UST 1578; TIAS 6116; 197 UNTS 3

Depositary: United Nations

Agreement on the importation of educational, scientific and cultural materials, with protocol.

Done at Lake Success November 22, 1950.

Entered into force May 21, 1952; for the United States November 2, 1966.

17 UST 1835; TIAS 6129; 131 UNTS 25

Depositary: United Nations

Convention for the promotion of inter-American cultural relations.*
Signed at Caracas March 28, 1954.
Entered into force February 18, 1955; for the United States October 3, 1957.
8 UST 1903; TIAS 3936
Depositary: Organization of American States

Note:
* Replaces as between contracting parties the convention of December 23, 1936 (51 Stat. 178; TS 928; 3 Bevans 372; 188 LNTS 125). Parties to the 1936 convention not party to the 1954 convention are: Bolivia, Chile, Colombia, Cuba, Dominican Republic, Guatemala, Honduras, Mexico, Nicaragua and Peru.

Convention for the protection of cultural property in the event of armed conflict, with regulations for the execution of the convention.
Done at The Hague May 14, 1954.
Entered into force August 7, 1956; for the United States March 13, 2009.
TIAS
Depositary: UNESCO

Statutes of the International Centre for the Study of the Preservation and Restoration of Cultural Property.
Done at New Delhi November–December 1956; revised April 24, 1963, and April 14–17, 1969.
Entered into force May 10, 1958; for the United States January 20, 1971.
22 UST 19; TIAS 7038
Depositary: International Centre for the Study of the Preservation and Restoration of Cultural Property

Convention on the means of prohibiting and preventing the illicit import, export and transfer of ownership of cultural property.
Done at Paris November 14, 1970.
Entered into force April 24, 1972; for the United States December 2, 1983.
TIAS; 823 UNTS 231
Depositary: UNESCO

Convention concerning the protection of the world cultural and natural heritage.
Done at Paris November 23, 1972.
Entered into force December 17, 1975.
27 UST 37; TIAS 8226
Depositary: UNESCO

Protocol to the agreement on the importation of educational, scientific and cultural materials of November 22, 1950.
Done at Nairobi November 26, 1976.
Entered into force January 2, 1982; for the United States November 15, 1989.
TIAS
Depositary: United Nations

International convention against doping in sport, with annexes and appendices. With prohibited list and therapeutic use exemptions.
Adopted at Paris October 19, 2005.
Entered into force February 1, 2007; for the United States October 1, 2008.
TIAS
Depositary: UNESCO

DEFENSE

Inter-American treaty of reciprocal assistance (Rio Treaty).
Done at Rio de Janeiro September 2, 1947.
Entered into force December 3, 1948.
62 Stat. 1681; TIAS 1838; 4 Bevans 559; 21 UNTS 77
Depositary: Organization of American States

Agreement for mutual defense assistance in Indochina, with three annexes.
Signed at Saigon December 23, 1950.
Entered into force December 23, 1950.
3 UST 2756; TIAS 2447; 185 UNTS 3

Parties:
Cambodia
France
Laos
United States
Vietnam [1]

Note:
1 The listing for Vietnam, the Republic of Vietnam (South Vietnam), the Democratic Republic of Vietnam (North Vietnam), the Provisional Revolutionary Government of the Republic of South Vietnam, and the Socialist Republic of Vietnam are based on the last notice received by the United States Government from the depositary for the treaty or agreement in question. The United States has been informed by the Socialist Republic of Vietnam that "... in principle, the Government of the Socialist Republic of Vietnam is not bound by the treaties, agreements signed by the former Saigon administration. However... the Government of the Socialist Republic of Vietnam will consider the agreements, on an individual basis, and will examine adherence to those agreements, treaties which are in the interests of the Vietnamese people . . ."

Security treaty (ANZUS Pact).
Signed at San Francisco September 1, 1951.
*Entered into force April 29, 1952.**
3 UST 3420; TIAS 2493; 131 UNTS 83
Depositary: Australia

Notes:
* As of September 17, 1986, the United States suspended obligations under the treaty as between the United States and New Zealand.

Southeast Asia collective defense treaty, with protocol (SEATO).*

Signed at Manila September 8, 1954.
Entered into force February 19, 1955.
6 UST 81; TIAS 3170; 209 UNTS 28

Depositary: Philippines

Notes:

* By decision of the SEATO Council of September 24, 1975, the Organization ceased to exist as of June 30, 1977. The collective defense treaty remains in force.

Memorandum of understanding for the cooperative support of the 76/62 OTO Melara Compact Gun (OMCG), with annexes.

Done at Rome October 24, 1978.
Entered into force October 24, 1978; for the United States July 17, 1979.
TIAS

Amendments:

June 13, August 23, and December 3, 1985, and June 5, 1986
May 30, June 22, August 24, and November 8, 1990
June 14, July 5, October 9, and December 3, 1991, and February 5, 1992
May 11, 25, & 29 and June 2 & 8, November 9, 2004 and September 2, 2005

Parties:

Australia
Canada
Denmark
Germany
Greece
Italy
Netherlands
Norway
Spain
Turkey
United States

Memorandum of understanding concerning cooperative full-scale engineering development of an advanced surface-to-air missile system, with annexes.

Signed April 24, May 9, 18 and July 6, 1979.
Entered into force July 6, 1979.
TIAS 12256

Amendment:

December 23, 1999

Parties:

Denmark
Germany, Federal Republic of [1]
United States

Note:

1 See note under GERMANY in Section 1

Agreement regarding the status of foreign forces in the former territory of the German Democratic Republic.

Exchange of notes at Bonn September 25, 1990.
Entered into force October 3, 1990.
TIAS

Memorandum of understanding for the production of STANDARD missile, with annexes.

Signed at Koblenz, The Hague, and Washington October 20, October 21, and December 3, 2004.
Entered into force December 3, 2004.
TIAS 04-1203.1

Parties:

Germany
Netherlands
United States

Memorandum of understanding concerning the establishment, administration, and operation of the combined joint operations from the sea center of excellence, with annexes.

Signed at Norfolk May 31, 2006.
Entered into force May 31, 2006.
TIAS 06-531.1

Parties:

Canada
France [1]
Germany
Greece
Italy
Netherlands
Norway
Portugal
Romania
Spain
Turkey
United Kingdom
United States

Note:

1 With reservation.

Memorandum of understanding concerning strategic airlift capability, with annexes.

Signed at Stockholm, Budapest, Sofia, Vilnius, Washington, Ljubljana, Brussels, Helsinki, Oslo, Tallinn, Warsaw, and Bucharest March 11, March 31, May 7, May 30, June 11, June 12, June 19, June 20, June 27, July 15, and July 30, 2008.
Entered into force September 23, 2008.
TIAS

Parties:

Bulgaria
Estonia
Finland
Hungary
Lithuania
Netherlands
Norway
Poland
Romania
Slovenia
Sweden
United States

Agreement concerning exchange of secured software-defined radio (SSDR) research and development information.

Signed at Washington, Warsaw, Bagneux, Rome, Stockholm, Madrid, and Helsinki August 17, 20 and 23, September 8, 15 and 16, and October 1, 2010.
Entered into force October 1, 2010.
TIAS 10-1001

Parties:
Finland
France
Italy
Poland
Spain
Sweden
United States

Memorandum of understanding concerning multinational Test and Evaluation Program (TEP) cooperation, with annexes.

Signed at Washington, Australia Capital Territory (ACT), London, Wellington, and Ottawa April 17, April 22, May 11, June 5, and August 19, 2015.
Entered into force April 22, 2015.
TIAS 15-422

Parties
Australia
Canada
New Zealand
United Kingdom
United States

NORTH ATLANTIC TREATY ORGANIZATION (NATO)

Note: The depositary for the North American Treaty Organization is the United States, unless otherwise noted. If the parties are explicitly listed, the agreement does not provide for a depositary.

North Atlantic Treaty.

Signed at Washington April 4, 1949.
Entered into force August 24, 1949.
63 Stat 2241; TIAS 1964; 4 Bevans 828; 34 UNTS 243

Agreement between the parties to the North Atlantic Treaty regarding the status of their forces.

Signed at London June 19, 1951.
Entered into force August 23, 1953.
4 UST 1792; TIAS 2846; 199 UNTS 67

Agreement on the status of the North Atlantic Treaty Organization, national representatives, and international staff.*

Done at Ottawa September 20, 1951.
Entered into force May 18, 1954.
5 UST 1087; TIAS 2992; 200 UNTS 3

Notes:
* See also NORTH ATLANTIC TREATY ORGANIZATION in Section 1.

Protocol to the North Atlantic Treaty on the accession of Greece and Turkey.

Done at London October 17, 1951.
Entered into force February 15, 1952.
3 UST 43; TIAS 2390; 126 UNTS 350

Protocol on the status of international military headquarters set up pursuant to the North Atlantic Treaty.

Signed at Paris August 28, 1952.
Entered into force April 10, 1954.
TIAS 2978; 5 UST 870; 200 UNTS 340

Protocol to the North Atlantic Treaty on the accession of the Federal Republic of Germany.

Signed at Paris October 23, 1954.
Entered into force May 5, 1955.
6 UST 5707; TIAS 3428; 243 UNTS 308

Agreement to supplement the agreement of June 19, 1951 between the parties to the North Atlantic Treaty regarding the status of their forces with respect to foreign forces stationed in the Federal Republic of Germany, with protocol of signature.*

Signed at Bonn August 3, 1959.
Entered into force July 1, 1963.
14 UST 531; TIAS 5351; 481 UNTS 262

Amendments:
October 21, 1971 (24 UST 2355; TIAS 7759)
May 18, 1981 (34 UST 405; TIAS 10367)†
March 18, 1993
March 18, 1993
May 16, 1994

Notes:
* For the agreement implementing paragraph 5 of article 45, see 14 UST 670; TIAS 5351; 481 UNTS 551. For administrative agreement to implement article 60, see 14 UST 677; TIAS 5351; 481 UNTS 565. See also TIAS 5352 under GERMANY – DEFENSE in Section 1.
† Effective April 1, 1974.

Agreement between the parties to the North Atlantic Treaty for cooperation regarding atomic information.

Done at Paris June 18, 1964.
Entered into force March 12, 1965.
16 UST 109; TIAS 5768; 542 UNTS 145

Agreement on the special conditions applicable to the establishment and operation of the International Military Headquarters in the Federal Republic of Germany, with protocol and exchange of notes.

Signed at Paris March 13, 1967, by the Federal Republic of Germany and the Chairman of the Delegation of the Supreme Headquarters Allied Powers in Europe.
Entered into force December 21, 1969.
29 UST 879; TIAS 8854

Depositary: Germany

Agreement regarding making available by the armed forces of the United States and the United Kingdom of accommodation to International Military Headquarters of North Atlantic Treaty Organization in the Federal Republic of Germany.

Done at Bonn February 7, 1969.
Entered into force December 21, 1969.
20 UST 4050; TIAS 6791; 737 UNTS 175

Depositary: Germany

Agreement regarding the status of personnel of sending states attached to an International Military Headquarters of North Atlantic Treaty Organization in the Federal Republic of Germany.

Done at Bonn February 7, 1969.
Entered into force December 21, 1969.
20 UST 4055; TIAS 6792; 737 UNTS 161

Depositary: Germany

North Atlantic Treaty Organization agreement on the communication of technical information for defense purposes.

Done at Brussels October 19, 1970.
Entered into force February 7, 1971.
22 UST 347; TIAS 7064; 800 UNTS 5

Memorandum of understanding for the international development of the North Atlantic Treaty Organization sea gnat system, with annexes

Dated December 8, 1976.
Entered into force January 10, 1977.
28 UST 8897; TIAS 8776

Parties:

Germany, Federal Republic of [1]
Norway
United Kingdom
United States

Note:

1 See note under GERMANY in Section 1.

Memorandum of understanding for the cooperative support of the NATO seasparrow surface missile system, with addendum and exhibit.

Done May 20, 1977.
Entered into force May 31, 1977.
29 UST 1103; TIAS 8870

Amendment:

December 23, 1999

Parties:

Belgium
Denmark
Germany, Federal Republic of [1]
Italy
Netherlands
Norway
United States

Note:

1 See note under GERMANY in Section 1

Agreement concerning helicopter pilot training in the United States under the scope of EURO/NATO training, with annexes.

Signed at Washington July 14, Bonn August 10, The Hague September 1, Copenhagen September 27, and Oslo October 10, 1977.
Entered into force October 10, 1977.
29 UST 5555; TIAS 9128

Parties:

Denmark
Germany, Federal Republic of [1]
Netherlands
Norway
United States

Note:

1 See note under GERMANY in Section 1.

Memorandum of understanding for international collaboration on the NATO explosion resistant multi-influence sweep system (ERMISS).

Done April 5, 1978.
Entered into force April 25, 1978; for the United States August 24, 1978.
30 UST 1170; TIAS 9244

Parties:

France
Germany, Federal Republic of [1]
Netherlands
United Kingdom
United States

Note:

1 See note under GERMANY in Section 1.

Memorandum of understanding concerning the EURO-NATO Joint Jet Pilot Training (ENJJPT) Program.

Signed at Brussels December 9, 1980.
Entered into force December 9, 1980.
32 UST 4259; TIAS 9947

Amendments:

December 6, 1991
April 15, 1993
October 4, 1994
September 19, 1995 (TIAS 12692)

Parties:

Belgium
Canada
Denmark
Germany, Federal Republic of [1]
Greece
Italy
Netherlands
Norway
Portugal
Turkey
United Kingdom
United States

Note:

1 See note under GERMANY in Section 1.

Protocol to the North Atlantic Treaty on the accession of Spain.
Signed at Brussels December 10, 1981.
Entered into force May 29, 1982.
TIAS 10564

Memorandum of understanding for the project definition phase of a NATO frigate replacement for the 1990s (NFR 90).
Signed October 20, 1987, January 23, 1988, and January 25, 1988.
Entered into force January 25, 1988.
TIAS
Parties:
Canada
France
Germany, Federal Republic of [1]
Italy
Netherlands
Spain
United Kingdom
United States

Note:
1 See note under GERMANY in Section 1.

International support agreement concerning primary logistical and administrative support for NATO units at Ramstein, Kindsbach, and Bann, with annexes.
Signed at Ramstein May 18, 1988.
Entered into force May 18, 1988.
TIAS
Parties
Allied Air Forces Central Europe
Supreme Headquarters Allied Powers, Europe
United States

Agreement to provide for the accession of Spain to the memorandum of understanding of May 20, 1977, for the cooperative support of the NATO seasparrow surface missile system.
Signed at Hamburg October 4, 8, and 14, 1991.
Entered into force October 14, 1991.
TIAS
Parties:
Australia
Belgium
Canada
Denmark
Germany
Greece
Italy
Netherlands
Norway
Portugal
Spain
Turkey
United States

Administrative agreement to implement article 60 of the agreement of August 3, 1959, as amended, to supplement the agreement between the parties to the North Atlantic Treaty regarding the status of their forces with respect to foreign forces stationed in the Federal Republic of Germany.
Done at Bonn March 18, 1993.
Entered into force March 29, 1998.
TIAS

Agreement on the status of missions and representatives of third states to the North Atlantic Treaty Organization.
Done at Brussels September 14, 1994.
Entered into force March 28, 1997.
TIAS
Depositary: Belgium

Memorandum of understanding concerning the establishment, mission, financing, administration and status of Headquarters 5 Allied Tactical Air Force (HQ 5 ATAF), with annexes.
Signed at Casteau September 25, 26, and 29, and October 2, 1995.
Entered into force October 2, 1995; effective January 1, 1994.
TIAS 12694.
Parties
Germany
Greece
Italy
Supreme Headquarters Allied Powers, Europe
Turkey
United States

Agreement among the States Parties to the North Atlantic Treaty and other States participating in the Partnership for Peace regarding the status of their forces.
Done at Brussels June 19, 1995.
Entered into force January 13, 1996.
TIAS 12666

Agreement between the parties to the North Atlantic Treaty for the security of information, with annexes.
Done at Brussels March 6, 1997.
Entered into force August 16, 1998.
TIAS

Protocol to the North Atlantic Treaty on the accession of the Czech Republic.
Signed at Brussels December 16, 1997.
Entered into force December 4, 1998.
TIAS 98-1204

Protocol to the North Atlantic Treaty on the accession of Hungary.
Signed at Brussels December 16, 1997.
Entered into force December 4, 1998.
TIAS 98-1204.1

Protocol to the North Atlantic Treaty on the accession of Poland.
Signed at Brussels December 16, 1997.
Entered into force December 4, 1998.
TIAS 98-1204.2

Memorandum of understanding concerning the manning, funding and support of NATO Southern Regional Maritime Special Entities, with annexes and appendices.
Signed at Mons November 30, 1999.
Entered into force September 1, 1999.
TIAS

Parties

Greece
Italy
Spain
Supreme Headquarters Allied Powers, Europe
Turkey
United Kingdom
United States

Protocol to the North Atlantic Treaty on the accession of the Republic of Bulgaria.
Signed at Brussels March 26, 2003.
Entered into force February 27, 2004.
TIAS 04-227

Protocol to the North Atlantic Treaty on the accession of the Republic of Estonia.
Signed at Brussels March 26, 2003.
Entered into force February 27, 2004.
TIAS 04-227.1

Protocol to the North Atlantic Treaty on the accession of the Republic of Latvia.
Signed at Brussels March 26, 2003.
Entered into force February 27, 2004.
TIAS 04-227.2

Protocol to the North Atlantic Treaty on the accession of the Republic of Lithuania.
Signed at Brussels March 26, 2003.
Entered into force February 27, 2004.
TIAS 04-227.3

Protocol to the North Atlantic Treaty on the accession of Romania.
Signed at Brussels March 26, 2003.
Entered into force February 27, 2004.
TIAS 04-227.4

Protocol to the North Atlantic Treaty on the accession of the Slovak Republic.
Signed at Brussels March 26, 2003.
Entered into force February 27, 2004.
TIAS 04-227.5

Protocol to the North Atlantic Treaty on the accession of the Republic of Slovenia.
Signed at Brussels March 26, 2003.
Entered into force February 27, 2004.
TIAS 04-227.6

Protocol to the North Atlantic Treaty on the accession of the Republic of Albania.
Signed at Brussels July 9, 2008.
Entered into force March 27, 2009.
TIAS

Protocol to the North Atlantic Treaty on the accession of the Republic of Croatia.
Signed at Brussels July 9, 2008.
Entered into force March 30, 2009.
TIAS

DIPLOMATIC & CONSULAR RELATIONS

Convention for the establishment of the right of protection in Morocco.*
Signed at Madrid July 3, 1880.
Entered into force May 1, 1881; for the United States March 9, 1882; effective July 3, 1880.
22 Stat. 817; TS 246; 1 Bevans 71

Parties:

Belgium
Denmark
France
Italy
Morocco
Netherlands
Norway
Portugal
Spain
Sweden
Union of Soviet Socialist Republics [1]
United Kingdom
United States

Notes:

* Extraterritorial jurisdiction in Morocco relinquished by the United States October 6, 1956. Article 15 relating to Moroccan nationality is obsolete and without effect.

1 See note under UNION OF SOVIET SOCIALIST REPUBLICS in Section 1.

Convention relating to the duties, rights, prerogatives, and immunities of consular agents.
Signed at Habana February 20, 1928.
Entered into force September 3, 1929; for the United States February 8, 1932.
47 Stat. 1976; TS 843; 2 Bevans 714; 155 LNTS 291
Depositaries: Cuba, Organization of American States

Vienna convention on diplomatic relations.
Done at Vienna April 18, 1961.
Entered into force April 24, 1964; for the United States December 13, 1972.
23 UST 3227; TIAS 7502; 500 UNTS 95
Depositary: United Nations

Optional protocol to the Vienna convention on diplomatic relations concerning the compulsory settlement of disputes.
Done at Vienna April 18, 1961.
Entered into force April 24, 1964; for the United States December 13, 1972.
23 UST 3374; TIAS 7502; 500 UNTS 241
Depositary: United Nations

Convention on consular relations.
Done at Vienna April 24, 1963.
Entered into force March 19, 1967; for the United States December 24, 1969.
21 UST 77; TIAS 6820; 596 UNTS 261
Depositary: United Nations

Treaty of amity and cooperation in Southeast Asia.
Done at Denpasar February 24, 1976.
Entered into force July 15, 1976; for the United States July 22, 2009.
TIAS
Amendments:
December 15, 1987
July 25, 1998

Depositaries: Indonesia, Malaysia, Philippines, Singapore, Thailand

ENERGY

Agreement concerning the establishment of a coordinating group to direct and coordinate development of international cooperation in the field of energy, and related matters.
Communiqué issued at Washington February 13, 1974.
Entered into force February 13, 1974.
25 UST 223; TIAS 7791
Parties:
Belgium
Canada
Denmark
European Community
France 1
Germany, Federal Republic of [2]
Ireland
Italy
Japan
Luxembourg
Netherlands
Norway
Organization for Economic Cooperation and Development
United Kingdom
United States

Notes:
1 France does not accept point 9 and first three paragraphs of point 10.
2 See note under GERMANY in Section 1.

Memorandum of understanding concerning cooperative information exchange relating to the development of solar heating and cooling systems in buildings.
Formulated at Odeillo, France October 1-4, 1974.
Entered into force July 1, 1975.
26 UST 2932; TIAS 8202
Parties:
Australia
Belgium
Canada
Denmark
France
Germany, Federal Republic of [1]
Greece
Israel
Italy
Jamaica
Netherlands
New Zealand
Spain
United Kingdom
United States

Note
1 See note under GERMANY in Section 1.

Agreement on an international energy program, including establishment of the International Energy Agency.
Done at Paris November 18, 1974.
Entered into force provisionally November 18, 1974; definitively January 19, 1976.
27 UST 1685; TIAS 8278; 1040 UNTS 271
Amendment:
February 5, 1975 (27 UST 1817; TIAS 8278)

Depositary: Belgium

Long-term cooperation program in the field of energy.
Done at Paris January 30, 1976.
Entered into force March 8, 1976.
27 UST 231; TIAS 8229
Parties:
Australia
Austria
Belgium
Canada
Denmark
Germany, Federal Republic of [1]
Greece
Ireland
Italy
Japan
Luxembourg
Netherlands
New Zealand
Norway
Portugal
Spain
Sweden
Switzerland
Turkey
United Kingdom
United States

Note:
1 See note under GERMANY in Section 1.

Agreement for cooperation in energy science and technology, with annexes.
Signed at Victoria July 23, 2007.
Entered into force July 24, 2008.
TIAS 08-724

Parties:
Canada
Mexico
United States

Agreement on International Renewable Energy Agency (IRENA).
Signed at Bonn June 29, 2009
Entered into force April 3, 2011.
TIAS

Depositary: Germany

The following agreements implement the agreement on an international energy program, including the establishment of the International Energy Agency, signed November 18, 1974 (27 UST 1685; TIAS 8278; 1040 UNTS 271). Unless otherwise noted, the depositary for these agreements is the International Energy Agency.

Implementing agreement for the establishment of a project on the fluidised combustion of coal, with annexes.
Done at Paris November 20, 1975.
Entered into force November 20, 1975.
33 UST 2131; TIAS 10177

Implementing agreement for the establishment of the economic assessment service for coal, with annex.
Done at Paris November 20, 1975.
Entered into force November 20, 1975.
32 UST 1337; TIAS 9775

Implementing agreement for a program of research and development on energy conservation in buildings and community systems, with annexes.
Done at Paris March 16, 1977.
Entered into force March 16, 1977.
TIAS 10553

Implementing agreement for a program of research and development on energy conservation in heat transfer and heat exchangers, with annexes.
Done at Paris June 28, 1977.
Entered into force June 28, 1977.
TIAS

Implementing agreement for a program of research and development on wind energy conversion systems, with annexes.
Done at Paris October 6, 1977.
Entered into force October 6, 1977.
TIAS

Implementing agreement for cooperation in the development of large scale wind energy conversion systems.
Done at Paris October 6, 1977.
Entered into force October 6, 1977.
TIAS

Implementing agreement for a program of research and development on man-made geothermal energy systems, with annex.
Done at Paris October 6, 1977.
Entered into force October 6, 1977.
33 UST 2157; TIAS 10178

Implementing agreement for a program of research and development on the production of hydrogen from water, with annexes.
Done at Paris October 6, 1977.
Entered into force October 6, 1977.
TIAS

Implementing agreement for the establishment of a project on the treatment of coal gasifier effluent liquors, with annexes.
Done at Paris October 17, 1977.
Entered into force October 17, 1977, effective October 1, 1976.
33 UST 2229; TIAS 10181

Implementing agreement for a program of research and development on wave power, with annex.
Done at Tokyo April 13, 1978.
Entered into force April 13, 1978.
33 UST 2253; TIAS 10182

Implementing agreement for a program of research, development and demonstration on forestry energy, with annex.
Done at Tokyo April 13, 1978.
Entered into force April 13, 1978.
TIAS

Implementing agreement for the establishment of the biomass conversion technical information service.
Done at Paris May 24, 1978.
Entered into force May 24, 1978.
TIAS

Implementing agreement for a program of research and development on advanced heat pump systems, with annex.
Done at Paris July 27, 1978.
Entered into force July 27, 1978.
33 UST 2279; TIAS 10183

Implementing agreement for a program of research and development for energy conservation in cement manufacture, with annex.
Done at Paris July 27, 1978.
Entered into force July 27, 1978.
33 UST 2305; TIAS 10184

Implementing agreement for a program of research and development on energy conservation through energy storage, with annex.
Done at Paris September 22, 1978.
Entered into force September 22, 1978; for the United States February 21, 1979.
33 UST 2325; TIAS 10185

Implementing agreement for a program of research and development on high temperature materials for automotive engines, with annex.
Done at Paris May 22, 1979.
Entered into force May 22, 1979.
33 UST 2383; TIAS 10187

Implementing agreement for a program of research, development and demonstration on geothermal equipment.
Done at Paris May 22, 1979.
Entered into force May 22, 1979.
33 UST 2359; TIAS 10186

Implementing agreement for a program of research, development and demonstration on enhanced recovery of oil, with annex.
Done at Paris May 22, 1979.
Entered into force May 22, 1979.
TIAS

Implementing agreement for a program of energy technology systems analysis, with annex.
Done at Paris November 13, 1980.
Entered into force November 13, 1980.
TIAS

Implementing agreement for a program of research and development and demonstration on energy conservation in the pulp and paper industry, with annexes.
Done at Paris February 18, 1981.
Entered into force February 18, 1981.
TIAS 10525

Implementing agreement for a program of research, development and demonstration on coal/oil mixtures, with annex.
Done at Paris March 23, 1981.
Entered into force March 23, 1981.
TIAS

ENVIRONMENT & CONSERVATION

Convention on nature protection and wildlife preservation in the Western Hemisphere, with annex.
Done at the Pan American Union, Washington, October 12, 1940.
Entered into force April 30, 1942.
56 Stat. 1354; TS 981; 3 Bevans 630; 161 UNTS 193
Depositary: Organization of American States

Convention on wetlands of international importance, especially as waterfowl habitat.
Done at Ramsar February 2, 1971.
Entered into force December 21, 1975; for the United States December 18, 1986.
TIAS 11084; 996 UNTS 245
Amendment:
December 3, 1982 (TIAS 11084)

Depositary: UNESCO

Convention for the conservation of Antarctic seals, with annex.
Done at London June 1, 1972.
Entered into force March 11, 1978.
29 UST 441; TIAS 8826
Amendment:
September 12–16, 1988

Depositary: United Kingdom

Agreement on the conservation of polar bears.
Done at Oslo November 15, 1973.
Entered into force May 26, 1976; for the United States November 1, 1976.
27 UST 3918; TIAS 8409
Depositary: Norway

Convention on international trade in endangered species of wild fauna and flora, with appendices.
Done at Washington March 3, 1973.
Entered into force July 1, 1975.
27 UST 1087; TIAS 8249; 993 UNTS 243
Amendment:
June 22, 1979 (TIAS 11079)

Depositary: Switzerland

Convention on the conservation of Antarctic marine living resources, with annex for an arbitral tribunal.
Done at Canberra May 20, 1980.
Entered into force April 7, 1982.
33 UST 3476; TIAS 10240
Depositary: Australia

United Nations framework convention on climate change, with annexes.
Done at New York May 9, 1992.
Entered into force March 21, 1994.
TIAS
Amendment:
December 11, 1997

Depositary: United Nations

Establishment agreement for the Center for International Forestry Research (CIFOR), with constitution.
Done at Canberra March 5, 1993.
Entered into force March 5, 1993;for the United States May 3, 1993.
TIAS 11960
Depositary: Australia

North American agreement on environmental cooperation, with annexes.
Signed at Mexico, Washington and Ottawa September 8, 9, 12 and 14, 1993.
Entered into force January 1, 1994.
TIAS
Parties:
Canada
Mexico
United States

United Nations convention to combat desertification in those countries experiencing serious drought and/or desertification, particularly in Africa, with annexes.
Done at Paris June 17, 1994.
Entered into force December 26, 1996; for the United States February 15, 2001.
TIAS
Depositary: United Nations

Inter-American convention for the protection and conservation of sea turtles, with annexes.
Signed at Caracas December 1, 1996.
Entered into force May 2, 2001.
TIAS ; 2164 UNTS 29
Depositary: Venezuela

Memorandum of understanding regarding a secretariat for submissions on environmental enforcement matters under the United States-Peru Trade promotion agreement.
Signed at Lima June 9, 2015.
Entered into force March 23, 2016.
TIAS
Parties:
OAS
Peru
United States

The Paris agreement regarding the United Nations Framework Convention on Climate Change.
Adopted at Paris December 12, 2015.
Signed by the United States April 22, 2016.
Entered into force November 4, 2016.
TIAS 16-1104
Depositary: United Nations

FINANCE

Articles of agreement of the International Bank for Reconstruction and Development, formulated at the Bretton Woods Conference July 1–22, 1944. *
Opened for signature at Washington December 27, 1945.
Entered into force December 27, 1945.
60 Stat. 1440; TIAS 1502; 3 Bevans 1390; 2 UNTS 134
Amendment:
August 25, 1965 (16 UST 1942; TIAS 5929)

Depositary: United States

Notes:
* Applicable to all territories

Articles of agreement of the International Monetary Fund, formulated at the Bretton Woods Conference July 1–22, 1944.
*Opened for signature at Washington December 27, 1945.**
Entered into force December 27, 1945.
60 Stat. 1401; TIAS 1501; 3 Bevans 1351; 2 UNTS 39
Amendments:
May 31, 1968 (20 UST 2775; TIAS 6748)
April 30, 1976 (29 UST 2203; TIAS 8937)
June 28, 1990 (TIAS 11898)

Depositary: United States
Notes:
* Applicable to all territories.

Convention on the Organization for Economic Cooperation and Development, with supplementary protocols Nos. 1 and 2 and memorandum of understanding on the application of Article 15.
Signed at Paris December 14, 1960.
Entered into force September 30, 1961.
TIAS 4891; 12 UST 1728; 888 UNTS 179
Depositary: Organization for Economic Cooperation and Development

Convention on international interests in mobile equipment.
Done at Cape Town November 16, 2001.
Entered into force April 1, 2004; for the United States February 1, 2005.
TIAS 06-301.2
Depositary: UNIDROIT

Protocol to the convention on international interests in mobile equipment on matters specific to aircraft equipment.
Done at Cape Town November 16, 2001.
Entered into force March 1, 2006.
TIAS
Depositary: UNIDROIT

WORLD WAR II RELATED AGREEMENTS

Accord relating to the liquidation of German property in Switzerland.
Exchange of notes at Washington May 25, 1946.
Entered into force June 27, 1946.
13 UST 1118; TIAS 5058
Parties:
France
Switzerland
United Kingdom
United States

Agreement relating to German assets in Sweden.
Exchanges of letters at Washington July 18, 1946.
Entered into force March 28, 1947.
61 Stat. 3191; TIAS 1657; 4 Bevans 88; 125 UNTS 119
Parties:
France
Sweden
United Kingdom
United States

Memorandum of understanding regarding German assets in Italy.
Signed at Washington August 14, 1947.
Entered into force August 14, 1947.
61 Stat. 3292; TIAS 1664; 4 Bevans 552; 138 UNTS 111
Parties:
France
Italy
United Kingdom
United States

Agreement relating to the resolution of conflicting claims to German enemy assets.

Done at Brussels December 5, 1947.
Entered into force for the United States January 24, 1951.
2 UST 729; TIAS 2230

Amendments and Extensions:
February 3, 1949 (2 UST 785; TIAS 2230)
May 10, 1950 (2 UST 791; TIAS 2230)
January 24, 1951 (2 UST 795; TIAS 2230)
April 30, 1952 (3 UST 4254; TIAS 2569)

Parties:
Belgium
Canada
Cuba
Denmark
Haiti
Honduras
Luxembourg
Netherlands
Nicaragua
United States [1]

Note:
1 With reservation.

Agreement relating to prewar external debts of the German Reich and the debt arising out of economic assistance furnished since May 8, 1945.

Exchange of letters at Bonn March 6, 1951.
Entered into force March 6, 1951.
2 UST 1249; TIAS 2274; 106 UNTS 141

Parties:
France
Germany, Federal Republic of [1]
United Kingdom
United States

Note:
1 See note under GERMANY in Section 1.

Agreement concerning German property in Switzerland, with related notes.

Signed at Bern August 28, 1952.
Entered into force March 19, 1953.
13 UST 1131; TIAS 5059; 175 UNTS 69

Parties:
France
Switzerland
United Kingdom
United States

Agreement on German external debts.

Signed at London February 27, 1953.
Entered into force September 16, 1953.
4 UST 443; TIAS 2792; 333 UNTS 3

Depositary: United Kingdom

Letter-agreement relating to restitution and liquidation of confiscated property recovered in Italy from German forces ("Rome Treasure").

Letter of April 27, 1954, from Administrator, Paris Reparation Refugee Fund, to the American Ambassador, Rome, accepted by the United States, the United Kingdom, and Italy on July 23, 1954.
Entered into force July 23, 1954.
5 UST 2170; TIAS 3080

Memorandum agreement relating to the disposition of certain German assets in Thailand.

Signed at Bangkok January 31, 1957.
Entered into force January 31, 1957.
8 UST 129; TIAS 3747; 278 UNTS 105

Parties:
France
Thailand
United Kingdom
United States

Memorandum of understanding regarding German assets in Italy, with exchange of notes.

Signed at Rome March 29, 1957.
Entered into force March 29, 1957.
8 UST 445; TIAS 3797; 283 UNTS 137

Parties:
France
Italy
United Kingdom
United States

Protocol terminating obligations arising from the accord of May 10, 1948 (62 Stat. 2061; TIAS 1773) regarding German assets in Spain, with exchange of notes.

Signed at Madrid August 9, 1958.
Entered into force July 2, 1959.
11 UST 2274; TIAS 4606; 351 UNTS 398

Parties:
France
Spain
United Kingdom
United States

Agreement relating to German assets in Portugal and to certain claims regarding monetary gold.

Signed at Lisbon October 27, 1958.
Entered into force October 24, 1959.
351 UNTS 303

Parties:
France
Portugal
United Kingdom
United States

MULTILATERAL FUNDS

Articles of agreement of the International Finance Corporation.

Done at Washington May 25, 1955.
Entered into force July 20, 1956.
7 UST 2197; TIAS 3620; 264 UNTS 117

Amendments:
September 1, 1961 (12 UST 2945; TIAS 4894; 439 UNTS 318)
August 25, 1965 (24 UST 1760; TIAS 7683)

Depositary: World Bank

Agreement establishing the Inter-American Development Bank, with annexes.
Done at Washington April 8, 1959.
Entered into force December 30, 1959.
10 UST 3029; TIAS 4397; 389 UNTS 69

Amendments:
January 28, 1964 (21 UST 1570; TIAS 6920)
March 31, 1968 (19 UST 7381; TIAS 6591)
March 23, 1972 (23 UST 2455; TIAS 7437; 851 UNTS 283)
June 1, 1976 (27 UST 3547; TIAS 8383)
January 27, 1977 (35 UST 3645; TIAS 10875)

Depositary: Organization of American States

Indus Basin Development Fund agreement, with annexes.
Done at Karachi September 19, 1960.
Entered into force January 12, 1961; effective from April 1, 1960.
12 UST 19; TIAS 4671; 444 UNTS 259
Depositary: Int'l Bank for Reconstruction and Development

Indus Basin development fund (supplemental), 1964.
Done at Washington March 31, 1964.
Entered into force April 6, 1964.
15 UST 396; TIAS 5570; 503 UNTS 388
Depositary: Int'l Bank for Reconstruction and Development

Articles of agreement establishing the Asian Development Bank, with annexes.
Done at Manila December 4, 1965.
Entered into force August 22, 1966.
17 UST 1418; TIAS 6103; 571 UNTS 123
Depositary: United Nations

Proces-verbal of rectification of the agreement establishing the Asian Development Bank.
Signed at New York November 2, 1967.
18 UST 2935; TIAS 6387; 608 UNTS 380
Depositary: United Nations

Tarbela Development Fund agreement.
Done at Washington May 2, 1968.
Entered into force May 2, 1968.
19 UST 4866; TIAS 6492; 637 UNTS 4
Depositary: Int'l Bank for Reconstruction and Development

Agreement establishing the African Development Fund, with schedules.
Done at Abidjan November 29, 1972.
Entered into force June 30, 1973; for the United States November 18, 1976.
28 UST 4547; TIAS 8605
Depositary: African Development Bank

Tarbela Fund (Supplemental) agreement, 1975.
Done at Washington August 15, 1975.
Entered into force August 15, 1975.
26 UST 2751; TIAS 8193
Depositary: Int'l Bank for Reconstruction and Development

Agreement establishing the International Fund for Agricultural Development.
Done at Rome June 13, 1976.
Entered into force November 30, 1977.
28 UST 8435; TIAS 8765

Amendment:
December 11, 1986 (TIAS 12068)

Depositary: United Nations

Agreement establishing the African Development Bank*, with annexes.
Adopted by the Board of Governors at Abidjan May 17, 1979.[Ψ]
Entered into force May 7, 1982; for the United States January 31, 1983.
TIAS
Depositary: United Nations

Notes:
* The agreement establishing the African Development Bank, done at Khartoum, August 4, 1963, entered into force September 10, 1964 (510 UNTS 3 and 569 UNTS 353 (corr.)).
Ψ The amendments to the agreement, which provide for non-regional membership, were adopted at Abidjan by resolution 05-09 of May 17, 1979, of the Board of Governors and concluded at Lusaka on May 7, 1982.

Agreement establishing the Inter-American Investment Corporation, with annex.
Done at Washington November 19, 1984.
Entered into force March 23, 1986.
TIAS 12087
Depositary: Inter-American Development Bank

Convention establishing the Multilateral Investment Guarantee Agency (MIGA) with annexes and schedules.
Done at Seoul October 11, 1985.
Entered into force April 12, 1988.
TIAS 12089
Depositary: World Bank

Agreement concerning the international fund for Ireland, with annexes.
Done at Washington September 26, 1986.
Entered into force September 26, 1986.
TIAS 11401

Parties:
Ireland
United Kingdom
United States

Agreement establishing the European Bank for Reconstruction and Development, with annexes.
Done at Paris May 29, 1990.
Entered into force March 28, 1991.
TIAS
Depositary: European Bank for Reconstruction and Development

FISHERIES

Convention for the regulation of whaling
Concluded at Geneva September 24, 1931.
Entered into force January 16, 1935.
49 Stat. 3079; TS 880; 3 Bevans 26; 155 LNTS 349
Depositary: United Nations

International convention for the regulation of whaling with schedule of whaling regulations.
Signed at Washington December 2, 1946.
Entered into force November 10, 1948.
62 Stat. 1716; TIAS 1849; 4 Bevans 248; 161 UNTS 72
Depositary: United States

Convention for the establishment of an Inter-American Tropical Tuna Commission, with exchange of notes of March 3, 1950.
Signed at Washington May 31, 1949.
Entered into force March 3, 1950.
1 UST 230; TIAS 2044; 80 UNTS 3
Depositary: United States

Protocol to the international convention for the regulation of whaling.
Done at Washington November 19, 1956.
Entered into force May 4, 1959.
10 UST 952; TIAS 4228; 338 UNTS 366

2016 Schedule
https://archive.iwc.int/pages/view.php?ref=3606&k=

Depositary: United States
Note: For information on previous schedules, see United States depositary website.

Convention on fishing and conservation of the living resources of the high seas.
Done at Geneva April 29, 1958.
Entered into force March 20, 1966.
17 UST 138; TIAS 5969; 559 UNTS 285
Depositary: United Nations

Amended agreement for the establishment of the Asia-Pacific Fishery Commission.*
Approved at the 11th Session of the Conference of the Food and Agriculture Organization, Rome, November 23, 1961.
Entered into force November 23, 1961.
13 UST 2511; TIAS 5218; 418 UNTS 348
Depositary: Food and Agriculture Organization

Notes:
* Formerly the Indo-Pacific Fisheries Council.

International convention for the conservation of Atlantic tunas.
Done at Rio de Janeiro May 14, 1966.
Entered into force March 21, 1969.
20 UST 2887; TIAS 6767; 673 UNTS 63
Amendments:
July 10, 1984
June 5, 1992

Depositary: Food and Agriculture Organization

Convention on future multilateral cooperation in the northwest Atlantic fisheries.
Done at Ottawa October 24, 1978.
Entered into force January 1, 1979;
for the United States November 29, 1995.
TIAS
Depositary: Canada

Convention for the conservation of salmon in the North Atlantic.
Done at Reykjavik March 2, 1982.
Entered into force October 1, 1983.
35 UST 2284; TIAS 10789
Depositary: Council of the European Union

Memoranda of understanding concerning salmonid research and enforcement of the international convention for the high seas fisheries of the North Pacific Ocean.
Signed at Vancouver April 9, 1986.
Entered into force April 9, 1986.
TIAS
Parties
Canada
Japan
United States

Treaty on fisheries with certain Pacific Islands States, with annexes and agreed statement.
Done at Port Moresby April 2, 1987.
Entered into force June 15, 1988.
TIAS 11100
Amendment:
May 14, 1992

Depositary: Papua New Guinea

Convention for the prohibition of fishing with long driftnets in the South Pacific, with protocol.
Done at Wellington November 24, 1989.
Entered into force May 17, 1991; for the United States February 28, 1992.
TIAS
Depositary: New Zealand

Convention for the conservation of anadromous stocks in the North Pacific Ocean, with annex.
Done at Moscow February 11, 1992.
Entered into force February 16, 1993.
TIAS 11465
Depositary: Russia

Agreement to promote compliance with international conservation and management measures by fishing vessels on the high seas.
Done at Rome November 24, 1993.
Entered into force April 24, 2003.
TIAS
Depositary: Food and Agriculture Organization

Convention on the conservation and management of pollock resources in the central Bering Sea, with annex.
Done at Washington June 16, 1994.
Entered into force December 8, 1995.
TIAS
Depositary: United States

Agreement for the implementation of the provisions of the United Nations Convention on the Law of the Sea of December 10, 1982, relating to the conservation and management of straddling fish stocks and highly migratory fish stocks, with annexes.
Done at New York August 4, 1995.
Entered into force December 11, 2001.
TIAS
Depositary: United Nations

Agreement on the international dolphin conservation program, with annexes.
Done at Washington May 21, 1998.
Entered into force February 15, 1999.
TIAS 12956
Depositary: United States

Convention for the conservation and management of highly migratory fish stocks in the Western and Central Pacific Ocean, with annexes.
Done at Honolulu September 5, 2000.
Entered into force June 19, 2004; for the United States July 27, 2007.
TIAS 13115
Depositary: New Zealand

FOREIGN ASSISTANCE

Constitution of the United Nations Food and Agriculture Organization.
Signed at Quebec October 16, 1945.
Entered into force October 16, 1945.
12 UST 980; TIAS 4803 (Composite Text, as amended to 1957)
Amendments:
October 30–November 24, 1961 (13 UST 2616; TIAS 5229)
November 16–December 5, 1963 (14 UST 2203; TIAS 5506)
November 20–December 9, 1965 (17 UST 457; TIAS 5987)
November 4–23, 1967 (18 UST 3273; TIAS 6421)
October 30–November 27, 1969 (21 UST 1464; TIAS 6902)
November 6–25, 1971 (23 UST 74; TIAS 7274)
November 16–26, 1973 (25 UST 928; TIAS 7836)
November 26, 1975 (27 UST 2381; TIAS 8318)
November 29, 1977 (29 UST 2868; TIAS 8982)
November 18, 1991 (TIAS 12134)

Depositary: Food and Agriculture Organization

Agreement relating to the assumption by Indonesia of all responsibilities and obligations of the Netherlands incurred under the economic cooperation agreements of July 2, 1948, as amended, and April 26, 1949, as amended, and the loan agreements of October 28, 1948 and December 22, 1949; and memorandum of understanding.
Signed at Washington February 11, 1952.
Entered into force February 11, 1952.
3 UST 2989; TIAS 2484; 165 UNTS 77
Parties:
Indonesia
Netherlands
United States

Articles of agreement of the International Development Association.*
Done at Washington January 26, 1960.
Entered into force September 24, 1960.
11 UST 2284; TIAS 4607; 439 UNTS 249
Depositary: World Bank

Notes:
* Applicable to all territories

Agreement for economic and technical assistance to the programs of Central American Integration.
Signed at Guatemala October 30, 1965.
Entered into force September 28, 1967.
18 UST 2770; TIAS 6362
Parties:
Costa Rica
El Salvador
Guatemala
Honduras
Nicaragua
United States

Agricultural commodities agreement for the sale of wheat, with memorandum of understanding.
Signed at Dar-es-Salaam February 18, and at Nairobi February 19, February 22, and March 4, 1966.
Entered into force March 4, 1966.
17 UST 628; TIAS 6010; 578 UNTS 57
Parties:
East African Common Services Organization
Kenya
Tanzania
Uganda
United States

Agreement for the establishment of the International Development Law Organization.
Signed at Rome February 5, 1988.
Entered into force April 28, 1989.
TIAS
Amendments:
June 30, 2002; November 30, 2002

Depositary: International Development Law Organization

Agreement establishing the Inter-American Institute for Global Change Research.
Done at Montevideo May 13, 1992.
Entered into force March 12, 1994.
TIAS
Depositary: Organization of American States

HEALTH & MEDICAL COOPERATION

The Pan American sanitary code.*
Signed at Habana November 14, 1924.
Entered into force June 26, 1925.
44 Stat. 2031; TS 714; 2 Bevans 483; 86 LNTS 43
Depositary: Cuba

Notes:
* Articles 2, 9, 10, 11, 16 to 53 inclusive, 61 and 62 replaced by the international health regulations, adopted at Boston, July 25, 1969 (TIAS 7026).

Additional protocol amending the Pan American sanitary code of November 14, 1924.
Signed at Lima October 19, 1927.
Entered into force July 3, 1928.
45 Stat. 2613; TS 763; 2 Bevans 648; 87 LNTS 453
Depositary: Cuba

Constitution of the World Health Organization.
Done at New York July 22, 1946.
Entered into force April 7, 1948; for the United States June 21, 1948.
62 Stat. 2679; TIAS 1808; 4 Bevans 119; 14 UNTS 185
Amendments:
May 29, 1959 (TIAS 4643)
May 23, 1967 (26 UST 990; TIAS 8086)
May 22, 1973 (28 UST 2088; TIAS 8534)
May 17, 1976 (35 UST 4280; TIAS 10930)
May 12, 1986 (TIAS 12049)
May 16, 1998 (TIAS 12953)

Depositary: United Nations

Protocol for the termination of the Brussels agreement for the unification of pharmacopoeial formulas for potent drugs.
Done at Geneva May 20, 1952.
Entered into force May 20, 1952.
3 UST 5067; TIAS 2692; 219 UNTS 55
Depositary: Belgium

Statute of International Agency for Research on Cancer.
Done at Geneva May 20, 1965.
Entered into force September 15, 1965.
16 UST 1239; TIAS 5873
Amendment:
May 19, 1970 (21 UST 1567; TIAS 6919)

Depositary: World Health Organization

World Health Organization nomenclature regulations, 1967.*
Adopted at Geneva May 22, 1967.
Entered into force January 1, 1968.
18 UST 3003; TIAS 6393
Depositary: World Health Organization
Note:
* In force for all members of the World Health Organization with the exception of the Federal Republic of Germany which has made a reservation that the nomenclature regulations, 1967, will not enter into force in the Federal Republic until the Director-General of the World Health Organization has been notified that the domestic prerequisites have been fulfilled. The World Health Organization Regulations No. 1 of July 24, 1948 (7 UST 79; TIAS 3482) regarding nomenclature remain in force as regards parties to them which are not yet parties to the 1967 regulations.

International health regulations, with annexes and appendices.*
Adopted at Geneva May 16-25, 2005.
Entered into force June 15, 2007; for the United States July 18, 2007.
TIAS
Depositary: World Health Organization

Note:
* Replaces as between States bound by these regulations the international sanitary conventions, 1951 and the international health regulations, 1969, and any subsequent amendments to those conventions.

HUMAN RIGHTS

General Act for the repression of the African slave trade.*
Signed at Brussels July 2, 1890.
Entered into force August 31, 1891; for the United States April 2, 1892.
TS 383; 27 Stat. 886; 1 Bevans 134
Depositary: Belgium

Notes:
* Replaced, as between contracting parties to the later conventions, by the convention of September 10, 1919 (49 Stat. 3027; TS 877), except for the stipulations contained in article I of the 1919 Convention, and by the convention of the same date on the subject of the liquor traffic in Africa (46 Stat. 2199; TS 779).

Agreement for the suppression of the white slave traffic.
Signed at Paris May 18, 1904.
Entered into force July 18, 1905; for the United States June 6, 1908.
35 Stat. 1979; TS 496; 1 Bevans 424; 1 LNTS 83
Amendment:
May 4, 1949

Depositary: United Nations

Convention to suppress the slave trade and slavery
Concluded at Geneva September 25, 1926.
Entered into force March 9, 1927; for the United States March 21, 1929.
46 Stat. 2183; TS 778; 2 Bevans 607; 60 LNTS 253
Depositary: United Nations

Inter-American convention on the granting of political rights to women.

Done at Bogota May 2, 1948.

Entered into force December 29, 1954; for the United States May 24, 1976.

27 UST 3301; TIAS 8365

Depositary: Organization of American States

Convention on the prevention and punishment of the crime of genocide.

Done at Paris December 9, 1948.

Entered into force January 12, 1951; for the United States February 23, 1989.

TIAS

Depositary: United Nations

Protocol amending the international agreement for the suppression of the white slave traffic, signed at Paris May 18, 1904, and the international convention for the suppression of the white slave traffic, signed at Paris May 4, 1910.

Done at Lake Success May 4, 1949.

Entered into force May 4, 1949; for the United States, a party only to the 1904 agreement, August 14, 1950; annex amending 1904 agreement entered into force June 21, 1951.

2 UST 1997; TIAS 2332; 92 UNTS 19

Depositary: United Nations

Convention on the political rights of women.

Done at New York March 31, 1953.

Entered into force July 7, 1954; for the United States July 7, 1976.

27 UST 1909; TIAS 8289; 193 UNTS 135

Depositary: United Nations

Protocol amending the slavery convention signed at Geneva on September 25, 1926, with annex.

Done at New York December 7, 1953.

Entered into force December 7, 1953; for the United States March 7, 1956.

7 UST 479; TIAS 3532; 182 UNTS 51

Depositary: United Nations

Supplementary convention on the abolition of slavery, the slave trade and institutions and practices similar to slavery.

Done at Geneva September 7, 1956.

Entered into force April 30, 1957; for the United States December 6, 1967.

18 UST 3201; TIAS 6418; 266 UNTS 3

Depositary: United Nations

International convention on the elimination of all forms of racial discrimination.

Done at New York December 21, 1965.

Entered into force January 4, 1969; for the United States November 20, 1994.

TIAS; 660 UNTS 195

Depositary: United Nations

International covenant on civil and political rights.

Done at New York December 16, 1966.

Entered into force March 23, 1976; for the United States September 8, 1992.

TIAS

Depositary: United Nations

Convention on the civil aspects of international child abduction.

Done at The Hague October 25, 1980.

Entered into force December 1, 1983; for the United States July 1, 1988.

TIAS 11670

Depositary: Netherlands

Convention against torture and other cruel, inhuman or degrading treatment or punishment.

Done at New York December 10, 1984.

Entered into force June 26, 1987; for the United States November 20, 1994.

TIAS

Depositary: United Nations

Optional protocol to the convention on the rights of the child on the sale of children, child prostitution and child pornography.

Done at New York May 25, 2000.

Entered into force January 18, 2002; for the United States January 23, 2003.

TIAS 13095

Depositary: United Nations

Optional protocol to the convention on the rights of the child on the involvement of children in armed conflict.

Done at New York May 25, 2000.

Entered into force February 12, 2002; for the United States January 23, 2003.

TIAS 13094

Depositary: United Nations

INTELLECTUAL PROPERTY

Convention for the protection of inventions, patents, designs
and industrial models.

Signed at Buenos Aires August 20, 1910.

Entered into force July 31, 1912.

38 Stat. 1811; TS 595; 1 Bevans 767; 155 LNTS 179

Depositary: Argentina

Convention on literary and artistic copyrights.*

Signed at Buenos Aires August 11, 1910.

Entered into force October 31, 1912.

38 Stat. 1785; TS 593; 1 Bevans 758

Depositary: Argentina

Note:

* Replaces the convention of January 27, 1902 (35 Stat. 1934; TS 491; 1 Bevans 339), which remains in force as between the contracting parties and El Salvador.

General inter-American convention for trademark and commercial protection.*
Signed at Washington February 20, 1929.
Entered into force April 2, 1930; for the United States February 17, 1931.
46 Stat. 2907; TS 833; 2 Bevans 751; 124 LNTS 357.
Depositary: Organization of American States

Note:
* Replaces as between contracting parties the convention of August 20, 1910 (39 Stat. 1675; TS 626; 1 Bevans 772) and the convention of April 28, 1923 (44 Stat. 2494; TS 751; 2 Bevans 395).
Parties to the 1923 convention not party to the 1929 convention are: Brazil, Dominican Republic and Uruguay.
Parties to the 1910 convention not party to the subsequent conventions are: Bolivia and Ecuador.

Accord relating to the treatment of German-owned patents.
Done at London July 27, 1946.
Entered into force November 30, 1946.
3 UST 552; TIAS 2415; 90 UNTS 229.
Depositary: United Kingdom

Protocol amending the Accord relating to the treatment of German-owned patents of July 27, 1946.
Done at London July 17, 1947.
Entered into force July 17, 1947.
3 UST 560; TIAS 2415; 90 UNTS 246
Depositary: United Kingdom

Agreement relating to German-owned patents in Italy.
Signed at Rome November 29, 1950.
Entered into force November 29, 1950.
2 UST 553; TIAS 2204; 88 UNTS 221
Parties:
Canada
France
India
Italy
Norway
United Kingdom
United States

Universal copyright convention with three protocols annexed thereto.
Done at Geneva September 6, 1952.
Entered into force September 16, 1955.
6 UST 2731; TIAS 3324; 216 UNTS 132
Depositary: UNESCO

Agreement among parties to the North Atlantic Treaty for the mutual safeguarding of secrecy of inventions relating to defense and for which applications for patents have been made.
Done at Paris September 21, 1960.
Entered into force January 12, 1961.
12 UST 43; TIAS 4672; 394 UNTS 3
Depositary: United States

First revision of implementing procedures to the North Atlantic Treaty for the mutual safeguarding of secrecy of inventions relating to defense and for which applications for patents have been made.
Done at Paris March 15, 1967.
Entered into force March 15, 1967; for the United States September 3, 1969.
20 UST 3062; TIAS 6786
Depositary: North Atlantic Treaty Organization

Convention revising the Paris convention of March 20, 1883, as revised, for the protection of industrial property.*
Done at Stockholm July 14, 1967.
Articles 1–12 entered into force May 19, 1970; for the United States August 25, 1973.
Articles 13–30 entered into force April 26, 1970; for the United States September 5, 1970.
21 UST 1583; 24 UST 2140; TIAS 6923
Amendment:
October 2, 1979

Depositary: World Intellectual Property Organization

Convention establishing the World Intellectual Property Organization.
Done at Stockholm July 14, 1967.
Entered into force April 26, 1970; for the United States August 25, 1970.
21 UST 1749; TIAS 6932; 828 UNTS 3
Amendment:
October 2, 1979

Depositary: World Intellectual Property Organization

Patent cooperation treaty, with regulations.
Done at Washington June 19, 1970.
Entered into force January 24, 1978.
28 UST 7645; TIAS 8733
Amendment:
October 2, 1979

Depositary: World Intellectual Property Organization

Strasbourg agreement concerning the international patent classification.
Done at Strasbourg March 24, 1971.
Entered into force October 7, 1975.
26 UST 1793; TIAS 8140
Amendment:
October 2, 1979

Depositary: World Intellectual Property Organization

Universal copyright convention, as revised, with two protocols annexed thereto.
Done at Paris July 24, 1971.
Entered into force July 10, 1974.
25 UST 1341; TIAS 7868
Depositary: UNESCO

Berne convention (with appendix) for the protection of literary and artistic works of September 9, 1886, completed at Paris May 4, 1896, revised at Berlin November 13, 1908, completed at Berne March 20, 1914, revised at Rome June 2, 1928, at Brussels June 26, 1948, at Stockholm July 14, 1967, and at Paris July 24, 1971, amended in 1979.
Done at Paris July 24, 1971.
Entered into force for the United States March 1, 1989.
TIAS
Depositary: World Intellectual Property Organization

Convention for the protection of producers of phonograms against unauthorized duplication of their phonograms.
Done at Geneva October 29, 1971.
Entered into force April 18, 1973; for the United States March 10, 1974.
25 UST 309; TIAS 7808; 866 UNTS 67
Depositary: UNESCO

Second revision of implementing procedures to the North Atlantic Treaty for the mutual safeguarding of secrecy of inventions relating to defense and for which applications for patents have been made.
Done at Brussels September 5, 1973.
Entered into force September 5, 1973.
25 UST 1203; TIAS 7853
Depositary: North Atlantic Treaty Organization

Budapest treaty on the international recognition of the deposit of microorganisms for the purposes of patent procedure, with regulations.
Done at Budapest April 28, 1977.
Entered into force August 19, 1980.
32 UST 1241; TIAS 9768
Amendments:
September 26, 1980
January 20, 1981 (33 UST 955; TIAS 10078)

Depositary: World Intellectual Property Organization

Nice agreement, as revised, concerning the international classification of goods and services for the purposes of the registration of marks.*
Done at Geneva May 13, 1977.
Entered into force February 6, 1979; for the United States February 29, 1984.
TIAS
Amendment:
October 2, 1979

Depositary: World Intellectual Property Organization

Notes:
* The 1977 agreement replaces as between contracting parties the agreement concerning the international classification of goods and services to which trademarks apply done at Nice June 15, 1957 (23 UST 1336; TIAS 7418; 550 UNTS 45), as revised at Stockholm July 14, 1967 (23 UST 1353; TIAS 7419; 828 UNTS 191).

Protocol relating to the Madrid Agreement concerning the international registration of marks.
Done at Madrid June 27, 1989.
Entered into force December 1, 1995; for the United States November 2, 2003.
TIAS
Depositary: World Intellectual Property Organization

International convention for the protection of new varieties of plants of December 2, 1961, as revised.
Done at Geneva March 19, 1991.
Entered into force April 24, 1998; for the United States February 22, 1999.
TIAS
Depositary: International Union for the Protection of New Varieties of Plants

Trademark law treaty and regulations.
Done at Geneva October 27, 1994.
Entered into force August 1, 1996; for the United States August 12, 2000.
TIAS; 2037 UNTS 35
Depositary: World Intellectual Property Organization

WIPO copyright treaty.
Adopted at Geneva December 20, 1996.
Entered into force March 6, 2002.
TIAS
Depositary: World Intellectual Property Organization

WIPO performances and phonograms treaty.
Adopted at Geneva December 20, 1996.
Entered into force May 20, 2002.
TIAS
Depositary: World Intellectual Property Organization

Singapore treaty on the law of trademarks, with regulations and attachments.
Signed at Singapore March 28, 2006.
Entered into force March 16, 2009.
TIAS 09-316.1
Depositary: World Intellectual Property Organization

Patent law treaty.
Signed at Geneva June 1, 2000.
Entered into force April 28, 2005; for the United States December 18, 2013.
TIAS
Amendment
May 15, 2008

Depositary: World Intellectual Property Organization

LABOR

Note: The depositary for agreements in this section is the International Labour Organization, unless otherwise noted. For agreements where parties are listed, no depositary was designated in the agreement.

Convention (ILO No. 53) concerning the minimum requirement of professional capacity for masters and officers on board merchant ships.
Adopted at the 21st session of the General Conference of the International Labor Organization, Geneva, October 24, 1936.
Entered into force March 29, 1939; for the United States October 29, 1939.
54 Stat. 1683; TS 950; 3 Bevans 281; 40 UNTS 153

Convention (ILO No. 55) concerning the liability of the shipowner in case of sickness, injury or death of seamen.
Adopted at the 21st session of the General Conference of the International Labor Organization, Geneva, October 24, 1936.
Entered into force October 29, 1939.
54 Stat. 1693; TS 951; 3 Bevans 287; 40 UNTS 169

Convention (ILO No. 58) fixing the minimum age for the admission of children to employment at sea (revised 1936).
Adopted at the 22nd session of the General Conference of the International Labor Organization, Geneva, October 24, 1936.
Entered into force April 11, 1939; for the United States October 29, 1939.
54 Stat. 1705; TS 952; 3 Bevans 294; 40 UNTS 205

Convention (ILO No. 74) concerning the certification of able seamen.
Adopted at the 28th session of the General Conference of the International Labor Organization, Seattle, June 29, 1946.
Entered into force July 14, 1951; for the United States April 9, 1954.
5 UST 605; TIAS 2949; 94 UNTS 11

Instrument for the amendment of the Constitution of the International Labor Organization
Dated at Montreal October 9, 1946.
*Entered into force April 20, 1948; reentered into force for the United States February 18, 1980.**
62 Stat. 3485; TIAS 1868; 4 Bevans 188; 15 UNTS 35

Amendments:
June 25, 1953 (7 UST 245; TIAS 3500; 191 UNTS 143)
June 22, 1962 (14 UST 1039; TIAS 5401; 466 UNTS 323)
June 22, 1972 (25 UST 3253; TIAS 7987)

Note:
* The Instrument for the amendment of the Constitution of the International Labor Organization, 1946, entered into force for the United States April 20, 1948. By letter dated November 5, 1975, the United States informed the ILO Director-General of its intention to withdraw from the Organization. The withdrawal became effective November 6, 1977. By letter dated February 15, 1980, the United States informed the Director-General of its decision to resume membership in the organization and accordingly accepted the obligations of the ILO Constitution; which became effective February 18, 1980.

Convention (ILO No. 80) for the partial revision of the conventions adopted by the General Conference of the International Labor Organization at its first twenty-eight sessions (Final articles revision convention, 1946).
Adopted at the 29th session of the General Conference of the International Labor Organization, Montreal, October 9, 1946.
Entered into force May 28, 1947; for the United States June 24, 1948.
62 Stat. 1672; TIAS 1810; 4 Bevans 183; 38 UNTS 3

Convention (ILO No. 105) concerning the abolition of forced labor.
Adopted at the 40th session of the General Conference of the International Labor Organization, Geneva, June 25, 1957.
Entered into force January 17, 1959; for the United States September 25, 1992.
TIAS; 320 UNTS 291

Convention (ILO No. 144) concerning tripartite consultations to promote the implementation of international labor standards.
Adopted at the 61st session of the General Conference of the International Labor Organization, Geneva, June 21, 1976.
Entered into force May 16, 1978.
TIAS

Convention (ILO No. 147) concerning minimum standards in merchant ships.
Adopted at the 62nd session of the General Conference of the International Labor Organization, Geneva, October 29, 1976.
Entered into force November 28, 1981.
TIAS

Convention (ILO No. 150) concerning labor administration: role, functions and organization.
Adopted at the 64th session of the General Conference of the International Labor Organization, Geneva, June 26, 1978.
Entered into force October 11, 1980; for the United States March 3, 1996.
TIAS

Convention (ILO No. 160) concerning labor statistics.
Adopted at the 71st session of the General Conference of the International Labor Organization, Geneva, June 25, 1985.
Entered into force April 24, 1988; for the United States June 11, 1991.
TIAS

North American agreement on labor cooperation, with annexes.
Signed at Mexico, Washington and Ottawa September 8, 9, 12 and 14, 1993.
Entered into force January 1, 1994.
TIAS

Parties:
Canada
Mexico
United States

Convention (ILO No. 176) concerning safety and health in mines.

Adopted at the 82nd session of the General Conference of the International Labor Organization, Geneva, June 22, 1995.

Entered into force June 5, 1998; for the United States February 9, 2002.

TIAS

Convention (ILO No. 182) concerning the prohibition and immediate action for the elimination of the worst forms of child labor.

Adopted at the 87th session of the General Conference of the International Labor Organization, Geneva, June 17, 1999.

Entered into force November 19, 2000; for the United States December 2, 2000.

TIAS 13045

Agreement on the appointment of the International Mines Rescue Body (IMRB), with attachment.

Signed at Bytom, Poland May 29, 2001.

Entered into force May 29, 2001.

TIAS 13150

Parties:

Australia
Czech Republic
France
Germany
Romania
Slovak Republic
South Africa
United Kingdom
United States

LAW ENFORCEMENT

Convention for the establishment of an International Commission of Jurists.

Signed at Rio de Janeiro August 23, 1906.

Entered into force August 26, 1907; for the United States March 9, 1908.

37 Stat. 1554; TS 565; 1 Bevans 547.

Depositary: Brazil

Convention on extradition.*

Signed at Montevideo December 26, 1933.

Entered into force January 25, 1935.

49 Stat. 3111; TS 882; 3 Bevans 152; 165 LNTS 45

Depositary: Organization of American States, Uruguay

Notes:

* Article 21 provides that the convention "does not abrogate or modify the bilateral or collective treaties, which at the present date are in force between the signatory States. Nevertheless, if any of said treaties lapse, the present Convention will take effect and become applicable immediately among the respective States . . ." The United States has bilateral extradition treaties with each of the other parties which antedate the convention, except for those with Argentina, Colombia and Mexico.

Protocol on uniformity of powers of attorney which are to be utilized abroad.

Done at the Pan American Union, Washington, February 17, 1940.

Entered into force for the United States April 16, 1942.

56 Stat. 1376; TS 982; 3 Bevans 612; 161 UNTS 229

Depositary: Netherlands, Organization of American States

Single convention on narcotic drugs, 1961.*

Done at New York March 30, 1961.

Entered into force December 13, 1964; for the United States June 24, 1967.

18 UST 1407; TIAS 6298; 520 UNTS 204

Depositary: United Nations

Notes:

* The single convention on narcotic drugs replaced as between the contracting parties the following conventions to which the United States is a party: **(a)** Convention of January 23, 1912, relating to the suppression of the abuse of opium and other drugs (38 Stat. 1912; TS 612; 1 Bevans 855; 8 LNTS 187), as amended by the protocol of December 11, 1946 (61 Stat. 2230, 62 Stat. 1796; TIAS 1671, 1859; 4 Bevans 267; 12 UNTS 179).

(b) Convention of July 13, 1931, for limiting the manufacture and regulating the distribution of narcotic drugs (48 Stat. 1543; TS 863; 3 Bevans 1; 139 LNTS 301), as amended by the protocol of December 11, 1946 (61 Stat. 2230, 62 Stat. 1796; TIAS 1671, 1859; 4 Bevans 267; 12 UNTS 179).

(c) Protocol bringing under international control drugs outside the scope of the convention of July 13, 1931, as amended (see above) (2 UST 1629; TIAS 2308; 44 UNTS 277).

(d) Protocol for limiting and regulating the cultivation of the poppy plant, the production of, international and wholesale trade in, and use of opium (14 UST 10; TIAS 5273; 456 UNTS 3).

Parties to (or otherwise obligated under) the above conventions and protocols which are not parties to the single convention of 1961 include:

Albania (1912, 1931, 1948); Central African Republic (1912, 1931, 1948, 1953); Estonia (1912, 1931); Tanzania (1931, 1948);

Samoa (1948, 1953).

Convention on the taking of evidence abroad in civil or commercial matters.

Done at The Hague March 18, 1970.

Entered into force October 7, 1972.

23 UST 2555; TIAS 7444; 847 UNTS 231

Depositary: Netherlands

Convention to prevent and punish the acts of terrorism taking the form of crimes against persons and related extortion that are of international significance.

Done at Washington February 2, 1971.

Entered into force October 16, 1973, for the United States October 20, 1976.

27 UST 3949; TIAS 8413

Depositary: Organization of American States

Convention on psychotropic substances.

Done at Vienna February 21, 1971.

Entered into force August 16, 1976; for the United States July 15, 1980.

32 UST 543; TIAS 9725; 1019 UNTS 175

Depositary: United Nations

Protocol amending the single convention on narcotic drugs, 1961.
Done at Geneva March 25, 1972.
Entered into force August 8, 1975.
26 UST 1439; TIAS 8118; 976 UNTS 3
Depositary: United Nations

Convention on the prevention and punishment of crimes against internationally protected persons, including diplomatic agents.
Done at New York December 14, 1973.
Entered into force February 20, 1977.
28 UST 1975; TIAS 8532; 1035 UNTS 167
Depositary: United Nations

Inter-American convention on letters rogatory.
Done at Panama January 30, 1975.
Entered into force January 16, 1976; for the United States August 27, 1988.
TIAS
Depositary: Organization of American States

Additional protocol to the Inter-American convention on letters rogatory, with annex.
Done at Montevideo May 8, 1979.
Entered into force June 14, 1980; for the United States August 27, 1988.
TIAS
Depositary: Organization of American States

International convention against the taking of hostages.
Done at New York December 17, 1979.
Entered into force June 3, 1983; for the United States January 6, 1985.
TIAS 11081
Depositary: United Nations

United Nations convention against illicit traffic in narcotic drugs and psychotropic substances, with annex and final act.
Done at Vienna December 20, 1988.
Entered into force November 11, 1990.
TIAS
Depositary: United Nations

Declaration of Cartagena concerning the production of, trafficking in and demand for illicit drugs.
Signed at Cartagena February 15, 1990.
Entered into force February 15, 1990.
TIAS 12411
Parties:
Bolivia
Colombia
Peru
United States

Memorandum of understanding concerning cooperation in the fight against illicit trafficking of narcotic drugs through the use of equipment and personnel based at Great Inagua and such other bases as may be established in the Turks and Caicos Islands, with annexes.
Signed at Washington July 12, 1990.
Entered into force July 12, 1990.
TIAS
Parties:
Bahamas
Turks and Caicos Islands
United States

Inter-American convention on mutual assistance in criminal matters.
Done at Nassau May 23, 1992.
Entered into force April 14, 1996; for the United States June 24, 2001.
TIAS
Amendment:
June 11, 1993

Depositary: Organization of American States

Inter-American convention on serving criminal sentences abroad
Done at Managua June 9, 1993.
Entered into force April 12, 1996; for the United States June 24, 2001.
TIAS
Depositary: Organization of American States

Inter-American convention against corruption.
Done at Caracas March 29, 1996.
Entered into force March 6, 1997; for the United States October 29, 2000.
TIAS
Depositary: Organization of American States

International convention for the suppression of terrorist bombings.
Adopted at New York December 15, 1997.
Entered into force May 23, 2001; for the United States July 26, 2002.
TIAS
Depositary: United Nations

Convention on combating bribery of foreign public officials in international business transactions, with annex.
Done at Paris December 17, 1997.
Entered into force February 15, 1999.
TIAS
Depositary: Organization for Economic Cooperation and Development

Agreement establishing the Group of States against Corruption (GRECO), with appendix.
Done at Strasbourg May 1, 1999.
Entered into force May 1, 1999; for the United States September 20, 2000.
TIAS
Depositary: Council of Europe

International convention for the suppression of the financing of terrorism, with annex.
Done at New York December 9, 1999.
Entered into force April 10, 2002; for the United States July 26, 2002.
TIAS 13075
Depositary: United Nations

United Nations convention against transnational organized crime, with supplementary protocols.
Done at New York November 15, 2000.
Entered into force September 29, 2003; for the United States December 3, 2005.
TIAS 13127
Depositary: United Nations

Convention on cybercrime.
Done at Budapest November 23, 2001.
Entered into force July 1, 2004; for the United States January 1, 2007.
TIAS 13174
Depositary: Council of Europe

Inter-American convention against terrorism.
Done at Bridgetown June 3, 2002.
Entered into force July 10, 2003; for the United States December 15, 2005.
TIAS
Depositary: Organization of American States

United Nations convention against corruption.
Signed at Merida December 9, 2003.
Entered into force December 14, 2005; for the United States November 29, 2006.
TIAS
Depositary: United Nations

International convention for the suppression of acts of nuclear terrorism.
Done at New York April 13, 2005.
Entered into force July 7, 2007; for the United States October 30, 2015.
TIAS
Depositary: United Nations

MARITIME MATTERS

Convention for the unification of certain rules of law with respect to assistance and salvage at sea.
Signed at Brussels September 23, 1910.
Entered into force March 1, 1913.
37 Stat. 1658; TS 576; 1 Bevans 780
Depositary: Belgium

International convention for the unification of certain rules relating to bills of lading for the carriage of goods by sea, with protocol of signature.
Done at Brussels August 25, 1924.
Entered into force June 2, 1931; for the United States December 29, 1937.
51 Stat. 233; TS 931; 2 Bevans 430; 120 LNTS 155
Depositary: Belgium

Convention on the Intergovernmental Maritime Consultative Organization.*
Signed at Geneva March 6, 1948.
Entered into force March 17, 1958.
9 UST 621; TIAS 4044; 289 UNTS 48

Amendments
September 15, 1964 (18 UST 1299; TIAS 6285; 607 UNTS 276)
September 28, 1965 (19 UST 4855; TIAS 6490; 649 UNTS 334)
October 17, 1974 (28 UST 4607; TIAS 8606)
November 14, 1975 (34 UST 497; TIAS 10374)
November 17, 1977 (TIAS 11094; 1380 UNTS 268)
November 15, 1979 (TIAS 11094; 1380 UNTS 288)
November 7, 1991 (2557 UNTS 190)
November 4, 1993 (2199 UNTS 113)

Depositary: United Nations

Notes
* The title of the Convention was changed to the Convention on the International Maritime Organization by amendment adopted by the Organization November 14, 1975, effective May 22, 1982.

Convention on the high seas.
Done at Geneva April 29, 1958.
Entered into force September 30, 1962.
13 UST 2312; TIAS 5200; 450 UNTS 82
Depositary: United Nations

Convention on the territorial sea and the contiguous zone.
Done at Geneva April 29, 1958.
Entered into force September 10, 1964.
15 UST 1606; TIAS 5639; 516 UNTS 205
Depositary: United Nations

Inter-American convention on facilitation of international waterborne transportation, with annex.
Signed at Mar del Plata June 7, 1963.
Entered into force January 11, 1981.
TIAS 12064
Depositary: Organization of American States

Convention for the International Council for the Exploration of the Sea.
Done at Copenhagen September 12, 1964.
Entered into force July 22, 1968; for the United States April 18, 1973.
24 UST 1080; TIAS 7628; 652 UNTS 237

Amendment:
August 13, 1970 (27 UST 1022; TIAS 8238)

Depositary: Denmark

Convention on facilitation of international maritime traffic, with annex.
Done at London April 9, 1965.
Entered into force March 5, 1967; for the United States May 16, 1967.
18 UST 411; TIAS 6251; 591 UNTS 265

Amendment:
November 19, 1973 (TIAS 11092)

Depositary: International Maritime Organization

International convention on load lines, 1966.
Done at London April 5, 1966.
Entered into force July 21, 1968.
18 UST 1857; TIAS 6331; 640 UNTS 133
Depositary: International Maritime Organization

Proces-verbal of rectification of the international convention on load lines, 1966.
Signed at London January 30, 1969.
20 UST 17; TIAS 6629
Depositary: International Maritime Organization

Proces-verbal of rectification of the international convention on load lines, 1966.
Signed at London May 5, 1969.
20 UST 2577; TIAS 6720
Depositary: International Maritime Organization

International convention on tonnage measurement of ships, 1969, with annexes.
Done at London June 23, 1969.
Entered into force July 18, 1982; for the United States February 10, 1983.
TIAS 10490
Depositary: International Maritime Organization

Convention on the international regulations for preventing collisions at sea, 1972.*
Done at London October 20, 1972.
Entered into force July 15, 1977.
28 UST 3459; TIAS 8587

Amendments:
November 19, 1981 (TIAS 10672)
November 19, 1987
October 19, 1989
November 4, 1993
November 29, 2001

Depositary: International Maritime Organization

Note:
* The 1972 convention replaces and abrogates the international regulations for preventing collisions at sea, 1960 (16 UST 794; TIAS 5813).
Parties to the 1960 regulations not parties to the 1972 convention are: Lebanon, Libya, Madagascar, Paraguay, Philippines, and Suriname.

International convention for safe containers (CSC), with annexes.
Done at Geneva December 2, 1972.
Entered into force September 6, 1977; for the United States January 3, 1979.
29 UST 3707; TIAS 9037; 1064 UNTS 3

Amendments to annexes:
April 2, 1981 (33 UST 3238; TIAS 10220)
June 13, 1983 (35 UST 4156; TIAS 10914)
May 17, 1991

Depositary: International Maritime Organization

Note:
* The 1972 convention replaces as between contracting parties the customs convention on containers, 1956 (20 UST 301; TIAS 6634; 338 UNTS 103).

International convention for the safety of life at sea, 1974, with annex.*
Done at London November 1, 1974.
Entered into force May 25, 1980.
32 UST 47; TIAS 9700

Amendments:
November 20, 1981
June 17, 1983
April 21, 1988
October 28, 1988
November 9, 1988
April 11, 1989
May 25, 1990
May 23, 1991
April 10, 1992
December 11, 1992
May 23, 1994
May 24, 1994
December 9, 1994
May 16, 1995
June 4, 1996

Depositary: International Maritime Organization

Note:
* Replaces the convention of 1960 as between contracting parties.

Protocol of 1978 relating to the international convention for the safety of life at sea, 1974.
Done at London February 17, 1978.
Entered into force May 1, 1981.
32 UST 5577; TIAS 10009

Amendments:
November 20, 1981
November 10, 1988

Depositary: International Maritime Organization

International convention on standards of training, certification and watchkeeping for seafarers, 1978.
Done at London July 7, 1978.
Entered into force April 28, 1984; for the United States October 1, 1991.
TIAS

Amendments:
May 22, 1991
May 23, 1994
July 7, 1995
June 4, 1997
December 9, 1998
May 20, 2004
December 9, 2004
May 18, 2006

Depositary: International Maritime Organization

International convention on maritime search and rescue, 1979, with annex.
Done at Hamburg April 27, 1979.
Entered into force June 22, 1985.
TIAS 11093

Amendments:
May 18, 1998
May 20, 2004

Depositary: International Maritime Organization

Agreement concerning interim arrangements relating to polymetallic nodules of the deep sea bed.

Done at Washington September 2, 1982.
Entered into force September 2, 1982.

TIAS 10562; 1871 UNTS 275

Parties:

France
Germany, Federal Republic of [1]
United Kingdom
United States

Note:

1 See note under GERMANY in Section 1.

Proces-verbal of rectification to the international convention for the safety of life at sea, 1974.

Done at London December 22, 1982.

TIAS 10626

Depositary: International Maritime Organization

Notes

* Replaces the convention of 1960 as between contracting parties.

Provisional understanding regarding deep seabed matters, with memorandum of implementation, joint record, and related exchanges of notes.

Signed at Geneva August 3, 1984.
Entered into force September 2, 1984.

TIAS 11066

Parties:

Belgium [1]
France
Germany, Federal Republic of [2]
Italy [1]
Japan
Netherlands [1 3]
United Kingdom
United States

Notes:

1 With declaration.
2 See note under GERMANY in Section 1.
3 For the Kingdom in Europe only.

Convention for the suppression of unlawful acts against the safety of maritime navigation.

Done at Rome March 10, 1988.
Entered into force March 1, 1992; for the United States March 6, 1995.

TIAS

Amendment:

October 14, 2005

Depositary: International Maritime Organization

Protocol for the suppression of unlawful acts against the safety of fixed platforms located on the continental shelf.

Done at Rome March 10, 1988.
Entered into force March 1, 1992; for the United States March 6, 1995.

TIAS

Amendment:

October 14, 2005

Depositary: International Maritime Organization

Protocol of 1988 relating to the international convention on load lines, 1966, with annexes.

Done at London November 11, 1988.
Entered into force February 3, 2000.

TIAS

Amendments:

May 26, 2000
December 2, 2000
May 24, 2002
December 9, 2004
December 8, 2006
October 12, 2007
May 16, 2008
December 4, 2008
June 5, 2009
December 10, 2010

Depositary: International Maritime Organization

Protocol of 1988 relating to the international convention for the safety of life at sea, 1974, with annex.

Done at London November 11, 1988.
Entered into force February 3, 2000.

TIAS

Depositary: International Maritime Organization

International convention on salvage, 1989.

Done at London April 28, 1989.
Entered into force July 14, 1996.

TIAS

Depositary: International Maritime Organization

Convention for a North Pacific Marine Science Organization (PICES).

Signed at Ottawa December 12, 1990.
Entered into force March 24, 1992.

TIAS

Depositary: Canada

Memorandum of understanding on the avoidance of overlaps and conflicts relating to deep seabed areas, with annexes.

Signed at New York February 22, 1991.
Entered into force February 22, 1991.

TIAS

Parties

Belgium
Canada
China
Germany
Italy
Netherlands
United Kingdom
United States

Memorandum of understanding on the avoidance of overlaps and conflicts relating to deep sea-bed areas, with annexes.

Done at New York August 20, 1991.

Entered into force August 28, 1991; effective August 20, 1991.

TIAS 11825

Parties:

Canada
Czech Republic
Germany
Italy
Poland
Union of Soviet Socialist Republics [1]
United Kingdom
United States

Note:

1 See note under UNION OF SOVIET SOCIALIST REPUBLICS in Section 1.

Agreement concerning cooperation in suppressing illicit maritime and air trafficking in narcotic drugs and psychotropic substances in the Caribbean area.

Signed at San Jose April 10, 2003.

Entered into force September 18, 2008.

TIAS

Depositary: Costa Rica

Agreement on cooperation on aeronautical and maritime search and rescue in the Arctic.

Signed at Nuuk May 12, 2011.

Entered into force January 19, 2013.

TIAS 13-119

Parties:

Canada
Denmark
Finland
Iceland
Norway
Russia
Sweden
United States

MIGRATION & REFUGEES

Convention between the American Republics regarding the status of aliens in their respective territories.

Signed at Habana February 20, 1928.

Entered into force August 29, 1929; for the United States May 21, 1930.

46 Stat. 2753; TS 815; 2 Bevans 710; 132 LNTS 301

Depositary: Organization of American States

Constitution of the International Organization for Migration.

Adopted at Venice October 19, 1953.

Entered into force November 30, 1954.

6 UST 603; TIAS 3197; 207 UNTS 189

Amendment:

May 20, 1987

Depositary: International Organization for Migration

Agreement constituting an International Commission for the International Tracing Service.

Signed at Bonn June 6, 1955.

Entered into force May 5, 1955.

6 UST 6186; TIAS 3471, pp. 18-37; 219 UNTS 79

Extensions and Amendments:

August 23, 1960 (12 UST 463; TIAS 4736, pp. 18-24; 377 UNTS 402)
April 27, 1972
May 6, 2006

Depositary: Germany

Agreement relating to the operation of the International Tracing Service.

Exchange of notes between the United States and the Federal Republic of Germany at Bonn and Bonn-Bad Godesberg June 6, 1955

Operative May 5, 1955.

6 UST 6169; TIAS 3471, pp. 2-6; 315 UNTS 155

Extensions and Amendments:

April 28 and May 5, 1960 (12 UST 445; TIAS 4736, pp. 2-5)
May 24, 1968

Depositary: Germany

Agreement providing for the administration and direction of the International Tracing Service by the International Committee of the Red Cross.

Exchange of notes between the United States and the President of the International Committee of the Red Cross at Bonn–Bad Godesberg and Geneva June 6, 1955.

Entered into force May 5, 1955.

6 UST 6175; TIAS 3471, pp. 7-17

Extensions and Amendments:

May 9 and 12, 1960 (12 UST 452; TIAS 4736, pp. 5–18)
May 31 and July 25, 1968.

Depositary: International Committee of the Red Cross

Protocol relating to the status of refugees.*

Done at New York January 31, 1967.

Entered into force October 4, 1967; for the United States November 1, 1968.

19 UST 6223; TIAS 6577; 606 UNTS 267

Depositary: United Nations

Note

* Protocol incorporates articles 2 through 34 of the convention relating to the status of refugees of July 28, 1951. (189 UNTS 150). States parties to the convention but not parties to the protocol are: Madagascar and Monaco. The United Kingdom also extended application of the convention to various territories for the international relations of which it was responsible.

NONPROLIFERATION

(See also Arms Control)

Additional protocol I to the treaty of February 14, 1967, for the prohibition of nuclear weapons in Latin America.*
Done at Mexico February 14, 1967.
Entered into force December 11, 1969; for the United States November 23, 1981.
33 UST 1792; TIAS 10147; 634 UNTS 362
Depositary: Mexico

Additional protocol II to the treaty of February 14, 1967 for the prohibition of nuclear weapons in Latin America.*
Done at Mexico February 14, 1967.
Entered into force December 11, 1969; for the United States May 12, 1971.
22 UST 754; TIAS 7137; 634 UNTS 364
Depositary: Mexico

Note:

* The United States is not a party to the treaty for the prohibition of nuclear weapons in Latin America (the Treaty of Tlatelolco). For the English text of the treaty, see 22 UST 762; TIAS 7137; for the text in other languages, see 634 UNTS 281.

Treaty on the non-proliferation of nuclear weapons.
Done at Washington, London, and Moscow July 1, 1968.
Entered into force March 5, 1970.
21 UST 483; TIAS 6839; 729 UNTS 161
Depositary: Russia, United Kingdom, United States

Convention on the physical protection of nuclear material, with annexes.
Adopted at Vienna October 26, 1979.
Entered into force February 8, 1987
TIAS 11080
Amendment:
July 8, 2005 (TIAS 16-508)

Depositary: International Atomic Energy Agency

Protocol on the provisional application of the agreement of November 27, 1992 establishing an international science and technology center.
Signed at Moscow December 27, 1993.
Entered into force March 2, 1994.
TIAS
Depositary: International Science and Technology Center Secretariat

Agreement to establish a science and technology center in Ukraine.
Done at Kiev October 25, 1993.
Entered into force July 16, 1994.
TIAS 17-124.1
Parties:
Canada
Ukraine
United States

Agreement on technological safeguards associated with the launch of the INMARSAT–3 satellite.
Signed at Washington February 14, 1994.
Entered into force August 19, 1994.
TIAS
Parties:
Kazakhstan
Russian Federation
United States

OCCUPATION & PEACEKEEPING

Convention on the settlement of matters arising out of the war and the occupation, with annex.
Signed at Bonn May 26, 1952.
Entered into force May 5, 1955.
332 UNTS 219; 6 UST 4411
Parties:
France
Germany
United Kingdom
United States

Protocol on the termination of the occupation regime in the Federal Republic of Germany, with five schedules and related letters.*
Signed at Paris October 23, 1954.
Entered into force May 5, 1955.
6 UST 4117; TIAS 3425; 331 UNTS 253
Depositary: Germany

Notes:

* Schedules II, III, and V terminated July 1, 1963, by the agreement of August 3, 1959 (TIAS 5351, p. 156). Schedule I as it relates to postal matters and telecommunications terminated November 1, 1968.
See also agreements of May 26, 1952 (TIAS 3425).

1 See note under GERMANY in Section 1.

Agreement concerning United States participation in the Multinational Force and Observers established by Egypt and Israel.
Exchanges of letters at Washington August 3, 1981.
Entered into force August 3, 1981.
TIAS 10556
Parties:
Egypt
Israel
United States

Agreement concerning the convention of October 23, 1954, on the presence of foreign forces in the Federal Republic of Germany.

Exchange of notes at Bonn September 25, 1990.
Entered into force September 25, 1990.
TIAS

Amendment:
September 12, 1994

Parties
Belgium
Canada
Germany, Federal Republic of [1]
Netherlands
United Kingdom
United States

Notes
1 See note under GERMANY in Section 1.

Agreement concerning the convention of May 26, 1952, as amended, on relations between the Three Powers and the Federal Republic of Germany and the convention of May 26, 1952, as amended, on settlement of matters arising out of the war and the occupation.

Exchange of notes at Bonn September 27 and 28, 1990.
Entered into force September 28, 1990.
TIAS; 1656 UNTS 29

Parties:
France
Germany, Federal Republic of [1]
United Kingdom
United States

Notes:
1 See note under GERMANY in Section 1.

PEACE

Joint Declaration, known as the Atlantic Charter, by the President of the United States and the Prime Minister of the United Kingdom, made on August 14, 1941.
55 Stat. 1600; EAS 236; 3 Bevans 686

States which have signified their acceptance of the purposes and principles embodied in the Charter:
Australia
Belgium
Bolivia
Brazil
Canada
Chile
China [1]
Colombia
Costa Rica
Cuba
Czechoslovakia [2]
Dominican Republic
Ecuador
Egypt
El Salvador
Ethiopia [3]
France
Greece
Guatemala
Haiti
Honduras
India
Iran
Iraq
Lebanon
Liberia
Luxembourg
Mexico
Netherlands
New Zealand
Nicaragua
Norway
Panama
Paraguay
Peru
Philippines
Poland
Saudi Arabia
Slovak Republic
South Africa
Syrian Arab Republic
Turkey
Union of Soviet Socialist Republics [4]
United Kingdom
United States
Uruguay
Venezuela
Yugoslavia [5]

Notes:
1 Pre-1949 agreement, applicable only to Taiwan.
2 See note under CZECHOSLOVAKIA in Section 1.
3 See note under ETHIOPIA in Section 1.
4 See note under UNION OF SOVIET SOCIALIST REPUBLICS in Section 1.
5 See note under YUGOSLAVIA in Section 1.

Agreement concerning an armistice with Romania, with annex and protocol.
Signed at Moscow September 12, 1944.
Entered into force September 12, 1944.
59 Stat. 1712; EAS 490; 3 Bevans 901

Parties:
Romania
Union of Soviet Socialist Republics [1]
United Kingdom
United States

Armistice agreement with Bulgaria, with protocol.
Signed at Moscow October 28, 1944.
Entered into force October 28, 1944.
58 Stat. 1498; EAS 437; 3 Bevans 909; 123 UNTS 223

Parties:
Bulgaria
Union of Soviet Socialist Republics [1]
United Kingdom
United States

Armistice agreement with Hungary, with annex and protocol.
Signed at Moscow January 20, 1945.
Entered into force January 20, 1945.
59 Stat. 1321; EAS 456; 3 Bevans 995; 140 UNTS 397

Parties:
Hungary
Union of Soviet Socialist Republics [1]
United Kingdom
United States

Note:
1 See note under UNION OF SOVIET SOCIALIST REPUBLICS in Section 1.

Agreement regarding Japan.
Signed at Yalta February 11, 1945.
Entered into force February 11, 1945.
59 Stat. 1823; EAS 498; 3 Bevans 1022

Parties:
Union of Soviet Socialist Republics [1]
United Kingdom
United States

Note:
1 See note under UNION OF SOVIET SOCIALIST REPUBLICS in Section 1.

Protocol of the proceedings of the Crimea conference.
Signed at Yalta February 11, 1945.
Entered into force February 11, 1945.
3 Bevans 1013; Foreign Relations: The Conferences at Malta and Yalta, 1945, p. 975ff

Parties:
Union of Soviet Socialist Republics [1]
United Kingdom
United States

Note:
1 See note under UNION OF SOVIET SOCIALIST REPUBLICS in Section 1.

Act of military surrender. Terms between the United States and other Allied Powers and Germany.
Signed at Rheims May 7 and at Berlin May 8, 1945.
Effective May 8, 1945.
59 Stat. 1857; EAS 502; 3 Bevans 1123

Parties:
Germany
Union of Soviet Socialist Republics [1]
United Kingdom
United States

Note:
1 See note under UNION OF SOVIET SOCIALIST REPUBLICS in Section 1.

Protocol of the proceedings of the Berlin conference.
Signed at Berlin August 2, 1945.
Entered into force August 2, 1945.
3 Bevans 1207; Foreign Relations: Conference of Berlin (Potsdam) 1945, Vol. II, p. 1478ff

Parties:
Union of Soviet Socialist Republics [1]
United Kingdom
United States

Note:
1 See note under UNION OF SOVIET SOCIALIST REPUBLICS in Section 1.

Communiqué on the Moscow conference of Foreign Ministers.
Signed at Moscow December 27, 1945.
Entered into force December 27, 1945.
60 Stat. 1899; TIAS 1555; 3 Bevans 1341; 20 UNTS 259

Parties
Union of Soviet Socialist Republics [1]
United Kingdom
United States

Note
1 See note under UNION OF SOVIET SOCIALIST REPUBLICS in Section 1.

Treaty of peace with Italy.*
Signed at Paris February 10, 1947.
Entered into force September 15, 1947.
61 Stat. 1245; TIAS 1648; 4 Bevans 311; 49 and 50 UNTS

Depositary: France

Notes:
* For agreements between the United States and Italy regarding implementation of the peace treaty and release of Italy from certain of its obligations thereunder, see under ITALY, PEACE TREATIES in Section 1.

Treaty of peace with Romania.
Signed at Paris February 10, 1947.
Entered into force September 15, 1947.
61 Stat. 1757; TIAS 1649; 4 Bevans 403; 42 UNTS 3

Depositary: Russian Federation

Treaty of peace with Bulgaria.
Signed at Paris February 10, 1947.
Entered into force September 15, 1947.
61 Stat. 1915; TIAS 1650; 4 Bevans 429; 41 UNTS 21

Depositary: Russian Federation

Treaty of peace with Hungary.
Signed at Paris February 10, 1947.
Entered into force September 15, 1947.
61 Stat. 2065; TIAS 1651; 4 Bevans 453; 41 UNTS 135
Depositary: Russian Federation

Protocol of agreements reached between the Allied High Commissioners and the Chancellor of the German Federal Republic.
Signed at Bonn November 22, 1949.
Entered into force November 22, 1949.
3 UST 2714; TIAS 2439; 185 UNTS 307
Depositary: Germany

Treaty of peace with Japan.
Signed at San Francisco September 8, 1951.
Entered into force April 28, 1952.
3 UST 3169; TIAS 2490; 136 UNTS 45
Depositary: United States

Declaration by Japan with respect to the treaty of peace.
Signed at San Francisco September 8, 1951.
3 UST 3306; TIAS 2490; 136 UNTS 146, 160

Agreement for the settlement of disputes arising under article 15(a) of the treaty of peace with Japan.
Done at Washington June 12, 1952.
Entered into force June 12, 1952; for the United States June 19, 1952.
3 UST 4054; TIAS 2550; 138 UNTS 183
Depositary: United States

Agreement concerning a military armistice in Korea, with annex.
Signed at Panmunjom July 27, 1953, by the Commander-in-Chief, United Nations Command; the Supreme Commander of the Korean People's Army; and the Commander of the Chinese People's Volunteers.
Entered into force July 27, 1953.
4 UST 234; TIAS 2782

Agreement relating to certain German libraries and properties in Italy.
Signed at Rome April 30, 1953.
Entered into force May 1, 1953.
4 UST 376; TIAS 2785; 175 UNTS 89
Parties:
France
Germany, Federal Republic of [1]
Italy
United Kingdom
United States

Note:
1 See note under GERMANY in Section 1.

The Pacific Charter.
Signed at Manila September 8, 1954.
Entered into force September 8, 1954.
6 UST 91; TIAS 3171; 209 UNTS 23
Parties:
Australia
France
New Zealand
Pakistan
Philippines
Thailand
United Kingdom
United States

Agreement concerning storage of, access to and release of information from the archives of the Allied High Commission and connected tripartite agencies.
Signed at Bonn June 30, 1954.
Entered into force June 30, 1954.
5 UST 1598; TIAS 3036; 204 UNTS 99
Parties:
France
United Kingdom
United States

Memorandum of understanding regarding the free territory of Trieste, with two annexes.
Initialed at London October 5, 1954.
Entered into force October 5, 1954.
5 UST 2386; TIAS 3099; 235 UNTS 99
Parties:
Italy
United Kingdom
United States
Yugoslavia [1]

Note:
1 See note under YUGOSLAVIA in Section 1.

Convention on the presence of foreign forces in the Federal Republic of Germany.
Signed at Paris October 23, 1954.
Entered into force May 6, 1955.
6 UST 5689; TIAS 3426; 334 UNTS 3
Depositary: Germany

Memorandum concerning understandings supplementing the protection afforded by the provisions of the Austrian State Treaty with respect to United States and British owned property in Austria.
Done at Vienna May 10, 1955.
Entered into force May 10, 1955.
7 UST 803; TIAS 3560; 273 UNTS 121
Parties:
Austria
United Kingdom
United States

State treaty for the reestablishment of an independent and democratic Austria.

Signed at Vienna May 15, 1955.
Entered into force July 27, 1955.
6 UST 2369; TIAS 3298; 217 UNTS 223

Parties:

Australia
Austria
Brazil
Czechoslovakia [1]
France
Mexico
New Zealand
Poland
Union of Soviet Socialist Republics [2]
United Kingdom
United States
Yugoslavia [3]

Notes:

1 See note under CZECHOSLOVAKIA in Section 1.
2 See note under UNION OF SOVIET SOCIALIST REPUBLICS in Section 1.
3 See note under YUGOSLAVIA in Section 1.

Penal administrative agreement with exchanges of notes dated November 1 and December 20, 1955, and notes of the German Chancellor dated October 14 and November 7, 1953.

Done at Bonn September 29, 1955.
Entered into force May 5, 1955.
7 UST 663; TIAS 3549

Parties:

France
Germany, Federal Republic of [1]
United Kingdom
United States

Note:

1 See note under GERMANY in Section 1.

Memorandum of understanding regarding German trademarks in Italy.

Signed at Rome July 5, 1956.
Entered into force July 5, 1956.
7 UST 1989; TIAS 3601; 258 UNTS 371

Parties:

France
Italy
United Kingdom
United States

Declaration and protocol on the neutrality of Laos.

Signed at Geneva July 23, 1962.
Entered into force July 23, 1962.
14 UST 1104; TIAS 5410; 456 UNTS 301

Parties:

Burma
Cambodia
Canada
China, People's Republic of
France
India
Laos [1]
Poland
Thailand
Union of Soviet Socialist Republics [2]
United Kingdom
United States
Viet-Nam, Democratic Republic of [3]
Viet Nam, Republic of [3]

Notes

1 Party to protocol only.
2 See note under UNION OF SOVIET SOCIALIST REPUBLICS in Section 1.
3 See Vietnam footnote under DEFENSE: agreement of December 23, 1950 (3 UST 2756; TIAS 2447; 185 UNTS 3).

Agreement concerning the administration of the archives of the Arbitral Commission on property, rights and interests in Germany.

Exchange of notes at Bonn and Bad Godesberg August 12 and 26, 1971.
Entered into force December 31, 1971.
23 UST 590; TIAS 7317

Parties:

France
Germany, Federal Republic of [1]
United Kingdom
United States

Note:

1 See note under GERMANY in Section 1.

Act of the International Conference on Viet-Nam.

Done at Paris March 2, 1973.
Entered into force March 2, 1973.
24 UST 485; TIAS 7568; 935 UNTS 405

Parties:

Canada
China, People's Rep.
France
Hungary
Indonesia
Poland
Provisional Revolutionary Government of Republic of South Viet-Nam [1]
Union of Soviet Socialist Republics [2]
United Kingdom
United States
Viet-Nam, Democratic Republic of [1]
Viet-Nam, Republic of [1]

Notes:

1 See Vietnam footnote under DEFENSE: agreement of December 23, 1950 (3 UST 2756; TIAS 2447; 185 UNTS 3).
2 See note under UNION OF SOVIET SOCIALIST REPUBLICS in Section 1.

Treaty on the final settlement with respect to Germany, with agreed minute and related letters.
Done at Moscow September 12, 1990.
Entered into force March 15, 1991.
1696 UNTS 115

Parties:

Germany, Federal Republic of [1]
France
Union of Soviet Socialist Republics [2]
United Kingdom
United States

Notes

1 See note under GERMANY in Section 1.
2 See note under UNION OF SOVIET SOCIALIST REPUBLICS in Section 1.

Declaration suspending the operation of quadripartite rights and responsibilities.
Signed at New York October 1, 1990.
Entered into force October 3, 1990.
TIAS

Parties:

France
Union of Soviet Socialist Republics [1]
United Kingdom
United States

Notes

1 See note under UNION OF SOVIET SOCIALIST REPUBLICS in Section 1

Agreement on a comprehensive political settlement of the Cambodia conflict, with annexes.
Done at Paris October 23, 1991.
Entered into force October 23, 1991.
TIAS

Depositary: Indonesia; France

Agreement concerning the sovereignty, independence, territorial integrity and inviolability, neutrality and national unity of Cambodia.
Done at Paris October 31, 1991.
Entered into force October 31, 1991.
TIAS

Depositary: Indonesia; France

POLLUTION

International convention relating to intervention on the high seas in cases of oil pollution casualties, with annex.
Done at Brussels November 29, 1969.
Entered into force May 6, 1975.
26 UST 765; TIAS 8068

Depositary: International Maritime Organization

Convention on the prevention of marine pollution by dumping of wastes and other matter, with annexes.
Done at Washington, London, Mexico City, and Moscow December 29, 1972.
Entered into force August 30, 1975.
26 UST 2403; TIAS 8165; 1046 UNTS 120

Amendment:

October 12, 1978 (incineration)
November 12, 1993

Depositaries: Mexico, Russia, United Kingdom, United States

Protocol relating to intervention on the high seas in cases of pollution by substances other than oil.
Done at London November 2, 1973.
Entered into force March 30, 1983.
TIAS 10561

Amendments:

July 10, 1996
October, 2002

Depositary: International Maritime Organization

Protocol of 1978 relating to the international convention for the prevention of pollution from ships, 1973, with annexes and protocols.*

Done at London February 17, 1978.
Entered into force October 2, 1983.
TIAS

Amendments:

September 7, 1984
December 5, 1985
December 1, 1987
October 17, 1989
November 16, 1990
July 4, 1991
March 6, 1992
October 30, 1992
September 14, 1995
July 10, 1996
September 25, 1997
April 27, 2001
April 1, 2004
October 15, 2004
July 22, 2005
March 24, 2006
October 13, 2006
July 13, 2007
July 17, 2009
March 26, 2010
July 15, 2011
March 2, 2012

Depositary: International Maritime Organization

Note:

* The 1978 protocol supersedes the international convention for the prevention of pollution of the sea by oil of May 12, 1954 (TIAS 4900) as between contracting parties to the 1978 protocol.
* The 1978 protocol incorporates with modifications the provisions of the international convention for the prevention of pollution from ships, including its annexes and protocol, signed at London November 2, 1973. The 1973 convention is not intended to enter into force and be applied on its own. Accordingly, as of October 2, 1983, the regime to be applied by the states parties to the 1978 protocol will be the regime contained in the 1973 convention as modified by the 1978 protocol.

Annex III entered into force July 1, 1992.
Annex IV entered into force September 27, 2003.
Annex V entered into force December 31, 1988

Convention on long-range transboundary air pollution.

Done at Geneva November 13, 1979.
Entered into force March 16, 1983.
TIAS 10541

Depositary: United Nations

Convention for the protection and development of the marine environment of the wider Caribbean region, with annex.

Done at Cartagena March 24, 1983.
Entered into force October 11, 1986.
TIAS 11085

Depositary: Colombia

Protocol concerning cooperation in combating oil spills in the wider Caribbean region, with annex.

Done at Cartagena March 24, 1983.
Entered into force October 11, 1986.
TIAS 11085

Depositary: Colombia

Protocol on long-term financing of the co-operative programme for monitoring and evaluation of the long-range transmission of air pollutants in Europe (EMEP).

Done at Geneva September 28, 1984.
Entered into force January 28, 1988.
TIAS 12086

Depositary: United Nations

Convention for the protection of the ozone layer, with annexes.

Done at Vienna March 22, 1985.
Entered into force September 22, 1988.
TIAS 11097

Depositary: United Nations

Convention for the protection of the natural resources and environment of the South Pacific Region, with annex.

Done at Noumea November 24, 1986.
Entered into force August 22, 1990; for the United States July 10, 1991.
TIAS

Depositary: Pacific Island Forum Secretariat

Protocol for the prevention of pollution of the South Pacific Region by dumping, with annexes.

Done at Noumea November 24, 1986.
Entered into force August 22, 1990; for the United States July 10, 1991.
TIAS

Depositary: Pacific Island Forum Secretariat

Protocol concerning cooperation in combatting pollution emergencies in the South Pacific Region.

Done at Noumea November 24, 1986.
Entered into force August 22, 1990; for the United States July 10, 1991.
TIAS

Depositary: Pacific Island Forum Secretariat

Montreal protocol on substances that deplete the ozone layer, with annexes.

Done at Montreal September 16, 1987.
Entered into force January 1, 1989.
TIAS

Amendments and Adjustments:

June 29, 1990
June 19-21, 1991
November 23–25, 1992
December 7, 1995
September 15-17, 1997
December 3, 1999

Depositary: United Nations

Protocol to the 1979 Convention on long-range transboundary air pollution concerning the control of emissions of nitrogen oxides or their transboundary fluxes, with annex.
Done at Sofia October 31, 1988.
Entered into force February 14, 1991.
TIAS 12086
Depositary: United Nations

Protocol concerning specially protected areas and wildlife to the convention for the protection and development of the marine environment of the wider Caribbean region.
Done at Kingston January 18, 1990.
Entered into force June 18, 2000; for the United States April 16, 2003.
TIAS
Depositary: Colombia

International convention on oil pollution preparedness, response and co-operation, 1990.
Done at London November 30, 1990.
Entered into force May 13, 1995.
TIAS
Depositary: International Maritime Organization

OECD Council decision on the control of transfrontier movements of wastes destined for recovery operations.
Adopted at Paris March 30, 1992.
Entered into force March 30, 1992.
TIAS 11880
Parties:
Australia
Austria
Belgium
Canada
Denmark
Finland
France
Germany
Greece
Iceland
Ireland
Italy
Luxembourg
Netherlands
New Zealand
Norway
Portugal
Spain
Sweden
Switzerland
Turkey
United Kingdom
United States

Protocol to amend the international convention for the prevention of pollution from ships, 1973, as modified by the protocol of 1978 relating thereto.
Done at London September 26, 1997.
Entered into force May 19, 2005; for the United States January 8, 2009.
TIAS
Depositary: International Maritime Organization

Protocol to the 1979 Convention on long-range transboundary air pollution on heavy metals, with annexes.
Done at Aarhus June 24, 1998.
Entered into force December 29, 2003.
TIAS 12966
Depositary: United Nations

Protocol concerning pollution from land-based sources and activities to the convention for the protection and development of the marine environment of the wider Caribbean region.
Done at Oranjestad, Aruba on October 6, 1999.
Entered into force August 13, 2010; for the United States August 13, 2010.
TIAS
Depositaries: Colombia; the Caribbean Environment Programme

Protocol to the 1979 Convention on long-range transboundary air pollution to abate acidification, eutrophication and ground-level ozone.
Done at Gothenburg November 30, 1999.
Entered into force May 17, 2005.
TIAS 13073
Depositary: United Nations

International Convention on the control of harmful anti-fouling systems on ships, 2001.
Done at London October 5, 2001.
Entered into force September 17, 2008; for the United States November 21, 2012.
TIAS 12-1121
Depositary: International Maritime Organization

Agreement on cooperation on marine oil pollution preparedness and response in the Artic.
Done at Kiruna May 15, 2013.
Entered into force March 25, 2016.
TIAS 16-325
Depositary: Norway

POSTAL MATTERS

UNIVERSAL POSTAL UNION

Note: The depositary for agreements in this section is the Universal Postal Union.

Constitution of the Universal Postal Union, with Final Protocol.*
Done at Vienna July 10, 1964.
Entered into force January 1, 1966.
16 UST 1291; TIAS 5881; 611 UNTS 7

Additional protocol to the constitution of the Universal Postal Union of July 10, 1964.
Done at Tokyo November 14, 1969.
Entered into force (except Article V) July 1, 1971; Article V entered into force January 1, 1971.
22 UST 1056; TIAS 7150; 810 UNTS 7

Second additional protocol to the constitution of the Universal Postal Union of July 10, 1964.
Done at Lausanne July 5, 1974.
Entered into force January 1, 1976; definitively for the United States April 14, 1976.
27 UST 345; TIAS 8231; 1005 UNTS 9

Third additional protocol to the constitution of the Universal Postal Union of July 10, 1964, general regulations with annex, and the universal postal convention with final protocol and detailed regulations.
Done at Hamburg July 27, 1984.
Entered into force January 1, 1986; definitively for the United States June 6, 1986.
TIAS

Fourth additional protocol to the constitution of the Universal Postal Union of July 10, 1964, general regulations and the universal postal convention with final protocol.
Done at Washington December 14, 1989.
Entered into force January 1, 1991.
TIAS

Fifth additional protocol to the constitution of the Universal Postal Union of July 10, 1964, with general regulations and the universal postal convention with final protocol.
Done at Seoul September 14, 1994.
Entered into force January 1, 1996; definitively for the United States May 20, 1998.
TIAS

Sixth additional protocol to the constitution of the Universal Postal Union of July 10, 1964, with general regulations and the universal postal convention with final protocol.
Done at Beijing September 15, 1999.
Entered into force January 1, 2001; definitively for the United States April 10, 2001.
TIAS

Seventh additional protocol to the constitution of the Universal Postal Union of July 10, 1964, with general regulations and the universal postal convention with final protocol.
Done at Bucharest October 5, 2004.
Entered into force January 1, 2006; definitively for the United States June 20, 2006.
TIAS

Eighth additional protocol to the constitution of the Universal Postal Union of July 10, 1964, with general regulations and the universal postal convention with final protocol.*
Done at Geneva August 12, 2008.
Entered into force January 1, 2010; definitively for the United States July 28, 2010.
TIAS

Note:
* Unless otherwise indicated by the depositary, all states parties to the constitution of the Universal Postal Union signed the final act of the Universal Postal Congress, Geneva, 2008. The General Regulations and Universal Postal Convention adopted at Geneva replaced those adopted at Bucharest October 5, 2004, which in turn replaced those adopted at previous postal congresses.

Postal payment services agreement.
Done at Geneva August 12, 2008.
Entered into force January 1, 2010; definitively for the United States July 28, 2010.
TIAS

POSTAL UNION OF THE AMERICAS AND SPAIN

Note: The depositary for agreements in this section is Uruguay

Constitution of the Postal Union of the Americas and Spain, with final protocol.
Done at Santiago November 26, 1971.
Entered into force July 1, 1972.
23 UST 2924; TIAS 7480

Additional protocol to the constitution of the Postal Union of the Americas and Spain.
Done at Lima March 18, 1976.
Entered into force October 1, 1976.
30 UST 337; TIAS 9206

Second additional protocol to the constitution of the Postal Union of the Americas and Spain, with general regulations.
Done at Managua August 28, 1981.
*Entered into force January 1, 1982.**
TIAS

Notes:
* While the United States has acceded to the second additional protocol most of the other parties have not yet done so. Even though not formally ratified, these agreements are customarily applied administratively.

PRIVATE INTERNATIONAL LAW

Protocol embodying a declaration on the juridical personality of foreign companies.
Done at the Pan American Union, Washington, June 25, 1936.
Entered into force for the United States July 10, 1941.
55 Stat. 1201; TS 973; 3 Bevans 274; 161 UNTS 217
Depositary: Organization of American States

Statute of the International Institute for the Unification of Private Law.
Done at Rome March 15, 1940.
Entered into force July 15, 1955; for the United States March 13, 1964.
15 UST 2494; TIAS 5743
Amendments:
June 15-16, 1965 (19 UST 7802; TIAS 6611)
December 18, 1967 (20 UST 2529; TIAS 6716)
February 18, 1969, for articles 5, 11 and 16 (30 UST 5663; TIAS 9519)
November 9, 1984, for article 16

Depositary: Italy

Statute of The Hague Conference on Private International Law.
Done at the 7th session of the Conference at The Hague October 9–31, 1951.
Entered into force July 15, 1955; for the United States October 15, 1964.
15 UST 2228; TIAS 5710; 220 UNTS 121
Amendment:
June 30, 2005

Depositary: Netherlands

Convention abolishing the requirement of legalisation for foreign public documents, with annex.
Done at The Hague October 5, 1961.
Entered into force January 24, 1965; for the United States October 15, 1981.
33 UST 883; TIAS 10072; 527 UNTS 189
Depositary: Netherlands

Convention on the service abroad of judicial and extrajudicial documents in civil or commercial matters.
Done at The Hague November 15, 1965.
Entered into force February 10, 1969.
20 UST 361; TIAS 6638; 658 UNTS 163
Depositary: Netherlands

PUBLICATIONS

Convention for the international exchange of official documents, scientific and literary publications.
Concluded at Brussels March 15, 1886.
Entered into force January 14, 1889.
25 Stat. 1465; TS 381; 1 Bevans 107
Depositary: Belgium

Convention for the immediate exchange of the official journals, parliamentary annals, and documents
Concluded at Brussels March 15, 1886.
Entered into force January 14, 1889.
25 Stat. 1469; TS 382; 1 Bevans 110
Depositary: Belgium

Convention relating to the exchange of official, scientific, literary and industrial publications.
Signed at Mexico January 27, 1902.
Entered into force July 16, 1902.
TS 491-A; 1 Bevans 335
Depositary: Mexico

Agreement for the repression of the circulation of obscene publications.
Signed at Paris May 4, 1910.
Entered into force September 15, 1911.
37 Stat. 1511; TS 559; 1 Bevans 748
Depositary: France

Convention on interchange of publications.
Signed at Buenos Aires December 23, 1936.
Entered into force April 1, 1938; for the United States October 23, 1939.
54 Stat. 1715; TS 954; 3 Bevans 378; 201 LNTS 295
Depositary: Organization of American States

Protocol amending the agreement for the suppression of the circulation of obscene publications signed at Paris May 4, 1910, with annex.
Done at Lake Success May 4, 1949.
Entered into force May 4, 1949; for the United States August 14, 1950.
1 UST 849; TIAS 2164; 30 UNTS 3
Depositary: United Nations

Convention concerning the international exchange of publications.
Adopted at Paris December 3, 1958.
Entered into force November 23, 1961; for the United States June 9, 1968.
19 UST 4449; TIAS 6438; 416 UNTS 51
Depositary: UNESCO

Convention concerning the exchange of official publications and government documents between States.
Adopted at Paris December 3, 1958.
Entered into force May 30, 1961; for the United States June 9, 1968.
19 UST 4467; TIAS 6439; 398 UNTS 9
Depositary: UNESCO

Proces-verbal relating to the convention concerning the exchange of official publications and government documents between States.

Signed at Paris October 18, 1960.

19 UST 4485; TIAS 6439

Depositary: UNESCO

Statutes of the International Center for the Registration of Serial Publications.

Done at Paris November 14, 1974

Entered into force January 21, 1976;

provisionally for the United States March 31, 1978.

TIAS

Amendment:

October 11 and 12, 1976

Depositary: UNESCO

REGIONAL ISSUES

Convention providing for creation of the Inter-American Indian Institute.

Done at Mexico City November 29, 1940.

Entered into force December 13, 1941.

56 Stat. 1303; TS 978; 3 Bevans 661

Depositary: Mexico

Agreement establishing the South Pacific Commission.

Signed at Canberra February 6, 1947.

Entered into force July 29, 1948.

2 UST 1787; TIAS 2317; 97 UNTS 227

Amendments:

November 7, 1951 (3 UST 2851; TIAS 2458; 124 UNTS 320)
April 5, 1954 (5 UST 639; TIAS 2952; 201 UNTS 374)
October 6, 1964 (16 UST 1055; TIAS 5845; 542 UNTS 350)
October 2, 1974 (26 UST 1606; TIAS 8120)
October 20, 1976 (33 UST 585; TIAS 10051)
October 7–12, 1978 (33 UST 590; TIAS 10052)

Depositary: Australia

Charter of the Organization of American States.

Signed at Bogota April 30, 1948.

Entered into force December 13, 1951.

2 UST 2394; TIAS 2361; 119 UNTS 3

Amendments:

February 27, 1967 (21 UST 607; TIAS 6847)
December 14, 1992
June 10, 1993

Depositary: Organization of American States

REGULATORY COOPERATION & STANDARIZATION

Convention concerning the creation of an international office of weights and measures, regulations and transient provisions.

Signed at Paris May 20, 1875.

Entered into force January 1, 1876; for the United States August 2, 1878.

20 Stat. 709; TS 378; 1 Bevans 39

Depositary: France

Convention amending the convention relating to weights and measures

Dated at Sevres October 6, 1921.

Entered into force June 23, 1922; for the United States October 24, 1923.

43 Stat. 1686; TS 673; 2 Bevans 323; 17 LNTS 45

Depositary: France

Convention establishing an International Organization of Legal Metrology.

Done at Paris October 12, 1955.

Entered into force May 28, 1958; for the United States (as amended) October 22, 1972.

23 UST 4233; TIAS 7533; 560 UNTS 3

Amendment:

January 18, 1968

Depositary: International Organization of Legal Metrology (France)

RULES OF WAR

Convention regarding the rights of neutrals at sea.

Signed at Washington July 22, 1854.

Entered into force October 31, 1854.

10 Stat. 1105; TS 300; 11 Bevans 1214

Parties:

Nicaragua [1]
Union of Soviet Socialist Republics [2]
United States

Notes:

1 Declaration of accession by Nicaragua signed at Granada June 9, 1855 (7 Miller 139).
2 See note under UNION OF SOVIET SOCIALIST REPUBLICS in Section 1.

Convention with respect to the laws and customs of war on land, with annex of regulations.*

Signed at The Hague July 29, 1899.

Entered into force September 4, 1900; for the United States April 9, 1902.

32 Stat. 1803; TS 403; 1 Bevans 247

Depositary: Netherlands

Notes

* Replaced by convention of October 18, 1907 (TS 539; 36 Stat.2277), as between contracting parties to the later convention. Sections II and III of the regulations are supplemented by convention of August 12, 1949 (TIAS 3365; 6 UST 3516), relative to protection of civilians in time of war, as between contracting parties to both conventions; chapter II of the regulations is complemented by convention of August 12, 1949 (TIAS 3364; 6 UST 3316), relative to the treatment of prisoners of war, as between contracting parties to both conventions.

Convention for the exemption of hospital ships, in time of war, from the payment of all dues and taxes imposed for the benefit of the state.

Done at The Hague December 21, 1904.

Entered into force March 26, 1907.

35 Stat. 1854; TS 459; 1 Bevans 430

Depositary: Netherlands

Convention respecting the limitation of the employment of force for the recovery of contract debts.
Signed at The Hague October 18, 1907.
Entered into force January 26, 1910.
36 Stat. 2241; TS 537; 1 Bevans 607
Depositary: Netherlands

Convention relative to the opening of hostilities.
Signed at The Hague October 18, 1907.
Entered into force January 26, 1910.
36 Stat. 2259; TS 538; 1 Bevans 619
Depositary: Netherlands

Declaration prohibiting the discharge of projectiles and explosives from balloons.
Signed at The Hague October 18, 1907.
Entered into force November 27, 1909.
36 Stat. 2439; TS 546; 1 Bevans 739
Depositary: Netherlands

Convention respecting the rights and duties of neutral powers and persons in case of war on land.
Signed at The Hague October 18, 1907.
Entered into force January 26, 1910.
36 Stat. 2310; TS 540; 1 Bevans 654
Depositary: Netherlands

Convention concerning bombardment by naval forces in time of war.
Signed at The Hague October 18, 1907.
Entered into force January 26, 1910.
36 Stat. 2351; TS 542; 1 Bevans 681
Depositary: Netherlands

Convention relative to the laying of automatic submarine contact mines.
Signed at The Hague October 18, 1907.
Entered into force January 26, 1910.
36 Stat. 2332; TS 541; 1 Bevans 669
Depositary: Netherlands

Convention relative to certain restrictions with regard to the exercise of the right of capture in naval war.
Signed at The Hague October 18, 1907.
Entered into force January 26, 1910.
36 Stat. 2396; TS 544; 1 Bevans 711
Depositary: Netherlands

Convention concerning the rights and duties of neutral powers in naval war.
Signed at The Hague October 18, 1907.
Entered into force January 26, 1910; for the United States February 1, 1910.
36 Stat. 2415; TS 545; 1 Bevans 723
Depositary: Netherlands

Convention respecting the laws and customs of war on land, with annex of regulations.*
Signed at The Hague October 18, 1907.
Entered into force January 26, 1910.
36 Stat. 2277; TS 539; 1 Bevans 631
Depositary: Netherlands

Notes:
* Sections II and III of the regulations are supplemented by convention of August 12, 1949 (6 UST 3516; TIAS 3365), relative to protection of civilians in time of war, as between contracting parties to both conventions; chapter II of the regulations is complemented by convention of August 12, 1949 (6 UST 3316; TIAS 3364), relative to treatment of prisoners of war, as between contracting parties to both conventions.

Convention for the adaptation to maritime warfare of the principles of the Geneva Convention.*
Signed at The Hague October 18, 1907.
Entered into force January 26, 1910.
TS 543; 1 Bevans 694
Depositary: Netherlands

Notes:
* Replaces as between contracting parties the 1899 convention.

Treaty to avoid or prevent conflicts between the American States.
Signed at Santiago May 3, 1923.
Entered into force October 8, 1924.
44 Stat. 2527; TS 752; 2 Bevans 413; 33 LNTS 25
Depositary: Chile

Convention on the rights and duties of states in the event of civil strife.
Done at Habana February 20, 1928.
Entered into force May 21, 1929; for the United States May 21, 1930.
46 Stat. 2749; TS 814; 2 Bevans 694; 134 LNTS 45
Depositary: Organization of American States

Convention on maritime neutrality.
Signed at Habana February 20, 1928.
Entered into force January 12, 1931; for the United States March 22, 1932.
47 Stat. 1989; TS 845; 2 Bevans 721; 135 LNTS 187
Depositary: Organization of American States

Treaty providing for the renunciation of war as an instrument of national policy.
Signed at Paris August 27, 1928.
Entered into force July 24, 1929.
46 Stat. 2343; TS 796; 2 Bevans 732; 94 LNTS 57
Depositary: United States

Notes:
* All provisions of this treaty with the exception of Part IV, which relates to rules of international law in regard to the operations of submarines or other war vessels with respect to merchant vessels, expired on December 31, 1936. Under the terms of article 23, Part IV "shall remain in force without limit of time".

Convention on rights and duties of states.
Done at Montevideo December 26, 1933.
Entered into force December 26, 1934.
49 Stat. 3097; TS 881; 3 Bevans 145; 165 LNTS 19
Depositary: Organization of American States

Convention for the maintenance, preservation, and reestablishment of peace.
Signed at Buenos Aires December 23, 1936.
Entered into force August 25, 1937.
51 Stat. 15; TS 922; 3 Bevans 338; 188 LNTS 9
Depositary: Argentina

Additional protocol relative to non-intervention.
Signed at Buenos Aires December 23, 1936.
Entered into force August 25, 1937.
51 Stat. 41; TS 923; 3 Bevans 343; 188 LNTS 31
Depositary: Argentina

Treaty on the prevention of controversies.
Signed at Buenos Aires December 23, 1936.
Entered into force July 29, 1937.
51 Stat. 65; TS 924; 3 Bevans 357; 188 LNTS 53
Depositaries: Argentina, Organization of American States

Convention to coordinate, extend and assure the fulfillment of the existing treaties between the American States.
Signed at Buenos Aires December 23, 1936.
Entered into force November 24, 1938.
51 Stat. 116; TS 926; 3 Bevans 348; 195 LNTS 229
Depositary: Argentina

Agreement for the prosecution and punishment of the major war criminals of the European Axis.
Signed at London August 8, 1945.
Entered into force August 8, 1945.
59 Stat. 1544; EAS 472; 3 Bevans 1238; 82 UNTS 279
Depositary: United Kingdom

Charter of the International Military Tribunal for the Far East
Dated at Tokyo January 19, 1946, amended April 26, 1946.
TIAS 1589; 4 Bevans 20

Convention relative to the treatment of prisoners of war.*
Dated at Geneva August 12, 1949.
Entered into force October 21, 1950; for the United States February 2, 1956.
6 UST 3316; TIAS 3364; 75 UNTS 135
Depositary: Switzerland

Notes:
* The 1949 conventions on the amelioration of the condition of the armed forces on the field and on prisoners of war replaced the conventions of July 27, 1929 (47 Stat 2021 and 2074; TS 846 and 847) as between contracting parties.

Convention for the amelioration of the condition of the wounded and sick in armed forces in the field.*
Dated at Geneva August 12, 1949.
Entered into force October 21, 1950; for the United States February 2, 1956.
6 UST 3114; TIAS 3362; 75 UNTS 31
Depositary: Switzerland

Notes:
* The 1949 conventions on the amelioration of the condition of the armed forces on the field and on prisoners of war replaced the conventions of July 27, 1929 (47 Stat 2021 and 2074; TS 846 and 847) as between contracting parties.

Convention for the amelioration of the condition of the wounded, sick, and shipwrecked members of armed forces at sea.
Dated at Geneva August 12, 1949.
Entered into force October 21, 1950; for the United States February 2, 1956.
6 UST 3217; TIAS 3363; 75 UNTS 85
Depositary: Switzerland

Convention relative to the protection of civilian persons in time of war.
Dated at Geneva August 12, 1949.
Entered into force October 21, 1950; for the United States February 2, 1956.
6 UST 3516; TIAS 3365; 75 UNTS 287
Depositary: Switzerland

Convention on the prohibition of military or any other hostile use of environmental modification techniques, with annex.
Done at Geneva May 18, 1977.
Entered into force October 5, 1978; for the United States January 17, 1980.
31 UST 333; TIAS 9614
Depositary: United Nations

Convention on the transfer of sentenced persons.
Done at Strasbourg March 21, 1983.
Entered into force July 1, 1985.
35 UST 2867; TIAS 10824
Depositary: Council of Europe

Additional Protocol III to the Geneva Conventions of August 12, 1949, relating to the adoption of an additional distinctive emblem, with annex.
Signed at Geneva December 8, 2005.
Entered into force January 14, 2007; for the United States September 8, 2007.
TIAS 07-908
Depositary: Switzerland

Note:
* The 1949 conventions on the amelioration of the condition of the armed forces in the field and on prisoners of war replaced the conventions of July 27, 1929 (47 Stat. 2021 and 2027; TS 846 and 847) as between contracting parties.

SCIENTIFIC & TECHNICAL COOPERATION

Convention of the World Meteorological Organization, with related protocol.
Done at Washington October 11, 1947.
Entered into force March 23, 1950.
1 UST 281; TIAS 2052; 77 UNTS 143

Amendments:

April 11, 1963 (16 UST 2069; TIAS 5947)
April 27, 1963 (16 UST 2073; TIAS 5947)
April 11 and 26, 1967 (18 UST 2795; TIAS 6364)
April 26, 1967 (18 UST 2800; TIAS 6364)
April 28–May 25, 1975 (26 UST 2580; TIAS 8175)
May 24, 2007 (TIAS)

Depositary: United States

Convention on the International Hydrographic Organization, with annexes.
Done at Monaco May 3, 1967.
Entered into force September 22, 1970.
21 UST 1857; TIAS 6933; 751 UNTS 41

Depositary: International Hydrographic Organization, Monaco

Agreement establishing the Middle East Desalination Research Center.
Signed at Muscat December 22, 1996.
Entered into force December 22, 1996.
TIAS

Parties:

Israel
Japan
Korea
Oman
United States

SPACE

Treaty on principles governing the activities of states in the exploration and use of outer space, including the moon and other celestial bodies.
Done at Washington, London, and Moscow January 27, 1967.
Entered into force October 10, 1967.
18 UST 2410; TIAS 6347; 610 UNTS 205

Depositary: Russia, United Kingdom, United States

Agreement on the rescue of astronauts, the return of astronauts, and the return of objects launched into outer space.
Done at Washington, London, and Moscow April 22, 1968.
Entered into force December 3, 1968.
19 UST 7570; TIAS 6599; 672 UNTS 119

Depositary: Russia, United Kingdom, United States

Convention on international liability for damage caused by space objects.
Done at Washington, London, and Moscow March 29, 1972.
Entered into force September 1, 1972; for the United States October 9, 1973.
24 UST 2389; TIAS 7762; 961 UNTS 187

Depositary: United States

Convention on registration of objects launched into outer space.
Done at New York January 14, 1975.
Entered into force September 15, 1976.
28 UST 695; TIAS 8480; 1023 UNTS 15

Depositary: United Nations

Memorandum of understanding concerning cooperation in an experimental satellite-aided search and rescue system, with annex.
Signed at Washington, Ottawa and Paris July 16, 19 and August 27, 1979.
Entered into force August 27, 1979.
TIAS

Parties:

Canada
France
United States

Understanding concerning in a joint experimental satellite-aided search and rescue project.
Signed at Leningrad November 23, 1979.
Entered into force August 13, 1980.
TIAS

Parties:

Canada
France
Union of Soviet Socialist Republics[1]
United States

Note:

1 See note under UNION OF SOVIET SOCIALIST REPUBLICS in Section 1.

Understanding concerning participation by Norway in an investigation of the demonstration and evaluation of an experimental satellite-aided search and rescue system.
Signed at Ottawa, Paris, Washington, and Oslo September 25, September 30, October 19, and November 13, 1981.
Entered into force November 13, 1981.
TIAS 12378

Parties:

Canada
France
Norway
United States

Memorandum of understanding concerning cooperation in a search and rescue satellite system, with annex.

Signed at London September 27, 1984.
Entered into force February 20, 1985.
TIAS

Parties:

Canada
France
Union of Soviet Socialist Republics [1]
United States

Note:

1 See note under UNION OF SOVIET SOCIALIST REPUBLICS in Section 1.

International COSPAS–SARSAT program agreement.

Done at Paris July 1, 1988.
Entered into force August 30, 1988.
TIAS; 1518 UNTS 209

Parties:

Canada
France
Union of Soviet Socialist Republics [1]
United States

Note:

1 See note under UNION OF SOVIET SOCIALIST REPUBLICS in Section 1.

Memorandum of agreement concerning the SARSAT Space Segment.

Done at Washington September 11, 1995.
Entered into force November 10, 1995.
TIAS 12690; 2026 UNTS 187

Parties:

Canada
France
United States

Agreement concerning cooperation on the civil international space station, with annex.

Signed at Washington January 29, 1998.
Entered into force March 27, 2001.
TIAS 12927

Depositary: United States

Arrangement concerning application of the space station intergovernmental agreement pending its entry into force.

Signed at Washington January 29, 1998.
Entered into force January 29, 1998.
TIAS 12927

Depositary: United States

Memorandum of understanding for cooperation in the ocean surface topography mission.

Signed at Washington, Darmstadt and Paris March 21, March 24, March 30, and April 7, 2006.
Entered into force April 7, 2006.
TIAS 06-407

Parties:

EUMETSAT
France
United States

TAXATION

Convention on mutual administrative assistance in tax matters.

Signed at Strasbourg January 25, 1988.
Entered into force April 1, 1995.
TIAS

Depositary: Council of Europe

Agreement on state and local taxation of foreign employees of public international organizations.

Done at Washington April 21, 1992.
Entered into force May 24, 1994.
TIAS 12135

Depositary: United States

TELECOMMUNICATION

Convention for protection of submarine cables, signed at Paris March 14, 1884, with declaration respecting the interpretation of articles II and IV.*

Signed at Paris December 1, 1886.
Entered into force May 1, 1888.
24 Stat. 989; 25 Stat. 1424; TS 380; TS 380 1; TS 380 2; TS 380 3; 1 Bevans 89; 1 Bevans 112; 1 Bevans 114

Depositary: France

Note:

* Applicable to all territories

Final Protocol of agreement fixing May 1, 1888 as the date of effect of the Convention concluded March 14, 1884, for the protection of submarine cables.

Signed at Paris July 7, 1887.
Entered into force May 1, 1888.
24 Stat. 989; 25 Stat. 1424; TS 380; TS 380 1; TS 380 2; TS 380 3;
1 Bevans 89; 1 Bevans 112; 1 Bevans 114

Depositary: France

Inter-American radio communications convention, with annexes.*

Signed at Habana December 13, 1937.
Entered into force July 1, 1938; for the United States: July 21, 1938 (Parts One, Three, and Four); April 17, 1939 (Part Two).
53 Stat. 1576; TS 938; 3 Bevans 462

Depositary: Cuba

Note:

* Part 2 of the convention (Inter-American Radio Office) terminated for all parties December 20, 1958.

Regional radio convention for Central America, Panama, and the Canal Zone.

Signed at Guatemala December 8, 1938.
Entered into force October 8, 1939.
54 Stat. 1675; TS 949; 3 Bevans 529; 202 LNTS 49

Depositary: Guatemala

Inter-American radio agreement, with annex, appendices, declaration, resolutions, and recommendations.*
Done at Washington July 9, 1949.
Entered into force April 13, 1952.
3 UST 3064; TIAS 2489; 168 UNTS 143
Depositary: United States

Note:
* The 1949 agreement replaces the agreement of January 26, 1940 (EAS 231; 55 Stat. 1482; 3 Bevans 611) which in turn replaced the arrangement of December 13, 1937 (54 Stat. 2514; EAS 200; 3 Bevans 480). The 1940 agreement remains in force as between the contracting parties (including the United States) and Brazil, Canada (with reservation), Chile, and Venezuela. The 1937 arrangement remains in force as between the contracting parties and Peru and Panama.

Agreement revising the telecommunications agreement signed at Bermuda December 4, 1945.*
Annexed to the Final Act of the United States–Commonwealth telecommunications meeting signed at London August 12, 1949.
Entered into force February 24, 1950.
3 UST 2686; TIAS 2435; 87 UNTS 131
Amendment:
October 1, 1952 (3 UST 5140; TIAS 2705; 151 UNTS 378)

Depositary: United Kingdom

Notes:
* Applicable to all territories

Multilateral declaration to denounce Part Two (Inter-American Radio Office) of the inter-American radio communications convention of December 13, 1937.*
Signed at Washington December 20, 1957.
Entered into force December 20, 1957.
9 UST 1037; TIAS 4079
Depositary: Cuba

Notes:
* A contract on the exchange of notifications of radio broadcasting frequencies between the Pan American Union and the Governments of Canada, Cuba, the Dominican Republic, Haiti, Jamaica, Mexico and the United States was signed at Washington on December 20, 1957, effective January 1, 1958. (For text see 9 UST 1050; TIAS 4079.)

Agreement on cooperation in intercontinental testing in connection with experimental communications satellites.
Exchanges of notes at Stockholm July 5 and 25, 1963, at Oslo
July 8 and September 11, 1963, and at Copenhagen July 2 and September 14, 1963.
Entered into force September 14, 1963.
14 UST 1278; TIAS 5431; 488 UNTS 121
Parties:
Denmark
Norway
Sweden
United States

Agreement relating to the International Telecommunications Satellite Organization, with annexes.
Done at Washington August 20, 1971.
Entered into force February 12, 1973.
23 UST 3813; TIAS 7532
Amendments
August 31, 1995
November 10, 2000
November 17, 2000

Depositary: United States

Convention on the international maritime satellite organization (INMARSAT), with annex.
Done at London September 3, 1976.
Entered into force July 16, 1979.
Amendments:
October 16, 1985
January 19, 1989
April 24, 1998

Depositary: International Maritime Organization

Convention relating to the distribution of programmer-carrying signals transmitted by satellite.
Done at Brussels May 21, 1974.
Entered into force August 25, 1979; for the United States March 7, 1985.
TIAS 11078
Depositary: United Nations

Radio regulations, with appendices and final protocol (WARC-79).
Done at Geneva December 6, 1979.
*Entered into force January 1, 1982; definitively for the United States October 27, 1983.**
TIAS
Depositary: International Telecommunication Union

Note:
* The 1979 Radio Regulations abrogate and replace the Radio Regulations adopted at Geneva December 21, 1959 (12 UST 2377; TIAS 4893) and partial revisions thereto: November 8, 1963 (15 UST 887; TIAS 5603); April 23, 1966 (18 UST 2091; TIAS 6332); November 3, 1967 (19 UST 6717; TIAS 6590); July 17, 1971 (23 UST 1527; TIAS 7435); June 8, 1974 (28 UST 3909) and March 5, 1978 (32 UST 3821; TIAS 9920), as between parties to the later Regulations. The 1959 radio Regulations were considered as annexed to the international telecommunication conventions of 1965 (Montreux) and 1973 (Malaga-Torremolinos) and as such binding upon parties to those conventions (see Notes to the international telecommunication convention 1982 (Nairobi)). The Taiwan authorities also adhered to the 1959 Radio Regulations and the 1963, 1966 and 1967 revisions thereto (see note under CHINA (TAIWAN) in Section 1).

Regional agreement for the medium frequency broadcasting service in Region 2, with annexes and final protocol.

Done at Rio de Janeiro December 19, 1981.

Entered into force July 1, 1983; for the United States April 6, 1993.

TIAS

Parties:

Argentina [1]
Brazil
Canada
Denmark
France
Netherlands
Suriname
United States

Notes:

1 With statement(s).

International telecommunication convention, with annexes and protocols.*

Done at Nairobi November 6, 1982.

Entered into force January 1, 1984; definitively for the United States January 10, 1986.

TIAS

Depositary: International Telecommunication Union

Notes:

* The 1982 convention has been abrogated and replaced in relations between contracting parties by the Constitution and Convention of the International Telecommunication Union adopted at Geneva December 22, 1992 (see below). Only those states parties to the 1982 convention that are not parties to the 1992 Constitution and Convention are bound. The 1982 international telecommunication convention replaced the Malaga-Torremolinos convention of October 25, 1973 (28 UST 2495; TIAS 8572), as between contracting parties to the later convention. Costa Rica, Grenada, Guinea-Bissau, Nauru, and Yugoslavia (see note under YUGOSLAVIA in Section 1) are parties to the 1973 convention but not parties to the later conventions. The Dominican Republic is a party to the Montreux convention of November 12, 1965 (18 UST 545; TIAS 6267) but not a party to the later conventions.

Partial revisions of Radio Regulations (Geneva, 1979): Relating to mobile services (MOB-83).

Done at Geneva March 18, 1983.

Entered into force January 15, 1985; for the United States April 6, 1993.

TIAS

Depositary: International Telecommunication Union

On the use of the geostationary-satellite orbit and on the planning of space services utilizing it (WARC ORB-85).

Done at Geneva September 15, 1985.

Entered into force October 30, 1986; for the United States April 6, 1993.

TIAS

Depositary: International Telecommunications Union

Inter-American convention on amateur radio service.

Done at Lima August 14, 1987.

Entered into force February 21, 1990; for the United States March 20, 1991.

TIAS

Depositary: Organization of American States

1987 partial revision of the radio regulations (Geneva, 1979), Relating to mobile services (MOB-87).

Done at Geneva October 17, 1987.

Entered into force October 3, 1989; for the United States April 6, 1993.

TIAS

Depositary: International Telecommunications Union

On the use of the geostationary-satellite orbit and on the planning of space services utilizing it (WARC ORB-88).

Done at Geneva October 6, 1988.

Entered into force March 16, 1990; for the United States April 6, 1993.

TIAS

Depositary: International Telecommunications Union

Regional agreement for the use of the band 1605–1705 kHz in Region 2, with annexes and final protocol.

Done at Rio de Janeiro June 8, 1988.

Entered into force July 1, 1990; for the United States April 6, 1993.

TIAS

Parties:

Canada
Denmark
France
Netherlands
United States [1]

Notes:

1 With declarations.

International telecommunications regulations [telegraph and telephone], with appendices and final protocol (WATTC-88).

Done at Melbourne December 9, 1988.

*Entered into force July 1, 1990; definitively for the United States April 6, 1993.**

TIAS

Depositary: International Telecommunications Union

Note:

* Ratification of or accession to the Constitution and Convention of the International Telecommunication Union adopted at Geneva
December 22, 1992 (see article 54 of the Constitution) and predecessor international telecommunication conventions (Nairobi, 1982; Malaga-Torremolinos, 1973) typically involves acceptance of the telegraph and telephone regulations which are considered annexed thereto. The 1988 regulations replace the 1973 regulations (28 UST 3293; TIAS 8586) as between the contracting parties. The 1958 regulations (10 UST 2423; TIAS 4390) remain in force as between the contracting parties and the Dominican Republic. The Taiwan authorities have also adhered to the 1958 regulations (see note under CHINA (TAIWAN) in Section 1).

Constitution and Convention of the International Telecommunication Union, with annexes.*
Done at Geneva December 22, 1992.
Entered into force July 1, 1994; definitively for the United States October 26, 1997.
TIAS

Amendment:
October 14, 1994
November 6, 1998
October 18, 2002

Depositary: International Telecommunication Union

Notes:
* The 1992 Constitution and Convention replaced the international telecommunication convention adopted at Nairobi November 6, 1982, as between the contracting parties to the Constitution and Convention. For the position of states which have signed but not ratified the Constitution and Convention, see article 52 of the Constitution.

TERRITORIAL ISSUES

Convention to adjust amicably questions between the United States, Germany, and the United Kingdom in respect of the Samoan group of islands.*
Signed at Washington December 2, 1899.
Entered into force February 16, 1900.
31 Stat. 1878; TS 314; 1 Bevans 276

Parties:
United Kingdom
United States

Note:
* The German Samoan islands became a mandate of New Zealand on May 7, 1919, Germany having renounced rights and titles to them, effective August 4, 1919 (articles 22, 119, and 288, Treaty of Peace with Germany signed at Versailles June 28, 1919). Subsequently these islands were administered by New Zealand, first under a League of Nations mandate, then as a United Nations Trust Territory. On January 1, 1962, Western Samoa acquired the status of an independent state. In July 1997, the name became Samoa.

Treaty relating to Spitzbergen (Svalbard), with annex.
Done at Paris February 9, 1920.
Entered into force August 14, 1925.
43 Stat. 1892; TS 686; 2 Bevans 269; 2 LNTS 7

Depositary: France

Treaty relating to insular possessions and insular dominions in the region of the Pacific Ocean, with declaration.
Signed at Washington December 13, 1921.
Entered into force August 17, 1923.
43 Stat. 1646; TS 669; 2 Bevans 332; 25 LNTS 184

Parties:
France
Japan
United Kingdom
United States [1]

Note:
1 With reservation.

Agreement supplementary to the treaty relating to insular possessions and insular dominions in the region of the Pacific Ocean.
Signed at Washington February 6, 1922.
Entered into force August 17, 1923.
43 Stat. 1652; TS 670; 2 Bevans 372; 25 LNTS 196

Parties:
France
Japan
United Kingdom
United States

Declaration and protocol of the conference on the status of Tangier.
Signed at Tangier October 29, 1956.
Entered into force October 29, 1956.
7 UST 3035; TIAS 3680; 263 UNTS 165

Parties:
Belgium
France
Italy
Morocco
Netherlands
Portugal
Spain
Sweden
United Kingdom
United States

TRADE & INVESTMENT

Convention concerning the formation of an International Union for the Publication of Customs Tariffs, regulations of execution, and final declarations.
Signed at Brussels July 5, 1890.
Entered into force April 1, 1891.
26 Stat. 1518; TS 384; 1 Bevans 172

Depositary: Belgium

General act of the international conference at Algeciras, with an additional protocol.*
Signed at Algeciras (Spain) April 7, 1906.
Entered into force December 31, 1906.
34 Stat. 2905; TS 45 6; 1 Bevans 464

Depositary: Spain

Notes:
* Extraterritorial jurisdiction in Morocco relinquished by the United States October 6, 1956.
1 See note under UNION OF SOVIET SOCIALIST REPUBLICS in Section 1.
2 With reservation and understanding.

Convention revising the duties imposed by the Brussels convention of June 8, 1899 on spirituous liquors imported into certain regions of Africa.*
Signed at Brussels November 3, 1906.
Entered into force December 2, 1907.
35 Stat. 1912; TS 467; 1 Bevans 551

Depositary: Belgium

Notes:
* Replaced by convention of September 10, 1919 (46 Stat. 2199; TS 779), as between contracting parties to the later convention.

Revision of the General Act of Berlin of February 26, 1885, and the General Act and Declaration of Brussels of July 2, 1890.

Signed at St. Germain-en-Laye September 10, 1919.
Entered into force July 31, 1920; for the United States October 29, 1934.
49 Stat. 3027; TS 877; 2 Bevans 261; 8 LNTS 27
Depositary: France

Convention relating to the liquor traffic in Africa.

Signed at St. Germain–en–Laye September 10, 1919.
Entered into force July 31, 1920;
for the United States March 22, 1929.
46 Stat. 2199; TS 779; 2 Bevans 255; 8 LNTS 11
Depositary: France

Treaty relating to the principles and policies to be followed in matters concerning China.*

Signed at Washington February 6, 1922.
Entered into force August 5, 1925.
44 Stat. 2113; TS 723; 2 Bevans 375; 38 LNTS 278
Depositary: United States

Notes:
* Pre-1949 treaties, applicable only to Taiwan.

Treaty relating to the Chinese customs tariff.

Signed at Washington February 6, 1922.
Entered into force August 5, 1925.
44 Stat. 2122; TS 724; 2 Bevans 381; 38 LNTS 268
Depositary: United States

Notes:
* Pre-1949 treaties, applicable only to Taiwan.

Convention on publicity of customs documents.

Signed at Santiago May 3, 1923.
Entered into force July 10, 1925.
44 Stat. 2547; TS 753; 2 Bevans 420; 33 LNTS 11
Depositary: Chile

Agreement to refrain from invoking the obligations of most-favored-nation clause in respect of certain multilateral economic conventions.

Done at the Pan American Union, Washington, July 15, 1934.
Entered into force September 12, 1935.
49 Stat. 3260; TS 898; 3 Bevans 252; 165 LNTS 9

Parties:
Cuba
Greece
United States

Protocol modifying the convention of July 5, 1890 relating to the creation of an International Union for the Publication of Customs Tariffs.

Done at Brussels December 16, 1949.
Entered into force May 5, 1950; for the United States September 15, 1957.
8 UST 1669; TIAS 3922; 72 UNTS 3
Depositary: Belgium

Convention establishing a Customs Cooperation Council, with annex and protocol.

Done at Brussels December 15, 1950.
Entered into force November 4, 1952; for the United States November 5, 1970.
22 UST 320; TIAS 7063; 157 UNTS 129; 160 UNTS 267
Depositary: Belgium

International convention to facilitate the importation of commercial samples and advertising material.*

Done at Geneva November 7, 1952.
Entered into force November 20, 1955; for the United States October 17, 1957.
8 UST 1636; TIAS 3920; 221 UNTS 255
Depositary: United Nations

Notes:
* Pursuant to articles 3(2) and 23 of the A.T.A. carnet convention of December 6, 1961 (TIAS 6631) the United States gave notice on May 19, 1969, of acceptance of A.T.A carnets for goods temporarily imported under the 1952 samples convention.

Convention on the recognition and enforcement of foreign arbitral awards.

Done at New York June 10, 1958.
Entered into force June 7, 1959; for the United States December 29, 1970.
21 UST 2517; TIAS 6997; 330 UNTS 3
Depositary: United Nations

Customs convention on the temporary importation of professional equipment, with annexes.

Done at Brussels June 8, 1961.
Entered into force July 1, 1962; for the United States March 3, 1969.
20 UST 33; TIAS 6630; 473 UNTS 153
Depositary: World Customs Organization

Customs convention on the A.T.A. carnet for temporary admission of goods, with annex.

Done at Brussels December 6, 1961.
Entered into force July 30, 1963; for the United States March 3, 1969.
20 UST 58; TIAS 6631; 473 UNTS 219
Depositary: World Customs Organization

Convention on the settlement of investment disputes between states and nationals of other states.*

Done at Washington March 18, 1965.
Entered into force October 14, 1966.
17 UST 1270; TIAS 6090; 575 UNTS 159
Depositary: World Bank

Note:
* The convention is applicable to all territories for whose international relations a Contracting State is responsible, except those which are excluded by such State by written notice to the depositary . . ." (Article 70).

Convention on transit trade of land-locked states.
Done at New York July 8, 1965.
Entered into force June 9, 1967; for the United States November 28, 1968.
19 UST 7383; TIAS 6592; 597 UNTS 42
Depositary: United Nations

Agreement on the international carriage of perishable foodstuffs and on the special equipment to be used for such carriage (ATP), with annexes.
Done at Geneva September 1, 1970.
Entered into force November 21, 1976; for the United States January 20, 1984.
TIAS; 1028 UNTS 121
Depositary: United Nations

Customs convention on containers, 1972, with annexes and protocol.*
Done at Geneva December 2, 1972.
Entered into force December 6, 1975; for the United States May 12, 1985.
TIAS 12085; 988 UNTS 43
Depositary: United Nations

Notes:
* Replaces as between the contracting parties the convention of May 18, 1956 (20 UST 301; TIAS 6634; 338 UNTS 103).

International convention on the simplification and harmonization of customs procedures, with annexes, as amended.*
Done at Kyoto May 18, 1973.
Entered into force September 25, 1974; for the United States January 28, 1984.
TIAS
Amendment
June 26, 1999

Depositary: World Customs Organization

Notes:
* The convention has thirty-one annexes, not all of which have entered into force and many of which are in force only for certain parties.

Convention on the limitation period in the international sale of goods.
Done at New York June 14, 1974.
Entered into force August 1, 1988; for the United States December 1, 1994.
TIAS
Amendment:
April 11, 1980

Depositary: United Nations

Customs convention on the international transport of goods under cover of TIR carnets, with annexes.*
Done at Geneva November 14, 1975.
Entered into force March 20, 1978; for the United States March 18, 1982.
TIAS; 1079 UNTS 89
Amendments to annexes:
October 20, 1978
October 18, 1979
July 3, 1980
October 23, 1981
October 28, 1983
October 12, 1984

Depositary: United Nations

Notes:
* Replaces as between parties to the convention the customs convention
of January 15, 1959 (20 UST 184; TIAS 6633). Japan is a party to the 1959 convention (with reservations) but not a party to the 1975 convention.

Agreement on trade in civil aircraft.
Done at Geneva April 12, 1979.
Entered into force January 1, 1980.
31 UST 619; TIAS 9620; 1186 UNTS 170
Amendments (Annex):
January 17, 1983 (TIAS 10673)
January 27, 1984 (TIAS 11531)
January 1, 1985 (TIAS 11531)
December 2, 1986

Depositary: World Trade Organization

United Nations convention on contracts for the international sale of goods.
Done at Vienna April 11, 1980.
Entered into force January 1, 1988.
TIAS; 1489 UNTS 3
Depositary: United Nations

International convention on the harmonized commodity description and coding system.
Done at Brussels June 14, 1983.
Entered into force January 1, 1988; for the United States January 1, 1989.
TIAS
Amendment:
June 24, 1986

Depositary: World Customs Organization

North American free trade agreement, with notes and annexes.
Signed at Washington, Ottawa, and Mexico December 8, 11, 14 and 17, 1992.
Entered into force January 1, 1994.
TIAS
Parties
Canada
Mexico
United States

The following agreements comprise the 1986 – 1994 Uruguay Round negotiations of the GATT/World Trade Organization. These agreements were signed at the Marrakesh ministerial meetings in April of 1994, and entered into force January 1, 1995.

Depositary: World Trade Organization

- Marrakesh agreement establishing the World Trade Organization (WTO).
- General Agreement on Tariffs and Trade, 1994.
- Agreement on agriculture.
- Agreement on the application of sanitary and phytosanitary measures.
- Agreement on textiles and clothing.
- Agreement on technical barriers to trade.
- Agreement on trade-related investment measures.
- Agreement on implementation of Article VI (Anti-Dumping) of the General Agreement on Tariffs and Trade 1994.
- Agreement on implementation of Article VII (Customs Valuation) of the General Agreement on Tariffs and Trade 1994.
- Agreement on preshipment inspection.
- Agreement on government procurement.
- Agreement on rules of origin.
- Agreement on import licensing procedures.
- Agreement on subsidies and countervailing measures.
- Agreement on safeguards.
- General agreement on trade in services and annexes, with protocols.
- Agreement on trade-related aspects of intellectual property rights.
- Understanding on rules and procedures governing the settlement of disputes.
- Trade policy review mechanism.
- International bovine meat agreement

Grains trade convention (part of international grains agreement), 1995.
Done at London December 7, 1994.
Entered into force July 1, 1995; for the United States May 21, 1999.
TIAS
Depositary: United Nations

Fourth protocol to the general agreement on trade in services.*
Signed at Geneva April 15, 1997.
Entered into force February 5, 1998.
TIAS
Depositary: World Trade Organization
Note:
* The United States is not a party to the first three protocols of the general agreement on trade in services.

Fifth protocol to the general agreement on trade in services.
Signed at Geneva December 1, 1998.
Entered into force March 1, 1999.
TIAS
Depositary: World Trade Organization

Agreement on mutual acceptance of oenological practices, with annex.
Done at Toronto December 18, 2001.
Entered into force December 1, 2002.
TIAS 13179.
Depositary: United States

The Dominican Republic-Central America-United States free trade agreement.
Signed at Washington August 5, 2004.
Entered into force March 1, 2006.
TIAS
Amendments:
December 1, 2006
August 6, 2007

Depositary: Organization of American States

Agreement on duty-free treatment of multi-chip integrated circuits (MCPs).
Done at Brussels November 28, 2005.
Entered into force January 4, 2006.
TIAS
Depositary: European Union

Cooperative agreement to foster trade, investment and development.
Signed at Washington July 16, 2008.
Entered into force July 16, 2008.
TIAS 08-716.2
Parties:
Botswana
Lesotho
Namibia
South Africa
Swaziland
United States

Food assistance convention.
Signed at London April 25, 2012.
Entered into force January 1, 2013.
TIAS 13-101
Depositary: United Nations

TRANSPORTATION

Convention for the unification of certain rules relating to international transportation by air, with additional protocol
Concluded at Warsaw October 12, 1929.
Entered into force February 13, 1933; for the United States October 29, 1934.
49 Stat. 3000; TS 876; 2 Bevans 983; 137 LNTS 11
Depositary: Poland

Convention on the Pan American highway.
Signed at Buenos Aires December 23, 1936.
Entered into force July 29, 1937.
51 Stat. 152; TS 927; 3 Bevans 367; 188 LNTS 99
Depositary: Organization of American States

Convention on the regulation of inter-American automotive traffic, with annex.
*Open for signature at the Pan American Union, Washington, December 15, 1943.**
Entered into force July 25, 1944; for the United States October 29, 1946.
61 Stat. 1129; TIAS 1567; 3 Bevans 865
Depositary: Organization of American States

Notes:
* Replaced by convention of September 19, 1949, on road traffic (3 UST 3008; TIAS 2487), as between contracting parties to the later convention.

Convention on international civil aviation.*
Done at Chicago December 7, 1944.
Entered into force April 4, 1947.
61 Stat. 1180; TIAS 1591; 3 Bevans 944; 15 UNTS 295
Amendments:*
June 14, 1954 (8 UST 179; TIAS 3756; 320 UNTS 21)
September 15, 1962 (26 UST 2374; TIAS 8162; 1008 UNTS 213)
July 7, 1971 (26 UST 1061; TIAS 8092)
October 16, 1974 (32 UST 322; TIAS 9702)[Ψ]
September 30, 1977
September 30, 1977
October 6, 1989

Depositary: United States

Notes:
* Applicable to all territories. Protocols of amendment to the Convention are legally binding only on those states which ratify or otherwise accept them; however, the above amendments are all of an organizational character and thus in effect for all ICAO members. The United States is not a party to the protocols of May 26, 1947 (418 UNTS 161) and June 14, 1954 (320 UNTS 209).
Ψ This amendment increased the size of the ICAO council and supersedes the protocols of June 21, 1961(13 UST 2105; TIAS 5170; 514 UNTS 209) and March 12, 1971(24 UST 1019; TIAS 7616).

International air services transit agreement.*
Signed at Chicago, December 7, 1944;
Entered into force January 30, 1945; for the United States February 8, 1945.
59 Stat. 1693; EAS 487; 3 Bevans 916; 84 UNTS 389
Depositary: United States

Notes:
* Applicable to all territories.

Convention on the international recognition of rights in aircraft.
Done at Geneva June 19, 1948.
Entered into force September 17, 1953.
4 UST 1830; TIAS 2847; 310 UNTS 151
Depositary: International Civil Aviation Organization

Convention on road traffic, with annexes and protocol.
Done at Geneva September 19, 1949.
Entered into force March 26, 1952.
3 UST 3008; TIAS 2487; 125 UNTS 22
Depositary: United Nations

Convention concerning customs facilities for touring.
Done at New York June 4, 1954.
Entered into force September 11, 1957.
8 UST 1293; TIAS 3879; 276 UNTS 230
Amendment:
June 6, 1967 (19 UST 4684; TIAS 6461; 596 UNTS 542)

Depositary: United Nations

Customs convention on the temporary importation of private
road vehicles.
Done at New York June 4, 1954.
Entered into force December 15, 1957.
8 UST 2097; TIAS 3943; 282 UNTS 249
Amendment:
July 2, 1984 (TIAS 11936)

Depositary: United Nations

Protocol to amend the Convention for the unification of certain rules relating to international carriage by air signed at Warsaw on October 12, 1929.
Done at The Hague September 28, 1955.
Entered into force August 1, 1963; for the United States December 14, 2003.
TIAS
Depositary: Poland

Agreement on the joint financing of certain air navigation services in Greenland and the Faroe Islands.
Done at Geneva September 25, 1956.
Entered into force June 6, 1958.
9 UST 795; TIAS 4049; 334 UNTS 89
Amendments:
June 4, 1963 (14 UST 874; TIAS 5369)
June 14, 1976 (27 UST 4013; TIAS 8421)
April 6, 1977 (29 UST 1188; TIAS 8872)
June 8, 1977 (29 UST 1188; TIAS 8872)
September 27, 1979 (31 UST 5570; TIAS 9673)
November 3, 1982 (TIAS 11533)

Depositary: International Civil Aviation Organization

Agreement on the joint financing of certain air navigation services in Iceland.
Done at Geneva September 25, 1956.
Entered into force June 6, 1958.
9 UST 711; TIAS 4048; 334 UNTS 13

Amendments:
March 27, 1975 (26 UST 1630; TIAS 8122)
September 27, 1979 (31 UST 5570; TIAS 9673)
November 3, 1982 (TIAS 11534)

Depositary: International Civil Aviation Organization

Convention on offenses and certain other acts committed on board aircraft.
Done at Tokyo September 14, 1963.
Entered into force December 4, 1969.
20 UST 2941; TIAS 6768; 704 UNTS 219
Depositary: International Civil Aviation Organization

Protocol on the authentic trilingual text of the convention on international civil aviation with annex.*
Done at Buenos Aires September 24, 1968.
Entered into force October 24, 1968.
19 UST 7693; TIAS 6605; 740 UNTS 21
Depositary: United States

Note:
* States becoming parties to the convention after the entry into force of the protocol are deemed parties to the protocol.

Proces-verbal of rectification to the protocol of September 24, 1968 on the authentic trilingual text of the convention on international civil aviation.
Done at Washington April 8, 1969.
Entered into force April 8, 1969.
20 UST 718; TIAS 6681
Depositary: International Civil Aviation Organization

Convention for the suppression of unlawful seizure of aircraft. (Hijacking)
Done at The Hague December 16, 1970.
Entered into force October 14, 1971.
22 UST 1641; TIAS 7192; 860 UNTS 105
Depositary: Russia, United Kingdom, United States

Convention for the suppression of unlawful acts against the safety of civil aviation. (Sabotage)
Done at Montreal September 23, 1971.
Entered into force January 26, 1973.
24 UST 564; TIAS 7570; 860 UNTS 105
Depositary: Russia, United Kingdom, United States

Montreal Protocol No. 4 to amend the Convention for the unification of certain rules relating to international carriage by air, signed at Warsaw on October 12, 1929, as amended by the Protocol, done at The Hague on September 28, 1955.
Done at Montreal September 25, 1975.
Entered into force June 14, 1998; for the United States March 4, 1999.
TIAS
Depositary: Poland

Protocol on the authentic quadrilingual text of the convention on international civil aviation, with annex.*
Done at Montreal September 30, 1977.
Entered into force September 16, 1999.
TIAS
Depositary: United States

Note:
* States becoming parties to the convention after the entry into force of the protocol are deemed parties to the protocol.

Protocol for the suppression of unlawful acts of violence at airports serving international civil aviation, supplementary to the convention of September 23, 1971.
Done at Montreal February 24, 1988.
Entered into force August 6, 1989; for the United States November 18, 1994.
TIAS; 1589 UNTS 474
Depositaries: International Civil Aviation Organization, Russia, United Kingdom, United States

Convention on the marking of plastic explosives for the purpose of detection, with technical annex.
Done at Montreal March 1, 1991.
Entered into force June 21, 1998.
TIAS
Depositary: International Civil Aviation Organization

Agreement to ban smoking on international passenger flights.
Done at Chicago November 1, 1994.
Entered into force March 1, 1995.
TIAS 12578
Parties:
Australia
Canada
New Zealand
United States

Arrangement on the joint financing of a North Atlantic Height Monitoring System.
Signed at Montreal July 31, August 11, 18 and 23, September 28, October 25 and December 12, 1995.
Entered into force December 12, 1995.
TIAS
Parties:
Canada
International Civil Aviation Organization
Iceland
Ireland
Portugal
United Kingdom
United States

Agreement concerning the establishing of global technical regulations for wheeled vehicles, equipment and parts which can be fitted and/or be used on wheeled vehicles, with annexes.
Done at Geneva June 25, 1998.
Entered into force August 25, 2000.
TIAS 12967
Depositary: United Nations

Convention for the unification of certain rules for international carriage by air.
Done at Montreal May 28, 1999.
Entered into force November 4, 2003.
TIAS 13038
Depositary: International Civil Aviation Organization

Multilateral agreement on the liberalization of international air transportation, with annex and appendix.
Done at Washington May 1, 2001.
Entered into force December 21, 2001.
TIAS 13148
Depositary: New Zealand

UN & RELATED ORGANIZATIONS

Declaration by United Nations.
Signed at Washington January 1, 1942.
Entered into force January 1, 1942.
55 Stat. 1600; EAS 236; 3 Bevans 697

Parties:

Australia
Belgium
Bolivia
Brazil
Canada
Chile
China [1]
Colombia
Costa Rica
Cuba
Czechoslovakia [2]
Dominican Republic
Ecuador
Egypt
El Salvador
Ethiopia [3]
France
Greece
Guatemala
Haiti
Honduras
India
Iran
Iraq
Lebanon
Liberia
Luxembourg
Mexico
Netherlands
New Zealand
Nicaragua
Norway
Panama
Paraguay
Peru
Philippines
Poland
Saudi Arabia
Slovak Republic
South Africa
Syrian Arab Republic
Turkey
Union of Soviet Socialist Republics [4]
United Kingdom
United States
Uruguay
Venezuela
Yugoslavia [5]

Notes:

1 Pre-1949 agreement, applicable only to Taiwan.
2 See note under CZECHOSLOVAKIA in Section 1.
3 See note under ETHIOPIA in Section 1.
4 See note under UNION OF SOVIET SOCIALIST REPUBLICS in Section 1.
5 See note under YUGOSLAVIA in Section 1.

Charter of the United Nations with the Statute of the International Court of Justice annexed thereto.*
Signed at San Francisco June 26, 1945.
Entered into force October 24, 1945.
59 Stat. 1031; TS 993; 3 Bevans 1153

Amendments:

December 17, 1963 (16 UST 1134; TIAS 5857; 557 UNTS 143)
December 20, 1965 (19 UST 5450; TIAS 6529)
December 20, 1971 (24 UST 2225; TIAS 7739)

Depositary: United States

Convention on the privileges and immunities of the United Nations.
Done at New York February 13, 1946.
Entered into force September 17, 1946; for the United States April 29, 1970.
21 UST 1418; TIAS 6900; 1 UNTS 16
Depositary: United Nations

WEAPONS

Convention on assistance in the case of a nuclear accident or radiological emergency.
Done at Vienna September 26, 1986.
Entered into force February 26, 1987; for the United States October 20, 1988.
TIAS
Depositary: International Atomic Energy Agency

Convention on early notification of a nuclear accident.
Done at Vienna September 26, 1986.
Entered into force October 27, 1986; for the United States October 20, 1988.
TIAS
Depositary: International Atomic Energy Agency

www.ingramcontent.com/pod-product-compliance
Lightning Source LLC
Chambersburg PA
CBHW052129020426
42334CB00023B/2652

* 9 7 8 1 5 9 8 0 4 8 6 5 0 *